THE AMERICAN CULTURE OF WAR, 2ND EDITION

The American Culture of War presents a sweeping, critical examination of every major American war of the late twentieth century: World War II, Korea, Vietnam, the First and Second Persian Gulf Wars, through to Operation Enduring Freedom. Lewis deftly traces the evolution of U.S. military strategy, offering an original and provocative look at the motives people and governments used to wage war, the debates among military personnel, the flawed political policies that guided military strategy, and the civilian perceptions that characterized each conflict.

Now in its second edition, *The American Culture of War* has been completely revised and updated. New features include:

* Completely revised and updated chapters structured to facilitate students' ability to compare conflicts
* New chapters on Operation Iraqi Freedom and the current conflict in Afghanistan
* New conclusion discussing the American culture of war and the future of warfare
* Over fifty maps, photographs, and images to help students visualize material
* Expanded companion website with additional pedagogical material for both students and researchers.

The American Culture of War is a unique and invaluable survey of over seventy years of American military history, perfect for any student of America's modern wars..

For additional information and classroom resources please visit *The American Culture of War* companion website at **www.routledge.com/cw/lewis**.

Adrian Lewis is Professor of History at the University of Kansas. He has taught at the Naval War College and at West Point, and is a retired United States Army Major. He is the author of *Omaha Beach: A Flawed Victory*.

THE AMERICAN CULTURE OF WAR

THE HISTORY OF U.S. MILITARY FORCE FROM WORLD WAR II TO OPERATION ENDURING FREEDOM

ADRIAN R. LEWIS

Routledge
Taylor & Francis Group

NEW YORK AND LONDON

BRIEF TABLE OF CONTENTS

PART III
THE NEW AMERICAN PRACTICE OF WAR 309

FULL TABLE OF CONTENTS

ACKNOWLEDGMENTS

I am indebted to a great many scholars whose works are dutifully noted. This study covers more than sixty years of American history. It is, thus, a synthesis of a great many works. It is also an analysis of the American conduct of war based on primary documents, the official and unofficial publications and documents of the services, the professional journals of services, and the spoken and written words of the historical actor: from privates to generals, from secretaries to presidents, and from private citizen to professors. I have endeavored to provide a cultural explanation for the American behavior in peace and war from World War II through Operations Iraqi Freedom and Enduring Freedom. To provide a more complete explanation I have used anthropological and political science theories, and historical methods. I have endeavored to be fair to all concerned by letting the historical actors speak for themselves; delineating the published, historical arguments; and presenting all sides of the various issues. While endeavoring to present the various sides of the historical issues addressed I have not failed to render an opinion based on my analysis. However, if I have erred in judgment of fact, the fault is mine. Please note, readers can find the complete bibliography on the companion website for the book: www.routledge.com/cw/lewis.

Special thanks are due my professors, mentors, and friends, Michael Geyer at the University of Chicago and John Shy at the University of Michigan. I owe them much. John Shy provided many insightful comments on my first draft that caused me to rethink and rewrite. I am grateful for his knowledge, time, perspective, and understanding. Katherine Barbieri, my friend and colleague, now at the University of South Carolina, has read every word. She edited this book and made numerous significant recommendations. I greatly appreciate her many contributions. Thanks are also due my former colleagues in the Department of History at the University of North Texas whose support, knowledge, and friendship I have benefited from over the years, specifically, Ronald Marcello, Randolph Campbell, Marilyn Morris, Laura Stern, Geoffrey Wawro, Richard Golden, Pete Lane, Alfred Hurley, and Alfred C. Mierzejewski. Thanks is also due to my colleagues and friends at the University of Kansas, particularly Theodore Wilson, William Tsutsui, and Paul Kelton.

The generous, professional people at the following institutions assisted in finding materials necessary for this study: the National Archive and Record Center in College Park, Maryland; the Military History Institute at the US Army War College in Carlisle, Pennsylvania; the US Army Center of Military History at Fort McNair in Washington, DC; the US Air Force, Office of Air Force History in Washington, DC; the US Army Training and Doctrine Command in Fort Monroe, Virginia; the Vietnam Center and Archive at Texas Tech University in Lubbock, Texas; the Eisenhower Library and Archive in Abilene, Kansas; the Military Oral History Center at the University of North Texas in Denton, Texas; the Naval Oral History Program at the US Naval Institute at the US Naval Academy in Annapolis, Maryland; the US Marine Corps University Archive in Quantico, Virginia; the Institute of Land Warfare, Association of the US Army in Arlington, Virginia; and the Main Library at the U.S.M.A. at West Point, New York.

I have benefited from the analytical exchange with students at the U.S.M.A, UC Berkeley, UNT, and the University of Kansas. A number of my graduate students at UNT deserve recognition: Donald K. Mitchener,

Josh Montandon, Sylvia Stastny, Mervyn Roberts, and Peter Kaiser. Four of my graduate students at KU assisted in the preparation of this second edition: Christopher Carey, Marion Mealey, Nicholas Sambaluk, and Christopher Rein. Many thanks are also due the many fine soldiers with whom I have had the privilege to serve. The list is too long to publish; however, special recognition is due Generals Richard Cavazos, Dave R. Palmer, James E. Mace; Colonels Monte R. Bullard, Patrick L. Hatcher, Franklin D. Young, and David Foye; Major James Sullivan; and First Sergeants Kahiki, Meno, McSpadden, and Mobley; and Sergeant Karen W. Kennedy. My assistants in the Office of Professional Military Graduate Education at the University of Kansas, Dawn Tallchief and William Steele, made it possible for me to leave the office and work at home to complete this book. I am grateful for their time, energy, and professionalism.

Thanks are also due Routledge Press and the many professional people there that made this work possible, especially Rebecca Novack. Special thanks are due my friend, mentor, and editor Kimberly Guinta, who edited this work and provided numerous helpful comments.

Finally I must thank my smart, talented, wonderful, beautiful daughters, Alexandria, Allison, Aubrey, Anastasia, and Angelica. They produce the joy and purpose in my life.

Adrian R. Lewis
Professor, University of Kansas

LIST OF ABBREVIATIONS

This listing is incomplete. Acronyms that are used infrequently are not listed.

AAF	Army Air Force
AD	armor division
ARVN	Army Republic of Vietnam
BCT	brigade combat team
CAP	combined action program
CAS	close air support
CCF	Chinese Communist Forces
CENTCOM	US Central Command
CFLCC	Coalition Force Land Component Commander
CFSOCC	Combined Forces Special Operations Component Commander
CG	commanding general
CIA	Central Intelligence Agency
CIB	combat infantry badge
CIDG	civilian irregular defense groups
CINCFE	Commander in Chief of the Far East
CINCSAC	Commander in Chief, Strategic Air Command
CINCUNC	Commander in Chief of the United Nations Command
CJCS	Chairman Joint Chiefs of Staff
COMUSMACV	Commander, US Military Assistance Command, Vietnam
CORDS	Civil Operations and Revolutionary Development and Support
CPA	Coalition Provisional Authority
CPV	Chinese People's Volunteers
DIA	Defense Intelligence Agency
DOD	Department of Defense
DPRK	Democratic People's Republic of Korea
DRV	Democratic Republic of Vietnam
EU	European Union
EUCOM	European Command
EUSAK	Eighth US Army Korea
FDL	fast deployment logistics ship
FEAF	Far East Air Force

FEC	Far East Command
FMF	fleet marine force
FSS	fast sealift ship
G1	general staff personnel officer or office
GWOT	global war on terrorism
HES	Hamlet Evaluation System
IAEA	International Atomic Energy Agency
ICBM	intercontinental ballistic missile
ID	infantry division
IDF	Israeli Defense Force
IRBM	intermediate-range ballistic missile
JCS	Joint Chiefs of Staff
JFACC	Joint Forces Air Component Commander
JFC	Joint Forces Commander
JFCOM	Joint Forces Command
JSOC	Joint Special Operations Command
KATUSA	Korean Augmentations to the US Army
KIA	killed in action
KTO	Kuwait Theater of Operation
LOC	lines of communication
MAAG	Military Assistance and Advisory Group
MACV	Military Assistance Command, Vietnam
MEF	marine expeditionary force
METL	mission essential tasks list
MIA	missing in action
MOOTW	military operations other than war
MPS	maritime prepositioning ships
NASA	National Aeronautic and Space Administration
NATO	North Atlantic Treaty Organization
NCW	network-centric warfare
NG	National Guard
NKPA	North Korean People's Army
NLF	National Liberation Front
NME	national military establishment
NMP	National Media Pool
NMS	national military strategy
NSC	National Security Council
NSS	National Security Strategy
NTC	National Training Center
NVA	North Vietnam Army
ODS	Operation Desert Shield/Storm—Iraq
OEF	Operation Enduring Freedom—Afghanistan
OIF	Operation Iraqi Freedom—Iraq
OJC	Operation Just Cause—Panama
ORC	organized reserve corps
ORHA	Office of Reconstruction and Humanitarian Assistance
OSD	Office of the Secretary of Defense

PAVN	People's Army of Vietnam
PGM	precision-guided munitions
PLA	People's Liberation Army
PLAAF	People's Liberation Army Air Force
PME	professional military education
PMF	private military firms
PPBS	planning-programming-budgeting system
PRC	People's Republic of China
PSYOP	psychological operations
RAF	Royal Air Force
RMA	revolution in military affairs
ROK	Republic of Korea
ROKA	Republic of Korea Army
RVN	Republic of Vietnam
SAC	Strategic Air Command
SAM	surface-to-air missile
SAMS	School of Advanced Military Studies
SEATO	Southeast Asia Treaty Organization
SLBM	submarine-launched ballistic missile
SOCOM	US Special Operations Command
SU	Soviet Union
SVN	South Vietnam
TAC	Tactical Air Command
TF	task force
TO&E	table of organization and equipment
TRADOC	US Army Training and Doctrine Command
UCP	Unified Command Plan
UN	United Nations
UNSCR	United Nations Security Council Resolution
USAF	United States Air Force
USASOC	US Army Special Operations Command
USSOCOM	United States Special Operations Command
USSR	Union of Soviet Socialist Republics
VC	Viet Cong
VTOL	vertical take-off and landing
WMD	weapons of mass destruction (chemical, biological, and nuclear)

MILITARY MAP SYMBOLS

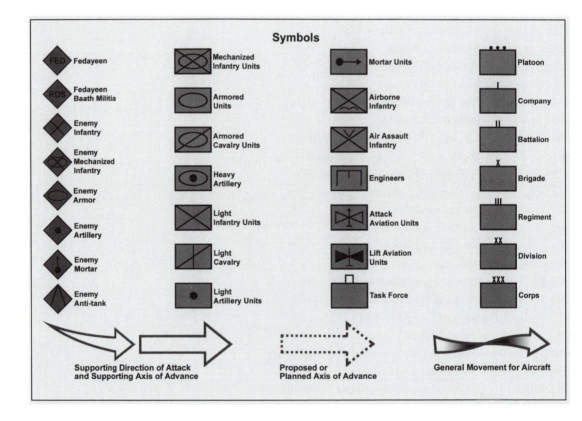

Symbols

Symbol	Label
FED	Fedayeen
RDS	Fedayeen Baath Militia
	Enemy Infantry
	Enemy Mechanized Infantry
	Enemy Armor
	Enemy Artillery
	Enemy Mortar
	Enemy Anti-tank
	Mechanized Infantry Units
	Armored Units
	Armored Cavalry Units
	Heavy Artillery
	Light Infantry Units
	Light Cavalry
	Light Artillery Units
	Mortar Units
	Airborne Infantry
	Air Assault Infantry
	Engineers
	Attack Aviation Units
	Lift Aviation Units
	Task Force
	Platoon
	Company
	Battalion
	Brigade
	Regiment
	Division
	Corps

Supporting Direction of Attack and Supporting Axis of Advance

Proposed or Planned Axis of Advance

General Movement for Aircraft

LIST OF ILLUSTRATIONS: PHOTOS, MAPS, AND CHARTS

INTRODUCTION

After four years of limited, low-intensity war in Iraq, Army Chief of Staff, General George W. Casey, before the Senate Armed Service Committee, stated:

> While we remain a resilient and committed professional force, our Army is out of balance for several reasons. The current demand for our forces exceeds the sustainable supply. We are consumed with meeting the demands of the current fight and are unable to provide ready forces as rapidly as necessary for other potential contingencies. ... Current operational requirements for forces and limited periods between deployments necessitate a focus on counterinsurgency to the detriment of preparedness for the full range of military missions. Soldiers, families, and equipment are stretched and stressed by the demands of lengthy and repeated deployments with insufficient recovery time. ... Army support systems including health care, education, and family support systems that were designed for the pre-9/11 era are straining under the pressure from six years at war. Overall, our readiness is being consumed as fast as we can build it.[1]

The current American practice of war is unsustainable. It fails to provide a sufficient number of soldiers to achieve political objectives. It wastes billions of dollars annually on unnecessary technologies and bases, the duplication of capabilities, and private military firms. It disassociates and disconnects the American people from the decisions for, conduct of, and human costs of war. And after the commitment of enormous resources, including the expenditure of lives, it too frequently fails to achieve, or only partially achieves, political objectives. Why and how did the current American practice of war evolve? And why, in a nation of 308 million people, is the Army continuously "out of balance," too small to do all that is asked and required of it?

This study delineates and analyzes the American conduct, practice, of war from World War II to Operation Enduring Freedom. It explains why Americans fight the way they do. The thesis is that culture influences the way nations fight. To understand the American practice of war, we have to identify and understand the cultural tenets that motivate actions. Culture influences the organization of the national command structure, force structure, strategic and operational doctrines, national and theater strategies, research and development, the procurement of soldiers, the acquisition of technology, civil-military relations, and the actions of soldiers in battle.

Using culture as one of the major determining factors in historical change, I argue that the traditional American practice of war was no longer valid in the wake of World War II. The traditional American system for procuring soldiers and equipment and fighting war no longer functioned as a result of: (1) the US becoming a superpower, responsible for the security of the "Free World"; (2) the advent of *artificial limited war*, a result of the development of nuclear weapons; (3) the "revolution in warfare," a result of advances in airpower, missile, and other technologies; (4) expanded American expectations from life, a result of unparalleled growth in wealth and consumption; and (5) a new American militarism, a result of the military becoming a major industry, institution, and lobby in American lives. From World War II until the end of the Vietnam War, Americans tried to adapt traditional cultural tenets and traditional ways of thinking and acting to the new national mission and the Cold War environment. Ultimately, this adaptation process failed. In Vietnam, it collapsed. What emerged was a new American practice of war—a practice that virtually eliminated the American people from the conduct of war.

*   *   *   *   *

In the wake of World War II, the political objectives that had directed US national and military strategies and the energies and intellect of the American people for two hundred years radically changed. In that aftermath of the war, as American power and influence grew to stretch around the Earth, as technologies and trade connected the world in new ways, as old Europe collapsed under the weight of two world wars, and as the Cold War emerged and the threat from the Soviet Union grew, the United States necessarily assumed new responsibilities and new roles in world affairs. By the end of the Second World War, the United States became in essence a European power *and* an Asian power, responsible for the security of over two hundred million people in Asia, Europe, and other parts of the world. Americans were responsible for defending people who were racially and ethnically different from themselves, people for whom they had little or no cultural affinity. The new political objectives of the US were to stop the spread of Communism, deter nuclear war, implant American capitalism, and transplant American culture. Permanent readiness for war and defensive national strategy and doctrine were the results of these new political objectives. However, this new mission and strategy were not in accord with the traditional American practice of war and not in accord with American thinking about the nature and conduct of war.

The justifications advanced by political and military leaders for adopting new strategies and doctrines after World War II were difficult to explain and comprehend. From whom and what was America defending these foreign people? And more importantly, did it rise to the level of grievance required to produce a unified war effort? Theoretically, Americans

were defending the "Free World" from Communism—an economic theory and ideology about the nature of human interaction and development. The ideology the Unites States sought to contain was difficult to grasp and understand, particularly when it only indirectly threatened Americans. Thus, the axioms of Communism were typically expressed in simplistic terms. Americans understood that they were better off than people living under the Communist system; they had more things and greater freedom. But, this was not sufficient reason to sacrifice their sons and daughters in war to save the people of Seoul or Saigon. As a consequence, in the early days of the Cold War, a fissure developed between the American people (*the nation*) and their understanding of war, and the United States (*the state*) and its new practice of war.

In addition, the state asked the American people to risk their lives and sacrifice in *artificial limited wars*. In 1953, Robert Oppenheimer, the man most responsible for the production of the atomic bomb, concluded that: "We may anticipate a state of affairs in which the two Great Powers will each be in a position to put an end to the civilization and life of the other, though not without risking its own. We may be likened to two scorpions in a bottle, each capable of killing the other, but only at the risk of his own life."[2] By eliminating military engagements between the two superpowers, the "scorpions," and placing restraints on engagements of surrogate forces and in peripheral areas, the superpowers endeavored to preclude annihilation blows with nuclear weapons.[3] These restraints, however, were self-imposed. *Artificial limited war* required *states* to place voluntary restraints on their actions and restraints on the objectives sought; the weapons and manpower employed; the geographic areas of hostility; and the emotions, passions, and intellectual commitment of its people, *the nation*.

While artificial limited war was necessary in the age of nuclear weapons, it was and is nonsense to most of humanity, because there is nothing limited about dying and killing. Limited war is limited at the strategic and operational levels of war, and it was only limited for the superpowers and major Western nations. At the tactical level of war, where the killing, dying, and suffering take place, there is nothing limited about limited war. Weapons produce the same effect in "limited war" as they do in "total war." They destroy life. To ask Americans to commit their most valued possession to war, and then hold back resources that would hasten its end, was inexplicable. The restraints in limited war were artificially imposed, and because everyone understood this, there was an internal illogic to war. Political and military leaders accepted and fought limited wars, but the American people and many of the soldiers who fought never accepted the doctrine or strategy of limited war. Defensive wars of attrition—a function of the limitation imposed on war—were un-American, and could not be reconciled with long-held cultural norms. Artificial limited war expanded the fissure between the American people, their understanding of war, and the US Government and its practice of war.

"Revolutionary technologies" held the promise of sealing the fissure, but instead only expanded it, because these technologies never achieved what the government and military claimed they could. Jet aircraft, missiles, radar, nuclear, and other technologies, and the nation's commitment to them, told the American people that in future wars armies would be obsolete—there would be no human commitment and no sacrifices to make in dirty, nasty ground wars. Americans were constantly told that: the fundamental nature of war had changed. They approved expenditures of billions of dollars annually on aircraft, missile, and naval technologies. They were constantly shown the capabilities of these amazing, new technologies, and observed with a sense of awe. And the American people were constantly told that this was the future of war. Yet, after all the claims of airpower, it took Army ground forces to save South Korea, and that war was more primitive than World War II. Later, it took Army ground forces to stabilize South Vietnam; and the most advanced airpower on earth could not stop the flow of weapons, men, and supplies down the Ho Chi Minh Trail. And the Vietnam War was more primitive than the Korean War. There was a contradiction between the realities of war and the imagined, futuristic, technological vision of war sold to the American people by the US Government. The promises of technology were never fulfilled. Decade after decade Americans were told a revolution in warfare had taken place only to be surprised later by a nasty, costly ground war. The most recent example of this was

Operation Iraqi Freedom. Stealth fighters and bombers, precision weapons, and advanced communication technologies supposedly changed the nature of warfare, causing a "revolution in military affairs." However, after the destruction of the poorly equipped, poorly motivated Iraqi Army, the war degenerated into an insurgency war, a war that required Army ground forces, and another relatively primitive war.

Because the government could not explain Communist ideology and the threat it posed, because it could not explain why American sons and daughters should fight to defend the people of South Korea and South Vietnam, and because it could not explain this new form of limited war, Americans came to oppose the draft and war as never before. *Artificial limited war and fighting against ideas and for people that were not directly related to the security of the United States violated major American cultural tenets for war.* From 1945 to 1975 a great many Americans grew to oppose this new form of artificial limited war, but endeavored to adapt their culturally imbued understanding of war to this new situation and environment. During peace their opposition only simmered. And, in the early days of the "Cold War," when there was palpable fear in the air, when China was "lost" to Communism and the Soviet Union exploded its first atomic bomb, the relationships between conscription, the human cost of war, and national security were evident. However, as American technology expanded, as Americans expended billions of dollars on the most advanced war machines ever produced, and as the palpable nature of the threats receded and Americans turned their attention towards the pursuit of "happiness" and "peace and prosperity," they became less and less able to see the links between the commitment and sacrifices of their sons and daughters and national security, and less and less willing to fight artificial limited war. During hot, limited wars, when Americans were fighting and dying on foreign battlefields, opposition mounted at home. The Korean War ended before this opposition reached critical mass. However, during the Vietnam War, a critical mass was achieved, resulting in an implosion that ended the citizen-soldier Army, and the traditional American practice of war.

The Vietnam War marked two important, related transformations in the American practice of war. It was the first war in American history in which ground forces were subordinate to airpower. Under the doctrine of "graduated response," airpower was supposed to be decisive. The US Army fought the entire war on the strategic defense, limited to the borders of South Vietnam. New technologies, operational doctrine, and strategic plans created the belief that the US could achieve its political objectives without a strategically offensive ground war. The second important transformation took place in the closing days of the Vietnam War. The citizen-soldier army dissolved, effectively removing the American people from the wars of the United States. By the time of the Persian Gulf Wars the American people had no legal, positive duties. The terrorist attacks on 9/11, and the Global War on Terrorism did not change this. When the Army, fighting two long wars in Iraq and Afghanistan, was grossly under strength, no effort was made to call upon the American people to serve.

With the demise of the citizen-soldier Army, one of the principal institutions of the modern nation-state no longer existed. The "Clausewitzian" remarkable trinity, the marriage between the government, the armed forces, and the people, which was required to fight total wars and major limited wars, had been transformed. Many of the most significant attachments between them were severed, giving each greater freedom, but this freedom also meant separation and disunity. The responsibility of the White House to limit the use of the armed forces to actions acceptable to the American people was greatly diminished. The White House had greater freedom to go to war. The White House and Pentagon had greater freedom to fight wars as they saw fit. And, the American people had greater freedom to pursue the American dream, to accumulate wealth and debt and to consume. At the dawn of the twenty-first century, America's wars resembled the wars of the seventeenth-century monarchs, where kings elected to go to war, a small professional army fought them, and the people were uninvolved.

The first Persian Gulf War only partially tested the new professional forces. However, some of the results of the new American practice of war became evident. The long-serving men and women of the armed forces formed a distinct "military cluster" with values, ethics, and beliefs that were different from those of the people they served.[4] After the Vietnam War, the armed services developed doctrines for war that endeavored to mitigate or eliminate the need for the support of the people. They sought to *not* fight another war dependent on the will of the American people, which many military and political leaders believed failed them during the Vietnam War. The former Chairman of the Joint Chiefs of Staff, General Colin Powell, and Commander in Chief Central Command, General H. Norman Schwarzkopf, while voicing the importance of the support of the people, planned and fought the first Persian Gulf War without them. It was to be a short, intense war. Under the "Weinberger/Powell Doctrine," overwhelming force was employed. Airpower was to be the primary means for the destruction of the enemy's main forces. It was a war in which the emotions, feelings, and passions of the American people had no time to manifest.

In 2003 President Bush "elected" to go to war in Iraq. He endeavored to isolate the war to a struggle against Saddam Hussein alone. He did not want war with the Iraqi people. He planned to fight the war primarily with airpower employing another new operational doctrine, "shock and awe" or the "Rumsfeld doctrine." While American technology created the illusion of victory, the war rapidly morphed from a conventional war into an insurgency war, creating the need for large numbers of ground forces. The war Bush elected to fight was a "true chameleon"—its nature was only slowly revealed. Within weeks of Bush's dramatic arrival on the decks of the *USS Abraham Lincoln* and his declaration of an "end to major hostilities," American soldiers and the Iraqi people were being killed in growing numbers in an insurgency war. As American technology proved less and less useful, the demands for ground combat forces increased, causing the redeployment of Army and Marine forces.

Leaders from the Army and Marine Corps—and a few senators—cautioned that the insurgency war was growing in strength and vigor, that ground combat forces were too few to stem the tide of the insurgence and provide security throughout the country, and that security was essential to win the support of the Iraqi people. Yet during the presidential debate of 2004, between President Bush and Democratic candidate Senator John Kerry, both men felt compelled to promise the American people that there would be no draft, that there would be no new taxes to pay for the war, and that, in fact, there would be additional tax cuts. In the midst of the global war on terrorism (GWOT), the President of the United States promised the American people they would not be called upon to fight or to sacrifice. Rather than call upon the American people to serve—an act that both Bush and Kerry considered political suicide—the Bush Administration chose to increase the burden on active duty, reserve, and National Guard personnel. The Administration extended tours of duty and rotated soldiers and marines back to Iraq after a relatively brief dwell time at home. This was a first for the United States, confirming the separation between state and nation.

In the months just prior to 9/11, the Rumsfeld Pentagon was planning to deactivate two of the Army's ten remaining divisions, in part to secure additional funding for *three* new jet fighters, one for each air service.[5] Had this reduction in force taken place, the US would have been incapable of fighting the wars in Iraq and Afghanistan, as well as defending Korea and Europe and maintaining its other commitments around the world. And while billions of dollars of airplanes sat idly on runways, soldiers purchased their own body armor, purchased communication equipment from Radio Shack, and "jerry rigged" armor plating for their military vehicles in an effort to reduce casualties.

The Bush Administration accepted greater risks in Iraq, Afghanistan, Korea, Eastern Europe, and other parts of the world by reducing troop strength. It "outsourced" the war. It employed private military firms (PMFs), American and foreign contractors and subcontractors, to provide security and support to American forces in Iraq and Afghanistan. It endeavored to replace soldiers with technology by employing UAVs, satellites, aircraft, and information technologies. It employed Special Forces to carry out missions normally conducted by much larger units. It employed surrogate forces, which held no loyalty to the United States or its political objectives. And it lived with the prospect of failure in the insurgency war in Iraq.

The United States, with all its great power, was stretched thin in the type of power applicable to the wars it was fighting in Iraq and Afghanistan. The consequence was that soldiers and marines died and were unnecessarily wounded in an insurgency war that might have been avoided had the Bush White House and the Rumsfeld Pentagon listened to the advice of Army Chief of Staff, General Eric Shinseki, and deployed sufficient numbers of troops at the outset to win the peace.[6] The most advanced aircraft known to man proved incapable of stopping an insurgent with a rifle or a suicide bomber, was incapable of discriminating between a determined enemy soldier and a frightened child, and was incapable of establishing the kinds of relationships with indigenous people required to win their confidence and support. And while the US invested billions of dollars to develop and manufacture the most advanced aircraft ever produced, to replace the most advanced aircraft ever produced, it was incapable of fighting an insurgency war, a people's war, in only one of the small countries targeted by the Bush Administration in the GWOT. And, to be sure, the world and our enemies watched, concluding that much of the power of the United States was an illusion. While there were voices that called for a more traditional response to war, voices that called for conscription and taxes to pay for the war, they were too few to form a chorus large enough and loud enough to influence policy. Out of 308 million Americans, less than one percent carried the burden of the GWOT. This is the new American practice of war, and it is not sustainable.

*   *   *   *   *

This work is divided into in three sections. The first section covers the Truman years from World War II to the end of the Korean War, the period when the traditional American practice of war was no longer capable of achieving political objectives, and a new vision of war emerged. The second section covers the Eisenhower, Kennedy, Johnson, and Nixon years—the Vietnam War Era—the period of attempted adaptation of the traditional, cultural norms to the new practices of war. The final section covers the new American practice of war, from the end of the Vietnam War to the present. The common themes that run throughout each section include national strategy, national military strategy, the defense and foreign policies of administrations, civil-military

PART I

TRADITION AND THE ENVISIONED FUTURE COLLIDE

1.
CULTURE, GENES, AND WAR

Whether one accepts or rejects Karl Wittfogel's thesis that the organization of agriculture and irrigation provided the model for military command, it is clear that disciplined, hierarchical fighting forces, once developed, were not only ideal means of aggression but imposing instruments of social control. So man's first political agenda was set; he became an imperial ape and a soldier, a conqueror and an organizer. And this, it would seem, is how and why war was born. . . . War is and always was a cultural phenomenon among humans. What we learned to do, we can choose to stop doing. . . . Our fate is in our hands. Technology, particularly nuclear technology, has rendered war, man's most powerful social institution, obsolete. If we recognize this in time, we will probably remain alive. . . .[1]

Robert L. O'Connell, "The Origins of War"

Political actors are predisposed to learn certain things over others. In the modern global system, realist folklore has provided a guide and cultural inheritance for Western states that has shaped and patterned the behavior of major states in certain situations. . . . War is an institution within the modern global political system that serves an important political function—the resolution of intractable issues. Until there is a functional equivalent to this institution, war will remain a way of handling certain situations. War and the steps and practices that lead to it must be seen as part of a culture of violence that has given birth to these practices.[2]

John A. Vasquez, *The War Puzzle*

The conduct of war is decisively influenced by culture.[3] In fact, it is impossible to understand the behavior of a nation in war without some understanding of its culture. A nation is a *cultural* entity. A state is a *political* entity. The modern nation-state combines these two forms of human organization to produce a single entity that is capable of generating enormous power. The noted anthropologist, Bronislaw Malinowski, wrote:

> In the terminology here adopted, we can say that the tribe as a cultural entity can be defined as a federation of partly independent and also coordinated component institutions. One tribe, therefore, differs from the other in the organization of the family, the local group, the clan, as well as economic, magical, and religious

teams. The identity of institutions; their potential cooperation due to community of language, tradition, and law; the interchange of services; and the possibility of joint enterprise on a large scale—these are the factors which make for the unity of a primitive, culturally homogeneous group. This, I submit, is the prototype of what we define today as nationality: a large group, unified by language, tradition, and culture. To the division as we find it between primitive culturally differentiated tribes there correspond today such divisions as between Germans and Poles, Swedes and Norwegians, Italians and French.[4]

The modern nation-state is the most powerful historic force since the decline of the absolute monarch. The concept of *nation* takes us beyond the legal considerations of the individual as a subject of states. The people of a given nation are connected by a common identity, a common culture, and it is their connectedness that creates the cohesion that makes possible total effort in war. However, the political entity, the state, can cause the cultural entity, the nation, to act in ways that are culturally irregular, and by so doing, diminish its power to achieve objectives through war. The difficult task in understanding the actions of a people in war is identifying the cultural tenets that are operative at a given time, and then which tenets exert the dominant influence. But before discussing the tenets that inform the American practice of war, a working understanding of cultural theory is necessary.

Culture

Culture has been defined in many ways. And there are a number of anthropological schools of thought with varying definitions of culture and explanations of how culture is produced and reproduced. In these pages no effort is made to delineate these arguments. However, a generally accepted working definition of culture and an explanation of how it influences behavior and is reproduced by succeeding generations is required.

Clifford Geertz, in his work *The Interpretation of Cultures*, wrote: "Believing, with Max Weber, that man is an animal suspended in webs of significance he himself has spun, I take culture to be those webs, and the analysis of it to be therefore not an experimental science in search of *law* but an interpretive one in search of *meaning*."[5] By finding meaning in the individual fibers of the web, insight into and understanding of actions and behaviors is gained. Culture has been defined in various ways:

> Culture, the total pattern of human behavior and its products embodied in thought, speech, *action*, and artifacts [technologies] and dependent upon man's capacity for learning and transmitting knowledge to succeeding generations through the use of tools, language, and systems of abstract thought; the body of customary beliefs, social forms, and material traits constituting a

distinct complex of tradition of a racial, religious, or social group . . . a complex of typical behavior or standardized social characteristics peculiar to a specific group, occupation or profession, sex, age, grade, or social class. . . .[6]

> Culture . . . refers to the ways of life of people in a given society, to their social heritage. According to the classic definition by the anthropologist Tylor, culture is "that complex whole which includes knowledge, belief, art, morals, law, custom, and any other capabilities acquired by men as a member of society." In any society there exists a body of knowledge, ideas, values (conceptions of desirability), attitudes, customs, myths, prejudices, and the like, which make up the nonmaterial aspects of the culture at that time and place.[7]

> Culture refers to the socially transmitted habits of mind, traditions, and preferred methods of operations that are more or less specific to a particular geographically based security community. Culture may be qualified for more precise usage, as in strategic culture or political culture. . . . Strategic culture is the result of opportunities, of resources, of the skill with which those opportunities and resources have been managed, and of the lessons which a society decides its unfolding history should teach. To a considerable degree societies are prisoners of their past. Policymakers have been educated both formally and by life experiences in their particular society to expect certain relationships generally to hold true. . . .[8]

While these definitions are useful, they fall short, because they fail to explain how culture influences behavior. Pierre Bourdieu's *Outline of a Theory of Practice* is useful in this regard.[9] In his work, each individual is an *agent*. Agents interact in societies using accepted *practices*, actions that have specific objectives and meaning. *Practices* are based on culturally accepted *strategies* for operating in a particular environment at a particular time. Practice, then, is the objectification of a selected strategy. Strategies are a function of social *structures*, sets and systems of norms of thought that have historical context and content. Structures help human beings make sense of their environment. When faced with a given structure people select and employ a strategy or strategies that are culturally acceptable and achieve the desired result. History, the physical environment, and technologies determine the content of structures. Successful practices are reproduced when confronted with objective conditions, in a particular environment, that fit into identifiable structures that have been culturally learned. In the mind, the objective conditions are placed into familiar structures, which enable people to act appropriately, that is, to select the most fitting strategy, and then to put it into practice.

However, agents do not simply reproduce practices based on the objective world, the structures they elicit, and the accepted strategies. They sometimes employ culturally unacceptable strategies, adapt strategies to nuances in the environment, and improvise new strategies, which result in new practices. Bourdieu refers to this ability to organize strategies, to adapt, innovate, and improvise as the *habitus*. The habitus is a cognitive process that identifies strategies and reproduces practices based on the objective perceptions of the real world. It produces variations of practices and strategies based on the variations and nuances of the objective world, the degree of individual inculcation of particular structures, the degree to which a selected strategy achieves the results desired, the willingness and motivation to improvise, and the unique make-up of each individual. However, unless one of these factors shifts significantly, agents tend to reproduce successful strategies and practices that fit the known structures.

Structures are identified in the environment all around us. They operate at different levels of consciousness. Some structures form durable dispositions that cause practices that are a function of unintentional thought. Bourdieu explained:

> The habitus, the durably installed generative principle of regulated improvisations, produces practices ... while adjusting to the demands inscribed as objective potentialities in the situation, as defined by the cognitive and motivating structures making up the habitus.... The habitus is the source of these series of moves which are objectively organized as strategies without being the product of a genuine strategic intention ...[10]

For example, the construct "manhood" consists of multiple structures that operate at numerous levels

of thought, which form a complex web that inform men of the expected strategies and practices, and motivate them to select the appropriate strategy and reproduce those practices acceptable to the society. These practices and strategies are reproduced at various levels of thought. For example, one structure of the construct manhood is "honor." Bourdieu observed:

> ... the point of honour is a permanent disposition, embedded in the agents' very bodies in the form of mental dispositions, schemes of perception and thought, extremely general in their applications ... and also, at a deeper level, in the form of bodily postures and stances, ways of standing, sitting, looking, speaking, or walking. What is called the *sense of honour* is nothing other than a cultivated disposition, inscribed in the body schema and in the schema of thought, which enables each agent to engender all the practices consistent with the logic of challenge and riposte....[11]

Thus, at one level, the sense of honor motivates behaviors that are automatic responses. At another level, the sense of honor goes beyond bodily posture and way of speaking, to the decision-making process, to considerations of whether to fight, and to considerations of peace or war. American ideas about manhood, in part, shaped the American understanding about how the nation, political leaders, and soldiers should and should not act in war.

For example, Richard Maxwell Brown, in his work *No Duty to Retreat*, recorded how the myth of the "old west" influenced Dwight D. Eisenhower:

> No one more directly stated the social philosophy of standing one's ground than President Dwight D. Eisenhower in a nationally televised speech in 1953. President Eisenhower, the leader of the "Free World" in a time of cold war ... expressed the ethos of *no duty to retreat* when he informed his nationwide audience that as a boy in Abilene, Kansas, he had been reared to "prize" the code of Abilene and "our Marshal," the renowned gunfighter Wild Bill Hickok. The President still believed in that code, which, he proudly declared, was "meet anyone face to face with whom you disagree"; "if you meet him face to face and took the same risk he did, you could

get away with almost anything as long as the bullet was in the front."[12]

Eisenhower saw this as an honorable way to behave on the playground or the battlefield, and an honorable way for the nation to act in war or other international matters.[13] The history, legends, and myths of the "Old West," the Civil War, and the American Revolution are incorporated into American culture, and are passed down by individuals and institutions that shape, in part, the personalities, beliefs, ethics, and actions (practices) of men, such as Truman, MacArthur, Bush, Patton, Halsey, Powell, and other political and military leaders.

In 1893, Frederick Jackson Turner advanced the thesis that, "American social development has been continually beginning over again on the frontier. This perennial rebirth, this fluidity of American life, the expansion westward with its new opportunities, its continuous touch with the simplicity of primitive society, furnished the forces dominating American character."[14] More recently Colin Gray advanced a similar thesis:

> If the cultural and stylistic proclivities of Americans were not so important for the consideration of basic national security policy, they would be excluded from discussion here. But those policy choices *are* considered by an American people distinctive in its strategic culture from other security communities. The American people are geopolitically conditioned as Americans to think and feel in a reasonably distinctive American way about those choices. The roots of American strategic culture lie in a frontier tradition, an experience and expectation of success in national endeavors, experience with an abundance of resources for defense, a dominant political philosophy of liberal idealism, and a sense of separateness—moral and geostrategic—from the evil doings of the Old World.[15]

Gray argues that American policy choices in matters of national security cannot be understood without some understanding of American culture. Gray concludes that "all human beings are culturally educated or programmed" and that "culture embraces both ideas and behavior and that it is inescapable."[16] The word "programmed" implies that people have to act in accordance with their programming; hence, if you understand the program you can predict the behavior. But people and nations do not always act in accordance with cultural norms. People do innovate, improvise, and create; and cultural norms frequently conflict, causing a wide range of actions and the evolution of culture. (For the purposes of this study, structures that produce consistent, durable strategies are called "cultural tenets.")

Political scientists also employ anthropological methods to advance arguments on the causes and conduct of war, noting that there exists within Western nations a "culture of war." John Vasquez, in his analysis of the causes of war writes:

> The hard-liners' [agents] cognitive map of the world tends to be simple rather than complex. Hard-liners tend to be nationalistic and hold a militaristic view of the world. The hard-liner as a type is hostile toward and distrustful of the other nation, and feels unable to control events. In a crisis they are risk-takers. In personal relations they are prone to dominance. Except for the last, which is a personality characteristic, it is clear that the characteristics hard-liners share are something they have learned from their experience or imbibed from the culture around them.[17]

Hard-liners are predisposed to see specific structures in the objective environment, and are inculcated with strategies and cultural tenets that recognize war as an acceptable and possibly preferred practice. Vasquez concludes that: "hard-liners can be defined as individuals who have a personal disposition (due to their beliefs) to adopt a foreign policy that is adamant in not compromising its goals and who argue in favor of the efficacy and legitimacy of threat and force."[18]

New agents (individuals) mature in "webs" of culture. When confronted with objective events in the real world, agents from different cultures can see very different structures, and what they see will tend to limit them to specific strategies, which result in practices acceptable to their own culture. Agents learn multiple strategies and practices acceptable for success in the various structures of their society. They form cultural dispositions that inform and motivate behaviors at all levels of consciousness, and pass this culture on to the next generation. Again, consider Vasquez's analysis on the dissemination of culture:

> To determine whether a domestic political context is initially more favorable to the influence of hard-liners or accommodationists, all one has to do is look at the "lessons of the past" that prevail in the national political culture. This is not a difficult task since these lessons are reflected in the popular media and the publications of the intelligentsia. The crucial question is: where do these lessons come from? It seems that in all societies these lessons are derived from the most traumatic experiences that the society as a whole goes through. For most, this is the last major war. Subsequent events, particularly more limited wars, will affect those lessons, but for the generation that lived through the traumatic experience, only another major war will lead to an opportunity for rethinking the lessons. Using a general learning model … one can assume that these lessons will be passed on to the next generation through socialization and will be accepted, although with less emotional attachment.[19]

Culture makes the objective world comprehensible by inculcating structures and constructs. It influences behavior by providing agents with strategies and establishing boundaries between the normal and the abnormal, between the permissible and the impermissible. It makes possible more complete communication than is possible with language alone. Demeanor, disposition, facial expressions, dress, and other nonverbal forms of communication are culturally learned, and often communicate more than words. Culture creates cohesion between people of same community, and barriers between people of other cultures, other communities. Culture, in part, creates the mental disposition that enables some people to sacrifice for the good of the larger cultural unit—the tribe, the nation, and/or the service. Culture can be studied, enabling outsiders to better comprehend the behaviors of a particular people or nation.

War is a series of structures that together form the construct of "war" in the minds of agents before it is objectified as actions and practices in the real world. It is a complex web of countless culturally regular tenets that generate specific strategies and motivate specific practices. The construct informs the various agents—men, women, the aged, and the young—of what is expected of them. The construct of war involves additional complexities, because it does not stand alone; it is intermingled with other constructs, such as manhood, citizenship, and other complex concepts. Obviously, determining the influence of culture on war is an exceedingly difficult task, not easily reduced to useable paradigms. However, some interpretation of culture is absolutely necessary to understand behavior, practices, and strategies, as well as the continuity of practices and strategies among a given people over time. In other words, cultural comprehension is a prerequisite for any in-depth understanding of war.

* * * * *

Military organizations develop doctrines and technologies to employ their forces in battles and campaigns in ways that are culturally regular and achieve the desired results. Nations recruit soldiers in ways that are culturally regular and produce sufficiently effective fighting forces that produce the desired results. The strategies by which forces are employed in sustained wars require the willing support of the people and have to be consistent with the cultural norms of the society and to achieve the results desired by the people. Doctrines, recruiting systems, and military strategies that are culturally regular, that repeatedly fail to achieve the desired results, motivate change. Failure motivates improvisation, adaptation, and/or innovation: the development of new, or the amendment of accepted strategies and practices. Major changes in strategies and practices are caused by major shifts in structures and constructs.

During World War II, and in the post-war period, significant changes in technologies and national strategies called into question culturally regular, accepted American doctrines, national strategies, military strategies, and recruiting systems. These major constructs of the American practice of war that held two centuries of cultural content were exposed to revolutionary new technologies, a radically changed foreign policy, and a new environment that engendered constant high levels of threat. As a consequence, the American cognitive processes incorporated a new practice of war.

Axioms of Cultural Theory

For the purposes of this study a number of axioms deduced from cultural theory require clarification.

—*Culture is manifested in very concrete ways that can decisively influence the outcome of war.* Victor Davis Hanson observed that:

> The culture in which militaries fight determines whether thousands of mostly innocent young men are alive or rotting after their appointed hour of battle. Abstractions like capitalism or civic militarism are hardly abstract at all when it comes to battle, but rather concrete realities that ultimately determined . . . whether Athenian cobblers and tanners could return home in safety after doing their butchery at Salamis or were to wash up in chunks on the shores of Attica.[20]

—*Culture is timeless and ubiquitous, existing in and influencing all nations at all times.* John Lynn emphasized the uniqueness of each nation-state: "A cultural interpretation is most likely to grant individuals and peoples their full personal, social, and cultural character."[21] Each nation is unique, with varying abilities to adapt, adopt, and learn. Geography and history insure that no two nations have identical constructs of war, that no two nations comprehend war in exactly the same way.

Hanson advanced the argument that there exists a uniquely Western way of war, born of the campaigns of the ancient Greeks, and that the superior performance of Western nations in war over centuries is the primary reason for the dominance of Western culture and Western civilization. He identified the attributes of Western culture that produced superior performance:

> . . . the Greeks fought much differently than their adversaries and that such unique Hellenic characteristics of battle—a sense of personal freedom, superior discipline, matchless weapons, egalitarian camaraderie, individual initiative, constant tactical adaptation and flexibility, preference for

shock battle of heavy infantry—were themselves the murderous dividends of Hellenic culture at large. The peculiar way Greeks killed grew out of consensual government, equality among the middling classes, civilian audit of military affairs, and politics apart from religion, freedom and individualism, and rationalism.[22]

The American way of war is an outgrowth of the Western way of war. Hanson's thesis supports that of Russell Weigley, who noted: "The frontier interpretation of American history applies only minimally to war; American ways of war were offshoots of European ways of war, and American strategic thought was therefore a branch of European strategic thought."[23] While Weigley disagrees with Turner, Gray, and others on the influence of the frontier on American culture, he and Hanson have identified the contributions of Europe to American thinking and conduct of war.[24] The frontier experience, the Western military tradition, and numerous other factors influenced the American practice of war. While common elements can be found in the American and German practices, a complete description of the attributes of each nation would show the uniqueness of each, as a function of their individual histories, military experiences, geographic circumstances, long-held political institutions and objectives, roles in world affairs, and the specific evolution of each culture.

Again, these theories are not limited to Western culture. Norvell De Atkine, in an essay entitled, "Why Arab Armies Lose Wars" and Kenneth Pollack, in a comprehensive study, *Arabs at War*, concluded that Arab culture decisively limits the military effectiveness of Arab states. Atkine wrote:

> Mindful of walking through a minefield of past errors and present cultural sensibilities, I offer some assessment of the role of culture in the military training of Arabic-speaking people. . . . It may well be that these seemingly permanent attributes result from a culture that engenders subtlety, indirection, and dissimulation in personal relationships [that, in part, explains] why Arab armies lose wars.[25]

Atkine should have specified: "lose conventional wars." Pollack wrote: "certain patterns of behavior fostered by the dominant Arab culture were the most important factors contributing to limiting the military effectiveness of Arab armies and air forces from 1945 to 1991...."[26] Conversely, it can be argued that tenets of Arab culture enhance the ability of Muslim people to fight insurgency wars and to employ terrorism. Pollack later wrote:

> Four areas of military effectiveness stand out as consistent and crippling problems for Arab forces: poor tactical leadership, poor information management, poor weapons handling, and poor maintenance. These complications were present in every single Arab army and air force between 1948 and 1991. All had significant and identifiable effects on the performance of Arab armed forces. These were, without question, the principal sources of Arab misfortune in war during this period of history. The lack of initiative, improvisation, adaptability, flexibility, independent judgment, willingness to maneuver, and ability to integrate the various combat arms effectively meant that Arab armies and air forces were regularly outfought by their adversaries.[27]

The inability of Arab nations to fight conventional wars against Western nations, and their repeated failures, caused them to search for new military and political doctrines and strategies.[28] Terrorism and insurgency are alternative, unconventional strategies for war, and guerrilla warfare and terrorism are operational and tactical doctrines. These strategies and doctrines have been adopted by some Arab nations, in part, because of their inability to succeed in conventional war against Western nations. Arab nations have had to adapt.

Nations have varying abilities to adapt, yet they can never escape their culture. It is impossible to ignore the fact that the Japanese adopted many of the attributes of the Western practice of war, demonstrating their mastery at Pearl Harbor, in the Philippines, and in Singapore. But, it is equally impossible to understand the suicidal banzai and kamikaze attack tactics—a horrendous misuse of human resources—without some understanding of Japanese culture.[29] While the Japanese adopted Western technologies and ways of fighting, they did so in a distinctly Japanese way. And while the Japanese followed

paradigms provided by Western states, they ultimately could not escape centuries of cultural learning.

—*Culture is not static, and all historical events are not equal.* Certain events exert greater, more lasting, and more persistent influence than others. The American practice of war—like the culture that formed it—is continuously acquiring and discarding. John Shy observed that the "... explanatory importance of events should be reckoned not by *proximity*, but by *priority* in historical time."[30] Thus, certain battles and wars have priority in historical time, and the learning that took place during them "rippled" through time, influencing behavior and decisions in the present.

American beliefs about war are a function of the extraordinary events that left deep scars in the nation, that required enormous sacrifices, that consumed vast resources, and that produced significant casualties directly touching the lives of numerous individual families and communities. Hence, the American experience in the Civil War exerted a more comprehensive, intensive, and sustained influence on American thinking about the conduct of war than the more recent American experiences in insurgent, guerrilla warfare in the Philippines War (1899–1902) or attrition, trench warfare in World War I (1917–1918). Aspects of Civil War thinking were reproduced during World War II, reinforcing tenets learned a century before.

Traumatic events in the life of a nation can produce rapid changes in cultural thinking about war. The effects of Hiroshima and the Tet Offensive were felt decades later, and are still creating waves of influence. Both were reinforced, *not* by similar historical events, but by other cultural tenets, which strengthened their influence. Both events, in very different ways, damaged the martial spirit of the American people, and influenced subsequent decisions on war. The spirit of a nation and its attitudes and willingness to engage in war can change significantly in relatively short periods of time, particularly if they are reinforced by other cultural tenets.

—*The armed forces of nation-states have to conduct significant wars, limited and total, in ways that are culturally regular.* Doctrine is defined as the "authoritative fundamental principles by which military forces guide their actions in support of objectives." Doctrine is a modern concept in military literature, but it is as old as war, existing throughout most history without discussion or delineation. The vast majority of the people of any given nation cannot define or describe the doctrines that make up the operational art or their armed forces. Nevertheless, these doctrines have to be culturally regular for the people to accept them. Army operational and tactical doctrines and national, strategic doctrines that deviate too far from culturally accepted norms do not retain the support of the people. Doctrines are a function of technology, resources, geography, national military strategy, historical experiences in war, service culture and traditions, individual genius, and national cultures. Doctrines are prevalent at the strategic, operational, and tactical levels of war. Each service of armed forces has it own operational and tactical doctrine.

—*In war it is necessary for a nation to understand the tenets, dynamics, frictions, divisions, and exigencies of its own primary culture to maximize its power.* For example, because cultures vary significantly among nations and within states, the martial spirit is not constant, and the martial spirit can be diminished or enhanced by numerous factors.[31] The willingness of the people of a nation to risk their lives in battle varies from nation to nation and war to war, and it can be argued that certain cultures have maintained through the centuries a stronger martial spirit than other nations. The frequency of war, the type of war, geographic circumstance, the wealth of the nation, the quality of life, the political system, and numerous other factors influence the martial spirit of a nation. The martial spirit may or may not explain success or failure in war. However, it is a necessary element to fight war, and one of the factors necessary to generate combat power. Ancient Sparta, medieval Prussia, and modern Germany have historically been considered nations with a strong martial spirit.[32] While the martial spirit has not always brought these states military or political success, it was nevertheless an important constituent in their ability to fight. As long as wars are made up of battles that require men to enter the battlefield, the martial spirit will be an essential component of a nation's ability to fight a war. Hence, political leaders need to understand and protect the martial spirit of its people.

—*Political leaders and governments can act intentionally and unintentionally in ways that are inconsistent with the accepted cultural norms of its people, thereby diminishing their capacity to make war.* The state and the nation are not always in agreement. The American conduct of World War II was culturally regular, consistent with American belief, expectations, values, ethics, attitudes, and institutional norms. The *state*, the political entity, and the *nation*, the cultural entity, were in agreement. The American conduct of the Vietnam War was not culturally regular. For example, a strategically defensive ground war was not in keeping with the American understanding of war. There was a considerable divide between the state and the nation over the conduct of the Vietnam War. The problem is to identify the cultural norms exerting the greatest influence on the behavior of a people during a given war. The more limited the war, the greater the possible deviation from cultural norms.

—*The cultural tenets active in a given nation to some degree conflict and reinforce other active tenets. Cultural tenets operate with varying degrees of strength, and some tenets are dormant until specific events activate them.* Michael Desch, in an essay entitled "Explaining the Gap: Vietnam, the Republicanization of the South, and the End of the Mass Army," wrote:

> ROTC programs have been discontinued at a number of elite schools, primarily in the Northeast, but many new programs have been established in other schools, primarily in the South, where 49 percent of Army, 41 percent of Air Force, and 41 percent of Navy ROTC programs are currently located.... The net effect was to produce an ROTC cadet pool that was more Southern and more likely to produce career officers than before. There is abundant evidence that graduates of ROTC programs are very different from the rest of civilian society.[33]

In 2001 the majority of US military officers came from the eleven states of the south. Arguably, southern culture placed greater premium on military service than the regional cultures of the northeast or midwest. The cultural tenets that produce soldiers conflict with other more salient tenets prevalent, for example, in the northeast states. However, the picture is more complex. Modern Western nation-states have evolved into multi-cultural states, with varying values, ethics, and beliefs.

—*Within a state there can exist multiple nations, cultural entities, and the greater the fragmentation of the political body, the state, the less able it is to conduct total war or significant limited wars.* The former Yugoslavia was a state comprising many nations that almost immediately went to war with one another in 1991 following the destruction of the ruling power that had kept them peaceful, the Soviet Union. Iraq is a state comprising three major nations, the Kurds, Sunnis, and Shia. The US is also a state with many nations. Michael Weiss, in his work *The Clustered World*, observed:

> For a nation that's always valued community, this breakup of the mass market into balkanized population segments is as momentous as the collapse of Communism. . . . Today, the country's new motto should be "*E pluribus pluriba*": "Out of many, many." Evidence of the nation's accelerated fragmentation is more than anecdotal. According to the geodemographers . . . American society today is composed of sixty-two distinct lifestyle types—a 55 percent increase over the forty segments that defined the U.S. populace during the 1970s and 80s. . . . These lifestyles represent America's modern tribes, sixty-two distinct population groups each with its own set of values, culture and means of coping with today's problems. . . . Increasingly, America is a fractured landscape, its people partitioned into dozens of cultural enclaves, its ideals reflected through differing prisms of experience. . . . This process has left too many Americans alienated from each other, divided by a cultural chasm.[34]

The American war effort in Iraq in 2003 was not a national effort. The military cluster fought the war. This process of partitioning into clusters that form enclaves in all parts of the country has been under way for decades, and because of the great mobility of the American people, enclaves with cultural values more like those of the northeast can also be found in the suburbs of Dallas or Houston.[35] While the breakup of America into enclaves is evident, regional and national core cultures still exert influences, albeit sometimes not as much influence as the culture of a particular cluster. More traditional, core cultural tenets are held with varying degree of significance in various clusters.

—*Organizations with long life spans, such as the US Army and Navy, possess subcultures that influence behavior and the decision-making of indoctrinated individuals.* Soldiers and sailors develop identities that are in part a function of the culture and history of the service in which they are trained and indoctrinated. The officer corps of the services were, and are, required to inculcate the culture of their service in order to succeed. The more closely agents inculcate the structures and practice the core strategies of their service, the greater their chances for successful careers.

—*To maximize a nation's combat power, that nation must understand the culture of its enemy.* The consequence for failing to understand your enemy's practice of war can be defeat. The Japanese attack on Pearl Harbor demonstrated a total failure to comprehend American culture. The attack, while a tactical success, was strategically a major blunder. It created the cohesion necessary for the American people to produce a total effort in war. Likewise, American political and military leadership demonstrated little understanding of the cultural tenets that influenced the North Vietnamese and Viet Cong during the Vietnam War, nor did they understand the cultural tenets that motivated the actions of the Iraqi people. Norvell De Atkine noted:

> But how does one integrate the study of culture into military training? At present, it has hardly any role. Paul M. Belbutowski, a scholar and former member of the US Delta Force, succinctly stated a deficiency in our own military education system: "Culture, comprised of all that is vague and intangible, is not generally integrated into strategic planning except at the most superficial level." And yet it is precisely "all that is vague and intangible" which defines low-intensity conflicts. The Vietnamese Communists did not fight the war the United States had trained for, nor did the Chechens and Afghans fight the war for which the Russians had prepared.[36]

—*A nation's practice of war is a cultural inheritance informing servicemen—not determining—how they ought to act in battle, and how the nation, the people, and their political leadership ought to conduct war.* Only culturally cohesive nation-states are capable of fighting total war. Conformity to accepted national strategies and doctrines for war is more important in total war, where the mobilization of enormous national resources is required, and hence public support is required, than in limited war. Most of America's small wars did not require the mobilization of significant national resources, or the support of the American people. They were carried out by the regular Army or Marine Corps, and attracted relatively little public attention. Hence, the military services and political leaders have conducted all types of campaigns and small wars. However, the more protracted the war, the more national resources required, the higher the casualties, the more intense the fighting, the greater the public awareness and attention. In essence, the more total the war, the greater is the pressure to reproduce core cultural strategies and practices that have traditionally produced successful outcomes.

Genes and Culture

Culture influences the range between the permissible and the impermissible. Genetics determine the range between the possible and the impossible. Genetics and culture combine to establish parameters of behavior. In the lifetime of an individual, their genetic makeup will not change. However, because culture is not static, the parameters are always being redefined to some degree. Hence, the ability of nation-states to produce combat soldiers at any given time is fixed by nature/genetics and nurture/culture.

The United States has been little concerned with its ability to produce combat soldiers, assuming that all American men could serve equally well. This, however, is a dangerous fallacy. All men cannot serve effectively as soldiers in combat, a fact that is contrary to the American cultural tenets about manhood, equality, and military service—tenets that had their origins in the formative period of the nation's history, when it was believed that citizen militia possessed the wherewithal to fight and win wars against French and British regular soldiers.

While geneticists have shown that 99.9 percent of human DNA, the building blocks for life on Earth, is the same for the 7 billion people on Earth, that 0.01 percent difference produces enormous variations and enormous diversity.[37] It can be argued that from this diversity individuals exhibit abilities, skills, and talents

at slightly different or unique levels of proficiency from other human beings. Slight differences in skills, types of intelligence, ambition, instincts, tolerance of conditions, acuity of eyesight, reflexes, speed, musculature, height, and other human qualities produce enormously different outcomes in the physical world. These variations in human abilities can make the difference between life and death. Everyone, regardless of cultural tenets, cannot serve effectively as combat soldiers, just as everyone cannot play in the National Football League or participate in Ph.D. programs.

The ability of nations to produce human beings capable of becoming combat soldiers is a function of two related factors, *nature* and *nurture*. Which factor produces the greatest influence has been debated for decades. However, today we know that the brain is not a clean slate at birth, waiting to receive structures and strategies, and that nature is greatly influenced by the quality and character of nurturing. In other words the hardwiring of the brain, like the physical development of the body, is not fixed when a child is born. The quality of nurturing influences the quality of the final product. Consider the words of the Nobel laureate, Francis Crick:

> The genes we receive from our parents have, over many millions of years been influenced by the experience of our distant ancestors. These genes, and the process directed by them before birth, lay down much of the structure of the parts of our brain. The brain at birth . . . is not a *tabula rasa* but an elaborate structure with many of its parts already in place. Experience then tunes [introduces structures and strategies] this rough-and-ready apparatus until it can do a precision job. . . . Thus the mature brain is the product of both Nature and Nurture.[38]

Nurturing completes the hardwiring of the brain. Hence, the cultural norms of the civilization in which an individual is nurtured and matures influence, in many ways, his or her ways of thinking, dispositions, attitudes, abilities, and beliefs. An individual born with a brain that had the qualities of Einstein, who was nurtured in a remote tribe in the Amazon, would never have developed the abilities or the disposition to produce works comparable to Einstein's theories on the makeup of the universe. The mental and physical development of human beings is influenced by the quality of nurturing. Nurturing, in part, forms character, establishing the range of the permissible and the impermissible, likes and dislikes.

Given the new knowledge available through the science of genetics, it has been argued that there are genes that predispose people for certain behaviors, for example, ambition, shyness, aggressiveness, and risk-seeking. People such as Bill Clinton, Condoleezza Rice, Martha Stewart, and Oprah Winfrey are said to possess the ambition genes.[39] Similarly, it is clear that some people are willing and able to take more and greater risks than other people. The "risk-seeking genes" or "novelty-seeking genes" produce a chemical reaction in the brain that creates positive responses under conditions of risk. Risk-seeking genes produce individuals willing to put themselves in harm's way, willing to venture across unexplored oceans, into space, or to the moon. Such individuals have been a necessary element in human progress. When the war trumpets sound, some individuals run toward the sound, while others run away from it. Those that run away tend to be endowed with "anxiety-seeking genes" that create negative responses under conditions of risk. David Hackworth, a highly decorated veteran of the Korean and Vietnam Wars, in reference to the Korean War wrote:

> My adrenaline was running fast and I wanted to be where the action was. I couldn't stop talking about it. Every day I'd warn Prazenka to treat me nice—I was going to Korea and I might just give him all my medals when I came back. I was ready to try out my warrior wings. I wanted to prove myself, I wanted to win the Combat Infantryman's Badge (CIB), I just wanted to go—so badly it hurt.[40]

Another veteran of the Korean War, Henry G. Gole, wrote: "I left college to volunteer for the draft in 1952 because I wanted to be the Audie Murphy of the Korean War." After several months of combat experience he observed:

> I went on over twenty combat patrols that either were wildly exciting or stupidly executed. I did not think much of the leadership skills or guts of my platoon leader nor of the platoon sergeant,

but perhaps they were told to avoid casualties. In any event, they always played it safe. In my own case, I think I was suspect for being too "gung-ho." *It is my impression that some 10 percent of the troops*—the Audie Murphy aspirants—shared my views. The majority of the troop, including the leadership, concentrated on survival and getting home.[41]

Gole and Hackworth possessed risk-seeking genes.[42] The number of genetic risk-takers in a given population is probably a constant. While the exact percentage is unknown, 10 percent appears to be a reasonable estimate. Since we are working with a sequence of genes, not a single gene, there are degrees of risk-takers. However, a certain threshold is required to take that final step onto the battlefield where people are being killed. And, for that percentage of a population whose genetic makeup puts them near the boundary, culture can make the difference, pushing them to one side or the other.

It is probable that throughout the long history of warfare, in the vast majority of wars, less than 15 percent of a given population took part in the actual fighting. That percentage has probably remained fairly consistent among nations, and racial and ethnic groups, until the nineteenth and twentieth centuries, when modern means of transportation made it possible for large groups of people to migrate. Those most willing to cross oceans into an uncertain world, to migrate, were the risk-takers. The movement of people around the planet and the creation of nations comprising many races and ethnic groups have probably altered the percentage of risk-takers in some nation-states.

No single ability produces good combat soldiers. More is required than the risk-seeking genes, such as the ability to live with ambiguity and uncertainty; the ability to tolerate discomfort, exposure to the weather, and harsh living conditions; and the ability to serve as part of a team. Thus, the picture is more complex than indicated above. However, the risk-seeking genes are absolutely necessary for individuals to risk their lives in battle.

If modern man, *homo sapiens*, has lived in tribal societies for the vast majority of his roughly 150,000 to 200,000 years of existence, it can be argued that human beings are genetically predisposed to perform certain, specific functions necessary for the survival of the *tribe*, and by extension the survival of humanity.[43] Thus, it can be argued that those with the anxiety-seeking genes are equally as important to the survival of humanity as those with the risk-seeking genes. If it is accepted that the personalities of people are influenced by their genetic makeup, it can be argued that there is such a thing as a "natural born leader," better able to direct the energy of people; a born politician, better able to bring about compromise; a born inventor, better able to create tools; a born hunter, better able to sense and react to the movement of prey; and a born soldier, better able to risk his life in battle and to kill other men.

Individuals, no matter how great their talents, could not live without the benefit of the combined talents of the tribe.[44] Humans in tribal societies had to adapt to the various roles mandatory for the continued existence of the community.[45] It is, thus, reasonable to conclude, given our current understanding on the origins of humanity and civilization, that people have a genetic predisposition for certain, necessary roles in communities. It is the combined talents of the members of a community that insured the survival of the tribe. An absence of toolmakers or hunters or compromisers jeopardized the survival of the tribe. Given human nature, soldiers were absolutely essential to the survival of any grouping of human beings.

Genetic factors go beyond mental disposition, preferences, and capacity for certain types of skills. Professional football and basketball players are born with the physical attributes necessary to play these sports at the highest level. People without these physical attributes, no matter how hard they try, will never be basketball players in the NBA. Individuals with "fast-twitch" muscles that allow for rapid acceleration, with high tolerances for pain, a keen sense of smell, great peripheral vision, rapid response reflexes and other such attributes make better hunters than the majority of a population. Consider these words written just after the end of hostilities in 1946:

Another personnel situation peculiar to the ground forces arose in 1943 when it became apparent that conditions under which ground soldiers trained in this country and under which

they lived and fought overseas were too demanding physically for many men. AGF [Army Ground Forces] recommended that only the most physically able inductees be assigned to ground arms in the future. The system known as the Physical Profile Plan was adopted and AGF received eighty-two per cent of its personnel allocation from the top category of physically qualified inductees.[46]

Combat soldiers required considerable endurance. While the range of potential soldiers is not nearly as narrow as the range of individuals who can play in the NFL, it is a fact that not everyone can perform well as a soldier.

Nurturing in a given culture influences the production of combat soldiers as well. In other words, society and culture can suppress or enhance the tendencies of individuals with risk-seeking genes. Individuals with risk-seeking genes can be taught and encouraged to *not* take risks, "to play it safe." And individuals with risk-seeking genes can be taught and encouraged to take greater risks. In other words, individual human beings, properly motivated, are capable to some degree of overcoming nature, just as they are able to overcome culture. However, while culture influences behavior, suppressing or enhancing certain genetic predisposition, it cannot completely override the genetic attributes of an individual. Culture can influence those who are partially qualified, pushing them one way or the other. One World War II study on "war neuroses" concluded that:

The individual's personality can be fortified by training, modified by experience, weakened or strengthened by leadership. But it can never be completely changed. The reaction of the individual soldier to the situation of battle will be either normal, when he carries on his duties regardless of fear of discomfort, or abnormal, when he develops neurosis and became a psychiatric casualty. . . . Many of the infantrymen should never have been assigned to a combat unit. Because of emotional instability, or physical defects, they were certain to crack up in battle. Medical and administrative channels were ineffective in removing these men, largely because of scarcity of replacements.[47]

Lord Moran in his study, *Anatomy of Courage*, provided the following insight:

When an army is being trained to fight it must begin by weeding out those whose character or temperament makes them incapable of fighting. Ideally such men would be rejected by a recruiting board before they became part of the Service. If that is found to be impossible the army must fall back on daily observation of the recruit during training to detect signs of instability. If both fail to expose the latent weakness of the young soldier it is left to war itself to strip the mask from the man of straw, which it will do with a quite ruthless precision of its own.[48]

Charles B. MacDonald, a combat veteran of World War II and student of warfare, wrote:

It's easy to get out of combat even after you're there. Lag behind in an attack; get lost on a patrol; feign combat fatigue (they're suckers for that one); or better still, just refuse to fight. What the Articles of War can do to you isn't necessarily dying. Besides, after the war, emotions will cool and you'll get off light.[49]

And, Audie Murphy, the Army's most highly decorated World War II soldier, wrote:

Olsen is the first to crack up. He throws his arms around the company commander, crying hysterically, "I can't take any more." The harassed captain tries to calm him, but Olsen will not stop bawling. So he is sent to the rear, and we watch him go with hatred in our eyes. "If I ever throw a wingding like that, shoot me," says, Kerrigan. "Gladly," I reply. "In North Africa, I thought he was one tough boy." "Yeah. He threw his weight around plenty." "He seemed to be everything the War Department was looking for. He was my idea of a real soldier. . . ." "Yeah. I'll never judge a man by his appearance again."[50]

Eisenhower, while inculcated with the American beliefs about manhood and the tenet that all men were created equal, nevertheless, recognized the inequality of war:

Early in the North African campaign it became evident that the emotional stamina and spiritual strength of the individual soldier were as important in battle success as his weapon and training. Combat neuroses among the troops developed on an alarming scale as the intensity of our offensives increased.

He further noted that: "In the rear, hospitals and camp facilities were necessarily set aside for those suffering from self-inflicted wounds, from hysteria and psychoneuroses and from venereal disease, sometimes, according to the doctors, deliberately contracted."[51] In the weeks and days prior to the Normandy invasion thousands of men eliminated themselves, one way or another, from the invasion force. Some individuals were psychologically injured before they entered the battlefield. Simply waiting for the Normandy invasion, the ambiguity and uncertainty caused unsustainable fear and mental breakdowns.[52] These, however, are not the stories people want to hear or read. These are not the stories that form myths and legends of nations; hence, people always have a distorted understanding of war and manhood.

Killing extracts something from men of conscience. And risking one's life erodes something in men. Combined, they create a disease. It can be argued that combat causes the development of a disease, currently called "post-traumatic stress disorder." In the past it was called "shell shock." Few men are completely immune to the disease. Others take a long time for its effects to develop and emerge, and still others cannot tolerate exposure at all. Thus, the selection process should ideally eliminate those individuals with low tolerance to the disease, either for genetic or cultural reasons. Cultural norms, however, frequently preclude individuals from acknowledging low tolerance, and individuals may not fully understand their level of intolerance until they are in battle. Such was the case with Olsen. Those who recognize their intolerance find ways to avoid serving in the armed forces, or in combat arms, or in combat. As a rule, and there are exceptions, men who do not want to serve in combat find ways to avoid it.[53]

From the American Revolution to the present very few men have had to serve in combat. There have always been ways to get out of serving in the armed forces during war. And if service could not be avoided, serving in the Army or Marine Corps, where typically 80 to 90 percent of the deaths and casualties took place, could be avoided by joining the Navy or Air Force. And if service in the Army could not be avoided, then there were always means to avoid serving in combat units—most occupations in the army are not combat related. And, if for some reason an individual wishing to avoid combat was not able to avoid serving in combat units, then once in a combat zone there were always ways to avoid fighting. Finally, once in combat, there were always ways for an individual to make himself unwanted or unavailable.

The process of enculturation takes place each day of an individual's life, expanding and/or diminishing his or her range of possibilities. To produce men with the wherewithal to defend the nation, the Army and Marine Corps are always engaged in a process of transculturation: "a process of cultural transformation marked by the influx of new culture elements and the loss or alteration of existing ones."[54] Consider the words of Lieutenant General Victor H. Krulak, USMC:

> The third thing they [the American people] believe about the Marines is that our Corps is downright good for the manhood of our country; that the Marines are masters of a form of unfailing alchemy which converts unoriented youths into proud, self-reliant stable citizens—citizens into whose hands the nation may safely be entrusted.[55]

Marine Corps culture transformed individuals, developing, enhancing, diminishing, and eliminating certain traits and qualities. Krulak believed that the qualities the Marine Corps brought out in men were good for the nation. Army culture, while different from Marine culture, put men through a similar process. Because culture is not static, a nation's ability to produce combat soldiers and marines changes at a rate consistent with the rate of significant cultural change.

War and Human Nature

War is primal, a function of human nature and the human condition. War is an historical force, and

arguably, a necessary force in human development. War has influenced every aspect of human life. It is said that "war is an ugly thing," but one cannot find a nation or state that was not shaped by it. The political geography of the earth is primarily a function of war. War is a destructive force, but it is also a creative force. War has destroyed nations, states, and empires, and reformed them. War has configured and reconfigured the borders between states. War has destroyed political and social systems and created the conditions for new systems to grow and develop. War created the conditions under which the vast majority of the peoples have lived throughout recorded history, including the city-states of ancient Greece; the Empire of Rome; the imperialist systems the British and French imposed on Africa, the Middle East, India, and Southeast Asia; the Communist system of the People's Republic of China and the former Soviet Union; the constitutional democracy of Japan and Germany; and the American "superpower" empire. Every major political, social, and economic system on Earth has been shaped in multiple ways by war.

War causes adaptation. War created the conditions for great advances in technology, including ships capable of traversing oceans, buildings capable of sustaining hurricane force winds, and vehicles capable of orbiting planets. Nuclear energy, jet and rocket propulsion systems, antibiotic drugs, the Internet, and numerous other technologies are primarily a function of war. Without war men would not traverse oceans in hours, travel in space, or microwave popcorn.

War is also a social force. War turned Prussians into Germans, peasants into Frenchmen, slaves into citizens, Arabs into Palestinians, and Virginians into Americans. War formulated, defined, and structured paradigms of human behavior. Constructs such as manhood and patriotism were formed and reformed, defined and redefined, through war. War placed real value and meaning on concepts such as duty, honor, freedom, and equality. War created the myths, legends, and symbols that informed and motivated the actions of people. War is a major historical force, destroying, forming, creating, recreating, changing, and influencing almost every facet of human life. If there is one eternal force that governs the interactions of human, political bodies on Earth, it is war and the constant change it creates. All people ultimately have recourse to war, and the life of every human on Earth has been, and will continue to be, influenced by war.

A long view of history, a study of war, and an objective, honest look at unchanging facets of human nature and the human condition reveal a number of facts:

First, as Plato has told us, "Only the dead have seen the end of war." War is a function of human nature and the human conditions. It will come to an end only when humanity comes to an end. To be sure, Western democracies will again fight total wars, ones which will require the active, willing support and participation of the people. Democracy, capitalism, and free trade have not, and will never, eliminate war. As long as there are weak and strong, and as long as people covet, there will be war.[56] The question for each nation throughout history has not been whether there will be another war, but when war came, whether the people, their government, and their armed forces were ready to face the challenges; whether there was sufficient will, spirit, cohesion, resolve, love of country, selflessness, and trained men ready to meet the crisis; and whether there was sufficient technological achievement and production capability to sustain the nation during the period of crisis.

Second, nations and states rise and fall through war. The United States became a "superpower" through war, and has retained that status because of war. And it is a fact that the United States will not always be a superpower, or even the dominant power on Earth. Like Rome and Britain, it too will ultimately be diminished, and war will be one of the major factors that cause or influence its decline.

Third, man, not the machines that men make, is the dominant weapon on the planet. The human body is the most resilient, precision weapon ever produced. The human brain, spirit, will, and ability to bond with other human beings and courageously sacrifice even one's self for the good of the community are the attributes that make man the dominant weapon on Earth. Humans are the most adaptable instrument and animal on Earth. The human ability to adapt—physically,

psychologically, intellectually, and emotionally—has made humanity the most successful species. And while war motivates men to adapt by creating and producing tools and machines, it is man himself—not his tools or machines—that is the ultimate instrument of war.

Fourth, humans are social animals that form the bonds of cohesion that make war possible. Political and/or cultural bodies make war. War is the function of the combined effort of a people. Something—some system of beliefs, common identity, and/or shared culture—has to hold people together to make it possible for them to fight a war.

Fifth, the very nature of war causes trauma, which causes delusion. The destructive nature of war, the pain and suffering it causes, the heinous act of killing, and the emotional response to death and carnage, causes people on both sides of the battlefield to believe and feel they are *not* the aggressor but the aggrieved, causes people to project unique, dehumanizing qualities on to their enemy, and causes people to seek remedies in Gods, miracle weapons, "invincible technologies," laws of war, international bodies, "undefeatable doctrines," and extraordinary men. American cultural beliefs about men and war, and faith in science and technology delude them about the true nature of war, causing them to consistently prepare to fight the wrong war and to underestimate the will, tenacity, and capabilities of people in developing nation-states. In reality, even the greatest empires, the greatest leaders, the most successful armies, the most advanced weapons, and the most effective doctrines have fallen under the weight of time through delusions about the nature of war.

*   *   *   *   *

This book argues that the most significant transformation in the American practice of war in the latter half of the twentieth century—with the exception of nuclear technology—was a function of cultural change and adaptation.

2.
TRADITIONAL AMERICAN THINKING ABOUT THE CONDUCT OF WAR

Americans hate war. But once they are provoked to defend themselves against those who threaten their security, they mobilize with unparalleled swiftness and energy. While the battle is on there is no sacrifice of men or treasure too great for them to make. Once hostilities are over, Americans are as spontaneous and as headlong in their eagerness to return to civilian life. No people in history have been known to disengage themselves so quickly from the ways of war. This impatience is the expression of a deeply rooted national ideal to want to live at peace. But tragic experience following World War I taught us that this admirable trait could lead to catastrophe. We needed to temper and adjust the rate of the demobilization of our forces so we would be able to meet our *new* obligations in the world.[1]

President Harry Truman

The American Revolutionary War thus became in the national memory and imagination paradigmatic of how America saved itself from being like, and part of, Europe and Europe's problems. . . . Americans, never ready for war, often surprised by it, were repeatedly brought to their knees by the first battles and campaigns. At best gallant, at worst disorganized and demoralized, they came close to complete defeat again and again. Never, however, did they give up. And beyond the humiliation of Brooklyn and the Brandywine lay Saratoga and Yorktown—or Quebec, New Orleans, Gettysburg, Missionary Ridge, Omaha Beach, Leyte Gulf, and Inchon. The Revolutionary War told the story so that all could remember and later repeat it.[2]

John Shy, *The American Military Experience*

Truman, Shy, and others identified significant practices of the American national strategy and doctrines that were no longer sustainable, because of the new world order created by World War II, the acceptance of United States government of new political objectives, and the invention of nuclear technology. Cultural tenets, which had sustained the nation in war for two hundred years, were no longer capable of producing the expected political outcomes.

Traditional Practices No Longer Worked

In the post-World War II period many students of America's wars concluded that the traditional American practice of war and the cultural tenets that sustained it were no longer applicable. Historians John Shy, Russell Weigley, and T.R. Fehrenbach; political scientists Morris Janowitz, Samuel Huntington, Bernard Brodie, Henry Kissinger, and Robert Osgood; Presidents Truman and Eisenhower; and soldiers Matthew B. Ridgway, Maxwell Taylor, and William Westmoreland have all endeavored to describe and explain the traditional American way of war and identify the major tenets that were no longer valid in the post-World War II era. Their arguments were motivated by what each perceived to be a failure of the United States to adapt to a new environment. Robert E. Osgood, writing in the late 1950s, wrote:

On the one hand, the United States has demonstrated an impressive ability to defeat the enemy. Yet, on the other hand, it has been unable to deter war; it has been unprepared to fight war; it has failed to gain the objects it fought for; and its settlements of war have not brought satisfactory peace. The blame for these failures must be shared by circumstances beyond American control; but to the extent that they were avoidable, they must be attributed not to a weakness in the basic elements of national power but to deficiency in the political management of power. And this deficiency stems … from the faulty habit of mind that regards war as a thing in itself rather than as a continuation of political intercourse. War as something to abolish, war as something to get over as quickly as possible, war as a means of punishing the enemy who dared to disturb the peace, war as the crusade—these conceptions are all compatible with the American outlook. But war as an instrument for attaining concrete, limited political objectives, springing from the continuing stream of international politics and flowing toward specific configurations of international power—somehow this conception seems unworthy to a proud and idealistic nation.[3]

Osgood recognized that the policy of containment arrived at after WWII called for a new national strategy: a defensive strategy, sustained readiness for war, and a willingness to fight wars short of total war. The political objectives of the American government were to stop the spread of communism and deter nuclear war. However, permanent readiness for war, defensive national strategy and doctrine, and fighting major limited wars went against significant cultural tenets. Fehrenbach, in his study of the Korean War, *This Kind of War*, wrote:

The Truman Administration accepted the limitation of the war to Korea. … But that Administration must have wished for Frederick's legions, his forty thousand iron grenadiers—for there was never any hope that the men of the fields and the merchants of America could continue undisturbed. In addition to restraint of objective, the second necessary ingredient of limited war is a professional army large enough to handle any task. In 1950, even to fight an undeveloped nation in Asia, America had to fall back upon her citizens. And in this, above all else, lies the resulting trauma of the Korean War. The far frontier is not defended with citizens, for citizens have better things to do than to die on some forsaken hill, in some forsaken country, for what seems to be the sake of the country.[4]

Much of America agreed with Fehrenbach's assessment. When the nation went to war, the cultural norms for war were reactivated: many Americans rallied around the flag, many answered the call to arms, and dormant aspects of patriotism were reactivated. However, limited war looked too much like peace, and the government's actions to limit the war nullified much of the war fervor and many of the traditional practices. Limited war caused consternation and uncertainty: Were the traditional American cultural tenets for war being reactivated or not? Were we mobilizing for war in accordance with cultural norms or not? Were we investing the lives of the nation's young men to achieve strategic victory or not? Major limited wars caused the development of cultural contradictions. The cultural norms for both peace and war are both active during major limited wars, resulting in internal pressures that threaten the war effort and domestic tranquility. However, this internal pressure was only evident during hot wars, major limited wars in which Americans were fighting and dying. During the Cold War the internal contradictions remained, but were for the most part dormant. The Korean War was too short to cause a complete disruption of cultural norms for fighting war; however, the pressure against the new form of limited war increased with each year of fighting.

Fehrenbach believed that the citizen-soldier army was organized to defend America, not Korea or Vietnam, and that in total war, where the nation's security was directly threatened, the citizen-soldier army was the correct instrument because a national effort was required. However, in more limited, defensive wars, on the "frontier," a professional army was required. As Truman noted, Americans hate war. The reason for this is that they value, above all else, the lives of the men who have to fight the war and historically war has been an aberration. In limited war,

Americans found it hard to justify the return on their investment. The direct relationship between national security and the sacrifices required in war were not evident.

Truman, Shy, Osgood, Fehrenbach, and others argued that the traditional American approach to war was no longer applicable in the post-World War II environment, and that the failure to recognize and respond to the new environment was damaging America internationally and domestically. The US was not only failing to achieve its political objectives, but in two limited wars it was creating significant divisions in the country.

* * * * *

What was the traditional American way of war? As noted above, others have answered this question and there is considerable consistency in their views. No effort is made here to recreate previous work. The effort here is to develop a synthesis of these assessments.

Geography, history, cultural heritage, and long-held national political objectives influence the American conduct of war. American values, beliefs, ethics, and philosophies of government, war, and progress are, at least in part, inherited from European ancestors and reshaped by the experience of conquering the North American continent. Until World War II, the United States maintained remarkable consistency in its political objectives. These were, in part, continental sovereignty; expansion and incorporation of the West (Manifest Destiny); prosperity, economic growth, acquisition, and trade (capitalism); security in the Americas (the Monroe Doctrine); and "the pursuit of happiness" through peace, freedom, equality, the accumulation of wealth, and increased consumption. Americans were isolationists, and armed forces were a necessary evil to be minimized to the extent possible. Two great oceans and the limitation of technology protected the United States. Because America has traditionally been unprepared for war, lacking a large body of professionally trained soldiers, it has depended on citizen-soldiers, its small, professionally trained officer corps, its wealth of resources, and its ability to improvise, adapt, and manage affairs in a crisis environment—"American ingenuity."

At the outbreak of war, national strategy required a period of crisis mobilization. Mass armies were assembled from the civilian population. The US Army has traditionally been a citizen-soldier army, meaning that not only the militia or National Guard and Reserves, but also the regular army, was rapidly assembled from volunteers and draftees. As late as 1957 an Army colonel in a memorandum to the Chief of the Officer Assignment Division wrote:

> Since the Revolutionary War, the national defense policy of the United States has been one which calls for a small standing Regular Army as a continuous force in peace which in time of national emergency could be augmented by a large militia of citizen soldiers. The size and strength of the Regular Army Establishment is not a constant nor has it been so affixed. The Regular Army is charged, with keeping abreast of the changing concepts of war during times of peace; it forms the nucleus of the larger citizen army in time of war.
>
> The Reserve Force are Federal forces composed of officers and enlisted men, organized, trained, and employed by the United States Army. The role and purpose of the Reserve as announced in Section 262, Chapter II, Title 10 provides for trained units and qualified persons to be available in time of war or national emergency. The law envisions the <u>supplementary</u> and <u>temporary</u> role (on active duty) of Reserve units and personnel.[5]

At the *political* and *strategic* levels, Americans have traditionally believed the following regarding the conduct of total wars: The US is a unique nation-state, unbound by the rules that govern other nations. War is serious business and ought *not* to be entered into lightly.[6] Major wars are a national endeavor involving the resources of the nation. Wars ought to be conducted in a professional, expeditious, and unrelenting manner to bring them to quick and successful conclusions. War ought to be strategically and doctrinally offensive and short. The aim of war ought to be the destruction of the enemy's main army, followed by the occupation of the country; and finally, the transformation of the defeated nation politically, economically, socially, and, ultimately, culturally. The objective is to produce a state that more closely resembles the United States—a capitalist democracy. Americans believe that war is fighting, that fighting ought to commence as soon as possible following the outbreak of war and proceed continuously and aggressively until victory is achieved. Americans optimistically believe that when fully mobilized there is nothing their fighting forces cannot achieve. Americans believe that fighting ought to produce demonstrative progress and ultimately decisive results. Compromise solutions are un-American and do not justify the human cost of war or achieve the nation's political objectives, which tend to be more absolute. Americans believe that the exigencies of battle ought to dictate the course and conduct of war, and that political matters should not impede the efficient use of force and the expeditious prosecution of war. This is the only way to immediately minimize the loss of life. Americans believe in equality of sacrifice, that the burden of war ought to be fairly distributed among the male population. They believe that the nation's human capital is its most precious resource, and that while Americans are fighting and dying, no other resource should be spared to bring the war to a rapid, successful conclusion. Americans, thus, endeavor to fight highly organized, systematic, material, and technology-based wars. Americans believe that war is an aberration that upsets the American tenet that man is *not* a means to an end, but the end— "the pursuit of happiness." Americans believe in acting unilaterally and aggressively in the international environment. They believe that nations, like individuals, are responsible for their own status, and that nations and men ought to be judged on their accomplishments and failures. Sustained warfare is un-American—potentially damaging to American democracy. Americans do not accept defeat. They increase effort, employ more resources, improvise, adapt, and/or seek new solutions.[7] Defeat is un-American. While no description of a nation's practice of war is complete, these are major tenets that have traditionally influenced American thinking about the conduct of war.

Osgood, Fehrenbach, Shy, and others recognized that during the nation's first artificial limited war, in its new role as superpower, the traditional American practice of war was no longer valid. Something new was needed. When strongly held cultural tenets conflict or no longer achieve their desired results, they create strong internal pressure for change.

The Culture of Equality of Sacrifice

The tenet that all men are created equal and, therefore, equally capable of the same level of achievement has been a staple of American culture.[8] Eisenhower, in his inaugural address, emphasized the importance of the tenet of "equality":

> At such a time in history, we who are free, must proclaim anew our faith. This faith is the abiding creed of our fathers. It is our faith in the deathless dignity of man, governed by eternal moral and natural laws. This faith defines our full view of life. It establishes, beyond debate, those gifts of the Creator that are man's inalienable rights, and that make all men equal in His sight. In the light of this equality we know that the virtues most cherished by free people—love of truth, pride of work, devotion to country—all are treasures equally precious in the lives of the most humble and of the most exalted. The men who mine coal and fire furnaces and balance ledgers and turn lathes and pick cotton and heal the sick and plant corn—all serve as proudly and as profitably, for America as the statesmen who draft treaties or the legislators who enact laws. This faith rules our whole way of life.[9]

This tenet of equality has been a strong force in American life. It was necessary to transform Anglo-Saxons, Germans, French, Italians, Poles, Russians, and other European ethnic groups into Americans. The tenet of equality was necessary to produce a culturally homogeneous national identity. The tenet also gave the nation an ideal towards which to strive. Over time, outside ethnic groups, such as the Irish, Jews, and Poles, were incorporated into the main political body of the United States.[10] The tenet of equality was extended to all facets of American life, even the battlefield.

While Americans believed strongly in equality of opportunity, including equality of opportunity to fight and possibly die in war, they did not believe in equality of outcome. In America's competitive capitalist economy there were winners and losers. Herbert McClosky and John Zaller, in their book, *The American Ethos: Public Attitudes toward Capitalism and Democracy*, wrote:

As the data show, most Americans strongly—even overwhelmingly—support the notion that everyone should have the same chance to 'get ahead,' but they are uniformly negative toward suggestions that everyone must end up with the same economic rewards. Indeed, the distinction between equal opportunity and equality of outcomes could scarcely be drawn more sharply than it is in these data.[11]

In reference to the statement: "Everyone in America should have equal opportunities to get ahead" public opinion polls showed that 98 percent of Americans "agree" and 2 percent "disagree." Opinion polls, to some degree, are distorted by the desire of people to demonstrate their acceptance of values and beliefs in vogue at a given period of time—"political correctness"—or their acceptance of some perceived universal truth that has not been practiced universally.[12] Nevertheless, the overwhelming affirmation of this cultural tenet, plus the historical context, supports the conclusion that Americans strongly supported the concept of equality.

American beliefs about equality were deeply integrated into beliefs about the nation's conduct of war. The American military experience and tradition created tenets about manhood, military service, and war. These tenets are part of American culture and influence the ability of the nation to produce combat soldiers. The tenet that all American men could perform equally well on the battlefield was born during the formative period of the nation, the colonial and revolutionary period, and reinforced during the War of 1812, when Andrew Jackson developed his "gifted amateur" thesis, which held that American militia men, while poorly trained in the conduct of war, were better soldiers than British regulars. Ever since, this tenet has informed American thinking about the conduct of war. During the colonial and revolutionary periods the nation relied on militiamen to fight Indians, maintain internal security, and fight the French and British regulars. Militiamen frequently failed the test of battle, angering men such as George Washington, who wrote:

> Militia, you will find, Sir, will never answer your expectations, no dependence is to be placed upon them; They are obstinate and perverse,

they are often egged on by the Officers, who lead them to acts of disobedience, and when they are ordered to certain posts for the security of stores, or the protection of the Inhabitants, will, on a sudden, resolve to leave *them*, and the united vigilance of their officers can not prevent them.[13]

Washington's contempt for the militia may have caused him to overstate the case. Regulars also failed in battle; however, because of self-selection, a more rigorous elimination process, and better training, regulars consistently performed at a higher level of proficiency. Alexander Hamilton expressed views similar to Washington. Hamilton fought with George Washington at Long Island, White Plains, Trenton, and Princeton. He wrote:

> Here I expect we shall be told that the militia of the country is its natural bulwark, and would at all times be equal to the national defence. This doctrine, in substance, had like to have lost us our independence. . . . The facts which, from our own experience, forbid a reliance of this kind, are too recent to permit us to be the dupes of such a suggestion. The steady operations of war against a regular and disciplined army can only be successfully conducted by a force of the same kind. Considerations of economy, not less than of stability and vigor, confirm this position. The American militia, in course of the later war, have, by their valor on numerous occasions, erected eternal monuments to their fame; but the bravest of them feel and know that the liberty of their country could not have been established by their efforts alone, however, great and valuable they were. War, like most other things, is a science to be acquired and perfected by diligence, by perseverance, by time, and by practice.[14]

Nevertheless, the myth that militia won the Revolution, defeating British regulars, was forever embedded in American history and legend, creating the cultural tenet that all American men could serve in combat with relatively equal levels of performance.

In the War of 1812, the militia was again called upon and again, in many cases, failed the test of war, but in victory only successful battles dominated the minds of Americans. Russell F. Weigley noted that:

In military affairs, not Chippewa and Lundy's Lane [battles won by the regular army] but Andrew Jackson's victory at New Orleans came to symbolize the new egalitarian attitudes. New Orleans was interpreted as a triumph of the natural American—strong precisely because he was unschooled and therefore natural—over the trained and disciplined but therefore artificial and effete European. "Their system, it is true," said one congressman of the heroes of New Orleans, "is not to be found in Vauban's, Steuben's or Scott's military tactics, but it nevertheless proved to be quite effective." Jackson himself viewed his victory in a similar light: "Reasoning always from false principles, [the British] expected little opposition from men whose officers even were not in uniform, who were ignorant of the rules of dress, and who had never been caned into discipline. Fatal mistake! A fire incessantly kept up, directed with calmness and unerring aim, strewed the field with the brave officers and men of the column, which slowly advanced, according to the most approved rules of European tactics, and was cut down by the untutored courage of the American militia."[15]

During the formative period of the nation the belief that all American men could perform effectively in combat was enshrined in history and culture. A second tenet grew out of this one: if all American men fight equally well in combat, then there is no need to maintain a large standing, professional army, which is expensive and considered a threat to the republic. Washington, Hamilton, and other military leaders recognized the fallacy of these tenets. Writing a century later Emory Upton, a Civil War General and military theorist, restated their concerns:

Our military policy, or, as many would affirm, our want of it, had now been tested during more than a century. It has been tried in foreign, domestic, and Indian wars, and while military men, from painful experience, are united as to its defects and dangers, our final success in each conflict has so blinded the popular mind, as to induce the belief that as a nation we are invincible. ... History records our triumph in the Revolution, in the War of 1812, in the Florida War, in the Mexican War, and in the Great Rebellion, and as nearly all of these wars were largely begun by militia and volunteers, the conviction has been produced that with us a regular army is not a necessity.[16]

This conviction was also prevalent in World War II. Consider the words published in *Infantry Journal* in 1946:

Army Ground Forces found him a civilian—a clerk, a mechanic, a student—and turned him out a better fighting man than the professional Nazi or the fanatical Japanese. The American ground soldier was rushed to a maturity for which he had not planned or even dreamed. Yet, so strong were his native hardihood, his resourcefulness, his competitive spirit—and so skillfully were these American traits fostered and fashioned by Ground Forces leaders—that he conquered, on the ground, face to face and weapon to weapon, those Axis warriors whose military upbringing had been foreseen and unhurried.[17]

While this sort of proclamation was good for the national ego and morale, it devalued the relatively small percentage of combat soldiers and marines who were, in fact, self-selected, and were ultimately the product of an elimination process that started before they entered the Army or Marine Corps and continued to the first battle. Americans grew to maturity believing that the average American man could do the job of fighting the nation's wars. As a consequence of these beliefs, combat soldiers, as a whole, have been historically undervalued. In the American mind, if every man could perform this task, there was no need to maintain professional forces or a large standing army. *However, this was a myth, which for a number of reasons is changing.*

The myth survived because it was rarely tested against significant states. The myth survived because of two great oceans and an absence of powerful states in the Americas. The Germans, French, and Russians have a much better understanding of the value of well-trained and equipped combat divisions. Hitler and Stalin understood better than Churchill and Roosevelt the relationship between the security of the nation-state and the quality and quantity of the divisions that guaranteed it. In World War II, by every measure, the Eastern Front was the major theater of operation. For the Americans and British, the relationship between soldiers and security was indirect. Naval forces, and later air forces, protected their homelands. For the French, Germans, and Russians, the relationship was direct and nothing was more important to the continued existence of the state than strong army fighting forces. In the post-World War II era, America's empire stretched across the two great oceans, radically changing the security requirements of the United States. As the Korean War demonstrated, the continued existence of South Korea was directly related to the quality and quantity of divisions the US could immediately put into battle. If it were not for the four Infantry Divisions of the Eighth US Army, South Korea would not exist today.

In the formative years of the nation, when brave souls crossed the Atlantic to get to the new world, it may have been that colonial America possessed a high percentage of men and women with the risk-seeking genes and that the ambient environment influenced culture in such a way as to maximize the enculturation of men capable of performing as combat soldiers. Still, combat soldiers have never been as plentiful as American history and culture has caused Americans to believe. Culturally, having a professional or large standing Army is un-American. Culturally, all American men are capable of fighting war. These cultural tenets are false and based on a misreading of history. *Thus, culturally, Americans have undervalued their combat soldiers and failed to understand their significance in war.*

The cultural tenets that "all American men serve equally well in combat" and "equality of sacrifice" served the nation well in total wars. For example, in World War II these tenets made it possible for the Selective Service System to function efficiently, producing 6.7 million ground force soldiers, from which hundreds of thousands of combat soldiers were culled.[18] Consider Weigley's analysis:

> By 30 June 1945, the American armed forces numbered 12,123,455, and the Army 8,267,958 [including the AAF]. But the ground combat power of the Army resided primarily in the approximately 5,000 combat riflemen per infantry division, along with similar numbers for the cutting edge of the sixteen armored divisions.

Out of a population of 132,699,275 residing in the continental United States in 1940, only about 5,000 men in each of eighty-nine Army divisions, 445,000 men, carried the principal weight of the Army's ground combat strength at any one time, at a maximum. The country's military leadership had acquiesced in an extraordinary disproportion between the American population at large and the segment of it that had to do much of the hardest fighting.[19]

There were 27,139,138 draft-age men in 1940. Thus, at any given time during one of the *most* total wars in American history less than two percent of the draft-age male population was engaged in combat, and this includes the six Marine Corps divisions. The reality was quite different from the myth. All men cannot and did not serve as combat soldiers.[20] And when war actually came and the prospect of being drafted loomed large, most men recognized this and avoided service, or avoided service in the Army and Marine Corps, where 80 to 90 percent of casualties were sustained, or avoided service in a war zone, or avoided service in combat arms—infantry, armor, artillery, and combat engineers. During World War II, and every war since, a large number of the enlisted men who served in the Air Force and Navy volunteered to do so to avoid being drafted into the Army. Those individuals who did not avoid combat service but who were unfit to serve were soon eliminated.

Within the US Army and Marine Corps there has always been a secret. It is that men who are believed to be unfit for combat are eliminated on a regular basis. While the Army and Marine Corps cannot re-create the conditions of combat, which vary in each war, they are experts at pushing men to their limits during training to reveal many of their qualities, or lack thereof. The elimination of soldiers from combat arms was (is) routine. The administrative means of elimination were long ago established and institutionalized. The system for producing combat soldiers from the point of entry into service to the battlefield was (is) a constant process of weeding out. The weeding process starts at the basic level, with sergeants making the initial call for elimination or transfer to a more civilian-like occupational skill. For the most part, this process was not spoken of outside the combat arms system, embarrassing no one and maintaining the American myth. Even in the late 1960s and early 1970s, when the nation and Army were desperate to find and draft men to send to Vietnam, the Army recognized that some men were "un-trainable" and eliminated them.

The Culture of Inequality of Outcome

Because soldiering was considered an innate ability of all American men, those who served in the Army during peacetime were considered losers, individuals incapable of succeeding in America's competitive capitalist economy. In 1952, the Secretary of the Army, Frank Pace, Jr., in a lecture entitled, "Public Service, Present and Future" on the values of military service, particularly serving as an Army officer, given to an audience of students at Princeton University, delineated "a number of misconceptions about government service":

> *Another misconception is that government offers fine careers for the incompetent.* I suggest that it will be an eye-opening experience for those who still believe this to examine the caliber of the young men entering Federal, state, and local governments today. . . .
>
> *Yet a third misconception is that government experience is a non-transferable commodity.* This is patently false. The opportunity to deal with broad problems makes the man in government often invaluable to business and industry.
>
> *And the final misconception has to do with loyalty and moral and ethical integrity.* No matter what some sensational headlines of the day may say, the overwhelming majority of those who work in government are scrupulously honest, hardworking, loyal and normal men and women who come from every walk of life. . . .[21]

Pace went on to make the case for service as an Army officer; however, he had a tough sell. The nation was in the midst of the Korean War, the conduct of which the American people were growing increasingly dissatisfied. Nevertheless, after almost two hundred years of history, the culturally held beliefs inculcated in the formative years of the nation were still in effect.

In 1954, a US Navy commander, D.J. Carrison, published an article entitled, "Our Vanishing Military Profession," in which he argued:

> Our military leaders should fight the unwise developments of present law, which encourage employers and educators to conduct rigorous campaigns to obtain exemptions or deferments for young men who aspire to a college education. A career labeled 'unworthy of superior talent' by a large influential segment of our country's leaders gives impressionable young men the idea that a commission in the Armed Forces is not a privilege but an admission of inability to face civilian competition in industry.[22]

In peacetime, military service was not considered a promising career for talented young men with other options. In total war, it was expected that *all* would serve when called upon. And while Americans in the 1950s came to respect and value the service and professionalism of the highly skilled Air Force and Navy pilots, Army ground combat forces occupied a particularly loathsome place.

In limited war, only a small fraction of the manpower of the nation was required. Who would sacrifice? How would they be selected? Could the nation justify committing one individual and not another? Could the nation justify committing its men, but not employing the full resources of the nation to bring the war to a swift and victorious conclusion? How was the nation to reconcile its tenet of equality, while committing some men literally to death and others to college campuses? What did such practices say about American nationalism, about American democracy, about the American people? What was fair? While the system for selecting and recruiting soldiers for war has never been completely fair and unbiased, it was close enough to the American expectation of equality to function with the support of the people. In limited war the inequities of the system went against the tenet of equality and were too obvious to ignore. Limited war created significant cultural contradictions for Americans.

In limited war, which looked a lot like peace to the vast majority of Americans, the tenet of "equality of sacrifice" conflicted with the tenets of "inequality of outcome" and "military service is for the least talented." In total war the latter tenets are almost completely supplanted by the former. But in limited war it became permissible for those considered to be the privileged, the talented, and/or the educated to avoid war by any legal means available without too much public outrage, feelings of guilt, or opprobrium. In fact, those individuals that were able to avoid serving in limited war, particularly Vietnam, quietly considered themselves smarter and better than those that served.[23] The cultural tenet that the talented did not serve in the armed forces, particularly the Army, was not the dominant tenet in all "clusters," but it was the dominant tenet in the US. Therefore, while it was un-American to avoid war when called upon to fight, it was acceptable to engage in means of avoidance during limited war.

In the late 1940s and early 1950s, Army leadership not only expressed concern for the state of readiness of the Army, but also for the willingness of the American people to accept the new duties that went along with the new responsibilities of American foreign policies, and their willingness to meet the new threat presented by international Communism and Soviet expansion. Lieutenant General Manton S. Eddy, who commanded the 9th Infantry Division ("Old Reliable") in North Africa, Sicily, and the Normandy invasion during World War II, in an address to the Rhode Island Legislature in February 1950, expressed his concerns:

> Of all the instruments of policy, the United States has consistently had the least understanding of the use of armed strength. In a world where military power plays a bigger role than ever before, this Nation dare not remain on its habitual course of blindness toward the fact that, like it or not, force is the final authority of policy. . . . But how many Americans see in it an urgent demand for personal action . . .? We still tend to seek an easy out for this military part of our obligation to humanity. . . . National policy on military matters can rise no higher than its source, and that source is the people. . . .
>
> At this early stage in allied defense planning there is one fact [for] which there is universal agreement. It is that the combined land forces of the Allies, including the United States, are far from sufficient. In air and sea power the Allies are relatively well off. On the ground they are definitely inferior. . . . The dominant military forces in

Europe today are the armies of the Communist nations. . . . As a nation, we are the greatest single force for peace in the world today. Our greatest danger will lie in any inclination to forget or dodge the responsibilities which are ours. If the philosophy of the people does not include a spirited and realistic military attitude, then there is little hope that we can live up to our obligations.[24]

Eddy and other Army leaders believed the power of the United States to prevent the spread of communism rested primarily on the will of the American people, not simply its technology, material wealth, or even the size of the Army. This was a common theme for Army leaders during the early years of the Cold War. The abstract nature of the "Cold War" and the indirect nature of the Communist threat placed a new equation for the use of military force before the American people, who were accustomed to overt, blatant acts of aggression that demonstrated the need for mobilization for war.

Without the willing support of the people, the Selective Service System could not function efficiently. In the latter half of the twentieth century, because of nuclear weapons, limited war became the only form of war between the major power blocs. The tenets that produced combat soldiers in total wars, especially that of equality of sacrifice, failed to function in limited war. The tenets remained, but they functioned very differently in limited war. The peacetime tenet that war *was for the least talented* was invoked in limited war, but it conflicted with the cultural tenet of *equality of sacrifice*. Many Americans strongly opposed the draft in limited war. They also opposed it in peace, but in limited war the opposition became louder and more virulent. The unresolved conflict distorted the Selective Service System, eroded support for the war, and impeded the recruitment and retention of soldiers. This cultural conflict, however, was resolved in 1973 when the citizen-soldier Army came to an end and the professional, all-volunteer force came into existence.

The Culture of Wealth and Consumption

A student of the Roman practice of war, Flavius Vegetius Renatus, writing during the last days of the empire, observed that: "The chief strength of our armies, then, should be recruited from the country. For it is certain that the less a man is acquainted with the sweets of life, the less reason he has to be afraid of death."[25] The less a man has the more easily he can be transformed into a soldier. The martial spirit is easier to implant in those individuals who are more poorly educated because they have a limited vision of the world and fewer options in life. Men who toil in fields or labor in industry are physically and psychologically more adaptable to the toils of the battlefield. And, the poverty of one's social and physical condition is more easily transferred to the poverty of the battlefield. A student of the US Army in the Korean War observed:

[N]o army can change entirely—either for better or for worse—the civilians to whom it issues uniforms, supplies, and rifles. As a man has lived as a civilian so can he be expected to fight as a soldier. Americans in Korea displayed prodigious reliance on the use of firepower; they became unduly concerned with putting in their time and getting out; they grew accustomed to fighting on a level of physical luxury probably unparalleled in world history to that time. In stark contrast to the American reverence for the programs of "R&R" (rest and recuperation) and the "Big R" (rotation back to the US), Chinese Communist soldiers fought—much as they had lived—with little hope of leaving the frontline until the war ended or until they became casualties. *Whether the US can maintain the requisite balance between a liberal society which is the master of its armed force and a professional soldiery which is free to preserve the military ethic is the vital question to which the American way of war in Korea offers limited but significant testimony.*[26]

The affluence of much of modern America is diametrically opposed to the destitute conditions of the battlefield. Two of the things that make life most precious are the expectations from life and the finality of death. Fighting at the edge of the battlefield, where the killing takes place, is ultimately a selfless endeavor. The culture of wealth, which emphasizes selfishness, is diametrically opposed to the culture of soldiers, which requires selflessness. Success in modern America's competitive, capitalist society is ultimately a selfish endeavor. Self-interest is the bedrock of capitalism. Many argue that greed is good for the economy, and hence, good for America. But without individuals willing to act selflessly, nations cannot provide for their defense. Thus, cultural tenets conflict, and it is the most significant cultural learning and the prevalent conditions that determine how such conflicts are resolved. The character and quality of enculturation influences the ability of a people to produce individuals with the wherewithal to act selflessly and serve during war. Consider the words of Robert E. Osgood, writing during the 1950s:

Quite aside from the moral odium of war, the fear of violence and the revulsion from warfare are bound to be strong among a people who have grown as fond of social order and material well-being as Americans. War upsets the whole scale of social priorities of an individualistic and materialistic scheme of life, so that the daily round of getting and spending is subordinate to the collective welfare of the nation in a hundred grievous ways—from taxation to death. This accounts for an emotional aversion to war, springing from essentially self-interest motives, which is quite as compelling as the moral aversion to war. And, like the moral aversion, it tends to put a premium upon military considerations at the expense of limited political objectives in the conduct of war.[27]

In 2008, another student of American life, Andrew Bacevich, wrote:

For the United States the pursuit of freedom, as defined in an age of consumerism, has induced a condition of dependence—on imported goods, on imported oil, and on credit. The chief desire of the American people, whether they admit it or not, is that nothing should disrupt their access to those goods, that oil, and that credit. The chief aim of the US government is to satisfy that desire, which it does in part through the distribution of largesse at home (with Congress taking the leading role) and in part through the pursuit of imperial ambitions abroad (largely the business of the executive branch).[28]

In 2008, *US News & World Report* reported that:

America is incredibly indebted. The debt in the financial world went from 21 percent of a $3 trillion gross domestic product in 1980 to 120 percent of a $13 trillion GDP in 2007, reflecting an astonishing accumulation of as much as $30 of debt for every $1 of equity in many firms. . . .[29]

Consumption is necessary for human existence—food, clothing, and shelter. Consumption is a self-centered activity. America's wealth produced levels of consumption few have known in human history. Such levels of consumption influenced culture and the way people live and think. The American economy in the latter half of the twentieth century helped shape a society in which people are told to consume from birth to death. Americans devote a great deal of their time and energy to the self-centered endeavor of consumption, which informs people that life is about them. No people in the history of the world have been marketed to as Americans have. In the 1950s, television entered American homes. By the end of 1952, there were 19 million TV sets marketing to Americans. Two years later television was the largest advertising medium in the country. As David Halberstam noted: "*Ten years later television had begun to alter the political and social fabric of the country, with stunning consequences.*"[30] Television viewing influences consumption and consumption influences every aspect of American life, including the nation's ability to produce combat soldiers.

During the Cold War wealth was one of the primary indices Americans used to explain the difference between their democratic capitalist system and the Communist system. In 1953 Assistant Secretary of Defense, John A. Hannah, lamented: "Yet ask the average person to define the struggle—the dominant fact shaping his life today—and . . . the most common definition will emphasize, 'We're better off here. We have finer homes, clothes, food, labor saving devices, television, automobiles, and so forth.'"[31]

American affluence grew considerably during the fifties. The value of each American life in terms of dollars grew enormously, exceeding that of all other people on Earth. Home, automobile, and television ownership increased. The interstate highway and commercial airline systems made Americans more mobile than any other society in history. Individual

freedoms, freedom from needs, and the freedom of time gave Americans a standard of living new to mankind. American expectations from life grew as the state prospered, and the definition of the "good life" changed. Eisenhower noted:

> In 1953 we had seen the end of the Korean War. In 1954 we had won out over the economic hazard of a recession. With these problems behind us, we in the United States entered a new era of unprecedented peace and unprecedented prosperity. The slogan "Peace, Progress, and Prosperity," which was applied to the first-term years and was used in the campaign of 1956, perhaps seemed platitudinous. But compared with any years of the two preceding decades, these surely must have seemed miraculous to most Americans. Not in the lifetime of millions of our citizens—children, adolescents, and men and women entering adult life—had we previously had peace, progress, and prosperity all at one time.[32]

Wealth created new cultural tenets. The cultural tenets required to produce miraculous peace, progress, and prosperity conflicted with cultural tenets required to produce soldiers for war, facilitating the transformation in American thinking about the conduct of war. Wealth in America created importance and privilege, which in many affluent clusters diminished the sense of duty to the state, and the willingness and ability to perform the labors of soldiers. Those clusters with less wealth aspired for and aggressively sought the importance and privileges of those with wealth.[33] Families changed. The number of children per family declined. More children meant less wealth and less time. Arguably in the latter half of the twentieth century more and more Americans became too "important" to fight war, particularly limited war. When measured against the lifetime earning potential of a North Korean, Chinese, Vietnamese, or Iraqi, American lives were worth many times more. While certain affluent clusters continued their traditional roles, other clusters scrupulously avoided service. In the American pecking order, the lives of some citizens were valued more highly than those of others. This was an aspect of American life that was not publicly acknowledged; nevertheless, it was, and is, a fact.[34]

Eisenhower further explained the transformation in American life:

> One dramatic feature of the expanding middle class was the increase in the number of white-collar workers and professional people. Widespread schooling, increasing domestic and international travel . . . and reasonable prosperity had helped turn people away from becoming laborers, while technology was making many unskilled and semiskilled jobs obsolete. More and more people were working in 'services,' because more and more people could afford to pay others to do work for them—from shining shoes to surgery.[35]

This analysis cannot be directly applied to the conduct of war. However, the physical aspects of work—getting dirty, the use of muscles, the tolerance for physical discomfort, the stamina and endurance required for manual labor, and the psychological disposition of laborers—were all practices that better prepared a man to become a soldier than did the paper-pushing practices performed by sedentary white-collar workers.

With each subsequent decade of the latter half of the twentieth century, the American people became physically and psychologically less capable of fighting wars. As the service industry expanded, the manufacturing industry contracted. In the 1990s ROTC departments around the country complained that new recruits couldn't run a half mile. New physical training programs were initiated to get potential cadets up to the minimal physical condition required for service, a standard that was far below that required in infantry units. Recruiters had the same problem. Too many Americans were too overweight to qualify for service. In 2002 most Americans, 64 percent, were overweight or obese.[36] The percentage of the American population capable of becoming combat soldiers was considerably lower in 2005 than in 1945. In February 2009 *US News & World Report* reported that:

> Our expanding girth is America's most visible health problem [and national security problem]. Not only are most adults too heavy, but obesity rates for children have more than doubled in the past 30 years. Excessive weight is a significant factor in four of the six leading causes of death; heart disease, cancer, stroke, and diabetes.[37]

This is an issue of national security. People who are overweight or obese lack the motivation, energy, confidence, and physical capabilities to serve in war. They also lack the will and confidence to volunteer for military service. The article concluded that: "Every year, in fact, an estimated 900,000 people die from avoidable causes: because they failed to maintain a healthy weight, eat nutritiously, and exercise, or because they smoked or drank excessively, for example. That's roughly 40 percent of all U.S. deaths." This is more Americans than were killed in all theaters of World War II. It is hard to imagine how the United States can remain a superpower with a significant portion of its population suffering from the debilitating effects of obesity.

The Culture of Science and Technology

From World War II to Operation Iraqi Freedom the preferred American approach to war has been to substitute technology for manpower. Consider the words published in *Infantry Journal* in 1945:

> What the Infantryman has done in this war—what he has had to do, and done—has come as a development, unexpected not only by most of the American people, but also by some of our commanders. The people thought, back in 1940, 1941 and 1942, that there could be no need of a "mass Army." They believed that men in planes and men in tanks could do practically all the hard combat work there would be to do. Back of this belief was the hope that we could win without great cost, that American sons and husbands could fight from within machines with far more safety than they could by fighting on the open fields of battle. And there were commanders, too, who believed at first that men in machines could handle the heaviest parts of the task. But by 1944 it was clear to all that the Infantryman would have to be there in the center of battle, in large numbers, taking the worst of it as he fought. . . .[38]

These words were as applicable in 2003 as they were in 1945. The United States Army ran out of infantrymen in both years, and the ultimate cost in lives was higher than it needed to be. The unnamed author of this piece concluded with a question that can now be answered:

> Once again, the men of the Army are wondering whether the nation will this time, the seventh time, realize the vital and continuing need for the ablest military leaders, for the same flexible yet indomitable type of mind and spirit that has been able to go forward with utmost energy, speed and expansion, physical and intellectual, to win the war just finished.

A mere five years later as the US Army deployed to fight the Korean War, it was evident that the nation had again failed to maintain adequate ground fighting forces, had again endeavored to substitute technology for manpower, and had again suffered near defeat for want of trained infantry. When it comes to war the American cultural preference for technological solutions dwarfs all other cultural tenets; and the outcomes of the battles and campaigns have had little or no influence on that preference.

The American culture of science and technology can be traced back to the formative years of the United States, and is closely linked to the cultures of equality and wealth. A student of American culture and history, Alexis de Tocqueville, in his 1835 work, *Democracy in America*, wrote:

> Equality begets in man the desire of judging of everything for himself; it gives him in all things a taste for the tangible and the real, contempt for tradition and for forms. . . . To minds thus predisposed, every new method that leads by a shorter road to wealth, every machine that spares labor, every instrument that diminishes the cost of production, every discovery that facilitates pleasures or augments them, seems to be the grandest effort of the human intellect. It is chiefly from these motives that a democratic people addicts itself to scientific pursuits, that it understands and respects them. . . . You may be sure that the more democratic, enlightened, and free a nation is, the greater will be the number of these interested promoters of scientific genius and the more will discoveries immediately applicable to

productive industry confer on their authors gain, fame, and even power.[39]

The cultures of equality and wealth made possible the American *addiction* for advanced technologies and for the biggest and most scientifically sophisticated weapon systems. In the latter half of the twentieth century the United States has out-spent all other states on Earth in search of the most advanced technologies for war. Americans expend hundreds of billions of dollars to replace the most advanced systems on the planet with other systems just slightly more advanced. Americans expend hundreds of billions of dollars on systems that don't work. Why? Science and technology held out the promise to alleviate all human suffering, to make all men and women equal, to create a paradise where no individual wanted, needed, or suffered anything. Americans embraced this promise with fervor.

During World War II the pace of scientific research and technological development increased substantially, driven by the desire to reduce American casualties and the need to defeat Nazi Germany and Imperial Japan. In World War II, only the British and the Americans invested vast sums and vast human resources in an unproven theory, which was manifested in a doctrine of war known as *Strategic Bombing*.[40] To explain why, Richard Overy, wrote:

> Public opinion in both states [the UK and US] was unusually susceptible to the science-fiction view of air power, first popularized by writers such as H.G. Wells, whose *War in the Air*, published in London as long ago as 1908, painted a lurid picture of 'German air fleets' destroying 'the whole fabric of civilization'. Wells was father to a whole generation of scaremongers, who traded on popular anxiety that bombing was somehow a uniquely unendurable experience.[41]

In December 1931, in an American journal titled *Liberty*, Colonel Fitzmaurice described what war from the air might look like:

> A hideous shower of death and destruction falls screeching and screaming through space and atmosphere to the helpless, thickly populated earth below. The shock of the hit is appalling.

Great buildings totter and tumble in the dust. . . . The survivors, now merely demoralized masses of demented humanity, scatter caution to the winds. They are seized by a demoniacal frenzy of terror. They tear off their gas masks, soon absorb the poisonous fumes, and expire in horrible agony, cursing the fate that did not destroy them hurriedly and without warning in the first awful explosions.[42]

Long before Gene Rodenberry created Captain Kirk and the *Starship Enterprise*, the ideas of decisive war from the air were prevalent. (Each new generation of technology created a new version of air war theory.) The specter of World War I, of trench warfare, weighed heavily on the British. The carnage experience at the Somme and Passchendaele, and witnessed at Verdun, were enough to motivate extreme efforts to avoid this type of warfare.[43] The vision of war created by science-fiction writers, such as H.G. Wells, and the predictions of airpower enthusiasts, such as Douhet and Billy Mitchell, not only planted seeds, ideas for a better, smarter way of war, they also added to the fears, anxieties, and concerns created during the Great War.[44]

Airpower was also seen as an instrument for projecting power across great oceans and to maintain empire. The British and US Navies had responsibilities in all the oceans around the globe. Airpower was another means to secure possessions thousands of miles from the homeland. It expanded the reach of ground and naval forces. Technological competition was (is) a tenet of the Western way of war. All sides tried to gain advantage through advances in technologies. The airplane was a versatile instrument for reaching deep into enemy countries. In 1940, after the Fall of France, when Britain stood alone, airpower dominated the war effort. Before the Wehrmacht could invade Britain it had to control the air above the invasion beaches. The survival of Britain depended on the capabilities of the Royal Air Force's Fighter Command. At the same time the British were fighting for their survival, the only means for them to strike back at Germany was airpower. Hence, in the early days of World War II airpower played a decisive role. Churchill and Roosevelt never lost sight of this fact. Airpower saved Britain. In the days that followed the victory of the RAF, the Americans and British built a

great fleet of heavy bombers, and initiated the *Strategic Bombing* campaign, the first such campaign in history. Proponents of airpower claimed that airpower had won the war, and that had it been employed more effectively, the ground campaign would have been unnecessary.[45] By the end of World War II, the American people had firmly embraced air war theory. This was the future of warfare.

After World War II the pace of technological competition did not abate. The "Cold War," and later the "Space Race," became the new driving forces. The technological advances of the Soviet Union produced fear and anxiety in the United States. After the launch of Sputnik in 1957, the first Earth-orbiting satellite, many Americans said "never again," and demanded that the United States maintain the lead in all forms of technology: military, space, medicine, genetics, physics, and all other disciplines. Technology also appeared to offer a way to eliminate the inequality of limited war, and perhaps even end the human sacrifices demanded by war—at least on the American side.

In the post-World War II era, the intense search for advanced weapon technologies became a major tenet of American culture, producing ways of thinking, strategies, and practices independent of other cultural tenets. The atomic bomb, long-range strategic bombers, jet aircraft, rockets, guided missiles, radar, and other technologies developed during World War II "revolutionized warfare."[46] The evidence seemed overwhelming until the Korean War. One of the ironies of America at the dawn of the twenty-first century was that in the midst of the greatest wealth of war machines and advanced military technologies ever produced by man, the American people were at the lowest ebb of martial spirit and ability to fight war in the nation's history.

Tenets of American Culture

A comprehensive description of American culture is beyond the range of this study and not required for its purposes. However, a summary of American thinking about the conduct of war is pertinent to this study:

1. Americans value human life, particularly that of Americans, above all else. As a consequence,

Americans have been willing to spend considerable portions of the nation's wealth on technologies, policies, and strategies that limit the expenditure of American lives. The most fundamental tenet of American life, written into the nation's constitution, is that man is not a means to an end, but the end itself. War, which requires men to become a means of state policy, is thus an aberration, a break from the norm that cannot be sustained indefinitely.

2. Equality of opportunity, and in total wars, equality of sacrifice, has been an important and consistent American cultural tenet from the Colonial/Revolutionary period to the Civil Rights Movement. Equality of opportunity was the primary tenet that produced Americans. While for some Americans equality was a dream—the American Indians, African Americans, Asian Americans, and other outside groups—over time these groups have moved closer to the dream. The move towards greater equality for all has been a significant historical force in America.

3. Equality of outcome is un-American. A person's status—wealth and quality of life—was believed to be based on his own talents, abilities, tenacity, innovativeness, and willingness to work hard. Inequality of outcome produced the unique American traits of individualism, unilateral behavior, and aggressiveness.

4. It is an American cultural belief that all male citizens are capable of performing effectively on the battlefield. This tenet of American life is closely connected with the tenet of equality, all men are created equal, and has informed American military policy for two centuries. It provides one of the arguments against maintaining a larger professional army and is the basis of legitimacy for the Selective Service Administration.

5. Americans have tended to believe that military service in peacetime was a poor use of human ability and talent; hence, only losers served in the Army during periods of peace. The smartest, most intelligent, and most competitive Americans went into business and pursued wealth.

6. Americans covet wealth and the symbols of wealth. Americans pursue wealth with tenacity and aggressiveness. Wealth in America creates importance, opportunities, prestige, influence, access, and exception. Wealth has produced an unacknowledged inequality, and a psychological and physical disposition that, arguably, diminishes the nation's ability to fight war.

7. Americans have taken considerable pride in being the most technologically advanced nation on the planet. They expect to maintain this position. This tenet of American life also supports the first tenet—the substitution of technological means for human effort.

8. Americans are optimistic. They expect change, and prefer the new to the old. Americans always expect things to get better. Better means newer, bigger, faster, easier, more glamorous, and more powerful.

9. Americans have tended to be isolationist and unilateral. The isolation of the US from significant enemies by two great oceans enabled Americans to look inward until World War II. American individualism tends to cause Americans to believe that each nation ought to make it on its own, the way the US did, and the way individual Americans did. World War II, and the advent of the "Cold War," required the American people to adopt a new perspective toward international relations. Still, aspects of the unilateral tenet remained and were evident in the latter part of the twentieth century in American attitudes toward the United Nations and other world organizations that it was believed were impinging on American sovereignty.

10. Americans have accepted the position of the most powerful nation-state on the planet—militarily, economically, culturally, and politically—but not all the implications that came with it. Power produces chauvinism and the wherewithal to exploit the resources of other nations and states. Americans believe in the exceptional position of the United States in the world. They believe that the US has a unique place in world affairs, and that the rules that govern the behavior of other states are not applicable to the US. They believe the US is a force for good. They believe that ultimately, the rest of the world will evolve to look like America, accepting American ways, values, ethics, and beliefs. Americans export

American culture. Americans believe that the power of the United States can transform other nations and regions of the world through political policies, economic means, and if necessary, the use of military force.

* * * * *

It would be folly to believe that the American culture of war could be reduced to a few pages. The objective here is much less ambitious. I am arguing that the American behavior in war in the latter half of the twentieth century is incomprehensible without some understanding of American culture, and that the demise of the citizen-soldier Army and the adoption of a new American way of war were caused primarily by cultural conflicts between strongly held tenets—first, that man is not a means to an end, and second, that equality of opportunity is the natural right of human beings. Limited war, as constructed in the post-World War II period, went against these basic cultural tenets. Limited war looked too much like peace to motivate the selflessness evident in total war. Americans have fought many wars, but war has always been an aberration, not a permanent condition. Thus, for relatively short periods of time, Americans have accepted war as a means for the

ends of the state, to achieve objectives that preserved and possibly spread the basic tenets of American life. Americans were capable of fighting all types of wars for short periods of time, given the state of readiness of the nation and the exigency of the situation. However, Americans ultimately fought *strategically offensive* wars with *offensive strategic doctrine*, the aim of which was the destruction of the enemy's main forces. This was the only way to envision an end to the conflict and a return to normalcy. War based on *defensive strategy and doctrine* could not produce decisive results. Hence, the termination of hostilities could not be predicted. Protracted, strategically defensive wars were un-American.

The demise of the citizen-soldier Army started at the end of World War II when the United States became a superpower and took on new political objectives, strategies, and doctrines for war. The new role of the US created cultural conflicts that were most evident during the Korean and Vietnam Wars, but were prevalent throughout the Cold War as well. The Vietnam War caused the cultural conflict to emerge into a full-blown domestic war, which ended with defeat in Vietnam and the end of the citizen-soldier Army in 1973. However, the cultural conflict is still prevalent.

3.
THE LEGACY OF WORLD WAR II:
MAN VERSUS MACHINE

Man–the Ultimate Factor. In the nature of the Army's mission it is the soldier himself who, as a tactical entity of combat, must fight and control the battle. To wield the power of his hardware he must enter the battle personally; indeed, no means are likely ever to be developed which will permit him to control the battlefield without entering and occupying it. He is the ultimate factor in victory. The Army must therefore continuously devote substantial scientific resources to research on human factors in warfare–developing improved methods of selecting men for combat; assuring that their equipment are compatible with their innate and trained aptitudes and battle skills ... and improving methods for training in the complex knowledge and skills of the soldier's profession.[1]

Lieutenant General Arthur G. Trudeau, 1959
US Army Chief of Research and Development

War has become vertical. We are demonstrating daily that it is possible to descend from the skies into any part of the interior of an enemy nation and destroy its power to continue the conflict. War industries, communications, power installations and supply lines are being blasted by attacks from the air. Fighting forces have been isolated, their defenses shattered and sufficient pressure brought by air power alone to force their surrender. Constant pounding from the air is breaking the will of the Axis to carry on. .... Strategic air power is a war-winning weapon in its own right, and is capable of striking decisive blows far behind the battle line, thereby destroying the enemy's capacity to wage war.[2]

General Henry Arnold, 1943
Commander Army Air Forces

World War II ushered in the new age of airpower, and by doing so initiated a process of transformation that would ultimately end with the elimination of ground forces as major combatants in war. Henceforth, wars were to be won entirely from the air. This school of thought has dominated air-war thinking since the introduction of the big, four-engine, heavy bomber in the 1930s, and the first serious effort to develop doctrine to win a war with strategic bombing. The most fundamental tenet that informs this thinking and gives life to the practices of the US Air Force is that airpower technology is the decisive instrument for the conduct of war. In 2003 during Operation Iraqi

Freedom, while employing the most technologically advanced aircraft, munitions, and doctrine ever produced, the basic thesis was the same: the war could be won entirely from the air. However, the air-war thesis, in the Army's view, has never proven successful. The Army provided the other school of thought, which held that man is the decisive instrument for the conduct of war. This fundamental tenet informs the thinking and animates the practices of the Army.

The Army and Air Force have never reconciled these beliefs that form the very core of their cultures. Not until the end of the twentieth century were serious efforts made toward joint doctrine. The inability of the Army and Air Force to produce joint doctrine damaged the ability of the nation to effectively use military power to achieve political objectives, and arguably, caused the nation's first defeat in war.

World War II, for four years, reinforced the cultural norms of the traditional American practice of war. At the same time, it created a new practice of war, based on new technologies that, in the last days of the war, unequivocally informed Americans that their traditional way of war was obsolete. Airpower and nuclear weapons exerted enormous influence on American thinking about the conduct of war. These technologies seemed to offer a way to finally end the psychological and physical destruction caused by face-to-face combat. They seemed to offer an end to the mass armies that turned men into instruments of the state. And they seemed to offer an end to enormous expenditure of resources required to fight total wars. If a few men in an airplane could cause the incredible destruction witnessed at Hiroshima in a single attack, surely there was no need for mass armies! However, core cultural tenets tend to change slowly.

The US Army held firm to its most basic cultural beliefs that man is the dominant instrument on the battlefield; that new technologies and doctrines only enhance firepower; that war is much more than simply killing; and that, at the end of the day, when total war stripped a nation bare of its resources, it was the adaptability, spirit, and character of men that would make the final decision on the survival of a way of life, if not a people.

Culture and technology were the driving forces that initiated a transformation in American thinking about the conduct of war after World War II. In America, men were not a means to an end, but the end. In America, all men were created equal. Whereas ground war with mass armies very nearly obliterated these fundamental tenets of American culture, airpower and nuclear weapons appeared to preserve them, appeared to maintain the cultural norms and cultural balance. All the technologies, doctrines, strategic thinking, and reinforcing and conflicting cultural tenets required for the demise of the citizen-soldier Army and the emergence of a new American practice of war were evident in World War II. This story starts in World War II, but it is still unfolding.

WWII Air War Doctrine vs. WWII Ground War Doctrine

While World War II was rich in new technologies and doctrines, at the end of the war, four offensive campaign-winning doctrines claimed decisiveness. The US Marine Corps and Navy, and the British, independently, developed *amphibious warfare doctrines*—the methods and principles to employ land craft and ship technologies to land combat forces on hostile shores. The British and US Navies developed *aircraft carrier task force doctrine*—the methods and principles to use aircraft carrier technologies to project naval and airpower across vast oceans against enemy forces. The Germans developed *"Wolf Pack" submarine doctrine*—the methods and principles to employ submarine technologies to destroy the enemy's merchant ship fleet. And the British and American navies developed *Anti-Submarine Warfare (ASW) doctrine*—the methods and principles to employ destroyers, aircraft carriers, and land-based aircraft technologies to find and destroy enemy submarines that preyed on allied merchant ships. While these doctrines contributed to the outcome of the war, none of them had the potential to be decisive in war. British and Marine Corps amphibious warfare doctrines created access to enemy forces and ultimately the enemy's homeland, but neither had the potential to destroy Imperial Japan or Nazi Germany. Navy aircraft carrier task force and ASW doctrines created passages to the battlefields, and kept strategically important logistical sea lanes open, but neither could destroy the enemy's main forces. Once the passage had been made and access to the battlefields achieved, either the Army air forces and/or the Army ground forces had to complete the destruction of the enemy's main forces.

The US Army employed two offensive campaign-winning doctrines in World War II, *Infantry* and *Armor*. The pioneering work of the Germans in armor warfare was copied by all major nations that fought in World War II, with variations that were a function of their own culture, industrial and technological capabilities, the paucity or abundance of their resources, geographic circumstances, and the disposition and intellect of their leaders. The Army's primary doctrine for fighting the war was its traditional Infantry doctrine, which in World War II was a strategic, operational, and tactical doctrine. The US Army planned to win the war by fighting successive, successful, offensive Infantry battles that produced successful campaigns of strategic importance, the cumulative effect of which would produce victory by destroying the German Army.

"The Arnold vision" of war from the air was first articulated in World War I:

> . . . the day may not be far off when aerial operations with their devastation of enemy lands and destruction of industrial and populous centers on a vast scale may become the principal operations of war, to which the older forms of military and naval operations may become secondary and subordinate.[3]

The German bombing campaign against England caused many observers to conclude that airpower could be decisive by destroying the will of the people or the enemy's industrial centers.[4] However, the technology in aircraft and munitions did not exist in 1917 to greatly influence the outcome of the war. Still, the idea was born, and Giulio Douhet, the Italian airpower theorist and author of the influential book *Command of the Air*, and Hugh Trenchard, the first Chief of the Royal Air Force, insured that it survived the interwar period. While many consider Douhet the "father of strategic air power doctrine," it was Trenchard who fought successfully for the survival of the RAF, in part, by maintaining the vision of the potential of airpower to break the stalemate of attrition and exhaustion warfare that produced the then unprecedented destruction and carnage of the First World War. By the 1930s advances in aircraft and munitions technologies had made possible new *strategic bombing doctrines*. The dominance of the Army's ground warfare doctrine was challenged by these new doctrines.

The air forces of Britain and the United States pioneered two different *strategic bombing* doctrines that they believed had the potential to produce victory independent of a ground war. The British strategic bombing doctrine was based on the theory that the civilian population was the center of gravity, the point of decision. British Bomber Command believed that bombing people would break their will, the *morale*

effect, and that as a consequence they would rebel against their government and/or stop working. In either case, the war would come to an end because the people were no longer producing the machines, equipment, and supplies necessary for war. American strategic bombing doctrine was based on the theory that it was possible to destroy the enemy's means of production, the *materiel effect*, by the concentrated bombing of major production nodes; that is, a system or industry whose destruction would cause the breakdown of the entire industrial sector.

While most students of the air war in Europe have concluded that airpower did *not* decide the outcome of World War II, they acknowledged that it contributed greatly to the Allied victory. It is further argued by some that had it been employed more effectively—more closely in line with doctrine—it could have produced decisive results. With the employment of the atomic bomb, and the development of jet aircraft and missile technologies, the theory of airpower became firmly inculcated in the minds of Americans.

In the post-war period, most Americans believed Army ground forces and doctrines were obsolete. Infantry doctrine, in particular, was considered an old and unnecessary practice of war. Ever since, the Army has been on the defensive. Airpower appealed to the American imagination. It was new technology. It was glamorous. It was continuously changing, continuously offering revolutionary transformations. Airplanes were sleek, sexy, and they offered enormous promise for a better future. No argument the Army could make had the potential to reverse the idea of airpower.

The Army's Practice of War

The history of the US Army is the history of the United States, and the history of the American people. At every critical moment in the nation's history, from the American Revolution, through the Civil War, to the destruction of Nazi Germany, the US Army was there, a major determinant in the unfolding of history and the shaping of the nation. No other institution in the United States has had a more profound role in the shaping the nation. The US Army has many faces: that of Western explorer, settler of Indians, engineer of waterways, deliverer of relief in emergencies and natural disasters, manager of the overseas empire, protector of allies, and others. However, the primary purpose of the US Army is to fight the nation's wars. The history of the US Army in peace and war is well documented.[5] No effort is made in these pages to summarize this extensive body of work.[6] The objective here is to identify core cultural tenets that influenced Army thinking in the post-World War II period. In World War II, technologies greatly influenced the Army's conduct of war. Army ground forces integrated new technologies into its traditional doctrine of war, and developed a separate armor warfare doctrine. It also developed airborne infantry, mechanized infantry, and Ranger infantry.[7] Still, the Army retained core cultural beliefs that went back to the Civil War and the formative years of the nation.

The Army's way of war prior to the invention of the tank was based on historical experiences. Infantry battles won all of America's wars prior to World War II. The primary instrument for the conduct of battles until World War II was a soldier armed with an individual weapon organized into regiments and divisions. The principal mission of the Army was to close with and destroy the enemy's main army in battle. This was the way the most traumatic events in the nation's history—the American Revolution, Civil War, and World War II, were ultimately fought and brought to a conclusion. Because the US typically entered war unprepared, its initial strategy, doctrine, and pursuit of battle were constrained by paucity of resources, training, and skilled leadership.[8] However, once mobilized, the Army tended toward the employment of offensive strategy, operations, and doctrine. War was to be fought in a continuous unrelenting manner.[9] Wars were to be won by a series of offensive campaigns and campaigns won by a series of offensive battles. The two most fundamental tenets for the US Army's approach to war were that *successful battles and campaigns win wars*, and that *man is the dominant instrument on the battlefield*. It can be argued that both are tenets of the "Western Way of War." Nevertheless, the way they were executed was uniquely American.

FM 100–5, *Field Service Regulations: Operations* (22 May 1941), contained the principal Army doctrine for the conduct of World War II. (Arguably, it also contained the cultural inheritance of the Army from the American Revolution to World War II. Doctrine is function of culture and technology. Technology, as a norm, changes faster than culture. Culture is thus constantly adapting to new technologies.) The thinking delineated in FM 100–5 was reflected in other Army doctrine manuals, such as, FM 31–5 *Landing Operations on Hostile Shores*. The United States Army in World War II was primarily an infantry army. The infantry divisions were the primary instruments for the destruction of the enemy's main forces. And the Army's most senior leaders were primarily infantry officers. FM 100–5 stated, "No one arm wins battles. The combined action of all arms and services is essential to success." Still, the emphasis was on the infantry. Of the eighty-nine divisions organized to fight World War II, seventy four were fundamentally infantry (66 infantry, 5 airborne, 1 mountain, 2 cavalry). Only sixteen armored divisions were formed, and they typically contained as many infantry battalions as tank battalions.[10] While infantry divisions were combined arms organizations containing tank and artillery units, their primary means of destroying the enemy was intended to be the infantry. FM 100–5 outlined the basic thinking of the Army:

> The Infantry is essentially an arm of close combat. Its primary mission in the attack is to close with the enemy and destroy or capture him. ... Infantry fights by combining fire, movement, and shock action. By fire, it inflicts losses on the enemy and neutralizes his combat power; by movement, it closes with the enemy and makes its fire more effective; by shock action, it completes the destruction of the enemy in close combat. Infantry is capable of limited independent action through the employment of its own weapons. Its offensive power decreases appreciably by an organized defensive position. Under these conditions or against a force of the combined arms, the limited firepower of Infantry must be adequately reinforced by the support of artillery, tanks, combat aviation, and other arms. ... The principal weapons of Infantry are the rifle and bayonet, the automatic rifle, and the machine gun. Other weapons include mortars, pistols, grenades, light antitank weapons, and antitank guns.[11]

Battles were to be won primarily by the infantry, supported by artillery, tanks, air power, and naval gunfire. FM 100–5 emphasized that: "*Man is the fundamental instrument in war; other instruments may change but he remains relatively constant. . . . In spite of the advances in technology, the worth of the individual man is still decisive. . . . The ultimate objective of all military operations is the destruction of the enemy's armed forces in battle.*"[12] This was an immutable cultural tenet of the US Army. FM 22–10, *Leadership*, published during the Korean War, restated this tenet: "Man is the fundamental instrument of war. Other instruments may change, new weapons may be created and new modes of defense may be devised, but man, the fundamental instrument, remains constant."[13] In 1959, General Trudeau restated these words. And a reading of World War I manuals reveals similar wording. No tenet was more basic to the mission and purpose of the US Army. This tenet has been heard again and again in numerous wars and in numerous ways on numerous battlefields. It is repeated in after actions reports, training memorandum, doctrinal publications, and other forms of communications.

In March 1943 Major General Walter B. Smith, Chief of Staff Allied Forces Headquarters, published a training memorandum for all Army forces in the North African-Mediterranean Theater, which, in part, stated:

> War is a dirty business, and anyone who engages in it must face the facts. It is simply a question of killing or being killed. It cannot be impersonal. To wage successful combat there must be a burning desire to come to grips with the enemy, and to kill him in mortal combat. There is no other way to win against a determined enemy. . . . Battles, large and small, cannot be won entirely by maneuver, or by artillery or air action. Well trained troops cannot be shot or bombed out of a position. They can be "softened" by such action, but it remains for the Infantry; conversed by its supporting arms, to close with the enemy and by use, or threatened use, of the bayonet to drive him from his position. . . . There is no other formula. . . . A weakling or unskilled soldier simply will not stand up to it. The required physical conditioning and skill can only be developed by training . . . in the same manner that a football

team is developed, or a boxer prepares for a fight. He must be particularly proficient with the bayonet. . . . And when accompanied by battle cries they have seemed to strike terror to his heart. *The object of war is to kill the enemy. . . .* And the more ruthlessness with which that object is pursued the shorter will be the period of conflict.[14]

This memorandum contained Army cultural beliefs about war and American cultural beliefs about manhood and honorable behavior. Ground warfare required men to close with the enemy on relatively equal terms and kill him. American superiority was seen in the quality of its men, not the quality of its weapons. War was still the ultimate test of manhood. Smith's memorandum was a reflection of American history and culture, "the Indian war cry" or "the rebel yell," beliefs about equality (with the proper training all American men can perform well in combat), meeting the enemy face-to-face, team spirit, physical battle, the bayonet, and the fight to the death. War, according to Americans and its principal instrument for war, the US Army, meant closing with the enemy and killing him much the way it was done in the American Revolution and Civil War. Smith recognized that the uniquely American game of football was the quintessential reflection of American thinking about the conduct of war: two teams with an equal number of players, under the relatively equal conditions, lined up to face one another on an agreed upon field for physical battle. Human attributes, not technological sophistication, made the difference. Victory was based on talent, skill, physical strength, tenacity, the will to win, and intelligence—all character traits highly valued in America's competitive, capitalist society.

* * * * *

Between doctrine and reality there is always a gap. Gaps always exist between what an army believes war should look like and what it actually is, between the expected performance of men and their actual performance, and between cultural standards of manhood and human nature. Throughout history, advances in technology brought about by science and engineering have increased the range, accuracy, rate of fire, and lethality of weapons; and thus, the carnage of war. Since the invention of the first gunpowder weapon, the capabilities and complexities of weapons have increased with no apparent limitations in sight. The optimal scientific approach to war, then, is to employ the most advanced technologies available, to kill the enemy as efficiently as possible, while sustaining as few casualties as possible.

The Army, as a subculture of the larger American culture, was imbued with tenets that, in some ways, conflicted with its most basic tenet, which held that man was the dominant instrument on the battlefield. One of the greatest strengths of American culture is its adaptability. The American capitalist system and the extraordinary freedoms enjoyed by Americans create the uniquely American individualism and adaptability that produces exceptional performance. However, it can also be argued that Americans have a preference for the way they adapt, and that the single-minded preference for adaptation using technology is in fact a weakness. Americans place enormous faith in the ability of science and technology to solve the problems of humanity, including war. The technological solution has tended to be the best solution for Americans. Americans also place the highest value on the lives of their young men. The logical conclusion of the convergence of technological trends and American cultural tenets is the elimination of man from the battlefield, using technologies that make possible the engagement of targets from beyond the limits of the battlefield.

At times the Army has confused firepower, which simply kills, with combat power, which achieves victories. While arguing for the primacy of man, the Army also developed technologies and ways of fighting designed to reduce the number of men required on the battlefield. The Army relied heavily on firepower, as a substitute for manpower, to win battles. Throughout World War II the Army's use of firepower from artillery, armor, naval gunfire, and airpower increased. Similar developments took place in the Pacific Theater. There were multiple reasons for this shift toward greater use of firepower, but the primary reason was to reduce casualties and save lives. Still, there were other reasons for the continuous increase in the use of firepower.

In the initial days of fighting during World War II, the Army had to go through a shakeout. Until initial exposure, the fighting qualities of a soldier are unknown. Tactically, American company and platoon size infantry units lacked the firepower of comparable German units. German squads and platoons were capable of generating greater firepower than equivalent American formations. Joseph Balkoski wrote:

> U.S. Army field manuals emphasized the importance of fire superiority, but in truth, the Yanks found it difficult to achieve without supporting artillery. American infantrymen simply were not provided with enough firepower to establish battlefield dominance. Each 29th Division [basic U.S. Army infantry division] rifle company of 193 men had only two machine guns, both of which were in an independent weapons platoon. On the other hand, a German infantry company of only 142 men had fifteen machine guns. The German company's firepower was further enhanced by its twenty-eight submachine guns. The 29ers had no weapons of this type. The American rifle company was dependent on its nine BARs for rapid fire, but these weapons could not stand up to the MG 42s. Instead of forcing the Germans to keep their heads down with a large volume of M1 and BAR fire, as the American manual demanded, it was usually the Yanks who got pinned. ... The MG 42's rate of fire was three times as fast as comparable American machine guns ... [and] could expend ammunition more freely than an American BAR man, since the rest of the German squad was devoted almost entirely to feeding the ravenous MG 42.[15]

And Russell Weigley observed: "The inadequacy of the battlefield power generated by the standard infantry division accounted for the custom of attaching one of the separate tank battalions to almost every infantry division. The attached tank battalions were to prove essential to the forward advance of the infantry against recalcitrant opposition. ..."[16] Because of superior German firepower at the small unit level, and the failure of senior Allied leaders to adequately consider terrain, US Army infantry tactical doctrine typically did not work; new doctrine had to be worked out as the situations changed and experience was gained. The Army had to adapt, and it did so primarily with technology. It came to rely on artillery and armor in support of infantry to overcome deficiencies in firepower at the squad and platoon level.

Training also influenced the ability to generate combat power. The German squads and platoons were not only capable of generating greater firepower; they were also better trained than most American formations. For example, the 29th Infantry Division entered battle for the first time on 6 June 1944. It fought its first battle against the veteran 352nd Division at the water's edge at Omaha Beach. German soldiers and formations had fought for five years at that point. Tactical doctrine had been refined on the Eastern Front in hard-fought campaigns. German soldiers understood well how to fight and survive on the battlefield.

The shortage of infantry divisions and the Army's individual replacement system, as opposed to unit rotation, also damaged the ability of the infantry to generate combat power. Typically, ninety percent of casualties were in infantry units. The Army organized, equipped, and trained too few divisions to rotate them in and out of combat. As a consequence, units stayed in line long after they should have been rotated out. The 1st ID, between D-Day, 6 June 1944 and the end of the war in May 1945, suffered 29,630 total casualties, almost twice its authorized strength. The 9th ID suffered 33,000; the 29th ID suffered 20,620; and the 28th 16,762. Many other divisions suffered casualties one and a half times their authorized strength. The 1st ID was in combat in Europe for 317 days. The 2nd ID was in combat 303 days; the 9th ID, 304 days; and 82nd Airborne Division, 422 days of combat. The Texas 36th NG Divisions saw 400 days of combat; the 45th Oklahoma-Colorado NG Division, 511 days; and the 29th Maryland and Virginia NG Division, 242 days. This type of sustained combat brutalizes men, causing psychological trauma. It also causes divisions to go through performance peaks and valleys, but overall diminishes combat effectiveness.

Late in 1944, the US Army was desperately short of infantrymen. Eisenhower converted tank-destroyer units, antiaircraft units, cooks, drivers, clerks, and other rear-echelon personnel into infantrymen. He even took measures to partially integrate the Army, creating black rifle platoons to serve in white infantry companies. Training again became a problem for veteran units. The shortage of infantry caused an increase in the use of artillery and airpower. Finally, a paucity of well-trained and selected small unit leaders diminished the ability of the Army to generate combat power at the edge of the battlefield. Leadership was developed through on-the-job training. It must be remembered that when World War II started in Europe in 1939, the US Army numbered 187,893 soldiers. The US Army that fought in World War II was an emergency-assembled citizen-soldier force that adapted and fought well given its lack of pre-war preparation.

As a consequence of the disparity in firepower, training, leadership, and other factors at the small unit level, the Army depended on greater firepower from artillery and airpower. An intelligence report from Army Group B outlined the German impression of the US and British Armies:

> Strong use of equipment, preservation of manpower. . . . Exceptionally strong massing of artillery, lavish expenditures of munitions. Before attacks begin, systematic, lengthy artillery preparations. Infantry and tanks advance behind a heavy curtain of mortar and machine gun fire. The artillery is divided into three groups. The first supports the attack with a rolling barrage; the second fires in support of individual calls-for-fire from the infantry in the main battle area; the third conducts counterbattery fire (with effective use of aerial observers). Multiple smoke screens obscure the attack zone in order to obscure defensive weapons and observation posts; in some cases a smoke screen is placed immediately forward of the front at the beginning of the attack.
>
> Little massing of infantry; mostly battalion or regimental strength. . . . Tanks attack in support of the infantry. . . . The infantry attack only after the strongpoints have been neutralized. . . . The attack goes according to a well-timed and organized plan. Piece after piece of the defensive line is broken. Less value is placed on initiative than on coordinated fire support.[17]

Senior Army leaders became airpower enthusiasts. Eisenhower, Montgomery, and Bradley accepted many of the claims of airpower advocates. In their operations it was clear that they placed great faith in the destructive power of air forces. In Operation Neptune, the Normandy invasion; Operation Goodwood, the attempted British breakout from Caen; and Operation Cobra, the American breakout from St. Lo, as well as other major battles, they relied heavily on airpower to generate the combat power needed to succeed.[18]

In World War II, the Army acquired a new offensive ground warfare campaign-winning doctrine. The tank was developed in World War I. However, it did not prove decisive in war until World War II. In May 1940, the Wehrmacht decisively defeated the French Army in a short, intensive war employing combined arms, maneuver warfare doctrine, frequently called "blitzkrieg"—the methods and principles for employing tanks, mechanized infantry, artillery, and close air support (CAS) as an integrated combat team, that relied on speed, maneuver, communications, and audacity to break into the enemy's rear areas to destroy his command, communications, and logistic centers and to encircle his forces.[19] Armor technology and doctrine appeared to be a form of warfare that had the potential to replace the Army's infantry campaign-winning doctrine. Consider the thinking of Lieutenant General Crittenberger, who wrote during the final days of the Korean War:

> Today everyone realizes that war is a national effort in which the Armed Forces, of necessity, must base their effectiveness on the country's national resources and capabilities. In the United States that means we must capitalize on our outstanding position in industry, including design and manufacture. In particular it means that we must capitalize on our predominant position in the automotive field, in the sphere of aviation and in electronics. And that is where and why American Armor comes into the picture, for Armor puts a premium on certain distinctive American characteristics. . . .
>
> Here in the United States the spirit and the entire concept of Armor is American in character. It is an arm of opportunity. It conforms to the American principle of moving in fast and getting the job done. . . . Looking at Armor objectively, it is alive, it is vital, it is modern. . . . Armor is characteristically a weapon of the young man. In design, manufacture concept, it is modern—just

as the young man is modern in outlook. It is also a weapon of opportunity. That, too, personifies youth. . . . It is not an arm of centuries of tradition. Instead, it is the vital, growing contemporary of American fighting men. It does not live in the past. It looks to greater opportunities and accomplishments, to new ideas and further prestige. And it will be more decisive, more effective as time goes on.

> In tempo and spirit, American Armor has moved forward as dynamically in its development as it moved decisively in combat. A spirit of change and constant improvement has been its motivating force. In ten or fifteen years, we have gone from. 30 and. 50 caliber machine guns for tanks on up to 90-mm and 120-mm, guns. . . . Advances in electronics, ballistics, and communications . . . have greatly enhanced Armor's effectiveness. Advancements . . . in techniques for full utilization of television and radar are all of vital concern.[20]

These words reveal virtually all the cultural tents noted in the previous chapter, and other tenets of American life: change, optimism, growth, faith in technology, faith in American power, equality, and others. In many of the claims outlined here for armor, the Air Force and Navy could have substituted "aircraft." The tank had many of the same appeals to the Army as aircraft had for the Air Force and Navy. If it can be argued that the Army had a glamour weapon, it was the tank. The tank was a technological means of killing, with greater range and more protection than any other instrument of land warfare. It had speed and cross-country mobility. It made war more destructive, increasing the intensity and pace. The tank thus had the potential to bring about a more rapid conclusion to war than traditional infantry warfare.

While all the attributes of the tank had great appeal to American thinking about the conduct of war, the tank tended to make the Army act more like the Air Force and Navy. The Air Force and Navy fight machines with machines. They endeavor to perfect their performance in the employment of technology. The Army traditionally fights men. It endeavors to perfect men and teamwork, to improve the human skills that facilitate the killing of other men. As General Smith noted, "It cannot be impersonal." The kinds of courage required by soldiers and marines is very different from the kinds of courage required in the Navy and Air Force, which is why the culture of the Army has to be very different from that of the other services. Nevertheless, the tank gave the Army another subculture that emphasized technology in much the same manner as the Air Force.

While the Army emphasized the decisive role of man and closing with the enemy, it substituted firepower for manpower at every opportunity. Firepower reduced casualties and reduced the number of frontline soldiers required to achieve tactical objectives. The urgency of war; the available technologies; the American preference for cutting-edge weapons; and the value Americans placed on human life caused the Army to seek technological solutions. However, firepower is only one aspect of combat power. And it is combat power, not firepower, that wins wars.[21]

The Army has at times been at war with itself. While recognizing that it had to produce a certain type of soldier to enter the battlefield and come face-to-face with the enemy in order to kill him, at the same time, it pursued ways of war that removed men from the battlefield, diminished their exposure to the enemy, and killed with technology from afar. In the 1950s this internal contradiction caused the Army to engage in counterproductive competitions with the Air Force, caused it to assume missions that were better left to the Air Force, caused it to use its limited funds on weapons systems that did not enhance the conduct of ground warfare, and caused it to move away from its primary mission of ground combat.

Airpower: A New Practice of War

Airpower dominated post-war thinking about the conduct of war. There were two accepted theories for the employment of strategic air forces, and one unofficial, unspoken theory. The first theory stated that the primary objective of airpower was the destruction of the will of the people, the bombing of cities and towns to destroy the willingness of people to work and support the government. The destruction of the will of the people, it was argued, destroyed the productive capacity of the state by psychologically removing the manpower required to run the nation's industries. The second theory stated that the primary

objective of airpower was the destruction of the means of production; that is, destroying the enemy's ability to make war by bombing key industries essential to the operation of a modern industrial economy. The third theory, *extermination warfare*, was never officially acknowledged. However, it has been argued that it was evident in the bombing campaigns of both Britain and the United States during World War II.

The bombing of civilians, the first theory, had a second objective, to affect the will of political leaders. The intent was to kill enough of the people to convince their political leaders to surrender. In the war against Japan, the atomic bomb ultimately achieved this end. However, there is a fine line between bombing to destroy the will of the people and bombing to destroy *people*. At what level of carnage does bombing to destroy the will of the people become bombing to exterminate people? The potential end result of targeting people themselves is genocide. Other reasons for bombing people included retaliation, revenge, anger, racism, the desire to demonstrate the efficacy of strategic airpower, shifting values and ethics caused by prolonged exposure to carnage, the desire to bring the war to a rapid conclusion to save lives, friction between allies, and other uniquely human factors, as well as technological limitations and resource constraints. The stated, official objective of the British strategic bombing campaign was the destruction of the will of the people. The stated, official objective of the American strategic bombing campaign was the destruction of the enemy's means of production.

Consider first the British approach. In 1919, Trenchard proclaimed that: "At present the moral effect of bombing stands undoubtedly to the material effect in a proportion of 20 to 1."[22] Trenchard had no evidence upon which to base this conclusion; nevertheless, the concept had considerable staying power. The 1928 RAF War Manual ('Operations' section) stated: "Although the bombardment of suitable objectives should result in considerable material damage and loss, the most important and far-reaching effect of air bombardment is its moral effect." The RAF and other services discussed various theories of air war during the inter-war period, but without the funding to build aircraft and test doctrine, all their theories were academic. In the 1930s, when the post-World War I agreements started to break down, Britain started to re-arm to compete with the growing military strength of Germany. Technology, however, limited what was possible. In the early days of the war the British tried both accepted theories, ultimately deciding on the destruction of the will of the people, which, as the war progressed, moved inexorably towards extermination warfare.

In May 1940, airpower was one of the factors that saved Britain, by persuading Churchill, the royal family, and the nation to continue to fight. After the "Fall of France," Britain faced the Nazi juggernaut alone. Given the development of the previous five years and the collapse of the French Army, Britain had few reasons to believe it could prevail. At this juncture, some in Britain believed it wise to consider some form of peace with Germany that might save the Empire. A number of factors influenced the decision-makers in Britain: the "miracle at Dunkirk," which saved more than 300,000 British soldiers and perhaps more importantly, British military leadership; the English Channel and the Royal Navy, which had historically saved Britain; the belief, fate, and personality of Churchill; the belief that the "new world," the United States, would come to the rescue of the old world; and faith in the new technology of airpower. On 17 May 1940, a report to the Cabinet from the Chiefs of Staff Committee on "British strategy in a certain eventuality," asserted that the combined bombing of Germany and German-controlled Europe with a vigorous naval blockade could create the conditions for a revolt against Germany.[23] Churchill lifted all restrictions on bombing, noting that: "an absolutely devastating, exterminating attack by very heavy bombers upon the Nazi homeland" was the only way to defeat Hitler.

Churchill accepted this vision of war from the air. In a "memorandum" to the Minister of Supply written on 3 September 1940, the Prime Minister outlined his thinking:

The Navy can lose the war, but only the Air Force can win it. Therefore, our supreme effort must be to gain overwhelming mastery in the air. The Fighters are our salvation, but the Bombers alone provide the means of victory. We must, therefore, develop the power to carry an ever-increasing volume of explosives to Germany, so as to pulverize the entire industry and scientific structure on which the war effort and economic life of the enemy depend, while holding him at arm's length from our island. In no other way at present visible can we hope to overcome the immense military power of Germany, and to nullify the further German victories which may be apprehended as the weight of their force is brought to bear upon African or Oriental theatres. The Air Force and its action on the largest scale must, therefore, subject to what is said later, claim the first place over the Navy or the Army.[24]

Churchill adopted the vision of victory through airpower, in part, out of an absence of other options. On the defense, the Navy, Army, and fighter command could save Britain by not losing the war, but only through offensive actions could Nazi Germany be defeated. And at this juncture, an amphibious invasion and ground war were far beyond the capabilities of Britain and its Empire. While Churchill believed airpower offered the potential for victory, his major objective was to get new allies. In June 1941, Hitler invaded the Soviet Union, and in December, Japan attacked the United States. These events totally changed the strategic situation, yet Churchill retained his faith in airpower.

To explain why Britain was willing to invest its fate in the unproven doctrine of airpower, Marshal of the RAF Arthur Harris, commander-in-chief of Bomber Command, wrote:

The idea was a natural one for a country which had never maintained an army of Continental proportions, has a large empire which must be defended as cheaply as possible, and has in the past largely won its wars by the strategic use of sea power working as an independent weapon; the same principle of strategy that made England a sea power in the past had only to be applied to the new weapon which had rendered obsolete the old one, the battleship.[25]

From this assessment, it can be deduced that ground forces were the equivalent of the "battleship." Throughout the war, senior British airpower leaders believed that strategic bombing alone could win the war and that the heavy bomber was the dominant weapon in the conduct of modern war.

In 1940, when the British initiated the strategic bombing campaign, the ability to hit small targets at altitudes of 20,000 to 25,000 feet did not exist. Hence, the ability of Bomber Command to destroy German production facilities was severely limited. The British also lacked the resources in bombers, trained crews, intelligence on German production facilities, and bombs with sufficient explosive power to do long-term damage to German facilities. Other problems, such as weather, the exigencies of naval and ground war, friction over the allocation of resources, and, most important, German defensive measures impeded the efforts of Bomber Command. The British were forced to bomb at night, and had great difficulty finding designated targets. As a consequence, and perhaps out of a sense of urgency to show results and some desire for revenge, the British emphasized the destruction of the "will of the people" through the killing of civilians. In April 1942, Churchill wrote to the Secretary of State for Air:

> We are placing great hopes on our bomber offensive against Germany next winter, and we must spare no pains to justify the large proportion of the national effort devoted to it. The Air Ministry's responsibility is to make sure that the maximum weight of the best type of bombs is dropped on the German cities by the aircraft placed at their disposal. Unless we can ensure that most of our bombs really do some damage it will be difficult to justify the pre-eminence we are according to this form of attack.[26]

Churchill was convinced that the destruction of German cities would produce results, and, technologically, Bomber Command was incapable of doing anything else.

British targeting reveals a desire to kill as many people as possible as opposed to killing those members of the state whose death and suffering was most likely to produce the desired political outcome:

> Early in 1942 he [Professor Lindemann, also known as Lord Cherwell and a member of the Cabinet] produced a cabinet paper on the strategic bombing of Germany. . . . It described, in quantitative terms, the effect on Germany of a British bombing offensive in the next eighteen months (approximately March 1942—September 1943). The paper laid down a strategic policy. The bombing must be directed essentially against the German working-class houses. Middle-class houses have too much space round them, and so are bound to waste bombs; factories and "military objectives" had long since been forgotten, except in official bulletins, since they were much too difficult to find and hit. The paper claimed that—given a total concentration of effort on the production and use of bombing aircraft—it would be possible, in all the larger towns of Germany (that is, those with more than 50,000 inhabitants), to destroy 50 percent of all houses. . . . Strategic bombing, according to the Lindemann policy, was put into action with every effort the country could make.[27]

As the war progressed, moral qualms evaporated. And, it must be remembered that the British war started two years before the American war. It was known that "working-class houses," particularly at night when the British attacked, had people in them—families, women and children. The British terminology, "de-housing," was deceptive. The British sought to maximize the number of casualties per bomb. In July 1943, the British carried out incendiary night attacks against the urban center of Hamburg, Germany, killing an estimated 45,000 people. Was this extermination warfare?[28]

In November 1944, the United States Secretary of War directed that a major study be carried out to evaluate the effects of bombing. The study resulted in *The US Strategic Bombing Survey*, which found that:

> The mental reaction of the German people to air attack is significant. Under ruthless Nazi control they showed surprising resistance to the terror and hardships of repeated air attack, to the destruction of their homes and belongings, and to the conditions under which they were reduced to live. Their morale, their belief in ultimate victory or satisfactory compromise, and their confidence in their leaders declined, but they continued to work efficiently as long as the physical means of production remained. The power

of a police state over its people cannot be underestimated.[29]

"Ruthless Nazi control" was not the primary cause for the behavior of the German people.[30] The assessment of the "surprising resistance" of the German people also applied to the people of Britain, Japan, Korea, and Vietnam. What other option did they have? Bernard Brodie concluded that:

> From at least the beginning of 1944 the average German had become disillusioned with the Nazi leadership, increasingly frightened by war's toll and its potential threat to himself and his family, and persuaded with growing certainty that all would end in defeat. Yet he stuck to his job and his machine for as long as it was physically possible to do so, and in so doing kept a disastrous war going to its ultimate ruinous conclusion. Why did he do so? The answer is to be found in need combined with habit, in coercion, and in propaganda—in descending order of importance— all adding up to the plain circumstance that the German worker had no real alternative open to him.[31]

Another student of strategic bombing, Robert A. Pape, noted:

> ... the citizenry of the target state is not likely to turn against its government because of civilian punishment. The supposed causal chain—civilian hardship produces public anger which forms political opposition against the government— does not stand up. One reason it does not is that a key assumption behind this argument—that economic deprivation causes popular unrest—is false. As social scientists have shown, economic deprivation does often produce personal frustration, but collective violence against governments requires populations to doubt the moral worth of the political system as a whole, as opposed to specific policies, leaders, or results. Political alienation is more important than economic deprivation as a cause of revolutions.[32]

The British strategic bombing doctrine did not destroy the will of the people, and it did not destroy the will of the government. In the mind of Hitler and his senior leaders who accepted Nazi ideology, people existed only to serve the state—particularly working-class people. After the horrendous battle of Stalingrad in which the Germans lost between 250,000 and 300,000 men, Hitler stated: "What is life? Life is the nation. The individual must die any way. Beyond the life of the individual, is the nation."[33]

Still, the British airpower historian, Richard Overy, concluded that the "impact of bombing was profound." Overy wrote:

> Industrial efficiency was undermined by bombing workers and their housing. ... [I]n the Ford plant in Cologne, in the Ruhr, absenteeism rose to 25 per cent of the workforce for the whole of 1944. ... A loss of work-hours on this scale played havoc with production schedules. Even those who turned up for work were listless and anxious.[34]

Thus, the bombing campaign killed workers and their families, caused absenteeism, and lowered the morale of those that continued to work, all of which reduced productivity. Bombing did in fact lower morale, diminish hope, create pessimism, and traumatize the people, but the vast majority of survivors continued to work. Overy also concluded that: "The naïve expectation that bombing would somehow produce a tidal wave of panic and disillusionment which would wash away popular support for war, and topple governments built on sand, was exposed as wishful thinking."[35] The British strategic bombing campaign was not decisive.

*   *   *   *   *

The US Army Air Corps, later Army Air Force (AAF), also concluded that airpower was the decisive instrument for the conduct of war. However, it pursued and developed a uniquely American strategic bombing doctrine—precision bombing. In its struggle to separate itself from the US Army, and in its battle to remain separate from the RAF's Bomber Command, the AAF argued that "precision bombing" alone was a war-winning doctrine. General Arnold stated: "The Army Air Forces' principle of precision bombing ... aimed at knocking out not an entire industrial area, nor even a factory, but the most vital parts of

Germany's war machine, such as the power plants and machine shops of particular factories. . . ." This doctrine greatly preceded the development of the technologies required to carry it out. At 25,000 feet, at 150 mph, using the Norden bombsight, flying flat in box formations, the B–17 and B–24 heavy bombers were totally incapable of destroying "the power plants or machine shops of particular factories." In fact, the AAF was incapable of consistently hitting point targets, factory buildings.

In 1918, the US Army Air Service conducted an independent study of the British World War I bombing campaign, in which they criticized the RAF for "the lack of a predetermined program carefully calculated to destroy by successive raids those industries most vital in maintaining Germany's fighting force." While American investigators accepted the theory that the "moral effect" of bombing was of strategic importance, they concluded that: ". . . the enemy's morale was not sufficiently affected to handicap the enemy's fighting force in the field . . .;" that, "The policy as followed out by the British and French in the present war of bombing a target once or twice and then skipping to another target is erroneous . . .;" and that, "Bombing for moral effect alone . . . which was probably the excuse for the wide spread of bombs over a town rather than their concentration on a factory, is not a productive means of bombing."[36] The objection was not with the theory of bombing to destroy the will of the people, but with the method.

In the 1930s at the Air Corps Tactical School (ACTS) at Maxwell Field in Alabama, the doctrine of precision bombing was advanced by an inspired group of young airmen. Donald Wilson, Harold George, and Robert Webster produced much of the pioneering work on precision bombing.[37] The Air Force's official history noted that:

> The Air Corps Tactical School proceeded to preach that offensive air operations offered the most direct avenue to victory. The ACTS faculty taught its 1934–35 class that "loss of morale in the civilian population is decisive" in war and that air power alone could directly affect this key factor. The instructors played down the advantages of population bombing because international sentiment opposed this method and because air

officers believed destruction of an adversary's industrial base, raw materials transportation system, and energy supplies would be a more efficient way to induce peace. The ACTS's "Air Force" text was a bit uncertain whether the foe's air force should be wiped out before launching a campaign against his economy, but it eventually resolved that if the hostile air arm was a threat it must first be neutralized. The text nevertheless made it clear there were no air missions more important than these two in bringing about the enemy's defeat.[38]

Thus, in the interwar years the Army Air Corps officers learned lessons that would hinder their ability to work with the rest of the Army. They learned that close air support, interdiction, and supporting ground forces operations were the least productive use of airpower. The Army Air Corps all but ignored the War Department's policy that the airpower was to operate "as an arm of the mobile Army," placing such missions low on the list of priorities. The uncertainty about air superiority combined with the drive to demonstrate the decisive role of bombers and the perceived defensive capabilities of the B–17s and B–24s, caused costly doctrinal mistakes in the initial phase of the air campaign. And, while the Air Force text gave priority to bombing for material effect, it did not eliminate bombing for moral effect.

A year before the outbreak of war in Europe, the 1938 text for the "Air Force" confirmed the thinking of American airmen:

> . . . the economic structure of a modern highly industrialized nation is characterized by the great degree of interdependence of its various elements. Certain of these elements are vital to the continued functioning of the modern nation. If one of these elements is destroyed the whole of the economic machine ceases to function. . . . Against a highly industrialized nation air force action has the possibility for such far reaching effectiveness that such action may produce immediate and decisive results.

Historians disagree on the extent to which the AAF deviated from its official doctrine of precision bombing in the European Theater. However, out of necessity the AAF did bomb for "moral effect," that is, area bombing, in concert with its precision-bombing campaign.

The AAF's basic instincts for material bombing were at times overcome by technological limitations, weather conditions, enemy antiaircraft systems, the urgency to produce results, and competition with the British. In the Pacific Theater, difficulties in initiating the campaign, anger, racism, some desire for revenge, and a general loosening of moral restraints, moved the Air Force to adopt the British practice of bombing city centers. Still, in reference to the air war in Europe, Conrad Crane concluded: "most AAF airmen did live up to the spirit of [precision-bombing]. [The] USSTAF did resist the temptation to attack morale directly and to kill civilians to attain that end."[39]

The AAF initiated its strategic bombing campaign with a number of assumptions that proved to be false. The AAF assumed that the heavily armed B–17s and B–24s flying in tight formations could penetrate German air space and defend themselves against German fighters and antiaircraft defense systems. It assumed that the Norden bombsight could produce a high degree of accuracy. It assumed that once a target was attacked it was destroyed, rendered inoperable. It assumed that the vital centers of an industrial society could be determined and systematically destroyed. And, it was assumed that escort fighter aircraft were unnecessary. The AAF failed to examine objectively the lessons learned from the British experiences in the first two years of the war. The fear of amalgamation into the British bombing program and the compulsion for independence from the Army drove the AAF to establish itself as a unique, decisive instrument of war. Its doctrine became dogma, and in its initial daylight raids the bombers suffered heavy losses. On 5 September 1942, the Eighth Air Force attacked the Rouen-Sotteville marshalling yard. Eighty percent of its bombs fell outside the marshalling yard, killing as many as 140 civilians and wounding another 200. A student of the air war, W. Hays Parks, wrote:

> Eighth Air Force's claims of 'precision' bombing were not particularly appreciated by the French, who were justifiably skeptical about the ability to bomb accurately from 25,000 feet. It was a prob-lem that would plague US heavy bombers striking targets in proximity to friendly civilians or Allied ground forces throughout the war; high-altitude formation bombing was not a precision tool.[40]

Parks concluded that: "The USA leadership underwent a philosophical change of heart in October 1943," because of the difficulties in destroying point targets, the heavy losses suffered in daylight deep penetration bombing of Germany, perceived British success in area bombing of German cities, and advances in radar technology. On 1 November 1943 General Arnold ordered the heavy bomber forces to carry out radar-assisted bombing attacks against selected targets, typically rail yards located in cities, when it was not feasible to bomb point targets visually. This was in essence area bombing. The AAF took part in the bombing of Hamburg, Dresden, and twenty-five other German cities. Still, Parks' conclusions are a bit off the mark. The AAF retained its belief in daylight precision bombing of selected strategically important targets, and throughout the war conducted precision bombing attacks.

By the end of 1943, adjustments were being made that facilitated precision bombing. New tactics and technologies were employed. Fighter escorts accompanied the bombers. The range of fighters was extended, enabling them to penetrate deep into Germany. New fighters were put in service. And the size of the Eighth Air Force increased. In February 1944, the AAF was capable of putting 1,046 bombers in the air over Germany. Six months later it almost doubled this capability, putting more than 2,000 in the air. By concentrating on the destruction of German aircraft industry, oil production facilities, and air defense systems, air superiority was gained. By the end of 1944 the Army Air Force and Bomber Command could fly wherever they wanted, whenever they wanted. With air superiority the strategic air forces were able to concentrate destructive power on key industries, such as oil production facilities or the German national railway system.

How effective was the American strategic bombing campaign in damaging the ability of Germany to make war? The authors of the *US Strategic Bombing Survey* wrote:

Because the German economy through most of the war was substantially undermobilized, it was resilient under air attack. Civilian consumption was high during the early years of the war and inventories both in trade channels and consumers' possession were also high. These helped cushion the people of the German cities from the effects of bombing. Plants and machinery were plentiful and incompletely used. Thus it was comparatively easy to substitute unused or partly used machinery for that which was destroyed. While there was constant pressure throughout for German manpower for the Wehrmacht, the industrial labor supply, as augmented by foreign labor, was sufficient to permit the diversion of large numbers to the repair of bomb damage or the clearance of debris with relatively small sacrifice of essential production.[41]

German production rose throughout most of the war, and only in late 1944 did it start to decline as a result of the strategic bombing campaign. National industrial economies were not easily brought to collapse by bombing. The resilience of the German economy disproved the AAF's axiom that: "... air force action has the possibility for such far reaching effectiveness that such action may produce immediate and decisive results." Excess capacity, greater efficiencies, extended hours of operation, increased labor, the shift in production from civilian to military goods, the substitution of products, the ability to repair damaged facilities, and numerous other factors precluded the AAF from achieving the decisive victory it sought.

A student of the German economy, Alfred C. Mierzejewski, concluded that the Allies concentrated their efforts on the wrong target late in 1944. He noted that: "Oil was not crucial to German industry ... assault on Germany's petroleum resources could not have harmed the Reich's basic industrial economy."[42] German industry was fueled by coal. Mierzejewski concluded that, given the geographic divisions in the German economy, the National Railway, the "Reichsbahn," was essential to the continued survival of Nazi Germany. He wrote: "... the Reichsbahn distributed the economy's life blood—coal. The coal/transport nexus was the very core of the division of labor. As long as it functioned, the

mechanism could continue to produce. If it were severed, then the economy would necessarily, though not immediately, crash to the ground." Thus the final collapse of the German economy was delayed by the failure to identify the decisive target. Mierzejewski's work demonstrates the difficulty in determining what was decisive in a modern industrial economy. It can be argued that modern industrial economies were extremely resilient and flexible, adapting quickly to numerous difficulties, and that the destruction of the Reichsbahn would have caused further adaptation. In addition, each state organized its system of production differently. Hence, what was decisive in one state was not necessarily decisive in another.

While it cannot be argued that either the British or American strategic bombing doctrines proved decisive, strategic bombing contributed mightily to the war effort. The heavy bombers destroyed large parts of the German aircraft industry helping the Allies gain air superiority. They carried out the "Transportation Plan" that destroyed key junctions in the French transportation system that supported the movement of forces into and out of Normandy. They attacked the V–1 "Buzz Bomb" sites, stopping the terror bombing of London. They assisted the tactical air forces in the destruction of the German ground forces. And, they destroyed large parts of Germany's ability to produce fuel, ultimately causing their tanks to run dry in the Battle of the Bulge. While it cannot be argued that strategic bombing destroyed the will of the German people, it can be argued that, albeit late in the war, it damaged the morale of the German people, creating pessimism and loss of hope. Still, airpower was not decisive in World War II. The offensive ground war in the east and west destroyed the German Army. Airpower facilitated the ground war. However, the cost of precision bombing in men and aircraft was high. At war's end 40,000 airmen had been killed in combat—more men than were killed in the entire Marine Corps in World War II—and 6,000 aircraft had been destroyed.

The bombing practices of the British and Americans were not static during the war. Bomber Command moved closer to the American practice of precision bombing, improving its ability to hit small targets in darkness and daylight. And the AAF adopted British practices employing radar bombing against targets in the heart of German cities—area bombing.[43] Still, the AAF held tenaciously to the doctrine of precision bombing of selective targets, and in regard to the future of warfare, it was this doctrine that had the potential of making the greatest contribution to the conduct of war. However, when the war ended, the AAF was still incapable of the precision it claimed.

*   *   *   *   *

To explain the differences in the American approach to the strategic bombing of Japan, Crane wrote: "Yet it is undeniable that for a number of reasons strategic-bombing principles and precedents from Europe contributed to 'the slide to total war' in the bombing of Japan."[44] In both theaters, the AAF fought total wars, employing all its resources to bring the war to an end, and sought a total war objective, the destruction of the enemy government. However, the air war against Japan reached new levels of destruction, and new levels of barbarism.

On the night of 9–10 March 1945, 325 B–29 superfortresses from the AAF's Twenty-first Bomber Command dropped 1,665 tons of incendiary bombs into a ten square mile target area in Tokyo, Japan.[45] The napalm and magnesium created a huge hurricane of fire that killed an estimated one hundred thousand people. Ninety percent of the structures in Tokyo were constructed of wood, which fueled and intensified the fire. Many people were completely incinerated. Entire families disappeared. Tornadoes of fire sucked the oxygen out of the air, causing people to suffocate. Those individuals that found shelter underground or in hardened structures were baked to death. One account went as follows:

The entire building had become a huge oven three stories high. Every human being inside the school was literally baked or boiled alive in heat. Dead bodies were everywhere in grisly heaps. None of them appeared to be badly charred. They looked like mannequins, some of them with a pinkish complexion. . . . But the swimming pool was the most horrible of all. It was hideous. More than a thousand people, we estimated, had jammed into the pool. The pool had been filled to its brim when we first arrived. Now there

wasn't a drop of water, only the bodies of the adults and children who had died.[46]

The success of the attack on Tokyo motivated similar attacks on other Japanese cities. As the months went by, General Curtis LeMay's air forces grew stronger in men and bombers. By the end of the war he was capable of putting nearly a thousand B–29s in the air, and more than sixty Japanese cities had been attacked, many of them repeatedly. Cumulatively, the fire bombing was far more destructive than the atomic bomb. Still, a student of the bombing campaign and the decision to employ the atomic bomb concluded:

There might seem to be some solace from the million aggregated horrors of this night in Tokyo to believe that it played some significant role in persuading the Emperor that the war was not only lost but must be halted soon. The story of the events to follow [the event that led to the final surrender], however, admits of no such ready consolation.[47]

In his book, *Mission with LeMay*, LeMay explained his thinking:

General Arnold needed results. Larry Norstad had made that very plain. In effect he had said: "You go ahead and get results with the B–29. If you don't get results, you'll be fired. If you don't get results, also, there'll never be any Strategic Air Forces of the Pacific. . . . If you don't get results it will mean eventually a mass amphibious invasion of Japan. . . .

Let's see . . . Could use both napalm and phosphorus. . . . They say that ninety per cent of the structures in Tokyo are built of wood. That's what Intelligence tells us, and what the guidebooks and the *National Geographic* and things like that. . . . So if we go in low—at night, singly, not in formation—I think we'll surprise the Japs. . . . But if this first attack is successful, we'll run another, right quick. . . . And then maybe another. . . .

Of course magnesium makes the hottest fire, and it'll get things going where probably the napalm might not. But the napalm will splatter farther, cover a greater area. We've got to mix it up. We're not only going to run against those inflammable wooden structures. We're going to run against masonry too. That's where the magnesium comes handy. . . .

No matter how you slice it, you're going to kill an awful lot of civilians. Thousands and thousands. But, if you don't destroy the Japanese industry, we're going to have to invade Japan. And how many Americans will be killed in an invasion of Japan? Five hundred thousand seems to be the lowest estimate. Some say a million. . . .

We're at war with Japan. We were attacked by Japan. Do you want to kill Japanese, or would you rather have Americans killed . . .? I hope you're right Curt. . . . Crank her up. Let's go.[48]

These passages offer insight into LeMay's thinking about the conduct of the air war. LeMay's strategic bombing campaign had four main objectives: first, to prove the effectiveness and dominance of strategic bombing over ground and naval forces; second, to destroy the will of the government of Japan to continue the war; third, to destroy the ability of the Japanese to make war by destroying its industry; and fourth, to destroy the Japanese people who made possible the production necessary to continue the war. While the stated objective of the fire bombing campaign was to destroy the ability of the Japanese to make war and to destroy Japanese industry, LeMay's words and actions indicate that the objective was also to destroy the will of the Japanese government. Killing Japanese facilitated the accomplishment of all objectives.

Unlike the American strategic bombing campaign in Europe that emphasized the targeting of specific industries, the air campaign against Japan targeted cities—"industrial cities." Precision bombing was abandoned. LeMay essentially adopted the British approach to the strategic bombing of Germany—area bombing. He, however, had bigger, more capable aircraft and munitions. Factories and other production sites are typically made up of concrete and steel. Napalm would have little effect on such targets. High-explosive bombs would have performed better against industrial sites containing heavy machinery. Hence, even if we accept the argument that "cottage industries," "the feeder industries" that provided the components for the major industrial sites existed throughout

Tokyo and other industrial cities, LeMay's interest in the construction material used in Japanese homes reveals his purpose. This was the same thinking that motivated the British to target the houses of working-class families in Germany. The campaign was designed to kill large numbers of Japanese, and by doing so, destroy the will of the Japanese. While publicly, Arnold stated he abhorred "terror bombing," he told his subordinate airmen that "this is a brutal war and . . . the way to stop the killing of civilians is to cause so much damage and destruction and death that the civilians will demand that their government cease fighting."[49]

Ideas of racism, social Darwinism, and imperialism; emotions of hate, anger, and revenge; and strong desires to limit American casualties and demonstrate the dominance of airpower mixed with the limitations of men, aircraft, and munitions to produce the strategic bombing campaign against the Japanese. John Dower noted:

> Prejudice and racial stereotypes frequently distorted both Japanese and Allied evaluations of the enemy's intentions and capabilities. Race hate fed atrocities, and atrocities in turn fanned the fires of race hate. The dehumanization of the Other contributed immeasurably to the psychological distancing that facilitates killing, not only on the battlefield but also in the plans adopted by strategists far removed from the actual scene of combat. Such dehumanization, for example, surely facilitated the decisions to make civilian populations the targets of concentrated attacks, whether by conventional or nuclear weapons. In countless ways, war words and race words came together in a manner which did not just reflect the savagery of the war, but contributed to it by reinforcing the impression of a truly Manichaean struggle between completely incompatible antagonists. The natural response to such a vision was an obsession with extermination on both sides— a war without mercy.[50]

While Dower's argument does not adequately take into consideration the influence of Japanese culture— the inability to surrender and the willingness to die for the emperor—he identified American cultural norms that motivated behaviors and influenced the conduct of the strategic bombing campaign against Japan. Race mattered. Just how much it mattered is hard to know, but Americans drew sharp distinctions between their Japanese enemy and their German enemy. An article published in *Marine Corps Gazette* in November 1944 made the following distinctions:

> The savageries committed by Nazi Germans throughout Europe show that even the most civilized people can relapse into barbarism within a short time. But while German "rebarbarization" is a recent phenomenon produced by the Hitler madness and may be expected to pass with it, Japanese savagery is deep and primordial, and an integral part of the Japanese character through the ages. It is no newly acquired characteristic, but a product of inheritance which has been carefully nurtured and preserved by Japanese religion, tradition, and political indoctrination. . . . Yet beneath the trappings of modernity the Japanese have remained what they always were—barbarians. . . . Japan's conduct is the result of savage, warlike racial traits shaped to a code of barbarism.[51]

The author believed that racially: ". . . the average Japanese soldier embodying the characteristics of his nation is a savage, dirty, and treacherous, but also tough and fanatic—and at times a wholly fantastic—fighter. . . ." Still, this was only one of many factors, and it was *not* the major factor that motivated the decisions to carry out the fire bombing campaign and to employ the atomic bomb.[52]

By war's end, LeMay's B–29s had produced 2.2 million casualties, 900,000 of whom were killed, a figure that exceeds Japanese combat casualties. Sixty-eight of Japan's largest cities were attacked, scorching 178 square miles, or 40 percent of urban areas. This unparalleled destruction caused Arnold and LeMay to conclude that the strategic bombing campaign had effectively destroyed the will of the Japanese: "the Japanese acknowledged defeat because air attacks, both actual and potential, had made possible the destruction of their capability and will for further resistance." The question that was never answered is: at what level of killing does the effort to influence the will of the people become mass murder, genocide?[53]

Cultures in which hereditary rulers are considered Gods could suffer horrendous loss without revolt. The Japanese people were culturally, psychologically, and emotionally disposed to accept genocide. Brodie wrote:

> In Japan there was no more tendency than there was in Germany for the low morale to find expression in any organized popular movement to revolt, or in manifest pressure upon the government to surrender. On the contrary, the Emperor's announcement of the surrender was apparently greeted by a majority of the population with stunned disbelief and dismay.[54]

In Japanese culture, it was considered an honor to die for the emperor, and a dishonor to surrender. A Japanese soldier explained: "When a Japanese surrenders . . . he commits dishonor. One must forget him completely. His wife and his poor mother and children erase him from their memories. There is no memorial placed for him. It is not that he is dead. It is that he never existed."[55] Unconditional surrender meant the occupation of the nation-state by foreign troops, the destruction of the accepted government, and the complete subjugation to the will of a foreign people and culture—an intolerable situation for most of humanity. People, once hostilities have started, tend to have few options in total war, except to support the leaders in power.

The argument that LeMay's objective was to destroy the will of the people is only partially correct. The objective was also to destroy the will of the Japanese political leaders with the belief that the hopelessness of the situation, the systematic destruction of their homeland, and the suffering and deaths of their people would influence their decision-making. Conventional bombing, however, had very little potential to influence the will of political leaders who believed that people are nothing but instruments of the state. The British bombing of German cities and the American fire bombing of Japan did little to influence the will of Hitler or the Emperor and ruling oligarchy in Japan. Rather than surrender, they would have accepted the deaths of millions of their people. Pape concluded:

> The evidence shows that it is the threat of military failure, which I call denial, and not

threats to civilians, which we may call punishment, which provides the critical leverage in conventional coercion. ... governments are often willing to countenance considerable civilian punishment to achieve important territorial aims [or to survive]. Consequently, coercion based on punishing civilians rarely succeeds. The key to success in conventional coercion is not punishment but denial, that is the ability to thwart the target state's military strategy for controlling the objectives in dispute.[56]

Pape's work has been controversial. He argued that neither the fire bombing, nor the atomic bomb, caused Japan to surrender: "In comparison to the Soviet entry, the atomic bomb had little or no effect on the Army's position."[57] He further argued that it was the American victory at Okinawa and the Soviet invasion of Manchuria that caused Japan to surrender. The argument that the atomic bomb did not influence the decision-making in Japan does not stand up under scrutiny. Premier Suzuki in December 1945 wrote: "They [the Army] proceed [ed] with that plan [Ketsu-Go to defend Japan] until the Atomic Bomb was dropped, after which they believed the United States ... need not land when it had such a weapon; so at that point they decided that it would be best to sue for peace."[58] Frank, in his comprehensive study, concluded: "... the Soviet intervention was a significant but not decisive reason for Japan's surrender. ... [T]he atomic bomb played the more critical role because it undermined the fundamental premise that the United States would have to invade Japan to secure a decision."[59] Still, the conclusion that the firebombing of Japan had little effect on the ruling oligarchy is correct.

The tenacity of political leaders, and their willingness to accept human losses, is not something that can be objectively measured. Human nature, cultures, history, ideologies, the political systems, and the personalities of the rulers influence the ability of a people and government to sustain bombing. The percentage of a people that would have to be killed to destroy the will of a government or a people varies with each nation. And modern nationalism has been a strong force in motivating the actions of people. To base the outcome of war on the numbers of civilian men, women, and children one can kill is not only

inhumane, it is impractical. This doctrine of war taken to its extreme is genocide. In the latter half of the twentieth century, with the doctrines of "massive retaliation," with nuclear weapons, the US and Soviet Union adopted a doctrine of mutual extermination. But, no side wins such a war. The strategic bombing doctrine carried out by the British and the Americans in World War II was a version of this thinking, and was limited only by the technology of the time. Had the British and Americans possessed limitless supplies of atomic bombs in World War II, there is little doubt that they would have used them. Truman addressed the nation shortly after the employment of the first atomic bomb:

> Sixteen hours ago an American airplane dropped one bomb on Hiroshima, an important Japanese Army base. ... The Japanese began the war from the air at Pearl Harbor. They have been repaid many folds. And the end is not yet. With this bomb we have now added a new and revolutionary increase in destruction to supplement the growing power of our armed forces. In their present form these bombs are now in production and even more powerful forms are in development. It is an atomic bomb. It is a harnessing of the basic power of the universe. The force from which the sun draws its power had been loosed against those who brought war to the Far East. ... We are now prepared to obliterate more rapidly and completely every productive enterprise the Japanese have above ground in any city. We shall destroy their docks, their factories, and their communications. Let there be no mistake; we shall completely destroy Japan's power to make war.[60]

Truman's words were poorly chosen. They created the impression that the atomic bomb was used for revenge, when in fact it saved hundreds of thousands of lives, possibly millions. Truman's words have provided too many shortsighted historians with the information they needed to charge him with racism, and the unnecessary destruction of more than 200,000 Japanese lives. As a consequence, too many Japanese and Americans fail to understand that the atomic bomb saved lives, and was absolutely the best outcome the Japanese could have expected or achieved in 1945.

The results of the strategic bombing campaign in World War II mattered little to American beliefs about the future potential of airpower. America's belief in airpower was so strong and so infectious that it drove post-war developments. This vision of airpower was reinforced by fundamental cultural tenets, specifically the tenet that man was not a means to an end, but the end. Ground war upset this tenet. Airpower offered a means to diminish this misuse of humanity. Hence, the effectiveness of the British and American campaigns in World War II was only of secondary importance. The dream, the vision had been created. And there was no turning back. One student of airpower wrote:

> Historians who have studied the impact of aviation on Western imagination are unanimous in their amazement at the full magnitude of cultural forces sweeping Western society and unlocking primordial yearning and passion as a result of the advent of human flight. This fascination is most clearly evident through its reflection in popular culture, for the fantastic visions soon found voice through thousands of novels, poems, movies, and works of art, each extolling the virtues of flight and awakening expectations of deliverance from all manner of ills plaguing the human race.[61]

Airpower was the answer to future wars, too many believed.

The Navy and Marine Corps

The missions of the United States Navy in World War II were not too dissimilar from those of the Athenian Navy during the Peloponnesian War or those of the British Navy during the Napoleonic Wars: to seek out and destroy the enemy's navy; to seek out and destroy the enemy's merchant fleet; to control strategically important sea lines of communication; to seize advanced bases, which made it possible to project power deep into enemy space; and to deploy, support, and sustain land forces. During World War II, the US Navy also adopted a vision of war dominated by airpower. After the impressive Japanese attack on Pearl Harbor in 1941 and the Battle of Midway in June 1942, the aircraft carrier became the dominant platform for the conduct of naval warfare, replacing the battleship. Navy aircraft carriers task force doctrine made possible the Central Pacific campaign, which gave the Army and Army Air Force access to the main Japanese islands. The aircraft carrier also made it possible for the Navy to move beyond its traditional wartime missions. Air superiority, close air support, air interdiction of land forces, air reconnaissance, and even strategic bombing became naval aviation missions, extending the Navy's reach well beyond coastal regions and deep into the interior of enemy nations. Shortly after the cessation of hostilities, Admiral Ernest J. King, Chief of Naval Operations, reported:

> Our fleet in World War II was not solely engaged in fighting enemy fleets. On numerous occasions a large part of the fleet effort was devoted to operations against land objectives. A striking example is the capture of Okinawa. During the three months that this operation was in progress our Pacific Fleet—the greatest naval force ever assembled in the history of the world—was engaged in a continuous battle which for sustained intensity has never been equaled in naval history; yet at this time the Japanese Navy had virtually ceased to exist—we were fighting an island, not an enemy fleet.[62]

Admiral Chester W. Nimitz, Commander-in-Chief Central Pacific Theater, added his prestige to this expanded vision of the role of naval aviation:

> Fleets do not exist only to fight other fleets and to contest with them the command of the sea. Actually, command of the sea is only the means to an end. Wars cannot be concluded by naval action alone or by air action alone. Wars are conducted and concluded by the combined action of sea, land, air, diplomatic, and economic effort. . . .[63]

Aviators ultimately came to dominate the Navy. The US Navy wisely and out of necessity advanced a more Julian Corbett *Maritime Strategy*, than an Alfred T. Mahan *Naval Strategy*.[64]

The Navy's efforts to expand its role in war were in part out of the necessity, and desire to employ all resources available to bring the war to a rapid conclusion. However, the long-range strategic bomber presented new institutional challenges to the Navy. Alexander P. De Seversky in his work, *Victory Through Air Power*, published in 1942, wrote:

> Clearly the time is approaching when even the phrase 'sea power' will lose all real meaning. All military issues will be settled by relative strength in the skies. At that time, I dare to foresee, by the inexorable logic of military progress, the Navy as a separate entity will cease to exist. The weapons it represents will have atrophied to the point where it is, at best, a minor auxiliary of air power.[65]

The atomic bomb that ended the war strengthened the argument that airpower provided by the Air Force could replace the need for naval forces. As a result, the Navy was put on the defensive shortly after the war ended, and to insure its continued existence, the Navy sought new missions and roles, specifically part of the nuclear strategic bombing mission that the Air Force claimed exclusively for itself. Thus, before the war ended, the conflict between the Air Force and Navy that would last into the twenty-first century was framed.

* * * * *

During World War II, the Marine Corps became the Navy's primary army for fighting the Central Pacific campaigns of Admirals King and Nimitz. Prior to World War II, the Marine Corps had a rich tradition in fighting America's "small wars" south of the US border.[66] However, its experiences in World War II exerted the dominant influence on Marine Corps culture. The Marine Corps is first and foremost a light infantry force. The most fundamental tenet of Marine Corps culture is that man is the dominant instrument on the battlefield. The second most fundamental tenet is that marines are better fighting men than soldiers. The primary reason for this permanent disposition was survival. The Marine Corps has always felt the need to justify its existence. The Army has at times argued that the Marine Corps was unnecessary, that the Army performed the same missions and had the same capabilities. By asserting that marines were better fighting men and the Marine way of war was uniquely different the Marine Corps established itself

as the *anti-Army*. During World War II, the Marine Corps established itself in opposition to the Army, a better alternative to the Army. The Marine Corps constructed and cultivated an image of an elite fighting force. To be elite, it had to compare itself to some norm, some point of reference against which elite status could be determined. The US Army was that norm and point of reference.

The Marine Corps has long had a dilemma. To justify its existence it needs to demonstrate that it is not just better than, but also different from, the Army, that it provides something the Army does not, at the same time it has to be sufficiently like the Army to fight on the same battlefield. Since the Army has the primary mission of fighting the nation's ground war, and the Marine Corps cannot sit out a war, it has to be capable of fighting alongside the Army under Army command. This has proven to be a difficult line to walk, particularly in limited war. The disposition of "better than" and "different from," yet seeking to fight "alongside," on the "same battlefields with the Army" has caused enormous friction, diminishing the ability of the two services to cooperate, fight, and achieve synergy on the same battlefields. Whereas the Army has traditionally been too small to do all that was asked of it and Marine divisions have augmented Army combat power, greater unity of effort and unity of command; and consequently, greater combat power and economy would have been achieved by simply maintaining a few more Army infantry divisions. This peculiarity of the American practice of war—essentially maintaining two armies and three air forces—has in too many campaigns and wars destroyed the ability of the United States to achieve political objectives.[67]

Never comprising more than two corps, Marine Corps thinking focused primarily on the operational and tactical levels of war. At the strategic level the Navy dominated Central Pacific planning.[68] The Central Pacific campaign was strategically significant in providing access to Japan, making possible the strategic bombing campaign, the employment of the atomic bomb, and had it been necessary, the invasion of Japan. Besides fighting the Central Pacific campaign, the Marine Corps' greatest strategic contribution to World War II was the development of amphibious warfare doctrine in concert with the US

Navy, a fact that is too frequently forgotten.[69] The doctrine developed by the Marine Corps and Navy made possible the Central Pacific campaign. (The US Army employed British amphibious warfare doctrine in the Mediterranean and European theaters.) While the Marine Corps influenced the outcome of battles and campaigns, it has never been the decisive element in the conduct of war. The outcomes of World War II, the Korean and Vietnam Wars, and Operations Desert Storm and Iraqi Freedom would have been the same with or without the Marine Corps.

Marine divisions were *not* designed, organized, trained, or equipped to fight Western armies. The Marines maintained no infantry divisions capable of fighting on the European continent, no armor or mechanized divisions, and no airborne and Ranger forces.[70] Marine divisions lacked the artillery, engineer, air defense artillery, armor, transportation, and supply units common to Western armies, and had no capability to conduct mechanized, maneuver warfare. Marine divisions were deployed and sustained by the Navy. This situation continued throughout the Cold War, and existed in Operations Desert Storm and Iraqi Freedom. Marines have little experience in fighting other Western cultures. In World War II, Marines fought Japanese forces, who tended to fight to the last man but were incapable of generating the combat power of major Western armies. The war in the Pacific was more primitive and visceral than the war in Europe, but a Japanese division could not generate the combat power of a German division.

During World War II, geography, in part, dictated the character of Marine operations. Marines fought in one theater of war, across a vast expanse of eight thousand miles of ocean. Marine operations were typically short, intense, hard-fought, bloody affairs. For example: the 2nd Marine Division (MD) that opened the Central Pacific campaign fought for Tarawa for five days, from 20 to 24 November 1943. It did not see combat again until 15 June, the campaign for Saipan, which lasted twenty-five days. From Tarawa to the end of the war the 2nd MD fought a total of thirty-eight days. Including the fight for Guadalcanal, it was in combat for 208 days.[71] The 3rd MD, activated on 16 September 1942, saw a total of forty-five days of combat. It fought at Guam from 12 July to 15 August 1944, twenty-one days, and at Iwo Jima from 21 February to

16 March 1945, twenty-four days. The 4th Marine Division fought in four battles and saw a total of seventy days of combat.[72] The 5th Marine Division was in combat just over a month, 35 days. And the 6th Marine Division saw eighty-two days of combat. The 1st Marine Division, with 382 days of combat, was the exception. Its longest campaign was at Guadalcanal, 152 days. Short, direct, intense, bloody combat came to characterize the Marine practice of war. Marines put forth a maximum effort for relatively short periods of time, armed with the knowledge that battle would last a few months at the most, and that the enemy was isolated and could not be reinforced.

Consider Navy and Marine Corps Central Pacific operations. Battles were based on the principles of mass, firepower, and speed. The Navy isolated the battlefield, the island, and naval gunfire provided the firepower required for the marines to get ashore. Following an intensive bombardment, the Marines conducted a direct frontal assault continuously supported by naval gunfire and marine and naval aviation. As the war progressed, the Japanese defensive doctrine evolved. To compensate for the enormous firepower superiority provided by naval gunfire, the Japanese moved their main defensive line inland, away from exposed beaches, and underground. As Japanese defensive doctrine adapted, the blood toll increased. The Marine solution to this was increased firepower. A study of Marine and Navy amphibious doctrine reveals that both the number of ships and the length of the bombardment increased throughout the war.

While the Marines fought some very difficult and bloody battles at places such as Tarawa and Iwo Jima, the outcome of the campaigns was never in doubt. The Japanese had no way to reinforce, no way to resupply, no way to retreat, no way to equal the firepower of the US Navy, and typically no airpower. The Japanese recognized their fate. However, their objective was not to achieve victory in the traditional sense. Their objective was to inflict as many casualties as possible on American forces, to hold out as long as possible, and to prolong the war. The Japanese believed they could *destroy the will of the American people*. They concluded, partly on the basis of racism, that Americans lack the tolerance to fight a long, bloody war, and that at some undefined level of attrition they would seek a negotiated settlement.[73] This strategy was also based on the assumptions that the Germans would defeat the Russians and the British, leaving the US isolated and alone; and that the primary interests of the US were in Europe.[74] Faced with this situation and a protracted bloody war of attrition in the Pacific, the Japanese believed the US would negotiate a favorable peace, making it possible for the US to refocus all its resources on the most dangerous threat, Nazi Germany.

At Iwo Jima, Peleliu, and Okinawa the Japanese inflicted sufficiently heavy casualties to convince senior Navy leaders in the Pacific that an assault on the main Japanese islands would produce unacceptable casualties. Nimitz argued against the operational and tactical doctrines he had employed repeatedly in the advance across the Central Pacific, noting that:

> it would be unrealistic to expect that such obvious objectives as a southern Kyushu and the Tokyo Plain will not be as well defended as Okinawa. ... Unless speed is considered so important that we are willing to accept less than the best preparation and more than minimum casualties, I believe that the long range interest of the U.S. will be better served if we continue to isolate Japan & to destroy Jap forces & resources by naval and air attack.[75]

By convincing Nimitz that the strategic bombing and the naval blockade campaigns ought to be continued and the invasion postponed, at least until Japanese forces could be further attrited, the Japanese had in part achieved their objective. However, Generals MacArthur and Marshall rejected this view.[76] The Army in the southwest Pacific had suffered fewer casualties than the Marine Corps. As a percentage of total forces deployed, the Army had achieved its objectives at Leyte, Luzon, and other Pacific battlefields with considerably fewer casualties. This fact influenced Marshall and MacArthur's decision. Had it not been for the atomic bomb, the invasion of Japan would have taken place at horrendous cost to both sides.

Marine Corps casualties can be explained in part by the types of operations it fought. Operations in the Pacific frequently left Navy and Marine planners with no choice: On islands such as Tarawa, the entire campaign was necessarily one continuous assault. However, Peleliu and other campaigns show that the Marine practice of war tended to produce the bloodiest solution.[77] General Holland Smith, USMC, characterized Marine thinking, "The way to beat these bastards is to hit them hard. Gain contact all along the front and then never let go. Keep after them all the time, give them no chance to rest or reorganize and they can't take it. ...."[78] He later wrote:

> Since I first joined the Marines, I have advocated aggressiveness in the field and constant offensive action. Hit quickly, hit hard and keep right on hitting. Give the enemy no rest, no opportunity to consolidate his forces and hit back at you. ... I stressed the need for heavy and concentrated support from naval gunfire, a subject I cannot refrain from mentioning time and time again because of its vital bearing on the success of amphibious warfare. ... The stronger the defenses the heavier, more prolonged and more effective should be the bombardment, over periods as short as three days and as long as ten days.[79]

Marine General O.P. Smith characterized the operations of Col. Chesty Puller, who at Umurbrogol Ridge on Peleliu rejected the opportunity to attack the enemy's flank and instead decided to attack the enemy's strength: "[Puller] believed in momentum; he believed in coming ashore and hitting and just keep on hitting and trying to keep up the momentum." Later, while surveying the battlefield, Smith stated: "there was no finesse about it, but there was gallantry and there was determination."[80] This unconcealed admiration for bloody solutions was part of Marine culture, which emphasized firepower, speed, offensive operations and tactics, the direct approach, and tenacity. At Peleliu the Marine culture of war rendered the 1st MD combat ineffective. After 30 days of combat it had to be relieved.[81]

Marines preferred to operate independent of the Army.[82] Craig Cameron in his book, *American Samurai*, a study of Marine attitudes, beliefs, and culture, wrote: "The largest and most serious inter-service conflict developed between the Army and Marine Corps over their different approaches to the conduct of ground operations in the [Central] Pacific theater. These invidious comparisons have continued to this day and remain, at best, thinly disguised."[83] According to the Marine historian, Allan Millett, Marines believed that "the Corps embodied standards of bravery, success, and economy not found in the Army."[84] (Given the Marine expenditure on Osprey and other technologies, "economy" can no longer be claimed.) Another Marine noted "My answer as to why the Marines get the toughest jobs is because the average leatherneck is a much better fighter. He has far more guts, courage and better officers. . . ."[85]

The presence of the Army in the Pacific Theater distorted the Marine conduct of battle. Cameron noted, "resentment and animosity toward the Army were deeply ingrained . . . and from the outset of the planning, he [Repertus, Commander the 1st Marine Division] wanted the capture of Peleliu to be solely a Marine venture. . . . [H]e wanted no support from the 81st Infantry Division."[86] In other words, Marine disdain for the Army, at times, caused irrational behavior. During World War II, these attitude and beliefs hardened into cultural tenets that have influenced the relationship between the Army and Marine Corps for the remainder of the twentieth century making it impossible for the two services to achieve synergy on the battlefield. Inter-service rivalry and animus between the services distorted their approach to war, damaging the ability of the US to achieve political objectives and maintain the support of the American people. It has also caused enormous waste and duplication of capabilities. It has been argued that competition between the services improved their performance. But, marginal improvements in the tactical and operation performance could not compensate for the strategic failures that result from inter-service rivalry, a fact that was evident to Senator Goldwater in the wake of defeat in the Vietnam debacle.

*　*　*　*　*

The allocation of the nation's human and material resources for total war reveals American thinking about war. In March 1945 the Army reached its peak strength of 8,157,386 men. Of these forces, the Army Air Force accounted for 2,290,573, and Army Service Forces accounted for 1,644,141. Army ground forces accounted for 3,147,837 men. However, only 1,968,500 of these were combat soldiers, and

of these forces all did not participate in combat. Only fifty-five percent of Army divisions were combat soldiers, when limited to men in companies, batteries, and troops of the combat arms.[87] Russell Weigley observed:

> In some ways, to be sure, the United States actually fought World War II with the wealth of resources implied by the country's overall abundance and by the American popular perception of the war. The Army Ground Forces were thin in combat strength partly because so much of the Army's manpower occupied logistical and administrative positions intended to assure plentiful supplies and as high as possible a standard of living for the troops. . . . Nonetheless, the picture remains one of the allocation of a remarkably thin share of World War II wealth and manpower of the United States to ground combat. The contrast with another of the aspects of the war, upon which American wealth was in fact brought to bear, is stark, while the Army staggered through much of the war in Europe with barely enough divisions, the Navy in the Pacific enjoyed by 1944 and 1945 a wealth of aircraft carriers and other warships that formed carrier task groups to create more than enough strength to overshadow and overwhelm the Imperial Japanese Navy several times over.[88]

Americans preferred to fight wars with technological and material abundance. Therefore, American national strategy and national military strategy reflected these tenets of American culture. American strategic planners sought to minimize the contribution of the Army's ground combat forces to the war effort. Roosevelt's "arsenal of democracy" and lend-lease strategy kept the allies, the British, Russians, and Chinese, fighting. The emphasis on airpower and naval forces consumed enormous resources.

Robert R. Palmer noted: "If the United States, with 12,000,000 men in its armed services, including those under the Navy Department, can produce less than 100 divisions including those in the Marine Corps, this fact must be considered by all concerned in a future global war, and will certainly be considered by any possible enemies."[89] It was a well thought-out policy to employ other resources as substitutes for ground combat forces. The policy was a function of cultural tenets and was reflected in all aspects of American strategy.[90] While the Army's most basic tenet was that man was the ultimate weapon on the battlefield, ground combat was the least desirable form of combat power. American beliefs about manhood, battle, and war were at odds with the value placed on young American lives, a value that compels Americans to expend every resource, almost unconditionally, to remove man from the battlefield.

In the post-World War II era new options existed that made possible adherence to the more basic, more deeply held tenets of American life, principal among them, that man is not a means to an end, but the end itself. War for centuries has upset this tenet of American life, making American citizens a means to an end. Airpower and other technologies offered new alternatives that the Army could not ignore.

4.
TRUMAN, THE COLD WAR, AND THE CREATION OF A NEW MILITARY ESTABLISHMENT, 1945–1950

In an instant many of the old concepts of war were swept away. Henceforth, it would seem, the purpose of an aggressor nation would be to stock atom bombs in quantity and to employ them by surprise against the industrial fabric and population centers of its intended victim. Offensive methods would largely concern themselves with the certainty, the volume, and the accuracy of delivery, while the defense would strive to prevent such delivery and in turn launch its store of atom bombs against the attacker's homeland. Even the bombed ruins of Germany suddenly seemed to provide but faint warning of what future war could mean to the people of the earth.[1]

—General Dwight D. Eisenhower, *Crusade in Europe*, 1948

You may fly over a land forever; you may bomb it, atomize it, pulverize it and wipe it clean of life—but if you desire to defend it, protect it, and keep it for civilization, you must do it on the ground, the way the Roman legions did, by putting your young men into the mud.[2]

—T.R. Fehrenbach, *This Kind of War*, 1963

In August 1945, the most significant innovation in the conduct of war in human history was revealed to the world. Two small atomic bombs were dropped on the Japanese cities of Hiroshima and Nagasaki, bringing World War II to an abrupt end. The war ended not with the destruction of the Japanese main army on the field of battle, not with the clash of mighty armies, but with two small nuclear devices and two lone B-29 bombers. These technologies caused many military thinkers to believe that armies were obsolete, that their value in future wars would be to mop up after airpower destroyed the enemy, and that a revolution in warfare had taken place, forever transforming the conduct of war. General Maxwell Taylor recalled discussing this new technology with Generals Marshall and Patton. He wrote:

> General Patton and I looked at each other in silence, both meditating upon the awful

significance of Marshall's words. . . . What if we had had such things to clear our way across Europe? Think of the thousands of our brave soldiers whose lives might have been spared. Now, indeed, I thought, we have a weapon which can keep the peace and never again will a Hitler or a Mussolini dare to use war to impose his will upon the Free World.[3]

Thus, before the atomic bomb was even used against the Japanese, it had created hopes and dreams for saving lives, for winning wars without ground combat, and for deterring future war. Eisenhower wrote:

> All the developments in method, equipment, and destructive power that we were studying seemed minor innovations compared to *the revolutionary impact of the atom bomb*. . . . [E]ven without the actual experience of its employment, the reports that reached us after the first one was used at

Hiroshima on August 6 left no doubt in our minds that a new era of warfare had begun.[4]

In this new era, the role of armies was uncertain, and whatever part they played in future wars, their status would never again equal that achieved in World War II.

Truman, the Policy of Containment, and National Strategy

President Truman is the only human being in history to order the employment of nuclear weapons against human beings. Truman was President during one of the most momentous and traumatic periods of world history. His actions during the events that took place laid the foundation not only for US foreign and military policies, but also for the structure of world politics, and war in the latter half of the twentieth century. During

his presidency World War II came to an end and the "Cold War" began. The Soviet Union became a nuclear power, and China became a Communist nation aligned with it. Under Truman's leadership, the strategic vision of the "policy of containment" and the strategic doctrine of "massive retaliation" were advanced. NATO was formed, the Marshall Plan enacted, and the Truman Doctrine, giving military and economic assistance to nations fighting Communist insurgencies, implemented. Truman initiated the reorganization and attempted unification of the Armed Forces, which resulted in the creation of the Air Force, Department of Defense, and CIA. Thus, Truman arguably exerted greater influence on the political and military affairs of the planet in the latter half of the twentieth century than any other human being. However, he did not create the world in which he made the critical decisions. He accepted the world as it was, and instituted policies

Fig 4.1 President Harry S. Truman signs the Armed Forces Day Proclamation making 19 May Armed Forces Day for 1951, during a brief ceremony in the White House. Among those present for the signature ceremonies are Secretary of Defense George C. Marshall (seated at the President's left). Rear row, left to right: Lieutenant General Merwin H. Silverthorn, Assistant Commandant of Marine Corps; Admiral Forrest P. Sherman, USN, Chief of Naval Operations; General Hoyt S. Vandenberg, Chief of Staff, US Air Force; Secretary of the Army Frank Pace, Jr.; Secretary of the Navy Francis P. Matthews; Secretary of the Air Force Thomas K. Finletter; General of the Army Omar N. Bradley, Chairman of the Joint Chiefs of Staff; and General J. Lawton Collins, Chief of Staff, US Army. US Army photography, 2 April 1951.

and strategy to preserve the American way of life and that of other Western nations. He too, however, fell prey to the hope that technology could replace man on the battlefield. What did he inherit?

For most of its history, the US had looked inward, focused on incorporating the land mass between the Atlantic and the Pacific Oceans. However, at the end of the nineteenth century the US stretched into the Pacific, acquiring an overseas empire, which included the Philippines. In 1917, the US entered the First World War to help preserve Europe's capitalist democracies. After the Great War, Americans again turned inward, becoming isolationists, eschewing military involvement in European affairs. Witnessing the rise of Nazism, President Franklin D. Roosevelt concluded that isolationism had been a mistake. He believed that World War II was, at least in part, caused by the failure of the "great powers" to act in world affairs. He advanced the formation of the United Nations, and in 1941, in a document known as *The Atlantic Charter*, along with Winston Churchill of Great Britain, committed the US to defeating Nazi Germany, preserving European capitalist democracies, and taking an active part in world affairs until mankind had reached some new level of political organization that guaranteed peace and security for all states, large and small:

> [T]hey believe that all the nations of the world, for realistic as well as spiritual reasons, must come to the abandonment of the use of force. Since no future peace can be maintained if land, sea, or air armaments continue to be employed by nations which threaten, or may threaten, aggression outside of their frontiers, they believe, pending the establishment of a wider and permanent system of general security, that the disarmament of such nations is essential. They will likewise aid and encourage all other practicable measures which will lighten for peace-loving peoples the crushing burden of armaments.[5]

Churchill interpreted this objective as follows: "Finally, not the least striking feature was the realism of the last paragraph, where *there was a plain and bold intimation that after the war the United States would join with us in policing the world until the establishment of a better order.*"[6] In the *Atlantic Charter*, Roosevelt committed the United States to maintaining the world order that had previously been maintained by Britain and France, but also to improving that order through the United Nations and the exportation of "Americanism." Roosevelt was a strong advocate for the UN, pressuring Stalin to support the new organization.

Following Roosevelt's death, President Harry S. Truman accepted the new role for the US in world affairs—the special place of the United States among nations, the dominance of the power of the Unites States, and the burden of leadership it created. In 1945 in a "Special Message to the Congress," he told the American people:

> Whether we like it or not, we must all recognize that the victory which we have won [World War II] has placed upon the American people the continuing burden of responsibility for world leadership. The future peace of the world will depend in large part upon whether or not the United States shows that it is really determined to continue in its role as a leader among nations. It will depend upon whether or not the United States is willing to maintain the physical strength necessary to act as a safeguard against any future aggressor. Together with the other United Nations, we must be willing to make the sacrifices necessary to protect the world from future aggressive warfare. In short, we must be prepared to maintain in constant and immediate readiness sufficient military strength to convince any future potential aggressor that this nation, in its determination for a lasting peace, means business.[7]

Truman, while accepting this new responsibility for the nation, was slow to fully understand the duties that went along with it. Historically, the US had not maintained a large standing force immediately ready for war. This new level of commitment of national resources to the defense of foreign shores marked a major change in US foreign policy and national strategy. The rapid collapse of the British Empire, the advance of Communism, and the Soviet acquisition of the atomic bomb placed expanding new demands on the US. However, not until North Korea attacked South Korea did Truman fully comprehend and accept the new duties placed upon the United States; and even after the start of hostilities the American people were uncertain about their new duties in world affairs.

The fight that was the "Cold War" created the environment and the conditions for the transformation of American thinking about the use of military force and the conduct of war. The "Cold War" (1945–1990) was a period when the two most powerful nation-states on the planet, the United States and the Soviet Union, continuously prepared to go to war with one another, and indirectly fought wars through surrogate, peripheral, non-aligned states. It was a period when these two "superpowers" formed strategic mutual defense alliances, such as NATO and the Warsaw Pact, to strengthen their ability to defend themselves and destroy their opponents. It was a period when the two superpowers competed for allies to make their bloc stronger, and fought political, diplomatic, and espionage wars to undermine and weaken their opponent's bloc and alliances. It was a period of global turmoil, when the exertions of World War II caused the collapse of European imperialism, and nationalism spread to India, Pakistan, China, Indo-China, African nations, Middle East nations, and other parts of the world. It was a period of great suffering and carnage in developing states racked by wars as they tried to achieve statehood, establish legitimate political systems, reconcile borders that were drawn based on the concerns of European imperialist powers, redress racial and ethnic divisions and discrimination, and recover and reorganize after decades and centuries of European rule. It was a period during which the extinction of humanity became a real possibility, because each "superpower" acquired nuclear arsenals capable of destroying the other, and ultimately civilization, several times over, employing armies of scientists and engineers in a race to develop the most destructive weapons and invincible delivery systems. It was a period when the world expended vast resources on armies, navies, and air forces, and militarism invaded the social and political fabric of nations. It was a period when the US maintained armies, navies, and air forces forward-deployed in nations and states around the world, influencing their economies and internal politics, and Americanizing their culture. It was a period of distrust, uncertainty, and anxiety, punctuated by moments of high fear and tension; a period of ideological entrenchment, when paranoia invaded governmental institutions and American society, and the specter of the "police state" threatened democracy and individual freedoms. It was also a period of great prosperity in the United States, during which Americanism spread around the globe, and American culture adjusted to the norms of being in a perpetual state of preparing for war or fighting war. *The Cold War was ultimately a fight over the political, economic, social, and cultural systems that would dominate Earth going forward.* During this long, costly, and difficult fight, all parties were transformed, politically, geographically, socially, culturally, economically, and militarily.

The Cold War is well documented, and no effort is made here to reintroduce in a comprehensive manner the history of its origins; however, it is necessary to reiterate the basic ideas and policies that prevailed throughout the latter half of the twentieth century.

In 1947, George F. Kennan, a foreign area analyst of Russia and the Soviet Union, in the State Department, published an article that helped shape American foreign and military policies and strategies for the next four decades. In that article, Kennan described the "policy of containment" later adopted by the Truman Administration and every subsequent administration until the collapse of the Soviet Union in 1990. Kennan wrote:

> In these circumstances it is clear that the main element of any United States policy toward the Soviet Union must be that of *a long-term, patient but firm and vigilant containment* of Russian expansive tendencies. . . . It is clear that the United States cannot expect in the foreseeable future to enjoy political intimacy with the Soviet regime. It must continue to regard the Soviet Union as a rival, not a partner, in the political arena. It must continue to expect that Soviet policies will reflect no abstract love of peace and stability, no real faith in the possibility of a permanent happy coexistence of the Socialist and capitalist worlds, but rather a cautious, persistent pressure toward the disruption and weakening of all rival influence and rival power.
>
> Balanced against this are the facts that Russia, as opposed to the western world in general, is still by far the weaker party, that Soviet policy is highly flexible, and that Soviet society may well contain deficiencies which will eventually weaken its own total potential. This would of itself warrant the United States entering with reasonable confidence upon a policy of firm containment, designed to confront the Russians with

unalterable counter-force at every point where they show signs of encroaching upon the interests of a peaceful and stable world.[8]

There were three important axioms in Kennan's thesis: first, Communism is not a status quo-oriented ideology. Marx, Lenin, and other Communists believed that they had identified a universal truth about the human condition, and that ultimately all nations would go through the same sequence of transformations. Communist ideology thus predicted the collapse of capitalism. Many advocates of Communism pursued this change with the zeal and tenacity of religious conviction, willing to expend resources to transform other states. Second, Russia was historically an expansionist state, as indicated by its large geographic boundaries and the diversity of it racial and ethnic groups. Finally, Communist ideology contained internal contradictions that could not be reconciled with human nature; therefore, the Communist state would ultimately collapse under the weight of its own ideas. Kennan correctly predicted that Communism would implode, but when? This neither he nor anyone else could determine. As a consequence, he called for a specific type of containment: "a long-term but firm and vigilant containment."

Kennan also presented the American administration with a problem of interpretation. What did "unalterable counterforce at every point" mean? Did this mean the US had to go to war to stop every type of incursion? Nations have many types of power: political, geographic, diplomatic, economic, military, leadership, and others. Any combination of these powers could be employed in a given situation. But when was the use of military power appropriate? What constituted the necessary conditions for war? *Containment destroyed the centuries-old determinants for major American wars, and put in place a new set and system of determinants.* Although the determinants for war changed, the US left in place its traditional system for fighting war, its citizen-soldier Army. No one asked whether the cultural tenets upon which the citizen-soldier Army functioned were still applicable given the new set and system of determinants for war. The Korean and Vietnam Wars were fought under this new equation of determinant factors. Further, each administration had to figure out what "every point" of "unalterable counterforce" meant to it. However,

beyond their size, the questions regarding the quality and character of ground forces required to police the world were never seriously discussed.

* * * * *

The causes of the Cold War have been greatly debated. The collapse of the Soviet Union and access to Soviet sources has only intensified the debate.[9] A full discussion of the issue is beyond the scope of this work; however, in the aftermath of World War II, the "Cold War" was inevitable. All the seeds of the Cold War are evident in World War II. Nations, a people, can experience severe traumas that cause psychological damage that impedes or prevents them from seeing the world as it really is, and hence, acting in a balanced, responsible manner. Russians in the wake of World War II were severely traumatized. The unprecedented carnage, the unparalleled loss of 25 to 30 million lives, the enormous suffering, the incredible destruction of cities and homes and places of work, the sights and sounds of the battlefield everywhere, the presence of brutal, foreign soldiers occupying cities and towns, the direct experience of killing, the personal losses and injuries to family members, and the total absence of normalcy caused post-traumatic stress disorder (PTSD) on a national scale.[10] It was impossible for the Russian people and leadership to act in an objective, balanced, rational manner in the aftermath of the war. This enormous pain and suffering traumatized the Russian people, influencing their thinking and decision-making process for generations. The American Psychiatric Association (APA) defines PTSD as follows:

> the development of characteristic symptoms following exposure to an extreme traumatic stressor involving direct personal experience of an event that involves actual or threatened death or serious injury, or other threat to one's physical integrity; or witnessing an event that involves death injury, or a threat to the physical integrity of another person; *or learning about unexpected or violent death, serious harm, or threat of death or injury experienced by a family member of other close associate.*[11]

After World War II the Russian people and leadership had an abnormally high need for security guarantees. They needed buffer zones in Eastern Europe to protect their home front from future invasions. They needed large armies to defend their frontier. They needed a large, trained strategic reserve, and well-equipped forces, including the most modern tanks and airplanes. They needed industry to continue at near a wartime production schedule. They needed intelligence on American military and scientific activities. They needed nuclear weapons. And they needed the employment that military service provided hundreds of thousands of Russian men. "Never again" were the words that constantly filled the mind of every Russian who lived through "the Great Patriotic War." They were not in a position to trust, particularly the Americans, who, while providing enormous resources to the Soviet Union through lend-lease, continuously delayed a much needed "second front" in Europe.

The trauma experienced by the American people during the war, while substantial, was not of the quality, character, or intensity of that experienced by the Russian people.[12] Still, Americans also learned important lessons from the war. Foremost among them was that the *power in existence had to be balanced*. The US could not depend on Europe to fight the first years of a war while it readied itself. And many political and military leaders believed that the lack of a credible deterrent on the part of the French and British and the "policy of appeasement," which was a function of that lack of preparedness, caused the greatest conflagration in human history. In the years that followed the war, a secret intelligence report informed Truman that the Soviet Union was more powerful than Germany and Japan combined, and that its military power was expanding. The Soviet acquisition of nuclear weapons in 1949 confirmed this report. These two conditions, the extraordinarily high need of the Russian people for security guarantees, and the necessity for the United States to take over the role of declining European powers and to balance the substantial forces maintained by the Soviet Union, made the "Cold War" unavoidable.

While the effects of psychological trauma diminish over time, it must be understood that traumatic events live on in the lives of subsequent generations, shaping how they see the world, influencing their decisions, and motivating their actions.

The experience of pain and suffering that causes PTSD does not only influence a people for the rest of their lives, it can be passed on to the next generation, and the next generation. The violence, death, and destruction of World War II were unparalleled in human history. The APA diagnostic manual states: "The disorder may be especially severe or long lasting when the stressor is of human design (e.g., torture, rape)." The severity of trauma influences the extent of the damage, and consequently the degree of variation in behavior and thinking from the norm. It is possible to identify behaviors, such as "feeling constantly threatened," that are related to specific historical events in the current disposition, behavior, and attitudes of a people.[13]

*   *   *   *   *

The Cold War and the "policy of containment" meant that the armed forces of the United States should remain in a permanent state of military readiness to provide the counter-force required to maintain peace and/or fight war until the Soviet Union collapsed from its "deficiencies." The Truman Administration and the Congress, however, opposed spending the money required to maintain American forces at the state of readiness the service chiefs believed was necessary given the Soviet threat and world-wide responsibilities. Memories of the Great Depression ran deep, and in the aftermath of World War II, given the totality of that war, it was difficult to imagine a ground war that would *not* escalate into nuclear war. Therefore, strategic airpower had become the decisive instrument and doctrine for the conduct of American wars. It appeared to offer the US the means of maintaining a high state of readiness without wrecking the economy or placing an enormous burden of debt on the American people. Airpower and the atomic bomb gave the United States a deterrent, and in the event of war, a means of devastating the enemy's homeland. Truman also believed that American security was enhanced by diplomatic offensives and economic support to allies. Collective defense agreements, such as the North Atlantic Treaty Organization (NATO) and the Military Assistance Program, were means of enhancing the security of the United States without maintaining a large standing army.

On 12 March 1947, the "Truman Doctrine" was promulgated. This was the first installment of various military assistance programs, eventually expanded into hundreds of billions of dollars, which made the United States the biggest arms producer and distributor on Earth. Specifically, Truman requested funds from Congress to provide military and economic assistance to Greece and Turkey with the objective of helping them defeat Communist guerrillas supported by the Soviet Union. In a larger sense, Truman initiated a program that committed the United States to "help free peoples to maintain their free institutions and their national integrity against aggressive movements that seek to impose on them totalitarian regimes." The Military Assistance Program (MAP), part of the Truman Doctrine, was a derivation of Roosevelt's "arsenal of democracy," the lend-lease program of World War II, a program that provided military aid and assistance to nations fighting Nazi Germany and Imperial Japan. Roosevelt effectively substituted America's material wealth for its human wealth. Truman too accepted this policy, and all subsequent presidents adopted similar MAPs. However, these commitments linked the United States in significant ways to the security of the people to whom they were providing assistance. The United States now had a say in the outcome of every struggle it provided resources to support.

In September 1949, Army Chief of Staff General Bradley, before the House Foreign Affairs Committee, outlined the military strategy of the United States:

These factors are the foundation of a sound strategy for collective defense. . . . In our approach to this arms aid program, the Joint Chiefs of Staff have followed the principle that the man in the best position, and with the capability, should do the job for which he is best suited. Further, our recommendations for this program have been predicated upon this basic principle, and upon the following assumed factors:

First, the United States will be charged with the strategic bombing. We have repeatedly recognized in this country that the first priority of the joint defense is our ability to deliver the atomic bomb.

Second, the United States Navy, and the Western Union naval powers, will conduct essential naval operations, including keeping the sea lanes clear. Western Union and other nations will maintain their own harbor and coastal defense.

Third, we recognize that the hard core of the ground-power-in-being will come from Europe, aided by other nations as they can mobilize.

Fourth, England, France, and the closer countries will have the bulk of the short-range attack bombardment, and air defense. We, of course, will maintain the tactical air force for our own ground and naval forces, and for United States defense.

Fifth, other nations, depending upon their proximity or remoteness from the possible scene of conflict, will emphasize appropriate specific missions.

The essence of our overall strategy is this: There is a formidable strength, and an obvious economy of effort, resources, and manpower in this collective strategy, when each nation is capable of its own defense, as part of a collective strategic plan.[14]

Bradley was arguing for the Military Assistance Program, which passed Congress late in 1949. The Congress appropriated $1,314,010,000 for military assistance to North Atlantic Treaty countries, to Greece and Turkey, to Iran, Korea, and the Philippines, and to the general China area. This program, along with the Marshall Plan, was to get Western Europe back on its feet after World War II so it could defend itself. American airpower and nuclear capabilities would provide deterrence. This strategy allocated no major role for Army ground forces. European ground forces were to defend Europe. Secretary of Defense Louis Johnson supported the program of aid to European allies, while at the same time advocating further cuts in the budget for the armed forces of the United States. Johnson, in an appearance before the House Foreign Affairs Committee, stated:

The three fundamentals of military preparedness are: manpower, materials—and suitable positions from which to employ them in the event of attack. The Western European members of the North Atlantic Pact generally have substantial manpower resources. They also have positions of self-evident strategic importance to the defense of the North Atlantic community, including the United States. However... they lack the equipment.... Under this program, no United States troops will be sent abroad to employ the equipment we will provide. This Military Assistance Program is solely an equipment and a technical and training assistance program. The only United States personnel involved will be a strictly limited number of technical and training specialists to assist and advise the participating countries.[15]

Truman substituted America's *material wealth* for its *human wealth*. But, how far could the administration take such a program, and what degree of control did it give the President to influence events around the world?

Technological wealth, primarily in the form of airpower, was also a means of defraying the human cost of war. Throughout the period of 1945 to 1950, Truman reduced the size of the Army. Bradley and other senior Army leaders did not accept this part of the President's national strategy. Bradley argued for a combat-ready Army that was immediately deployable:

> Because too many Americans are searching for an easy and popular way to armed security through top-heavy trust in air power at the sacrifice of our remaining arms, we are in danger of reckoning our safety on fantasy rather than fact. I do not ... deny that the threat of instant retaliation through air offensive is our greatest deterrent to war today. But I must part company with those enthusiasts who ascribe to air power limitless capabilities in winning an instant decision.... However crippling air attack can be, I am convinced beyond any reasonable doubt that, should this Nation be forced into still another conflict, we shall once more be forced to gain the inevitable victory over our dead bodies—those of our soldiers on the ground. If I did not believe that war in the future will still thrust its eventual burden on the soldier who fights on the ground, then I would readily recommend abolition of the Army....[16]

Senior Army leaders were constantly on the defensive, trying to defend the Army from further crippling cuts and make the argument that airpower, while important, was not the panacea claimed. Bradley wrote:

> Because the Army cannot subscribe to the thesis that air power is a self-sufficient power capable of single-handed victory in a global war, I am dismayed that those who dare question it should be tagged as ox-cart soldiers in an atomic age. And I am alarmed that the Army's insistence on a combined defensive force should be distorted in the minds of some Americans as stubborn opposition to the strengthening of air power.[17]

Strategic Airpower and National Military Strategy

In 1947, the President established an Air Policy Commission to develop recommendations on the employment of airpower in future wars. Following an intensive five-month study, the commission presented a 166-page report, which emphasized the importance of airpower, the concept of massive retaliation, sustained readiness and modernization, and the willingness to discard the old ways of war:

> Relative security is to be found only in a policy of arming the United States so strongly (1) that other nations will hesitate to attack us or our vital national interests because of the violence of the counterattack they would have to face, and (2) that if we are attacked we will be able to smash the assault at the earliest moment. This country, if it is to have even relative security, must be ready for war. Moreover, it must be ready for modern war. It must be ready not for World War II but for a possible World War III. To realize this double-barreled policy will be as difficult a task as this country has ever taken on. Nothing less than a reversal of our traditional attitudes towards armaments and national sovereignty can make it succeed.
>
> Heretofore the United States has been able to make most of its preparations for war after war began. This will not be the case in a future war.... This means an air force in being, strong, well equipped and modern, not only capable of meeting the attack when it comes but, even

more important, capable of dealing a crushing counteroffensive blow on an aggressor.[18]

The authors of the report recognized that the way Americans thought about war had to change, and that the pre-World War II national strategies no longer worked. They believed that the US Air Force had to be ready for war on 1 January 1953. It was assumed that other nations would have sustained nuclear weapons programs by the end of 1952. Hence, they argued for an intensive effort: "The United States must press most energetically and immediately its basic and applied research and development programs in aerodynamics, power plants, electronics, and related fields with a view to developing at the earliest possible date the most effective piloted aircraft and guided missiles and the defenses against them." The commission recommended that the counteroffensive force be constructed around fleets of bombers, accompanying planes, and long-range missiles. They also recommended the construction of a radar defensive system that would create a protective ring around North America. Recognizing that these recommendations would be enormously expensive, the authors cautioned against the continued investment in World War II technology and outmoded thinking:

> We view with great anxiety the pressures from many sides directed towards the maintenance of yesterday's establishment to fight tomorrow's war; of unwillingness to discard the old and take on the new; of a determination to advance the interest of a segment at the sacrifice of the body as a whole. All this is understandable. For it comes in large part from loyalty of each Service to its traditions. But we can no longer afford the waste it involves.[19]

The recommended strategy and doctrine were clear. Airpower was the future of warfare. Ground forces were the past. Technology had rendered them obsolete. Airpower was new and modern, and eliminated mass armies and the casualties they produced. Joint doctrine was not considered. The report stressed again and again that: "We must have in being and ready for immediate action a counteroffensive force built around a fleet of bombers . . . The strength

of the counteroffensive force must be such that it will be able to make an aggressor pay a devastating price for attacking us." Common usage of the term "massive retaliation" started during the Eisenhower Administration, but the ideas were born during the Truman Administration.

In 1948, General Carl Spaatz, Chief of Staff of the USAF, rendered a report to the Secretary of the Air Force, delineating his thinking, which was in concert with the assessments of the Air Policy Commission:

> The primary role of military air power is to attack—not other aircraft, but targets on the ground that comprise the source of an enemy's military strength. In the main, those targets are industrial: oil refineries, steel mills, engine factories, electric power plants, aluminum smelters, or whatever may be important to military effort. From them flow the arms and weapons, the fuel and ordnance—in short, everything necessary to maintain a fighting force in the field, on the sea, or in the air. Because air power can cut off the flow of the enemy's military strength at its source it can be decisive in war.[20]

This was the "precision bombing" theory of war that the Army Air Force advanced in World War II. However, throughout the 1950s the Air Force was completely incapable of hitting point targets. Hence, the only way to rapidly destroy these targets was with nuclear weapons. In "the world of air power" Spaatz envisioned, the bomber was the primary aircraft, and its targets were the "eight great industrial areas in the world today of sufficient productivity to be significant factors in a full-scale war"—Japan, central Siberia, the Ural Mountains, Moscow, the Don Basin, western Europe, the British Isles, and the northeastern United States. Spaatz concluded that:

> In World War II, it was clearly shown that a determined attacking force cannot be stopped short of its target. . . . While defensive air power can do much to minimize the effectiveness of an aerial attack, the present capabilities of air weapons do not alter this World War II lesson. . . . The ultimate defense available [as a consequence] to the United States for protection from aerial

attack from over the top of the world lie in the maintenance of a striking-force-in-being that could answer aerial aggression with a smashing *retaliatory attack*.... The fact, accepted by all military thinkers, that a future major war would commence with an aerial attack is given particular importance because, if such an attack were carried out with atomic bombs, its results might well be decisive.[21]

The Air Power Commission and Spaatz's vision of the future of war were accepted by Truman. Limited wars, major conventional wars, and Communist insurgencies in peripheral regions were minor considerations. Truman wrote:

I was firmly committed to the position that, as long as international agreement for the control of atomic energy could not be reached, our country had to be ahead of any possible competitor. It was my belief that, as long as we had the lead in atomic developments, the great force would help us keep the peace.[22]

To maintain this lead, Truman had to increase investment in the production and development of nuclear weapons and their delivery systems, which in the late 1940s and early 1950s meant strategic bombers. Yet, between May 1945, the end of the war in Europe, and May 1947, the Air Force dropped from 2,253,000 men to only 303,614. Force modernization lagged, and for the fiscal year 1952, only forty-two air groups were planned. Inter-service rivalry in an environment of declining budgets hindered the modernization of all the armed forces. In July 1949, a Special Committee of the National Security Council argued that, "production of atomic weapons should be stepped up." It also recommended that, "the newly developed B-36 bomber be given a priority second only to atomic weapons." The B-36 was the delivery system, a long-range intercontinental bomber capable of dropping the latest atomic weapons. The Air Force was also developing a new command, Strategic Air Command (SAC), for its strategic bomber. In this vision of future wars, what role would the Army fulfill?

On 25 March 1948, Secretary of Defense Forrestal addressed the Senate Armed Services Committee. He delineated his views of the type of military forces necessary to keep the peace:

I abhor war, as do all Americans. Because of that abhorrence, I propose today a specific program which is solely designed to achieve one great objective—to avert war. ... [W]e cannot afford to sit by while these countries [Hungary and Czechoslovakia] fall, one by one, into the Soviet orbit, until we are left virtually alone and isolated in a Communist world.... If we make it plain and clear that the United States will not tolerate the destruction of the Western civilization of Europe we shall have peace.... We need a strong Air Force, capable of striking sustained blows far beyond the peripheral bases which we now hold; an Air Force capable of the air defense of homeland and our protective bases, and capable of seeking out and destroying an enemy that might impose war. ...

We need ground forces to protect our air bases from hostile attack, which it takes much more than airplanes to resist. We need ground forces to seize and hold more distant bases, should the attack fall upon us, in order to take the war to the enemy and not suffer its ravages here in America. Such bases, as well as our great cities here at home and our key production centers, require antiaircraft protection, which is provided by the Army. And a strengthened Air Force will require enlargement of those Army elements which service and support its operations.[23]

Thus two of the Army's primary missions were to seize advanced bases from which air attacks could initiate, and defend America's cities from air attacks. The Army was to become, in part, the "Marine Corps" of the Air Force.

At the end of the nineteenth century, the US Navy was the primary service for projecting American power across the oceans. The Navy recognized that to protect the newly acquired American empire across the vast Pacific it required advanced maintenance and supply bases to service and protect the fleet. From these advanced bases the Navy could project power around the world and into the enemy's home waters. To secure these bases the Navy needed ground forces, and in the event of war it needed ground forces to seize and secure advanced bases from which the fleet could further project power. This mission gave new life and purpose to the Marine Corps, and initiated the development of Central Pacific amphibious warfare doctrine.

In the late 1940s and early 1950s many believed that the Air Force had become the primary service for projecting power. However, the limited range of aircraft and the inability to refuel in the air created a problem for the Air Force similar to that faced by the Navy fifty years earlier. Hence, the Army was to become the "Marine Corps" of the Air Force. The Army was no longer the decisive instrument of war, but an auxiliary tool designed to facilitate the accomplishment of the primary instrument for war, the Air Force. Some argued that the Army should recognize its new role and become subordinate to the Air Force, forming a relationship similar to that of the Navy and Marine Corps.

Army leadership accepted the new role of air power, and the missions delineated for the Army by the Air Force. In January 1947, in an address entitled "The Postwar Military Establishment and its Manpower Problems," Lieutenant General J. Lawton Collins, "Lightning Joe," who landed his VII Corps on the beaches of Normandy on 6 June 1944, delineated his understanding of the threats to the security of the United States and his vision of the future of warfare:

I think, personally, that the outstanding military lesson gained from the past war is that airpower is the dominant factor of present day warfare.... We believe that the next war may come with a heavy surprise attack against us and will come by air.... I would like to picture for you one man's concept of the possible pattern of a war that might be launched against us.... With seapower as the chief means of transporting men and supplies, wars of the past have always gone East to West or West to East around the world. We believe that the development of airpower will alter the latitudinal direction of future wars and causes them to be fought "longitudinally" over the "top" of the world.... From Siberia, for example, you could take an airplane with a range of 5,000 miles and cover the whole of the United States....[24]

Collins also outlined the types of weapons that the US might have used against it:

Before discussing what might be the possible targets for an atomic attack I would like to cover briefly some of the other scientific developments which might be employed in a future war. The possibility of biological warfare must be considered since it has the capability of destroying people without destroying buildings or other facilities. Biological warfare could be used not only against our armed forces but also against the great mass of people in our large cities. It is also possible that some long-range guided missiles with a range of up to 3,000 miles and one-ton pay load may be developed. However, the outstanding weapon of mass destruction at the present time is the atomic bomb.[25]

Collins, like many others, was incapable of clearly seeing the future of war. However, while accepting the Air Force's vision of the future of warfare, Collins concluded that balanced forces were required, that armies and navies were still necessary, that the demobilization of the Army had gone too far, and that to meet future requirements the size of the Army had to be increased. He told his audience "when you think in terms of disarmament remember that we have already largely disarmed. Our Army had demobilized 90 percent." The Army also argued for the maintenance of a tactical air force capable of supporting ground operations. The Air Force had almost eliminated its Tactical Air Forces, envisioning little need to support ground forces.

A number of crises between 1947 and 1949 caused serious reflection on the state of readiness of the Army. In February 1947, the Soviet takeover of Czechoslovakia shocked the Western World. The US Army in Europe under General Lucius D. Clay could only watch. The Army numbered fewer than 1.4 million soldiers deployed across the planet. In Europe were five of the Army's sixteen remaining divisions— three in Germany, one in Austria, and one in Italy. Bradley noted: "The Army had almost no combat effectiveness.... The Army was thus in no position whatsoever to backstop a get-tough policy of containment vis-à-vis the Soviets. Actually, the Army of 1948 could not fight its way out of a paper bag."[26] On 30 March, the Soviets imposed a blockade of all land transportation into and out of Berlin. Through diplomacy the Soviets at first relented, but in June they again imposed the blockade. The Berlin airlift made it possible for the US and Europe to sustain the inhabitants of the city during the two-year crisis. On 12 May 1949, the blockade ended—277,804 sorties had delivered 2,325,809 tons of food and supplies over a twenty-six-month period. While the crisis was managed and viewed as a victory for the Truman Administration, the status of the Army continued to decline.

On 14 April 1948, Army Chief of Staff General Omar N. Bradley addressed the House Armed Services Committee. He presented his views of the Army's role in national defense:

> Success in modern war can come only through a carefully planned employment of balanced land, sea, and air forces operating as a team. Air bases will unquestionably be necessary. These bases are defensive, to prevent attack on our homeland, and offensive, to permit the air effort to be carried to the enemy. This being so, the land forces—the Army—will be responsible for seizing and holding bases from which the air effort may be most effectively launched.... The Army will also play a large part in preventing the enemy from holding bases from which he can attack our bases and the United States itself....
>
> At the outbreak of an emergency, or before it takes place, the Army must be prepared: to occupy those areas from which air attacks could be launched against our industrial cities; it must be prepared to give protection against bombing, sabotage, and fifth column attacks to the most vital installations, including the atomic energy plants; and, it must be able to seize the overseas areas of vital importance to our communications and to our Air Forces. The units for this job must be in being, up to strength, fully equipped, and trained. Advanced bases are essential to an enemy if he is to bomb our cities.... The only certain and safe guarantee against enemy air attack is to seize and hold the bases from which his aircraft would fly.[27]

Bradley argued unsuccessfully for an increase in Army strength from 542,000 soldiers to 822,000. He wanted a "mobile strike force" of 223,000 soldiers to perform the missions outlined above, and he recognized that the Army was fully employed carrying

occupation duties in Germany and Japan. In the nuclear age, Bradley too accepted the advanced base strategic airpower doctrine as the primary mission for the Army. Bradley, however, did not lose focus of the traditional Army role:

> ...we anticipate many vital objectives, such as scattered guerrilla forces, against which the air weapons will not be effective. Only trained land forces can reduce such opposition. Furthermore, there will unquestionably be situations wherein the full effect of air power will be felt only in conjunction with land forces which can dominate enemy land forces.

When Bradley made this argument the term "limited war" had not entered the lexicon of strategic analysts; however, that is exactly what Bradley and other senior Army leaders argued for—a force capable of fighting limited war, small-scale conflicts in disputed regions of the world. After the Korean War, the first major limited war in the nuclear age, the Army formed the Strategic Army Corps (STRAC) to rapidly respond to limited wars in peripheral regions; however, again, commitments in Europe and Asia and instabilities in Army manpower made it difficult to sustain a three-division corps at a high state of readiness for deployment.

In the "First Report of the Secretary of Defense," December 1948, James Forrestal cautioned Americans and the President:

> If the Army is to function as an effective member of the national security team, there must be a clear public understanding that land forces will continue to be indispensable as a primary fighting arm. This fact has been obscured since World War II by a host of collateral functions which have precluded the Army from preparing itself for an emergency. The Army's fighting role should not be overlooked or underrated as a result of a public misconception that air power replaces land power.[28]

Forrestal was considered a Navy man, but he argued for a balanced force. At this point, however, Bradley and Forrestal were fighting a losing battle. American faith in airpower was firm. The Navy too had suffered under the new vision of war. However, Forrestal had managed to maintain the Navy at a reasonable level of combat-readiness at the cost of his job. Truman, doubting his loyalty and perhaps angered at the continuing budget debates, requested his resignation on 1 March 1949. On 28 March, Forrestal resigned.[29] Louis A. Johnson replaced him. At the dawn of the Cold War he was exactly the wrong man for the job.

In this atmosphere, charged with expectations of the miracles to be performed by airpower and the money to be saved by cutting ground forces, the Army argued for universal military training. Brigadier General George A. Lincoln, chief of Army plans, remembering the surprise attack at Pearl Harbor, told the Congress in 1948, "we will not have the time to mobilize we had from 1939 onward. Adequate forces in readiness must be immediately available and there may be little warning."[30] The debate on universal military training (UMT), a plan that would require all men of a given age to receive some military training, had been in progress since the end of World War II. Congress had rejected it several times and briefly, with the support of the President, allowed the draft to expire in 1947. Peacetime conscription was considered by many in Congress un-American. However, the realities of the Korean War caused the Army to once again advocate for the program, which now had the support of the President, George Marshall, Dwight D. Eisenhower, Mark W. Clark, Omar Bradley, Henry L. Stimson, and James Forrestal. Before the Senate Armed Services Committee on the Problem of Military Manpower Bradley stated:

> If this country is to survive, our citizens will have to face the hard fact that the conditions under which we labor [the Cold War] may persist for 10, 15 or 20 years and that our only sensible military answer to these conditions is to have our citizens adequately prepared and organized to take up our defense. This is the cold and unalterable fact.[31]

General Collins, Army Chief of Staff, added his voice to those supporting UMT:

> [T]here is a recurring tendency to believe that the advance of science and its application to warfare have decreased the requirement for manpower.

We are ever mindful of the need for young scientists both in civil life and in the armed forces. But I should like to emphasize that wars are still tough slugging matches. Korea has proved once again that we still need men as well as the implements with which they fight. The core of our ability to fight is trained manpower. I cannot stress too strongly the fact that democracies must be defended by citizen-soldiers. It seems to me there is only one solution, dictated by the lessons of the past.... It is the program of Universal Military Training designed to provide a steady flow of trained men.... Universal Military Training would necessarily require some sacrifices by all of us.... But if we are to continue our own free way of life we must be prepared to accept sacrifices. If we are to continue as leaders of free men we cannot shirk the responsibilities that go with leadership.... We face a future in which our military needs cannot be met by voluntary means alone.[32]

The Army had sought to avoid the poor state of readiness it faced in 1940, but in 1950 it was again unprepared for war. UMT was enormously unpopular with the American people. Civilian educational, religious, labor, pacifist, and farm groups opposed it. Compulsory military duty in peacetime was unacceptable to large parts of America.[33] And because Americans were convinced that airpower would be the decisive instrument of war, what they wanted was a "seventy-group" Air Force, not another Army division.[34] Prior to the Korean War, Collins and Bradley argued futilely that war was still the dirty, nasty business that it had been in World War II, the Civil War, and the Revolutionary War. However, they were fighting an idea with considerable appeal to any people, but especially to the American people, who viewed war as an aberration, possessed enormous faith in science and technology, and disdained the idea of man becoming a permanent instrument of the state. Since no one could predict an end to the Cold War, in essence, the Army was asking the American people to become a means to an end indefinitely.

In February 1950, months before the outbreak of the Korean War, the Chairman of the National Security Resource Board and former Secretary of the Air Force spoke at Baylor University in Texas and explained America's security situation:

It is our belief that if any democracy attempted to maintain in peacetime a *comparable regular armed force*, the free economy of that democracy would be wrecked.... Here are three facts which every American should know because this is the world in which we live. Behind the Iron Curtain there has been an atomic explosion. Behind that curtain is the air equipment capable of delivering a surprise atomic attack against any part of the United States. And, we have no sure defense against such an attack.... Would any of us like to forfeit either the capacity to defend ourselves as best possible against sudden atomic air attack, or the strategic air capacity necessary for instant effective *retaliation* against those who would make a surprise move against this country?" It is a basic dilemma of our time that those who menace our way of life may force arms expenditures of a magnitude [that would] cripple our economy and imperil our free institutions.... If reports received from behind the Iron Curtain are correct, in a short time Russia will be at its strongest position in armaments, and under its present program that position will increase steadily year by year.[35]

The Secretary's message was clear: the United States could not afford to maintain conventional forces to counter those of the Soviet bloc. To do so would bankrupt the country, wreck the economy, and imperil our free institutions. The only logical solution was, therefore, airpower and nuclear weapons. On 29 August 1949, the Soviet Union exploded its first atomic bomb, ending the American monopoly.[36] And in October, the Chinese Communist Forces of Mao Tse Tung defeated the Nationalist Forces of Chiang Kai Shek, creating the People's Republic of China (PRC).[37] The Soviet acquisition of the atomic bomb and the creation of the PRC gave a further boost to the proponents of airpower and nuclear weapons in the US. In January 1950, Truman authorized accelerated research and development on the "super bomb," the hydrogen bomb. (On 1 November 1952, the US tested the first hydrogen bomb at Enewetak Atoll in the Marshall Islands. On 27 November 1955, the Soviet Union tested its first hydrogen bomb.)

The events of 1949 convinced Secretary of State Dean Acheson that the Soviet Union had the initiative around the world, that American nuclear and conventional forces were inadequate and had to be built up rapidly to deter war, that the US had to be able to fight wars short of nuclear war, and that the new world-wide responsibilities of the United States required a new world-wide military establishment.[38] The US could not go back to the pre-World War II paradigm for national defense, or rely purely on airpower. In the early months of 1950, NSC-68, a classified National Security Council policy document, advanced by Acheson and Paul H. Nitze, was discussed at the highest level of government.[39] The policy paper in summary stated:

The issues that face us are momentous, involving the fulfillment or destruction not only of this Republic but of civilization itself.... With conscience and resolution this government and the people it represents must now take new and fateful decisions.... One of the most important ingredients of power is military strength. In the concept of "containment," the maintenance of a strong military posture is deemed to be essential for two reasons: (1) as an ultimate guarantee of our national security and (2) as an indispensable backdrop to the conduct of the policy of "containment." Without superior aggregate military strength, in being and readily mobilizable, a policy of "containment"—which is in effect a policy of calculated and gradual coercion—is no more than a policy bluff ... We have failed to implement adequately these two fundamental aspects of "containment". In the face of obviously mounting Soviet military strength ours has declined relatively....

[W]e must, by means of a rapid and sustained build-up of the political, economic, and military strength of the free world, and by means of an affirmative program intended to wrest the initiative from the Soviet Union, confront it with convincing evidence of the determination and ability of the free world to frustrate the Kremlin design of a world dominated by its will. The whole success of the proposed program hangs ultimately on recognition by this Government, the American people, and all free peoples, that the cold war is in fact a real war in which the survival of the free world is at stake.[40]

NSC-68 was a simplistic formulation designed to be easily understood. It divided the world into good and evil. Undiscriminating global anticommunism became the major force in American foreign and military policy. Kennan's tenet of "counter-force at every point" was defined in NSC-68. It was designed to be a blunt instrument to move Truman and his Secretary of Defense to increase defense spending to $35 billion, $5 billion above that requested by the JCS, and $20 billion more than Truman and Congress planned to spend. The President ended up requesting $14,241 million to be divided almost evenly between the services.[41] However, in April Truman discussed and analyzed NSC-68 with his principal advisers. Still, budget concerns and the economy dominated the thinking of the President and the new Secretary of Defense, Louis A. Johnson. The President wanted additional information. He wanted a second committee formed to study the implications of NSC-68 on the economy. This committee was scheduled to report its findings in August 1950.

On 25 June 1950, the North Korean People's Army (NKPA) invaded the Republic of Korea (ROK) and Truman committed the nation to a war the services were ill-prepared to fight, even the Air Force. The Air Force's emphasis on strategic bombing left it in a poor state of readiness to carry out conventional missions such as air superiority—fighter-to-fighter—close air support of forces on the ground, interdiction, and strategic and operational air mobility. In 1950, the Army had fewer than 600,000 men and ten active divisions. Its primary missions were: the occupation and rehabilitation of Germany and Japan; the maintenance of forces in the US to support occupation; and the provision of the US component of the United Nations security force.[42] In other words, the Army was little more than a police force responsible for the lives of 125 million people. Training for war was a secondary mission. All the services went to war in Korea with equipment from World War II, much of which was obsolete. As a result of this lack of foresight, the failure to understand eminent threats, concerns about the economy, and the over-reliance on airpower and nuclear weapons, the Armed Forces of the United States, particularly the Army, were not prepared to fight the war in Korea, and men died as a result of these failures.

General Curtis LeMay, US Air Force, lamented:

In 1945 we had possessed the largest and best trained and most experienced and most effective Army and Navy in our history. In 1948 we were going around explaining to the world that we really didn't mean it; we were so sorry; and our bazookas had all been taken to the city dump, and our airplanes had been smashed into junk. And Gus had gone back to the diner, and George had gone back to the real estate office. . . . And please forget that we ever tried to be soldiers, sailors, and airmen. It was the prevailing psychology of the year. The maintenance of a puissant force was regarded as a national aberration.[43]

LeMay's words and tone expressed his frustration and anger, and that of other senior military leaders who questioned the extent of the disarmament in the face of a growing Soviet military threat. Still, LeMay identified an important aspect of American thinking about the conduct of war. The maintenance of powerful military forces was an aberration. The tradition of maintaining a small standing Army, with the Navy as the first line of defense, secure behind the vast Pacific and Atlantic Oceans, was again put into practice after World War II, with the new dimension of airpower.

Secretary Acheson noted:

The dispatch of the two divisions to Korea, removed the recommendations of . . . NSC-68, from the realm of theory and made them immediate budget issues. . . . I urged that the President ask for an immediate increase in authorized forces of all services, for substantial appropriations—too much rather than too little—for increased military production and powers to allocate and limit uses of raw material, and state that this was to increase the capabilities not only of our own forces but of allied forces as well. The President agreed. . . .[44]

A few days after the outbreak of the Korean War the President went to Congress to get approval for increased military spending and authorization to increase the size of the Army. In a message to Congress, Truman explained his actions:

The attack on the Republic of Korea . . . was a clear challenge to the basic principles of the United Nations Charter and to the specific actions taken by the United Nations in Korea. If this challenge had not been met squarely, the effectiveness of the United Nations would have been all but ended and the hope of mankind that the United Nations would develop into an institution of world order would have been shattered. Prompt action was imperative.[45]

Truman called for a rapid increase of the Armed Forces and a partial call-up of reserves to support MacArthur, to strengthen strategic reserves in the United States, and to assist the armed forces of allied nations.

When war came, the Army was too small, with too many missions, dispersed in too many parts of the world. The US Army Eighth Army in Korea faced one humiliating tactical defeat after another, until it was surrounded in the Pusan Perimeter, facing strategic defeat. Few Americans back home suffered during the Korean War. It was a limited war, and few people were asked or required to sacrifice. But soldiers died because the Army was unprepared for a war they'd been asked to fight. As Ridgway noted:

> We were, in short, in a state of shameful unreadiness when the Korean War broke out, and there was absolutely no excuse for it. The only reason a combat unit exists at all is to be ready to fight in case of sudden emergency, and no human being can predict when these emergencies will arise. The state of our Army in Japan at the outbreak of the Korean War was inexcusable.[46]

Congress shares responsibility with the President for the state of the armed forces. General Collins recalled a report by the House Appropriations Committee on the Army's budget:

> [T]he committee's careful scrutiny of the estimate of manpower, equipment, and missions to be performed leads to the conclusion that the estimates of funds required are out of proportion to the actual needs on the basis of the Army's predictions of requirements. While the committee does not propose to reduce the size of the Army below numbers estimated by the military authorities as requisite or the amount of equipment and supplies necessary to maintain such an Army, it is well aware of the fact that it is the

habit of the services to estimate their fund requirements generously in order that they may be able to meet all contingencies. This is a sound policy to follow during actual warfare and the Congress at that time approved it but there is no sound reason why the Army cannot be administered in peacetime with more regard for dollars than apparently is their custom or intent.[47]

Neither Congress nor the American people understood the cost in treasure and blood the "Cold War" was to extract. The Congress voted authorization of $13.222 billion for the entire Department of Defense, $1 billion less than that requested by the frugal Truman Administration. The services' lack of preparedness dictated American strategy and doctrine for the conduct of the Korean War, initiating the chain of events and creating the conditions for the major strategic decisions that brought the United States into war with the People's Republic of China. The entry of Chinese Communist Forces into the Korean War in November 1950 triggered an expanded mobilization resulting in twenty active divisions, temporarily reversing the move toward almost exclusive reliance on airpower and nuclear weapons.

Considering the decisions made by Truman, Congress, the American people, and the armed forces, it can be argued that they all were responsible for the sorry state of the armed forces in June 1950, which needlessly cost so many American lives. The Truman Administration had placed its trust in nuclear weapons and strategic bombing, in mutual defense treaties, and in military aid and assistance to nations fighting Communism. The Congress had cut the budget of the armed forces beyond that recommended by the Truman Administration. The American people had opposed universal military training and were dissatisfied with conscription under the Selective Service System during times of peace. Army demobilization was completed on 30 June 1947 with the discharge of the last non-volunteer forces. The total strength of the Army on 1 July was 989,664, including 364,000 Air Forces personnel who would form the US Air Force. Congress and the American people also had not supported the Organized Reserve Corps (ORC) and National Guard (NG). The ORC consisted of 68,785 officers and 117,756 enlisted men at the outbreak of hostilities in Korea. In 1945 the Army had planned for a force of 1.75 million organized into twenty-five divisions. Ground NG forces numbered 324,761, organized into just under 5,000 units. The twenty-seven NG divisions were at roughly fifty percent of their go to war TO&E (table of organization and equipment—manpower, weapons, vehicles, and other equipment) strength, and averaged only forty-six percent of their TO&E equipment.[48] Finally, the armed forces had not helped themselves. In the post-war period without the exigencies of war, the services competed in a zero-sum game for resources. This system motivated behaviors that damaged the integrity of the services. The so-called "revolt of the admirals" was only one such episode of a service placing its own interests ahead of those of the country.[49] The inability of the services to develop joint strategy and doctrine eroded their influence. This situation became critical during the Vietnam War, when Kennedy, Johnson, and McNamara virtually ignored the advice of the Joint Chiefs of Staff.

However, if instead of looking at the decisions made by the various agents as decisions based primarily on the exigencies of the time, they are looked at through the prism of strongly held American cultural tenets, then those decisions are coherent. They make sense because they follow traditional, culturally imbued strategies and practices. This is probably the best explanation for American behavior at the dawn of the Cold War. Cultural learning can be unlearned; however, the more basic the tenets, the more difficult the unlearning. America's political leaders learned little during the Korean War regarding the future of warfare. The war was too short and unpopular to cause the type of reflection required to change deeply held patterns of behavior. President Eisenhower, like his predecessor, had enormous faith in airpower. By the latter half of the 1950s, the increased range and speed of bombers, more lethal nuclear weapons, the forward deployment of American airpower to bases in the UK and Europe, and the technology to refuel in the air had greatly increased the capabilities of airpower, and by so doing diminished the apparent need for ground forces. While a conventional sustained bombing campaign still required advanced bases, few military theorists at the time contemplated such a campaign. With conventional bombs, numerous sorties were necessary. Such a campaign could not be carried out from the borders of the United States. The logistical, maintenance, and human requirements necessitated bases in foreign countries. The Army's advanced bases mission died having never been used.

Army Opposition

The Army never fully accepted the theory of strategic airpower. Starting in the late 1940s and throughout the 1950s, Army Chiefs of Staff and senior Army leaders argued against the new vision of war from the air with nuclear weapons. In defense of the Army, leaders such as Dwight D. Eisenhower, Omar N. Bradley, J. Lawton Collins, Mark W. Clark, Matthew B. Ridgway, Maxwell D. Taylor, James M. Gavin, Lyman L. Lemnitzer, Manton S. Eddy, Bruce C. Clarke, and others argued for the retention of significant ground combat forces to meet the growing Communist threat. Ironically, in 1948, Eisenhower, in his final report as Army Chief of Staff, was one of the first to raise the alarm. Eisenhower had witnessed the Army's decline from 6 million men in 1945 to 552,239 men as of 1 July 1948, from eighty-nine divisions to ten divisions.[50] Eisenhower reported:

> The Army phases of a balanced air-sea-ground organization require special stress at a time when many voice the opinion that land forces have been made obsolete by the advance of aviation, the development of rockets, and the atomic bomb. Today the only element of the military establishment that can hold a defensive position, seize for exploitation a major offensive base, exercise direct complete control over an enemy population—three fundamental purposes of armed effort—is, as always, the foot-soldier. The introduction of the plane and the atomic bomb has no more eliminated the need for him than did the first use of cavalry or the discovery of gunpowder.[51]

Armies exist for two basic purposes: first to generate the combat power necessary to destroy enemy forces and thereby win wars; and second, to deter war through their demonstrative ability to generate combat power. Eisenhower recognized that the Army was primarily performing occupation duty, and hence, was not ready to fight. He further noted that the Army's lack of preparation for war invited war:

The budget of the Army and its numerical strength are devoted largely to the consequences of victory. Occupation is both worthy and necessary, but it must be seen as preventive rather than as positive security. Moreover, its physical magnitude and manifold problems demand such concentrated effort that relatively few men and little time are left for the Army's primary job. The purely security mission—organizing, training and sharpening for national defense—has necessarily taken second place. By no stretch of the facts can the United States Army, as it is now manned, deployed, and engaged, be considered an offensive force. It is not ready to respond to an emergency call because its global distribution not only leaves it weak in every sector but prevents the concentration of anything beyond the merest handful for possible tactical use. This virtually complete dispersion of our ground strength cannot be permitted to continue over any considerable period, because there are elements in both the world situation and our own strategic position that demand the constant availability of respectable land forces....[52]

Eisenhower then assessed the readiness of Army equipment:

Even our existing Regular Army is underequipped with such modern weapons. The occupation mission, consuming more than two billion dollars of the Army's annual budget, plus other budgetary limitations, has left almost no money for current procurement. Unless this defect is remedied we will shortly have to acknowledge that in weapons and equipment our ground troops may prove inferior to a modern offensive force.[53]

In 1948, Eisenhower and other senior Army leaders told the Secretary of Defense and the President that the Army was incapable of generating sufficient combat power to win a major war, and, as a consequence, was failing in its mission to deter war. The Truman Administration, by its military policies, communicated to the world that the United States would not defend the new Republic of Korea. It signaled to the world that it was disarming, and hence, would only defend occupied countries. The Truman

Administration had an accurate assessment of the Army's state of readiness, and the potential dangers. A few months after the initiation of hostilities in Korea Bradley wrote:

It is now apparent that the aggression in Korea was well planned and well prepared and the militant international Communism inspired the northern invaders. It is also apparent that Communism is willing to use arms to gain its ends. This is a fundamental change and it has forced a change in our estimate of the military needs of the United States. [W]e have finally drawn the line.... We may in this way succeed in forcing the respect which we now know conciliation, appeasement and weakness can never bring. The cost will be heavy—but not as heavy as the war which we are now convinced would follow our failure to arm. [I]t is now evident that we must have an even greater flexibility of military power in the United States itself—not only for our own protection, but also to give us a ready, highly mobile standby force which we can bring to bear at any threatened point in the minimum time....[54]

These were strong words, uncharacteristic of Bradley. The term "appeasement" was loaded with memories of the failures of British and French foreign and military policies in the 1930s, and knowledge of the sacrifices of World War II. Bradley, however, had good reason to stress this point. Truman and his advisors ignored the warnings, and as a consequence, share as much of the blame for the causes of the Korean War, as the British for the causes of World War II, which, many people believe, was the result of their "policy of appeasement." Bradley had argued for a rapid deployment force before the war in Korea, and he knew that sacrifices were again being made by servicemen in Korea—sacrifices that might have been avoided had the Army retained the "respect" it had at the close of World War II. Now, he hoped that events in Korea would convince political leaders to reverse the policies of the last five years that had so devastated the Army. Bradley could have also noted that it was geography that saved South Korea. The proximity of the four US Army divisions in Japan to the battlefield is all that made possible the continued existence of South Korea. The Army did not have significant rapid deployment force, and airpower could not stop the advancing North Korean Army, nor could the Navy and Marine Corps. Had US forces deployed from the west coast they would have arrived too late to save South Korea.

General Fredrick J. Kroesen observed:

> I have never read a comprehensive survey of why and how the deterioration of the World War II Army was allowed to happen. I was in it and I had no idea of how bad it was and only much later came to the realization that the destruction of the force could not have been accomplished more thoroughly if it had been deliberate—in fact being a government program, a deliberate attempt at destruction could not possibly have been so successful.[55]

Clay Blair in his work, *The Forgotten War*, agreed with General Kroesen's assessment. Blair believed that Truman deliberately gutted the Armed Forces because the Army, and then the Navy, had rejected him. He was refused admittance to West Point and Annapolis in his youth, primarily because of his bad eyesight. Blair used Truman's own words to make the point:

> "You always have to remember when you're dealing with generals and admirals, most of them, they're wrong a good deal of the time. . . . They're most of them just like horses with blinders on. They can't see beyond the ends of their noses. . . ." Half to three quarters of all generals were "dumb." Besides that, he said, "No military man knows anything at all about money. All they know how to do is spend it, and they don't give a damn whether they're getting their money's worth or not. . . . I've known a good many who feel that the more money they spend, the more important they are. . . ." The basic fault of both generals and admirals was the education they received at West Point and Annapolis: "It seems to give a man a narrow view of the things."[56]

Blair concluded: "By June 25, 1950 Harry Truman and Louis Johnson had all but wrecked the conventional military forces. . . . The fault was Truman's alone. . . . Truman's trench-level military

outlook combined with his fiscal conservatism and contempt for the generals and admirals had led him to weaken gravely the armed forces. . . ." Blair's words are caustic and inflammatory; nevertheless, beyond the personal attack on Truman, he was correct. It was Truman's policies that so damaged the ability of the armed forces to deter and fight war. And his reductions in the strength of the armed forces were not accompanied by commensurate reductions in missions. Truman, however, along with the rest of America, had suffered through the Great Depression, and this was probably his primary motivation.

Between 1945 and 1950 the Army tried to increase the combat power of its divisions through new developments in training based on lessons learned in World War II, and by the limited acquisition of more lethal weapons. The Army maintained its traditional system of basic training, small unit training, combined unit training, and finally field training. Field training, combined unit training, and joint training with the other services had typically been neglected. The cost of large maneuvers and the problems of coordinating with the other services typically precluded such training. However, in January 1950, General Clark, Chief, Army Field Forces, could report: "The most extensive and diversified peacetime maneuver training program in our history is now under way." Clark noted the following benefits from the training:

> There are many features of maneuver training that can be obtained by no other means. Realism of training, the introduction of non-combatant functions, the test of our combat doctrine and the development of new doctrine—in varying degrees each large-scale exercise offers all of these. In addition each provides for testing our equipment. . . .[57]

Some stateside units were, in fact, well trained. The 11th Airborne Division at Camp Campbell and the 82nd Airborne Division at Fort Bragg were two such units. Clark's words rang with an air of confidence and assurance that the Army was on the right track. However, the majority of the Army was not prepared for war. All the reductions in the size of the Army, all the missions and responsibilities, all the overseas deployments, and all the budget cuts made it impossible for the Army to train in a comprehensive manner. The Army, with all this turbulence, had difficulty maintaining cohesive combat units. Speaking during the war, the Army Chief of Staff, General Collins, endeavored to remind the American people of the many duties their Army was carrying out at that moment:

> This Army . . . is deployed over the face of the world—with sizable forces located in forty-nine countries on six continents. In addition to the men of our great Eighth Army fighting in the mud and mountains of Korea, soldiers are keeping watch along the iron curtain in Berlin and Vienna, are participating in atomic tests in the Nevada desert, are standing guard along our northern approaches in Iceland, Greenland and

Alaska, are assisting in the defense of Japan, are protecting our essential outposts in Panama and the Caribbean and on islands of the Pacific, and are providing advice and military assistance to our friends along the periphery of the Soviet empire in Europe, the Middle East and Asia. Within the continental United States, Army anti-aircraft units are deployed to defend our cities and key industrial facilities and other Army forces are stationed in all of the forty-eight states.[58]

Army leaders believed the Korean War proved the fallacy of the argument that nuclear weapons and airpower alone could keep the peace and advance American interests around the world. They retained their belief that man was the ultimate weapon on the battlefield, and advanced the concept of limited war.

5.
THE KOREAN WAR, THE OPENING PHASES, 1950–1951

Conditions today are sufficiently turbulent that war might be visited upon the world without the impetus of planning or deliberate policy. One isolated action might precipitate conflict, and, once started in a critical area, war leaps across new borders and quickly involves other nations whose whole desire is for peace. Our future security depends on American willingness to combat unceasingly the conditions that provoked war and on our readiness to defend America and its principles should war break out despite preventive measures. Our task is to convince any possible aggressor that he can choose war only at the risk of his own destruction. A grim outlet it may be, but it is inescapable.

General Dwight Eisenhower
Army Chief of Staff, 1948

The Korean War meant entry into action "as is." No time out for recruiting rallies or to build up and get ready. It was move in–and shoot. This put the bulk of the burden on the G.I. The story of the infantry soldier is an old and honorable one. He carries his home with him–and often his grave. Somehow, he has to bring along the whole paraphernalia of fighting, as well as domesticated living: the grocery store, the ration dump; the hospital, the Medical Corps; the garage, the motor pool; the telephone, the Signal Service. He must sleep and eat and fight and die on foot, in all weather, rain or shine, with or without shelter. He is vulnerable day and night. Death has his finger on him for twenty-four hours, in battle, going toward it, or retreating from it. It is a wonder that the morale of those uniformed gypsies never falters.[1]

General of the Army, Douglas MacArthur
Reminiscences, 1964

The Korean War was an infantry war. All the advances in technologies, airpower, nuclear power, naval power, missiles, and other machines of war contributed, but they were not decisive, nor did they have the potential to be. Short of extermination warfare, they could *not* deter or stop the advance of the North Korean People's Army (NKPA). It took soldiers, infantrymen, fighting a primitive war in the heat, stench, rain, mud, and frigid conditions of the Korean peninsula with individual weapons, to stop the NKPA and the Chinese People's Volunteers (CPV) and save the new Republic of Korea (ROK).[2] With all the billions of dollars invested in technologies, with all the intellectual

energy focused on airpower and nuclear weapons, with all the human capital invested in the search for new weapons of war, the ROK would not exist today if it were not for the exertions and sacrifices of the American soldier. And, as is the American tradition, the Army received the least attention, the least money, and was maintained at the lowest possible manpower.

In 1950, the majority of the Army's overseas units were undermanned, dispersed throughout the occupied countries, poorly trained and equipped, and intellectually and psychologically unprepared for war. To some degree the size and state of the US Army influenced the thinking of Soviet leaders, expanding the range of permissible behavior of its client states. Knowledge of American airpower and nuclear capabilities did not deter limited wars in peripheral regions. In the immediate post-World War II period the Truman Administration sent the wrong signals. Eisenhower concluded that:

> Military weakness on our part cannot be hidden. The transparency of our governmental process, the public discussion of military matters, the information our citizens must have to arrive at a sound public opinion—all these assure to any nation that seeks it a factual knowledge of our day-to-day military position. Moreover, they afford great advantage to a conspirator against the peace, since he is given full notice of our intentions and ample warning of any decision in the international sphere.

In Korea, the Army and the nation rose to the challenge, but the cost of unpreparedness was high, and, as always, soldiers paid the highest price.

The Korean War also demonstrated that a small developing state could place such a heavy burden on the armed forces of the United States that they were unable to respond adequately to threats in other parts of the world, leaving the nation vulnerable to diplomatic, political, and military setbacks elsewhere.

*   *   *   *   *

During the Korean War, a significant, but unnoticed transition in the American way of war took place. In 1951, as the war became a stalemate, the American citizen-soldier Army stopped employing offensive strategy, the Army's traditional campaign-winning doctrines. Instead, the Army assumed a strategic defense, and airpower became the primary offensive arm. *The citizen-soldier Army of the United States would never again fight a major war with offensive strategy and doctrine.* In 1951, "major limited war" came to mean a strategically defensive ground war in which the Army was *not* supposed to produce victory. The situation would remain this way until the end of the Cold War. Airpower became the primary and only strategically offensive arm, and it was employed to achieve essentially negative objectives; that is, to convince the enemy they could not win.[3]

This new approach to war, initiated in Korea, was culturally un-American. Strategically defensive wars

of attrition would never be acceptable to the American people, particularly with a citizen-soldier Army. Especially when the demonstrated nuclear capabilities that ended World War II, the impressive array of aircraft and technologies, the claims of airmen and enthusiastic political leaders, the billions of dollars of taxpayer money expended on airpower, and the strategic doctrines of the Truman and later Eisenhower Administrations told the American people that armies were either obsolete, or auxiliaries of the Air Force. In the age of nuclear weapons, jet aircraft, and missiles, *conscription* made little sense; as a consequence, the ground wars in Korea and Vietnam made little sense. It was inexplicable to the American people to possess all this power and not use it. Thus, the American citizen-soldier Army, which depended on the support of the people, could not adapt to this new strategy and doctrine, particularly in nation-states with no cultural affinity with the American people. However, the Korean War ended before the cultural conflict reached a critical point.

The Korean War

In 1905, the Japanese defeated the Russians in a short, bloody war, and occupied Korea. In 1910, Korea was annexed and became a province of Japan. For thirty-five years, Japan ruled Korea. On 6 August 1945, the United States dropped the first atomic bomb on Hiroshima. Two days later the Soviet Union declared war on Japan. This declaration made it possible for the USSR to intervene in the war in Asia, to take the surrender of the veteran Kwantung (Japanese) Army in China, to support the Communist Chinese under Mao Tse-Tung, and to take part in the post-war reorganization in the region. On 9 August, the US dropped the second atomic bomb on Nagasaki, bringing World War II to an end, and initiating the "Cold War." Had there been no atomic bomb, there would have been no South Korea. The rapid surrender of Japan made the military support of Soviet forces unnecessary, creating the conditions for US forces to enter Korea.

On 15 August 1945, US General Order Number One called for the US Army to take the surrender of Japanese forces south of the 38th parallel in Korea. The armed forces of the USSR took the surrender of Japanese forces north of the 38th parallel. The division of the Korean peninsula was a temporary expedient; however, as relations between the US and USSR deteriorated and political divisions in Korea moved toward civil/revolutionary war, the border at the 38th parallel became militarized, a point of contact between the Communist left and the Western-oriented capitalist right.[4] On 15 August 1948, the Republic of Korea (ROK) was formed in Seoul, Korea under the leadership of President Syngman Rhee. Less than a month later, 9 September, the Democratic People's Republic of Korea (DPRK) was formed in Pyongyang under the leadership of Kim Il Sung.

Geography greatly influenced the conduct of the Korean War, facilitating the ability of the United States, United Nations, the People's Republic of China (PRC), and the Soviet Union (USSR) to contain and limit the war to a relatively small geographic area. Korea is a peninsula, roughly 600 to 650 miles long from its northern border with Manchuria to its southern tip. It varies in width from 125 miles to 200 miles and covers 84,000 square miles. Korea is funnel shaped in the northern half, and has contiguous borders with the PRC and the former USSR in the north. The Yalu and Tumen Rivers delineate Korea's

Fig 5.1 Korea, Area of Operations.

Fig 5.2 Korea, Nature of Terrain.

450 miles long border with the PRC. Japan lies just over a hundred miles to the southeast across the Korea Straits. Thus, Korea is strategically situated in the center of a triangle between three traditional rivals. As a consequence, Korea has been both the spoils of and an invasion route for these larger, more dominant states in their competitions. Korea's common borders with the PRC and USSR made it possible for these states to intervene directly in the Korean War with supplies, equipment, and conventional and/

or insurgency forces in support of the North Korean Communists. Geography, thus, eliminated exhaustion and annihilation strategies.

Short of war with the PRC or USSR, there was no way to isolate the battlefield, to stop the flow of supplies, equipment, and other material into North Korea. Geography also enabled NKPA to cross the Yalu into China, precluding their complete destruction. These forces could rest, refit, and reenter Korea when ready to continue the war. The PRC or USSR could also intervene at will with so-called "volunteer forces" or with their regular forces. Hence, in a war in which the PRC and USSR participated, passively or actively, there was no way to complete the destruction of the enemy's army—through annihilation strategy. In addition, the resources, population, and geographic proximity of the PRC and USSR to Korea made it possible for them to provide manpower almost indefinitely. In a limited war with the slow drain of resources, the US and the UN could not match the combined resources of the two communist giants. It was not possible to exhaust or annihilate communist forces in Korea, leaving only one strategy—attrition. Given these geographic circumstances, from a military point of view, the US should not have fought the Korean War.

Because Korea is a peninsula, the US Navy could dominate three sides of the fields of battle. And once forces were stretched across the waist of the peninsula certain forms of maneuver with significant forces became impossible. Without airborne and/or amphibious forces it was not possible to conduct envelopment/flanking movements, or turning movements. Offensive operations were necessarily front attacks, penetrations, or infiltrations; thus, the geography of Korea favored defensive operations. These restrictions on the forms of maneuver caused by the narrowness of the peninsula and the dominance of the US Navy made it possible for the US to employ limited manpower to control the peninsula and balance the superior numbers of the enemy. However, the funnel shape of North Korea limited this effect. The further north US forces traveled, the greater the number of soldiers required to defend the lines of communication (LOC). With each mile traveled north, the demand for soldiers increased.

The Korean War was more primitive than World War II. In 1950, Korea lacked the infrastructure of European nations. There were few large cities and little industry. Lines of communications, rail and road were generally poor, and cross-country movement by vehicle, tracked and wheeled, was difficult. There was no space in Korea for the heavy armor and mechanized divisions that characterized World War II in Europe. This was an infantry war. Mobility in some parts of the country was restricted to foot movement. One main road and one main rail system linked the entire country. Korea has a spine of mountains running almost its entire length. The mountainous terrain was primarily in eastern parts of the country, and was excellent for defensive and infiltration tactics. The flat areas were covered with rice fields that channeled vehicular transportation. The terrain in most parts of Korea reduced engagement ranges, and diminished the technological advantages of US forces.

The climate went from one extreme to the other. During the winter months, October to March, the weather was severe, approaching arctic conditions. The summers were hot, with temperatures reaching over 100 degrees F. The mountainous terrain, heat, and heavy loads carried by soldiers combined to produce heat casualties and to erode the mobility and combat power of the Eighth Army. In the summer months, a stench emanated from the ubiquitous rice fields fertilized with human waste. Ridgway wrote:

> There is one feature of Korea that every fighting man will remember—the smell. The use of human excrement—night soil—to fertilize the fields, the husbanding of that commodity in pails and barrels, and in leaky wagons, give to the atmosphere of the country a fragrance so overpowering that the soul at first rebels.[5]

War in Korea made enormous demands on the human body and spirit. Yet, Korea is a beautiful country, with 30 million people (roughly 20 million in the South and 10 million in the North) who culturally rank among the most industrious, adaptable, and enterprising on Earth. The character and tenacity of the Korean people contributed mightily to the survival of the Republic of South Korea.

*　*　*　*　*

In the early months of 1950, Kim Il Sung petitioned Stalin and Mao Tse-Tung to support the invasion of South Korea with the objective of reuniting the peninsula. Stalin was deeply concerned about US intervention, and would only "consent" with Mao's approval and support of the plan. To convince Stalin and Mao, Kim Il Sung argued that the US would not intervene, that his forces would achieve strategic surprise and complete the destruction of South Korean forces in three days. He explained that there would be an uprising of 200,000 communists against the Rhee government, that his guerrilla forces had penetrated into the southernmost provinces of South Korea and were in position to support the invasion, and that if the US did decide to react they would encounter a fait accompli.[6] The Korean War was, at least in part, the function of miscalculations on all sides. Secretary of State, Dean Acheson, had in fact indicated publicly that South Korea did not fall within the defensive perimeter of the US, drawing the line at Japan. By so doing, he strengthened Kim Il Sung's argument.

At 04.00 on 25 June 1950, the NKPA attacked across the 38th parallel, executing a well-developed invasion plan, achieving tactical and strategic surprise. The NKPA numbered roughly 120,000 men. It was organized into ten divisions, five separate infantry brigades, and one armor brigade with 120 Soviet-made T34 tanks. North Korean forces also included a large, well-equipped, well-trained guerrilla force that had infiltrated into South Korea to instigate an insurgency.[7] Substantial numbers of Soviet advisors assisted the NKPA. The ROK was taken by surprise, and its armed forces were ill equipped to halt the invasion. The ROK Army was organized into eight divisions with approximately 98,000 soldiers. US military assistance to the ROK had been intentionally restricted to the development of defensive capabilities. The objective was, in part, to preclude South Korea, under the aggressive leadership of Rhee, from attacking North Korea. Nationalism and the desire to reunite the peninsula influenced leaders on both sides. The ROK Army had no combat aircraft, tanks, or heavy artillery. The ROK Air Force and Navy were insignificant.

In response to the attack, the United Nations Security Council immediately convened. The Security Council approved a US-sponsored resolution calling for "... all members of the United Nations to furnish such assistance to the Republic of Korea as may be necessary to repel the armed attack and to restore international peace and security in the area." On 27 June, President Truman authorized General Douglas MacArthur, Commander-in-Chief, Far East (CINCFE) to use air and naval forces to assist the ROK in slowing the advance of the NKPA. At the same time, he ordered the US Seventh Fleet, under the command of Vice Admiral Arthur D. Struble, to blockade Korea and defend the Formosan Straits—placing the US between the Chinese Communists on the mainland and the Chinese Nationalists on the island of Taiwan. Truman also accelerated military assistance to the French forces and "Associated States" fighting the Communists in Indo-China (Laos, Cambodia, and Vietnam). By ordering the Seventh Fleet into the Straits of Formosa, the US intervened directly in the Chinese civil war, an act interpreted by the PRC as "armed aggression" and a "blatant violation of the United Nations Charter." The Chinese could legitimately argue that US actions were an act of war. That same day, in a news conference, Truman informed the American people of his actions and explained why they were necessary:

> In Korea the Government forces, which were armed to prevent border raids and to preserve internal security, were attacked by invading forces from North Korea. The Security Council of the United Nations called upon the invading troops to cease hostilities and to withdraw to the 38th parallel. This they have not done, but on the contrary have pressed the attack. The Security Council called upon all members of the United Nations to render every assistance to the United Nations in the execution of this resolution. In these circumstances I have ordered United States air and sea forces to give the Korean Government troops cover and support.[8]

This was the first use of the UN to give US actions legitimacy. The day following Truman's announcement, Seoul fell to the NKPA. MacArthur flew to Korea to assess the situation. He wrote:

> The South Korean forces were in complete and disorganized flight. We reached the banks of the Han just in time to be caught up in the last rearguard action to defend its bridges. Seoul was

already in enemy hands. Only a mile away, I could see the towers of smoke rising from the ruins of this fourteenth-century city. I pushed forward toward a hill a little way ahead. It was a tragic scene. . . . I watched for an hour the pitiful evidence of the disaster I had inherited. In that brief interval on the blood-soaked hill, I formulated my plans. They were desperate plans indeed, but I could see no other way except to accept a defeat which would include not only Korea, but all of continental Asia.

The scene along the Han was enough to convince me that the defensive potential of South Korea had already been exhausted. There was nothing to stop the Communists from rushing their tank columns straight down the few good roads from Seoul to Pusan at the end of the peninsula. All Korea would then be theirs. Even with air and naval support, the South Koreans could not stop the enemy's headlong rush south. *Only the immediate commitment of ground troops could possibly do so. The answer I had come to seek was there. I would throw my occupation soldiers into this breach. . .*[9]

While MacArthur's account is a bit dramatic, and Ridgway has challenged the accuracy of his recollection of these events, three key points are irrefutable: Seoul had fallen to the NKPA, the ROK Army was in retreat, and incapable of reversing the situation; US air and naval power had not and could not stop or reverse the rapid advance of the NKPA; and therefore, the only way to preclude a Communist victory was to employ US Army ground forces.[10] MacArthur's words also indicate the significance he placed on actions in Korea. Not only was Korea at stake, but "continental Asia." His words indicate that the Chinese Communist victory over the Nationalists in 1949 might still be undone.

Upon returning to his headquarters in Japan, MacArthur sent Truman an urgent message, which concluded with:

The only assurance for holding the present line, and the ability to regain later the lost ground is through the introduction of United States Ground Combat Forces into the Korean battle area. To continue to utilize the forces of our air and navy without an effective ground element cannot be decisive. . . . Unless provision is made for the full utilization of Army-Navy-Air teams in this shattered area, our mission will at best be needlessly costly in life, money and prestige. At worst, it might be doomed to failure.[11]

A day later, Truman authorized the use of US ground forces in Korea, without a declaration of war, or a joint resolution from Congress. Truman never questioned whether he had the authority to order the use of air, sea, or ground forces in war. However, MacArthur in his *Reminiscences*, noted that:

I could not help being amazed at the manner in which this great decision was being made. With no submission to Congress, whose duty it is to declare war, and without even consulting the field commander involved, the members of the executive branch of the government agreed to enter the Korean War.[12]

Truman acknowledged that: "This was the toughest decision I had to make as President. What we faced in the attack on Korea was the ominous threat of a third world war."[13] The "policy of appeasement" that many believed caused World War II was on the President's mind as he made the decision for war.

Truman's initial strategic objective, and that of the UN, was to restore the status quo on the Korean peninsula and prevent World War III. "I wanted to take every step necessary to push the North Koreans back behind the 38th parallel. But I wanted to be sure that we would not become so deeply committed in Korea that we could not take care of such other situations as might develop."[14] Truman planned from the very outbreak of war to fight a limited war, even if that meant the loss of South Korea. Still, the Army started the Korean War the way it started World War II, World War I, and the Civil War—unprepared, with all resultant loss of life.

The Korean War can be divided into three strategic and six operational phases. Each strategic phase represented a change in strategic objectives. The first objective was to restore South Korea, to kick the NKPA out of South Korea—a limited war objective. The second objective was to reunite Korea and roll back Communism. In essence, to destroy North Korea as a separate political entity—a total war objective. After the PRC intervened, the objective was once again to restore and defend South Korea—back to the limited war objective. Operationally the war can be divided into six phases, each designed to achieve strategic objectives: delay and defend (the Pusan Perimeter); the offensive turning movement (the Inchon Landing); pursuit and exploitation (crossing the 38th parallel and the advance to the Yalu); retreat, delay, and defend (war with China); attack to regain the 38th parallel (Ridgway's offensive); and negotiating while fighting (the static, defensive war of attrition).

The Opening Phase: Walker's Battle for Pusan

MacArthur's initial strategic objective was to secure the port of Pusan, on the southeast tip of the peninsula. To do this, he had to stop the advance of the NKPA.[15] If the port of Pusan were lost, the war between North and South Korea would be over. If Pusan were lost, the restoration of the situation would require the mounting of a major amphibious operation that would take years to prepare, given the poor state of readiness of the Armed Forces of the US. And once the entire peninsula was in Communist hands, the President and the United Nations may have accepted the loss of Korea, as they had the loss of China, a year earlier. Hence, holding Pusan was of strategic importance.

In Japan, MacArthur, now Commander-in-Chief United Nations Command (CICUNC), had Lieutenant General Walton "Johnnie" Walker's Eighth Army available for deployment. It consisted of four of the Army's ten divisions, the 1st Cavalry Division (an infantry division), and the 7th, 24th, and 25th Infantry Divisions (ID). Walker was a well respected, highly decorated, experienced soldier. In 1944 and 1945 his XX Corps had frequently led Patton's Third Army in its campaigns across Europe. To Walker, Patton once stated: "Of all the corps I have commanded, yours has always been the most eager to attack and the most reasonable and cooperative."[16] Walker, however, coming from the European Theater, was not one of MacArthur's chosen few, which created some friction. Walker had assumed command of the Eighth Army in September of 1948 with the mission to improve its combat readiness. One student of Army training wrote: "the Eighth Army experienced a paradigm shift in its basic responsibilities in 1949. The change of focus from constabulary

functions to combat readiness reflected Army-wide trends, accelerated throughout 1949 and the first half of 1950...."[17] Still, Walker and his Army faced numerous obstacles that impeded their ability to improve combat effectiveness.[18] The divisions were considerably below wartime strength in personnel and had high turnover rates that damaged continuity and stability. On 30 June 1950, the 24th ID had 757 officers (OFF) and 11,398 enlisted men (EM), and was over a 1,000 men short of its authorized strength. The 25th ID had 836 OFF and 14,113 EM, and was more than 500 men short of its authorized strength. The 1st Cavalry Division had 689 OFF, and 11,605 EM, and was more than 100 men short of its authorized strength. Finally, the 7th ID had 818 OFF, and 12,970 EM, and was almost 1,000 men short of authorized strength.[19]

The authorized strength of each division was well below the wartime strength of 18,900 officers and enlisted men. Each regiment had eliminated one of its three battalions, with the exception of the all-black 24th Infantry Regiment. This meant the divisions could not fight in accordance with established doctrine. The divisions lacked equipment, supplies, space, and time to train. The divisional tank battalions had been reduced to tank companies, and artillery battalions were short one battery. And while the focus and quality of training had improved, many units were psychologically unprepared for battle. General Roy K. Flint, observed:

> For young soldiers . . . life in Japan was an adventure. Not only were they learning to live in the Army, but a new and strange culture beckoned just outside the camp gates. [M]any young privates lived with Japanese women just outside the camp. . . . Their only natural enemy was venereal disease. . . . Heavy drinking was a problem in all units and all ranks.[20]

In war-torn Japan, a sergeant was a wealthy man, and a private could supplement his income by black market trading. Japanese houseboys performed many of the routine duties of soldiers, providing them with additional free time. Still, with all the impediments to training, the Eighth Army was better trained than most historians and soldiers have recognized. Under Walker, the military training program had progressed from individual training through squad, platoon, and company

Fig 5.3 Arrival of General Collins and General Vandenberg: L–R: G/A Douglas MacArthur, C in C FEC; Col. Laurence E. Bunker, Aide-de-Camp to General MacArthur; and Lieutenant General Walton H. Walker, Commander of the Ground Forces in Korea, await the arrival of General J. Lawton Collins, Chief of Staff, US Army, and General Hoyt S. Vandenberg, Chief of Staff, USAF at Haneda AFB, Tokyo, Japan. General Collins and General Vandenberg will confer with General MacArthur regarding the situation in Korea. US Army photography by Sgt. Girard, 13 July 1950.

training to battalion, and in some units, to regimental training. Still, Walker was well aware of the state of his army. He understood that his Army was not prepared to fight as divisional teams, and many were not prepared to fight as regimental teams. The Eighth Army possessed a few very good units and leaders; however, the quality of training had been uneven. Overall, the Eighth Army needed another six to twelve months of training to reach a sufficient level of combat-readiness.

To bring the other divisions to approximate fighting strength, the 7th Infantry Division was stripped of personnel and whole units. MacArthur informed Truman that individual replacements and entire divisions were needed. MacArthur also cautioned Truman that his request was based on war with North Korea alone, and that if the Chinese or Soviets intervened, "a new situation would develop which is not predictable now." Truman and the Pentagon were initially slow to respond to MacArthur's requests. They were uncertain about what they faced. Was the invasion an isolated conflict, or part of a general war, with the Korean invasion simply a feint to draw US forces into the region, and away from the major theater in Europe? Truman, after further analysis and discussion, released the 2nd ID, the 3rd ID (the latter of which had fewer than 5,000 men) and the 5th Regimental Combat Team and the 187th Regimental Combat Team of the 11th Airborne Division. However, their deployment would take time, and, MacArthur needed still more forces, requiring a call-up of National Guard forces, as well as conscription. On 1 September 1950, Oklahoma's 45th and California's 40th National Guard Divisions were federalized.[21] These eight Army divisions along with one Marine division, the ROK Army, and Korean augments to the US Army (KATUSAs) fought the Korean War.

The first Army unit deployed to Korea was Task Force (TF) Smith—a composite unit based on the 1st Battalion, 21st Infantry, of the 24th ID—commanded by Lieutenant Colonel Charles B. (Brad) Smith. The Commanding General (CG) of the 24th ID, Major General William F. Dean, wrote:

> No commander likes to commit troops piece-meal, and I'm no exception, but Smith was defi-nitely the man for the job if it had to be done. He had a fine World War II record in the South Pacific and was a natural leader. So he and his 406 riflemen, plus a few artillerymen, were on the way to a landing field outside Pusan on July 1.[22]

TF Smith was to move north by train, and then, based on intelligence from the ROK Army, put in a defensive position on the main road to block the advance of the NKPA. On 5 July 1950, Task Force Smith engaged a superior enemy force in the vicinity of Osan. In an uneven battle, TF Smith was destroyed as an organized fighting force. It delayed the enemy only a few hours.

The 24th ID deployed piecemeal. Units from the division advanced as far north as possible and then fought desperate delaying actions without the support of tanks and adequate artillery and antitank weapons. One account written during the war read:

> Some 10 days after the initial elements of the United States 24th Infantry Division were com-mitted in Korea, the remainder of that under-strength division was engaged with the enemy . . . every battalion was attempting to defend a front greater than that normally allocated to a full-strength division. Artillery was spread so thinly that it frequently could reach the flanks of its supported unit with only one or two pieces. Engineers were employed as infantrymen. . . . This inadequate force suffered many defeats, but still managed to regroup, pull together, and fight again over the long road from Osan to Taejon.[23]

The NKPA used envelopment tactics, finding the flanks of the American line, moving around them, and thereby forcing the unit to withdraw to another defen-sive position along the main arteries, where this pro-cess started again. As more American forces entered the theater, a defensive perimeter was formed.

The opening phase of the war was a race for time and space. The Eighth Army's objective was to deploy and build up sufficient forces to stop the NKPA as far north as possible, to establish a defensive line from which the situation could be stabilized, and finally to conduct offensive operations to retake the Korean peninsula up to the 38th parallel. In the initial phase, at a minimum, the Port of Pusan had to be retained. To do this, forces had to be deployed piece-meal. The Eighth Army could not wait to ready itself for war. The NKPA's objective was to complete as rap-idly as possible the destruction of the ROK Army, and push US forces back into the sea before significant US forces could be deployed.

On 13 July, Walker formally took command of the Eighth US Army in Korea (EUSAK), establishing his headquarters in Taegu. On 15 July, President Syngman Rhee placed ROK forces under MacArthur's command, extending that command to Walker. By 20 July Walker had deployed the 25th ID and 1st Cavalry Division, and redeployed the ROK Army, which consisted of the 1st, 3rd, 6th, 8th, and Capital Divisions. In late July the 1st Marine Brigade joined the battle, bringing the Eighth Army forces into rough parity with the NKPA. By early August, the Eighth Army's troop strength had risen to 92,000 (45,000 US and 47,000 ROK). At the same time the strength of the NKPA had declined to an estimated 80,000 troops. (This was a considerable loss of forces, indicating the ROK Army had performed better than it was given credit.) South Korea would continue to exist, but the enemy still held the initiative, and Walker was unaware of enemy troop strength, and still uncertain about the performance of his Korean allies.

By the end of July, the Eighth Army had with-drawn into a position that became known as the "Pusan Perimeter." It was engaged on two sides with its back to the sea forming a rectangular area on the south-east tip of the Korean Peninsula, stretching roughly 100 miles from the vicinity of Taegu south along the Naktong River to the Korean Straits, and east, roughly 50 miles, to the Sea of Japan. Walker ini-tially lacked the manpower to establish a continuous defensive perimeter, or fight in accordance with Army doctrine. He used a system of strong point defenses on dominating terrain, and counterattack tactics to maintain the perimeter. The timely arrival of Army regiments and the 1st Marine Provisional Brigade provided needed reserves for counterattacks. Walker used these forces as "fire brigades," plugging holes in the defense where enemy breakthroughs threatened.

On 31 July, Walker ordered:

> There will be no more retreating, withdrawal, readjustment of lines or whatever else you call it. There are no lines behind which we can retreat. This is not going to be a Dunkirk or Bataan. A retreat to Pusan would result in one of the greatest butcheries in history. We must fight until the end. We must fight as a team. If some of us must die, we will die fighting together.[24]

Throughout the month of August Walker rushed troops from one threatened sector to another; however, he had a number of advantages. The Eighth Army's troop strength increased steadily as more United Nations forces arrived. A railway system and road network gave him interior lines, and the ability to reinforce his separated units faster than his enemy. Tactical communication intelligence provided Walker with the locations and time of almost every major attack, enabling him to start the movement of forces to the threatened area before the attack took place. Air reconnaissance provided detailed information. Control of the air, close air support, and the ability to interdict the enemy's supply lines, which extended from North Korea, diminished the enemy's combat power. And North Korean generalship was unimpressive. Instead of concentrating the combat power of the NKPA against a single front and focal point, the generals dispersed it. Still, soldiers and marines fought desperate battles to retain or retake hilltops, and communication between positions was frequently broken by enemy penetrations.

Navy and Marine aviators became the heroes of the close air support war. They assisted soldiers and marines in plugging holes in the line and fighting off breakthrough attacks. Marine and Navy aircraft, because of their proximity to the battlefield, also had a longer loiter time over the battlefield than Air Force aircraft. Flying off aircraft carriers or from within the perimeter, they could answer urgent calls more rapidly. They were effectively integrated into the battle as forces continued to arrive from the US and other United Nations countries. In regard to air interdiction General Almond wrote that:

> ... despite concentrated air efforts by the Marines, the Navy, and the Air Force thus far in the fighting, it had been impossible to prevent the North Koreans from moving tremendous quantities of supplies to the support of their forces then some 300 miles south of the 38th parallel. The interdiction of roads, railroads, and bridges had no decisive effect on their overall movements.[25]

Airpower was not decisive, but it was important. By the end of August, the Eighth Army, with the support of the Far East Air Force (FEAF), had stabilized the situation. In September, MacArthur was ready to go on the offense. Walker's delay and defend operation had succeeded in stopping the advance of the NKPA.

However, the performance of the soldiers of the Eighth Army had in too many cases been poor. Some units exhibited "bug-out fever" when under enemy attack. The Eighth Army had been thrown into battle psychologically, emotionally, physically, and materially unprepared to fight. Units had been pieced together in an effort to get them up to strength. Some leaders took command the week they went into battle. To compensate for the lack of trained infantry, firepower from artillery and airpower was used extensively. In *Training Bulletin No. 1*, it was noted:

> General Van Fleet has stated many times that one of our major advantages over the Reds is our ability to mass supporting fires rapidly on any target. In X Corps in late 1950 and early 1951 we found that ability primarily in the artillery; the infantry was not making maximum utilization of the weapons available. For example, we found attack after attack where the recoilless rifles were never placed in position because it was too much of an effort to hand-carry the guns and ammunition up the rugged mountains. Our company and platoon orders too often merely mentioned the attachment of support of crew-served weapons—no targets or areas of fire were assigned, with the consequence that many infantry weapons were never used in the attack. To reduce casualties and add effectiveness to our

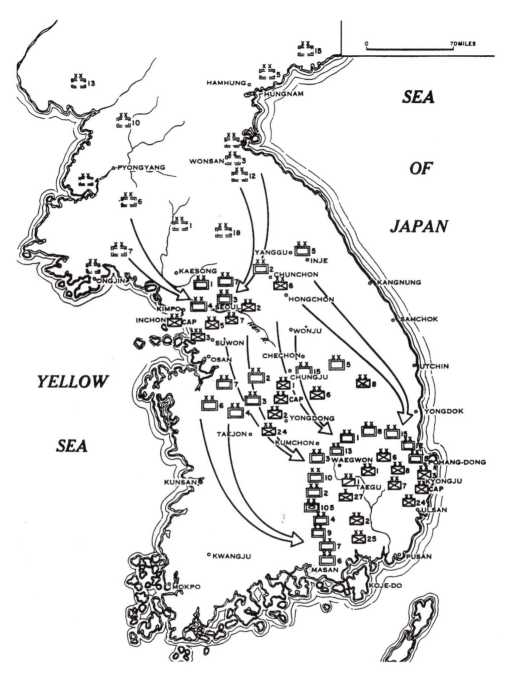

Fig 5.4 Attack of North Korean Forces.

attacks, we must get the crew-served weapons 100 per cent into the game. We are often too anxious to get the job over with as soon as possible; consequently, we tend to tackle the job with comparatively little time spent in planning.... Full utilization of all weapons requires considerable time for planning and movement of weapons.[26]

The Army improved as it gained experience, and as more cohesive, better-trained units arrived from the United States. However, when it met its most severe test against the CPV it was still not proficient in many of the skills required to succeed on the battlefield. Many units were simply incapable of fighting as teams. They lacked the unit training required to perform essential combat operations. Too much of the

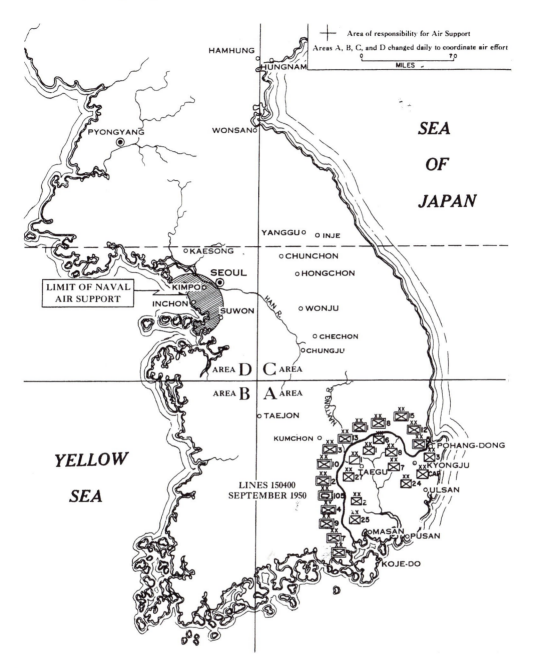

Fig 5.5 South Korea, The Pusan Perimeter.

Army was in a poor state of physical readiness, incapable of sustained marches carrying the fifty to sixty pounds of weapons and equipment necessary to fight. The result was higher casualties and decreased combat effectiveness.[27]

In 1950, the armed forces of the United States were still segregated. While many Army units had "bug-out fever," a tendency to turn away from the enemy and flee, the criticism of the all-black 24th Infantry Regiment was particularly severe. Given the racial climate at the time and the prevalence of Jim Crowism, objective consideration was impossible. Nevertheless, the inferior status of the 24th Infantry placed burdens on the unit that were difficult to overcome. As a consequence, some elements of the 24th did in fact perform poorly. Others, however, fought well.[28]

The Eighth Army achieved its first strategic objective. It retained control of the port of Pusan.

And, given the suddenness of the deployment and the poor state of the Army, Walker and his soldiers and marines deserve great credit for their conduct of the defense. Walker, however, has received considerable criticism for his conduct of operations in Korea, particularly the initial "delay and defend" phase. Clay Blair wrote:

> Walker made many mistakes, especially in the early days of the war. The first was to underestimate vastly and even to ridicule his enemy. That led to the second mistake: the decision to commit the green 24th Division, battalion by battalion, well forward of the Kum River. The ensuing decision to defend Taejon in the hope the 1st Cav Division could reach there in time was another mistake.[29]

Blair concluded: "it was the mistakes of NKPA generals and squad-level courage rather than superior American generalship that 'won' the Battle of the Pusan Perimeter." Another historian argued that: "The Americans' lack of imagination in their scheme of maneuver and their failure to employ existing doctrinal concepts cost them heavily in both lives and lost opportunities."[30] It has also been argued that given the Eighth Army's overall superiority in forces, by late August Walker should have taken the offensive.

There were, in fact, numerous defects in the performance of the Army. However, context is important. The psychological shock of being thrown into battle; the knowledge of having inadequate equipment, training, and forces; the lack of comprehension about why they were there, why they were fighting; and a lack of affinity for the nation they were trying to save damaged the ability of soldiers to generate combat power. Before an army that has been defeated and has retreated can take the offensive, the minds of the men that have to do the fighting must first make the transformation to the offense. Both the ROK Army and US Army had received severe blows that damaged their fighting spirit. The transformation required could not take place overnight. In Korea, the Americans did what they do best; adapted, improvised, and advanced. And while, arguably, Walker may not have been the best general for the job, he did what was most important. He won.

The Inchon Landing

On 23 July 1950, MacArthur cabled Washington:

> Operation planned mid-September is amphibious landing of a two division corps in rear of enemy lines for purpose of enveloping and destroying enemy forces in conjunction with attack from south by Eighth Army. I am firmly convinced that early and strong effort behind this front will sever his main lines of communication and enable us to deliver a decisive and crushing blow. The alternative is a frontal attack which can only result in a protracted and expensive campaign.[31]

This was classic MacArthur. He had used similar maneuvers against the Japanese. He always preferred going in the back door. The operation was a deep *turning movement* designed to land forces in the enemy's rear, sever his lines of communication, and force him to fight in two directions. The X Corps summary noted:

> The plan boldly called for the committing of the GHQ Reserve and the 1st Marine Division in an amphibious operation to seize the Inchon-Seoul area and cut the main line of the enemy communications and supply to his armies in the south. In conjunction with this seaborne envelopment, Eighth Army was to launch a major offensive from the south, and driving in a northwesterly direction along this axis Taegu-Taejon-Suwon, to effect a juncture with the amphibious forces at Seoul. (2) The Navy (3) and the Air Force had important roles of transportation, security, naval gunfire support, carrier aircraft support, and strategic bombing. The tactical air cover was to be furnished by the 1st Marine Air Wing ... and some naval carrier aircraft support. The objective of Plan 100 B was the destruction of the North Korean Army. ...[32]

The JCS, the Navy, Marines, and the Army Chief of Staff, General Collins, initially opposed MacArthur's invasion plan, fearing it was too risky.[33] The Navy and Marine Corps presented the strongest arguments against it. Speaking to Colonel Donald H. Galloway, one of MacArthur's staff officers, the Navy's amphibious expert in the Far East, Rear Admiral James H. Doyle stated: "Don, if you think a plan like that would work, you ought to have your head examined."[34] Doyle believed that MacArthur was "oblivious of the enormous technical hazards," and sought to inform and dissuade the Supreme Commander. Navy amphibious doctrine identified seven criteria for landing on a given piece of terrain: 1. Ability of naval forces to support the assault and follow-up operations; 2. Shelter from unfavorable sea and weather; 3. Compatibility of the beaches and their approaches; 4. Offshore hydrography (i.e., water depths and bottom configuration); 5. The extent to which anti-ship mines could be employed; 6. Conditions that may affect the enemy's ability to defeat mine-clearance efforts; and 7. Facilities for unloading shipping. After an analysis of MacArthur's Inchon plan a member of Doyle's staff concluded: "We drew up a list of every natural and geographic handicap—and Inchon had 'em all."

General Lemuel C. Shepherd Jr., Commander Fleet Marine Force Pacific, and General Oliver P. Smith, Commander 1st Marine Division, also registered their objections to the plan. They concluded that there was "a complete lack of understanding at GHQ concerning the manner in which amphibious operations were mounted out." And in fact, the amphibious doctrine envisioned for the Inchon Landing was *not* in accordance with Navy and Marine Corps World War II Central Pacific amphibious doctrines, which was based on firepower. Surprise was to be the decisive factor in the Inchon Landing. This doctrinal approach was more in accord with British Amphibious warfare doctrine, the doctrine the US Army employed in World War II.[35] The Navy and Marines wanted and recommended a less ambitious plan.

At a meeting on 23 August, attended by Army Chief of Staff J. Lawton Collins and Chief of Naval Operations Admiral Forrest Sherman, Admiral Doyle presented the Navy's arguments against the Inchon invasion. He delineated all the problems that could cause disaster. The littoral and hydrographic conditions at Inchon were considered too dangerous for an amphibious assault. The tidal range at Inchon, among the largest in the world, varied so greatly (thirty-three feet) that the Navy's ability to support the landing, and, if necessary, evacuate the assault force, was severely limited.[36] The tides dictated the date and time of the landings. With the ebb and flow of the tide came strong currents up to eight knots that hampered the maneuver

of ships and equaled the maximum speed of some small landing craft. The channel to the port was so narrow, a single deepwater lane, that the movement of ships was severely restricted, particularly during low tides. Wolmi, a small, fortified island with a long narrow causeway, protected the port. It had to be secured before the landing could take place. Instead of attacking onto a beach, marines at one landing site had to attack over a fifteen-foot protective seawall, which required ladders to traverse. Additionally the marines were attacking into urban terrain, the city of Inchon, with a population of 250,000. Each house was a potential fighting position. The invasion site was not in supporting distance of the Eighth Army (180 miles from the Pusan perimeter) and if the element of surprise were lost, the X Corps might find itself surrounded and alone. In addition, Walker's Eighth Army was to be reduced in strength by the removal of the 5th Marine Regiment, which was to land at Inchon. These and other factors caused the Navy and Marines to conclude that MacArthur's plan was fatally flawed. The Navy, thus, proposed an alternate landing site further south.

MacArthur, after listening to the Navy's presentation, spoke:

> Admiral, in all my years of military service, that is the finest briefing I have ever received. . . . you have taught me all I had ever dreamed of knowing about tides. . . . I have a deep admiration for the Navy. From the humiliation of Bataan, the Navy brought us back. I never thought the day would come that the Navy would be unable to support the Army in its operations.

MacArthur continued:

> The bulk of the Reds are committed around Walker's defense perimeter. The enemy, I am convinced, has failed to prepare Inchon properly for defense. The very arguments you have made as to the impracticabilities involved will tend to ensure for me the element of surprise. For the enemy commander will reason that no one would be so brash as to make such an attempt. Surprise is the most vital element for success in war. . . . The Navy's objections as to tides, hydrography, terrain, and physical handicaps are indeed substantial and pertinent. But they are not insuperable. My confidence in the Navy is complete,

and in fact I seem to have more confidence in the Navy than the Navy has in itself. The Navy's rich experience in staging the numerous amphibious landings under my command in the Pacific during the late war, frequently under somewhat similar difficulties, leaves me with little doubt on that score. . . .[37]

MacArthur's appeal to the Navy's pride probably had little influence in changing Admiral Sherman's assessment of the plan. Saving the Navy, particularly Navy aviation, and the Marine Corps were probably the major incentives for Sherman's reversal. One student of the Inchon Landing, Ronald Carpenter, wrote:

For an ostensible age of atomic war, the Air Force received major budgetary support under Truman. The Navy had 'its back to the wall, while the Marine Corps was literally fighting for existence . . .' Secretary of Defense Louis Johnson cut 'fat out of the Armed Forces' with 'most of his trimming on the Navy and Marines.'

While the Army had taken more substantial cuts, Johnson's attitude and approach to the Navy had been particularly hostile. Just a year earlier, he had cut the Navy's supercarrier from the defense budget, initiating the "revolt of the admirals." And Truman, in a letter to a Congressman, wrote: "The Marine Corps is the Navy's police force and as long as I am President that is what it will remain. They have a propaganda machine that is almost equal to Stalin's."[38] Truman later apologized. Still, the Marine Corps at 97 percent strength at the outbreak of the Korean War numbered only 64,279 men. The 1st Marine Division (FMF Pacific) numbered 7,779 men, and the 2nd Marine Division (FMF Atlantic) numbered 8,973 men. The go-to-war strength of a Marine division was 22,000 men.[39] To form a full division, the Marine Corps had to reassign units from the 2nd Division to the 1st Division and called up Marine Corps reserves.

Sherman viewed the Korean War and the Inchon Landing as an opportunity for Navy aviation and the Marine Corps to prove that the nation still needed them. Carpenter concluded:

MacArthur need not prove to Sherman what the Navy could do, but Sherman could prove to Washington what the Navy and its Marines could do. . . . Along with defeating North Korea, success at Inchon could restore Navy and Marine Corps prestige and ensure their stronger position in the US defense establishment.[40]

It cannot be argued that the Navy or the Marine Corps suffered more substantial cuts than the Army in the post-war period, nor can it be argued that since the battles of Midway or Iwo Jima the prestige of the Navy and Marine Corps had been damaged. All the services, even the Air Force, were ill prepared for war in Korea because of the austere budgets of the Truman Administration and the concentration of spending on strategic forces, long-range bombers and nuclear weapons. Nevertheless, success in war had the potential to restore service budgets, demonstrate capabilities, regain the attention and affection of the nation, and thus, prove that these forces were still relevant and necessary.

It took someone of MacArthur's stature, prestige, and confidence to overcome the opposition to his plan. Short of Eisenhower, there was not another general or admiral in the armed forces that could have gotten this plan approved. At Inchon, MacArthur gambled and won. The landing, "Operation Chromite," was an unmitigated success. On 15 September, Major General Edward M. (Ned) Almond's X Corps, consisting of the 1st Marine Division, which led the assault, and the 7th ID, conducted an amphibious assault at the Port of Inchon. The amphibious assault phase of the operation was under Navy command. Strategic surprise and operational surprise were achieved. The NKPA had no major forces in position to oppose the landing or counterattack. UN forces enjoyed enormous naval gunfire and air superiority. The bombing, which started on 10 September, precluded tactical surprise; however, this level of surprise was not necessary. Resistance was light. Some landings were unopposed, and the NKPA fought without determination. The official history of the Marine Corps concluded:

. . . it was obvious that the North Koreans had abandoned Inchon in haste during the night [of D-Day]. . . . Communications were destroyed, so that NKPA defense force fought or fled as isolated units. Adequate reserves were not at hand initially, with the result that stop-gap detachments were fed piecemeal into battle, only to be flattened by the Marine steamroller. In short, the North Koreans lost control. And when they attempted to regain it, time had run out.... Resistance on the [Inchon] peninsula proved negligible, although once again the capture of prisoners and material revealed enemy potential unused.[41]

On D-Day, the Marine landing force suffered twenty killed in action, one missing in action, and 174 wounded.[42] MacArthur had been right, and everyone else wrong. The Inchon Landing facilitated the destruction of the NKPA, and restored South Korea to its pre-war geographic borders.

The Inchon Landing has not escaped controversy, however; Robert Debs Heinl, a Marine veteran of the campaign at Iwo Jima, in his work, *Victory at High Tide*, advanced what has become the traditional interpretation: "The operation which MacArthur had in mind was, above all, a naval operation; without the Navy's ships and support, without the Marines' amphibious troops, and without the professional know-how of both Navy and Marines, the landing at Inchon ... could never become reality."[43] Stanley Sandler advanced the idea that the Inchon Landing was unnecessary and that the risk of failure has been exaggerated:

> If X Corps had been combined at the perimeter with Eighth Army it seems unlikely that the North Koreans could have contained UN forces for much longer. Furthermore, even had the NKPA been forewarned of the landings, or had the working out of the tide tables gone awry, given UN absolute control of the air over the landing sites it is difficult to see how the North Koreans could have done much more than harass the landing. A beached UN armada on the Inchon mud flats would have been an embarrassment but hardly a disaster.[44]

The low casualty count supports Sandler's assessment. While getting to Inchon required considerable knowledge, skill, and talent, the assault phase of the operations was relatively easy. At Inchon the NKPA was unprepared to defend, and UN firepower was overwhelming. And at Pusan UN forces had won the buildup race, and it was simply a matter of time.

The Inchon Landing damaged the confidence of the Joint Chiefs of Staff and other senior military leaders. Their willingness to challenge MacArthur was destroyed. In reference to MacArthur's plan for a second amphibious landing at Wonsan, Ridgway observed that, "Had he suggested that one battalion walk on water to reach the port, there might have been someone ready to give it a try."[45] MacArthur's perceived infallibility and the diffidence of the JCS ultimately led to the debacle in North Korea and the relief of MacArthur.

Operationally the X Corps was not placed under Walker's command. MacArthur retained command. This was the first of a series of mistakes made by MacArthur. This arrangement violated the principle of unity of command. Initially this arrangement made sense. Walker's preoccupation with the defense of and breakout from the Pusan perimeter, the geographic separation of the forces, and the location of the planning in Tokyo, were initially justification for this chain of command. However, once the X Corps was in Korea, it should have been placed under Walker's command.

The day after the invasion, Inchon was secured and the Eighth Army initiated its breakout attack. The NKPA fought tenaciously, not fully realizing its lines of communication (LOC) were in danger. Three days after the attack began, MacArthur was growing concerned at the lack of progress. He started developing plans for a second amphibious landing.[46] However, this proved unnecessary. The NKPA soon broke. Its lines of communications had been severed, causing it to run low on ammunition and supplies. The morale of many NKPA units, which had been sustained by success and savage discipline, collapsed. One observer wrote:

> Many conscriptees were sent into combat unarmed, with instructions to pick up weapons on the battlefield. In the attack, these draftees were forced into the leading elements by North Korean regulars who followed behind and shot them if they faltered or attempted to desert. Under such circumstances, it is natural that a large number would desert at the first opportunity.[47]

Walker endeavored to use envelopment tactics to capture and destroy the NKPA. Both US and ROK

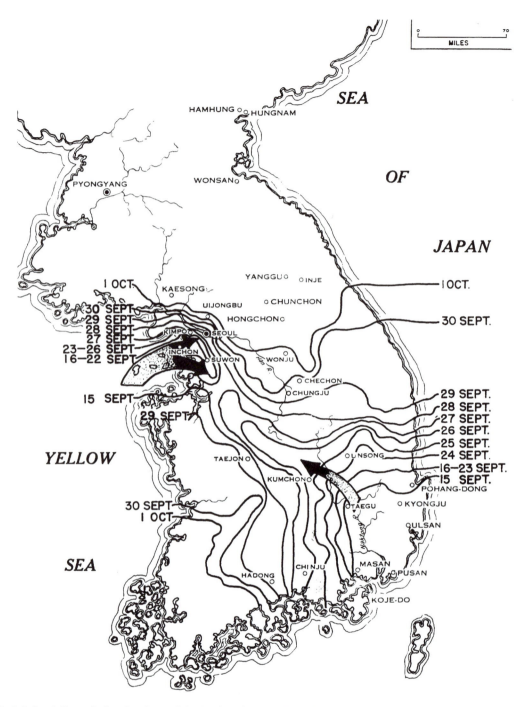

Fig 5.6 South Korea, Inchon Landing and the Breakout from the Pusan Perimeter.

forces "were ordered to destroy the enemy by penetrating deeply and, through enveloping and encircling maneuvers, getting astride of his lines of withdrawal to cut his attempted retreat."[48] MacArthur, however, wanted Walker to move fast. He pushed Walker to advance as rapidly as possible. As a consequence,

enemy forces were bypassed, and many survived to fight another day. Speed in the advance is not always the best approach. The systematic destruction of the NKPA was not facilitated by speed.

On 26 September, the X Corps captured Seoul and linked up with the Eighth Army in the vicinity of

Osan. On 30 September, the city of Seoul was formally restored to the ROK. UN forces had recaptured most of the territory of South Korea, and were "mopping" the final resistance. The same day MacArthur returned control of Seoul to President Rhee, Chou En-lai, Foreign Minister of the PRC, warned that, "The Chinese people will not tolerate foreign aggression, nor will they supinely tolerate seeing their neighbor being savagely invaded by the imperialist."

Total casualties as reported up to 30 September were 19,474. The total strength of the UN force, including EUSAK, USAF, British Army, Korean Augmentation, and Republic of the Philippines, was 102,372. ROKA strength was 174,465.

Crossing the 38th Parallel and the Chinese Intervention

By the end of September 1950, the UN forces had achieved Truman's initial political objective of restoring the pre-war situation in Korea. Success, however, caused Truman to change the political objective to rolling back Communism and the reunification of the Korean peninsula. In 1949 Truman had been charged with the "loss of China." The Communists defeated the Nationalists, exiling them to the island of Taiwan. Now was Truman's opportunity to advance democracy and capitalism. The decision to cross the 38th parallel was a search for a total solution to the problem in Korea. It was a decision in keeping with the traditional American practice of war. The advance across the parallel was what Americans expected—the complete destruction of the enemy's army and unconditional surrender. The achievement of a unified non-Communist Korea would justify the cost in American lives; maintenance of the status quo would not. From the American perspective, it made little sense to go to war and leave in place the same situation that caused the war. Truman's generals in the Far East Command and JCS supported the move. They argued that it was necessary to complete the destruction of the enemy's army, and that "from the point of view of the military operations [the 38th parallel] . . . has no more significance than any other meridian."[49] It was, in fact, an artificial barrier, but politically it held great significance. Still, in the minds of the JCS, the military objective of completing the destruction of the

enemy's main forces became the primary objective. Thus, for political and military reasons, the decision was made to cross the 38th parallel into North Korea. The euphoria and optimism created by the success of the Inchon Landing, and America's natural political and military inclinations, overrode America's global strategy, established international priorities, and common sense. Euphoria and opportunism motivated new instructions to MacArthur from the JCS. On 27 September he received the following authorization:

> Your military objective is the destruction of the North Korean armed forces. In attaining this objective, you are authorized to conduct military operations, including amphibious and airborne landings and ground operations north of the 38th Parallel in Korea, *provided that at the time of such operations there has been no entry into North Korea by major Soviet or Chinese Communist Forces, no announcement of intended entry, nor a threat to counter our operations militarily in North Korea.* Under no circumstances, however, will your forces cross the Manchurian or U.S.S.R. borders of Korea and, as a matter of policy, *no non-Korean ground forces will be used in the northeast provinces bordering the Soviet Union or in the area along the Manchurian border.* Furthermore, support of your operations north or south of the 38th Parallel will not include air or naval action against Manchurian or against U.S.S.R. territory.[50]

Given these instructions, UN Forces should have never crossed the 38th parallel. The PRC had already issued warnings to the US and UN. In addition, the Army had numerous reports of the movement of substantial Chinese forces into Manchuria. MacArthur's intelligence officer estimated that a Chinese army totaling 246,000 troops had moved in to the provinces bordering North Korea.[51] As UN forces approached the Chinese border, the warning intensified, and Chinese People's Volunteers moved across the Yalu into North Korea. Truman was concerned about starting World War III. He had considerable respect for Soviet forces, and took measures to insure that US forces did not become engaged with them. Commanders in the field were informed that "if major USSR combat units should at any time during military operations in the Korea area of hostilities engage or clearly indicate their intention of engaging in hostilities against US and/or friendly forces, the US should prepare to minimize its commitment in Korea and prepare to execute war plans." The USSR was an Asian and a European power. War in Korea with the USSR might also mean war in Europe. Truman was unwilling to start a total war in Korea. He was willing to give up his limited commitment to Korea if the USSR intervened.

Truman and his military advisors did not have the same respect and concern for the PRC. It was believed that the People's Liberation Army (PLA) was the most effective "oriental" fighting force, but that it was not up to "western standards."[52] Hence, Truman amended the initial directive of the JCS to MacArthur, "Hereafter in the event of the open or covert employment anywhere in Korea of major Chinese Communist units, without prior announcement, you should continue the action as long as, in your judgment, action by forces now under your control offers a reasonable chance of success."[53] Following these instructions was a note from Secretary of Defense Marshall: "We want you to feel unhampered strategically and tactically to proceed north of the 38th Parallel."[54]

On 1 October the ROK Army's 3rd Division crossed the 38th parallel. Two days later Chou En-lai again warned the US and UN that, "... American intrusion into North Korea would encounter Chinese Resistance." On 7 October, the UN General Assembly adopted a resolution that changed one of the major political objectives of the war. The resolution called for: "All appropriate steps be taken to ensure conditions of stability throughout Korea. All constituent acts be taken, including the holding of elections, under the auspices of the United Nations, for the establishment of a unified, independent and democratic Government in the sovereign State of Korea...."[55] In other words, the UN sought the unification of the peninsula with military force. It authorized the use of UN forces north of the 38th parallel. That same day, before the completion of mopping-up operations, the US 1st Cavalry Division crossed the 38th parallel into North Korea. The next day, Mao Tse-tung ordered Chinese "volunteer forces" to "resist the attacks of US imperialism." And on 9 October, UN forces initiated an offensive to complete the destruction of the NKPA. The operation was exploitation and pursuit. The NKPA was broken. It was now time to exploit the success already achieved by destroying the remaining enemy forces before they could reorganize and establish an effective defense. The advance of the ROKA towards Wonsan had precluded the NKPA from organizing a coherent defense. The Eighth Army attacked towards the capitol of Pyongyang. Meanwhile the X Corps moved to conduct an amphibious landing at Wonsan on the west coast. At Wonsan the X Corps joined with ROKA forces and advanced north.

On 15 October, Truman and MacArthur met at Wake Island. MacArthur informed the President that, "We are no longer fearful of their [Chinese] intervention.... If the Chinese tried to get down to Pyongyang there would be the greatest slaughter."[56] It can be argued that rational, intelligent analysis of relative combat power informed the decisions of MacArthur and the JCS, that in regard to force structure, technology, leadership, and training US forces were superior to the PLA. However, a quick head count, a glance at a map, a little understanding of geography and terrain, and some memory of recent operations, such as the performance of Task Force Smith, should have caused them to reconsider. Western arrogance, racism, flawed analysis of intelligence, and faulty assumptions caused US and UN leaders to disregard their strategy and plans to preclude World War III. They also disregarded the Chinese warnings, and underestimated the capabilities of the PLA.

The FEC and JCS concluded that the Chinese would not enter the war because they feared war with the United States, and an alliance between the US and the Chinese Nationalists on Taiwan. The PRC had also missed the best opportunity to influence the situation in Korea. If they had planned to intervene, it was reasoned, they would have done so before the total collapse of the NKPA. Still, there was no excuse for the deployment and disposition of American and UN forces in October 1950 in the face of a superior enemy. Fear did in fact motivate the Chinese. It motivated them to fight.

The Eighth Army and X Corps raced up the Korean peninsula separated by a spine of mountains. The X Corps was on the east and the Eighth Army on the west. There was no unity of command. MacArthur denied Walker's request to place the X Corps under

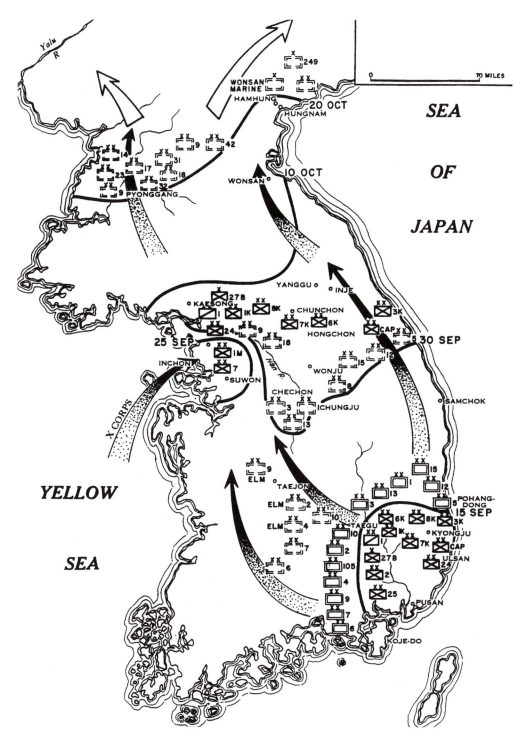

Fig 5.7 Korea, Exploitation across the 38th Parallel.

his command, and to slow the advance until the supply situation had improved. O.P. Smith, the commander of the 1st Marine Division, was also uneasy about the pace and organization of the advance. The Eighth Army and X Corps advanced at their own speed with little regard to the disposition of the other. They were directed and coordinated from MacArthur's headquarters in Tokyo, Japan. The Eighth Army consisted of three corps. I Corps of Major General Frank W. Milburn consisted of the

American 1st Cavalry Division, the 24th ID, ROK 1st Division, and 27th Commonwealth Brigade, a primarily British command with one Australian battalion. The ROK II Corps consisted of the 6th and 8th Divisions. And IX Corps of Major General John B. Coulter consisted of the 2nd ID and 25th ID, and the ROK 7th Division. Lieutenant General Edward M. Almond commanded the X Corps in the western half of North Korea. It consisted of the 1st Marine Division, the 7th ID, and the ROK 3rd Division.

On 16 October, Chu Teh, commander of the People's Liberation Army, ordered the "People's Volunteer Army," under the leadership of Generals Peng Te-huai, Lin Piao, and Chen Yi, to secretly cross the border into North Korea.[57] UN forces continued their advance and on 26 October the ROK 6th Division reached the Yalu River, where it was attacked by the CPV. On 1 November, US forces arrived in the vicinity of the Yalu River. They were attacked that night. The lead elements of the 1st Cavalry Division suffered heavy casualties. "I heard a bugler," said a lieutenant from the Cav, "and the beat of horses' hooves in the distance. Then as though they came out of a burst of smoke, shadowy figures began shooting and bayoneting everybody they could find." The initial CPV attacks were warnings. The CPV broke off the attack and vanished into the mountains. Thus, Walker and MacArthur had the opportunity to re-evaluate the disposition of the Eighth Army, the command structure, and current operations. Walker understood that he was facing a new enemy. He understood that this was not the broken NKPA, but the organized, disciplined CPV. He also understood that his LOC stretched almost the entire length of the Korean peninsula, and that his Army had exposed flanks because of the funnel-shaped geography of North Korea, the separation between the Eighth Army and X Corps, and the pursuit mission.

On 6 November, MacArthur concluded, "A new and fresh army now faces us, backed by a possibility of large alien reserves. Whether and to what extent these reserves will be moved forward to reinforce units now committed remains to be seen and is a matter of greatest international significance."[58] Still, the decision was made to continue the attack north to the border of the PRC, and, as darkness fell on the night of 25 November, the Chinese launched a powerful,

coordinated attack. The size and ferocity of the attack caught the Eighth Army and X Corps by surprise. MacArthur reported to the JCS:

> All hope of localization of the Korean conflict to enemy forces composed of North Korean troops with alien token elements can now be completely abandoned. The Chinese forces are committed in North Korea in great and ever increasing strength. No pretext of minor support under the guise of voluntarism or other subterfuge now has the slightest validity. We face an entirely new war.[59]

Was this what MacArthur wanted? His critics say, "yes."

There was no military justification for the disposition of the Eighth US Army given the repeated warnings from China, the considerations of geography and terrain, and the intelligence on the size and capabilities of enemy forces in the border regions. North Korea is funnel-shaped. At the narrowest point of the funnel, the area roughly from Pyongyang to Wonsan, the Eighth Army, in a well-developed, deliberate defense, could have held. At the narrowest point, the Eighth Army possessed sufficient forces to stretch across the peninsula from sea to sea. No matter how large the Chinese Army, on the offense the funnel shape geography forced it into a narrow frontage where the only option was frontal attacks. UN forces controlled the sea and the air. The Eighth Army, in a good defensive posture at the narrowest point on the peninsula, with airpower, possessed the firepower to stop the attack of hundreds of thousands of Chinese. In the Pusan Perimeter, in a *hasty defense*, with fewer personnel, the Eighth Army demonstrated the wherewithal to defend a one hundred and fifty mile front. In a *deliberate defense* it could have held a similar front against a Chinese force three or four times as large. However, this was not possible in the northern-most provinces. In this region, the top of the funnel, the Eighth Army would have had to cover an area more than three times larger than the Pyongyang to Wonsan corridor, to form a continuous defensive line. Given the size of the Eighth Army, this was beyond its capabilities. The more mountainous terrain in the northern-most provinces also increased the manpower requirements. North Korea was lost because of the disposition of the Eighth Army, not because of its manpower, training, or equipment. MacArthur's operational decisions strategically and politically shaped the destiny of the Korean people, and the security needs of the US into the twenty-first century.

The Joint Chiefs of Staff, particularly the Chairman, Omar Bradley, were derelict in their duties. They tolerated a chain of command that damaged the ability of the Army and the other services to fight. They watched MacArthur divide his forces in the face of a numerically superior enemy and said nothing. They allowed him to advance into the indefensible border regions, and into terrain that soaked up manpower. They were silent when he bypassed the most defensible terrain and geographic region without constructing a fallback defensive position. They permitted him to advance without opening up more reliable supply lines, and without building up sufficient supplies to fight the threatening Chinese. All of this was sacrificed for the sake of speed. The JCS bear considerable responsibility for the subsequent failures in Korea. W. Averell Harriman, advisor to President Truman during the crisis in Korea observed, "General Bradley and the Chiefs of Staff were afraid of General MacArthur, I think; they were very timid about it."[60]

On 30 November, UN forces initiated a general retreat. Thousands of UN soldiers became casualties, prisoners of war, or went missing in action. The CPV used infiltration and envelopment tactics. Once in the rear of UN forces they set up roadblocks, forcing the surrounded units to fight their way through while simultaneously fighting rear guard actions. When major units, whole regiments, were incapable of breaking through they abandoned their vehicles and equipment and tried to escape through the mountains in smaller units of squads and platoons. Many were captured. Major units became combat ineffective. The objective of the CPV was not to push UN forces back to the 38th parallel, but the total destruction of the US Eighth Army.

On 3 December, MacArthur informed Washington that twenty-six Chinese divisions had been identified and that another 200,000 enemy soldiers were in the vicinity to support the attack. He wrote: "This small command, actually under present conditions, is facing the entire Chinese nation in an undeclared war, and unless some positive and immediate action is taken,

hope for success cannot be justified and steady attrition leading to final destruction can be reasonably contemplated." The following day on 4 December, the CPV recaptured Pyongyang, the capital of North Korea. By the 15th, UN forces were back in the vicinity of the 38th parallel. Washington had no intention of initiating a general war in Korea. On 15 December Truman addressed the American people in a broadcast from the White House:

> Then, in November, the Communists threw their Chinese armies into the battle against the free nation. By this act they have shown that they are now willing to push the world to the brink of a general war to get what they want.... That is why we are in such grave danger. The future of civilization depends on what we do.... We have the strength and we have the courage to overcome the danger that threatens our country. We must act calmly and wisely and resolutely.
>
> We are expanding our Armed Forces very rapidly.... We have a large Navy. We have a powerful Air Force. We have units around which a strong Army can be built. But measured against the danger that confronts us, our forces are not adequate.... On June 25, when the Communists invaded the Republic of Korea, we had less than 1½ million men and women in Army, Navy, and Air Force. Today, the military strength has reached about 2½ million. Our next step is to increase the number of men and women on active duty to nearly 3½ million.
>
> As a part of the process of achieving a speedier buildup, the number of men to be called up under the Selective Service System had been raised, and two additional National Guard Division are being ordered to active duty in January.[61]

This was the traditional American response to the expanding needs of war. On 29 December, the JCS directed MacArthur to hold in Korea, informing him that:

> We believe that Korea is not the place to fight a major war. Further, we believe that we should not commit our remaining available ground forces to action against the Chinese People's Volunteers.... However, a successful resistance to the Chinese-North Korean aggression at some position in

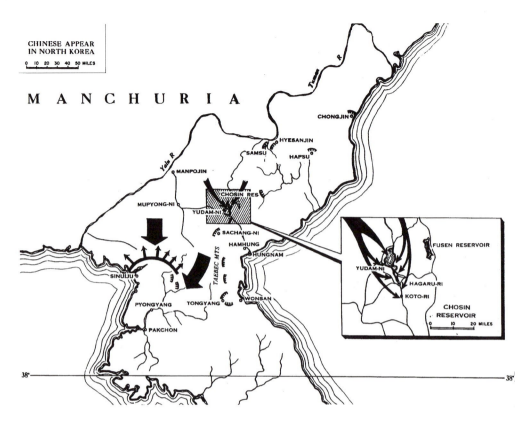

Fig 5.8 North Korea, Chinese Attack in North Korea.

Korea and a deflation of the military and political prestige of the Chinese Communists would be of great importance to our national interest.[62]

MacArthur responded with his own proposal:

Should a policy determination be reached . . . to recognize the state of war which has been forced upon us by the Chinese authorities and to take retaliatory measures within our capabilities, we could (1) blockade the coast of China; (2) destroy through naval gunfire and air bombardment China's industrial capacity to wage war; (3) secure reinforcements from the Nationalist garrison on Formosa to strengthen our position . . .; and (4) release existing restrictions upon the Formosan garrison for diversionary action, possibly leading to counter-invasion against vulnerable areas of the Chinese mainland.[63]

The JCS after "careful consideration" rejected MacArthur's proposals, and concluded with: "Should

it become evident in your judgment that evacuation is essential to avoid severe losses of men and material you will at that time withdraw from Korea to Japan."[64] This was not what MacArthur expected. This was not the traditional American response. Artificial limited war changed the American practice of war. The United States and the Army, because of the talent, tenacity, character, and professionalism of General Matthew B. Ridgway, never faced the ignominy of defeat in Korea.

Ridgway Takes Command: The Ground War

On 23 December, General Walton H. Walker was killed in a vehicle crash. He was succeeded by Lieutenant General Matthew B. Ridgway, who had commanded the famed 82nd Airborne Division in the Sicily and Normandy invasions, and the XVIII Airborne Corps in the Battle of the Bulge. Ridgway, responding to a reporter in 1952, outlined his approach to command:

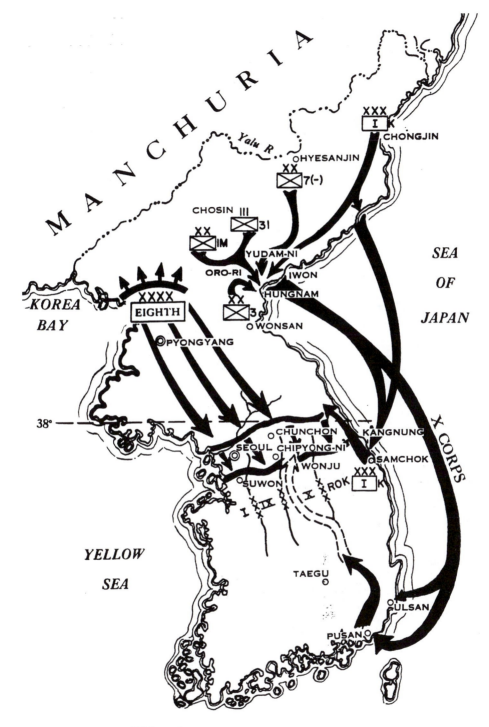

Fig 5.9 Korea, Eighth Army and X Corps Retreat.

When you get a new job to do, spend most of your time discovering exactly what your new mission is. Then break it down into workable units. Establish an organization that will enable each unit to accomplish its particular mission. Then try to find good men to fill the key spots. Give them full authority for individual action, but check them relentlessly to see they speed the main job. And if they don't produce, fire them.[65]

Fig 5.10 Mao Tse Tung and the Red Chinese Hordes, 11 December 1950. Reprinted with permission from Time, Inc.

He further noted that, "The one thing I demand in a man is loyalty," and that, "I am a soldier and a soldier's job is to obey orders."

When Ridgway met with MacArthur on 25 December he was given command of the entire Eighth Army: "The Eighth Army is yours, Matt. Do what you think is best.... I will support you. You have my complete confidence."[66] The following day Ridgway flew to Korea and issued his first general order:

> I have with little notice assumed heavy responsibilities before in battle, but never with greater opportunities for service to our loved ones and our Nation in beating back a world menace which free men cannot tolerate. It is an honored privilege to share this service with you and with our comrades of the Navy and Air Force. You will have my utmost. I shall expect yours.[67]

Thus, Ridgway's first action as Commander of the Eighth Army was to tell his soldiers why they were fighting. In an artificial limited war, in which the President's decision for war did not enjoy the full support of the American people, Ridgway found it necessary to keep telling soldiers why they were fighting. He had to compete with dissenting opinions that made their way into the newspapers and other sources of information read by soldiers.

Ridgway arrived in Korea just in time for the CPV offensive across the 38th parallel. As the CPV advanced, their LOC grew longer and more vulnerable to attack from the air. Seoul was captured on 3 January, and the Eighth Army continued its retreat. Ridgway faced one of the most difficult military tasks in war, assuming command of a defeated, retreating, broken army, in the face of a superior force. Ridgway had to halt the retreat, establish a defense, reinvigorate his army, and then attack to restore South Korea to achieve the political objectives of the United States. Ridgway's first task was to assess the situation, his subordinate commanders, and the status of troops—mentally, physically, and emotionally—as well as the status of supplies and equipment:

> My concern in this conference [with corps commanders] was to devise every means we could to make an immediate improvement in the Eighth Army's combat potential, for I was determined to return to the offensive just as quickly as our strength permitted.... But before the Eighth Army could return to the offensive it needed to have its fighting spirit restored, to have pride in itself, to feel confidence in its leadership, and have faith in its mission. These qualities could not be assessed at secondhand, and I determined to make an immediate tour of the battle-front to meet and talk with the field commanders in their forward command posts and to size up the Eighth Army's spirit with my own eyes and senses. Fighting spirit is not something that can be described or spelled out to you. An experienced commander can feel it through all his senses, in the posture, the manner, the talk, the very gestures of the men on the fighting front.[68]

Ridgway's ability to assess "fighting spirit" was a function of cultural learning, of understanding what an effective soldier looked like. Ridgway visited front-line positions in an open jeep to talk with corps, division, battalion, company, and even platoon commanders. "I rode in an open jeep, and would permit no jeep with the top up to operate in the combat zone. Riding in a closed vehicle in a battle area puts a man in the wrong frame of mind." Ridgway's inspections gave him an understanding of the quality and character of the defense, the status of equipment and morale, and an assessment of leaders. Reporting to General Collins, Ridgway wrote: "I have so far found only one or two cases where a division has shown any appreciable resourcefulness in adapting its fighting tactics to the terrain, to the enemy, and to conditions in this theater."[69] He found that too many units of the Eighth Army lacked the know-how to carry out their missions and duties. They were deficient in small unit tactics and too many leaders were not fulfilling their responsibilities. He concluded that the fighting spirit was too low to generate the combat power needed to reverse the situation:

> I must say, in all frankness, that the spirit of the Eighth Army as I found it on my arrival there gave me deep concern. There was a definite air of nervousness, of gloomy foreboding, of uncertainty, a spirit of apprehension as to what the

future held. . . . It was clear to me that our troops had lost confidence. I could sense it the moment I came into a command post. I could read it in their eyes, in their walk. I could read it in the faces of their leaders, from sergeants right on up to the top. They were unresponsive, reluctant to talk. I had to drag information out of them. There was a complete absence of that alertness, that aggressiveness, that you find in troops whose spirit is high. . . . [T]hey seemed to have forgotten, too, a great many of the basic, unchanging principles of war. They were not patrolling as they should. Their knowledge of the enemy's location and his strength was pitifully inadequate. There are two kinds of information no commander can do without—information pertaining to the enemy, which we call combat intelligence, and information on the terrain. Both are vital. . . . All intelligence could show me was a big red goose egg out in front of us, with 174,000 scrawled in the middle of it.

Ridgway immediately initiated actions to improve the welfare and morale of soldiers, to retrain them, and to restore their fighting spirit. He ordered immediate and aggressive patrolling to gain knowledge of the terrain, maintain contact with the enemy, and restore fighting spirit. He removed commanders that exhibited defeatism or who lacked the physical stamina to serve in combat units, cautioning others that "heads would roll if my orders [are] not carried out." He insured that soldiers had everything they needed to fight in the harsh Korean winter, and enforced supply discipline rules. He increased the firepower of the Eighth Army by requesting that the Pentagon expedite the deployment of ten battalions of artillery. He requested thirty thousand Korean laborers from President Rhee to dig fighting positions and string barbed wire in order to add depth to his defense. He also requested that the ROK National Guard be organized and equipped as a civilian transportation corps for logistical support of the frontline units. Nine companies were available by 26 March 1951 to haul ammunition and supplies to the front using the traditional Korean "A" frames. By mid-June, 85 companies, 30,589 carriers, were assisting the Eighth Army move supplies over the rugged terrain and rain-soaked roads.[70] Ridgway initiated programs to retrain

soldiers. He rotated units out of combat for training and rest, and then back into combat. He led by personal example. He looked and acted like a soldier, wearing a web belt and harness with a hand grenade attached. Ridgway later noted: "I held to the old-fashioned idea that it helped the spirits of the men to see the Old Man up there, in the snow and sleet and mud, sharing the same cold, miserable existence they had to endure."[71]

Ridgway did a lot of talking. He explained to his subordinate commanders what he expected:

> Then I talked a little about leadership. I told them their soldier forebears would turn over in their graves if they heard some of the stories I had heard about the behavior of some of our troop leaders in combat. The job of a commander was to be up where the crisis of action was taking place. In time of battle, I wanted division commanders to be up with their forward battalions, and I wanted corps commanders up with the regiment that was in the hottest action. If they had paper work to do, they could do it at night. By day their place was up there where the shooting was going on. The power and the prestige of America was at stake out here, I told them, and it was going to take guns and guts to save ourselves from defeat. I'd see to it they got the guns. The rest was up to them, to their character, their competence as soldiers, their calmness, their judgment, and their courage.[72]

Ridgway also issued a lot of orders communicating his intentions to attack, to go on the offensive, "I skinned Eighth Army staff officers individually and collectively many times to have them do as I wanted. . . ." He informed all that, "I am going to attack. . . . We are interested only in inflicting maximum casualties to the enemy with minimum casualties to ourselves. To do this we must wage a war of maneuver—slashing at the enemy when he withdraws and fighting delaying actions when he attacks."[73]

Ridgway soon recognized he had another problem. The Korean War was the subject of debate back home, and soldiers knew it. The President's policies in Korea did not have the quality and character of support that was prevalent in World War II. And press coverage of the war was damaging the morale of the forces fighting in Korea. Ridgway acted to counter the negative effects of the press coverage and the debate in the United States. He sought to explain to soldiers what they were fighting for:

> To me the issues are clear. It is not a question of this or that Korean town. Real estate is, here, incidental. It is not restricted to the issue of freedom for our South Korean allies. . . .
>
> The real issues are whether the power of Western civilization, as God has permitted it to flower in our own beloved lands, shall defy and defeat Communism; whether the rule of men who shoot their prisoners, enslave their citizens, and deride the dignity of man, shall displace the rule of those to whom the individual and his individual rights are sacred; whether we are to survive with God's hand to guide and lead us, or to perish in the dead existence of a Godless world. . . . This has long since ceased to be a fight for freedom for our Korean Allies alone and for their national survival. It has become, and it continues to be, a fight for our own freedom, for our own survival, in an honorable, independent national existence.
>
> The sacrifices we have made, and those we shall yet support, are not offered vicariously for others, but in our own direct defense. In the final analysis, the issue now joined right here in Korea is whether Communism or individual freedom shall prevail; whether the flight of fear-driven people we have witnessed here shall be checked . . . or be permitted step by step to close in on our homeland and at some future time, however distant, to engulf our own loved ones in all its misery and despair. These are the things for which we fight.[74]

Ridgway echoed concerns prevalent in the Army since the outbreak of the Cold War. In limited war, the connections between the sacrifices that soldiers were required to make and the security of the United States were indirect and difficult to perceive. In limited war, it was more difficult to produce the national consensus that was the norm in more total wars. Limited wars required the Army to acknowledge and understand the national debate and the effects it was having on the motivation of soldiers. It required the Army to actively, tenaciously work to counter the negative influences of the press and the national debate on the morale and discipline of soldiers. Ridgway's words were an acknowledgment of this problem, and a palpable example of his efforts to maintain the fighting spirit of his army. Ridgway believed in the American soldier. He knew what was possible, and was thus able to re-ignite the fighting spirit of the Eighth Army, turn it around, and attack.

*   *   *   *   *

The enemy the US fought in Korea was unlike that fought in Europe. Army infantry operation and tactics doctrine had to adapt to new conditions and a new enemy:

> In Korea, Americans encountered unfamiliar enemy tactics along with rugged terrain that hampered full employment of the World War II mechanized doctrine. North Korean tactics, and those of the Chinese, differed from the European-style warfare to which Americans had grown accustomed. The more fluid enemy tactics in Korea resembled aspects of guerrilla warfare, notably in extensive use of infiltration and night attacks. The U.S. Army, on the other hand, had become conditioned to European battlefields, orienting doctrine, organization and weaponry in that direction. American soldiers had grown road bound and dependent upon extensive artillery support, elaborate communications, and endless supplies. Korea's rugged mountains, few roads, and harsh climate helped obstruct the effective employment of superior American military power.[75]

The engagement ranges in Korea were considerably shorter than those in Europe, and the enemy developed tactics to mitigate the effectiveness of American superior firepower and control of the air. Darkness and adverse weather conditions favored the enemy. Captured North Korean and Chinese documents emphasized the desirability of night attacks noting "the ineptness and distaste" of US forces for actions during darkness.[76] The Chinese used camouflage and concealment to close within two hundred meters of American lines, when possible, before initiating the attack. They were poor marksmen with individual weapons, but excellent with the use of the

7.62-mm light and medium machineguns, 60- and 82-mm mortars, "Chinese stick" grenades, and satchel and pole charges. CPV armor units were equipped with T 34 tanks, and initially few artillery units were deployed. CPV attacked in echelons concentrating on specific sectors of the defense, after probing attacks found the main defensive line. All their major weapons were in the first echelon. When a soldier fell, another soldier in the second or third echelons would pick up his weapon and continue the attack. One-third of the attacking unit was held in reserve to exploit breakthroughs. The much-discussed human wave tactics were not the norm for CPV, but they did take place. Once penetration was made, Chinese forces expanded to the flanks to enlarge the breach. They fought with great tenacity and zeal, using bugles and horns to confuse, intimidate, and terrorize the defenders, and to control their formations.[77]

To regain the initiative, restore confidence, and ultimately retake lost territory, Ridgway planned a series of limited offensives. However, first he had to stop the retreat, and gain an accurate picture of the enemy's disposition. In late January 1951, he ordered aggressive patrolling, and ordered the 2nd Infantry Division to turn around and advance north. On the night of the 13th and 14th of February, the 23rd Infantry "the Tomahawk Regiment," of the 2nd ID, fought desperate battles against Chinese human wave tactics to stop a major Chinese advance.[78] One assessment of the battles and Chinese tactics read:

> Now, while the entire perimeter of Chipyong-ni was under pressure, the main CPV blow fell against weakened George Company. George was piling up the dead by the hundreds, but too many of the enemy were getting in close with explosives and hand grenades. The artillery fired star shells and HE [high-explosives ammunition] alternately, riddling the Chinese, but still they came on. The Chinese washed up on the low ridge again and again, fighting a determined battle for each foxhole. Little by little, against violent resistance, they were chipping the ground away from the American defenders.... The Chinese kept pressing in. They did not try to overwhelm G with one rush, but continued to creep through the night, knocking out hole after hole. The 1st Platoon, near three o'clock in the morning, was

pushed back out of position.... The 23rd's perimeter was broken. The Chinese had a pathway into the vitals of the regiment. All they had to do was to exploit it.... The Chinese now demonstrated what would be proved again and again upon the Korean field of battle: they could crack a line, but a force lacking mechanization, air power, and rapid communications could not exploit against a force possessing all three.... [A]ir, armor, artillery, and redeployed infantry had plugged the hole.[79]

At daylight, the 23rd Infantry counterattacked, reestablishing its perimeter. The successful defense led to a sequence of offensive operations, "Thunderbolt," "Roundup," "Killer," and "Ripper," that started the Eighth Army back up the peninsula.[80] On 14 March, Seoul was recaptured. By the end of the month, UN forces were back in the vicinity of the 38th parallel. At this juncture, Truman changed the political objectives for the third and final time. The political objective reverted back to that of September 1950—restore the Republic of South Korea. This decision caused the Eighth Army to halt major offensive operations and establish a defense. Both armies dug in and the war entered its final phase—a fighting stalemate, a defensive war of attrition. Once the line was solidly drawn across the peninsula, and both armies were in well-established deliberate defenses, offensive ground operations were for limited gains, such as the next ridgeline. Airpower became the major source of UN strategically offensive combat power. Still, the Eighth Army reached its peak performance under Ridgway in the spring of 1951, regaining the initiative against the formidable People's Liberation Army. During the strategic defense phase of the Korean War, the Army relied primarily on firepower to destroy enemy forces and break up planned offensives. Huge artillery parks were constructed, with the ability to mass tremendous fires almost immediately. Maneuver warfare had come to an end, and greater reliance was placed on artillery and airpower. An Army *Training Bulletin* noted:

> Under cover of our artillery fire, units could move with relative ease from a LD [line of departure] to the assault position; however, numerous failures occurred after artillery fire lifted or shifted—particularly covering the final fifty yards. Chief

reason for this was failure to use all available weapons that could fire during this period, such as rifles and hand grenades, machine guns, recoilless rifles, flame throwers, tanks and smoke. . . . There is not enough aimed shoulder fire.[81]

From World War II until the end of the century the Army's reliance on firepower from sources other than those of the infantry increased.

In hindsight it can be argued that it was a mistake to stop the forward progress of the Army. The war continued for two more long years, while negotiations were carried out. By assuming the defense, the Eighth Army surrendered the initiative, and political leaders robbed themselves of their most important negotiation tool—success on the battlefield. During this "negotiating while fighting phase" forty percent of the total casualties of the war were sustained. Geography, the battlefield situation, the President's promise, and the credibility of the US should have influenced the political decisions of the President. The President had made a commitment to the Korean and American people. The prestige and credibility of the People's Republic of China and the United States were engaged in the struggle for Korea. The outcome of the war would affect world opinion for decades, diminishing or expanding influence. The most defensible geographic location and terrain were a hundred miles to the north. And, both Ridgway and Van Fleet believed that forward progress was still possible. Therefore, within the range of limitations established by the President—to fight a war within the confines of the Korean Peninsula with American forces no greater than eight American divisions—there was still room for action. There was still the potential to achieve a better outcome. However, by no means did the Eighth Army possess the combat power to push to the Yalu River. Geography, the size of China's population, along with the People's Liberation Army and the combined resources of the PRC and Soviet Union precluded military victory on the Chinese border, short of total war. Truman, who probably regretted his decision to cross the 38th parallel, sought what he believed was the most expeditious means to end the war. However, by stopping the Eighth Army, he actually prolonged the war, and in the process, created a new, major power, the PRC, which had demonstrated

to the world its ability to fight the US to a stalemate. This new prestige would influence future wars.

The American way of life, with all its abundance, produces cultural arrogance that diminished the ability of American soldiers in Korea to identify with the people they were trying to save. Americans believe they live in the greatest country in the world, which means all other countries are somehow less great. Power to some degree produces contempt and the behavior of too many American soldiers in various parts of the world has reflected poorly on the United States, contributing to the alienation of the people we are trying to save. Some soldiers exhibited considerable contempt for Koreans and their way of life. Rene Cutforth, a Korean Catholic priest, gave his impression of American soldiers:

> Do you know that if you held a plebiscite in South Korea, the Communist vote would be more than seventy-five percent? We are sick of war and ruin. . . . Your armies have not behaved well to the people, and we dislike you all cordially. It is impossible to keep these great theories of freedom in front of the eyes of simple people. They are afraid of the bombs and the burning and the raping behind the battle line. The Chinese understand us much better, I'm afraid. Your cause is good, but you have lost our good will, and though you all appear to despise us, that is a big thing to lose. In this country, manners count for everything.[82]

It is important to understand the culture of the people whose "hearts and minds" we are trying to influence.

*   *   *   *   *

The assumption of strategic defense marked an important change in the American way of war. Two hundred years of American warfare came to an end. An Army that retained significant offensive combat power in the midst of a shooting war in which Americans were fighting and dying voluntarily went on the strategic defense. Political leaders decided not to pursue victory. The citizen-soldier Army of the United States would never again employ the Army's traditional offensive campaign-winning infantry doctrine. Once the Army went over to the defense, a psychological transformation started, not only in the

Army, but also in the United States. A static war of attrition was not the type of war Americans expected. Support for the war deteriorated. And as soldiers came to realize that victory was no longer sought and that there was no way to bring the war to an end through ground combat operations, through their own efforts, other priorities rose in importance. A decade later, the precedents established in Korea were reenacted in Vietnam. The threat of direct intervention by the PRC caused the US to fight a strategically defensive war of attrition, a war that from the start the Army could not win.

6.
THE KOREAN WAR, THE FINAL PHASES, 1951–1953

When they [the B–29s] got back to their base–Here was a case of man bites dog. A communication had just come in. . . . The message said to the B–29 people: "Our congratulations and our thanks. The First Cavalry Division is now across the Naktong River." What they had done was to completely erase the enemy artillery concentrations on those hills west of the Naktong. With all their people and artillery . . . destroyed . . . there was no possibility of the enemy's resisting. . . .

This was the old Attack technique . . . and the original dream of Army commanders who saw in the new-fangled airplane only an extension of ground firepower. "Flying Artillery" once more. It worked. . . . But that wasn't what B–29's were trained for, nor was it how they were intended to perform. The B–29's were trained to go up there to Manchuria and destroy the enemy's potential to wage war. They were trained to bomb Peking and Hankow. . . . The threat of this impending bombardment would, I am confident, have kept the Communist Chinese from revitalizing and protracting the Korean War. . . . The great tragedy is that even these 157,000 [American] casualties were mostly unnecessary. *That war . . . could have been terminated almost as soon as it began. I will always believe this.*[1]

General Curtis LeMay, USAF

General Curtis LeMay was confident that strategic bombing alone could have won the war in Korea, and saved thousands of American lives. He believed that the US possessed the technology to dictate the course and conduct of the war, and that it was a waste of precious American lives to engage in an unnecessary ground war. This vision of war was communicated to the American people in numerous ways, and they accepted it. However, it made the Korean and Vietnam Wars difficult to understand. If LeMay was right, why were we committing our young to bloody infantry battles? And LeMay, and other proponents of airpower had to be right, otherwise, why we would be spending billions of dollars annually on bombers and bombs?

LeMay also believed that it was a mistake to employ strategic airpower, a limited resource, in support of ground tactical operations. LeMay commanded SAC throughout most of the 1950s, and it was his belief that airpower was the decisive instrument for the conduct of war—all wars. The Army disagreed. The Army argued that in the early days of the war, airpower demonstrated that it was incapable of stopping the advance of the NKPA and that the employment of ground forces had been necessary to achieve this objective. Both arguments were a function of the service culture from which they were derived. However, in the new age of nuclear weapons, jet aircraft, and missiles, the argument that best fit the American vision of war, was that of the Air Force. The actual conduct of the war meant little in this environment. The American people would ultimately consider the Korean War a mistake, a dirty, little infantry war in which the United States did not achieve its strategic objective of total victory. The Korean War, however, foretold the future of warfare, and restated the history of warfare.

Fig 6.1 General Curtis LeMay, US Air Force Strategic Air Command, 4 September, 1950. Reprinted with permission from Time, Inc.

World War II strategic bombing doctrines did not have the potential to achieve decisive results in limited wars, where airpower was restricted to a single geographic region and the enemy's means of production and the population centers that produced war materials were outside of that region. By 15 September 1950, General George E. Stratemeyer, Commander Far East Air Force (FEAF), was able to report: "Practically all of the major military industrial targets [in North Korea] strategically important to the enemy forces and to their war potential have now been neutralized."[2] In the official history of *The USAF in Korea*, Robert Futrell concluded that the strategic bombing of North Korea "made an appreciable contribution to the United Nations victory south of the 38th parallel," but he hastened to add that, "the campaign lacked decisiveness."[3] Without a willingness to fight a more total war, the strategic bombing doctrines of the Air Force could not destroy the enemy's means of production, will to fight, and/or people, all of which were outside of the confined theater of war. The Air Force well understood this, but LeMay was willing to expand the war to the cities of the People's Republic of China. He, like MacArthur and other senior military leaders, was willing to fight a more total war.

World War II strategic bombing doctrines also did not work because developing countries such as North Korea lacked a large working and/or middle class population to bomb into submission. Hence, the ability to win the war by destroying the will of the people was almost nonexistent. Peasant based, poorly educated, near subsistence level societies were unaccustomed to the rights of citizens in the Western tradition—unaccustomed to revolt, to challenging the government, to recognizing any rights, except the right to exist. Of all the people on the planet, they were the least likely to be bombed into submission. And, extermination warfare could not be justified. In limited war none of the World War II strategic bombing doctrines were capable of producing decisive results.

Strategic airpower and nuclear weapons *did* provide the deterrent power that precluded limited wars from developing into a more total war, and, it was hoped, the deterrent power to keep other nation-states from entering the localized war. But henceforth,

it was in limited war and in missions restricted to specific geographic areas and by the political parameters set in Washington that the Air Force endeavored to prove the decisiveness of airpower. This was not the type of war the Air Force envisioned or planned to fight. A student of the air war in Korea wrote: "It was a phony war, too because the United Nations Air Forces always fought with one hand tied behind their back."[4] Another student of strategic airpower noted: "The three years of FEAF Bomber Command operations in Korea were rich in ironies. A plane designed to carry all-out war to the industrial heart of enemy nations served in a limited, localized, peripheral conflict."[5] Most of the American people would have agreed with LeMay. Artificially imposed restrictions were difficult to explain and accept when Americans were fighting and dying. However, Truman's decision to fight a limited war, a war without the employment of nuclear weapons, even in the face of the Chinese onslaught and threat to the Eighth Army, established a precedence that has been followed ever since, by every leader of every state with nuclear weapons. This was the most significant decision of the twentieth century.

Given the limitations imposed, the Air Force searched for targets, doctrine, and technologies that might prove decisive. For the remainder of the twentieth century the Air Force fought campaigns circumscribed and constrained by political leaders. Still, while not decisive, airpower made significant contributions to the survival of South Korea.

The Air War

General LeMay observed: "This may come as a surprise to the reader: we never lost a single man on the ground to enemy air action in Korea.... No ground soldier is known to have lost his life during enemy air action. Not one."[6] The US Air Force controlled the skies over battlefields on which UN ground forces fought. Not since World War II had American ground forces suffered a significant air attack. As a consequence of American dominance in the air and seas, naval and air forces devoted greater efforts and resources to fighting the ground war, either independently or in concert with ground forces, than in fighting in their own environments. Airpower greatly influenced the situation on the ground in Korea; however, the same driving forces that precluded the Army and Army Air Forces from cooperating and achieving synergy at places such as Sicily and Normandy precluded them in Korea.

The Air Force entered the Korean War unprepared to fight the type of war required of it by political leaders.[7] The Tactical Air Command was too low on the Air Force's list of priorities to adequately prepare for a limited war; in fact, by January 1949 TAC had been demoted to a planning headquarters stripped of its units and absorbed into the Continental Air Command. Army protests and the arguments within the Air Force caused the restoration of the TAC in July 1950.[8] Nevertheless, the Strategic Air Command had been the primary focus of the Air Force, receiving the majority of resources—energy, intellect, budget, talent, and prestige. By experience, training, doctrine, technology, and culture the Air Force was geared and oriented toward strategic bombing and more total war. In limited wars, the Air Force could not fight the way it was designed or had planned. The Air Force, thus, had to adapt its strategic bombers and other technologies to conduct tactical missions.

Early in the war came the first restrictions from Washington. Major General Emmett O'Donnell, commander of Bomber Command, and a veteran of the air war against Japan, developed the initial strategic bombing plan for the Korean War:

> It was my intention and hope … that we would be able to get out there and to cash in on our psychological advantage in having gotten into the theater and into the war so fast by putting a very severe blow on the North Koreans, with an advance warning, perhaps telling them that they had gone too far in what we all recognized as being an act of aggression … and [then] go to work *burning* five major cities of North Korea to the ground, and to destroy completely every one of about 18 major strategic targets.[9]

The firebombing of North Korea's five major industrial cities and other industrial complexes was not approved. Washington was concerned that the Communists would exploit the fire raids for propaganda purposes. And henceforth, limiting civilian

casualties and the destruction to civilian property would be a legitimate concern in war. Proportionality was *not* a tenet of the Air Force's practice of war in World War II. But, it would be, in future wars. Ultimately this requirement pushed the Air Force to develop precision-guided munitions. Arguably, the development of these technologies was delayed more than a decade because of the narrow focus on strategic bombing and nuclear war. The future employment of airpower would be measured to correspond to the limited political objectives sought.

* * * * *

In the initial phase of the war, the exigencies of the situation dictated the employment of airpower. Because of the urgency of the situation on the ground, MacArthur would not approve the use of the twelve available B–29s in a strategic bombing campaign. They were needed to destroy targets that facilitated the conduct of the ground war. However, the Air Force was eager to initiate the strategic bombing campaign, and deployed additional air resources, medium and heavy bombers, to the FEAF. SAC deployed the 22nd and 92nd Bombardment Groups and the 31st Strategic Reconnaissance Squadron from the US to back up the FEAF's own 19th Bombardment Group. Together they formed the FEAF Bomber Command (Provisional). On 8 August General George E. Stratemeyer ordered O'Donnell to initiate the strategic bombing campaign. However, once the Air Force determined that its civilian political bosses would not permit it to win the war employing its strategic bombing doctrine, it sought a new campaign-winning doctrine to win the war without the Army. Allan Millett noted:

> On the day he assumed command [of the FEAF] Weyland wrote Vandenberg that Korea offered an unparalleled opportunity to show how tactical air power could win a conventional war. The Air Force, therefore, should "fully exploit its first real opportunity to prove the efficacy of air power in more than a supporting role…." The Korean War experience might provide positive guidance for the USAF force structure and help formulate concepts for the defense of Western Europe, *but that experience should come in a massive commitment to interdiction, not to close air support.*[10]

In limited war, tactical airpower doctrine became the Air Force's primary campaign-winning doctrine. The Air Force concluded that air attacks on enemy forces, lines of communication, and logistical centers had the potential to produce decisive results. In limited war many of the missions that the Army Air Force believed were the least productive in World War II became the only way for airpower alone to prove decisive. After gaining its independence from the Army, the Air Force was still determined to prove it could win wars without the Army.

The Air Force and Army also labored against attitudes and perspectives that were the legacies of World War II. In World War II, the Air Force viewed close air support as its least productive mission, believing that the Army should rely on its own artillery out to its maximum effective range. Millett noted:

> . . . the Army saw artillery as dominant within its range, and air power the principal weapon outside artillery range. In Korea, for example, the 'bombline,' the geographic limit upon air strikes not under positive control, tended to coincide with the outer limits of the effective range of corps artillery. . . . In sum, the Army did not expect integrated close air support, and the Air Force did not intend to deliver it except under carefully circumscribed conditions. . . .[11]

Army tactical commanders ultimately concluded the Navy and Marine Corps provided a more timely and accurate close air support system than the Air Force. This greater cooperation was a function of joint service cultures and the dominance of one service over the other. Consider the words of Admiral Charles D. Griffin:

> It was interesting to observe that the Army liked to get ground support from the Navy and Marine Corps, much in preference to getting it from the Air Force. My Army friends, many of them who were over there in Korea, would comment very forcibly on this particular point. They felt that the Navy-Marine Corps system was a system that was developed to bring out the best in the total military effort. The Army and the Air Force seemed to have grown steadily separated, rather

than having a closely-knit organization. The Army would make a request for some air support. However, in many cases they had no way of knowing whether they'd ever get it or not. In many respects, it wasn't very satisfactory.[12]

Because of the Air Force's long struggle to separate itself from the Army, the two services had in fact "grown steadily separate." And this was much more than procedural. This was in attitudes and ways of thinking.[13] Airpower was integrated into Marine Corps battles. Marine aviators were marines first. They were dedicated to fighting the ground war. And the glamour and glory of Navy aviation was not strategic bombing. After achieving the air superiority mission, they too were dedicated to assisting marines on the ground. The Air Force wanted to fight its limited war campaigns unencumbered by Army demands. Marine aviation was a resource the Army greatly envied, and in Vietnam the Army constructed its own air forces.

In addition, the Air Force/Army system for requesting and directing tactical air support, which was based on systems developed in the European Theater of Operation, was slow and cumbersome.[14] The Navy and Marine Corps entered the war with a system that provided greater flexibility and more rapid response. Marine Corps and Navy aviation also did not suffer from the shortages in personnel and equipment, particularly radios and radio operators, that plagued the Army. The Army could not support the communication nets required by doctrine. During the years of occupation duty many key components of the system had been eliminated and had to be reestablished. Many Army units had to rely on the Air Force's tactical air control parties radio net to request air support, which caused problems because it bypassed the approving authority. After many of the initial shortages were overcome, some senior Army commanders still believed that the tactical air control system was unresponsive.[15] General Almond, Commander of the X Corps, outlined the problem:

> The chief objection I had to the support that we received in Northeast Korea was the fact that the Air Force's high command desired notification of tactical air support requirements 24 hours in

advance. I explained to General Partridge, the 5th Air Force Commander ... that this was impossible. Our requirements for immediate air support were not always predictable 24 hours in advance; we needed an Air Force commitment to respond to unplanned tactical air support requests within 30–50 minutes of the initial request so that the enemy located by ground units could not be moved to a different place and probably better concealed. This was my chief complaint and my constant complaint. The Air Force required requests for the support too far ahead of the use to which it was to be put. . . .[16]

In the early days of World War II the Army encountered similar problems. Not until late in 1944 was the Army Air Force capable of the responsiveness the Army required in unplanned, tactical situations. Some lessons of war have to be relearned in every war. Culturally preferred ways of operating cause the neglect of some of the more mundane, but essential, functions of war.

*   *   *   *   *

Air forces flew out of bases in Japan, Okinawa, and Korea, and the waters surrounding the Korean peninsula. The size and capabilities of the FEAF increased throughout the war, particularly in the first year of the war. From the outbreak of war to the signing of the armistice the FEAF grew from 33,625 officers and airmen to 112,188. At war's end it consisted of seventy squadrons, including seven Marine and three foreign squadrons, having grown from forty-four. When the war started, the FEAF possessed 657 aircraft, and 1,441 when it ended. It employed a wide range of aircraft, from World War II B–29 and B–26 bombers, to the most technologically advanced jet aircraft, including the F–80 Shooting Star and F–84 Thunderjet fighter-bombers, and the F–86 Sabre air-superiority fighters.[17] Because the Korean War was the first jet aircraft war, many lessons had to be learned.

The Korean War gave the Air Force its first opportunity to manage and coordinate all the air assets in a theater of war. The FEAF in Japan consisted primarily of Bomber Command (Provisional), and the Fifth Air Force. The Twentieth Air Force in Okinawa and the Thirteenth Air Force in the Philippines were subordinate command. The Navy's Seventh Fleet air resources consisted of 1st Marine Air Wing (1st MAW), and Task Force 77, composed of the Navy's carrier air groups, which typically had two to three carriers conducting operations. Foreign air forces from Australia, New Zealand, and South Africa provided additional resources. The FEAF operated under the command of Far East Command. MacArthur, Ridgway, and Clark each placed different demands on the FEAF; however, each faced different situations. While the FEAF commanded and directed the overall air effort, priorities had to be worked out with the Army, and agreements made with the Navy and Marine Corps. The priorities and agreements were negotiated and then renegotiated during the war, and each service had the option of appealing up the chain of command, all the way to Washington if necessary. Millett noted: "The interservice compromise, finished on July 15 [1950] to no one's complete satisfaction, gave FEAF operational control of all land-based aviation in the theater but limited Stratemeyer to 'coordination control' of carrier aviation in the war zone."

The Navy believed that the Air Force was incapable of treating it fairly. Admiral John J. Hyland, Jr., observed that the Air Force tended to "give the Navy the poorest and least important strikes and take the most profitable ones for themselves. So the Navy has always been worried about getting itself under somebody else's control and not be able to operate the Navy to its best effectiveness."[18] In varying degrees, all the services held this view. It was also difficult for the Air Force to communicate with the Navy. Navy and Air Force communications and encryption procedures were dissimilar and incompatible, and the Navy tended to maintain radio silence during operations.[19] The FEAF, thus, exerted little operational control of navy aviation, and the US in effect fought two air wars. The services preferred to fight their own separate wars, to perfect their own technology and doctrine independent of the other services, cooperating only on the periphery. Marines believed that Marine Corps aviation was to support their operations. When they did not get the support they believed necessary (because of Army requests or utilization) they went up both of their chains of command, bypassing the Army. These efforts usually produced the desired results.[20]

The Air Force objected to the employment of strategic bombers in tactical support of ground forces (a repeat of the World War II argument between the Army and Army Air Force). They believed that such missions were better left to the Fifth Air Force—the Tactical Air Force, commanded by Major General Earle E. "Pat" Partridge, employing fighter-bombers, light bombers, and fighters—and that the heavy bombers were best used for the strategic bombing campaign. The Air Force won the argument, and after the crisis of the Pusan Perimeter and the Inchon Landing, the heavy bombers were primarily devoted to strategic bombing. Bomber Command began the systematic attack on the enemy's supply lines, Operation Strangle, flying 54,410 interdiction sorties between January and June 1951. However, air power failed to stop the flow of men and materiel out of the PRC and Soviet Union and into the Korean peninsula. Later in Vietnam, the Air Force faced a similar problem trying to stop the flow of resources down the Ho Chi Minh Trail.

*   *   *   *   *

On 17 December 1950 in the northern-most sector of North Korea, Lieutenant Colonel Bruce Hinton, in a North American F–86 Sabre, shot down a Soviet MiG–15 piloted by a Russian, initiating the air superiority campaign. This was the first jet air-to-air combat. According to the USAF the Sabre won. According to the Soviet/Russian Air Force the MiG won. General William W. Momyer, USAF, noted:

> Our Fifth Air Force contained the North Korean Air Force (NKAF). Of course the NKAF was not all Korean, but basically Chinese with Russian and Polish pilots as well. Further, there is substantial reason to believe that most of the fighter squadrons actively engaging the F–86's were Soviet squadrons....[21]

Stalin was slow to provide Communist forces fighting in Korea with Soviet airpower; however, in November, he acquiesced to the pleas of Mao Tse Tung and Kim Il Sung, sending Russian air and ground forces to defend the PRC border regions. At the same time, a Russian diplomatic offensive, which charged the UN air forces with violations of Chinese air space, kept Washington's focused on containing the war.

Sabre pilots of the 4th Fighter Interceptor Group and MiG pilots of the 64th Fighter Aviation Corps both fought defensive campaigns. Soviet/Chinese air bases located in Manchuria were off limits to UN forces. The Sabres officially had to wait for the enemy to attack across the Yalu River into North Korea to engage. Similarly, for most of the war, the MiGs were restricted to the air space over North Korea. Unofficially the air campaign took place over both sides of the Yalu. A major part of the aerial campaign was fought in a well-defined air space in the northeast corner of North Korea that became known as "MiG Alley." According the Air Force's official history, in aerial combat the FEAF claimed to have destroyed 900 MiGs, 792 of which were MiG–15s; to have damaged 973; and to have "probably" destroyed another 168 Soviet aircraft. The FEAF claimed to have suffered only 139 aircraft destroyed, of which seventy-eight were Sabres.[22]

American pilots tended to believe the Sabre was the superior aircraft. The MiG had a faster rate of climb than the Sabre, but was not as responsive or maneuverable. The canopy of the Sabres permitted greater visibility than the MiG, making it possible for Sabre pilots to detect and engage targets faster. Some US Air Force pilots judged the two aircraft "roughly equal," attributing the higher kill ratio to the superior skill and aggressiveness of American pilots. More recent scholarship challenges the official assessment of the US Air Force. Xiaoming Zhang, in his work, *Red Wings Over the Yalu*, wrote:

> [R]ecent revelations of Soviet involvement in Korea [following the collapse of the Berlin Wall] offers a contrary picture: It was the Soviet air force, not the PLAAF [People's Liberation Army Air Force], that went head-to-head with UN air forces from the beginning of the Chinese military intervention. The Soviets claimed the destruction of more than 1,000 UN aircraft against only some 300 losses of their own.... The 64th IAK claimed that its fighter units were responsible for 1,106 enemy planes destroyed, and antiaircraft artillery units were credited with 212 planes downed. In return it acknowledged the loss of 335 MiGs and

120 pilots, plus sixty-eight antiaircraft gunners killed in action.[23]

American and Soviet/Russian figures cannot both be right. Stalin's deployment of the 324th and 303rd Interceptor/Fighter Air Divisions (IAD) in April 1951, it is argued, reversed the trend towards UN dominance in the air over North Korea. These fighter divisions consisted of veteran World War II pilots who had amassed considerable experience in the MiG–15s. The Russians believed that the MiG–15 was superior to the Sabre. The Soviets also rotated their air divisions, and because of uneven training and skill, some divisions performed considerably better than others. Zhang wrote:

> When the armistice was signed on July 27, 1953, Moscow had rotated twelve fighter air divisions (twenty-nine fighter air regiments), ranging from 150 to three hundred fighter planes, throughout Korea. More than forty thousand Soviet troops . . . served in Korea, with a peak figure of twenty-six thousand from July 1952, to August 1953. The Communist air force flew more than ninety thousand sorties, of which more than two-thirds were made by the Soviets, and the rest were by Chinese and North Korean pilots.[24]

Later in the war Stalin pushed the development of the Chinese PLAAF and, in the last years of the war, they took a more active role in the air war. Zhang concluded: "the most productive Soviet contribution to the air war in Korea involved the creation of the Chinese air force. . . ." The Chinese air forces eventually became the third largest air force on the planet.

*   *   *   *   *

The Air Force performed numerous missions during the war that made it possible for the UN to achieve its ultimate political objectives. The Air Force dropped 476,000 tons of bombs on Korea. Airpower interdicted lines of communications (railroads, marshaling yards, roads, and bridges), destroyed supply and equipment depots, troop concentration, industrial areas, and airfields. Almost half of the Air Force's sorties (47.7 percent) were interdiction missions. Airpower limited the ability of CPV to conduct

offensive operations. The FEAF flew close air missions that facilitated the conduct of ground operations, and maintained pressure on the CPV and NKPA by attacking "sensitive" targets, including command and control facilities and headquarters. In addition, it provided operational and strategic intelligence through aerial reconnaissance, conducted emergency transport of American personnel out of and into Korea, and carried out psychological warfare operations, for example, dropping propaganda leaflets. The FEAF carried out sustained campaigns that ultimately influenced the CPV decision to sign the armistice.

*   *   *   *   *

Since the defeat of the Imperial Japanese Navy in World War II the US Navy has been unchallenged in surface warfare. The US surface fleet no longer fought other fleets. It has dominated the waters around all battlefields on which the US ground forces have fought since 1945, and participated in the air and land battles with naval aviation and gunfire. The Navy and Marine Corps conducted forty-one percent of the air sorties flown during the Korean War, and dropped 202,000 tons of bombs (Navy 120,000 and Marine Corps 82,000). This included forty percent of interdiction missions and more than fifty percent of all close air support.[25] (Navy aircraft could not carry the bomb load of Air Force aircraft.) They also suffered the loss of 1,248 aircraft, 564 of which were downed by enemy action. Admiral Andrew Jackson, who joined Task Force 77 in January 1952, described naval operations:

> Task Force 77 was furnishing air cover and air support for the Marines in particular. We were also attacking targets in the north, North Korea, mostly logistic lines of supply, the main one, of course, being the railroad that ran down the east coast of North Korea, which we tried to keep out of commission. And we did keep it out of commission to a large extent. . . . [W]e would go in one afternoon and tear up the railroad track line, take pictures of it, and come back. The next morning we'd send a photographic plane in and take pictures, and the line had all been repaired during the night. What the North Koreans did was keep supplies right alongside, or close alongside, rails and ties and so forth, and they had a

bottomless supply of coolies who would repair the lines during the night, and what they could do was unbelievable . . . The other thing that was our prime target was locomotives. . . . We frequently had night operations because this was when the trains would run. They wouldn't run in the day-time, they'd stay in the many tunnels. . . . We would let them have a few nights off to get run-ning and then we would gear up and do a lot of night flying and try to catch them.[26]

The Navy operated from privileged sanctuaries with no threat from the air or sea. MiGs did not ven-ture out to confront American carriers. The Korean War was credited with reestablishing the utility of the aircraft carrier. In the aftermath of the Korean War, the Navy got its supercarrier.[27]

CPV and NKPA forces responded to American air dominance by moving underground and into the mountains, transporting supplies at night, camouflag-ing and concealing facilities and resources, moving forces and attacking under the cover of darkness, dig-ging World War I type defensive positions that could withstand bombing attacks, and pouring their ample supply of manpower into the fight. The advantage of having privileged sanctuaries, logistical and other bases, just across the border in China, facilitated CPV operations. The Communists were able to sustain themselves throughout the war in the face of vastly superior American airpower. One observer concluded:

The Korean conflict thus showed that the prevail-ing modern concept that air superiority is a nec-essary prerequisite to the launching of an offensive is not always true. . . . The United Nations air forces could never entirely stop the movement of the opposing land forces in spite of having what was tantamount to complete air superiority.[28]

Americans, however, would not learn this lesson. For Americans this conclusion only meant that we needed better technology.

The Korean War made new, unanticipated demands on the Air Force, and it endeavored to adapt and improvise, always with the objective of showing the decisiveness of airpower. General Weyland wrote:

It [the Korean War] has been a laboratory study of limited military action in the support of a very difficult political situation. Furthermore it has provided the air forces in particular with an opportunity to develop concepts of employment beyond the World War II concepts of tactical and strategic operations. . . . It is most important for us to understand that the last two years of the war were fought to secure favorable terms under which to cease hostilities. With this kind of objec-tive the door is open for completely new patterns of air employment. The war to date has repre-sented a short step in the direction of using air power as a persuasive force to attain limited objectives.[29]

By the time the US entered the Vietnam War, with the emphasis on "massive retaliation" during the Eisenhower presidency, the Air Force had returned to its old patterns of behavior, the focus on strategic air-power at the expense of tactical airpower. A decade later in Vietnam the learning had to start anew.

Censorship, the Media, and Public Opinion

Public opinion is formed, molded, and continuously reshaped by what people read, hear, and see. News organizations operate under the principle of "the public's right to know," and the belief that "the free-dom of the press" safeguards the freedom of individ-uals and democratic forms of government. Of course these axioms are based on the assumption that news agencies are unbiased, objective, and detached from special interests, including the influence of the own-ers. This is never quite the case. News organizations operate under the influence of their owners and the stress of competition. They seek to be first, with the most sensational information, stories, and images for their audience. The reporter's job is to get the latest news to his audience before his competitor "scoops" him. Accuracy has often been sacrificed for the sake of being first. And retractions rarely receive the atten-tion of the initial story. In addition, individual report-ers tend to lean towards the right or the left, the Republicans or the Democrats. Artificially limited war, in which the national unity characteristic of more total war is absent, greatly intensifies partisanship in reporting. The news, which influences public opinion, at times constricts the actions of political and military leaders. Hence, what is best for the country can be, and has been, restricted and obscured by the news. General William T. Sherman recognized this friction between the services and the media when he stated: "I hate newspapermen. They come into camp and pick up their camp rumors and print them as facts. I regard them as spies, which in truth, they are. If I killed them all there would be news from Hell before breakfast." Given the objectives of the armed forces and their need for operational security, and the objectives of the media, and their need for access and openness, a natural antagonism exists at all times between the two. However, the relationship does not have to be a win/lose situation. And, because people's opinions are of strategic importance to government, the relationship between the services and press is vital to the achievement of political objectives.

*   *   *   *   *

On 26 June 1950 the Secretary of Defense designated the Department of the Army as the executive agency responsible for maintaining and coordinating the briefing for the Department of Defense. The Department of Defense operated under the belief that: "No matter how large or how skilled the Defense Department's staff of military and civilian specialists, they must be supported by an enlightened citizenry, fully aware that they are partners in the overall organization for national defense."[30] Major General Floyd L. Parks, the Army's Chief of Information, was in charge of the program. Both in Tokyo and Washington the Army endeavored to take the initiative in public relations, greatly increasing the number of public information officers, creating new centers to distribute news, and establishing objectives and guidelines. The Department of the Army's Office of the Chief of Information delineated the following objectives:

1. To foster public pride in the United States Army and to bolster the soldier's pride in himself and the Army.
2. To broaden the impact area of Army public information by providing publications, radio, and television with information about the Army which they do not receive through news services.

3. To support and explain the personnel actions of the Department of the Army with particular respect to civilian components, rotation from Korea, assignments and world-wide commitments.
4. To explain and support the Army's procurement program, including the Salvage Rebuild Program and the Cost Consciousness Program.
5. To support the training program.[31]

The Army actively sought the cooperation and goodwill of the press. It communicated with the public through the media by issuing "news releases;" "immediate releases;" official communiqués (official comments from senior leaders); the distribution of thousands of pictures and newsreels; motion picture films, such as, "Go For Broke," "Battleground," "Breakthrough," and "Force of Arm;" television film series, such as *The Big Picture*; the official monthly Army magazine, *Army Information Digest*; the Home Town News Center, and Public Information Offices.[32] The Army established Public Information Offices in New Jersey, Missouri, and California, to distribute news and stories to newspaper, radio, and television. In addition, the Army responded to requests from television personalities such as Edward R. Murrow, whose program *See It Now* was broadcast on CBS, and Dave Garroway, whose program *Today* ran on NBC; and assisted radio writers in the production of programs, such as *Report from the Pentagon, You and the World, Mutual Newsreel, Time for Defense, The Kate Smith and Mary Margaret McBride Show, Cavalcade of America* and others. The Army also assisted in the production of feature films.

In the opening days of the war, MacArthur decided against formal censorship. The Public Information Office of the FECOM in Tokyo introduced a "voluntary code" of censorship to the press and radio representatives. The code delineated specific information that was not to be made public, including troop movements, names and locations of units, names of commanders, and other specific information that might provide the enemy with useable intelligence. However, within two weeks of promulgating the code, MacArthur was charging correspondents with failing to adhere to it, specifically exaggerating casualty figures, insisting that the Army figures were inaccurate, and disclosing the locations of units. He also believed that some of the stories published were prejudiced to the United Nations Command and the war effort. Still, MacArthur resisted censorship, fully realizing it had been used throughout World War II. He noted: "There is probably no more misused or less understood term than press censorship. Contrary to what many believe, no precise rule can make it effective, nor were any two military censors ever in agreement on detail."[33] MacArthur well understood the power of the press, and sought to use it to gain support for the war effort, maneuver political leaders in Washington, and gain recognition of the sacrifices being made by United Nations forces.

Public support for the war—particularly in a citizen-soldier army—had a direct influence on the morale of soldiers; and thus, combat effectiveness. MacArthur took measures to insure that his chain of command reported accurately all significant changes in the situation: ". . . casualty records now flow swiftly to Army headquarters in Korea, then to Tokyo and on to the Adjutant General's Office where they are made ready for the Department of Defense to disseminate to news media after the emergency addresses have been notified."[34] With the President's decision to commit US forces to war in Korea reporters from all parts of the world converged on Tokyo. They came from Australia, Belgium, Canada, Formosa, Cuba, Denmark, the United Kingdom, Germany, France, Greece, Indonesia, Italy, Norway, the Philippines, Turkey, from all parts of the United States, and from numerous other nations. From 25 June to late August the number of accredited reporters grew from seventy-seven to 330, and the number continued to rise for the remainder of the year as dramatic events such as the Inchon Landing and the attack of the Chinese People's Volunteers captured the attention of the world. By late August 1950, 206 reporters were in the combat zones, the Pusan Perimeter. These reporters had the power to influence world opinion, and world opinion had the power to influence the quality, type, and quantity of support in material and manpower resources.

World opinion—for better or worse—created parameters for actions. In the twentieth century all major wars were coalition wars. Nations needed other nations to conduct war. The Army provided reporters with travel orders, post exchange (PX) cards, authorization to buy field clothing, courier airplane reservations, and numerous other accommodations. Reporters accompanied divisions into action, typically attaching themselves to the division headquarters where they waited for briefings, listened for reports of major actions, requested transportation to those actions, and requested to visit particular areas or units. The Army assigned a public information officer to guide, direct, and respond to informational requests from reporters. They also arranged billets, mess facilities, communication lines, interviews, and other logistical matters. In the opening days of the war there were shortages of everything—transportation, telephone lines, time, and patience. To get stories out of Korea, reporters sometimes flew to southern Japan where lines were available. Others entrusted their stories to pilots flying between Korea and Japan. From Tokyo, stories were transmitted to major cities around the world. The combat zone was a dangerous place and after six months of war there were twelve reporters confirmed killed, twenty-three had received wounds, two were listed as missing, and two were confirmed captured.

By mid July 1950, General Walker's headquarters was established in Taegu. A schoolhouse in close proximity was requisitioned to house reporters. The Signal Corps installed telephone lines and two teletypes. A mess hall was established nearby. At peak volume, copy over the teletypes in radio exceeded 80,000 words, of which roughly one-third was edited and filed by the public information staff on behalf of reporters.[35] As the Army moved, so too did reporters, and the accommodations in Taegu were not matched until the Army again stopped. Thus, after the Inchon Landing, reporters followed the Eighth Army north. At Seoul, Walker established his headquarters, and the Army recreated the conditions in Taegu. When the Army crossed the 38th parallel, so did reporters.

Reporters found it difficult to adhere to the voluntary code. In December 1951, when General Walker was killed, the news of his death was flashed immediately around the world—a significant violation of Army security at a critical time in the fighting. A censor in FECOM, Major Karl A. Von Voigtlander, wrote:

"*Then and there, after six months of trial and error, voluntary censorship ended and compulsory censorship began. There was no mourning for the voluntary code. Most correspondents agreed that it had failed to do an effectively consistent job of safeguarding vital information.*"[36]

Both MacArthur's headquarters and the Eighth Army headquarters initiated censorship. They used approximately the same criteria. The Press Advisory Division in Tokyo and Korea read and cleared the stories of correspondents. Many reporters were pleased to get rid of the temptation the voluntary code caused. However, with censorship came an added benefit to the Army. In addition to eliminating material and stories that might provide the enemy with useable intelligence, censors eliminated stories that "*would cause embarrassment to the United States, its allies or neutral countries, as well as those* [stories] *of a critical nature which might bring our forces or those of our allies into disrepute. . . .*"[37] Such stories obviously should not have been censored. The purpose of censorship was not to permit the services to disguise unpleasant facts, mistakes, criminal behaviors, or setbacks. Censorship based on this criterion defeated the purpose of an open, free press. The Army, at times, was not completely honest with reporters, and thus, the American people. Still, a high level of trust was maintained between the services and reporters throughout the war.

All the services provided censors to safeguard their information. The Press Advisory Office worked around the clock. Each story was assigned a serial number and logged into a registry with a note on actions taken. This enabled censors to go back and check what they had released against what was published. Reporters could be kicked out of the country for trying to get around the censors. Censors could not make changes, only deletions; however, they could, and did, recommend revisions. Reporters were allowed to make the necessary changes and resubmit. Photographers, newsreel cameramen, and radio broadcasters with tape recorders created additional problems, as they were subject to the same restrictions. No military censorship of the mail or of commercial wire or radio facilities was imposed. However, few reporters tried to circumvent the system.

War is the most complex human endeavor. Reporters frequently don't know what they are looking at, and unlike the new, young soldier who has never seen war, there is no senior NCO or officer there to explain it to them. The result is that the people back home are being educated by novices. Thus, services had to take an active role in telling their story. When things were going well, reporters were quick to predict the end of war. When the CPV entered the war, reporters were quick to call the Army's retreat a "rout" and doom and gloom became the front-page story. There was a tendency to exaggerate the good and the bad. This was not malicious behavior; it was human nature.

Probably the worst reporting of the war took place in December 1950, as the Eighth Army withdrew under pressure. The situation was fluid and uncertain. The location and status of some units were unknown. The 1st Marine Division and elements of the 7th ID of the X Corps were cut off and fighting their way out. The reporters' demand for information and the public's right to know conflicted with operational security, amplifying the tensions that were normal between reporters and the military. In war, it takes time for the situation to develop; however, the reporters' imperative of getting the story out as quickly as possible did not allow them the time to fully understand what was taking place. A tactical defeat, the loss of a battle, might be reported as the destruction of an Army—a strategic debacle. Tactically, in fact, for some units, the Chinese offensive was a major catastrophe; however, too often reporters portrayed the story as a rout of the Eighth Army, which was inaccurate and unfair. General Ridgway assessed the situation:

> The Eighth Army was pulling back toward the 38th parallel, while X Corps began its withdrawal from its beachhead positions around Hungnam. News reports at this time, or at least news headlines, gave the impression that the UN forces had suffered a major catastrophe, when actually they had performed a magnificent withdrawal in the face of unremitting attacks by overwhelming superior forces—and thanks to some extremely gallant fighting, particularly by the 1st Marine Division and the US 2nd Infantry Division, had kept their losses to a minimum.[38]

Without doubt the Army suffered a major operational defeat at the hands of the Chinese; however, tactical catastrophes did not equal an operational catastrophe, and reporters tended not to understand the difference. Reporters observing the situation and conditions of one tactical unit, company or battalion, could not see the big picture. In addition, perceptions and even professional opinions vary. The Army tended to view its actions and responses more favorably than reporters; a natural, healthy, and unavoidable occurrence.

Public opinion continued to be of strategic importance. The services could not leave it to reporters to educate the American people on the course and conduct of the war. To get the big picture, reporters had to rely on the Army that was constantly receiving reports from all units engaged in combat. Trust between the services and reporters was of the utmost importance. General Parks, in a message to Army commanders, wrote:

We of the Armed Forces should frankly recognize that we have something to sell—service to the Nation.... It is an axiom that you must have complete frankness and a reputation for honesty in dealing with news media. I learned early that newsmen were smarter individually than I was, and collectively I could not hope to compete in the same league. I wanted no battle of wits with them; the only logical course of action was to be straightforward, honest and to tell the truth. Therefore if the story is bad, I admit it; if it is good, I try to see that the good points are known—and speedily.[39]

During the Korean War in Washington, Tokyo, and Korea, the Army took the initiative to get the story right, but still, public support declined during the latter years of the war. There were many reasons for this. A stalemated, limited war that imposed restraints on the use of force was not what Americans expected. Korea was an undeclared war, more than 8,000 miles from American shores. There was no direct threat to the security of the United States. One had to use abstract reasoning to find justification for the war. Americans knew little about Koreans, and there was a lack of cultural affinity. These, however, were factors beyond the control of the armed forces.

Finally, there was another side to the equation of democracies at war—the active participation of the people. On 22 January 1953, in an address to the Armed Forces Staff College in Norfolk, Virginia, Major General Julius Ochs Alders USAR, Commanding General of the 77th ID, and Vice President and General Manager of *The New York Times*, concluded that:

[A]s a nation we [Americans] are not well informed. One could make a strong case for the thesis that there is more ignorance than information prevalent today among our fellow citizens. Let me cite one or two examples from a typical opinion poll. Three thousand persons were asked, "What do you know about the Bill of Rights?" Thirty-one percent said they had never heard of it or were not sure what it was. Only 21 percent had reasonably accurate answers. Another group was asked what was meant by "balancing the Federal budget." More than half did not know.... *It does not suffice for us to be strong and well-intentioned if we, as a people, are hazy about the important events now occurring throughout the world and if we do not understand the issues and principles at stake and their relationship to us....* Unfortunately, citizenship in a free society is not that easy. Democracy throws the ball to us. It asks us to make up our own minds independently on the basis of the facts as we know them. How much more simply they arrange those matters in Russia.[40]

Too many Americans are too poorly informed to participate intelligently in the debates on war and peace. In the decades after the Korean War, this problem grew worse.

The Relief of General Douglas MacArthur

On 11 April 1951, President Truman relieved General Douglas MacArthur as Supreme Commander Allied Power, Commander in Chief United Nations Command, and Commander in Chief, Far East. MacArthur learned of his relief from his wife, who was informed by an aide, who had heard the news on a radio broadcast.[41] Four days earlier, Truman had sought the advice and recommendation of his primary advisors: Secretary of State Dean Acheson, Secretary of Defense George C. Marshall, Mr. Averell Harriman, and CJSC General Omar N. Bradley.[42] In the initial discussion, Acheson and Harriman recommended relief. Marshall and Bradley recommended "against such action." Bradley believed the matter could be dealt with without the extreme and public measure of relief of the popular general.[43] The President, who had probably already made up his mind, directed Bradley to seek the opinions of the JCS. They too recommended the relief of MacArthur, and delineated their reasoning:

> By numerous official communications and also by public statements, he had indicated that he was in opposition to the decision to limit the conflict to Korea.
>
> In the very complex situation created by the decision to confine the conflict to Korea and to avoid the third World War, it was necessary to have a Commander-in-Chief more responsive to control from Washington.
>
> He failed to comply with directives requiring that speeches, press releases, or other public statements concerning military and foreign policy be cleared by the appropriate department before being issued, and for officials overseas to refrain from direct communication on military or foreign policy with newspapers, magazines, or other publicity media in the United States.
>
> He had proposed direct armistice negotiations with the enemy military commander in the field, and had made a public statement in connection therewith, after being informed that a Presidential announcement on the same subject was being planned.
>
> There was also discussion to the effect that General MacArthur's independent actions were publicly derogating control of the military by the constituted civil authorities.[44]

These discussions and further reflections convinced Marshall and Bradley that the relief of MacArthur was in the best interest of the United States. With the unanimous support of his senior advisors the President directed Bradley to assist in preparing the necessary relief statement and press releases.

The arguments outlined by the JCS can be summarized into three major reasons: General MacArthur disobeyed the President's directives governing public statements, took measures to undermine the President's foreign policy initiatives, and was incapable of conducting the war with the limitations imposed upon him. However, all of the reasons delineated

were a function of one more basic reason: the Truman Administration was not conducting the war in accordance with the traditional American practice of war, and MacArthur knew only one way to fight war. MacArthur in his speech before Congress after his relief, explained his actions:

> While no man in his right mind would advocate sending our ground forces into continental China and such was never given a thought, the new situation did urgently demand a drastic revision of strategic planning if our political aim was to defeat the new enemy as we had defeated the old.
>
> Apart from the military need as I saw it to neutralize the sanctuary protection given the enemy north of the Yalu, I felt that military necessity in the conduct of war made mandatory:
>
> 1. The intensification of our economic blockade against China;
> 2. The imposition of a naval blockade against the China coast;
> 3. Removal of restrictions on air reconnaissance of China's coastal area and of Manchuria;
> 4. Removal of restrictions on the force of the Republic of China on Formosa with logistic support to their effective operations against the common enemy.[45]

MacArthur intended to fight more total war, one that would have moved the US closer to direct confrontation with the People's Republic of China, and possibly the Soviet Union. MacArthur believed the conflict with the PRC had already started and that more total war was unavoidable. It is important to understand that the PRC also fought a limited war. It employed a subtle but essential subterfuge to keep the war limited. Its forces in Korea were designated "volunteers." This lie precluded official war between the People's Liberation Army (PLA) and the US Army. In other words, the US Army and the PRC Army never officially engaged each other in war. Unofficially, however, they killed each other in large numbers.

MacArthur sought a total solution to the problem in Korea that would have upset the balance that Truman and the PRC and SU were trying to maintain. MacArthur believed that sufficient means were available to achieve total victory, and that those resources ought to be fully applied, as they had been in other wars. MacArthur saw Communist China as a threat to Western democracies. He believed that the failure to liberate all of Korea was a betrayal of a promise made to the Korean people by the United States and the United Nations. He believed that Chiang Kai-Shek and the Nationalist Chinese (Kuomingtang) on Formosa were the United States' natural allies, and that those forces available on Formosa should be armed and equipped, and launched directly at the PRC. He believed that airpower should be used to attack military targets in China to destroy privileged sanctuaries just over the border and to attack lines of communication in China. He believed the US possessed air, land, and sea forces it was not fully employing, and that as long as American soldiers were fighting and dying in battle it was unconscionable to deprive them of these resources. MacArthur stated: "I called for reinforcements, but was informed that reinforcements were not available. . . . Why, my soldiers asked of me, surrender military advantages to an enemy in the field? I could not answer."[46]

MacArthur believed that he understood the "Asian mind" better than anyone in Washington. He had spent decades in the Asian Pacific realm, as a boy, as a soldier and general, and even in his first retirement. He felt that because of his superior knowledge and understanding, the government in Washington should defer to his judgment. MacArthur also believed that he understood war better than any man alive. He had greater experience in war, in leading soldiers, in winning battles and wars than any other American at that particular point in history. MacArthur sought decisive actions, not "prolonged indecision." And, in fact, until the Chinese entered the war, the US had fought a traditional American war. It fought the way Americans expected. War to MacArthur and the American people meant the employment of all the means necessary to bring the fighting to a quick and decisive end. Loyalty to soldiers demanded nothing less. MacArthur was convinced that he had acted professionally in making his requests.

MacArthur concluded that: ". . . once war is forced upon us, there is no other alternative than to apply every available means to bring it to a swift end. War's very object is victory. . . . In war, indeed, there can be no substitute for victory."[47] MacArthur forgot, or did not understand, that war is a political act, and that the conduct of the war could not take precedence over the political objectives of war. He also forgot that, in the United States, elected political leaders establish the political objectives of war. MacArthur was over seventy years old. He was the product of his generation, and incapable of the transition required by the realities of a new world created by nuclear weapons, "superpowers," and the "Cold War." After the CPV intervened, the Truman Administration's political objective was no longer victory. The traditional American way of war, as practiced by MacArthur, was replaced by the new reality of artificial limited war, of fighting for limited objectives, compromised solutions, and employing limited means. In the age of nuclear weapons, limited war was the only rational approach to war. Still, the question was how limited of a limited war to fight?

The Truman Administration, the CJCS, the JCS, and the Army Chief of Staff were largely at fault for the civil-military crisis that led to MacArthur's relief. The natural inclination of Truman, and all Americans, was to fight a more total war, a war with a clear victory. The natural inclination of Americans was that when soldiers are fighting and dying in war, the nation owes it to them to apply all its resources to bring the war to a quick and decisive end. Truman, by authorizing US/UN forces to cross the 38th parallel, was acting on the traditional American approach to war. He was making a commitment to the American people that the war would end in a clear victory. He was also making a commitment to the Korean people that the peninsula would be reunited. Truman, too, sought a total solution to the Korean War. Truman and the JCS repeatedly gave MacArthur the go-ahead to fight a more total war. After the Inchon Landing they did not restrain or question MacArthur's actions, even when he sent two independent American columns racing toward the Chinese borders in violation of the principles of war and common sense and in violation of JCS directives to use only South Korean forces in the regions bordering the PRC. *Thus, it was in the midst of the Korean War that the American government learned that it had to fight a new type of war that required compromise solutions and the application of limited means.* The problem was: how could such a war be explained to the American people? American beliefs about the conduct of war were more in accord with General MacArthur, and most senior leaders in the US Army. Lieutenant General Edward M. Almond, the commander of X Corps in Korea, stated: "I am against war until we get into it. When we get into it, I think we ought to fight it with everything we have in the best possible manner."[48] This is what most Americans believed. Nevertheless, limited war was the future of warfare. Responding to MacArthur, Truman outlined his thinking:

> But you may ask: Why can't we take other steps to punish the aggressor? Why don't we bomb Manchuria and China itself? Why don't we assist Chinese Nationalist troops [from Formosa] to land on the mainland of China?
>
> If we were to do these things we would be running a very grave risk of starting a general war. If that were to happen, we would have brought about the exact situation we are trying to prevent.
>
> If we were to do these things, we would become entangled in a vast conflict on the continent of Asia and our task would become immeasurably more difficult all over the world. . . .[49]

Ridgway replaced MacArthur, and General James Van Fleet eventually replaced Ridgway. Ridgway was a true professional. He adopted the President's vision of limited war.[50] Van Fleet tended more towards the MacArthur vision of war. These conflicting visions created some friction, resentment, and harsh feelings.

MacArthur's defiance of the President was wrong. His behavior was unprofessional, and the President took the appropriate actions to defend and preserve the Constitution. MacArthur, however, was the wrong man for the job from the beginning. On 26 January 1950 he was seventy years old. Truman and the JCS should have retired him, or created a new command, a ground force commander, to conduct the war. However, MacArthur's arguments indicate that he understood one important aspect of war that was partially lost in the following decade. He

understood that loyalty down the chain of command was just as important as loyalty up the chain of command. He understood that when you asked men to commit their lives to an endeavor, the nation not only owes them the best it can provide, it owes them clear, firm political objectives of strategic importance to the United States, a coherent strategy to fight the war, and the tenacity and the will to see it through to completion. MacArthur failed to understand that the "best" had to be limited by the political objectives sought, and that the President established the objectives. However, political objectives achieved through war are measured in lives, and political leaders, to maintain an effective citizen-soldier army in the field, must be able to explain to soldiers and citizens that the objectives of the nation are worth the sacrifices they are required to make. Presidents too need to understand loyalty down the chain of command. Changing political objectives twice in the middle of a war sent conflicting messages.

New Personnel Policies: The Results of Transformation

The Army and nation adopted new personnel policies to conduct the Korean War. Throughout the war the Army faced severe personnel problems. Truman did not mobilize the nation for war. There was a limited call-up of National Guard and Reservist personnel and units, but, for the most part, manpower requirements were met through the Selective Service System, the draft. In 1947 the Selective Service System went out of existence. In 1948 Army strength dropped to less than 600,000 soldiers. To stop the decline in troop strength, on 15 March 1948, the Joint Chiefs of Staff recommended the immediate reenactment of the draft.[51] This legislation had the support of the President and on 24 June 1948, Congress passed the Selective Service Act (SSA). The SSA had been out of existence a mere fifteen months before it was determined that the nation could not maintain its defense establishments without conscription. Still, in June 1950 the SSA was about to go out of existence again. The JCS again made an argument for retention of the system. Collins argued: "A Selective Service Act. . . would be a deterrent to aggression. It would demonstrate the determination of the people of the United

States to maintain peace and stability by standing behind their commitments and encouraging the free people of the world to defy aggression." Bradley argued that, "Selective Service machinery in operation . . . will probably save four or five months in a critical period of preparation for any future war."[52] These arguments may have garnered the necessary support; however, on 25 June Truman committed the US to the defense of South Korea, and on 24 June Congress acted to continue the SSA.

Under the 1948 SSA, the term of service was less than two years, twenty-one months (later increased to twenty-four months), and the object was to provide for an Army of 837,000 soldiers to maintain twelve active divisions and six National Guard divisions.[53] However, Congress failed to increase the Army's authorized strength and allocate the funds for the increase in personnel. As a result, no one was drafted in 1949. The draft did, however, motivate young men to volunteer for service, making it possible for the Navy, Air Force, and Marine Corps to meet their manpower requirement without conscription. Still, the Army entered the war in Korea with 591,487 soldiers, only slightly better off than in 1948. After deciding to go to war, Truman "authorized the Secretary of Defense to exceed the budgeted strength of military personnel for the Army, the Navy and the Air Force, and to use the Selective Service System to such extent as required in order to obtain the increased strength we must have."

At the outbreak of war, the Army rushed soldiers and equipment to Korea and undertook various means to rectify its personnel problems. The General Reserve and the continental armies were stripped of men, companies, battalions, and regiments in order to get experienced and trained personnel into the theater.[54] The Army experienced a severe reduction in combat effectiveness as units were patched together in Korea, and poorly trained units entered the battlefields. In 1952, the Army Chief of Staff, General Collins, addressed the situation:

> We had to strip units remaining in the zone of interior [continental United States] in order to strengthen the units in Korea. At one time there remained in the Regular Army in this country only one division, the 82nd Airborne, in

readiness to fight. We dared not reduce our last divisions to impotency, even though the Eighth Army in Korea still was desperately in need of men. To meet further pressing needs, we had to order more than two thousand company-size National Guard and Organized Reserve Corps units into the active military service. But these reserve component units also were short of trained men. The only sources of manpower to fill them were the Selective Service System. . . . The dreadful experience of rushing understrength units into action, of early emergency recalls for combat veterans with family responsibilities, of long delays in training our citizensoldiers—all these stark deficiencies *hold for us a solemn warning which we must not ignore. . .*[55]

On 16 December 1950, Truman proclaimed a state of national emergency, which allowed the services to refuse to accept resignations, and suspend any statutory provisions prescribing mandatory retirement or separation of regular Army officers. This made it possible to some extent to stabilize units. Still, by the end of 1951 roughly one-third of enlisted men were "regulars" and two-thirds were "inductees." The authorized strength of the Army was increased several times during the war; on 1 July 1950 to 1,081,000; in September to 1,263,000; and by the end of 1951 to 1,552,000. With a two-year term of service this meant that in 1953 in an Army of a little more than 1,500,000 men, almost 750,000 men would leave the service. The Selective Service was to provide the Army with another 750,000 new inductees as replacements.[56] Collins explained this turnover in personnel in civilian terms:

> What would the average business and professional man do if he were suddenly asked to release half of his trained employees in less than one year's time—workers, accountants, skilled technicians and the like—and to hire new personnel, train them and, at the same time, continue to conduct an efficient, economical operation in the face of keen competition which did not have those problems? That is exactly what the Army must do.[57]

He might have added that the lives of soldiers, the ability of the Army to generate combat power, and, as a consequence, the security of the nation were directly affected by the turbulent nature of the policies for manning the Army.

Throughout the war the Army used an individual replacement system. Soldiers were sent to Korea through a poorly organized pipeline that had a negative effect on their morale.[58] One study noted:

> Chief factors thwarting the delivery of replacements to their destinations in good physical condition were the necessity for speed in processing and moving them and deficiencies in transportation facilities; and long periods of time in a casual status without knowledge of future assignments, the many stations along the way in the replacement system, and numerous other inconveniences lowered the morale of replacements.

At a number of these stations in the early days of the war there was limited ability to provide soldiers with basic subsistence.

The Korean War soldier was younger than the World War II soldier. In World War II the average draftee was twenty-six, and approximately ten percent of the Army was twenty-one or under. In the Korean War fifty percent of soldiers were twenty-one or under, and had two years of high school. Of the Korean War draft, General Alexander M. Haig, Jr., wrote:

> Our Army in Korea was not a cross section of America. . . . At first, because they were members of an all-volunteer Army, and later, due to the inequities of a draft that facilitated the exemption of members of the more educated classes. . . . Korea was the first, though not the last, case in my lifetime in which we chose to believe that American troops could fight a major conflict while large sectors of the home front made no material sacrifices or moral commitment to the struggle.[59]

Charles C. Moskos, Jr. in his study, *The American Enlisted Man*, noted: ". . . because of the operation of the Selective Service System and the manpower allocation policies of the armed services, the bulk of ground combat forces was mainly drawn from lower socioeconomic groups. Also, at home, things went on

pretty much as usual."[60] The argument for deferments was based on the World War II experience. The scientific community, with the support of a number of skilled politicians, argued that too many of the nation's best and brightest had been sent off to war, hurting the nation's ability to produce the scientists needed to construct the new technologies required. This argument convinced the President. Equality of sacrifice was subordinated to the inequality of talent and intelligence. The questions then were: What type of talent? What type of intelligence? And, how were they to be measured?

On 9 July 1950, Collins notified General Mark W. Clark, Chief of Army Field Forces, to be prepared to recommend National Guard units for deployment. He recommended a corps size organization of three divisions. Collins indicated that the President was anxious to avoid the mobilization of the Guard units, but given the situation he concluded that a limited call-up was necessary.[61] National Guard units belonged to the states. They were available to the President during national emergencies. State governors, US senators, and representatives were always willing and ready to personally intervene and argue on the behalf of their units, particularly in limited war, creating political problems for the President and the Army. The National Guard Association also exerted political influence. Truman also did not want to create a state of emergency in the United States, and the call-up of the National Guard was an indication that the regular Army could not handle the situation in Korea, and perhaps that the President had erred in judgment. Nevertheless, on 19 July Truman announced a partial mobilization for twenty-one months. It was later extended to twenty-four months.

National Guard divisions had difficulty mobilizing and training. They too were stripped of trained, experienced personnel who were then sent directly to Korea to fill existing units.[62] The Army would have saved time and resources had these divisions been deployed as cohesive units. Not until the winter of 1952 would two entire National Guard divisions enter combat in Korea: the Oklahoma-Colorado 45th Infantry Division and the California 40th Infantry Division. And within months of arriving in Korea some guardsmen were on their way home having reached the end of their active service duty. The

Selective Service System provided replacements. On 5 September 1950 the 28th ID from Pennsylvania, the 43rd ID from Rhode Island, Vermont, and Connecticut were federalized. They were rushed to Germany to strengthen NATO. Later the 31st ID, "the Dixie Division" from Georgia, Alabama, and Florida, the 37th from Ohio, the 44th from Illinois and the 47th ID from Minnesota and North Dakota were also called to active duty; however, they were never deployed to Korea. They were used to maintain a strategic reserve, until the end of the war when they were demobilized.

In February 1951, General Biederlinden, the G1, Personnel Office for FEC in Japan, summarized his efforts to produce more combat soldiers:

> Combat divisions still remain 3,000 (the equivalent of one regiment) understrength.... [S]ince October, despite the development of a planned program, the Department of the Army has consistently failed to meet promised monthly quotas....The failure to provide adequate replacement support had a deleterious effect on the entire Korean operation. Every expedient was employed to close the gap and maintain combat divisions at effective fighting strength. Thousands of service enlisted men had to be reclassified and sent to combat units without retraining. Wounded men were returned to the front lines again and again without sufficient recuperation to assure full recovery. Combat units were combined, stripping personnel from one to fill another. Republic of Korea, UN forces, indigenous personnel, and incapacitated limited service—all were exploited to the maximum.... The end result of such personnel planning must inevitably be reflected in extended frontages, the inability to develop full combat effectiveness, all resulting in adjustments in tactical planning combined with abnormal casualties.[63]

This unwillingness to call upon the American people in sufficient numbers to provide for a more equitable personnel system that would have improve combat effectiveness and thereby reduce casualties, without some understanding of American culture, was inexplicable. That same month MacArthur sent General Collins a message, again, protesting the paucity of manpower:

> The continuous lack of combat replacements for the seven months of combat is a matter of grave concern to me. The expedients of local conversion of Service personnel and attachment of ROK'S [Korean Augmentations to the US Army] have been fully exploited. There is no acceptable substitute for trained combat fillers and no compromise measure will equal the effectiveness of a full strength unit. Furthermore, no rotation is permitted. To date, Army divisions have been fighting from 20% to 50% below authorized strength in infantry and artillery units....Necessary extended frontages are susceptible to infiltration, exposing combat elements as well as supply and communication lines, resulting in abnormal rear area casualties.[64]

Due to this critical personnel shortage the Army could not fight according to its doctrine, and could not achieve its personnel objectives vital to the retention of good soldiers.[65] To make up for the shortage MacArthur decided to assign large numbers of South Koreans to the ranks of the Army. In August 1950 thousands of Korean Augmentations to the US Army (KATUSA) were integrated into the 24th, 25th, and 7th Infantry Divisions, and later into other divisions.[66] KATUSAs ultimately made up approximately thirty-six percent of the Eighth Army's strength, totaling 30,000 soldiers with roughly 7,800 per division. South Koreans fighting in American units contributed mightily to the war effort. KATUSAs, however, were only a partial solution to the Army's personnel problems.

* * * * *

As a result of this personnel trauma and the advent of limited war the Army enacted two major personnel policies that were part and parcel of the transformation of American thinking about war, and that had long-term effects on the nation and the Army's ability to generate combat power and fight wars. In February 1951, the decision was made to rotate personnel in Korea. The rationale for the rotation was:

> Although relief of combat veterans from the pressure of long duty on the line generally has been regarded primarily as a means of conserving manpower, it also has been considered as a

form of morale service, a matter of humanity, and a question of military expediency. World War II experience indicated that after periods of sustained combat, soldiers sometimes became careless, sometimes overly careful, and sometimes even indifferent to their personal safety; in any event, an infantryman's chance of survival after six months in combat was about 30 percent. FEC, working on the basis of World War II experience, pioneered in the field of wholesale rotation.[67]

Department of the Army studies on World War II casualties indicated that a soldier reached his peak performance in the fourth or fifth month of combat.[68] Numerous studies from World War I and World War II concluded that combat soldiers had a relatively short life span that could be extended by a rotation system. The term post-traumatic stress disorder was not used during the Korean War; nevertheless, it has been a crucial factor in war since men first started to fight. An Army Ground Forces study of casualties explained what happens to soldiers over time:

> While it is true that the infantry soldier will eventually wear out in combat, it being simply a question of length of time determined by how he is used, the thoughts and feelings of the infantryman at battalion level may provide a key to his more efficient use. First and foremost, the infantryman feels he is hopelessly trapped. He wants a 'break.' Under present policy, no man is removed from combat duty until he has become worthless. *The infantryman considers this a bitter injustice. . . .*He feels that the command does not distinguish between him and the base area soldier, and is actually less concerned for his welfare. . . .After some months in combat . . . *the infantry rifleman feels he has 'done his share.'* Around him are new faces; his old comrades in arms have thinned out . . . and the old tie is gone. He has proved his courage. More and more, he feels that it is not a question of IF he gets hit but of WHEN and HOW BAD. There is no escape.[69]

In World War II the Army fielded 89 divisions. In the initial victory plan it was estimated the US had the manpower potential to field 215 divisions (10 percent of 140 million people, 14 million) without eroding the industrial base.[70] Not a few Army divisions sustained over 100 percent casualties during the war. The flow of replacements through the division exceeded the authorized strength of the division. Some Army divisions were under combat conditions for more than 365 days. An effective rotation system undoubtedly would have improved the combat effectiveness of divisions, and prolonged, and perhaps saved, the lives of soldiers. However, not even in a total war where the nation was united in a common cause could the US government institute an equitable, effective system of military service. And as noted some soldiers came to recognize that they had "done their share" and that the system was unjust. While they sacrificed, others sat safely at home.

The 1st ID that landed at Omaha Beach had also landed in North Africa and Sicily. Samuel Stouffer in his study, *The American Soldier: Combat and its Aftermath*, revealed:

> At the time a survey was made of the combat veterans in ten rifle companies of the 1st Division, just arrived in England after successful campaigns in North Africa and Sicily. The study showed that these veterans, while exhibiting a rather fierce pride in their outfit, were more embittered than perhaps any other soldiers who had been studied by the Research Branch. The majority felt that they had done their share as compared with other soldiers—a few of them repeating a mot current in the division. "The Army consists of the 1st Division and eight million replacements."[71]

Soldiers were inculcated with the American sense of equality and fairness, and understood the burden of war was falling on relatively few. In limited war the problem of manpower procurement was magnified many times. Nevertheless, it was proven in two World Wars that the longevity of soldiers was improved by rotating them. The questions were: What type of rotation system best met the needs of the Army and how best to implement it? Could the Army implement a rotation system without the support of the Truman Administration and Department of Defense? And would the Administration implement such a policy without the support of the American people, which in limited war was not consistently united behind the war effort? Collins, speaking in 1953, explained the Army's thinking:

> Of course our rotation program contributes to the difficulties, but we must continue it for the sake of our men. Too often in past wars most of our front-line soldiers had to continue fighting until killed or wounded. In times past, they envied the airmen who knew that they could return home after a certain number of missions. . . . In Korea, our combat soldier knows that after a certain number of months of front-line duty he can go home. To date we have returned more than a half million men from the Far East. . . . We are literally rebuilding it [the Army] in the face of the enemy for the third time.[72]

Thus, in three years of war the United States deployed three different armies. The objective of rotation was for *no* combat soldier to serve more than one winter in Korea: After six months with a combat division or a similar unit in Korea, or twelve months in Korea in a supporting unit, a man was eligible for rotation, if a suitable replacement had arrived. This last criterion was the most difficult to achieve. The first ship of personnel who served their time in war departed for the United States on 22 April 1951. A "point" system was developed. It was revised several times but soldiers in combat units received more points per month than soldiers in support units. Infantry soldiers received more points per month than artillery soldiers. Once a soldier had accumulated the required number of points he was supposed to go home.

The American forces of the Eighth Army consisted of six regular Army divisions, two National Guard divisions, and one Marine division. The continuous rotation of troops in the Army, that in January 1951 numbered 231,125 soldiers, required between 20,000 and 30,000 fresh Army personnel per month, the equivalent of almost two Army divisions. The Army was too small, and too committed in other parts of the world, to fully support the rotation system, causing discontent and anger among those soldiers who anticipated rotation, but because of the shortage of personnel, were forced to remain in Korea beyond their time. Even with the Army's efforts to massage the system, combat units remained

understrength throughout the war. In other words, the Army implemented a manpower program it could not support. General Mark Clark, who had an intimate understanding of the problem, wrote:

> During two terrible wars I, as a commander of American ground troops in action, was obliged to face up to the manpower problem which is an ever-increasing threat to the security of our nation. In Italy and again in Korea I was obliged to scrimp and save, to "cannibalize" rear area outfits in order to beef up our front-line combat units so as to make them more effective. During an all-out war, such as World War II, there could be no thought of rotation. Men had to be put into uniform for the duration, and the combat infantryman had to fight for the duration. Our enemy in Korea fought like that. There was no rotation for a Chinese or North Korean except in a wooden box or without a leg. But rotation for us in Korea meant that we no sooner got a team working effectively than key men were through with their part of the war and were sent home, to be replaced by recruits from the United States or, at times, by Koreans. . . .[73]

While the rotation system did improve the morale of individual soldiers, the replacement system that made it possible damaged combat effectiveness.[74] What were the objectives of rotations? Was it to improve the fighting ability of the Army, the combat power of the Army, through higher morale? Or was there another reason?

With a little imagination a system of rotating *units* could have been put in effect. Such a system would have maintained unit cohesion and fostered teamwork, resulting in increased combat effectiveness. *Units*—cohesive, trained companies or battalions or regiments—could have been rotated in and out of combat, maintaining the basic core of the formations for years without degradation of combat effectiveness. The individual rotation system was *not* designed to increase combat effectiveness, and it was well known that it did not. The reasoning behind rotation was more fundamental to American cultural beliefs. How does a nation in limited war, employing a draft system, decide whose lives will be risked with the full knowledge that men are going to die? What do

National Guard forces contribute? Should they be called up before men are drafted who have made no commitment to the service? What is fair? What is equitable? Fundamentally, how do democracies decide who will live and who will die in a limited war?

While acknowledging that the rotation system eroded combat effectiveness, Clark identified the more fundamental reason for the system:

> Rotation was necessary for the kind of limited war we fought in Korea. It was necessary because it would have been unthinkable to call on a tiny percentage of young American manhood to carry the entire burden of the Korean War. The rotation system made it possible for us to achieve some degree of equalization of sacrifice.[75]

The rotation system gave the impression of equality. It was supposed to insure that the burden and sacrifice of war was distributed fairly across the male population of the United States of certain age groups. A working rotation system, however, could not simply be an Army program. It had to be a national program. It required the support of the President, Congress, the Selective Service Administration, and the American people. The war ended before the system received the kind of support required to function effectively, and it was unlikely that the Army would have ever received the political and public support required to make the system work in a limited war.

There was another reason for the new personnel policy, perhaps not fully perceived. The Army's rotation policy went into effect when the Army shifted from strategically offensive operations to defensive operations. On the strategic defense the United States Army was going to deteriorate. Neither the Truman Administration nor the Army could explain to soldiers why an American Army that retained significant offensive combat power was sitting on the defense. Defensive wars of attrition were un-American. Americans accepted that soldiers were tools of the state, to achieve specific, positive political objectives. They understood that this was a short-term condition that would end in months or a few years at the most. Indefinite, protracted war was un-American and unacceptable. On the offense, soldiers could envision a termination point. They could see progress. They knew the war was coming to an end. Soldiers that are moving forward have the moral high ground. They hold the initiative, and they know that through offensive actions the US is seeking positive objectives. As a consequence, they are willing to commit themselves to the war to hasten its end. On the defense the Army lost the moral high ground. It could not predict victory. It lost the initiative. The defense bred doubt and uncertainty. It caused soldiers to ask, "Why am I here? If we are at war why aren't we fighting it more aggressively? Why aren't we trying to get it over with? Why aren't we using all our resources? Why am I risking my life when the country is not committed to winning the war and bringing it to a rapid end?" The American citizen-soldier Army could not indefinitely fight a limited, strategically defensive war of attrition. It created an untenable cultural contradiction. Rotation gave soldiers expectations of an end point. It created some sense of fairness, but it was not enough.

Rotation also had unforeseen influence on soldiers. It communicated to them that winning the war was a secondary consideration. If the Army and the nation were willing to sacrifice combat effectiveness for the principle of equality, then soldiers too could downgrade the importance of the war.[76] To be sure, survival, minimizing risks, has always been of the utmost importance to soldiers in combat, but this was different. Because soldiers were not committed for the duration of the war, their primary objective changed. No longer was the objective to achieve victory, to end the war as quickly as possible by destroying the enemy's main Army, which meant that everyone got to go home. The objective under a rotation system was to survive a specified tour of duty, be it six months, or twelve months. An Army study found that: "For the combat man enduring the rigors of Korea, the rotation criteria on an individual basis gave him something to look forward to—a goal to be reached. To him rotation was a very personal thing, and one in which he, as an individual, had a vital interest."[77]

The Army introduced to combat a system based on self-interest. Soldiers were no longer vested in the outcome of the war, and their attachments to their units and buddies were degraded. S.L.A. Marshall, in his classic study of men in battle in Korea, observed:

Upon arriving in the Theater I began to hear pessimistic reports about how gravely our musical chairs rotation policy had down-graded the fighting spirit of the average young American in the combat line. Worried senior officers expressed the view that if the war's pace changed and the pressure rose suddenly, troops might be found lacking in the old drive and guts. Line captains told me that morale had so far deteriorated that when units came under full attack more men died from taking refuge in the bunkers than from fighting their weapons in the trenches.[78]

Anthony B. Herbert, a veteran of the war, wrote:

With the peace talks going full swing, a rotation system was instituted, and with that, there came a chance that I might make it home. I had given up on the idea long before, and the possibility was like a new lease on life. Like others, I began to fight a little more cautiously, to take fewer chances than I had before.[79]

The personal nature of war was changed. Of course, all soldiers want to win the war to see victory achieved, but it did not matter in their personal lives. The United States was not going to be attacked. Their homes and families were not directly threatened, and, they were going to go home after a certain period of time no matter what, whether the war was won or lost.

Unit cohesion was also damaged. Soldiers form buddy teams, a relationship of mutual dependence. One or two soldiers rotated out of the unit, leaving their buddies, who were forced to find new buddies. In a short period of time these relatively new relationships too were dissolved. Thus, relationships that could be the most important in an individual's life, or death, were formed and dissolved in a matter of weeks or months. Combat units were in a constant state of turbulence, forming and dissolving. Within infantry units the system resulted in the continued presence of new, untested men.[80] Combat effectiveness declined, and men died that should not have. An Army study found that:

. . . for the commander in the field individual rotation and replacement brought many headaches. The rapid turn-over of men within their units and

their subsequent replacement with men largely only basically trained presented many problems in maintaining combat efficiency. Supervision and discipline suffered because of a lack of unit training; feelings of "aloneness" and a "cog in a machine" attitude developed among the troops. Frequently the top level personnel required to replace the key men rotated out of units to the U.S. were siphoned off before reaching the lower echelons. If a commander allowed a key man to rotate, he had no assurance of receiving a comparable replacement. Conferences with regimental, battalion and company commanders of the 25th and 2nd Infantry Divisions disclosed a general desire for replacement on a unit basis. . . .[81]

Under the individual rotation system, soldiers became interchangeable parts in a large machine. One soldier was as good as another in the eyes of the system. The system did not understand how long it took to train and develop a good machine gunner, one of the most important men in the squad, or how long it took to find good men with the strength and endurance to hump and fire anti-tank weapons, or to find a soldier who had an intuitive ability to read maps and determine locations with a high degree of accuracy. Unit cohesion at the small unit level was difficult to maintain. An officer who fought in Korea observed:

You can't maintain Squad, Platoon, Company, Battery, Battalion and Divisional teams with constantly-rotating personnel. . . . There was no knitting of a mutual confidence in one another through association in strife and danger, through fire and movement, such as one gets in realistic peacetime field work or actual combat. Without that mutual confidence and trusting interdependence all the way, up and down, there are no truly aggressive and effective units.[82]

In Korea the Army allowed the norms of American society to design a personnel system that, while achieving some degree of equality of sacrifice, ultimately damaged combat effectiveness. The reduction in combat effectiveness meant a higher expenditure in American lives, increased use of firepower to substitute for the loss in effectiveness, and as a consequence, greater destruction and deaths in South Korea.[83] The Army had argued for universal military training and for increases in its strength. The Congress decided against those recommendations. During the Korean War, Americans started to view war as a national endeavor carried out by a system that functioned independently of them, a system that functioned without their participation. The resources of the United States were so vast that limited war could be carried out by only a fraction of the nation's manpower.

Writing in 1953 an American journalist who had recently traveled the country observed: "In Army, Navy, Marine Corps and Air Force installations all over the country, chaplains, noncommissioned officers and psychologists told me the same story: 'The biggest trouble we have is that so many men do not want to serve. In a dozen different ways they all say the same thing—let somebody else serve. Why me?'" To explain this attitude he wrote:

> In the first place, most men resent having military service break into the progress of their lives from school to jobs to marriage to children. . . . In time of all-out war men are willing to accept this interruption, but in times of half-war or Cold War they resent it. They resent it because they are not convinced the sacrifice they make is necessary. When Pearl Harbor was bombed every American felt immediately, desperately threatened—and overnight everyone wanted urgently to do whatever he could. But the Korean attack was farther away and the threat was not to United States homes, but to United States ideals, and to the idea that the free nations must all hang together or they would all hang separately.[84]

Americans questioned the need for service in limited wars. And the questioning grew in intensity when the nation's most precious resource started coming home in flag-draped coffins. The Army was at a particular disadvantage. As General Parks noted: "There is nothing glamorous about training in the mud, much less being shot at in the same eternal element."[85] In the "Womble Report on Service Careers" published immediately after the Korean War in 1954, it was noted that:

Public Respect for Constituted Authority has Declined. There is ample evidence of a lack of understanding on the part of the people concerning the necessity for implementing our present national military policy. It appears that a portion of this unfavorable attitude stems from the recent conduct of hostilities in Korea. Certainly these hostilities were conducted without the degree of support afforded to two preceding world-wide conflicts. Continued operation of Selective Service is equally distasteful. Until the public is made to understand and accept a public responsibility of military service, the situation is not likely to improve.[86]

The situation never improved. The public never understood or accepted its responsibilities for military service in limited war, where the threats were indirect and ambiguous. American distaste was not for Selective Service that had proven successful in two World Wars, but for the lack of substantiated need. Clausewitz postulated:

> Will this always be the case in the future? From now on will every war in Europe be waged with the full resources of the state, and therefore have to be fought only over major issues that affect the people? Or shall we again see a gradual separation taking place between government and people?[87]

In Korea the "gradual separation" was initiated.

*   *   *   *   *

The second major personnel policy instituted during the Korean War was the integration of the US Army. The US Army became the first major American institution to integrate. Blacks, after fighting for two hundred years in segregated units with white officers, were finally accepted as almost equals in ground warfare. Why? What caused one of the nation's most conservative institutions, which was traditionally decades behind the larger American society in social change, to take the lead and jump ahead of the rest of the country? The change was motivated by military effectiveness. The shortage of manpower was eroding the ability of the Army to fight. Blacks were a source of manpower. General Ridgway explained:

While I was still in command of the Eighth Army I had received from Major General William B. Kean, then commander of the U.S. 25th Division, an earnest and thoughtful recommendation for the integration of white and Negro troops. Kean had had full opportunity to observe Negro troops both in peacetime, at Fort Benning, and in Korea, where the all-Negro 24th Infantry Regiment was part of his command, and he felt that, both from a human and a military point of view, it was wholly inefficient, not to say improper, to segregate soldiers this way. This coincided precisely with my own views and I had planned in mid-March to seek authorization from General MacArthur, who would in turn sound out Washington, to commence integration at once.[88]

Ridgway, surprisingly, made no mention of Truman's July 1948 Executive Order 9981, which stated: "It is hereby declared to be the policy of the President that there shall be equality of treatment and opportunity for all persons in the armed services without regard to race, color, religion or national origin. This policy shall be put into effect as rapidly as possible...."[89] This directive for the integration of the Armed Forces was virtually ignored by all the Armed Forces.[90] "Rapidly as possible" was ill defined, and thus, could be interpreted to mean decades. Eisenhower had argued against its implementation, "In general, the Negro is less well educated than his brother citizen that is white and if you make a complete amalgamation, what you are going to have is in every company the Negro is going to be relegated to the minor jobs ... because the competition is too rough."[91]

The fact that the Army waited until it was in the midst of the Korean War, facing severe personnel problems, explains much. Military effectiveness was the primary reason for the adoption of this new personnel policy. Ridgway continued:

It was my conviction, as it was General Kean's, that only in this way could we assure the sort of esprit a fighting army needs, where each soldier stands proudly on his own feet, knowing himself to be as good as the next fellow and better than the enemy. Besides it had always seemed to me

Fig 6.2 Black American Soldier with 75MM Recoilless Rifle Guarding the Approach to Command Post on the Front Line in Korea. US Army photograph.

both un-American and un-Christian for free citizens to be taught to downgrade themselves this way, as if they were unfit to associate with their fellows or to accept leadership themselves.[92]

American culture did in fact educate black people to believe that they were inferior to white people. Inferior people could not stand up to their supposedly superior opponents on the battlefield. This argument was used for centuries to preclude or limit the number of black people in combat units. However, the personnel shortage in Korea made integration necessary.

While decisions were starting to be made on the integration of blacks, South Koreans had already been integrated into the Army in large numbers through KATUSA units. It was hard to justify the continued segregation of black Americans when foreigners were granted equal status in the US Army. In July 1951, three years after Truman's Executive Order was promulgated, the Eighth Army, in the midst of war in Korea, became the first major command in the armed forces to integrate. Proportionately more blacks saw combat duty in Korea than in World War II, constituting thirteen percent of all US forces.[93] Approximately forty percent of all blacks assigned to Korea served in combat units; however, of the 131 Medal of Honors awarded, only two went to blacks. The acceptance of blacks as soldiers initiated social changes that profoundly influenced the nation. The first black men in powerful positions in the United States were officers in the Army and Air Force. It is interesting to note that American racism was exported to Korea and Japan. Koreans and Japanese adopted the same prejudices, based on what they learned from white soldiers.

The Final Phase of the War: Defensive War of Attrition

In April 1951, Lieutenant General James Van Fleet took command of the US Eighth Army in Korea. At that time, American forces numbered 253,250 soldiers; UN forces 28,061; and ROK forces 260,548. In addition, there were 12,718 Korean Augmentations to the US Army (KATUSA).[94] Van Fleet was given the following orders from Ridgway:

Your mission is to repel aggression against so much of the territory (and the people therein) of the Republic of Korea as you now occupy and, in collaboration with the Government of the Republic of Korea, to establish and maintain order in the territory. In carrying out this mission you are authorized to conduct military operations, including amphibious and airborne landings, as well as ground operations in Korea north of the 38th parallel, subject to the limitations. . . .

In the execution of this mission you will be guided by the following prescriptions:

(1) Advance of major elements of your forces beyond the general line: Junction of IMJIN and HAN Rivers—CHORWON—HWACHON RESERVOIR—TAPEPO—RI, *will be on my orders only.* [This was the WYOMING LINE.]
(2) You will direct the efforts of your forces towards inflicting maximum personnel casualties and material losses on hostile forces in Korea, consistent with the maintenance of all your major units and the safety of your troops.[95]

Ridgway believed he was giving Van Fleet, "the latitude his reputation and my high respect for his ability merited," given the limitations of the directives of the President. Van Fleet, however, working from the perspective of World War II, believed his prerogative, as commander, had been severely restricted, and that the Eighth Army could have driven the Chinese from the Korean peninsula.[96] Ridgway, by drawing a line across the peninsula, beyond which the Eighth Army was not to advance, had taken away the initiative of his field commander. This was obviously a political decision. So Van Fleet fought a defensive war of attrition, restricted to operations within the confines of the geographic boundaries of South Korea. This decision eliminated other forms of strategy. On the defense it was impossible to destroy the enemy's army, the will of its people, or its government. In other words there was no way to win. On the defense the only option was to not lose, to fight defensively until the other side decided to negotiate a settlement, or offensive airpower produced a decision.

The Korean peninsula, the geographic configuration of the battlefield, limited both armies to frontal attacks. The confinement of the peninsula, the restrictions imposed by geography, made this strategy manageable. Still, surrendering the initiative eliminated the possibility of a quick solution to the war. The most important incentive to motivate the PRC to compromise at the peace table was voluntarily given up.

Ridgway, gauging American support for the war, was convinced that the right decision had been made. He reflected, "The seizure of the land between the truce line and the Yalu . . . would have lengthened our own supply routes, and widened our battlefront from 110 miles to 420. Would the American people have been willing to support the great army that would have been required to hold that line?"[97] He concluded the answer was "no." On 12 May 1952, Ridgway left Tokyo to relieve Eisenhower as the new NATO Supreme Commander of Allied Forces in Europe. General Mark Clark relieved Ridgway. General Eisenhower had decided to run for President.

By early summer 1951 both armies were well entrenched. Major offensive operations produced only limited results—the next ridgeline. The situation

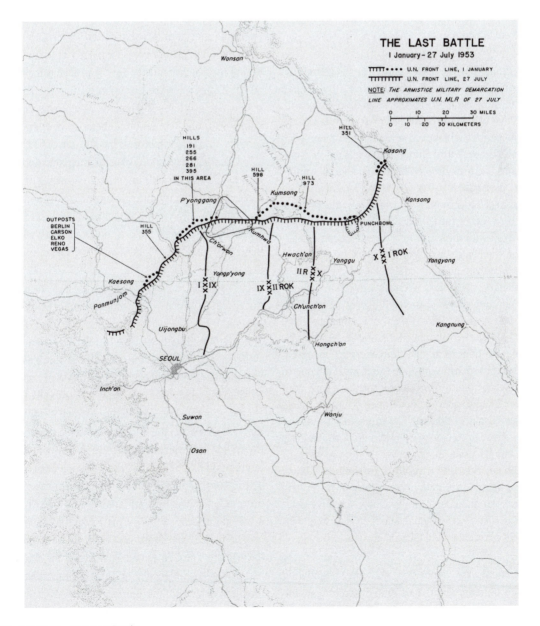

Fig 6.3 Korea, The Last Battle.

on the ground created the conditions for armistice talks. On 24 June 1951, Jacob A. Malik, the Soviet Union's United Nations representative, in a radio speech, advocated a ceasefire, to which Ridgway responded on 30 June. On 10 July, negotiations of the Korean Armistice Conference opened at Kaesong, later moved to Panmunjom. The negotiations broke down repeatedly. The withdrawal of foreign troops, the ceasefire line, the repatriation of prisoners, and other issues extended the talks. And, while the talks went on, soldiers continued to fight and die. Admiral Charles Turner Joy, the Chief of the United Nations Command delegation to the Korean Armistice Conference, wrote:

> When the Red Chinese plunged into the fray, the controlling political objective of the United States became a desire to avoid all-out war with China. When the Soviets suggested an armistice, the political objectives in Korea became an honorable cease-fire. During the armistice negotiations, we took on a political objective of gaining a propaganda victory over Communism in respect to prisoners of war. Thus the political objectives of the United States in Korea weathervaned with the winds of combat, accommodating themselves to current military events rather than constituting the goal to be reached through military operations. Consequently, the delegation, and indeed General Ridgway, never knew when a new directive would emanate from Washington to alter our basic objective of obtaining an honorable and stable armistice agreement. In such circumstances it is most difficult to develop sound plans, to present one's case convincingly, to give an appearance of unmistakable firmness and finality. It seemed to us that the United States Government did not know exactly what its political objectives in Korea were or should be. As a result the United Nations Command delegation was constantly looking over its shoulder, fearing a new directive from afar which would require action inconsistent with that currently being taken.[98]

Admiral Joy concluded that the negotiating strategy he was directed to employ prolonged the war and thereby caused unnecessary losses in lives. More than 40 percent of American casualties were sustained during the final defensive phase of the war.

Airpower was employed to facilitate negotiations. General Clark approved a bombing campaign to destroy dams that provided irrigation to rice fields in northwest Korea. The campaign flooded vast areas. The dam-busting campaign, the destruction of North Korean cities, and the continuing interdiction campaign caused considerable hardship and suffering. FEAF Formal Target Committee, meeting in April 1953, concluded that the punishing air campaign had been decisive in bringing the negotiations to a successful conclusion: "... the damage inflicted upon the enemy as a result of this application [of airpower] has been the only military pressure placed on the enemy during the past months and ... is probably the force which has caused the Communists to ... put forth new peace overtures."[99] General Weyland supported this conclusion: "Our around-the-clock air operations brought to all North Korea the full impact of war. The material destruction wrought, the panic and civil disorder created, and the mounting casualties in civilian and military populations alike became the most compelling factors in enemy accession to an armistice."[100] Other factors, however, had greater influence on the Communists' decision-making process.

The armistice negotiations outlasted the presidency of Truman. In November 1952 Dwight D. Eisenhower was elected President of the United States. A month later he flew to Korea to survey the situation, and to discuss the war with his commanders in the field. Shortly after his inauguration in January, Eisenhower made it known that he was considering a new strategy. He considered removing some of the limitations of the Truman Administration, and expanding the war effort to include the use of the atomic bomb. On 5 March 1953, Joseph Stalin died. The Soviet Union had not recovered from the severe destruction and carnage suffered in World War II, and it had no constitutional norms for the accession to power; hence, the death of Stalin created political uncertainty. The Chinese recognized that the situation had changed dramatically, and that for the most part they had achieved their primary objectives in Korea. The armistice document was signed on 27 July 1953 at Panmunjom. Eisenhower and his Secretary of

Fig 6.4 President Dwight D. Eisenhower, 12 February 1951. Reprinted with permission from Time, Inc.

State, John Foster Dulles, concluded that the threat of the atomic bomb had caused the Chinese to reach a final settlement. Others argued that the death of Stalin created conditions of uncertainty in the Soviet Union and China, causing domestic political matters to take first priority. And still others argue that the conventional air campaign produced the final decision.

The inability of the Chinese and the Americans to reach a decision on the ground with the forces deployed created the conditions for the armistice. Conventional airpower alone could not force a decision, and the death of Stalin would not have caused the shift in priorities if the situation on the ground had not been stabilized. Had China continued to feel threatened by the advance of the Eighth Army, the war would have continued. Eisenhower's threat and great credibility, coupled with the death of Stalin, probably influenced the immediacy, the timing, of the Communist decision; however, the Communists had achieved their major political objectives—the removal of American forces from the Chinese border and the survival of Communist North Korea. They also gained enormous prestige and confidence by fighting the most powerful nation on the planet to a standstill. At the same time, the American position in world affairs had diminished. The threat of the atomic bomb would not have produced an armistice agreement had the Eighth Army been on the Yalu River. Multiple factors influenced the Chinese decision-making process; foremost among them, they had achieved their primary objectives.

US forces remain in Korea. And given the unstable nature and hostile disposition of the North Korean dictatorship, and its acquisition of nuclear weapons and intermediate-range missile technology, US forces will remain in South Korea into the foreseeable future. No permanent peace agreement was ever signed, and the 38th parallel is one of the most heavily armed borders on Earth. The armistice agreement established a demilitarized zone (DMZ) between the two nations, a Military Armistice Commission, and the Joint Observation Teams that patrol the DMZ. Most importantly, however, it required the exchange of prisoners of war, the major obstacle to an early agreement. Between 20 April and 3 May 1953, during Operation Little Switch, 6,670 Communist soldiers

were exchanged for 684 UN soldiers, 149 of which were Americans. Between 5 August and 23 December, during Operation Big Switch, 75,823 Chinese and North Korean soldiers were exchanged for 12,773 UN soldiers.

The United States mobilized 5,720,000 officers and men to fight the Korean War, secure Europe, and provide a strategic reserve. These forces were allocated to the services as follows: Army, 2,834,000; Navy, 1,177,000; Air Force, 1,285,000; and the Marine Corps, 424,000. The Army fielded twenty divisions, eight of which fought in Korea. Of the 33,741 Americans killed in the Korean War, 82 percent were in the Army, roughly the same percentage as World War II. The Army suffered 27,731 battle deaths and 77,596 wounded; the Air Force 1,238 battle deaths, and 368 wounded. The Marine Corps suffered 4,262 battle deaths, and 23,744 wounded; the Navy 505 battle deaths, and 1,576 wounded. Better than 94 percent of the battle deaths in Korea were in the ground combat forces. It is estimated that the US sustained a total of 103,284 wounded in action.[101] South Korea suffered 415,000 military KIA or MIA, an estimated 429,000 WIA, and 500,000 to 1 million civilians dead. The Chinese suffered an estimated 142,000 KIA or MIA, and 238,000 WIA. North Korea sustained 1.5 million military and civilian KIA or MIA. Thirteen allied nations contributed ground combat units, ranging from a division to a platoon. The allies suffered 3,063 dead, and 11,817 wounded.

The Korean War was the first war fought by the United States in the nuclear age. Hence, it was the first artificial limited war, albeit, with the potential to become World War III and the world's first nuclear war. Truman deserves great credit for keeping the war limited. Technology, the radically changed environment of the 1950s, and the new role of the US in maintaining the world order initiated the process of transformation in American thinking about war. However, American culture influenced the unfolding of American military policies, strategies, and doctrines in the years and decades that followed. The preferred American way of war had come to an end. General Douglas MacArthur, who believed in a more total war strategic doctrine, where fighting continued until victory was attained, was incapable of making the transition to this new form of limited war.

MacArthur's thinking was more in concert with the thinking of the American people than Truman's. As General Collins noted: "The American public in November of 1951 was not yet fully resigned to a peace without military victory."[102] When the war was over, the American people still were not resigned to limited war and negotiated settlements. And this clearly was not the type of war they expected in the age of airpower and nuclear weapons. The Korean War was a dirty infantry war that failed to produce the outcome the American people expected. Thus, the war further eroded American faith in conventional forces. The fact that the war ended in a stalemate seemed to indicate the ineffectiveness of ground forces, influencing American perception about the Army and its place in national defense. The Army, however, believed that it had performed well under the most difficult circumstance and that: "The communist aggression in Korea ... marked the beginning of a new military policy for the United States. ..." And, that: "The final recognition of this fact by the American people made it possible to start the rebuilding of the armed forces to the minimum strength required. ..."[103] The Army was wrong.

PART II

THE EFFORT TO ADAPT

7.
EISENHOWER, THE COLD WAR, AND MASSIVE RETALIATION, 1953–1960

The fighting there [in Korea] was finally stopped last July on terms which had been proposed many months before. That result was achieved, at least in part, because the aggressor ... was faced with the possibility that the fighting might, to his own peril, soon spread beyond the limits and methods which he had selected, to areas and methods that we would select [the atomic bomb]. In other words, the principle of using methods of our choice was ready to be invoked, and it helped to stop the war which the enemy had begun and had pursued on the theory that it would be a limited war, at places and means of its choosing.[1]

–John Foster Dulles, Secretary of State, 12 January 1954

Thus, to many Americans SAC of the Air Force seemed a panacea. Here was a massive and potentially decisive military instrument, well calculated to achieve absolute success and to spare us the long drawn-out agony of mass ground warfare. We saw and understood the vital importance of maintaining it at top efficiency ... but more than that its compatibility with our military concepts led us to overlook some of the limitations both of the instrument itself and the philosophy of warfare that it represented. Therefore, the Korean conflict caught us emotionally unprepared. We fought with an uneasiness and a sense of frustration new to us. ... The urgent requirement in Korea were first to hold and then to retake ground, and we found ourselves called on to fight just the type of a tough ground force action that much of the Nation had come to feel was somehow obsolete.

–James E. Cross, *Military Review*, June 1956

In 1953, Eisenhower was President and in the position to enact his vision of the national security policy, but before he could implement his vision he had to end the war in Korea. On 27 July 1953, an armistice agreement was signed ending three years of bloody war. Eisenhower and his Secretary of State, John Foster Dulles, believed that the threatened use of the atomic bomb brought the Chinese to the peace table and to their acceptance of terms very similar to those previously offered during the Truman Administration.

Through ongoing armistice talks, foreign embassies, the media, and the redeployment of strategic forces, the Eisenhower Administration communicated to the Chinese that the war would be expanded in ways and means beyond the abilities of the PRC to control if an agreement were not concluded.[2] To emphasize this point, Eisenhower deployed B–29s to the Philippines with undercarriages specially designed to drop nuclear weapons within strike range of North Korea and China. The deployment was made public. Eisenhower and Dulles concluded that their initiatives had worked, had brought peace. However, the death of Stalin, conflicting views on strategy between the PRC and Soviet Union, internal divisions in the Communist Party of the PRC, and the fact that North Korea had been saved also influenced the armistice decision. The single most critical factor was not the

Fig 7.1 President Dwight D. Eisenhower.

Eisenhower and Dulles did not believe the United States and its allies could match the human and material resources of the enemy; hence, the reliance on armies was considered unreasonable. It was also believed that the effort to match the Communists with conventional forces would bankrupt the country. Eisenhower was concerned with the cost of defense. He believed that the way to defeat the Soviet Union was to demonstrate that the American way of life created the greatest good for the greatest number of people. Economic success, not military success, was the way to defeat the Soviet Union. Maintaining a large standing Army was expensive. Thus, the major question facing the US, according to Dulles, was: "How should collective defense be organized by the free world for maximum protection at minimum cost? The heart of the problem is how to deter attack." The answer was nuclear weapons and airpower. The US adopted a "first use" doctrine that emphasized complete destruction. Dulles wrote:

> This, we believe, requires that a potential aggressor be left in no doubt that he would be certain to suffer damage outweighing any possible gain from aggression. This result would not be assured, even by collective measures, if the free world sought to match the potential Communist forces, man for man and tank for tank, at every point where they might attack. The Soviet-Chinese bloc does not lack manpower and spends it as something that is cheap. If an aggressor knew he could always prescribe the battle conditions that suited him and engaged us in struggles mainly involving manpower, aggression might be encouraged. He would be tempted to attack in places and by means where his manpower superiority was decisive and where at little cost he could impose upon us great burdens. If the free world adopted that strategy, it could bankrupt itself and not achieve security over a sustained period.
>
> The free world must devise a better strategy for its defense, based on its own special assets. Its assets include, especially, air and naval power and atomic weapons which are now available in a wide range. . . . The free world must make imaginative use of the deterrent capabilities of these new weapons. . . . Properly used, they can produce defensive power able to retaliate at once and effectively against any aggression.[4]

atomic bomb, but the fact that the Chinese had achieved their political objectives through ground combat. It is ironic that the very instrument that saved South Korea, the US Eighth Army, was diminished in Korea, and airpower, which proved indecisive, was elevated. America learned the wrong lessons from the Korean War.

Eisenhower's Vision of War: The New Look

Dulles promulgated Eisenhower's strategic doctrine, "massive retaliation," and military policy, "the new look," tasks that more appropriately belonged to the Secretary of Defense, Charles E. Wilson. With the birth of the PRC the theory of the "Communist monolith" was born. Dulles wrote:

> The Soviet menace does not reflect the ambitions of a single ruler and cannot be measured by his life expectancy. . . .The Soviet Communists have always professed that they are planning for what they call 'an entire historical era.' The assets behind this threat are vast. The Soviet bloc of Communist-controlled countries . . . represents a vast central land mass with a population of 800 million.[3]

Eisenhower's defense and military policies were delineated in National Security Council position paper, NSC 162/2, on 30 October 1953:

Defense Against Soviet Power and Action. In the face of these threats, the United States must develop and maintain, at the lowest feasible cost, requisite military . . . strength to deter and, if necessary, to counter Soviet military aggression against the United States or other areas vital to its security. The risk of Soviet aggression will be minimized by maintaining a strong security posture, with emphasis on adequate offensive retaliatory strength and defensive strength. This must be based on massive atomic capability, including necessary bases; an integrated and effective continental defense system; ready forces of the United States and its allies suitably deployed and adequate to deter or initially to counter aggression, and to discharge required initial tasks in the event of general war; and an adequate mobilization base; all supported by the determined spirit of the US people.[5]

While Eisenhower supported the use of American forces in Korea, he would not have fought the Vietnam War.[6] Eisenhower had a different answer to Kennan's "counter-force at every point" axiom. In 1954, before the French defeat at Dien Bien Phu, Eisenhower considered military assistance to the French that would have brought the US into the war. After careful analysis, he and his advisors concluded that Vietnam, while important to the national interest of stopping the spread of Communism, was not of sufficient strategic importance to warrant the commitment it would take to sustain a non-communist country. In his view, limited wars in nations with contiguous borders to the PRC were strategically unwise. In his view, only industrial powers were real threats to the security of the United States—nation-states that had legitimate nuclear targets. Eisenhower wrote:

My feeling was then, and still remains, that it would be impossible for the United States to maintain the military commitments which it now sustains [during the Korean War] around the world (without turning into a garrison state) did we not possess atomic weapons and the will to use them when necessary.[7]

In Stephen Ambrose's portrait, *Eisenhower: The President*, the relative importance that Eisenhower placed on ground combat forces and nuclear weapons was elucidated:

At a mid-December meeting with the Republican congressional leaders, Eisenhower explained his strategy. "The things we really need are the things that the other fellow looks at and respects," he declared. The Russians did not respect the handful of American divisions in Europe, but they did respect the bomb. Eisenhower said the United States "must take risks in certain areas," and "must make a long-term effort," so that "we do not get to the point where we must attack or demobilize." Asia-firsters among the Old Guard congressmen protested against the planned reductions in ground strength in Korea. Eisenhower told them that he did not believe "Korea will be stabilized greatly by the continued presence of ground troops. We must put more dependence on air." He said that if the Communists broke the armistice, "we go all out" in nuclear retaliation.[8]

In a televised news conference, when asked about his "new look" military policy, Eisenhower stated:

You cannot possibly say that the kind of a unit and organization that I took to war or took over across the Channel in 1944 would have any usefulness today whatsoever. For example, you will recall we landed on June 6; we got out of that narrow little beachhead on about July 25. All right; behind that we built up two artificial harbors and we were landing over the beaches. What would two atomic bombs have done to the whole thing?

Eisenhower went on to delineate his thoughts on the Army and war:

Let me point this out: I hear people say "bigger army." *Now, our most valued, our most costly asset is our young men.* Let's don't use them any more than we have to. For 40 years I was in the Army, and I did one thing: study how can you get an infantry platoon out of battle. The most terrible job in warfare is to be a second lieutenant leading a platoon when you are on the battlefield. If we can do anything to lessen that number—remember this: we are planning right now the greatest peacetime army we have ever held, one million men in time of peace.[9]

Eisenhower was well imbued with basic American cultural tenets. He identified the nation's "most valued asset," and substituted technology for manpower. He also reduced the Army considerably below a million men.

Secretary of Defense, Charles Wilson, adopted Eisenhower's visions. Before a Senate Subcommittee for Appropriations on 15 March 1954 he stated:

> ... the integration of new weapons systems into military planning creates new relationships between men and material which emphasize air-power and permit overall economies in the use of manpower. ... The Fiscal Year 1955 budget incorporates the new air force's objectives and continues a rapid buildup of air strength. ... As we increase the striking power of our combat forces by the application of technological advances and new weapons and by the continuing growth of airpower, the total number of military personnel can be reduced.[10]

This was a fundamental belief prevalent from World War II to the dawn of a new century.

Eisenhower was also concerned about the cost of defense and militarism. In a discussion with Emmett John Hughes, one of his speechwriters, Eisenhower stated:

> The jet plane that roars over your head costs three-quarters of a million dollars. That is more money than a man earning ten thousand dollars every year is going to make in his lifetime. What world can afford this sort of thing for long? We are in an armaments race. Where will it lead us? At worst, to atomic warfare. At best, to robbing every nation and people on earth of the fruits of their own toil. Now there could be another road before us—the road of disarmament. What does this mean? It means for everybody in the world bread, butter, clothes, homes, hospitals, schools, all the good and necessary things for decent living. So let this be the choice we offer.[11]

Eisenhower had a vision and the confidence of having led the largest invasion in history, of having defeated in combat the most powerful armies ever arrayed in battle. He understood war, and he hated it. Eisenhower believed it would be impossible to avoid using nuclear weapons in war with the Soviet bloc. He was convinced that war had fundamentally changed, that the advent of air and nuclear power caused a revolution in warfare. He believed that technology could replace the man on the battlefield, that mankind had entered a new age. He would only commit to war if America's vital interests were directly threatened, and he understood the power of geography. Any state that deployed forces on the "Chinese continent" had to be willing to go to war with China, and possibly fight World War III. Eisenhower knew the Army was forward deployed, spread across the planet from Korea, to Japan, to Panama, to parts of Europe. He did not plan to use it. Eisenhower believed the nation had to take risks. The US, and particularly the Army, could not be all things, at all times, to all the peoples of Earth. Thus, his strategy was not to man the Army to counter the capabilities of Soviet ground forces, and he would not man the Army based on its missions and roles around the globe, but also he would not reduce those missions and roles. Eisenhower wrote:

> National security does not mean militarism or any approach to it. Security cannot be measured by the size of munitions stockpiles or the number of men under arms or the monopoly of an invincible weapon. That was the German and Japanese idea of power which, in the test of war, was proved false. Even in peace, the index of material strength is unreliable, for arms become obsolete and worthless; vast armies decay imperceptibly while sapping the strength of the nations supporting them. Monopoly of a weapon is soon broken. But adequate spiritual reserves, coupled with understanding of each day's requirements, will meet every issue of our time.[12]

The presence of the US Army in a foreign state represented the commitment of the US. In other words, the Army was simply an ostentatious line telling the enemy not to cross. Eisenhower understood that only certain well-identified nation-states possessed the wherewithal to fundamentally challenge American security, and the threat of the atomic bomb would keep them in check. In keeping with his strategic outlook, Eisenhower emphasized airpower, reducing the Army's budget, and to a lesser extent the Navy's budget. He knew that the US and its allies, whose power to influence world affairs was still declining, could not match the Communist bloc man for man, and that it was foolish and too expensive to try. He feared such a strategy would bankrupt the country. Eisenhower counseled the American people not to listen to their fear. He believed that the situation was not out of control, and that the Soviet threat was manageable. His confidence, steadiness, experience, and credibility were in themselves a considerable military asset and deterrent to war. No other president in the twentieth century commanded the respect and credibility due Eisenhower. Eisenhower, the person, enhanced America's security. In the 1950s, Americans were taught to live with risk, to live with less than perfect security.

Eisenhower worked to keep Americans out of war, not only by strategy but also by doctrine. Eisenhower promulgated his officially accepted strategic doctrine, "massive retaliation," to the entire world. He insured that the Soviets understood his doctrine. He wanted no ambiguity. The world will never know if he was bluffing, but for a man who professed to hate war, who took pains to keep men out of it, it is at least questionable whether he would have actually initiated Armageddon. As Senator Kennedy noted: "No civilized, peace-loving nation is enthusiastic about initiating a nuclear holocaust—an Armageddon which would unleash on both sides enough destructive power to devastate the world many times over."[13] Perhaps Eisenhower believed that the bluff alone—the magnitude of the threat—would keep the peace. If so, he gambled and won. However, to make the threat real Eisenhower had to make the capability real. He had to know the vision of airpower espoused by airmen such as Arnold, Spaatz, and LeMay could achieve all that was predicted, before he could sell the vision to the Soviets, hence, the emphasis on airpower. And to demonstrate his conviction, his confidence in massive retaliation, perhaps, he intentionally reduced the size of the Army, demonstrating to the Soviets his resolve.

Eisenhower's biggest gamble was in the peripheral areas of the world, areas not firmly in the Soviet or US bloc. In these regions Eisenhower's strategy was ambiguous. He depended on the threat of massive retaliation; however, the threat was not viable, as the war in Vietnam later demonstrated. Eisenhower well understood that non-aligned nations lacked the wherewithal to directly influence American security. Such areas of the world added to the power and prestige of a given bloc, but did not fundamentally change the balance of power. Eisenhower used the atomic threat, mutual defense treaties, indigenous local forces as substitutes for US ground forces, American economic and military assistance, American political and diplomatic clout, the show of force, the forward deployment of conventional forces, and his great credibility and prestige to keep peace and achieve American objectives in peripheral areas important to the United States. Eisenhower's "massive retaliation" threat, in regard to peripheral areas, was not viable.

It is peculiar and worth noting that Eisenhower adopted a vision very different from that of the other senior ground (infantry) combat commanders that served under him in World War II. It is peculiar because of their shared background, the immersion in Army culture, and the similarity in learning experiences of these senior leaders—West Point, Infantry Basic Course, Command and General Staff College, War College, World War II, extensive professional and social communications, and so on. It is also peculiar because Eisenhower exhibited little loyalty to the service in which he matured as a leader and through which he became President. Eisenhower deduced lessons from World War II and the Korean War, and adopted a vision of war that was diametrically opposed to those of Ridgway, Clark, Taylor, Bradley, Collins, and the vast majority of Army leaders. Why? Eisenhower's actions may have also been designed to show that he was in fact a joint Commander-in-Chief of the Armed Forces of the United States, that he favored no one service. Still, Eisenhower did a disservice to the Army, not by his frugal policies, but by his failure to insure that the Army retained its center and fighting spirit, that it remained fundamentally a ground combat force designed to close with the enemy and kill them. It is one of the great ironies of twentieth-century American history that the man whose very being was so deeply associated with the US Army, whose character was shaped by the institution, was President of the United States, with the power to move the Army in any direction he desired, when the Army lost its compass. Still, Eisenhower can only be charged with neglect. The Army itself was responsible for safeguarding its most basic tenets.

During the Eisenhower Administration the American ideology regarding the use of military force continued its process of transformation. The belief that wars could be fought exclusively from the air, that mankind in technologically advanced societies had finally moved beyond the dirty business of ground warfare was firmly established. Armies of the future would simply mop up the battlefield, occupy the defeated country, or attempt to restore order in cities destroyed by nuclear weapons. However, not everyone agreed with this vision of war.

The Army's Fight Against the New Look and the Doctrine of Massive Retaliation

All the services are engaged in a constant battle for funding, mission, and relevance in the current political and international environment. During much of the Cold War the fights between the services for limited resources were zero-sum games, meaning a gain for one service was a loss for another. General Mark Clark, who commanded Allied Forces in Italy during World War II and the United Nations Command in the Far East during the last year of the Korean War, writing in 1954, challenged the current thinking of the Eisenhower Administration:

> There is much talk these days about push-button warfare and the fact that the technical experts have developed such weapons of mass destruction that the role of the infantryman is now secondary. There has been great technical development in weapons and I hope our experts in research and development will continue to make improvements. However, in my opinion, and without in any way disparaging the vital roles of the Air Force and the Navy, the infantryman remains an indispensable element in any future war. Certainly he must be supported by the Air and the Navy and every kind of technical weapons, but he never will be relegated to an unimportant role. He is the fellow with the stout heart

and a bellyful of guts, who, with his rifle and bayonet, is willing to advance another foot, fire another shot and die if need be in defense of his country.[14]

The Army maintained its most fundamental belief that man was the dominant instrument on the battlefield. During the mid to late 1950s, Generals Ridgway and Taylor were the most vocal, tenacious advocates of limited war, and they had the experience of the Korean War to support their arguments. Ridgway believed that the lessons of the Korean War were that air and naval power alone could not stop a determined enemy. The air and naval components had not stopped the Communist advance down the Korean peninsula. In addition there were no nuclear targets in Korea, or later in Vietnam. The regions of the world where conflicts were most likely possessed no vast industrial areas to destroy; hence, the employment of the atomic bomb in these regions was a form of extermination warfare. The use of such weapons of mass destruction in poor and undeveloped regions of the world would have been a crime against humanity. It had taken ground forces to stop and then take back South Korea from the NKPA and PLA.

Ridgway and Taylor envisioned a range of wars from limited to total. Ridgway wrote:

> The basic point at issue, I think, lay in differing concepts of how, in the event of war, the doctrine of 'massive retaliation' should be applied. My belief was simply this: that we must possess the power of swift and devastating retaliation. At the same time we must possess the capability for 'selective' retaliation, the capacity to use one arm, or two, or all three—land, sea, and air combined—to apply whatever degree of force a particular situation demanded.[15]

Another lesson of Korea was that the US Army had been unprepared and as a consequence had needlessly expended the lives of American servicemen. Ridgway, in reference to the Korean War, wrote:

> It was the bitter lesson, learned through our experience in Korea at such a cost in blood and national prestige, that steeled me in my resolution later, when as Chief of Staff, I protested with

greatest vehemence against 'economies' which would have placed us in the same relative state of ineffectiveness.[16]

Ridgway's experiences in Korea reinforced convictions formed in World War II—another war the US entered unprepared—and influenced his words and actions as Army Chief of Staff. In Ridgway's view the Army should maintain a large, well-trained, well-equipped, strategically deployable force to meet contingencies around the world. And they should not be a "trip wire force" for the initiation of nuclear war:

It was a time to give a soldier deep concern, for in that period following the end of World War II, there was a growing feeling that in the armies of the future the foot soldier would play only a very minor role. Two factors stimulated this thinking—the earnest desire of the nation to cut down on its military expenditures, and the erroneous belief that in the atomic missile, delivered by air, we had found the ultimate weapon.... My arguments regarding air power ... were in no sense a protest against emphasis on the air arm. They were in protest against what I sincerely believed to be an overemphasis on one form of air power, the long-range bomber, to the neglect of other means by which the magnificent weapon, the combat airplane, can be employed.

My strongest arguments, in fact, were for a greater and more varied development of air power. It was clear to me, as to every other even moderately intelligent infantry officer, that the army of the future must be very greatly dependent upon aircraft of one form or another. As I have pointed out ... it must be an air-transportable army, possessed of long- and short-range mobility far beyond anything ever known in war before. To fight the war of the future we must possess the capability not only to transport the nuclear bomb for great distances, and drop it with fine accuracy on a target. We must also possess the capability to lift whole armies, armed with nuclear weapons, and put them down upon any spot on the earth's surface where their tremendous, and selective, firepower will be needed.[17]

Ridgway was an airborne soldier. His experiences in commanding the 82nd Airborne Division and XVIII Airborne Corps in World War II shaped his

perspective of the Army. Ridgway also accepted the thesis that in future wars airpower would be the dominant factor. However, he envisioned a very different form and use of airpower. Ridgway believed that it was possible to develop an Army that was totally deployable by air. He argued that:

the Army plans to place increasing emphasis upon airborne, air-transportability and air-ground support techniques. For it is only by air that we can combine maximum mobility and maximum firepower. This of course will entail very close cooperation between Army troops and the Air Force and air elements of the Navy.[18]

Ridgway stressed the need for *joint operations* and *joint doctrine*, recognizing that the Army lacked strategic mobility, the ability to rapidly deploy to battlefields. The Army was the only service that had to depend on the other services to get to the battlefield. And, the Army was virtually alone in this vision. Half a century later the Army was still making the same arguments, and the nation was still incapable of rapidly projecting major ground combat units into troubled regions of the world by air. Given this vision of war, the placement of strategic air transports under the Air Force in 1947 was a major mistake. The focus of the Air Force and its priorities greatly impeded the development of such a capability.[19]

*　*　*　*　*

In 1954 the eight National Guard divisions mobilized for the Korean War—the 28th, 31st, 37th, 40th, 43rd, 44th, 45th, and 47th IDs—returned to state control. In the years that followed, the 5th ID, 7th Armored Division, and 101st Airborne Division were deactivated. Cutting the Army's strength was an attractive way to reduce the defense budget, or to reallocate funds to high-tech weapon systems. The Army had the lowest technology budget, but the highest manpower budget. The deactivation of an Army division could fund the research and development of new aircraft. The majority of the American people tended to support this policy, not fully recognizing the need for the Army in a world where airpower and nuclear weapons were considered the decisive

Fig 7.2 General and Mrs. Matthew B. Ridgway bid farewell to General George C. Marshall, Secretary of Defense, as he leaves Haneda Airbase, Tokyo, Japan, for the United States. US Army photograph, 11 June 1951.

instruments for the conduct of war. In addition, defense contractors lobbied Congress and the American people to gain their support for the latest aircraft or related technologies. By reducing the size of the Army and thereby its intrusion into the lives of Americans, protests against the citizen-soldier Army were limited. The Army was still defending hundreds of millions of foreigners in various parts of the world, but there was no war and the Army was in reality too small to actually defend the areas it occupied. Indigenous forces carried the heaviest burden for their own defense, with help from military assistance programs.

While most Congressmen tended to support a national strategy based on advanced technologies, the Army received some Congressional support. Senator John F. Kennedy was a supporter of the doctrine of limited war, and tried, along with other senators, to prevent cuts in Army strength:

Back in 1954, when these manpower cuts began, I offered an amendment to prevent a cut in Army divisions from nineteen to seventeen. Senators Gore, Mansfield, Symington, Humphrey, Monroney, and Lehman joined in sponsoring the amendment, and a majority of Democratic Senators supported it. But the amendment lost—and so did the cause of our ability to fulfill far-flung commitments in Berlin, the Middle East, the Far East, and throughout the world. And we lost, General Gavin told us once he left the Army, because "Congress was assured that our combat strength was not being reduced. We were simply cutting the fat . . . [But] the contrary was the case."[20]

While recognizing the need to fight limited war, Ridgway and Taylor also believed that the Army had to develop a new doctrine to fight on the atomic battlefield. In the late 1940s and 1950s, infantry officers, specifically airborne infantry officers, dominated the top levels of the Army. They envisioned an army that was strategically deployable by air, an army that could put significant combat power on the ground anywhere in the world, but also an Army with greater tactical and operational mobility, an Army with its own air force that was capable of fighting on the atomic battlefield.

Ridgway's tenure as Army Chief of Staff came to an end in 1955. He passed the responsibility for transforming the Army to Taylor. In reference to his tenure as the Army's top leader in the Pentagon, Ridgway wrote:

> Throughout my service as Chief of Staff three great tasks confronted me: First, to preserve the spirit and pride of an Army which top-level efforts steadily sought to reduce to a subordinate place among the three great services that make up our country's shield; second, to deploy this waning strength in such a way that ground combat units would be as effective as possible in the event of war; and third, to lay the foundations for a totally different Army … an Army trained, equipped, and organized to fight and win in an atomic war.[21]

In the 1950s, the Army Chief of Staff had considerably greater power and authority than in 2010. Ridgway was in a constant battle with his political bosses, who pressured him to reduce the strength of Army divisions, deactivate units, and reduce the Army's budget. Ridgway concluded: "I did not feel during my tour in the Pentagon there was any real understanding of the Army's needs, or any real recognition of what would be required in men, money, arms and equipment to carry out the missions the Army was asked to be ready to perform."[22] Ridgway's opposition to the Secretary of Defense and President ultimately cost him his job. With the loss of Ridgway, the Army lost not just the battle, but also the war to advocates of airpower.

The spirit of the Army was severely damaged in the 1950s. The Army's position as the nation's primary war-winning service was usurped by the Air Force. And, many came to believe that the Army's campaign-winning infantry doctrine was obsolete. In an article published in *Military Review* in April 1956,

entitled, "In Defense of the Army," Lieutenant Colonel Wallace C. Magathan, a member of the faculty at the US Army Command and General Staff College, responded to an argument that advocated that the Army become an auxiliary of the Air Force, a view delineated in *Army Combat Forces Journal* in August 1955:

> It had become clear that the Army is now an auxiliary service.... Of course everyone admits that ground forces are still needed.... Why not make the Army a branch of the Air Force? … it is hoped that many officers will begin to be attracted by the … honor that the Nation will accord us for closing up an unmodern and expensive service.[23]

Magathan noted that the fact that these words were written indicated the extent of the "uneasiness in the Army officer corps on the true role of the Army in the thermonuclear missile era."

In an article entitled, "What is the Army's Job?" published in *Military Review* in 1956, the supporting role of the Army and the transformation of American thinking about war were identified:

> Today, the United States is maintaining more powerful ground forces than ever before in her peacetime history. Paradoxically, the country is less certain than ever before of why it is maintaining these forces. They are no longer our primary deterrent against large-scale enemy attack, and they no longer constitute our primary weapon for waging large scale war. The massive long-range striking force of the Strategic Air Command (SAC) has come to fill these roles, while the ground forces and, to a large extent, the naval forces are now cast in supporting roles. To the average citizen these supporting roles, particularly that of the Army, are vague and poorly defined. He is confused as to the types of wars his country is prepared to fight. Worse, he senses that his leaders share his confusion.[24]

And, as late as 1959, Major General H.P. Storke felt compelled to write: "too many false impressions—impressions which some day could endanger the security of our Nation—have been permitted to spread unchallenged." He continued:

Those who proudly wear the Army Green find it extremely difficult to understand the apparent belief that the Army would be of little use in modern warfare. Nevertheless, many—too many—Americans do believe this to be true. These patriotic Americans, whose very existence some day may depend on the Army's fighting men and who today are paying heavy taxes to guarantee the defense of that existence, have been poorly informed of the missions and capabilities of our modern Army.... By them, the Army too often is regarded as a lethargic, land-bound, mud-slogging body of miserable men with rifles—an anachronism with no place in a push-button war fought with supersonic airplanes, missiles, and atoms. This is a false image of our modern Army ....[25]

The Army lost the battle for the public imagination. Charles C. Moskos, Jr., observed:

... attitudinal surveys conducted during the Cold War period showed Americans consistently giving highest prestige to the Air Force followed, in order by the Navy, Marine Corps, and Army. These surveys also found specific stereotypes associated with each of the services: Air Force, technical training and glamour; Navy, travel and excitement; Marine Corps, physical toughness and danger; Army, ponderous and routine.[26]

The Army's own internal surveys revealed that Army personnel also believed the Air Force was "the most modern and glamorous" service, and that the Army was "traditional-bound and routinized."

Ridgway concluded:

All the reductions in the Army's strength, all the failure to provide for the Army the mobility and the aerial fire support it needs, is merely a reflection of ... the erroneous attitude that air is all powerful and the foot soldier is obsolete. There are many people, and they have great influence, who continue to shout that a new war would be over very quickly—that air power alone could fight it, in a matter of weeks, and control the peace thereafter.[27]

The psychological effects of the airpower ethos were cumulative. The mental disposition it created could not be reversed in 1964 when decisions were made again to fight a ground war. The Vietnam War was lost between 1945 and 1960. Airpower created a false vision of war. Airpower made it seem that wars could be fought and won cheaply in terms of American lives. Americans came to view wars of the future as primarily air wars. Therefore, they expected airpower, not the Army's ground forces, to be the decisive instrument for the conduct of the Vietnam War. The Army was to defend and wait, to fight a strategically defensive war of attrition while airpower secured victory through strategically offensive operations. *Vietnam was the first war in the nation's history in which Army ground forces were not the primary instrument for defeating the enemy.* The Navy, too, emphasized airpower. The aircraft carrier became a symbol of American naval power, almost exclusively.

*   *   *   *   *

Taylor was selected to replace Ridgway with the specific understanding that he would not openly oppose the President's defense programs, that he would instead support the President's position. During Taylor's tenure as Chief of Staff (1955–1959), the Army's position continued to deteriorate. Taylor noted that, "As I had feared, the only way to relieve the pressure acceptable to the 'New Look' was to cut military power, particularly that of the Army." In 1959 the defense budget was $41 billion, of which almost half went to the Air Force. Twenty-eight percent went to the Navy, and 23 percent to the Army.[28] In 1957 the Army consisted of 20 active duty divisions, 14 infantry, 4 armor, and 2 airborne. Forty percent of the Army was deployed overseas, with 4 infantry divisions and 1 armor division forming the Seventh US Army in Europe, and 2 infantry divisions in Korea forming part of the Eighth Army. Eight divisions formed the Strategic Army Forces (STRAF).[29] These were combat-ready forces with missions to reinforce the forward-deployed units. Roughly 46 percent of the defense budget throughout this period went to the Air Force.

Taylor also opposed the strategic doctrine of massive retaliation, which he argued:

... could offer our leaders only two choices, the initiation of general nuclear war or compromise and retreat. From its earliest days, many world events have occurred which cast doubt on its validity and expose its fallacious character. Korea, a limited conventional war, fought by the United States when we had an atomic monopoly, was clear disproof of its universal efficacy.

Taylor believed the proof of the great fallacy was ample: "The many other limited wars which have occurred since 1945—the Chinese civil war, the guerrilla warfare in Greece and Malaya, Vietnam, Taiwan, Hungary, the Middle East, Laos, to mention only a few—are clear evidence that . . . it [the atomic bomb and airpower] has not maintained the Little Peace . . . ."[30]

In the latter half of the 1950s, Taylor and the Army became the leading advocates of the doctrine of limited wars.[31] During the Eisenhower Administration, Taylor was fighting a losing battle, as his predecessor had. Taylor noted:

> In the climate of the Eisenhower Administration, it was hard to make the case for limited war to the satisfaction of the decision-makers. Limited war suggested Korea, a thought which was repulsive to officials and the public alike. . . . The resources needed for limited war were largely ground forces using unglamorous weapons and equipment—rifles, machine guns, trucks and unsophisticated aircraft—items with little appeal to the Congress or the public.[32]

The Army's budget reflected the attitude and priorities of the time. Instead of investing in the basic requirements for land warfare, the Army was pushed to go into the high-tech business. Taylor recalled that, "Secretary Wilson once sent back an Army budget to get us to substitute requests for newfangled items with public appeal . . . ."

During Taylor's tenure, the Army went through one of the most radical transitions in operational and tactical doctrine in its long history. It transitioned from its World War II and Korean War infantry and armor campaign-winning doctrines to the Pentomic doctrine. Army divisions were reorganized to fight the atomic battle. The Army developed tactical nuclear weapons—artillery, rockets, and a mortar—and sent them down to division level. The Army sought new innovative technology to increase operational and tactical mobility. It sought to develop air-deployable

divisions that produced greater combat power than its traditional divisions. While the Pentomic doctrine and organization were discarded in the early 1960s, the Army produced weapons systems that would be used for the next two decades, and some of them far beyond. The first generation of tactical nuclear weapons that were later deployed to Western Europe were produced. The helicopter, M–60 tank, M113 armored personnel carrier, M–60 machine gun, 90-mm recoilless rifle, 81-mm mortar, and other systems were developed.[33]

Throughout the 1950s, the Army wrestled with the problem of fighting war on the nuclear battlefield, and keeping up with the Russians. Testifying before the Senate, Taylor noted that the Soviet Communists had equipped their army "with a complete family of modern weapons and equipment and continue to maintain it in an excellent state of combat readiness." Taylor concluded that the US Army was behind, that it was possible to fight on the nuclear battlefield, but that it would take considerably greater mobility, radio communications, individual initiative, force protection, and atomic firepower. Taylor wrote:

> In the first place, it [Army divisions] should be adaptable either to a nonnuclear limited war on the Korean model or to war in a European theater of operations where the use of nuclear weapons might be expected. To have this dual capability, it must be able to disperse into small units capable of independent action and to reassemble swiftly when it was safe to concentrate without danger of attack by nuclear weapons.[34]

By dispersing and hiding, Taylor believed the likelihood of Army formations being targeted with nuclear weapons was greatly reduced. Yet to fight and exploit opportunities created by nuclear firepower they had to be capable of rapidly concentrating: "The ability to disperse and hide, coupled with the ability to converge and fight, required mobility of a kind we have only begun to appreciate." The technology that Taylor required to perform these operations simply did not exist in the 1950s. And important parts of the capabilities Taylor sought still did not exist at the end of the century. The logistical requirements of a division were enormous. It was not possible to make these supply trains airmobile, nor was it possible for the division to operate without them. Colonel Mataxis noted:

> ... this [a single-type Pentomic division structure] will not be practicable until new developments permit the capability for sustained combat, air transportability, and battlefield mobility to be incorporated in a single division without prohibitive costs. Viewed realistically, this is a 'long-long range' goal.[35]

The Army undertook a major effort to develop the new technologies required to dramatically increase tactical and operational mobility. Writing in 1958 Major General Paul F. Yount, Chief of Transportation, outlined some of the programs under development:

> Within the combat zone the Army is rapidly increasing its organic capability for air transport of troops, equipment, and supplies. The Army is developing a family of STOL (Short Take-off and Landing), VTOL (Vertical Take-off and Landing), and helicopter aircraft capable of performing a myriad of transportation tasks varying from moving combat troops across obstacles to the more routine movement of supplies from the Army maintenance area forward to the combat units.
>
> Some of the items of inventive genius, now under development, which may be expected to enable the Army of the future to meet the challenge include: Hiller Flying Platform, Delackner Aerocycle; Sky Hook, a radio-controlled flying pallet; Flying Crane, a heavy lift helicopter designed to lift 8 to 16 tons for short distances at low speeds; an aerial vehicle capable of performing all tasks commonly associated with the land jeep: the Bell XV–3 utilizing the tilting rotor principle; the XV–1 Convertiplane; and a nuclear-powered, remote-controlled cargo-carrying device with VTOL capabilities.[36]

With the exception of the heavy lift helicopter, none of these items existed in the Army's inventories at the dawn of the new century. The technology simply did not exist to perform the tasks of mobility the Army sought with its Pentomic doctrine. The Army's efforts to get back into America's hearts and minds and remain relevant led it astray. The Army too was

inculcated with the American faith in science and technology as a means of solving all of humanity's problems.

In 1957, Taylor outlined the requirements for the new Pentomic doctrine:

> In developing future Army forces adaptable to the atomic battlefield we are impressed with the need to accomplish four things. First, we must increase our ability to locate atomic targets on the battlefield. Second, we must increase our ability to deliver nuclear fires. Third, we must reduce our susceptibility to detection by the enemy. Fourth, we must increase our ability to exploit our own firepower.[37]

Taylor envisioned a doctrine that in the 1950s and 1960s was technologically impossible. In the 1990s some parts of Taylor's vision were realized. Satellite technologies made it possible for the US and Soviet Union to detect "atomic targets," collect intelligence, and much more. Precision-guided munitions technologies "have increased our ability to deliver nuclear [and conventional] fires." Stealth technologies have "reduced susceptibility to detection." Operationally and tactically with helicopters the Army moves infantry forces considerably faster than in the late 1950s. Armor forces, however, are still only marginally faster than the Army of the 1950s, and strategically the logistical requirements of an Army division had increased enormously. Hence, the ability of the Army to strategically deploy, to cross oceans to get to the battlefield, had actually declined.

Taylor's Pentomic division eliminated the triangular division structure of the Army. (From World War II through the Korean War Army divisions consisted of three regimental combat teams and each regiment consisted of three battalions.) The Pentomic division consisted of five battle groups. The level of command, the regimental headquarters, was eliminated. The battle groups consisted of five companies. Each battle group was capable of independent actions. The strength of an Infantry Division was reduced from approximately 17,000 to 14,000. The division had nuclear capable 8-inch howitzers, rockets, guided missiles, and even a small rocket that looked like a mortar, with a miniature nuclear warhead called the *Davy Crockett*. Nuclear firepower was one of the few parts of Taylor's vision that was attainable. And, the question always present was: would the employment of tactical nuclear weapons lead to the exchange of strategic nuclear weapons—would the war escalate?[38] Amazingly Taylor reorganized infantry, airborne, and armor divisions before the doctrine was adequately tested and proven.

General Westmoreland, who commanded the 101st Airborne Division when it was converted to the new Pentomic organization, observed that:

> Because the Pentomic Division was a creature of the Chief of Staff, few in the Army were about to criticize it. During its test period with the 101st, the slogan was: "Our job is not to determine whether it *will* work—it is to make it *work*!" Because test officers were reluctant to tell their bosses that the organization was unsound, the concept was adopted and remained standard for several years, a prime example of the difficulty that "yes-men" can cause . . . .[39]

Westmoreland, after gaining some experience with the new organization and doctrine, recommended abolishing the Pentomic Division, noting that, "in view of the way the Army had to operate in Vietnam . . . we would have been in real trouble with the Pentomic Division."

To defend itself the Army tried to become something it wasn't. It bought into pop culture, science fiction, the *Star Trek* vision of war, and a different set of values. It tried to compete with the Air Force by becoming more like the Air Force. The Army went into the high-technology business; the nuclear business; the missile business; and the research and development business for cutting-edge, high-speed, exotic technologies. The Army believed that it needed high-tech weapons, particularly nuclear weapons and missiles, to survive. The Army tried to create a Hollywood image that it could sell to Congress and the American people. Taylor wrote:

> In early October 1957, when Sputnik I was placed into orbit by the USSR, the Army was ready to compete in the space race with the Jupiter C missile. In early November of that year, the Army was directed to place a satellite in orbit without delay. Eighty-four days later, on

31 January 1958, the Army successfully placed Explorer I in space. . . . Currently the Army is developing a 1½ million pound thrust space vehicle booster for the Advanced Research Project Agency (ARPA) of the Department of Defense; it will provide a number of scientific satellite launching vehicles to the National Aeronautical and Space Administration (NASA); and it will test 10 NASA space capsules. . . . The Army has pressed forward with an urgent requirement for the very small, close range atomic weapons with yields in the order of tons, rather than kilotons. These are essential for use in close proximity to friendly forces with little or no danger. . . . The Army has broadened its program to provide a family of nuclear power plants for supplying heat and electricity . . . Programs have been undertaken for developing nuclear propelled special land vehicles. An example is the Army Overland Train . . . .[40]

In a losing endeavor to compete with the Air Force, Army leaders undertook efforts to remake the Army into something that deviated from its fundamental purpose. And while trying to adjust to the new reality of nuclear war the Army lost its focus. James E. Hewes, Jr., in his study of the Army, noted:

> The Army's own modernization program emphasized the development of missiles and Army aviation at the expense of conventional weapons and equipment . . . In an era of financial austerity the Army's major overhead operating costs, the operations and maintenance program, suffered most. More and more equipment was useless for lack of spare parts. Deferred maintenance seriously impaired the Army's combat readiness. Local commanders often had to transfer operations and maintenance funds intended for repairs and utilities for more urgent missions, and illegal transactions made possible by the thin dividing line that existed in practice between procurement activities and overhead operations.[41]

The Army's expenditure in missiles and nuclear technology damaged its efforts to modernize its ground forces to fight limited wars. Andrew Bacevich concluded that:

... taken as a whole the Army's missile program reflects a preoccupation with an excessively narrow concept of war—despite the Service's theoretical appreciation for a broader spectrum of conflict. This enormous investment in missile development shows that in practice the Army assumed that atomic weapons would be used in any future war and would determine its outcome.[42]

While the Army searched for the technology to fight on the nuclear battlefield, its ability to fight a limited or general conventional war deteriorated. And the Army, by trying to become something it was not, contributed to the demise of the public's understanding of war. The Army itself seemed to no longer believe the basic tenet that man was the ultimate weapon on the battlefield.

In the December 1956 issue of *Military Review*, Professor Harry H. Ransom of Harvard University published an article entitled "Scientific Manpower and National Strategy," in which he outlined the dominant perspective of the time: "United States Armed Forces today are engaged in a technological race with the Soviets. The outcome may affect national survival. . . . this contest may be won or lost in the field of research and development, and ultimately in the Nation's classroom."[43] Ransom believed that there were rapidly increasing numbers of scientists, engineers, and technicians in the Soviet Union, and growing shortages of the same in the United States. On 4 October 1957, it seemed all of America accepted Ransom's assessment. The Soviet Union had placed the first man-made object in orbit around the Earth, *Sputnik*, initiating a series of firsts in the space race. *Sputnik* and other Soviet firsts caused fear and a "crisis of confidence" in the United States that intensified the space, technology, and military races, and the transformation in American thinking about the use of force. One witness of the event wrote:

Watching Sputnik traverse the sky was seeing history happen with my own eyes. To me, it was as if Sputnik was the starter's pistol in an exciting new race. I was electrified, delirious, as I witnessed the beginning of the Space Age. . . . The Russian satellite essentially forced the United States to place a new national priority on research science. . . . Politically, Sputnik created a

perception of American weakness, complacency, and a "missile gap," which led to bitter accusations, resignations of key military figures, and contributed to the election of John F. Kennedy, who emphasized the space gap and the role of the Eisenhower-Nixon Administration in creating it. . . . Within weeks America had begun to use Sputnik to reinvent itself.[44]

Soviet successes in space were considered a direct challenge to American leadership in science and technology, and created a sense of urgency. George Kennan noted: "It caused Western alarmists . . . to demand the immediate subordination of all other national interests to the launching of immensely expensive crash programs to outdo the Russians in this competition. It gave effective arguments to the various enthusiasts for nuclear armament in the American military-industrial complex." It caused Americans to invest billions into the advancement of science. It caused the creation of new institutions such as the Advanced Research Projects Agency (ARPA), in 1958, known today as DARPA, the enactment of new legislation such as the National Defense Education Act to provide loans to college students studying science and provide grants to universities. It caused the creation of the National Aeronautics and Space Administration (NASA). And it motivated Kennedy to spend billions of dollars to insure that an American was the first human being to walk on the moon. It also ignited the imaginations of thousands of American youth, creating the dreams of space travel and technological solutions to all human problems. *Sputnik*, thus, intensified the transformation in American thinking about the use of military force, and exerted greater pressure on the Army to become something new and modern.

*   *   *   *   *

In June 1959, Taylor passed the responsibilities of the Army Chief of Staff to General Lyman L. Lemnitzer. It was now his duty to defend the Army by explaining why the nation needed it, and by advocating limited war doctrine in which the Army still played the primary role:

The question [has] existed in the minds of many concerning the usefulness of ground forces in a nuclear war. The military requirements which exist and will continue to exist to meet the military challenge which could confront us, in the form of either general or limited war, and the essential requirement to seize, occupy, and hold ground before victory can be won, eliminate all doubt concerning the indispensable function of the Army as a fundamental element in providing national security. While the Army has been regarded in some circles as at best obsolescent, it is in fact very much in step with the needs of the times.

In reviewing the history of limited wars which have occurred in a wide variety of places and circumstances since 1945, it becomes evident that despite many points of difference in these wars, they have possessed a common distinguishing characteristic. This was combat operations on land—in most cases, sustained combat—for the purpose of securing control of land areas and the people in them. Thus, it is in this field of limited war capability that I believe we must continue to improve in order that we may confront the *entire spectrum* of threats posed by the Communist bloc with the optimum degree of appropriate force to meet the varying situations.[45]

Lemnitzer adopted the Bradley, Ridgway, and Taylor vision of limited war. The best argument for maintaining a large, combat-ready army was not fighting on the nuclear battlefield, a doctrine of war that was ultimately discredited, but recognition of the type of wars the United States was most likely to fight—limited war. General Bruce C. Clarke, Commander of US Army Continental Army Command, writing in 1959, noted:

Despite an initial nuclear monopoly and a continuing superiority in atomic strike power on the part of the United States, Communism managed in the ten year period between 1946 and 1956 to gain control of more than five million square miles of territory inhabited by more than six hundred million people. All of this was accomplished by means short of general war.

Clarke believed the Soviets were expanding their efforts to turn developing states, recently liberated

from European imperialism, into Communist states. He then outlined the type of Army needed:

We need deployed forces in being in critical areas of the world to provide the Soviets with convincing evidence of our determination, to bolster the morale of our allies, and fight in place, or be redeployed rapidly if necessary . . . .

We need to extend the effect of these deployed forces by providing assistance in material and training to indigenous forces . . . .

We need a mobilization base sufficient to maintain a general war posture even while participating in limited wars. This places particular emphasis on the requirements for reserve component forces in a high state of training and properly equipped.

We need a flexible logistic support system with required overseas stockage to permit support of forces deployed anywhere in the world.

We need joint and combined plans and doctrine for limited war. This includes the need for joint training exercises on a frequent basis . . . .

Finally, we need a strategic strike force sufficient to enable rapid reaction by use of measured force where and when required. This force must be capable of accomplishing assigned tasks with or without the use of atomic weapons.[46]

Remarkably, four decades later the Army was still making the same arguments. In 1959 the United States was in the early stages of its commitment to the war in Vietnam. US Army advisors were in the new republic providing military assistance against the communist insurgency. The reality of Vietnam conflicted greatly with the vision of the nuclear battlefield, and since no nuclear weapons had been employed since World War II, the Pentomic doctrine, which was based on technology that did not exist, came into question.

For fifteen years, from 1945 to 1960, Army leaders fought against the vision that airpower had fundamentally changed the nature of war and that henceforth armies were obsolete. With the election of President Kennedy it seemed that the Army had won its case. The policies of the Truman and Eisenhower Administrations did much to damage the ability of the Army to generate combat power and damaged the Army's spirit, and by extension the spirit of the nation.

Americans learned to live with the terror of nuclear holocaust, retained their vision of total, unconditional war, and accepted the Eisenhower thesis that airpower dominated the planet.

The ability of the armed forces of the United States to conduct joint operations actually declined during the Truman and Eisenhower years. The exigencies of total war that forced cooperation in World War II were gone. The limited budgets; the Administration's emphasis on the Air Force; the conclusion drawn by many that the Army, and to a lesser extent the Navy, were obsolete; and the services' efforts to maintain their campaign-winning technologies and doctrines increased the competition between the services. The United States entered the decade of the 1960s with four separate armed forces, each seeking to duplicate the capabilities of the other, each seeking more and broader missions.

The Chaotic Array of Nuclear Technologies

In the late 1950s numerous ideas were considered, tested, and developed. Each service was developing missile technology, nuclear weapons, and nuclear-powered vehicles. The Navy and Air Force were developing several types of strategic nuclear capabilities. The Navy sought strategic nuclear missions for its primary instrument of war, the aircraft carrier, and for the submarine. The Air Force sought land-based continental missile technology, primarily to compete with the Army and keep the missile program in the Air Force; in addition, it continued to develop strategic aircraft to deliver nuclear weapons and a nuclear-powered aircraft. The Army too was developing strategic missile technology. It developed the Redstone and Jupiter missiles for strategic deterrence and for putting satellites in orbit. The Army also advanced the development of tactical nuclear weapons. Congress was asked to fund myriad programs. However, the services, to get the mission, would initially fund programs out of their service budgets. The driving force was more psychological than real. The cost of making Americans feel secure, the cost of making the nation's nuclear threat credible to Americans, its allies, and the world, caused the enormous expenditures, not the real capabilities of the Soviet Union, which were only partially known.

The 1950s might be considered "the wild, wild west of nuclear technology." The array of uses the services envisioned for nuclear energy was astounding. No other people on the planet were as predisposed as Americans to pursue such an enormous array of atomic technologies. The services competed and invested in all sorts of ideas: nuclear airplanes; nuclear trains; nuclear-powered, remote-controlled cargo-carrying devices with vertical takeoff and landing capabilities; atomic mortars and artillery; and numerous other ideas. Yet, in the late 1950s the SU did not have the resources to initiate a first strike against the US that would cause sufficient damage to preclude retaliatory attacks. To clarify these issues and make sense of this chaotic environment, some understanding of the nation's strategic nuclear capabilities at the end of the Eisenhower Administration is necessary.

Throughout the 1950s the strategic bomber was the primary delivery system for nuclear weapons and the main deterrent to nuclear war. The three major technological considerations for a strategic bomber were range, speed, and payload. Other considerations were cost, reliability, and maintenance requirements. New weapon systems required the services to lobby Congress, since that is from where the money came. In 1948, the B–36 Peacemaker, a long-range bomber, with an unrefueled range of 6,500 miles or a combat radius of 3,000 miles, entered service. The aircraft was too slow to outrun enemy fighters, and lacked the range to bomb the Soviet Union from the borders of the United States. But, the B–36 was a compromise. It represented the transition from the internal combustion engine to the jet engine. It was powered by six combustion engines and four jet engines, and was the largest bomber ever to enter service. It was also the Air Force's last propeller-driven bomber. In 1949 SAC understood that the next generation of fighter aircraft would make the B–36 obsolete. In October 1951, the medium-range B–47 Stratojet bomber entered service, and the US Air Force entered the jet age.[47] The B–47 was powered by six General Electric jet engines, and had a relatively short radius of 1,700 miles; hence, it had to be forward-deployed to the UK, and depended on air-to-air refueling. In 1953, a B–47 flew from the US to England in record time: 3,120 miles in five hours and thirty-eight minutes.

By 1955, 1,260 of SAC's 2,800 aircraft were B–47s organized into twenty-three wings. The aircraft remained in front-line service throughout the 1950s and early 1960s.

However, the mainstay of the SAC throughout the Cold War and the successor to the B–36 was the Boeing B–52 Stratofortress. The first production B–52A rolled out of a Boeing plant in Renton, Washington, in March 1954. The aircraft entered operational service the following year.[48] In 2003, in Operation Enduring Freedom, the B–52 was still carrying out combat missions. It has a range of 8,000 miles and air refueling capabilities. It was originally designed to drop nuclear bombs, but was later modified to drop conventional bombs and cruise missiles. In this capacity it was also used extensively in Vietnam. Over its service life the aircraft has been refitted and upgraded numerous times, to adjust to the changing environment and advances in technology.

In the late 1950s, the B–58 supersonic bomber entered service. At a speed of Mach 2, a range of 5,000 miles, air-to-air refueling capability, and a delta-winged design, the B–58 was the most impressive aircraft in SAC. However, the aircraft saw a mere ten years of service. The Air Force experimented with other supersonic aircraft in the late 1950s and early 1960s, but the argument for missile-based deterrence, technical problems with supersonic aircraft, and the high cost of manned aircraft caused the cancellation of these experimental aircraft. Evolving missile technology threatened manned bombers.

In 1956 the SAC argued that there was a "bomber gap," that the Soviet Union had developed and deployed long-range bombers capable of attacking the US and was producing them in large numbers. Based on this assessment, SAC concluded that it needed more B–52s and atomic bombs to provide deterrent and adequate retaliatory force. SAC had little proof to back up its claims. However, to them the prospects were too dangerous to neglect. The lack of intelligence sharing between governmental agencies precluded the decision-makers in Washington from getting a clear picture of the threat. There was a growing concern for the vulnerability of the deterrent force to a first-strike nuclear attack, which would leave the US defenseless.

To get a better picture of the situation in the Soviet Union, in 1954 Eisenhower approved the development of a high-flying, long-range aerial reconnaissance aircraft—the Lockheed U–2, secretly built at "Skunk Works" in Burbank, California. The U–2's capabilities so exceeded that of all other aircraft it was considered invulnerable. It was loaded with data collection devices, cameras that scanned through seven apertures, and monitors, which received radio and radar transmissions. Eisenhower approved overflights of Soviet Union territory in 1956. The CIA operated the U–2. Thus, the intelligence it collected went through the NSC to the President. The Soviets protested the overflights, but the U–2s provided "ninety percent of our hard intelligence information about the Soviet Union." They revealed that there was no "bomber gap." In fact, the Soviet Union had very limited capability to strike the US from its borders in the mid and late 1950s. And, according to Michael Beschloss, a student of the U–2 affair, they "reassured the President that Soviet boasts about a mammoth bomber and missile buildup were no more than boasts. This helped to persuade Eisenhower to hold down defense spending against almost unbearable public pressure."[49] Overflights did not provide continuous images of Soviet alert status or preparations for surprise attacks. Eisenhower had to personally approve each overflight, and fewer than two hundred flights were continually conducted. Eisenhower closely managed the program. He sought to improve relations with the SU and he recognized the overflights were a considerable source of friction. They angered Soviets, who were making rapid strides in missile technology, with emphasis on surface-to-air, antiaircraft missiles.[50]

In the latter half of the 1950s, the TAC acquired tactical nuclear weapons, and aligned itself more closely with the SAC. Given resource constraints—training time and money, and aircraft maintenance—the nuclear mission took precedence over conventional tactical missions. The lessons TAC learned from the experience in Korea were lost. Many came to believe that Korea was an aberration, and that under the Eisenhower doctrine of massive retaliation the most likely war would take place in Europe against the Soviet Union—clearly the most dangerous threat. Conrad Crane concluded that:

Weyland [former commander of FEAF] and his TAC successors struck a Faustian bargain with the atomic Mephistopheles, transforming the organization into a 'junior SAC' concentrating on the delivery of small nuclear weapons. The F–105 Thunderchief, which replaced the F–84 and would bear the brunt of tactical air support in the early years of Vietnam was designed to deliver a nuclear bomb after a high-speed, low altitude approach. It was unsuitable both for air combat and for true close air support.[51]

As a result of emphasis on the nuclear mission the TAC entered the Vietnam War much the way it entered the Korean War—psychologically, technologically, and doctrinally unprepared.

*   *   *   *   *

While the Air Force's strategic bombers were Eisenhower's primary means for deterring war, the Navy too sought part of the nuclear deterrent mission. In the 1950s aircraft carriers and submarines were developed with the capability to deliver nuclear weapons. The submarine would ultimately prove to be the launch platform least vulnerable to a Soviet first strike. The submarine's unique capabilities almost guaranteed the ability of the US to suffer a first strike and still deliver a devastating blow to the SU.

Before World War II came to an end, the Navy had identified a role for the aircraft carrier in the strategic bombing mission. Shortly after the atomic bombs were dropped on Hiroshima and Nagasaki, the Navy sought the ability to employ atomic bombs. On 24 July 1946 acting Secretary of the Navy, John L. Sullivan, wrote the President:

> …the atomic bombing of Hiroshima and Nagasaki and the first Bikini [island] tests have amply demonstrated that the atomic bomb is the most effective single instrument of mass destruction ever developed.
>
> The high mobility of the Naval Carrier Task Force combined with its capacity for making successive and continuous strikes in almost any part of the world make this force a most suitable means of waging atomic bomb warfare. Carrier Forces are particularly effective during the early phases of a war when fixed shore installations may be temporarily immobilized by

planned surprise attack in force. Increased range of carrier aircraft … will further increase the areas accessible to attack by carrier based aircraft. Also, the Carrier Task Force can provide a fleet of fighters to escort its bombers throughout their tactical range and thus insure maximum probability of successful accomplishment of the bombing mission.

Sulivan concluded: "I strongly urge that you authorize the Navy to make preparations for possible delivery of atomic bombs in an emergency in order that the capabilities of the Carrier Task Forces may be utilized to the maximum advantage for national defense."[52] Truman permitted the Navy to initiate the modifications to existing carriers and aircraft to employ the atomic bomb. Because of the size and weight of the plutonium bomb, Fat Man (60-in diameter, 10,000-lb), dropped on Nagasaki, the Navy had few aircraft capable of being modified. Nevertheless, the Navy was determined to present the President and the Secretary of Defense a *fait accompli*. With the capability already proven and operational, the Navy not only secured for itself nuclear weapons and a piece of the strategic mission, but also created the need for new aircraft and carriers to accommodate nuclear weapons.

In March 1949, the Navy had demonstrated the capability to launch an aircraft from a carrier and deliver a simulated atomic bomb over three thousand miles from the carrier. In April 1949, Secretary of Defense Louis Johnson cancelled the Navy's proposed supercarrier, the *USS United States*, causing the "revolt of the admirals." However, a student of naval warfare, Norman Friedman, concluded that: "From 1953 onward nuclear as well as non-nuclear components were deployed at sea, the navy having, in effect, won the battle symbolized by the *United States*."[53] The acquisition of the mission, and acknowledgement and acceptance of that mission by the Department of Defense, Congress, and the executive branch created the conditions for the further development of carriers and aircraft capable of delivering atomic bombs. The Navy suffered a setback with the cancellation of the *United States*, but it won the war for a strategic nuclear capability, and continued to lobby and argue for a new supercarrier.[54]

With the outbreak of the Korean War, Congress was willing to fund a scaled-down version (60,000 ton) of the *USS United States* (80,000 tons). On 1 October 1955, the first *Forrestal* class aircraft carrier was delivered to the Navy. It was one of four that joined the fleet between 1955 and 1959. It incorporated all the design features in use at the end of the twentieth century; however, the size and displacement of these vessels increased almost with each new ship.[55] Since the innovations of the 1950s, most of which were British, the aircraft carrier has changed little.[56] The aircraft carrier became a symbol of American power. Its impressive size and technologies inspired awe. It had a psychological effect on Americans, ultimately becoming the central character in movies and television programs. The aircraft carrier was also a source of deterrent. Its mere presence caused potential enemies to rethink their actions.

In 1954, the Navy launched its first nuclear-powered submarine (SSN), the *Nautilus*. It was followed a year later by the *Seawolf*. In 1960, the first *Polaris* class submarine entered service. The *Polaris* was the first submarine capable of employing submarine-launched ballistic missiles. The *Polaris* submarines revolutionized nuclear strategy. The vastness of the ocean, the stealth characteristics of the submarine, the ability to move throughout the oceans of the world to geographic locations in close proximity to the SU, and the ability to launch while submerged produced a new level of capabilities. The Soviets developed a similar capability. The range of the solid-fuel rockets, the accuracy of the warhead, and the number of warheads (multiple independently targeted re-entry vehicles—MIRVs) that could be placed on a single rocket increased in the following decades, as the size of submarines and the numbers of missiles carried also increased. As a result, the nuclear-powered ballistic missile submarine became the most destructive weapon system ever produced, and its captain the most powerful man on the planet.

Land-based missiles, ICBMs, had the potential to replace the strategic bomber as a delivery system. They were seen as a threat to piloted aircraft. They were less vulnerable than bombers, required less maintenance, and eliminated much of the human factor on the ground and in the air. However, once launched they could not be recalled, and they could not shift targets. Thus, aircraft offered greater flexibility, but more uncertainty. The services pursued both routes of delivery.

At the end of World War II, the Army secured a number of German V–1 pilotless bombs and V–2 guided missiles. The V–1 was essentially a cruise missile, flying within the earth's atmosphere using aerodynamic lift to overcome gravity. The V–2 was the first guided missile, a rocket with a warhead and guidance system. The US pursued the development of both systems. In addition to securing German technology, the Army secured German plans and scientists. The Soviet launch of *Sputnik* on 4 October 1957 created a sense of urgency. In November the Soviets launched *Sputnik II*, which was a larger, heavier satellite. If the Soviets could put an 1,100-pound satellite in orbit, it could hit the US with a nuclear weapon. The ability to put a satellite in orbit did not equate to the ability to destroy America's nuclear capabilities in a first strike. Still, the Soviet achievement had profound implications for reconnaissance, communications, and navigation, and a profound psychological effect on Americans.

The American missile problem was insufficient range. The initial developments in rocket technology produced systems incapable of being launched from the United States and hitting targets in the Soviet Union. Intermediate-range ballistic missiles (IRBM) were developed and forward-deployed to the UK and Alaska. In 1960 the first "true" intercontinental ballistic missile (ICBM) entered service. The Air Force's *Atlas* missile had a range of 8,700 miles. The *Atlas* was launched in the open from fixed launch pads. It took considerable time to mount and prepare the rocket for launch. Time was a key factor in the event of nuclear war. The Air Force activated several squadrons of *Atlas* ICBMs, providing the nation a new deterrent force.

Writing in 1959, Bernard Brodie concluded:

> The criterion of costs being 'within reason' invokes a subjective judgment, but the requirement to reduce the vulnerability of the retaliatory force deserves such priority that if necessary certain other kinds of military expenditures should be sacrificed to it; secondly, there is no question that this country can afford, if it must, a

8.
THE NEW NATIONAL MILITARY COMMAND STRUCTURE, CIVIL-MILITARY RELATIONS, AND THE GROWTH OF MILITARISM, 1945–1975

In the creation of a sound military force for the armed defense of the nation, there is no place for free competitive enterprise among the separate services in the business of fighting a war. Security is a cooperative venture; it is not a competitive race. To forewarn aggressors and to construct effective military might, we are in need of partnership, not partisanship; concern for the safety of this nation, not the survival of our arms.[1]

—General Omar N. Bradley, US Army, 1949

However desirable the American system of civilian control of the military, it was a mistake to permit appointive civilian officials lacking military experience and knowledge of military history and oblivious to the lessons of Communist diplomatic machinations to wield undue influence in the decision-making process. Over-all control of the military is one thing; shackling professional military men with restrictions in professional matters imposed by civilians who lack military understanding is another.[2]

—General William C. Westmoreland, US Army, 1976

The National Security Act of 1947 set up the most dysfunctional, worst organizational approach to military affairs one can possibly imagine. In a near-perfect example of the Law of Unintended Consequences, it created a situation in which the biggest rival of any US armed service is not a foreign adversary but one of its sister services.[3]

—General Anthony C. Zinni, USMC, 2000

There are many organizations and systems around the world for the command and control of armed forces, ranging from the World War II British committee system, under which power at the highest levels was diffused, to the German General Staff system, under which power was more centralized and concentrated. The development of the German General Staff—possibly the most proficient, professional organization for the conduct of war ever developed—was an outgrowth of Prussia/Germany's geographic circumstances, no natural defensible borders; the prevalence of significant, strong states with contiguous borders; the relatively impoverished state of Prussia; the greed and competitiveness of the European monarchy system; the growth of the standing army; the experience of the suffering and devastation caused by the Thirty Years' War; and the perennial nature of war in Europe.[4] The continued existence of the Prussian state was a function of the continuous efficiency, professionalism, and effectiveness of the Prussian Army. The state existed because the Army existed.[5]

The organization and system for the command and control of armed forces instituted by a nation-state is in part a function of its historical experiences, culture, military traditions, geographic circumstances, political and social systems, myths and legends, and the values, ethics, and beliefs of its people, who, in the age of the modern nation-state, support and maintain the armed forces. No system of command, control, and planning for the maintenance and employment of armed forces is perfect—maximizing combat effectiveness and achieving synergy at minimum cost to the people. As in all aspects of life, tradeoffs and compromises have to be made. Maximizing combat effectiveness was not a primary objective for some nation-states, and was a secondary or tertiary consideration for others that were primarily concerned with priorities such as civilian control of the military, and the non-interference of the military in the lives of the people. Of course, military ineffectiveness caused by the system of command and control is a luxury of nation-states that are not directly threatened by other significant powers.

Prior to World War II, the US enjoyed this luxury. Protected by two great oceans and a world order maintained by the British and French Empires, the United States possessed a level of security the German and Russian-speaking people have never enjoyed. And that luxury made possible systems of military command and control that could survive with extraordinary waste, diffused power, neglect, and military incompetence. The survival of the United States, for most of its history, was *not* tied to the survival and capabilities of its armed forces. Thus, the American cultural norm was to institute systems for command, control, and administration that intentionally failed to maximize military effectiveness. For almost two hundred years maximizing combat effectiveness was not an objective of the United States; in fact, it was un-American to do so. While cultural change can take place rapidly under the conditions of war or some other traumatic event, as a rule, cultural change takes place slowly. Changes in the American system for administrating and deploying the armed forces have taken place at various periods throughout the nation's history; however, more fundamental changes in the system have taken considerable time. Such was the case in the post-war period.

For half a century, observant senior military and civilian leaders have argued that the national command structure for the maintenance and employment of the armed forces of the United States instituted in the early days of the Cold War damaged the ability of the United States to fight war and, as a consequence,

impeded and/or precluded it from achieving political objectives. It has also been argued that the national command structure institutionalized militarism, wasted billions of dollars, and more importantly wasted lives. The National Security Act of 1947 and the Amendments of 1949, which created the US Air Force, the Department of Defense, the Secretary of Defense, the Joint Chiefs of Staff, the Chairman of the JCS, the National Security Council, the Central Intelligence Agency, and the system of competing services with overlapping responsibilities and capabilities, decisively destroyed the ability of the services to cooperate and produce comprehensive policies, strategies, and joint doctrines. As General Zinni noted, the legislation created a persistent environment in which the biggest rivals of a service is its sister services. The inability of the armed forces to develop joint doctrine, unified chains of command, and coherent strategy facilitated defeat in Vietnam, and ultimately the destruction of the citizen-soldier Army.[6] The inability of the American people to accept artificial limited war was, in large part, a function of the inability of the armed forces to effectively fight it.

The tests of any system of command are fourfold: First and foremost, does it achieve its political objectives, does it win wars? Second, does it maximize the capabilities of the forces employed? Third, does it preserve the fighting forces—physically, emotionally, and psychologically? And fourth, can the nation-state maintain it, politically, economically, and socially? Does it impose an unsustainable burden on the people? By these standards the National Security Act of 1947 was an abysmal failure. This fact was evident before and during the Korean War; however, the system as executed during the Vietnam War was a national disgrace, eroding the potential combat power of all the services. The 1947 Act survived because the services, the administrations, the Congress, the American people, and the defense industry wanted it. In a limited war, where the homeland was not threatened, a nation-state as powerful as the US did not have to rationalize its resources. War could be carried out with gross inefficiencies because of the great wealth and power of the US. However, watching the poor performance of the military and the government in Korea and Vietnam and in other operations damaged the credibility of the services, eroding American faith in their armed forces and government. The result was that the American people said "yes" to the production of military hardware, research and development, and even the incredible waste that parts of the system produced; but "no" to their sons and daughters, "no" to conscription.

The National Military Command Structure

In 1947, 1949, 1953, 1958, and 1986 the US Congress passed legislation to reorganize the national defense organization, and in 2003 additional changes were recommended. The body of written material on this topic is extensive and no effort is made here to reproduce it. However, the major arguments for and against and the objectives of these Acts are delineated and discussed.

The impetus for the unification of the services grew out of the experiences of World War II. The inability of the United States to present a united front to its British ally in strategic planning; the inter-service disputes over operations, doctrine, resources, and command; and the desire of the President to have the armed forces speak with one voice when recommending strategic options created the driving forces for the unification of the services at the highest level. In the years that followed, the high cost of new technologies and the cost of maintaining four separate services became additional incentives for unification. And, in the years following the war in Vietnam, defeat became another motivator. These motivating factors, however, never overcame vested interests.

Truman recognized that unification was a long-term process, and that the process required much more than changes in organizational structures: "It will require new viewpoints, new doctrine, and new habits of thinking throughout the departmental structure." Significant change in the cultures of the services was required to produce "new habits of thinking," and long after Truman's death this objective was still unrealized. Truman understood too that there was considerable opposition from some senior officers, particularly the admirals, and that the undertaking would present the "greatest difficulty." Still, he concluded that when the task was completed, "we shall have a military establishment far better adapted to carrying out its share of our national program for achieving peace and security." Truman advanced nine recommendations (also see Truman's letter in appendix):

1. We should have integrated strategic plans and a unified military program and budget.
2. We should realize the economies that can be achieved through unified control of supply and service functions.
3. We should adopt the organizational structure best suited to fostering coordination between the military and the remainder of the Government.
4. We should provide the strongest means for civilian control of the military.
5. We should organize to provide parity for air power.
6. We should establish the most advantageous framework for a unified system of training for combined operations of land, sea, and air.
7. We should allocate systematically our limited resources for scientific research.
8. We should have unity of command in outlying bases.
9. We should have consistent and equitable personnel policies.[7]

The National Security Act of 1947 accomplished, affirmatively, only two of these recommendations, the separation of the Air Force from the Army and the establishment of unified commands. Other recommendations were partially implemented. In subsequent legislation the civilian control of the military was strengthened by increasing the power of the Secretary of Defense. With the 1958 legislation almost all deployed forces were placed under unified commands, and operational control was removed from the service chiefs. The Secretary of Defense issued orders to the unified and specified commands through the Chairman of the Joint Chiefs of Staff, who was not officially in the chain of command. Other recommendations were accomplished a decade later under McNamara, specifically item numbers 1, 2, and 7—the consolidation of the budgeting process, and the creation of a semi-unified supply system, and the consolidation of research and development programs. Since World War II, the defense agencies have been moving incrementally toward greater centralization. The objective is centralized planning and decision-making, while maintaining the initiative for field commanders in the operational and tactical environments— decentralized execution. However, centralization is not unification. The services never developed the kind of joint thinking and joint culture of which Truman spoke. At the end of the twentieth century, the two biggest defects remained: the armed forces of the United States rarely trained together; and second, there was no joint culture or mutual comprehension and acceptance of the cultures of the separate services. The services could fight on the same battlefield, but not as cohesive combat teams with joint doctrine capable of achieved synergy. And, as late as 1983, during the invasion of Grenada, dumb things, such as incompatible radio systems, hindered the ability of the Army and Navy to communicate. Since World War II, the United States has fought enemies vastly inferior in every way that mattered. These nation-states did not directly threaten the lives of Americans. As a consequence, with the exception of the Vietnam experience, there has been little incentive to change.

*   *   *   *   *

On 9 April 1946, the Senate Military Affairs Committee introduced S. 2044, which followed closely the President's recommendations. A month later, 9 May, the Chairman of the Senate and House Naval Affairs Committee promulgated a letter that outlined the Navy's objections to the bill.[8] The authors of this document appealed to traditional American fears of the Army taking over the country; of violating the constitutional divisions of powers; of enacting undemocratic practices; and of creating an all-powerful, German-type chief of staff. The major concerns, however, were more basic, and represent the same thinking that precluded the armed forces from operating with maximum combat effectiveness in Vietnam and other wars. The larger concerns were items (A) "the bill would concentrate too much power in the hands of too few;" (F) "the equitable distribution" of the military budget, and (G) "representation in the Cabinet." The Navy was primarily concerned about its autonomy, believing that the newly independent Air Force would dominate a unified command structure, and that it and the Marine Corps would suffer as a result. The Navy was also concerned about access to the President and Congress, and expanding the missions and roles of Navy aviation and the Marine Corps.

When this letter was prepared, "the equitable distribution of funds" was a major concern. The Air Force and Navy were engaging in a bitter feud and the Navy concluded that Air Force doctrine and technology were consuming the defense budget. The Air Force's share of the budget was damaging the Navy's efforts to construct a supercarrier. The Soviet Union, which would be the nation's principal enemy for the next forty years, had no major navy for the US Navy to fight. The Air Force thus argued the big expensive aircraft carriers were unnecessary, and argued for increases in the number of air groups. The Navy too recognized that control of the sea was no longer a mission that justified the expenditure of vast resources to build aircraft carriers. The Navy needed a new mission. It needed part of the strategic bombing mission. It needed atomic weapons—the technology in vogue. To deliver these atomic weapons it needed heavier, jet aircraft. World War II carriers had limited capabilities to accommodate such aircraft. Hence, the Navy needed a supercarrier, and new aircraft. The Navy viewed this as a fight for the life of naval aviation.

The Marine Corps too concluded that Truman, with the help of the Army, was planning to eliminate the Marine Corps along with the Navy. Allan Millett wrote:

> Determined to save the FMF as a team of divisions and aircraft wings, Vandergrift quickly developed the Corps position of unification.... The air-ground FMF must be preserved as the amphibious element of the Navy's "naval campaign" fleet organization; the Marine Corps must be recognized as an independent service; and defense decision-making must not be centralized under either a single, powerful civilian secretary or a single chief of all the armed forces. Instead the 1945 pattern should continue, for the "greatest advantage of the current organization from a national point of view is that it is responsive to the control of Congress and the people...." Vandergrift urged the Congress not to eliminate the positive benefits of interservice rivalry in designing military techniques.[9]

Vandergrift gave a speech before Congress full of emotion, indignation, and anger that went against the President's proposal—something done primarily when a service felt threatened. He concluded with:

> The Marine Corps, then, believes that it has earned this right—to have its future decided by the legislative body which created it—nothing more. Sentiment is not valid consideration in determining questions of national security. We have pride in ourselves and in our past but we do not rest our case on any presumed gratitude owing us from the nation. The bended knee is not a tradition of our Corps. If the Marine as a fighting man has not made a case for himself after 170 years of service, he must go. But I think you will agree with me he has earned the right to depart with dignity and honor, not by subjugation to the status of uselessness and servility planned for him by the War Department [the Army].[10]

The Secretary of the Navy, and the first Secretary of Defense (September 1947 to April 1949), James Vincent Forrestal, with the political support and lobbying of the Navy and Marine Corps, also opposed the unification plan advanced by the President and the Army, believing that it concentrated too much power into too few hands. Forrestal accepted the Navy's horizontal system of command, which depended, in part, on voluntary coordination and cooperation.[11] On 16 April, a day after listening to General Eisenhower testify in support of the legislation before Congress, Forrestal outlined his thinking in his diary:

> . . . I was somewhat shaken by the recurring evidence of the Army's intransigence in regard to the chain-of-command concept (when, as a matter of fact, during the war they had not been able to issue a single order to MacArthur—and they couldn't now). I said my whole attitude in the bill was that unless the civilians who were named to the various jobs outlined would work together in complete harmony, the operation of the bill would be a mess. And by the same token, I said that unless the Services were led by officers who were determined to make the thing go, there would be the same chance of a mess. I said the difficulty I had all along was the Army's genial

assumption that by writing a chart and drafting a law you could get discipline, when as a matter of fact I had seen very little of it in the Army itself. Cooperation and harmony take constant effort and work as well as imagination to foresee the things that will create friction.[12]

Because officers are formed and permanently shaped by the cultures of their service, it was impossible to produce the type of officers Forrestal believed were necessary. And, because civilian leaders rapidly adopt the culture, perspective, norms, and exigencies of the service they represent, they too were incapable of the kind of job performance that maximized effectiveness and produced synergies. Forrestal himself was an example of civilian leadership adopting the culture of the service they represented. During World War II, Forrestal frequently appeared in the field wearing navy khaki uniforms.[13] In all matters, particularly budgetary, Forrestal was a "Navy man."[14] This outlook made him incapable of representing the other services as Secretary of Defense. Forrestal's willingness to advance the Navy's position ultimately caused the President to conclude he was disloyal and to remove him. Nevertheless, Forrestal, the Navy, Marine Corps, and other legislators were able to shape the bill to insure that the United States retained a system of competing services. All the services wanted to survive to preserve their technologies, doctrines, missions, and traditions. All the services were proud organizations with distinguished histories. And all the services regularly placed the needs of their institution above the needs of the country as defined by the President. This was a form of militarism.

World War II and the Cold War moved the services into the forefront of American institutions. They had greater responsibilities than ever before, but resources were still limited. All the services demanded more resources. All the services sought and fought for a larger role in national defense, which meant more resources. In the process they managed to alienate and create enemies of one another. Each could argue that their technologies and doctrines were in the best interest of the country and the most efficacious for achieving political objectives. And not even war could overcome the pull of service loyalty. Not even defeat in war could change the services. In matters where service interests conflicted with national interests, the services always won.

Exactly what did the National Security Act of 1947 achieve? The 1947 Act established the National Military Establishment (NME) under the Secretary of Defense. The NME consisted of the Departments of Army, Navy, and Air Force, completing the divorce between the Army and the Army Air Force. The Marine Corps became a separate service within the Navy Department, and retained all its World War II duties. Millett noted: "When the National Security Act of 1947 finally passed both houses and went to Truman for signature, the Marine Corps believed it had won the ultimate legislative sanction for its role as both amphibious assault specialist and force in readiness."[15] The NME was not an executive department. The services retained command authority over their forces and budget authority. The Secretary of Defense was "the principal assistant to the President in all matters relating to the national security." He was to supervise the budget process and provide direction; however, he had little control over the services. The service secretaries still exercised considerable authority as cabinet members. The Secretary of Defense created another layer of civilian authority between the President and his senior military advisors, and with the addition of the Air Force Chief of Staff, and later the Commandant of the Marine Corps, the advice the President and Secretary of Defense received was further diluted, creating greater opportunities for friction. The new status of the Marine Corps increased the clout of the Navy. No President since the passage of the Act has had the quality of advice, relationship, and trust enjoyed by Roosevelt, Marshall, and King in World War II. And no service chief since has had the access to the President that King and Marshall enjoyed.

The JCS provisionally established during World War II was made a permanent part of the NME. It consisted of the Chiefs of Staff of the Army and Air Force and the Chief of Naval Operations. Its duties were to prepare strategic plans, to provide strategic direction to the military forces, to establish unified commands in strategic areas, to formulate policies for joint training, to act as principal military advisors to the President and Secretary of Defense, and to carry out the duties directed by the President and the Secretary of Defense. The National Security Act also provided for Joint Staff, made up of approximately equal numbers of officers from all the services, and the National Security Council. The purpose of the NSC was "to advise the President with respect to the integration of domestic, foreign, and military policies relating to the national security so as to enable the military services and the other departments and agencies of the Government to cooperate more effectively in matters involving the national security."[16] The NSC under the guidance of the President developed and promulgated strategic military doctrine and national strategy. The NSC consisted of the President, Secretary of State, Secretary of Defense, the service secretaries, and other advisors appointed by the President. The Act also created the Central Intelligence Agency (CIA) and established a legal basis for unified and specified commands.

In less than a year of service as Secretary of Defense, Forrestal was dissatisfied. The 1947 legislation had failed to produce the quality of unified decision-making he expected from the JCS, particularly in the budgeting process. Thus, Forrestal had the Chiefs conference at the Key West Naval Base, Florida, in March 1948 for a "free and frank discussion" on the roles and missions of the services. The conference produced the Key West Agreement; however, it did not produce a corporate body capable of acting responsibly in a joint capacity, and it added nothing to the status quo. Forrestal departed the conference with the following understanding:

1. For planning purposes, Marine Corps to be limited to four divisions *with the inclusion of a sentence in the final document that the Marines are not to create another land army.*

2. Air Force recognizes right of the Navy to proceed with the development of weapons the Navy considers essential to its function *but with the proviso that the Navy will not develop a separate strategic air force, this function being reserved to the Air Force.* However, the Navy in the carrying out of its function is to have the right to attack inland targets—for example, to reduce and neutralize airfields from which enemy aircraft may be sortying to attack the Fleet.

3. Air Force recognizes the right and need for the Navy to participate in an all-out air campaign.[17]

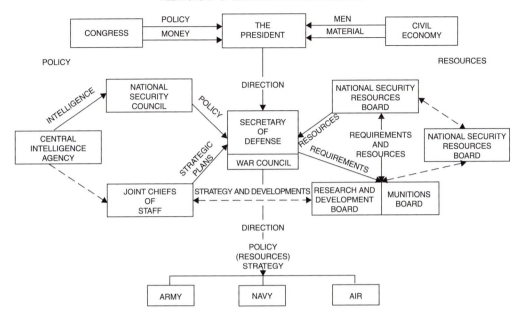

Fig 8.1 This 1947 chart shows the relationship of major elements of the National Security—resources, civil economy, foreign policy, strategy, and military effort. It charts functional, rather than organizational, relationships.

Forrestal's report to the President added, "Navy not to be denied use of A-bomb;" and "Navy to proceed with the development of 80,000 ton carrier and development of HA [high altitude] aircraft to carry heavy missiles there from . . ."[18] The Air Force and Army had not agreed to this. Bradley and Blair wrote: "Contrary to his later assertions, Forrestal did not ask the JCS to 'vote' for or against the Navy's supercarrier. . . . Had we been asked to vote in a formal sense, Spaatz, Van [Hoyt S. Vandenberg, Spaatz's designated replacement] and I would probably have spoken against it. . . ."[19] Forrestal was dishonest. In his drive to achieve Navy objectives he was willing to use subterfuge.

The services could have organized based on missions, or based on domain—air, sea, land, and littoral regions. As it was, they organized based on both. The Navy and Marine Corps organized based on missions. They were, therefore, better able to focus on the threat, and refocus to meet new threats. They were more adaptable than the Army and the Air Force. The Navy and Marine Corps were also more adaptable because they worked together, and maintained the capability to operate with organic force in every domain, air, sea, and ground. The Army and Air Force

organized based on domain, and both were very much stuck on their World War II missions, all-out ground offensive and strategic bombing, respectively. The Air Force was determined that the Army possess no combat aircraft, no major transport aircraft, and a very limited number of aircraft for reconnaissance and other miscellaneous functions. The Air Force was of the opinion that ground forces were, or were in the process of, becoming auxiliary forces. Hence, the Air Force did not seek an organic ground force capability. Everything could be done from the air. The Air Force also argued against funding the Navy's supercarrier, concluding that in the nuclear age it was a highly vulnerable platform and hence a poor use of limited resources. The Air Force also recognized that with this carrier the Navy planned to attain part of the Air Force's strategic air mission. While the dispute between the Air Force and Navy was the most visible and hotly debated, the Army was the biggest loser in 1947 and 1948.

The Army and Air Force would have performed significantly better in the latter half of the twentieth century had they organized based on missions. The Army should have retained the tactical air forces, those air resources that provided close air support, and the Army also should have retained their air transport resources, not only for its airborne divisions, but also to rapidly deploy significant forces to the battlefield. Both missions—close air support and strategic mobility for the Army—were low on the Air Force's list of priorities. At a time when Ridgway, Taylor, and Gavin were trying to build an Army that could be deployed and sustained by air, a force of three to five divisions, the Air Force was arguing there was a strategic bomber gap and that more B–52s and B–47s were needed, and Eisenhower was enforcing fiscally conservative budget policies. When the Army lost its ability to strategically deploy to battlefields around the world, it created the conditions for its own obsolescence and possible demise. When World War II started, the Army had fewer than 200,000 men, but owned transport ships and aircraft. During the war it acquired landing craft and developed schools to train soldiers in small boat operations for amphibious landings. Later in the war the ships and landing craft were transferred to the Navy. The Army was the only service that could not get itself to the battlefield, and because each service was engaged in competition to prove the combat effectiveness of its major weapon systems, to demonstrate to the American people and political leaders their superiority over the other services, the Army was at a major disadvantage. This was no small matter. It was not simply a selfish service concern. It was (is) a matter of national security, as all subsequent wars have proven.

South Korea would not exist today had it not been for the close proximity of four Army divisions stationed in Japan. *It literally would not exist today.* The ability to respond rapidly with substantial ground forces—force far beyond the capabilities of the Marine Corps—is all that saved South Korea. Over the decades the inability of the United States to rapidly put major ground forces into foreign lands has precluded the achievement of political objectives, and has required efforts above and beyond what would have been necessary had the US possessed this capability. The Army has made this same argument every decade of the latter half of the twentieth century. In 1956 a student at the Army War College wrote:

air transport is the key to both the tactical and strategic mobility of the Army. It is difficult for

the Army to obtain aircraft; as long as the Army is dependent on the priority whims of other services for the means to make it effective it will be without the needed effectiveness. Lack of adequate funds and unrealistic interservice priorities are hamstringing the Army.[20]

This problem has never been fixed.[21]

The Army's air defense mission functionally belonged to the Air Force. A brief study of the "Battle of Britain" reveals the importance of an integrated system. In 1940 following "the Fall of France," Britain fought an air campaign that saved Britain from a German invasion. The British developed an integrated system that included fighter command, radar systems, command and control headquarters, and the antiaircraft command. This organization greatly multiplied the combat power of various components. The US Air Force is responsible for the defense of North America, controlling the early warning system of radar and communication installations, and the fighter aircraft. The strategic air defense systems constructed by the Army around America's major cities and the operational air defense systems of the Air Force would have functioned more effectively as part of an integrated air defense system. The US strategic air defense system was never tested in war. Nevertheless, organizations based on mission produced the integration of resources from each domain, creating greater adaptability and cohesion, and, thus, superior operational performance.

The Marine Corps emerged from World War II and Korea with an outstanding record of service to the nation. Its demonstrated capabilities secured and insulated its position in the national defense structure. The Marine Corps developed and cultivated a mystique, a way of war, and a distinct mission that appealed to the American people and Congress. Victor H. Krulak explained why the American people maintained and supported the Marine Corps:

Essentially, as a result of the unfailing conduct of our Corps over the years, they [the American people] believe three things about the Marines. First, they believe that when trouble comes to our country there will be Marines—somewhere—doing something useful about it, and doing it *at once.* . . . Second, they believe that when the Marines go to war they invariably turn in a performance that is dramatically and decisively successful—not most of the time, but always.... The third thing they believe about the Marines is that our Corps is downright good for the manhood of our country....[22]

The Marine Corps became the nation's rapid reaction force—"first to fight." It developed the capability to respond to emergencies in the various corners of the world, considerably faster than the Army, which also meant it was more active and in the public eye. The Marine Corps created, cultivated, and marketed an image of boldness, aggressiveness, readiness, and eagerness to fight. The Marine Corps carved out a unique place for itself in national defense, but also formed a second land army that endeavored to insure that it always looked better than the primary land force. While maintaining its focus on amphibious operations, Marines fought in independent units in large-scale protracted ground combat—in Korea, Vietnam, and the Persian Gulf. Still, at some level it was necessary for the Marine Corps and Army to cooperate. The Marine Corps used equipment developed primarily by the Army, artillery, tanks, etc; trained at Army installations; and fought in campaigns alongside the Army; hence, some coordination and agreement on doctrine was necessary.

The small size and outstanding reputation of the Marine Corps made it the most stable, institutionally secure, politically untouchable service. In the latter half of the twentieth century the influence and roles of the Marines in national defense increased with each decade. A 1952 Amendment to the NSA gave the Commandant of the Marine Corps (CMC) co-equal status on the JCS on Marine Corps issues. In 1978, the CMC became a full member of the JCS. And, in 2005, General Peter Pace became the first Marine Chairman of the JCS, the nation's most senior military leader.

The Key West Agreement did not improve the situation of the Secretary of Defense, who lacked the power and the staff to impose decisions on the services. During Forrestal's tenure as Secretary of Defense, he negotiated with the services to no one's satisfaction. Truman gave him a budget ceiling and it was his responsibility to divide it between the services. In his final days as Secretary of Defense, and the final days of his life, Forrestal, in testimony before the Senate Armed Services Committee, concluded:

> After having viewed the problem at close range for the past 18 months, I must admit to you quite frankly that my position on the question has changed. I am now convinced that there are adequate checks and balances inherent in our governmental structure to prevent misuse of the broad authority which I feel must be vested in the Secretary of Defense.[23]

*   *   *   *   *

In 1949, the National Security Act was amended and the NME became the Department of Defense (DOD). The amendment significantly increased the powers of the Secretary of Defense. DOD was an executive department. The services were placed under its authority and control. The three military department Secretaries were reduced from cabinet rank and removed from the NSC. The individual services were demoted in power and status. The Secretary of Defense was given the "direction, authority, and control" of the Department of Defense. He was given greater power over the budgetary process. Lines of authority were clarified. And he was given a larger staff. Still, the amendment provided for the separate administration and operation of the three military departments under the service secretaries. And the Secretary of Defense was not given operational control of combat forces. The chain of command for units in the field still went through the service chiefs; thus, during the Korean War MacArthur's unified command was administered through the Department of the Army. Nevertheless, Forrestal's replacement, Louis Johnson, concluded: "Eighty per cent of the problems that had beset unification immediately disappeared when the President signed the bill increasing the authority and the responsibility of the Secretary of Defense for unification."[24] He was too optimistic, as subsequent legislation demonstrates.

A new position of comptroller was authorized. The individual occupying this position was designated one of the Assistant Secretaries of Defense. He was to be responsible for supervising the preparation of the DOD budget. He was to work with the comptrollers from each of the departments. The Secretary of Defense had final approval of the budget. The objectives of the amendment were "to provide for their [the services] authoritative coordination and unified direction under civilian control of the Secretary of Defense but not to merge them . . . ."[25] These were the stated objectives. The unstated, and possibly the main objective, was to force compliance from the services in budget and other matters. Louis Johnson, shortly after the signing of the 1949 Amendment, wrote:

> The cost of our Armed Forces comes high; too high in fact. We are determined to cut it at the rate of about a billion dollars this year. . . . We are going to make the savings by eliminating waste and duplication. We have declared war on these two enemies of efficiency and we will wage it with vigor and determination. . . . When we come before the Congress today our budget represents a coordinated, integrated estimate of the needs of the Department of Defense as a whole. There is not enough taxpayers' money available to give each of the three services everything that each of them feels it may need. . . . We are evaluating the weapons and the systems of attack and defense of the three services and bringing them into a cohesive whole. . . . We are combining facilities and services whenever possible and are taking advantage of specialized abilities and techniques developed in the respective services.[26]

Johnson's optimism was not justified. Congress ultimately made many of the decisions he claimed. However, closing or consolidating facilities and services was extremely difficult, because it meant a loss for a given state. The cancellation of the Navy's "supercarrier" and the Korean War created crisis situations that caused the services and nation to revert to traditional relationships, and behaviors. The Korean War destroyed Johnson's frugal budget, and ultimately his career. The first two Secretaries of Defense were *not* successful.

The amendment also created the position of Chairman of the Joint Chiefs of Staff, who would serve as the most senior officer in the armed forces. Eisenhower was offered the position, but rejected it.

General Omar N. Bradley was the first to officially serve in this position. Bradley was reluctant to accept the position, and wrote in his diary: "[I] wanted no part of the job." Bradley later noted:

> My reasons for demurring were the same as those I had advanced for declining Forrestal's invitation to become his principal military adviser. There was still much to be done to salvage the Army. Moreover, I did not relish the prospect of winding up my professional service moderating bitter debates between the Air Force and Navy.[27]

Eventually, Bradley was persuaded to take the job, and, on 16 August 1949, he was sworn in. Bradley explained his decision:

> I changed my mind. . . . The main reason for my change of heart was my deep concern about the state of the military establishment. Owing to the cancellation of the supercarrier, there was a vicious mutiny afoot in the Navy. With his crazy bull-in-china shop approach, Johnson was in no way fit to deal with it. . . . A Navy mutiny could conceivably tear apart the Department of Defense, possibly tempting the Kremlin to capitalize on our military disarray. A firm but fair JCS Chairman . . . might be the moderating force that could prevent a crippling brawl.[28]

Bradley was incapable of serving as an "honest broker." He had accepted the Air Force's vision of the future of warfare based on strategic bombers and nuclear weapons. He, thus, could not represent the Navy's interests. The outbreak of the Korean War challenged the major tenets of Bradley's strategic thinking, and all of those who believed the next war would be fought with airpower and nuclear weapons.

The uniforms the service chiefs wore tended to limit their vision of war to the campaign-winning operational doctrines of their service. And their dual role as chief advocate for their service and advisor to the Secretary of Defense and President on matters of strategic planning, conflicted. The role of service chief generally won the struggle. The powers of the chairman were insufficient to produce an integrated, uniformly accepted strategic plan. The chairman was to preside over the JCS, provide the agenda for meetings, inform the Secretary of Defense, and "when appropriate" the President of "those issues upon which agreement among the Joint Chiefs of Staff has not been reached . . . ." The chairman, however, had no vote. He was to:

> . . . provide for the effective strategic direction of the armed forces and for their operation under unified control and for their integration into an efficient team of land, naval, and air forces but not to establish a single Chief of Staff over the armed forces nor an armed forces general staff.[29]

Congress gave the chairman responsibilities, but little authority.

In 1953 the Act was again amended to clarify and further define lines of authority and control, to improve the machinery for strategic planning for national security, and to realize greater efficiencies and reduce waste. The powers and authority of the Secretary of Defense and the Chairman of the JCS were expanded. Various defense organizations that operated independently of the Secretary of Defense were either eliminated or placed under his authority. And the Joint Staff was placed under the control of the Chairman of the JCS, as opposed to the JCS. The amendment also gave the chairman a vote.

In 1958, the Department of Defense Reorganization Act was passed. The objective of this legislation was to provide a comprehensive program for the future security of the United States:

> to provide for the establishment of integrated policies and procedures for the departments, agencies, and functions of the Government relating to the national security; to provide that each military department shall be separately organized under its own Secretary and shall function under the direction, authority, and control of the Secretary of Defense; to provide for their unified direction under civilian control of the Secretary of Defense but not to merge these departments or services; *to provide for the establishment of unified and specified combatant commands, and a clear and direct line of command to such commands*; to eliminate unnecessary duplication in the Department of Defense, and particularly in the field of research and engineering by vesting

overall direction and control in the Secretary of Defense; to provide more effective, efficient, and economical administration in the Department of Defense; *to provide for the unified strategic direction of the combatant forces, for their operation under unified command, and for their integration into an efficient team of land, naval, and air forces* but not to establish a single Chief of Staff over the armed forces nor an overall armed forces general staff.[30]

The 1958 legislation again strengthened the direction, authority, and control of the Secretary of Defense. The military departments were removed as executive agents. Chief of Naval Operations was, in fact, no longer the chief of naval operations. The Departments of Army, Navy, and Air Force lost control of their major field commands, such as the Strategic Air Command, a specified command, and European Command, a unified combatant command. Unified and specified commands were also given greater command authority. They were responsible for the performance of military missions assigned them by the Secretary of Defense with the approval of the President. They were responsible for determining the force structure of their combatant commands, Army, Navy, Air Force, and Marines. They commanded all the forces in their assigned area of operation, and were responsible to the President through the Secretary of Defense for the performance of military missions. They also acquired political responsibilities. They were required to meet and know the political leaders in their region, and understand the political and military situations that might cause war, or were of strategic importance to the United States. They, thus, had to coordinate with the Department of State and CIA.

The chain of command went from the President to the Secretary of Defense to the unified and specified commands. The Joint Staff assisted the Secretary of Defense in exercising direction over unified commands. The departments could not transfer forces assigned to unified and specified commands. Only the Secretary of Defense could assign or transfer major units assigned to these commands. The service departments had been again demoted. However, they retained responsibility for the individual training and administration of their personnel assigned to unified and specified commands.

This legislation was also intended to merge and control the research and development competitions, primarily between the Army and Air Force. The Army's Jupiter and the Air Force's Thor intermediate-range missile programs were obvious examples of unnecessary duplication. The duplication of effort and the failure to share research was costing the nation billions of dollars.

The power of the Secretary of Defense increased with every legislative act regarding the national command structure. The most senior advisor to the President on military matters and war was a civilian. The service chiefs administered and trained their services. The Joint Chiefs of Staff developed military strategy under the leadership of the Chairman of the JCS, with the approval of the Secretary of Defense; however, because of the service hats they wore, they were rarely capable of achieving consensus. The 1958 legislation was a significant evolution in the command structure of the armed forces. This was the organizational structure that unsuccessfully fought the Vietnam War. From 1958 to 1986 the organization of the Department of Defense remained unchanged by the Congress. But, this was not the end of the story. In the 1980s further amendments were debated and enacted, and again the Navy and Marine Corps were the biggest opponents to the legislation.

Given the new roles and missions of the armed forces and the United States, given the Cold War environment and the enormous expenditure of national resources, no observer can argue that the Congress rationalized the system for the organization and control of the national defense to meet the new threats. Congress was as much a part of the problem as the services. The waste, duplications, conflicts of interests, and the inability of the Pentagon to produce a coherent national military strategy, joint doctrine, or unified command system damaged the nation's ability to fight. The chiefs were smarter than that. However, service culture pulled them inexorably toward a position that placed the needs of their service above the needs of the war. And congressmen with vested interests in a particular service accepted these gross inefficiencies. The structure and outlook that Truman sought was never achieved.

By statute the principal military advisors to the President, the National Security Council, and the Secretary of Defense are the Joint Chiefs of Staff, consisting of the Chairman—who outranks all other officers of the Armed Forces while holding office—the Chief of Staff of the Army; the Chief of Naval Operations; the Chief of Staff of the Air Force; and the Commandant of the Marine Corps. The Joint Chiefs of Staff, subject to the authority and direction of the President and the Secretary of Defense, are assigned (among others) the functions of:

(1) preparing strategic plans and providing for the strategic direction of the Armed forces;
(2) establishing unified commands in strategic areas.

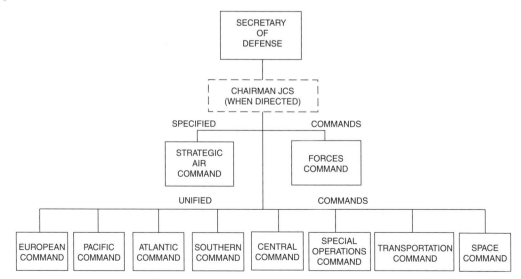

Fig 8.2 Chart of the Joint Chiefs of Staff.

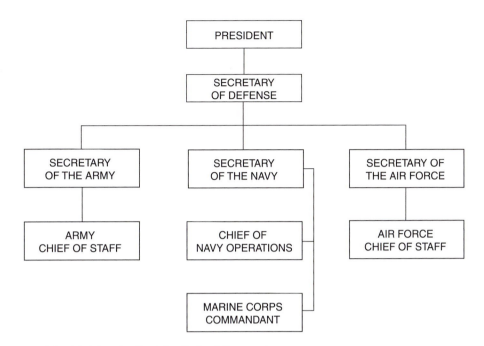

Fig 8.3 Chart of the Administrative/Logistics Chain of Command.

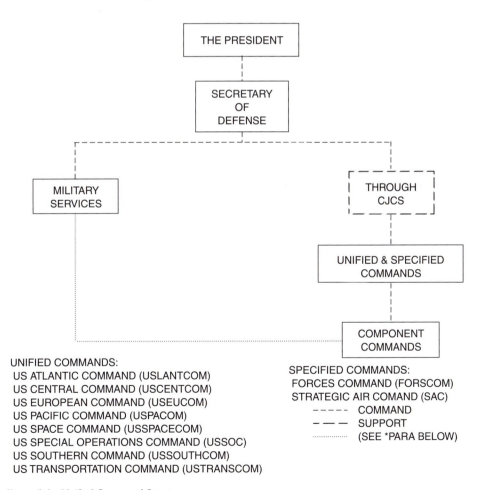

UNIFIED COMMANDS:
US ATLANTIC COMMAND (USLANTCOM)
US CENTRAL COMMAND (USCENTCOM)
US EUROPEAN COMMAND (USEUCOM)
US PACIFIC COMMAND (USPACOM)
US SPACE COMMAND (USSPACECOM)
US SPECIAL OPERATIONS COMMAND (USSOC)
US SOUTHERN COMMAND (USSOUTHCOM)
US TRANSPORTATION COMMAND (USTRANSCOM)

SPECIFIED COMMANDS:
FORCES COMMAND (FORSCOM)
STRATEGIC AIR COMAND (SAC)
– – – – – COMMAND
– – – SUPPORT
· · · · · · · · · (SEE *PARA BELOW)

Fig 8.4 Chart of the Unified Command Structure.

Civil-Military Relations: Conflicting Loyalties

As the Cold War emerged, generals and admirals sought additional funds to meet the very real and growing communist threat. The President outlined a policy of containment that required the US to assume a defensive strategy in non-Communist parts of the world. The armed forces did not question the President's policy. However, to carry it out required more resources, larger forces, and modern technology. The rapid, irresponsible demobilization; the knowledge of Soviet military potential; the fear of Communist expansion; the emotional memories of the turmoil, uncertainty, and unpreparedness that accompanied the outbreak of World War II; and loyalty to men and women of the armed forces caused the generals and admirals to seek a level of peacetime military expenditures unimaginable to most Americans and their political leaders. On 2 October 1950, in an article entitled, "Why Was the US Unarmed?" *Time Magazine* endeavored to explain to the American people the reason for the poor state of its armed forces in the opening weeks of the Korean War:

> When war began in Korea, Americans had good reason to believe that the sinews of their war machine were tough & thick; never in peacetime had US coin been spent so lavishly on the armed forces of the nation. In the five years after World War II, the US had poured out a staggering $90 billion for the Army, Navy and Air Force. . . . In 1949, the defense bill came to $100 for every man, woman and child in the US, v. only $8 apiece in 1938. . . . Yet the first agonizing weeks in Korea proved well enough that all this coin had failed to develop the sinews of war. Said one military man: "The fist is still there, but the muscles of the arm have been wasted away." For its $90 billion the US got—not a powerful fighting force—but only ten combat divisions. And even those were sadly understaffed, full of green troops, and underequipped. US tanks, almost all left over from World War II, were obsolescent; antitank weapons were out of date. Most of World War II's mighty Navy lay cocooned, prepared to fight off rust rather than an enemy. Even the Air Force, the strategic bombing darling of military planners, had to scramble to find planes

to give ground troops limited tactical support. Faced by the shocking weakness of its armed forces many an American bleakly asked: Where did the $90 billion go . . .? *How much will it cost to guarantee reasonable security in the future?*[31]

Objectively the answer to this last question was unknowable. But, what was obvious in the first battles for Korea was that the Truman Administration was far off the mark. Truman's defense policies and budgets put the services on the defensive. The administration's foreign and fiscal policies conflicted with its military policies, creating a serious conflict of interests and conflict of loyalties for the generals and admirals. The policies of the administration and politics in Washington exacerbated inter-service rivalry. Truman placed little value on the advice of the JCS, believing that they were incapable of working together to fashion a reasonable budget, that they always sought more and larger forces, and that they did not understand the economic situation of the country that he had to manage.[32] Truman's impressions and attitude were created, in part, by his observation of the behavior of the generals and admirals.

Issues of loyalty were, and are, extremely complex. While service culture clearly limited the vision of war of senior military leaders, it would be wrong to conclude that they were not men of integrity, or that they acted purely out of arrogance, ignorance, or selfishness. The twentieth edition of the *Officer's Guide* informed new Army officers that: "Loyalty is demanded in all ways from military officers. He must be loyal to his men, to his brother officers, his organization, his commander, the Army, and to the Nation he has sworn to protect."[33] However, the actual working of the system of loyalties was not simply hierarchical, and there was little agreement on which loyalty required the highest devotion.[34] A brief study of the concept of "loyalty" reveals that there was no consensus in the Army. In 1950 S.L.A. Marshall wrote, "His [the Army officer's] ultimate commanding loyalty at all times is to his country and not to his service or his superior." In 1967 Matthew B. Ridgway wrote: "While the loyalty he (the officer) owes his superiors is reciprocated with equal force in the loyalty owed him from above, the authority of his superiors is not open to question." And, in 1970 General W.R. Peers wrote: "An officer's highest loyalty is to the Army and the nation." The Army, the nation, and superiors all laid claim to the highest loyalty. Loyalties conflict. Loyalty to one's service could, at times, conflict with loyalty to the President, country, subordinates, and/or career. During the Korean War General Douglas MacArthur, who was relieved by Truman, made the argument that he was acting on a higher loyalty than that owed the President. He was acting on loyalties to the country, and to the men under his command. Consider the problem:

In 1950 Secretary of Defense Louis Johnson cut the defense budget three times until it was less than half the $30 billion the JCS requested and believed necessary. At the same time Acheson and Nitze were arguing for a major increase in the defense budget, Army Chief of Staff, J. Lawton Collins, with full knowledge that the Truman budget did not meet the needs of the Army, or the other services, loyally went before Congress to defend Truman's Fiscal Year 1951 budget of $4 billion, which reduced the already under-strength Army by another 37,000 soldiers. Collins, standing before Congress, painted an optimistic picture of the current state of readiness of the Army:

> We have units that are ready to move right now in case of aggression; we have the best men in the Army today that we have ever had in peacetime, and although we have a number of critical equipment problems yet to solve, *I can assure you that our troops, with the equipment that they have, would give a good account of themselves, if we were attacked.* The recent reductions in our occupation commitments have enabled us to concentrate more of our efforts upon strengthening the combat units which form the hard core of our fighting force. We are giving our divisions and other combat units more officers and men, some items of better weapons and equipment, and improved training under field conditions.[35]

Collins' words were not an accurate assessment of the current state of readiness of the Army, and he knew it. Collins, in response to questions regarding the adequacy of the size of the Army, in essence lied to Congress. He justified his position by placing the burden of war on National Guard and Reserves, the other services, and American industry:

> We realize that if there is anything that gives any nation pause today with respect to starting a possible war, it is less the actual military strength of the United States than the tremendous industrial potential of this country. . . . We can safely reduce to approximately this number only if we maintain a high state of readiness in our National Guard and Organized Reserve Corps. However, we are supporting this budget that will provide only 10 divisions because we realize the necessity to integrate Army requirements with those of the other Services within our national budget.[36]

Collins had not told Congress what he honestly believed. His primary duty, as he understood it, was to support the President's defense program, and he loyally carried out this responsibility. The cost of this loyalty was high. Collins later lamented:

> From this record it is clear that members of the JCS, including General Bradley and myself, shared with the President, the Administration, and the Congress the responsibility for the reductions in JCS estimates of military requirements, which so hampered our conduct of the Korean war.

It was much worse than "hampered." He further noted that:

> It has sometimes been argued . . . that the JCS should submit its estimates of military requirements without any consideration of their impact on the national economy. There may be some theoretical merit to this idea, but it is contrary to our American system and, in fact, contrary to the Budget and Accounting Act of 1921. This act requires that officers and employees of the executive branch of the government support the President's budget recommendations and offer "no request for an increase in an item . . . unless at the request of either House of Congress." The prescribed procedure in the Department of the Army in my day was that an Army witness was bound to present and support all budget items unless specifically asked by a Committee member for the witness' personal views.[37]

Generals and admirals were to support the President's policies and budget directives whether they agreed with them or not. This practice continued into the twenty-first century. Collins concluded that:

> Looking back, perhaps the JCS should have taken a firmer stand in defending its $30 billion estimate for the fiscal year 1950, even in the face of broad public concern for the mounting national debt, the lessening purchasing power of the dollar, and the insistent demands for economy in government . . .[38]

In the opening days of the Korean War, Americans died who should not have. Strategy was implemented that should not have been. Operations were at risk that should not have been. And political objectives were changed that should not have been. Collins recognized that the cost of the President's fiscal policy had been high.

Words similar to those of Collins were spoken years later by senior Army leaders, who after the tragic results of the Vietnam War wished they had done more to change policies and strategies they knew were deeply flawed and had little chance for success.[39] Collins' loyalty to the service and the President's policy of containment conflicted with his loyalty to the President and the President's fiscal policy. The loss of life, credibility, and prestige that accompanied the succession of defeats in the opening phase of the Korean War; the loss of half of Korea, and the cost of all the subsequent difficulties that the communist half of Korea created for the remainder of the century, while primarily the fault of President Truman, weighed heavy on men such as Bradley, Collins, and Ridgway, who had recognized the dangers but were powerless to change the situation.

The service chiefs also share the blame with Truman because they had damaged their credibility with the President by their inability to develop a unified command and force structure, produce comprehensive strategies and plans, develop joint doctrine, or fight on the same battlefield as teams. War is the most serious business of mankind. The survival of South Korea, and the quality and character of the lives of people of North Korea, were determined by the strength—or lack thereof—of the armed forces of the United States, particularly the Army.

On the other hand, perceived disloyalty to a President could end a career, as General Ridgway, who earned the ire of Eisenhower, learned. By pressing too strongly for additional resources, changes in strategy and/or doctrine, and/or for particular programs and weapon systems, a general or admiral could end his career. Loyalty to the administration became one of the prerequisites for service at the highest levels of the armed forces. However, loyalty to one's service was a prerequisite for achieving high rank. And loyalty to the administration was not necessarily the same as loyalty to the service. Just as loyalty to one's career was not necessarily the same as loyalty to one's service. The services had to learn how to circumvent and manipulate the system. They had to learn to cope with a system that constantly put them in situations where their loyalties conflicted.

There was another dynamic that influenced the behavior of civilian and military leaders: the desires of administrations to show unanimity in public discourse, to demonstrate that they had the support of the nation's most senior military leaders. Consider the words of Ridgway:

> I then reiterated my previous stand—that I would not order reductions in Army units in potential combat areas unless I had direct orders to do so. That Mr. Wilson [Secretary of Defense] had the authority to issue such orders I did not question. But the responsibility for the consequences, I felt must also rest on his shoulders. Throughout my tour there was never any lack of willingness on the part of the Defense Department to exercise full authority. Frequently though, this was not accompanied by an equal willingness to assume responsibility for actions taken.
>
> On the other hand there seemed to me to be a deliberate effort to soothe and lull the public by placing responsibility where it did not rest, by conveying the false impression that there was unanimous agreement between civilian authorities and their military advisers on the form and shape the military establishment should take.
>
> As a combat soldier I have been shot at from ambush, and bombed by planes which I thought

to be friendly, both of which are experiences that are momentarily unsettling. I do not recall, however, that I ever felt a greater sense of surprise and shock than when I read in President Eisenhower's State of the Union message in 1954 that: "The defense program recommended for 1955 . . . is based on a new military program unanimously recommended by the Joint Chiefs of Staff." As one member of the Joint Chiefs of Staff who most emphatically had not concurred, I was nonplused by his statement.[40]

This subterfuge influenced the ability of the nation to prepare for war and conduct war by inhibiting, or in some cases precluding, the nation's seniormost military leaders from speaking their mind, responding honestly. This requirement caused a credibility gap between the administration and Congress, the administration and the American people, and between the military and the American people. This credibility gap, during war, eroded American support for the war—the greater the gap, the greater the erosion of the goodwill and faith of the American people. General Maxwell Taylor, Army Chief of Staff, 1956–1960, characterized the situation:

> The new Chiefs [under the new Eisenhower Administration] were regarded as members of the Administration "team," working for the objectives of that team under the guidance of their civilian superiors. In formulating their military advice, it was hoped that they would take into account the views and feelings of these superiors and avoid submitting contentious or embarrassing recommendations. They were expected to accept public responsibility for the actions of the Administration in the field of military policy, regardless of their own views and recommendations. They were to avoid any impression of disunity in public or before Congress. That dissent might invoke sanctions was clearly implied by appointing the new Joint Chiefs of Staff for no specified term, with the stated intention to review all appointments after two years.[41]

Since the enactment of the National Security Act in 1947, every administration has expected and demanded the loyalty of the chiefs. Thus, when the chiefs speak in public, the American people and

Congress cannot trust, cannot believe that they are hearing an honest assessment based on their years of experience and service. In fact, their spoken words are sometimes not their own, but prepared statements, "talking points," for programs and policies the administration is endeavoring to sell to Congress and the American people. And, because under the Constitution of the United States Congress is responsible for organizing, equipping, and funding the armed forces, the match between means and objectives has been easily lost or distorted. The requirement for "team players" was in part a requirement for "yes-men" primarily in the areas of national military strategy, strategic doctrine, and strategy for a given war. A few senior officers have publicly broken with administrations on various issues of national strategy. But as a rule, they have hurt or ended their careers in the process.[42] General Westmoreland explained how this system hurt the nation during the Vietnam War:

> Secretary Rusk admitted on television that "we don't expect these men to sit there like hypnotized rabbits waiting for the Viet Cong to strike," but he went on to intimate that they were outside their bases only to keep the enemy off balance and prevent major attacks against installations. The President's press secretary said flatly, "There has been no change in the mission of the United States ground combat units in Vietnam in recent days or weeks. The President has issued no order of any kind in this regard to General Westmoreland recently or at any other time." On the other hand, he explained, "General Westmoreland also had authority within the assigned mission to employ these troops in support of Vietnamese forces faced with aggressive attack when in his judgment the general situation urgently requires it."
>
> It was not falsehood, but it was a masterpiece of obliquity, and I was unhappy about it. To my mind the American people had a right to know forthrightly, within the actual limits of military security, what we were calling on their sons to do, and to presume that it could be concealed despite the open eyes of press and television was folly. This was either the start of or a contribution to a troublesome, divisive credibility gap that was long to plague the Administration and

eventually to affect the credibility of some of my own pronouncements.[43]

The dishonesty of an administration automatically became the dishonesty of the loyal Chiefs of Staff. Westmoreland, like Collins, felt the pull of conflicting loyalties:

> Yet it was difficult to differentiate between pursuit of a military task and such related matters and the morale of the fighting man, who must be convinced that he is risking death for a worthy cause. I myself as the man perhaps most on the spot may have veered too far in the direction of supporting in public the government's policy; an instinct born of devotion to an assigned task even more than to a cause and of a loyalty to the President as Commander in Chief.[44]

Collins, Ridgway, Taylor, and Westmoreland all voiced their concerns that the system promoted conflicting loyalties, and destroyed honest discussion and openness. How can a nation that cannot honestly address problems successfully fight a war? How can a nation in which loyalty to the President conflicts with loyalty to the mission and the fighting men, successfully conduct a war? Clearly some level of conflict is natural, and even healthy; however, at some point it becomes destructive, and when conflicts are *not* honestly faced their negative effects are multiplied.

The problem of command, control, and planning was still more complicated. Under certain conditions senior military leaders have openly challenged the authority of the administration. In 1993, the military historian Russell Weigley wrote:

> The era of the Cold War brought an unprecedented frequency of decisions to be made at that political-diplomatic-strategic intersection. Of necessity, this Cold War circumstance also produced an unprecedented mingling of civilian and military leaders in the course of the policy-making process. The consequent familiarity of leaders on both sides of the civil-military boundary with each other almost certainly reduced the distanced respect of the military for the civil authorities that rendered the military almost excessively self-deprecating as late as the preparations for war with Japan in 1940–41, and that

declined but still managed to prevail throughout the four subsequent years of war. As usual, familiarity bred if not necessarily contempt, then at least a sure reduction of awe and even respect.[45]

Weigley advanced the thesis of Samuel Huntington, published in his classic study *The Soldier and the State: The Theory of Politics of Civil-Military Relations*. Weigley believed that a system of "subjective civilian control" was operative at the highest levels of government, as opposed to the ideal "objective civilian control."[46] Huntington noted that subjective control presupposed the involvement of the military in institutional, class, and constitutional politics. Power was subjective based on the personalities and influence of given leaders, and the boundaries between military and civilian authority were blurred.

There is evidence that by the late 1940s the "awe" and "excessively self-deprecating" nature of the officer corps had already started to disintegrate. In the early days of the Cold War some very senior officers concluded that they would overtly, directly challenge the authority of the President. The most outstanding example of this came in 1951, when General Douglas MacArthur undertook to rewrite the foreign and military policies of the United States to fit his strategic vision and was relieved of duty and retired. However, MacArthur was not alone in challenging presidential authority. In 1949 Secretary of Defense Louis A. Johnson, with the approval of President Truman, cancelled the Navy's supercarrier, the *USS United States*, a $200 million vessel. The cancellation caused an episode known as the "revolt of the admirals." In 1956 General Maxwell Taylor opposed President Eisenhower's "new look" policy, and took steps, similar to those of the admirals, to undermine it. One student of the "revolt of the admirals" wrote:

> In the aftermath of the cancellation, naval frustrations were at an extremely high level as many top officials, most notably aviators, concluded that the existence of their branch was at stake. In this charged atmosphere they began preparing for a battle they perceived as essential to save their service from a severe crippling at best and extinction at worst. By this time the Navy had pinpointed its three major adversaries: President

Truman, whose insistence on a total military budget of under $15 billion for fiscal years 1949 and 1950 was making all the squeezing necessary; Secretary of Defense Johnson, who seemed determined to build up the Air Force at the expense of the Navy ... and the Air Force, which was misrepresenting what airpower could do and what the Navy could not do in providing for the nation's defense.[47]

Bradley, the new Chairman of the Joint Chiefs of Staff, was also targeted because he sided with the Air Force. The Navy executed a deliberate, coordinated plan to subvert the will of elected political leaders, whom they believed were attacking their service. Because the nation was not at war, this plot was not as potentially destructive as MacArthur's insubordination. However, in regard to civil-military relations it was a greater threat because it involved numerous senior officers engaged in an organized plot. Naval officers lied, spread inaccurate rumors, and engaged in personal attacks, demonstrating that their service loyalty, on specific issues, took precedence over loyalty to the President. The Navy's charges against the Air Force led to congressional hearings, during which Bradley argued:

I stressed these points: That inasmuch as the surface navy of the Soviet Union was "negligible," it was grossly wasteful to fund a US Navy beyond what was needed to cope with the growing Soviet submarine threat. That inasmuch as the Air Force had been assigned the primary responsibility for strategic bombing, it was militarily unsound to build supercarriers when the money was required for "other vital needs." That aircraft carriers could not be justified to support future amphibious operations. I predicted that "large-scale amphibious operations" such as those in Sicily and Normandy "will never occur again." I added: "Frankly, the atomic bomb properly delivered almost precluded such a possibility. That no one could abolish the Marine Corps without congressional approval. I did not recommend that it be abolished but directly and indirectly I challenged the need for a large Marine Corps. I pointed out to those who believed that a "tremendous Marine Corps" was essential for amphibious operations, that at Sicily and Normandy, "two of the largest

amphibious assaults ever made," no Marines were present ....[48]

Bradley, like other senior military leaders of the time, was fixated on total nuclear war. He demonstrated little understanding of the future roles of the Navy in limited war. (Bradley has been much maligned by historians and Navy and Marine officers for his comments about amphibious operations; however, he was right. The Inchon Landing was in no way comparable to the landings at Sicily and Normandy, where eight divisions were put ashore in a period of 24 to 48 hours. There has been nothing comparable in size, scale, and significance to the invasions in the Mediterranean and European Theater since. And in the 1950s and early 1960s the Marine Corps also accepted the Bradley thesis on amphibious operations.[49]) General Eisenhower, witnessing the "revolt," wrote:

I believe the President has to show the iron beneath the pretty glove. Some of our seniors [military leaders] are forgetting that they have a Commander in Chief. They must be reminded of this, in terms of direct, unequivocal language. If this is not done soon, some day we're going to have a blowup.... [The President and Secretary of Defense] are going to have to get tough—and I mean tough.[50]

Eisenhower as President would face another revolt of his own service. In February 1950, Secretary of Defense, Louis Johnson, reminded officers of their duty and responsibilities:

It is a praiseworthy trait and a splendid tradition that every military man should be loyal to his service and have faith in his weapons, but all them should bear in mind that they are working together with their companion services for a common objective—the security of the United States. We have always tried to instill a sense of loyalty to his own service in every soldier, sailor, marine and airman, but we all owe an even higher allegiance to our country. The common cause of national security transcends the interest of any service, and each service must make concessions for the benefit of all.... I have made it clear ... that harmful competition among the military services for headlines and publicity will not be tolerated.[51]

Johnson equated loyalty to the administration with loyalty to the country, which, in most cases, is correct. Elected political leaders, in theory, promulgated the general will of the people. The Navy's revolutionaries and MacArthur wrongly separated these loyalties.

This behavior was very different from that of Collins, Ridgway, and Westmoreland, who disagreed with the policies of an administration, argued against them, implemented means and manipulated resources to mitigate their influence, but took no steps to deliberately undermine presidential policies. They recognized that the administration was using them, by attributing assessments and policies to them that they did not support. But they served at the pleasure of the President. They could always quit, resign their commission, and then protest presidential policies. Ridgway followed this path, publishing excerpts from his book *Soldier* that were highly critical of the President's "new look." However, openly opposing presidential policies was opposing presidential authority, and thus, the Constitution of the United States, and, in theory, the will of the people.

The Navy and Marine Corps believed that Johnson was out to gut them and possibly eliminate them. Admiral Conolly recorded a conversation with Secretary Johnson:

> Admiral, the Navy is on its way out. Now, take amphibious operations. There's no reason for having a Navy and a Marine Corps. General Bradley . . . tells me that amphibious operations are a thing of the past. We'll never have any more amphibious operations. That does away with the Marine Corps. And the Air Force can do anything that the Navy can do nowadays, so that does away with the Navy.[52]

There is no reason to doubt Conolly's recollection. Secretaries of Defense do *not* have the power to eliminate a service. However, they possessed the power to do considerable harm, and it would be wrong to assume that the men who have held this position were free of preferences, prejudices, and loyalties to a specific service. And, it is a fact that Secretaries of Defense, at various times, have damaged individual services. While the insubordination of the Navy cannot be justified, the Navy's assessment of Johnson was reasonably accurate. To be sure, the Navy was not alone in trying to undermine the will of the President and Secretary of Defense, frequently colluding with supportive senators and congressmen. As noted, Taylor undertook a similar course of action in 1956. Taylor's attempted revolt did not go as far as that of the Navy, but he was required by Secretary of Defense Wilson to publicly show his support for the 1957 New Look budget: "I have taken the position of going along with and supporting the present budget for 1957 and there is no revolt in the Army."[53] All the services have engaged in this practice to various degrees, with varying degrees of political skill and success. (In 1955 the Navy got its carrier. It commissioned a slightly scaled down version of the "supercarrier," the Forrestal class. The Navy's acquisition of part of the strategic bombing mission and the Korean War demonstrated a continuing need for naval aviation.[54] This would have taken place without the revolt.)

The institutional learning that took place in the late 1940s and early 1950s became accepted practice for the services. Nick Kotz, in his book, *Wild Blue Yonder: Money, Politics, and the B–1 Bomber*, traces the history of the development of the B–1 bomber. He wrote:

> On October 1, 1986, the US Air Force proudly hailed a victory for which its generals had valiantly fought for thirty years. A new strategic bomber called the B–1 was taking its place in the American nuclear arsenal. . . . At a cost of more than $28 billion for the hundred-plane force, the B–1 was the most expensive airplane in aviation history. . . . Prodded by congressional investigators, the Air Force admitted that, despite the fanfare, not a single bomber had been battle-ready that October day. The B–1 was instead snarled in technical problems—problems the Air Force had known about for more than a year. The most serious malfunction would take at least four years to correct—handicapping the B–1 precisely during the critical period for which the Air Force had

contended the plane was most needed. . . . The American public had been misled; so had the Congress and Secretary of Defense Casper Weinberger. Even the National Military Command Center at the Pentagon, responsible for the nation's secret war plan, was unaware that the B–1s were not ready for battle.[55]

A congressional investigation revealed that:

the B–1 bomber's chances of completing a wartime mission were only half as good as intended. "Frankly, the Air Force screwed it up," said committee chairman Les Aspin. . . . "They screwed it up and didn't tell us about it." Aspin predicted it would take more than $3 billion and four years to deal with the problems, "some of which are correctable at a price and more are question marks, where a solution isn't in sight at any price."

Loyalty to the Air Force took precedence over loyalty to the administration. The services learned that it was better to have a faulty weapon system than no weapon system at all. After having spent billions of dollars on an aircraft or ship, it was almost impossible to close the program. For better or for worse, the technology had to be fixed. This was the case with the B–1 bomber. It had to be fixed, and the Air Force knew it. Hence, from the Air Force's perspective, the duplicity was worth the goal. The Air Force got its bomber.

Both the Air Force and Navy secured the weapon systems that maintained their service in its current organization and operational doctrine, which changed little from World War II to Vietnam. The services, particularly the Navy and Air Force, were based on primary weapons systems that virtually dictated their operational doctrine. Without these primary weapons systems, the services lost their identity. The Navy's identity was based on the aircraft carrier. The Air Force's identity was based on the strategic bomber. Strategic bombing was a primary Air Force operational doctrine and strategy for war. The missions associated with strategic bombing formed the service's reason for being. They formed the service's history, self-image, and culture. The aircraft carrier was the Navy's strategic bomber. These primary weapon systems dominated service thinking. In war these systems had to be employed, their basic missions had to

be performed. The weapon system, the technology, thus, dictated operational doctrine, influenced strategy, and made it difficult to develop joint doctrine. The absence of joint doctrine precluded the services from producing synergy in war, damaging their credibility with the American people, and their ability to achieve political objectives.

Administrations came and went, but the Army, Navy, Air Force, and Marine Corps were forever. What one administration was unwilling to do, the next might be convinced to do through political persuasion, economic incentives, coalition building, threats, and coercion. The services in the latter half of the twentieth century regularly mounted campaigns to subvert the will of the President. The Marine Corps' V–22 Osprey, an aircraft with the vertical lift capabilities of a helicopter and the in-flight capabilities of an airplane, was cancelled by Secretary of Defense Cheney during the George H.W. Bush Administration. The George W. Bush Administration decided to build it.[56] In 2002 Secretary of Defense Donald Rumsfeld, who time and again demonstrated personal animus towards the Army, cancelled the Army's Crusader Artillery system, causing the Army to appeal to Congress and mount a campaign to save the system. The Army lost the battle. Still, the system that the Army had spent billions of dollars on was not completely dead. The practice of undermining the decisions of Presidents and Secretaries of Defense by lobbying and marketing to the Congress and the American people became an accepted practice.

However, these practices were primarily in matters directly influencing the internal workings of the services. There was no "revolt of the admirals," or the generals, over the strategy and strategic doctrine for the conduct of the war in Vietnam. Threats to the primary weapons systems and operational doctrines of the services generated far greater response than failed strategy and fatally flawed strategic doctrine. The history of the post-World War II era reveals that in matters involving the primary weapons systems and operational doctrines of the services and the autonomy, internal workings, and culture of the services, they were less willing to compromise and accept the decisions of the administration. The services produced officers willing to fight tenaciously for their service, to the point of undermining the will, policies, and authority of the administration. However, in matters of strategic doctrine, national strategy, and strategy for the conduct of war, they were flexible, concerned primarily with the employment of the primary weapons systems and perfecting their operational doctrines. As a consequence of this outlook, the services were incapable of providing administrations with the quality of strategic advice they needed and expected.

The tests of the 1947 Act were the outcome of wars, and military effectiveness and the maintenance of forces during war. After the Vietnam War it was evident that the system had failed in all areas. In a book entitled, *Dereliction of Duty: Lyndon Johnson, Robert McNamara, The Joint Chiefs of Staff, and the Lies that Led to Vietnam*, H.R. McMaster argued that the inability of the Joint Chiefs of Staff to provide the President with quality, effective advice was the major cause for the nation's defeat in Vietnam. He wrote:

> The war in Vietnam was not lost in the field, nor was it lost on the front pages of the *New York Times* or on the college campuses. It was lost in Washington, D.C., even before Americans assumed sole responsibility for the fighting in 1965 and before they realized the country was at war; indeed, even before the first American units were deployed. The disaster in Vietnam was not the result of impersonal forces but a uniquely human failure, the responsibility for which was shared by President Johnson and his principal military and civilian advisers. The failings were many and reinforcing: arrogance, weakness, lying in the pursuit of self-interest, and above all, the abdication of responsibility to the American people.[57]

The Vietnam War was arguably lost in 1947 with the passage of the National Security Act, which amplified inter-service rivalries, and thus exaggerated human weaknesses, such as selfishness, pride, and arrogance. McMaster concluded that the Joint Chiefs of Staff had been derelict in their duty as advisers to the President in military affairs, strategic planning, and the conduct of war; and as loyal servants of the people of the United States. President Kennedy too came to this conclusion following the Bay of Pigs

debacle. In a meeting at the Pentagon on 27 May 1961, Kennedy told the JCS that:

> I must say frankly that I do not think that the JCS gave me the support to which the President is entitled . . . While the CIA was in charge of it [the Cuban invasion operation], I would say that you should have been continuously scrutinizing the military soundness of their plan and advising them and me as to your views. The record as I know it does not show this kind of watchfulness. . . . The advice you owe me as Commander-in-Chief . . . should come to me directly. I imagine that there will be times when the Secretary of Defense will not agree with your advice to me, in which case I would naturally expect him to tell me so and why.[58]

Kennedy's opinion of the JCS further deteriorated following the Cuban Missile Crisis. It was not that the men who formed the JCS lacked knowledge or comprehension of military affairs, or were personally selfish. In fact, the men that occupied the offices of the Chiefs of Staff were proven leaders of courage *within* their services. However, the uniforms that they wore pulled them inexorably towards their service, and the organizational structure established in 1947 did nothing to mitigate the effects of service loyalty, but in fact amplified the problem.

In 1983 Senator Barry Goldwater, a general officer in the Air Force reserve, on the floor of the United States Senate stated:

> I regret to conclude after years of observing this process that the system is such that the members of the Joint Chiefs rarely override their individual Service allegiances. When the rope from the individual Services pulls in one direction and the rope from the Joint Chiefs pulls in the other direction, the individual Services invariably win the tug-of-war. The Services win the tug-of-war, but the country loses. . . . Reports commissioned by the Executive branch in 1949, 1960, 1970, and 1982, reached the same conclusion: the Joint Chiefs do not provide useful and timely military advice.[59]

In the post-World War II period, the armed forces of the United States did not fight war. They fought weapon systems. War was not viewed as a comprehensive experience, but the perfection of the deployment of a particular weapon system. In this sense, the services were like a professional team of superstars, each individually displaying unparalleled skill and capable of generating greater power than any single opponent in that field, but incapable of producing synergy, incapable of functioning as a team, incapable of supplanting service ego for the good of the whole; and, as a consequence, incapable of maximizing their potential power and usefulness to the nation. The defects of the system were well known and studied; however, the system itself took precedence over the missions and objectives of the armed forces, the political objectives of the United States, and the men and women under their command who selflessly committed their lives for the good of the nation. The result was the destruction of the goodwill and faith of the American people during the Vietnam War, and defeat in Vietnam.

The American political system adapted during the Cold War to support and sustain inter-service rivalry, and production of military means for reasons other than national security.

The Iron Triangle and the Growth of Militarism

Militarism in one form or another exists in just about all human communities. The creation and maintenance of states, nations, and empires requires military forces. With these forces, inevitably, came some form of militarism. The questions are: To what degree does militarism exist in a nation-state? How powerful is its influence? How pervasive is its influence? How many institutions and agencies, governmental and civilian, does it touch and inspire? And how profoundly does it shape the behavior of the people?

Militarism distorts American culture and its conduct of war.[60] Alfred Vagts explains that:

Militarism . . . covers every system of thinking and valuing and every complex of feelings which rank military institutions and ways above the ways of civilian life, carrying military modes of acting and decision into the civilian sphere. . . . Militarism . . . presents a vast array of customs, interests, prestige, actions, and thoughts associated with armies and wars and yet *transcending true military purpose. Indeed, militarism is so constituted that it may hamper and defeat the purpose of the military. . . .* An army [navy and air force] so built that it serves military men [Congressmen and their constituents], not war, is militaristic; so is everything in an army which is not preparation for fighting . . . .[61]

Militarism is the inculcation of military values, ethics, and belief into the thinking of a people. It is the preference for military ways and means and military solutions to problems, international and domestic. Militarism promotes military strategies and practices above other forms of engagement. Vagts further observes that "Militarism . . . has meant also the imposition of heavy burdens on a people for military purposes, to the neglect of welfare and culture, and the waste of the nation's best man power in unproductive army service."[62] Militarism is the expenditure of resources for military means beyond that needed for national security. Militarism is the maintenance and acquisition of military facilities, equipment, and units beyond that required for national security. Militarism does not necessarily mean the love of war.[63] However, it can also mean the love of the instruments of war, the technologies of war, the bombers, fighters, aircraft carriers, and so on, and the sense of power and prestige they produce. Militarism is a predisposition, an attitude, a way of looking at and thinking about the world that emphasizes military perspectives and means, military behaviors, and solutions.

The Cold War made defense big business. The United States is the biggest producer and exporter of arms on the planet. The National Security Act of 1947 institutionalized selfishness, not only among and between the services, but also in the Senate, in the House of Representatives, in industries, and in communities across the country. It created competition between the services for limited resources and at the same time permitted them to pursue their own interests and objectives, almost exclusive of the other services. Other agents embraced this system, in large part because of the economic incentives it produced. Spending tens, then hundreds of billions of dollars annually on defense, some of which went to each agent, caused the growth of militarism. Producing weapons to sell to allies, such as Britain and Germany, and then "allies," such as Saudi Arabia and Iran, produced enormous wealth, facilitating the growth and continuation of militarism.

In the 1950s an "iron triangle" emerged.[64] It consisted of congressmen and their constituents, the American people, the military and civilian leaders in the Department of Defense, and defense contractors, "military industries." Congress controls "the purse." It controls military expenditures and weapons procurement. It also controls foreign military sales. Each point of the triangle has a vested interest in a procurement system. The services became deeply involved in politics. They lobby congressmen to protect their interests and to secure and maintain particular technologies, weapon systems, and bases.[65] To sell themselves, the services maintain congressional liaisons, public affairs offices, and lobby groups made up of senior retired officers. They publish position papers, target specific legislation through mailing campaigns, sponsor conferences, court congressmen, and petition the media for coverage of specific concerns or weapons. Over the years the services became adept at sponsoring key weapons systems and policies, using all forms of communication, television, newspapers, magazines, email, and even public appearances to get their positions across.

Congressmen and women use their influence and votes to maintain military facilities and weapon systems that support their states and districts, programs that keep their constituents financially happy. And industry lobbies the military to buy certain weapon systems and specific numbers of weapons. Industry appeals to communities to gain public support for its weapons. Communities lobby tenaciously to keep bases, weapon systems, research and development programs, and other programs that have little to do with the ability of the armed forces to fight war in their areas. Military bases and technologically sophisticated production facilities create good, high-paying jobs and pump money into local economies. Some of these efforts end up forcing unwanted technologies, including weapons, on the services, cause the maintenance of facilities that hindered the ability of a service to deploy and train, and caused the

services to maintain facilities and equipment they did not need. The American defense industry influenced local, state, regional, and the national economy. The American defense industry serves not only the security needs of the United States, but also the economic needs of communities throughout the country and helps the US balance of trade. War is not just security, it is also big business—which has the priority is frequently hard to know.

*   *   *   *   *

How do the armed forces, political leaders, and the nation decide on the procurement of weapons, the adoption of strategic and operational doctrine, the allocation of resources among the services, and the delineation of the responsibilities and functions of the services? American cultural tenets influence the relationship between the services, and between the services and the American people. The competitive, capitalist nature of American society, American faith in science and technology, the American drive for more and more consumption, and the American readiness, eagerness to discard the old for the newer, for the bigger and more modern, influenced the military force structure and the procurement of technologies. The services are always engaged in an information campaign directed at the American people. The ability of a service to create a vision of war acceptable to the American people is a major factor in force design and resource allocation. For that vision to be acceptable it has to hold cultural contents. Real, proven effectiveness is less important than cultural acceptability. Michael S. Sherry in his book, *The Rise of American Air Power: The Creation of Armageddon*, argues that:

> . . . the danger of nuclear armageddon, as well as perceptions of that danger, was created less by the invention of nuclear weapons than by the attitudes and practices established before 1945. . . . I . . . concentrate on what Americans have expected of and learned from strategic bombing. *Their perspectives on the bomber are crucial, for the warplane was created in imagination before it was invented as a practical weapon.* The bomber was the product of extravagant dreams and dark foreboding about the role it might play in war and peace. . . . The bomber in imagination

is the most compelling and revealing story. . . . I emphasize that practical developments were usually secondary to imagination in shaping strategic air war. . . . I suggest that among policy makers, if not the public at large, a technological fanaticism often governed actions, an approach to making war in which satisfaction of organizational and professional drives loomed larger than the overt passion of war.[66]

In World War II the United States adopted an unproven doctrine of war. It expended enormous resources in time, intellect, men, and material to test and prove an idea—strategic bombing doctrine. The nation accepted the claims of air enthusiasts that airpower would be the decisive instrument in the conduct of the war, and committed vast resources in search of a dream. Thus, the American approach to war was not based solely nor primarily on rational calculation of the capabilities of men and machines. Other, sometimes profoundly irrational, factors influenced the allocation of resources, the organization of the armed forces, and strategic and operational doctrines.

In 1954, Army Chief of Staff Ridgway concluded that the Army had to do a better job of selling itself to the American people, that it had to reverse long-held philosophies:

> Our long-range objective must be to inform the American public of genuine military activities and accomplishments . . . in order to instill confidence in Army personnel, policies and management, and to widen public understanding that the Army is performing loyally and intelligently in support of national aims and the public interest. To accomplish this objective, we must modify the philosophy which has for years guided the Army's action in the field of public relations. This philosophy has influenced officers to remain aloof from the public and reticent on their few appearances. We must become more articulate and develop a positive public relations attitude throughout the Army. Too many officers look upon public relations as a defensive operation rather than a living, dynamic one.[67]

Senior Army leaders throughout the 1950s advanced Ridgway's argument that the Army had to

change its approach to the media and the public. One colonel wrote: "The Army in general has not yet accepted the fact that, whether it wills it or not, it is engaged in the battle for men's minds as truly as any other enterprise. . . ." He further noted that the Army was at a disadvantage: "Today, because of the world tensions, we must maintain an Army of greater size than can be accomplished by voluntary service. This involves two concepts that are traditionally unpopular with the American people—a large standing Army and peacetime conscription."[68] He might have added that the Army was at a further disadvantage because of the American penchant for high technology and big, glamorous weapon systems. He concluded: "Officers must learn to seek, rather than to shun, contact with the public." The Army got better at telling its story, but, with its innate disadvantages, never as good as the other services.

In 1955, General Maxwell D. Taylor replaced Ridgway as Army Chief of Staff. He recognized that telling the Army's story was not enough. The story had to be packaged in a manner that would make people want to buy. The glamour factor was important, and the Army was the least glamorous service. Taylor explained how the Army's budget was determined during his tenure as Chief of Staff:

> In the climate of the Eisenhower Administration, it was hard to make the case for limited war to the satisfaction of the decision-makers. . . . The resources needed for limited war were largely ground forces using unglamorous weapons and equipment—rifles, machineguns, trucks and unsophisticated aircraft—items with little appeal to the Congress or the public. Secretary Wilson once sent back an Army budget to get us to substitute requests for newfangled items with public appeal. . . . It was partly a misguided response to this urging which drew the Army into a costly and losing competition with the Air Force in producing an Intermediate Range Ballistic Missile (IRBM) at a time when the ammunition reserves for basic Army weapons were far too low for comfort. It also led me to conjure up the Madison Avenue adjective, "pentomic," to describe the new Army division which was designed on a pentagonal rather than triangular pattern with atomic-capable weapons in its

standard equipment.... nuclear weapons were the going thing and, by including some in the division armament, the Army staked out its claim to a share in the nuclear arsenal.[69]

The requirement to sell the Army and Army programs to the American people influenced the organization, equipment, and doctrine of the Army. This was also true of the other services. However, how well a service "played the game" had little to do with the combat effectiveness of American forces in the next war.[70] By the end of the 1950s the services were committed to marketing themselves. Arguably, the better the public image, the larger the service budget. The services ultimately became as good at marketing themselves as General Motors and Ford. They learned that whether they get a particular weapon system is greatly influenced by public perceptions, which influences congressional support. In the 1950s the Air Force was the biggest winner. It scored the highest in public opinion polls and received the lion's share of the defense budget. The Air Force received significant support from industry. Consider the thinking of Eisenhower, quoted and expanded upon by Peter Boyle, a student of the Eisenhower Presidency:

Eisenhower felt that much of the pressure for increased defense spending came from special interests, especially arms manufacturers and military figures, who had lobbied for pet projects, which had been underfunded or had been refused funding. He told Republican legislative leaders that, when he saw advertisements for Boeing and Douglas, he was "getting sick of the lobbies of the munitions makers.... You begin to see this thing isn't wholly the defense of the country, but only more money for some who are already fat cats." He commented that "the munitions makers are making tremendous efforts toward getting more contracts and in fact seem to be exerting undue influence over the senators."[71]

This approach to national defense is now well established and developed. It is rarely questioned. Boeing and other defense manufacturers now lobby the American people directly. (They now advertise weapons systems on television and the Internet.) Senator Goldwater noted: "The aircraft industry has probably done more to promote the Air Force than the Air Force has done itself." The Navy came in second. The image of a supercarrier launching aircraft produces feelings of pride and patriotism in many Americans. Systems such as aircraft carriers and bombers appeal to the American imagination, but also to the American myth and self-image. Great nations possess great weapon systems—the greater the nation, the bigger and more technologically sophisticated its military hardware.

The weapon systems that won the hearts and minds of the American people tended to win American dollars. The weapon systems that won the American dollars were the biggest, most glamorous, and technologically advanced weapons mankind was capable of producing. However, the service and weapons systems that won in the American marketplace were not necessarily those best suited to win in the jungles of Southeast Asia, the mountains of Afghanistan, the cities of Iraq, or in other foreign lands. Americans designed and purchased weapons systems to fight the war they wanted to fight, not the war they were most likely to fight. This is a form of militarism. During the 1950s, the weapon systems that dictated the operational doctrines of the services did not facilitate the nation's ability to fight limited wars and achieve political objectives in developing states we needed to stop the spread of Communism. In 1959, General Weyland, Commander of the Tactical Air Command, warned that "the Pentagon's preoccupation with strategic bombing and long-range missiles may soon leave us unprepared to fight a limited war."[72] The United States entered the Vietnam War, *not* with a joint air and ground team, and *not* with the joint strategic and operational doctrines required to fight a limited war. The same was true decades later.

From World War II to Operation Enduring Freedom there has been an overall failure to match means to objectives, because the force structure of the United States has not been based on rational calculations of the threats and forces needed to fight conventional, limited wars or counterinsurgency wars, the most likely wars, but on systems that won in the marketplace. In America, a vision of counterinsurgency or light infantry warfare could never compete with a vision of air war fought with very advanced, very expensive aircraft. It did not matter that multi-million-dollar aircraft were being used to attack an old truck moving down the Ho Chi Minh trail, a task that could have been better performed by a slow-moving World War II P–51 Mustang. The American force structure was *not* based on the exigencies of war, the realties of geography, or political dynamics of the region, but the exigencies of the marketplace, the dictates of the Iron Triangle, and the preferred American cultural vision of war. A decade of successful marketing could only end with a strategic doctrine of limited war based on the systems that won in the marketplace. The doctrine that lost the Vietnam War, graduated response, was based on airpower technologies. The strategic doctrine and strategy for the Vietnam War were so flawed that not even the abundance of the US could compensate for its deficiencies.

Congressmen regularly join the services and campaign to advance particular programs, installations, and weapon systems, the success or failure of which can directly influence their political careers. Collusion between congressmen and the services has become commonplace. The higher the technology, the more sophisticated the weapon, the greater the cost, and the greater the profits for defense contractors and the communities that produced them—therefore, the more successful the congressmen. However, this relationship erodes civilian control of the military. Congressmen who conspire with the services over bases and equipment not only diminish the respect due highly elected officials, but establish a relationship that destroys their objectivity. On matters of national defense they are biased before the issues are known. And, the services know to whom they can go for support on this or that issue. National defense, as a consequence, is somewhat of a game, played by the services and Congress. Unfortunately, the outcome of the game frequently has little to do with the next war.

The inability of the armed forces of the United States to work together became obvious to the American people during the 1950s and 1960s. And, while inter-service rivalry and the "Iron Triangle" eroded their faith and confidence in the services, it did not motivate a national call for change. The American people were, in fact, a part of the Iron Triangle. The jobs produced by bases and expensive weapon systems, the billions of dollars servicemen pumped into communities, and political and economic clout that accompanies major military projects, cause people to act in their own financial interest. Thus, the American people have been in a rather odd situation. They recognized that the system fails to produce the best military organizations, the best strategy, and the best doctrine, but they have had economic and other incentives to leave the system alone and to support it. The lack of confidence in the system damages the ability of the nation to produce and retain the goodwill and faith of the American people, and the ability of the armed forces to recruit their young sons and daughters, but the system encourages parents to vote for administrations and congressmen and women who supported strong defense and particular weapon systems that directly influence their communities, county, and state. The American response was thus: "yes" on technology, but "no" on our sons and daughters. The American people have a vested interest in maintaining the Iron Triangle; the conduct of war is a secondary issue at best.

The marriages that produced the Iron Triangle concerned and worried Eisenhower, prompting him to issue his now famous warning to the American people in January 1961:

> The conjunction of an immense military establishment and a large arms industry is new in the American experience.... The total influence—economic, political, even spiritual—is felt in every city, every statehouse, every office of the federal government.... In the councils of government, we must guard against the acquisition of unwarranted influence, whether sought or unsought, by the military-industrial complex. The potential for the disastrous rise of misplaced power exists and will persist.[73]

Eisenhower meant "the military-industrial-congressional complex." He concluded that this complex must never be allowed to "endanger our liberties or democratic processes. We should take nothing for granted."

The American political, economic, military system in the latter half of the twentieth century transcended true military purposes. It served many needs beyond the necessities for war and national security.

9.
KENNEDY, McNAMARA, AND ARTIFICIAL LIMITED WAR, 1961–1963

Unfortunately, our past reliance upon massive retaliation has stultified the development of new policy. We have developed what Henry Kissinger has called a Maginot-line mentality—dependence upon a strategy which may collapse or may never be used, but which meanwhile prevents the consideration of any alternative. When that prop is gone, the alternative seems to many to be inaction and acceptance of the inevitability of defeat. After all, once the Soviets have the power to destroy us, we have no way of absolutely preventing them from doing so. But every nation, whatever its status, needs a strategy. Some courses of action are always preferable to others; and there are alternatives to all-out war or inaction.[1]

Senator John F. Kennedy,
"The Missile Gap" 14 August 1958

The Kennedy Administration—unlike the Eisenhower Administration, which relied on massive retaliation—accepted two strategic doctrines: massive retaliation and limited war doctrine. Kennedy also adopted a doctrine advanced by the Army under the leadership of General Maxwell Taylor, called "flexible response." The Army had argued throughout the 1950s for a limited war doctrine to augment the doctrine of massive retaliation, which had the effect of deterring more total war, but could *not* produce positive effects in peripheral areas where total war was unjustified. Flexible response required the United States to maintain forces capable of fighting the entire range of possible wars, from local "brushfire" war, to general conventional war, to limited nuclear war, to total nuclear war. Flexible response caused a renaissance in the Army. However, a decade of misdirection and uncertainty could not be undone all at once.

Kennedy imbued his administration with a romanticized vision of American power and goodness, a strong sense of American optimism, and a belief in the special role of the United States in world affairs. Kennedy was born into a family that had great expectations for its sons, that had a strong sense of public responsibility and duty, and that had the wealth and status to shape their political careers. Kennedy was the second of nine children. His oldest brother was killed in World War II. John inherited the responsibilities of the senior son. Kennedy's father, Joseph, the grandson of an Irish Catholic immigrant, exerted considerable influence on the careers of his sons. John was Harvard educated, and during World War II, served in the Navy commanding a PT boat—a small torpedo patrol boat. He saw action in the South Pacific, and was nearly killed when a Japanese destroyer rammed his boat.

John was considered an intellectual. He kept company not only with the social elite, but also the intellectual elite. During the 1950s, national strategic doctrine and military affairs became, in part, the province of America's intellectuals. University professors and researchers from semi-independent think-tanks, such as the RAND Corporation, published numerous works on the causes of war, nuclear strategy, civil-military relations, defense organization, military professionalism, weapon systems, and numerous other topics related to

Fig 9.1 President John F. Kennedy signs General Dwight D. Eisenhower's Commission as General of the Army, as others look on during a ceremony at the White House. (L to R, standing): Secretary of the Navy John B. Connally, Jr.; Deputy Secretary of Defense Roswell Gilpatric; Secretary of Defense Robert S. McNamara; Vice President Lyndon B. Johnson; Secretary of the Army Elvis J. Stahr, Jr.; and Secretary of the Air Force Eugene Zuckert. Washington, DC, 24 March 1961. US Army photograph.

the military and national defense. Economists, political scientists, anthropologists, psychologists, sociologists, and historians all developed theories to explain the outbreak of war, and how to fight war. This new elite ventured into areas that had been considered the exclusive province of the services—the strategic, operational, and tactical doctrines of the services. Part of the reason for this new development was the carnage produced in two world wars, making the twentieth century the bloodiest in all of human history. A second reason was the revolutionary nature of nuclear power and missile technology, which, when combined, created a weapon that could wipe out vast numbers of human beings in an instant. A third reason was the tremendous cost of national defense. For the first time in the nation's history, in peacetime, it was expending tens and later hundreds of billions of dollars on defense during peacetime. How best to spend our limited resources for defense was intensely debated in Congress, the halls of universities, and the streets of America. All Americans were aware of the threat of nuclear weapons and the debates over how best the nation could defend itself and its interests

abroad. *Sputnik*, and later the Cuban Missile Crisis, caused fear and uncertainty that intensified this interest.

Kennedy believed his experiences, education, and research provided him with an in-depth understanding of American national security policies, the Soviet threat, nuclear warfare doctrines, and the Communist challenge from developing, peripheral nations. He had a vision of what the national defense establishment ought to look like, what it ought to be capable of achieving, and what objectives it ought to pursue. As a senator, he had concluded that the military policies of the Eisenhower Administration were dangerous to the security of the United States. His message during the presidential campaign in 1959 had a sense of urgency. He believed that unless the situation was reversed within the next five years, the US might have to accede to Soviet demands and influence in parts of the world threatened by Communism. Kennedy moved aggressively to transform the American military establishment—to create a stable nuclear environment and implement limited war strategic doctrine. He appointed Robert McNamara as his agent for change.

Theories of Artificial Limited War

Modern limited war was an *artificial* creation caused by the development of nuclear weapons. The limited wars of the past, those prior to the advent of the modern nation-state, were limited because they lacked social and political organization, cultural cohesion, nationalistic ideology, military organization and theory, and the industrial, logistical, and technological capabilities to fight more total wars. Modern limited war required nation-states to place *artificial restraints* on the conduct of war to preclude it from escalating into more total war, nuclear war. Artificial limited war required nations to place limitations on the objectives sought, weapons and manpower employed, the time, terrain, and geographic area of hostilities, and the emotions, passions, energy, attention, and intellect committed. However, those restraints could be removed at any time. They were fictional barriers that Western nation-states endeavored to observe. Clausewitz noted:

> The bounds of military operations have been extended so far that a return to the old narrow limitations can only occur briefly, sporadically, and under special conditions. The true nature of war will break through again and again with overwhelming force, and must, therefore, be the basis of any permanent military arrangement.[2]

Nuclear weapons created the "special conditions" that created artificial limited war. And, the ever-present danger in limited war was that the "true nature" of war would reemerge, with all the death and destruction made possible by nuclear weapons. Nuclear weapons, exclusively under the control of the dominant Western powers, eliminated total wars, and created limited war. However, given human nature and the inevitable distribution of technology, it is by no means certain that this pattern of behavior will continue, particularly as these weapons move beyond the control of Western nation-states that seek to maintain the status quo into non-Western, developing nation-states that seek to redress the balance of world power.

Clausewitz further explained the natural order of men in war. He wrote:

> The maximum use of force is in no way incompatible with the simultaneous use of the intellect.

If one side uses forces without compunction, undeterred by the bloodshed it involves, while the other side restrains, the first will gain the upper hand. That side will force the other to follow suit, each will drive its opponent toward extremes, and the only limiting factors are the counterpoises [elements that man does not control] inherent in war.[3]

This, in fact, is more than the use of the "intellect" and "compunction." This was basic human behavior for one simple reason: *there is nothing limited about dying.*

It was not limited war that was intolerable to Americans; it was the *artificial nature* of limited war. Arguably all artificial limited wars are optional. Political leaders made a decision to fight. The security of the nation-state was not directly threatened. What was not optional to Americans were the lives of their sons and daughters who were drafted to fight these artificial limited wars. War by its very nature is unlimited. "Total war" and "war" are the same term to most people. For most of humanity limited war is an oxymoron—a combination of contradictory and incongruous ideas. Limited war is limited at the strategic and operational levels of war. At the tactical level of war where the battles are fought and the wounding, suffering, and dying takes place, there is no such thing as "limited war." Weapons produce the same effect in "limited war" as they do in "total war." They kill. Limited war was an artificial, intellectual creation of the superpowers. There was nothing limited about the Korean War for Koreans. There was nothing limited about the Vietnam War for the Vietnamese. And there was nothing limited about both wars for dead Americans and their families.

In 1952, the United States tested the hydrogen bomb. It was immediately evident that this weapon was almost useless as a means for achieving political objectives. It was many times more powerful than the bombs dropped on Hiroshima and Nagasaki in World War II, but it had absolutely no tactical or operational value, and its strategic value was questionable because once employed there was nothing left to be victorious over. The only value of this weapon was in deterring nuclear war and total conventional war between major powers. In the 1950s, two forms of limited war were analyzed and debated: limited nuclear war and limited conventional war.

The development of tactical nuclear weapons in the mid 1950s made possible nuclear war that fell short of total nuclear holocaust. Theorists from the academic community, men such as Henry Kissinger, Bernard Brodie, Robert Osgood, Herman Kahn, and others debated the logic and illogic of fighting a tactical nuclear war. Some theorists believed that tactical nuclear weapons could be employed on battlefields without necessarily escalating to total strategic nuclear war. Given the natural inclinations of mankind this thinking was deeply flawed. And, while the US deployed tactical nuclear weapons to Europe and NATO member nations, under this doctrine of limited, nuclear war they were never used; and in the late 1950s and early 1960s it became highly unlikely that the government of the US would have ever authorized their use. As the capabilities of the Soviet nuclear arsenal increased, the fear of retaliation and uncontrolled escalation also increased, creating a "balance of terror."

Tactical nuclear weapons were deployed to Europe as a deterrent to conventional invasions from the countries of the Warsaw Pact, and as a placebo for European allies. Neither Europe nor the US believed it was possible to match the conventional armed forces of the Warsaw Pact countries, man for man, tank for tank. The cost was prohibitive. Hence, tactical nuclear weapons were deployed to Europe under the theory that it was possible to fight a tactical nuclear war, that it was possible to climb the rungs of nuclear escalation, from the employment of a single weapon to demonstrate willingness, to everything short of nuclear holocaust. This was a fiction of strategic importance. It made Europeans believe that the US was fully committed to their security, and that the US would in fact use its nuclear arsenal in defense of Europe. Still, in reality, at that particular juncture in history, nuclear weapons eliminated all forms of nuclear war. Tactical nuclear weapons were supposed to be targeted at the enemy's forces, not the enemy's cities. However, the spread of urban areas across Central Europe and the yield of tactical nuclear weapons made it impossible for these areas to escape destruction. And, in fact, there was little to distinguish some tactical nuclear weapons from strategic nuclear weapons. The bomb dropped on Hiroshima had an explosive yield in the range of kilotons, yet it was of strategic significance to the war. Bernard Brodie explained:

One frequently meets reference to 'tactical' nuclear weapons as distinct from 'strategic' ones with the implication that there are marked intrinsic differences between them or the factors governing their use. The most common belief is that the former are necessarily of small yield and the latter of large. These ideas are completely erroneous.... Those, therefore, who insist that they want to use only the very smallest atomic bombs tactically should be clear that they are talking about a restriction which will have to be arbitrarily imposed. ...

Brodie concluded that: "*between the use and non-use of atomic weapons there is a vast watershed of difference and distinction, one that ought not be cavalierly thrown away, as we appear to be throwing it away, if we are serious about trying to limit war.*"[4] The British military theorist Liddell Hart seconded this conclusion:

But once any kind of nuclear weapon is actually used, it could all too easily spread by rapid degrees, and lead to all-out nuclear war. The lessons of experience about the emotional impulse of men at war are much less comforting than the theory—the tactical theory which has led to the development of these weapons.[5]

The doctrine of limited nuclear war was another form of deterrent, one that consumed a lot of academic interest and billions of dollars. Nuclear weapons in a bipolar world eliminated all forms of nuclear war. As the man primarily responsible for the development of the atomic bomb, Robert Oppenheimer, noted in 1953:

We may anticipate a state of affairs in which the two Great Powers will each be in a position to put an end to the civilization and life of the other, though not without risking its own. We may be likened to two scorpions in a bottle, each capable of killing the other, but only at the risk of his own life.[6]

Conventional limited war theories are complex and poorly understood. Theorists held very different ideas about the employment and effectiveness of these doctrines, further complicating comprehension. Limited war doctrine was also employed differently by the various administrations. Unlike the Korean War, where limits were set primarily at the strategic level of war, a point beyond which no additional resources would be committed, in Vietnam, the strategic military commitment was ill defined and "open-ended." Limitations were imposed primarily at the operational and even tactical levels of war. As a consequence, over time, the American commitment grew with no correlation to the political objectives of the nation. Strategically the American commitment increased each year from 1961 to 1969, as if the political objectives were unlimited. America's commitment to Vietnam was out of proportion with Vietnam's significance to our national security. Limited war theories were primarily a function of the Korean War. It was in the wake of the Korean War that military professionals, the academic community, politicians, and intellectuals cultivated these new theories.

The Army defined limited war in relatively simple terms: "A war prosecuted by a belligerent who voluntarily exercises restraints of the means, objectives, geographical area, or time."[7] Ridgway defined limited war and identified the problem Americans had with comprehending its tenets:

> One mistake we avoided in Korea was an insistence on "total victory" or "unconditional surrender ..." before talking peace. But in the light of many of the slogans that fill the air and the public prints nowadays, I am moved to wonder if all our citizens have come to understand the concept of limited war. A limited war is not merely a small war that has not yet grown to full size. It is a war in which the objectives are specifically limited in the light of our national interest and our current capabilities. A war that is "open-ended"—that has no clearly delineated geographical, political, and military goals beyond "victory"—is a war that may escalate itself indefinitely, as wars will, with one success requiring still another to insure the first one.

Ridgway understood that the traditional American thinking about the conduct of war was an impediment to comprehension:

> An insistence on going all-out to win a war may have a *fine masculine ring*, and a call to 'defend freedom' may have a *messianic sound* that stirs our blood. But the ending of an all-out war in

these times is beyond imagining. It may mean the turning back of civilization by several thousand years, with no one left capable of signaling the victory.[8]

Total war arouses the passions of the people, invokes cultural concepts of manhood, and produces the belief that the war is for some great and noble cause, which in fact some wars are. American culture predisposes Americans to "go all-out to win," even though this disposition sometimes alienates allies and magnifies the fears of enemies.

In 1954, during Ridgway's tenure as Army Chief of Staff, US Army FM 100–5, *Field Service Regulations Operations* delineated the new American approach to war:

> Limitations. Military forces are justifiable only as instruments of national policy in the attainment of national objectives. Since war is a political act, its broad and final objectives are political; therefore, its conduct must conform to policy. *Victory alone as an aim of war cannot be justified, since in itself victory does not always assure the realization of national objectives.* If the policy objectives are to be realized, policy and not interim expediency must govern the application of military power.[9]

This thesis of war may have been acceptable to some in the Army, for sure a minority, but it was totally unacceptable to the American people and not in concert with Eisenhower's massive retaliation doctrine. National political objectives that required war, the commitment of the citizen-soldier Army, had to be of sufficient significance to warrant the sacrifices war extracted, and if those sacrifices had to be made, Americans expected tangible results. They expected victory.

In the August 1949 edition of FM 100–5, there was no discussion or definition of limited war. Under the principle of war "objective" was the following definition:

> The ultimate objective of all military operations is the destruction of the enemy's armed forces and his will to fight. The selection of intermediate objectives whose attainment contributes most decisively and quickly to the accomplishment of

the ultimate objective at the least cost, human and material, must be based on as complete knowledge of the enemy and theater of operations as is possible . . . .[10]

This was the way Americans expected to fight war. The Korean War showed to Army leaders that more total war had gone away and limited war was the way of future war. However, while the Army endeavored to make this intellectual transformation, the American people held to traditional cultural norms for the conduct of war. The 1949 version of FM 100–5 was the culturally accepted American way of war.

Henry Kissinger and Robert E. Osgood were two of the most influential theorists of limited war. They studied the Korean War and recognized the new reality of war created by nuclear weapons. Kissinger, in an article published in 1955, "Military Policy and Defense of the 'Grey Areas,' " wrote:

> Thus our capacity to fight local wars is not a marginal aspect of our effective strength; it is a central factor which cannot be sacrificed without impairing our strategic position and paralyzing our policy. The risk involved in an all-or-nothing military policy are so fearful that if we follow it our resolution will weaken and leave the initiative to the other side.[11]

The growing nuclear arsenal of the Soviet Union convinced Kissinger, Osgood, and others that nuclear stalemate would transform the power relationship, rendering massive retaliation ineffective in the peripheral areas where total nuclear war could not be justified. In 1957 Kissinger published a book titled, *Nuclear Weapons and Foreign Policy*, in which he argued that:

> Limited war is not a cheap substitute for massive retaliation. On the contrary, it must be based on the awareness that with the end of our atomic monopoly it is no longer possible to impose unconditional surrender at an acceptable cost. The purpose of limited war is to inflict losses or to pose risks for the enemy out of proportion to the objectives under dispute. The more moderate the objectives, the less violent the war is likely to be.[12]

Robert Osgood, in his study, *Limited War: The Challenge to American Strategy*, published in 1957,

defined and developed the theory of limited war that greatly influenced the Kennedy and Johnson Administrations:

> A limited war is one in which the belligerents restrict the purpose for which they fight to concrete, well-defined objectives that do not demand the utmost military effort of which the belligerents are capable and that can be accommodated in a *negotiated settlement*. Generally speaking, a limited war actively involves only two (or very few) major belligerents in the fighting. The battle is confined to a local geographical area and directed against selected targets—primarily those of direct military importance. It demands of the belligerents only a fractional commitment of their human and physical resources. It permits their economic, social, and political patterns of existence to continue without serious disruption. . . . Furthermore, a war may be limited from the perspective of one belligerent, yet virtually unlimited in the eyes of another.[13]

Osgood believed that this was the most important issue of the day involving not only the security of the United States, but also the survival of Western civilization. He believed that the US was not using its power properly and as a result had suffered a number of setbacks from the Communists, including the loss of a unified Korea. He believed that the reason the US had not used its military power more effectively was because of a flawed concept of war: "In practice, the limitation of war is morally and emotionally repugnant to the American people." Osgood sought to help the US move beyond its "traditional approach to war" by advancing a theory of limited war. He delineated the traditional American approach to war, outlined the problems of that approach in a world of nuclear weapons, and formulated principles for the conduct of limited war, many of which corresponded with Kissinger's thinking and were later adopted by the Kennedy and Johnson Administrations. Osgood wrote:

> The administration, like Americans in general, sensed the unprecedented nature of the nation's course in world politics, and it was disturbed by its inability to reconcile this course with America's traditional image of itself as a bold and idealistic nation untrammeled by the moral

ambiguities, the restraints and frustrations, of controlling, balancing, and moderating national power. Its response to this contradiction between reality and predisposition was to try to maintain a rhetorical bridge between them by invoking the inspirational phrases of "collective security" while depreciating the strategy that actually created an unbridgeable gulf [containment strategy]. This placed it at the double disadvantage of raising expectations that did not correspond with the facts and then defending the facts by throwing cold water on the expectations. The effect was not to build a bridge between reality and predisposition but rather to create the illusion of a bridge, which only compounded public frustration and bewilderment.[14]

Nation-states live with many illusions that influence their actions. During the Cold War the US lived with many illusions of strategic importance that damaged the ability of the US to achieve its political objectives through the use of military force. One was that technology had radically changed the nature of war. Osgood identified another illusion: while Americans accepted the "policy of containment," they did not accept the limited war strategy, which was inextricably part of it. The illusion of unlimited war, of fighting war the traditional American way, remained in place. Containment was a defensive policy. It required the US to prepare and to fight small and possibly large conventional wars using multiple means in various regions of the world that were not traditionally considered important to the security of the United States in order to counter Communist expansion. To contain Communism the US had to forward-deploy forces on the continent with the two most significant enemy nation-states, the USSR and the PRC. Americans accepted the policy but not the national strategy and doctrine it required. And there were consequences. Osgood noted:

> The United States would have been in a far better position to achieve its objectives in Korea if it had had a military establishment capable of handling an expanded war without rendering itself defenseless in every other part of the world. With another four divisions to expend, the UN forces might even have succeeded in unifying Korea ... for the

Chinese were committed to their full capacity.... Certainly the lesson here is that the greater our capacity for local defense, the more capable we shall be of resisting aggression at a cost commensurate with limited political objectives.[15]

Kissinger also advanced this thesis, noting that the US could not realistically contemplate actions in peripheral regions without more significant conventional forces.[16]

Kissinger and Osgood both believed it was possible to fight a defensive, limited war of attrition in Southeast Asia, if the US had the will and employed its resources effectively. Osgood's rules for limited war were:

> 1. Statesmen should scrupulously limit the controlling political objectives of war and clearly communicate the limited nature of these objectives to the enemy. 2. Statesmen should make every effort to maintain an active diplomatic intercourse toward the end of terminating the war by a negotiated settlement on the basis of limited objectives. 3. Statesmen should try to restrict the physical dimension of war as stringently as compatible with the attainment of the objectives at stake.[17]

Osgood believed that "military force was a rational instrument of national policy." He drew heavily from the works of Clausewitz. Osgood assumed that both opponents were rational actors. He recognized that one side could be engaged in a total war while the other was fighting a limited war, but he failed to understand that the emotions, passion, hate, and anger of the actor fighting more total war made those actions more irrational. He failed to understand that for the side fighting unlimited war, certain objectives, such as independence, could not be compromised. He failed to understand the quality and level of punishment a nation fighting a total war was willing to endure. To communicate limitations, to enter into negotiations that were not dictated by success on the battlefield, and to impose rigid limitations on geography was to surrender the initiative and communicate a lack of will to fight, thereby strengthening the enemy's resolve. In other words, Osgood's rules eliminate the strategic threat of survival, giving the enemy no need to fear for its continued existence. This took much of the uncertainty out of the war for the enemy, surrendering an enormous strategic advantage. Osgood and Kissinger also advanced the strategy of defensive wars of attrition. Osgood wrote:

> In the gray areas America's superior mobility, training, equipment, and firepower most readily compensate for numerical deficiency in manpower. Even if Chinese manpower were really 'inexhaustible,' as we commonly assume, China's supply of trained and equipped manpower and its ability to sustain them in combat are certainly limited, as the latter stages of the Korean War clearly demonstrated. If we anticipate a "war of attrition," that would be precisely the kind of war in which our superior production and economic base would give us the greatest advantage. As one writer has observed, "A war of attrition is the one war China could not win [a quote from Kissinger]."[18]

Osgood and Kissinger evinced a very healthy dose of American arrogance. Their attrition strategy was based on the assumption that the enemy would attack continuously until exhausted of manpower or the will to expend its manpower. Defensive attrition strategy cannot win wars. It can only preclude defeat. Without strategically offensive operations, positive actions, victory cannot be predicted. Of course, arguably, in limited war victory was not sought, only an acceptable stalemate. However, how was the war to be brought to a conclusion? Without offensive operations of strategic importance there was no way to force an end to the war, and permanent war was unacceptable to Americans, particularly with a drafted Army.

Osgood read the works of Mao Tse-tung, noting that, "Mao Tse-tung has expounded the principles of revolutionary warfare more comprehensively and systematically than any other Communist writer—notably in his work *On the Protracted War* (1939)."[19] Osgood believed that Americans could also fight a protracted war of attrition, a strategy later adopted in the Vietnam War. Mao's theory of war in its final phase, however, was strategically offensive, requiring positive actions by primarily conventional military forces. Students of Mao theory tend to de-emphasize

or forget the final phase of his theory on war, which ultimately predicted decisive results. Osgood's theory depended on the enemy's acknowledging the maintenance of the status quo. It sought negative objectives, including convincing the enemy they cannot win. In such a war, the end of hostilities cannot be predicted, and the enemy dictates the course and conduct of the war. Osgood also did not adequately consider Mao's theory of insurgency war and the battle for the hearts and minds of the people. For Osgood and Kissinger, limited war meant primarily defensive, conventional wars of attrition. This is ultimately what it also came to mean to the Kennedy and Johnson Administrations. They witnessed the last two years of the Korean War and concluded that this was the future of warfare. However, limited war did not have to be a strategically defensive war of attrition. Neither Ridgway nor Taylor restricted limited war to one form of strategy. Limited offensive war was possible, as the first year of the Korean War demonstrated.

Osgood also advanced a theory of "graduated deterrence," noting that: ". . .in order to facilitate a strategy of limited war . . . it may be wise to announce our adherence to a policy of graduated deterrence in the gray areas."[20] This doctrine was defined:

> Thus the first requirement of deterrence is that it be credible to the potential aggressor; and credibility, in turn, requires that the means of deterrence be proportionate to the objective at stake. This commensurability may be difficult to achieve in practice, but the underlying principle is simple enough: it is the principle of economy of force, without which the reciprocal self-restraints essential to limited war cannot exist.[21]

There are a number of problems with this thesis: first, the side fighting a more total war for unlimited objectives may not recognize the "self-restraints" that Osgood expects both sides to observe. Second, graduated deterrence destroys credibility by announcing a limited, partial commitment. Third, it is almost impossible to measure combat power and the ability of the enemy to sustain punishment accurately. Finally, Osgood did not understand the principle of "economy of force," defined as, "allocating minimum essential combat power to *secondary efforts*." The part that was not understood was the "secondary effort."

On the primary effort the principle of war "mass" was applicable. For example, on his primary objective, Napoleon employed the maximum force available, everything he had, to produce the quickest, most decisive results. In war it is necessary to destroy the enemy's main forces in order to render him helpless or convince him that his cause is hopeless and to therefore accept the terms offered. This fact of war did not change with the invention of the atomic bomb. Mass was required in the main effort because it was impossible to accurately measure the will of the enemy to resist. On secondary efforts combat power could be measured against the enemy's combat power to employ just enough force to maintain the situation, and to free up as many forces as possible for the primary effort. The secondary effort was not where the decision on the outcome of the campaign or war would be made. Osgood took the secondary objective for the primary objective, and thus, believed it was possible to measure combat power precisely enough in a major conventional war to just achieve the objective. This is an extremely risky way to fight war, and ultimately failed.

Osgood also poorly understood the importance of coalition warfare and the legitimacy provided by the United Nations and significant allies. While advancing a limited war theory he too was very "American" in his approach to war, believing that: "the United States intervened unilaterally in Korea to promote what it regarded as a vital national interest."[22] Containment was a vital *Western* interest. Without Europe, Britain, and other Western nations as well as Japan, the policy could not have been implemented. And the advent of limited war did not change the fact that in the twentieth century all major wars were coalition wars. Even a nation-state as powerful as the US—which had to maintain a high level of domestic production—was severely taxed by a major limited war halfway around the planet. And the legitimacy provided by the support of allies was an intangible resource of potentially enormous power, particularly in a world where communication technologies were rapidly making public opinion a direct element of combat power. However, two hundred years of history had produced cultural tenets that tended to make Americans more unilateral in their thinking and behavior.

Osgood and Kissinger argued that the US could fight a protracted war of attrition in Southeast Asia, with certain preconditions. Kissinger wrote:

> We thus might say that these are two prerequisites of effective local action by the United States: indigenous governments of sufficient stability so that the Soviets can take over only by open aggression, and indigenous military forces capable of fighting a delaying action. If these conditions are met, the American contribution to the defense of the 'grey area' will involve the creation of a strategic reserve (say in the Philippines, Malaya, or Pakistan) capable of redressing the balance and of a weapons system capable of translating our technological advantage into local superiority.[23]

Kissinger and Osgood believed that in modern attrition war material and technology were more important than manpower, will, and the principles of war. Kissinger noted that, "there would appear to be little likelihood that a state with a steel production of less than 10,000,000 tons annually could win a contest with the United States." He also believed American airpower would greatly restrict the movement of Chinese forces. Osgood and Kissinger were very American in their outlook on war, emphasizing the material aspects of war, and American technology, and de-emphasizing the human factor, character, tenacity, the will to resist, beliefs worth dying for, and other elements of humanity that are intangible, but, at times produce super-human effort, that may make the difference between victory and defeat. The ideas of Kissinger and Osgood greatly influenced the Kennedy and Johnson Administrations, and later, the conduct of the Vietnam War. It is ironic that one of the primary authors of limited war theory negotiated the final ignominious peace treaty for the Vietnam War.

Osgood wrongly predicted the outcome of the transition required of the American people. He wrote:

> . . . that insofar as the United States had failed to anticipate and counter the Communist military and political threat as effectively as objective circumstances might have permitted, it has failed, fundamentally, because of a deficiency in American attitudes and conceptions rather than

because of a lack of native intelligence, technical competence, or material power. But although this deficiency is deep-rooted [in American culture] and, one might say, almost inevitable, considering the nature of American predispositions and experience in international politics, it is not irremediable and it need not be fatal.

But, it was fatal. It was fatal to the people of North Korea, South Vietnam and the entire Indochina peninsula, and it was to the nation's primary instrument for fighting conventional, limited war—the citizen-soldier Army. Culturally, Americans could not adjust to limited, defensive wars of attrition, but they could change the nature of the army they fielded, and the way the United States fought limited war. The citizen-soldier Army was incapable of supporting limited war as conceived by Osgood and Kissinger, and later practiced by Johnson and McNamara. And had the Korean War been a ten-year war, the citizen-soldier Army would have died in the late 1950s. The American citizen-soldier Army could fight limited *offensive war*, war in which the end of hostilities was based on the positive actions of the nation, and thus, termination could be predicted. But permanent war would never be acceptable to the American people.

While Osgood identified the major problem of limited war for the American people, he and Kissinger developed a theory of limited war that conflicted with basic American cultural tenets and violated basic principles of war. In the 1950s there was a national propensity to discard the old and to think anew. There was a belief that as a result of advances in technology everything had changed so radically that nothing from the past mattered. There was also a belief that American power so exceeded that of other nations that the rules that governed past wars no longer mattered to the US. These beliefs and attitudes influenced the development of limited war theories.

Kennedy: The Adoption of New Doctrines for War

Kennedy's thinking on national defense was influenced by the writings of Henry Kissinger, Bernard Brodie, Albert Wohlstetter, Herman Kahn, Robert E. Osgood, and others.[24] During his six years in the House of Representatives and eight years in the Senate, he had listened to the views of the services, and was particularly impressed with the arguments advanced by Kissinger and Osgood, and by Ridgway and Taylor on limited war.[25] He also was profoundly influenced by the Soviet advances in space, primarily *Sputnik*. Kennedy concluded that American thinking about war was based on assumptions that were no longer valid:

> Among the assumptions to be invalidated will be the following ten, which probably are most fundamental to our thinking in the twentieth century:
>
> 1. American arms and science are superior to any other in the world.
> 2. American efforts for world-wide disarmament are a selfless sacrifice for peace.
> 3. Our bargaining power at any international conference table is always more vast and flexible than that of our enemy.
> 4. Peace is a normal relation among states; and aggression is the exception—direct and unambiguous.
> 5. We should enter every military conflict as a moral crusade requiring the unconditional surrender of the enemy.
> 6. A free and peace-loving nation has nothing to fear in a world where right and justice inevitably prevail.
> 7. Americans live far behind the lines, protected by time, space, and a host of allies from attack.
> 8. We shall have time to mobilize our superior economic resources after a war begins.
> 9. Our advanced weapons and continental defense systems, established at a tremendous cost and effort, will protect us.
> 10. Victory ultimately goes to the nation with the highest national income, gross national product, and standard of living.[26]

Kennedy's "assumptions" outlined many of the same tenets delineated by Osgood.[27] Kennedy recognized and acknowledged traditional American thinking and practices in war, while also recognizing the revolutionary nature of missiles and nuclear weapons. Kennedy believed there was a "missile gap"—that the

US was behind the Soviet Union in the development of missiles and other technologies. He believed that in order to reach parity and surpass the Soviet Union, large increases in the defense budget were required. Kennedy believed that the Cold War was a permanent state of hostilities, and that the political environment was chaotic and needed to be stabilized. He believed that American military policy was not adequately linked to its foreign policy, noting that: "We have extended our commitments around the world, without regard to the sufficiency of our military posture to fulfill those commitments." Kennedy found the risks that Eisenhower was willing to take unacceptable. He did not accept Eisenhower's thesis that nuclear power alone could maintain the peace, and that American forces forward-deployed in Korea, Europe, and other parts of the world were simply "trip-wires" for nuclear war. Kennedy believed that the United States possessed the wherewithal—in concert with allies in Europe and Asia—to maintain conventional combat forces capable of meeting the Communist threat without the employment of nuclear weapons. He also believed the US could maintain a conventional warfare capability to fight and win the little wars, to contest Communist advances.

Kennedy had opposed cuts in Army strength recommended and carried out by the Eisenhower Administration. In a speech delivered at Lake Charles, Louisiana, on 16 October 1959, he stressed the importance of ground forces and conventional weapons:

> No problem is of greater importance to every American than our national security and defense. And no aspect of our defense capabilities under this [the Eisenhower] Administration should be cause for greater concern than our lag in conventional weapons and ground forces. . . . in practice our nuclear retaliatory power is not enough. It cannot deter Communist aggression which is too limited to justify atomic war. It cannot protect uncommitted nations against a Communist takeover using local or guerrilla forces. It cannot be used in so-called "brush-fire" peripheral wars. It was not used in Korea, Indochina, Hungary, Suez, Lebanon, Quemoy, Tibet, or Laos. In short, it cannot prevent the Communists from gradually nibbling away at the fringe of the Free World's

territory and strength, until our security has been steadily eroded in piecemeal fashion—each Red advance being too small to justify massive retaliation with all its risks. And history demonstrates that this is the greater threat—not an all-out nuclear attack.[28]

Kennedy accepted the primacy of the nuclear deterrent forces, but believed they were not enough. He supported the strategic vision of General Maxwell D. Taylor, as articulated in his book, *The Uncertain Trumpet*. Taylor advocated a new strategic doctrine:

> The strategic doctrine which I would propose to replace Massive Retaliation is called herein the *Strategy of Flexible Response*. This name suggests the need for a capability to react across the entire spectrum of possible challenges, for coping with anything from general atomic war to infiltrations and aggressions such as threaten Laos and Berlin in 1959. The new strategy would recognize that it is just as necessary to deter or win quickly a limited war as to deter general war. Otherwise, the limited war which we cannot win quickly may result in our piecemeal attrition or involvement in an expanding conflict which may grow into the general war we all want to avoid.[29]

"Flexible response" was ultimately adopted as the strategic military doctrine of the United States by the Kennedy Administration. Flexible response required the United States to maintain the entire range of military options from guerrilla warfare, to limited conventional warfare, to general conventional warfare, to limited nuclear warfare, to total nuclear war. Taylor's strategic doctrine violated none of the principles of war—mass, economy of force, objective, surprise, and so on. However, Kennedy's Secretary of Defense, Robert McNamara, later translated "flexible response" into "graduated response," a conventional air war doctrine that violated numerous principles of war.

In 1959, theorists on nuclear strategy took a new direction, and the simple deterrent formulations of the Eisenhower era were challenged. Albert Wohlstetter wrote: "The notion that a carefully planned surprise attack can be checkmated almost effortlessly, that, in short, we may resume our deep pre-Sputnik sleep, is wrong and its nearly universal acceptance is terribly dangerous."[30] New technologies and dramatic increases in the number of weapons available caused an evolution in thinking about nuclear war. Thus, Bernard Brodie wrote in 1959:

> ... it seems inescapable that the first and most basic principle of action for the United States in the thermonuclear age is the following: a great nation which has forsworn preventive war *must* devote much of its military energies to cutting down drastically the advantage that the enemy can derive from hitting first by surprise attack. This entails doing a number of things, but it means above all guaranteeing through various forms of protection the survival of the retaliatory force under attack.[31]

Brodie had articulated this concept as early as 1954; however, the nation at that time depended primarily on one nuclear delivery system—the strategic bomber—and the Soviet nuclear threat was considerably less capable. Advances in missile technology led to new capabilities and new thinking. *Sputnik* dramatically demonstrated the potential of missile technology, and the Soviets had developed and demonstrated a hydrogen bomb. Wohlstetter's and Brodie's new nuclear doctrine was that the US had to maintain the ability to destroy the Soviet Union after suffering a surprise nuclear attack, a "second-strike" capability. If both the US and the Soviet Union maintained the capability to retaliate after receiving the initial strike, in other words, if neither side was capable of achieving in a "first strike" the destruction of the enemy's retaliatory second-strike force, the incentive to conduct a surprise attack was greatly diminished. Mutually assured destruction theoretically created the condition of nuclear stability. If the US and the Soviet Union could substantially diminish the potential of a surprise strategic nuclear attack, they could compete around the world with conventional forces, surrogate forces, guerrilla forces, and other forms of warfare. Kennedy accepted the strategic doctrine of mutually assured destruction as a replacement for massive retaliation.

In 1961, when Kennedy assumed the office of President of the United States, he had a well-established vision of where he wanted to take the nation's defense programs. After less than six months in office he was faced with the Berlin Crisis, during which he delineated his assessment of the international environment and the challenges ahead:

> The immediate threat to free men is in West Berlin. But that isolated outpost is not an isolated problem. The threat is worldwide. Our effort must be equally wide and strong, and not be obsessed by any single manufactured crisis. We face a challenge in Berlin, but there is also a challenge in Southeast Asia, where the borders are less guarded, the enemy harder to find, and dangers of communism less apparent to those who have so little.... We do not want to fight—but we have fought before. And others in earlier times have made the same dangerous mistake of assuming the West was too selfish and too soft and too divided to resist invasions of freedom in other lands.... We cannot and will not permit the communists to drive us out of Berlin.... For the fulfillment of our pledge to that city is essential to the morale and security of Western Germany, to the unity of Western Europe, and to the faith of the entire Free World. Soviet strategy has long been aimed, not merely at Berlin, but at dividing and neutralizing all of Europe, forcing us back to our shores. We must meet our oft-stated pledge to the free peoples of West Berlin—and maintain our right and their safety, even in the face of force—in order to maintain the confidence of other free peoples in our word and our resolve.... For the choice of peace or war is largely theirs....[32]

From the time Kennedy entered office, he was on the defense against Communism in numerous regions of the world. He faced one crisis situation after another. Kennedy lacked the confidence, experience, patience, steadiness, credibility, and, perhaps, wisdom of Eisenhower. Nevertheless, he possessed certain qualities of character, tested and honed in the South Pacific in war, which enabled him to serve the nation well during a period of intense threat of global nuclear war. The nuclear capabilities of the Soviet Union were real and rapidly expanding, and Khrushchev had adopted a more aggressive foreign policy.

Secretary of Defense Robert S. McNamara

In 1961 President Kennedy started the process of implementing the new strategic doctrines of "flexible response" and "mutual assured destruction." Taylor became an advisor to the President, given a new position in the White House created specifically for him, the Military Representative of the President. A year later Taylor became Chairman of the Joint Chiefs of Staff. Robert S. McNamara was selected for the position of Secretary of Defense. It became his primary responsibility to implement the new strategic doctrine and military policies of the President.

McNamara is widely considered the most powerful Secretary of Defense in the history of the institution. He reorganized the Department of Defense, the Army, and to a lesser degree the other services. He implemented policies that some considered "revolutionary." He instituted planning and management procedures that remained in effect at the end of the twentieth century. He reorganized major commands, formed joint commands, and centralized major functions common to the services. He cancelled some major weapons programs, and advanced others. And he was primarily responsible for the strategy employed in the war in Vietnam. While it is generally argued that presidents are responsible for what happens or fails to happen during their tenure, it can be argued that because McNamara served two presidents during turbulent periods of transition, including the inauguration of the inexperienced Kennedy Administration, the Berlin Crisis, the Bay of Pigs fiasco, the Cuban Missile Crisis, the assassination of the President, the advent of the Johnson Administration, and the critical decision points that moved the nation into war in Vietnam, he bore greater responsibility than anyone else as the primary source of continuity for the nation's defense and for the later debacle in Vietnam.

In the Pentagon, McNamara instituted a reorganization to put in place management organizations similar to those at Ford Motor Company. He established the Systems Analysis Office in 1961. McNamara's inner group in the Pentagon also became known as "the whiz kids." They had little or no military experience and believed it was unnecessary in regard to strategic planning and force design. McNamara made decisions with greater rapidity than the Pentagon was accustomed. He was less willing to listen to committees, less willing to compromise, and expected results quickly, noting that: "The individual in the position of responsibility must make the

decision and take the responsibility for it." If McNamara did not get the results he wanted when he wanted them, he put someone else in charge. He cared little for the traditions of the service, and was unafraid to make changes. The expertise of uniformed military leaders did not impress him. He did not bow to their superior knowledge in various fields of specialization. He required the service chiefs to justify with comprehensive data major systems and programs. If he was not convinced of the need for a particular system or program he cancelled it based on his assessment, and often in opposition to the position of the requesting service. He expected loyalty from civilian and military leaders in the Department of Defense, and when he did not get it he endeavored to remove the impediments. McNamara's character and management style caused considerable friction with and among the services.

On 10 January 1962, McNamara issued an executive order on the reorganization of the Army. At the end of March, McNamara instructed the Secretary of the Army, Elvis J. Stahr, to accelerate the process. The Secretary of the Army considered this directive an unreasonable intrusion into the affairs of the Army. On 2 May he resigned. McNamara had one of his close advisors, Cyrus Vance, supervise the final stages of the reorganization. In July, Vance became Secretary of the Army, in effect making the Secretary of the Army an extension of the Office of the Secretary of Defense.[33] In 1963, the Chief of Naval Operations, Admiral George W. Anderson, testified before a congressional committee on an experimental weapon system. The Admiral disagreed with McNamara's plan to combine the development process for this system with that of the Air Force, arguing that the Navy had specific requirements. He gave his honest opinion, igniting a conflict between the Admiral and Navy on one side, and McNamara and his whiz kids on the other. Breaking with the loyalty clause for flag rank, Anderson publicly stated:

> . . . we feel emotionally aroused as well as dispassionately concerned if the recommendations of the uniformed chiefs of our services, each backed up by competent military and civilian professional staffs, are altered or overruled without interim consultation, explanation and

discussion. ... the operations analyst—properly concerned with 'cost effectiveness'—seems to be working at the wrong echelon—above the professional military level rather than in an advisory capacity to the military who should thoroughly appreciate this assistance. Specialists cannot, without danger, extrapolate their judgments into fields in which they do not have expert knowledge. Unfortunately, today in the Pentagon an unhealthy imbalance has resulted because at times specialists are used as experts in areas outside their fields.[34]

The "Anderson affair" ended with the appointment of the Admiral to Portugal as Ambassador. From military leaders, McNamara wanted loyal yes-men.[35] He also tried to remove Air Force General Curtis LeMay, who was also known for speaking his own mind. LeMay wrote: "Fact is, I was engaged in a protracted struggle with the President's appointee, Secretary McNamara. ... We were diametrically opposed in policy. Our contention, easily recognizable in 1962, had emerged again almost a year later in testimony before the House Armed Services Committee."[36] LeMay believed: "there was another obligation inherent in the job. It was required that I give my candid opinion to the Congress when asked to do so." All administrations rejected this idea. Johnson, however, in this case, rejected McNamara's initiative, allowing the old war hero to finish out his term. LeMay served as Air Force Chief of Staff from 30 June 1961 to 31 January 1965.

One of McNamara's whiz kids, Dr. Alain C. Enthoven, Deputy Assistant Secretary (Comptroller), in his book, *How Much is Enough?*, responded to Admiral Anderson's charge:

One of the main traits of career military officers is a preoccupation with means rather than ends—with performance rather than effectiveness. This is because careers are largely built around particular military means, not around the identification and solution of broad military problems by whatever means seem most appropriate. Retired General Curtis LeMay spent his career in long-range bombers and throughout his career, remained an unabashed advocate of strategic bombing as the solution to most of the military problems facing the United States.

Vice-Admiral Hyman Rickover is a naval nuclear power-plant expert who would solve US antisubmarine warfare problems by buying more nuclear-powered ships. ... The normal military career is built around the mastery of a particular means of waging war, and when an individual reaches the top levels of his Service, he is likely to continue to look to that means to solve the problems that arise.[37]

Enthoven further noted that intra-service competition caused the services to develop and support "unrealistic and unresponsive" plans, programs, and budgets. He noted that within the Navy, the surface fleet, naval aviation, and submarine forces competed for resources; and within the Air Force the Tactical Air Command competed with the Strategic Air Command. A similar situation existed between the major combat arms of the Army: infantry, armor, and artillery. The services were not only at war with each other, but also at war with themselves. As a consequence of this competition all alternatives presented to the Secretary from the services were the result of compromises within the service. Enthoven concluded that: "the Secretary cannot depend on the Services and the JCS to develop for his consideration alternatives that are responsive to his interests, if his interests are perceived to be contrary to those of the military."[38]

Enthoven pointed out that the primary contributors to military theory and strategy in the 1950 and 1960s were civilian scholars, such as Bernard Brodie, Herman Kahn, Henry Kissinger, Samual Huntington, Robert E. Osgood, Thomas Schelling, Albert Wohlstetter, and others. Enthoven's own assessment was in concert with the views held by these scholars. For example, Bernard Brodie wrote:

The basic fact is that the soldier has been handed a problem that extends far beyond the expertise of his own profession. ... when it comes to military questions involving political environment, national objectives, and the vast array of value-oriented propositions that might be made about national defense, his liaison with peoples who are relatively expert in these fields leave much to be desired.[39]

He later wrote:

... the professional military, with exceedingly few exceptions, contributed little but resistance ... and have continued ever since to contribute little or nothing to the understanding of the basic strategic-political problems of our times. That is not to be wondered at, because they have been improperly educated.... They have, in fact, a trained incapacity for dealing with it, and their performance in Vietnam should be all the proof we need.

The argument that military leaders lacked understanding because their education had not prepared them for the responsibilities of force design, the development of strategic doctrine, and strategic planning ignored the fact that General/Secretary of Defense Marshall saw the US through two wars, that General/President Eisenhower was responsible for national security for almost a decade, and that General Ridgway outlined a strategic limited war doctrine before Kissinger and Osgood. And this list is not fixed in time. George Washington, Zachary Taylor, and Ulysses S. Grant literally shaped the nation. General/Secretary of State Colin Powell, and General/Foreign Envoy Anthony C. Zinni (USMC) have greatly influenced not only the course of America's wars but also the course of America's foreign policies.[40] These men were better qualified by experience to plan for and conduct war and to formulate the peace that ideally follows the war. They also were uniquely prepared for strategic planning and force design. War, short of total nuclear war, was still a cultural and human endeavor. This was an aspect of war that Enthoven, Brodie, McNamara, and others from the intellectual elite failed to understand.

Enthoven, however, correctly identified that senior military leaders are culturally impaired, and tend to place loyalty to their service above all else, and that a lifetime commitment to a particular piece of technology—bomber, aircraft carrier, or tank—tended to limit the range of strategic vision.[41] Military leaders also labored under a system that promoted service selfishness, that inhibited cooperation, and that almost precluded comprehension of the cultures of other services. This environment caused friction and compromises that failed to maximize the capabilities of the armed forces. The inability of the services to develop comprehensive strategies and military policies facilitated the ability of McNamara and the whiz kids to implement policies and dominate planning.

At times the JCS simply became a backdrop for decisions made by the administration. In November 1965, the first year of the Vietnam War, the JCS, Army General Earl Wheeler, Chairman of the JCS, Army General Harold K. Johnson, Admiral David L. McDonald, Air Force General John McConnell, and Marine Corps General Wallace Greene, received a long-sought meeting with the President and his Secretary of Defense to discuss the strategy for the conduct of war. They were dissatisfied with the strategy, and sought changes. Then Colonel Charles G. Cooper attended the meeting as the map holder for this high level discussion. In an article entitled, "The Day It Became the Longest War," he wrote:

> Normally, memories are dimmed by time—but not this one. My memory of Lyndon Johnson on that day remains crystal clear. While General Wheeler, Admiral McDonald, and General McConnell spoke, he had been attentive, apparently listening seriously, communicating only with an occasional nod. After General McConnell finished, General Wheeler asked the President if he had any questions. Johnson waited a moment or so, then turned to Generals Johnson and Greene, who had remained silent during the briefing, and asked, "Do you fully support these ideas?" ... Both generals indicated their agreement with the proposal. Seemingly deep in thought, President Johnson turned his back on them for a minute or so, then suddenly, losing the calm, patient demeanor he had maintained throughout the meeting, he whirled to face them and exploded.
>
> I almost dropped the map. He screamed obscenities, he cursed them personally, he ridiculed them for coming to his office with their "military advice." Noting that it was he who was carrying the weight of the free world on his shoulders, he called them filthy names— sh__heads, dumbsh__s, pompous assh__s— and used "the F-word" as an adjective more freely than a Marine at boot camp. He then accused them of trying to pass the buck for World War III to him. It was unnerving. It was degrading.[42]

McNamara had ambushed and cowed the JCS. The chiefs failed to do the job that the nation expected and legislation demanded during the Vietnam War. The nation's Vietnam experience was the function of multiple failures at the highest levels of government. Their failing was, in part, a function of the civilian leadership in the Pentagon and White House; in part, a function of the system instituted with the 1947 National Defense Act; and, in part, a function of the service cultures that impeded their ability to think strategically and comprehensively.

McNamara and his whiz kids were not strategic thinkers, accustomed to integrating broad concepts of foreign and defense policies. Nor were they politicians capable of compromise and forming consensus. A student of McNamara's leadership wrote:

> strategic thought was not a congenial process for the mind of Robert McNamara. There was nothing in his previous experience . . . to provide him with a grasp of high strategy and international political-military relations. Moreover, Mr. McNamara gathered around him in 1961 men who did not complement his own intellectual processes so much as reinforce them. In Beaufre's terms, 'logistic thought' was the mode of the new management.[43]

In essence, no one in the Kennedy and Johnson Pentagon was thinking strategically. McNamara and his whiz kids were scientific managers, technicians involved in fixing and perfecting systems. They were efficiency experts primarily concerned with measuring capabilities at all levels and insuring that the US possessed capabilities to match or surpass those of the enemy at the least cost. They applied the same methods to all problems endeavoring to quantify certain aspects of war that produced little useable data. They were intellectually strong in the use of logic, quantitative methods, and deductive reasoning. They were intellectually weak in the use of common sense, an understanding of humanity, and a comprehension of the totality of war, and their moral compass was considerably underdeveloped. McNamara and Enthoven failed to understand that war is a human endeavor. Hate, anger, indignation, envy, passions, emotions, desires, values, beliefs, patriotism, tenacity, and other uniquely human qualities and characteristics influence the conduct of war from the tactical level to the strategic level. The willingness of people to fight cannot be measured in the numbers of bombs dropped and bodies counted. Bombs kill men and help win battles. But men win wars. The inability of McNamara and his whiz kids to comprehend this was their biggest failure, the roots of all their other failures. McNamara, too late, acknowledged that, they "totally misjudged" and "misunderstood" the situation in Vietnam. They, however, did not have to pay the cost for their failures.

*   *   *   *   *

In 1968, a year after he left the Office of the Secretary of Defense, McNamara published a book entitled, *The Essence of Security: Reflections in Office*, in which he endeavored to outline his accomplishments and the thinking behind his actions while serving as the eighth Secretary of Defense. McNamara believed that he based "all major defense decisions" on seven "core conclusions":

> That the security of the United States must continue to rest on a firm commitment to the policy of collective security . . . .
>
> That although our strategic nuclear capability is absolutely vital to our security and to that of our allies, its only realistic role is deterrence of all-out nuclear or non-nuclear attacks since it is now impossible for either the United States or the Soviet Union to achieve a meaningful victory over the other in a strategic nuclear exchange.
>
> That the doctrine of massive retaliation is therefore useless as a guarantee of our security, and must continue to give way to both the theory and the practice of flexible response.
>
> That the direction of the Department of Defense demands not only a strong, responsible civilian control, but a Secretary's role that consists of active, imaginative and decisive leadership of the establishment at large, and not the passive practice of simply refereeing the disputes of traditional and partisan factions.
>
> That the dynamics of efficient management in so complex an institution as the Defense Department necessarily require the use of modern managerial tools and increasing efforts to determine whether the "cost" of each major program and each new project is justified by the "benefit" or strength it adds to our security.

That the Department's primary role of combat readiness is fully consistent with innovative programs designed to utilize at minimal cost its potential for significantly contributing to the solution of the nation's social problems.

And that finally the security of this Republic lies not solely or even primarily in military force, but equally in developing stable patterns of economic and political growth both at home and in the developing nations throughout the world.[44]

What is remarkable about McNamara's "core conclusions" is the absence of a statement about the employment of soldiers, marines, sailors, and airmen for strategic national interests; about the cost to the nation in terms of the lives of servicemen; about the men and women who have to fight the wars and how he planned to insure that their lives were safeguarded by every means possible consistent with achieving the nation's political objectives; and about the political circumstances that might justify the employment of ground combat forces. McNamara's "cost-benefit" analysis, at the strategic, nuclear level of war, was based primarily on units of money per kiloton or megaton of survivable destructive power; in limited war it was based primarily on units of money per divisions and per units of destructive power of weapon systems. It is not evident that he understood the concept of combat power, which is based not only on technology and numbers of ships, aircraft, and divisions, but also intangibles such as morale, *esprit de corps*, unit cohesion, the ability of the services to operate as teams on the battlefield, tenacity, courage, leadership, generalship, confidence in the chain of command, the importance of the task to national security, the ability to demonstrate and articulate "why they fight," public support, and other intangible factors not easily quantified. The most efficient use of money does not always produce the most combat power. And because Americans could see and touch technology, but were unable to see or discern the combat power a squad or battalion or division can generate, there was a tendency to equate technology with combat power. Policies and programs that maximize efficiency may in fact damage the ability of a service to generate combat power. This problem became evident in Vietnam.

McNamara accepted the strategic doctrine of flexible response. However, he significantly modified the concept: "Thus security for the United States and its allies can only arise from the possession of a range of *graduated deterrents*, each of them fully credible in its own context."[45] He envisioned war as a series of gradients from guerrilla to nuclear, and sought to insure that at each gradient the US had the capability to fight and win. Graduated deterrent meant the US could escalate from one level of deterrent to the next higher level, for example, from general conventional war to tactical nuclear war.

Flexible response in the initial Ridgway and Taylor conceptions meant the US had to be able to fight a range of wars, including limited war. Limited war placed restrictions and limitations on the use of force, means, resources, geography, and objectives. In limited war the nation decided how much of its defense resources it wanted to commit to achieve specific objectives in a given peripheral region of the world, given all its other commitments. Once that level of commitment was reached no more resources were provided. Limited war did not mean escalation to the next higher level of war. It meant placing definite limitations on the level of commitment. Truman placed strategic limitations on the Korean War. He determined that he would not initiate World War III in Korea, and told his field commander that if they could not achieve the objectives with the forces allocated, given minor adjustments, he would send the Navy to evacuate the peninsula. Limited conventional war pertained primarily to peripheral regions of the world necessary to contain the Soviet Union and the People's Republic of China. This doctrine did not apply to Europe, to NATO. *Graduated deterrence and flexible response are not the same concepts, nor the same doctrine.*

McNamara's most significant and lasting contribution to national defense may have been his reorganization of the way the Department of Defense conducted business. McNamara put in place management tools that better enabled the President, Secretary, and the services to make certain types of decisions. Kennedy instructed McNamara to determine and provide what was needed to safeguard national security without arbitrary budget limits, but to do so as economically as possible. McNamara determined that congressional legislation gave him sufficient authority to carry out his duties, but that there was an "absence of the essential management tools." McNamara brought to the Pentagon sophisticated business methods used by major firms. He consolidated the budgets of the services; that is, instead of each service submitting a budget with no consideration to those of other services, he required an integrated approach, which revealed a number of significant deficiencies and inconsistent practices.

Charles J. Hitch, the Defense Comptroller, was responsible for revising the budgeting process. He budgeted jointly for specific functions, such as strategic retaliatory forces, continental air and missile defense forces, general purpose forces, research and development, and reserve and guard forces. McNamara put into practice a five-year budgetary process called, "planning-programming-budgeting system" (PPBS) out of which the annual five-year defense program was constructed, linking long-range planning with the annual budgets. A Systems Analysis Directorate under Alain C. Enthoven was created to provide the Secretary with the information needed to evaluate major weapons and programs without depending on the assessments of the services. Certain functions of the services were consolidated. For example, elements of the intelligence agencies of the services were combined to form the Defense Intelligence Agency (DIA). The Defense Supply Agency was formed, consolidating eight separate agencies. McNamara placed all active duty, deployable combat forces under unified or specified commands, removing them from service departments. He believed this improved operational efficiency. He concluded that his reorganization eliminated literally tens of thousands of man-hours of labor, saved more than $14 billion over a five-year period, and increased efficiency.

One of McNamara's first actions was to rationalize the armed forces, and to separate strategic forces from all other kinds of forces. Strategic forces require survivable systems, early warning, and reliable command and communication systems. McNamara pushed forward the development of the second generation of ICBM, the *Minuteman*, and slowly retired the older liquid-fuel *Atlas* and *Titans I* and *II*. To secure them, hardened underground silos, dispersed in

regions of the country that were not near population centers, were constructed. Multiple independently targeted re-entry vehicles were placed on each rocket. Nuclear missiles fired from aircraft, trains, and trucks were researched to reduce the vulnerability to a Soviet first strike; however, the hardened silo remained the accepted means of deployment. Between 1961 and 1967 the number of land-based ICBMs increased from 28 to 1,054. Under McNamara's watch 41 Polaris submarines with 656 missile launchers became operational. McNamara did not support the construction of the new B-70 supersonic bomber to replace the B-52, a severe blow to the Air Force, but he implemented an expensive modification program to extend the service life of the B-52. McNamara maintained 40 percent of roughly 600 long-range bombers on 15-minute alert status. ICBMs, SLBMs, and SAC formed the triad system, which guaranteed the US a second-strike capability. For better control of strategic, nuclear resources, a new integrated National Military Command System was established. It included airborne control systems.

McNamara's Reorganization of the Army

To give Kennedy the strategic flexibility to meet Soviet aggression in arenas other than nuclear war required an Army considerably more capable than that left by the Eisenhower Administration. One of McNamara's gradients of deterrent was limited ground war. McNamara acknowledged the difficulty of impressing upon the American people the need for such a capability. The persistence of the American dream born at the end of World War II that airpower and atomic bombs were the last word in warfare had to be overcome. He noted:

> Today our nuclear superiority does not deter all forms of Soviet support of Communist insurgency in Southeast Asia. What all of this has meant is that we, and our allies as well, require substantial non-nuclear forces in order to cope with levels of aggression that massive strategic forces do not, in fact, deter. This has been a difficult lesson both for us and for our allies to accept. There is a strong psychological tendency to regard superior nuclear forces as a simple and unfailing solution to security and an assurance of victory under any set of circumstances. What

must be understood is that our nuclear strategic forces play a vital and absolutely necessary role in our security and that of our allies, but it is an intrinsically limited role. Therefore we and our allies must maintain substantial conventional forces, fully capable of dealing with a wide spectrum of lesser forms of political and military aggression.[46]

McNamara could not reverse this "psychological tendency," which was a function of deeply held cultural tenets. As American technology advanced and defense budgets grew, the American faith in technology only deepened, and the willingness to use men as instruments of war declined.

New missions and counterinsurgency doctrines meant the resurrection of the Army. The Army was reorganized and refocused on conventional ground warfare. Space and intercontinental missiles became the primary domain of the Air Force and NASA. While the Army continued to develop tactical nuclear weapons and missiles, and to maintain the thousands of nuclear weapons deployed to Europe in the late 1950s, it redirected its primary efforts to conventional, non-nuclear operations. The Pentomic Division went away and an organizational structure similar to the World War II triangular division was reinstated. The size of the Army was increased, and new equipment and technology came into the inventories. Major Army commands were consolidated. New commands and organizations came into existence, among them the air-mobile division.

Kennedy and McNamara prepared the Army to fight a limited war, but not in Vietnam. Their strategy was to maintain strong ground forces forward-deployed in Europe, Korea, and Japan and to maintain a healthy mobile strategic reserve in the United States that could actually fight a limited war. However, the orientation was still primarily on Europe with an emphasis on mechanized forces. To increase the strategic mobility of the Army, the Air Force was pushed to develop the C-130, C-141, and C-5A, and fast-deployment logistic ships were also researched.

Under the McNamara Pentagon, the Army Chief of Staff General George H. Decker approved a reorganization plan that refocused the Army on the conduct of traditional ground warfare—a return to the fundamentals of the campaign-winning infantry and armor doctrines of World War II. The Army retained much of the doctrinal thinking designed to fight on the nuclear battlefield; however, the emphasis had changed. The Army's reorganization plan was based on studies conducted by the Army's Command and General Staff College, and the US Continental Army Command (USCONARC).[47] The latter study was entitled, "Reorganization Objectives Army Division (ROAD) 1965." The Secretary of the Army and Defense approved the plan, and in May 1961 the President approved the reorganization.

ROAD adapted the triangular division of World War II to current Army missions and technology. The brigade headquarters replaced the World War II regimental headquarters and the battle group headquarters of the Pentomic Division. The brigade headquarters had no organic combat forces. Under the brigade headquarters were three infantry battalions. The brigade headquarters was designed to command two to five battalions. Battalions could be attached and detached under standard operational procedures. The system was designed to be flexible, to allow the Army to task-organize forces, for specific missions. The battalions consisted of five companies, three infantry line companies, a combat support company (which contained the heavy and specialized weapons of the battalion), and a headquarters company. Companies, like battalions, could be attached and detached forming task forces or simply reinforcing.

With the return of the triangular division, battalion command was reestablished. Lieutenant colonels commanded battalions and colonels commanded brigades. The division downgraded its tactical nuclear missions. It retained its nuclear-capable 8-inch howitzer and Davy Crocket rockets. The time and resources devoted to training to fight on the nuclear battlefields was refocused on traditional offensive and defensive combat operations, and greater emphasis was given to guerrilla warfare.

The basic building blocks of divisions were uniform across the Army; hence, the brigade from one division could be attached to another division with little loss in effectiveness. This was the unique feature of the new organization—the ability to task-organize at every level from division to company without the loss of combat effectiveness.[48] The typical infantry division consisted of eight infantry and two tank battalions; airborne divisions of nine infantry battalions; mechanized divisions of seven mechanized infantry and three tank battalions; and an armor division of six tank and five mechanized infantry battalions. The division's artillery consisted of three battalions of 105-mm howitzers, and two battalions of 155-mm howitzers, and a company of 8-inch howitzers. A support command completed the division organization. The division was the smallest unit in the Army capable of independent combat operations, and the largest unit in the Army trained to fight as a team.

The helicopter, armored personnel carrier, and tank increased the tactical and operational mobility of Army divisions, but reduced its strategic mobility. As the numbers of armored vehicles, tanks, and helicopters increased, so too did the logistical support they required. As a result, the ability to get divisions to battlefields across oceans declined. However, once on the battlefield the ROAD division was capable of generating considerably more combat power than a World War II division. It was faster, more flexible, and capable of absorbing greater shock. It was capable of defending larger frontage, in greater depth, and striking deeper into enemy forces. These new capabilities were a function of advances in technology and organization.

Army Aviation: the Helicopter

On 1 July 1965 the 1st Cavalry Division (Airmobile) was activated. On 27 August the advance party of the division arrived at An Khe, Vietnam. The remainder of the division—over 400 aircraft, nearly 16,000 soldiers, and over 1,600 vehicles—was deployed by sea by the US Navy and the Military Sea Transportation Service. Helicopters were loaded on the deck of the aircraft carrier *USS Boxer* for transport. On 3 October the entire division was assembled and assigned a 150-mile square area of operation in the central highlands. In November 450 men of the 7th Cavalry, a battalion size organization, were dropped into the Ia Drang Valley by helicopter, where they fought an intensive battle against elements of three regiments of the regular PAVN forces. During the course of the battle the 7th Cavalry was reinforced, resupplied, and provided close air support by helicopters. Wounded

and dead soldiers were evacuated by helicopter. The helicopter facilitated command and control by the brigade and division commanders. Observation helicopters conducted reconnaissance, providing the chain of command with immediate intelligence. Close air support and artillery were coordinated and adjusted from helicopters. And, when the battle was over the cavalry rode back to An Khe in helicopters. The Army had proven the capabilities of this technology. The driving force behind Army aviation was the demand for greater operational and tactical mobility. Small units could move further and faster than ever before, increasing combat effectiveness.

In 1939 Igor Sikorsky demonstrated the helicopter to the Army; however, the technology was in its infancy and played no part in World War II. In August 1945, the US Army Air Force dropped two atomic bombs on Japan, bringing the war to an end. The advent of nuclear weapons caused the service to rethink their doctrines and technology. Allan Millett's research revealed that Marine Corps initiated the development of air-assault doctrine before it had helicopters. He wrote:

> With a thunderous roar the nuclear device denoted beneath the center of Bikini lagoon … cast doubt on the Marine Corps's main function, the amphibious operation. The shock wave of Operation Crossroads, a series of Navy-directed nuclear tests in the summer of 1946, reached Headquarter Marine Corps and stimulated General Vandergrift to call for a reanalysis of amphibious doctrine.... The board concluded that a Japanese nuclear weapon would have destroyed the two divisions that assaulted Iwo Jima before they reached the beaches. But it believed it saw a solution to the ship-to-shore problem: The initial assault waves would land behind the beach defenses, dropped into weak points in the enemy positions by helicopter. Flying from well-dispersed carriers, the helicopter forces would both close with the enemy rapidly.... Both the board and Vandergrift quick concluded that the "vertical envelopment" assault … gave new life to the amphibious operation....[49]

When it was argued that nuclear weapons made amphibious assault obsolete, the Marine Corps began a search for technologies and doctrines that made it relevant in the prevailing conditions. The helicopter had the capability to rapidly disperse and mass forces. It had the potential for over the horizon vertical envelopment—that is the ability to lift off from aircraft carriers out of sight of land because of the curvature of the Earth and land forces behind enemy lines. However, in 1946 helicopter technology was not yet ready for service. It made its formal debut into the inventories of the services in Korea.

On 2 August 1950 the helicopter accompanied the 1st Marine Brigade into combat in Korea. It was used for command and liaison flights, rescue missions, reconnaissance, evacuation of casualties, and drops of food and water. In the early days of the war the helicopter helped maintain vital links between units that were cut off by North Korean forces. In the summer of 1951 the Marine Corps activated the first helicopter transport squadron.[50] A British observer wrote:

> [T]he helicopter has earned in Korea its permanent place in the pattern of air power. The US Marine Corps were able to test under combat conditions their theories on the value of the helicopter as assault transport. Entire companies of fully-equipped Marines were flown in 10-seat HRS-1 (S.55) helicopters to almost inaccessible mountainside positions in the front lines. Days of marching were avoided. Troops arrived in the line fresh. On occasion, telephone lines to headquarters were laid from the helicopter as they delivered the soldiers.[51]

The Army and the Air Force quickly adopted the helicopter and expanded its use throughout the war. It was used to evacuate wounded personnel, for limited resupply, and limited transport of troops. During the war helicopters evacuated an estimated 25,000 casualties—many of whom would have never survived on land transportation.

During the Korean War the Army was also dissatisfied with the close air support provided by the Air Force. The helicopter was an opportunity for the Army to reacquire organic close air support; however, its most important function was tactical and operational mobility. Men such as General James M. Gavin advocated the extensive use of helicopter and other

aircraft for the atomic battlefield. However, feuding between the Army and Air Force slowed the development of the helicopter. An agreement between the Army and Air Force, 23 March 1950, gave the Air Force responsibility for the procurement of Army aircraft and aircraft equipment, for research and development, and for the classification of types of aircraft. As the speed, reliability, and lift capacity of the aircraft increased, the Army's interest in its utility in the tactical and operational role increased. Agreements between the Army and Air Force were then renegotiated, with the Army gaining greater control with each round.

After the Korean War the Army started arming helicopters. Grenade launchers and rocket launchers were attached to helicopters. And in 1959 Bell Helicopter Company armed an OH-13 helicopter with a wire-guided anti-tank missile. Exercises were conducted to test the technology in various roles. In the mid 1950s, the Sky Cav concept was tested at Fort Rucker, the home of the Army's Aviation School and Fort Benning, Georgia, the home of the infantry. Units were formed to develop and test doctrine. It was determined that to transport troops and land them in hostile terrain, the helicopter had to be armed. The Army's search for technology and doctrine to fight on the nuclear battlefield advanced the development of the helicopter. The requirement of the Pentomic Division to rapidly disperse and reassemble created new missions for the helicopter. In July 1958 Army aviation put on a demonstration for 400 of the nation's top military and industrial leaders, including Secretary of the Army Wilbur Brucker. Three H-37 Sikorsky helicopters landed an "Honest John" missile, crew, and tons of equipment. The unit was fully operational shortly after landing. In the late 1950s the Army published FM 57–35, *Army Transport Aviation—Combat Operations*. This manual delineated basic tactics and techniques for air assault operations. General Tolson, one of the authors of the manual, noted: "this manual stood the test of time and would be vindicated in the tests of the 11th Air Assault Division and in Vietnam."[52]

In the late 1950s the XH-40 Bell Utility Helicopter was tested. It was the first helicopter with a turbine engine, and its potential was quickly recognized. To bridge the gap between the Army and Air Force, the

Army developed the Army Aircraft Development Plan. It was a plan for the expansion of Army aviation and provided guidance for research and development. In December 1961 two Army transport helicopter companies were deployed to Vietnam on the recommendations of General Maxwell Taylor. The Army acquired valuable experience supporting the ARVN.

In 1961 McNamara undertook a study of Army aviation. He wanted the Army to justify its need. The Army provided the required information; however, McNamara was not satisfied. Major General Hamilton H. Howze was appointed to head the Army Tactical Mobility Requirement Board, which ultimately became known as the Howze Board. Howze was an Army aviator who was certain to produce a report favorable to Army aviation; however, civilian Pentagon officials were added to the board to insure that quantitative methods were used to determine the efficiency of airmobile doctrine. The most important recommendation of the Howze Board was the formation of an air assault division consisting of more than 450 helicopters. The board concluded: "Adoption by the Army of the airmobile concept ... is necessary and desirable. In some respects, the transition is inevitable, just as was that from animal mobility to motor."[53] To counter the board the Air Force formed its own board, to demonstrate that the Air Force could meet the Army's needs.[54] Throughout the 1950s the Air Force argued against the Army's development and acquisition of substantial helicopter forces, and in the early 1960s was still determined to keep the number of aircraft in an Army division to a minimum. A student of Army aviation, Frederic A. Bergerson, noted: "The Air Force fought bitterly during this period to prove its superiority in matters of air support ... Air Force-Army test ... stressed the mobility of the Air Force's C-130."[55] Nevertheless, McNamara supported the development of an air assault division, and in February 1963, the 11th Air Assault Division (Test) was activated at Fort Benning, Georgia. This organization ultimately led to the formation of the 1st Cavalry Division. McNamara wrote:

> Much improved mobility, especially for our forces oriented toward underdeveloped areas, was obtained through greater emphasis on helicopters. In 1961 the Army and Marine Corps had

about 3,100 helicopters, all but 200 of which had piston engines. By the end of fiscal 1970 ... we will have about 7,500 modern turbine helicopters, with much greater capacity and speed and higher possible utilization rates than the ones they replaced.[56]

General Howze noted: "never has it been suggested that the proposed Army airmobile units are competitive, in any of their capabilities, with Air Force units. As recommended by the Mobility Board in its report, the air assault division will depend on the Air Force for almost all close air support."[57] These words could not disguise the fact that Howze envisioned an air assault division capable of providing considerable close air support to soldiers on the ground, and operating independently to destroy enemy forces on the ground. Howze wrote: "The air assault division commander must be able to counter three varieties of assault ... airborne, armored, and infantry, plus of course combinations of the three.... [N]ew enemy airheads would be particularly susceptible to the rocket and machine gun firing helicopters...."[58] Each service preferred to rely on its own resources to achieve military objectives.

Howze's vision was only partially realized. He envisioned multiple air assault divisions combined with an airborne division, acting under a corps headquarters capable of a wide-range of operations. He believed the helicopter would revolutionize warfare:

> I am equally prepared to list a few of the advantages of the Air Assault Division. Most importantly, I believe, is the ability of the new division to turn upside down the problem of the terrain obstacle, a problem which through all history has governed ... all ground combat tactics. In taking to the air the new division suddenly finds that most terrain obstacles work for it, whether the action is offense, defense, or retrograde. It is quite impossible to exaggerate the effect of this advantage, to overestimate the contrast between one side's ability to leap barriers in minutes by helicopter, and the other side's requirement to proceed by long hours of days of foot movement. And in battlefield supply the contrast is just as great.
>
> Related to the first advantage is the second: the willingness with which the air assault division may

... thoroughly muck up the terrain—well behind its own forward positions, when necessary—by blowing all the bridges and culverts, and infesting all bypasses, roads and trails with mines . . . .

Third in importance is the great flexibility of employment which derives from mobility. The air assault commander has open to him a far greater variety of feasible courses of action in the attack, a new latitude of choice as respects both point of thrust and direction of thrust—which in turn permits him to attack enemy weakness and avoid enemy strength—and vastly greater possibilities of surprise . . . .

This discussion of advantages can be expanded to include many others: the inherent capability of airmobile forces to ambush conventional forces, the new mobility of direct firepower, the reduction of artillery ammunition expenditure common to slow conventional attack, the utility of the stay-behind forward observer, the comparative efficiency of air-to-ground and air-to-air communications, the relative invulnerability of our own lines of communication and rear area logistic system, the ease with which air assault formations can fatigue and confuse their opponents, the speed with which they can react to unexpected opportunity, and the manner in which they can minimize their own casualties while inflicting heavy punishment on the enemy.[59]

This did not complete Howze's list of capabilities and advantages, and while he recognized disadvantages including cost, weather, and vulnerability to surface-to-air rockets, Howze never identified the full range of factors that limited the usages of the helicopter. He also did not comprehend the psychological effects of the helicopter on soldiers. The Army never organized more than one air assault division, and never attained the range of capabilities identified by Howze. Still, the air assault division became a permanent part of the Army's force structure.[60] The capabilities of aircraft greatly enhanced the ability of the Army to see, fight, resupply, redeploy, and evacuate.[61] In the 1990s, the Marine Corps with the development of vertical takeoff and landing (VTOL) aircraft, the V-22 Osprey, pushed these concepts and doctrine to new levels of capability, greatly expanding operational mobility and, with sufficient number of aircraft, creating strategic mobility.

Communist Revolutionary War Doctrine and Army Counter-Revolutionary War Doctrine

Without some understanding of insurgency war doctrine and "people's war" strategy, it is not possible to understand the Vietnam War. The literature on this subject is vast, and no effort is made to duplicate it. However, because of the significance of this form of war and America's efforts to counter it, some discussion is necessary.[62] Between 1945 and 1950 the United States recognized the effectiveness of Communist insurgency and guerrilla warfare doctrine.[63] In Eastern Europe, China, and Indochina this doctrine caused the defeat and overthrow of governments supported by the West. Bernard B. Fall identified the significance of this form of war in the post–World War II era:

If we look at the twentieth century alone we are now in Viet-Nam faced with the forty-eighth small war. Let me just cite a few: Algeria, Angola, Arabia, Burma, Cameroon, China, Columbia, Cuba, East Germany, France, Haiti, Hungary, Indochina, Indonesia, Kashmir, Laos, Morocco, Mongolia, Nagaland, Palestine, Yemen, Poland, South Africa, South Tyrol, Tibet, Yugoslavia, Venezuela, West Iran, etc.

The magnitude of this transformation was not fully understood by the West because it was taking place primarily in developing states. Fall concluded that, "This . . . is quite fantastic. In fact, if a survey were made of the number of people involved, or killed, in those forty-eight small wars it would be found that these wars . . . involved as many people as either one of the two world wars, and caused as many casualties."[64]

An *insurgency* is an organized movement to overthrow an established government by eroding public support through political indoctrination, subversion, indirect and direct military operations, terrorism, and control of the population. The people are the objective in insurgency warfare. In theory, a government cannot long survive without the support of the people. Clausewitz identified three ways to win a war: destruction of the enemy's main armed forces, destruction of the will of the people, and the destruction of the enemy government. Insurgencies concentrate on the destruction of the government through the destruction of the will of the people that support it. Governments function most effectively with the willing support of the people. And at a minimum the acquiescence of the people is necessary for a government to function. Hence, the primary objective of an insurgency is to erode and ultimately destroy the legitimacy of the government, and its acceptance by and support of the people. Fall described this complex form of war:

> One of the problems one immediately faces is that of terminology. Obviously "sublimited warfare" is meaningless, and "insurgency" or "counterinsurgency" hardly define the problem. But the definition that I think will fit the subject is "revolutionary warfare" (RW). Let me state this definition: RW=G+P, or "revolutionary warfare equals guerrilla warfare plus political action." This formula for revolutionary warfare is the result of the application of guerrilla methods to the furtherance of an ideology or a political system. . . . The Communists, or shall we say, any sound revolutionary warfare operator . . . most of the time used small-war tactics, not to destroy the . . . Army, of which they were thoroughly incapable; but to establish a competitive system of control over the population. . . . the military aspect, definitely always remained the minor aspect. The political, administrative, ideological aspect is the primary aspect.[65]

Clausewitz, who witnessed and studied the first modern "people's war" during the French occupation of Spain in the Napoleonic era, concluded that the following conditions were required to carry out a people's war, a "revolutionary war":

1. The war must be fought in the interior of the country.
2. It must not be decided by a single stroke.
3. The theater of operations must be fairly large.
4. The national character must be suited to that type of war.
5. The country must be rough and inaccessible, because of mountains, or forests, marshes, or the local methods of cultivation.[66]

Guerrilla forces are paramilitary forces that operate in the interior of enemy-held territory. Guerrillas are civilians recruited and trained to fight an enemy

among the population to which they are native. Guerrillas have the ability to move undetected among the people. They operate at the local, regional, and national levels. They use their anonymity to carry out operations against the government, to win supporters, to recruit fighters, collect intelligence, kill collaborators, undermine the government, and terrorize and/or control the population. Their objective is to gain the support of the people. Communism as an economic system did not work; however, Communism as an ideology in peasant societies proved a considerable force, particularly when combined with the force of nationalism, the drive for statehood, and the desire for self-determination. Communism, which emphasized the community, proved far superior to capitalism, which emphasized the individual, in mobilizing and motivating people in peasant, agricultural societies. Ideology is an important component in "revolutionary war theory." It creates cohesion, motivates actions, directs resources and energy, and guides decision-making.

Communist insurgents initially endeavor to persuade, to convince through disciplined behavior, political indoctrination, and demonstrations of the impotence of the government. If this does not work they use intimidation, terrorism, selective and mass murder. Westmoreland characterized the operations of the Viet Cong in Vietnam:

> This enemy also uses terror—murder, mutilation, abduction, and the deliberate shelling of innocent men, women, and children—to exercise control through fear. . . . A typical day in Viet-Nam was last Sunday. Terrorists near Saigon assassinated a 39-year-old village chief. The same day in the delta, they kidnapped 26 civilians assisting in arranging for local elections. The next day the Viet Cong attacked a group of Revolutionary Development workers, killing 1 and wounding 12 and in another they opened fire on a small civilian bus and killed 3, wounded 4 of its passengers. These are cases of calculated enemy attack on civilians to extend by fear that which they cannot gain by persuasion.[67]

By killing the leadership (village chiefs), by demonstrating the government could not protect the people (kidnapping, killing, and wounding), and by demonstrating that the institutions of the government did not work (the election system and the transportation system), the VC endeavor to gain the support of the people.

Guerrillas need outside support to function. They require external resources, guidance, and coordination. In Vietnam the "National Liberation Front," also known as the Viet Cong (VC), formed the guerrilla force. North Vietnam provided the external resources and direction they needed to carry out the insurgency. The PRC and USSR provided the external resources required for North Vietnam to carry out the war. The People's Army of North Vietnam (PAVN) provided the primary regular army forces required to permit the VC to operate.

Mao Tse-tung read Clausewitz. And while much is made of Mao's emphasis on the political task, winning the support of the people through disciplined cadres who possess the correct ideological perspective, the political objective, his strategic formulation also emphasized the importance of the military task, and the significance of regular, trained forces in battle—the military objective. He was in this sense an adherent of the thesis of Clausewitz. Mao, under the heading of "The Object of War," wrote:

> Here we are dealing with the elementary object of war, as "politics with bloodshed", as mutual slaughter by opposing armies. It should be pointed out that destruction of the enemy is the primary object of war and self-preservation the secondary, because only by destroying the enemy in large numbers can one effectively preserve oneself. Therefore attack, the chief means of destroying the enemy, is primary, while defence, a supplementary means of destroying the enemy and a means of self-preservation, is secondary. In actual warfare the chief role is played by defence much of the time and by attack for the rest of the time, but if war is taken as a whole, *attack remains primary*. . . . This is precisely why we say that attack, which is basically a means of destroying the enemy, also has the function of self-preservation. It is also the reason why defence must be accompanied by attack and should not be defence pure and simple.[68]

Mao understood that the defense was the strongest form of war—a people under attack fight harder

than a people projecting power beyond their borders to attack—and that the weaker opponent should initially assume the strategic and tactical defense and fight a war of attrition and exhaustion. This was phase one of his "people's war theory"—the survival phase. During this phase regular forces and guerrilla forces (local and regional) avoided battle, conserved strength, organized administratively and logistically, acquired foreign assistance, conducted propaganda (information and misinformation) campaigns, and overall emphasized the political task of gaining the support of the people, tasks that increased the military capacity of regular and guerrilla forces. Geography and terrain were important factors in avoiding battle and concealing logistical bases. Cultural affinity and understanding were necessary to win the support of the people. During phase two, revolutionary forces remained on the strategic defense, but went over to the tactical offense. Small unit operations, battalion size and below, were carried out to discredit the government, and demonstrate to the people that the government was impotent. Revolutionary forces (local and regional guerrilla forces) attacked and killed government officials, infiltrated the government bureaucracy, undermined government programs, and stole government resources and secrets. Small unit operations by regular forces were also carried out. The political task of gaining the support of the people continued. Revolutionary forces built their strength until "gradually changing the general balance of force and preparing the conditions for our counter-offensive."[69] At this point, Mao understood that to achieve decisive results in war, regular forces had to go over to the strategic offense and destroy the enemy's main army in battle, which was phase three, annihilation strategy. Clausewitz observed that "the essence of war is fighting, and since the battle is the fight of the *main force*, the battle must always be considered as the true center of gravity of the war."[70] The US ground forces never fought the "main force" in Vietnam, and never conducted major strategically offensive operations beyond the borders of South Vietnam. The US Army fought the entire war on the strategic defense.

The Communist North Vietnamese under the leadership of Ho Chi Minh and Vo Nguyen Giap adapted Clausewitz's and Mao's theories to their unique situation.[71] Douglas Pike, a student of North Vietnamese doctrine, concluded that:

> ...the Vietnamese communists conceived, developed, and fielded a dimensional new method for making war; that in forty years they honed this method into a brilliant innovative strategy that proved singularly successful against three of the world's great powers; and, most important, *that it is a strategy for which there is no known proven counterstrategy....* They invented nothing, discovered nothing, but they synthesized what had been learned about war and politics.

Pike explained Giap's strategic plan to defeat the United States:

> Briefly, Giap's answer was to develop two armed *dau tranh* tactics, or what he called "fighting methods" (*cach danh*). The first was the occasional small military blockbuster that he labeled the "coordinated fighting method" (*cach danh hop dong*), a medium-sized attack against a relatively important target, an enemy battalion headquarters, for instance. The essence of its success lies in its being perfectly planned and flawlessly executed. The target is destroyed with surgical precision, and the impact on the enemy is not military so much as psychological. The second tactic General Giap termed the "independent fighting method" (*cach danh doc lap*), sometimes the "gnat-swarm technique." This involves mounting dozens of daily small-scale actions, no single one being important but cumulatively raising the enemy's anxiety level and destroying his self-confidence. High casualties can be taken, and attacks need not be entirely victorious so long as they pin down the enemy and reduce his initiatives. Then the two techniques are combined—timing in this appears to be a master of intuition—into a single intensive campaign in which military activity steadily escalates into a "comprehensive offensive." At its peak there is delivered the final psychological capper, what might be called the Dein Bein Phu gambit, a massive assault on some politically or psychologically important target, which, when captured, destroys the enemy's will to continue warfare.[72]

Dien Bien Phu destroyed the French will to continue the war. And, arguably the Tet Offensive in 1968 destroyed the American will. The US Army under the Kennedy and Johnson Administrations never developed an effective counterinsurgency doctrine.

*   *   *   *   *

Not willing to cede peripheral states to the Communists, the US under the Eisenhower Administration used other means short of war. The CIA, with support from the Pentagon, sought to shape governments in Africa, the Middle East, Asia, and Central and South America. The CIA, in fact, produced another American campaign-winning doctrine. The CIA had noted success; however, its methods and ability to gain access were not always successful. The White House and Pentagon recognized the need for a doctrine to counter insurgencies and guerrilla warfare. The Army during the Eisenhower Administration made a limited commitment to this form of war.

Under the Kennedy Administration, counterinsurgency warfare received its greatest emphasis. Kennedy believed that Communist-inspired "wars of national liberation" in "Third World nations" posed a threat to American interests. To counter Communist insurgencies required new doctrine, and some would argue a new type of American soldier. A former commander of the 1st Special Forces Group (Airborne) and the chair of the committee that produced the Army's "first definitive approach" to counterinsurgency, Colonel Francis John Kelly, noted:

> It was at this point [the activation of the 5th Special Forces Group in 1961] that President Kennedy began to display particular interest in the Special Forces. His enthusiasm, based on his conviction that the Special Forces had great potential as a counterinsurgency force, led him to become a very powerful advocate for the development of the Special Forces program within the Army. President Kennedy himself made a visit to the Special Warfare Center in the fall of 1961 to review the program, and it was by his authorization that Special Forces troops were allowed to wear the distinctive headgear that became the symbol of the Special Forces, the Green Beret.[73]

Kennedy believed that with effective counterinsurgency doctrine, and highly trained, motivated, dedicated, unorthodox, innovative, elite soldiers to vigorously implement it, the tide of Communism that was moving through developing nations could be turned back. Hence, he took a personal interest in the creation and expansion of Special Forces units. The Army selected Colonel William P. Yarborough to be commander of the Army Special Warfare Center and School in 1961.[74] Kennedy pressured the reluctant US Army to reorient its thinking toward counterinsurgency warfare. Special Forces and the Special Warfare Center became the primary instrument for conducting this new campaign-winning doctrine.

New groups, oriented toward Southeast Asia, Africa, and Latin America, were formed.[75] Their primary objective was to educate and train indigenous security forces, to make them self-sufficient, willing and able to fight effectively against insurgent and regular forces, to defend the people, and to support and defend the government. To achieve this objective it was necessary to identify and kill the guerrillas; to root out the infrastructure that supported them; to secure the population; to educate and train indigenous government agencies; to provide security forces with weapons, vehicles, and other resources required to defend themselves; to provide the people with the means and resources required to make a living; and to demonstrate an affinity, a connection with the plight of the people that would gain and maintain their loyalty and support. The latter tasks were part of the "nation building" mission, and involved governmental agencies and civilian organizations as well as the military. Succinctly, Special Forces organized, equipped, and trained paramilitary forces, counterinsurgency/counter-guerrilla forces, and regular forces to defeat insurgent and regular enemy forces.

To achieve these objectives Special Forces and other units and organizations involved in counterinsurgency warfare had to physically live among the people. To produce individuals with the wherewithal to carry out such operations required years of training, dedication, and an enormous human investment. Language skills, cultural understanding, adaptability, physical endurance, the ability to work with native forces, and a high degree of military skills were required. The average soldier or marine was not well suited for this type of war. It required time and patience, cultural humility, subordination, and adaptability. It required respect and understanding of other cultures. It required empathy, the ability to identify with the people they were trying to help. The political task of winning and maintaining the loyal support of the people could not be accomplished with American scientific management techniques, technology, efficiency, and cultural arrogance. Paddock described Special Forces operations in Vietnam:

> A typical A detachment worked with a counterpart Vietnamese Special Forces detachment to recruit, arm, and train several hundred personnel in self-defense and carried out extensive civic action and medical activities. Early Special Forces A detachments sometimes engaged in combat, but primarily in the context of training and while employing their tribal "strike forces" in raids, patrolling, ambushes, and camp defense. By training indigenous cadre—who then assisted in training additional self-defense forces—detachments achieved both the "force multiplier" effect and the indirect application of force. Initially efforts proved so successful in denying certain areas to Viet Cong influence that the CIA requested additional assistance from Special Forces to expand what became known as the Civilian Irregular Defense Group (CIDG) program.[76]

In a limited war in a far away land, such as Vietnam, that did not have the attention of the American people, it was possible for the US to successfully carry out counterinsurgency, counter-guerrilla war. By *not* "Americanizing" the war; by keeping American forces restricted to small numbers of highly trained, highly motivated personnel; by continuing to place the burden of defense on indigenous security forces; by training and equipping these forces; by requiring the government to sustain itself; by providing only technologies the country could maintain; by keeping the American "footprint" so small that it attracted little public attention and mitigated the charge of imperialism; and finally by limiting American objectives and commitments, the US could have fought a counterinsurgency war almost indefinitely.

Counterinsurgency and nation-building operations required enormous patience and perseverance. Once American main force units were employed and the attention of the nation focused on the war, it became impossible for the United States to fight this type of war. One of Clausewitz's criteria for a people's war was that: "the national character must be suited to that type of war," recognizing that war is a cultural endeavor. Americans fought an American war, not a Mao Tse-tung or Giap war. The Army and Marine Corps could have fought an insurgency war. They have done so before. But, when the war became an American war, not an Army or Marine Corps war, then the war had to conform to the American cultural norms for the conduct of war.

Over 40,000 armed and trained irregulars in eight camps took part in the CIDG program. Special Forces acted as advisors to an additional 40,000 regional forces and popular forces. They took part in the MACV Studies and Operation Group (SOG), an organization that conducted operations in North Vietnam to develop an indigenous resistance movement, and conduct reconnaissance operations in Laos and Cambodia. In 1963 the CIA's CIDG program came under Army command. MACV changed the mission and redeployed Special Forces to have "Special Forces camps and their indigenous paramilitary personnel participate in border surveillance tactics to help seal off infiltration of supplies and troops from North Vietnam down the Ho Chi Minh Trail." In other words, the Army redirected Special Forces toward more traditional military missions.

The US Army resisted the President's vision of Special Forces and counterinsurgency wars. Andrew F. Krepinevich, Jr., in his book, *The Army in Vietnam*, wrote:

> Thus the Special Forces' role in the Army's force structuring for counterinsurgency was not to spearhead an imaginative program designed to generate the counterinsurgency capability necessary if the Army was to meet its assigned mission. Rather, the Special Forces became the Army's only force (and ill-employed force, at that) dedicated to the newly acquired counterinsurgency mission. More than anything else, they would be cited as proof that the Army was doing something to prepare for low-intensity

contingencies. Their primary function, therefore, would be to provide the Army with a front behind which it could continue to develop forces for the familiar European contingency.[77]

And Douglas S. Blaufarb, in his book, *The Counterinsurgency Era: US Doctrine and Performance: 1950 to the Present*, wrote:

> What filled the gap was a largely military response which paid obeisance to such "people oriented" concepts as military civic action and improved propaganda, but in strategic and tactical terms focused largely upon measures to transform the Vietnamese armed forces into an effective military apparatus, mobile and professionally managed, able to concentrate its force effectively when required to strike a massive blow. It was believed that such a force—if properly supported by a competent intelligence effort—could easily meet and disperse the poorly armed insurgents as a "lesser included capability" of its newfound proficiency. Indeed, that view is the only fully endorsed official doctrine of counterinsurgency the United States Army has ever accepted.[78]

Army culture proved incapable of adapting to this form of warfare, and substituted its infantry campaign-winning doctrine for an authentic counterinsurgency campaign-winning doctrine; however, the Americanization of the war completely destroyed any chance of successfully employing counterinsurgency doctrine. The Army was geared to fight other armies. Once American regular forces were deployed to Vietnam in 1965, the Army relegated the ARVN, Special Forces, counterinsurgency, and nation-building to tertiary in importance. The primary task became finding, fixing, and destroying the enemy's main forces, an impossible task on the strategic defense. And the Army made the additional mistake of creating a Vietnamese army in its own image.

Armed with "counterinsurgency" and "counter-guerrilla" doctrines; with a resurrected Army capable of fighting limited war and influencing the political situation in peripheral regions; armed with a profound sense of rightness in the American cause, Kennedy extended and expanded the nation's commitment to the war in Vietnam. Kennedy was richly endowed with American culturally imbued optimism, aggressiveness, and arrogance.

*   *   *   *   *

The Army of 1965 that went into Vietnam was larger, better equipped, better trained, and better organized than the Army of 1959 and the Army that went into Korea. It had readopted aspects of its World War II campaign-winning infantry and armor doctrines, but had improved them based on the capabilities of new technology and reorientation on the European Theater. The Army, however, was not better led. It did not have senior leaders of the quality of World War II and Korea. It did not have a President or Secretary of Defense that valued the advice and recommendations of the most senior military leaders. It did not have a reflective, comprehensive strategic planning body. It labored under the 1947 National Security Act, which promoted competition between the services, and a system of command and control that impeded its ability to generate combat power. The services were incapable of fighting with synergy. They each had a different vision of how to fight war. Finally, the Army was recovering from a decade of misdirection, of trying to justify its existence, of trying to compete with the Air Force and Navy in the technology and nuclear business.

10.
THE VIETNAM WAR, THE OPENING PHASES, 1955–1967

The last units of Brigadier General Chu Huy Man's B–3 Front crossed into Cambodia. They were beyond reach now. They would reinforce, reequip, rest, and rehabilitate their surviving soldiers, and then, at a time of their choosing in the spring of 1966, reenter South Vietnam and resume their attacks.

Major Norm Schwarzkopf watched them go and was disgusted with the US policy that permitted the creation of North Vietnamese sanctuaries across the border in supposedly neutral Cambodia [and Laos]. He was not the only military man in the field who was angered by a policy that tied the hands of the American and South Vietnamese forces.

Major General Harry Kinnard [Commander of the 1st Cavalry Division] and his boss, Lieutenant General Stanley (Swede) Larsen, both appealed to General Westmoreland and US ambassador Henry Cabot Lodge to do everything in their power to persuade Washington to review and revoke the restrictions on American freedom of action along and across the border. . . .

−Lieutenant General Harold Moore, 1992
We Were Soldiers Once . . . And Young

The appeal was made but the policy remained in effect, causing Kinnard to conclude: "the American military surrendered the initiative to North Vietnam. What it said . . . was that this war would never end in an American victory. Initiative had been sacrificed to the polite diplomatic fiction that Cambodia was sovereign and neutral and in control of its territory."[1] When Johnson committed the United States to war in Vietnam he had two fully developed conventional war strategic doctrines: the Army's offensive infantry warfare doctrine, and the Air Force's offensive strategic bombing doctrine. He also had a partially developed counterinsurgency, counter-revolutionary war doctrine. He decided not to use the Army's or Air Force's offensive war doctrines. Johnson and McNamara decided to develop a new defensive-ground war/offensive-air war strategic doctrine, "graduated response." This doctrine was supposed to create the conditions for the success of the third element of Johnson's strategy, nation-building. Westmoreland described the doctrine of graduated response:

> The President announced that we would not broaden the war. This set for us a defensive strategy on the ground and gave the enemy great latitude for action. Johnson's administration formulated a strategy briefly described as: Hold the enemy, defeat him in the South, help build a nation, bomb war-related targets in the North on a gradual escalating basis until the enemy gets the message that he cannot win, and thus will negotiate or tacitly accept a divided Vietnam.[2]

The Johnson Administration planned to fight a protracted, limited defensive war of attrition on the ground in South Vietnam, and to win the war with offensive airpower by bombing North Vietnam. This air war doctrine was not in accordance with accepted Air Force doctrine. And the ground war doctrine was not in accordance with Army war-fighting doctrine. The Johnson Administration, because of its fear that the PRC would intervene, as it had during the Korean War, surrendered the strategic initiative in the ground war to the Communists in Hanoi, and endeavored to implement a new form of strategic bombing doctrine. Neither worked.

There was no way to win the war in Vietnam without fighting an offensive ground war, which would have meant a wider and more total war that would have involved, at a minimum, the commitment of PRC ground forces, possibly as volunteers, and the commitment of greater Soviet resources, possibly just short of ground forces. As in 1950, the PRC was unwilling to have American forces on its border, and the awe of American power that existed in the aftermath of World War II was gone. America's nuclear arsenals were a deterrent to more total war, and to direct confrontation between the two superpowers, but in peripheral regions it totally failed to deter aggression. The security and economic advantages received in return for a democratic, non-communist South Vietnam was not worth the risk of World War III. The Vietnam War should have never been fought. And this is not an assessment that is a function of hindsight. It is an assessment that is based on an understanding of geography, history, culture, the nature of American military power, and relative, potential combat power.

Geography and Strategy

Vietnam is a long, narrow "S" shaped country that stretches approximately 850 miles from north to south. It varies in width from 50 to 350 miles, and has a landmass of about 330,000 square miles. Vietnam is located on the east side of the enormous Indochina peninsula. The geography and terrain of the country influenced the implementation of strategy and application of military power during the war. To the north, North Vietnam shares a border with the PRC, making it possible for the PLA to directly intervene. In geopolitical terms, this was the same situation that caused a stalemate in the Korean War in 1951. The border with

the PRC eliminated *exhaustion strategy* because the border could not be closed without a much larger war. Short of using nuclear weapons, it was impossible to stop the flow of equipment and supplies from China into North Vietnam. To the west, South Vietnam shared an extensive border with Laos and Cambodia. The length of the border made it almost impossible to close. Unlike Korea, which, because of its narrowness, restricted enemy forces to a front of less than two hundred miles, the western border of South Vietnam, with its nonlinear shape, stretched almost a thousand miles. The length, vegetation, and terrain made it virtually impossible to stop infiltration, or any other form of maneuver. Cambodia and Laos also provided the VC and NVA with sanctuaries, which eliminated *annihilation strategy*. The Communist forces could cross the border into these supposedly sovereign states, and US forces could not follow. This artificial line eliminated strategically offensive operations, as well as pursuit and exploitation, and thus, the ability to complete the destruction of enemy forces. To the east, Vietnam's coastline stretched about 1,400 miles, all of which could be controlled by the US Navy. While the Navy could close the front door, the back door was wide open. In Korea, the Navy could control the vast majority of the area around the battlefield, leaving only two hundred miles of front for the Army to control. With the elimination of *annihilation* and *exhaustion* strategy, all that was left was *attrition* strategy—culturally the most un-American practice of war.

Ground forces could not employ traditional strategies to achieve victory. They could not complete the destruction of the enemy's main forces, capture the enemy's capital and destroy its government, or destroy the will of the people. Airpower could not destroy the means of production because they were not in North Vietnam. And airpower could not destroy the will of the people because North Vietnam was a peasant society with no urban middle class and working classes to bomb into submission. However, it was believed that airpower had the potential to destroy the will of the government through punishing the people of North Vietnam. This was a strategy for war that had never been proven. It was strategy based on American faith in technology. A study of World War II reveals that after the tremendous firebombing of

Fig 10.1 South Vietnam, US Corps Tactical Zone Boundary.

Japan, the Japanese government was unwilling to surrender. A study of the British air campaign against Germany reveals a similar outcome. And these nations had substantial upper class and middle class people to punish. This analysis shows there was no way to win the war without a strategically offensive ground war, or an extermination air campaign. The US Air Force probably could have eradicated life in North Vietnam without using nuclear weapons. However, an offensive ground war would have meant a more total war, almost certainly war with the PRC, or Chinese volunteers. A larger, offensive ground war risked World War III. Kennedy, Johnson, and Nixon did not believe South Vietnam was worth the risk.

The final strategic option was a permanent defensive ground war of attrition. While it was impossible for US ground forces to win the war on the strategic defense, it was also impossible for them to lose. In other words, the forces of North Vietnam would never have the capacity to defeat the armed forces of the United States in a ground war. Hence, the US could have sustained South Vietnam on the strategic defense indefinitely. Given the region of the world, and the geographic circumstance of South Vietnam, nation-building was never going to produce a viable state, one that could stand on its own without substantial, active military assistance from the US. It has been argued that had the Army adopted the right counterinsurgency doctrine, it could have destroyed the Viet Cong and produced a stable democratic South Vietnam.[3] Without destroying the will of the government and people of North Vietnam, there was no way to secure South Vietnam. The insurgency was sustained from the North. No matter how many men and resources the US committed to nation-building and the insurgency war, no matter how effective or ineffective Army and Marine Corps counterinsurgency doctrines and tactical doctrines, as long as the ground war was restricted to the boundaries of South Vietnam, there was no way to stop North Vietnam from supporting the VC. Without the sustained active support of American forces, South Vietnam was *never* going to be able to stand up to the North Vietnamese and VC forces supported by the combined resources of the PRC and Soviet Union.[4]

In 1946 Ho Chi Minh informed the Western world, "You can kill ten of my men for every one I kill of yours, but even at those odds, you will lose and I will win." And Giap, the Vietnamese general that orchestrated the defeat of the French at Dien Bien Phu, stated: "Every minute, hundreds of thousands of people die on the earth. The life or death of a hundred, a thousand, tens of thousands of human beings, even our compatriots, means little." When asked how long he would continue to fight he stated: "Another twenty years, maybe a hundred years, as long as it took to win, regardless of the cost."[5] While the US fought a limited war for limited objectives, the

North Vietnamese and Viet Cong fought a total war for total objectives. Geographic circumstances and the culture and history of the Vietnamese people made defeat inevitable in a limited, defensive war of attrition.

American ground forces fought on the strategic defense, with the knowledge that they could not bring about an end to the war, and that they were not supposed to win the war. The result was the deterioration of the morale of the Army and the support of the American people—the same conditions that developed during the final years of the Korean War after the US assumed the strategic defense.

The Vietnam War: Explaining American Involvement

The Vietnam War was in part a function of the result of World War II, the advent of the Cold War, the emergence of the Soviet Union and the United States as the world's dominant "superpowers," the growth of Asian nationalism, the example of the Japanese in World War II, the demise of European imperialism, the demise of the awe of Europeans, the expansion of Communism, the dynamics of French domestic politics, and the dynamics of US domestic politics. The loss of China, the half-victory in Korea, and concerns about the security of Japan also influenced American thinking.

US involvement in Vietnam started shortly after World War II with military assistance to the French. In August 1945, following the surrender of the Japanese, who had occupied French Indochina in September 1940—and by so doing demonstrated the superiority of Japanese (Asian) arms over French (European) arms—the Viet Minh declared independence. Before a cheering crowd of 500,000 Vietnamese assembled in Hanoi, Ho Chi Minh—the leader of the nationalist, Communist movement—proclaimed the Democratic Republic of Vietnam (DRV) a sovereign, independent nation-state. The French-Indochina War started in 1946, when France, which had suffered humiliating defeat in the opening days of World War II, returned to Indochina to reclaim part of its former empire, and part of its former great nation status.[6] The mutually exclusive objectives of the Viet Minh and the French led to war.

The USSR and PRC recognized the new Communist nation, establishing the conditions for military and economic assistance. On 8 May 1950, responding to the French requests for military and economic assistance, Secretary of State Dean Acheson announced that Truman had decided that the United States would support the French war in Indochina. Acheson explained the reasoning behind this new policy:

> As we saw our role in Southeast Asia, it was to help toward solving the colonial-nationalist conflict in a way that would satisfy nationalist aims and minimize the strains on our Western European Allies. This meant supporting the French 'presence' in the area as a guide and help to the three states in moving toward genuine independence within (for the present, at least) the French Union. It was not an easy or a popular role.[7]

A strong France facilitated American security and economic objectives in Europe.

The security and economic recovery of Japan also influenced decision-makers. A joint Department of State and Defense report in January 1950 concluded: "Continuing, or maintaining, Japan's economic recovery depends upon keeping Communism out of Southeast Asia, promoting economic recovery there and in further developing those countries, together with Indonesia, the Philippines, Southern Korea and India as the principal trading areas for Japan." Shortly after Acheson's announcement of US support, Secretary of Defense George C. Marshall approved the establishment of a 128-man Military Assistance and Advisory Group (MAAG) in Saigon.[8] Its mission was to supervise the delivery of material, monitor and assess the situation, collect intelligence, and coordinate American assistance with the French. Over the next four years the US provided $2.6 billion in aid to France.

Still, in 1954, French forces were defeated at Dien Bien Phu. Eisenhower was an adherent to the "domino theory," which predicted the collapse of a sequence of nations in a given region to Communism once the first nation—domino—fell. Eisenhower stated:

> Strategically, south Viet-Nam's capture by the Communists would bring their power several

hundred miles into a hitherto free region. The remaining countries in Southeast Asia would be menaced by a great flanking movement. The freedom of 12 million people would be lost immediately and that of 150 million others in adjacent lands would be seriously endangered. The loss of south Viet-Nam would set in motion a crumbling process that could, as it progressed, have grave consequences for us and for freedom.[9]

Eisenhower also emphasized the importance of this region to the economies of the West. Still, while recognizing that the US had vital interests in the region, he decided that the security value of Indochina was not worth the direct involvement of US forces.[10]

Eisenhower understood the cost of intervention. In 1954, Army Chief of Staff, Matthew B. Ridgway, on his own initiative, sent a team of senior soldiers to Vietnam to study the problems of war in Indochina. Ridgway's analysis may have influenced the President's thinking. At a minimum it provided him with well-reasoned arguments for *not* going to war. Ridgway wrote:

> In the spring of 1954 ... we very nearly found ourselves involved in a bloody jungle war in which our nuclear capability would have been almost useless. It was during the time a gallant French garrison, made up mainly of mercenaries of the Foreign Legion—for France had lacked the will to draft its own young men for service in Indo-China—was making its brave but futile stand at Dienbienphu. To military men familiar with the maps of Indo-China, the outcome of that siege was a foregone conclusion. . . .
>
> Soon I was deeply concerned to hear individuals of great influence, both in and out of government, raising the cry that now was the time, and here, in Indo-China, was the place to "test the New Look," for us to intervene, to come to the aid of France with arms. At the same time that same old delusive idea was advanced—that we could do things the cheap and easy way, by going into Indo-China with air and naval forces alone. To me this had an ominous ring. For I felt sure that if we committed air and naval power to that area, we would have to follow them immediately with ground forces in support.

I also knew that none of those advocating such a step had any accurate idea what such an operation would cost us in blood and money and national effort. I felt that it was essential therefore that all who had any influence in making the decision on this grave matter should be fully aware of all the factors involved. To provide these facts, I sent out to Indo-China an Army team of experts in every field. . . . They went out to answer a thousand questions that those who had so blithely recommended that we go to war there had never taken the trouble to ask. . . .

Their report was complete. The area, they found, was practically devoid of those facilities which modern forces such as ours find essential to the waging of war. . . . The land was a land of rice paddy and jungle—particularly adapted to the guerrilla-type warfare at which the Chinese soldier is a master. This meant that every little detachment, every individual, that tried to move about the country, would have to be protected by riflemen. . . .

If we did go into Indo-China, we would have to win. We would have to go in with a military force adequate in all its branches, and that meant a very strong ground force—an Army that could not only stand the normal attrition of battle, but could absorb heavy casualties from the jungle heat, and the rots and fevers which afflict the white man in the tropics. . . . We could have fought in Indo-China. We could have won, if we had been willing to pay the tremendous cost in men and money that such intervention would have required. . . .

That error, thank God, was not repeated. As soon as the full report was in, I lost no time in having it passed on up the chain of command. It reached President Eisenhower. To a man of his military experience its implications were immediately clear. The idea of intervening was abandoned, and it is my belief that the analysis which the Army made and presented to higher authority played a considerable, perhaps decisive, part in persuading our government not to embark on that tragic adventure.[11]

Long before Kennedy and Johnson committed US forces to war in Vietnam, the issues of war in this region had been studied, and war rejected, by no less than the Supreme Allied Commander for the invasion of Europe. Ridgway's study concluded that it would take 500,000 to 1 million men. The British had also studied the problem and concluded that Vietnam was the wrong war at the wrong place at the wrong time.[12]

The Geneva Accord of 20 July 1954 ended the fighting, and divided Vietnam into two states at the 17th parallel. The Communists controlled the northern part of the country, and the French retreated temporarily to the southern part. The division of the country was to be a temporary arrangement pending the election in July 1956, which was supposed to reunite the country under one government. The US never formally acknowledged the Geneva Accord, but in a separate unilateral declaration agreed to adhere to the terms of the agreements, cautioning that, "it would view any renewal of aggression in violation of the. . . agreement with grave concern and as seriously threatening international peace and security."[13]

On 26 October 1955, south of the parallel, the Republic of Vietnam (RVN) was proclaimed. Ngo Dinh Diem became its first President. He repudiated the elections, in violation of the agreement, and the Eisenhower Administration initiated programs to provide direct assistance to the new government. Thus began America's direct involvement in Vietnam. And, once committed, American prestige, credibility, resolve, integrity, and honor became important reasons for staying the course.

Kennedy had great admiration for the struggle for freedom in Vietnam, enormous faith in American power, great optimism about American willingness to sacrifice, and unbridled confidence in American intelligence and ingenuity. In 1956 Senator Kennedy wrote:

We shall not attempt to buy the friendship of the Vietnamese. Nor can we win their hearts by making them dependent upon our handouts. What we must offer them is a revolution—a political, economic, and social revolution far superior to anything the Communists can offer— far more peaceful, far more democratic, and far more locally controlled. Such a revolution will require much from the United States and much from Vietnam. We must supply capital to replace that drained by centuries of colonial exploitation; technicians to train those handicapped by deliberate policies of illiteracy; guidance to assist a nation taking those first feeble steps toward the complexities of a republican form of government. We must assist the inspiring growth of Vietnamese democracy and economy, including the complete integration of those refugees who gave up their homes and their belongings to seek freedom. We must provide military assistance to rebuild the new Vietnamese Army, which every day faces the growing peril of Vietminh Armies across the border. This is the revolution we can, we should, we must offer to the people of Vietnam....[14]

The realities of geography, manpower, and resources were not insurmountable difficulties in Kennedy's view. He believed the Eisenhower Administration had not done enough, and that the quality, character, and quantity of American assistance had to change, had to increase. Kennedy had a comprehensive view of what he believed needed to be done. However, he misunderstood the nature of American power, and the cultural tenets on which the citizen-soldier Army was built. He also did not understand the culture of the Vietnamese, and the legitimacy earned by the Communists. Consider the words of General Maxwell Taylor, who served as one of Kennedy's close advisors:

> The risk of backing into a major Asian war by way of SVN are present but are not impressive. NVN is extremely vulnerable to conventional bombing, a weakness which should be exploited diplomatically in convincing Hanoi to lay off SVN. Both the DRV and the Chicoms would face severe logistical difficulties in trying to maintain strong forces in the field in SEA, difficulties which we share but by no means to the same degree. There is no cause for fearing a mass onslaught of Communist manpower into SVN and its neighboring states, particularly if our airpower is allowed a free hand against logistical targets. Finally, the starvation conditions in China should discourage Communist leaders there from being militarily venturesome for some time to come.[15]

Taylor, Kennedy, and Johnson grossly underestimated the will and capabilities of the Vietnamese and Chinese. The experience of the Korean War was forgotten. In testimony before the Senate Committee on Foreign Relations in 1966, Taylor explained why the US was in Vietnam:

> A simple statement of what we are doing in South Viet-Nam is to say that we are engaged in a clash of purpose and interest with the militant wing of the Communist movement represented by Hanoi, the Viet Cong, and Peking. Opposing these Communist forces, in the front ranks stand the Government and people of South Viet-Nam, supported primarily by the United States but assisted in varying degree by some 30 other nations.
>
> The purpose of the Hanoi camp is perfectly clear and has been since 1954. It is to absorb the 15 million people of South Viet-Nam into a single Communist state under the leadership of Ho Chi Minh and his associates in Hanoi. In the course of accomplishing this basic purpose, the Communist leaders expect to undermine the position of the United States in Asia and to demonstrate the efficacy of the so-called "war of liberation" as a cheap, safe, and disavowable technique for the future expansion of militant communism.[16]

Kennedy and Johnson accepted this assessment. President Johnson believed that:

> If we are driven from the field in Vietnam, then no nation can ever again have the same confidence in American promise or in American protection. In each land the forces of independence would be considerably weakened and an Asia so threatened by Communist domination would certainly imperil the security of the United States.

Johnson, like Kennedy, had available the same information Eisenhower used to make his decisions. He also had the assessment of some of his closest advisors. In 1965, George Ball, who had cautioned Kennedy that committing American ground forces to the war would be a grave mistake, informed Johnson that:

> The South Vietnamese are losing the war to the Viet Cong.... No one has demonstrated that a

white ground force of whatever size can win a guerrilla war—which is at the same time a civil war between Asians—in jungle terrain in the midst of a population that refuses cooperation to the white forces.... *The Question to Decide*: Should we limit our liabilities in South Vietnam and try to find a way out with minimal long-term costs? The alternative—no matter what we may wish it be—is almost certainly a protracted war involving an open-ended commitment of US forces, mounting US casualties, no assurance of a satisfactory solution, and a serious danger of escalation at the end of the road.... Once we deploy substantial numbers of troops in combat it will become a war between the US and a large part of the population of South Vietnam, organized and directed from North Vietnam and backed by the resources of both Moscow and Peiping.... Once we suffer large casualties, we will have started a well-nigh irreversible process. Our involvement will be so great that we cannot—without national humiliation—stop short of achieving our complete objectives. *Of the two possibilities I think humiliation would be more likely than the achievement of our objectives— even after we have paid terrible costs.*[17]

Others also opposed escalation. Regarding a July 1965 discussion on the war, Johnson wrote:

At this session my old friend Clark Clifford was in a reflective and pessimistic mood: 'I don't believe we can win in South Vietnam,' he said. 'If we send in 100,000 more men, the North Vietnam will meet us. If North Vietnam runs out of men, the Chinese will send in volunteers. Russia and China don't intend for us to win the war.'[18]

Ball's and Clifford's analysis reflected an accurate understanding of the geography of the region.

Truman, Eisenhower, Kennedy, and Johnson each in turn committed the United States to the security of South Vietnam, with increasing vigor. Each President believed that the security of the United States was tied to the survival of the Republic of South Vietnam. Each believed that once committed, American prestige, credibility, and resolve were called into question; and as a consequence, America's ability to influence allies and enemies around the world.

However, it was not until the Kennedy and Johnson Administrations that the cost of American involvement started to exceed the security value of Vietnam. And, it was Johnson who crossed the line by Americanizing the war.

The Advisory Phase

The American war in Vietnam is best understood by dividing it into three phases: the advisory phase (1954 to 1964), the Americanization phase (1965 to 1968), and the Vietnamization phase, 1969 to 1975.

On 1 October 1954, Eisenhower sent then Prime Minister Ngo Dinh Diem a message, which offered, "to assist the Government of Viet-Nam in developing and maintaining a strong, viable state, capable of resisting attempted subversion or aggression through military means."[19] Diem had rejected the Geneva agreement, refusing to participate in the nationwide election, and the Eisenhower Administration, accepting Diem's leadership and strategy, initiated the flow of men and material. On 19 February 1955, the Southeast Asia Collective Defense Treaty (SEATO), with a protocol that covered South Vietnam, Cambodia, and Laos, went into effect. Under Article IV, the treaty in part stated:

Each Party recognizes that aggression by means of armed attack in the treaty area against any of the Parties or against any State or territory which the Parties by unanimous agreement may hereafter designate, would endanger its own peace and safety, and agrees that it will in that event act to meet the common danger in accordance with its constitutional process.... It is understood that no action on the territory of any State designated ... shall be taken except at the invitation or with the consent of the government concerned.[20]

The SEATO gave the US the legal foundation to provide direct assistance to the RVN.

In 1956, the Military Assistance and Advisory Group (MAAG) was reorganized to manage the increased flow of equipment, supplies, and advisors into Vietnam. The US used subterfuge to violate the limitations imposed by the Geneva Accord.[21] The immediate concern was an invasion from the North by conventional forces. The US, thus, directed its efforts to prepare the RVN to fight a conventional war, and since the equipment provided was American, the ARVN learned to fight with American operational and tactical doctrines—a way of war based on the abundance of the United States.

In 1957, the Communist insurgency began in the South. The insurgency was designed to undermine and eventually overthrow the government of the RVN through political mobilization, persuasion, intimidation, threats, terrorism, selective killing, and mass murder. The objective was to gain the loyal support of the majority of the people of SVN, and by doing so destroy the "illegitimate" American-sponsored government. The Ho Chi Minh Trail opened in 1959. This line of communication provided direct support from North Vietnam (NVN) to the insurgency in the South. A year later the National Liberation Front (NLF), also known as the "Viet Cong" (VC), was formed to lead, organize, support, motivate, and coordinate the insurgency. In 1960, the last year of the Eisenhower Administration, the US had 700 advisors in Vietnam.

On 19 January 1961, President-elect Kennedy and senior cabinet members met with President Eisenhower and his cabinet to discuss Southeast Asia. Clark Clifford, Kennedy's "transition planner," had arranged the meeting. Clifford recorded the following in his notes:

> At this point, President Eisenhower said, with considerable emotion, that Laos was the key to the entire area of Southeast Asia. He said that if we permitted Laos to fall, then we would have to write off all the area. He stated we must not permit a Communist take-over. . . . He said that the United States should accept this task with our allies, if we could persuade them, and alone if we could not. He added, 'Our unilateral intervention would be our last desperate hope in the event we were unable to prevail upon the other signatories [of SEATO] to join us.'[22]

The accuracy of Clifford's note is open to question. The assessment of "considerable emotion" and the term "last desperate hope" sound pessimistic and uncharacteristic of Eisenhower, who had had ample opportunity to invest greater resources in the region.

Still, President Kennedy almost immediately came under considerable pressure from the press and opinion leaders not to "lose" Southeast Asia, as Truman had lost China. In January 1961, Premier Nikita Khrushchev challenged the new President. He publicly committed the SU to support national liberation movements, specifically in Vietnam and Algeria. At the same time, the situation in Laos was rapidly deteriorating. In a press conference on 23 March, the President informed the American people that:

> Soviet planes, I regret to say, have been conspicuous in a large-scale airlift into the battle area— over . . . 1,000 sorties since last December 13th, plus a whole supporting set of combat specialists, mainly from Communist North Viet-Nam . . . all with the clear object of destroying by military action the agreed neutrality of Laos. . . .

In May, Kennedy sent Vice President Lyndon B. Johnson to South Vietnam to consult with President Diem. Shortly thereafter, Kennedy increased military assistance to Vietnam. On 2 August 1961, Kennedy stated that, "the United States is determined that the Republic of Viet-Nam shall not be lost to the Communists for lack of any support which the United States can render."

In October 1961, Kennedy sent Maxwell Taylor, Walt Rostow, and other advisors to Vietnam to assess the situation. They concluded that the situation was deteriorating, and recommended a large increase in American advisors and an expanded role for US servicemen in combating the insurgency. Taylor informed the President that "there can be no action so convincing of US seriousness of purpose and hence so reassuring to the people and Government of SVN and to our other friends and allies in SEA as the introduction of US forces into SVN." He later told the President that he did not believe that the program to save SVN would succeed without the deployment of the 8,000 troops he recommended. In a letter to Diem, dated 14 December 1961, Kennedy promised that the United States was "prepared to help the Republic of Viet-Nam to protect its people and to preserve its independence." He further wrote: "We shall promptly increase our assistance to your defense effort. . . . I have already given the orders to get these programs underway."[23] Kennedy authorized an increase in the size of MAAG and increased its responsibilities.[24] US advisors increased from 700 to 1,200. The CIA was authorized to initiate new programs to broaden the counterinsurgency effort by developing the paramilitary potential of certain minority groups. The Civilian Irregular Defense Group (CIDG) was established to implement and manage these programs, and US Army Special Forces became the primary tool for executing them.[25]

On 21 September 1961, the 5th Special Forces Group, 1st Special Forces was activated at Fort Bragg, North Carolina. It was ultimately responsible for all Special Forces operations in Vietnam. In November, the first Special Forces soldiers were deployed to provide assistance to the Montagnard tribes in the strategically important Central Highlands. The 5th Special Forces Group would eventually reach a strength of approximately 2,500 soldiers, leading an Army of roughly 50,000 tribal fighters who patrolled the border region to collect intelligence, impede enemy infiltration, and secure the population in these isolated regions.

Increasing tension between the US and USSR precluded Kennedy from de-escalating in Vietnam. The USSR was competing with the US in nuclear, rocket, airpower, space, and ground forces technologies. Premier Khrushchev committed the USSR to support communist insurgencies in developing countries, and initiated the Berlin crisis. And, for domestic political reasons, Kennedy could not appear "soft" on Communism.

* * * * *

The year 1963 was difficult for the people of the US and the RVN. It started with a major, humiliating defeat for the US-trained and equipped ARVN 7th Division in the battle of Ap Bac. The senior US advisor, Lieutenant Colonel John Paul Vann, had planned and hoped for a major victory.[26] The ARVN forces outnumbered the Viet Cong, and had greater firepower and operational mobility. The Viet Cong, however, were more determined, better trained and led, had superior tactical mobility and good intelligence. The performance of the ARVN's 7th Division was abysmal. Some commanders refused to fight. They would not advance to support units in contact, or

follow the guidance of the American advisors. Cowardice, incompetence, and a lack of discipline characterized the performance of the ARVN. David Halberstam, a reporter who witnessed the aftermath of the battle, wrote:

> Ap Bac was to be as close to a golden opportunity as there ever was in Vietnam; instead, it was a battle which demonstrated on a grand and dramatic scale all the tiny failings of the system, all the false techniques, evasions and frauds which had marked the war in Vietnam. It was also typical of the atmosphere existing at that time in Vietnam: having suffered a stunning defeat, the American military headquarters referred to it as a victory. Also, headquarters officers became angry not with the system which produced the defeat, nor with the Vietnamese commanders who were responsible for it, but with the American advisers who observed and criticized it and with the American reporters who wrote about it.... To us and to the American military advisers involved, Ap Bac epitomized all the deficiencies of the system: lack of aggressiveness, hesitancy about taking casualties, lack of battlefield leadership, a nonexistent chain of command. The failure at Ap Bac had been repeated on a small scale every day for the past year, and if not corrected quickly, they boded even greater trouble for the future.[27]

The inability of the government of Vietnam to field an effective army made it impossible to secure the population, and frustrated American advisors who became increasingly critical. Without security, it was impossible to win the support of the people. And without the support of the people it was impossible to win the revolutionary war against the VC. ARVN soldiers were also noted for their mistreatment of the civilian population in hamlets and villages. They too frequently stole, cheated, and molested the people there. The failures of the ARVN and the success of the VC placed peasants in some provinces in positions where they had no other option but to support the VC. Well before the deployment of US ground combat forces, the government of Vietnam had demonstrated the inability to unite the people, or motivate the army to fight. One option remaining was to change the government.

In November, disloyal generals, acting on what they believed was the approval of the Kennedy Administration, assassinated President Diem. Many senior political and military leaders in the Kennedy Administration had concluded that the Diem government was the primary cause for the failures in Vietnam. Corruption, nepotism, the alienation of various groups, the inability to gain the support of the people, and weak military leadership were among its many failings. Halberstam believed that:

> South Vietnam became, for all intents and purposes, a Communist-type country without Communism. It had all the controls, all the oppressions and all the frustrating, grim aspects of the modern totalitarian state—without the dynamism, efficiency and motivation that Communism had brought to the North. It was a police state, but it was unique in that its priorities were so haphazard; as a result, it was hopelessly inefficient.[28]

Diem was also growing increasingly independent and resistant to American guidance and demands for political and domestic reforms.

Repression and persecution of Buddhists brought matters to a head. The self-immolation of seven Buddhist monks, and the government raids on pagodas in Hue and Saigon caught on television cameras shocked the world. In August, George Ball, with the approval of the President, instructed the US Ambassador to the RVN in Saigon, Henry Cabot Lodge (1963–1964, 1965–1967), to provide support to "appropriate military commanders..." and "urgently examine all possible alternate leadership and make detailed plans how we might bring about Diem's replacement if this should become necessary." Through Lodge, the generals interpreted this as the approval to overthrow the Diem government. On 1 November 1963, they initiated the coup. The following day, Diem and his brother Nhu were dead. Kennedy did not direct the assassination of Diem. However, his support for a change in government led to it.

On 22 November, Kennedy was assassinated in Dallas, Texas.[29] Lyndon Baines Johnson became President. He retained Kennedy's cabinet and foreign and military policies. The Kennedy Administration had greatly expanded American involvement in, and commitment to, South Vietnam. At the time of Kennedy's death, over 16,000 soldiers were serving in Vietnam with expanding roles in combat operations, and the US had expended over $500 million in direct aid. Yet the situation in SVN continued to deteriorate. By 1964 the Communists controlled the Northern provinces and were stepping up military operations in the central part of the country. The Ho Chi Minh Trail remained open. And regular NVA units were appearing in greater numbers and frequency. To meet these growing threats, Johnson continued to expand the duties, responsibilities, and size of US forces. In the first year of the Johnson Administration, American forces in Vietnam increased to 23,000. On 15 May 1964, the Military Assistance Command, Vietnam (MACV), which was activated on 6 February 1962, took over the resources, responsibilities, and missions of the MAAG, which was deactivated. And on 20 June 1964, General William C. Westmoreland took command of MACV.

In August 1964, two US destroyers on patrol in the Gulf of Tonkin reported coming under attack. North Vietnamese patrol boats had allegedly fired on the *USS Maddox* on 2 August, and the *Maddox* and *Turner Joy* on 4 August, "without provocation." No one was killed or wounded, and evidence shows that the second incident never took place.[30] Edwin Moise wrote, "The report of tired men under stress who, while looking out into a dark night that they were convinced hid attacking PT boats, thought that they had glimpsed those PT boats or evidence of their presence, cannot begin to counterbalance the impossibility of this version of events."[31] Nevertheless, the attacks prompted Johnson to retaliate with air strikes. And on 5 August, Johnson went before the Congress and, in part, said:

> Last night I announced to the American people that the North Vietnamese regime had conducted further deliberate attacks against the US naval vessels operating in international waters, and that I had therefore directed air action against gunboats and supporting facilities used in these hostile operations.... Our policy in southeast Asia has been consistent and unchanged since 1954. I summarized it on June 2 in four simple propositions:

1. *America keeps her word.* Here as elsewhere, we must and shall honor our commitments.
2. *The issue is the future of Southeast Asia as a whole.* A threat to any nation in that region is a threat to all, and a threat to us.
3. *Our purpose is peace.* We have no military, political, or territorial ambitions in the area.
4. *This is not just a jungle war, but a struggle for freedom on every front of human activity.* Our military and economic assistance to South Vietnam and Laos in particular has the purpose of helping these countries to repel aggression and strengthen their independence.... As President of the United States I have concluded that I should now ask the Congress on its part, to join in affirming the national determination that all such attacks will be met, and that the United States will continue in its basic policy of assisting the free nations of the area to defend their freedom.[32]

Congress gave the President the support he requested. "The Gulf of Tonkin Resolution" passed the Senate with only two dissenting votes, and the House of Representatives with a vote of 416 for and 0 against. Johnson believed that Truman had made a mistake in going to war in Korea without the expressed support of Congress. Theoretically the support of Congress meant the support of the American people, and in fact, in the early years of the war, Johnson had the support of the majority of the American people. The unknown factor was the quality, character, and depth of that support. Theoretically Congressional support also shielded the President from partisan attacks on his Vietnam foreign policy and conduct of the war. The resolution in part stated:

Whereas naval units of the Communist regime in Vietnam, in violation of the principles of the Charter of the United Nations and of international law, have deliberately and repeatedly attacked United States naval vessels lawfully present in international waters, and have thereby created a serious threat to international peace; and Whereas these attacks are part of a deliberate and systematic campaign of aggression that

the Communist regime in North Vietnam has been waging against its neighbors and the nations joined with them in the collective defense of their freedom.... Resolved by the Senate and House of Representatives of the United States of America in Congress assembled, That the Congress approves and supports the determination of the President, as Commander in Chief, to take all necessary measures to repel any armed attack against the forces of the United States and to prevent further aggression.

The United States regards as vital to its national interest and to world peace the maintenance of international peace and security in Southeast Asia. Consonant with the Constitution of the United States and the Charter of the United Nations and in accordance with its obligations under the Southeast Asia Collective Defense Treaty, the United States is, therefore, prepared, as the President determines, to take all necessary steps, including the use of armed force, to assist any member or protocol state of the Southeast Asia Collective Defensive Treaty requesting assistance in defense of its freedom.[33]

The resolution, which was in part written by Johnson, gave the President all the authority needed to take the nation to war and carry it out as he saw fit. The SEATO Treaty also supported US actions in Vietnam.

In November 1964 Johnson defeated Senator Barry Goldwater in the presidential election. With that behind him, secure in the approval of Congress and the support of the American people, Johnson took parts of the nation to war. With the Gulf of Tonkin Resolution, the Johnson Administration, with McNamara as the point man, initiated a policy of misleading the American people and Congress as to the nature of the war and the character of American involvement. This policy eventually caused a credibility gap between the government/military and the press/American people.

Johnson and the Americanization Phase

Late in 1964 and early in 1965, the VC carried out a series of attacks against US installations and personnel, attacking the Bien Hoa Air Base in November, the Brinks officer billet in Saigon in December, and the American barracks at Pleiku in February. Johnson's advisors recommended retaliation, initiating the air war and the first deployment of US ground forces for combat operations in Vietnam.

McNamara's strategic doctrine for the conduct of the war in Vietnam became known as "graduated response," a doctrine that was very different from the "flexible response" doctrine envisioned by Ridgway, Taylor, and other senior Army leaders. Graduated response was not a doctrine developed by the military. Many senior military leaders opposed it. They believed it violated too many of the principles of war to succeed. Graduated response was a "whiz kid" approach to war: an approach to war based on logic, deductive reasoning, arrogance, and erroneous assumptions about the nature of power and human behavior.

Graduated response was an incremental approach to war that centered on the erosion of the enemy's will to resist by slowly ratcheting up the degree of destruction via airpower. It was believed that when the level of pain, suffering, and destruction reached the right intensity the enemy would change his behavior and acquiesce to American demands. Airpower was viewed as the best instrument for producing controlled, precise, measured pain. Airpower eliminated the passion of war, limited the involvement of the American people, and caused far fewer casualties than ground operations. It was clean, neat, and could be employed by highly skilled technicians. This was the vision of war inculcated into the American people throughout the 1950s.

The Army was deployed to Vietnam in an administrative manner. Westmoreland commanded a Military Assistance Command, not an Army. This was a mistake. The Eighth Army in Korea belonged to someone. Armies existed to engage and destroy other armies; and command creates a unique, personal relationship. It creates ownership, a mental disposition of attachment, and a mental framework of shared responsibilities for soldiers and the commanding general. The Army failed to create such relation-

ships in Vietnam. Instead, the Army administered the war.

While American strategy and strategic doctrine were hopelessly flawed, the armed forces of the United States violated basic principles of war from the beginning to the end of American involvement. Unity of command did not exist. A Joint Chiefs of Staff study of unified commands concluded:

> Command arrangements for the Vietnam War were complex and unsatisfactory. The Army failed to gain approval either for creating a Southeast Asia Command or for raising Military Assistance Command, Vietnam (MACV), to a unified command with PACOM in a supporting role. Instead, under CINCPAC, the Commander, US Military Assistance Command, Vietnam (COMUSMACV), largely controlled forces and operations within South Vietnam; CINCPAC delegated to its Service components, Pacific Air Forces (PACAF) and Pacific Fleet (PACFLT), responsibility for conducting air and naval operations against North Vietnam and Laos; PACFLT also retained control of 7th Fleet forces providing gunfire support and air strikes on targets in South Vietnam. Control of B–52s remained under the Commander in Chief, Strategic Air Command (CINCSAC), but targets in Vietnam were selected by COMUSMACV, refined by CINCPAC, and approved in Washington. CINCPAC's domination of command arrangements created resentment among senior Army and Air Force officers. In 1972 the Army Chief of Staff was General William Westmoreland.... He nominated and pressed for the current COMUSMACV, General Abrams, to become CINCPAC. Westmoreland's effort failed.[34]

The chain of command in Vietnam not only violated the principle of war unity of command; it violated common sense. Part of the problem was that air and ground forces defined the principle of unity of command differently. For the Army it meant all resources from all the services were placed under a single operational ground force commander. For the Air Force it meant that airpower fights a separate war against North Vietnam, and that all air resources be placed under its command, the system that was

Fig 10.2 President Lyndon B. Johnson and General William C. Westmoreland, Commander, US Military Assistance Command, Vietnam, present SSG Charles Morris, 173rd Abn Div. with the Distinguished Service Cross, 26 October 1966. US Army photograph.

employed in the Korean War. In Vietnam, however, Navy aviation reported to the Pacific Fleet in Hawaii. And Marine Corps aviation resources reported to the Marine Corps in Vietnam, which was supposed to report to Westmoreland, but in reality, like the rest of Marine Corps, did pretty much as it wanted. And Marine aviation always had recourse to its own chain of command, through the Navy to the Pacific Fleet, which was theoretically also Westmoreland's higher headquarters, but in reality both the Commander-in-Chief Pacific and the Commander of MACV reported to the Pentagon. The system was modified during the war, but unity of command was never established. While it is too much to say that the armed forces of the US fought four separate wars in Vietnam, it is not far from the situation that prevailed. Each service concentrated on winning the war primarily with its own resources, strategy, and doctrine, in its own

separate domain. The US had gone backwards in its war practices.

The Air War: Graduated Response

The Vietnam War was first and foremost an air war. Airpower was supposed to generate the decisive combat power needed to destroy the will of the North Vietnamese Communists to continue the war in the South. This was the first such war in American history. However, the air war was not fought in accordance with Air Force doctrine. Instead, the doctrine employed was the "graduated response" doctrine developed by McNamara and his "whiz kids." In 1966, before the Senate Committee on Foreign Relations General Maxwell Taylor, the US Ambassador to Vietnam, explained the strategic objective of the bombing campaign, "Rolling Thunder."

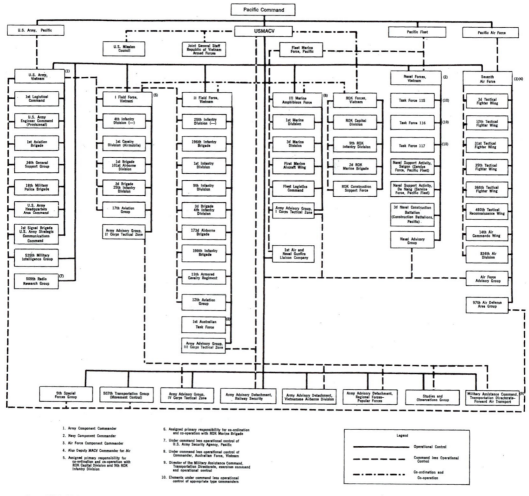

Fig 10.3 Chart of Pacific Command, 1967. George S. Eckhardt, *Command and Control 1950–1969.*

The ... reason for the decision to use our air-power was to provide a sobering reminder to the leaders in Hanoi that progressively they must pay a mounting price for the continuation of their support of the Viet Cong insurgency. In spite of their defiant statements of determination to endure these attacks forever, I for one know from experience that no one derives any enjoyment from receiving incoming shells and bombs day after day, and I have no doubt that the warning message is getting through to the leadership of Hanoi. In a very real sense, the objective of our air campaign is to change the will of the enemy leadership. We hope that, in due course, the combination of the Viet Cong failure to win victory on the ground in South VietNam and the effect of continued air attacks will present to the Hanoi leadership a situation so disadvantageous that they will decide that it is in their interest to halt their aggression, redefine their aims, and join with us in discussing ways and means of improving the lot of all VietNam.[35]

The Vietnam War presented the Air Force with a unique opportunity to demonstrate the decisive nature of airpower. Many airmen believed that even under the doctrine of graduated response the overwhelming power of American air forces would produce victory. However, "Operation Rolling Thunder" (2 March 1965—31 October 1968), the campaign that was supposed to achieve American objectives in Vietnam, failed.[36]

On 10 February 1965, McGeorge Bundy, Special Assistant to the President for National Security Affairs, wrote to the President, informing him that without new US action a Vietnam defeat "appears inevitable."[37] Two days later, Johnson gave the order to prepare the bombing campaign, and in the first week of March operations commenced. Airpower was easier and politically safer to employ than troops. For retaliation, it appeared to be a perfect weapon. Johnson made no major address to inform the American people of the change in strategy. He decided to fight the war in a manner that caused the least attention. He had a domestic agenda, "The Great Society," that required his political capital and the attention of the American people.

Admiral U.S.G. Sharp, thousands of miles from the battlefield at his headquarters in Hawaii, directed the air campaign. The primary objective of the campaign was to "communicate" with the enemy, to inform the Communists in Hanoi that they could not win; to inform them of American commitment and resolve; to cause them to understand the futility of continued defiance; and to cause just enough pain to make them cease their support for the insurgency in South Vietnam, without which it was believed the VC could not survive. A secondary objective was to slow the flow of men and material down the Ho Chi Minh Trail. The bombing campaign also communicated to the people of South Vietnam. It told them that the Americans were there to stay and that the Americans were fully committed and would see the war through to a successful end. McNamara declared: "When the day comes that we can safely withdraw, we expect to leave an independent and stable South Vietnam, rich with resources and bright with prospects for contributing to the peace and prosperity of Southeast Asia and the world."[38] Finally, airpower was also used to support the ground war, to kill enemy forces.

Washington tightly controlled the air campaign, not only to closely measure the pain inflicted, but also out of lingering fears. Washington feared that the SU and PRC would enter the war. It feared the American people would either turn against the war or demand a more total war, creating the possibility for war with the PRC and SU. It feared the portrayal of the United States as an aggressive, corrupt power, using its advanced technology to kill peasants, women, and children. It feared the response of the international community, particularly the condemnation of Europe. And it feared the propaganda advantage bombing gave North Vietnam. As a consequence of these fears, target selection was based on four criteria: military significance, risk to pilots and aircraft, danger of civilian casualties, and the risk of widening the war. Initially Washington decided which targets to attack, the number and types of planes to employ, the tonnage and types of munitions to drop, the date and time of the attack, and sometimes the direction of approach to the target area. If an attack was cancelled due to adverse weather, Washington had to be notified, and had to approve rescheduled attacks. These policies angered and frustrated the airmen. In addition, the drive for centralized strategic planning and decision-making over the past decade had resulted in centralization of operational and tactical decision-making, and as a consequence some loss of initiative. Pilots and field commanders were severely limited in the planning of operations and the development of theater strategy. The Pentagon primarily wanted the services to faithfully execute their orders. This was Enthoven's vision of war.

The air forces fought three major campaigns in Vietnam: the strategic bombing of the North, the interdiction campaign against the Ho Chi Minh Trail, and the war in the South, fought in coordination with the ground war. The air forces conducted numerous types of missions in Vietnam, including training the air force of South Vietnam, defoliation operations, counter-guerrilla operations in conjunction with Special Forces, reconnaissance missions, in-theater transport of troops and supplies, as well as the traditional strategic bombing, interdiction, and close air support missions. Innovations abounded, from new aircraft to new weapons, from new technologies to new tactics. A number of these innovations held great significance for the future of warfare. An Air Force pilot who fought the air campaign in Vietnam wrote:

The air war over North Vietnam was the first 'modern' air war—one where missiles were the main weapons in air combat. . . . The air war over North Vietnam was different; it was the one area of the Vietnam War that had military significance in the global balance of power. Both the United States and the Soviet Union put some of their best weapons into play in the skies over North Vietnam.[39]

The US Air Force flew out of bases in Vietnam, Thailand, and Guam. The 2nd Air Division (later, in April 1966, the 7th Air Force) was established in Thailand under Lieutenant General Joseph H. Moore. He was primarily responsible for implementing Operation Rolling Thunder. From roughly 1,000 personnel and eighty-three aircraft in early 1965, the command and its air resources grew to 35,000 personnel and 600 aircraft operating on six large runways in 1968. In South Vietnam only three airfields could accommodate the Air Force's heavy bomber: Bien Hoa, Tan Son Nhut, and Da Nang. Because these fields were consistently under observation, Hanoi generally knew when bombing raids were initiated from South Vietnam. The Air Force employed a wide array of aircraft, many of which had to be adapted to the Vietnam environment. The F–105 Thunderchief, the controversial General Dynamics F–111, the F–4 Phantom adopted from the Navy, the B–52s, on loan from SAC, the C–130 and new AC–130 Spectre gunship, reconnaissance, command and control, and rescue planes were among the primary aircraft employed.

Air Force pilots had to fly 100 missions to go home. Some never made it. Hundreds were shot down, and many of them became prisoners of war. F–105 pilots flying out of Thailand had a four- to five-hour mission to attack Hanoi. Hanoi was known as "Route Package 6," and was the Air Force's most difficult and dangerous mission. A mission commander with his "flight" of four F–105s typically flew from Thailand over South Vietnam, refueled over the Gulf of Tonkin, and then into Hanoi. The mission commander had to find the target. He commenced his attack at about 16,000 feet, aircraft 30 seconds apart. Targets were typically airfields, railroad yards, barracks, and key bridges. Two rail lines that ran from the

PRC to Hanoi carried the majority of North Vietnam's war materiel. North Vietnam had very little other industry to destroy. The border areas with the PRC were off limits, as were Soviet ships that provided Hanoi's second major source of materiel. Walter Boyne wrote:

> The extreme difficulty of the Pack 6 mission is more obvious when one analyzes just how inherently hazardous any combat mission was. Just taking off in a heavily loaded aircraft on a typical hot Southeast Asia day was dangerous in itself, as were the multiple in-flight refuelings. Missions to the other Route Packages and to Laos became increasingly hazardous. North Vietnam continually moved Anti-Aircraft Artillery south, particularly along the Ho Chi Minh Trail, and a careless pilot could easily and quickly become a dead pilot.[40]

The North Vietnamese employed Soviet-made aircraft, MiG 15s and 17s from the Korean War era, and the later model MiG 21 air-superiority fighter capable of speeds in excess of 1,300 mph. The MiGs were primarily employed defensively in the vicinity of Hanoi to intercept American aircraft. They tended to be smaller, more maneuverable, and slower than American aircraft. They were armed with heat-seeking air-to-air missiles and guns. Peter Lane, an Air Force pilot who flew 104 missions over North Vietnam and Laos in 1967, noted that the MiGs were "more of an annoyance factor rather than a real threat." The major limitation of the MiGs was the pilots who lacked training and experience. Some of the Communist pilots were believed to be Chinese and Russians. The Air Force downed 137 MiGs and the Navy 57. Because the MiGs were on the defensive, they had the advantage of flying within the field of their early warning radar system. Their operations were integrated into the actions of the ground-based anti-aircraft guns and surface-to-air missiles. If a MiG or the anti-aircraft system could not shoot down an aircraft they might cause the pilot to deviate from his planned course, or possibly jettison his bomb load short of his target. Of the 1,099 Air Force planes lost during the Vietnam War, the vast majority were brought down over North Vietnam. Seventy percent of Air Force and Navy POWs were captured during missions over North Vietnam.[41]

The North Vietnamese also employed Soviet-made anti-aircraft artillery and surface-to-air missiles (SAM). During the war their technology improved. The Soviets made adjustments to the weapons systems to counter American capabilities. The SU provided Hanoi with a comprehensive system, including early warning radar and target acquisition radar linked to anti-aircraft guns.

Initially Americans flew high-altitude missions to get above the enemy's small caliber anti-aircraft guns. In 1965, the SU provided Hanoi with the SA–2 SAM, large caliber anti-aircraft guns, and radar systems. This technology made it possible for the North Vietnamese to shoot down American aircraft. The Americans responded by flying low and then developing and employing electronic jamming equipment; aircraft specially designed to attack radar systems with missiles that locked on to the source of radar waves and destroyed the system; rudimentary "smart" bombs (laser-guided bombs and computer-directed, electro-optically guided bombs) with greater accuracy, range, destructive power, and safety for the pilot who released the weapon at greater distances from the target; night observation devices; and other technologies designed to defeat Soviet equipment and Hanoi's tactics.

To protect their radar systems, Hanoi also developed new tactics. They moved systems constantly, switching from one station to another, and turned them on and off to create confusion. They increased the number of systems and changed the frequencies regularly. Hanoi's early warning radar network ultimately expanded to cover North Vietnam, Laos, and the Gulf of Tonkin between 3,000 and 30,000 feet, eliminating the American advantage of surprise. American aircraft that came into the target areas under the radar screen below 3,000 feet ran into a barrage of anti-aircraft fire. American rules of engagement and target selection also gave Hanoi an advantage. Because American air forces were restricted to certain areas, and certain types of targets, Hanoi was able to adjust. Sharp noted, "Since we were forced to move target selections from the southern part of North Vietnam up toward the heartland in small steps over a protracted period, the enemy could predict

with reasonable accuracy when the important targets would be hit."[42] Thus, they were able to concentrate their anti-aircraft guns around high-value targets. American air forces also had to be concerned about killing Soviet advisors; hence, according to the rules of engagement, only SAM sites that were operational were attacked. On one operation Navy pilots identified 111 SAMs neatly packed on railcars. They were not given permission to destroy the target, causing one pilot to note, "We had to fight all 111 of them one at a time."

While Hanoi and the SU devoted considerable resources to the air war, the US still controlled the air over Vietnam. American air forces attacked targets in North Vietnam with a high degree of confidence. Hanoi continued to adjust its tactics and acquire Soviet technology, and because the US never mounted a sustained effort to destroy the North Vietnamese defense system, they had some successes, but in the final analysis the defenders were unable to prevent American airpower from attacking and destroying targets.

The Air Force, after mounting protests that echoed all the way to the White House, eventually gained greater operational freedom. And over the years, Rolling Thunder was expanded as more aircraft and pilots entered the theater. Washington was still involved in the target selection process and closely monitored operations, but the air forces of the United States had the opportunity to produce enormous destruction, even taking into consideration McNamara's graduated pressure doctrine and Johnson's periodic bombing halts designed to give Hanoi opportunities to accept his offers to negotiate. An Air Force study concluded that by mid 1966:

> . . . Rolling Thunder had taken a heavy toll on enemy equipment, destroying or damaging several thousand trucks and watercraft, hundreds of railway cars and bridges, many ammunition and storage supply areas, and two-thirds of the enemy's POL [petroleum, oil, and lubricants] storage capacity. Many sorties were flown against AAA, SA–2, and other air defense facilities, thousands of cuts were made in enemy road and rail networks. To counter this air campaign, Hanoi was forced to divert an estimated 200,000 to 300,000 full and part-time workers to repair roads, railway

lines, bridges, and other facilities, and to man its air defenses.[43]

Still, the Air Force did not achieve the strategic objective of destroying the will of Hanoi. The North sustained considerable destruction to its industrial facilities and transportation systems, but continued to operate effectively. Besides, their war effort was not dependent on these resources. The bombing did not destroy the morale of the people of North Vietnam. It did not stop the infiltration of forces and supplies into South Vietnam. And it did not destroy the enemy's main forces. Air attacks destroyed much, killed tens of thousands, disrupted life, and caused enormous pain and suffering. However, as soon as the bombing stopped, the people went back to work. They buried their dead, removed the wreckage, repaired the damage, rebuilt their infrastructure, transferred production to other facilities, moved underground, acquired new resources from the PRC and SU, and simply managed the situation, the same way the British did in 1940, and the Germans did in 1943, 1944, and 1945.

*   *   *   *   *

In South Vietnam, the quality of support the Air Force provided the Army and ARVN was vastly superior to that provided in Korea. Greater acceptance of the tactical role of airpower; a new commitment to soldiers on the ground; advances in technology; and an older, more confident and mature Air Force were the primary reasons. The challenge of Army aviation in close air support missions may have also influenced Air Force behavior. Consider the words of a Special Forces soldier who fought in Vietnam:

> Support by the US Air Force in the Republic of Vietnam was superb. The tactical air force and airlift command elements performed outstanding feats in support of Special Forces. For example, airlift for the first three combat parachute assaults concluded by the Special Forces in South Vietnam consisted of nine C–130 aircraft. These planes were assembled, rigged, operationally prepared, spotted, and ready for take-off within a few hours after the approval of the

operation was given. The first aircraft crossed the intended drop zone exactly on the minute prescribed. In October 1966 tactical aircraft, hastily scrambled, provided the firepower to rescue a sizable contingent of Special Forces in the Plei Trap Valley. Without these fighters, the force stood to receive staggering casualties. Tactical aircraft provided instant response to missions generated by the mobile guerrilla forces, including resupply of vital necessities. Airlift command was largely responsible for the movement each month of 17,000,000 pounds of supplies in 500-pound lots to Special Force camps throughout Vietnam. The armed C–47 gunship was a tremendous help to camps under attack and accounted for the continued existence of camps many miles removed from the immediate relief forces of firepower.[44]

The Air Force, as in World War II and Korea, deployed its heavy strategic bombers in tactical roles in concert with ground forces and independent of them. An Air Force study concluded:

> After US ground troops took over the war late in 1965, air power continued to contribute heavily to enemy attrition in South Vietnam at an extremely low cost in US loss of life. During the ensuing 2 years, the Air Force flew about 25 percent of its tactical strike sorties (46,000) and 30 percent of its B–52 sorties (3,300) in supporting 73 successful major US ground offensives against the Viet Cong and North Vietnamese troops. The remaining 150,000 strike sorties and 7,700 Arc Light sorties were consumed in other actions against both enemy soldiers and supplies within the country. On many of these occasions, the fighters, working in concert with FACs and gunships, destroyed enemy troops that had been fixed in position by allied ground forces. President Johnson's characterization of the air effort in the siege of Khe Sanh as "the most overwhelming, intelligent, and effective use of air power in the history of warfare" was a contemporary recognition of the decisive nature of tactical, B–52, and airlift missions in preserving the Marine base.[45]

While this was not the mission for which the B–52 was built, and this employment was not in concert with Air Force doctrine, the Air Force operation in South Vietnam contributed significantly to the conduct of battles and campaigns. Still, the primary effort was reactive. The enemy held the initiative, deciding when and when not to fight.

*   *   *   *   *

The 7th Fleet's Task Force 77 conducted air operations over Vietnam from the decks of the *Coral Sea, Ranger, Hancock, Midway, Constellation, Ticonderoga, Enterprise, Kitty Hawk*, and other carriers. Seventeen carriers participated in the war, making seventy-three cruises lasting a total of 8,248 days. Typically, three to four attack carriers were "on-line" with the task force operating from patrol areas called Dixie and Yankee Station. At times as many as five carriers were conducting operations. Of the 7.6 million tons of bombs dropped on Vietnam, Laos, and Cambodia between 1964 and 1973, Navy and Marine Corps aviators dropped 1.5 million. Naval aircraft included the F–4 Phantoms, A–1 Skyraiders, A–4 Skyhawks, A–6 Intruders, A–7 Corsairs, E–2A Hawkeyes, and various other aircraft. Carriers operated between 70 and 80 planes. Navy aircraft could not carry the bomb load of Air Force aircraft, but they had a much shorter turnaround time. Many navy missions could be carried out in an hour. The Navy lost 531 aircraft in combat and 299 in accidents. Three hundred and seventeen naval aviators were killed in action.

In addition to the strategic bombing of North Vietnam and supporting ground operations in South Vietnam, the Navy maintained a blockade along the coast of South Vietnam with destroyers and air patrols. Task Group 70.8 included cruisers, destroyers, and, at times, the battleship *New Jersey* with its 16-inch guns. The Navy controlled the entire coast of Vietnam, providing naval gunfire in direct support of marines, counter-battery fire, and bombardment of targets spotted by aircraft or other means. The Navy also conducted Mobile Riverine Force operations in cooperation with the Army in the Mekong Delta region. The Navy formed the Riverine Assault Force, Task Force 117, which consisted of the 9th and 11th River Assault Squadrons. These units worked with the Army's 9th Infantry Division against an estimated twenty-eight VC battalions and sixty-nine separate companies. This was not a joint command. Army and Navy commanders had to agree on operations.

*   *   *   *   *

The air war doctrine in Vietnam has been much debated, and no effort is made here to reproduce that debate; however, some discussion of air war doctrine is required. Graduated response violated Air Force strategic bombing doctrine, which was based on the use of overwhelming offensive airpower to destroy the ability of the enemy to wage war. The Air Force's initial objective was to destroy the enemy's means of production. General John P. Connell, who replaced General Curtis LeMay as Air Force Chief of Staff on 1 February 1965, developed a plan to destroy ninety-four targets of strategic importance in North Vietnam. This plan was rejected. The strategic bombing plan developed by McNamara created greater risk for pilots for considerably less "bang for the buck;" nevertheless, it was implemented. Walter J. Boyne, a retired Colonel USAF, wrote:

> The basic flaw in the design of the missions was that they were striking the wrong end of the North Vietnamese/Viet Cong supply line, sometimes losing $3 million aircraft in attacks against trucks worth 6,000 rubles and carrying bags of rice. The frustration of Air Force leaders and the men flying the missions was extreme; they understood perfectly well that it was far less risky and far more efficient to sink a ship in Haiphong harbor carrying 300 trucks with one mission than to have to spend 1,000 mission to try to destroy those same trucks on the Ho Chi Minh Trail. This was hard intelligence, obtained by the pilots who flew north, were shot at, and returned with an acute awareness of the risk versus return. Unfortunately, they were never able to communicate this intelligence to the highest level in DOD, because the communication lines ran in one direction only: down.[46]

The Air Force and the Army recognized that the strategy and doctrine for the employment of airpower was not likely to achieve decisive results. Many airmen ultimately came to believe that they failed because they were not allowed to conduct the campaign in accordance with Air Force doctrine. The political leaders in Washington were at fault. Their "go-slow" approach eliminated surprise, and allowed the enemy to adjust, recover, and develop strategies and means to counter the American air campaign.[47] The White House and Pentagon imposed restrictive rules of engagement. As the war progressed the rules of engagement grew into pages of detailed instructions governing the actions of pilots. The White House and Pentagon selected and approved targets to apply gradual pressure. Johnson was reported to have said on more than one occasion: "They can't hit an outhouse without my permission."[48] Later Admiral Sharp sought to answer the question, "How did we fail?":

We had superior forces; why didn't we win? The world was amazed that North Vietnam was able to hold off the United States for so many years and to make progress with their aggression in South Vietnam.... My explanation rests in a simple but grave tragedy: we were never allowed to move decisively with our tremendous air and naval power. Once the decision was made to participate in this war and engage Americans in the military conflict, I believe we should have taken the steps necessary to end the war successfully in the shortest possible time. It was folly to commit Americans to combat and then force them to fight without utilizing the means we so richly possessed to win an early victory. It is my firm belief, however, that we did exactly that by not using our air and naval power to its full effectiveness. Instead, we lapsed into a concept of gradualism. Slowly, very slowly, we increased the pressure on North Vietnam in a series of nibbles that permitted them to build up their defenses and to anticipate every move we made.... This policy resulted only in a long and drawn-out war with far too many killed and wounded unnecessarily.[49]

Air Force officers tended to share Sharp's assessment. Some Army officers also accepted this thesis. Westmoreland in the aftermath of the war wrote:

Even after introduction of American combat troops into South Vietnam in 1965, the war still might have been ended within a few years, except for the ill-considered policy of graduated

response against North Vietnam. Bomb a little bit, stop it a while to give the enemy a chance to cry uncle, then bomb a little bit more but never enough to really hurt. That was no way to win.[50]

The Senate Armed Services supported this assessment:

That the air campaign has not achieved its objectives to a greater extent cannot be attributed to inability or impotence of airpower.... It attests, rather, to the fragmentation of our air might by overly restrictive controls, limitations, and the doctrine of 'gradualism' placed on our aviation forces, which prevented them from waging the air campaign in the manner and according to the timetable which was best calculated to achieve maximum results.[51]

Some Air Force leaders offered other explanations for failure to destroy the will of the people, drawing conclusions similar to those delineated in the World War II strategic bombing survey. Air Force Major General Edward Lansdale observed that a police state could maintain sufficient control of its population to preclude social disintegration.[52] Other observers drew the opposite conclusion. Senate Majority Leader Mike Mansfield, in a discussion with Johnson over expansion of the bombing campaign, stated: "Yeah, but Hanoi and Haiphong are spit clean, and have been for months. You bomb them, you get nothing. You just build up more hatred. You get these people tied more closely together because they are tied by blood...."[53]

In fact, there was no way to win with airpower alone. No strategy and no doctrine, short of extermination warfare, that the Air Force could have developed was capable of producing a stable, non-Communist South Vietnam given the geographic circumstances, the social and economic base of North Vietnam, and the limited, defensive, ground war strategy of the White House. Both World War II airpower doctrines were incapable of producing a decision in Vietnam. Bombing could not destroy the will of the North Vietnamese, a largely peasant society accustomed to hardship and years of war, and it could not destroy their means of production, most of which came from the SU and PRC.

The Ground War: The Marine Corps vs. the Army

In March 1965, Johnson approved McNamara's recommendation to deploy two battalions of Marines to Vietnam to protect the American airbase in Danang. Johnson reasoned, "I'm scared to death of putting ground forces in, but I'm more frightened about losing a bunch of planes from a lack of security." While one can question the logic of Johnson's cost–benefit analysis, the deployment introduced US ground combat forces directly into the war, and started the process of escalation. A month later, Westmoreland requested nine battalions, causing Johnson and McNamara to analyze their options.

McNamara reasoned:

> . . . none of us feel that the Chinese are likely to come in, in the near term. They are reasonably optimistic that over the next three to six months, with additional US combat troops in there. . . they feel that they can sufficiently stiffen the South

Vietnamese and strengthen their forces to show Hanoi that Hanoi cannot win in the South. It won't be that the South Vietnamese can win. But it will be clear to Hanoi that Hanoi can't win. And this is one of the objectives we're driving for.[54]

Johnson was, at times, pessimistic. He did not believe the air or the ground war would produce decisive results:

> It's going to be difficult for us to . . . prosecute . . . a war that far away from home with the divisions we have here. . . . I'm very depressed about it. Because I see no program from either Defense or State that gives me much hope of doing anything, except just praying and grasping to hold on . . . and hope they'll quit. I don't believe they're ever going to quit. And I don't see . . . any . . . plan for victory—militarily or diplomatically.[55]

Still, Johnson approved the deployment of troops. He endeavored to do the bare minimum

Month of Arrival	Year	Unit
March/May	1965	3rd Marine Division
May	1965	173rd Airborne Brigade
July	1965	1st Brigade, 101st Airborne Division
September	1965	1st Cavalry Division (Air-mobile)
October	1965	1st Infantry Division
January/May	1966	1st Marine Division
March	1966	25th Infantry Division
August	1966	196th Infantry Brigade
August/December	1966	5th Marine Division (elements)
September	1966	4th Infantry Division
December	1966	1st and 2nd Brigades, 9th Infantry Division
December	1966	199th Infantry Brigade
September	1967	23rd Infantry Division (America!) (formed in Vietnam of various units already present)
October	1967	198th Infantry Brigade
November	1967	2nd and 3rd Brigades, 101st Airborne Division
December	1967	11th Infantry Brigade
February	1968	3rd Brigade, 82nd Airborne Division
July	1968	1st Brigade, 5th Infantry Division
July	1969	3rd Brigade, 9th Infantry Division
December	1970	2nd Brigade, 25th Infantry Division (separate)

Fig 10.4 Major US Combat Units in South Vietnam.

Administration	Role		Year	Added (or subtracted) During Year	Year-end Totals
Dwight D. Elsenhower	A D V I S O R Y		1960	+ 327	700
John F. Kennedy			1961	+ 2,500	3,200
			1962	+ 8,800	12,000
			1963	+ 4,500	16,500
Lyndon B. Johnson	C O M B A T		1964	+ 6,500	23,000
			1965	+ 158,000	181,000
			1966	+ 204,000	385,000
			1967	+ 101,000	486,000
			1968	+ 50,100	536,100
Richard M. Nixon	C O M B and A T	W I T H D R A W A L	1969	−62,100	474,000
			1970	−138,200	335,800
			1971	− 135,800	140,000
			1972	−116,000	24,000
			1973	March 29: Last troops leave	

Note: With rotations, a total of 2,594,000 Americans served in Vietnam.

Fig 10.5 US Troops in Vietnam.

necessary to sustain the situation. Yet he placed no upper limitation on the number of troops he was willing to deploy. Johnson, unlike Truman in 1951, never definitively decided at what level of commitment Vietnam exceeded its strategic value to the United States.

In November 1965, the US 1st Cavalry Division, the Army's only airmobile, air assault division, inserted two battalions into the Ia Drang Valley, where they fought the first major battles against regular regiments of the NVA. The engagements were intense and bloody. Both sides fought well. Consider the actions of the twenty-seven soldiers of the 2nd Platoon of Bravo Company, 1st Battalion, 7th Cavalry:

The predicament of the isolated force ... grew progressively worse. 2nd Lieutenant [Henry T.] Herrick and his men sorely needed the reinforcements that Colonel [Harold] Moore was

attempting to send. The North Vietnamese laced the small perimeter with fire so low to the ground that few of Herrick's men were able to employ their entrenching tools to provide themselves cover. Through it all the men returned the fire, taking a heavy toll on the enemy. Sergeant Savage, firing his M16, hit twelve of the enemy himself during the course of the afternoon.

In midafternoon Lieutenant Herrick was hit by a bullet which entered his hip, coursed through his body, and went out through his right shoulder. As he lay dying, the lieutenant continued to direct his perimeter defense, and in his last few moments he gave his signal operation instructions book to S. Sgt. Carl L. Palmer, his platoon sergeant, with orders to burn it if capture seemed imminent. He told Palmer to redistribute the ammunition, call in artillery fire, and at the first opportunity try to make a break for it. Sergeant Palmer, himself already slightly wounded, had no sooner taken command than he too was killed.

The 2nd Squad leader took charge. He rose on his hands and knees and mumbled to no one in particular that he was going to get the platoon out of danger. He had just finished the sentence when a bullet smashed into his head. Killed in the same hail of bullets was the forward observer for the 81-mm mortar. The artillery reconnaissance sergeant, who had been traveling with the platoon, was shot in the neck. . . .

Sergeant Savage, the 3rd Squad leader, now took command. Snatching the artilleryman's radio, he began calling in and adjusting artillery fire. Within minutes he had ringed the perimeter with well-placed concentrations, some as close to the position as twenty meters. The fire did much to discourage attempts to overrun the perimeter, but the platoon's position still was precarious. Of the 27 men in the platoon 8 had been killed and 12 wounded, leaving less than a squad of effectives.[56]

Under the most difficult circumstances, the platoon fought well, in accordance with Army tactical doctrine and training. This was not Task Force Smith, the poorly equipped, understrength unit that entered South Korea in June 1950. The Army of 1965 had progressed significantly from the early days of the Korean War and the dark days of the Eisenhower Administration. The platoon suffered additional casualties, but was recovered—the living and the dead. The Ia Drang battles were bloody and costly, both sides sustained heavy losses; however, when it was over the kill ratio was ten to one in America's favor—enemy KIA 834 bodies counted, estimated enemy KIA 1,215, POW 6; 1st Cavalry KIA 79 and WIA 125 (no estimate of enemy WIA).[57] If the NVA and VC, under the leadership of General Vo Nguyen Giap, continued to fight in this manner, Westmoreland reasoned, they would bleed themselves to death—attrition warfare. The battle confirmed for Westmoreland the validity of his offensive, operational doctrine "search and destroy."[58] Others, however, concluded that the final act of the Ia Drang campaign foretold a very different outcome.[59]

Giap learned from the battle of the Ia Drang as well. He recognized that he lacked the firepower to engage the US forces in head-to-head contests, and

that other tactics had to be developed. The People's Army of Vietnam (PAVN) and VC were tactically lighter and faster than US forces, had a better grasp of the terrain, and thus, were usually able to avoid battles on American terms, or disengage when the flow of battle went against them. American forces rarely completed the destruction of enemy forces engaged in battle. In addition, the PAVN and VC had excellent intelligence. VC had infiltrated the Saigon government and worked for the US Army in various capacities in all parts of the country. Civilian employees of the US also provided intelligence to the VC and PAVN, and the movements of Army units and aviation resources were easily observed.

A month after the battle of Ia Drang, the 12th Plenum of the Party Central Committee met in Hanoi to reassess its strategy and the new situation created by the deployment of significant American forces. According to the official History of the PAVN, the following decisions were made:

> The Party Central Committee decided that the strategic formula for our resistance war is still protracted warfare, but we will vigorously strive to "concentrate the forces of both North and South Vietnam and seek an opportunity to secure a decisive victory within a relatively short period of time." North Vietnam must defeat the air war of destruction being conducted by the American imperialist, must protect the cause of building socialism, and must mobilize human and material resources for the war to liberate South Vietnam. We must at the same time make vigorous preparations in all areas to be prepared to defeat the enemy should he be so rash as to expand his "limited war" strategy to the entire nation.[60]

The Plenum decided to continue to fight a protracted war of attrition. However, some political and military leaders argued for a more direct approach to the war. They believed they possessed the men and materiel to fight the US the way the battle of Dien Bien Phu had been fought. At this juncture, the protracted war coalition won the strategic argument. However, the debate did not end, and in 1967, the Plenum shifted its strategy, initiating the Tet Offensive. The Plenum in 1965 and 1966 was uncertain about

Fig 10.6 Men of the 1st Cavalry Division on a landing zone.

US actions, and decided to proceed cautiously as it took steps to increase the size of the PAVN, secure greater support from the PRC and USSR, and expand the efforts of the VC. In the early years of Americanization, Communist leaders recognized that it was still possible for the US to invade North Vietnam and fight a more total war.

The Plenum also claims to have identified the major American weakness:

> The American imperialists are the strongest economic and military power in the imperialist camp. The general world situation and the domestic situation in the United States, however, will not allow them to fully utilize their economic and military power in their war of aggression in Vietnam. Politics has always been the enemy's weak point, and it is still the basic weakness he has not been able to overcome.[61]

The situation in Vietnam consumed the attention and energy of Plenum. The domestic political situation in the US—the will of the American people to continue the war—was not a major consideration in 1965.

As the tempo of the war increased, so did the number of American forces. By the end of 1965, the US had committed 181,000 personnel. During the next two years, US troop strength increased by over 100,000 soldiers a year, hitting a peak of 536,100 troops in 1968. The Republic of Korea Army (ROKA) provided an additional 50,000 soldiers.[62] The vast majority of American forces were committed to support roles or nation-building activities. The battlefields of Vietnam, however, had no frontlines. As more American forces arrived in-country, Westmoreland committed them to combat. While strategically limited to the defense, Westmoreland acted aggressively to kill the enemy whenever and wherever possible. In March 1966, the MACV reorganized the command structure, establishing the I and II Field Force, Vietnam and equivalent commands, the III Marine Amphibious Force and the Republic of Korea (ROK) Forces, Vietnam. Each major command was assigned an area of operation.

Westmoreland's strategy for the conduct of the ground war was a "protracted war of attrition." Because ground combat operations were confined to SVN, Westmoreland could not attack the enemy's center of gravity—"the hub of all power and movement, on which everything depends."[63] The center from which Communist power emanated was not in South Vietnam. The White House, graduated response, and geography mandated a protracted war of attrition. Westmoreland well understood these limitations, and explained them to his superiors:

> Thus, the ultimate aim is to pacify the Republic of Vietnam by destroying the VC—his forces, organization, terrorists, agents, and propagandists—while at the same time reestablishing the government apparatus, strengthening GVN military forces, rebuilding the administrative machinery, and re-instituting the services of the Government. During this process security must be provided to all of the people on a progressive basis.[64]

Westmoreland's "search and destroy" operational doctrine consisted of three types of operations that were to be carried out sequentially in phases in a defined area. The first operation was "search and destroy," to find, fix, and fight the enemy's "big units," battalion size and above. This was followed by "clearing operations," phase II, to seek out and find guerrilla forces in an area in which big units no longer operated because of the success of the search and destroy operations. The final phase consisted of "securing operations" to eliminate local VC, and create and maintain a stable environment in which the pacification program could advance. Westmoreland described the process as follows: "A sledge first has to break the boulder into large fragments; groups of workers then attack fragments with spalling tools; then individuals pound the chips with tap hammers until they are reduced to powder and the boulder ceases to exist."[65]

Westmoreland has been criticized for failing to link combat operations to security operations. Archer Jones wrote:

> These operations bore no systematic relation to the South Vietnamese government and army's pacification program. Hence it failed to support

this defensive and offensive persisting strategy to give security to the areas they dominated nor their effort to acquire control of villages within the insurgent sphere of control. By adopting a raiding strategy, General Westmoreland avoided having any significant impact on the enemy's logistics. On the other hand, a persisting strategy, by gradually reconquering the Commnuists' base area, would have deprived them of supplies and recruits as well as circumscribing their base area in which to maneuver.[66]

Westmoreland argued that in the early years of the war he had too few forces to spread around the country, placing squads in every village for security; that there were significant, large NVA and VC units that had to be fought; and that a prerequisite for gaining the security and the support of the people was the removal of these forces. To provide security, major enemy forces had to be eliminated first. Thus, Westmoreland emphasized the first phase, ground combat operations, search and destroy.

Westmoreland's buildup of forces was matched by Hanoi. Fearing an invasion, Hanoi rapidly expanded the size of the NVA and VC. Helicopters made it possible for American forces to respond to almost every crisis, but Westmoreland never had sufficient numbers of forces to secure South Vietnam by permanently stationing small units in each village and hamlet. Westmoreland understood that he had to fight the "other war," the war for the hearts and minds of the people. However, he placed considerable responsibility for winning the other war in the hands of the government of SVN. In his opinion, the Popular Forces and the ARVN were primarily responsible for carrying out securing operations.

The US Marine Corps disagreed with Westmoreland's operational doctrine. Lieutenant General Victor H. Krulak, USMC, Commanding General Fleet Marine Force Pacific, concluded that, "Every man we put into the hunting for NVA was wasted." He advanced an "enclave strategy," in which small units—companies and platoons—worked closely with Vietnamese Popular Forces and the people within a given enclave, "tactical areas of responsibility," to provide security 100 percent of the time, and to form close bonds of trust with the people that would eliminate their support of the VC. By early 1966, the Marines had activated nineteen combined action units. By the end of 1967, seventy-nine units were operational. The Marines reasoned that the VC could not survive without the support of the people. They believed that the primary objective was to win "the other war," or "the war within the war," the war for the hearts and minds of the Vietnamese people.[67] Krulak wrote:

> The Vietcong had enjoyed a free ride in the Vietnamese hamlets because of the general incompetence of the Popular Forces and the consequent uncertainty of the people. The Combined Action idea was an effective answer to the problem, helping to free the people to act, speak, and live without fear. . . . the Marines' concept, from the start, involved fighting the Vietnam battle as a multipronged effort. They aimed to bring peace and security to the people in the highly populated coastal regions by conducting aggressive operations against the guerrillas and expanding the pacified areas as rapidly as they were totally secure. At the same time, they planned to train the local militia and to support the Vietnamese Armed Forces in their fight against the Vietcong. Finally, the Marines were determined to go after the larger organized units whenever they could be definitely located and fixed.[68]

The Marines initially experimented with combined action companies (CAC) and later settled on combined action platoons (CAP) as the primary unit. A CAP consisted of:

> A Marine squad composed of carefully screened volunteers who already had some combat experience was given basic instruction in Vietnamese culture and customs and then combined with a Popular Force platoon. The Marine squad leader—a sergeant or corporal—commanded the combined force in tactical operations, and the Popular Force platoon leader was his operational assistant. The remaining Marines were distributed through the unit in subordinate leadership positions.[69]

The Marine Corps endeavored to win the people with superior political, economic, social, and ideological movements. They believed these operations would deny the insurgency basic resources. Major William C. Holmberg, USMC explained:

> People and their productivity serve as basic resources for the conduct of insurgency. . . . Through the people, the insurgents also obtain financial support through contributions, taxation, and terroristic measures; protection through their ability to move or locate undetected among the populace; information used to conduct military, guerrilla or terroristic operations; additional manpower to serve as insurgents, active supporters or passive supporters of the insurgency. If the insurgent ideological cause is sufficiently strong, manpower augmentation and replacement will be automatically provided by the local social environment.[70]

The Marine Corps' basic thesis to counter the insurgency was correct. Both the battles had to be fought and won—the military battles, and the battle for the support of the people. However, was the combined action program the best solution? This issue has been greatly debated and a perusal of *Marine Corps Gazettes* during the Vietnam War shows that many Marines placed great hope in the program not just for Vietnam, but also for fighting insurgencies in other developing countries.[71] While no definitive assessment is offered in these pages, consider the following difficulties:

The Marine Corps' combined action operational doctrine required specially selected marines with combat experience and special training in Vietnamese culture. Given a thirteen-month tour of duty in Vietnam, a fully qualified marine would have had six to eight months left in-country before his tour came to an end. With an eight-month turnover rate it was difficult to build the kind of trust required for a Vietnamese peasant to risk his life openly supporting the Marines. The Vietnamese that responded to the program always knew that the Marines with whom they had developed personal relationships would leave shortly. During the average tour of a marine, it was only possible to gain a superficial knowledge of the Vietnamese language and culture. And, given that the individuals that took part in the combined action program were specially selected, the program could only be implemented on a small scale. The cultural arrogance of the average American and the lack of

Fig 10.7 General Westmoreland with Lieutenant General Robert E. Cushman (USMC), CG III MAF, and General Wallace M. Greene, Commandant of the Marine Corps.

cultural affinity with Asian people made it difficult to find Marines who could genuinely develop the type of relationship required for this program. And pacification was not what the average marine signed up to do.[72] To implement the program on a large scale would have required enormous numbers of personnel, and once American forces were committed, the American people expected the war to be fought the American way. Hundreds of thousands of military personnel devoted to pacification for years would have been extremely difficult for the Pentagon and a President to explain to the American people. Finally, at some point, pacified areas had to be turned over to the government of Vietnam. No pacification program had the potential to succeed without a stable government capable of sustaining the support of the people. Thus, the government of South Vietnam was ultimately responsible for the success or failure of the pacification programs. And without the substantial support provided by the US, the government of SVN was incapable of sustaining the support of the people against the insurgency supported from North Vietnam. Still, the Marines were vested in the civic action programs and enjoyed some success. Archer Jones wrote:

> The cheering-section behavior exhibited the degree to which the platoon had become part of the community. On their part, the marines displayed a comparable allegiance to their platoons. So in spite of having three chances in four of being wounded while on duty in one of the platoons, 60 percent of the marines serving in these units volunteered for an additional six months of service in Vietnam to continue with their platoons. The Vietnamese displayed a similar dedication when none deserted the combined

action platoon in 1966, compared with the 25 percent desertion rate for normal Popular Force platoons. Moreover, that no village that had a combined action platoon reverted to Communist control testifies to their effectiveness.[73]

In 1968, the First Civic Affairs Group, FMF, was activated in Camp Pendleton. General Lewis W. Walt noted, "we are developing a steadily increasing staff capability through the school training of some 40 officers a year. We are developing doctrine and plans which have, as their basic consideration, the premise that civil affairs are, and will continue to be for the foreseeable future, an integral part of our responsibilities." The Marine Corps had a long history of fighting "small wars." It demonstrated a greater willingness to adapt and adjust its tactics and operations to the circumstances of Vietnam than did the Army.

Finally, it should be noted that some senior Army leaders were in agreement with the major tenets of Marine counterinsurgency operational doctrine. Army Chief of Staff, General Harold K. Johnson, believed that Westmoreland was fighting the wrong war. General William E. DuPuy, Westmoreland's Operations Officer, noted that Johnson:

> was a counterinsurgency man 100 percent. He thought, and there were a lot of people in Washington that agreed with him, that Westmoreland and DuPuy and his other henchmen out there didn't understand the war, that the war was a counterinsurgency and that . . . we were trying to get prepared for a big bashing of the North Vietnamese Army.[74]

Johnson initiated a study entitled *A Program for the Pacification and Long-Term Development of Vietnam.* It was published in March 1966, and became known as the PROVN study. It concluded that:

> the objective beyond the war should be the restoration of stability with the minimum of destruction, so that the society and lawful government may proceed in an atmosphere of justice and order. . . . The United States . . . must redirect the Republic of Vietnam—Free World military effort to achieve greater security. . . . The critical actions are those that occur at the village, the district and

provincial levels. . . . This is where the war must be fought. . . .

Westmoreland read the PROVN study, and rejected it.[75] He was optimistic that his search and destroy doctrine would produce the most significant results in the shortest time.

The Marine Corps, while given some freedom of action, implemented its strategic vision in opposition to Westmoreland's operational doctrine. The Army fought one war and the Marines another. To motivate Army and Marine commanders to fully and aggressively implement his search and destroy operational doctrine, Westmoreland imposed management tools such as body counts, battalion days in the field, the hamlet evaluation system (HES), and other measures that he believed assessed the performance of combat units, individual commanders, and the achievement of objectives.[76] Several of these measures corrupted the system, causing commanders to seek objectives that were only tangentially related to defeating the VC and NVA.[77] Statistical performance measures in some cases motivated the unnecessary destruction of homes, hamlets, and the lives of innocent civilians; the expenditure of enormous quantities of ammunition for insignificant body counts; and the promotion of careerism within the officer corps. David H. Hackworth, one of the most highly decorated soldiers in the Vietnam War, wrote:

> The emphasis on body count, a system already . . . obsolete. . . was also taking its toll on the war effort by making everyone a bounty hunter and a liar. . . . Yet, with the passage of time, the reliance on it among the top brass of the military, the Defense Department bureaucrats, and the politicians would only increase. The more bodies we counted, went the thinking, the better we were doing. In fact, my experience with Slam [S.L.A. Marshall who was studying combat operations in Vietnam] revealed that the pressure for a high and instant body count interrupted the flow of battle, tied up communications, and created unnecessary casualties among troops tasked with the job of doing the counting during a fight. Body count was also well on its way to destroying whatever was left of the moral code of soldiers and officers in the zero-defect Army.

Leaders did not challenge suspected figures reported by subordinate units (who themselves knew the importance of a significant count) and too often actively inflated their scores to please their ER [evaluation report] raters or just to get higher HQ off their backs. Sometimes a body count was completely made up to mask a screwed-up mission.[78]

Colin Powell supported this view:

Our senior officers knew the war was going badly. Yet they bowed to groupthink pressure and kept up pretense, the phony measure of body counts, the comforting illusion of secure hamlets, the inflated progress reports. As a corporate entity the military failed to talk straight to its political superiors or to itself.[79]

Nevertheless, no matter how effective or ineffective Westmoreland's and Krulak's operational and tactical doctrines, victory could not be predicted or attained on a battlefield restricted to South Vietnam. In Vietnam, no matter how brilliantly conceived and flawlessly executed the tactics and operations, the war could not be won because the strategy was fatally flawed. As Clausewitz notes, to achieve decisive results requires offensive strategy and operations. On the strategic defense, the United States could not achieve decisive results. All the Army, Marine Corps, and ARVN could do was preclude defeat—a negative objective. Offensive operations would have risked war with China, a cost too high for the Johnson Administration. Consider the resources the United States would have committed had the Soviet Union or China initiated operations in Mexico. War in China's backyard was a bad idea.

The Vietnam War did not fit the American experiences of past wars, or their expectations of future wars. Americans expected decisive war from the air, possibly employing nuclear weapons, or a repeat of World War II with lines drawn on maps delimiting the advances of armies, consistently depicting progress, and reports on destruction of enemy cities or production facilities. They expected decisive actions and victory from both approaches to war. Instead they got a protracted defensive war of attrition, with the only measure of progress being the body count. Still, by the end of 1967, Westmoreland, with 485,000 military personnel under his command, was predicting victory.

*   *   *   *   *

Tactics in Vietnam varied by time and location. Operations in the Mekong Delta were very different from those in the Central Highlands. Airmobile units operated very differently from light infantry units. Operations in dry season (summer and fall) were different from those in monsoon season (winter and spring). And, operations in 1965 were very different from those in 1969. Hence, no detailed analysis is offered. However, there were several major trends regarding combat motivation and technology that are outlined here. In 1965, soldiers learned quickly that they were not going to be permitted to complete the destruction of the enemy forces. They learned that they were not in charge of their destiny. This influenced combat motivation. In 1969 they learned that the Army was withdrawing unilaterally with or without victory, and no soldier wanted to be the last man to die in Vietnam. In between, technology evolved rapidly, influencing the conduct, the tactical performance of soldiers in unforeseen ways.

In Korea, in the last two years of the war, the objective was not to complete the destruction of the enemy's main army, and it was not to conquer and hold terrain. Thus, if there was no plan to win the war with ground forces, there was no need to risk the lives of soldiers if the defensive mission could be achieved primarily by firepower. This was also the situation in Vietnam. As a consequence of the adoption of defensive strategy in a limited war in which the objective was not victory, the role of the Army and infantry changed. Some units adopted the practice of finding the enemy and then calling in artillery or airpower to destroy him. General Palmer, a veteran of the war, concluded that Army tactical commanders in Vietnam spent firepower as if they were millionaires and husbanded their men's lives as if they were paupers. He further noted that:

Like the changing opinions of the proper role for modern weaponry ... tactical concepts of fire and maneuver also underwent a complete flip-flop during the war. Prior to the introduction of

American ground combat units in 1965, US Army doctrine called for—and advisors so urged their counterparts—closing with the enemy and destroying him in place, for maintaining close and continuous contact, for pursuit.... But that began to change in 1965: by 1967 only a foolhardy or a desperate commander would ever engage hostile elements by any means other than with firepower.... As the months of the war of attrition bled by, the new tactics quickly became standard. Infantry units were all but forbidden to practice their traditional mission of closing with and killing the enemy. Instead, maneuver elements found the foe while firepower eliminated him. B–52 usage, for instance, leaped from sixty sorties a month in 1966 to over eight hundred monthly in 1967. When contact was made, American units, preoccupied with avoiding casualties, generally fell back into a defensive perimeter to call for air and artillery.[80]

Because tactics varied, a note of caution is due. Lieutenant Colonel Roy K. Flint (later Brigadier General) disagreed with Palmer's assessment. As the Commander of the 3rd Battalion, 22nd Infantry, of the 25th Infantry Division that operated in III Corps Tactical Zone (III CTZ) in the vicinity of Saigon, he described his operations in February 1968:

Well, I think it's a tremendous idea if it works, but I've never found one case yet where firepower alone destroys the enemy force. I'd say—with one notable exception—that that is our general method of operation. We try to make contact in such a way that we retain our freedom of movement and minimize our casualties. You realize, of course, that the biggest problem of fighting here is to walk up on an unseen bunker and have a man hit. Then you have that horrible problem of extracting him under fire before you can bring the firepower in on the bunker. Therefore the key is to get off the first shot or cause the enemy to open fire prematurely. Well—this sounds great—but it's a matter of patient movement. All right—that's Part I—find the enemy. Part II is being in a position yourself when you find him where you have no casualties or perhaps so lightly wounded that you have freedom of movement. Now if you've got that, I agree 100% with pull back a safe distance and bring in every bit of available

firepower—artillery, air strike, CS and everything else we can to kill him in his position.[81]

Flint was emphatic that killing by fire alone was not a common practice in the 25th Infantry Division: "... as I said earlier, I've never done this and found every enemy soldier dead—and the fact of the matter is, surprisingly few of them are killed, particularly in a well-bunkered area—so the infantry has still got to go in."

Still, the ammunition expenditure in Vietnam exceeded that of all other wars fought by the United States. The use of bombs and artillery rounds show that the practice of employing enormous firepower reached new levels in Vietnam. How effective or counterproductive this firepower was, is another question. Instead of using soldiers to go into villages and dwellings, identify the bad guys and kill only them, leaving the women and children unharmed, too many units tended to go into the village, identify suspected enemy locations, and called in artillery or airpower to destroy it. Hence, the famous words of an American soldier fighting at Ben Tre during the Tet Offensive, "We had to destroy the town to save it."[82]

American infantry units in the field were chronically understrength. One soldier noted, "Because we were so understrength, we heavily depended on our firepower, the artillery, and air strikes."[83] This was a problem that went back to World War II. The American conduct of war was very destructive to the civilian populations whose "hearts and minds" it was trying to win. Consider the words of Lieutenant Morgan Sincock:

Infantry officers are taught to prioritize their situation, with their mission taking priority over their men. This is the necessary philosophy to wage war. Men do get killed and wounded. To put the men first diminishes the chance of accomplishing the mission. In war, you risk lives. To many of us, the risk became unacceptable when we were unable to utilize the resources at our disposal. Some battles were fought with timidity and caution rather than abandon and commitment because we could not rationalize the sacrifice of men's lives in order to protect civilian property.... Many, although not all, officers shared my philosophy that it was wisest to use maximum firepower and minimum frontal assaults by infantry. We would often make contact, pull back a few meters, and continue to engage the enemy with small-arms fire while we began a massive pounding of the enemy positions with all available firepower.[84]

The strategically defensive nature of the war caused greater reliance on firepower. Infantry is a maneuver force. If there were no major operational maneuvers of strategic importance, why risk lives? The Army's traditional infantry doctrine was not employed in Vietnam, and the Americans' use of firepower transmitted messages of strategic importance to the enemy: It told the Vietnamese and the world that American lives were more valuable than those of the Vietnamese people they were there to save. And, it communicated to the enemy that Americans, employing a citizen-soldier Army, cannot take casualties. Americans cannot stand the sight of body bags coming home in large numbers, and thus, the will of the American people is vulnerable. The Communists did not fully realize and acknowledge this vulnerability until after the Tet Offensive in 1968. However, a discussion with the Chinese who fought the Americans in Korea might have revealed it sooner.

*   *   *   *   *

Technology greatly influenced the conduct of war; however, its unintended effects sometimes diminished its intended effects. Such was the case with much of the technology employed in Vietnam, foremost among them, the helicopter.

The helicopter gave the US Army superior operational mobility, greater flexibility and speed, faster response time, increased firepower, and interior lines—the ability to reinforce separated units faster than the enemy. The vertical ascent and descent capabilities allowed the Army to put soldiers on the ground anywhere in Vietnam, including dense jungle. Landing zones could be cleared in hours. On 28 June 1965 the 173rd Airborne Brigade conducted the largest air assault operation in Army history up to that time. It was highly successful. Some 1,494 helicopter sorties were flown. Fifty-six Viet Cong were killed and twenty-eight taken prisoner. Tons of supplies and numerous documents were discovered. Brigadier General Ellis

W. Williamson, the commander of the 173rd, recognizing the significance of helicopters, stated:

> In all candor I must admit that I did not expect to find as many enemy in that area as we did. . . . We did a lot of things that we could not even have considered six weeks ago. As you recall when we first arrived in Vietnam we started off doing one thing at a time. On this operation, at the extraction time, we took 3,000 troops out of three different landing zones in three hours and ten minutes. We wouldn't have moved troops that fast or afford to bring our troops that close together at one time unless we had a lot going on at one time. . . . As I looked at it from above, it was a sight to see. We were withdrawing from the center LZ while some friendly troops were still in the western LZ. We had a helicopter strike going in a circle around the center LZ. The machine gun and rocket firing helicopters kept making their circle smaller and smaller as we withdrew our landing zone security. Just to the west side we had another helicopter strike running north to south. We also had something else that was just a little hairy but it worked without any question, the artillery was firing high angle fire to screen the northern side of the landing zone. The personnel lift helicopters were coming from the east, going under the artillery fire, sitting down in the LZ to pick up troops and leaving by way of the southwest. In addition to that, we had an air strike going to the northeast. All of these activities were going on at the same time. We could not have done that a few weeks ago.[85]

The helicopter greatly increased the pace of operations. The same force was capable of performing multiple missions in a relatively small period of time with air mobility. The range of missions was also greatly expanded. And as helicopter technology improved and specialized aircraft entered the Army inventories, the firepower, lift capacity, and overall capabilities of the Army in Vietnam expanded. Westmoreland noted:

> Suppose that we did not have helicopters and air-mobile divisions today. How many troops would we have needed to accomplish what we have achieved in South Vietnam . . .? No finite answer

is possible because our tactics in Vietnam were based on massive use of helicopters.... What would we do without helicopters? We would be fighting a different war, for a smaller area, at a greater cost, with less effectiveness. We might as well have asked: 'What would General Patton have done without his tanks?'[86]

The helicopter greatly facilitated the conduct of Army operations. However, the Army's adaptation of this technology was influenced by American cultural tenets and other factors. General Palmer recorded the thoughts of an astute outside observer who noted that the helicopter "exaggerated the two greatest weaknesses of the American character—impatience and aggressiveness." Palmer concluded that: "for better or for worse, American soldiers in Vietnam became firmly wedded to technology. It was the equalizer in a war, which seemed in so many other ways to favor the enemy. Eventually, it came to dominate Allied tactical thinking and to dictate the very manner of fighting."[87] This is an overstatement. However, the helicopter produced a number of unintended behaviors. It changed the way the Army thought about operations. It made it possible for the Army to operate more like the Air Force and Navy. For some airmobile/air assault units, war became, in a sense, an 8 to 5 job. Soldiers could load up in the morning, spend the day hunting bad guys, and return to camp in the evening for a hot dinner and cold beer. For regular infantry units, the helicopter tended to tie soldiers to landing zones. Landing zones became the umbilical cord, conveying all the resources needed to sustain units in the field. It also became a life-giver, enabling units to rapidly reinforce or evacuate, and quickly transport wounded personnel. In jungle, this meant the further a unit moved away from an LZ the further it was from its lifeline. Hence, there were strong motivations to stay relatively close to LZs.

The helicopter influenced the functioning of the chain of command. A veteran of the war wrote:

The ubiquitous helicopter damaged the chain [of command] severely since the temptation to deal with subordinates several layers down was too great to resist. Indeed, the war became known as the 'small unit commander's war,' quarterbacked by a senior commander circling overhead. With a

platoon leader, for example, getting precise instructions from a division commander, the teamwork and leadership development between the platoon leader, the company commander, the battalion commander, and the brigade commander were bound to be disrupted.[88]

Tactically, the helicopter announced when the Army was moving, the direction of movement, and the size of the force being employed. The enemy, thus, decided if and when he wanted to fight.

Other technologies also influenced operations in Vietnam. Powell noted:

We were ... deluded by technology. The enemy was primitive, and we were the most technologically advanced nation on earth. It therefore should be no contest. Thus, out of the McNamara shop came miracles like the 'people sniffer,' a device that could detect concentrations of urine on the ground from an airplane.... If the urine was detected in likely enemy territory, we now had an artillery target. But woe to any innocent peasants or water buffalo that happened to relieve themselves in the wrong place.[89]

The people sniffer never produced the results expected. Yet, it was another example of American thinking about war: excessive faith in technology, excessive use of firepower, the prodigious waste of resources, and little concern for the indigenous population. Another stillborn technological solution was Agent Orange. The objective was defoliation, to eliminate the enemy's ability to use terrain to camouflage and conceal his activities, and to increase the effectiveness of American firepower.

General Bruce Palmer, General Westmoreland's Deputy Army Commander in Vietnam, noted that within the Army, two cultural tenets prevalent since World War II were still operative: first, that technology was a substitute for manpower; and second, that the Army and particularly infantry were for the "least talented" Americans:

... it is widely recognized that American armies, particularly in the twentieth century, have relied heavily on the technological superiority of their arms and equipment.... And so the allegation is frequently made that the US Army pins its hopes for battle success on heavy, massed firepower rather than on the professional skill and tenacity of its infantry, who in the final analysis must close with the enemy and finish him off. This explains why the Army tends to put its more highly educated and qualified personnel into artillery and armor units rather than infantry. . . . In my parochial view, such attitudes are seriously flawed. The training of truly professional infantry is more complex and difficult than many military men realize, and all too often it is relatively neglected. In fact, good, solid, realistic training is the only way that the American Army can overcome its tendency to rely on the weight of firepower to compensate for any lack of professional skill in the art of maneuver.[90]

The Army sought technological solutions to the problems of fighting in Vietnam. Firepower and other technologies were substituted for manpower. As the range, accuracy, rate of fire, and lethality of artillery and airpower increased, the Army relied more and more on firepower.

The Vietnam War damaged the spirit of the Army. It caused the slow disintegration of professionalism. No proud Army wants to fight the type of war the US Army was required to fight in Vietnam. To bleed with no culminating objective and no end in sight was folly, and ultimately intolerable. The United States Army deployed to Vietnam was the best trained, best equipped army of any deployed to war in the twentieth century. It was the first fully integrated US Army deployed to war since the American Revolution. It was a traditional American citizen-soldier Army, the last to be deployed by the United States in the twentieth century.

11.
THE VIETNAM WAR, THE FINAL PHASES, 1967–1975

For the first time in modern history, the outcome of a war was determined not on the battlefield, but on the printed page and, above all, on the television screen. Looking back coolly, I believe it can be said (surprising as it may still sound) that South Vietnamese and American forces actually won the limited military struggle. They virtually crushed the Viet Cong in the South ... and thereafter they threw back the invasion by regular North Vietnamese divisions. None the less, the War was finally lost to the invaders after the US disengagement because the political pressure built up by the media had made it quite impossible for Washington to maintain even the minimal material and moral support that would have enabled the Saigon regime to continue effective resistance.[1]

–Robert Elegant, "How to Lose a War," 1981

Most of the public affairs problems that confronted the United States in South Vietnam stemmed from the contradictions implicit in Lyndon Johnson's strategy for the war. ... Doing just enough to placate scattered but vocal prowar elements in Congress and the news media, it would also preserve options for the president that might disappear if the so-called hawks gained ascendancy. Johnson had his way, but at the cost of his own credibility. By postponing some unpopular decisions while making others only after weighing how the press and public might react, he indeed hardened the American people and Congress to the necessity for military action. ... Yet in the process he also peppered the public record with so many inconsistencies and circumlocutions that he prompted one commentator to observe that the record of his administration's "concealments and misleading denials ... is almost as long as its impressive list of achievements."[2]

–William Hammond, *The Military and the Media*, 1988

The role of the media in the Vietnam War has been greatly debated. It has been argued that the media played a decisive role, that the will of the American people to fight the war was destroyed by the distorted, inaccurate, one-sided, anti-military, liberal press. The services have tended to accept this argument. This was evident later in Operation Desert Storm, during which the Central Command denied reporters direct access to tactical formations and formed media pools that were tightly controlled by public affairs officers.[3] The services modified their behaviors and policies towards the media based on their perceptions of its performance in Vietnam. General Westmoreland believed that the press in Vietnam acted irresponsibly; that it misrepresented the actions of the armed forces of the United States and ARVN, particularly during the 1968 Tet Offensive, which the press inaccurately portrayed as a major defeat for US and ARVN forces. He also believed that the press exerted too much influence on President Johnson and other politicians, recognizing that they frequently made decisions based on public opinion polls. While many in the military developed a profound distrust of the media, later studies have argued that the problems in Vietnam were a function of the duplicity of the White House and Pentagon; their efforts to hide the true nature of the war and America's involvement; deeply flawed, contradictory strategy; the efforts of the Army to conceal unpleasant information and reveal only half-truths; and that in fact the preponderance of coverage was either favorable or neutral.

The major scholarly works are unanimous in their conclusion that the media *did not* decisively influence the war.[4] William M. Hammond, in the Army's official history, concluded: "they [the Johnson Administration] forgot at least two common-sense rules of effective propaganda: that the truth has greater ultimate power than the most pleasing of bromides and that no amount of massaging will heal a broken limb or a fundamentally flawed strategy." However, where one stood determined their perspective. Works on the role of the media in Vietnam are too numerous to fully consider in these pages; however, some assessment is required.

Censorship, the Media, and Public Opinion

The Vietnam War was not lost in Vietnam. The armed forces of the United States could not win the war under the strategy and doctrine of the Johnson Administration, but arguably they also could not lose it. The war was lost in the United States when the American people concluded that the war could not be won following the policies and strategies of the Johnson Administration; and consequently, withdrew their support.

Public knowledge, understanding, and opinions are formed by what people read, see, and hear. Those that control these forms of communications thus influence public opinion. Between the Korean War and the Vietnam War, a number of factors came together to change the relationship between the press and the military that had been built during World War II and the Korean War. During both wars the press accepted censorship. In 1950 television entered the homes of Americans. News became abbreviated, but influenced greater numbers of people than ever before. News anchors became influential, respected commentators who addressed Americans nightly. The advent of modern communications systems and the ubiquitous

television greatly increased the speed and strength of the media by bringing images of war directly into living rooms. Television cameras became smaller, more mobile, and rugged, able to go wherever the action was. The ability to transmit news across oceans and continents at the speed of light meant Americans could see the horrors of war much sooner than before. New technologies enabled producers to edit film to tell the story they thought they saw. The network news organizations became powerful forces, exerting political influence and shaping public opinion. They could change public perceptions overnight. The competitions between networks for ratings and audience share also influenced the quality of reporting.

Young reporters were eager, ambitious, and unable to make sense of what they saw in Vietnam. The press started with two contradictory outlooks. On the one hand, they were motivated by patriotism —the desire to support the troops, acceptance of the correctness of America's stand against Communism, and a willingness to accept and support the words and policies of the President. On the other hand, reporters write to win the approbation of their peers. They tend to distrust the government, believing that it is their job and responsibility to uncover government wrongdoing. They have attitudes, values, and ethics that run counter to those of the military. And, getting the scoop, "the big story," before their competitors, for too many, was more important than accuracy.

In Vietnam, censorship was not employed. A voluntary system was established with fifteen ground rules designed to protect military intelligence. Reporters were forbidden to reveal planned offensive operations, troop movements, and other information that might be valuable to the enemy. If the rules were violated, a reporter could lose his MACV accreditation. Still, after several breaches of the rules, Westmoreland concluded that censorship was necessary. In 1965, following the initiation of the sustained bombing campaign, Westmoreland told the Joint Chiefs of Staff that a conference was necessary to establish new policies for dealing with the press: "Since the rules of the game are changing rapidly, it seems to me that we should consider arrangements similar to those exercised during the Korean conflict. This would involve providing for accredited war correspondents (we might want to give them another name) and censorship in some limited form."[5] Westmoreland's request was repeated several times; however, it was ultimately denied.

Hammond noted:

> Officials at the US mission ... remained convinced that neither censorship nor voluntary restraints on the press would do much good. The US forces were operating from a sovereign country, Ambassador Taylor observed, in which newsmen were free to travel by other than US military means and to file dispatches through cables and telephones operated by the South Vietnamese.[6]

Vietnam was considered too open to effectively impose censorship. Foreign correspondents from all over the world were free to travel to Vietnam. The Vietnamese government was considered a fully functioning, sovereign government, and only it could regulate the movement of foreign correspondents. In addition, attempts to impose restraints on the American media had met with stiff opposition. News agencies in the United States had enormous, expanding power. They published editorials criticizing the MACV for limiting access to bases, pilots, and information. The White House, particularly, seemed to fear the press. Censorship was rejected:

> [R]epresentatives of all US government agencies concerned with the war in South Vietnam— concluded that the uproar [caused by the imposition of restraints] prefigured what was likely to happen if the Johnson Administration decided to impose a restrictive press policy. American success in South Vietnam depended upon the support of the public, they noted in their final report, and that support was likely to waiver if "any significant number of our people believe ... they are being misled." Working from that premise, the group rejected any form of field press censorship, opting firmly for the system of voluntary cooperation.[7]

A number of reasons were given for rejecting censorship: it required "the legal underpinnings of a declaration of war;" considerable logistical and administrative resources; jurisdiction over all communications and transportation facilities; large numbers of multilingual military personnel; control over teletypes, radios, and telephone systems; and the cooperation of the government of South Vietnam. It was believed that there were too many ways for the press to get around censorship, too many reporters (about 600 accredited correspondents in January 1968), multiple means of communication, a huge volume of information that flowed to foreign countries, the ability to purchase information from Vietnamese officials, leaks within MACV and ARVN headquarters, and numerous other factors that created enormous control problems.

Through the correspondent accreditation process, by providing transportation and other forms of support, by granting access to commanders and servicemen, by formal briefings, and various other measures, it was believed that the press could be managed and used to support the war effort. However, the search for the sensational, the inexperience of many correspondents, difficulties with the Vietnamese language, and Western cultural arrogance damaged the ability of the press to report objectively on the war. And, once an adversarial relationship developed, the press challenged and questioned every move, every operation, every figure, and every pronouncement of the military.

Before the first division entered combat in Vietnam, the Army had a public relations problem. The Vietnam War was not what Americans expected or wanted to see. Between the Korean War and Vietnam War, America had undergone significant technological, economic, cultural, and social changes. Its interests had been focused on the space race, the arms race, and the rapid advances in science and technology, all of which reinforced the new vision of war from the air and space. Americans were wealthier and enjoying a higher standard of living than ever before. They were also more mobile and better educated. Throughout the 1950s, a gap had developed and grown between the Army and the American people, as many came to believe the Army was no longer necessary. In Vietnam, the Army was *never* going to be able to paint the picture Americans expected and wanted to see. Americans could not see the air war, and did not understand political restraints that meant that the Army was not supposed to win the war.

The Vietnam War is considered the first "television war." With the advent of television, the power of the media soared. Films of battles were shown in the US less than twenty-four hours after they were recorded. Footage was transmitted from Tokyo to the United States via satellite. The footage, however, painted only half the picture. (There were no images of the war from the perspective of the enemy.) And the who, the what, the when, the where, and the why were frequently unclear. Americans could not distinguish between a dead VC and a dead citizen of South Vietnam. Film editors cut and pasted footage together to tell a story the way they believed would be most significant, and the way they believed it ought to be told, sometimes in contradiction to what the commanders on the ground had told the journalist.

Film produced tunnel vision through which the rest of the situation was imagined. The viewer saw what the cameraman thought was important. The cameraman inevitably shot what was most shocking, and what was most likely to produce the most visceral, emotional effect. From these images the viewer extrapolated and generalized about the overall conduct of the war. In addition, news agencies showed the same footage, the most shocking events, again and again, reinforcing and magnifying the effects. As a consequence of repeatedly viewing film of the sensational deaths of Americans, with few images of the deaths of the VC and NVA, as well as the destruction caused by American forces, with no comparable images from the Communist side, Americans got a distorted picture of the war. Still, according to the vast majority of scholarly research on the media in Vietnam, it did not decisively influence public opinion against the war. John Mueller wrote:

> Many have seen Vietnam as a "television war" and argued that the vivid and largely uncensored day-by-day television coverage of the war and its brutality made a profound impression on public attitudes. The poll data used in this study do not support such a conclusion. They clearly show that whatever impact television had, it was not enough to reduce support for the war below the levels attained by the Korean War, when television was in its infancy, until casualty levels had far surpassed those of the earlier war.[8]

Of course, the way one constructs a poll influences the data it produces. If television images did not influence public opinion, marketers and politicians would not use it to sell their products or themselves. While it is too much to argue that the media was decisive, it is equally too much to argue that it did not influence public opinion. The character and quality of that influence can and has been debated. However, the media possessed the potential to strategically influence war. Information matters. The Army, more so than the other services, needed the media to tell its story. The media was the link between the Army and the American people, and the Army, in fact, had a great story to tell.

The armed forces did not always help themselves in their dealings with the media. Imbued with a "can do" attitude, they endeavored to put the best face on every situation, and were too often incapable of calling an "ambush" an "ambush."[9] Instead they engaged in double-speak, which the press quickly saw through. The media was able to collect information from multiple sources at different levels of command and from different locations. When the stories they received conflicted, they concluded, sometimes rightly, sometimes wrongly, that they had intentionally been misled. The White House and Pentagon also, at times, intentionally misled, tried to conceal the truth, and lied. A credibility gap developed that did enormous harm to the US and its war effort.

New Personnel Policies: The Result of Transformation

In 1965 Lieutenant Colonel Harold G. Moore's 1st Battalion, 7th Cavalry deployed from Fort Benning, Georgia, to war in Vietnam as if it were deploying for a training exercise. It went into battle the same way. Moore wrote:

> Unfortunately, my battalion and every other in the division now began to suffer the consequences of President Johnson's refusal to declare a state of emergency and extend the active-duty tours of draftees and reserve officers. The order came down: Any soldier who had sixty days or less left to serve on his enlistment as of the date of deployment, August 16, must be left behind.

We were sick at heart. We were being shipped off to war sadly understrength and crippled by the loss of almost a hundred troopers in my battalion alone. The very men who would be the most useful in combat—those who had trained longest in the new techniques of helicopter warfare—were by this order taken away from us. It made no sense then; it makes no sense now.[10]

When Moore's battalion fought regiments of the regular army of North Vietnam in the Ia Drang it was at two-thirds of its operational go-to-war strength—platoons that were designed to fight with forty-one men entered combat with as few as twenty-seven soldiers. Unlike Truman, who initiated a partial call-up of the National Guard and Reserves, and declared a state of emergency that in the early days of the war precluded trained soldiers from retiring or ending their contractual term of service, Johnson sought to fight the war as if the nation was not fighting a war. His actions created an enormous chasm between the realities of war—the wounded and dead soldiers and marines, the huge defense expenditures, and the images shown on the evening news—and the actions of Americans at home, who, for the most part, were asked to do nothing. In addition, Truman had an environment of fear, caused by the Soviet test of an atomic bomb and the loss of China to the Communists in 1949, and he had a blatant act of aggression, a major land invasion against a state sponsored and supported by the United States. While stopping considerably short of the mobilization that took place for World War II, Truman took actions that were more appropriate for a nation at war. Johnson sent the wrong signals to the American people. He did not have the element of fear or the blatant act of aggression, and he endeavored to hide the war, and to disguise the deployment of combat forces. By so doing he created the conditions for the ultimate collapse of the will of the American people. Johnson's conduct of the war had more to do with the destruction of the will of the American people during the Tet Offensive in 1968, than the actions of Hanoi, the NVA, and VC. The Johnson Administration did not psychologically prepare the nation for war. The American people have suffered such setbacks before, and always in the past they have rallied together to produce what was

needed for victory. The problem was not in Hanoi. It was in Washington.

Johnson refused the Army's request to call up the National Guard and Reserves. The Army was more dependent on reserves than the other services. Army contingency plans were based on the call-up of reserve forces. In a meeting with Secretary of Defense McNamara in 1965, Army Chief of Staff Harold K. Johnson stated:

I haven't any basis for justifying what I am going to say, but I can assure you of one thing, and that is that without a call-up of the reserves that the quality of the Army is going to erode and we're going to suffer very badly. I don't know at what point this will be, but it will be relatively soon. I don't know how widespread it will be, but it will be relatively widespread.[11]

McNamara ignored Johnson, whose assessment was confirmed within a few years. The President had decided to fight the war in "cold blood."[12] He did not want to arouse the passions or ire of the American people, who might force him to fight a more total war, and he did not want to signal to the world a major commitment to Vietnam. He was most worried about the signals sent to the PRC and SU. He did not want them to go through the process of developing plans and mobilizing forces to counter US forces in Vietnam. He did not want a repeat of the Korean War experience. The National Guard and Reserves thus became safe havens for those wishing to avoid military service in Vietnam. Johnson and McNamara sacrificed combat effectiveness and the psychological preparation of the nation for war, for the appearance of normalcy that they hoped would keep the Chinese and Soviets out of the war. But their actions also spoke loudly to soldiers and marines fighting the ground war, and to the American people who could *not* associate the images on national television with the actions of their government. There was an internal contradiction in the American conduct of war that grew in intensity each year of the war.

To spread the burden and limit the protests of the war, a one-year tour of duty was instituted, much like the rotation system the Army tried to put into effect during the Korean War. Old soldiers responded negatively to this policy. General Bruce Palmer, Jr., Westmoreland's Deputy in Vietnam and a veteran of the campaigns in New Guinea and the Philippines in World War II, believed that:

> In Vietnam the one-year tour policy had the same effect as a rotation system and badly damaged unit cohesion. It also greatly compounded the Army's problem of maintaining strength in combat units, especially rifle companies. In both Korea and Vietnam rifle companies were rarely if ever at full authorized strength and operated routinely at strengths as low as 60 percent of authorized. In Korea rifle companies sometimes fought with musters as low as 25 percent authorized strength.[13]

The one-year tours of duty improved the morale of individual soldiers, but damaged unit cohesion, *esprit de corps*, and the ability of the Army to maintain authorized unit strength. Military proficiency, particularly in an Army trained and equipped to fight on European battlefields, was also a problem:

> Reports from Vietnam that the enemy was a mighty jungle fighter . . . caused the military service schools to juggle hastily the instructional units in the curriculum to accommodate this type of foe. Despite these efforts, the elemental lessons of infiltration, scouting and patrolling, reconnaissance, ambush tactics, night fighting, and unorthodoxy in tactics and logistics had to be learned and relearned on the ground in Vietnam. The twelve-month tour of duty operated against any one commander's accumulating very much experience or passing it on to his successors.[14]

Communist soldiers throughout the war had greater experience, understanding of the nature of their enemy, and understanding of the ground on which they fought, than did American soldiers. Each year of the war, the US deployed a different Army. Units rarely enjoyed the advantages of teams of combat soldiers with more than a few months of experience. In addition, American soldiers had no vested interest in the outcome of the war. They were going to leave Vietnam at a specified time no matter what happened. As soldiers got closer to the end of their tours their willingness to participate in combat operations understandably diminished. The same arguments were made during the Korean War. And, again, the White House, the American people, and some in the Army accepted the cultural tenet of equality of sacrifice by rotating personnel, over the military axiom of maximization of combat effectiveness.

The Army's own studies, from World War II and Korea, had revealed that the combat effectiveness of soldiers declined after six months of sustained combat, and that the one-year tour improved and sustained the morale of soldiers. The one-year tour of duty was the right answer. However, a more thoughtful application of this policy could have greatly improved combat effectiveness. The Army knew that combat effectiveness was improved by rotating units, battalions, regiments, brigades, or divisions. In the wake of the Korean War, with full knowledge of all the personnel deficiencies that damaged combat effectiveness, a discussion took place within the Army, and a unit rotation system called "Operation Gyroscope" was developed. The plan went into effect in 1956, and was believed to have the following benefits:

> Gone will be the days when a man who had built up a required number of points, packed his gear, bid adieu to his outfit, and moved on to an assignment at home, perhaps never to rejoin the regiment or battalion which had come to be "his own. . . ." GYROSCOPE will allow an individual an opportunity to remain in the same combat unit for the entire length of his Army career, spend an equal amount of time overseas and in the States, and serve in all of the overseas theaters. By stabilizing individuals in combat units, individual morale and unit esprit de corps will benefit. Pride in organization—a fundamental human trait—will grow as the traditions and history of the regiment and division became not merely an intangible concept in a discussion period, but an actuality in the form of battle streamers, unit citations and decorations, to be cherished by every member. . . . It is a historic fact that soldiers remaining in a unit over periods of time develop extraordinary loyalties to their outfit, to their leaders and their comrades-in-arms. Such intense loyalties are a means of developing team fighters who will fight to the death if necessary for the reputation of their

organization and their individual prestige within it. . . . An objective analysis indicates that division rotation is possible—that it will be a decided improvement over the individual replacement system, and that it will outweigh the disadvantages and inconveniences caused during the transition period.[15]

The Army identified additional benefits: "Reenlistment rates may be expected to increase as a result of the advantages in career service and the increased morale and pride in unit. Thus, the cost of training new men for relatively short terms will be reduced and greater efficiency will be achieved."[16] The Army initially tried to rotate divisions. However, in 1958 Gyroscope was revised, and smaller units, battle groups and battalions, were to be rotated instead.[17] However, reductions in force, the deactivation of units, the reorganization of the Army, and general instability within the Army damaged the ability of the Army to sustain even a scaled-down version of the program. The expanding diversity of Army units, in part a function of technology, also made rotation difficult. Still, it was well known that the rotation of units improved combat effectiveness. In war, the Army recognized that it would need both systems: the individual replacement to maintain units in combat at an operational strength, and the rotation system for units that had been in sustained combat for six months to a year. In Vietnam, given the constraints imposed by the Johnson Administration, all that was possible was the individual replacement system.

The personnel shortages Moore and the rest of the Army in Vietnam experienced were not simply a function of decisions made in Washington. The way the Army operated in Vietnam required large numbers of soldiers to remain in the rear at the numerous bases to provide security and carry out the daily maintenance and administrative requirements. Hence, even when a division was at 95 percent of its operational strength, a 188-man infantry company could typically put 100 to 120 men in the field.[18] The US Army in Vietnam consumed more resources per soldier than any army in American history. This consumption produced an enormous requirement for administrative and logistical personnel. General Bruce Palmer, Jr., noted: "the overall manpower problem

was being aggravated (as was the case in Vietnam) by overly elaborate construction of base areas and a standard of living that was inappropriate for an active theater of operation."[19] By focusing more narrowly on combat missions, and restricting one-year tours to only *combat* soldiers, and better yet, combat units, the Army could have improved combat effectiveness. The vast majority of soldiers in Vietnam were not in "sustained combat." Hence, it was not necessary to rotate service support personnel and some combat support personnel.

Officer leadership in Vietnam typically served six months in command of combat units and then rotated out to staff positions. Changes of command ceremonies were held almost weekly. Brigadier General Douglas Kinnard, a veteran of the war, in his work, *The War Managers*, explained the thinking behind this command policy:

> There were many more competent officers available for command positions in Vietnam than there were commands. . . . However, to allow officers to spend their entire tour in command would have restricted the number of command opportunities. Also it was alleged that a one-year tour of command in combat would make too great physical and perhaps emotional demands on an officer. (I doubt it.) Therefore, the command tour was set at six months, with commanders constantly rotating.[20]

Kinnard noted that this policy promoted careerism: "Once in command, the aspirant had to look good in a very short period of time. . . . What happened was that, as one general put it, 'There were too many battalion and brigade commanders getting their ticket punched rather than trying to really lead.'" Combat effectiveness was subordinate to the administration of the officer promotion system, causing some officers to place loyalty to their career above loyalty to the service and the soldiers under their command. As a result of these personnel policies, Americans suffered higher casualties from inexperience. These policies also resulted in more than 2,594,000 Americans serving in Vietnam, a figure that is one-third larger than the size of American ground forces that fought World War II.

No personnel system is perfect. The Army had to work within the constraints of the national personnel system. Anything was possible if the White House and American people supported it. However, it was decided to maintain Army personnel at the bare minimum, requiring it to prioritize administrative efficiency over combat effectiveness. While the Army too was at fault by endeavoring to provide soldiers with all the amenities of home, and for putting in place the six-month command tour for officer leadership, the larger problem was the decision made in the White House. America's personnel policies wore out professional soldiers, ultimately decimating the NCO Corps, without which the Army could not function properly. Unit cohesion, morale, discipline, and fighting spirit all deteriorated during the war.

* * * * *

The implementation of the Vietnam draft became a source of controversy, anger, and protests that ultimately ended the draft. The charges of class, race, and age discrimination were levied against the Selective Service System. The literature on the Vietnam draft is too extensive to be fully examined in this work. Much of it is based on emotion and anger, not facts and well-reasoned arguments. However, the basic arguments are outlined here.[21] There are two schools of thought. The dominant, or standard, view was developed during the war. In April 1966, *Newsweek* published an article entitled "The Draft: The Unjust vs. the Unwilling," in which it was argued that "the [draft] boards have favored the affluent over the poor by granting student deferments to youths whose families can afford to send them to college."[22] Numerous articles and books advanced this argument of class, race, and age discrimination—that the poor, blacks, and the young bore the heaviest burden of the war. One researcher argued that: "Roughly 80 percent [of Vietnam enlisted men] came from working-class and poor backgrounds. Vietnam, more than any other American war in the twentieth century, perhaps in our history, was a working class war."[23] Equality of sacrifice was a strongly held tenet of American culture. The Vietnam War appeared to violate it in a particularly egregious manner. And perceptions, right or wrong, mattered.

The men that fought the Vietnam War, officers and enlisted men alike, tended to support the argument that the implementation of the draft was unfair. General Colin Powell concluded:

I particularly condemn the way our political leaders supplied the manpower for that war. The Policies—determining who would be drafted and who would be deferred, who would serve and who would escape, who would die and who would live—were an antidemocratic disgrace. I can never forgive a leadership that said, in effect: These young men—poorer, less educated, less privileged—are expendable (someone described them as "economic cannon fodder"), but the rest are too good to risk. I am angry that so many of the sons of the powerful and well placed . . . managed to wangle slots in Reserve and National Guard units. Of the many tragedies of Vietnam, this raw class discrimination strikes me as the most damaging to the ideal that all Americans are created equal. . . .[24]

General Alexander Haig Jr., based on his observations of the war in Vietnam, supported this assessment:

I had observed in Vietnam that the war was largely being fought, as the Korean War had also been fought, by young people from the lower end of the socioeconomic scale. The sons of what was then just beginning to be called "the white upper-middle class" were effectively exempted from the dangers of combat by a draft system based on the unspoken assumption that their lives were somehow more valuable than those of other young Americans who were less well educated and less well-to-do. Those who could afford to go to college or otherwise exploit the system's loopholes to obtain deferments did not go into the Army; those who could not come up with the cash went in their place.[25]

Many enlisted soldiers who fought in Vietnam also expressed their contempt for the draft. One soldier wrote:

That fucking draft. How unfair that damn thing was. We young people didn't know any better. We just went on. But I can't believe that older people would let a draft work like that. It was so obvious. If you had money or connections, you could get out or join the National Guard or reserves. I have more respect for the people who went to Canada than I do for the people who went into the reserves: They were the draft-dodgers. At least the people who went to Canada knew they might be punished.[26]

Another soldier wrote: "We were fighting the Communists. But everybody I was with over there out in the field were poor white, black, or Chicano men; eighteen and nineteen years old.... Didn't see any senators' sons or doctors' sons or lawyers' sons or upper-middle-class children."[27] It is further argued that those sons of the upper classes that did show up for the war tended to see more paperwork than combat. Because they were typically better educated, they were siphoned off for administrative jobs, unless they specifically asked for combat, which a few did. Still, the National Guard and reserves became "safe havens from Vietnam.... Discrimination and favoritism were the norm for precious slots.... Slots often were made available for the sons of prominent individuals."[28] There is evidence to support the argument of class discrimination. D. Michael Shafer, in an essay entitled, "The Vietnam-Era Draft: Who Went, Who Didn't, and Why It Matters," found that:

Between 1964 and 1973, 53 million Americans reached draft age, 26.8 million of them men. Of these, 60 percent escaped military service. Of the remaining 40 percent, only one-quarter, 10 percent of the male age-cohort, served in Vietnam and of these, only approximately 20 percent—or 2.0 percent of the male age-cohort—served in combat. Within these totals, draftees never constituted a majority except among those who served in combat. The draft, however, led many to become "reluctant volunteers" in order to control their service assignments and avoid Vietnam [or the Army and Marine Corps]. Reluctant volunteers ultimately outnumbered draftees about two to one.... Of the nearly 16 million young men who did not serve, 15.4 million were exempted or disqualified, 570,000 evaded the draft illegally (of whom 360,000 were never caught, 198,000 had their

cases dismissed, 8,750 were convicted and 3,250 received jail terms), and 30,000 (perhaps as many as 50,000) fled the country.[29]

Shafer noted that:

Between 1962 and 1972, Harvard and M.I.T. graduated 21,593—14 died in Vietnam. During the same period, some 2,000 young men came of draft age in South Boston, a working-class neighborhood not far from Harvard and M.I.T.—25 died in Vietnam. Coming from South Boston meant being 20 times more likely to die in Vietnam than going to Harvard or M.I.T.[30]

And:

A study of Chicago's Vietnam War dead found that men from poor neighborhoods were three times as likely to die in Vietnam as those from rich neighborhoods, while those from neighborhoods with low educational levels were four times more likely to die than those from neighborhoods with high educational levels.[31]

The US Government, it is argued, produced a draft system that favored certain classes of people over others, and that this eroded the legitimacy of the Selective Service System. In the years before the citizen-soldier Army was legislated out of existence, the system that produced it deteriorated. Marilyn Young described one of the manpower procurement programs:

Between 1966 and 1972, a special Great Society program—Project 100,000—scooped up over 300,000 young men previously considered ineligible for the military because of their low test scores. Project 100,000, Secretary of Defense Robert McNamara declared, was the "world's largest education of skilled men." With lower admissions scores, the "subterranean poor" would have an opportunity to serve their country in Vietnam; simultaneously, the program had the advantage of avoiding the politically unpleasant alternative of requiring students or reservists to do the same.... In its first two years of operation, 41 percent of those brought into the military through Project 100,000 were black,

80 percent had dropped out of high school, 40 percent could read at less than sixth-grade level, and 37 percent were put directly into combat.[32]

These men suffered casualties twice those of regular Army soldiers. In the US Army's Historical Series, *The US Army's Transition to the All-volunteer Force 1968–1974*, Robert K. Griffith, noted that: "although it was never so stated, the program increased the pool of men eligible for induction even as the buildup for Vietnam was getting under way."[33] President Johnson, in a discussion with Secretary of Defense McNamara, gave his assessment of the value of a social program that brought the poor and the poorly educated into the Army:

> Looks to me like what it would do for [Senator] Russell is move all these Nigra boys that are now rejects and sent back on his community, to move them [into the Army], clean them up, prepare them to do something, and send them into Detroit. . . . You have to tell him. . . . We'll take this Nigra boy in from Johnson City, Texas, and from Winder, Georgia, and we'll get rid of the tapeworms and get the ticks off of him, and teach him to get up at daylight and work till dark and shave and to bathe. . . . We'll put some weight on him and keep him out of a charity hospital . . . and keep him from eating off the old man's relief check. And when we turn him out, we'll have him prepared at least to drive a truck or bakery wagon or stand at a gate. . . . How many do you think you would take of these second-class fellows?[34]

Johnson was a complex man. He did more to advance Civil Rights for African Americans than any other President. Yet, he was imbued with the cultural stereotypes about blacks that characterized much of the South. And his conclusion, that military service was for "second-class fellows," was held by most Americans. It was a tenet of American culture that was only suppressed during more total war. Class and racial discrimination was real (gender discrimination was also real. Women too served in Vietnam, primarily in the Army Nurse Corps.)[35] The Truman Administration had reinforced the tenet that the best and the brightest ought to be excluded from serving in war, because they were needed to provide the talent for the sciences and other highly skilled fields. While draftees were always a minority in Vietnam, in 1969 nine of every ten draftees were in Vietnam. In 1970, draftees filled the majority of combat assignments in the Army. Thus, by volunteering for service in the Navy or Air Force, the National Guard or Reserves, or the Army in Europe or Korea, an individual could avoid service in combat in Vietnam. Those with greater resources and hence better educations knew this better than the poor from Detroit, Johnson City, or Winder. Studies have shown that between 40 and 60 percent of all volunteers were draft induced.[36]

To avoid service altogether, thousands of men fled the country, moving to Canada, and thousands more found ways around the draft by failing the physical examination or the Armed Forces Qualification Test (AFQT). President Bush senior observed: "A generation of Americans had been acclaimed for refusing to serve. Those who did serve often returned home, not to gratitude and praise, but to ridicule—even while the draft-dodgers and the protester were considered by many to be courageous, even heroic."[37] The Vietnam War destroyed the American consensus, the social contract and the spirit of laws. The system could not function without legitimacy.

*   *   *   *   *

In 1967, Dr. Martin Luther King, Jr., opposed the war and the draft, in part because it was unfair to African Americans. In a speech entitled, "The Declaration of Independence from the War in Vietnam," he wrote:

> Perhaps the more tragic recognition of reality took place when it became clear to me that the war was doing far more than devastating the hopes of the poor at home. It was sending their sons and their brothers and their husbands to fight and to die in extraordinarily high proportions relative to the rest of the population. We were taking the young black men who had been crippled by our society and sending them 8,000 miles away to guarantee liberties in Southeast Asia which they had not found in Southwest Georgia and East Harlem. So we have been repeatedly faced with the cruel irony of watching Negro and white boys on TV screens as they kill and die together for a nation that has been unable

to seat them together in the same schools. So we watch them in brutal solidarity burning the huts of a poor village, but we realize that they would never live on the same block in Detroit. I could not be silent in the face of such cruel manipulation of the poor.[38]

It is *not* true that blacks, as a proportion of the population, died in greater numbers in Vietnam than whites. How then was this perception created? In 1966, black soldiers made up 13 percent of the Army and 8 percent of the Marines, but suffered close to 23 percent of the casualties in Vietnam. In 1967, in the 1st Cavalry Division black soldiers suffered 26 percent of the casualties, twice the percentage of blacks assigned to the division.[39] In 1968, blacks made up 11 percent of all enlisted men in Vietnam, but 22.4 percent of all killed. These figures caused concern in the black communities, and the charge of institutional racism was levied against the Army. This, however, was not the major cause for the higher casualties suffered by African Americans in the early years of the war. In their work *Stolen Valor*, B.G. Burkett and Glenna Whitley concluded:

> Blacks were not in Vietnam because an evil government drafted them out of the ghettoes to use as cannon fodder; they were there because of the courage and patriotism of young black men, despite the fact they lived in a country where they frequently experienced racism. The early units to go into the war were elite troops of the Marine Corps, the Special Forces, and the 173rd Airborne, units almost exclusively populated by highly motivated volunteers—including higher proportions of blacks. Seventy-five percent of blacks who served in Vietnam volunteered to go. In fact, blacks tended to volunteer for combat at higher rates than whites. Twenty blacks received the Medal of Honor, almost one hundred received the Distinguished Service Cross.[40]

The search for opportunities that were denied blacks in the civilian world, a long-held African American affinity for military service, particularly in the Army, as the great equalizer, the limited number of positions in the service for which blacks were qualified, and desire to serve their country caused the initial discrepancies in casualties. While the Army offered blacks greater access to education, health care, job security, and leadership positions than they could find outside of it, they were limited by the quality of their education. During the Vietnam War, blacks reenlisted at more than twice the rate of whites, 32 percent of blacks and 13 percent of whites. And African Americans frequently volunteered to serve in the more elite, prestigious combat units; units that they were not allowed to serve in during World War II and the early days of the Korean War. Still, in 1967, the Army took steps to insure balance. At war's end, the number of black casualties almost exactly equaled the percentage of African Americans in the population, 13 percent. However, balance in the number of casualties should *never* be an Army objective. To achieve balance, the Army has to discriminate. The true objective is equality of sacrifice. And that is a national problem, not an Army problem.

* * * * *

More recent scholarship, the revisionist school, argues that the upper and middle class did in fact fight the war. One group of researchers argued that: "Per capita death rates apparently were only slightly lower in affluent American communities than in others (A plausible estimate of the deficit is 15%). . . . Vietnam was not a class war."[41] George Q. Flynn, in his detailed study of the draft, wrote: "The SS [Selective Service] argued in vain that few escaped entirely from service through education [deferments]. In 1966, 56 percent of men who attended college eventually served, while only 46 percent of noncollege men served."[42] Of course, statistics can be used to support any view the researcher wants to advance. It is how they are interpreted that matters. The pool of "noncollege" men was considerably larger. And those men with college educations who could not avoid service were not likely to end up in combat with an infantry platoon in Vietnam. No definitive answer as to the "per capita death rate" is offered here. However, college students received deferments and the poor and working classes were much less likely to attend college. President Johnson targeted "second-class fellows," and since Americans from different socioeconomic groups were treated differently, those from affluent families were more likely to receive favorable treatment. The men that did fight the war tended to believe there were few from the affluent among their ranks and those with higher educations received the majority of the non-combat jobs. Individuals from the upper classes definitely had more options, and the system ultimately lost legitimacy in the eyes of the American people.[43] A survey taken in February 1970 found that, "not one son or grandson of any US Senator or Representative has ever been killed or missing in this Vietnam War."[44] Finally, those individuals from affluent families that did fight were from unique affluent clusters, for example, Southerners tended to have a stronger military culture, a stronger martial spirit than Americans from the Northeast; hence, they produced more officers and more soldiers.

The primary concern of the draft was to disrupt American society as little as possible. Providing the armed forces with the best men possible was a secondary consideration. The vast majority of Americans were removed from the conduct of war. The Army that fought in Vietnam, however, was the best educated and healthiest ever deployed to war. It reflected the higher standard of living attained during the Eisenhower years.[45] It was not an Army of losers, drug addicts, and racists as it is frequently portrayed in films and books. It did have these problems, particularly in the latter years of the war when no one wanted to be the last man to die in Vietnam. Still, it was, for the most part, an Army of good, patriotic men and women, the vast majority of whom served honorably. It was primarily an Army of the working class. Some of the "affluent" showed up too, but not in the numbers that reflected their percentage of the population. No matter how the draft is viewed, the Selective Service System damaged the ability of the Army to fight; and hence, the ability of the United States to win. General Powell described some of the negative effects of the "national personnel system":

My Lai [the site of the massacre of over a hundred unarmed women, children, and old men by American soldiers] was an appalling example of much that had gone wrong in Vietnam. Because the war had dragged on for so long, not everyone commissioned was really officer material. Just as critical, the corps of career noncommissioned officers was being gutted by casualties. Career noncoms form the backbone of any army, and producing them requires years of professional soldiering. In order to fight the war without calling up the reserves, the Army was creating instant noncoms. Shake-and-bake sergeants, we called them. Take a private, give him a little training, shake him once or twice, and pronounce him an NCO. It astonished me how well and heroically some of these green kids performed. . . . Still, the involvement of so many unprepared officers and noncoms led to breakdowns in morale, discipline, and professional judgment—and to horrors like My Lai. . . .[46]

The President sought to fight the war without raising taxes, without disturbing the affluent, and without the National Guard and Reserves. And still, antiwar movements formed. In 1967, in San Francisco, a group of anti-draft men delineated their argument:

We Refuse to Serve. In the past few months, in many parts of the country, a resistance has been forming ... a resistance of young men—joined together in their commitment against the war. . . .

We will renounce all deferments and refuse to cooperate with the draft in any manner, at any level. We have taken this stand for varied reasons:

Opposition to conscription
Opposition only to the Vietnam War
Opposition to all wars and to all American military adventures.[47]

The antiwar, anti-draft movements damaged the ability of the nation to conduct war. Support for the war deteriorated rapidly after 1967. Divisions in society made the will of the American people more vulnerable to efforts from the Communists to undermine it. The Civil Rights Movement, the Free Speech Movement, the Sexual Revolution, the drug culture, the Hippie Movement, the Women's Liberation Movement, the Gay Liberation Movement, the Antiwar Movements, and the entire counterculture phenomenon that tore the country apart in the 1960s and 1970s, severely damaged the ability of the United States to fight a war.[48]

McNamara Changes Course

In November 1967, the Gallup Poll showed that 57 percent of the American people disapproved of the President's handling of the war, and only 28 percent approved.[49] Divisions in Washington exacerbated divisions in the country. Months earlier, McNamara had come to the conclusion that the strategic doctrine that he helped design and implement in Vietnam was not working. He recommended changes that deepened the chasm between him and the JCS. The JCS recommended further escalation, an increase in the number of troops, a partial call-up of the National Guard and Reserves, an expanded bombing campaign with fewer restrictions, and other measures that they believed would bring the war more rapidly to a successful conclusion. McNamara, however, opposed further escalation. In a memorandum to the President dated 19 May 1967 he, in part, wrote:

> This memorandum is written at a time when there appears to be no attractive course of action.... Continuation of our present moderate policy, while avoiding a larger war, will not change Hanoi's mind, so is not enough to satisfy the American people; increased force levels and actions against the North are likewise unlikely to change Hanoi's mind, and are likely to get us in even deeper in Southeast Asia and into a serious confrontation, if not war, with China and Russia.... So we must choose among imperfect alternatives.
>
> The Vietnam war is unpopular in this country. It is becoming increasingly unpopular as it escalates.... Most Americans do not know how we got where we are, and most, without knowing why ... are convinced that somehow we should not have gotten this deeply in. All want the war ended and expect their President to end it. Successfully. Or else. This state of mind in the US generates impatience in the political structure of the United States. It unfortunately also generates patience in Hanoi.
>
> [In Vietnam] the "big war" in the South between the US and the North Vietnamese military units (NVA) is going well.... Regrettably, the "other war" against the VC is still not going well. Corruption is widespread. Real government control is confined to enclaves. There is rot in the fabric.... The population remains apathetic.... The Army of South Vietnam (ARVN) is tired, passive and accommodation-prone....
>
> There continues to be no sign that the bombing has reduced Hanoi's will to resist or her ability to ship the necessary supplies south. Hanoi shows no signs of ending the large war and advising the VC to melt into the jungles. The North Vietnamese believe they are right ... they believe the world is with them and that the American public will not have staying power against them.... They believe that, in the long run, they are stronger than we are for the purpose.
>
> There is no reason to doubt that China would honor its commitment to intervene at Hanoi's request, and it remains likely that Peking would intervene on her own initiative if she believed that the existence of the Hanoi regime was at stake.
>
> Proponents of the added deployments in the South believe that such deployments will hasten the end of the war.... The addition of the 200,000 men, involving as it does a call-up of Reserves and an addition of 500,000 to the military strength would ... almost certainly set off bitter Congressional debate and irresistible domestic pressures for stronger action outside South Vietnam.
>
> The use of tactical nuclear and area-denial-radiological-bacteriological-chemical weapons would probably be suggested at some point if the Chinese entered the war in Vietnam or Korea or if US losses were running high while conventional efforts were not producing desired results.[50]

McNamara accurately summarized the situation in Vietnam and the US. For all his declared brilliance, it took him seven years to figure out what Ridgway and Eisenhower knew from simply looking at a map. Geography dictated the military situation on the ground. To win, the US had to be willing to fight a more total war, a war with the PRC. It had to be willing to invade North Vietnam and accept battle with Chinese forces. The security value obtained from a democratic non-Communist South Vietnam was not worth the price the US and the world would have to pay. McNamara feared that "escalation threatens to spin the war utterly out of control." He, therefore, argued for limitations on troop deployments, restriction or a unilateral halt on bombing, limited ground offensives, and an end to "search and destroy" operations. None of these recommendations were in concert with the vision of the JCS, and it was rumored that they considered resigning en masse if McNamara's recommendations were accepted.[51]

The conflict between McNamara and his generals hit the press and became a matter of public debate: the hawks against the doves. Johnson was torn. He too feared escalations and the reactions of China and the Soviet Union. He sought no wider war; however, he could not abandon South Vietnam after so much loss of life and treasure, and the commitment of American prestige and credibility. Yet, staying the course meant a long war with the patience of the American people deteriorating. There were no good alternatives. However, at this juncture Johnson tended towards his generals.

Westmoreland insisted that the war was progressing according to plan. However, he could not predict an end to the war, even with an additional 200,000 soldiers. Nor could the Air Force predict victory with additional resources and fewer restrictions on bombing. As long as the United States remained on the strategic defense in the ground war, there was no way to predict an end to the war and consequently, no way to explain to the American people how the nation was going to achieve its objectives in South Vietnam. Geographically, and in terms of resources provided by China and the SU, there was no way to stop Hanoi from supporting the war in the South without invading North Vietnam or using nuclear weapons. The US had to physically threaten the survival of North Vietnam; that is, seek the destruction of the PAVN and Hanoi government, to save South Vietnam. To go to war on a continent that included China, and not expect to fight China, particularly given the experience of the Korean War, was not only the height of arrogance, it defied common sense, and bordered on stupidity—as our European allies, who failed to support us, recognized. The nuclear arsenal of the United States precluded direct confrontation with the Soviet Union; however, its deterrent value did not extend into peripheral areas in limited war, particularly those in the enemy's backyard.

The Chinese had taken the measure of US forces in Korea, and were not in awe of American power. And just as the US would not have tolerated Communist Chinese forces in Mexico, China was not willing to accept the presence of US forces on its borders. Xiaoming Zhang, in an article entitled, "The Vietnam War, 1964–1969: A Chinese Perspective," argued that China was extensively involved in the Vietnam War, providing weapons, supplies, men for the construction of transportation arteries, and strategic planning assistance. He concluded that had the US taken the offensive and invaded North Vietnam, the Chinese would have entered the war. He wrote:

> China's determination to offer material and manpower support for the DRV was based on a mixture of strategic and ideological considerations. Chinese leaders comprehended Vietnam's strategic importance to the security of China's southern border. Beijing regarded Vietnam along with Korea and Taiwan as the most likely places where the United States might establish bases and possibly initiate hostilities.[52]

In 1962 alone, the PRC provided the North Vietnamese with 240,000 individual weapons, 2,730 artillery pieces, fifteen planes, twenty-eight naval vessels, and 175 million rounds of ammunition—a movement of materials American intelligence could not have missed. China gave priority to the war in Vietnam, taking weapons and equipment from its own People's Liberation Army to support the People's Army of Vietnam. The PRC provided equipment to meet specific threats and crises, such as antiaircraft guns for the air war, and tanks for the conventional invasion in 1972. Not every request from the DRV was fulfilled. Still, the Chinese were committed.

Given China's behavior in Korea, where it too fought a limited war, its most probable course of action in Vietnam would be to intervene with a "volunteer force." China was not likely to seek a direct confrontation between the US Army and the People's Liberation Army if it could be avoided. It was still recovering from failed economic policies of "the Great Leap Forward," and the internal disorder caused by the "Cultural Revolution." The Chinese government of 1965 was very different from that of

1951, but many of the same leaders were still making the decisions, and the situation they faced in Vietnam was very similar to that in Korea. The Chinese government had solidified its position on the mainland, and the Nationalist Army in Taiwan was no longer a major threat. However, the fear and desperation that caused China to act in 1951 were still prevalent. War with China was a major consideration for the US entering war in Vietnam. If the US was not willing to fight the PRC, it should not have been willing to Americanize the fight in South Vietnam.

The lack of American willingness to attack North Vietnam also communicated weakness to Hanoi, Beijing, and Moscow. Eisenhower's willingness to expand the war in Korea, at least in part, influenced decision-making in Beijing and Moscow in 1953. Kennedy's willingness to threaten a larger war in the Cuba Missile Crisis influenced decision-makers in Moscow. Johnson's unwillingness to contemplate offensive actions against North Vietnam, and his verbal acknowledgement of such, also influenced decision-making in Hanoi and Beijing, creating the conditions for the ultimate destruction of South Vietnam. Even if the Johnson Administration had no intention of invading North Vietnam, it was a mistake to communicate this to the enemy.

McNamara's conversion to the "dove" camp caused him to fall into disfavor with the President. Late in 1967 he accepted an appointment to head the World Bank; however, by the time McNamara departed, the war was already lost.

The Tet Offensive

In 1967 the Communist leadership in the North, armed with the knowledge that there would be no major US offensive across the 17th parallel, again decided to step up operations in SVN. They planned a major offensive designed to bring the war to a decisive end. The plan called for a logistics buildup, diversionary attacks in the border areas to draw American forces out of the cities, the infiltration of men and materiel into the cities, and finally a simultaneous uprising across the entire country to overthrow the government.

Hanoi believed the people of South Vietnam would support them, and once the Americans were

handed a *fait accompli* they would have no other option but to leave. Late in 1967 enemy attacks on the border areas commenced. These attacks, particularly the battle for Khe Sanh, greatly worried Johnson, who believed that Hanoi was trying to create another Dien Bien Phu, the battle that decisively destroyed French forces in 1954.

In January 1968, the Tet Offensive began. The attack shocked America, particularly after Westmoreland had informed the nation that victory was in sight. Westmoreland, in his official report, acknowledged that MACV had been surprised:

> Even though by mid-January we were certain that a major offensive action was planned by the enemy at Tet, we did not surmise the true nature of the scope of the countrywide attack . . . It did not occur to us that the enemy would undertake suicidal attacks in the face of our power.

Westmoreland gave his estimate of the situation:

> The enemy's main attack was launched late on the 30th and in early morning of the 31st of January, employing about eighty-four thousand Viet Cong and North Vietnamese troops. . . . In addition to Saigon, initial assaults were mounted against thirty-six provincial capitals, five of the six autonomous cities, sixty-four of the two hundred and forty two district capitals and fifty hamlets. . . . This enemy's attack in Saigon began with a sapper assault on the American Embassy, a move of dubious military value but psychologically important.

Tactically and operationally, Tet was a major victory for the US and SVN. Westmoreland believed "the Tet Offensive had the effect of a Pearl Harbor; the South Vietnamese government was intact and stronger; the armed forces were larger, more effective, and more confident; the people had rejected the idea of a general uprising; and enemy forces, particularly those of the Viet Cong, were much weaker." He concluded:

> In the main, the Tet offensive was a Vietnamese fight. To the ARVN, other members of the South Vietnamese armed forces, the militia, the National Police—to those belonged the major share of credit for turning back the offensive. . . .

When put to a crucial test, no ARVN unit had broken or defected. The South Vietnamese had fully vindicated my trust. From the premature start on January 29 through February 11, the Communists lost 32,000 killed and 5,800 captured, close to half the troops actively committed. American forces lost 1,001 killed; South Vietnamese and Allied forces, 2,082. By the end of February, as American and ARVN troops swept the environs of the towns and cities, the enemy toll rose to 37,000 killed.... Nothing remotely resembling a general uprising of the people had occurred. It all added up to a striking military defeat for the enemy on anybody's terms.[53]

Paradoxically, Tet was a major political, psychological, diplomatic, and strategic defeat for the armed forces of the United States, and the government and people of South Vietnam. Tet and the events that followed destroyed the will of the American people and the Johnson Administration. Why has been greatly debated. While the US and ARVN forces fought well, quickly restoring the situation, the media portrayed the campaign as an overwhelming defeat for the US. On the evening news, Americans watched the battle outside of the American Embassy, and the bloody battles in Saigon, Hue, and Khe Sanh—the four battles that produced the most significant and influential films of the war. They listened to the esteemed news anchor, Walter Cronkite, explode with "What the hell is going on? I thought we were winning the war."[54] Later in a television special on the war, he told the American people: "It seems now more certain than ever that the bloody experience of Vietnam is to end in a stalemate...." He advanced the argument that as "an honorable people" the US should seek a "negotiated settlement."[55] Westmoreland was shocked and alarmed by the power and influence of the media over the White House and the American people: "President Johnson stated that when he lost Walter Cronkite he lost Middle America. What a frightening realization ... for in the long run public support proved to be our Achilles heel."

Such coverage strengthened the will of Hanoi, making them more determined. The media also identified a new strategy for Hanoi, direct psychological attacks on the will of the American people. Peter

Braestrup, a veteran of the Korean War, reporter, and author of the most comprehensive study on the media during Tet, *The Big Story*, wrote: "Hanoi did not claim a victory—psychological, symbolic, or otherwise—at the embassy. But American newsmen were quick to award Hanoi a major "psychological" triumph there, if only because they—the newsmen—and Lyndon B. Johnson had been taken by surprise. It was a portent of journalistic reactions to come."[56]

The coverage of the Tet Offensive by the American media was dishonest, inaccurate, unprofessional, and irresponsible. First, the American people were told the VC had entered the American Embassy, which was inaccurate. And then they were told what to think—this was an event of "symbolic" and "psychological" significance.[57] The VC never entered the Embassy. The American people were told repeatedly that Khe Sanh was becoming another Dien Bien Phu, in contradiction to what the Marine commander on the spot and Westmoreland told them. Given American airpower and ability to reinforce it, it was impossible for NVA to produce another Dien Bien Phu. Americans were shown the horrendous images of General Loan, the National Chief of Police, summarily executing a VC officer in the streets of Saigon. However, the images were shown out of context. Peter Rollins noted:

> Although General Loan's indiscretion was an important Tet story, it was not necessarily a representative microcosm. Editing supplied new ingredients or removed essential ones.... Omission of such opening visuals might have indicated to viewers that reporters had not been present during the preceding street fighting and thus were not aware of the pitch of emotions for both slayer and slain. More significantly, Howard Tucker's "stand-upper" after the execution was removed. Ron Steinman, NBC's Saigon Bureau Chief, believed that such verbiage would be "anticlimactic." Tucker's comments would have placed the act in a human context. Loan was indeed the national police chief, a significant fact in relation to recent events: his capital city had become a maelstrom of fighting—passions were intense, revenge for the execution of families was on the minds of those fighting in the streets. Within this context, Loan's cryptic comments to

the foreign correspondent Tucker were not irrelevant ... [H]e observed: "Many Americans have been killed these last few days and many of my best Vietnamese friends. Now do you understand? Buddha will understand."[58]

While not an excuse, Loan's actions in the middle of battle are more understandable. Context matters. At Hue the destruction caused by the Marines and US airpower were shown without the context of the stubborn tenacity of the enemy and without stories of the atrocities of the NVA and VC, who killed thousands of unarmed people, including women and children. Inaccuracy can be expected in a complex war; however, this went beyond that. This was dishonesty. In the aftermath, the press did little to correct the views it had created. Braestrup concluded: "rarely has contemporary crisis-journalism turned out in retrospect, to have veered so widely from reality." Many Americans watched other Americans being killed and wounded. They observed the behavior of the South Vietnamese. And they concluded that their government was lying to them, that Vietnam was not worth saving, and that the war could not be won. Westmoreland determined that: "Unfortunately, the enemy scored in the United States the psychological victory that eluded him in Vietnam, so influencing President Johnson and his civilian advisers that they ignored the maxim that when the enemy is hurting, you don't diminish the pressure, you increase it."[59]

The White House and the Pentagon did little to counter the picture created by the media. Braestrup noted: "What was striking—and important—about the public White House posture in February and March 1968 was how defensive it was. In retrospect, it seems that President Johnson was to some degree 'psychologically defeated' by the threat to Khe Sanh and the onslaught on the cities of Vietnam."[60] Johnson lacked the confidence and vigor to counter the impression created by the media. Physically he was a sick man, and was unable to summon the energy and fortitude required to counter the picture of defeat painted by the media.

The Tet Offensive and subsequent request for an additional 200,000 troops were the decisive blows to the will of the American people. Americans lost confidence and trust in their government and armed forces, and the war they were conducting. Students of the war, however, disagree about the role of the media in creating the impression of defeat. Elegant observed:

> But never before Viet Nam had the collective policy of the media—no less stringent term will serve—sought by graphic and unremitting distortion the victory of the enemies of the correspondents' own side. Television coverage was, of course, new in its intensity and repetitiveness; it was crucial in shifting the emphasis from fact to emotion. And television will play the same role in future conflicts—on the Western side, of course. It will not and cannot expose the crimes of the enemy who is too shrewd to allow the cameras free play.[61]

The media did not accept this verdict. Braestrup wrote: "there is no evidence of a direct relationship between the dominant media themes in 1968 and changes in American mass public opinion vis-à-vis the Vietnam war itself." Braestrup, like Hammond, placed the blame squarely on the policies and strategy of the Johnson Administration, noting:

> In a sense, the inherent contradictions of his limited-war policy came home to roost. Between escalation (politically and economically very costly) and a 'phase down,' Johnson did not choose. Essentially, he sought to buy time for 'more of the same.' This approach led to two months of Presidential inaction in the face of a perceived 'disaster,' at least in public. ... He emphasized the need to stand firm, but he did not spell out what this meant, or how the battlefield situation was changing, as he saw it, in Vietnam. He left a big void, which others hastened to fill.[62]

Opinion polls support this assessment. In 1965, opinion polls show that 61 percent of Americans supported the President's policies in Vietnam. By November 1966, support had fallen to 51 percent. By November 1967, the eve of the Tet Offensive, the majority of Americans no longer supported the war, with 46 percent against and 44 percent for. Johnson had actually lost the support of the majority of the American people before Tet. However, the Tet Offensive, and the subsequent request for an additional 200,000 troops, further damaged the President's position, making it almost impossible for Johnson to regain the initiative. Vietnamization was initiated in the wake of the Tet Offensive. Americans began coming home, turning the war over to the South Vietnamese.

The President of the United States has enormous power to influence the American people, to shape and form public opinion. Presidents are also responsible for the national military strategy. Therefore, it was the White House that failed during and after Tet. The American people respond positively to decisive actions. Had the President, himself, not been psychologically and emotionally defeated, he could have taken actions that had the chance of reversing public opinion. The Vietnam War was lost in the United States when the will of the American people and the Johnson Administration collapsed. Still, it took four more years of fighting before the last American soldier left Vietnam.[63]

It is commonly believed that the US, and the government of South Vietnam, lost the war because they failed to win the support of the people of South Vietnam. Yet during the Tet Offensive there was no mass uprising against the Americans and South Vietnamese government of President Nguyen Van Thieu. In fact, the ARVN fought well. Consider the response of General Lewis W. Walt, USMC, who commanded III, MAF in Vietnam from May 1965 to June 1967, to a letter from a young marine captain who was critical of the performance of the Vietnamese during the Tet Offensive:

> You refer in your letter to the "open hostility of the population and the dramatic success of the TET offensive." How can you describe the reaction of the Vietnamese people as "openly hostile" when there are numerous incidents on record where whole families or groups of South Vietnamese were put to death because they refused to aid the VC and NVA forces during the offensive? In the Danang area, the 2nd NVA Div's planned attack was thwarted by the people who reported the plans and movements of the enemy. The South Vietnamese people did not rally to the Communist "liberators," but rather, developed an even deeper hatred for the North Vietnamese who had violated the sacred TET Holy Day, and

who had committed countless acts of terrorism and murder against innocent civilians. The South Vietnam soldiers did not defect to the Communists, but stood and fought, and gained an immeasurable degree of esprit and confidence in so doing. The political cadre who accompanied the enemy soldiers brought complete tools of government with them and yet, in not one single instance, were they able to seize governmental control.[64]

President Thieu, on television, speaking in broken English, also acknowledged the fact that the people did not revolt: "What they have realized in the city [was] that the people was against them. So I believe, the general uprising they have hope, have not happen. They have met with the anti-communist sentiment from the people in the city. So they failed in both the country-side and the city."[65] Ambassador Ellsworth Bunker noted that the ARVN had fought well: "I think we're stronger on a number of accounts here. I think the Vietnamese Armed Forces, for example, have demonstrated their capability. I think they have turned in an excellent performance. I think they have gained confidence in themselves."[66] The people, government, and armed forces of South Vietnam came out of the Tet Offensive more hopeful and confident than ever. The Viet Cong that rose up were identified, killed or captured; the NVA and Hanoi had suffered a major defeat; American support and military presence was at its height; and American support seemed firm.[67]

While the absence of a revolt did not mean that the Americans and government of South Vietnam had won the hearts and minds of the people, it *did* mean that the Communists had *not won* the hearts and minds of the people. When the US changed its strategy and political objectives in Vietnam in 1968, the balance of general support from the people had tilted, if only slightly, in favor of South Vietnam. Hence, if in fact the US lost the support of the South Vietnamese people, it was during the period 1968 to 1973, the years of Vietnamization, during which it became evident that the US was leaving. However, the war in Vietnam was not lost in Vietnam.

* * * * *

The final American phase of the war began in 1968, the last year of the Johnson Administration. On

1 March 1968, Clark Clifford assumed the duties of Secretary of Defense. Clifford, who was selected because of his hawkish stance on Vietnam, quickly became a dove. After studying classified intelligence reports, discussions with the JCS on American strategy, and Westmoreland and Wheeler's request for an additional 200,000 troops, and discussions with Dean Acheson, Averell Harriman, Paul Nitze, and others who opposed further commitment and favored de-escalation, Clifford concluded that the war could not be won in any predictable time frame, and that the US ought to develop plans to extricate itself from the war. Clifford's assessment was correct. On the strategic defense, an end to hostilities could not be predicted. Even after suffering the terrible losses during the Tet Offensive, the Communists were able to cross into their privileged sanctuaries, heal their wounds, and come back the next year. In 1969, Clifford published an essay describing his remarkable transformation. Through a series of "colloquial style" meetings he was given the following information:

> "Will 200,000 more men do the job?" I found no assurance that they would. "If not, how many more might be needed—and when?" There was no way of knowing. . . . "Can the enemy respond with a build-up of his own?" He could and he probably would. . . . "Can bombing stop the war?" Never by itself. It was inflicting heavy personnel and material losses, but bombing by itself would not stop the war. When I asked for a presentation of the military plan for attaining victory in Viet Nam, I was told that there was no plan for victory in the historic American sense. Why not? Because our forces were operating under three major political restrictions: The President had forbidden the invasion of North Viet Nam because this could trigger a mutual assistance pact between North Viet Nam and China: the President had forbidden the mining of the harbor at Haiphong ... because a Soviet vessel might be sunk; the President had forbidden our forces to pursue the enemy into Laos and Cambodia, for to do so would spread the war, politically and geographically. . . . These and other restrictions . . . were wisely designed to prevent our being drawn into a larger war.[68]

After listening to these gloomy conclusions Clifford was "convinced that the military course we were pursuing was not only endless, but hopeless." He thus developed a policy to "level off our involvement, and to work toward gradual disengagement." Clifford had some support. Acheson, Harriman, and Nitze argued that other parts of the world were more important to American security, that Europe was being neglected, and that too many resources needed in other areas were pouring into Vietnam. Clifford succeeded in convincing the President to change course, and on 31 March 1968, the President made his new policy known to the American people. He established a troop ceiling of 549,500. He made a commitment to speed up aid and assistance to South Vietnam's armed forces, to enable them to take over more responsibility. And, in a message to Hanoi, he restricted bombing of the North. This was an invitation to enter into peace talks. Johnson ultimately considered Clifford's conversion a betrayal, but he had won the battle in Washington. Plans to increase troop strength were abandoned, and plans to de-escalate were implemented.

The failure of the Tet Offensive in Vietnam, the bombing campaign, and Johnson's open pledge to negotiate motivated Hanoi to adopt a new strategy—negotiating while fighting. This new strategy enabled Hanoi to focus on what it now perceived to be decisive—the will of the American people. Hanoi sought to erode American support for the war, forcing the administration to abandon the Saigon government. On 13 May 1968, formal talks opened in Paris. On 3 July, General Creighton Abrams replaced General Westmoreland as commander of MACV.[69] Abrams had been deputy commander since May 1967. Because of the losses suffered by the Communists in 1968, Abrams faced a different environment and situation. The Tet Offensive, the assassinations of Dr. Martin Luther King, Jr., and Robert Kennedy, the Civil Rights Movement, and the anti-war/anti-draft protests, all coming in quick succession, shook the confidence of the President and the nation. Johnson decided not to run for a second term.

Nixon and the Vietnamization Phase

In November 1968, Richard M. Nixon was elected President, defeating Vice President Herbert H.

Fig 11.1 Secretary of Defense Robert S. McNamara and Secretary of Defense-designate Clark M. Clifford, 7 February 1968, Washington, DC. US Army photograph.

Humphrey. The major issue of the presidential campaign was the war in Vietnam. Nixon did not plan to abandon Vietnam:

> Abandoning the South Vietnamese people ... would threaten our long-term hopes for peace in the world. A great nation cannot renege on its pledges. A great nation must be worthy of trust.... If we simply abandoned our effort in Vietnam, the cause of peace might not survive the damage that would be done to other nations' confidence in our reliability.... If Hanoi were to succeed in taking over South Vietnam by force— even after the power of the United States had been engaged—it would greatly strengthen those leaders who scorn negotiation, who advocate aggression, who minimize the risks of confrontation with the United States. It would bring peace now but it would enormously increase the danger of a bigger war later.[70]

President Nixon concluded:

> As I saw it, however, this option [unilateral withdrawal] had long since been foreclosed. A precipitate withdrawal would abandon 17 million South Vietnamese, many of whom had worked for us and supported us, to Communist atrocities and domination. When the Communists had taken over North Vietnam in 1954, 50,000 people had been murdered, and hundreds of thousands more died in labor camps. In 1968, during their brief control of Hue, they had shot or clubbed to death or buried alive more than 3,000 civilians whose only crime was to have supported the Saigon government. We simply could not sacrifice an ally in such a way. If we suddenly reneged on our earlier pledges of support, because they had become unpopular at home, we would not be worthy of the trust of other nations and we certainly would not receive it.[71]

The Democratic candidate for President, Humphrey, was too closely tied to the failed policies of the Johnson Administration, and Nixon implied that he had a "secret plan to end the war."[72] Nixon later outlined his thinking on the conduct of the war, denying that he had advanced a "secret plan":

I wanted the war to end. . . . I felt that there were a number of unexplored avenues to probe in finding a way to end the war. I believed that we could use our armed strength more effectively to convince the North Vietnamese that a military victory was not possible. We also needed to step up our programs for training and equipping the South Vietnamese so that they could develop the capability of defending themselves. Most important, I believed that we were not making adequate use of our vast diplomatic resources and powers. The heart of the problem lay more in Peking and Moscow than in Hanoi. As a candidate it would have been foolhardy, and as a prospective President, improper, for me to outline specific plans in detail. . . . I was asking the voters to take on faith my ability to end the war. A regular part of my campaign speech was the pledge: "New leadership will end the war and win the peace in the Pacific." I never said that I had a "plan," much less a "secret plan," to end the war. . . . As I told AP on March 14, 1968, there was "no magic formula, no gimmick."[73]

In January 1969, the Nixon Administration took office. Melvin Laird replaced Clark Clifford as Secretary of Defense, William Rogers replaced Dean Rusk as Secretary of State, and Henry Kissinger replaced Walt Rostow as National Security Advisor. *Vietnamization* was the cornerstone of Nixon's strategy. Nixon developed and initiated plans to increase the size and capabilities of the armed forces of South Vietnam, and to withdraw US ground forces. Using "the carrot and the stick" tactic, he entered into secret negotiations with Hanoi, and intensified the bombing campaign. Nixon believed that Eisenhower had ended the Korean War by threatening to expand the war in ways and means beyond the capabilities of the PRC. He planned to demonstrate the same willingness to use American airpower.

He planned a *quid pro quo* diplomatic offensive to neutralize China and the Soviet Union, and secure their assistance to influence Hanoi. He sought to give them something they wanted—trade, arms limitation, diplomatic agreements, and other incentives—in exchange for their assistance in pressuring Hanoi to negotiate. Finally, Nixon planned a two-part public relations offensive to influence American opinion, "the silent majority," and to discredit the antiwar movement and others who opposed his initiatives. Nixon planned to fully utilize the economic, political, diplomatic, and military power of the United States to

Fig 11.2 President Richard M. Nixon and President of South Vietnam Nguyen Van Thieu, 30 January 1969.

bring the war to an end. He believed he could succeed where Johnson had failed: "I'm not going to end up like LBJ, holed up in the White House afraid to show my face on the street. I'm going to stop that war. Fast."[74]

Hanoi rejected Nixon's initial offers for a negotiated settlement. To demonstrate his resolve and willingness to use force, Nixon initiated a secret bombing campaign against PAVN and VC sanctuaries in Cambodia, expanding the war. In "Operation Menu" B-52s dropped more than 100,000 tons of bombs over a fifteen-month period. The secret eventually became public, increasing antiwar protests, Congressional debate, and the call for unilateral withdrawal.

In March 1969, Abrams fundamentally changed the ground war operational strategy.[75] Lewis Sorley concluded that:

Abrams's most significant impact as the new MACV commander was in his conduct of the war—his concept of the nature of the war itself, the "one war" response to that perception, identification and exploitation of the enemy's dependence on a logistics nose, emphasis on security of the populace and the territorial force improvements that provided it, effective interdiction of the enemy infiltration, and development of more capable armed forces for the South Vietnamese.[76]

Sorley argued that Abrams had a new, more comprehensive vision of the war that refocused and integrated the resources of MACV and the ARVN.

Abrams based his operational and tactical doctrine on a study conducted by the Army staff in 1966, *A Program for the Pacification and Long-Term Development of South Vietnam* (PROVN Study). Abrams adopted what he called the "one-war" approach, combining the more conventional war of finding, fixing, and fighting the enemy with security and pacification operations. He eliminated search-and-destroy operational and tactical doctrine, and reliance on body count. He emphasized "secure and

Fig 11.3 General Creighton Abrams, who had been one of General George Patton's tank commanders in World War II, took over from General Westmoreland on 3 July 1968.

Republic of Vietnam Armed Forces Strength [a]

	Army	Air Force	Navy	Marine Corps	Total Regular	Regional Forces	Popular Forces	Total Territorial	Grand Total
1954–55	170,000	3,500	2,200	1,500	177,200	54,000 [b]	48,000 [b]	102,000	279,200
1959–60	136,000 c	4,600	4,300	2,000	146,000	49,000 [c]	48,000	97,000	243,000
1964	220,000	11,000	12,000	7,000	50,000	96,000	168,000	264,000	514,000
1967	303,000	16,000	16,000	8,000	343,000	151,000	149,000 [c]	300,000	643,000
1968	380,000	19,000	19,000	9,000	427,000	220,000	173,000	393,000	820,000
1969	416,000	36,000	30,000	11,000	493,000	190,000	214,000	404,000	897,000
1970	416,000	46,000	40,000	13,000	515,000	207,000	246,000	453,000	968,000
1971–72	410,000 c	50,000	42,000	14,000	516,000	284,000	248,000	532,000	1,048,000

[a] All figures are approximate only.
[b] Civil Guard (later Regional Forces) and Self-Defense Corps (later Popular Forces) were officially authorized only in 1956.
[c] Decline due to increased desertions and recruiting shortfalls.

Fig 11.4 Republic of Vietnam Armed Forces Strength.

hold." Abrams wanted the population secured—in the hamlets, the villages, and the provinces—and he wanted them held, defended. He endeavored to cut off the flow of resources to the VC and NVA in South Vietnam through interdiction operations. He fought whenever and wherever the enemy could be found. He sought to end the divisions between the ARVN and the US Army by eliminating the separation of missions. He endeavored to refocus the ARVN on security missions, on small unit operation, and on working with and among the people. Abrams sought to improve the leadership of the ARVN and build its morale and aggressiveness. His strategic and doctrinal thinking moved the Army closer to that of the Marine Corps. In April 1970, Abrams' staff, in a report entitled, "The Changing Nature of the War," felt sufficiently optimistic to conclude that: "For the first time in the war, the enemy's traditional bases of power are being directly challenged—his political organization and his control of the population." As late as 1972, Abrams believed that the war could be won and that South Vietnam could survive as a free, independent nation capable of defending itself.

Those who believed that winning the hearts and minds of the people, "the other war," was the key to success thought that if Abrams' new approach had been implemented in the early years of the war, the outcome might have been different. Others argue that the only reason Abrams could implement his new

approach was because the Tet Offensive and Westmoreland's search and destroy operations had taken such a heavy toll on the enemy, almost eliminating the combat effectiveness of the VC, and greatly diminishing the ability of the PAVN to conduct major offensive operations. Because Hanoi was forced to change its strategy, Abrams was able to implement his vision. Jeffrey Clark, in the official history of the US Army in Vietnam, noted that: "Westmoreland had already outlined this new orientation in January, when the Tet offensive had suddenly upset his plan. Abrams now intended to put his predecessor's proposal into effect."[77] Abrams' "new" strategy had the potential to strengthen the government and armed forces of South Vietnam, but not to destroy the will of Hanoi, complete the destruction of the PAVN, stop the flow of resources from the PRC and USSR, or restore the will and support of the American people.

In 1970, the pro-American government of Prime Minister Lon Nol overthrew the government of Prince Sihanouk of Cambodia, creating new military opportunities. George Herring wrote:

The Cambodia crisis represented yet another effort on the part of a profoundly insecure individual [Nixon] to prove his toughness to an ever widening list of enemies, real and imagined, an opportunity he felt he must seize to demonstrate his courage under fire and show his adversaries that he would not be intimidated.[78]

There were, however, legitimate political and military reasons for US and ARVN military operations in Cambodia. Cambodia's sovereignty and neutrality were fiction. The PAVN and VC had conducted operations from Cambodia since the 1950s. Abrams and the JCS had identified significant enemy forces and supply storage facilities in Cambodia. These locations were used as staging bases for attacks into South Vietnam. Abrams recommended operations against Communist forces in Cambodia to secure the borders of South Vietnam. On 25 April, against the recommendation of his Secretary of Defense and Secretary of State, Nixon ordered US and ARVN forces into Cambodia to destroy enemy sanctuaries and assist the government. Nixon recognized that the Cambodian incursion would further inflame the antiwar movement. However, he saw this as an opportunity to demonstrate to Hanoi that he would not shrink from the employment of significant military force because of the antiwar movement in the United States.

The Cambodian incursion was the largest operation since the Tet Offensive, involving 30,000 US and 50,000 ARVN soldiers. During the operations, an estimated 11,349 Communists were killed, 2,328 captured, and enough supplies captured or destroyed to equip fifty-four battalions.[79] The operation was a major setback for the PAVN and VC. However, in the United States it sparked a new and more severe round of protests. Protests erupted across the United States. At Kent State, the Ohio National Guard killed two students in an antiwar protest. Congress, angered by the expansion of the war, revoked the 1964 Gulf of Tonkin Resolution and passed legislation that prohibited expenditures for US forces outside of Vietnam. Ultimately, Cambodia suffered horrendous deaths as the Communists rallied and attacked the Lon Nol government.

By December 1970, US troop strength had declined to 335,800, and in 1971 to 140,000. General Abrams protested reductions in forces, arguing that the withdrawal of troops failed to take into consideration the military situation on the ground. Nevertheless, the unilateral withdrawals continued.

In March 1972, Hanoi again escalated, launching a massive, conventional, three-pronged offensive with 125,000 men in fourteen divisions and twenty-six separate regiments, supported by tanks and artillery. The objective of the "Easter Offensive" (the Nguyen Hue Campaign) was total victory. By March, US forces in Vietnam had declined to approximately 95,000, of which only 6,000 were combat troops. The coming election and the antiwar protests in the United States appeared to have tied the President's hands. In addition, the ARVN looked vulnerable following the 1971 offensive into Laos, while the PAVN, with increased Soviet support in conventional weapons—tanks, artillery, and anti-aircraft missiles—appeared capable of swift victory. Given this situation, Hanoi was optimistic that what it could not win through negotiations could be won on the battlefield. General Giap planned for three major attacks, in the northern, central, and southern parts of South Vietnam. The initial attacks went well. However, most ARVN units, with their backs to the wall, fought tenaciously. Sensing that the attacks were timed to embarrass him in his efforts towards a peace agreement and diplomatic efforts with the PRC and USSR, and in the face of political opposition and antiwar protesters, Nixon unleashed American airpower, stating, "The bastards have never been bombed like they're going to be bombed this time."

Nixon ordered the US Air Force and Navy to quickly augment their forces in Southeast Asia to meet the threat and punish the NVA. From March to April, US aircraft sorties increased from 4,237 to 17,171, and in May rose to 18,444. The "Linebacker" air operation dropped approximately 150,000 tons of explosives on North Vietnam.[80] The naval historian John Darrell Sherwood noted:

> Only a small number of Air Force aircraft, a handful of Army advisers, and the Navy carriers in the Gulf of Tonkin were on hand to aid the South Vietnamese in stemming the tide of the Communist onslaught. In the end, naval air power proved vital during the epic struggle because of its ability to surge rapidly to confront a developing threat. In a matter of a few short weeks, the Navy's carrier presence in the Gulf of Tonkin jumped from two to six ships and Navy aircraft flew the majority of strikes during the critical early days of the offensive.[81]

Herring noted that the public outrage at the escalation was manageable because: "The American public had always considered bombing more acceptable than the use of ground forces."[82]

In addition, Nixon ordered the mining of the Port of Haiphong. With American and Vietnamese helicopter forces, the ARVN had the advantage of interior lines and was able to quickly redeploy forces, and reinforce troops fighting in threatened areas. Helicopter gunship and artillery provided the ARVN with needed firepower. In units that failed, ARVN political generals were sacked and replaced with professional, talented leaders. The Soviet Union, seeking new agreements with the United States, publicly continued its support for Hanoi, but privately cautioned the government to reach a peace agreement. By June it was evident that the offensive had failed, even though the fighting continued. According to data compiled by the Nixon Administration, the PAVN suffered over 100,000 dead, 450 tanks destroyed, and heavy losses in artillery, trucks, and other equipment. Facilities and installations in North Vietnam also sustained heavy damage.[83] South Vietnam survived its first major challenge without large numbers of US ground forces. The ARVN had proven itself, and the policy of Vietnamization seemed successful. American airpower also deserved much of the credit for turning the tide. Thus, the big question remained: could the ARVN defend the country without American support?

The failure of the NVA campaign facilitated Kissinger's negotiations in Paris with Le Duc Tho. However, in October 1972, Le Duc Tho prematurely announced that an agreement had been reached, causing the surprised government of South Vietnam to reject it. Hanoi broke off talks and the war continued. In November 1972, Nixon was reelected president. By December, US troop strength in Vietnam had declined to 24,200. To motivate Hanoi back to the table and to conclude the peace agreement, Nixon initiated an intense "Christmas bombing" campaign, Linebacker II. To emphasize his intent, he told Admiral Moorer, CJCS: "I don't want any more of this crap about the fact that we couldn't hit this target or that one. This is your chance to use military power effectively to win the war, and if you don't I'll consider you responsible." In eleven days, flying 729 sorties, B-52s

dropped 15,237 tons of bombs. An additional 5,000 tons were dropped by fighter bombers. On 2 January 1973, talks resumed, and before the month ended, the US, RVN, NLF, and DRV signed the Paris Peace Accords. Linebacker II gave the impression that airpower had been decisive in compelling Hanoi to accept the peace agreement, and the assumption became that had it been used more effectively earlier in the war, victory would have been achieved.[84] A similar argument was made to explain the final armistice in Korea. However, in both wars, the enemy achieved the primary objective. The terms of the final agreement were only slightly different from those offered in October, and with the withdrawal of US forces Hanoi achieved victory. It was just a matter of time.[85]

The President of RVN, Nguyen Van Thieu, accepted the final agreement because he had no other options. Nixon promised and delivered massive military and economic assistance, promised to enforce the agreement, and threatened to abandon him if he did not accept the agreement. In a letter to Thieu dated 14 November 1972, Nixon wrote:

> But far more important than what we say in the agreement on this issue is what we do in the event the enemy renews his aggression. You have my absolute assurance that if Hanoi fails to abide by the terms of this agreement it is my intention to take swift and severe retaliatory action.[86]

When Nixon wrote these words he may have believed them. It was possible to back them up with airpower. However, the US Congress and the American people would have never accepted another major deployment of ground forces.

The peace agreement called for the complete withdrawal of US forces, but left the PAVN in South Vietnam. It was not possible to secure peace with 150,000 enemy soldiers in-country. The entire peace arrangement was orchestrated subterfuge. Nixon, in a televised speech from the White House, told the American people: "We today have concluded an agreement to end the war and bring peace with honor in Vietnam." The agreement was a means for the United States to extricate itself from the war. However, there was no "honor." Hanoi saw the agreement as a means to get the US out of Vietnam so it could complete the destruction of the ARVN and Saigon government. Hanoi also knew the US was not coming back. Nevertheless, Thieu was out of options. Nixon announced a halt to all US offensive operations in Vietnam, the end of the military draft, and in March, 591 American prisoners of war came home. Nevertheless, the war continued.

Between 1973 and 1975, the PAVN launched several major offensives with regular forces. The ARVN initially fought well, but suffered from a lack of confidence. The US had created a dependent army, psychologically incapable of sustained, independent military operations, even with billions of dollars of US equipment. The complete withdrawal of American forces caused enormous damage to the morale and will of the South Vietnamese. The government of SVN requested the military assistance the United States had promised during the peace negotiations. Nixon and Kissinger, however, were unable to keep their promises. The Watergate scandal had paralyzed the nation in the meantime. In May 1973, the House voted to cut off funds for air operations in Indochina. The following month Congress passed an amendment requiring the cessation of all military operations in and over Indochina, and in November passed the War Powers Act, requiring the President to notify and acquire Congressional approval for the deployment of armed forces in sustained operations. Congress acted to limit the power of the President to make war. In August 1974, Nixon resigned. Gerald R. Ford became President, and he too lacked the power to render the assistance the US had promised. In April 1975, the government of SVN fell to the PAVN. The war had finally come to an ignominious ended.

* * * * *

In Vietnam, the US spent an estimated $200 billion, more than half of which went to the air war, and suffered its first defeat. The US sustained 47,382 killed in action, 10,811 deaths from other causes, and 153,303 wounded in action. Of those killed, 65.8 percent were soldiers, 25.5 percent Marines, 4.3 percent Navy, primarily aviators, and 4.3 percent Air Force, primarily pilots. But the death toll from war is never fully known.[87] Months, years, and decades after the end of hostilities, men were still dying from physical and psychological wounds received during the war. In the Vietnam War, the psychological wounds—post-traumatic stress disorder—were deep and took a higher toll than in most wars. The Vietnam War was the first war the US lost, making the sacrifices of servicemen seem futile. It was an unpopular war which lacked the support of the American people. Servicemen were not welcomed home. They were treated with hostility and disrespect. Agent Orange and diseases contracted in Vietnam, such as hepatitis, also took a toll on the lives of the men that served.

It was estimated that the RVN sustained 223,748 killed, and 570,600 wounded, and 415,000 civilian deaths. The estimates of RVN casualties vary widely and an accurate assessment will never be known. It was estimated that North Vietnam suffered over 666,000 killed. However, in April 1995, Hanoi declared that 1.1 million combatants had died, and 600,000 were wounded between 1954 and 1975.[88] These figures include Viet Cong guerrillas, Communist South Vietnam soldiers, and PAVN soldiers. The Vietnamese Communists suffered human losses that exceeded by two times the number of Americans killed in World War II. The period of American withdrawal and abandonment of the RVN, 1972–1975, was one of the most disgraceful periods of American history. And the suffering in the region continued long after the withdrawal of US forces.

The US went to war in Vietnam without the United Nations, without its traditional European allies, without mobilizing the National Guard and Reserves, without a sustained effort to gain and maintain the support of the American people, and with only a small fraction of the nation. Americans placed great faith in technology to win the war. Airpower was supposed to win the war. America failed in Vietnam, lost its first war, placed the burden of fighting the war on those with the least political clout, and, some would argue, betrayed an ally who had sacrificed much and whose government was the direct result of US intervention. The vast majority of Americans were unwilling to pay "any price" for the "success of liberty" in a foreign country that was incapable of posing any real threat to the US, and that had no significant natural resources, and no cultural affinity with the American people. Worse, however, was the fact that many in the military came to believe that when American servicemen were fighting and dying in a foreign land in pursuit of national political objectives, the American people failed to give them their full support. General Colin Powell wrote, "In Vietnam, we had entered into a halfhearted half-war, with much of the nation opposed or indifferent, while a small fraction carried the burden."[89]

In an effort to capture the attitudes and mood of the nation in the immediate aftermath of the Vietnam War, a young Army Reserve Captain, in an article entitled, "Down the Road to Armageddon?" wrote:

> In the history of every great power there comes a moment when its strength recedes. We are witnessing the decline of the American Empire. The most significant factor in the diminution of America's international position will be the shift in values of a new generation of young Americans. It is my thesis that future US security will be endangered because elite youth will draw "lessons" from the recent past which shall be misapplied later. We will, in effect, psychologically disarm.... Recent Defense Department survey reveals that about 60 percent of American youth desire no association with the military, "no time, nowhere, no how." It is exactly such attitudes in a world of flux and uncertainty that may create a period of maximum danger.... The crucial fact about the evolving establishment is that we lack the political will to make sacrifices in the furtherance of national security goals.... Amid the anguish of our epoch—the convulsions, the mindless violence, the deteriorating international scene—the ebb tide of American power is evident.[90]

Werner was wrong in his conclusion, but he was right about the willingness of America's youth to serve the nation in war. The Vietnam War damaged the martial spirit of the American people.[91] Adam Smith in *The Wealth of Nations* wrote: "The security of every society must always depend, more or less, upon the martial spirit of the great body of the people...." Smith meant security from external threat,

but that security, he understood, was based on the cultural cohesion of the nation. Under President Ronald Reagan, the United States recovered from the Vietnam debacle, but the citizen-soldier vanished, and the responsibility for defense of the United States fell to fewer and fewer.

Americans were unwilling to fight war indefinitely with a drafted Army. It took thirty years to figure out that the US needed an expeditionary, professional Army. The end of the Vietnam War marked the end of attempts to adapt traditional American thinking about the conduct of war to the new realities of artificial limited war. Americans experienced the war as a dirty, bloody infantry war that failed to produce victory. Ironically it was the first war in the history of the United States where the decisive arm for the conduct of the war was supposed to be airpower. In the post-Vietnam War era airpower continued to dominate American thinking about the conduct of war.

The outcome of the Vietnam War dealt the myth of America a severe blow. Americans grew up thinking their armed forces were unbeatable. This was the nation that defeated Germany and Japan simultaneously. This was the nation that in World War II outproduced all other nations. This was the nation that invented the atomic bomb, and advanced many other technologies, such as radar and airpower. Americans grew up believing their ingenuity and technology could overcome all obstacles and that their government through two centuries of progress had institutionalized integrity, honor, and moral correctness. Americans believed that they, as a people, were morally right and courageous. Vietnam called all this into question. There seemed to be an irreconcilable difference between America's beliefs about itself and the realities revealed during the Vietnam War: the defeat by a poor, undeveloped nation; the massacre at My Lai; the chronic, extensive mendacity of the Johnson and Nixon Administrations; and numerous signs of corruption and deterioration that eroded Americans' faith in America.

12.
THE RECOVERY AND REORGANIZATION OF THE ARMED FORCES OF THE UNITED STATES, 1975–1990

It [Army Airland Battle Doctrine] is based on securing or retaining the initiative and exercising it aggressively to accomplish the mission. The object of all operations is to impose our will upon the enemy—to achieve our purpose. To do this we must throw the enemy off balance with a powerful blow from an unexpected direction, follow up rapidly to prevent his recovery and continue operations aggressively to achieve the higher commander's goals. The best results are obtained when powerful blows are struck against critical units or areas whose loss will degrade the coherence of enemy operations in depth, and thus most rapidly and economically accomplish the mission. From the enemy's point of view, these operations must be rapid, unpredictable, violent, and disorienting. The pace must be fast enough to prevent him from taking effective counteractions.[1]

–US Army, FM 100–5, *Operations*, 1986

So the one thing the Gulf war did: the tank-plinking made everybody understand the importance of precise delivery of weapons for hitting a fielded enemy army. In other words, it showed that air power could very methodically and rapidly decimate a ground force if it had the accuracy of fairly small and conventional weapons. This was a significant turning point.[2]

–General Buster Glosson, *War With Iraq*, 2003

In the aftermath of the Vietnam War, the services, particularly the Army, had to recover, reorganize, rebuild, and rethink the conduct of war, and the actions and behaviors of their officer corps. The outcome of the Vietnam War was *not* in keeping with the military tradition of the United States. Obviously something was very wrong, but, what?

Recovery would take time, tenacity, and intelligence. It would also take money and a vision of the future. The process of recovery and transformation could not be completed until an administration was willing to expend the resources required. It was President Ronald Reagan who finally provided funds and created the environment for recovery of the armed forces, noting that, "defense is not a budget issue. You spend what you need."

The post-Vietnam War malaise and defeatist attitude, and the chasm between the American people and the military were to some degree overcome during the Reagan Administration. Reagan not only expended the resources necessary to rebuild the armed forces, he showed that he trusted the military, and that he was willing to use them. He clarified the confusion that held America in near paralysis. He created a world that Americans could understand, a world of good vs. evil. Americans wore the white hats, sat tall in the saddle, and were the good guys. The Soviet Union, Communist leaders and their military, wore the black hats and were the "evil empire," the bad guys.[3] This was a simplistic view of a complex world, but it resonated with, and inspired, Americans. Reagan restored the American military, and the morale and spirit of the American people. Reagan, however, could not and did not attempt to undo the transformation in the American procurement of soldiers, and the resultant changes in the standards for use of military force. An all-volunteer professional military force would fight the next war. The American people had successfully removed themselves from the conduct of artificial limited war.

In the post-Vietnam War era there was much talk about the services cooperating and working together to achieve political objectives and synergy on the battlefield. While there was some progress toward joint doctrine, and while the Army and Air Force entered into informal agreements on operational doctrine, the Air Force still sought technologies and doctrines that would render ground forces obsolete, and the Army still believed that ground forces were necessary and decisive in war.

The "Revolution" in Strategic Bombing Doctrine

In the aftermath of the Vietnam War, some argued that strategic bomber doctrine had undergone a stealth and precision "revolution." In the 1990s, two new aircraft were revealed to the world: the F-117 stealth fighter and the B-2 stealth bomber.[4] These aircraft were capable of penetrating enemy air space undetected by radar, and they employed precision weapons. The military's objective was no longer to destroy the will of the people through the mass bombing of the population, or to destroy the enemy's means of production through the mass bombing of factories, transportation networks, or energy sources. In the age of artificial limited war, it was no longer possible to destroy the enemy's means of production. Iraq, like North Korea, North Vietnam, and other future enemies did not produce the war machines it employed; hence, there was no way to destroy its means of production with precision or dumb bombs. And, because of advanced communication technologies, including the ability to beam images and sounds into space and back to any part of the Earth at the speed of light, the mass destruction of a people with bombing became politically unacceptable. Any such action would be headline news almost immediately. Thus, in the wake of the Vietnam War,

World War II strategic bombing doctrines became obsolete.

The new doctrine of strategic bombing applied precision weapons to the enemy's strategic centers of gravity. Consider the thinking of Air Force Brigadier General Buster Glosson, the man who planned the air campaign for Operation Desert Storm:

> Intelligence was critical for precision targeting and that would be the assignment of the F-117s that I knew would be the key to the campaign. Arguing for this philosophy put me to the test within my own service, because not everyone believed in the F-117 like I did. That day Horner [Joint Forces Air Component Commander] told me he did not think the F-117s would work the way I thought they would. Every instinct I had told me he was dead wrong. *'Mass is a thing of the past,'* I scribbled in my notes. *'We are in a precision world.'*[5]

Glosson's faith in technology was culturally regular, reflecting the attitudes and beliefs of the American people. He built the air war plans for Operation Desert Storm around the capabilities of the F-117. He believed this aircraft could win the war without the Army, without a ground war—a consistent tenet of American thinking about the use of armed forces since World War II. Glosson's strategic centers of gravity in order of priority were: governmental leadership; nuclear, biological, and chemical capabilities; state infrastructure; and the enemy's armed forces, which in the case of Iraq consisted of air force fighters, Scud missiles, the Republican Guard, and the regular Army.[6] Enemy ground forces, in accordance with traditional Air Force thinking, were last on the Air Force's list of priorities. But there was something new. With precision weapons the Air Force concluded that it had the means to destroy enough of the enemy's combat force to make a decisive difference—a strategic difference. In other words, the physical destruction of the enemy's ground forces, without the Army, became a strategic capability. In all previous wars airpower had been a tactical capability employed in concert with ground forces. Consider each strategic center of gravity:

The objective in Operation Desert Storm was to restore Kuwait to the sovereignty of its monarch. The objective was not regime change in Iraq. However, the achievement of the latter assured the success of the former objective. In his list of critical lessons learned, Glosson emphasized that the "political leadership of a country and the force that permits it to govern must be destroyed. All other centers of gravity become insignificant unless the central 'cog' is destroyed."[7] Precision weapons made it possible to conduct "decapitation strikes," to target governmental buildings, command and control facilities, and the homes of political leaders without destroying entire cities. After the war, Glosson observed: "This wasn't devastated Germany in the spring of 1945. We'd hit only selected facilities, and hit them hard, but we'd caused Iraq, as a nation, no lasting damage." Many Iraqis would disagree with this assessment, but Glosson was right. This was not war-torn Germany. What Glosson did not understand was that killing governmental leadership was a real center of gravity only when fighting *states*. In wars between *nations* the destruction of a particular group of governmental leaders is not decisive. New leaders rise. Another government is immediately formed to take its place, and many actions are decentralized, requiring no orders or direction from a central government. The destruction of the government in Hanoi would not have stopped the Vietnam War.

Precision destruction of enemy ground combat forces independent of friendly ground forces represented a new strategic capability for air forces. Glosson believed the precision revolution had forever changed the conduct of ground warfare:

> Nobody had ever looked at it from that standpoint before. They always looked at air power taking away the capability of an enemy army by destroying the logistics base of the division, interdicting them and impeding their ability to move in daylight, cutting off the supplies and all that crap. This is good, it's necessary, but nobody had ever looked at actually destroying the division itself and halting its maneuver in short order.[8]

Destruction of the enemy's armed forces with precision weapons, while a new strategic capability, was no small task, nor was it cheap. Intelligence sources have to identify the exact location of each

tank, infantry-fighting vehicle, and artillery piece. And airpower has to destroy thirty to forty percent of the forces of each major command to render them combat ineffective. This calls for a lot of airplanes, flying a lot of sorties, and expending a lot of very expensive missiles. This approach requires time, but because of the standoff range, considerably less risk to pilots than with dumb bombs. While ground forces could do the job considerably faster and more thoroughly, they incurred greater risk, because they had to enter the battlefield. And of course, minimizing risk has always been the second most important factor, immediately behind winning, in the American approach to war. Glosson well understood this, "Winning—there is no substitute; minimum loss of life—there is no compromise."

What Glosson failed to understand was that the destruction of the enemy's war machines might not destroy his will to fight. Machines may be destroyed or abandoned, but infantrymen or insurgents armed with rifles, and the tenacity that comes from nationalism, religious convictions, hate, anger, and insult may take up the fight. It is interesting to note that the limited war doctrine of the 1950s that recognized outcomes short of complete victory was gone. Against developing nations that were not backed by the Soviet Union or PRC, there was no need for the US to settle for anything less than complete victory.

The destruction of a state's infrastructure is problematic. This can be an attack on the government, or an attack on the will of the people. If actions are directed at severing the lines of communication between the government and its armed forces, this approach can cause some degree of paralysis, which facilitates the destruction of the government or the armed forces, but simply severing the links alone will not produce decisive results. The government or armed forces still have to be attacked. Glosson wrote:

> I believed the majority of everything important to Saddam could be taken away from him with the strategic attacks in Phase I of the war [which lasted the entire war]. My philosophy was I want there to be a purpose for everything that we're doing, every bomb we drop. *Now, there are some cases where you have to send political messages to the leadership and to the people, for psychological reasons.* I bombed things Saddam was proud of,

including his nuclear, biological and chemical weapons research sites and apparatus. I bombed police stations, intelligence facilities, and places where I knew the Iraqi regime tortured people. ... I wanted to destroy things that were associated with Saddam's fake mystique, the aura he tried to keep up in front of people, linking himself to the lineage of the ancient ruler Nebuchadnezzer. I wanted Saddam to feel the pressure.[9]

The political messages directed at the Iraqi people could only be decisive if they convinced the people to overthrow the government. The political messages directed at the leadership could only be decisive if they convinced that leadership it could not win and thus had no other option but to quit the war and go home. Because the life of the government is tied to the outcome of the war, political bombing, short of nuclear weapons, has never proven decisive. Political bombing to send a message to people, which does not punish the people but demonstrates the impotence of the political and military leadership, might encourage the people to overthrow the government, but there is no guarantee. In a police state, no matter how impotent the government may appear, as long as its police force and army are loyal and functioning, the people may feel they have no opportunities to rebel.

Actions directed at the destruction of power plants, water and sewage plants, dams, public transportation and communication networks, and other public works are in essence indirect attacks on the people. History has shown that in more total war, in wars between *nations*, punishing the people has had little influence on the decisions of political leaders. Against *nations* this approach produces the same results as the bombing of London in 1940. It creates solidarity. Against *states*, which are incapable of fighting more total war because they lack the willing support of the people, punishing the people may cause them to withdraw what little support the government has, facilitating the collapse of the armed forces; and hence, the collapse of the government. However, punishing the people will have little or no influence on the decision-making of dictators, such as Saddam Hussein, particularly if he believes his survival is tied to the outcome of the conflict. No degree of

destruction of the infrastructure of Iraq was going to influence the decision-making of Hussein. The infrastructure of the enemy state is not a strategic center of gravity. Attacking the infrastructure of a state or nation cannot produce decisive results. It can only facilitate the destruction of the government or the armed forces, the real strategic centers of gravity.

Nuclear, biological, and chemical capabilities comprise a center of gravity only in the sense that they are not used to attack friendly strategic forces, or centers of gravity. Their destruction is defensive. Only through offensive actions are decisive results achieved.

With stealth and precision technology the Air Force had two ways to win: destroy the enemy government, or destroy its armed forces. In Iraq the target of the most strategic significance was Saddam Hussein. Killing him would end the war.[10] The problem was getting accurate intelligence on his location. In Saddam Hussein's closed system, which was based on personal loyalties, this problem was insurmountable. Hence, the next priority should have been the destruction of the Iraqi ground forces. Destroying the Iraqi infrastructure and punishing the Iraqi people could never be decisive.

Glosson predicted that in the Gulf War: "The ability to penetrate defended airspace and drop precision weapons was going to be more useful ... than a thousand F-16s." He concluded that while ground forces had been deployed, airpower had been decisive. He believed that "by the end of 1990, the Air Force had gone through a precision revolution," and that "strategy should always be air and special operations first—followed by ground operations as necessary to reach political and military objectives." He emphasized, "that military leaders should not permit their thought processes to get preoccupied with 'massive and overwhelming force.' Instead, their focus should be on 'decisive force.'"[11]

At the start of the war, not all airmen agreed with Glosson's doctrine or shared his complete faith in stealth technology. In Vietnam, the Air Force had provided the Army with the most responsive, comprehensive, and effective support in the history of the two services. Some airmen believed that airpower working in concert with ground forces was the best solution. Glosson was impatient, and even scornful of the "non-believers." He wrote: "The non-believers made their case early and often. On August 29, I briefed Major General Royal Moore, commander of Marine air units arriving in the Gulf. Another brute force advocate, he believed the F-117 had failed in Panama and would miss its targets again in the Gulf."[12] Glosson was particularly critical of the Air Force staff:

The standard, default mindset of the Air Force staff planner was to start at the edge of the enemy military mass and beat down defenses and eventually get where you have total control. Only then could you focus on what you were really going to take away from the nation-state that you were fighting against. It was believed that getting total control of the air would take a fair amount of time, so until you had that, you didn't do anything toward your real objective. It was the same mindset as the Eighth Air Force in World War II. I'm not criticizing them—that's the only choice they had. But I sure didn't have to go down that road, because technology had changed things in the intervening fifty years. I was not going to follow the same blueprint and mold they had been following in previous wars.[13]

Glosson's charge was not fair to strategic planners on the Air Force staff. His words, however, are indicative of the friction that hampered Air Force operations, and the friction between the Air Force staff in the Pentagon and Central Command Air Force (CENTAF) in Saudi Arabia. Vietnam weighed heavily on Glosson and Horner, both of whom were determined that the war would not be run from Washington, targets would not be selected in the Pentagon, and CENTAF would not be reduced to simply executing missions planned thousands of miles away. Glosson observed that Horner was concerned that "the Air Staff back in Washington was trying to dictate to him how he was going to run the campaign. The last thing he wanted was for someone else to come up with a plan, then issue it to him."[14] Diverging views between CENTAF and the Air Force staff was more a function of disagreements over jurisdiction than disagreements over strategic air doctrine.

The Air staff, under the leadership of Colonel John A. Warden III, the deputy director for warfighting concepts, developed the initial air plan, codenamed "Instant Thunder." It called for attacks on the government and infrastructure in Baghdad. Warden stated his doctrinal thinking:

Although we tend to think of military forces as being the most vital in war, in fact they are means to an end. That is, their only function is to protect their own inner rings [of leadership] or to threaten those of an enemy. . . . The essence of war is applying pressure against the enemy's innermost strategic ring—its command structure. . . . It is pointless to deal with enemy forces if they can be bypassed, by strategy or technology, either in the defense or offense.[15]

This approach was not that different from Glosson's. And, the thinking of Warden's and Glosson's reflected Army Air Force World War II thinking. "All that was needed was to find that one key industry (oil, railroad, or steel), or find that one key piece of technology (ball bearings) on which all else depended. Destroy that, and declare victory." In fifty years, the more basic tenets of American airpower theorists had actually changed little. What was different in 1990 was the technology.

The real world is always more complex than the models constructed by advocates of a particular piece of technology. And men who fight with machines habitually fail to understand the human factor in war. Years of training to perfect the employment of one type of technology divorces them from the full spectrum of war. They are, in effect, partially blind. In more total war, in a people's war, Warden's and Glosson's airpower theories were deeply flawed. Ho Chi Minh's death did not end the Vietnam War. And even if the Air Force could have killed significant numbers of Vietnamese leaders, others would have risen to take their place. The death of Mao Tse Tung would not have ended the Chinese Revolution. And the death of Stalin in World War II would not have ended the war on the Eastern Front. The destruction of significant numbers of tanks and artillery pieces does not necessarily mean the destruction of the will of people, or the end of the war. In "people's wars," destroying the enemy's fighting machines may simply end the first phase of the war. People's wars, wars that only *nations* are capable of fighting, are not won by killing one person, or group of leaders; or by the domination of one type of technology over another. They are about ways of life—the issues of freedom, self-determination, the end of exploitation, and/or the end of foreign rule, objectives that cannot be compromised away. And, people are the most adaptable and resilient weapon on Earth.

To Rebuild an Army: Back to the Future

In the wake of the Vietnam War, the Army refocused on conventional war in Europe against the Warsaw Pact—the type of war it most wanted to fight, not the type of war it was most likely to fight. In July 1973, the Army activated a new command under General William E. DePuy, the US Army Training and Doctrine Command (TRADOC). TRADOC was to take the lead in remaking the Army: new technology, new doctrine, new training, and a new sense of professionalism. To emphasize the importance of this new command and its mission, DePuy, a four-star general, one of the Army's most respected leaders, was given command and responsibility for changing the Army.[16] With the return to the European battlefields, the experiences of the Israelis in the 1973 Yom Kippur War seemed more applicable than those of the Army in Vietnam.[17] The experience of Israel had revealed the effectiveness of a new generation of technology. DePuy concluded that, "because of the cost of and preoccupation with the Vietnam war, the Army lost a generation of modernization." The Soviets had indeed improved the quality and capabilities of their weapon systems. And the Soviet buildup in the late 1960s and 1970s gave them a substantial numerical superiority over NATO forces. The Army would have to fight outnumbered. To make up for the relative equality in technology, and the enemy's superior numbers, the Army had to be better trained and led with superior operational and tactical doctrines.

In the Yom Kippur War of 1973, the dominance of the tank came into question. Relatively inexpensive wire-guided missiles fired from distances as far as two kilometers by infantrymen were capable of destroying tanks, which cost nearly a million dollars per vehicle. Surface-to-air missiles challenged the dominance of bombers and ground attack aircraft. The pace and lethality of war had so increased that traditional concepts of mobilization, logistics, replacement vehicles, and the significance of the first battle were no longer

valid. Either a nation was ready for war on day one, or it would suffer defeat on the battlefield. War was "come-as-you-are." During its short war, Israel had required a major emergency resupply of primary weapons systems from the US in order to continue. Joint doctrine had been required for the success of the Israeli Defense Force (IDF) in this new, intense, lethal battlefield.

In the late 1970s and early 1980s a controversial debate raged throughout the Army on conventional operational doctrine.[18] Based on assessments of the lessons of the Yom Kippur War and estimates of relative combat power in the European theater, the Army developed a doctrine called the "active defense." Having just lost a strategically defensive war in Vietnam, many in the Army rejected this doctrine. The active defense was not purely defensive, but it de-emphasized offensive operations and emphasized firepower over maneuver. In July 1977, General Don Starry took command of TRADOC. Starry promulgated a vision of war that emphasized the extended battlefield, out to 150 kilometers, and included offensive operations, speed, and maneuver.[19] He also emphasized the human factors: training, leadership, courage, and character. Starry believed the Yom Kippur War taught the following lessons:

> First, we learned that the US military should expect modern battlefields to be dense with large numbers of weapons systems whose lethality at extended range would surpass previous experience by nearly an order of magnitude. Direct-fire battle space would be expanded several orders of magnitude over that experienced in World War II and Korea.
>
> Second, because of numbers and weapons lethality, the direct-fire battle will be intense, resulting in enormous equipment losses in a relatively short time. Significantly, we noted, combined tank losses in the first six critical days of the Yom Kippur War exceeded the total US tank inventory deployed to NATO Europe....
>
> Third, the air battle will be characterized by large numbers of highly lethal aerial platforms—both fixed- and rotary-wing—and by large numbers of highly lethal air defense weapons.
>
> Fourth, the density-intensity-lethality equation will prevent domination of the battle by any single

weapons system; to win, it will be necessary to employ all battlefield systems in closely coordinated all-arms action.

Fifth, the intensity of battle will make command and control at the tactical and operational levels ever more difficult. Effective command-control will be further degraded by the presence of large numbers of radio-electronic combat systems aimed at inhibiting effective command-control.

Sixth, at both the tactical and operational levels the complexity of modern battle demands clear thinking. Thinking takes time, and in battle there is no time to think. Therefore, to the extent possible, likely battle circumstances must be thought through in advance to reduce the chance of surprise and to ensure prompt, timely, and relevant decisions.

Finally, regardless of which side outnumbers the other, regardless of who attacks whom, the outcome of battle at the tactical and operational levels will be decided by factors other than numbers and other than who attacks and who defends. In the end, the side that somehow, at some time, somewhere during the battle seizes the initiative and holds it to the end is the side that wins. More often than not, the outcome of battle defies the traditional calculus employed to predict such outcomes. *It is strikingly evident that battles will continue to be won by the courage of Soldiers, the character of leaders, and the combat excellence of well-trained units—beginning with crews and ending with corps and armies.*[20]

Starry concluded that:

For those of us who crafted new doctrine to reflect the new environment, one single statement became the goal: The US military must decide how to fight outnumbered and win the first and succeeding battles of the next war at the tactical and operational levels ... without having to resort to the use of nuclear weapons to offset the military's likely numerical disadvantages. . . .

The Army now had been wrestling with this problem for more than three decades. Technology has not changed the Army's fundamental belief that man is the dominant weapon on the battlefield. Following an intense debate, the Army developed AirLand Battle

doctrine, and sought the Air Forces' approval of this doctrine.

AirLand Battle doctrine was first introduced in FM 100–5 *Operation* 1982. In 1983 the Army started emphasizing and studying the operational level of war. At Fort Leavenworth, the School of Advanced Military Studies (SAMS) was established to educate mid-level officers on operational art, and to continue to develop operational doctrine. The SAMS contributed to the 1986 edition of FM 100–5, which described AirLand Battle doctrine:

Our operational planning must orient on decisive objectives. It must stress flexibility, the creation of opportunities to fight on favorable terms by capitalizing on enemy vulnerabilities, concentration against enemy center of gravity, synchronized joint operations, and aggressive exploitation of tactical gains to achieve operational results. Our tactical planning must be precise enough to preserve synchronization throughout the battle. At the time it must be flexible enough to respond to changes or to capitalize on fleeting opportunities to damage the enemy. Success on the battlefield will depend on the Army's ability to fight in accordance with four basic tenets: *initiative, agility, depth, and synchronization.*[21]

AirLand Battle doctrine was designed to defeat Soviet technology and doctrine. Because the Soviets attacked in echelons, Army doctrine was designed to defeat each echelon, not one at a time, but simultaneously. AirLand Battle doctrine placed great importance on airpower fighting the "deep battle" to destroy conventional second and third echelon attacking forces well beyond the range of Army ground weapon systems.[22] The Army would defeat the first echelon, and attack to complete the destruction of the second and third echelons, which should have been substantially attrited by airpower.

AirLand Battle doctrine was not revolutionary. It also was not a rewrite of German blitzkrieg maneuver warfare doctrine. FM 100–5 identified the five forms of maneuver, envelopment, turning movement, infiltration, penetration, and frontal attack. The preferred maneuvers were envelopment and turning movement. Under penetration it was noted that: "Penetration is used when enemy flanks are not assailable and when time does not permit some other form of maneuver." What was always unclear about AirLand Battle doctrine was when or where the war or campaign was won? Given that in the 1980s the enemy was the Soviet Union, was the objective Moscow, the Soviet border, the Warsaw Pact borders, the destruction of the enemy's forces in Eastern Europe, or the Russian frontier? The Germans in 1941 never adequately answered this question.

The Army committed billions of dollars to develop attack helicopters for the deep strike missions. A "revolution" in precision weapons was taking place and aircraft, Air Force and Army, were now capable of engaging tanks and other vehicles with tremendous accuracy. The Air Force unofficially accepted AirLand Battle doctrine, which enabled the two services to work together. While still emphasizing the European battlefield, the Army maintained a versatile force structure consisting of five types of infantry—light, airborne, air assault, Ranger, and mechanized—as well as Special Forces. However, because the European battlefield was the Army's priority, the focus was on heavy divisions—mechanized and armor. Insurgency wars and guerrilla wars received little attention. The Army wanted to forget Vietnam.

Under Starry's leadership, the Army also underwent a "training revolution."[23] It constructed new training facilities and developed new methods of training. The National Training Center (NTC) was established at Fort Irwin, California, with the most advanced American equipment, and even some Soviet equipment, acquired primarily from the Israelis. The Joint Readiness Training Center (JRTC) was established at Fort Polk, Louisiana, for training light forces. And the Combat Maneuver Training Center was established at Hohenfels, Germany. New technologies, such as the multiple integrated laser engagement system (MILES), were designed and employed. However, the most significant change was the elimination of subjective evaluation systems and the introduction of objective systems that measured performance. The Army developed Military Qualification Standards (MQS) for individual training and "Mission Essential Tasks Lists" (METL) for unit training. For every job in the Army, MQS were developed; and for every mission and every unit, METLs were developed. MQS

broke down major jobs into required, observable tasks. Each task had to be performed and verified to receive a passing "GO." Failure to complete the required list of tasks resulted in a "NO GO," and additional training to the get individuals up to standards. Unit training was also conducted as objectively as possible. The Army Training and Evaluation Program (ARTEP) broke down every mission into performance measures. With MILES equipment, trainers could objectively assess casualties. The Army's new training method eliminated doubt. Either an individual or unit was training on specific tasks or missions, or they were not. Training was based on real-world capabilities of Soviet forces. The MQS, ARTEP, and METL were revised as new information was gained, or new methods evolved. The system was flexible, designed to incorporate change and integrate new technology. One of the most important things the Army did was to emphasize *battle drills*. Battle drills for every eventuality imagined were developed and practiced until they became reflex actions. A high level of proficiency was attained through the use of battle drills.

The Army also revised its professional military education (PME) programs, for officers and NCOs, expanding the time they spent in classrooms. The Army expended enormous effort addressing the problem of professionalism, endeavoring to fix the problems that created "careerism" in Vietnam. The Army War College was directed to study this issue. It produced a number of studies designed to measure the quality of Army professionalism. Information attained from these studies was used to evaluate the Army's personnel and education systems. Ethical and moral education were integrated into all the Army's PME programs, from cadet to colonel, from ROTC to USMA, and from the Command and General Staff College to the War College. The Army was very sensitive to charges made against it in countless books and articles. Works with titles such as: *Crisis in Command, Self-Destruction,* and *Army in Anguish* hurt Army pride, reinforcing the "never again attitude."

The Army also concluded that it could not fight a war without the Air Force and decided to seek joint doctrine and training. FM 100–5, *Operations,* April 1977, emphasized that: "*the Army cannot win the land battle without the Air Force.*" In 1978, the Air Staff and Army Staff began to work out procedures for integrating their forces on the battlefield. This effort produced an agreement between TRADOC and US Air Force Tactical Air Command. In 1982, the joint attack of the second echelon (J-SAK) doctrine was published. This semi-official doctrine made it possible for Air Force and Army to operate on the same battlefield.[24] The Air Force, with its A-10 Warthog, close support and battlefield interdiction aircraft, participated in joint training at Forts Irwin, Lewis, and other Army installations. The Army's Operations FM continued to emphasize the importance of joint operations with the Air Force, a subsequent manual stated: "*the requirement for an air-ground communications system and an agreed employment concept (followed by joint training in operation procedures and frequent exercises) is absolutely essential.*" The Army, recognizing the "interdependency of the Army and Air Force," sought and planned to fight single, unified battles in the next war. However, in the late 1980s, a controversial debate took place within the Air Force over the A-10 and the close air support (CAS) mission. In fact, this debate had gone on since World War II. This was just the latest chapter, and an indicator of how little had really changed in the thinking of the two services. The CAS mission had always been the least significant to the Air Force, and in the 1980s the Air Force endeavored to get rid of its A-10s, which were developed exclusively for close support and interdiction, and again questioned the need for CAS.[25]

With the elimination of the draft the significance of technology increased. The Army recognized that in the next war it would probably fight outnumbered, and that there would be insufficient time to draft, train, and equip divisions before the war was over. Technology was a combat multiplier. The Army experimented with new technologies, seeking to replace the generation of technology developed in the late 1950s and early 1960s, eventually producing and deploying the M1 Abrams main battle tank, the M2/M3 Bradley Infantry Fighting Vehicles, the AH-64 Apache attack helicopter, the UH-60 Black Hawk utility helicopter, the HMMWV (high-mobility multipurpose wheeled vehicle), and the HEMTT (heavy, expanded-mobility tactical truck). The Army also replaced all its individual weapons. These were the primary technologies with which the Army would fight the next major war.

Fighting outnumbered, Army doctrine required greater speed and survivability from Army technology. The Army could not exchange battalion for battalion, brigade for brigade, and division for division, with the Warsaw Pact, and win. Each Army unit had to fight multiple Soviet units equal in size to survive. Army technology and doctrine were designed with the idea that speed would give the Army tactical and possibly operational interior lines, the ability to reinforce separate units faster than the enemy. The ability to fight a battle, destroy enemy forces and/or disengage, and then move rapidly to another "battle position" where a break through was threatened and fight another battle, with the same forces, was the intent. This thinking went into the design of the M1, M2, and the logistical resource systems required to support them.[26] Two of the most important innovations incorporated into the M1 were Chobham armor and a turbine engine.[27] The M1 can run at speeds better than 40 mph. And the M2 Bradley, while not as fast, was designed to keep up with it. Army armor and mechanized forces were the fastest on Earth. This speed included the logistical ability to support the forces with fuel, ammunition, food and water, and repairs.

The Army, with minor modifications, maintained the organizational structure developed in the early 1960s, when ROAD division replaced the Pentomic division. The Army maintained a flexible organization and was able to task-organize for particular operations employing a wide range of force and capabilities, from air assault and light infantry forces; to airborne infantry, Rangers, and Special Forces; to heavy armor and mechanized divisions.

The Army took a serious and honest look at itself, and made important changes to improve its combat effectiveness and give the American people a first-class organization. It and the other services inexorably rebuilt, but it was the Army that had been the most severely damaged by the experience of the Vietnam War and the end of conscription. It was the Army that had the longest way to go.[28] The journey was accomplished with professionalism, love of service, and the motivation that comes from defeat. Not since the reorganization and transformation of the Prussian Army after its defeat at Jena in 1806 by the Grand Army of Napoleon has an Army gone through such extensive change. Ironically, in many ways, the transformation the Prussians sought was the exact opposite of that the US Army sought. The Prussians endeavored to produce a *national army* that was motivated by patriotism, out of the *professional army* of the old regime, the absolute monarch. The US endeavored to transform its *national army* into a *professional, long-service Army* that was *not* reliant on patriotism and the will of the people. Both succeeded.

The Marine Corps's "New" Maneuver Warfare Doctrine

In the years between the end of the Vietnam War and Operation Desert Storm the Marine Corps, like the Army and Air Force, endeavored to rethink the way it fought. It promulgated a "new maneuver warfare doctrine;" however, Marine culture, as in the case with the Army and Air Force, created the parameters for that doctrine. Historically and traditionally the Marine Corps has been a light infantry force. While the Navy provided it strategic mobility, once on the ground the marines were limited to the rate of speed of the infantry, three to four miles per hour. Operational mobility, intra-theater mobility, was also limited, primarily to littoral regions.

Since WWII, the concept of maneuver warfare has been associated with heavy armored and mechanized forces that move at fifteen to thirty miles per hour. German blitzkrieg operations were a form of maneuver warfare. The Marine Corps force structure was not designed for this type of maneuver warfare. Thus, it either had to reformulate the concept of maneuver warfare or change its force structure. It did both. It sought new technology and new air units.[29] However, the primary means for implementing this new doctrine was to rethink the way the Marine Corps fought.

In 1989 the Marine Corps published FMFM1 *Warfighting*. It delineated Marine Corps thinking about the conduct of war:

> The Marine Corps concept for winning under these conditions is a warfighting doctrine based on rapid, flexible, and opportunistic maneuver. But in order to fully appreciate what we mean by *maneuver* we need to clarify the term. The traditional understanding of maneuver is a spatial

one; that is, we maneuver in space to gain a positional advantage. However, in order to maximize the usefulness of maneuver, we must consider maneuver *in time* as well; that is, we generate a faster operational tempo than the enemy to gain a temporal advantage. It is through maneuver in *both* dimensions that an inferior force can achieve decisive superiority at the necessary time and place.[30]

The Marine Corps developed the following definition: "Maneuver warfare is a warfighting philosophy that seeks the enemy's cohesion through a series of rapid, violent, and unexpected actions which create a turbulent and rapidly deteriorating situation with which he cannot cope." This concept was further qualified:

> From this definition we see that the aim in maneuver warfare is to render the enemy incapable of resisting by shattering his moral and physical cohesion—his ability to fight as an effective, coordinated whole—rather than to destroy him physically through incremental attrition, which is generally more costly and time-consuming.... By our actions, we seek to pose menacing dilemmas in which events happen unexpectedly and faster than the enemy can keep up with them. The enemy must be made to see his situation not only as deteriorating, but deteriorating at an ever-increasing rate. The ultimate goal is panic and paralysis, an enemy who has lost the ability to resist.... By definition, maneuver relies on speed and surprise, for without either we cannot concentrate strength against enemy weakness. Tempo is itself a weapon—often the most important. The need for speed in turn requires decentralized control.... The object of maneuver is not so much to destroy physically as it is to shatter the enemy cohesion, organization, command, and psychological balance.

Marine doctrine and thinking about war was and is, in large part, a function of its history, the enemies it has fought. The Marine Corps has not fought a Western army since World War I, and even that was a brief experience. Its doctrine was designed to fight non-Western armies, non-Western cultures—Asian, and Central and South American cultures. Its doctrinal thinking was also oriented towards "small wars." In some ways, Marine Corps thinking resembled that of the Air Force. Instead of finding, fixing, fighting, and destroying the enemy's main force in battle, it sought to circumvent it, to find a center of gravity that destroyed the enemy's cohesion. This required some way to get at the enemy's "inner rings," to get beyond the enemy outer ring of combat forces, to his center of gravity. How this was to be done was unclear.

In 1990, the Marine Corps further refined its thinking. It published FMFM 1–1 *Campaigning*. Under the heading "Maneuver" it stated:

> Typically, we think of maneuver as a function of relational movement and fire on a grand scale, but this is not necessarily the case. The Combined Action Program, begun by III Marine Amphibious Force under General Lewis Walt in 1965 during the Vietnam War, is an example of unconventional maneuver at the operational level. The program sought to make the Viet Cong guerrillas' position untenable by attacking their essential base of popular support through the pacification of South Vietnamese villages.[31]

With such a definition of "maneuver" almost anything could be defined as maneuver warfare.

Arguably both the Army and Marine Corps went back to their roots, went back and reoriented on the types of war they had historically fought and culturally preferred to fight. In the European Theater of Operation or against the Soviet Union the idea "to pose menacing dilemmas" or of causing "panic and paralysis" seemed nonsense; however, against a guerrilla force in an insurgency, or in a small war in Central or South America it made a great deal of sense. While the Army refocused on fighting another Western power of equivalent or greater power, the Marine Corps refocused on it cultural norms.

The Marine Corps has traditionally been a light infantry force. Infantrymen dominate its top leadership. Marines pride themselves on their "no-frills," "bare-bones" approach to war. America's heavy formations, which required long logistic trains, were in the Army, and the Marine Corps had no desire to look like the Army. As a rule, the Marines hated receiving assistance from the Army. They hated adopting or

complying with Army strategy, operational plans, organization, and doctrine. However, the Middle East posed a new and considerable problem for the Marine Corps. How to fight in open desert against an enemy's heavy, armored force? How to fight, for example, Saddam Hussein's Republican Guard equipped with Soviet T-72 tanks and BMP infantry fighting vehicles, and possibly chemical weapons? The force structure of the Marine Corps was not designed for such a fight. While promulgating a unique form of maneuver warfare doctrine, the Marine Corps had not developed a classic maneuver warfare force structure. As a consequence, to fight in Operation Desert Storm it had to make a number of adjustments to its organization. It had to form hybrid units, modify its doctrine, and depend on attached Army forces. The Marine Corps lacked sufficient numbers of tanks and the combined arms doctrine to fight armor forces on the European or Middle East battlefield. It also lacked an infantry fighting vehicle, a vehicle equivalent to the BMP or M2 Bradley, and its tanks were a generation behind. It had not yet transitioned from the M60A1 tank to the latest generation of the M1A1, and some in the Marine Corps believed there was no need to do so. One student of the marine operations, Kenneth W. Este, wrote:

> The tank, LAV, and AAV units came into their own as the 1st and 2nd Marine Divisions girded themselves for classic desert warfare. Unfortunately, no new progress in doctrine and training had occurred in the previous ten years, and the tank battalions had to "hold school" for the infantry regiments and their attachments on an ad hoc basis. In the end, each division and regiment developed its own procedures for joining AAV, infantry, engineer, tank, and anti-tank units into combined arms teams. All the active and most of the reserve armored vehicle battalions were sent to the force. These provided sufficient resources for each division to field two mounted regiments.[32]

For the Marine Corps, the tank was first and foremost an infantry support weapon. On the armored warfare battlefield in 1991, the 1st and 2nd Marine Divisions could not generate as much combat power as a single Armed Cavalry Regiment. However, on the insurgency and the urban terrain battlefields one marine regiment could generate more combat power than an entire armor division. However, force structure, equipment, and doctrine never determine the deployment of forces in wars fought by the US; interservice rivalry and Pentagon politics determine the order of battle. The Marine Corps did not belong on a mechanized warfare battlefield, but they could not sit out a war.

The Weinberger Strategic Doctrine: No More Graduated Response

With the recovery of the armed forces came new/old ways of thinking about war. The strategic doctrine adopted by the Reagan Administration might be characterized as "back to the future." World War II soldiers would have identified and been comfortable with it. After suffering trauma, humans tend to want to return to their roots, to their foundation. This is what the armed forces did. On 28 November 1984 Secretary of Defense Caspar Weinberger at the National Press Club in Washington, DC, promulgated "the Weinberger doctrine," which was intended to delineate the criteria for the deployment of American forces in war. The Weinberger doctrine was a Pentagon—more accurately an Army—response to the Vietnam War. Army Chief of Staff General Edward C. Meyer and Colonel Harry Summers greatly influenced it.[33] It was specifically designed to preclude another such war. However, its major emphasis was not on the criteria for war, but on the conduct of war.

This was an issue that many officers felt passionately about. Many of these men had dedicated their lives to the war in Vietnam, particularly regular Army and Marine officers and senior NCOs. Many had served multiple tours in Vietnam. They had lost and even witnessed the deaths of close friends. They had lived among the Vietnamese people, and formed multiple attachments. They had made promises to these people, based on promises political leaders had made to them. Many felt that the United States had betrayed the people of South Vietnam, particularly after Kennedy's approval of the overthrow of President Diem. Consider Westmoreland's words:

South Vietnam no longer exists; it has been gobbled up by North Vietnam following blatant aggression. The flicker of freedom there has been extinguished probably forever. Our erstwhile honorable country betrayed and deserted the Republic of Vietnam after it had enticed it to our bosom. It was a shabby performance by America, a blemish on our history and a possible blight on our future. Our credibility has been damaged. In our national interest, that unhappy experience should not be swept under the rug and forgotten.... There is ... one valid truth accepted by most: The handling of the Vietnam affair was a shameful national blunder.[34]

Westmoreland's words were angry and purposeful, but they reflected the sentiments of many officers who had served in Vietnam.[35] Westmoreland, and others, concluded that Kennedy was wrong when he stated in his inaugural address to the American people: "Let every nation know, whether it wishes us well or ill, that we shall pay any price, bear any burden, meet any hardship, support any friend, oppose any foe to assure the survival and the success of liberty." Westmoreland, in response, wrote: "*No one 'bore a burden, met a hardship' except those on the battlefield and their loved ones. In fact, if not for the sensational media coverage piped for the first time into homes of Americans, few would have appreciated that we were at war.*"[36] Similar words were written regarding the Korean War.[37] These profound, but for the most part unspoken, feelings of anger and betrayal were amplified back in the United States when the services were confronted with the anti-military attitudes and behaviors of many Americans and the government.

Few Americans outside of the military understand the trauma the Army experienced in the wake of the defeat in Vietnam. When the next war came, the Army, even though it had substantially rebuilt itself, was reluctant to fight. The Army retained a profound distrust of political leaders and the American people. The Army questioned their resolve and staying power. Just as the American people said "never again, no more Vietnams," many officers said the same. Some left the service, but others who stayed concluded that the government, and to some degree the American people, could not be trusted to conduct war in a manner that insured success. Hence, military leaders had to vigorously guide political leaders who typically lacked military experience.

The leaders of the services also operated with the knowledge that during the Vietnam War some senior military leaders were derelict in their duties as advisors to the commander-in-chief, possibly causing the nation's first defeat in war. In addition, it took decades to rebuild the Army, and no one wanted to see it deteriorate again for a lost cause. Thus, many senior military leaders were motivated by defeat, by a profound sense of loss, by love of country and service, by guilt, by a desire to rebuild and maintain their service, and by a desire to never let another Vietnam destroy America's confidence in America. This passion has to be understood to comprehend the conduct of the Persian Gulf War, and the behavior of senior Army leaders.

The Weinberger doctrine was supposedly written to establish the new rules of engagement; however, it went much further than that, and in many ways it was a return to culturally accepted tenets for war. It was also a strategy doctrine and strategy for war. Weinberger delineated "six major tests" to be applied when weighing the use of combat forces:

(1) FIRST, the United States should not commit forces to combat . . . unless the particular engagement is deemed vital to our national interest or that of our allies.

(2) SECOND, *if we decided it is necessary to put combat troops into a given situation, we should do so wholeheartedly, and with the clear intention of winning. If we are unwilling to commit the forces or resources necessary to achieve our objectives, we should not commit them at all.*

(3) THIRD, if we do decide to commit forces to combat overseas, we should have clearly defined political and military objectives. *And we should know precisely how our forces can accomplish those clearly defined objectives. And we should have and send the forces needed to do just that.* As Clausewitz wrote, "No one starts a war—or rather, no one in his senses ought to do so—without first being clear in his mind what he intends to achieve by that war, and how he intends to conduct it." *If we determine that a combat mission has become necessary for our vital national interests, then we must send forces capable to do the job—and not assign a combat mission to a force configured for peace keeping.*

(4) FOURTH, *the relationship between our objectives and the force we have committed—their size, composition and disposition—must be continually reassessed and adjusted if necessary. When they do change, then so must our combat requirements.* We must continuously keep as beacon lights before us the basic questions: "Is this conflict in our national interest?" "Does our national interest require us to fight, to use force of arms?" *If the answer is "yes," then we must win. If the answer is "no," then we should not be in combat.*

(5) FIFTH, before the US commits combat forces abroad there must be some reasonable assurance we will have the support of the American people and their elected representatives in Congress. . . . We cannot fight a battle with Congress at home while asking our troops to win a war overseas or, as in the case of Vietnam, in effect, asking our troops not to win, just to be there.

(6) SIXTH . . . the commitment of US forces to combat should be the last resort.[38]

MacArthur, in the dark, cold days of the Korean War, would have appreciated and endorsed these words. In fact, MacArthur would argue that the second and fourth tests of Weinberger's doctrine were paraphrases of his own words before the Senate after his relief. Much of the Weinberger doctrine was culturally American common sense, the kind of common sense that was used to fight World War II. However, the very reason for the development of limited war doctrines was to move away from this "all or nothing" approach to war. Ridgway and Taylor had argued against just this thinking. This was a long way from the "Clausewitzian" axiom that "the political objective—the original motive for the war—will thus determine both the military objective to be reached and the amount of effort it requires."[39] Weinberger's theory—like Reagan's rhetoric—postulated a black and white world with nothing in between. There were only two conditions: war or peace, victory or defeat. Hence, given the logic of this position, the Eighth Army in Korea would have had to complete the destruction of the Chinese People's Volunteer Army in North Korea, and advanced to the Yalu River. To do this the US would have had to use nuclear weapons. The "vital national interests" could not mean war short of "winning" a decisive victory. The Wienberger doctrine meant no war or more total war.

However, another way to interpret Weinberger's doctrine is to conclude that he meant the US would not fight another Vietnam War; the US would not get involved in another limited war on the periphery of the PRC or SU where they could directly intervene, because only the PRC and SU could force the US to fight a limited war where victory was not the objective. This was a practical doctrine that made enormous good sense. However, the phrasing left too much unclear, too much to the imagination.

Still, rather than being a test for the decision to go to war, the Weinberger doctrine was more accurately a doctrine for how to fight war. In the sentences in italics the issue is how to fight war. The use of force received considerably greater attention than the "support of the American people," and the "objectives" of war. Winning the war was the major issue. Among the tenets advanced were: supplying sufficient forces to rapidly achieve the objective; Americans *cannot* fight long wars; Americans *cannot* fight protracted wars of attrition; Americans *can* fight wars of annihilation. Wars had to be short, intense, and decisive. And a major part of the new American way of war was to fight the war in such a manner as to all but eliminate the American people from the equation. The wars the US elected to fight were all well within the capabilities of the standing forces. The American people were not to be disturbed. Wars were to be over before movements against them could develop. This required the use of overwhelming force; however, that force ideally was *not* to be generated by ground forces, where the vast majority of the casualties take place, eighty to ninety percent. It was to be generated by airpower in multiple forms, cruise-missiles, unmanned aerial vehicles, stealth aircraft, strategic bombers, fighter aircraft with long-range precision missiles, and helicopters. The US invested hundreds of billions of dollars in technology to remove man from the battlefield. The armed forces sought technologies to kill the enemy without risking American lives, an unspoken objective since the end of World War II.

The Weinberger doctrine evolved into the Colin Powell doctrine that was employed in Operation Just Cause, the 1989 invasion of Panama, and Operation Desert Storm, the 1991 invasion of Iraq.[40] Clearly defined obtainable political objectives, speed, overwhelming force, precision weapons, long-range engagements, airpower, Special Operations (including psychological warfare and civil affairs operations), so-called "exit strategies," the unspoken, non-involvement of the American people, and limited access for the media characterized American operational thinking in the post-Vietnam era. The armed forces wanted certainty, no ambiguity about objectives or the outcome; hence, the overwhelming employment of force in Operation Desert Storm.

The Goldwater Nichols Act: More Revision to the National Command Structure

Defeat in Vietnam, and subsequent operational failures, such as the failed hostage rescue operation in Iran in 1980, motivated another look at the national command structure, and ultimately the enactment of new legislation in 1986.[41] Yet, in 2000, General Anthony Zinni, USMC felt compelled to write:

> The National Security Act of 1947 set up the most dysfunctional, worst organizational approach to military affairs one can possibly imagine. In a near-perfect example of the Law of Unintended Consequences, it created a situation in which the biggest rival of any US armed service is not a foreign adversary but one of its sister services.[42]

Zinni's words were an indication that the last round of revisions had not produced the quality of cooperation and integration required to produce synergy in operations.

The National Security Act of 1947 and the Amendments of 1949 created a system of competing services with overlapping responsibilities and capabilities that damaged the ability of the United States to deploy forces, fight wars, and achieve political objectives. It contributed to the nation's first defeat in war, and facilitated the destruction of the citizen-soldier Army.[43] The services that had depended on the selfless service of the American people to function had proven incapable of acting selflessly during the latter half of the twentieth century. The inability of the American people to accept limited war doctrine was, in part, a function of the inability of the armed forces to effectively fight limited war. Thus, in 1982, the Congress of the United States again took up the issue of the organization of the national command structure. Numerous testimonies were heard. The Chairman of the Joint Chiefs of Staff, Air Force General David C. Jones, gave his assessment of the problems and delineated his recommendations. He started by outlining the historical development of the command structure, and continued with a frank admission of the failures:

> President Truman strongly urged the formation of an integrated Department of National Defense, but many within the War and Navy Departments and the respective Congressional Committee feared that integration would undermine the esprit and confuse the function of the established Services. Thus, the National Security Act of 1947 was a compromise that led to but limited integration of effort among our separate land, sea, and air arms. We have been trying ever since—with very limited success—to overcome this handicap.
>
> Vietnam was perhaps our worst example of confused objectives and unclear responsibilities. The organizational arrangements were a nightmare; for example, each Service fought its own air war. Since that time we have been concerned with how to react more effectively to contingencies, but have not as yet devised a way to integrate our efforts to achieve maximum joint effectiveness without undue regard to Service doctrine, missions and command prerogatives.
>
> Clearly our record has not been what it could and should have been. We got by in the past because of our industrial base and the factors of time and space which allowed us to mobilize that base. In the World Wars we had the buffers of geography and of allies who could carry the fight until we mobilized and deployed. After World War II we depended largely on our nuclear superiority to cover a growing imbalance of conventional capabilities and deter direct clashes with the Soviets.
>
> However, today we no longer have the luxury of the buffers which in the past had allowed us to mobilize, organize and deploy after a conflict began. . . . [W]e must free ourselves of the institutional and conceptual constraints of the past so

that we can develop better strategy and tactics and imaginative solutions to the defense problems of today and tomorrow. . . .[44]

Jones acknowledged that these problems were not new: "This latest study found very serious deficiencies in the joint system, but what is most striking is that, for the most part, those very deficiencies have been articulated by virtually every study conducted over the past twenty-four years, and in some cases much longer." The inability of America's political and military leaders to overcome cultural and bureaucratic norms, and inter-service animus has had profound costs to the nation. Jones delineated the problems:

> First, responsibility and authority are diffused, both in Washington and in the field. Because of this, we are neither able to achieve the maximum effective capability of the combined resources of the four Services nor to hold our military leadership accountable for this failure.
>
> Second, the corporate advice provided by the Joint Chiefs of Staff is not crisp, timely, very useful or very influential. And that advice is often watered down and issues are papered over in the interest of achieving unanimity. . . . Dissatisfaction with the corporate advice of the JCS was evident from the very beginning.
>
> Third, individual Service interests too often dominate JCS recommendations and actions at the expense of broader defense interests. . . . It occurs within the JCS because four of the five members are charged with the responsibility to maintain the traditions, esprit, morale and capabilities of their Services. . . . It has never been considered very beneficial for an officer's career to champion causes that lead to greater joint effectiveness at the expense of the institutional interests of his own Service.
>
> And fourth, a Service Chief does not have enough time to perform his two roles as a member of the Joint Chiefs and as the head of a Service—and these two roles have a built-in conflict of interest. . . . [T]he study group also confirmed that the conflict of interest problem still exists: "What the current system demands of the Chiefs is often unrealistic. They have one job that requires them to be effective advocates for their own Service; they have another that requires

them to subordinate Service interests to broader considerations; and they are faced with issues where the two positions may well be antithetical. It is very difficult for a Chief to argue in favor of something while wearing one of his 'hats', and against it while wearing the other. Yet that is what the current system often asks of the Service Chiefs.

None of this was new. Truman had made similar arguments. Not even war could overcome pull of service loyalty. In 1986, The Defense Reorganization Act became law. The objectives of the legislation were delineated:

> An Act to reorganize the Department of Defense and strengthen civilian authority in the Department of Defense, to improve the military advice provided to the President, the National Security Council, and the Secretary of Defense, to place clear responsibility on the commanders of the unified and specified combatant commands for the accomplishment of missions assigned to those commands and ensure that the authority of those commanders is fully commensurate with that responsibility, to increase attention to the formulation of strategy and to contingency planning, to provide for more efficient use of defense resources, to improve joint officer management policies, otherwise to enhance the effectiveness of military operations and improve the management and administration of the Department of Defense, and for other purposes. . . .[45]

The legislation strengthened the authority of the Chairman of the JCS: "The Chairman of the Joint Chiefs of Staff is the principal military adviser to the President, the National Security Council, and the Secretary of Defense." The duties of the JCS were transferred to the Chairman: "The Chairman shall establish procedures to ensure that the presentation of his own advice to the President, the National Security Council, or the Secretary of Defense is not unduly delayed by reason of the submission of the individual advice or opinion of another member of the Joint Chiefs of Staff." Members of the JCS that had views that differed from those of the CJCS had to go through the CJCS to render their opinion. Thus, by

law, the Chairman's military advice to the President was no longer circumscribed by the opinions of the other members of the JCS. The Chairman attended and participated in meetings of the National Security Council, subject to the direction of the President. Communication from the President and the Secretary of Defense to the unified combatant commands was to go through the Chairman. The Chairman was to facilitate communication between the President and the unified commanders, and serve as the spokesman for the commander of the unified combatant commands, particularly in operational requirements. The Chairman was not in the chain of command. It still went from the President to the Secretary of Defense to the unified and specified commanders. Still, the power of the CJCS was substantially increased.

The legislation provided for a Vice Chairman, and strengthened the authority of the unified and specified commanders. The Vice Chairman, in the absence of the Chairman, acts as the Chairman, and was considered to be training to become the Chairman. The Chairman and Vice Chairman could not be from the same service. Hence, no one service could again retain the Chairman position for more than the tenure of one officer. These amendments further demoted the position of the service chiefs. The legislation emphasized joint training. At a particular point in an officer's career it became mandatory for him/her to serve in a joint assignment: "officers may not be selected for promotion to the grade of brigadier general or rear admiral (lower half) unless the officer has served in a joint duty assignment." The objective was to promote inter-service understanding and cooperation, to overcome the bigotry produced by service culture. The Act imposed a new requirement on the President to "transmit to Congress each year a comprehensive report on the national security strategy of the United States," which included discussions on the worldwide interests, goals, and objectives of the US vital to national security; foreign policy, worldwide commitments, and national defense capabilities; the adequacy of the capabilities of the US to carry out national security strategy, and other such information as may be necessary to help inform Congress on matters relating to national security strategy.[46]

In 2005 the 16th Chairman of the JCS, Marine General Peter Pace, outlined his responsibilities:

The Chairman's role is to be a clear and independent voice, providing the best military advice in an apolitical, non-partisan manner.... The Chairman's responsibilities include strategy development, definition of roles and missions, contingency and strategic planning, programming and budgeting, and sustained readiness, along with other functions as delineated in US Code. The Chairman, and by extension the Joint Staff, is not in the operational chain-of-command and has no operational authority. Our task is to articulate the orders of our President and Secretary of Defense to those who do have that operational authority and to support the efforts of those empowered with it. We must be of assistance to the combatant commanders as they carry out the missions they have been assigned.

Pace concluded: "Consensus can be a worthy goal but not if the ultimate outcome is a recommendation that is so diluted it fails to satisfy the requirement or issue at hand."[47]

*   *   *   *   *

The Navy and Marine Corps opposed the Goldwater-Nichols legislation, and openly lobbied against it.[48] Secretary of the Navy, John Lehman, led the attack. In a letter to the Senate Armed Services Committee, Chaired by Senator Goldwater, he wrote: "I am surprised and disappointed that the serious effort that the service secretaries and the service chiefs devoted to your hearings seems to have largely been ignored in the staff effort." Lehman opposed the proposal strengthening the authority of the unified commanders, noting that the legislation would: "make the offices of the service secretary and service chief essentially ceremonial. In place of the former would be five CINC proconsuls [unified commands] freed from civilian control."[49] He also disagreed with strengthening the position of the CJCS and the position of Vice Chief of Staff.

The Commandant of the Marine Corps, P.X. Kelley, vehemently supported Lehman's position. He wrote:

If the 'draft bill' were to be enacted in its current form it would result in a significant degradation in the efficiency and effectiveness of the defense establishment—to the point where I would have deep concerns for the future security of the United States. In this regard, I know of no document which has concerned me more in my 36 years of uniformed service to my country.

Kelley noted that, "The 'draft bill' virtually destroys the corporate nature of the Joint Chiefs of Staff." He opposed strengthening the unified commands: "In my professional view, this chapter of the 'draft bill' would create chaos between the duties and responsibilities of the service chiefs and those of the CINCs. It provides a complex, unworkable solution to an ill-defined problem. This is an exceptionally dangerous chapter.... It will create more disharmony than jointness." Kelley concluded, "My opinion is that these proposals are alien to good logic and common sense, and the only 'consensus' is among the drafters themselves."[50]

While all the services voiced their disagreement with the legislation, James L. Locher III, who worked with Goldwater to pass the Act, noted the letters from the Army and Air Force were "less strident." He also noted that the Navy's establishment of an office to defeat the legislation particularly angered Goldwater: "Can you believe that? They're not supposed to lobby Congress on legislation."[51] In fact, this was a common and long accepted practice. The Navy and Marine Corps together had two votes in JCS deliberations. In 1978 the Commandant of the Marine Corps became a full member of the JCS. The Marine Corps was still under the Secretary of the Navy and dependent on the Navy. A CJCS that did not have to operate on consensus diminished the power of the Navy and Marine Corps. The Navy and Marine Corps concluded that the legislation would reduce their power to determine their future. However, their worries were as unnecessary as they were in the late 1940s and early 1950s.

On the other hand, for some senior Army officers the legislation did not go far enough. General Edward C. Meyer, US Army, disagreed with the approach of General Jones that was made law. He recommended that the advisory function of the JCS be separated from the responsibilities of the service chiefs, and other changes:

I believe that we must consider the feasibility of changes beyond the ones proposed by General

Jones creating a stronger chairman and Joint Staff. We must find a way to provide better balanced, sounder, and more timely advice from senior Service professionals in addition to strengthening the Chairman and the Joint Staff. . . . This "dual-hatting," dictated by law, confers real power with the Service Chief hat and little ability to influence policy, programming, and budget issues with the joint hat. This is the root cause of the ills which so many distinguished officers have addressed these past 35 years. . . . The JCS, while charged with the responsibility to conceive, plan, and organize a defense founded on a unified command structure, has never been provided the means to realize these plans. In particular, they continue to lack real linkages with the resource allocation process. . . . As currently worked in the resource allocation process today, we do not make a true horizontal examination. Rather, we focus on single Services or on functions—vertical slices—, which in aggregate yield less than what might otherwise be attainable.[52]

Meyer noted that: "All of this accounts for a long thread of continuity in the critiques of General Bradley, Gavin, Taylor, and Jones. . . ." Remarkably, the positions of the Army, Navy, and Marine Corps had not changed since World War II. Meyer recommended the separation of functions, the creation of a "National Military Advisory Council." The Joint Staff would work for the Chairman and the four generals on the council. The council would be responsible for strategic planning and operational planning. The service chiefs would administer and supervise the development, training, and sustainment of their individual services. Meyer's solution had the potential for greatly diminishing the problem of conflicting loyalties in matters of strategic and operational planning. Meyer's proposal was also not new. In 1952, when the 1953 legislation was being debated, a member of the Rockefeller Committee, Vannevar Bush, and General Omar Bradley had made a similar proposal, the establishment of a "National Military Council." They too believed that creation of a joint planning group of senior military leaders, divorced from their roles as service advocates, would produce integrated strategic plans as opposed to compromised, patchwork plans where each service did essentially what it wanted to do.[53] This solution, however, was too

radical. Thus, in the view of Meyer and Zinni, another partial fix was enacted. In 1947, 1949, 1953, 1958, and 1986 the US Congress passed legislation to reorganize the national defense structure, and in 2003 further change was recommended.

While the Goldwater-Nichols Act represented change, it did not fundamentally alter traditional relationships between the services. It did not fix the problem of the service chiefs serving in two capacities. It did not create a joint service culture, or significantly change the service cultures. It did not fix the problem of joint training. And most significantly, it did not alter the inexorable pull of service loyalty. The services did, however, endeavor to work together with greater cooperation, and initiated the development of joint doctrine—the new Joint Forces Command (JFC) was supposed to oversee the development of joint doctrine. Part of the reason for this was to keep civilian leaders from making crucial decisions. It was better to compromise on a decision than endure one that went completely against the objectives of one service. The services also recognized each other's right to exist, at least at the senior-most level; and thus, each service deserved a piece of the pie.

In the wake of the Goldwater-Nichols Act the Pentagon determined that the commander-in-chiefs of the nine unified/specified commands were, for the most part, interchangeable. Army, Air Force, or Marine general or an admiral could command Central Command, European Command, Special Operations Command, and so on. While the Navy managed to hang on to the Pacific Command, if this trend continued, a Marine or Air Force General could occupy this position. Is it true that service expertise matter little at the senior-most level? Is it true that an Army general could develop Pacific Theater strategy as well as a Navy admiral, or that a Marine general could develop theater strategy for the US Army's and NATO's heavy armor formations as well as an Army general, or that an Air Force officer could develop a plan for Special Operations Forces as well as an Army Special Operations general? The concept of jointness practiced at the dawn of the twenty-first century was still deeply flawed. However, this would not be transparent until the United States fought another major war.

*   *   *   *   *

After the failed hostage rescue operation in Iran, Congress passed the Cohen-Nunn Act, which created the United States Special Operations Command (USSOCOM), a four-star joint operational command.[54] It was believed that part of the reason for the failure was a lack of unity of command. Hence, all Special Operations Forces, including those of the Army, Navy, and Air Force, were placed under a single command, which provided the five geographic, combatant commanders with the units required to conduct special operations. However, in the aftermath of 9/11, unity of command again became a problem, as the Rumsfeld Pentagon sought ways to conduct operations in various parts of the world without going through the geographic, unified commanders. One problem was that to track down terrorists and find WMD, Special Forces had to cross the boundaries of geographic commanders. This created additional points of coordination where breakdowns in communications were possible. Another problem was that limited Special Operations resources had to be transferred from one geographic commander to another and from one operational environment to another, creating points of friction.

PART III

THE NEW AMERICAN PRACTICE OF WAR

13.
THE PERSIAN GULF WAR: OPERATION DESERT SHIELD, 1990–1991

No good soldier wants to go to war and would prefer instead to see all other options exhausted. . . . At the same time, our military never tried to avoid using force either, nor did they speak out against it. Colin Powell, ever the professional, wisely wanted to be sure that if we had to fight, we would do it right and not take half measures. He sought to ensure that there were sufficient troops for whatever option I wanted, and then the freedom of action to do the job once the political decision had been made. I was determined that our military would have both. I did not want to repeat the problem of the Vietnam War . . . where the political leadership meddled with military operations. I would avoid micromanaging the military.[1]

—George Bush and Brent Scowcroft, *A World Transformed*, 1998

In the Persian Gulf War in 1991, the Armed Forces of the United States demonstrated to the world their new capabilities, recovering a reputation that had been badly tarnished in Vietnam.[2] President Bush told the nation the "Vietnam syndrome" was finally behind us.[3] The short war, low casualties, and decisive defeat of one of the largest armies on the planet, was arguably a function of the Goldwater-Nichols Act, the Reagan military buildup, the Weinberger/Powell doctrine, the efforts of military leaders to reconstruct the armed forces, the type of civil-military relations practiced by President George Bush, and the new, more assertive and unified military leadership. However, the coalition led by the US fought a single, isolated, non-Western, developing *state* that depended on Western technology and know-how to maintain its armed forces. Arab states and Muslim cultures have militarily performed very poorly against Western *nations*. Operation Desert Storm was *not* a real test of the recently resurrected armed forces of the United States.

Operation Desert Storm was fought with the Cold War armed forces. The services had not had time to reassess the threats, and types of technology and doctrine needed in the new "world order." And the "peace dividend" had not yet eradicated forty percent of the Army, or significant forces of the other services. Operation Desert Storm was only possible because of the collapse of the Soviet Union, and the end of the Cold War. Had the Soviet Union existed and continued its support of Iraq, geographically it would have been a major, strategic blunder to go to war there, and it would have been impossible to redeploy the VII Corps from Europe to Iraq.

The US Army that went into the Persian Gulf War did so with a considerable lack of confidence. The majority of combat arms officers who were not serving in combat units did not rush to transfer back to the combat units they called home. They believed they would get their chance to fight soon enough. No one predicted a 100-hour ground war. Many officers believed that war in the deserts of the Persian Gulf, with the political objective to save Kuwait, was a bad idea. They saw the potential to alienate the entire Arab and Muslim world, and to end up fighting a very different war than that planned by the Bush Administration. They understood that, as in Vietnam, the American people had no cultural affinity to the people of Kuwait. They worried about the media and how it would portray the war. They worried that the Bush Administration would micro-manage the war, precluding them from using the full potential of their forces. They worried about the enemy's use of chemical or biological weapons, recognizing that US forces had never operated in such an environment, and were not fully equipped or trained to do so. They worried about operating in the deserts, recognizing that their forces were geared and equipped for war in Europe, and not designed, equipped, or conditioned for extended periods in extreme heat and sand. They worried about Iraqi defenses, fully understanding that the Army since World War II had demonstrated poor mastery of minefield breaching operations. Some officers pessimistically predicted thousands of casualties, even tens of thousands. While the Army had recovered materially, technologically, and qualitatively during the Reagan Administration, it had not completely recovered emotionally and psychologically. As a consequence, the Army greatly overestimated the combat potential of Iraqi forces, and underestimated its own capabilities. This lack of confidence definitely influenced the conduct of the war.

The Army's reliance on airpower to destroy and attrit enemy ground forces, a job it typically retained for itself, did not conform to Army history, culture, and doctrine, which held that ground forces were the fastest, most efficient means for destroying an enemy's main army. The air war plan called for the Air Force to destroy as much as fifty percent of Iraqi ground forces. This was unprecedented. The Army, as it had in Vietnam, accepted a doctrine and strategy in which the Air Force was supposed to be the decisive instrument for the conduct of the war.

Operation Desert Storm was in many ways an aberration. First, it was not a national effort. There was no draft, and for the most part the regular, active duty forces fought the war. Second, coming as it did at the end of the Cold War, the armed forces were supremely prepared to fight what was in essence a "Third World" state. The armed forces had only just started the process of the post-Cold War draw down when they were called upon to fight the fourth largest army on Earth. Third, the US fought a state, *not a nation*, not a culturally cohesive people with nationally accepted leaders. The US went to war against a

dictator and his army. And fourth, the US did not seek total victory. It sought very limited objectives. The war in Iraq was another artificial limited war, the first fought without the prevalence of the danger of Soviet or Chinese intervention. In 1991 the Army was not trying to build a nation, win the hearts and minds of the people, nor equip and train a national army. These factors greatly influenced the outcome of the war.

In terms of strategic outcomes, however, the Persian Gulf War was familiar. It looked, in many ways, like the Korean War. While saving Kuwait, the US failed to complete the destruction of the enemy's main army achieving only one of its two political objectives. This left significant enemy forces just across the Kuwaiti border, calling for continuous vigilance against further aggression, and the constant presence of US and British forces in the region. These surviving forces also made it possible for Saddam Hussein to retain political control of Iraq, by brutally suppressing the Kurds and Shia, who sought to overthrow his government. Still, the war was a significant victory that had important consequences for the region. One of the unexpected results of the war occurred at home, the complete restoration of the armed forces of the United States in the hearts and minds of the American people. Operation Desert Storm gave the American people an Army they could be proud of again. This was no small matter.

Saddam Hussein's Decision to Invade Kuwait

On 2 August 1990, the armed forces of Iraq invaded Kuwait. Saddam Hussein's objective was to incorporate the small, oil-rich kingdom into Iraq.[4] One study concluded that in the wake of the eight-year Iran-Iraq War, Iraq was near exhaustion and:

> it seems obvious that Iraq invaded its neighbor because it was desperate. It had a million-man army that it could not demobilize, because it had no jobs to send the men home to. It had no jobs because its economy had been ruined by the war. It could not get its economy going again until it demobilized. Thus, the Iraqi leadership saw itself trapped in a vicious dilemma. At the same time, Kuwait was fabulously wealthy, and Iraq—by seizing it—could hope to exploit its wealth to resolve its economic problems.[5]

Kuwait has a population of 2.3 million, of which approximately forty-five percent are native Kuwaitis; a geographic area of 6,880 square miles (about the size of New Jersey); and its major industry is oil. Kuwait possesses oil reserves of 94 billion barrels, the world's third largest.

Before the war with Iran, Iraq too was fabulously wealthy. The war paralyzed entire sectors of its economy as one-third of Iraqi workers went off to fight. Oil revenues dropped from $26 billion per year to $10 billion. To keep its economy from collapsing, Iraq "imported" nearly one million Egyptian workers. To finance the war, Iraq exhausted its surplus of over a hundred billion dollars, and borrowed tens of billions of dollars from Kuwait and Saudi Arabia. When the war ended in 1988, Iraq was deeply in debt to its neighbors. Saddam Hussein sought various means of debt relief, which failed. He tried to manipulate the price of oil by threatening OPEC member nations. However, the world's most influential and largest oil-producing nation, Saudi Arabia, with the support of Kuwait, was unmoved. Saddam Hussein sought to intimidate his neighbors. He charged Kuwait with stealing billions of dollars of oil. Kuwait and Iraq shared a "neutral zone," consisting of oil fields that were jointly owned. Saddam Hussein accused Kuwait of taking more than its share, and demanded debt release and tens of billion of dollars to help Iraq rebuild its war-damaged infrastructure. Saddam Hussein believed that Iraq had fought to secure not only Iraq, but also Kuwait and Saudi Arabia. He believed Iraq had stopped the spread of the Iranian-Shia fundamentalist revolution, and that Kuwait had failed to acknowledge its blood debt to Iraq. In July 1990, when Kuwait refused the relief that Iraq sought, Saddam Hussein's patience came to an end.

The impressive arsenal of modern weapons provided to Saddam Hussein during his war against Iran—by France, the Soviet Union, and to a lesser degree the US—played no small part in his decision for war. Between 1980 and 1988, Iraq spent an average of $6 billion dollars a year on weapons. By eagerly providing these weapons, the West created another regional superpower. Working under the thesis that Iraq was stopping the spread of the Iranian fundamentalist revolution, and under the doctrine that "the enemy of my enemy is my friend," US policy "tilted" toward Iraq. The US assisted Iraq in its search for modern sophisticated weapons by:[6]

(1) the provision of credit guarantees by the Agriculture Department's Commodity Credit Corporation (CCC) for the purchase by Iraq of American agricultural products (thereby freeing up Iraq funds for military purchases); (2) the secret handover of sensitive intelligence information of Iranian military positions (much of it gleaned from satellite photography); (3) the sale to Iraq of American 'dual-use' items with obvious military applications, such as transport planes, helicopters, heavy trucks and scientific gear; and (4) the transfer to Iraq of weapons given by the United States to its allies in the region, including Egypt, Jordan, Kuwait, and Saudi Arabia.[7]

Saddam Hussein developed the capability to produce ballistic missiles and chemical and biological weapons from technologies and machinery acquired from the West. He was also in the process of acquiring the ability to produce nuclear weapons. Western nations, including the US, influenced this effort by assisting Israel in its acquisition of nuclear weapons, creating the incentive for states such as Iraq and Iran to acquire the atomic bomb, and by indirectly providing Saddam Hussein with the knowledge and technologies required.

Saddam Hussein's arsenals influenced his decision not only because of the number and types of weapons he possessed, but also because of his perceptions of the quality of his technology. Saddam Hussein believed Iraq possessed first-class Soviet and French equipment, the same weapons deployed in NATO. He believed that his technology, his tanks and airplanes, were relatively equal to those of the US. Neither he, nor the rest of the world, grasped the enormous disparity between US technology and that of Iraq's sponsors. Indeed, military leaders in the US did not fully grasp the enormous qualitative differences. This perception of relative equality caused miscalculations on both sides.

Geography also influenced Saddam Hussein's decision. Kuwait was a prize not only because of its oil reserves, but also because it rounded-out Iraq, making it more defensible and providing greater access to the sea. Saddam Hussein claimed that Kuwait had historically and legitimately been part of Iraq, a claim that was also made in 1961, when Kuwait achieved independence from Britain.[8] Saddam Hussein endeavored to portray himself as a modern-day Saladin, the hero of the Islamic world, who, during the Middle Ages, fought against the invading Crusaders. Saddam Hussein argued that Iraq's struggle was the struggle of the entire Arab world against Western imperialism. He argued for a united Arab state: "We don't look on this piece of land here in Iraq as the ultimate limit of our struggle. It is part of a larger area and broader aims: the area of the Arab homeland and the aim of the Arab struggle."[9] It has been argued that Saddam Hussein was a madman, a megalomaniac who saw himself as the unifier of the Arab world. And, it is certain, Saddam Hussein endeavored to enhance his prestige and position in the Arab world through war. However, Saddam Hussein's actions were calculated.

Saddam Hussein endeavored to determine what actions the US would take if he invaded Kuwait. He knew American spy satellites had detected his redeployment of forces to the Kuwaiti borders, and that Washington was well aware of his threats and grievances towards Kuwait. Saddam Hussein summoned the US Ambassador to Iraq, April Glaspie, to discuss Kuwait. He asked that she return to Washington to voice his concerns about the recent deployments of US forces to the region and Kuwait. He was informed that: "The President personally wants to expand and deepen the relationship with Iraq...." And that: "we [the US] don't have much to say about Arab-Arab differences like your border differences with Kuwait.... All we hope is that you solve these matters quickly...."[10] In her report to Washington she concluded that, "we have fully caught his attention;" and recommended that "we ... ease off on public criticism of Iraq."[11] With this understanding, the supportive relationship that had developed between the US and Iraq, and the knowledge of the American experience in Vietnam, Saddam Hussein convinced himself that the US would take no significant military action. The Bush Administration, like the Truman and Johnson Administrations before it, had sent the wrong signals and underestimated the ambitions and will of the opponent. It had also failed in intelligence collection,

interpretation, and analysis. One student of the war, Michael T. Klare, wrote: "Not one to take risks needlessly, Saddam would have never given the green light to an invasion if he believed that the costs would be excessive. ... It was only because he determined that the risk of a counterattack was very low that he decided to go ahead."[12] On 1 August 1990, Saddam Hussein issued the order to invade Kuwait.

The UN responded quickly to the invasion of Kuwait, promulgating Resolution 660, which demanded that, "Iraq withdraw immediately and unconditionally all its forces to the position in which they were located on 1 August 1990." Saddam Hussein ignored the UN, and four days later the 82nd Airborne Division started deploying from Fort Bragg, North Carolina, to Saudi Arabia for what would become known as Operation Desert Shield. At the same time the UN Security Council passed a second resolution (661), which determined that "Iraq so far has failed to comply with ... resolution 660 and has usurped the authority of the legitimate Government of Kuwait ... determined to bring the invasion and occupation of Kuwait by Iraq to an end and to restore the sovereignty, independence and territorial integrity of Kuwait." The UN also imposed trade sanctions, and an embargo around Iraq. The questions were: would sanctions be enough, and how much time should be allowed for sanctions to work before military action was taken? With the support of the British, the UN, the Arab League, and European NATO allies, President George Bush formed and led a 37-nation coalition that had the limited objective of restoring Kuwait.

The West created the conditions and the monster it sought to destroy in 1990. Western nations, including the US, continued to support Saddam Hussein even when he employed chemical weapons against Iranians and his own people. One student of the war wrote: "One of the many ironies of this war lay in the fact that Saddam's worst atrocities were downplayed. ... His gassing of the Kurds and Iranians during the Iraq-Iran war brought only peripheral protest, because his fight then was directed against the then 'threat-of-the-moment'—Iran's Ayatollah."[13] The West's support of the Israeli nuclear program, willingness to look the other way when Saddam Hussein used WMDs, and willingness to provide weapons to both Iraq and Iran destroyed its credibility as a force for peace in the Middle East, and its argument for intervention on moral grounds.[14]

The Iraqi Army: Too Much Respect and Awe

The Iraqi Army in 1990 was a highly respected, well-equipped, combat-experienced fighting force. In 1980, Saddam Hussein attacked Iran, seeking to capitalize on the internal disorder to seize coveted land.[15] However, Iran, with a population of 45.2 million, was not as disabled as Saddam Hussein believed. The Iranians, using crude tactics, poorly trained soldiers, and poorly maintained American-made equipment, fought back tenaciously, causing Iraq to fully mobilize. Iraq, with a population of 19.1 million, built an armed force of 1 million men, with a reserve corps of 480,000 men. In 1988, Iran and Iraq signed a cease-fire agreement, and in November the following year, Saddam Hussein told the Iraqi people, "you entered the war with 12 divisions … now we have 70. The entire world has not seen such a development. Neither in World War I or World War II … has the world witnessed a country of 19 million producing 70 divisions."[16] While this proclamation was a bit of an exaggeration, it wasn't far from the truth.

The Iraqi Army was organized along Soviet lines. It fought primarily with Soviet technology. However, after eight years of war, Iraq had produced its own way of fighting, its own operational and tactical doctrine. The Army was organized into 7 regular army corps headquarters, 2 Republican Guard sub-corps, and 3 reserve crops. It had a total of 63 divisions, 9 heavy armored divisions (including 1 reserve and 2 Republican Guard), 5 mechanized divisions (including 2 Republican Guard), 18 motorized infantry divisions (including 8 Republican Guard, 5 of these newly formed), and 31 infantry divisions (including 14 reserve divisions). Iraq also employed 20 Special Forces brigades. The Iraqi Army could field between 4,000 and 5,000 main battle tanks, of which 500 were T–72M1s and 500 T–72Bs and –Gs. The latest model T–72 mounted a 125-mm smoothbore gun with a range of 2,000 meters. Still the majority of Iraqi armor consisted of older generations of Soviet and British tank technology; 3,000, T–54/55/62; 1,500 T–59/69; 150, British Chieftain. The Iraqi Army could field 4,000 infantry fighting vehicles, primarily

Soviet-made BMPs, and maintained an impressive artillery arsenal, possessing 122, 132, and 152-mm guns capable of firing high explosive, smoke, illumination, antipersonnel, and chemical munitions.[17]

The Iraqis had a well-developed chemical warfare doctrine. Chemical munitions were integrated into operation against Iran to good effect. In 1984, a chemical attack was used to block an Iranian attack. The Iraqis used nerve and mustard gas. A Marine Corps study noted: "The Iraqis developed their proficiency in chemical weapons gradually during the war with Iran. They were motivated to find a solution to the impact of Iranian human wave infantry attacks which—like that of the Chinese attacks on US forces in Korea—was devastating."[18]

The Iraqi Air Force was the sixth largest on the planet. It consisted of approximately 40,000 men and 10,000 air defense soldiers. It was equipped primarily with Soviet technology possessing roughly 1,000 aircraft, including fighters, fighter-bombers, and bombers. It was organized into twenty-two attack squadrons flying MiG 23s, French Mirage F1 EQ5s, and various other Soviet aircraft; 17 interceptor squadrons flying MiG 29s, 25s, 21s, French Mirage F1 EQs, and other Chinese and Soviet aircraft; two bomber squadrons flying Soviet Tu–22s, 16s, and Chinese H–6s; and one reconnaissance squadron flying MiG 25s, and 21s.[19] The Iraqis also employed almost 500 Soviet, French, and German attack helicopters. The Iraq Air Force in the air was no match for the US Air Force. However, Soviet air defense systems were impressive. They had tested and retested in the Vietnam War.

In the aftermath of two impressive, victorious wars against Iraqi conventional forces, it is difficult to recall the respect and even awe in which the Iraqi Army was held by the US military prior to Operation Desert Storm. It is difficult to remember how reluctant senior military leaders were to get involved. In a memorandum circulated through the Army by the Command and General Staff College, in the months prior to war, it was noted that:

> The Iraqi Army was in combat against the Iranians for eight years and developed into a battle-hardened force capable of conducting effective offensive and defensive operations. The Iraqi Army polished its offensive capability,

achieving good results during final operations against the Iranians. ... An elite force, the Republican Guard Forces command was initially organized to protect the Iraqi government. Later, this force was employed in highly successful offensive operations against the Iranians. Recently brigades of the Republican Guards conducted the Blitz type attack into Kuwait. ... The Iraqi soldier is a tough resilient foe equipped with modern weapons and capable vehicles.[20]

And a study conducted by the US Army War College, Strategic Studies Institute concluded:

Iraq's achievement in forcing Iran to accept a truce represents an authentic victory. The victory was attained because the Iraqis planned for and successfully executed complicated, large-scale military operations and shrewdly managed their resources. Claims that they won simply by using massive amounts of chemical weapons cannot be substantiated. ... The report further concludes that—contrary to general belief—Iraq's rulers enjoy significant popular support. The authors base this conclusion on the Ba'thists' ability to order a general call-up during what was perhaps the darkest period of the war. The willingness of the population to comply with the regime's order in effect confirmed its legitimacy. ...

In the specific sphere of military operations, the study concludes that a cadre of genuinely competent professional officers exists within the Iraq military. The group is fully capable of keeping pace with the latest innovations in weapons technology. The officer corps understands and is committed to the conduct of combined arms operations to include the integration of chemical weapons. It commands soldiers who, because of their relatively high education level, are able to carry out such operations.[21]

In *Army* magazine, in an article entitled, "The Republican Guards: Loyal, Aggressive, Able," it was noted that: "Iraq's Republican Guard Corps has grown to become a formidable armored and mechanized infantry force, well equipped, disciplined and blooded in combat."[22] And the soldiers of the VII Corps were told that, "Iraq was a third-rate power with a first-rate

army, toughened by eight years of hard combat experience...."

Marine Corps studies drew similar conclusions. A study produced in 1990 noted:

Iraq emerged from its war with Iran as a superpower in the Persian Gulf. ... Iraq achieved regional superpower status through a series of escalatory steps that were required to repel Iran's Islamic fundamentalist crusade. Iraqi leaders mobilized a diverse population, strengthened Iraq's armed force, and transformed its society to take the offensive and terminate the war with Iran.[23]

The Marine Corps' publication argued that the Iraqi Army was in fact a national army that had the support of the people: "Iraq fields a 'people's' army. The regime initiated a total call-up of available manpower in 1986. The response was good. No draft riots occurred; young men—even college students—reported without incident. The fact that the public answered the call tells us that Iraqis support their government." In fact, a large ethnic minority, the Kurds, hated Saddam Hussein, and did not serve. The Marine study further argued that: "Iraq's General Staff is not political. ... It is not interested in mixing in politics, and will not do so as long as the army's honor is upheld. One of the major changes wrought by the war was the weakening of political control over the army." The Marine study concluded that:

The army has high institutional self-esteem. Morale is good after the victory over Iran. The average soldier sees himself as the inheritor of an ancient tradition of warfighting—the Iraqis primarily spread the might of Islam in the 7th century. Officers are well trained and confident, and as long as Saddam does nothing to impair the dignity of the army, they will back him to the hilt.

With these words, the Army and Marine Corps bestow on the Iraqi Army the respect typically held only for extraordinary Western armies. Both the Army and Marine Corps concluded that Iraq was in fact a nation, that Saddam Hussein enjoyed the support of the Iraqi people, that they were willing to fight for him, and that Iraq had achieved "victory" in its war against Iran. They concluded that the Iraqi Army, after eight years of fighting, was a highly professional, well-led, competent military force, with a professional officer corps. They concluded that Iraqi forces were a combined arms army, capable of executing complex maneuvers, and that it was "superb" in defensive operations. They did not accept the verdict from the Arab-Israeli Wars, which held that, while Arab soldiers were tactically competent and courageous, their leadership, being selected primarily for political reasons, was, for the most part, mediocre, or worse, incompetent, that cultural norms impaired the ability of Arabs to master the Western way of war, and that operationally the military effectiveness of Arab forces lagged far behind that of Western nations, primarily because they were not meritocracies. The best people and best ideas could not rise to the top.

Chemical munitions and minefields presented unique, significant problems. For half a century the US Army demonstrated a minimal competency in breaching minefields, and while it possessed the capability to operate in a chemical environment, such weapons greatly impeded the conduct of operations, significantly slowing the movement of forces. The US Army had never conducted operations in a chemical environment of the magnitude it was believed the Iraqis were capable of producing. And the Army did not possess enough NBC equipment and trained personnel to service itself, the Marine Corps, and coalition forces. Had US forces fought in an NBC environment, its combat power in every aspect would have been significantly degraded.

In hindsight, the Iraqi Army was not as proficient as many in the Army and Marine Corps feared, and, at best, it had achieved a stalemate in the war against Iran. At the dawn of the twenty-first century, having the most powerful, modern armed force on Earth, it is difficult for Americans to remember how defeat in Vietnam and the failed Iranian hostage rescue operation had damaged the confidence and morale of American forces. Under Reagan, the armed forces had recovered materially and professionally. And in Operation Just Cause in 1989, they demonstrated a high level of competency. However, they had not fought a major "nation" since the defeat in Vietnam. The armed forces of the US did not go into Operation Desert Storm with the confidence it demonstrated

later in 2003 in Operation Iraqi Freedom. And the first Bush Administration went into the war with a little humility, and a genuine concern that it had the real support of allies, who ultimately pledged $50 billion to pay for the war. Schwarzkopf remembered the uncertainty: "Then I sat back to watch the victory unfold . . . while the politicians and military experts who had warned that dire things would happen if we went to war were eating their words."[24]

Fear caused by the Iranian counter-invasion in 1984 to some degree unified Iraq. However, there were deep cultural and religious fractures in Iraqi society that diminished its capacity to maintain that unity. Iraq was *not* a nation. It was a state, which lacked the potential to produce or maintain a modern army. Iraq produced neither the finished materials nor the sophisticated technologies required to construct a modern army. It was dependent on Russia and the West for its war-making capacity. Formed by the British in 1922, Iraq was essentially three nations. A quick study of the geography of the region reveals that political boundaries were imposed by external powers with no consideration given to natural geographic boundaries, the people of the region, or their history and culture. In 1932 the British granted Iraq its independence, but stayed to manage the country's affairs until 1958.[25] That year, military officers overthrew the monarchy. In 1968 the Ba'ath Party seized power. Saddam Hussein came to power in 1979. He immediately conducted a Stalin-like purge of his political competition, and created the fear required to maintain control in a police state. The next year he took the state to war. The Shias, the largest ethnic group, had no love or affinity for Saddam Hussein, a Tikrit, Sunni Muslim. Saddam Hussein was not a Mao Tse Tung or a Ho Chi Minh, authentic national leaders.[26] Nor was he a Hitler who was charismatic, but a fatalistic megalomaniac consumed by hate and bent on destruction. Saddam Hussein was more like Stalin, a ruthless opportunist who led by fear, distrusted his people, and periodically purged potential challengers to his leadership. Saddam Hussein led and maintained power through the Ba'ath Party, nepotism, internal security forces, and loyal, elite Army corps. He was not a mad man, as some have argued. He did not employ his chemical weapons capabilities against the US and coalition forces—demonstrating respect for

US nuclear arsenals. And after eight years of war he returned territory to Iran in exchange for its neutrality. Saddam Hussein was capable of rational behavior. He was not suicidal. His ignorance of the world outside Iraq, overconfidence in the capabilities of his forces, and lack of intelligence sources caused him to continuously miscalculate.

Saddam Hussein's war plans were based on his assessment of the Communist strategy in the Vietnam War. His strategic objective was to influence the will of the American people. He believed this was the center of gravity. He believed that Americans had a strong aversion to casualties, and that when the body bags started coming home in large numbers the American people would demand an end to the war. Saddam Hussein did not expect to defeat the armed forces of the US on the battlefield. He planned to bleed them until the American people cried, "Stop!"

While bestowing on the Iraqi Army the qualities of Western armies, some in the Army and Marine Corps took a few steps back toward the Israeli assessment, concluding that culture mattered, and that Arab culture limited Iraq's military effectiveness:

> In spite of this progress, the weaknesses of the Iraqi Army appear to remain the same. The Iraqis required detailed planning and careful execution to perform effectively. They are tenacious in the defense, but 'doctrinally inclined to fight set piece battles seeking to lure their enemy into prearranged killing zones where, once the artillery has broken the momentum of the attack, an armor heavy counterattack would be launched.' They have a short logistical tail, and have problems supporting extended drives. They are still beginners at effective cooperation between joint forces. And, there is always the tendency by the Ba'athist Party to politicize and rigorously control the armed forces to maintain Saddam Hussein 's grip on power.[27]

The Army's thesis was essentially the same as the thesis of this work: the Iraq Army, like the armed forces of the United States, could not override its cultural inheritance. It could improve, but it did so essentially along cultural lines. And, therein lay its major weakness. Its soldiers lacked initiative; its commanders were afraid to improvise; cooperation between the services was lacking; a system of promotion based on merit was only partially accepted, a requirement of war with Iran; relatively little attention was given to logistics; the NCO Corps did not perform adequately, serving as an intermediate body that translated and transmitted orders and information between decision-makers to those who executed the decisions; and armed forces operated best with specific, detailed instruction and with well-rehearsed tactics and operations. The fog of war significantly impaired the operational effectiveness of the Iraqi Army. Without an honest, competitive, meritocracy it is impossible for the most talented to rise to the top. Saddam Hussein's police state worsened the cultural disadvantages of the Iraqi Army. The Iraqi Army may have also suffered from an inferiority complex, recognizing that Arab armies had performed very poorly in conventional operations against Western nations, and that it faced the most powerful state on Earth. While there were varying assessments of the combat effectiveness of the Iraqi Army, the Army and Marine Corps tended to overestimate its professional attainment. In war, while it is much better to overestimate the combat effectiveness of one's enemy than to underestimate it, too much respect can influence the outcome of the war, causing victorious states to seek partial victory when a more complete victory was possible and in its grasp. Such was the case in Operation Desert Storm. The US settled for a partial victory.

Bush's War or America's War?

Why was the invasion Kuwait worth the lives of Americans? Why did we go to war? On 8 November, Bush decided on the offensive option. In discussions with his staff and allies he concluded that economic sanctions alone would be insufficient. Talking this problem over with Egyptian President Mohammed Hosni Mubarak, he noted:

> We also talked about the effect of sanctions on Iraq. Hosni was convinced that Saddam was in a tight political corner and it was unlikely he would or could simply withdraw from Kuwait under economic pressure. After eight years of fighting, thousands of casualties, and the expenditure of $200 billion, Iraq had little to show for its war with Iran. He predicted that if Saddam withdrew, he

would lose too much face. It would be suicide: his people would kill him. The foreign minister of Oman, Yusef Alawi, also insisted that Saddam would not bow under sanctions and argued for a military effort. I found these views discouraging.[28]

Bush sought UN and US Congressional resolutions for war, but believed he needed neither to go to war. The UN, however, gave the war international legitimacy, and helped secure the support of the collapsing Soviet Union and Islamic countries. Congressional support meant, in theory, the support of the American people. Since the end of the Vietnam War and the passage of the "War Power Act" in 1973, presidents have maintained that as Commander-in-Chief responsible for the security of the United States, they have the power to deploy American forces to war without congressional approval. Congress, however, has maintained that within sixty days of the initiating of hostilities congressional approval is in fact required, or those forces would have to be withdrawn. This conflict has never been resolved. However, presidents have sought congressional support, if not approval, before deploying forces. While Bush worked to get

resolutions for war, he issued the orders for the deployment of forces for offensive operations. He wanted everything in place to initiate hostilities by midnight 15 January 1991, the deadline set for Saddam Hussein to withdraw his force. On 28 November, Bush wrote in his diary:

> ... The final analysis: we will prevail. Saddam Hussein will get out of Kuwait, and the United States will have been the catalyst and the key in getting this done, and that is important. Our role as a world leader will once again be reaffirmed, but if we compromise and if we fail, we would be reduced to total impotence, and that is not going to happen. I don't care if I have one vote in the Congress. That will not happen ... I want the Congress involved. The big debate goes on about the declaration of war, but the big thing is, we need them, we want them; and I'll continue to consult.[29]

Bush received Congressional support, but just barely. Remarkably he had done a better job of convincing foreign nations, some of which he had to

Fig 13.1 President George Bush with Secretary of Defense Dick Cheney (left), National Security Advisor Brent Scowcroft, Chairman of the JCS, Colin Powell (right), and other members of JCS.

bribe, of the need for war, than the American people.[30] The ghosts of Vietnam still hung heavily in the
corridors of the Capitol, the halls of universities, and
living rooms of some American homes. Bush, in his
diary entry on 28 November noted: "Gephardt 'breaks'
with the President, saying 'no use of force, sanctions
must work. . . .' Its ironic, the isolationistic right lined
with the [old] Kingman Brewster left [voicing the]
Vietnam syndrome. Bob Kerry, a true war hero in
Vietnam and John Glenn, also a hero, 'no force, no
force.'"[31] Other senior American statesmen argued
against war and predicted high casualties, including
former Secretary of Defense Robert McNamara.

Bush could have fought the war without the support of the UN, the Congress, or the American people.
In 1991 there was one major difference in the way the
United States conducted war: the American people
would not be called upon to fight. The White House
and the Pentagon were not reliant on the will of the
American people. Still, Bush sought their support. Why
should Americans fight for Kuwait? Bush endeavored
to explain. First he told the American people this was
about "naked aggression," a larger country had attacked
its smaller neighbor. He argued there was a larger principle at stake: "I view it very seriously, not just that but
any threat to any other countries, as well as I view
very seriously our determination to reverse this awful
aggression. . . . This will not stand. . . ."[32] He argued that
the failure to act in the 1930s led to a larger war. He
compared Saddam Hussein to Hitler, drawing the most
heinous images possible. However, support for the war
remained weak. Later, he and his advisors argued that it
was about oil, and Secretary of State James Baker told
the American people it was about "jobs." Later still, the
Administration argued it was about weapons of mass
destruction, and that Saddam Hussein was producing
an atomic bomb and had chemical weapons. Bush was
concerned about the security of Saudi Arabia, and the
rise of Iraqi power. He also voiced concerns about the
place of the US in world affairs. The prestige, credibility,
and influence of the Untied States were at stake, a concern of Kennedy, Johnson, and Nixon. And finally there
was the moral issue, stopping the many atrocities
taking place in Kuwait. While a nation can pursue
multiple objectives in war, the inconsistencies in Bush's
information campaign damaged its ability to communicate and convince.

Americans had no affinity for Kuwaitis, ethnically,
culturally, or politically. Kuwait was an Arab,
Muslim, constitutional monarchy of enormous wealth.
Kuwaitis represented none of the values accepted by
Americans and delineated in the Constitution of the
US. However, Kuwaitis helped Bush make the argument for war. They spent $10 million dollars on a Wall
Street marketing campaign to convince Americans
that Saddam Hussein was the devil, evil incarnate, and
a baby killer. Bush and the Kuwaitis' campaign demon-
ized Saddam Hussein, creating the expectation that
when the war was over Saddam Hussein would no
longer be in power. This, however, was not the stated
political objective. Covertly, though, the CIA was
engaged in a campaign to remove Saddam Hussein.

The Bush Administration's interest in Kuwait was
not based on the principle of non-aggression, nor was
it based on moral concerns. The United States has
not been a force for democracy and freedom is this
region. In fact, the US has devoted enormous
resources to keeping royal families and dictators in
power, including Saddam Hussein. And, some understood that even if Saddam Hussein was the devil, Iraq
could not produce a tank, or a jet aircraft, lacking the
industry and technological wherewithal. And terrorism was not yet a major American concern. The
economies of the Western world ran on Persian Gulf
oil, and that oil, above all else, provided the reason for
Bush to intervene. Kuwait's ownership of almost ten
percent of the world's known oil reserves was one of
the primary reasons for war. Iraq already possessed
an estimated 100 billion barrel oil reserve. Combining
the reserves of Kuwait and Iraq would have produced
the second largest producer on Earth. Only Saudi
Arabia, with an estimated 261 billion barrels, twenty-
six percent of the world's supply, held greater
resources. Bush was also concerned about the security of Saudi Arabia, and the expansion of Iraq's political and military power. By going to war, Bush sought
to maintain the balance of power in the region. Oil,
however, could not be translated into a cause for
which Americans would be willing to fight—hence,
the superheated rhetoric, the demonization, the moral
arguments, and the principle of non-aggression.

In fact, Americans had no practical reason to risk
their lives for Kuwait. They would have paid an extra
dollar or two per gallon at the gas pump. No one

would have exchanged the lives of their sons and daughters for a few dollars saved on a barrel of oil. Had Iraq been a real nation, capable of fighting a more total war, capable of inflicting heavy casualties; had dead Americans by the hundreds per week returned to the US in flag-draped coffins; had the war gone on for years; and had there been a draft pulling young men out of colleges, workplaces, and homes, Bush would have found that he totally lacked the support to bring the war to a successful conclusion.

The outcome of the war was not just a function of US and coalition actions. It was also a function of poor Iraqi leadership, and divisions among the Iraqi people. Most importantly, by limiting the objectives of the war, Bush and Powell made sure they did not create a nation, that they did not create the conditions that united the numerous peoples of the Soviet Union in 1941. The pressure put on the peoples of the Soviet Union by the German invasion and its unprecedented brutality made the USSR a true nation, capable of enormous effort and sacrifices.[33] The war in Iraq did not evolve into a "people's war," which is one of the primary reasons US technology was so effective.

Bush did the right thing in Iraq, but not for the reasons he delineated. And the first Persian Gulf War was not an "American people's war." A principle is not a principle unless it is applied universally. Bush and Congress had no intention of expending American lives or resources to stop naked aggression in Africa, to stop genocide in Cambodia, to involve itself in regions of the world that lacked the significance of the Middle East. Moral issues were not a concern of the US. During the Iran-Iraq War, Saddam Hussein destroyed thousands of Kurdish homes and businesses, and killed between 150,000 and 200,000 Kurdish civilians, employing chemical weapons against them. The US did almost nothing to stop this attempt at genocide. War is an ugly thing, but it is not nearly as ugly when it is based on principles of human rights. Bush's war was based on pragmatic self-interest. He used other arguments to make the war palatable. Had there been a draft, had there been a citizen-soldier Army, he would have had a much harder sell.

On 12 January 1991, each House of Congress voted to support the joint resolution authorizing the use of force in accordance with the UN resolutions.

The Senate narrowly passed the resolution, 52–47. Bush had greater support in the House where the vote was 250–183. Memories of the Vietnam War and the Gulf Tonkin Resolution were on the minds of some senators and congressmen. Typical when the war tocsin sounds, congressmen and women rally around the flagpole and the debate on the war resolutions degenerates into patriotic rhetoric; however, not this time. This time a real debate took place.

On 16 January at 6:30 PM Bush addressed the nation, "The liberation of Kuwait has begun ... We will not fail." Almost concurrently, on 17 January in Saudi Arabia, coalition aircraft were rolling down the runways—their destination, Iraq.

Operation Desert Storm: Theater Strategy

Central Command (CENTCOM), under the command of General H. Norman Schwarzkopf, had overall responsibility for planning and directing operations. General Colin Powell, Chairman of the JCS, who possessed the new powers bestowed by the Goldwater-Nichols legislation, translated political directives into military orders, determined military objectives, provided the resource that Schwarzkopf requested, and provided guidance. However, it was the CENTAF Commander, Lieutenant General Charles A. Horner, who took the initiative and developed the CENTCOM plan, which in its embryonic form was primarily an air war.[34] Horner appointed Brigadier General Buster Glosson his principal planner. Glosson formed a planning cell in the basement of the Royal Saudi Air Force headquarters building, which became known as the "black hole."[35] It took the Pentagon's Air Staff initial plan "Instant Thunder," developed by John A. Warden III and others in the "Checkmate" planning division, and produced an executable operational plan, which included a retaliatory plan to be carried out if Saddam Hussein invaded Saudi Arabia.

The Army deployed a team from the School of Advanced Military Studies (SAMS) at Command and General Staff College, Fort Leavenworth, Kansas, to assist CENTCOM in the development of the ground war plan. Lieutenant Colonel Joe Purvis headed the team. Still, the final plans, air and ground, were Schwarzkopf's.

Fig 13.2 General H. Norman Schwarzkopf.

The initial objective was to "induce" Saddam Hussein to comply with UN Resolution 660 and unconditionally withdraw his forces from Kuwait. However, as the plan evolved, the destruction of the Iraqi Army became an objective. The CJCS, Powell, stated, "I don't want them to go home—I want to leave smoking tanks as kilometer fence posts all the way to Baghdad."[36] Powell later stated, "Cut it off, then kill it." His objective was to destroy the offensive capability of the Iraqi Army so that it could not threaten its neighbors. However, enough of the Iraqi Army had to be left to deter Iran from exploiting Iraq's weakness. An unspoken strategic objective was the elimination of Saddam Hussein.

The first priority of the US was the defense of Saudi Arabia. A US delegation of senior presidential advisors convinced the Saudi King to request US support—which, of course, Bush quickly granted, deploying light ground forces and air forces to serve as a deterrent until heavy armor forces could be deployed. Bush also warned the Iraqi leader that the invasion of the Saudi Kingdom would have grave consequences. Bush's warning and Saddam Hussein's knowledge of US military potential, particularly the

nuclear arsenals, probably had more of a deterrent effect than the deployment of the 82nd Airborne Division. However, the division showed that Bush was serious and committed.

Saddam Hussein had significant reasons for keeping the war and his objectives limited to Kuwait. As long as US and UN demands were limited to the evacuation of Kuwait, Saddam Hussein's position was not directly threatened. If he invaded Saudi Arabia, the limitations he sought might not survive the coming war, which also meant that Saddam Hussein might not survive the war. A more total war would have threatened Saddam Hussein's position. The Iraqi Army's one serious attack into Saudi Arabia at Khafji was not part of a major offensive to occupy the country.

The Persian Gulf War is typically divided into two major phases, the deployment-defensive phase, Desert Shield; and the second deployment-attack-liberation phase, Desert Storm. Each major phase of the war required an array of forces capable of achieving strategic and operational objectives. Each major phase was divided into sub-phases for ground and air operations. The Army deployed in two major phases, first to provide for the defense of Saudi Arabia, and second to develop offensive courses of action. The Air Force, by its very nature, could and did deploy and build up forces considerably faster than the Army. It was ready for offensive operations months before the Army. Glosson wrote: "I desperately wanted to start this war in late October, early November. I just thought it was the right time and that we didn't need the Powell build-up we were later forced to take."[37] In Glosson's view, an early initiation of hostilities would have given the Air Force more time to win the war without the Army.

In the offensive phases, Schwarzkopf listed his operational objectives: attack leadership and command and control; gain and maintain air supremacy; totally cut supply lines; destroy chemical, biological, and nuclear capability; and destroy Republican Guard. In Schwarzkopf's view, the Republican Guard was the operational center of gravity. Operation Desert Storm was divided into four phases. Phase IV was the ground and air war. Phases I, II, and III comprised the air war. The first priorities were to destroy command and control facilities, communication networks, and major headquarters to sever the line of communication between Saddam Hussein and his field forces; and it was hoped to kill Saddam Hussein. Other objectives were to destroy the nuclear, chemical, and biological warfare capabilities of Iraq. The second priority was air superiority over the battlefield, which would give the Air Force, Navy, Marine Corps, and Army air forces the freedom to attack any target in the Kuwait Theater of Operation (KTO) unchallenged. Air superiority meant more than destroying the Iraqi Air Force, it also meant destroying Iraq's integrated air defense system—missile systems, radar systems, command systems, and the communication systems that tied them together. Because this system was built, at least in part, by the French, intelligence on it was unprecedented. The third priority was the attrition or destruction of Iraqi ground forces. The final mission of airpower was during the ground assault phase. Airpower would continue to destroy enemy ground forces, but also provide close air support and interdict enemy forces. The Air Force was also tasked to carry out psychological warfare operations (PSYOPs). B–52s not only dropped bombs, but also leaflets.

Glosson did not agree with Schwarzkopf's four-phase approach. He believed there were in fact only two phases to the operational plan, strategic and tactical. He argued against the four-phase plan, and immediately after the war he wrote: "The mistake though, was to split the campaign in four phases. There were really only two phases: the strategic air campaign and the tactical support of the land campaign. Instead of finishing Phase I, we'd worked it right up to the last day." Glosson emphasized that the plan was Schwarzkopf's plan, indicating that he would have done things differently. The approach that Schwarzkopf demanded made it possible for the Army to redirect the air effort away from strategic targets and onto the enemy's ground forces. Prior to the Normandy invasion, Eisenhower had a very similar problem with the AAF. This issue caused considerable friction between Glosson and the Deputy CENTCOM Commander, Lieutenant General Calvin A.H. Waller, US Army. Glosson concluded, "Waller detested me." He also noted the Air Force carried on the strategic campaign to the last day, in opposition to Waller's directive.[38]

All airpower in the theater was doctrinally under CENTAF command—unity of command. However, this had never worked before, and in Korea and Vietnam, the Navy, Marine Corps, and Air Force each fought their own air war. Horner recognized this problem and was determined to make joint command work. Glosson observed:

> In theory Horner, as the Joint Force Air Component Commander [JFACC] for CENTCOM, was going to have control of all the air forces: Navy, Marine, Air Force and through the Coalition, the allies who joined us. But the reality was we'd never done it that way. Horner was adamant this would be a joint effort and we would not have the fractured set-up of Vietnam all over again with the Navy and the Air Force flying separate routes. But one thing for sure, parochialism was alive and well.[39]

Marine Corps air was concerned about supporting Marine Corps ground forces—no change since the Korean War. The Navy was concerned that the Air Force would take the most highly valued targets for itself—a complaint that was made after the war. And all three air services thought differently about doctrine. Glosson noted, "The Marines had been complaining that the retaliatory strikes and Phase I of the campaign did not leave their air assets available for other tasking direct from the Marine Expeditionary Force (MEF). . . . Then the Navy informed me that they wanted to back out of planned strikes near Baghdad." He also noted that his own staff was initially incapable of acting as a joint staff. On 26 August he wrote in his diary, "*parochialism out of control.*" And under critical lessons he concluded: "JFACC must be strengthened. He must be a true Joint Force Air Component Commander—there is not an alternative." CENTAF did in fact send air tasking orders (ATO) to the Navy and Marine Corps, and these missions were carried out. Navy air liaison officers were made part of the CENTAF planning cell in Riyadh. These officers represented the Navy's view, and forwarded the ATO. The system was not perfect, but it worked better than it did in Korea and Vietnam. Still, while much praise has been directed at CENTCOM for the successful "joint" campaign, Goldwater-Nichols had not yet significantly changed a half-century of cultural learning.[40]

On 13 September 1990, General Schwarzkopf's staff briefed Powell on CENTCOM's Desert Storm plan.[41] And on 11 October, the plan was briefed to the President. The ground war plan was significantly less developed than Horner's and Glosson's air war plan. And the White House was overall unimpressed. Brent Scowcroft wrote:

> I was not happy with the briefing. It sounded unenthusiastic, delivered by people who didn't want to do the job. The option they presented us, an attack straight up through the center of the Iraqi army, seemed to me to be so counterintuitive that I could not stay silent. I asked why not an envelopment to the west and north around and behind the forces in Kuwait to cut them off. The briefer's answer was that they did not have enough fuel trucks for so extensive an operation and the tanks would run out of gas on the shoulder of the encirclement. In addition, they did not know whether the shifting sands of the western desert would support an armored operation. Therefore it was not feasible. I was appalled with the presentation and afterwards I called Cheney to say I thought we had to do better. Cheney shared my concern and sent the planners back to the drawing board.[42]

Bush wrote: "The briefing made me realize we had a long way to go before the military was 'gung ho' and felt we had the means to accomplish our mission expeditiously, without impossible loss of life."[43] Bush and Scowcroft were probably thinking they needed new leadership. Powell, however, rose to the occasion. He calmed frayed nerves, and assured the President and his advisors that a better, more comprehensive ground war plan would be developed. Bush's impressions, however, were right—the Army was suffering from a lack of confidence. Another option advanced by one of Bush's advisors was an amphibious landing, a replay of the Inchon Landing. The Army immediately rejected this approach. Some marines also rejected this approach. Landing light infantry against armor forces was a bad idea.

To give the President the options he wanted, Powell and Schwarzkopf wanted overwhelming force, the Powell doctrine. On 15 October, back at his headquarters in Riyadh, Schwarzkopf directed Purvis to start developing a two-corps attack plan, actually a three-corps plan, including the MEF. The Army was slow to bring the Marine Corps into the planning, a serious mistake. Shortly thereafter, Powell requested one of the Army's three heavy armor corps and part of another. The entire VII Corps in Europe was to be deployed as well as two heavy divisions from the United States.[44] With these forces in the "order of battle," a new plan quickly took shape.

In hindsight, the Army's initial plan would have worked. Saddam Hussein's forces were not the highly trained, professional forces the Army and White House expected to fight, and Soviet technology was no match for the newest generation of American technology. One corps, the XVIII Airborne Corps, plus the MEF and air forces, forces that were already deployed for Operation Desert Shield, would have been more than sufficient to push Saddam Hussein's forces out of Kuwait. However, they were not sufficient to cut it off and kill it, an objective added by the US. When Powell added that mission, he increased the need for fast-moving armor divisions.

With separate air war and ground war plans in hand, the question became when to transition from the air war to the ground war. With precision technology, some in the Air Force believed it was possible to destroy the Republican Guard from the air, to make it combat ineffective. It was believed that this required the destruction of fifty percent of its forces. The Army accepted this. The initiation of the ground war became tied to this figure of fifty percent destruction, causing one student of the air war to conclude, "This prospect was so riveting it nearly became the only goal of concern in the minds of some."[45] To achieve this level of destruction, computer simulation showed that it would take 600 sorties per day for four days.[46] However, this level of destruction, even with precision weapons, seemed almost impossible—and it was.

* * * * *

During the Gulf War Schwarzkopf maintained control of the ground forces, essentially wearing two hats. Lieutenant General John J. Yeosock served as commander of the 3rd Army and Army Forces, US Central Command (ARCENT). Orders passed from Schwarzkopf to Yeosock to Corps commanders. The ground war plan called for attacks from the southern border of Iraq and Kuwait, with three major forces,

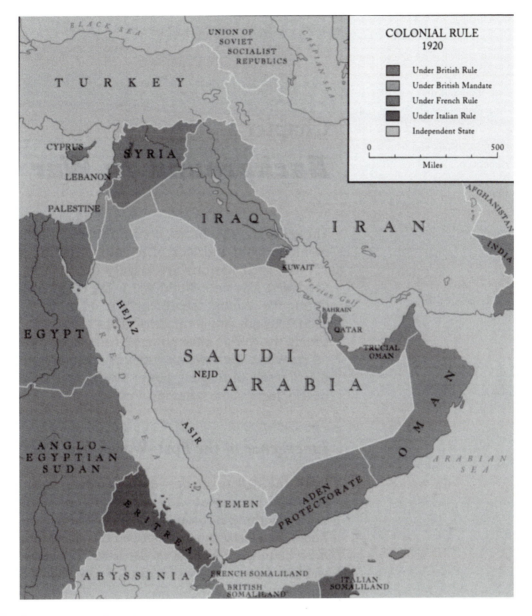

Fig 13.3 Persian Gulf War, Colonial Rule, 1920.

two supporting attacks, a main attack, and an amphibious feint. With the objective to liberate Kuwait and destroy the Iraqi Army, geography virtually dictated the conduct of the war.

Kuwait is a tiny country, from south to north just over a hundred miles at its longest point, and from east to west just under ninety miles at it widest point. Kuwait is bordered on the east by the Persian Gulf and on the west by Iraq. To the immediate north is also Iraqi territory, and not too far beyond, less than fifty miles, is Iran. Saudi Arabia forms the southern border of Kuwait and Iraq. Coalition forces necessarily attacked north. The Euphrates-Tigris River valley divides Iraq. It formed the northern-most line of advance for coalition ground forces. If Iraqi forces made it north of the valley they were out of range of coalition ground forces. At Basra, with the confluence of the two rivers and less than fifty miles from Kuwait, Iraqi forces had an escape route into the northern half of Iraq. Between Baghdad and Basra were forty-two bridges spanning the river valley. Destroying these bridges isolated the battlefield.

The climate also influenced operations. Kuwait's summers are intensely hot and dry, and the winters are short and cool. Operations during the summer months are extremely difficult for men and machines. Add dust and sand and you have a hostile environment, one that has to be fought right along with the enemy. Technology gave the US the edge. However, soldiers and marines had to adjust to a climate that Iraqi soldiers considered the norm.

Given the size of coalition forces, the space they required, the limited access, and their objectives, there were only three types of maneuvers possible attacking north out of Saudi Arabia: a direct frontal attack north into Kuwait, an envelopment or flanking attack from the south-west to the east into Kuwait, and a turning movement deep into Iraq to get into the enemy's rear

to block his retreat, cut his LOC, and force him to fight in two directions. The ground force plan did all three. The flat, slightly undulating terrain permitted all three forms of maneuvers. The operation consisted of two major supporting attacks and a main attack to destroy the Republican Guard divisions. The 1st and 2nd Marine Divisions under Lieutenant General Walt Boomer and the Arab Corps carried out the first supporting attacks. They attacked north directly into Kuwait to fix the enemy's main forces in place and to liberate Kuwait. It was expected that Iraqi forces would maneuver to attack. The XVIII Airborne Corps, consisting of the 82nd Airborne, 101st Airborne, and 24th Infantry Division (Mechanized), with the French 6th Infantry Division attached, conducted the second major supporting attack, a deep turning movement

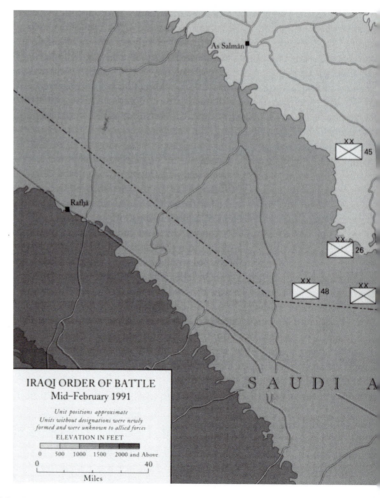

Fig 13.4 Persian Gulf War, Iraqi Order of Battle.

into Iraq to block the main supply route, Highway 8, from Basra to Baghdad along the Euphrates River. Once the blocking forces were in place the 24th Infantry Division was to attack east to cut off the enemy's retreat. Another major mission of the XVIII Airborne Corps was to screen the western-most flank of the invasion force. The forces of the XVIII Airborne Corps were located the farthest west and had the greatest distance to cover. Arguably, they should have kicked off the attack first, possibly 24 hours before the supporting attack of the marines, which had the shortest distance to cover. However, Schwarzkopf was very conservative. He wanted the 24th ID to advance at roughly the same pace as the VII Corps, the main attack force, to keep them within supporting distance of one another. Airmobile resources of the 101st

Airborne Division (Air Assault) carried out the initial movements of the XVIII Airborne Corps, securing airfields and establishing forward supply bases.

The VII Corps' objective was to "Conduct main attack ... to penetrate Iraqi defenses and destroy RGFC forces," the operational center of gravity.[47] The marine supporting attacks and breaching operations were to be initiated first. The attack with armor forces was to commence twenty-four hours later. The Marine Corps' attack was designed to convince the enemy it was the main attack, causing it to maneuver to engage. The 1st Cavalry Division located between the Marines and the VII was part of a deception plan designed to convince Republican Guard forces located in the vicinity of the western-most Kuwaiti border that the flanking maneuvers up Wadi al Batin was the main attack.

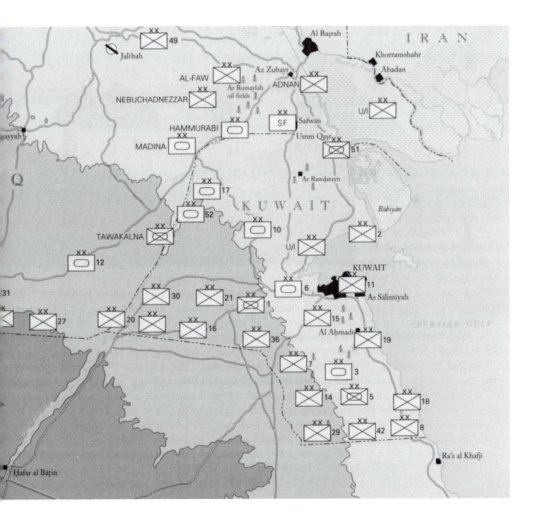

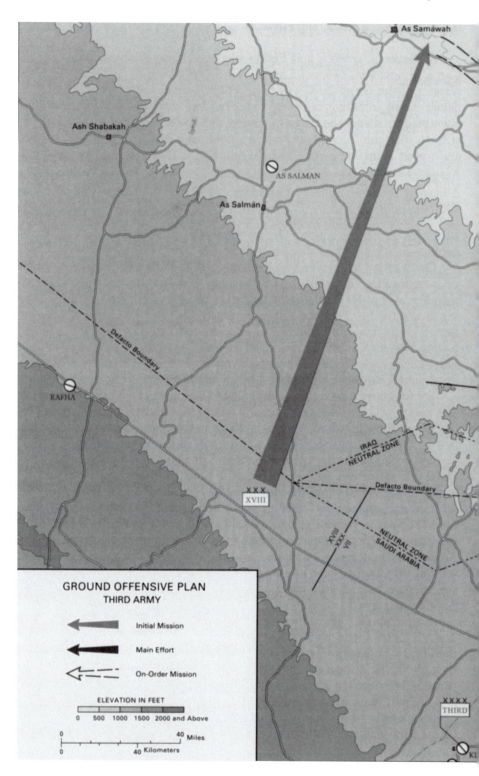

Fig 13.5 Persian Gulf War, The Ground Offensive Plan.

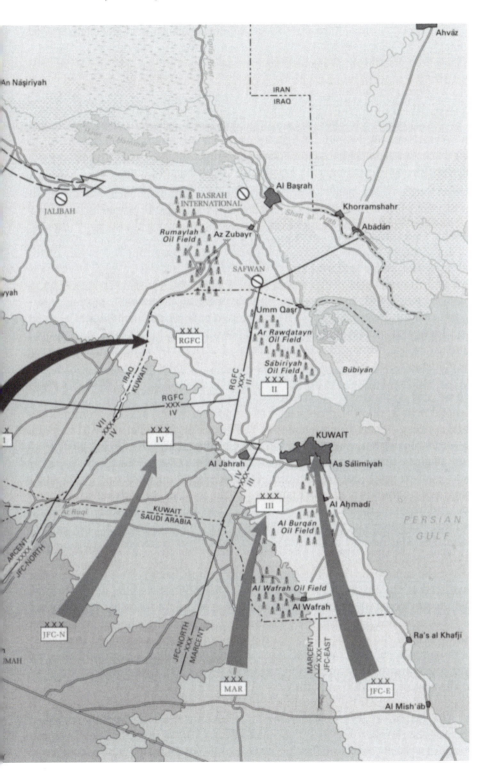

The objective of the Marines and the 1st Cavalry was to fix enemy forces in Kuwait in place, or better yet, cause them to maneuver south to attack. While the attacks of the Marines and the 1st Cavalry were taking place, the VII Corps was to advance deep into Iraq in an effort to envelop the Republican Guard forces. Schwarzkopf later observed: "We deceived our opponent into thinking that our main attack would be a frontal one against Iraqi defenses in occupied Kuwait." Another observer wrote: "the deception mission [of the 1st Cav] was a complete success; it froze an entire Iraqi Corps in place, and helped ensure the success of the VII Corps' left hook around the Iraqi defense."[48] An amphibious feint was part of a deception plan designed to cause the Iraqi Army to move forces toward the coast, reducing the combat power the Marines had to fight in the first twenty-four hours of battle.

The ground war plan was based on a number of assumptions: First, that the Iraqi Army, particularly the Republican Guard, was a "first class" outfit. Second, that the Iraqi main armor forces would maneuver to fight once it identified the main attack. Third, that the Russian T–72 was comparable to the M1. Fourth, that the Iraqi leadership was professional and competent. And fifth, that the US was fighting a nation, a culturally cohesive people. None of these assumptions was correct. Finally, Schwarzkopf's ground war plan had a major flaw. It failed to close the back door first. It failed to cut off the enemy's line of retreat before the supporting attack of the Marines started pushing Iraqi forces out of Kuwait. This made it impossible to achieve one of the major political objectives, the destruction of the Republican Guard, if Iraqi forces decided not to fight but to evacuate.

Put this in context of the Korean War. MacArthur's turning movement, the Inchon Landing, placed Marines behind the NKPA before the Eighth Army initiated its breakout from the Pusan Perimeter. While diverting too many forces to recapture Seoul, MacArthur endeavored to close the back door before the main attack took place. Schwarzkopf's plan did the exact opposite. The Marine and Saudi attacks from the south were to convince the Iraqis that this was the main attack. It was to kick off before the VII Corps' main attack and the XVIII Corps' turning movement, the forces that had the greatest distance to cover. Schwarzkopf's plan had the Marines pushing the Iraqis out of Kuwait before the turning movement could get behind it and the flanking movement could get a fix on it. Schwarzkopf's plan anticipated that the Iraqis would move to engage the Marines the way a Western army would, giving his other forces the time they needed to get into position. He was wrong. The

Iraqis started evacuating even before they were fully engaged with the Marines. Schwarzkopf's plan did not take into consideration Arab culture. A study of the Egyptian conduct of the 1973 Yom Kippur War would have provided him guidance on the enemy's behavior. Schwarzkopf's plan was a function of too much respect and awe for the Iraqi forces, and insufficient confidence in his own forces. Still, even under this plan, Schwarzkopf had two other ways, besides the heavy armor forces of the 24th ID, to cut off the enemy's line of retreat: airpower and air assault forces— the air and ground tank killing forces of the 101st. These forces, if quickly deployed and working with the Air Force, had the potential to close the back door. Schwarzkopf, however, was not Patton, and he was not willing to accept another Bastogne.[49]

The Air Force, alone, offered another potential means for closing the back door. The Air Force noted that: "some Republican Guard units escaped because a US Army corps commander set the fire support coordination line [FSCL] too far forward. To prevent accidental attack on his forces, the ground commander decided where to draw this line." This line, it was argued, prevented the Air Force from engaging escaping enemy force independent of the Army: "For many hours, the Air Force was not permitted to strike the Iraqi convoys headed toward Baghdad."[50]

Taking this analysis one step further, had airpower convinced Saddam Hussein he could not achieve some satisfactory conclusion to the war, he might have initiated the evacuation before the ground war started, saving his army, and robbing Bush and Schwarzkopf of a more substantial, observable victory. In hindsight, it was unnecessary to carry on a month-long air campaign before the ground war commenced. The Army had not yet recovered from defeat in Vietnam. The Air Force was being asked to destroy the enemy's ground force in a way never seen before. The old Army believed the destruction of the enemy's army was its job. The strategy employed in the Gulf War was not in accordance with Army history, or AirLand Battle doctrine, which envisioned the Army fighting the battle at the forward edge of the battlefield while the Air Force conducted deep strike operations. The Army, as it had in Vietnam, accepted the primacy of airpower.

14.
THE PERSIAN GULF WAR: OPERATION DESERT STORM, 1991

Simply (if boldly) stated, air power won the Gulf war. It was not the victory of any one service, but rather the victory of coalition air power projection by armies, navies, and air forces. At one end were sophisticated stealth fighters striking out of the dark deep in Iraqi territory. At the other were the less glamorous but no less important troop and supply helicopters wending their way across the battlefield. In between was every conceivable form of air power application, short of nuclear war, including aircraft carriers, strategic bombers, tactical and strategic airlift, and cruise missiles. . . . Indeed, while many analysts expected air power to influence the outcome of the war, few expected it to be the war's decisive force.[1]

–Richard P. Hallion, US Air Force Historian, 1992

"Cut if off–then kill it." With those words . . . Gen. Colin L. Powell . . . summed up the US strategy for defeating the 545,000-man Iraqi army. . . . The "cutting off" went on for some weeks [the air war]. The coalition air forces achieved the goal of air supremacy. . . . "Killing" the Iraqi armed forces was another matter. Only ground forces can defeat other ground forces in detail: only ground forces can seize and hold ground; only ground forces can attack, outmaneuver, encircle and defeat other ground forces. Only ground forces can occupy key enemy political, economic and administrative centers after the battle and keep the peace.

–Edward M. Flanagan Jr., Lieutenant General US Army, 1991

Both the Army and the Air Force claimed decisiveness in the Persian Gulf War. Air Force Chief of Staff, General Merrill A. McPeak, in a Pentagon briefing on 15 March 1991, stated, "My private conviction is that this is the first time in history that a field army has been defeated by airpower." And Air Force General Chuck Horner, Commander of Allied Air Forces in Operation Desert Storm, concluded that airpower had destroyed the will of the Iraqi armed forces to fight. General Schwarzkopf, while acknowledging the contribution of the Air Force, in a briefing on 27 February 1991, downplayed the role of the Air Force, arguing that its effectiveness diminished over the course of the campaign and that the Army was needed to complete the destruction of enemy ground forces. The Army argued that it physically destroyed the Iraqi Army in close combat. Both arguments had been made, in one form or another, in every major war since World War II. However, the Pentagon had again initiated a war where airpower was supposed to be decisive. The technology and doctrine had changed, but the objective was still the same, to fight and win a war exclusively from the air, to prove that ground forces were in fact obsolete. The Air Force's assessment, because it supported accepted and preferred American cultural tenets, carried the greatest weight. The impressive array of aircraft and precision weapons demonstrated in Iraq and shown again and again on nation-wide television reinforced American faith in technological solutions. In the wake of the first Persian Gulf War, six Army divisions were deactivated.[2] The other services also underwent reductions in force, but only the Army lost forty percent of its active strength.

While both the Army and the Air Force claimed decisiveness, the Iraqi Army deserved considerable blame for its defeat. It was one of the worst-led forces in one of the worst-fought wars in the history of warfare. Still, what was most important to the rapid destruction of the Iraqi Army was not its generalship, but the fact that Iraq was not a *nation*. It was a *state*, and hence, it was incapable of fighting a more total war. The Persian Gulf War was Saddam Hussein's war. It was not the war of the people of Iraq. In fact, had the US employed a good sniper and killed Saddam Hussein, there would have been no war. Iraq was a police state, and under Saddam Hussein it was irreconcilably divided. The Iraqi people were totally incapable of fighting a "people's war." Ethnic divisions (Kurds, Shias, Sunnis, and others) and hatred of Saddam Hussein made it impossible for Iraq to generate the combat power of a unified, culturally, politically cohesive people—a nation. The Iraqi people lacked the ideology, the passion, the cohesion, and the leadership of the Vietnamese Communists. As a consequence, coalition weapons were much more effective. Bombs that paralyzed much of the Iraqi fighting force had no such effect on the Viet Cong or NVA. The majority of the people of Iraq were not vested in Saddam Hussein's Iraq.

Decisiveness was also a function of the US's limited political objectives. More total objectives may have created a nation, and produced an authentic national leader. More total objectives may have turned one of the Iraqi tribal nations, for example, the Sunni Muslims, against coalition forces. More total objectives may have had the effect that the creation of Israel had on the Arab population of that region: the formation of a national identity and the unification of those people into the Palestinians, a nation. Bush's limited objectives, and American technology and doctrine, precision weapons, and targeting of military forces, which limited civilian casualties and suffering, insured that the formation of national identity did not take place. US and coalition forces did not produce sufficient carnage and anger to mobilize the Iraqi people against them. Limited political objectives, the absence of national unity, and the measured use of combat power provide better explanations for the rapid collapse of Iraqi armed forces than the arguments of the Army or the Air Force. And, in fact, the

Iraqi Army was not completely destroyed. The Republican Guard was severely crippled, but a significant number escaped destruction. These forces were sufficient in number to put down revolts, insuring the survival of the government of Saddam Hussein. They were also sufficient enough to continue to pose a threat to Kuwait. Their existence forced the US and the UN to maintain a military presence in the region. The presence of US forces, as in Europe and Korea, created stability. The cost of maintaining stability is considerably cheaper than the cost of war.

The Air War

Air Force Major General Buster Glosson sought to win the war from the air without ground forces. He believed that airpower alone was a war-winning technology, and that with stealth technology and precision weapons airpower had finally achieved the objectives established in the 1920s and 1930s. Glosson wrote:

> Precision was at the core of all my plans. I couldn't emphasize this enough. Precision was going to let me carve and dice Iraq's strategic capabilities and do it fast. With precision, I wouldn't have to wait to batter down defenses and chip away at targets. I could hit what I wanted and destroy what had to be destroyed faster and more efficiently than air power had ever done before.[3]

Glosson continued:

> The way I wanted to defeat Iraq was to craft our joint air power to do as much of the job as possible so Schwarzkopf would not have to throw coalition soldiers and Marines across the line unless he absolutely had to—and if they did go in, I wanted it to end up looking like a police action, not like Patton vs. Rommel. . . . I believed if we planned the right campaign, executed it well, and gave it time to work, we'd essentially defeat Iraq from the air. That did not mean follow-up ground action would not be required. It did mean any ground action would be quick, with minimum loss of life.[4]

In Operation Desert Storm, the Air Force had two doctrines, two opportunities to win the war without the Army. Strategically the coalition believed that it was possible to sever the "spinal cord" of Iraq, by destroying its communication systems and physically isolating its leadership so completely that it was impossible for Saddam Hussein and senior generals to control their military forces. They believed it was possible to kill Saddam Hussein and other senior civilian and military leaders, an objective that was never formally stated, but clearly attempted. The Air Force sent 260 missions against suspected locations of Saddam Hussein.[5] Finally it was believed that by destroying the infrastructure of Iraq, by punishing the people, Iraqis could be convinced to rise up and overthrow the Saddam Hussein government.

The Air Force's second doctrinal approach was to destroy the enemy's ground combat forces and destroy its morale and will to fight. The Air Force believed it was possible to win the war operationally and tactically from the air by destroying the Iraqi Army:

> Air Staff planners developed early plans to destroy the entire Iraqi Army in the KTO. Analysts studied the Iraqi Army and planned to exploit the vulnerabilities of an army arrayed in the desert. Operations would begin with attacks against key systems that would affect all Iraqi forces in the theater (command and control, logistics, air defense), continue with attrition of the Republican Guard, then shift to the rest of the Iraqi Army. . . . The product of these [Checkmate computer] calculations was a graph that predicted an impressive and rapid attrition of the Iraqi forces in the KTO when subjected to concentrated air attacks. These calculations reportedly led Checkmate to conclude that the attack on the Iraqi Army could negate the 15,000+ anticipated US casualties of a ground war, particularly if the requirement for the ground war could be obviated by air action.[6]

This was a doctrine in some ways akin to that employed in Korea, where geographic restrictions made it impossible for SAC heavy bombers to destroy the enemy's means of production. Hence, the Air Force had to refocus on the tactical war, which in 1950 meant attacks on enemy logistical centers and transportation arteries. The difference was that in 1991, the Air Force had the technology to directly attack the enemy's fighting forces with precision weapons.

Computer programs are only as good as the information that goes into them, and as in every war, friction, accidents, and the unknown destroy plans, typically within the first few days of battle. Poor intelligence; difficulties finding and identifying targets; difficulties assessing battle damage; inter-service friction; bureaucratic failures; bad weather; inexperience in desert environments; inexperience in high-altitude bombing; the diversion of resources; uncertainty about targets (civilian or military, friend or foe); aircraft and human limitations; the slope of the learning curve; and fixed doctrinal dispositions impeded the efforts of the Air Force, as they had in World War II and all subsequent wars.

Of the 2,614 aircraft deployed for the Persian Gulf War, the Air Force deployed 1,540 and the Navy, 450. The US provided seventy-six percent of the total coalition airpower. Saudi Arabia deployed 339 aircraft, mostly fighters, and Britain seventy-three aircraft, fifty-seven of which were fighter-attack planes. The US Air Forces deployed its full array of capabilities, including 144 A-10s, which flew 8,100 sorties; 249 F-16s, which flew 13,500 sorties; seventy-four B-52Gs, which flew 1,624 sorties and dropped thirty percent of the bomb tonnage. (The B-52s flew from bases in the US, Spain, Britain, the Middle East, and Diego Garcia in the Indian Ocean, demonstrating the worldwide reach of US of the Air Force.) The Air Force also employed F-117 Stealth Fighter/Bombers, F-15Es, Strike Eagles, F-15C Eagles, and F-111F Aardvarks combat aircraft.

The Air Force was also responsible for strategic airlift and air tanker refueling for all the services. Army and Marine forces and equipment not deployed by ships were strategically deployed on C-17s, C-141s, C-130s, and C-5Bs cargo aircraft. Commercial airlines augmented the strategic airlift capabilities of the Air Force as well. Air Force KC-13O, KC-135, and KC-10 tankers refueled Navy, Marine Corps, and coalition aircraft as well as Air Force aircraft. Air Force cargo aircraft and tankers made it possible for the US to respond rapidly to the Saudi request for assistance. Finally, Air Force MC-130s special operation aircraft supported Army and Navy Special Operation Forces.

The air campaign, instead of proceeding according to planned phases, "blended together, as targets from all phases were included in the first three days' ATO." For psychological reasons, Schwarzkopf wanted the Republican Guard attacked in the opening days of the air campaign. This job went to F-16s and B-52s. With a wide array of aircraft deployed, it was possible to strike multiple targets, to conduct strategic and tactical campaigns. Strategic targets, however, received the bulk of the air effort, as the Air Force tried to destroy the infrastructure of Baghdad, severing the spinal cord, and killing Saddam Hussein.

Chemical weapons and Scud missiles mounted on transporter-erector-launchers employed with "shoot and scoot" tactics greatly worried Washington. While Schwarzkopf argued that they were "militarily insignificant," forty-two Scuds fell on Israel. None were loaded with chemical weapons. They caused relatively minor physical damage and there were no direct fatalities. However, they had considerable psychological effect. They created conditions that bordered on panic in some areas of Israel, forcing the government to heighten its readiness posture and make preparations for retaliatory strikes. Scud missiles were therefore of strategic importance to Washington. Bush and Saddam Hussein both understood that the cohesion of the coalition was based on Israeli neutrality. No Arab state would fight alongside the much-hated Israelis. Saddam Hussein planned to provoke Israel into attacking, believing that once Israel retaliated, allied Arab states would have no option but to quit the coalition. Therefore, Bush did everything possible to assuage Israeli anger, and to protect Israel. He sent Patriot antimissile batteries to Israel to protect its cities, and personally called Prime Minister Yitzak Shamir to request that Israel stay out of the war.[7] He directed Schwarzkopf to divert the resources necessary to find and destroy Saddam Hussein's mobile Scuds.

Schwarzkopf employed the Army's Delta Force and Britain's Special Air Service (ASA) to locate and destroy the Scuds, and diverted coalition air forces to support those operations. Approximately 1,500 sorties were flown on these operations, but according to the *Gulf War Air Power Survey,* not one launcher was confirmed destroyed.[8] While some have challenged this conclusion, the effort clearly did not achieve the expected results. However, the effort itself was

probably of greater importance to the Israelis. Scuds were unsophisticated surface-to-surface missiles with a one-ton conventional explosive warhead and a range between 150 and 200 miles. Iraqis launched 88 of these missiles. One proved to be particularly deadly. On 25 February, a Scud warhead struck a US barracks in Dhahran, killing twenty-eight and wounding ninety-five. Scuds with chemical weapons would have caused considerably greater damage. However, the implicit threat of America's nuclear arsenal persuaded Saddam Hussein not to employ chemical weapons.

The Air Force had a number of major problems. One of them was obtaining intelligence. The Air Force had difficulty finding targets, and also wrestled with the problem of "effect versus destruction," recognizing that all targets did not have to be destroyed to be taken out of the fight, and that it was a waste of resources to try to completely destroy every target. In reference to intelligence, Glosson observed that, "just getting targeting data was a challenge. Intelligence was my number-one problem. Personalities, antiquated systems, Cold War mentality—the obstacles were too long to list." Precision weapons required highly accurate data on the location of enemy forces. Intelligence was frequently outdated by days, meaning that when aircraft arrived over the target location the enemy was no longer there, Glosson continued:

> CENTAF intelligence at the time had no capacity and no understanding of how to go about planning. It was absolutely the worst situation a human could imagine. . . . No matter how graphic I make it, no matter how emotional I make it, no matter how I choose my words, I cannot say how bad it was. I had never seen anything in my entire military service that was a parallel to the incompetence of CENTAF intelligence. Never.[9]

Another major problem was hitting the targets. Horner and Glosson, to diminish losses, raised the weapons release altitude for Air Force fighters and bombers. That meant that pilots were not fighting the way they had been trained. As a consequence, combat effectiveness declined. Glosson discovered that:

> The F-16s were showing disappointing results except for a few at night. Part of that was because

they were hitting the "pickle" switch to release their bombs at an altitude that was too high. I'd told them, "Until the ground campaign starts, I don't want any of you guys pickling below about 7,000 feet." Well, somehow they interpreted that guidance to mean that they were supposed to pickle so as to pull out of their dives above six or seven thousand feet. Their accuracy was out the wazoo. To pull out at 7,000 feet, they were pickling around 10,000. Some units were pickling above 20,000 feet! I wanted them to pickle at 7,000 feet and that meant they pulled out of their dives down at 5,000 feet.[10]

Glosson further noted: "The other thing that made the F-16s, A-10s, F/A-18s and other non-precision aircraft more accurate was the use of Killer Scouts. 'We need to go to FACs,' Joe Bob said. The trouble was, we didn't have any." In Vietnam, the Air Force employed forward air controllers to survey the battle area and identify targets. Once identified, the location of the target was passed on to strike aircraft operating in the vicinity. Glosson noted, "The Air Force was once full of pilots who knew the airborne FAC job, but I didn't have any in the Gulf." Instead, he put together a quick fix—"killer scouts"—but special slow flying aircraft with considerable loiter time over the battlefield were no longer in the Air Force's inventory (UAVs would ultimately take over this job). And there were other problems and glitches that made the accuracy of the Air Force's computer simulation "out the wazoo." Gordon and Trainor wrote:

> To pin down the Republican Guard, the Air Force ran twenty-four B-52 sorties a day against the forces. But the results were not good. . . . In an effort to improve the B-52s accuracy, a team of experts was secretly dispatched from the Strategic Air Command to work out some fixes. Part of the problem, it was later determined, had to do with discrepancies between the B-52s' targeting system and the intelligence data that the Black Hole was using. Programmed into the B-52s' computers was a geodetic map, essentially a grid that covered the world. While the bombing coordinates provided by the Black Hole used a map developed in 1984, the targeting systems in the B-52s were based on an older geodetic survey. . . . The problem was fixed, but none

of the air-war commanders pretended that it would make the B-52s a precision bomber. In the end, the B-52 was primarily a means of terrorizing the Iraqi ground troops, not killing them.[11]

Another problem was what Air Force General Jumper called the "kill chain," the time lapse between a sensor locating and identifying a target to the time it is engaged by a shooter. For example, the sensor-to-shooter time in a Scud hunt was approximately sixty minutes; too slow to kill the target.[12] The Air Force's objective of centralized control and decentralized execution did not produce the speed required to kill highly mobile targets.

After almost two weeks of bombing, the priority started to shift to the destruction of the Iraqi Army. The corps commanders, Luck and Franks, argued that the targets they had identified were not being attacked. As a consequence, after considerable discussion, greater attention was given to destroying Iraqi ground forces. However, the strategic air campaign was not stopped, although the Army and Air Force disagreed about the focus of the campaign. The Air Force, as in World War II, argued that it was a mistake to shift focus and that the war could be won from the air, striking strategic targets. However, the Army insisted on shifting to tactical targets. A General Accounting Office (GAO) study found that:

> In effect, several competing objectives existed under the broader umbrella of meeting the goal of reducing the Iraqi ground forces by 50 percent. For a while the commander in chief of the Central Command ordered that attrition against Iraqi frontline forces be maximized. This meant that fewer sorties were flown against the less-threatening "third echelon" Republican Guard divisions, and fewer against the Republican Guard heavy armor divisions, than against the infantry divisions closer to the front. As a result, destruction of the three 'heavy" Republican Guard divisions (holding the bulk of all the armor) was considerably less than that against either frontline forces. . . .[13]

Another source of friction was battle damage assessment. Air Force pilots claimed more kills than could be confirmed. The Army developed a formula that cut by half the claims of A-10 pilots. The Air Force disagreed with this method, and believed that the Army undercounted the number of kills from the air, while the Army concluded its system had proven to be fairly accurate.[14] The Army wanted the Air Force to "shape" the battlefield for the assault, primarily by the attrition of enemy tanks and fighting vehicles, and by isolating the battlefield, cutting off enemy logistical support and means of escape. While the strategic campaign had not proven decisive, the Air Force could still win the war by destroying the Iraqi Army on the ground, or at least its will to fight. The Army repeatedly encouraged the Air Force to purse this course.

To carry out the destruction of the Iraqi Army, the Air Force developed a tactic called "tank-plinking." Glosson described how it worked: "Tanks were Joe Bob's coup de grace. He suggested we use the F-111 and its Pave Tack laser targeting system with a 500-pound laser-guided bomb, the GBU–12, against individual Iraqi tanks—a technique we later called "tank-plinking."[15] Nearly fifty percent of the smart bombs employed by the Air Force were GBU–12. Each of these laser-guided bombs cost roughly $3,000, and packed more than enough explosive power to destroy a $900,000 Soviet T–72. Plinking proved to be the most effective and cheapest means to destroy tanks from the air. However, the Air Force also fired more than 5,000 Maverick (AGM–65) missiles, primarily from A-10s and F-16s. Each missile cost $70,000. Since the vast majority of Iraq's tanks were not top of the line T–72s, but much older T–54/55/62s, these weapons were used to destroy tanks that were worth considerably less than the missiles. The average Iraqi tank was worth less than $50,000. However, the most important costs of war are measured in lives, not dollars.

As the ground war approached, it became evident to some that the air campaign was not going to completely sever the spinal cord of Iraq, nor completely destroy the operational effectiveness of its main Army, nor completely destroy the Iraqi Army's morale and will to fight. After forty-one days of air attacks, there was still a war to fight. The Air Force wanted more time. Glosson wanted two to three more weeks of strategic bombing, believing it would produce decisive results. He wanted more time

to destroy Iraq's leadership and NBC facilities, and to convince the Iraqi people to overthrow Saddam Hussein. Powell, however, was pushing for the ground war.

* * * * *

The US Navy deployed carriers, submarines, battleships, cruisers, destroyers, frigates, amphibious ships, replenishment ships, and minesweepers— 124 ships took part in Operations Desert Shield and Storm.[16] Iraq had no navy to fight; hence, control of the sea and the ability to project power unimpeded were a given. A White Paper on the Sea Services' Role in Desert Shield/Storm noted:

> First on the scene … were two carriers, *Eisenhower* (CVN–69) and *Independence* (CV–62), with their supporting casts of combatants. By the time President Bush ordered US forces to the Middle East on 7 August, both were ready to undertake combat missions for as long as might be necessary. Ultimately, these two would be relieved by two others and, when hostilities commenced on 17 January, six carriers were launching aircraft against Iraqi targets. At conflict's end four would be operating in the Persian Gulf, a "first" for any navy.[17]

The Navy performed a number of significant missions during the war. Carrier-based aircraft supported the operations of the Air Force. The Navy launched cruise missiles from cruisers and submarines, carried out blockade operations with destroyers, conducted maritime interception operations, conducted special operations with Navy SEALs, and conducted an amphibious feint off the coast of Kuwait with amphibious assault ships. The Navy demonstrated the ability to "surge," by putting six of its twelve carriers into the war. The Navy was also able to respond rapidly with forces stationed in the Mediterranean and Persian Gulf. However, the Navy did not have time to organize itself for sustained operations. The Vietnam War and Korean War went on for years; the Persian Gulf War for months. As a consequence, the Navy did not carry the burden of the air war it had in previous wars. Part of the Navy's combat power was its psychological effect. Its mere presence was a combat multiplier.

However, the Navy in a hostile environment was *not* capable of devoting the majority of its airpower resources to fighting the war. Carriers have to defend themselves at all times. They are incapable of sustained high intensity operations. The term "surge" meant just that. For a limited period of time the Navy could put forward a maximum effort. The Navy could not continue that level of combat activity over months and years. Each of the six carriers deployed to fight Operation Desert Storm carried roughly seventy-five to eighty aircraft.

Geography stretched and limited the capabilities of the Navy. The further inland the area of operation was, the less capable naval aviation. In Korea and Vietnam, the area of operation was just off shore. In Iraq, some carriers operated from as far away as the Mediterranean, and even in the Persian Gulf naval aviators had to fly across Kuwait to attack targets in Iraq. These distances extended flying time, diminishing the number of sorties and amount of bomb load. And because of the limited capacity of ships, and their smaller, less capable aircraft, the Navy could not produce the quantities, or range of effects on target of similar numbers of Air Force aircraft. The Navy, for example, had no equivalent to the Air Force's F-117 Stealth Fighter or A-10 Warthog. The Navy also lacked tankers to project significant power far from carriers. While the Air Force supplemented the Navy's limited tanker capacity, it gave priority to its own operations.

During the war the Navy carried out 4,855 "theater-strike" sorties. Richard Hallion noted that: "The average number of theater-strike sorties that a carrier launched in the war was only 18.82 per day—equivalent, say, to launching only one or up to two squadrons of Navy A-6Es. This represented approximately 24 percent of a carrier's daily total of fixed-wing sorties."[18] In other words, the vast majority of naval sorties were *not* committed to winning the war. More effort was devoted to defending the aircraft carrier than fighting the war. This figure was far below the number of precision strikes the Navy believed was possible. Hallion continued: "On any particular day in the Gulf war, roughly 30 percent of a carrier's air operations were devoted strictly to fleet air defense duties, although in the more dangerous Persian Gulf this rose to 50 percent." Hallion concluded that:

in the first two weeks of Desert Storm—arguably the most critical weeks of the war—the Navy's six carriers averaged only 10.87 theater-strikes sorties per deck per day. Rounding this, and presuming that each airplane carried an average of four 2,000-pound bombs, means that each day . . . each carrier was only able to launch 44,000-tons of high explosives aimed at key targets in Iraq.[19]

The capabilities and missions of the US Navy have changed little since World War II. The Navy is inextricably tied to one type of platform with all its capabilities and limitations. Squadrons of shore-based, aircraft carrier-capable, Marine F/A-18s supported the war effort, making significant contributions.[20] It would have relieved stress on men and machine, and reduced the probabilities of accident had the Navy, once in theater and hostilities initiated, based its F/A-18s and other strike aircraft on shore at Air Force airfields or separately at Navy and Marine airfields. Such an arrangement would have also facilitated coordination and cooperation between the services and diminished maintenance requirement and the wear and tear on the aircraft carrier; however, the Navy would never permit such an arrangement, no matter how operationally effective.

*   *   *   *   *

The Air Force and Navy won the propaganda war. By employing precision weapons against Baghdad they effectively robbed Saddam Hussein of the destruction and civilian casualties he had hoped for, to win the worldwide condemnation of the American war effort. Saddam Hussein realized that world and American opinion had influenced decision-makers in Washington during the Vietnam War. He believed he could recreate these conditions. Some mistakes were made by the coalition forces. The Air Force struck a civilian bunker and a prison, which caused some concern in Washington, and greater scrutiny of targets by the Air Force. But, for the most part, Saddam Hussein lost the propaganda weapon he believed was of strategic importance.

On 8 February, Secretary of Defense, Richard "Dick" Cheney, and Chairman of the Joint Chiefs of Staff, Colin Powell, arrived in Riyadh to discuss the progress of the war with Schwarzkopf and his senior leaders, and specifically to ascertain when the ground war could be launched. The following day Horner, Boomer, and Vice Admiral Stan Arthur briefed Cheney and Powell, informing them that they were ready to attack. The Army needed an additional twelve days to move its forces into attack position, conduct additional reconnaissance into Iraq, and map out lanes through minefields and obstacles. Hence, the earliest day the attack could take place was 21 February. Schwarzkopf told Cheney and Powell:

> I think we should go with the ground attack now. We'll never be more ready—our guys are honed to a fine edge and if we wait much longer we'll degrade their preparedness. Also, at the rate we're consuming munitions, I'm not sure how much longer we could keep up the air attack. Assuming that our bombing has worn down the enemy to the extent we need, the optimum time has always been the middle of February.

Cheney asked for a date. Schwarzkopf responded, "The twenty-first. But I'll need three or four days of latitude because we've got to have clear weather to kick off the campaign."[21]

For the Army, bad weather conditions were best for a movement to contact and attack. Wind and rain concealed the movement of forces and kept the enemy buttoned up. The noise of rain and wind covered up the noise of advancing formations. Thermal sights enabled the Army to see through the darkness and rain. Global positioning technology made it possible for ground forces to know where they were at all times. Hence, while bad weather increased the misery of soldiers and marines, it was a plus for the attacking forces. The situation was different for Boomer and his marines. The Marine Corps was more dependent on airpower than artillery, and Marine and Navy aviation needed favorable weather to fly in support of the Marines. Cheney took Schwarzkopf's recommendation to the President, who gave his approval. And, Schwarzkopf endeavored to give the Marines conditions that favored their doctrine.

Bush had one significant problem in the international environment, President Mikhail Gorbachev of the collapsing Soviet Union. While supporting the coalition, Gorbachev sought compromise solutions

until the ground war started. Iraq was in debt to the Soviet Union for billions of dollars. Its Army had been trained and partially equipped by the SU. The reputation of the Soviet Army was in some ways tied to the performance of the Iraqi Army. Gorbachev pushed for other solutions to save a client state. His efforts threatened to derail Bush's war plan. The French, who were members of the coalition, were very likely to side with Gorbachev if he could find a solution short of the ground war. Gorbachev's search for a diplomatic outlet created time constraints for Bush. The sooner the ground war started the better.

The air campaign lasted forty-three days. When Iraq accepted the terms for ceasefire, which began at 8:00 am Saudi time on 28 February, over 110,000 sorties had been flown in the 1,012-hour air war. The major conclusions of the Air Force were:

> Air power can hold territory by denying an enemy the ability to seize it, and by denying an enemy the use of his forces. And it can seize territory by controlling access to that territory and movement across it. It did both in the Gulf War. . . . The results of this war can hold no comfort for armored vehicle advocates, for air attack rendered all categories of armored fighting vehicles superfluous—they were no protection to their occupants whatsoever, no matter how thick their armor. In sum, air power produces the conditions conducive to both defeat and victory—by destroying enemy points of resistance, communication, leadership, morale, and means of supply, among others.[22]

In other words, the Army's armor divisions were a poor use of taxpayer money. Glosson concluded: "We had revolutionized the way war would be fought in the future. . . ." He believed the F-117s had "carried the war."[23] However, the GAO in its comprehensive study, provides another assessment:

> Air power was clearly instrumental to the success of Desert Storm, yet air power achieved only some of its objectives, and clearly fell short of fully achieving others. Even under generally favorable conditions, the effects of air power were limited. Some air war planners hoped that the air war alone would cause the Iraqis to leave

Kuwait (not least by actively targeting the regime's political and military elite), but after 38 days of nearly continuous bombardment, a ground campaign was still deemed necessary. . . . Saddam Hussein was able to direct and supply many Iraqi forces through the end of the air campaign and even immediately after the war. . . .[24]

The GAO's study concluded that, "Many [of the Air Force's] claims of Desert Storm effectiveness show a pattern of overstatement." There was nothing new in these conclusions. They have been made since World War II.

The Ground War

The XVIII Airborne Corps commanded by Lieutenant General Gary E. Luck was initially responsible for the defense of Saudi Arabia. The Corps grew significantly between August and early November when General Schwarzkopf felt confident enough to report to the President that he had sufficient forces to defend Saudi Arabia. The XVIII Airborne Corps consisted of the 82nd Airborne Division, 24th Infantry Division (Mechanized), and 101st Airborne Division (Air Assault). Attached to it for Operation Desert Storm were the 197th Infantry Brigade, 3rd Armored Cavalry

Fig 14.1 M1 Abrams Main Battle Tank and M2 Bradley Fighting Vehicle.

Regiment, 1st Cavalry Division, 1st Brigade of the 2nd Armored Division, 11th Air Defense Artillery Brigade, III Corps Artillery, 12th Combat Aviation Brigade, and the 3rd Armor Division (aviation elements). These forces represented the first phase of the deployment. The light forces were deployed by air and were operational within weeks. The heavy forces moved by sea. And it was not until October that significant numbers of M1 tanks and M2 infantry fighting vehicles were on the ground.

Forces in the second phase of the deployment came primarily from American NATO forces in Germany. The VII (Jayhawk) Corps, the same corps that landed at Utah Beach during the Normandy invasion, commanded by Lieutenant General Fredrick M. Franks, consisted of the 1st and 3rd Armored Divisions, and the 2nd Cavalry Regiment. It had faced the Warsaw Pact for three decades. Now it was being redeployed to Iraq. These forces represented the strongest ground combat force on Earth. In addition, the 1st Infantry Division (mechanized) from Fort Riley, Kansas, was deployed and attached to the VII Corps. The Army also deployed Special Forces and Rangers. In all, the Army deployed more than

400,000 soldiers to Saudi Arabia, more than half of its personnel.

The Marine Forces, Central Command (MARCENT) consisted primarily of the 1st and 2nd Marine Divisions (reinforced) under the Command of Lieutenant General Walt Boomer. The Marine Corps had three active and two reserve tanks battalions. All were deployed. The Marine Corps was in the process of transitioning from the M60A1 to the M1A1 main battle tank when the first deployments for Operation Desert Shield took place. The transition had not been completed when the ground war started. Only one and a half of the Marine Corps' five tank battalions had converted to M1A1s.[25] The Army attached the "Tiger Brigade," 1st Brigade, 2nd Armor Division, equipped with M1A1 tanks to add to the Marine Corps's firepower. The Marines also deployed the 4th and 5th Marine Expeditionary Brigade, a force of more than 20,000 marines, to prepare for an amphibious landing or feint off the coast of Kuwait.

The British 1st Armor Division, the French 6th Light Armored Division, a Saudi Mechanized Infantry Division, and two Egyptian and a Syrian division

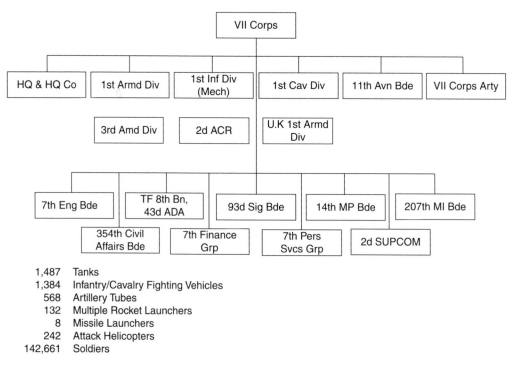

1,487	Tanks
1,384	Infantry/Cavalry Fighting Vehicles
568	Artillery Tubes
132	Multiple Rocket Launchers
8	Missile Launchers
242	Attack Helicopters
142,661	Soldiers

Fig 14.2 VII Corps, January 1991.

added to the coalition's combat power. The coalition force numbered 600,000, including: 35,000 British, 10,000 French, 35,000 Egyptians, 20,000 Syrians, 40,000 Saudi Arabians, 7,000 Kuwaitis, 1,000 Canadians, and 16,800 troops from other nations. This was a first—Arab divisions fighting alongside Western divisions.

On 22 August, Bush authorized the call-up of a limited number of National Guard and Reserve forces, and initiated "stop-loss" policies that precluded discharges and retirements of regular forces. Under the "total force concept" that Army Chief of Staff General Abrams put in place, it was almost impossible to deploy the regular Army without employing US Army Reserve and National Guard personnel. The same was true for the Air Force. Initially 40,000 personnel were brought on active duty, 25,000 of which were Army, for a period of ninty days with the option for a ninty-day extension. In November, Bush increased the authorization. Three National Guard combat brigades, the 48th Infantry from Georgia, the 155th Armored from Mississippi, and the 256th Infantry from Louisiana, were activated. In addition, two National Guard field artillery brigades were activated: the 142nd from Arkansas and Oklahoma and the 196th from Tennessee, Kentucky, and West Virginia. The 48th Infantry was supposed to be the "round-out brigade" of the 24th Infantry Division (mechanized) at Fort Stewart, Georgia.

The vast majority of National Guard combat forces mobilized for war came from the South. Had these forces gone into battle against a significant enemy, the South would have paid a very heavy cost. However, all three combat brigades required additional training and hence were sent to the National Training Centers for unit training. They were not ready on day one of the war, and hence, most of these units never saw combat.

The two artillery brigades were deployed in January and February. They provided fire support during Operation Desert Storm. Reserve and National Guard units are better able to maintain their proficiency if their primary function is fighting a machine, or employing some other piece of technology. Maneuver units require teamwork and trust, attributes that are acquired only through intense training. On 18 January 1991, Bush increased the authorization to 220,000

Reserve and National Guard forces for the period of twelve months. In Operation Desert Shield/Storm the Guard and Reserves fulfilled their traditional roles, serving honorably. By doing so they repaired reputations that were tarnished during the Vietnam War.

Between 6 August and 17 January, when operation Desert Storm started, the US deployed the equivalent of:

> the city of Atlanta, with all its population and sustenance, and moved it more than 8,000 miles to Saudi Arabia. Accomplishment of this feat required the unloading of 500 ships and 9,000 aircraft that carried through Saudi ports more then 1,800 Army aircraft, 12,400 tracked vehicles, 114,000 wheeled vehicles, 38,000 containers, 1,800,000 tons of cargo, 350,000 tons of ammunition, and more than 500,000 soldiers, airmen, marines, sailors, and civilians.[26]

Hospitals, police forces, clothing facilities, road construction machinery, sanitation facilities, water purification plants, offices and office equipment, computers, post offices, and numerous other facilities were deployed. This was no minor task.[27] It required professionalism, dedication, talent, and considerable tenacity.

* * * * *

The ground war commenced at 4:00 am on 24 February 1991. Bush informed the nation, "The liberation of Kuwait has entered the final phase." The Iraqi Army was not the fighting force Schwarzkopf and other American planners thought. It initiated the retreat well before main force units were engaged, and in many cases collapsed without a significant fight. It is estimated that as many as 200,000 deserted, surrendered, or decided not to fight. Which meant instead of fighting an army of over 500,000 in KTO, the coalition forces actually fought about 300,000 soldiers, still no small matter. The disintegration of Iraqi forces caused Schwarzkopf to revise his plan; however, not fast enough:

> Our primary force of heavy tanks—sixteen hundred of them—was waiting at the Saudi border to launch the main attack. It would have three key objectives: to free Kuwait City (the job of the pan-Arab corps of Egyptians, Syrians, and

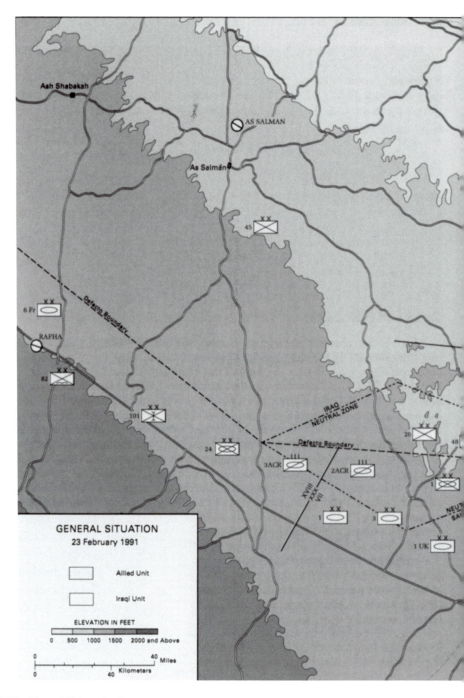

Fig 14.3 Persian Gulf War. "Jump Off Location."

Saudis, Kuwaitis, and other Arabs), to outflank and destroy the Republican Guard (the job of VII Corps), and to block the Iraqis' getaway routes in the Euphrates valley (the job of McCaffrey's division in the XVIII Airborne Corps). My battle plan called for this attack to be held off until dawn of the second day, in order to allow Boomer

twenty-four hours to breach the barriers and engage the defenders along the border. But Iraqi resistance seemed to be crumbling.[28]

As more information came in Schwarzkopf moved up the timetable for the main attack, and the turning movement. "So I gave the order to my

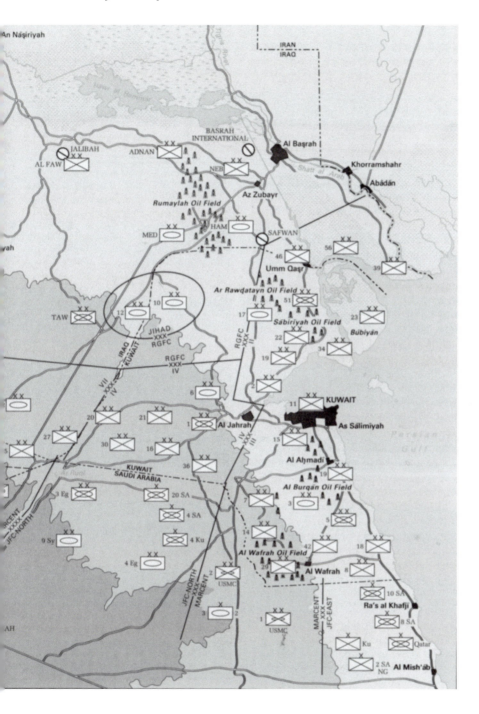

forces . . . at three that afternoon we let loose the main attack of Desert Storm." Others also recommended moving up the time for the main attack, sensing that fighting would not be as difficult as they initially believed. Schwarzkopf later worried, with good reason, that he would not have enough time to complete the destruction of the Iraqi Army before it evacuated into northern Iraq and beyond the range of ground forces.

Attacking forces crossed the line of departure, breaching the Iraqi defenses at multiple locations. Mine plows, mine rollers, various types of combat engineer vehicles (CEV) and armored combat earth-movers (ACE), line-charges, and marines with probing

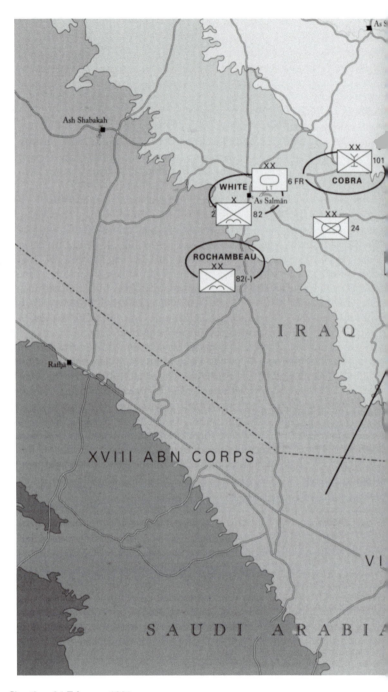

Fig 14.4 Persian Gulf War, Ground War Situation, 24 February 1991.

sticks were used to breach the minefields. Iraqi forces had had six months undisturbed to prepare defensive positions, construct obstacles, dig tank ditches, lay mines, construct hardened positions, develop a layered defense in depth, prepare kill zones, lay wire, and refine operational and tactical defensive plans. Yet any evaluation of the Iraqi defense has to rate it "poor." The Iraqi Army failed to use effectively its resources, manpower, time, geographic circumstances, and cultural strengths to construct the defense, a disgraceful lack of leadership. Breaching operations went faster than anyone expected and the coalition forces suffered few casualties. General Boomer, who had expected thousands of casualties,

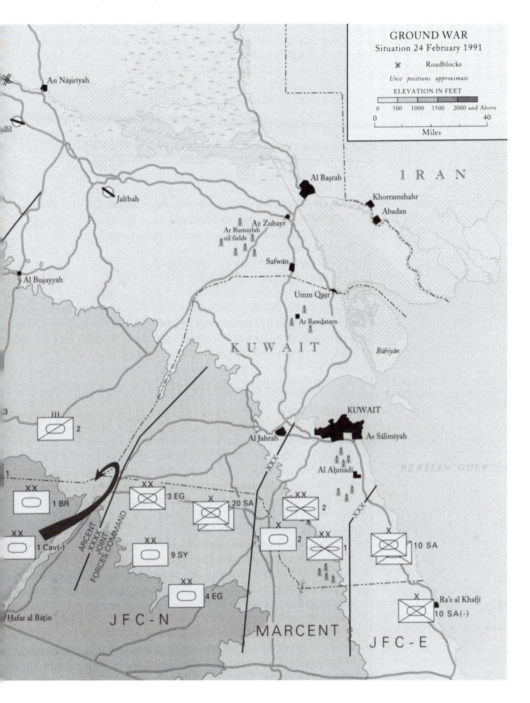

GROUND WAR
Situation 24 February 1991

✖ Roadblocks

Unit positions approximate

ELEVATION IN FEET

advanced virtually unopposed. In the first few hours of battle, the Marines had taken thousands of prisoners. Some fought, but most dropped their weapons and quit. The 1st ID allocated eighteen hours to breach lanes for the VII Corps's advance. It took two.

Fog, wind, rain, and sand delayed the airmobile attack of the 101st Airborne Division; however, within the first thirty-one hours of the ground war the 101st had established blocking positions on Highway 8; however, at Basra Iraqi forces could still cross in to the northern half of the country. The Air Force had destroyed a great many bridges, but not all. And pontoon bridges were quick to erect and repair. The 101st set up blocking positions with TOWs,

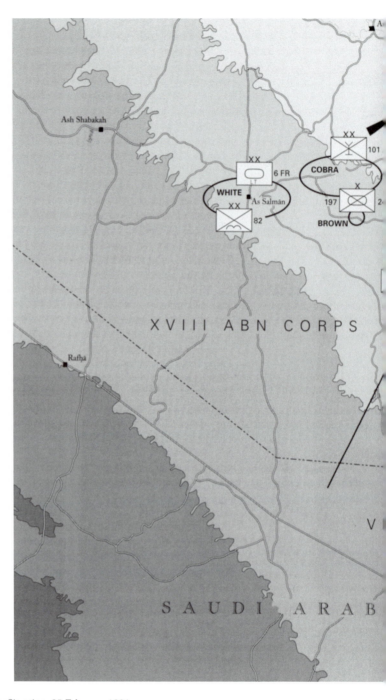

Fig 14.5 Persian Gulf War, Ground War Situation, 25 February 1991.

heavy antitank missiles with a range of over two kilometers mounted on HMMWVs. Each hour the strength of the positions grew. Apache helicopters were part of 101st's tank killing capabilities. The 101st's operation was the largest airmobile assault in history: sixty-six Blackhawks and thirty Chinooks established a forward operational base (FOB), from

which "Objective Sand" thirty miles short of Highway 8 was seized.

Through difficult terrain, General Barry McCaffrey's 24th ID made good progress towards its blocking position in the Euphrates valley. As it approached the Euphrates River Valley it fought through two Iraqi infantry divisions. On the evening of

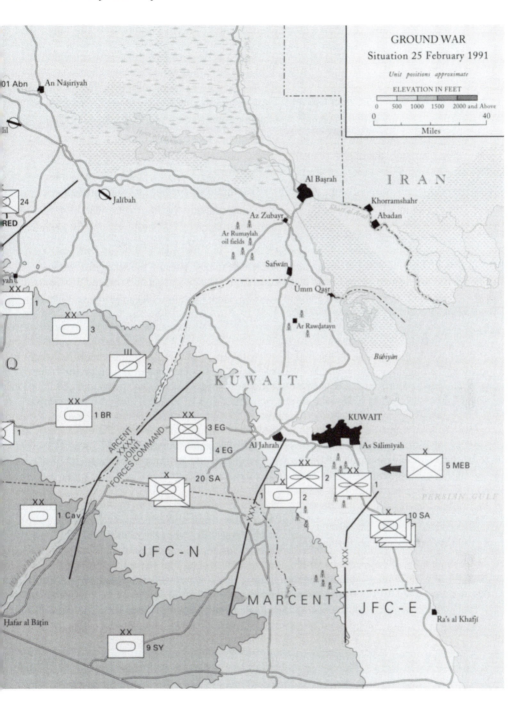

the 26th, the 24th ID established blocking positions on the highway, its armor greatly increasing the combat power of the 101st.

In VII Corps' area of operation, the covering force, the 2nd Armored Cavalry Regiment (ACR), quickly passed through the breaching units to assume the lead in this large-scale movement to contact. Unlike the two

supporting attacks that had terrain objectives, the VII Corps had to maneuver to find, fix, and fight the enemy. Intelligence from AWACs, U2s, and satellites provided General Franks with some information on the movement of enemy forces. However, these technologies did not entirely eliminate the fog of war. Franks had considerable doubts about the enemy's intents. VII Corps units, with 1,587 tanks and 1,502 Bradley fighting vehicles, following OPLAN Desert Saber, crossed into southern Iraq west of the Wadi Al Batin (see map), destroying elements of several divisions. The lead elements raced into Iraq at a pace of more than twelve miles per hour against light resistance. Franks wanted to keep his forces concentrated, and some of his elements were still passing through the initial breach points on the afternoon of the 25th, so he halted the advance of his lead formations on the night of the 24th.

Schwarzkopf had expected VII Corps to attack through the night, wheel to the east, and smash into the Republican Guard at the earliest opportunity: "I came into the war room early the next morning [the 25th] and hurried to the battle map to see how far we'd advanced during the night. 'What the hell's going on with VII Corps?' I burst out. Its lines had shifted backward."[29] Throughout the campaign Schwarzkopf expressed his dissatisfaction with Franks' plans and rate of advance. From the beginning to the end both men had very different visions of the operations.

The advance continued on all fronts throughout the 25th. Describing the operation, Franks stated:

> Our plan to outflank him [Hussein] was working. Elements of his forces were deploying to the south to face the 1st Cavalry. Iraqi forces were also deploying against our most westward forces. We were now deep into Iraq. On 25 February at 0841 I ordered the 1AD to shift northward and pass the 2ACR. 3AD was still behind 2ACR at that time. Early in the morning on 26 February at 0216 I gave a frag order to orient the force to the east. This meant the passing of the 3AD to the north between 1AD and 2ACR. By 0918 26 February the force was arrayed as follows: 1AD in the north, south of them 3AD, 2ACR and 1AD (UK). First Infantry [1ID] was in reserve behind 2ACR.

At this point, as the VII Corps turned 90 degrees to face east, the movement phase ended and the attack phase commenced. At 12:40, the 2nd ACR made contact with the Iraqi 12th Armored Division and elements of the Tawakalna Division (RGFC). At 1:30 the 1st AD hit the defensive perimeter of the Iraqi 26th Infantry Division. The 3rd AD, between the 2nd ACR and the 1st AD, also made contact with

enemy forces. Thermal sights, and the long range and accuracy of the main gun of the M1s gave US forces a tremendous advantage. The initial contacts were preliminary fights against blocking positions. Franks ordered his forces to keep moving. Small elements, battalions, were left behind to finish off opposition. Franks expected the main battle against the Republican Guard to take place on the evening of the 26th.

Around noon on the 25th, Schwarzkopf observed that in Kuwait City the Iraqi forces had blown up the desalinization plant. He interpreted this as a complete pullout. The Iraqi forces were evacuating Kuwait. Schwarzkopf decided to change the nature of the operation: "The campaign had shifted from deliberate attack to what tacticians call an exploitation, in which an army pursues a faltering enemy, forcing it to fight in hopes of precipitating a total collapse." Schwarzkopf, while noting that in his discussion with Yeosock, "I had determined to turn up the heat," he did not indicate that he issued new orders. In fact, he wrote: "While this pace was nowhere near as fast as I'd have liked, it was acceptable. Our intelligence showed that the Republican Guard was still holding its positions along Kuwait's northern border; as long as VII Corps moved out aggressively that day, it could still accomplish its mission."[30] Schwarzkopf concluded, "I began to feel as if I were trying to drive a wagon pulled by racehorses and mules." McCaffrey's 24th ID was the racehorse, and Franks' VII Corps was the mule. Schwarzkopf and Franks were fighting two very different operations. Franks continued to maneuver his forces for the attack while Schwarzkopf was in the pursuit and exploitation phase.

Schwarzkopf and Franks would later be criticized for failing to move to pursuit and exploitation fast enough, for failing to recognize after the fight for Khafji at the end of January that the Iraqi Army was not the first-class fighting outfit they had expected to fight.[31] During the battle for Khafji, it is argued, there was ample evidence that the Iraqi Army was still an Arab Army. Had the lessons of Khafji been learned Schwarzkopf would have attacked simultaneously along the entire front, or better yet, initiated the movement of the blocking forces first so they could get behind the Republican Guard, closing the escape route.

By 2:15 am on the 26th it was absolutely clear that Saddam Hussein was evacuating Kuwait. The evacuation message was aired over Baghdad radio. Saddam Hussein's forces did not leave Kuwait as they found it. Five hundred oil wells were set ablaze. Oil storage tanks were opened, their contents flowing into the Gulf. Kuwait's cities were looted.

On the afternoon of the 26th, Schwarzkopf's frustration over the pace of the advance exploded into threats. Yeosock informed Franks that Schwarzkopf wanted the tempo of the operation to speed up. Schwarzkopf's intelligence from electronic intercepts and aerial surveillance (JSTARS) informed him that Saddam Hussein's forces were trying to escape. From Schwarzkopf's view, this fact fundamentally changed the operation from what had been a *movement to contact* and *deliberate attack* to a *pursuit* and *exploitation.* Schwarzkopf wrote: "On the phone . . . 'John,' I said bluntly, 'no more excuses. Get your forces moving. We have got the entire goddamn Iraqi army on the run. Light a fire under VII Corps.' "[32] Schwarzkopf was wrong, as subsequent battles showed. In the Army's history of the VII Corps it was noted that:

> Within hours Schwarzkopf's intent, as Yeosock understood it, had changed, according to his executive officer, Lt. Col. John M. Kendall, from a 'slow and deliberate' pace 'to magic[ally moving] units forward.' Yeosock believed the theater commander had lost his appreciation of the 'time-distance factors associated with the movement of a heavy corps against enemy forces whose intent was still ambiguous.'[33]

The evacuation of Kuwait did not immediately change the situation that confronted Franks' VII Corps. While some Republican Guard divisions were retreating, others held their ground. They had to be fought. VII Corps was fighting and maneuvering to put four heavy divisions on line for the main attack against the Republican Guard. Tactically, Franks planned to conduct a double envelopment with two heavy divisions on each flank. Franks noted: "It is a fact of land warfare that you cannot have perfect knowledge of everything going on, so if you want to act, or think you need to act, then the higher you are, the more imperative it becomes to validate the information if your actions will affect the tactical battle." Franks continued:

The main problem that came out of all this was Riyadh's sense of our movement rate. On the one hand, there seemed to be a perception down there that all the Iraqi forces had been defeated virtually from the get-go (including the RGFC) and that all that was left was to pursue the defeated enemy and mop up (that nothing much was left for the Army and Marines to do but garrison the ruins). Well, the RGFC was still very much a fighting force, though greatly weakened. And we were not taking our own sweet time in getting ourselves to them—especially considering the lousy weather and the maneuver skills needed to put together a three-division fist. This wasn't some kind of a free-for-all charge, with tanks instead of horses and raised sabers. It was a focused maneuver involving several thousand fighting vehicles to concentrate combat power in a rolling attack against an enemy defending with tanks, BMP, and artillery.[34]

Franks was very sensitive to this criticism, which he believed reflected not only on his leadership, but also on the performance of the soldiers under his command. He concluded: "So give me a change in orders . . . or stay out of my way. Don't second-guess us at 600 kilometers from the fight." The fault was not completely VII Corps. Part of the problem was Schwarzkopf's plan.

Late on the 26th, VII Corps' main battle with the Republican Guard began. Franks maneuvered his force for the *attack* with four divisions and an armored cavalry regiment on-line, the 1st AD, 3rd AD, 2nd ACR, 1st ID, and the British 1st AD. For the next day and a half, until the ceasefire, the VII Corps was continuously in battle. At "73 Easting" grid line, the two lead cavalry troops of "Cougar Squadron" fought an intense tank battle.[35] Captain Herbert R. McMaster, one of the troop commanders, later stated:

> We pressed the attack east. The enemy had established a U-shaped defense and the troop had moved into the center of their position . . . tanks fired main guns and Bradley's fired TOW missiles at enemy tanks and personnel carriers forward of the 73 grid line. Violent explosions followed the impact of the perfectly aimed and guided fires. All vehicles were suppressing enemy infantry to the front who fired machine guns

at us and scurried back and forth among the endless sea of berms which comprised the enemy position.

The squadron took the position. However, the enemy tried to retake it:

> The enemy attempted a futile counterattack just before dark. Enemy tanks, BMP's, and MTLB's weaved between the berms to the troop's front attempting to close within range of their weapons capability. Tanks and Bradley's to the flanks, however, had relatively clear shots through the berms and the enemy effort was soon thwarted as, one by one, the enemy vehicles erupted into flames. TOW anti-tank missiles pursued and caught truck loads of enemy soldiers fleeing to the east. The Troop's mortar section was well into action now; dropping high explosive variable timed rounds which explode in mid-air and spray shrapnel down on the enemy infantry. We could see through the thermal sights that the mortars were exacting a heavy toll. The sun was setting. Continuous machine-gun and 25mm high explosive fire kept the enemy at bay and prevented him from organizing an effective counterattack. Enemy vehicles and bunkers continued to burn and the fire engulfed the troops in an eerie reddish glow which reflected off the heavy, low clouds. Occasionally, an enemy vehicle ammunition or fuel compartment erupted in a secondary, violent explosion.[36]

US forces had a number of advantages that were a function of Iraqi technology, training, and failure to adapt. The tank duels opened at a range greater than that expected by the Iraqis. As a consequence, their rounds repeatedly fell short, and the Iraqis failed to make the necessary adjustments. The same was true of artillery fire. Once the first rounds went down range, the Iraqis failed to make the necessary adjustment to bring the rounds on target. Iraqi tankers fired at the muzzle flash of American tanks and Bradleys, believing that the tank was, at least momentarily, stationary. The Iraqis fought as though they were fighting the previous generation of American tank technology, the M–60, which had to stop to accurately engage targets at great range. The main gun of the M1 operated with great accuracy on the move. Soviet advisors

were responsible, at least in part, for the poor level of Iraqi training.

An M1A1 Tank platoon leader, Lieutenant Richard M. Bohannon, recorded the action of his unit 1–37 Armor, 1st AD:

> On the night of February 26, 1991, we fought against the 29th Brigade of the Iraqi Tawakalna Division. The Tawakalna, part of Saddam Hussein's Republican Guard Division, was established in a blocking position in an attempt to allow retreating Iraqi forces to their rear an escape to the north. . . . Our mission was to attack in order to destroy the Republican Guard Medinah Division. . . . The discovery of such a large and previously undetected enemy force in our sector came somewhat as a surprise. . . . Visibility worsened, due to a sand storm mixed with rain. Thermal sights effectively cut through the haze, but identifying vehicles by type beyond 1500 meters was virtually impossible. . . . Task Force 1–37 and 7–6 both brought their teams/companies on line. . . . Meanwhile the pace of the fight began to accelerate. D/1–37 [a company] observed enemy troops 900 meters to its front advancing in 3–5 second rushes, and destroy them with coax [machine gun]. TF 7–6 and TF 1–37 reported additional troops and vehicles at 2000–4000 meters. They destroyed these targets with coax, TOW, 25mm, and tank min gun fire. . . .

Bohannon observed that: "The Bradley has proved to be a capable weapon system. Not only was its TOW an effective tank killer, but its 25 mm gun was also capable of destroying or disabling most Iraqi tanks and APCs." Bohannon continued:

> We advanced at a slow 5–10 kph rate. By 21.00, at least eight enemy vehicles were burning. . . . The attack continued toward the east. To our front we faced dismount troops in trenches and numerous armored vehicles in defilade, consisting predominantly of T–72s and BMP–1s. We fired at most of the vehicular targets at ranges of 2,200–2,800 meters, but engagements beyond 3,000 meters were not uncommon. One M1A1 on the move hit a BMP with HEAT round at 3,250 meters. The longest shot with a confirmed kill was 3750 meters. The Iraqis returned fire,

chiefly with small arms and machine guns, but also with T–72 main guns and/or dismounted antitank missile teams. Apaches joined in the fight. . . .

We fought a close battle on the objective. As we maneuvered around burning vehicles and bunkers, we lost four tanks to enemy fire. The first was D–24, which was struck in the left side. The explosion killed the engine and injured the loader and gunner. At 23:00, the infantry reported the area clear, and at 05:00 the next morning, the brigade reformed and continued the attack east. Final BDA [battle damage assessment] for TF 1–37's sector of the Battle of 73 Easting included 21 T–72s, 14 BMP–1s, two 57-mm AA guns, one T–62, and an MTLB destroyed, and over 100 EPWs [enemy prisoners of war]. Our personnel status was zero KIA, zero MIA, six WIA. TF 1–37 added two more successful battles to its history by 28 February.[37]

In every way—technology, training, leadership, and tenacity—Iraqi forces were outclassed. Iraqi ground forces were destroyed at an astonishing rate. An Iraqi tank battalion commander observed that after five weeks of war he had lost only two tanks to airpower. However, in less than six minutes of war with ground forces he had lost his entire command.[38] No armor or air forces in the history of warfare had gone through as many heavy formations as fast. At Medina Ridge on the morning of the 27th the 1st AD fought an intense battle, destroying over 300 tanks of the Republican Guard:

As they crested Medina ridge, Meigs ordered a halt when he realized the magnitude of the formation arrayed before him. To even the odds, he called for air support. Apache helicopters from 3–1st Aviation quickly took up station and hovered no more than 30 feet above TF 4–70th Armor's battle line before opening fire with Hellfires. Iraqi artillery immediately added background noise to the battle by dropping heavy fire behind Meigs' line of tanks. As usual, the artillery fired without adjustment and continued to land harmlessly in the same spot. Now Meigs' main tank guns added their own deadly tattoo to the crescendo of battle sounds. The farthest any had ever fired in training was 2,400 meters. Now,

when the pressure was really on, his tankers were regularly drilling sabot rounds through T–72s at 3,000 meters and beyond.[39]

The attack continued on all fronts throughout the day and into the night. By nightfall the VII Corps had destroyed five Iraqi heavy divisions. By this time the XVIII Airborne Corps had reinforced its position on the Euphrates, and the 24th ID with the 3rd ACR were advancing east towards the northernmost flank of the VII Corps. The 1st Cavalry Division, Army reserves, was placed under the operational command of the VII Corps, forming a five-division "fist." But Iraqi forces that had been pushed out of Kuwait and significant Republican Guard forces evacuated into northern Iraq, out of range of US ground forces. Anthony H. Cordesman concluded that on 1 March, Iraqi forces still had 842 tanks, 1,412 APCs/IFVs and 279 artillery pieces.[40] However, estimates of how many Iraqi forces escaped vary. At minimum four heavy divisions escaped; enough force for Saddam Hussein to crush any revolt. At 19:30 hours, the 1st ID and British 1st AD were directed to halt.

As Iraqi forces fled, the XVIII Airborne Corps destroyed a large convoy, supported by coalition airpower. The Air Force also destroyed a significant fleeing convoy. The next day, the 28th, at 8:00 am a ceasefire went into effect. The VII Corps was directed to secure Safwan airfield, where the armistice agreement was negotiated. On 2 March the ceasefire broke down, as a brigade from the Hammurabi Armored Division engaged Major General Barry McCaffrey's 24th ID. In an hour-long battle the Iraqi brigade was destroyed.

In four days the VII Corps advanced more than 150 miles, and destroyed an estimated 4,985 Iraqi vehicles, including 1,300 tanks, 1,200 infantry fighting vehicles and armored personnel carriers (APC), 285 artillery pieces, and 100 air defense systems. It captured 21,463 Iraqi soldiers, 600 tanks, 575 infantry fighting vehicles and APCs, 370 artillery pieces, 450 air defense systems, and 1,300 wheeled-vehicles. VII Corps suffered seven M1 tanks destroyed, four damaged; fifteen M2/M3 Bradley fighting vehicles destroyed and ten damaged; 2 M113 APC destroyed; one AH–64 Apache destroyed and one damaged. Twenty-eight VII Corps

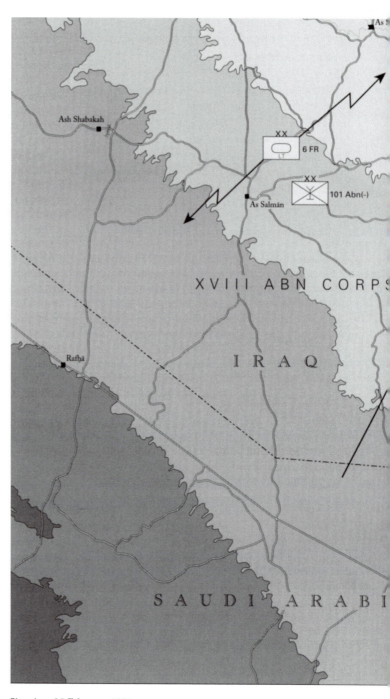

Fig 14.6 Persian Gulf War, Ground War Situation, 26 February 1991.

soldiers died in action. Could they have done more? According to one soldier who fought, the answer is: Yes. Colonel Douglas Macgregor wrote:

> The generals and colonels commanding the lead divisions and brigades in the VII Corps attack were much more concerned with what the

enemy *might* do to *them* than with what they could do to the enemy. Though their fears were never justified by the facts, their fears were real enough in their own minds to slow the VII Corps' movement to a snail's pace.

The fruits of victory, the total destruction of the Republican Guard, rotted on the vine while

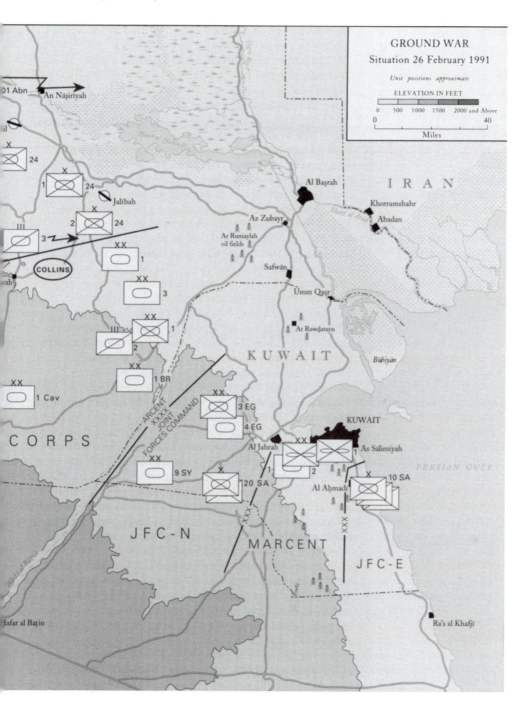

the commanding generals of the US Army's VII Corps wasted precious hours herding their division into a "tight fist" for a fight that was already passed. By the time the corps' divisions arrived and "attacked," little of the Republican Guard remained. . . .

What the soldiers of Cougar Squadron won on the battlefield—the opportunity to pursue and complete the destruction of Saddam Hussein's base of power, the Republican Guard Corps—was lost by the US Army chain of command that never saw the Iraqi opponent in a true light and never grasped the strategic implications of their actions. The result was the escape of the Republican Guard and its subsequent use by Saddam Hussein to destroy the Kurdish and

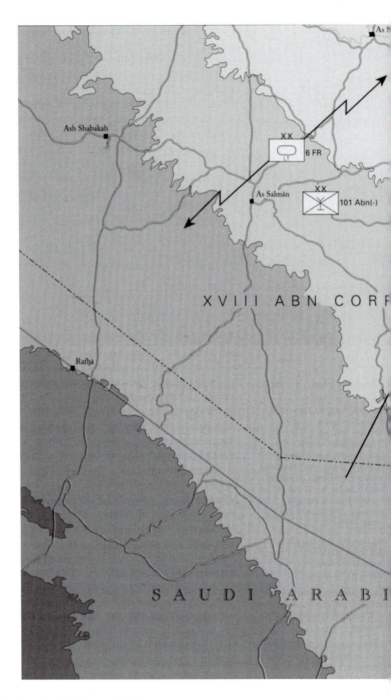

Fig 14.7 Persian Gulf War, Ground War Situation, 27 February 1991.

Shiite Arab insurrection that had been encouraged by the George H. W. Bush administration.[41]

The Army's failure to complete the destruction of the Republican Guard left Saddam Hussein in power. Franks made a number of significant mistakes, stopping on the night of the 24th, and failing to recog-

nize after the first couple of engagements that his Abrams, Bradleys, and Apaches were totally outperforming the Iraqis' Russian technology. It was not necessary to concentrate his forces. However, context is important. Franks' Corps had not seen battle. Franks' delay gave his men time to adjust to the battlefield. Franks also gave his soldiers a night to

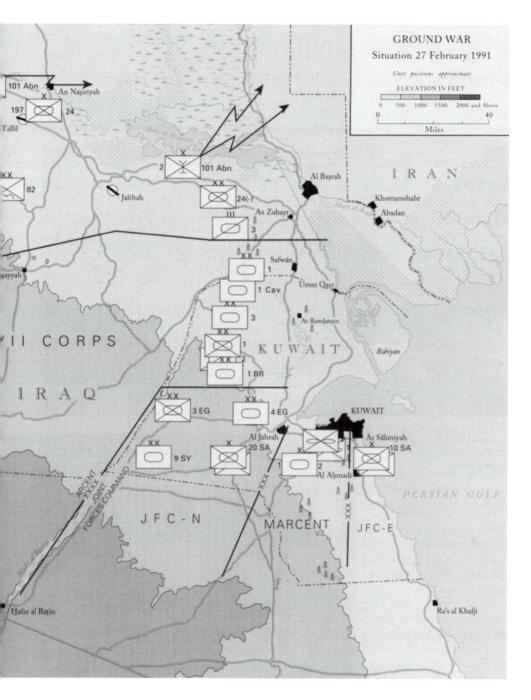

get a few hours of sleep before the main battle was joined. From the morning of the 25th to the morning of the 28th, his forces were constantly on the move and had the rest of the Iraqi forces turned to fight, the battle could have gone on for two more days. Franks may have taken a more cautious approach, but given the array of Iraqi forces fought, the potential of fleeing Iraqi forces to turn and fight,

the days of continuous operations in a stressful environment, the potential for the Iraqi forces to employ chemical weapons, and the fog of war, it is difficult to argue that his decisions were not justified. The decision to stop the war before the strategic objective of the destruction of the enemy's main army was achieved is another matter. But that was not Franks' decision.

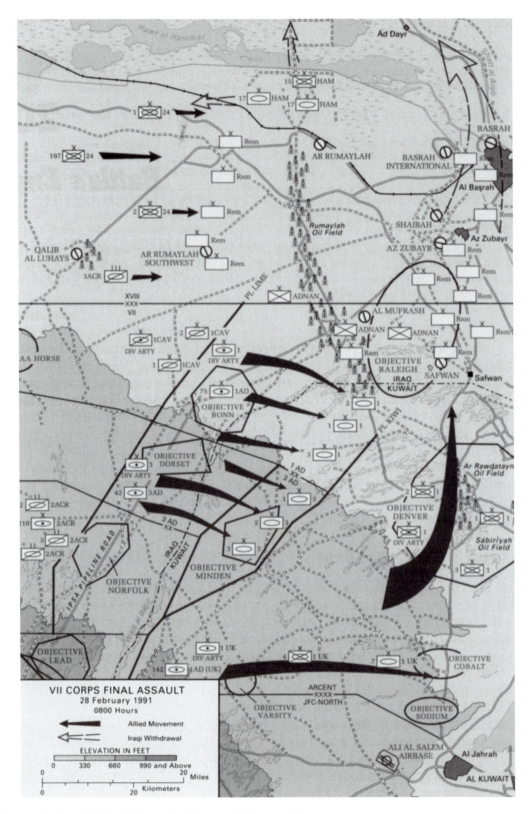

Fig 14.8 Persian Gulf War, VII Corps Final Assault, 28 February 1991.

In total, 246 coalition soldiers were killed. Of them 148 were Americans, thirty-five of whom were killed by friendly fire. Twenty-nine more Americans were killed when unexploded munitions blew up. In a television address on 28 February 1991, Bush declared, "Kuwait is liberated. . . . Iraq's army is defeated. . . . Our military objectives are met." The question quickly became: had the political objectives been achieved?

*   *   *   *   *

General Chuck Horner, USAF, wrote:

In the absolute final analysis, the ability of Coalition ground forces to defeat the Iraqi Army so rapidly and thoroughly may have little to do with destroying tanks and artillery. There is powerful evidence from the 88,000 POWs that air's most significant impact on Iraqi fighting strength was the destruction of morale.[42]

Iraqi forces folded after 100 hours of ground combat, causing many observers to conclude that the Air Force had won the war, and the Army had simply mopped up the battlefield. Horner continued:

Isolation of the battlefield denied the Iraqi soldier food and water, but he was at the same time worn down by the incessant air attacks, and by the PSYOPS campaign that held out hope in the form of surrender. He was also effectively disarmed, because by the time the ground war started, he and his companions feared going near their vehicles—APCs, tanks, and artillery pieces, which air attacks had made death traps.

Ground forces carried out the vast majority of the physical destruction of the Iraqi Army. During the ground war, of the 2,159 tanks destroyed, the ground forces destroyed 1,708 tanks, and the air forces 451; of the 521 APCs destroyed, the ground action accounted for 297, and air action 224; and of the 1,465 artillery pieces destroyed, the ground force eliminated 1,112, and air forces 353.[43] Given this data, it is difficult to argue that airpower won the war, even if one accepts Horner's argument of the destruction of Iraqi morale. To be sure, airpower destroyed the will and fighting spirit of some Iraqi units, but subsequent battles show conclusively that other Iraqi units fought with determination.[44] Like most armies, some units are better trained, led, equipped, and motivated than others. The Republican Guard units, and some Iraqi armor and mechanized divisions, were among the better units. Static infantry divisions, poorly trained formations, and those units that had little or no attachment to the regime had little reason to fight, and hence, collapsed with a little inducement and the promise of fair treatment.

The Army also rejected the argument that it won only because of its superior technology.[45] It is interesting to note that the Russians also rejected this argument, concluding that had Russian soldiers manned those T–72 tanks, which were considered the equal of the M1, the outcome would have been very different. The Army argued that it was better trained and led, and that the training revolution of the 1980s, which produced the NTCs, made the difference. While accepting this assessment and acknowledging that the Army deployed to the Gulf was the best-educated, best-trained army in its history, superior technology was no small factor in the outcome of the war. The M1A1 with its 120-mm main gun, laser range finder, upgraded computer system, thermal imaging sights, and cross-country speed gave the US forces considerable advantages. Other technologies such as the Apache and A-10 also contributed to the success. Arab culture was also a large factor. The Iraqi Army suffered from the same cultural disadvantages that the Egyptians, Syrians, Palestinians, and Jordanians suffered in all the Arab-Israeli Wars. Culturally, it was incapable of meeting Western standards of combat effectiveness and professionalism. Nevertheless, Americans could again feel proud of all the armed forces, and again believed the world had entered a new age. Most observers were convinced that American airpower technology had finally lived up to the claims of World War II, Korea, and Vietnam.

Military Victory and Political Failure

As soon as the Iraq War ended, the controversy began: had the war been stopped too soon? Did the US and UN achieve their political objectives? While the decision to halt the killing rested with President Bush, the Chairman of the JCS, Colin Powell, was the first to push for an end to hostilities. He explained why:

I had already spoken to Norm Schwarzkopf earlier in the morning and told him I sensed we are nearing endgame. The prisoner catch was approaching seventy thousand. Saddam had ordered his forces to withdraw from Kuwait. The last major escape route, a four-lane highway leading out of Kuwait toward the Iraqi city of Basrah, had turned into a shooting gallery for our fliers. The road was choked with fleeing soldiers and littered with the charred hulks of nearly fifteen hundred military and civilian vehicles. Reporters began referring to this road as the "Highway of Death. . . ."

Our forces had a specific objective, authorized by the UN, to liberate Kuwait, and we had achieved it. The President had never expressed any desire to exceed that mandate, in spite of his verbal lambasting of Saddam. We presently held the moral high ground. We could lose it by fighting past the "rational calculation. . . ." And as a professional soldier, I honored the warrior's code. "We don't want to be seen as killing for the sake of killing, Mr. President," I said. "We're within the window of success. I've talked to General Schwarzkopf. I expect by sometime tomorrow the job will be done, and I'll probably be bringing you a recommendation to stop the fighting."[46]

While the objective of the UN was the restoration of Kuwait, an objective that had been achieved, the US had also established the objective of the destruction of the Iraqi Army, and this job had not been completed. Still, Schwarzkopf supported the ceasefire decision even though he had earlier asked for an additional twenty-four hours. He wrote:

He [Powell] waited as I took a minute to think. My gut reaction was that a quick cease-fire would save lives. If we continued to attack through Thursday, more of our troops would get killed, probably not many, but some. What was more, we'd accomplished our mission: I'd just finished telling the American people that there wasn't enough left of Iraq's army for it to be a regional military threat. Of course, Yeosock had asked for another day, and I'd have been happy to keep on destroying the Iraqi military for the next six months. Yet we'd kicked this guy's butt, leaving no doubt in anybody's mind that we'd won decisively, and we'd done it with very few casualties.

Why not end it? Why get somebody else killed tomorrow? That made up my mind. "I don't have any problem with it."[47]

Schwarzkopf rationalized ending the war:

We hated the idea of sparing any Iraqi equipment, particularly Republican Guard T–72s: sooner or later those tanks would be put to malicious use. But from a purely military standpoint, and from the standpoint of our Arab allies, we weren't concerned. To reconstitute even a single effective division from what was left would take Iraq a long time.

Schwarzkopf was wrong. Saddam Hussein almost immediately used these forces and weapons to maintain political control.

Many scholars have since concluded that Powell was wrong for prematurely advancing a ceasefire, that Schwarzkopf was wrong for not arguing against it, and that Bush was wrong for accepting Powell's recommendation to cease hostilities, and for deciding not to force the Iraqi soldiers to walk home without their weapons and vehicles. Thomas G. Mahnken, in an essay entitled, "A Squandered Opportunity? The Decision to End the Gulf War," wrote: "Powell's fear of exceeding the culminating point of victory is . . . ironic, since, if anything, coalition forces stopped short of achieving a decisive victory, based at least in part upon his advice."[48] Bush missed the opportunity to remove a dictator, and by so doing laid the foundation for a second war in Iraq in 2003. Mahnken continued: "By contrast, halting too soon can yield an incomplete victory and leave in place a foe that is weakened but unchastened. Even though the Bush administration did an outstanding job of planning and conducting the Gulf War, it encountered considerable difficulty determining when to end it."[49] Michael R. Gordon and Bernard E. Trainor in their book, *The General's War*, also advanced this argument, adding that: "The United States also erred in renouncing any intention of going to Baghdad, a reassurance aimed at our Arab allies. This self-denial simplified things for Saddam Hussein when the ground war got under way. A 'survivor,' he then knew that he did not have to worry about the allies toppling him," a repeat of the Johnson mistake.[50]

Bush faced a situation similar to that faced by Truman following the Inchon Landing and the destruction of the NKPA. Whereas Truman decided to gamble and advance across the 38th parallel, Bush decided not to take Baghdad and occupy Iraq. Bush later wrote:

In my view, I told the country what we were going to do. The United Nations resolution authorized us to end the aggression. We tried to do it peacefully; and when that didn't work, we used force and we did, indeed, end the aggression. Our mission was not to kill Saddam and it darn sure was not to be an occupying power in that Arab country. It was simply to end the aggression, keeping our word along the way to our allies and the Coalition.

Bush and Scowcroft further noted:

Trying to eliminate Saddam, extending the ground war into an occupation of Iraq, would have violated our guideline about not changing objectives in midstream, engaging in 'mission creep,' and would have incurred incalculable human and political costs. Apprehending him was probably impossible. The coalition would instantly have collapsed, the Arabs deserting it in anger and other allies pulling out as well. Under those circumstances, there was no viable 'exit strategy' we could see. . . .

Bush concluded, "the United States could conceivably still be an occupying power in a bitter hostile land."[51]

Bush, unlike Truman, did not have to worry about major powers such as the Soviet Union or PRC entering the war. Hence, it can be argued that he had greater freedom to advance to Baghdad. However, Bush had formed a coalition that included Saudi Arabia, the nation that paid for most of the war, Egypt, and other Arab countries. For the first time in history, Arab Egyptian and Saudi divisions were fighting alongside American divisions. Bush had legitimate concerns about alienating these new allies that had stepped up to assist the United States. The Soviet Union and France also would not have supported a march on Baghdad. Bush also recognized the risks and difficulties in occupying an Arab nation.

Americans would be seen as an imperialist power. What started out as a limited war against a dictator had the potential to turn into a people's war against Iraqis and possibly other Arab states, and/or volunteer fighters from other Arab states. In this sense, Bush's decision carried risks similar to those faced by Truman. Then Secretary of Defense, Dick Cheney, defended Bush's decision:

If you're going to go in and try to topple Saddam Hussein, you have to go to Baghdad. Once you've got Baghdad, it's not clear what you do with it. It's not clear what kind of government you would put in place of the one that's currently there now. Is it going to be a Shia regime, a Sunni regime or a Kurdish regime? Or one that tilts toward the Ba'athists or one that tilts toward the Islamic fundamentalists? How much credibility is that government going to have if it's set up by the United States military when it's there? How long does the United States military have to stay to protect the people that sign on for that government, and what happens to it once we leave? [And, at what cost in lives and treasure?][52]

Bush was able to go against the American preference for total solution, absolute victory, in part, because the American people were not involved in the war effort. The "nation" was not at war. The military cluster fought the war. Nevertheless, an additional twenty-four hours, or the decision to make the Iraqis walk home without their weapons and vehicles, may have ended the reign of Saddam Hussein.[53] Was this the real mistake? While the Bush Administration proved adroit at gaining support for, planning, and fighting the war, it proved inept in planning the peace. And Bush should have consulted with his allies, particularly the British, who had very definite ideas about what the post-war peace ought to look like. It also would have been appropriate to consult with the UN.

The end of the coalition war signaled the start of another war in Iraq. The Kurds and Shia, with the encouragement of the White House, rose up to oppose Saddam Hussein. And, had coalition forces achieved a more complete victory, disarming Saddam Hussein, the rebellions might have succeeded. However, Saddam Hussein escaped the coalition war with significant combat power, and coalition forces stood aside and watched as he used them to retain power. Saddam Hussein used tanks and attack helicopters against unarmed people. Entire towns emptied as the inhabitants fled into the mountains. This was the shabbiest performance of the war. What principles, what moral laws, and what warriors' codes were at work that permitted this human catastrophe to take place? When George Bush left office, Saddam Hussein was still the dictator in Iraq, and Bush had reinstalled a monarchy, not a democracy, in Kuwait. Another opportunity squandered.

*   *   *   *   *

A few months after the end of hostilities, May 1991, the United Nations Special Commission on Disarmament (UNSCOM) arrived in Iraq to start the process of finding and destroying Iraq's WMDs, and identifying programs and facilities designed to construct them.[54] The International Atomic Energy Agency (IAEA), which had been in Iraq for a decade prior to the war, took part in the search for nuclear technologies and facilities. The IAEA was the UN body charged with enforcing the Nuclear Non-Proliferation Treaty. Signatories to the treaty were to permit inspections to insure that they were not developing or producing nuclear weapons.

When the world entered the nuclear age, it was acknowledged that only a few nations possessed the wherewithal to produce nuclear weapons. However, the knowledge to produce these weapons was not difficult to obtain. The acquisition of the production facilities, specific types of nuclear reactors required to produce plutonium and uranium 235, became the biggest obstacle. The oil-rich nations of the Middle East, while internally lacking the wherewithal to develop nuclear facilities, had the wealth to purchase them from any nation willing to sell the technology. Iraq had the desire and the wealth to acquire a nuclear weapons program, and the French and Russian governments were willing to assist. Israel, with the assistance of the US, had its own nuclear program. In 1981, the Israeli Air Force destroyed the Iraqi nuclear reactor before it went online. This action did not stop Iraq's search for nuclear weapons, and motivated other Middle East nations to initiate the search for nuclear technology to restore the regional balance of power that was lost with the Israeli acquisition of nuclear weapons.

In the wake of World War I, a war in which chemical weapons killed hundreds of thousands of combatants, the 1925 Geneva Protocol went into effect. It prohibited the use of gas and "bacteriological methods of warfare." In World War II, these terrible weapons were not used. However, the technology to produce these weapons spread beyond the borders of the Western developed nations. And some Middle East nations, with the assistance of the West, developed the means to produce and employ these weapons. In the aftermath of the Iran-Iraq War, during which Iraq employed these weapons with devastating effects against Iranian forces, the UN 1993 Chemical Weapons Convention prohibited the production, stockpiling, and use of chemical weapons and established inspection procedures. Other UN-sponsored laws, resolutions, and conventions were also designed to stop the spread of WMDs. However, the system went against the internationally accepted ideal of sovereignty—an ideal to which the US held firmly.

Iraq, in defeat, agreed to comply with UN measures governing WMDs and to submit to inspections. Resolution 687 went into effect immediately after the war. It required the "destruction, removal, rendering harmless of all chemical and biological weapons and all stocks of agents and all related subsystems and components and all research, development, support and manufacturing facilities related thereto; and all ballistic missiles with range greater than 150 kilometers [approximately 93 miles], and related major parts and repair production facilities." Saddam Hussein ignored Resolution 687. Instead of complying he engaged in games of subterfuge, misdirection, and "hide and seek." However, Dr. David Kay, the chief inspector for UNSCOM, was tenacious. His inspections were so aggressive and invasive that Saddam Hussein was forced to destroy large quantities of his stocks of chemical and biological weapons and the technology to produce them to preclude discovery. Saddam Hussein had significant enemies, both internal and external. If they perceived a weakness, or perceived that Saddam Hussein lacked the wherewithal to retaliate with substantial force, they might be motivated to attack or attempt to overthrow him. Hence, increasing the uncertainty about what weapons Iraq possessed was a form of security for Saddam Hussein. While UNSCOM was achieving its objectives, it was incapable of determining how much of this illegal material Saddam Hussein possessed or had destroyed. This intelligence gap was never breached, in part, creating the conditions that led to the second Gulf War in 2003.

The Media and Public Opinion

General Michael J. Dugan, US Air Force, observed:

> There is a good deal of ill feeling among members of the media over how they were treated by the military during the Persian Gulf War. The feeling seems to be mutual. In an interview with David Frost, Gen. Norman Schwarzkopf charged that during the war CNN was 'aiding and abetting an enemy. . . .'

In post-Vietnam War operations the Army and the other services, remembering the media's coverage of that war, tightly controlled the movement of the media, limiting its access.[55] The Bush Administration supported this policy. Bush believed that:

> Vietnam and Watergate had created an adversarial sense of cynicism among many in the press, who seemed convinced that all public servants could be bought or were incapable of telling the truth, that all were unethical in one way or another. The result was that every rumor is pursued no matter what the truth, no matter how hurtful to innocent parties.[56]

Given this lack of trust in the press, the armed forces, with the support of the President, took measures to control the movement of reporters. Instead of censorship, the services granted limited access, which achieved the same purpose. Still, the Center for Army Lessons Learned, After Action Report, Desert Storm, concluded: "Civilian news coverage contributed greatly to maintaining soldier morale during Desert Storm. The coverage was generally positive; the American people were behind the operation and soldiers felt this impact."[57] This assessment represented a shift in attitude that influenced the behavior

of the Pentagon, the White House, and the services in future wars.

Wars in the late twentieth century tended to be one major operation with numerous smaller operations carried out by the various branches of the service. The World War II equivalent would be the Normandy Invasion. The invasion, however, would be the entire war. Operations were fast and covered considerable distance. Hence, to cover an operation, reporters had to be transported and sustained by the major units that were moving with the flow of the battle. This gave the service considerable control over what reporters saw. And, the combat operations of the Air Force and Navy could only be viewed through the cameras of those services. In recognition of this new operational environment, in 1977 the Army disbanded the Army Field Press Censorship reserve units.

In Operation Urgent Fury in Grenada, 1983, the press was not permitted access to American forces, and for the first two days of the conflict they were not permitted on the island. The American people, who were growing more conservative, and less tolerant of the "left-wing, liberal press," tended to support the Pentagon's press policy. Nevertheless, after Grenada, the press complained loudly, causing General John W. Vessey, the Chairman of the Joint Chiefs of Staff, to form a panel to study how the needs of the press, to keep the American people informed, and the needs of the armed forces, to maintain operational security, could both be met. Major General Winant Sidle chaired the panel that came up with a number of recommendations, one of which was to select, provide security clearance, and train and equip a group of reporters that would be activated for a given military operation. Sidle explained how the system they developed was supposed to work:

> The press pool was envisioned as a small group of reporters, the size to depend on the situation. The group would be composed of representatives of the wire service, television, news magazines and daily newspapers, if possible. . . . The criterion used to select the news organizations gave precedence to those that cover the widest American audience. . . . Material generated by the pool would be made available to all interested agencies not included in the pool. . . . The

pool would be alerted shortly before an operation began, then transported to the scene at, or soon after, H-hour. Members would be briefed and provided with escort(s) and transportation to assist them in covering the story. They would also be provided with meals, billeting and a means to file their material back to their home offices. The panels also recommended that the largest possible pool should be used initially, and the pool would be replaced by "full coverage" as soon as feasible.[58]

In 1984 the DOD accepted the recommendations of the Sidle Panel, and in 1985 instituted the National Media Pool (NMP). DOD selected the networks and agencies, and they selected their "news media representatives," or reporters. The reporters received background checks, training, and accreditation, and became members of the Department of Defense National Media Pool. Members of the pool were on call in Washington, available for worldwide deployment.

After the NMP was formed, DOD conducted a number of rehearsals to identify and fix potential problems. The NMP was first employed in Operation Just Cause in Panama, December 1989. The system did not work as planned. Other reporters were on the scene before the NMP, and members complained that they were not granted the access required to make the effort worthwhile. Panama was a free and open country with a significant American presence. The major media networks had branches or affiliate stations in Panama. They were there before the operation started, and could travel throughout the country. Under these circumstances the only real privilege the NMP received was to witness parts of the deployment, and even there they were severely limited. The media could not cover many of the most impressive actions, those carried out by Rangers, Special Forces, and Navy SEALs.

In 1990, for Operation Desert Shield, the NMP was again activated. The Secretary of Defense, Dick Cheney, requested visas and access from the Saudi government for American reporters.[59] Access was granted provided the US military transport the reporters. In the initial deployments, a 17-person NMP accompanied US forces. CENTCOM, however, did not control the government of Saudi Arabia, and as the buildup of troops progressed, so did the buildup of reporters from all parts of the planet. In December, there were 800 correspondents in Saudi Arabia, and when the war ended, 1,600 reporters. Still, reporters could not accompany US forces during Operation Desert Storm without the approval of CENTCOM. And too many reporters hindered operations. Sidle explained:

> The press prefers to be on its own during battle but, as any military person who has seen combat knows, too many reporters on hand trying to cover an action can impair operational security and troop safety. Too many reporters on their own can impede the conduct of a battle. This is particularly true when the large majority of the correspondents are not experienced in covering combat, which was the case in Saudi Arabia. Some try to question troop leaders in the heat of a fight. Others draw unwarranted conclusions because they do not know or understand what is going on. Many are unfamiliar with the military tactics and, by their actions on the ground, can inadvertently create problems by exposing troop positions or movements, or by filing stories that will be helpful to the enemy.[60]

This is an old story. However, in World War II and Korea, the relationship was less adversarial. Footage from the Vietnam War reveals reporters interviewing soldiers and marines in the middle of the battles for Hue and Saigon during the 1968 Tet Offensive; absurd scenes of reporters sticking microphones to the mouths of soldiers in the middle of a firefight. Sidle recalled seeing a cable sent by a major television network to its Saigon bureau chief, which said: "When the Army does something well, it is not news. It is expected. So, concentrate on when the Army does something wrong. That's news." In 1991, Sidle concluded that, "Based on this network's current nightly news programs, the network is still sometimes operating by this principle." In addition, pseudo-news had become entertainment. The 24-hour news networks, talk radio, and news programs such as *Sixty Minutes, 48 Hours*, and others, had transformed news into entertainment, which significantly changed the journalistic ethics of reporters, producers, and anchors.

To accommodate the press CENTCOM formed 20 small press pools of roughly 17 reporters. Each was assigned to major commands for Operation Desert Storm. About half went to the Army and the other half to the Marines, Air Force, and Navy. DOD issued ground rules for reporters, and when Operation Desert Storm started, nearly 200 reporters were in place with combat units. Given that the services had to provide transportation, and other forms of support, this was no small task. Sidle noted that the ratio of reporters in the field compared favorably to other wars.[61] Still, reporters did not like being grouped together in this manner.

Public affairs officers reviewed stories to insure they were in compliance with the established ground rules. Operational security and force protection were the objectives of the "Media Ground Rules." They included for example:

> The following information should not be reported because its publication or broadcast could jeopardize and endanger lives. ... Any information that reveals details of future plans, operations or strikes. ... Information on operational or support vulnerabilities that could be used against US forces, such as details of major battle damage or major personnel losses of specific US or coalition units. ...[62]

In cases where the reporter and public affairs officer disagreed the problem was passed up the chain of command, and could go all the way back to the Pentagon. This review process could cause considerable delay, but neither the services nor the Pentagon had the power of censorship. Still, the press was never granted the type of access it had enjoyed in Vietnam. Reporters complained that they were being denied access, kept in groups, and were unable to investigate for themselves. In essence, they got the story the services wanted them to get.

US News and World Report concluded, "Because of the Pentagon's policy of refusing to permit reporters to freely accompany troops into battle, the four-day ground war was both sanitized and largely invisible."[63] To correct the historical record it published a book entitled, *Triumph Without Victory: The Unreported History of the Persian Gulf War*. In the type of war fought in the KTO it was not possible to have

reporters run around the battlefield independently, nor was it possible for the military to provide transportation, security, and PA officers for every reporter.

In Desert Storm, Americans could rightly conclude that the armed forces performed in an outstanding manner. However, if the press had been given free reign, the picture might have been somewhat different. Bad things happen in every war. In any large human endeavor where emotions and feelings run high, things are going to happen that people regret. The danger is when the minor stories of human failings come to dwarf the larger story of the human sacrifices that are being made to achieve some greater good. Still, the services and the Pentagon came away from the war with a more positive assessment of the press. In subsequent wars they instituted a policy of "openness." However, the antagonism between the two institutions remained.

During the war the media failed to question the validity of the stories "coming out of Kuwait," and the veracity of Kuwaiti officials. In fact, the media let itself be used as a propaganda instrument of the Kuwaiti government. It helped sell the war. To win the support of the American people, who had no affinity for Kuwaitis, stories were fabricated, taken out of context, and exaggerated. Stories about stolen incubators and babies being left on the floor to die, stories of mass rape and mass executions, and others, were clearly exaggerated to gain the moral support of the American people. The media failed to expose these inaccuracies.

The Verdict

The very success of the armed forces in Iraq paved the way for reductions in forces.[64] It was evident that the victory in Iraq could have been achieved with a considerably smaller Army. Immediately following Operation Desert Storm the Administration sought a "peace dividend." President Clinton was frequently blamed for "dismantling" the military. In fact he simply carried out the Bush cuts. The Cold War was over. It was time to get rid of the Cold War armed forces. More than a third of the Army was deactivated. The Bush Administration, even before the first missile was launched in Iraq, had started the deactivation of Army divisions. When the war started in Iraq the

Army was literally in the process of shutting down divisions. Deactivation was delayed to fight the war, but resumed immediately after it. Generous early retirement programs were implemented, a function of the new, high regard with which the American people held the armed forces in the wake of the Persian Gulf War. At the end of the Vietnam War no such programs were offered. And as before, there seemed to be no logic to the reduction in force. The light infantry forces, those units that would have been most useful in places like Afghanistan and Iraq, were eliminated. The 9th ID, 7th ID, and 6th ID furled their colors and went away. Hundreds of thousands of highly trained soldiers left the Army.

Unlike other reductions in force, the Army did not select the officers that departed. The Army offered generous retirement programs and other incentives, and those individuals who had the most options left. The Army lost many of its best soldiers and leaders, and shut down some of its most highly trained, motivated, and effective units. Light-infantrymen are a unique national resource that have been continuously undervalued in American culture, in part, by the erroneous belief that anybody can serve as a combat soldier. No other profession lives with the discomfort and the physical hardship experienced, accepted, and, in some cases, enjoyed, by infantrymen. It was this type of soldier the Army and the nation got rid of; the same breed that was required in Somalia, Afghanistan, Iraq, and other undeveloped regions of the world, where the physical comforts most Americans expect do not exist. This was the breed of soldier most needed to fight insurgent forces, conduct operations in urban and mountainous terrain, patrol borders, provide humanitarian relief, hunt down Osama Bin Laden, kill Taliban and al-Qaeda forces, contain regional warlords, carry out nation-building operations, and so on. No other fighting force is as flexible and can be moved as quickly to troubled regions. This was no small loss. But it went almost unnoticed until they were needed again.

Colonel Daniel P. Bolger, writing in 1999, echoed concerns voiced by Bradley, Collins, and Ridgway in the late 1940s and 1950s:

American military leaders [and political leaders] intentionally and systematically substituted firepower for manpower. ... With 91 active-duty infantry battalions (67 Army, 24 Marine) and the Army Special Forces, Navy SEALs, and Air Force combat control teams who also fight up close and personal, there are about 100,000 infantry types in the entire armed forces. ... The armed forces field 1.4 million men and women. Doing the math tells its own tale. For every rifleman or machine gunner, there are thirteen guys doing something else.[65]

The all-volunteer, professional force performed extraordinarily well in its first major war against a large force armed with much of the latest Soviet weaponry. And it did so without the American people, validating the new American way of war. In the wake of the war, after nearly fifty years of worry, Army leaders stopped voicing their concerns about the willingness of the American people to defend freedom in distant areas of the world. It was more effective to fight war without disturbing the American people. The victory also gave subsequent White House and Pentagon civilian leaders supreme confidence in the capabilities of the armed forces, and thus, the willingness to use them. The operational tempo of all the services increased considerably during the Clinton and second Bush Administrations. However, Operation Desert Storm was in many ways an aberration, coming when it did at the end of the Cold War. And, it is important to remember that contrary to the initial belief, the US did not fight a cohesive, culturally unified nation that was capable of fighting a more total, people's war. And President Bush, Secretary of Defense Cheney, and Chairman of the JCS Powell took extraordinary measures to insure that the US did not get bogged down in a war with the Iraqi people.

The Bush Administration handed power over to the "baby-boom" generation, the generation that had not experienced the Great Depression or World War II, that had benefited most from the great prosperity of the 1950s and rapid advances in technology, and that had experienced and participated in (one way or another) the nation's first defeat in war. These were very different Americans. The sacrifices, hardships, uncertainties, and fears that shaped the World War II generation were unknown to them.

*   *   *   *   *

In the aftermath of the Persian Gulf War American power, prestige, and influence were the highest they had been since World War II. The Berlin Wall had fallen, the Cold War was over, the Soviet Union was collapsing, and the US stood alone, as the world's only superpower, and it had just demonstrated that power to the world, creating considerable awe. Economically and technologically, the US had no equals. At this juncture, President Bush had a rare opportunity, one that comes along maybe once in a century, to articulate a new vision for the world to replace the Cold War world order. He had the political, military, and economic powers to put in place a "new world order." Bush, however, was not a man of vision, nor was he able to adopt the ideas of others. The opportunity passed. The awe was fleeting. Under the Bush leadership, or more accurately, absence of leadership, the US squandered an opportunity to reshape the world. In this vacuum created by the end of the Cold War, radical, anti-American elements grew. Their ideas and vision took hold in the Middle East, and other parts of the world. This lapse was one of the biggest political failures of the twentieth century.

15.
THE NEW AMERICAN PRACTICE OF WAR: WAR WITHOUT THE PEOPLE

Between the early centuries of the Republic's expansion, when the grant of citizenship was used again as a means to hold the state together, citizenship essentially was a status, which conveyed certain legal powers or benefits. It was also a moral demand in that, out of historical and contemporary ethical belief and practice, it placed before a man a schedule of his responsibilities toward the patria. . . . Historically, citizenship had called for a payment of taxes; now Rome was so rich those taxes were no longer required. Moreover, that same wealth did away with the military service every Roman owed his patria. Citizen mercenaries, recruited from the lower classes, now filled the ranks and gave their allegiance to Marius, Sulla, or some other general or politician who promised them good pay and retirement benefits.[1]

–Peter Riesenberg, *Citizenship in the Western Tradition*, 1992

Cultural dissonance has developed, to some degree, in communities all around the country. On the eve of the twenty-first century, America has become a splintered society, with multi-ethnic towns . . . reflecting a nation more diverse than ever. [T]he term cluster . . . refers to population segments where, thanks to technological advancements, no physical contact is required for cluster membership. . . . [T]he clusters simply underscore realities already apparent, such as the widening gap between the richest and poorest Americans. . . . Sociologists say global competition and the cyber-revolution have widened the gap that divides the haves from the have-nots. . . . "No longer are Americans rising and falling together, as if in one large national boat," former labor secretary Robert Reich observed. "We are, increasingly, in different, smaller boats." And not all are assured of life rafts.[2]

–Michael J. Weiss, *The Clustered World*, 2000

In the years following the Vietnam War, starting with the end of the draft, the armed forces of the United States formed a "military cluster" (0.5 percent of US households), a professional, long-serving fighting force with its own unique system and set of values, ethics, and beliefs. By default, they would fight the next war and the future wars of the United States assisted by various private military firms (PMFs). The most significant transformation in the American conduct of war since World War II and the invention of the atomic bomb was not technological, but cultural, social, and political: *the removal of the American people from the conduct of the wars of the United States.*

One of the essential elements of the modern nation-state, the citizen-soldier, the dual role of sovereign and subject, no longer exists in the United States. Clausewitz's trinity of war—the marriage between the people, the government, and the armed forces—no longer reflects reality in the United States. Professional armed forces and private military firms under the direction of the central government now conduct the wars of the United States. One observer concluded that:

The United States now has a mercenary army. To be sure, our soldiers are hired from within the citizenry, unlike the hated Hessians whom George III recruited to fight against the American Revolutionaries. But like those Hessians, today's volunteers sign up for some mighty dangerous work, largely for wages and benefits—a compensation package that may not always be commensurate with the dangers in store, as current recruiting problems testify.... Since the time of the ancient Greeks through the American Revolutionary War well into the 20th century, the obligation to bear arms and the privileges of citizenship have been intimately linked.... That tradition has now been all but abandoned.[3]

During the two long wars in Afghanistan (2001–present) and Iraq (2003–2010), the government has used reenlistment bonuses and other financial incentives to keep soldiers and marines on active duty, and to recruit new soldiers and marines. Those with the least are the most responsive to these financial incentives. However, patriotism still matters. It motivates and inspires our men and women in uniform. PMFs are in fact the modern equivalent of mercenary armies. If present trends continue, humanity may one day view the nineteenth and twentieth centuries as an aberration, the centuries of the rise and decline of the nation-states. What is transpiring in the United States is not unique to it. Other Western states, including Germany, France, Britain, and other socially and culturally Western states, such as Japan and Korea, are going through a similar transformation. Affluence and consumption is eroding the martial. Increased diversity has diminished national cohesion and the sense of nationalism. Advanced technologies have seemingly reduced the need for combat soldiers. What this may ultimately mean is an end of the ability of *Western* governments to fight more total war, to produce holocausts such as World Wars I and II. For without the willing support of the people, such carnage is not possible. This, however, will not bring an end to such wars. Much of the world has not embraced Western values and ethics. Much of world lives with trauma and in poverty. There will be wars, and the Western world will *not* be able to avoid them. The question is: will the evolving military system—a system almost devoid of the will and participation of the people—be

able to provide the security necessary to sustain the Western way of life?

* * * * *

With the collapse of the Soviet Union and Communism in Eastern Europe (circa 1989), the US Army and Air Force were partially out of work. They needed new missions, new direction, and transformation. The potentially catastrophic war the two services had prepared to fight for half a century would not take place in the foreseeable future. In the 1980s, the decade just prior to the Soviet demise, the Army had more than a third of its forces and the majority of its armor combat power in Europe—roughly 300,000 soldiers, two corps, the equivalent of more than five divisions. The Army's heavy divisions, its armored forces, now appeared to many people as obsolete. There was serious talk that the days of the tank had passed. The Air Force's strategic bombing and air superiority missions against the Soviet Union had shaped its doctrine and technology. The B1 and B2 bombers were designed to penetrate Soviet air space and deliver nuclear weapons. The Air Force's new F-22 Raptor was designed to defeat the best Soviet air superiority fighter. These missions no longer provided a reason for being. Both the Army and Air Force needed new missions to justify their force structure. The collapse of the Soviet Union had little influence on the Navy's surface fleet and the Marine Corps. The mission of the Navy's aircraft carrier fleet was little changed, and the Marine Corps had no significant forces in NATO. (The strategic mission of the Navy's fleet of missile-launch and attack submarines was also diminished by the demise of the Soviet Union.)

The Army and Air Force did not have to look far for new missions. Continuous crises in the Middle East, the attacks of 9/11, and two of Bush's "Axis of Evil" states, Iran and Iraq, provided new purpose and direction. However, gaining access to the region and the very different nature of the threat required the two services to reexamine their force structure, means for deployment, and operational doctrine. The transformation of the two services was, at least in part, a function of their changing roles and missions. The new orientation of the Army and Air Force caused them to collide with the Navy and Marine Corps, but there was more than enough work for all the services. The air forces and ground forces of the Navy and Marine Corps were based at sea. Thus, they did not have the problem of access that confronted the Army and Air Force. The Army needed bases in the Middle East. It needed lighter, faster, more strategically airmobile forces, and it needed a fleet of new C-17 transport aircraft to provided strategic mobility. It also needed greater operational intra-theater mobility—air and sea. It did not need large numbers of heavy armor formations. The new enemies had no equivalence to the Soviet Tank Corps. The Air Force also needed new bases and an expanded air refueling capacity. Air Force bombers had global reach; however, its fighters required numerous refuelings to stretch airpower from the US and Europe to the Middle East. Hence, the Air Force too needed advanced bases. Private military firms (PMF) provided the Army strategic mobility, transporting heavy armor forces from the US to the Middle East, and took care of the maintenance of tanks, infantry fighting vehicles, and other equipment on ships pre-positioned in the region. PMFs also provided some intra-theater mobility.

In the wake of the Persian Gulf War, Operation Desert Storm, it was believed that information, stealth, and precision technologies were "revolutionizing" the conduct of war. It was believed that a revolution in military affairs (RMA) was under way, toward a form of war called "network-centric warfare."[4] It was uncertain what the services would look like when transformed, and it was uncertain exactly how information destroyed the enemy's will to resist, his fighting forces, and/or his government. However, smaller, faster, more effective forces were the expected outcome of the RMA. While not fully implemented, the RMA proved ineffective in achieving political objectives in Iraq and Afghanistan. And, once again soldiers, not airpower, were needed to achieve the missions.

The Gulf War showed the effectiveness of stealth and precision technologies, and showed that the Army, which suffered few casualties in the ground war, could have destroyed the fourth-largest army on Earth with half the forces deployed. What this told Americans was that the all-volunteer force was working and effective, but that its ground forces were too large. It appeared that the US could get rid of substantial parts of the Army, more than a third, and experience little or no deterioration in capabilities.

The US could also increase its effectiveness by investing in new airpower technologies. No matter what the outcome of a war, Americans always learned the same lessons. Lessons are learned through the prisms of culture, which produces a strong preference for technological solutions and a strong disinclination to employ American manpower in artificial limited wars.

War Without the People: The Clustering of America

As a consequence of the increased cultural diversity of the American population, conflicting interests, and the fight for limited resources, "tribal nations" formed across the US. According to the 1990 census, Americans belong to 75 ethnic tribes, 600 Native American tribes, 70 Hispanic tribes, and many racial tribes. Between 1970 and 1990, 26.3 million immigrants became occupants of the US, creating new school districts in New York, Los Angeles, and Chicago. Over 100 different languages are spoken in the American school system. Given the diversity of the American population and the ways in which they form enclaves, it is more accurate to think of the United States as a composite state, made up of many diverse tribes, than a culturally cohesive nation. There are tribal nations in the United States that because of ethnic, racial, or religious heritage and attachments, consistently place the welfare of other nation-states before that of the US. Without cultural cohesion it is impossible to fight total war, or significant limited wars. Consider these words:

> Cultural uniformity in some degree must characterize the members of a society. The members need not be identical.... The members must, however, be in some respect similar. They must have some sentiments in common, or there can be no spiritual union. They must have some standardized responses to language and other means of communication, or there can be no obedience or leadership. They must have some common aims, or there can be no co-operation.[5]

With the end of the draft, one of the primary mechanisms for bridging the gap between cultural, racial, ethnic, and other groups was eliminated. The armed forces realized that the all-volunteer force enhanced professionalism, reduced turnover, and promoted homogeneity. The people who joined wanted to be there, and they stayed longer. Once indoctrinated with military values, ethics, and beliefs, and, hopefully, love of service, these individuals became life-long soldiers, sailors, airmen, and marines. They became part of a military interest group. Upon retiring or leaving the service—and with a twenty-year retirement program many officers and NCOs departed the military every year—they retained the attachments to their service. They joined and supported the many military organizations that lobby Congress, and advanced issues important to the services. Many worked in military towns or industries that supported major units or produced equipment and weapons for the military. Their numerous attachments to their service influenced how members of the military cluster viewed the world, how they thought, and how they voted. This cluster influenced the growth of militarism in American culture and society.

The demographic of the military cluster was not and is not representative of the nation. By the end of September 2000, forty-two percent of all recruits were from the South.

Consider the words of Secretary of Defense Robert Gates:

> The nearly four decades of all-volunteer force has reinforced a series of demographic, cultural, and institutional shifts affecting who is most likely to serve and from where. Studies have shown that one of the biggest factors in propensity to join the military is growing up near those who have or are serving. In this country, that propensity to serve is most pronounced in the South and Mountain West, and in rural areas and small towns nationwide—a propensity that well exceeds the communities' portion of the population as a whole. Concurrently, the percentage of the force from the Northeast, West Coast, and major cities continues to decline. I am also struck by how many young troops I meet who grew up in military families, and by the large number of our senior officers whose children are in uniform. . . .
>
> In addition, global basing changes in recent years have moved a significant percentage of the Army to posts in five states: Texas, Washington, Georgia, Kentucky, and . . . North Carolina. For otherwise rational environmental and budgetary

reasons, many military facilities in the northeast and west coast have been shut down, leaving a void of relationships and understanding of the armed forces. This trend also affects the recruiting and educating of new officers. The state of Alabama, with a population less than 5 million, has 10 Army ROTC host programs. The Los Angles metro area, population over 12 million, has four host ROTC programs. Chicago metro area, population 9 million, has three.

Gates concluded that: "there is a risk over time of developing a cadre of military leaders that politically and culturally, and geographically have less and less in common with the people they've sworn to defend." In 2000 the vast majority of military personnel and former military personnel (excluding African Americans) were Republicans. "Among those in both the elite military and active reserve groups, Republicans outnumbered Democrats by margins of approximately 8 to 1 and 6 to 1, respectively. In contrast, the civilian leaders were more evenly divided, with a strong plurality of the veterans preferring the Republicans. . . ."[6] It can be argued that in the hotly contested 2000 election between George W. Bush and Al Gore, the military pushed Florida into the Republican camp, securing a victory for Bush.

One student of civil-military relations, Thomas E. Ricks, wrote: "US military personnel of all ranks are feeling increasingly alienated from their own country, and are becoming both more conservative and more politically active than ever before."[7] Ricks recorded the feelings of several military leaders:

> 'Today,' says retired Admiral Stanley Arthur, who commanded US naval forces during the Gulf War, 'the armed forces are no longer representative of the people they serve. More and more, enlisted [men and women] as well as officers are beginning to feel that they are special, better than the society they serve. This is not healthy in an armed force serving a democracy.'

Retired Lieutenant General Bernard Trainor, USMC, explained the difference: "When I got out of boot camp, in 1946, society was different. It was more disciplined, and most Americans trusted the government. Most males had some military experience. It

Table 15.1 Sample demographics of three surveys of American soldier veterans of Iraq, Kuwait, and Haiti and US Army active duty soldiers

Demographics	Iraq soldiers Summer 2004 (n = 968)	Kuwait soldiers February 2003 (n = 185)	Haiti soldiers February 1995 (n = 522)	Active army demographics, 2004 (n = 494,291)
Gender				
Male	87.6	86.8	93.9	85.3
Female	12.4	13.2	6.1	14.7
Rank				
Junior enlisted	46.9	52.9	66.1	40.6
NCO	34.8	33.2	29.5	44.7
Officers	18.3	14.0	4.5	14.8
Race				
African-American	19.6	17.7	16.9	22.7
Asian-American	1.1	.6	—	—
Whites	55.7	55.4	62.5	60.1
East Indian-American	.1	—	—	—
Hispanic-American	11.7	7.4	8.1	10.3
Middle Eastern-American	.3	—	—	—
Native American	1.1	2.2	—	—
Pacific	1.7	.6	—	—
American Bi-Ethnic-American	2.7	8.6	—	—
Others	6.1	7.4	16.8**	6.9**
Age			Age	
17–19	3.5	7.8	— 17–19	7.0
20–22	23.1	23.5	— 20–24	34.0
23–25	23.1	25.1	— 25–34	35.0
26+	49.7	43.6	— 35–44+	24.0
Religious affiliation				
Christian	67.3	68.6	—	—
Others	22.7	15.2	—	—
None/Atheist/Agnostic	9.9	15.1	—	—
Married status				
Yes	51.4	51.5	55.0	51.0
No	48.6	48.5	45.0	49.0
Significant other (married, fiancé, dating, etc)				
Yes	74.8	79.8	75.2	—
No	25.2	20.2	24.8	—
Children				
Yes	43.6	45.3	43.6	46.0
No	56.4	54.7	56.4	54.0
Political affiliation				
Democrat	25.3	21.6	—	—
Republican	31.1	34.7	—	—
Other/None	43.6	43.7	—	—
Military branch (Officers Only)	—			
Combat	43.5	6.7	67.2	—
Combat Support	12.9	16.7	18.6	—
Combat Service Support	23.6	76.7	14.2	

Demographics	Iraq soldiers Summer 2004 (n = 968)	Kuwait soldiers February 2003 (n = 185)	Haiti soldiers February 1995 (n = 522)	Active army demographics, 2004 (n = 494,291)
Education				
Some high school/ diploma	37.7	47.8	52.6	76.0
Some college	40.0	38.6	41.6	7.0
4 Year college degree	16.9	9.2	3.9	11.0
Some graduate School/ degree	5.4	4.3	2.0	6.0
Previous military deployments	—			
Yes	59.6	66.6	39.3	—
No	40.4	33.4	60.7	

Notes

1 Columns may not equal 100 percent due to rounding error.

2 **Includes all except African-Americans, Whites, and Hispanics.

3 A dash ("—") implies the question was not asked or no data are available.

was an entirely different society—one that thought more about its responsibilities than its rights." Trainor's comments reveal not only his assessment of American society, but also a perception of how the American concept of citizenship has changed.

While Ricks' study is not scientific, and is based on analysis of a small group of marines, other studies support his conclusions. In the 2003 *Military Times* poll it was found that:

> Two-thirds [of surveyed military personnel] said they think military members have higher moral standards than the nation they serve.... Once in the military many said, members are wrapped in a culture that values honor and morality. 'Even if you don't have it when you enlist, they breed it into you to be a better person,' said Army Sgt. Kevin Blanchard. 'When you go home you see how you're different than the people you grew up with.'

It was also found that: "Respondents were evenly split on the question of whether civilian leaders have their best interests at heart."[8] Consider the words of a young marine corporal who served in Iraq in 2003:

We all came together
Both young and old
To fight for our freedom
To stand and be bold

In the midst of all evil
We stand our ground
And we protect our country
From all terror around

Peace and not war,
Is what some people say
But I'll give my life
So you can live the American way.

I give you the right
To talk of your peace
To stand in your groups
and protest in our streets.

But still I fight on,
I don't bitch, I don't whine.
I'm just one of the people
Who is doing your time.

I'm harder than nails,
Stronger than any machine.
I'm the immortal soldier,
I'm a US MARINE!

So stand in my shoes,
And leave from your home.
Fight for the people who hate you,
With the protests they've shown.

Fight for the stranger,
Fight for the young.
So they all may have,
The greatest freedom you've won.

Fight for the sick,
Fight for the poor,
Fight for the cripple
Who lives next door.

But when your time comes,
Do what I've done.
For if you stand up for freedom,
You'll stand when the fight's done.[9]

In fact, there was very little protest against Operation Iraqi Freedom (OIF). Most Americans were detached from it. Still, the contempt of this young marine is evident, and a conversation at any airport in America with veterans of the wars in Iraq or Afghanistan reveals similar attitudes. The men and women of the armed forces of the United States have not reflected mainstream American values, ethics, and beliefs since the advent of the professional force. The government and military have proven that they can prosecute limited wars achieving the stated political objectives without the participation of the American people. The obvious conclusion of these developments and Weiss's cluster theory is that a small, affluent, political cluster decides which wars the professional military cluster will fight, and the military cluster endeavors to dispassionately execute the wars with the most lethal array of weapons possible. The irony is that in the midst of the greatest wealth of military weapons and technologies the world has ever seen, in the midst of the most destructive power ever created by man, fewer and fewer Americans are involved in employing that power and making the decisions on when and against whom it will be used.

In 2003, when it became evident that the Army and Marine Corps were too small to carry out all assigned missions, the White House and Pentagon could not call upon the American people to make up for its miscalculations, flawed strategies, and intelligence and foreign policy failures. The military cluster instead bore the full burden of the nation's next two long wars. *Equality of sacrifice* was no longer a consideration in the nation's procurement of manpower.

This problem, that had plagued administrations since the Korean War and the advent of artificial limited war, had finally been rectified.[10] The removal of the American people from the war equation had a number of benefits for the administration. Because wars after 1973 cost the vast majority of the voting public nothing, there was no need for them to become involved in the decisions on the conduct of war. And they need not concern themselves with the causes of the war. The administration, consequently, need not concern itself in a major way with political pressure from the people on the issue of war. There would be little protest against the actions of the administration in regard to the causes and conduct of war, as long as the professional military cluster made all the sacrifices. While 9/11 created the conditions for war in 2001, the cause and conduct of the war in Iraq—which had nothing to do with 9/11—exerted very little political pressure in the 2004 presidential election.[11] Even when it was evident that the United States had gone to war for reasons other than those delineated by the Bush Administration, that the insurgency war was going badly, and that hundreds of billions of dollars were being spent in Iraq, other issues, such as taxes, gay marriages, and abortion rights exerted greater political pressures.

When President Bush debated the Democratic candidate, Senator John Kerry, both felt compelled to promise the American people that there would be no draft, that there would be no new taxes to pay for the war, and that, in fact, there would be additional tax cuts. In the midst of a "global war on terrorism," the President promised the American people they would not be called upon to fight. Rather the Bush Administration chose to increase the burden on active duty, Reserve, and National Guard personnel and to live with the prospect of failure in the insurgency war in Iraq for a lack of personnel. American support for Bush's war in Iraq did not translate into volunteers to fight it, support for the draft, nor support for taxes to pay for the war. After the terrorist attacks on 9/11, Bush said to the American people:

> Americans are asking: What is expected of us? I ask you to live your lives, and hug your children. I know many citizens have fears tonight, and I ask you to be calm and resolute,

even in the face of a continuing threat.... I ask your continued participation and confidence in the American economy. Terrorists attacked a symbol of American prosperity. They did not touch its source.[12]

In short, the President told the American people to go shopping.

With the end of the draft in 1973, the American people had been removed from the responsibility to fight the state's wars for over twenty-five years. This left significant questions unanswered: can these tribal nations that make up the United States come together to form a greater community in times of national crisis, and when external threats are real, palpable, and significant? What was to happen if the burden of war exceeded the capabilities of the military cluster? Would the government sacrifice the achievement of its political objectives? Would it reinstate the draft and call on the American people to fight America's wars, or would it use more lethal, more destructive weapons and tactics? Is the world a less dangerous place with the removal of the American people from the conduct of the state's wars? And did the professional military cluster make the decision to go to war easier for the administration? Consider the words of Jean Jaures: "Government will be far less ready to dream of adventurous policies if the mobilization of the army is the mobilization of the nation itself.... *The nation in arms is necessarily a nation motivated by justice.*"

Civil-Military Relations: Who's in Charge?

With the people, in large part, being removed from the nation's conduct of war, it can be argued that the triangular relationship became a bipolar relationship between political and military leaders. However, this would be only partially accurate. The third corner of the triangle, Congress—theoretically the political body that most represented the will of the American people—still functioned in the allocation of resources to the military. Congress was still involved in issues of base construction and closing; the production and purchase of ships, airplanes, and other equipment; the authorized manpower strength of the services; and the budgets of the services. Congressmen and women became much more animated and invested

considerably more time and energy on issues of base closings, and the location and production of aircraft and ships than the decision for war and the conduct of war. Issues of military installation and production facilities directly influenced the careers of many politicians.

Arguably, in the wake of Vietnam War, civilian control of the military has declined, and the services exerted greater influence over national strategy, national military strategy, and foreign policy than ever before. Consider the words of Richard H. Kohn, a student of civil-military relations:

> ... civilian control has deteriorated significantly in the last generation. In theory, civilians had the authority to issue virtually any order and organize the military in any fashion they choose. But in practice, the relationship is far more complex. Both sides frequently disagree among themselves. Further, the military can evade or circumscribe civilian authority by framing the alternatives or tailoring their advice or predicting nasty consequences; by leaking information or appealing to public opinion (through various indirect channels, like lobbying groups or retired generals and admirals); or by approaching friends in the Congress for support. They can even fail to implement decisions, or carry them out in such a way as to stymie their intent. The reality is that civilian control is not a fact but a process, measured across a spectrum—something situational, dependent on the people, issues, and the political and military forces involved. We are not talking about a coup here, or anything else demonstrably illegal; we are talking about who calls the tune in military affairs [which involves war] in the United States today.[13]

And Carl Builder concluded: "The most powerful institutions in the American national security arena are the military services—the army, navy, and air force—not the Department of Defense or Congress or even their commander in chief, the president." Builder argued the armed forces in fact produce American national strategy:

> The roots of modern American military strategies lie buried in the country's three most powerful institutions: the army, navy, and air force. Though many people outside the military

institutions, including academics and presidents may propose military strategies and concepts, these can be implemented only if and when military institutions accept and pursue them.[14]

Russell Weigley in 1992 argued that General Colin Powell, Chairman of the Joint Chiefs of Staff, violated the principle of civilian control of the military. He wrote:

When Congress, the 1992 presidential campaigners, and elements within the George Herbert Walker Bush administration were debating whether the United States ought to employ military force in Bosnia and Hercegovina in an attempt to save lives and to forestall the spreading of the war inside a splintering Yugoslavia to a wider area of the Balkans, General Powell interjected his judgment, purportedly based on his military expertise, that the available possibilities for inserting military force were unsound because, as the *New York Times* reported his views, "military force is best used to achieve a decisive victory." In the midst of the civilian policy debate, General Powell not only announced his views emphatically enough that he was quoted and paraphrased on the front page of the *New York Times*, but he summarized his reasons for opposing a Bosnian intervention on the op-ed page of the *Times* under his own name.[15]

Powell, with the Vietnam War in mind, stated: "As soon as they tell me it is limited, it means they do not care whether you achieve a result or not. As soon as they tell me, 'surgical,' I head for the bushes."[16] The "*they*" were Powell's civilian bosses, and as Weigley noted: "Such an assertion cannot possibly be an expression of professional military knowledge. . . . His opinions in the case were much more political than professional." Another student of civil-military relations, Oli Hosti, concluded:

If being "political" means competing for roles, missions, resources, and the likes, then that does not represent a recent or especially worrisome change, although questions might be raised about the propriety of the military using Congress, such interest groups as defense contractors or veterans organizations, the media, and the public to gain leverage. More generally, we can see two trends that have an important bearing on relations between the military and civilian authorities, and the principle of control of the former by the latter: through changes in professional education, the military are becoming more politically sophisticated and adept, while the number of political leaders in the executive and legislative branches with military experience is declining.[17]

The rise in the prestige of the armed forces in the wake of Operation Desert Storm did in fact increase the political power of the service. And it is a fact that military leaders have been increasingly adept in influencing Congress. Still, did this represent a fundamental change?

The Goldwater-Nichols Act of 1986, discussed in Chapter 12, in no way diminished the powers of the President or civilian control of the military. Civilian control of the military, like most human interactions, has never been an absolute. As Kohn noted, civilian control is "a process, measured across a spectrum. . . ." The pendulum swings back and forth, within a narrowly defined area, depending upon the strengths or weaknesses of individual leaders. There has always been some room for negotiations, descent, revisions, and redress. During the Truman Administration the services were frequently successful in derailing the President's directives and programs. Even Eisenhower was incapable of completely imposing his will on the armed forces. General George B. McClellan, during the Civil War, virtually ignored Lincoln's orders until *he* was fired. General Douglas MacArthur disagreed with Truman's strategy for the conduct of the Korean War until he was fired. General John K. Singlaub publicly disagreed with President Carter's plan to reduce the number of Army forces in Korea, effectively ending his military career. And, most recently, General Stanley McChrystal was relieved of command of NATO forces in Afghanistan for disloyal comments about the Obama Administration and its policies. Civilian control of the military is structurally well defined, but it is still a process that is contingent on a number of factors: the condition, peace or war; the personalities, character, and charisma of civilian and military leaders; knowledge of operations and doctrine; political skill; professionalism; the popularity of the President and his Secretary of Defense; the popularity of the generals and admirals;

the state of inter-service rivalry; personal relationships; and other factors. Still, generals and admirals could go only as far as presidents let them.

Second only to the Constitution, no other legislation has so thoroughly guaranteed civilian control of the military as the National Security Act of 1947. Prior to the Vietnam War, Samuel P. Huntington argued the civil control of the military was enhanced by inter-service rivalry: "Interservice controversy substituted for civil-military controversy.... Service rivalry permitted the civilian agencies to pick and choose."[18] The National Security Act of 1947 has maintained a system of competing services. In the aftermath of World War II, the services became big business, maintaining relatively large forces to fight the Cold War. As a consequence they have greater influence than in previous periods of American history. However, their influence is usually restricted to issues of technologies, doctrines, bases, funding of the services, and the conduct of war. And these issues actually increase the power of civilian leaders because they exacerbate the inter-service fighting.

McNamara developed the theater strategy and strategic doctrine for the air and ground wars in Vietnam. The services were divided and incapable of developing a comprehensive strategy for the conduct of the Vietnam War. Those divisions made McNamara the strategist and the senior-most operational commander. The Pentagon ran Operation Rolling Thunder to the point of selecting targets. Neither the Army nor the Air Force nor the Marine Corps would have fought the war the way it was conducted. However, as long as the services fought among themselves, political leaders had the power to "pick and choose," or to ignore them. President Johnson bragged on more than one occasion that the Air Force could not bomb an "outhouse" without his permission. Too many senior military leaders sat silent as the nation committed its young men to a war that they believed could not be won with the strategy employed. Defeat in Vietnam motivated the subsequent behaviors of many senior political and military leaders.

In the post-Reagan era, generals and admirals endeavored to exert greater influence over the conduct of war and the decision to go to war than during the Kennedy, Johnson, and Nixon Administrations. This was because presidents, such as Reagan and Bush, with the memories of Vietnam still fresh, were more willing to accept their professional advice and leadership, and generals and admirals were more aggressive in rendering it. Both parties feared another Vietnam debacle. Because of Vietnam, the pendulum swung toward greater military control. Unlike in the Vietnam War, the generals developed the theater strategy and strategic doctrines for the Persian Gulf War—as they had in the Korean War. When asked "Who picks the targets in Desert Storm?" General Schwarzkopf responded that President Bush had left the details of the war to his generals. Bush, he declared, had "allowed the commanders in the field to do what the commanders in the field think is correct. Obviously, we brief them on what we're doing. Obviously, if they thought we were doing something dumb, they'd tell us about it, and we'd change it."[19] The powers of the President to replace or relieve an officer, or an entire chain of command, to deploy forces, and determine how they would be used, had not changed.

In the wake of the Gulf War, the services still competed with one another for budgets, programs, and other limited resources. The Goldwater-Nichols Act did not change this. It did create a new level of "jointness," of cooperation and accommodation, but it did not fundamentally change the driving forces that animate the behavior of the services. The services still had to sell themselves, and there were still winners and losers. Political, military decisions still were *not* based on comprehension of the threats and maximizing the combat capabilities of the armed forces. Defeat in Vietnam did not change this. In the aftermath of the Persian Gulf War the Army fought the forty percent reduction in force. Still, six of its divisions were deactivated. The Army lacked the political clout to maintain its force structure.

The Clinton Administration arguably marked a new low for civilian control of the military in the twentieth century. This new low probably motivated the work of Weigley, Hosti, Kohn, and others. However, was this a function of military initiatives or the failure of the Clinton Administration to exert its power and authority? The most blatant recent example of a President permitting the military to bully him into acquiescing to its will was the enactment of the policy of "Don't Ask, Don't Tell," regarding homosexuals in the military. When campaigning for the presidency,

Clinton indicated that he would initiate actions to permit homosexuals to serve openly in the armed forces. In 1948, President Truman signed Executive Order 9981, requiring the integration of the armed forces of the United States.[20] All the services opposed the integration order, all argued against it, and all endeavored to impede its implementation. Nevertheless, Truman had the political courage to promulgate the order. And it must be remembered that in 1949, Jim Crowism was a strong force in America. Clinton not only had to deal with the military on this issue, but also the Congress. Thus, he had to take a different approach than Truman. Clinton faced considerable opposition. The services joined with influential Congressmen to try and block his initiatives. Still, Clinton did have the power to enact the policy.

Clinton, however, chose subterfuge. He initiated a policy that caused considerable confusion, and did not deliver what he had promised. Whether or not one agrees with the policy is not the issue. Clinton failed to exercise the powers of the President. This was more a function of Clinton's character than the actions of the services. Clinton's failure on this issue established the quality and character of his relationship with the military for the remainder of his presidency. And, while it is true that the respect and deference that senior military leaders have traditionally shown elected political leaders had declined in the wake of the Vietnam War, it is equally true that this was not new, and that this did not represent a fundamental change. General McClellan was frequently rude and insubordinate to President Lincoln.

The factors that influenced civil-military relations at the end of the century were: the Vietnam debacle, the belief of the American people that political leaders were most responsible for the first American defeat in war, the rise in the popularity of the armed forces during Operation Desert Storm, the decline of political leaders with military experience, the willingness of Congressmen and women to conspire with military leaders against presidents, the increasing political adroitness of the services and their lobbying organizations, and the personality and character of men such as Bill Clinton, George Bush, Colin Powell, John Shalikashvili, and other senior civilian and military leaders. The dynamic interaction of these and other factors influenced power relationships and, hence, decisions on the conduct of war. Still, there

were no fundamental changes in the system for civilian control. Civilian political leaders retained all the powers delineated under the constitution. The services were still fighting among themselves, enabling political leaders to "pick and choose."

Those who make the argument that the power of the military to determine national policy endangers civilian control of the military can point to no fundamental or structural change that supports this thesis, and no behaviors that do not have historical precedence. What they have is a brief period of time that does not represent the norm, but is a periodic aberration caused by the confluence of a number of factors. In Operation Iraqi Freedom, the Secretary of Defense, Donald Rumsfeld, greatly influenced the theater strategy, strategic doctrine, operational doctrine, and the deployment plan. He got involved in the operational and tactical decisions. And he would, in large part, be the cause of the major failures. In the wake of 9/11 the pendulum swung decidedly toward greater civilian control.

Bush, Rumsfeld, and Cheney frequently ignored the service chiefs and the CJCS. Two observers with close ties to the Pentagon, Michael Gordon and retired General Bernard Trainor, USMC, wrote:

> During his short tenure at the Pentagon, Rumsfeld had established himself as an indomitable bureaucratic presence. It was a commonplace among the Bush team that the military needed stronger civilian oversight, and Rumsfeld exercised control with the iron determination of a former corporate executive.... When he arrived at the Pentagon, Rumsfeld made clear that his goal was nothing less than to remake the US military to fashion a leaner and more lethal force....[21]

Rumsfeld's prejudice and biases, likes and dislikes, and strategic vision were soon evident in the leaders he selected and the policies and strategies he put in place. In 2003, there was no doubt about who ran the Pentagon and thus orchestrated the American conduct of war.

The Revolution in Military Affairs

On 5 March 1994, Army Chief of Staff Gordon R. Sullivan, in a letter to the Army's general officers, entitled "Force XXI," wrote:

Today, we are at a threshold of a new era, and we must proceed into it decisively. Today the Industrial Age is being superseded by the Information Age, the Third Wave, hard on the heels of the agrarian and industrial eras. Our present Army is well-configured to fight and win in the late Industrial Age, and we can handle Agrarian-Age foes as well. We have begun to move into Third Wave warfare, to evolve a new force for a new century—Force XXI.

Force XXI will synthesize the science of modern computer technology, the art of integration doctrine and organization, and the optimization of our quality people. The goal is to create new formations that operate at even greater performance levels in speed, space, and time. Force XXI—not "Division XXI," and there is a message there about breaking free of old concepts—will use command and control technology to leverage the power of the Information Age.... Force XXI will represent a new way of thinking for a new wave of warfare.[22]

At the dawn of the twenty-first century it was believed that new information technologies were revolutionizing warfare. The Army, like the other services, was caught up in a frenzy of activities inspired by the revolution in military affairs (RMA). The Army was going to do more with less. Every captain and sergeant was going to have a networked computer, which provided real-time situational awareness, instant intelligence updates, and instant communications. Every Army leader was going to have near-perfect, real-time battlefield situation awareness. Technology had again increased the rate, accuracy, and lethality of firepower. Some argued that the tank was obsolete; others maintained the traditional view that man was the dominant instrument on the battlefield; all sought to adapt the technological trends in vogue to their way of war. The greatest advances in technology, however, were primarily in the air war—stealth, precision, and space sensor technologies. And the Army's biggest problems were the same problems identified by Ridgway and Taylor in the 1950s: the inability to get to battlefields around the world in a timely manner, in days as opposed to months, and the American belief that everything can be achieved from the air with advanced technologies. This belief made administrations reluctant to employ ground combat forces. As a consequence, the US continued a pattern established in the 1950s of conducting successful battles and operations, but failing, or only partially achieving strategic and political objectives.

The most recent vision of the transformation of war was in fact not so new. In its objectives, it had changed little from the visions articulated in the 1940s, 1950s, 1970s, 1980s, and so on. Americans envisioned war without ground combat forces; war fought with technology; war carried out by highly skilled, highly trained technicians; war from the air; war from space; war that was clean and neat, where Americans were not exposed to the nastiness of killing and the trauma of death. But, again, war had not changed. In its basic form, in people's wars, it was and is the same dirty, nasty, bloody business it has always been. Consider these words:

> The staggering technological advances seemed to have altered the fact of military life overnight, and one natural result was the emergence of the Air Force as the Nation's first line of defense and weapon of offense. America accepted this development remarkably easily for a weapon system made up of the nuclear bomb and the long-range aircraft to deliver it suited our traditional way of thinking on how wars ought be waged.

These words were written in 1956, but by substituting "information technologies and stealth bombers" for "nuclear bomb and the long-range aircraft" they are as representative of American thinking in 2006 as they were fifty years ago. No state on the planet Earth has gone through as many so-called "revolutions in warfare" and "transformations" as the United States. No state has expended the resources comparable to the US in the search for the panacea for war. Consider these words:

> The more subtle and gradual forms of attack through infiltration, political persuasion, insurrection, and developing guerrilla war have found us with no adequate political or military answer. In struggles of this type there are seldom suitable targets for massive air strikes. Ground forces geared and equipped for large-scale war are notoriously ineffective against guerrillas. Militarily, such forces cannot bring their might to bear, and

their efforts are all too likely to injure and alienate indigenous populations and thus lose an equally important political battle. *In these situations national power has meaning only in terms of its immediate application. Today, unfortunately, the sum of applicable American power is not always impressive.*[23]

These words were also written in 1956, and they too were applicable in 2006. For half a century, the United States has planned and equipped itself to fight the type of war it wants to fight, not the type of war it is most likely to fight. American military leaders continuously fail to think strategically. All the services produce "operators" and "technicians"—men who perfect techniques for fighting conventional forces and nuclear war. And given the enormous imbalance in US military power *vis-à-vis* other states, these are the two least likely forms of war. The officers of the armed forces of the US, with few exceptions, don't study foreign cultures, don't study foreign languages, don't study human behavior, and don't study history beyond the battles and campaigns of successful Western military leaders. Courses at the War Colleges teach nothing of Muslim religion and culture, nothing of Chinese history and society, nothing of the history of Africa and its numerous people. In the officer corps of the US there is a profound and extraordinary ignorance of the world the US seeks to police. The corps is too busy mastering machines, methods, and operational doctrines to study the peoples of the world. *Ultimately it is the will of the people that has to be influenced, assuaged, incorporated, pacified, or destroyed in order to achieve political objectives.*

The United States, with all its great power, was stretched thin in the type of power "applicable" to the wars it was fighting in Iraq and Afghanistan. And as a consequence, too many soldiers and marines died or were wounded needlessly. Cultural consistency has been killing American soldiers and marines for half a century. And without a major cultural transformation in American thinking about the conduct of war, in 2025 Americans can again expect to expend too many of the lives of its young men and women because it has prepared to fight the wrong war, while wasting billions of dollars on the most advanced aircraft ever produced to replace the most advanced aircraft ever produced—aircraft that are incapable

of stopping a man on the ground with a rifle, of discriminating between a determined insurgent and a scared mother or child, or of establishing the kinds of relationships with indigenous people that win their confidence and support.

War is ultimately a human endeavor. It is more than killing. And the only thing that technology will ever do is make the act of killing more efficient. Unless the objective is extermination, a heinous objective, technology alone will never provide the answer to war. Technology alone will never stop a determined enemy. Man does not "make" the greatest weapon on the planet. Man "is" the greatest weapon in war. The human brain and the human spirit are the greatest weapons on the Earth. They enable people to adapt and produce the intelligence and tenacity to sustain themselves through war and other hardships.

Human tribes may suffer terrible losses, but extinction is rare. In the post-World War II period, given the magnitude of American political promises to states in all corners of the planet, even in peace, the US Army has been too small to do all that was asked and required. It has also been oriented towards the wrong type of war. American political leaders have continuously robbed themselves of solutions less destructive, more humane, and more effective. The best way to spread Americanism, the best way to transform other societies, is by the demonstrative superiority of the American way of life to produce prosperity for the greatest number of people, and by the stability created by the presence of US forces. Over-reliance on firepower and technology from World War II to Operation Iraqi Freedom has been, in large part, a function of too few soldiers to do the job, and too few soldiers trained to fight people's wars or irregular wars. Peter Mansoor, a brigade commander during OIF, acknowledged this problem:

> Hard lessons won at great cost [in Vietnam] collected dust on library shelves in the US Army's academic institutions. . . . The coalition lacked more than troops in Iraq. It lacked imagination and insight. Without an operational concept to guide the conduct of the war, Lieutenant General Sanchez and CJTF-7 lacked the link between strategic ends and tactical means that would ensure a successful outcome to the struggle, or even a calculation of the necessary means to

wage it. The succession of units responsible for al Anbar province—the heart of Sunni power and base of the budding insurgency—was symptomatic of this conceptual shortfall. One of my staff officers succinctly described the theoretical framework for the post-major combat operation campaign as 'ad hockery in action.' Division and brigade commanders answered CJTF-7's call for increased offensive operations to destroy the 'diehard' elements of the Ba'athist regime. Beyond that, there was no comprehensive plan.[24]

The US Army and the services failed to study the types of war they were most likely to fight. They failed to study insurgency warfare, terrorism, or guerrilla warfare. They failed to organize and equip themselves to carry out counterinsurgency operations, peacekeeping, and nation-building operations, until they were in the fighting and conducting these operations. And, they failed to learn the utter necessity of understanding the culture of the people they were fighting or trying to save from Communism, terrorism, or some dictators. To be sure, the Soviet threat was real and substantial. Meeting that threat required vigilance, dedication, and enormous time and energy. However, the United States has world-wide responsibilities, and what worked in Europe did not work in other regions of the Earth. A revolution in military affairs is badly needed, but not one based on new technologies—one based on an understanding of humanity, culture, languages, and people.

*   *   *   *   *

In the wake of the first Persian Gulf War many military theorists believed an RMA was taking place.[25] All the services emphasized transformation. However, they were not exactly sure what they were supposed to look like when the transformation process was complete. What was known was that American forces were to be "small, more lethal and nimble joint forces." Transformation was based on new digital communications technologies, precision-guided munitions, stealth technologies, reorganization, "jointness," and "network-centric" warfare doctrine.[26] It was believed that the US possessed the wherewithal to construct "the system of systems," a network that consisted of three major components: sensors, communications, and shooters.[27] The sensors were space-based observation

and other types of satellites, unmanned aerial vehicles, manned surveillance airplanes, joint surveillance target attack radar systems on aircraft, ground-based radar systems, Special Forces, Rangers, and even soldiers and marines. The sensors enabled all the services to cut through the "fog of war," see the battlefield in real time, to have almost complete "battlefield awareness," to focus on any "grid square" on Earth, and detect, track, and engage multiple targets simultaneously. The sensors provided "information dominance," the ability to see the battlefield far more accurately and completely than the enemy; and, as a consequence, to deprive the enemy of the information needed to effectively deploy, maneuver, and fight his forces. Sensors were linked through advanced communication channels to decision-makers and weapons capable of delivering precision destructive power on specific, individual targets, with measured lethality. The sensors, decision-makers, and shooters of all the services would all simultaneously, in real time, be able to see the exact same battlefield. On screens, indicators would show the locations of all enemy and friendly forces. American tanks and airplanes were all to be equipped with transponders that emitted signals that indicated their exact location. JSTARS, UAVs, space-based spy satellites, and other sensors provided the location of enemy forces. The ability to immediately detect enemy forces and destroy them with multiple shooters, and with measured lethality and precision, was the vision. Speed, responsiveness, accuracy, flexibility, decisiveness, and reduced vulnerability were the objectives.

Using the human body as an analogy, the objective of operations was to destroy the system of nerves that transmitted orders from the brain to the muscles, severing the links between the decision-makers and the fighting forces. The emphasis was also on destroying the brain. If the brain could be destroyed it might be unnecessary to destroy the nerve system, the communications infrastructure of a state, or the muscles, enemy forces. Severing the many links between the brain and the muscles was no small task. Numerous systems transmit signals. Hence, the task was to temporarily stop the flow of instruction, and then move rapidly, faster than the enemy could respond, to destroy the brain, or sufficient parts of the central nervous system to paralyze the enemy and thereby achieve military and political objectives. By controlling the flow of information to the enemy, by having almost complete information of enemy and friendly forces in real time, and through speed and precision destruction, victory could be achieved without the mass armies or the enormous destruction common in war. The objective was *not* to fight directly the enemy's main forces, the muscles. By operating faster than an enemy using superior information, the enemy's options were taken away. His decision-loop, the time it takes for him to react to changes on the battlefield, is too slow to compensate for the rate of change inflicted by fast-moving American forces, causing partial paralysis, which creates the opportunity for the decisive destruction of the center of gravity, the brain, i.e. the political and military leadership. Technology, operational doctrine, and new adaptive organizations were to come together in ways that created synergies that made possible the RMA. The problem with this thinking was that it left out the human beings. People are more than the sum of their parts. This doctrine diminished and hid the fact that wars are *not* won until the people accept defeat. If the people do not accept the outcome, the war is not over. The brain, the central nervous system, and the muscles can be destroyed, but if the people don't accept defeat, the struggle continues.

In 2005, in the midst of the growing insurgency war in Iraq, the services were working hard to achieve this RMA vision of war. As might be expected, the Air Force and Navy were leading the way in developing technologies and doctrine:

> With gathering momentum, the Air Force is moving to implement its vision of 'network-centric warfare' (NCW), working hard to extract as much information as possible from existing sources of data and streamline the means by which airmen can use the information in combat. . . . Finally, the Air Force is following a 'flight plan' that calls for USAF to realize even its most visionary NCW aims before 2014, potentially revolutionizing the way the services fight in less than a decade.[28]

After Operation Desert Storm, the Army started transforming its divisions into digitally linked forces. The 4th ID, then at Fort Hood, Texas, was the Army's first "digitized" heavy division. The Army also started investing in unmanned ground vehicles (UGV),

establishing the Robotics Program Office at the Army Research Laboratory, which entered into contracts with General Dynamics Robotic Systems division to develop families of UGVs that were capable of finding and attacking targets with no human direction, conducting reconnaissance, and providing logistical and ambulance support. (UGVs have to be smarter than UAVs because they have to negotiate numerous obstacles, and differentiate between combatants and noncombatants.) In an article entitled "Inside the Pentagon's Plan for a Soldier-Free Battlefield" it was noted that, ". . . the real goal for UGVs is autonomous operation with no human input whatsoever . . ."[29] It was further noted that according to the 2001 Defense Authorization Act, "one third of all operational ground vehicles are supposed to be unmanned by 2015." Billions of dollars were committed to achieve this objective. Still, the Army was a long way from realizing network-centric war. This was a futuristic vision of war. With the costs of the wars in Iraq and Afghanistan soaring, these programs have been substantially cut back. However, the vision has not gone away.

The concept of NCW, however, has a number of practical problems. Precision weapons are very expensive. In a high intensity environment against a substantial enemy, depletion is a concern. In Operation Desert Storm, nine percent of munitions were precision-guided, in Operation Iraqi Freedom, that figure was seventy percent. A bigger problem is the vulnerability of sensors and computer systems. The reconnaissance, communication, and global positioning satellites, on which network-centric warfare depends, are defenseless against missile attack. In 2009, the Chinese demonstrated the ability to destroy a satellite with a ground-based missile. The vast network of Department of Defense computers is also vulnerable at numerous points. Hackers implanting worms and viruses from across the globe have attacked the system.

NCW is a limited war strategic doctrine. In total wars, destroying the enemy's central nervous system and/or brain will not end the war. NCW doctrine will not work in an insurgency war, in people's wars. This fact was apparent throughout the war in Iraq, as Army, Marine, and Iraqi casualties mounted, and the most advanced technologies ever produced sat motionless on runways or on the decks of aircraft carriers. NCW worked best against states with highly centralized governments. Guerrilla and insurgency operations with highly decentralized chains of command, where the initiative rest with each fighter, were not vulnerable to network-centric doctrine. Terrorist networks functioned through open source communication networks, primarily through the Internet. Terrorist leaders, in many cases, recruit new fighters and motivate them to act without ever coming in physical contact them. American post-Cold War operational thinking did not reflect the realities of the new environment. While there has been an enormous body of official and unofficial scholarly work produced on the revolution in military affairs, the picture of what the armed forces were supposed to look like when transformed was still vague. Yet, there was one element of transformation that for Americans was as consistent as war itself. One *old* tenet of the new RMA was that technology could replace ground combat forces. This unbalanced preference for technological solutions continued to exert enormous influence on American thinking about the conduct of war, and have real consequences on the ground. In the first year of the George W. Bush Administration, the Rumsfeld Pentagon planned to cut two of the Army's ten remaining divisions—there were sixteen divisions in 1991 when the Army conducted Operation Desert Storm. Had these cuts been made before 9/11, it would have made it impossible to conduct simultaneous operations in Afghanistan and Iraq and also maintain worldwide commitments. At the same time Rumsfeld was planning to get rid of better than twenty percent of the Army, he was planning to spend billions of dollars on three new jet fighters—one for each service.[30]

Truman in the 1940s, Eisenhower in the 1950s, Carter in the 1970s, Bush in the 1980s and 1990s, and Bush in 2000, all sought to replace Army divisions with technology. Every decade, with the exception of the Vietnam War Administrations and the Reagan Administration, new administrations have endeavored to cut the Army to less than what was necessary given conservative estimates of the prevalent threats and worldwide commitments—the Army was forward-deployed in Germany, Korea, Panama, and the Middle East, as well as other parts of the world. For the past fifty years, no tenet of American thinking about the conduct of war has been as consistently reproduced

in policies and practice than the belief that airpower could replace manpower.

When the armed forces of the United States went to war in Iraq in 2003, the RMA was well under way. Precision-guided munitions, satellite global positioning, navigation technology, satellite reconnaissance advanced notification systems, satellite intelligence collection and early warning technologies, cruise missiles, unmanned aerial vehicles, advanced satellite communication systems, laser-guided and optical-guided technologies, airborne radar early warning and air control platforms, an unrivaled array of advanced aircraft, advanced anti-aircraft and anti-missile systems, thermo-imaging night observation technologies, and other impressive technologies gave the US the most advanced and expensive arsenals in the history of war. These advances enabled the armed forces to see more accurately and comprehensively; to engage targets at greater distances with greater precision; to respond with greater speed; to engage multiple targets simultaneously, employing a wide range of weapons systems, many of which did not require Americans to enter the battlefield; and to measure the lethality, the degree of destruction desired, with greater accuracy. And still the US was incapable of achieving quick, decisive victories in Iraq and Afghanistan, and ultimately had to deploy more soldiers and marines to fight the ground war.

The armed forces of the United States trained and organized themselves to perfect the conduct of operations and tactics. They worked hard to become skilled technicians and operators. Men, machines, organization, equipment, maximizing firepower, reducing casualties, accurate employment of weapons on target, all the palpable, physical, animated aspects of war were perfected. Strategic thinking, ethnic and sectarian divisions, traditional relationships, ideology, religion, attitudes, nationalism, beliefs, family structure, customs, culture, all the intangible human aspects of war were not studied, or were studied by only a few US Army Special Forces. The American way of war emphasized positive actions to achieve visible, almost instantaneous results. War, however, is a human endeavor and it is the intangibles that motivate people to fight.

* * * * *

Consider the American conduct of war prior to 11 September 2001: On 24 March 1999, the air forces of the United States (each service has its own air force), in concert with allied NATO forces, initiated combat operations in the failed state of Yugoslavia. The Clinton Administration sought to employ military forces to stop "ethnic cleansing" and restore peace in the Kosovo region. Clinton declared: "We and our 18 NATO allies are in Kosovo today because we want to stop the slaughter and the ethnic cleansing. We cannot simply watch as thousands of people are brutalized, murdered, raped, forced from their home, their family histories erased—all in the name of ethnic pride and purity."[31] Clinton and the nineteen members of NATO, initially decided the military task, and ultimately the political objective, could be achieved with airpower. They resisted putting ground forces into the region to physically and immediately stop the ethnic cleansing. One student of America's wars, Andrew J. Bacevich, wrote:

> In the annals of US military history the war for Kosovo stands out as a singularly peculiar episode. Among other things, the war produced more than its share of "firsts." It was, famously, the first war that US forces fought to its conclusion without sustaining a single combat casualty. Indeed, for the policymakers who conceived Operation Allied Force and the commanders who directed it, minimizing the risk to allied soldiers seemingly took precedence over both their obligation to safeguard Serb noncombatants and their interest in protecting the ethnic Albanians whose plight provided the ostensible rationale for intervention. American officials described that intervention as a *moral* imperative. Yet before the conflict had even ended observers were wondering if the United States had turned moral tradition on its head, with combatants rather than noncombatants provided immunity from the effects of fighting.[32]

The campaign that was supposed to take days, took months—78 days. And, had Slobodan Milosevic been Adolf Hitler, the Albanian Muslim population would have suffered a holocaust. The use of ground forces was considered, even threatened, but ultimately political leaders decided to supplement its airpower,

which was proving to be indecisive, with surrogate ground forces:

> In Kosovo the US utilized the KLA, which it had earlier denounced as terrorists, because it sought to win battles, and the KLA—criminals, terrorists, and all—was deemed indispensable. American officials had ample proof of this, but they made a pact with it despite deep apprehension because they needed the KLA's help against the Serbs.[33]

The United States and its NATO allies employed surrogate forces, on whose loyalty they could not depend, and airpower to achieve its objectives. Rather than employ their own ground forces they preferred to get in bed with the devil. Ethnic cleansing could not be immediately or effectively stopped at an altitude of 20,000 feet. Another student of the war, Michael Evans, wrote:

> The air war did not succeed in protecting the Kosovo population. Indeed, it worsened and accelerated the humanitarian crisis because the Serbs systematically depopulated the province of Albanians. While NATO struck at the heartland of Yugoslavia, Kosovo was subjected to mass terror reminiscent of German SS field units in Eastern Europe during World War II. In trying to prevent genocide, the West used a military method—air power—which accelerated it. In an extraordinary paradox, a war based on the notion of discriminate force using dazzling information-age technology—B-2 bombers, cruise missiles, and joint direct-attack munitions—sacrificed the Albanian Kosovars to indiscriminate death at the hands of Serb forces using methods we associate with the Dark Ages. In humanitarian terms, the air war was an unmitigated disaster, and a cautionary warning for the West in employing force in future intra-state conflicts.[34]

Evans correctly predicted that: "The humanitarian failure will not prevent Western air forces theorists from arguing that the war was a decisive victory for air power."[35] The American people had no part in the war, and little interest. Bacevich observed that, "By the time the war finally wound down in June, Americans had effectively decided that it no longer merited their attention.... Sports teams that lose the Super Bowl or the NCAA basketball championship receive a warmer welcome upon returning home than did the Americans who won the war in Kosovo."[36]

Jointness and Force Structure

In 2007 Brigadier General Sean MacFarland wrote: "the Al Anbar campaign was a model of joint operational effectiveness." Colonel MacFarland commanded an Army brigade in the fight for Anbar province in Iraq. He described his command as follows:

> One of the great legacies of the fight for Al Anbar province will be the enduring, mutual respect earned by the various service-members who fought side by side. This respect was nowhere more evident than in Ramidi, where our Army brigade combat team, the 1st BCT, 1st Armored Division (Ready First Combat Team), fought under the command of 1 Marine Expeditionary Forces (1 MEF). The Ready First was not a pure Army BCT. It contained US Marine Corps (USMC) elements, including a reinforced rifle battalion ..., a riverine patrol unit, an air and naval gunfire liaison platoon, and civil affair detachment. The Air Force supported the Ready First with an air liaison team.... The brigade staff itself was a de facto joint organization—it had Army, Navy, Air Force, and Marine officers and NCOs throughout. The electronic warfare officer, a Catholic Chaplain, and the head surgeon were all Navy commanders. The civil affairs and public affairs officers were Marines. Outside the brigade, support came from a Marine logistics group and 1 MEF's air combat elements. Numerous other external USMC units, including a platoon from a radio battalion, a postal unit, explosive ordnance disposal teams, fire-fighting teams, air traffic controllers, and military transition teams, also provided support. So did the Navy, in the form of surgical teams and corpsmen, SeaBee battalions, electronic warfare experts, and SEAL platoons from SEAL teams 3 and 5.[37]

MacFarland concluded: "The US Army and the US Marine Corps, each today without peer in its domain of land warfare, have not shared such a strong bond of common experience and understanding since the island campaigns of World War II. The services should nurture those bonds and sustain them over time." During OIF the services did in fact achieve a new level of joint interdependence. This was more a function of necessity than design. The Army and Marine Corps were too small to do all that was necessary to save Iraq and sustain Afghanistan. As a consequence, the Navy and Air Force had to take on new roles in land warfare and the Army and Marine Corps had to work closer than ever before. The questions are: Can this level of integration and cooperation be maintained? Is "joint interdependence," or "jointness," a fact, or a temporary expedient?

FM 3–0 Operations defines "joint interdependence" as: "the purposeful reliance by one Service's forces on another Service's capabilities to maximize the complementary and reinforcing effects of both.... Joint capabilities make Army forces more effective than they would be otherwise."[38] Force structure reveals much about the services. If the technologies, doctrines, and organizations of the services are evolving in such a way as to complement the strengths, diminish the weaknesses, and expand the capabilities of the other services, it can be argued that jointness has in fact taken hold in the cultures of the services. However, if the force structures of the services are evolving in such a way as to *duplicate* the capabilities of the other services, or to expand traditional service technologies into the domains of other services, then it can be argued that *competition* between the services trumps jointness. The story, however, is not completely black or white. In many areas the services are in fact moving toward greater integration and cooperation. Administrative functions, educational and training functions, medical facilities, and other non-combat-related activities have been more fully integrated in recent years. Budget issues are in part forcing this development.

Operational tempo also influenced joint interdependence. Following the collapse of the Soviet Union, the operational tempo of the services increased enormously as presidents took on commitments in all corners of the planet (Iraq, 1991; Somalia, 1992; Haiti, 1994; Bosnia-Herzegovina, 1995; Kosovo, 1999; Afghanistan, 2001; Iraq, 2003). The all-volunteer force met these requirements without significant increases in manpower. The increased operational tempo and the ever-increasing range of military operations other than war (MOOTW) placed greater demands on the services to coordinate, synchronize, and integrate operations, maximize the use of limited resources, and to exploit the unique abilities and technologies of a given service. Post Desert Storm doctrines emphasized joint operations, rapid force projection, advanced technologies as force multipliers, the ability to shift rapidly from one type of operation to another, and MOOTW. Joint doctrine was designed to respond to the "full spectrum" of potential operations, which included offensive, defensive, stability, and support operations, or more precisely under the heading of MOOTW, drug-trafficking, disaster relief, humanitarian assistance, and peacekeeping; and under the heading of war, regional conflicts, civil wars, insurgencies, terrorism, conventional conflict, and tactical nuclear war.[39] In this new, rapidly changing environment, joint training and joint doctrine were considered, by some, mandatory. The Joint Force Command was given the mission to "harmonize" the capability and resources of the services, and to coordinate and integrate their doctrine and training.[40]

However, the survival of the service and the protection of key weapon systems are still the most powerful motivators of action in the armed forces of the Unites States. Each service still seeks to expand its capabilities in traditional ways that do not enhance the capabilities of the other services. The individual service cultures are a function of technologies and missions that have been in existence since World War II. Cultural change is not easy. When the immediate emergencies have passed, and the situation in Iraq and Afghanistan is stabilized, the services are very likely to return to their most comfortable patterns of behavior—preparation for conventional war with their major weapon systems, the systems that form their operational cultures and determine how they fight. Consider the words of Secretary of Defense Robert Gates, spoken to a group of officers at Maxwell Air Force Base:

> And whether the issue was fixing outpatient care, getting better armored vehicles, or sending more ISR [intelligence, surveillance, and reconnaissance] capabilities into the theater, I kept running into the fact that the Department of Defense as

an institution—which routinely complained that the rest of the government are not at war—was itself not on a war footing, even as young Americans were fighting and dying every day.

For too long there was a view, or a hope, that Iraq and Afghanistan were exotic distractions that would be wrapped up relatively soon—the regimes toppled, the insurgencies crushed, the troops sent home. Therefore, we should not spend too much, or buy too much equipment not already in our procurement plans, or turn our bureaucracies and processes upside down. As a result, the kinds of capabilities that were most urgently needed by our warfighters in the theater were for the most part fielded ad hoc and on the fly, developed outside the regular bureaucracy and funded in supplemental appropriations that would go away when the war did—or sooner. The wars we are in clearly have not earned much of a constituency in the Pentagon as compared to the services' conventional modernization programs. That was the root of my frustration when I came here to Maxwell a year ago and spoke about "pulling teeth" to get more ISR.[41]

The ways in which the men and women of the armed forces think about war are deeply entrenched at each level from cadet to general. The mandatory joint education system has not changed the fundamental cultural tenets that influence the actions of leaders.

Jointness since Operation Desert Storm has meant that the services each get a fair share of the operational pie, without inter-service fighting that required civilian interference. In other words, the services have agreed to cooperate and recognize the right of the others to exist; and thereby minimize the involvement of civilian leadership. Having identified this new level of acceptance of one another, the services are not static. At the dawn of the new century, the Air Force and Marine Corps were in ascendancy, while the Army and the Navy were in decline. Operation Iraqi Freedom temporarily changed this. The Rumsfeld Pentagon was in the process of gutting the Army when it was called to fight the insurgency wars in Iraq and Afghanistan. The Army was ill-equipped and ill-prepared for the war it faced in Iraq and Afghanistan, having invested heavily in its heavy armor forces at the expense of its light infantry forces, the type most needed in the two long wars. As a result resources had to be reallocated across the services. The production of F/A 22 Raptors was cut back and the production of new mine-resistant ambus-protected (MRAP) V-shaped vehicles, designed to defeat improvised explosive devices for the Army and Marine Corps, was greatly expanded. However, all this took time, and time was costly in lives and trea-sure. And the Air Force is still committed to the pro-duction of F/A 22 Raptor. When the crises have passed, the fight for resources will begin again.

With the demise of the SU came the demise of the Air Force's primary mission, *strategic bombing*. This mission had for decades formed the very identity of the Air Force. The Air Force had to rethink, reori-ent, and reconfigure its forces. For example, the pri-mary missions for which the B-1 bomber was built—attacking the Soviet Union with nuclear weap-ons—no longer existed. The B-1 had to be reconfig-ured for conventional operations. The primary mission of the B-2 also had to be modified. Neither bomber was used in the first Persian Gulf War. The Air Force's strategic bombing mission, at least in the immediate future, was obsolete. In some ways the Air Force became like the Navy. The primary mission of the Navy, to fight other navies, arguably went away with the destruction of the Imperial Japanese Navy in World War II. While the Soviet Navy provided a rea-son for being, only its submarine fleet was a serious challenge to the US Navy.

The Air Force's *air superiority mission* while not completely eliminated was also greatly diminished. The US has not fought an air superiority war against nation-states capable of producing, maintaining, sus-taining, and training competitive fighter squadrons since the Korean War, and even that was a very lim-ited campaign. In Vietnam, the biggest challenge was from SAMs. With the demise of the Soviet Union, the air superiority mission, while not eliminated, was substantially diminished. Hence, some have argued the Air Force's new F-22 Raptor, which was designed for this mission, is no longer necessary.[42] It is also argued that in the not too distant future unmanned combat aerial vehicles (UCAV) will reach a level of technological sophistication to remove man from combat aircraft.[43] While the PRC, Russia, and the European Union provide rationale for the continued development of air superiority aircraft, in the global war on terrorism, and wars against developing "Third World" states, there has been little or no need for air-to-air combat fighters. Developing states and terror-ists prefer cheaper SAMs, which require little training. Hence, two of the Air Force's major missions no lon-ger had a reason for being. The US Navy no longer fights navies, and the US Air Force no longer fights air forces. That leaves only one dimension in which to fight, the ground war.

At the dawn of the twenty-first century, the pri-mary mission of the Navy and Air Force in active combat was to fight the ground war. There are three missions in which the two air forces can fight, one strategic, two tactical. These were the missions car-ried out in the Persian Gulf War. Strategic attacks against targets significant enough to influence the outcome of the war, and/or tactical attacks against enemy ground forces either independently or in con-cert with ground forces. Thus, there are two doctrines for achieving victory without ground forces. The stra-tegic mission of airpower has evolved in such a way that little risk is involved. The targets can be selected from space or other intelligence sources. Ships and submarines can launch cruise missiles from hundreds of miles away. B-52s and B-1s can do the same. B-2s and F-117s engage targets at distances greater than fifty miles, and UCAV and space are pointing the way to the future of strategic airpower. These are jobs that can be carried out by highly trained, highly skilled technicians. The attributes required by the men that flew B-17 missions over Nazi Germany, or F-105 missions over North Vietnam, are no longer required.

Arguably the primary missions of the US Navy have not changed since World War II. The Department of Defense identified the following "functions" for the Navy:

> seek out and destroy enemy naval forces and suppress enemy sea commerce; gain and main-tain general naval supremacy; control vital sea areas and protect vital sea lines of communica-tion; establish and maintain local superiority (including air) in an area of naval operations; seize and defend advanced naval bases; and conduct such land, air, and space operations as may be essential to the prosecution of a naval campaign.[44]

However, there are no serious naval challenges to the US Navy, and the armed forces of the US are forward-deployed all over the planet. Private firms are primarily responsible for deploying the Army and other forces. Hence, the major missions of the Navy are to conduct limited independent operations with its airpower, surface and submarine fleets (cruisers and submarine employing missiles); to provide rapid, emergency response to crises in various parts of the world; to maintain US presence in contested regions; to deter actions opposed by the US; to augment the Air Force in major wars; to deploy and support the Marine Corps; and to assist in the deployment of the Army.

The greatest strength of the Navy, arguably, is that it has greater access to all regions of the planet for sustained air operations than the Air Force. "Arguably" because the Air Force since the late 1940s has consistently challenged this thesis. In the wake of the first Persian Gulf War, however, it was believed that a new sense of jointness had changed the perspective of the Air Force towards the Navy's aircraft carrier. Commander James Paulsen, US Navy observed that: "Following Desert Storm, the Air Force recognized the aircraft carrier's contributions and the independence they offer to global presence. In light of the restrictions of deployable basing rights, the Air Force reversed its 50-year stance against the need for naval aviation."[45] Paulsen noted that:

> Operation Desert Shield and Desert Storm brought together the tactical capabilities of naval aviation and the strategic capabilities of the Air Force. The air-tanking assets of the Air Force and the strike assets of the Navy brought extended capabilities to the table. This development became an important element of the air war over Iraq in 1991 and the beginning of a new joint relationship for the next decade.

During the Persian Gulf War the Air Force was given the mission to provide air tanker support, "strat gas," to Navy aircraft. This new joint relationship was in effect in 2002–2003. Paulsen noted that: "When planning for Iraqi Freedom approached realization, it was clear the multicarrier presence being assembled would require vast numbers of tankers, and the Air Force would be called on to provide that airborne fuel." Had the Air Force, in fact, changed a view and position it has held for fifty years? Given the advancements in technology, the Air Force's argument against the aircraft carrier should have been substantially stronger in 2003 than in 1949. Consider the following:

The Air Force is forward-deployed in various regions of the world, and thus, is capable of responding almost immediately to crises in these regions. Second, the Air Force can rapidly forward-deploy to regions and countries that have the runway space required. With its C-17s and C-5 transports the Air Force can package, transport, and construct its expeditionary requirements for a sustainable airfield. In the first Persian Gulf war Saudi Arabia had the runways and other facilities required. All the Air Force had to do was occupy them. Third, the Air Force has demonstrated the ability to circumnavigate the Earth without landing. In other words, the Air Force with its B-2s and B-1s and aerial refueling capabilities can strike any point on the planet at any time with considerable firepower. The B-2, without anyone knowing it is there, from eight miles up, can strike any point on Earth with conventional or nuclear weapons within a 24-hour period. The B-1, while relying on its great speed as opposed to stealth, can do the same. Fourth, Navy aircraft carriers are not as independent as they appear. The high demands of 50 strike fighters; the limited storage capacity for munitions, jet fuel, and other resources on board; the relatively small number of logistical support ships; and the high-intensity of modern combat operations, tie carriers to land support sources. Fifth, the Navy aircraft lack the range of capabilities of Air Force aircraft. The Navy, because of its reliance on one combat aircraft, the F/A-18, cannot perform the missions of the Air Force's B-2s, B-1s, F-117s, B-52s, and other aircraft. Finally, while the Navy has demonstrated a remarkable ability to "surge," to commit its forces to an operation at a relatively high rate of intensity, it cannot sustain that rate for long periods of time. The Air Force, however, can sustain its forces at a high rate of intensity for the duration of the war. The hazards of aircraft carrier operations are not prevalent. While the Navy's capabilities in combat operations have changed little since the early days of the Cold War, the Air Force's capabilities have changed significantly since the collapse of the Soviet Union. However, neither service has figured out a substantial role for itself in insurgency warfare, where the will of the people is the center of gravity.

The Navy has capabilities the Air Force does not possess: it typically can respond more rapidly to emergency situations. It can, in some cases, launch aircraft and influence situations in minutes as opposed to hours. In some regions of the world, the Navy can provide sustained air support more effectively than the Air Force. And, the mere presence of an aircraft carrier can deter the outbreak of war and demonstrate US resolve in foreign policy objectives. In emergency situations, the Navy performs numerous military and humanitarian missions that are a function of its presence at sea and ability to move to and maneuver in the area of interest. Still, the Navy has shown little imagination in advancing carrier technology and capabilities. The only advances in carrier design since the 1950s have been to make them incrementally larger, continuously modernize aircraft, and add nuclear propulsion. The new level of jointness between the Navy and Air Force was a marriage of necessity. The Air Force and the Navy are committed to expanding their capabilities, with little consideration of the capabilities of the other.

*   *   *   *   *

The Army, like the Air Force, lost its primary enemy and mission with the collapse of the Soviet Union. The Army and Marine Corps serve much the same purposes in war. They both fight the ground war. The Marine Corps forms a second land army, which maintains a manpower strength of about forty percent of that of the Army's. In the 1950s it was roughly ten to twenty percent of the Army. Each service has a number of unique capabilities. The Army's airborne, air assault, armor/mechanized, and Special Forces have no equivalence in the Marine Corps. The Marine Corps' ability to deploy from the sea has no equivalence in the Army. Yet, both services are working hard to expand their missions into the domain of the other. The Marine Corps has created a new Special Operations capability, the Marine Corps Forces Special Operations Command. With the Osprey, it now has the capabilities of the Army Air Assault Division. The Army has acquired high-speed sea-going vessels to expand its expeditionary capabilities. The two services are organized differently, have different force structures, some different technology and doctrine, and different cultures. Still, in recent years the two services have grown more alike.

In the new world of "jointness" Army doctrine became joint doctrine; and thus, Marine doctrine. And Marine doctrine became joint doctrine; and thus, Army doctrine. For example, on 16 September 2002, Joint Publication 3–06, *Doctrine for Joint Urban Operations* was published. While the Marine Corps was the primary proponent of the publication, the document was produced in consultation with the Army and the other services, and was applicable to all the services. The Army was primarily responsible for the development of the counterinsurgency manual, F 3–24. However, the Marine Corps made significant contribution to the development of the manual.

In the aftermath of Operation Desert Storm, the Army expanded its expeditionary capabilities and the Marine Corps expanded its mechanized, maneuver warfare capabilities. In Desert Storm, the Marine Corps fought the largest tank battle in its history. However, Schwarzkopf wisely attached a heavy US Army armor brigade to General Boomer's Corps, so it fought that battle with considerable support from the Army. In the wake of the war, the Marine Corps reevaluated its force structure. It had promulgated a new maneuver war doctrine prior to Operation Desert Storm, but was unable to use it. Its force structure lacked the mobility to fight a classic war of maneuvers. In classrooms, the Marine Corps re-fought the war in Iraq, correctly concluding that it would again have to fight against Arab heavy armor formations. As a consequence, the Marine Corps expanded its ability to fight more traditional maneuver warfare. Two students of Marine Corps operations wrote:

> [U]nder Maneuver Warfare, the aim was to strike at the enemy's command and control center, leaving the soldiers on the bypassed blocks without leadership or cohesion. The doctrine also stressed the need for speed—speed of decision-making first and foremost, then speed of execution as well; since speed was always relative, it meant being faster than your enemy above all else. Almost a generation of Marine officers had grown up studying the new doctrine.[46]

To achieve speed in desert terrain, the Marine Corps need vehicles, armored vehicles. Hence, it added more track vehicles to its force structure. It replaced its aging M60 tanks with new M1A1. In 2003 the Marine Corps demonstrated the ability to maneuver more than three regiments across hundreds of miles of desert. In Operation Iraqi Freedom the Marine Corps had greater ability than ever before to fight armored formations.

The Marine Corps still did not have the equivalent of the Army Bradley infantry fighting vehicles, and had it gotten into a genuine tank battle its amphibious assault vehicles (Amtrac) would have proven inadequate. The Marine Corps also did not possess the tank-killing ability of the Army's AH-64 Apache Helicopter. It did, however, have its own fixed-wing air force. A Marine fighter pilot observed:

> For decades, Marines jealously have guarded Marine fixed-wing aviation for the near-exclusive use of the Marine air-ground task force commander. Operation Iraqi Freedom was no exception. As the war progressed from planning to execution, the maneuver commander had an impressive and at times overwhelming amount of coalition air supporting his scheme of maneuver.[47]

The Marine Corps depended on its air wing of vertical takeoff AV-8Bs Harriers (soon to be replaced with the Joint Strike Fighter), F/A 18s, and its Super Cobra helicopters, an improved Vietnam era helicopter. The Marine Corps did not neglect its infantry; however, instead of focusing on storming the beaches, it emphasized military operations in urban terrain, war in cities.

The Army in the aftermath of the Persian Gulf War was again concerned about survival. The Army needed a way to get to the battlefield. The Army needed to become an expeditionary force, more like the Marines. While the Army's Stryker brigades looked nothing like Marine Corps units, they were designed for rapid deployment. With the Air Force's new C-17s for strategic mobility, the Army started developing independent brigade-size organizations capable of generating more combat power than a World War II division and operating independently of a division headquarters. Each brigade had attached logistical support units and indirect fire resources. Sustainability once on the ground was still a major problem. The Army still depended on the Air Force and, to some degree, the Navy.

"Sea basing," the maintenance of several brigades and regiments of Army and Marine Corps equipment, pre-positioned float, provides the Army and Marine Corps with an answer to strategic mobility problems. Ships loaded with Abrams and Bradleys and the other equipment required for Army operations could be pre-positioned, greatly shortening the Army's deployment time. For intra-theater mobility the Army experimented with high-speed vessels (HSV), leasing two HSVs, the *Joint Venture* and *Spearhead*, for Operation Iraqi Freedom. They were employed to relocate Army pre-positioned stocks from Qatar to Kuwait and to carry out other intratheater logistic missions. One Navy observer noted: "The Army views the HSV as a theater support vessel with a focus on logistics.... The Army has driven much of the interest in high-speed ships to help shrink its deployment timeline."[48] The Navy too experimented with HSVs. In 2009 the Navy-Army High-Speed Ship Program initiated production of ten joint HSVs—five for the Army and five for the Navy.[49] JHSV-1 *The Spearhead* will enter service in 2011.[50] Arguably JHSVs are the Army's long-term solution of strategic and operational mobility. The US Army is now an expeditionary force.

While much time and attention has been devoted to "jointness," indicators show that this transformation had not yet penetrated the core cultures of the services.[51] The Air Force still argues that it can generate greater combat power, faster, and at considerably less cost than the Navy, which has to maintain expensive aircraft carriers, that long-range precision munitions and airpower are substitutes for many of the ground force capabilities of the Army and Marine Corps, and that ground forces were, for the most part, auxiliaries.[52] The Marine Corps organized its own mechanized maneuver warfare force, and has developed and procured vertical landing and take-off aircraft (V-22 Osprey) that make it possible to carry out operations deep into the interior of countries, expanding its operational mobility. Arguably the V-22 makes the Army's airborne and air assault divisions obsolete. Marines can now strike deep into the interior of a country, but also maintain the ability to support and extract their forces. The Marine Corps has also developed Special Forces.[53] The Army is developing theater support vessels (TSV), inter-theater shallow draft high speed sealift ships (SDHSS), JHSVs and Stryker brigades with wheeled fighting vehicles to quickly deploy rapid response forces that generate as much or more combat power than similar size marine units.[54] The Army has invested billions in helicopter and artillery technologies to eliminate its dependence on the Air Force for close air support, and is acquiring fixed-wing intra-theater transport aircraft. And if it were scientifically and technically possible, the Army, to be sure, would construct helicopters to provide strategic mobility. Jointness is an idea, not a fact.

Jointness needs to be redefined. Success in Operation Iraqi Freedom was considered a success of "jointness." Still, in operations conducted by the armed forces of the US, the first criterion is to insure that each service gets its piece of the operational pie. If the Air Force can perform the mission most effectively, naval aviation still has to be taken into consideration, and if possible a role found or created for it. The Marine Corps forms a second land Army. It is difficult to discern major differences in the missions and tasks required of the two services. General Tommy Franks initially wanted three heavy divisions to fight the war in Iraq. He got one, and one was at sea when the war commenced and ended. Whenever the Army is deployed for major operations, no matter what type of operation, no matter what the force structure of the enemy, the Marine Corps is also deployed. While observers are unanimous in their praise of the conventional campaign and assessments of the quality and character of the coordination, synchronization, and integration of forces between the services, some thought it absurd to see Marine Corps amphibious vehicles hundreds of miles inland, and recognized that for maintenance, logistical, supply, mobility, firepower, force protection, command and control, and air defense purposes, it made more sense to deploy another heavy Army division and possibly a brigade of light infantry.[55] Consider these words:

> By design, Marine Corps forces are not organized or equipped for sustained land combat, and

certainly not for a campaign ashore lasting months in an offensive hundreds of miles into the interior of a country with a poor infrastructure and virtually no coastline. Accordingly, the Army provided significant reinforcement.... At the time the Marines executed their initial operation ... in Iraq on 20 March 2003, the Army had attached more than 2,700 soldiers to 1 MEF to provide the capabilities not resident in Marine forces. These units contributed to the success of 1 MEF. ...[56]

In this environment, it made no sense to deploy amphibious tractors in Baghdad. Jointness as practiced by the Pentagon, shared the operational pie, but put soldiers, sailors, airmen, and marines at greater risk. After the war, Franks responded to criticisms that he went into Baghdad with insufficient forces:

> I will simply say that in this particular circumstance the force that entered Iraq—had it not had the 4th ID, the 1st Armored Division, and Armored Cav Regiment en route to and beginning to download its equipment in Kuwait—this would have been a gamble. But the fact [that] the force that entered Iraq was the lead element of additional substantial combat power, the piece of which were already beginning to unload, took the gamble out to the equation and placed the level at what I call prudent risk.[57]

In desert terrain, an Army armor or mechanized division generated considerably more combat power than an Army or Marine infantry division, with technology that was considerably more survivable.

The Goldwater-Nichols Act can be credited with producing senior officers with greater understanding of the culture and capabilities of each service. However, service loyalty in an environment of declining resources always trumps jointness. The services have overlapping responsibilities, and often duplicate the capabilities of one another. The services have continued the traditional practices of selling themselves, lobbying for weapons, conspiring with congressmen, and opposing changes to their force structure that are not in accordance with traditional ways of operating. Whether competition between the services makes them better is open to debate. What is known is that the competition is very expensive. And, that there are still winners and losers. In the period between Operation Desert Storm and Operation Iraqi Freedom, the Army was the loser, and as a consequence, the United States almost lost another war. With environmental security issues, a function of global warming, and globalization, the increased interconnectedness of the peoples of Earth, there will be plenty of conflicts in the developing world, and therefore, plenty of work for all the services. There are still too few soldiers and marines to do what is necessary.

16.
THE GLOBAL WAR ON TERRORISM AND THE WAR IN AFGHANISTAN: OPERATION ENDURING FREEDOM, 2001–2011

All these crimes and sins committed by the Americans are a clear declaration of war on God, his Messenger, and Muslims. . . . [T]he *jihad* is an individual duty if the enemy destroys the Muslim countries. . . . As for the fighting to repulse [an enemy], it is aimed at defending sanctity and religion, and it is a duty. . . . On that basis, and in compliance with God's order, we issue the following *fatwa* to all Muslims: The ruling to kill the Americans and their allies–civilian and military–is an individual duty for every Muslim who can do it in any country in which it is possible to do it.[1]

–Osama Bin Laden, 23 February 1998

The gravest danger our Nation faces lies at the crossroads of radicalism and technology. Our enemies have openly declared that they are seeking weapons of mass destruction, and evidence indicates that they are doing so with determination. The United States will not allow these efforts to succeed. We will build defense against ballistic missiles and other means of delivery. We will cooperate with other nations to deny, contain, and curtail our enemies' efforts to acquire dangerous technologies. And, as a matter of common sense and self-defense, America will act against such emerging threats before any fully formed. We cannot defend America and our friends by hoping for the best. So we must be prepared to defeat our enemies' plans, using the best intelligence and proceeding with deliberation. History will judge harshly those who saw this coming danger but failed to act. In the new world we have entered, the only path is the path of action.[2]

–President George W. Bush, "The National Security Strategy," 2002

In February 1998, the terrorist leader Osama Bin Laden again declared war on Americans. Since the late 1990s he had directed and deployed his army of al-Qaeda terrorists to carry out attacks against Americans in the United States and their interests in foreign countries to include: the bombing of US embassies in East Africa (Tanzania and Kenya, August 1998), an attack against the US Navy destroyer, the *USS Cole* (Yemen, 2000), attacks in the United States culminating with the attack on the Pentagon and the attacks in New York City that destroyed the World Trade Center on 11 September 2001 (9/11), and, after the commencement of operations in Afghanistan (2002) and Iraq (2003), suicide attacks against soldiers and marines.[3] These attacks had significant political, economic, social, psychological, and military costs and consequences for the American people.[4] On Sunday night, 1 May 2011, almost a decade after the 9/11 attacks, US Navy SEALs killed Osama Bin Laden with two shots—one in the chest and one to the head—in Abbottabad, Pakistan. A few hours later, President Barack Obama, who ordered the operation, announced to the American people:

> Tonight I can report to the American people, and to the world that the United States has conducted an operation that killed Osama Bin Laden, the leader of al-Qaeda, and a terrorist

who's responsible for the murder of thousands of innocent men, women, and children. It was nearly 10 years ago that a bright September day was darkened by the worst attack on the American people in our history. The images of 9/11 are seared into our national memory— hijacked planes cutting through a cloudless September sky, the Twin Towers collapsing to the ground, black smoke billowing up from the Pentagon, the wreckage of Flight 93 in Shanksville, Pennsylvania . . .

The President explained that:

After a firefight, they killed Osama Bin Laden and took custody of his body.[5] For over two decades, bin Laden had been al-Qaeda's leader and symbol, and has continued to plot attacks against our country and our friends and allies. The death of Bin Laden marks the most significant achievement to date in our nation's effort to defeat al-Qaeda. Yet his death does not mark the end of our effort. There is no doubt that al-Qaeda will continue to pursue attacks against us. We must—and we will—remain vigilant at home and abroad. . . . [H]is demise should be welcomed by all who believe in peace and human dignity.

With these words the President marked the end of a manhunt, but not the end of the wars to defeat terrorists and, more importantly, the sources that produced terrorism. US forces and intelligence agencies continued to fight in Afghanistan, conduct clandestine operations in Pakistan, Iraq, and other Middle East states, and work with allies and international organizations to find and kill terrorists and destroy their numerous sources. However, the death of Osama Bin Laden was a major benchmark in the war on terrorism. From Thucydides to Donald Kagan, it has been recognized that prestige, honor, and credibility were causes of war and preservers of peace.[6] These things influence the behavior and thinking of people and governments. The killing of Osama Bin Laden showed that America kept its promises, that the reach of the United States was world-wide, that American military professionalism and skill could reach into any state on Earth, and that the United States would not hesitate to act to kill enemies who killed Americans.

These are important lessons. The killing of Bin Laden was not the end, but it was a significant.

Al-Qaeda vs. The Bush Administration

The Bush Administration responded predictably to the terrorists' attacks on 9/11. It developed and promulgated a new national security strategy that called for "preemptive war," or more accurately, *preventive war*.[7] It then used the new "Bush doctrine" to go to war in Iraq, a state that had not attacked the United States. A Holy War that pitted the Muslim world against the United States was what al-Qaeda and other Islamic extremists wanted. In a work titled, "Al-Qaeda as an Adversary: Do We Understand Our Enemy?" D.L. Byman concluded that:

Al-Qaeda's leadership has a strategic view of terror. In addition to using violence to shock enemies and glorify God, Al-Qaeda leaders clearly seek to use the reactions of the United States and its other adversaries against them. For example, it is now clear that bin Laden sought to bring a heavy US military response to the September 11 attacks on Afghanistan, believing (so far, wrongly) that this would precipitate a broader clash between the West and Islam world. Although he clearly underestimated US resolve, power, and skill, in both his small and large actions he has attempted to manipulated and use the American response to suit his ends.[8]

Bin Laden sought to direct the energies of a billion angry Muslims who felt they had been unjustly treated by the West, men and women who were also angry at their status and the conditions and parameters of their lives. Bin Laden wanted war to diminish the United States and cause it to retreat from the Middle East. His objective was a much wider war than that in Afghanistan. He wanted to get the US to overextend itself militarily and financially, and to get other Muslim states and communities into the fight. Bin Laden wrote:

All that we have mentioned has made it easy for us to provoke and bait this administration. . . . [F] or example, Al-Qaeda spent $500,000 on the event, while America, in the incident and its aftermath, lost—according to the lowest estimate—more than $500 billion … which is evidence of the success of the bleed-until-bankruptcy plan—with Allah's permission.[9]

Bin Laden's objective was to weaken and diminish the United States, and ultimately to get it out of the Middle East.

Still, strategically Bin Laden and al-Qaeda failed. The war they sought did not take place. They underestimated the armed forces of the United States and the power and resources of the United States. They underestimated the strength and resilience of the alliance of Western democracies. And, they overestimated the willingness of Muslims to join their extremist movements, to accept their fundamentalist ideology and way of life, to kill other Muslims and destroy their homes, businesses, and communities. They overestimated the willingness of Muslims to hate Americans and others from the West, and to give up on their dreams and aspiration for a better way of life for themselves and their children. Muslims want the same things Americans want, the same things other human beings want. The war between the Muslim world and the United States did not emerge from the rubble of the World Trade Center, and history may ultimately reveal that by attacking the United States, al-Qaeda initiated a series of events that started democratic, capitalist revolutions across the Middle East.[10]

The attacks on 9/11 required war. The human male response to violence is most commonly, more violence. However, from violence opportunities emerge. The Bush Administration failed to see the nature of the unique opportunity in front of it. It was culturally blind. Goodwill towards the United States from a sympathetic world, which watched in astonishment and horror the collapse of the Twin Towers of the World Trade Center again and again, was destroyed or simply allowed to dissipate in less than a year by bad policies, poorly chosen words, and unnecessary actions. Bush's "*Top Gun* landing" on the *USS Abraham Lincoln* after the perceived victory in Iraq in May 2003 was a major mistake. This "Hollywood stunt" showed incredible arrogance and disrespect. It was completely unnecessary, and more importantly it angered and embarrassed many in the Arab world,

who had just watched the US Army and Marine Corps decimate the highly regarded Republican Guard of Saddam Hussein in a matter of weeks. No President could have avoided violent retaliation to the terrorist attacks of 9/11. Arguably, the most powerful nation on Earth had to have its "pound of flesh" for the insult and injury suffered at the hands of a small group of dedicated, organized, and determined terrorists. However, the United States was not attacked by a nation or a state, and the wars that followed 9/11 could have been fought without alienating peoples and governments in the Middle East and other regions, could have been fought in a manner that took advantage of this new sympathy from nations and states that have *not* traditionally been allied with or supportive of the United States. The Bush Administration was incapable of using and exploiting the wealth of sympathy and goodwill generated on 9/11. It was incapable of articulating a more inclusive vision of war and the peace that might follow. It thus wasted these rare and valuable resources. This failure made the costs of the wars much higher for Americans, particularly the soldiers and marines, sailors and airmen who had to fight it.

Nine days after the terrorist attacks, in a joint session of Congress, President George W. Bush committed the United States to the global war on terrorism (GWOT). He delineated the objectives of the United States: "Our war on terror will not end until *every* terrorist group of global reach has been found, stopped and defeated." These words, which played well with shocked and angry Americans, were poorly chosen. This grandiose objective was well beyond the resources of even the United States. Such an objective required the support and cooperation of much of the world, its peoples, governments, and armed forces. It required the support of non-traditional allies and former enemies. Bush in one moment called upon the peoples of the world to unite behind this great cause, and in the next threatened them with an ultimatum. He said: "This is not, however, just America's fight, and what is at stake is not just America's freedom. This is the world's fight. This is civilization's fight. This is the fight of all who believe in progress and pluralism, tolerance and freedom." These were positive and inclusive words. But then Bush added: "Every nation, in every region, now has a decision to make. Either you are with us, or you are with the terrorists. From this day forward, any nation that continues to harbor or support terrorism will be regarded by the United States as a hostile regime."[11] Bush divided the world. He made it black and white, good or evil. Either a nation-state was "with us," or it was a "hostile regime." The UN either supported the US or was irrelevant. Wars were either won or lost. Congressmen and women were either patriotic or unpatriotic. While such simplistic formulations are easy to explain to the American people and create a tough guy image that appeals to certain clusters of Americans, the world was and is considerably more complex. The order Bush tried to impose on the world caused friction with allies, alienated potential friends, and stirred anger that motivated some to fight. The world is not black and white. It has numerous shades of gray. And *no* government can control everything that goes on within its borders. Simplistic formulas to complex problems tend to fail. By not developing a more nuanced strategy to fight the war on terrorism, Bush lost opportunities that made the military task considerably more difficult.

Bush also sought to rally the American people and allay their fears. He made an emotional appeal, reminiscent of Churchill in the early days of World War II, when Britain stood alone against Nazi Germany and the Nazi-occupied Europe. Bush stated:

> Freedom and fear are at war. The advance of human freedom, the great achievement of our time and the great hope of every time, now depends on us. Our Nation—*this generation*—will lift a dark threat of violence from our people and our future. We will rally the world to this cause by our efforts, by our courage. We will not tire; we will not falter, and we will not fail.

But, Bush did not call upon the nation, the American people, *this generation*, to do anything. He did not ask them to serve. He did not seek to reinstitute the draft. He did not ask Americans to buy war bonds or plant "victory gardens." He did not ask Americans to contribute anything that required them to sacrifice. In fact, he made no demands on the American people. What he asked them to do was to continue to act in their own self-interest. He stated:

> Americans are asking: What is expected of us? I ask you to live your lives, and hug your children. I know many citizens have fears tonight, and I ask you to be calm and resolute, even in the face of a continuing threat.... I ask your continued participation and confidence in the American economy. Terrorists attacked a symbol of American prosperity. They did not touch its source.

How much fear Americans felt is questionable. Many Americans felt angry and wanted to do something, I among them. Bush had a wealth of highly motivated American energy at his call. It was his to harness and direct, but unlike President Roosevelt, who prepared the nation for global war in the days following the Japanese attack at Pearl Harbor, Bush believed his global war on terrorism could be fought without sacrifices from the American people. So he gave the American people tax cuts and told them to go shopping, to participate in the economy.

Years later, fighting two long wars, the US Army and Marine Corps were overextended. Soldiers and Marines were serving multiple tours in combat, and still there were insufficient forces to properly execute the joint counterinsurgency doctrine. In the face of an unprecedented national crisis, Bush confirmed this relatively new American practice of war: *war without the people*, and placed the burden of two long wars on less than one percent of the population. Selfless service to the nation was required of only the military cluster. To the military cluster Bush stated: "And tonight, a few miles from the damaged Pentagon, I have a message for our military: Be ready. I've called the armed forces to alert, and there is a reason. The hour is coming when America will act, and you will make us proud." Bush's words and actions confirmed that the Clausewitzian tenet of the "trinity of war"— the people, the government, and the armed forces— no longer functioned in the United States. While the vast majority of Americans did nothing, the men and women of the armed forces, particularly the Army and Marine Corps, were experiencing and suffering from post-traumatic stress disorder on a scale and depth never before witnessed in the United States.[12] There was no equality of sacrifice.

Strategy is the art and science of employing national resources to achieve political objectives.

Bush started his global war on terrorism by eliminating two of his greatest strategic resources, the American people and the peoples and governments of the world who lived in the gray areas, between the black and white worlds he tried to create. The war against terrorism will be won, but not because of the genius of US strategy. It will be won because the war initiated by al-Qaeda was unwinnable from the start. It will be won because Muslim people will reject the vision of life offered by al-Qaeda and other Islamic fundamentalists who have hijacked the Islamic religion. An ideology, or an interpretation of a religion, that moves too far from what human beings want and need, a system of belief that eliminates half the population (women) from participating in the social and political life of the community, that practices war that kills fellow citizens and alienates and destroys cohesion, is ultimately destine to fail. The greatest strength of the United States is not in its military or its government. It is in the demonstrative superiority of the American systems, the American way of life, to produce wealth and prosperity for the greatest number of people. American cultural norms, political and economic system are weapons of inestimable value in the war on terrorism. However, its true effects are largely unseen and are not easily measured; as a consequence, the government habitually fails to employ them strategically. The war on terrorism continues, but its outcome is inevitable.

Terrorism and Counterterrorism

Terrorism, according to the United Nations, is: "Criminal acts intended or calculated to provoke a state of terror in the general public, a group of persons or particular persons for political purpose." The US Foreign Relations Authorization Act of 1988 defined terrorism as: "Premeditated, politically motivated violence perpetrated against noncombatant targets by subnational groups or clandestine agents." The Department of Defense defines terrorism as: "The unlawful use of violence or threat of violence to instill fear and coerce governments of societies. Terrorism is often motivated by religious, political, or other ideological beliefs and committed in the pursuit of goals that are usually political." And, Army FM 3–0, *Operations*, defines terrorism as: "The calculated use of unlawful violence or threat of unlawful violence to inculcate fear, intended to coerce or to intimidate governments or societies in the pursuits of goals that are generally political, religious, or ideological." The definition of terrorism has been greatly debated, because it matters.[13] It helps determine the objectives of strategy, identify the resources needed to defend against it, identify the agency primarily responsible for destroying it, the development of strategic and operational doctrines to combat it, and the enactment of policies and strategies best suited to preclude or contain it. Political and military leaders, CIA, FBI, and officials from other agencies, academics and other researchers have had difficulties defining terrorism, and many disagreed with the strategy and policies the Bush Administration employed to combat it.

Terrorism is purposeful violence designed to influence the behavior of people and their government. However, it is not an objective nor is it a strategy. It is an instrument and a tactic, which can be employed to achieve strategic objectives. Acts of terrorism alone cannot destroy governments, armies, or nations. Terrorism is considered "the weapon of the weak." Terrorists seek change that they lack the strength to achieve with the overt use of force. The objective of terrorists is political and/or social change, the overthrow of governments or political systems and the establishment of a new government and possibly a new way of life based on their ideology, political, and religious beliefs. Terrorism is part of an information campaign. The immediate objective is to strike such fear in the hearts of a people that they are motivated to immediately place new demands on their government that will change the status quo. Terrorism has political, economic, social, psychological, and cultural consequences.[14] Terrorists target the *will*. They have five target audiences: the people of a particular state or nation in whom they hope to strike terror; the government(s) of that state, which is influenced by the people who are terrorized; angry or alienated groups that might be persuaded to join their cause; the peoples of the world whose governments might be influenced to provide resources overtly or covertly, or to remain neutral; and the fighters in their own ranks, whose skill and motivation are needed to sustain and advance the movement. Paul Pillar, former deputy chief of the CIA's Counter Terrorist

Center, identified the four basic elements of terrorism: 1. Pre-mediated, planned acts of violence; 2. politically designed to change the existing political order; 3. aimed at civilians, not military targets; 4. carried out by subnational groups, not by the armed forces of established states (states do sponsor terrorism). A fifth element is attention, the desire to gain as much world attention and shock effect as possible.

One of the problems of defining terrorism is the identity of the actor. States that commit violence against other states or their citizens are committing acts of *war*. Non-state actors or subnational groups who attack states or their citizens are not committing acts of war. They are committing crimes. And states do not go to war with criminals or subnational groups. They employ police forces and their criminal justice systems to enforce laws and to destroy organized criminal groups. Sir Michael Howard, the British military historian, believed the Bush Administration failed to properly identify the enemy, and that that failing caused others that had tragic consequences for the United States. He observed that: "When in the immediate aftermath of the attack on the World Trade Center the American Secretary of State Colin Powell declared that America was 'at war,' he made a very natural but a terrible and irrevocable error." He noted that:

> to use, or rather to misuse the term 'war' is not simply a matter of legality, or pedantic semantics. It has deeper and more dangerous consequences. To declare that one is 'at war' is immediately to create a war psychosis that may be totally counter-productive for the objective that we seek. It will arouse an immediate expectation, and demand, for spectacular military action against some easily identifiable adversary, preferably a hostile state. . . .

Arguably, George W. Bush declared war before he had a state to fight. Howard further noted that:

> To "declare war" on terrorists, or even more illiterately, on "terrorism" is at once to accord them a status and dignity that they seek and which they do not deserve. It confers on them a kind of legitimacy. Do they qualify as "belligerents"? If so, should they not receive the protection of the laws of war?

The Bush Administration had no intention of providing terrorists the refuge of international laws; hence, the employment of language meant for state-to-state confrontations diminished the credibility and legitimacy of the United States in the war on terrorism. Howard believed an alternate approach was possible:

> Could it have been avoided? Certainly, rather than what President Bush so unfortunately termed 'a crusade against evil', that is, a military campaign conducted by an alliance dominated by the United States, many people would have preferred a police operation conducted under the auspices of the United Nations on behalf of the international community as a whole, against a criminal conspiracy; whose members should be hunted down and brought before an international court, where they would receive a fair trial and, if found guilty, awarded an appropriate sentence.[15]

"Rogue states" or "weak states" may sponsor terrorism, or harbor groups that commit terrorism, but they are not terrorists. The Bush charge against Afghanistan was that it was a *weak state* that permitted terrorists to operate from the security of its borders. The Taliban government hosted Osama Bin Laden and his terrorist organization. The Bush charge against Iraq was that it was a *rogue state* that sponsored terrorism. Saddam Hussein, he argued, had connections with al-Qaeda, and was providing it with resources to attack Americans, potentially with weapons of mass destruction. The Taliban and Saddam Hussein facilitated terrorist activities. But they were not terrorists.

The comprehensive strategy against Islamic fundamentalist terrorist organizations required both a police response and a military response. Arguably the FBI, with its vast forensic capabilities and abilities to work with foreign police agencies, should have taken the lead. However, the FBI is primarily a domestic agency. It lacked the international connections and jurisdiction to function effectively in foreign countries. The CIA and State Department are responsible for state-to-state relationships, but they lacked the expertise of the FBI. State-to-state aggression—rogue and weak states—required military involvement. The fight against terrorism required the integration of the capabilities, expertise, and talents of numerous agencies. The fact is that no single agency had the resources, capabilities, and expertise required to defeat foreign terrorist threats. However, the war on terrorism was not a war that fit easily into the American cultural understanding of "war." The use of the term created expectation that could not be easily met, with a limited war against the weak state of Afghanistan.

*   *   *   *   *

Counterterrorism is defined in Army FM 3–0 *Operations* as: "Operations that include the offensive measure taken to prevent, deter, preempt, and respond to terrorism. Counterterrorism actions include strikes and raids against terrorist organizations and facilities outside the United States and its territories." In February 2003 the Bush Administration published the *National Strategy for Combating Terrorism*. The document was supposed to delineate a comprehensive strategy for the conduct of the war against terrorism. The introduction was borrowed from President Bush's 6 November 2001, speech, which in part stated:

> The struggle against international terrorism is different from any other war in our history. We will not triumph solely or even primarily through military might. We must fight terrorist networks, and all those who support their efforts to spread fear around the world, using every instrument of national power—diplomatic, economic, law enforcement, financial, information, intelligence, and military.

The documents delineate the resources required to defeat terrorism:

> The war on terrorism is asymmetric in nature but the advantage belongs to us, not the terrorists. We will fight this campaign using our strengths against the enemy's weaknesses. We will use the power of our values to shape a free and more prosperous world. We will employ the legitimacy of our government and our cause to craft strong and agile partnerships. Our economic strength will help failing states and assist weak countries in ridding themselves of terrorism. Our

technology will help identify and locate terrorist organizations, our global reach will eliminate them where they hide. And as always, we will rely on the strength of the American people to remain resolute in the face of adversity.[16]

These were good words. But the actions of the Bush Administration did not conform to them. The Bush Administration went first to the American practice of war. It relied first and foremost on military means and advanced technologies. It added to this mix the CIA. By so doing it alienated traditional and potential allies, and used words and methods that alienated the peoples of the countries whose support was most needed in the fight against terrorism. It took years for the US Government to adapt to the new realities of the global war on terrorism. New relationships with foreign countries had to be formed and other relationships strengthened. New relationships and alliances between governmental agencies had to be forged. Domestic agencies had become international agencies. Organizational cultures had to be transformed. New organizations had to be created.[17] Military forces had to be reorganized. New missions had to be taken on by all the services and the agencies of government. The role of the defense industry had to change to take on responsibilities previously considered exclusively military. Resources had to be reallocated. The emphasis on technology had to give way to the emphasis on manpower and human understanding. Training had to be reoriented away from conventional warfare and toward counterinsurgency and irregular warfare. The war against terrorism ultimately required more construction than destruction. This new direction required a profound shift in the thinking of the US government, its agencies, and the men and women of the armed forces. The perspective of a soldier at war in Afghanistan helps to clarify the issues and problems:

> Al-Qaeda still thrives in the ungoverned tribal areas along the border between the two countries [Afghanistan and Pakistan], and while many of its members have been killed, new recruits quickly take their place. US soldiers have learned that to deny al-Qaeda a foothold in Afghanistan will require the establishment of a government that Afghans can believe in, the security that

allows them to support it and jobs that provide an alternative to fighting. "We are not going to kill our way out of this war," says Lieut. Colonel Brett Jenkinson, commander of the US battalion stationed in Korengal Valley. "What we need is a better recruiting pitch for disaffected youth. You can't build hope with military might. You build it through development and good governance."[18]

Between 2003 and 2005 the United States and its allies expended vast resources in the fight against terrorism. But the essence of the problem and the nature of the wars escaped the Bush Administration until the Army and Marine Corps were well immersed in an insurgency war with insufficient forces and too few allies to achieve the political objectives. Only in 2005 did they start to grasp the essence and magnitude of the problem, and start to adapt to address the sources of terrorism: corrupt and failed governments, lawlessness, ethnic and sectarian divisions, the desire for revenge, religious prejudice and intolerance, perverse ideology, poverty, illiteracy, injustice, and hopelessness.[19] The GWOT required more construction than destruction. And, the primary focus of the armed forces of the United States from World War II to Operation Enduring Freedom, with the exception of a brief period during the Vietnam War, had been on the destruction of the enemy's main forces.

In failed and weak states that have frequently been ravaged by war, raw, basic emotions and desperate conditions were (are) rich soil for growing terrorists. Slowly the Bush Administration came to this realization. The services also came to this realization too slowly. Too much time and energy devoted to "network-centric warfare" and the "revolution in military affairs" created blunders. However, resources and energy were refocused, and, as a result, there was a new emphasis on human-to-human relationships, a new emphasis on counterinsurgency and stability operations, nation-building and economic development, cultural comprehension and language skills, information operations, inter-agency and non-governmental organization cooperation, and a new direction in military education. New organizations and learning were evident in the development of the human terrain system, provisional reconstruction teams, security force assistance programs, and inter-agency studies

programs, all of which were designed to win the hearts and minds, to build relationships that facilitated the accomplishment of strategic objectives.[20] Still, this was war. Policing was necessary, but organized, trained, well-armed enemy forces had to be fought. Al-Qaeda and Taliban leaders and soldiers were violent extremists who would not quit. They had to be fought and killed at close quarter. This was a job for the Army and Marine Corps. But, the military task was only a small part of the solution to the global problem of terrorism.

The Response: The GWOT and Bush Doctrine of Preemptive War[21]

On 17 September 2002 the Bush Administration published the new *National Security Strategy* of the United States. This NSC document was a prescription for *preventive* and *preemptive war*. Under the heading "Prevent Our Enemies from Threatening Us, Our Allies, and Our Friends with Weapons of Mass Destruction," it, in part, stated:

> We must be prepared to stop rogue states and their terrorist clients before they are able to threaten or use weapons of mass destruction. . . . Given the goals of rogue states and terrorist, the United States can no longer solely rely on a reactive posture as we have in the past. The inability to deter a potential attacker, the immediacy of today's threats, and the magnitude of potential harm that could be caused by our adversaries' choice of weapons do not permit that option. We cannot let our enemies strike first. . . . The greater the threat, the greater is the risk of inaction—and the more compelling the case for taking anticipatory action to defend ourselves, even if uncertainty remains as to the time and place of the enemy's attack. To forestall or prevent such hostile acts by our adversaries, the United States will, if necessary, act preemptively.[22]

Douglas Feith, Rumsfeld's Under Secretary of Defense for Policy, delineated the principles underlying the new policies, decisions, and actions of the Bush Administration. He wrote: "The Bush Administration's response to 9/11 was different from that of any previous US administration to a terrorist attack. It was based on five major thoughts":

First, the foremost purpose of the US response to the attack was not punishment or retaliation, but preventing the next attack—a point that argued for quick action to disrupt ongoing terrorist plans.

Second, we were at war with a global terrorist network of Islamist extremist groups, including state and nonstate sponsors—and the next attack might come not from al Qaida but from some other part of the movement. Our strategy has to target both those groups themselves and their key sources of actual and potential support—operational, logistic, financial, and ideological.

Third, our attacks were bent not on political theater but on mass destruction. This highlighted the possibility that terrorist might obtain chemical, biological, or nuclear weapons to maximize the death toll.

Fourth, a series of 9/11-typed terrorist attacks on the United States could change the nature of our country. Our national security policy extends beyond simply protecting people or territory. It includes securing our constitutional system, our civil liberties, and the open nature of our society—"our way of life," as President Bush expressed it.

This war aim brought us to the fifth strategic thought: In order to counter this threat successfully, we could not rely on a defensive strategy alone. The United States has so many rich targets that it would demand extraordinary measures to secure them individually—and the effort to do so would endanger our free and open society. These considerations necessitated a strategy of initiative and offense—of disrupting the terrorist network abroad.[23]

This doctrine provided a rationale for war with Iraq, Iran, and North Korea. Under this doctrine Bush promised *unilateral military actions*, to strike enemies before they could attack the US. Preemptive war doctrine was not necessary to go after al-Qaeda and other terrorist organizations. They were criminal organizations, and could be legally hunted, arrested and/or killed. The problem was access, getting to the terrorist who hid in sovereign, foreign countries. Bush and senior-most advisors believed that the United States could legitimately act without the support of

the United Nations, and without a resolution of support from Congress. They believed the power of the President in matters related to national security was almost absolute. They employed the CIA, for example, in a "rendition program" to kidnap suspect terrorists in foreign countries, interrogate them in a third country, using "enhanced interrogation" techniques, which some considered torture, and, sometimes, to imprison them offshore, at the Guantanamo Bay Detainment Camp at the US Naval Base in Cuba, where the laws of the United States had no power.[24] President Bush's Secretary of Defense Donald Rumsfeld, in support of the doctrine of preemptive war, wrote:

> In the twenty-first century, the idea that countries could be left alone unless and until they actually launched an aggressive war had to have exceptions. The lethality of modern weapons and the stated intent of terrorist to use them made it difficult to sustain that traditional view. Regimes with records of aggression and dishonesty, and which had or were working toward WMD capabilities, could inflict far more massive damage than ever before. And Iranian nuclear strike on the small state of Israel, for example, could destroy so much of the nation that Israel might be unable to survive as a viable state. Could a responsible Israeli prime minister allow that to occur by waiting until after a nuclear missile was launched? Nuclear or biological material covertly passed to a terrorist organization could be detonated or released in one or more cities, killing millions, bringing our economy to a halt, and effectively suspending our country's cherished civil liberties. Could an American president sit back, wait, and take that risk?[25]

This thinking is a function of the abundance of military power, weak and rogue state opponents, the environment of uncertainty created by the terrorist attack on 9/11, and a sense of righteousness that caused some to disregard precedence, traditions, and laws governing the behavior of states. Thomas Schelling in his book, *The Diplomacy of Violence*, wrote:

> With enough military force a country may not need to bargain. Some things a country wants it

can take, and some things it has it can keep, by sheer strength, skill, and ingenuity. It can do this *forcibly*, accommodating only to opposing strength, skill and ingenuity and without trying to appeal to an enemy's wishes.

Schelling concluded that: "Forcibly a country can repel and expel, penetrate and occupy, seize, exterminate, disarm and disable, confine, deny access, and directly frustrate intrusion or attack. It can, that is, if it has enough strength."[26] This was the underlying belief of the Bush Administration, that American military power was so great that it could dictate the course and conduct of the global war on terrorism. The Bush doctrine emphasized the unique status of the United States:

The United States possesses unprecedented—and unequaled—strength and influence in the world. Sustained by faith in the principles of liberty, and the value of a free society, this position comes with unparalleled responsibilities, and opportunity. The great strength of this nation must be used to promote a balance of power that favors freedom.

Many Americans had a visceral reaction to the concept of preventive war. They associated it with the Germans and the two world wars. They associated it with wars of aggression. During the 1950s in the early days of the Cold War the concept of preventive war was discussed intensely and each time it was rejected. In the first decade of the nuclear age, the United States, the inventor of the atomic bomb, had a clear superiority over the Soviet Union in nuclear technology and weapons. To prevent some future nuclear holocaust, some argued that the United States should go to war before nuclear parity was reached. This concept of war was rejected again and again. Bernard Brodie, in his book, *Strategy in the Missile Age*, first published in 1959, wrote:

the people of the United States have obviously made a decision, with little overt debate but quite remarkable unanimity, against any form of preventive war. The lack of active consideration of the matter confirms only the preordained nature of the decision, which accords profoundly with our national psychology and system of values.[27]

Michael Walzer, in his study *Just and Unjust War*, wrote:

A preventive war is a war fought to maintain the balance, to stop what is thought to be an even distribution of power from shifting into a relation of dominance and inferiority. . . . Preventive war presupposes some standard against which danger is to be measured. That standard does not exist, as it were, on the ground; it has nothing to do with the immediate security of boundaries. It exists in the mind's eye, in the idea of a balance of power.[28]

No weak or rogue states have ever come close to rivaling the power of the Soviet Union.

Preemptive war thinking was very different. When a threat was imminent a state could act preemptively to stop the attack or to create a more favorable military situation. In other words, a state could initiate war and still be on the defensive. This was acceptable to Americans. In a speech in Cincinnati on 7 October 2002, Bush made it clear he was thinking of *preventive war*, not *preemptive war*. "If we know Saddam Hussein has dangerous weapons today, and we do, does it make any sense for the world to wait to confront him as he grows stronger and develops even more dangerous weapons."[29] And, "does it make any sense for the world to wait to confront him as he grows even stronger and develops even more dangerous weapons?" No attack from Iraq was imminent. Bush did not believe this was a realistic requirement for war in the age of terrorism and the proliferation of WMDs.[30]

There were voices that argued against the Bush doctrine.[31] Arthur Schlesinger, Jr., a former advisor to President Kennedy, observed that: "One of the astonishing events of recent months is the presentation of preventive war as a legitimate and moral instrument of US foreign policy. . . . During the Cold War, advocates of preventive war were dismissed as a crowd of loonies." Jeffrey Record wrote: "Pursuit of the neoconservative agenda of permanent American primacy via perpetual military supremacy, and, as a matter of doctrine, an aggressive willingness to use force preemptively, even preventively, to dispatch threatening regimes and promote the spread of American political and economic institutions, invites perpetual isolation and enmity."[32] Brent Scowcroft, the senior Bush's national security advisor, who had argued against going into Baghdad and regime change in the first Persian Gulf War, was one of the most noted dissenters:

> Part of the Bush administration believes that as a superpower we must take advantage of this opportunity to change the world for the better, and we don't need to go out of our way to accommodate alliances, partnerships, or friends in the process, because that would be too constraining. [But relying almost solely on ad hoc] coalitions of the willing is fundamentally, fatally flawed. As we've seen in the debate about Iraq, it's already given us an image of arrogance and unilateralism, and we're paying a very high price for that image. If we get to the point where everyone secretly hopes the United States gets a black eye because we're so obnoxious, then we'll be totally hamstrung in the war on terror. We'll be like Gulliver with the Lilliputians.[33]

Offensive warfare and first strikes against a state that was growing militarily stronger was considered a war of aggression; and hence, un-American. However, in the post–9/11 environment Americans were more willing to accept un-American doctrines and policies. The Bush doctrine of "preemptive war" signaled to the world his intent to go to war. At the same time, within the Administration, it foreclosed discussions on the use of other forms of power and other forms of strategies. Jeffrey Record noted, "The Bush Doctrine rightly focuses on the principle of regime change as the most effective means of defeating threats posed by rogue and terrorist-hosting weak states, but actual regime change can entail considerable, even unacceptable, military and political risks, depending upon local, regional, and international circumstances." He further noted that: "The Bush Doctrine correctly dismisses the effectiveness of deterrence against suicidal terrorist organizations, but it may be mistaken in dismissing its effectiveness against rogue states."[34] By prematurely foreclosing the discussion on options, Bush eliminated potential solutions short of war. Prior to Bush's publication of his strategy, the world learned of his intent to invade Iraq. Arab states immediately

responded. On Tuesday 25 September 2001, the *Dallas Morning News* reported:

> Arab leaders warned Washington repeatedly over the past week that their governments would consider withdrawing from a US coalition to fight terrorism if Iraq is attacked.... "If Iraq is hit, it would really raise the street," Ali Abul Raghebo, Jordan's prime minister, warned in an interview. "If Iraq is hit for this reason, it might affect the level of cooperation of the Arab countries within the coalition."
>
> He and other Arab leaders say no hard evidence has surfaced publicly linking the Iraqi government to the Sept. 11 attacks. Many Arab governments have expressed nervousness about the popular reaction to any attack on Iraq, saying it would be viewed not as an attempt to halt terrorism but rather to exact revenge and settle old scores from the 1991 Persian Gulf War.
>
> "What we want is justice not revenge," said the Saudi Arabian foreign minister, Prince Saud al-Faisal, following a round of meetings in Washington last week. Arab League Secretary-General Amer Musa was more blunt. "Clearly we would never accept a strike against an Arab country, no matter what the circumstances," he told reporters.[35]

Arab leaders and states that lived in the gray areas, unseen by the Bush Administration, were ignored. Potential, silent allies became neutral observers at best and secret supporters of the terrorists at worse. Bush thus made the task of the armed forces considerably more difficult by alienating important, potential allies, whose people secretly supported terrorist operations in Iraq and Afghanistan. Pakistan is a case in point. While the US provided the government of Pakistan billions of dollars to fight the war on terrorism, US actions alienated the people of Pakistan, some of whom hid Osama Bin Laden and other terrorists. These are complex relations and many factors influence the behaviors of governments and people. However, the words, actions, and policies of the Bush Administration diminished support for the United States in important regions of the world. US forces were pushed to the limits of endurance by the two long wars in Afghanistan and Iraq. It might have been otherwise. Schelling's thesis addressed only one type of power: destructive military power. There are many types of power that influence the outcome of war, and the achievement of political objectives. The preponderance of American destructive military power obscured the need for the Bush Administration to more fully employ other types of power. The war on terrorism required more construction than destruction. It took us years to figure this out.

*   *   *   *   *

Leadership matters. We cannot get inside the head of a president to determine and assess his thinking; however, we can assess his actions and the external factors that may have influenced his decisions. And we can assess the character of the man, endeavoring to ascertain the values, ethics, and beliefs that informed his decisions. President George W. Bush is the son of President George H.W. Bush. And, there is no doubt that the successful political career of George W. Bush is a function of the life of President George H.W. Bush. The son lived in the shadow of the father.[36] The son selected senior cabinet leaders who had served his father. They guaranteed his success, under normal circumstances. Bush's method of leadership was to select senior, proven leaders for top cabinet posts and vice president, men and women whose conservative ideology reflected his own views, and to then delegate substantial authority to them.[37] On major issues these men presented ideas and solutions to Bush, and he made decisions based on his gut feelings and ideological beliefs. However, certain members of the Bush Administration exerted considerably more power than others. Dick Cheney was considered by many the most powerful Vice President in US history.[38]

Bush was, in part, motivated by his perceptions of the failings of the Clinton Administration, which he considered weak, immoral, and ineffective. He held considerable contempt for the behavior of the Clinton Administration, believing that it was, at least in part, responsible for the 9/11 attacks on the US. Bush believed that had Clinton responded to the threats of terrorism more vigorously and with greater force and determination, the attack of 9/11 could have been prevented. He told Bob Woodward: "The antiseptic notion of launching a cruise missile into some guy's, you know, tent, really is a joke."[39] Bush later stated

that, "I do believe there is the image of America out there that we are so materialistic, that we're almost hedonistic, that we don't have values, and that when struck, we wouldn't fight back. It was clear that bin Laden felt emboldened and didn't feel threatened by the United States."[40]

In his State of the Union address on 28 January 2003, Bush stated the "British government has learned that Saddam Hussein recently sought significant quantities of uranium from Africa." When these words were spoken they were known to be false.[41] An assessment of the Bush leadership published in *US News and World Report* concluded:

> At the heart of the new debate is a central fact of Bush's leadership: His philosophy of governing is as audacious as that of any president in the past half century. Following the formula of Ronald Reagan, Bush is governing in bold strokes of primary colors, not pastels. It is not a programmatic approach but—especially on national security issues—a way of thinking that is both fresh and risky. Bush's vision of the future is double edged, calling for strong conservatism at home and positing a far-reaching struggle abroad against forces he calls "the evildoers" of terrorism. What unsettles much of official Washington, however, is that this is essentially a gambler's philosophy. Bush has put down all his chips and is letting his presidency ride on the outcome, take it or leave it.[42]

A student of Bush's political career, reflecting on the President's words that "I feel no sense of the so-called heavy burden of the office," wrote, "There it is: A one-sentence character sketch." He continued:

> Other presidents have agonized over hard choices—think of Lyndon Johnson in the early days of Vietnam, wanting to get out yet knowing that he couldn't—but not Bush. "The best thing he does is make decisions," his longtime political guru, Karl Rove, told me during the gubernatorial years. Rove went on to say that it was more important for a leader to make a decision and stick by it than that the decision be absolutely right. Bush is comfortable with the burdens of the office because he doesn't feel them the way others do: He never looks back, never

second-guesses himself, never shows weakness, never admits a mistake, never reverses course.[43]

White House Chief of Staff Andy Card observed that:

> He [Bush] believes that leadership carries with it an obligation to think big and act big. And he does think big, and he's going to act big.... He has spread freedom to lands that no one thought would be able to enjoy it four years ago—in Afghanistan ... and the seeds of it have been sown in Iraq.[44]

By the end of 2003 many Americans, who had accepted Bush's "truth," were beginning to recognize that there was another, more accurate and balanced, truth. When no weapons of mass destruction were found in Iraq, many Americans concluded the President had lied about the primary cause of the war, and that the war had been unnecessary. On 21 July 2003, the cover of *Time* read, "Untruth and Consequence: How Flawed was the Case for Going to War against Iraq?" The 3 November 2003 cover of *Newsweek* read, "Bush's $87 Billion Mess: Waste, Chaos, and Cronyism, The Real Cost of Rebuilding Iraq," and the 25 September 2005 cover of *Time* read, "Iraq: Is it Too Late to Win the War?"[45] Yet, there was little public condemnation of the Bush Administration. Because the wars were not a national effort, because there was no draft, because there were no new taxes to pay for the war, and because the news media failed to adequately cover and investigate the war, the real costs of the wars were hidden. The American people are, for the most part, pacified.

* * * * *

The attacks on 9/11 initiated the most significant reorganization of government since the establishment of the Department of Defense (DOD) during the Truman Administration to fight the Cold War. On 25 November 2002, Congress established the Department of Homeland Security (DHS), a cabinet-level, executive department of the United States to fight the war on terrorism. The primary mission of the DHS is to:

> prevent terrorist attacks within the United States; reduce the vulnerability of the United State to

terrorism; minimize the damage, and assist in the recovery, from terrorist attacks that do occur within the United States; carry out all functions of entities transferred to the Department, including acting as a focal point regarding natural and man-made crises and emergency planning ...; ensure that the overall economic security of the United States is not diminished by efforts, activities, and programs aimed at securing the homeland; and monitor connections between illegal drug trafficking and terrorism, coordinate efforts to sever such connections, and otherwise contribute to efforts to interdict illegal drug trafficking.[46]

The Bush Administration initially resisted the establishment of a new governmental bureaucracy. It went against the philosophy of the Republican Party that smaller government was better government. However, the intelligence failure that led to 9/11, the lack of preparedness of the country to respond effectively to crises and disasters, and the failure of the numerous agencies of government to integrate their responses and share information convinced Bush to advance this restructuring of government. In June 2002, the White House promulgated a document titled, "The Department of Homeland Security." In the Introduction it stated:

> The President's most important job is to protect and defend the American people. Since September 11, all levels of government have cooperated like never before to strengthen aviation and border security, stockpile more medicine to defend against bioterrorism, improve information sharing among our intelligence agencies, and deploy more resources and personnel to protect our critical infrastructure.
>
> The changing nature of the threats facing America requires a new government structure to protect against invisible enemies that can strike with a wide variety of weapons. Today no one single government agency has homeland security as its primary mission. In fact, responsibilities for homeland security are dispersed among more than 100 different government organizations. America needs a single, unified homeland security structure that will improve protection against today's threats and be flexible enough to help meet the unknown threats of the future.

The President proposes to create a new Department of Homeland Security. . . by largely transforming and realigning the current confusing patchwork of government activities into a single department whose primary mission is to protect our homeland.[47]

The Department of Homeland Security incorporated many existing agencies and functions, such as: US Customs and Border Protection, US Immigration and Customs Enforcement, Federal Emergency Management Agency, US Coast Guard, US Secret Service, and others. It became responsible for the new Transportation Security Agency.[48] It became responsible for the coordination of the intelligence and law enforcement agencies, including the CIA, NSA, FBI, INS, DEA, DOE, Customs, DOT and other organizations. Finally, it became responsible for coordination with state and local governments and the private sector. In 2011, the Secretary of Homeland Security, Janet Napolitano, described the responsibilities of her department:

> DHS has a vital mission to secure the nation from the many threats we face. This requires the dedication of more than 230,000 employees in jobs that range from aviation and border security to emergency response, from cybersecurity analyst to chemical facility inspector. Our duties are wide-ranging, but our goal is clear—keeping America safe. Our mission gives us five main areas of responsibility: 1. Guarding against Terrorism, 2 Securing our Borders, 3 Enforcing our Immigration Laws, 4. Improving our Readiness for Response to, and Recovery from Disasters, and 5. Maturing and Unifying the Department.[49]

One responsibility of DHS requires special consideration, information analysis and infrastructure protection. DHS, according to Bush, would:

> fuse and analyze intelligence and other information pertaining to threats to the homeland from multiple sources. . . . The Department would merge under one roof the capability to identify and assess current and future threats to the homeland, map those threats against our current vulnerabilities, issue timely warnings, and immediately take or effect appropriate preventive and protective action.

To fuse and analyze intelligence the Office of Intelligence and Analysis was created. However, DHS still required the cooperation and support of the intelligence agencies, each with its own culture, history, and unique ways of operating. No edict from on high was going to immediately change the ways the CIA, NSA, FBI, and other agencies operated. What was required was a cultural change. To bring this about more legislation was necessary. Bush continued: "An important partner with the Department's intelligence and threat analysis division will be the newly formed FBI Office of Intelligence. The new FBI and CIA reforms will provide critical analysis and information to the new Department."[50] Many believed the attacks on 9/11 were the function of intelligence failures, and the lack of cooperation and information sharing between agencies. The DHS was supposed to fix this problem; however, the effectiveness of this reorganization remains to be seen.

The American response to the attacks of 9/11 was not too dissimilar from its response to the advent of the Cold War. It was to create a new department, give it broad authority through the legislative process, give it tens of billions of dollars and hundreds of thousands of personnel, give it research and development capabilities, and give it aggressive, highly motivated leadership.[51]

The War in Afghanistan: Operation Enduring Freedom, 2001–2008

On 11 September 2001, Islamic terrorists hijacked four jumbo jets loaded with fuel and American passengers.[52] They flew two of the jets into the twin towers of the World Trade Center in New York, one into the Pentagon, and the fourth crashed into a field in Pennsylvania after an onboard struggle during which passengers tried to regain control of the aircraft. The identities of the terrorists were quickly discovered. Most were from Saudi Arabia and all were members of the al-Qaeda terrorist organization led by Osama Bin Laden. Al-Qaeda operated from bases in Afghanistan and was protected by the Taliban regime. The Taliban would not surrender Osama Bin Laden nor deny his terrorist organization refuge, as the United States demanded. On 7 October 2001, the United States commenced Operation Enduring

Freedom (OEF-A), a joint campaign to destroy the Taliban regime and kill or capture Osama Bin Laden and his al-Qaeda terrorist fighters. On 14 November, the United Nations Security Council passed Resolution 1378 supporting US action. It, in part, stated:

> Condemning the Taliban for allowing Afghanistan to be used as a base for the export of terrorism by the Al-Qaida network and other terrorist groups and for providing safe haven to Usama Bin Laden, Al-Qaida and other associated with them, and in this context supporting the efforts of the Afghan people to replace the Taliban regime ... *Expresses* its strong support for the efforts of the Afghan people to establish a new transitional administration leading to the formation of a government ... [and] *Calls* on Member States to provide: support for such an administration and government.[53]

Afghanistan is called "the graveyard of empires."[54] In February 1989, the Soviet Union withdrew its combat forces from Afghanistan (the occupation had started in December 1979), accepting defeat.[55] The British withdrew from the region in the late 1940s, giving up colonial rule of India and creating the independent Islamic state of Pakistan. Afghanistan's rugged, mountainous terrain, lack of resources, poverty, drug economy, and largely illiterate population make it a difficult country to conquer and occupy. But, the larger question is, why would anyone want to conquer and occupy it? To understand the value of Afghanistan, a map of the political geography of the region is necessary. Afghanistan is a landlocked country with a population of 28,513,677. It is a triangular-shaped country with a geographic area of 249,935 square miles, about the size of Texas. It shares borders with Pakistan in the south and east

Fig 16.1 Map of Afghanistan.

(formerly part of the British Empire); Iran in the west; and Turkmenistan, Uzbekistan, and Tajikistan in the north (formerly part of the Soviet Union). Afghanistan through much of the nineteenth and twentieth centuries was located between two great empires, the British and the Russian/Soviet. As a consequence, it was a pawn in "the great game" of empires.[56] Afghanistan is not a nation. It is a state comprising many nations, some of which cross into other states with contiguous borders. The people of Afghanistan live in tribal societies. The population is forty-two percent Pashtun and twenty-seven percent Tajik. Hazara, Uzbek, Aimak, Turkmen, Baloch, and others make up the remaining population. Three major languages, Pashtu, Dari, and Turkic, and thirty minor languages are spoken in Afghanistan. The vast majority of the people, eighty percent, are engaged in agriculture. There is little industry. Afghanistan is the second-poorest state on Earth and the second-most corrupt. The per capita income was less than $700 (2003 estimate). Afghanistan produces wheat, fruit, and nuts; however, its most lucrative crop is poppy, opium. Afghanistan provides ninety-five percent of the heroin consumed on Earth. The drug trade supports the operations of the government, terrorist organizations, and sustains the lives of the people. Afghanistan does not possess the potential for growth and development prevalent in Iraq. One observer noted:

> A study of Afghanistan's recent history may help others understand the process involved in changing from a tribal society to a nation-state. In 1964 Afghanistan launched a democratic experiment, and today tries to create a constitutional monarchy within a parliamentary framework. . . . Created partly as a result of imperialism, but never a colony, Afghanistan, like all new states, now tries to build a stable nation, but with an overwhelming 90–95% non-literate population, a basically agrarian economy, and a peasant-tribal society with loyalties oriented locally and not nationally. The task of achieving stability may not be impossible, but it is certainly challenging.[57]

These words were written in 1973. For the latter half of the twentieth century the task of achieving stability and creating a modern nation-state was in fact impossible for Afghanistan. Is it now possible?

The Bush and Obama Administrations have committed enormous resources to transform Afghanistan from a tribal society into a democratic nation-state, but the chances for success are not good.

The Taliban is a Sunni, Pashtun, Islamic fundamentalist movement, organization, and, at one time, Afghan government. It was started by Mullah Mohammed Omar, who in 1994, leading a small group of fighters, the Taliban, "liberated" several villages in Afghanistan from local warlords.[58] The success of the Taliban motivated others to join the movement and its ranks. In 1994 the Taliban captured Kandahar. In 1995 it captured Herat, in 1996 Kabul, in 1998 Mazar-e-Sharif, and in 1999 Taloqan. By 2000 it controlled ninety percent of the country. This, however, did not end the civil war. With the capture of the capital, Kabul, came recognition from Pakistan, Saudi Arabia, and the United Arab Emirates.[59] They and other Arab nations provided the Taliban with weapons and other forms of support. India, Iran, Russia, and Central Asian states supported the opposition, the Northern Alliance. David Isby describes the Taliban as follows:

> The Taliban culture was built on the religious and political experience of the Afghan refugee camps, the political and societal frustrations of Pakistan's Pushtuns facing underdevelopment in their home districts and exclusion from state power, and Pushtun nationalism. It espouses violent anti-modern (especially as it relates to liberalism and globalism), anti-US, anti-Western, anti-woman, anti-education, anti-rational . . ., and anti-secular views. It embraces all possible (and impossible) conspiracy theories and international jihad as a concept.[60]

There was kinship between the Taliban and al-Qaeda. Both had been educated in the madrasahs that taught Islamic, fundamentalist ideology and doctrines. Both had fought and suffered under Soviet occupation. The Taliban, acknowledging the support of Osama Bin Laden during the war against the Soviet Union, gave al-Qaeda sanctuary within its borders.

*   *   *   *   *

One student of America's "new way of war," Norman Friedman, described US operations in Afghanistan as follows:

The Afghan War was both a test and a demonstration of an emerging new style of warfare, called network-centric or described as the outcome of a Revolution in Military Affairs. This type of war is characterized by the use of remote sensors, such as those aboard specialized aircraft, satellites, and UAVs, to allow both a headquarters and subordinate commanders to attack targets which the attackers often cannot see directly. The new style of warfare emphasizes quick operations to upset an enemy's timetable and, ideally, to drive him to a collective nervous breakdown. One hope is that a relatively few weapons, intelligently employed, can collapse an enemy. Clearly the older-style alternative, to bring mass forces and mass weaponry to bear, was impossible in Afghanistan, as least on the timetable the U.S government adopted.[61]

Freedman concluded that:

In effect, the initial air campaign, which concentrated on vital targets deep in Afghanistan, was a test of the pure form of network-centric theory. . . . It failed. . . . However, when a second element, a substantial force on the ground, was added, *the strategy proved brilliantly successful. Thus the Northern Alliance coalition troops made victory in much Afghanistan possible—when combined with a network-centric strike campaign.*[62]

Another student of the war concluded that:

Airpower, special forces, and indigenous troops (even those with relatively little training) form a powerful and robust combination. While events in Afghanistan and later in the northern Iraq demonstrate the costs and the benefit of using the model, when these are compared with the costs and benefits of deploying heavy divisions, and particularly the costs of creating new governments without indigenous war allies, the model performs well.[63]

Too many American experts were too quick to declare victory and the success of the Rumsfeld doctrine.

A decade after the initiation of OEF, in 2010, David Isby wrote: "In no way are the US and its coalition partners close to achieving the result they want,

and the potential for everything going up in flames in the face of unforeseen events remains very real."[64] The United States and its NATO allies ultimately had to deploy significant numbers of ground forces in Afghanistan to fight the Taliban insurgency and complete the destruction of al-Qaeda. Freedman and Andres, like many of the proponents of network-centric warfare, were wrong. In both Afghanistan and Iraq victory was declared prematurely. The true costs and the nature of the war were hidden from Americans. Almost a decade later, after the commitment of hundreds of thousands of soldiers and marines and hundreds of billions of dollars, the United States was still engaged in combat operations in both countries. And, it is very likely that the United States missed the opportunity to complete the destruction of the enemy by deploying too few soldiers and marines to do the job. The question was not "either this or that" in regard to the employment of airpower and other technologies. Nor was it a question of using indigenous forces to assist in the fighting or the formation of a new government. Of course they would be used. Nor was the issue the deployment of "heavy divisions," which were unnecessary given the capabilities of the Taliban and al-Qaeda. The question was whether sufficient numbers of US ground forces were deployed to achieve the political objectives. And the answer, again, is NO. We did it again.

Rumsfeld gave credit for what became known as the Rumsfeld doctrine to his Deputy Secretary Paul Wolfowitz:

Wolfowitz helped conceptualize the global war on terrorism as being broader than just Afghanistan. At that Camp David discussion Wolfowitz raised the question of Iraq, but Bush wanted to keep the focus on Afghanistan. Wolfowitz also suggested that whenever we struck first, our special forces should be a part of the military strategy. . . . Two weeks after 9/11, he wrote in a memo that "In addition to using Special Forces to attack targets associated with Al Qaida or the Taliban we should consider using those [Special Forces] as a kind of armed liaison with anit-Al-Qaeda or anti-Taliban elements in Afghanistan."[65]

The Bush Administration resisted deploying large numbers of American ground forces. It moved slowly and cautiously, and ultimately decided not to deploy significant numbers of soldiers and marines. It decided to deploy airpower and Special Forces. As a consequence, thousands of al-Qaeda and Taliban forces were allowed to escape into Pakistan and other parts of the country. They lived to fight another day. The Rumsfeld doctrine made minimum demands on US ground forces, and thereby minimized the political exposure of the White House. The White House seemed to fear the deployment of ground forces from 2001 to 2003. Reflection on the Vietnam War and the Soviet experiences in Afghanistan may have produced this fear.

The Rumsfeld doctrine, like other new operational doctrines since World War II, relied heavily on advanced airpower and precision weapons. The new element was the reliance on US Special Forces, and their ability to connect with and lead indigenous ground forces. The indigenous ground forces were the enemy of my enemy. The Special Forces negotiated agreements, deals, with the indigenous forces. They provided them with weapons, training, money, and other forms of assistance. The indigenous forces in turn agreed to continue the fight against their enemy, but with the assistance and direction of Special Forces. Special Forces fought alongside the indigenous forces, calling in airpower to break up enemy concentration, facilitate the advance, and guarantee success. Robin Moore, an observer of US Special Forces in Afghanistan, described the mission of the Green Beret as follows:

> The mission was quite simple—find the mysterious and elusive Commander Atta, train and supply his shoddy forces, lead them against far superior forces, capture a dozen cities, destroy ten thousand Taliban and al-Qaida terrorists, learn the Dari language in a day or two, and then storm the largest, most protected Taliban stronghold in Northwest Afghanistan, Mazar-e-Sharif. After they finished all that, they were to establish law and order and rebuild the shattered province. While they were resting or between laying siege to cities, they were to guide laser bombs and US aircraft against Taliban armor, vehicles, command posts, and whatever else happened to be in the way. . . . Their command assumed it would take more than six months for partial success in

completing their mission. They did it all in just a few weeks.[66]

While Moore's words are meant to be a humorous exaggeration, they are not far from the truth. Extraordinary demands were placed on US Special Forces, and they performed with extraordinary courage and professionalism, achieving the missions given. However, it was impossible for such a small force to do all that was necessary. It was impossible for it to control all phases of the operations, collect intelligence, and be present at the right place at right time. This form of warfare required trust that had not been earned.

On 19 September 2001, the first US Special Operations Forces and intelligence force entered Afghanistan. Their first tasks were to establish contact and relationships with the Northern Alliance (also known as the Afghan United Front) forces, led by generals Abdul Dostum and Ustad Atta Mohammad, and determine if they were willing and capable of fighting against the Taliban. Sean Naylor observed that "Once the A-teams got their feet on the ground and put their heads together with their chosen G-chiefs [Guerrilla-chiefs], the combination of American know-how and air power with the Northern Alliance muscle power proved unstoppable when opposed by the Taliban's ragtag army."[67] The first battle was for the northern city of Mazar-e-Sharif. US airpower directed by Special Forces on the ground facilitated the attacks of the Northern Alliance forces. On 10 November Taliban and al-Qaeda forces that had not been killed or captured gave up the city. On 13 November the Northern Alliance captured Kabul without a fight. Less than two weeks later, on 26 November, approximately 5,000 Taliban and al-Qaeda forces surrendered at Kanduz. On 10 December 2001, the Taliban deserted Kandahar, the last major city they controlled. In January, Operation Anaconda was initiated. In intense battles, significant numbers of Taliban and al-Qaeda forces were killed. Surviving enemy forces escaped into the mountainous terrain on the borders of Pakistan. However, in the mountainous region of Tora Bora, where Osama Bin Laden was believed to be hiding, some American officials and Afghan leaders believed he was allowed to escape.[68]

The objectives of the Northern Alliance and those of other local Pashtun militia recruited to fight the Taliban were different from those of the United States. In battles at places such as Kandahar and Tora Bora, enemy forces were too frequently able to escape because local militia forces were poorly trained and equipped, employed insufficient forces, and lacked the will to stop them. In some cases Taliban and al-Qaeda forces were simply released. Having no love for Americans, a kinship with their opponents, and centuries of operational methods that did not include the complete destruction of the enemy, militias acted pragmatically in their own best interests and in the process precluded the United States from achieving significant parts of its political objectives, the capture of Osama Bin Laden and the destruction of al-Qaeda. Sean Naylor wrote:

> The Dagger leaders assumed a portion of the Al Qaida force would fight to the death, but only to protect their comrades, including bin Laden and other senior leaders, as they tried to escape. This is exactly what happened. The Tora Bora base backed on to the porous Pakistan border, across which lay the Pushtun tribal areas of the Northwest Frontier Province, whose inhabitants were sympathetic to the Taliban and largely beyond the control of the central government in Islamabad. With no US conventional forces to block their escape hundreds of Al Qaida fighters slipped into Pakistan.[69]

In February 2002, US forces from the 10th Mountain and 101st Airborne Divisions deployed to Afghanistan to finish the job; however, it was too late. The enemy had dispersed in the border region of Pakistan, and the "mission creep" had expanded the role and responsibilities of US forces. In addition to hunting and killing al-Qaeda and Taliban forces, the new missions were to train Afghan Security Forces, conduct stability operations, and facilitate the formation of a democratic government that had the support of the people—no small task in a state as primitive as Afghanistan that did not control the territory within its borders.

*   *   *   *   *

On 20 December 2001, the United Nations Security Council established the International Security Assistance Force—Afghanistan (ISAF).[70] Its mission is:

in support of the Government of the Islamic Republic of Afghanistan, conducts operations in Afghanistan to reduce the capability and will of the insurgency, support the growth in capacity and capability of the Afghan National Security Forces (ANSF), and facilitate improvements in governance and socio-economic development, in order to provide a secure environment for sustainable stability that is observable to the population.[71]

Under the heading "Security," ISAF forces were to conduct "security and stability operations throughout the country together with the Afghan National Security Forces and are directly involved in the development of the Afghan National Army through mentoring, training and equipping." ISAF was administered through the North Atlantic Treaty Organization (NATO). This meant that European nations would share the burden of the war and reconstruction effort. But not until July 2003 was ISAF "NATO-ized," marking the first deployment of ground forces outside of Europe in the history of the alliance. For European nations, however, the war was still optional. They could decide what forces to contribute and how long they would stay. Forty-seven states ultimately contributed to, and participated in, the ISAF coalition. Lieutenant General John McColl, United Kingdom, was the first ISAF commander. Senior military leaders from Canada, France, Turkey, Italy, and Germany also commanded ISAF, until 2006, when the United States started to expand its commitment to Afghanistan and took command of operations.

On 5 December Hamid Karzai, who had supported the Mujahidin in its decade-long struggle against the Soviet Army, became chairman of the Interim Administration of Afghanistan. In June 2002 Karzai became President of the interim government. And in October 2004 he was formally elected President in a nation-wide election (in 2009 Karzai was reelected President; however, charges of corruption diminished his legitimacy with the Afghan people and allied nations). Elections did not mean the end of the civil war or that the people considered themselves citizens. The Taliban and al-Qaeda survived in the tribal areas of Pakistan, which shared a porous 1,400-mile-long border with southern Afghanistan.

The Federally Administered Tribal Areas (FATA) consist of seven tribal agencies in northwest Pakistan. Five million people, primarily Pashtun, lived in these tribal areas, which were only loosely controlled by the Pakistani government.[72] The Pashtun were a nation that straddled two states. In March 2002 the *New York Times* reported that: "One tribal leader, wagging his finger for emphasis, said that tribal elders saw America as the enemy and that his people would sacrifice their lives to keep American soldiers off their land." And, "A more moderate leader, a well-educated man, said more calmly that no foreigner may go into the tribal areas without permission. That warning must be taken seriously; ages ago Alexander the Great was turned back, and for the last 53 years, until December, no soldiers, not even Pakistanis, were allowed in."[73]

Some states have separate nations within their borders that they do not and cannot govern. Such was the case in Pakistan. Access to the region where the Taliban and al-Qaeda hide was a major problem for Pakistan and the United States. This problem caused enormous friction between the two governments and violence in Pakistan. Imtiaz Gul, in his book, *The Most Dangerous Place: Pakistan's Lawless Frontier*, wrote:

> The battle between the US-led coalition forces and the radical militants inspired by Al-Qaeda seems to have put Pakistan on fire. Statistics of the spiral of violence are mind-boggling. In 2009, militants staged almost ninety suicide attacks and carried out another five hundred bombings and ambushes, killing over three thousand people.[74]

The government of Pakistan was divided and had to walk a fine line between the demands of the Americans, who provided it with more than $2 billion in military and economic aid annually, and the opinions and attitudes of Pakistani people, which was, for the most part, hostile to the United States. Bob Woodward noted that:

> In the earlier briefing, [Mike] McConnell [Bush's director of national intelligence] had laid out the problem in dealing with Pakistan. It was a dishonest partner of the US in the Afghanistan War. "They're living a lie," McConnell had said. In exchange for reimbursements of about $2 billion

a year from the US, Pakistan's powerful military and it spy agency, Inter-Service Intelligence (ISI), helped the US while giving clandestine aid, weapons and money to the Afghan Taliban. They had an "office of hedging your bets," McConnell said.[75]

One of the consequences of Pakistan's duplicity was the employment of armed UAV and other sensor technologies to find terrorist and precision missile strikes to attack and kill them (primarily Predator and Reaper drones armed with AGM–114 Hellfire missiles). One source noted that:

> In 2007, hunter-killer drones were performing 21 combat air patrols at any one time, by the end of 2009 they were flying 38, and in 2011 they increased to about 54 ongoing patrols.... According to one estimate, by March 2011 as least 33 Al-Qaeda and Taliban leaders (high value targets) had been killed by the drones and from 1,100 to 1,800 insurgent fighters had been killed as well.[76]

Human intelligence from sources within Pakistan facilitated UAV operations. These methods, however, increased the friction between the US and Pakistan because they violated the sovereignty of the state, and too frequently killed innocent civilians.

David Kilcullen, a counterinsurgency expert, testifying before the House Armed Services Committee in April 2009, stated:

> Since 2006, we've killed 14 senior Al-Qaeda leader using drone strikes; in the same period, we've killed 700 Pakistani civilians.... The drone strikes are highly unpopular ... And, they've given rise to a feeling of anger that coalesces the population around the extremists.... The current path that we are on is leading us to loss of Pakistani government control over its own population.[77]

Pakistani anger at US methods hurt US efforts to win the hearts and minds of the Pakistani people, without which it was difficult to collect the quality of human intelligence required to find and capture al-Qaeda and Taliban leaders.[78] Money, however, was a motivator. The commitment of billions of dollars annually brought something. But, was it enough? The Pakistani government fears its people and the nation within. Consider these words:

> Stabilizing Afghanistan might well become crucial to preventing the far more terrifying prospect of an Islamist takeover in Pakistan. Says US Army Brigadier General John Nicholson Jr., who commands US and NATO troops in southern Afghanistan: "If the Pashtun population of Pakistan see a moderate, Islamic and Pashtun-led government in Afghanistan, well, it's hard to argue with. So we have potentially a greater impact in Pakistan with success in the east."[79]

Pakistan is uncertain about the quality of America's commitment. They fear the US will eventually abandon Pakistan, as it abandoned Afghanistan after the war with the Soviet Union.[80] This was not an unreasonable assessment. However, Pakistan is a nuclear power. It is known to possess about 100 nuclear weapons. The security of these weapons is a major concern for the United States.

After its initial defeat, the Taliban retreated into Pakistan where it reorganized, refitted, recruited, and then returned to the fight in Afghanistan. The Taliban survives in border regions of the two countries and governments. It also survives between Islamic extremist and the more moderate, secular elements in Pashtun society. The political and military revival of the Taliban was, in part, due to the assistance and acquiescence of the members of the Pakistani government. Members of Pakistan's military and intelligence services have a history of working with the Taliban that predates 9/11. The lines of communication, well-established friendships, shared ideological and religious beliefs, and networks of supply have been in operation for decades. With the number of forces the US and NATO have deployed to the region, it is not possible to control the border regions and destroy these relationships and networks, which assure the survival of the Taliban.

In 2003 the war in Afghanistan took a backseat to the war in Iraq. The vast majority of the White House and Pentagon's attention and resources were focused on the war in Iraq, which after the initial successes continued to deteriorate into chaos until 2006. The inability of the government of Afghanistan to enforce the laws, to secure the people and widespread corruption diminished the legitimacy of the Karzai government. By 2006 the Taliban had reorganized and were on the offensive, and they had a new strategy:

> By 2006 there were clear signs that the Taliban were becoming an integral part of a wider supranational jihadist movement, to a much greater extent than the "older Taliban" ever were. They increasingly appeared to believe that the decisive factor in winning the war would not be Western public opinion ..., but the support of their Muslim brethren. If this is true, some apparent irrationality in the Taliban strategy and goals could be explained: their priority would be to mobilize Muslim opinion worldwide as a source of funding, moral support, and volunteer.... Ultimately the belief is that victory will come with the overstretching of the enemy through the creation of "one, ten, a hundred Iraqs," rather than with country-specific strategies.[81]

The war is not over. The opportunity to complete the destruction of the enemy was lost when the United States turned its attention towards Iraq before finishing the war in Afghanistan. One observer concluded:

> The development of Afghanistan as a successful nation-state is at grave risk, and its failure could have a resounding strategic and economic impact on the United States and, indeed, the entire world. This summer will be a critical, as increasing instability threatens to unravel the initial successes achieved after the US invasion in 2001.
>
> Four major, interconnected problem threaten the stability of the country: a strong resurgence of the Taliban, a substantial increase in violence, an alarming growth in opium production, and a demoralized population with little faith that their quality of life will improve and serious misgivings about the conduct of the Afghan Government and NATO forces. At the same time, the United States had decreased its contribution for reconstruction and stabilization (R&S) air. Over the course of the War of Terrorism, R&S funding for Afghanistan has been minimal.... This "bare bones" spending policy is one of the factors threatening the stability of Afghanistan.[82]

The Karzai government is seeking accommodation with the Taliban. The Pakistan government continues to walk a fine line between its ally the United States and the anger of its people at the United States for its numerous violations of its sovereignty. US resources are not unlimited, and the patience of Congress, particularly in an environment where there is a sense of urgency to cut the federal budget, is also limited. There is a very high probability that the US will leave Afghanistan, without creating a viable new, democratic nation-state.

Osama Bin Laden failed. His movement has suffered enormous damage in its war of terror against the United States, but his strategy has caused enormous harm to the people of the United States and, arguably, had the potential to harness and direct the energies of the Muslim world against the West. The attacks of 9/11 were designed to ignite a movement throughout the Middle East. Bin Laden opposed the secular monarchies and dictators who led states such as Saudi Arabia, Egypt, Syria, Iraq, and other Muslim states. He correctly believed the United States helped sustain these governments. Hence, a prerequisite for change was elimination of the presence of the United States from the region. Bin Laden hoped to establish Islamic government, such as the Taliban, throughout the Middle East, and ultimately to unite those governments. Through war he and his followers hoped to separate the United States from its traditional allies, the United Nations, and other multinational and world organizations; get the US government to overcommit the armed forces of the United States and thereby drain its strength; caused the US to expend billions of dollars, possibly a trillion, and ruin its economy; sow seeds of discontent in the United States, separating the American people from their government and divide them among themselves. He planned to destroy the will of the American people to continue wars in foreign lands.

Bin Laden also sought to demonstrate to the world the ineffectiveness of US forces, military technologies, and intelligence agencies. He wanted US forces to over-react, destroying their legitimacy in foreign lands and alienating them from potential allies, host governments, and other sources of support. Through war he sought to recruit new members and sources of funding; elevate the morale of current fighters; and gain momentum in influencing world opinions. Without doubt, the terrorist attack on 9/11 achieved much, but ultimately it failed. It stretched American resources, but not to the breaking point. It did not sever the many relationships that unify Western democracies. And, it did not cause the United States to give up in the Middle East. But, probably most important, it did not inspire millions of Muslims to become terrorists to fight against the United States. The ideology espoused by al-Qaeda and the Taliban is incapable of producing the best for Muslims. At some level the peoples of the Middle East know this.

Obama's War in Afghanistan: Operation Enduring Freedom, 2008–2011

In 2008, Senator Barack Obama, in his "Plan for Ending the War in Iraq," under the heading "Resurgent Al-Qaeda in Afghanistan," stated:

> The decision to invade Iraq diverted resources from the war in Afghanistan, making it harder for us to kill and capture Osama Bin Laden and others involved in the 9/11 attacks. Nearly seven years later, the Taliban has reemerged in southern Afghanistan while Al-Qaeda used the space provided by the Iraq war to regroup, train and plan for another attack on the United States. 2007 was the most violent year in Afghanistan since the invasion in 2001. The scale of our deployments in Iraq continues to set back our ability to finish the fight in Afghanistan, producing unacceptable strategic risks.[83]

Few would disagree with this assessment. When President Obama assumed office, the situation in Afghanistan was deteriorating. The war in Iraq had consumed the time, energy, and resources of the Bush Administration and the American people. The US had just over 32,000 soldiers and marines fighting in Afghanistan, and 160,000 fighting in Iraq. NATO allies had contributed an additional 40,000 troops in Afghanistan. Still, the Army and Marine Corps were too small to do all that was required in both wars. The Obama Administration came into office with a plan to change this, to refocus resources on Afghanistan, and to drawdown US forces from Iraq.

Obama immediately initiated a review of strategy, and the deployment of an additional 12,000 combat troops to reinforce Afghanistan. To implement his new strategy for Afghanistan, the President needed a new leadership team.

Karl Eikenberry, a retired general, was appointed US Ambassador to Kabul, and in June 2009, General Stanley McChrystal took command of the International Security Assistance Force (ISAF) from General David D. McKiernan. McKiernan had spoken loudly about the resurgence of the Taliban and called for four additional brigade combat teams and an additional aviation brigade. His assessment of the situation in Afghanistan seemed to be in line with that of the new President. Nevertheless he was dismissed. Secretary of Defense Robert Gates simply noted that he wanted "fresh eyes." McChrystal had worked closely with the new CENTCOM commander General David Petraeus. And Obama was trying to form the most effective leadership team possible. Bush's team, who successfully implemented "the surge" strategy in Iraq, seemed to be a good place to start. Obama's change of leadership also indicated a change in focus and signaled a new, more aggressive strategy.

On 30 August 2009, General McChrystal published his first "Commander's Initial Assessment," in which he concluded:

> Important progress has been made, yet many indicators suggest the overall situation is deteriorating despite considerable efforts by ISAF. The threat has grown steadily. . . . The entire culture—how ISAF understands the environment and defines the fight, how it interacts with the Afghan people and government, and how it operates both on the ground and within the coalition—must change profoundly.[84]

McChrystal believed that "ISAF's center of gravity is the will and ability to provide for the needs of the population 'by which, and through' the Afghan government." He delineated a new strategy, and called for additional resources. He believe he needed an additional 40,000 troops to stabilize the situation and achieve NATO political objectives. McChrystal

Fig 16.2 President Barack Obama at West Point.

cautioned the President that: "Failure to provide adequate resources also risks a longer conflict, greater casualties, higher overall costs, and ultimately, a critical loss of political support. Any of these risks, in turn, are likely to result in mission failure."[85]

On 1 December 2009, after much public discussion, Obama announced that McChrystal would get what he needed, an Afghanistan surge of 30,000 troops. At the United States Military Academy at West Point, Obama told the corps of cadets and the American people:

> Afghanistan is not lost, but for several years it has moved backwards.... I have determined that it is in our vital national interest to send an additional 30,000 US troops to Afghanistan. After 18 months, our troops will begin to come home. These are the resources that we need to seize the initiative, while building capacity that can allow for a responsible transition for our forces out of Afghanistan.... Our overarching goal remains the same: to disrupt, dismantle, and defeat al-Qaeda in Afghanistan and Pakistan, and to prevent its capacity to threaten America and our allies in the future.[86]

Obama expected NATO allies to contribute an additional 5,000–10,000 troops to get McChrystal what he needed. However, the most controversial part of Obama's speech was his announced plan to start the drawdown of US forces in July 2011. By 2014 he expected to have all US forces out of Afghanistan. Obama's critics argued that the announcement of a withdrawal date was a strategic mistake. They argued that our enemies would simply conserve their forces and wait for us to leave. Senator John McCain of Arizona, the top Republican on the Senate Armed Service Committee and Obama's opponent in the presidential race, was the loudest critic of the Obama strategy. He stated: "The way you win wars is to break the enemy's will, not to announce dates that you are leaving."

The centerpiece of Obama's strategy, however, was the "Afghanization" of the war: to recruit, train, and hopefully impart some sense of nationalism to the Afghan National Security Forces (ANSF), and then turn the war over to them. (McChrystal planned to expand the target strength of the Afghanistan National Army (ANA) from 134,000 to 240,000; and the Afghan National Police to 160,000.) Another

Fig 16.3 2nd Battalion, 504th Infantry Paratroopers leaving a landing zone, Patika province, Afghanistan, 25 May 2005.

component of Obama's strategy was to strengthen the Pakistani government, military, and security forces to enable them to go after the terrorists who had taken sanctuary in their border regions. If both the Afghanistan and Pakistan governments and armed forces had the wherewithal to effectively hunt and kill terrorists, US forces could be safely withdrawn. The third component of Obama's strategy was a "civilian surge," to create the institutions of government necessary to control and govern the state. Speaking to the Karzai government, Obama stated:

> We will support Afghan Ministries, Governors, and local leaders that combat corruption and deliver for the people. We expect those who are ineffective or corrupt to be held accountable. And we will also focus our assistance in areas—such as agriculture—that can make an immediate impact in the lives of the Afghan people.[87]

The "civilian surge" would permit US forces to transition from the mission of counterinsurgency to counterterrorism. Counterinsurgency had a large nation-building component and required considerably more time and resources than counterterrorism, which emphasized the finding and killing of terrorists.

General McChrystal's job was to take the new resources he had been given and the guidance provided by the Obama Administration and translate them into effective combat and stability operations on the ground. In a document titled "Commander's Counterinsurgency Guidance," McChrystal delineated the "crucial next steps" needed to succeed in Afghanistan as follows:

> Gain the initiative by reversing the perceived momentum possessed by the insurgents.
> Seek rapid growth of Afghan national security forces—army and police. Improve their effectiveness and ours through closer partnering, which involves planning, living and operating together and taking advantage of each other's strengths as we go forward. . . .
> Address shortfalls in the capacity of governance and the ability of the Afghan government to provide rule of law.

> Tackle the issue of predatory corruption by some officials or by warlords who are not in an official position . . .
> Focus our resources and priorities in those areas where the population is most threatened. We do not have enough force to do everything everywhere at once, so this has to be prioritized and phased over time.

Seeking to benefit from the successful counterinsurgency strategy employed in Iraq by General Petraeus, McChrystal developed a new counterinsurgency strategy and doctrine for Afghanistan. He outlined the mission and his thinking on the conduct of the war: "ISAF's mission is to help the Islamic Republic of Afghanistan (GIRoA) defeat the insurgency threatening their country. Protecting the Afghan people is the mission."[88] He told his soldiers and marines that:

> The Afghan people will decide who wins this fight, and we (GIRoA and ISAF) are in a struggle for their support. . . . Essentially, we and the insurgents are [each] presenting an argument for the future to the people of Afghanistan: they will decide which argument is the most attractive, most convincing, and has the greatest chance of success. . . .

McChrystal believed that, "Nearly eight years of international presence has not brought the anticipated benefits. The Afghan people are skeptical and unwilling to commit active support to either side until convinced of a winning proposition." To win, McChrystal believed he had to win the hearts and minds of the Afghan people:

> We will not win simply by killing insurgents. We will help the Afghan people win by securing them, by protecting them from intimidation, violence, and abuse, and by operating in a way that respects their culture and religion. This means that we must change the way that we think, act, and operate. We must get the people involved as active participants in the success of their communities.

McChrystal placed the security of the people above the hunting and killing of al-Qaeda and Taliban forces. He also believed that the way the Army and Marine Corps operated created more insurgents than it killed. He wrote:

> First, an insurgency cannot be defeated by attrition, its supply of fighters, and even leadership, is effectively endless. Roughly seventy percent of the Afghan population is under age 25. Vast unemployment, illiteracy, and widespread political and social disaffection create fertile ground for insurgent influence and recruiting.
>
> The intricate familial, clan, and tribal connections of Afghan society turns "attrition math" on its head. From a conventional standpoint, the killing of two insurgents from a group of ten leaves eight remaining: 10–2=8. From the insurgent standpoint, those two killed were likely related to many others who will want vengeance. If civilian casualties occurred, that number will be much higher. Therefore, the death of two creates more willing recruits: 10 minus 2 equals 20 (or more) rather than 8. This is part of the reason why eight years of individual successful kinetic actions have resulted in more violence.[89]

McChrystal's strategy had four major components: first, winning the hearts and minds of the Afghan people; second, partnering with and training the ANSF; third, building governance capacity and accountability; and fourth, making the US Army in Afghanistan a learning, adaptable organization. In November 2009, General McChrystal promulgated his "Counterinsurgency (COIN) Training Guidance." Again he emphasized that: **"The People are the Prize."** He also emphasized the learning that had to take place: **"Language Training**. Everyone should learn basic language skills." And:

> **You must understand your Operational Environment**. Traditional Intelligence Preparation of the Battlefield (IPB) is insufficient and it is intimate knowledge of the Human Terrain that is paramount. Know the society's leadership system; learn the National Provincial, and district government structure. Understand the familial, clan and tribal cultures. What are the relationships and separate tensions among the separate groups?[90]

Ignorance of Arabic/Islamic culture damaged the American war efforts in Iraq and Afghanistan, just as ignorance of the Asian/Vietnamese culture damaged the American war effort in Vietnam. Such damage can be decisive and irreversible. McChrystal understood that cultural knowledge is essential to gain trust and respect, and to lead people in a specific direction. He understood that to formulate effective policies, strategies, and doctrines, knowledge of the culture of a people in the area of operations is absolutely essential. But he also recognized that American culture itself was a problem.

The cultures of the Army and Marine Corps can thwart the efforts to win the hearts and minds of people in foreign lands by alienating them. Again consider McChrystal's words: "When ISAF forces travel ... firmly ensconced in armored vehicles with body armor and turrets manned, they convey a sense of high risk and fear to the population. ISAF cannot expect unarmed Afghans to feel secure before heavily armed ISAF forces do."[91] Army culture teaches soldiers to be aggressive, to take initiative, to make decisions quickly, to not acknowledge mistakes, to accomplish one objective and move rapidly to the next, to be tenacious, to be impatient, to look people directly in the eyes, to speak with a firm voice, to stand straight, to wear uniforms and equipment in a certain way, and so on. In some Asian and Middle Eastern cultures this type of behavior can be viewed as aggressive and offensive. People who feel threatened, intimidated, or just ill at ease find it difficult to cooperate with foreigners. Without doubt the mere presence of soldiers or marines dressed and armed for battle is intimidating. McChrystal's words indicate that the culture of the Army and Marine Corps needed to change to be successful in Afghanistan. Setting the example, McChrystal did not wear battle dress uniform when he visited Afghan communities.

However, could soldiers and marines learn the language skills and cultural understanding necessary to make a difference in the villages of Afghanistan? The Army and Marine Corps were to some degree requiring soldiers and marines to become social workers, political scientists, and anthropologists. To learn and understand the history, the languages, the ideologies, the religious beliefs, the social structures, and the ethnic divisions, was no small task, and well beyond the ability of most combat organizations. What was necessary was the minimum essential knowledge required to be effective. In recent years the Army and Marine Corps have endeavored to "operationalize" the concept of culture to make it useful at the tactical level of war, where engagements between soldiers and indigenous peoples take place.[92] The Army has put considerable effort and resources into the development of a "human terrain system." It has organized, trained, and deployed human terrain teams (HTT) to work with brigade, regimental, and division commanders in Iraq and Afghanistan "by filling the cultural knowledge gap in the current operating environment and providing cultural interpretations of events occurring within their area of operation."[93] The Army's *Human Terrain Team Handbook* defines human terrain as follows: "Social Science research of a host nation's population produces a knowledge base that is referred to as the Human Terrain, or 'The elements of the operational environment encompassing the cultural, sociological, political and economic factors of the local population.'" It further notes that, "The local population in the area of conflict must be considered as a distinct and critical aspect of the Commander's assessment of the situation.... In an irregular warfare environment 'Commanders and planners require insight into cultures, perceptions, values, beliefs, interests, and decision-making processes of individual and groups....'"[94] In the streets of Fallujah or Khandahar such understanding can make the difference between hostile engagements and peaceful engagements, between reliable intelligence and ambush, between life and death.

These were smart things to do, but the Army and Marine Corps came late to this element of counterinsurgency warfare and hence had much to learn. Minor things such as having a little humility and respect, showing a little deference to community leaders, and knowing a few local customs and norms of behavior can make an enormous difference in the willingness of a people to cooperate and work with US forces. But, knowledge of foreign cultures cannot be acquired within the services or the Pentagon. The HTS was too little, too late. A new partnership with America's universities is necessary. Just as government agencies have become incorporated into strategic planning, America's universities, particularly their foreign

research centers, can provide much of the knowledge necessary for the services to become culturally competent in a given region of the world.[95] At the same time the Army and Marine Corps pursue greater cultural comprehension of the peoples in the lands in which they fight, they cannot become social workers or anthropologists. The warrior cultures of the services have to be protected.

Under the heading, "ANSF Partnership," McChrystal quoted Secretary Gates, "Arguably, the most important military component of the struggle against violent extremists is not the fighting we do ourselves, but how well we help prepare our partners to defend and govern themselves." The "Afghanization" of the war was the major component of the mission for the Obama Administration, which placed limits on US commitment, manpower, and time. Part of this mission was turned over to private military firms. As US forces draw down, private military firms can fill the vacuum. This is what took place, to some degree, in Iraq in 2010, when US forces were withdrawn.

Good governance is required to gain and maintain the support of the people. ISAF thus became deeply involved in helping the Karzai government build the institutions necessary to control the populations of the geographic area of Afghanistan. Corruption, however, is a major problem.[96] Corruption is part of the culture of any government in Afghanistan, and arguably all governments in the region. One of the appeals of the Taliban was that, while they were ruthless and primitive, they were just. Too many members of the Karzai government stole resources that should have gone to the people, and used them to maintain power, family, and friends. Too many members of the Karzai government were involved in the criminal gangs that run the huge Afghan drug industry. Corruption and criminal activities damage the legitimacy of the Karzai government. US efforts to change the culture of the government of Afghanistan will probably fail. What is needed in Afghanistan is generational change, and generational learning. We will not be there long enough to bring about such a change.

McChrystal's lack of respect and his contempt for the Obama Administration ended his command of ISAF and his military career. In June 2010, *Rolling Stone* magazine published an article titled "The Runaway General," in which McChrystal and his staff openly criticized the Obama Administration. Not since President Truman relieved General Douglas MacArthur in 1951 was a commanding general so publically relieved of duty. Obama selected General Petraeus, the CENTCOM commander, to replace McChrystal. On 4 July Petraeus took command with these words:

> This morning, as I look at the representatives of the organizations engaged here in Afghanistan, I feel privileged to be joining this critical effort as such a pivotal time. As each of you know well, we are engaged in a tough fight. After years of war, we have arrived at a critical moment. We must demonstrate to the Afghan people, and to the world, that Al-Qaeda and its network of extremist allies will not be allowed to once again establish sanctuaries in Afghanistan from which they can launch attacks on the Afghan people and of freedom-loving nations around the world. And with the surge in ISAF forces and the growth of our Afghan partners, we have a new opportunity to do just that.

> We are engaged in a contest of wills. Our enemies are doing all that they can to undermine the confidence of the Afghan people. In so doing, they are killing and maiming innocent Afghan civilians on a daily basis. No tactics are beneath the insurgents; indeed, they use unwitting children to carry out attacks, they repeatedly kill innocent civilians, and they frequently seek to create situations that will result in injury to Afghan citizens. In answer, we must demonstrate to the people and to the Taliban that Afghan and ISAF forces are here to safeguard the Afghan people, and that we are in this to win. That is our clear objective.

Petreaus accepted a demotion in position to take command in Afghanistan.[97] As the CENTCOM Commander, he had worked closely with McChrystal to develop the new "surge," population-centric, counterinsurgency strategy and doctrine, and to get McChrystal the resources and manpower he needed. When Petraeus took command of ISAF, he had

Fig 16.4 General David Petraeus.

119,819 soldiers from thirty different nations and states operating under his command.[98] This number included 78,430 US forces. In May 2011, after he'd been in the job less than a year, the Obama Administration announced that General Petraeus would be the next Director of the CIA, and that General John R. Allen, USMC, would take command of ISAF. This appointment represents another first. Both the strategic commander, CENTCOM, and the operational commander, ISAF, are Marines. Is this an indicator of the new level of jointness, or the success of the Marine Corps in the continuing rivalry between the services?

The war in Afghanistan continues, and the commanders closest to the situation are cautiously optimistic. In March 2011, before the Senate Committee on Armed Services, General Petraeus reported: "it is ISAF's assessment that the momentum achieved by the Taliban in Afghanistan since 2005 has been arrested in much of the country, and reversed in a number of important areas."[99] The NATO Supreme Allied Commander, Europe and Commander of United States European Command, Admiral James G. Stavridis, in an article titled, "The Comprehensive Approach in Afghanistan," wrote:

The Comprehensive Approach is ongoing in Afghanistan. Although it has proceeded by fits and starts, it has matured over the years and is functioning at a higher level now. As the conflict has changed over the years, more actors are involved, bringing more capabilities to the effort. This situation has stabilized and is changing for the better.

Stravidis believed that the "comprehensive approach" was succeeding, that the international effort, involving the resources and talents of forty-nine countries, and the whole of government approach, were earning the support of the people, building ANSF, growing the economy, and killing Taliban forces and legitimacy. Stavridis delineated the indicators of success: national elections in which forty percent of those eligible voted; growth in the ANSF to 260,000; reduction in the production of the drug crop, "20 of the 34 provinces are currently poppy-free;" the "53 percent growth in its agriculture sector;" the creation by the Karzai government of a Major Crimes Task Force and Sensitive Intelligence Unit to fight corruption; the discovery of "$1 to 3 trillion worth of minerals located under Afghan soil;" the efforts of the Karzai government to seek reconciliation with Taliban forces willing to "accept the constitution, lay down their weapons, sever ties to al-Qaeda, and become productive or participating members of society," and the continued commitment of the United States, United Nations, and international communities.

However, there is also considerable pessimism about the ultimate outcome of the struggle in Afghanistan. In 2010, retired General Volney F. Warner, one the Army's most respected retired leaders, wrote: "We need to husband the valor and dedication of our volunteer force and make certain our leaders do not turn to them for quick solutions by applying force to international problems that are better left to political resolution—such as Afghanistan/Pakistan."[100] Volney quoted an unnamed expert who had "30 years of in-theater experience and familiar with the language and culture of the Afghanistan":

Afghanistan is a country in the sense of real estate, but it is not a nation and has rarely been one except under a few periods of autocratic rule that extended out of Kabul a few hundred kilometers. With the cultural makeup of families and tribes driving any sense of cohesiveness from the bottom up, it is not likely to ever be a Westphalian nation-state. . . .

Volney's expert concluded: "The last thing that the United States needs is to be sold into continuing an unwinnable war in a non-nation against a religious confederation that belongs to no nation and is very adept at strengthening its ranks by planning the anti-Westerner theme."[101] In 2011 Lieutenant Colonel John J. Malevich, then at the US Army and Marine Corps Counterinsurgency Center, and Daryl C. Youngman, wrote:

We have preconceived notions about the nature of the insurgency that may be misguided or even false. We have a deeply flawed understanding of the Pashtun people and Pashtunwali, the way of the Pashtun. We do not understand the roles and importance of the tribes and elders, the influence of the mullahs and Islam, or the competition for power among the tribes, Islam, and the government. This seriously impedes our population-centric counterinsurgency.

Because of our eagerness to distribute aid money and our limited understanding of the internal power dynamics of Afghanistan, our good intentions are being manipulated, and we are being taken advantage of. The government of Afghanistan is not the Jeffersonian democracy we had hoped for.[102]

They called for a major shift in US strategy and concluded that we had to: "Stop trying to change Afghanistan's culture," and refocus. "The insurgency's root cause is not lack of economic opportunity, but the desire to establish an Islamic Emirate of Afghanistan under *Sharia* law." Bing West, in an article titled, "The Way out of Afghanistan," also concluded that US strategy was wrong. He wrote:

> In the net, neither side is winning. On the one side, the United States lacks the numbers to secure thousands of villages and the Afghan security forces lack confidence; on the other side, the Taliban cannot mass forces due to US firepower. The Taliban believe that after an American withdrawal, the rural districts will topple like dominos. . . . The counterinsurgency theory of persuading the population to turn against the Taliban has proven wrong in practice. . . . The primary US mission should be to transition to a hundred such advisor task forces, while reducing our total from 100,000 to 50,000.[103]

On Wednesday 22 June 2011, President Obama, in a national address to the American people, announced his decision to end the "surge" and to withdraw US forces from Afghanistan by the end of 2014. When these words were spoken, the US was fighting the longest war in its history, had roughly 100,000 troops in Afghanistan, and had suffered 1,522 killed. The President stated:

> Thanks to our extraordinary men and women in uniform, over civilian personnel, and our many coalition partners, we are meeting our goals. As a result, starting next month, we will be able to remove 10,000 of our troops from Afghanistan

by the end of this year, and we will bring home a total of 33,000 troops by next summer, fully recovering the surge I announced at West Point. After the initial reduction, our troops will continue coming home at a steady pace as Afghan security forces move into the lead. Our mission will change from combat to support. By 2014, this process of transition will be complete, and the Afghan people will be responsible for their own security.[104]

This news was welcomed by the majority of the American people, many of whom believed the mission had been accomplished with the death of Osama Bin Laden and the destruction of his al-Qaeda terrorist organization in Afghanistan. The length of the war, the downturn in the economy, and the cost of the war were also factors in America's war weariness. General Petraeus, Secretary of Defense Gates, and other senior military leaders loyally supported the President's decision, but argued for a smaller reduction in force. They worried that all the gains of the surge could be reversed if too many soldiers and marines were withdrawn too soon. President Karzai also supported Obama's decisions, stating that Afghan security forces were sufficiently trained and led to assume greater responsibility for the security of Afghanistan.

There is no shortage of debate or strategy proposals for ending the war in Afghanistan.[105] We are not going to build a modern, democratic nation-state there. The reason Afghanistan is called "the graveyard of empires" is not because empires have been defeated there, it is because empires have ultimately determined that there is nothing there worth the continued fight. In other words, the resources that were committed could not be justified, given the best possible outcome. What we have to do is preclude terrorist organizations from using Afghanistan as a safe haven from which to attack the US and its allies. We have to conduct narrowly focused combat operations in Afghanistan to kill and destroy terrorists, their training camps, and other facilities. We need to view this as a long-term commitment, a sort of "no-fly zone"—something we will be doing for decades if not longer. And we have to protect our precious, limited resources—the combat power produced by the ground forces of the United States.

17.

THE SECOND PERSIAN GULF WAR: OPERATION IRAQI FREEDOM I, THE CONVENTIONAL WAR, 2003

In official Washington, the ignorance of what was going on inside Iraq before the war was monumental. None of the proponents of the war, including the neo-conservatives, and also no one in the institutes and think-tanks that provided the intellectual fodder for the war's justification, had the faintest idea of the country that they were to occupy. The academics and researchers who congregated around Washington think-thanks and the vice-president's office, who had made Iraq their pet project, were blinkered by their dogmatic certainties or their bigotries. There was a fundamental misunderstanding about the nature of Iraqi society and the effects on it of decades of dictatorship.[1]

Ali A. Allawi, *The Occupation of Iraq*

Rumsfeld's team took over crucial aspects of the day-to-day logistical planning . . . and Rumsfeld repeatedly overruled the senior Pentagon planners on the Joint Chiefs of Staff. "He thought he knew better," one senior planner said. "He was the decision maker at every turn." On at least six occasions, the planner told me, when Rumsfeld and his deputies were presented with operational plans . . . he insisted that the number of ground troops be sharply reduced . . . When it [the time-phased force-deployment list, or TPFDL] was initially presented to Rumsfeld last year for his approval, it called for the involvement of a wide range of forces from the different armed services, including four or more Army divisions. Rumsfeld rejected the package, because it was "too big," the Pentagon planner said. He insisted that a smaller, faster-moving attack force, combined with overwhelming air power, would suffice.[2]

—Seymour Hersh, "Offense and Defense"

In March 2003, President George W. Bush and his closest advisors *elected* to go to war to remove Saddam Hussein and his "regime" from power. The war was unnecessary and the execution of post-conflict operations demonstrated a remarkable level of incompetence. Saddam Hussein was a threat to the security of the United States and other states in the region; however, he was *not* the threat the Bush Administration made him into, and there was nothing he possessed that could *not* be destroyed from the air.[3] Militarily, Saddam Hussein, while a threat, was contained. Charles Duelfer, who interviewed Saddam Hussein after his capture, wrote:

The problem posed by the Saddam regime was not diminishing. We now know he retained his aspiration for WMD. Saddam told us after the war that he would "do whatever is necessary" to respond to comparable threats from his neighbors such as Iran and Israel. However, even without WMD, Saddam could have caused major problems.[4]

Aspirations do not generate combat power, and Saddam Hussein, while a problem, had no WMDs and could have been managed without recourse to war. However, Saddam Hussein was not contained economically. UN sanctions and the Oil-for-Food program were not working. Charles Duelfer, Deputy Chairman of the UN Weapons Inspection Organization, wrote:

> But by 2001, it was becoming obvious that the sanctions path was leading to nowhere. Saddam was successfully manipulating people and governments in 1999–2002—when the price of oil averaged well under $30 a barrel.... Saddam channeled that illicit income into rebuilding his security services, regime structure, and weapons programs, including prohibited ballistic missiles.[5]

In the development of their strategy and plans, Bush and his advisors made a number of assumptions, which proved to be wrong. They believed the war would be short and easy, and that the military power of the United States was so overwhelming they could dictate the course of the war. They believed that unilaterally they could change the course of the history of a foreign state and culture, and, indeed, the entire Middle East region. They believed the war would pay for itself, with the oil wealth of the invaded state. They believed the Iraqi people would be grateful and greet them as liberators. They did not think it was necessary to understand the peoples whose lands they were invading, the dynamic of their social and political systems, or the condition of the infrastructure of the country. Nor did they seek to understand the nature of war against Muslims in the Middle East. They thought primarily of men and machines, technology and logistics, space and time, and their own plans. The war, however, was a chameleon. And by trying to impose their will upon Saddam Hussein's government, with too little attention to the people, the culture, the region, or the degraded state of Iraq, Bush and his senior-most advisors totally failed to see what they were looking at. They misjudged the situation, and the cost of the war. They missed and destroyed numerous opportunities to share the burden of the war with other states to preclude the insurgency war. The Bush Administration, like the Johnson Administration, placed too much faith in military solutions based on advanced technologies, and by doing so, it grossly misread the situation in Iraq.

The Arguments and Decision for War

There is no shortage of arguments on the causes of the second American war against Iraq. The problem is determining which argument or arguments provide the most accurate explanation. Because the primary documents needed to develop a definitive explanation will not be available for decades and because emotions are still influencing opinions, the best that can be achieved at this point is a brief survey of the various arguments, and an assessment of the events along the road to war. What *is* now known is that the primary reason advanced by the Bush Administration for the war, that Saddam Hussein possessed weapons of mass destruction and was working and plotting with al-Qaeda and other terrorist groups against the United States, was inaccurate. Evidence supports the conclusion that the Bush Administration distorted the intelligence about WMDs and Saddam Hussein's collusion with al-Qaeda. To explain the causes of the war, Bush, in his book, *Decision Point*, wrote:

> For more than a year, I had tried to address the threat from Saddam Hussein without war. We had rallied an international coalition to pressure him to come clean about his weapons of mass destruction programs. We had obtained a unanimous United Nation Security Council resolution making clear there would be serious consequences for continued defiance. We had reached out to Arab nations about taking Saddam into exile. I had given Saddam and his sons a final forty-eight hours to avoid war. The dictator rejected every opportunity. They only logical conclusion was that he had something to hide, something so important that he was willing to go to war for it.[6]

Such logic is a formula for continuous war. Other states, such as North Korea and Iran, are developing WMDs in plain sight. The terrorist attacks on 11 September 2001 created the condition and environment for war. However, the neoconservatives, an extreme element of the Republican Party, who had sought the removal of Saddam Hussein since Operation Desert Storm—a war they considered unfinished—made the initial and strongest arguments for war from within the Bush Administration. The neoconservatives provided the ideological and intellectual foundation for the Bush Administration and its war in Iraq. Consider the following arguments.

Some Middle East scholars and political scientists have predicted an eventual clash of civilizations, or a clash of cultures. Samuel P. Huntington, in an article in *Foreign Affairs*, wrote the "fault lines between civilizations are replacing the political and ideological boundaries of the Cold War as the flash points for crisis and bloodshed."[7] In his book, *The Clash of Civilization: Remaking the World Order*, he continued: "The central theme of this book is that culture and cultural identities, which at the broadest level are civilization identities, are shaping the patterns of cohesion, disintegration, and conflict in the post-Cold War world." He noted that, "The West's universalist pretensions increasingly bring it into conflict with other civilizations, most seriously with Islam and China ..."[8] Those who accept this thesis believe that the Western, secular world and the Muslim, religious fundamentalist world are on a collision course. While some believe that Huntington's thesis is too simplistic, devoid of substantial data and systematic analysis, others believe the struggle is already under way.

Bernard Lewis, Professor of Near Eastern Studies at Princeton University, in his book, *What Went Wrong? The Clash Between Islam and Modernity in the Middle East*, developed and advanced a similar argument. He wrote:

In the course of the twentieth century it became abundantly clear in the Middle East and indeed in all over lands of Islam that things had indeed gone badly wrong. Compared with its millennial rival, Christendom, the world of Islam had become poor, weak, and ignorant. In the course of the nineteenth and twentieth centuries, the primacy and therefore the dominance of the West was clear for all to see, invading the Muslim in every aspect of his public and—more painfully—his private life.[9]

Lewis concluded that the Muslim world had fundamental cultural problems that effectively destroyed its ability to adapt and integrate modern ideas, methods, technologies, and ways of thinking; and hence, to compete with the West. He wrote:

Inevitably their [the French and British] role as villain was taken over by the United States, along with other aspects of the leadership of the West. The attempt to transfer the guilt to America has won considerable support, but for similar reasons remains unconvincing. Anglo-French rule and American influence, like the Mongol invasions, were a consequence, not a cause of the inner weakness of Middle-Eastern states and societies.[10]

These arguments are always missing one fundamental fact about why people fight. During the Civil War a captured Confederate soldier was asked by a Union soldier, who believed he understood the causes of war: "Why are you fighting? You don't own any slaves." The Confederate soldier responded: "Because you're down here." There would be no "clash" if the West was not in the Middle East. People fight when they are invaded, which is why *defense is the strongest form of war*. People become passionate about defending their homes from invaders. When asked why the Americans and British are in the Middle East, Michael Klare, the author of *Blood and Oil*, responds:

And since cheap oil is essential to the nation's economic vigor, American leaders—of whatever party affiliation—have felt compelled to do whatever was necessary to ensure that enough was available to satisfy our ever-expanding requirements. . . . Oil, however has been treated far more seriously, as a resource so vital to American prosperity that access to it must be protected at any cost, including the use of military force. . . . In the name of national security, military force has frequently been used over the past fifty years to guarantee access to foreign petroleum and to protect such key suppliers as Saudi Arabia and Kuwait from internal and external attack. . . .[11]

The Bush Administration denied that oil was the motivation for war in Iraq. Secretary of Defense Donald Rumsfeld declared, "This is not about oil and anyone who thinks that, is badly misunderstanding the situation." To which Klare responded: "We know that such statements cannot be true—the entire history of US intervention in the Persian Gulf discredits them. . . ." Consider the Arab perspective. The Iraqi Ambassador to the United Nations, Mohammed

Aldouri, in October 2002, told the General Assembly that the United States was the aggressor, a hegemonic power:

> This American aggressive hysteria has nothing to do with putting an end to the proliferation of weapons of mass destruction in the world, for the United States of America is the state which owns the largest arsenal of weapons of mass destruction, and they have a long history which shows they have used these weapons against the people, starting with Hiroshima and Nagasaki and then Vietnam. . . . There will be many victims of this hegemonistic tendency if we do not put an end to it. The urgent task today is that of refusing Washington's attempt to hamper the return of the inspectors after Iraq has indeed adopted all the practical measures and arrangements and paved the way for the return of the inspectors to carry out their work easily.[12]

Ali A. Allawi, the first Iraqi post-war Minister of Defense, writing after the war wrote:

> No wonder that cynicism runs deep regarding America's true motives. Seizure of the oil fields, building Iraq as a base to subvert Iran, breaking up the country as part of a redesigned, fragmented Middle East, removing Iraq as a threat to Israel, these were all arguments held out as the 'real' motives behind America's push into Iraq. There was no 'American party' in Iraq, no people who were open advocates of an alliance with America because it was in the manifest interest of the country to have such an arrangement. America's only allies in Iraq were those who sought to manipulate the great power to their narrow advantage. *It might have been otherwise.*[13]

From the perspective of Arab and Muslim states who had suffered nearly a century under the rule of Western powers, the US was the newest imperialist power. The vision of war and the transformation of Iraq extolled by the Bush Administration harked back to the dawn of the last century when the concept of "the white man's burden" and "Manifest Destiny" influenced the actions of Western imperial powers, including the United States. During this final phase of European imperialism, the Western world believed it

was its duty to civilize the backward peoples of the world. From the perspective of the Middle East it appears that the United States has now "taken up" this "burden." Some American scholars also believed the United States was an aggressive imperialist power. In 2004, Rashid Khalidi, the Edward Said Chair in Arab Studies at Columbia University, published a book entitled *Resurrecting Empire: Western Footprints and America's Perilous Path in the Middle East*, in which he delineated the major causes for the war in Iraq. He wrote:

> This was a war fought firstly to demonstrate that it was possible to free the United States from subordination to international law or the U.N. Charter, from the need to obtain the approval of the United Nations for American actions, and from the constraints of operating within alliances. In other words, it was a war fought because its planners wanted to free the greatest power in world history from these Lilliputian bonds. . . . The Iraq War was fought secondly with the aim of establishing long-term American military bases in a key country in the heart of the Middle East: Pentagon officials still talk of retaining "fourteen enduring bases" in Iraq. . . . It was a war fought thirdly to destroy one of the last of the third world dictatorships that had at times defied the United States and its allies (notably Israel). . . . It was a war fought finally to reshape, along the radical free-market lines so dear to Bush administration ideologues, the economy of a country with the world's second-largest proven reserve of oil. This made Iraq a particularly attractive target for leading members of the administration . . . who had all been intimately involved with the oil business.[14]

In 2004, Chalmers Johnson published a work entitled *The Sorrows of Empire: Militarism, Secrecy, and the End of the Republic*, in which he argued that:

> By the time the Soviet Union collapsed in 1991, and with it the rationale for American containment policies, our leaders had become so accustomed to dominance over half the globe that the thought of giving it up was inconceivable. Many Americans simply concluded that they had "won" the Cold War and so deserved the imperial fruits

of victory. A number of ideologists began to argue that the United States was, in fact, a "good empire" and should act accordingly in a world with only one dominant power.... Americans may still prefer to use euphemisms like "lone superpower," but since 9/11, our country has undergone a transformation from republic to empire that may well prove irreversible.[15]

Johnson concluded that 9/11 changed the thinking of the leadership in Washington. However, others argued that the objectives of transforming Iraq and the Middle East was less a function of the 9/11 attacks and neoconservative ideology, and more a function of American foreign policy and worldview since the end of the nineteenth century when America became an empire with possessions in the Pacific. According to this view, the American empire seeks to spread Americanism. It is based on the belief that ultimately the rest of the world has to look like the United States. Globalization is, in fact, Americanization. Andrew Bacevich, a proponent of this thesis, argued that President Woodrow Wilson articulated the vision that has animated American policy and behavior for a century:

In a speech delivered to the US Senate in January 1917, but directed over the heads of foreign governments to people around the world, Wilson spelled out the details of his proposed New Diplomacy. Sketching out a preliminary version of what would emerge a year later as his Fourteen Points—to include self-determination, freedom of the seas, economic openness, disarmament, non-intervention, and replacement of the balance of power with a "covenant of cooperative peace...." Wilson assured Congress in his peroration, "These are American principles, American policies. We could stand for no other. "Indeed," he concluded, "they are the principles of mankind and must prevail."

Our own day has seen the revival of Wilsonian ambitions and Wilsonian certainty, this time, however, combined with a pronounced affinity for the sword. With the end of the Cold War, the constraints that once held American ideologues in check fell away. Meanwhile, in more than a few quarters, America's unprecedented military ascendancy, a by-product of victory in the Cold

War, raised the alluring prospect that there at last was the instrument that would enable the United States to fulfill its providential mission.[16]

Bacevich argued that both major political parties embraced this Wilsonian ideology, and that there was very little difference in their rhetoric and behavior in foreign policy.[17] He argued that the war in Iraq was, "undertaken with expectations that such a demonstration of American power offered the shortest route to a democratic Iraq and a more peaceful Middle East...." He further argued that a uniquely American form of militarism had infected the country, and that attributes of American culture influenced decisions for war:

Out of defeat ... emerged ideas, attitudes, and myths conducive to militarism. But this militaristic predisposition alone cannot explain the rising tide of American bellicosity that culminated in March 2003 with the invasion of Iraq. For that we must look also to interests and, indeed, to the ultimate in US national interests, which is the removal of any obstacles or encumbrances that might hinder the American people in their pursuit of happiness ever more expansively defined.[18]

American happiness is dependent on Middle East oil, because American consumption is dependent on Middle East oil. However, American security is ultimately dependent upon remaking the rest of the world in America's image. The final factor in this worldview is disarmament of the rest of the world. The United States is to be the only significant world military power, the final guarantee of American happiness. Roosevelt's Atlantic Charter was in many ways a rephrasing of the Wilsonian ideology that was embraced by Reagan, George H.W. Bush, and George W. Bush. The Huntington and Bacevich theses are not mutually exclusive. Both see the struggle in Iraq as part of a larger global war, with the effort directed at transformation, to remake the Middle East more in the image of the United States, or something acceptable to the United States.

In March 2006, Professor John Mearsheimer, a political scientist at the University of Chicago, and Stephen Walt, a Professor at Harvard University, published a controversial article entitled, "The Israel Lobby," in which they concluded that Jewish American lobbies and Israel played a decisive role in the decision for war:

> Pressure from Israel and the Lobby [the Jewish lobby organization in the US] was not the only factor behind the decision to attack Iraq in March 2003, but it was critical. [T]he war was motivated in good part by a desire to make Israel more secure. According to Philip Zelikow, a former member of the president's Foreign Intelligence Advisory Board, the executive director of the 9/11 Commission, and now a counselor to Condoleezza Rice, the 'real threat' from Iraq was not a threat to the United States. The 'unstated threat' was the "threat against Israel," Zelikow told an audience at the University of Virginia in September 2002. "The American government," he added, "doesn't want to lean too hard on it rhetorically, because it is not a popular sell."[19]

Mearsheimer and Walt also noted that "Israeli intelligence had given Washington a variety of alarming reports about Iraq's WMD programs. As one retired Israeli general later put it, 'Israeli intelligence was a full partner to the picture presented by American and British intelligence regarding Iraq's non-conventional capabilities'." They concluded:

> There is little doubt that Israel and the Lobby were the key factors in the decision to go to war. . . . If their efforts to shape US policy [continue to] succeed, Israel's enemies will be weakened or overthrown, Israel will get a free hand with the Palestinians, and the US will do most of the fighting, dying, rebuilding, and paying.[20]

In 2007, Mearsheimer and Walt published a book titled, *The Israel Lobby and US Foreign Policy*, in which they further developed their argument, noting that: "The real reason why American politicians are so deferential is the political power of the Israel lobby." They argued that "Washington's close relationship with Jerusalem makes it harder, not easier to defeat the terrorists who are now targeting the United States, and it simultaneously undermines America's standing with important allies around the world."[21] While Mearsheimer and Walt were severely criticized by

some scholars, their views were supported by others.[22] The British historian John Keegan observed:

> Many of the neo-conservatives were Jewish; almost all were Zionist and pro-Israeli. That was to prove unfortunate for it entangled their policies for the Middle East, which were generally rational and enlightened if not always realistic, with their ambitions for the future of the Jewish state, which were contentious and nationalistic. . . . They were particularly insistent that 'regime change' in Iraq, the focus of their antipathies, would foster change for the better in its neighbours, including Syria and Iran. Paradoxically, however, several of the neo-conservatives supported extremist politicians in Israel, who rejected compromise with the Palestinians; they wanted a larger and stronger Israeli state. . . .[23]

In the wake of the conventional phase of Operation Iraqi Freedom, Bush acknowledged the significance of Israel. He stated: "If you're a supporter of Israel, I would strongly urge you to help other countries become democracies. Israel's long-term survival depends upon the spread of democracy in the Middle East."[24]

The more immediate arguments for war came from within the Bush Administration. In an article published in the *New Yorker* magazine, it was noted that, "Wolfowitz has been a major architect of President Bush's Iraq policy and, within the Administration, its most passionate and compelling advocate."[25]

During the Clinton Administration as a member of a neoconservative organization, Project for the New American Century (PNAC), Wolfowitz promoted a policy of regime change in Iraq. In a letter to President Clinton dated 26 January 1998 from the PNAC, signed by Wolfowitz and Richard Perle, it was argued that:

> We are writing you because we are convinced that current American policy toward Iraq is not succeeding. . . . We urge you to seize that opportunity [the State of the Union Address] to chart a clear and determined course for meeting this threat. . . . That strategy should aim, above all, at the removal of Saddam Hussein's regime from power. . . . As recent events have demonstrated, we can no longer depend on our partners in the

Gulf War coalition to uphold the sanctions or to punish Saddam when he blocks or evades UN inspections. Our ability to ensure that Saddam Hussein is not producing weapons of mass destruction, therefore, has substantially diminished. Even if full inspections were eventually to resume … experience has shown that it is difficult if not impossible to monitor Iraq's chemical and biological weapons production.[26]

This letter was followed by a letter, dated 29 May 1998, to Speaker of the House, Newt Gingrich, and Senate Majority Leader, Trent Lott, advocating the same strategy and stressing the consequences for a failure to take action. In September 2000, PNAC published a document entitled, "Rebuilding America's Defense: Strategy, Forces and Resources For a New Century." Some argue that after 9/11, the Bush Administration adopted this document as its "blueprint for foreign and defense policy."[27] It is clear that many of the recommendations and proposals advanced in the neoconservative document were later implemented. The neoconservatives, led by Paul Wolfowitz and Richard Perlel, accepted the Huntington-Lewis thesis, but modified it. They argued that the only way to preclude a larger cataclysm was to transform the Middle East—a cultural transformation based on Western values, ethics, and beliefs. They believed that the US, with or without allied support, possessed the power to transform Iraq, and through Iraq the entire Middle East. They believed that Iraq was the focal point for cultural and political transformation, deducing that a democratic, secular, capitalist Iraq would influence Iran, Kuwait, Saudi Arabia, and other Muslim, Middle East states, transforming the entire region.

In January 2003, Wolfowitz gave a speech that linked Iraq to the 9/11 attacks on the United States:

As terrible as the attacks of September 11 were, however, we now know that the terrorists are plotting still more and greater catastrophes. We know they are seeking more terrible weapons—chemical, biological, and even nuclear weapons. In the hands of terrorists, what we often call weapons of mass destruction would more accurately be called weapons of mass terror. The threat posed by the connection between terrorist networks and states that possess these weapons of mass terror presents us with the danger of a catastrophe that could be orders of magnitude worse than September 11.

Iraq's weapons of mass terror and the terror networks to which the Iraqi regime are linked are not two separate themes—not two separate threats. They are part of the same threat. Disarming Iraq and the war on terror are not merely related. Disarming Iraq of its chemical and biological weapons and dismantling its nuclear weapons program is a crucial part of winning the war on terror.

Wolfowitz argued forcefully for war against Iraq. In an article published in the *New York Times*, entitled "Spy Case Renews Debate Over Pro-Israel Lobby's Ties to Pentagon," it was noted that:

The Pentagon Civilians, led by Paul D. Woflowitz, the deputy defense secretary, and Douglas J. Feith, the undersecretary for policy, were among the first in the immediate aftermath of the Sept. 11 attack to urge military action to topple the regime of Saddam Hussein in Iraq, an approach favored by Aipac [American-Israel Political Action Committee] and Israel. Mr. Wolfowitz and Mr. Feiith were part of a larger network of policy experts inside and out of the Bush administration who forcefully made the case that the war with Iraq was part of the larger fight against terrorism. The Pentagon group circulated its own intelligence assessments, which have since been discredited by the Central Intelligence Agency and by the independent Sept. 11 commission, arguing that there was a terrorist alliance between the Hussein regime and Al Qaeda. The group has also advocated that the Bush administration adopt a more aggressive policy toward Iran, and some members have quietly begun to argue for regime change in Tehran. . . .[28]

The Bush Administration accepted a modified Huntington-Lewis thesis, and adopted the worldview of the neoconservatives. In a speech before the American Enterprise Institute, a neoconservative group, Bush stated: "A liberated Iraq can show the power of freedom to transform that vital region by bringing hope and progress to the lives of millions. . . .

A new regime in Iraq could serve as a dramatic example of freedom for other nations in the region."[29] In the wake of the conventional war, in a speech before the UN he stated:

> Success of a free Iraq will be watched throughout the region. Millions will see that freedom, equality and material progress are possible at the heart of the Middle East. Leaders of the region will face the clearest evidence that free institutions and open societies are *the only path* to long-term national success and dignity. And a transformed Middle East would benefit the entire world.... Iraq as a democracy will have great power to inspire the Middle East.[30]

And his National Security Advisor Condoleezza Rice argued that, "a transformed Iraq can become a key element in a very different Middle East in which the ideologies of hate will not flourish."[31]

Another significant factor in the decision for war was the assessment of the Bush Administration that the war would be short, easy, and cheap. The Iraqi armed forces were only a third as powerful as they were in 1991, and Iraq was geographically and politically isolated. North Korea and Iran, the other two states in Bush's "Axis of Evil," were more significant threats than Iraq, yet Iraq was the target. Small nations that are politically and geographically isolated are vulnerable. Had the Soviet Union still existed and supported Iraq, the war would have been impossible. North Korea is safe because it has a contiguous border with the People's Republic of China. War against North Korea would require the approval of China. A ground war against Iran, a much larger nation, would not be cheap. The geographic and political isolation of Iraq, and the depleted condition of its armed forces, influenced the decision for war.

This summary of the arguments on the causes of the war is incomplete. Numerous books have been written on this issue and because many Americans ultimately concluded that the war was unnecessary, it remains controversial. The arguments are not mutually exclusive. It is more a matter of emphasis. The actions taken on the road to war clarify a number of issues.

*   *   *   *   *

In 2002, President George W. Bush, Vice President Dick Cheney, Secretary of Defense Donald Rumsfeld, Secretary of State Colin Powell, and National Security Advisor Condoleezza Rice initiated the actions necessary to take the country to war. Because there had been no overt act of aggression from Iraq, the first step was to convince the American people of the need for war. The atmosphere of fear created by the 9/11 terrorist attacks facilitated the Administration's push to convince the American people of the necessity for war. In a speech in Cincinnati on 7 October 2002, the President told the American people, "we cannot wait for the final proof, the smoking gun that could come in the form of a mushroom cloud." (Rice and Cheney repeated this "smoking gun" line frequently.) Using intelligence produced in the Pentagon, the President tied Saddam Hussein to al-Qaeda and the 9/11 attacks on the United States. He accused Iraq of supporting, training, financing, and equipping terrorist organizations.[32] Cheney was the Administration's "point man" and strongest advocate for war. He argued that:

> After his defeat in the Gulf War in 1991, Saddam agreed ... to U.N. Security Council Resolution 687 to cease all development of weapons of mass destruction. He agreed to end his nuclear weapons program. He agreed to destroy his chemical and his biological weapons. He further agreed to admit U.N. inspection teams into his country to ensure that he was in fact complying with these terms. In the past decade, Saddam has systematically broken each of these agreements. The Iraqi regime has in fact been very busy enhancing its capabilities in the field of chemical and biological agents. And they continue to pursue the nuclear program they began so many years ago. These are not weapons for the purpose of defending Iraq; these are offensive weapons for the purpose of inflicting death on a massive scale, developed so that Saddam can hold the threat over the head of anyone he chooses, in his own region or beyond.... [W]e now know that Saddam has resumed his efforts to acquire nuclear weapons.... Many of us are convinced that Saddam will acquire nuclear weapons fairly soon.... And far from having shut down Iraq's prohibited missiles, the inspectors found that Saddam had continued to test such

missiles, almost literally under the noses of the U.N. inspectors.[33]

In a later speech he said:

Simply stated, there is no doubt that Saddam Hussein now has weapons of mass destruction; there is no doubt that he is amassing them to use against our friends, against our allies, and against us. And there is no doubt that his aggressive regional ambition will lead him into future confrontations with his neighbors, confrontation that will involve both the weapons he has today and the ones he will continue to develop with his oil wealth.[34]

This was an argument for "preemptive war," more accurately "preventive war." To prove their argument Bush, Cheney, Rumsfeld, Rice, and other advisors told the world they had irrefutable intelligence from numerous sources, including spy satellites and aircraft, Iraqi defectors, weapons inspectors, and Iraqi purchases of technologies from abroad that it was believed could have only one purpose. They said their intelligence was confirmed and supported by British, UN, and other intelligence agencies. On *Meet the Press*, Paul Wolfowitz told the American people, "I've never seen the intelligence community as unified."

In November 2002, the US House of Representatives and the Senate passed a resolution authorizing the President to use military force to enforce UN resolutions and to disarm Iraq. The House voted 296 to 133, and the Senate 77 to 23. In the House, 126 Democrats and 6 Republicans voted against the resolution, while in the Senate the vote was 21 Democrats and 1 Republican against. The Senate "rubber-stamped" the war, as it had the war in Vietnam with the Gulf of Tonkin Resolution. Just as no congressman wanted to be seen as "soft on Communism" during the Cold War, after the attacks of 11 September 2001, no politician wanted to be seen as "weak on terrorism." The congressional debate that preceded the war resolution was remarkable for its hyperbole, superficiality, and absence of critical thinking.[35] While some senators and representatives were thoughtful, reflective, and articulate, others were an embarrassment to their states, constituents, and the country, demonstrating little

knowledge or understanding of the region or the issues. Saddam Hussein was compared to Hitler countless times, invoking the "policy of appeasement" that started World War II, yet few took notice of the fact that Iraq was not comparable to the technologically advanced, industrial nation-state of Germany; and thus, totally incapable of generating the combat power necessary to threaten the West.[36] In fact, Iraq could not produce the parts required to keep its tanks running.

Those who did argue against the resolution noted that there was no definitive proof that Saddam Hussein had supported the al-Qaeda terrorist network; that the Administration had provided little proof that Hussein possessed WMDs, and if he did he totally lacked the delivery systems to threaten the US; that Iraq had been effectively "contained," with UN sanctions and American and British airpower patrolling the skies over Iraq; that little had changed in the last couple of years to warrant such a major shift in US policy; that UN inspectors were making progress; that Bush had already achieved a major victory by getting the inspectors back into Iraq; and that the problem ought to be handled by the UN through diplomacy and other means short of war. It was further argued that other nations had WMDs and were more advanced in their goal to acquire nuclear weapons; that war would further alienate Arab and Muslim peoples, creating more terrorists and a greater threat; that war could destabilize the region and moderate Arab governments friendly to the US; that the US had a unique position of trust around the world, and had never used its power to take over another country without a significant act of aggression, and had *never* adopted a policy of "preemptive war;" and that the cost and course of the war was unknowable. Some feared a long-term commitment, a Vietnam-like quagmire, and the open-ended expenditure of billions of dollars.[37] The argument that the US was alienating its traditional European allies, and possibly creating new alliances between those allies and Russia and China, was given little attention. Issues of sovereignty and the American unilateral approach to issues of national security limited such discussions. The outcome of the vote was known before the debate took place. The President's popularity rating was high, fifty-eight percent, when the debate took place, rising to sixty to seventy percent when the war took place. The war had the support of the majority of Americans.

The Congressional Resolution was followed by UN Security Council Resolution 1441. The Security Council vote was 15–0. Even Syria, the only Arab nation on the Council, voted in favor. The resolutions gave the war and Bush legitimacy. There was debate over exactly what the UN resolution authorized. While some nations argued that an additional resolution was required for war, Bush interpreted it differently, noting that the phrase "will face serious consequences" was sufficient.[38] Bush had already decided on war, concluding that Saddam Hussein "has made the United Nations look foolish," and promising that, "If the United Nations doesn't have the will or the courage to disarm Saddam Hussein . . . the US will lead a coalition to disarm Saddam Hussein."[39]

In December 2002, Hussein readmitted inspectors. However, it was too little, too late. In a speech before the Veterans of Foreign Wars on 26 August 2002, Cheney stated: "A return of inspectors would provide no assurance whatsoever of his compliance with U.N. resolutions. On the contrary, there is a great danger that it would provide false comfort that Saddam was somehow 'back in his box.'"[40] The journalist Seymour Hersh argued that the decision for war was made as early as February 2002:

> There was little doubt among some White House insiders about what the President wanted to do, and about when he had made his decision. . . . White House talking points always noted that no decision had been made, the N.S.C. staff member added, but all involved knew it was a done deal. As of February 2002, he said, "The decision to go to war was taken."[41]

On 5 February 2003, Colin Powell, using his considerable prestige and credibility, made the final sell before the UN. Powell told the world that "every statement I make here today is backed up by sources, solid sources. . . . These are not assertions. What are we giving you are facts and conclusions based on solid intelligence." He noted the numerous sources of intelligence to include: intercepted telephone conversations, Iraqis who "risked their lives" to get information out of Iraq, satellite and aerial photography, and

US and foreign intelligence agencies, particularly the British.[42] Powell stated, "Hussein made no effort, no effort to disarm." He accused Iraqis of "concealing their efforts to produce more weapons of mass destruction." He accused Iraq of lying in its declaration. He played intercepted telephone conversations, none of which mentioned WMDs. He then interpreted these conversations, inserting what he believed they were talking about. He showed satellite photos cautioning the audience that it took years of study to be able to interpret these photos; hence, he had to interpret for them. Powell showed "active chemical bunkers," "decontamination vehicles," and "ballistic missile" production facilities, stating time after time they had been moved before the inspectors arrived. He accused Iraq of playing a "shell game," moving chemical weapons and missiles around the country to keep them hidden from inspectors. He showed what a tiny vial of the biological agent Anthrax looked like, and stated that Iraq had not accounted for 8,500 liters of this dangerous substance. He said, "This is evidence not conjecture." He stated Iraq has "sophisticated" mobile biological agent production facilities, and showed pictures of what they looked like. He stated he had eyewitness evidence of their existence. He said Iraq had modified jet engines to spray these deadly agents and had developed unmanned aerial vehicles to dispense them, technologies that even the US did not possess. He said Iraq had not accounted for hundreds of tons of chemical weapons, that it had dual-use chemical production facilities, that Iraq had reconstituted its infrastructure for its chemical weapons program, and that it was hiding these chemical weapons from the UNMOVIC.

Powell then turned to nuclear weapons and said Iraq had not abandoned its program to develop nuclear weapons. He said defectors had confirmed the existence of this program, and that Hussein had two of the three key components necessary to construct a nuclear bomb, the scientists with the required expertise, and a bomb design. All Hussein needed was the fissionable material. He showed aluminum tubes that he said were for a centrifuge that would be used to refine uranium to produce fissionable material. He concluded: "There is no doubt in my mind . . . Hussein is very much focused on putting in place the key missing piece from his nuclear weapons program, the ability to produce fissile material...." Finally he turned to terrorism and accused Hussein of training terrorists and providing al-Qaeda terrorists with sanctuary.[43]

It was a virtuoso performance that effectively sold war to the people of Earth. But it was, for the most part, a grossly distorted assessment.

Following the war to remove Saddam Hussein, the White House deployed teams of investigators to find Iraq's WMDs. After two years of searching, a bipartisan presidential commission had no option but to conclude that: "the intelligence community was dead wrong in almost all of its prewar judgments about Iraq's weapons of mass destruction.... This was a major intelligence failure." The commission endeavored to identify the main causes for the failure: "inability to collect good information about Iraq's WMD programs, serious errors in analyzing what information it could gather, and a failure to make clear just how much of its analysis was based on assumptions rather than good evidence." The US employs fifteen major intelligence agencies, and expends $40 billion annually to maintain them.[44] Very smart people worked in these agencies. The National Reconnaissance Office possesses the most sophisticated spy satellites, aerial photography aircraft and cameras, and the most talented, skilled, experienced photographic interpreters on Earth. The US possesses the most advanced nuclear physicists on Earth. How did they all get it wrong?

George Tenet, the Director of the CIA during the buildup of war in Iraq, in his book, *At the Center of the Storm*, concluded that:

> After 9/11, everything changed. Many foreign policy issues were now viewed through the prism of smoke rising from the World Trade Center and the Pentagon. For many in the Bush administration, Iraq was unfinished business. They seized on the emotional impact of 9/11 and created a psychological connection between the failure to act decisively against al-Qa'ida and the danger posed by Iraq's WMD programs. The message was: We can never afford to be surprised again. In the case of Iraq, if sanctions eroded and nothing were done ... we might wake up one day to find that Saddam possessed a nuclear weapon, and then our ability to deal with him would take

on an entirely different cast. Unfortunately, this train of thought also led to some overheated and misleading rhetoric, such as the argument that we don't want our "smoking gun to be a mushroom cloud."[45]

Tenet, while acknowledging pressure from the White House, particularly Dick Cheney, believed that the CIA never bowed to that pressure or produced intelligence to please its political bosses.[46] Tenet's basic argument is that the CIA got it wrong. It made intelligence mistakes regarding Iraq WMDs. However, in his view, it did not matter. The Bush Administration had already decided on war. He reflected, "Would we have gone to war with such conclusions?" and answered "I don't believe the war was solely about WMD, so probably yes." The CIA never acknowledged a connection between al-Qaeda and Saddam Hussein. Tenet wrote: "Let me say it again: CIA found absolutely no linkage between Saddam and 9/11."[47] Still, the CIA failed the country, and the men and women of the armed forces who depend on them to get it right.[48] To explain the failure, Tenet wrote:

> In retrospect, we got it wrong partly because the truth was so implausible.... Saddam was a genius at what the intelligence community calls 'denial and deception'—leading us to believe things that weren't true. But he was a fool for not understanding, especially after 9/11, that the United States was not going to risk underestimating his WMD capabilities as we had done once before.... Before the war, we didn't understand that *he* was bluffing, and he didn't understand that *we were not*.[49]

Operational Doctrine: Shock and Awe

On 19 March 2003, President Bush committed the US to a second war in Iraq.[50] The verdict on the conventional campaign has been unanimous—it was a stunning victory:

> Operation Iraqi Freedom (OIF) was one of the most decisive US victories. A dictatorial regime ruling a population of 25 million was defeated in only 21 days of fighting instead of the planned campaign of 125 days. US forces showed

remarkable improvement in their conduct of joint/combined warfare since the Gulf War in 1990/1991. New technological advances were integrated successfully with sound tactical and operational concepts. The coalition commanders displayed a high degree of operational flexibility and agility.[51]

Of course, the larger question is, did the United States and Bush's "coalition of the willing" achieve their political objectives? The immediate political objectives were to topple the dictatorship of Saddam Hussein and to eliminate Iraq's weapons of mass destruction. The larger objective was to establish a stable democratic, capitalist Iraqi nation-state. Saddam Hussein and his senior leaders were to be removed from power. The larger objective, however, has not yet been achieved, and in the years immediately following the conventional war, the violence escalated. The insurgency grew in strength and vigor, and there were signs the war was evolving into a civil war between the Sunni and Shia sects. On 26 September 2005, the cover page of *Time* magazine pessimistically asked, "Iraq: Is It Too Late to Win the War?" The conclusion could be deduced from the story: "Although US officers had known for months about the atrocities taking place in Tall 'Afar, they were powerless to do anything about them. Stretched thin, fighting rebels in places like al-Qaim and Mosul, the military dedicated just a single infantry battalion to an area twice the size of Connecticut."[52]

To fight the war in Iraq, the Pentagon put into practice *new* operational doctrine based on new technologies that were built on the long-held tenets of American culture. The second Bush Administration believed that our military, the most technologically advanced armed forces on the planet, would produce a quick, decisive victory in Iraq, as they had in 1991. However, the Rumsfeld Pentagon had no intention of fighting a war under the Weinberg/Powell strategic doctrine and AirLand Battle operational doctrines. Rumsfeld believed these doctrines represented the past, Cold War era thinking. With the revolution in military affairs (RMA) fully under way, he believed that with advanced technologies and new ways of operating, a small ground force could accomplish what was required of a much larger force a decade ago. The

Pentagon recognized that Iraqi forces were considerably less capable than they were in 1991, having suffered from the embargo, economic constraints, and a lack of technological knowledge and infrastructure. They also recognized that the Iraqi Army was in fact, culturally, an Arab army. The respect and awe bestowed on Iraqi forces in the days prior to Operation Desert Storm were gone. The Rumsfeld Pentagon well understood that in the first Gulf War there had been substantial overkill. The mission could have been accomplished with half the forces deployed. In addition, because of the "no-fly" zones, Special Forces and CIA operations, and large identifiable opposition groups (the Shia and Kurds), Iraq's defenses had been substantially weakened in the decade prior to OIF.

The mission in 2003 was also very different from that of 1991, when the objective was to restore Kuwait and destroy the armed forces of Iraq, both limited war objectives. Killing Saddam Hussein would have achieved one of the immediate objectives of OIF. Still, the political objective of removing a government was more total, entailing the march to Baghdad, the capture and occupation of the city, the removal of all Ba'athist political leaders, and the establishment of new government. The US did not want to fight the Iraqi armed forces if it could be avoided. However, the potential for a much wider war existed—a war with the Iraqi people, or one of the large ethnic, tribal groups, for example, the Sunnis. Still, the services and the Pentagon were considerably more confident of success in 2003 than in 1991. While the services were substantially smaller, they were the most respected forces on the planet. The Army, however, in 2003 was forty percent smaller than it had been in 1991, and it was more widely spread across the planet.

However, Rumsfeld did not plan to fight a conventional ground war. He planned to use a variant of the doctrine used in Operation Enduring Freedom, which relied heavily on Special Forces—airpower, surrogate forces, small, flexible ground forces, and the new concept, shock and awe:

> The goal of Rapid Dominance will be to destroy or so confound the will to resist that an adversary will have no alternative except to accept our strategic aims and military objectives. To achieve this outcome, Rapid Dominance must control

the operational environment and through that dominance, control what the adversary perceives, understands, and knows, as well as control or regulate what is not perceived, understood, or known.... To affect the will of the adversary, Rapid Dominance will apply a variety of approaches and techniques to achieve the necessary level of Shock and Awe at the appropriate strategic and military leverage points. This means that psychological and intangible, as well as physical and concrete effects beyond the destruction of enemy forces and supporting military infrastructure will have to be achieved.[53]

While all the axioms of "shock and awe" were not employed, this doctrinal thinking deeply influenced the actions of the Pentagon. Shock and awe was modified, and became known as "the Rumsfeld doctrine." It was based on speed, maneuver, shock effect, extensive covert preparation of the battlefield, precision strikes at strategically significant targets, and information dominance. This doctrine was based on the premise that the US was fighting a state, not a nation, and that it was possible to maintain the separation between the people and the government. Thus, the preservation of Iraq's infrastructure, the preservation of Iraq's oil fields, and the minimization damage to cultural facilities, homes, schools, and other public areas was of strategic importance.

Many in the Rumsfeld Pentagon believed that the awesome, overwhelming demonstration of US airpower attacking multiple targets simultaneously would strike such fear that the enemy was, to some degree, paralyzed. Intelligence sources would locate key leaders, including Saddam Hussein, who could then be targeted and killed with precision weapons, so-called "decapitation strikes." The destruction of the enemy's communication systems would deprive them of the information necessary to effectively employ their forces; and multiple intelligence sources and digital communication systems would allow US forces to act with a new level of situational awareness, and thus react faster than the enemy, and respond with greater agility and flexibility. Air Force General Richard Meyers, then CJCS, stated that US forces were going to deliver "such a shock on the system that the Iraqi regime would have to assume early on that the end is inevitable."[54]

It was further believed that psychological operations (PSYOP), and Saddam Hussein's own brutality, would separate the Iraqi people from the Iraqi armed forces, and the Iraqi Army from the "elite" Republican Guard and other special units loyal to Hussein, rendering them inactive or ineffective. It was believed that the use of indigenous, surrogate forces would facilitate the overthrow of the Hussein regime and win the support of the people, and that the shock created by the rapid advance of small, highly trained, ground forces, including Special Forces, would cause the enemy's will to collapse. The objective was not to destroy the enemy's main forces, but to destroy his will to fight by attacking and destroying "the brain," "the inner circle," and the "central nervous system" in a short, intense war.

Theater Strategy: Franks vs. Rumsfeld

Political and natural geography dictated the war plan. Basing rights, lines of communication, military overflight, temporary staging areas, and border crossings were greatly restricted. The access and support provided by Saudi Arabia in the first Gulf War was gone. Iran and Syria both were overtly hostile to the US, and very likely to provide covert support to terrorist and guerrilla forces fighting against the US within Iraq. Jordan, a friend of the US, had to maintain its neutrality, and would not provide access. This left only two strategic options for ground forces, Turkey and Kuwait. Turkey was a NATO nation and long-time ally of the US in the Cold War. Turkey had provided the US with permanent facilities for airbases, and radar and listening stations during the Cold War. The Bush Administration believed that with a $6 billion dollar aid package and political support for admittance of Turkey into the European Union, the government of Turkey could be persuaded to permit the passage of a US heavy division, the 4th ID, across its land to northern Iraq. However, anti-Americanism in the Islamic world was at an all-time high. While Turkey was a secular, democratic state, it was also a Muslim nation. On 1 March 2003, the Turkish Parliament sided with the nation, against the US. Thus, Kuwait provided the only strategic avenue of approach for ground forces. Iraq had a small area of coastline on the Persian Gulf, which made an amphibious assault

OPERATION IRAQI FREEDOM
Area of Operations Reference Map

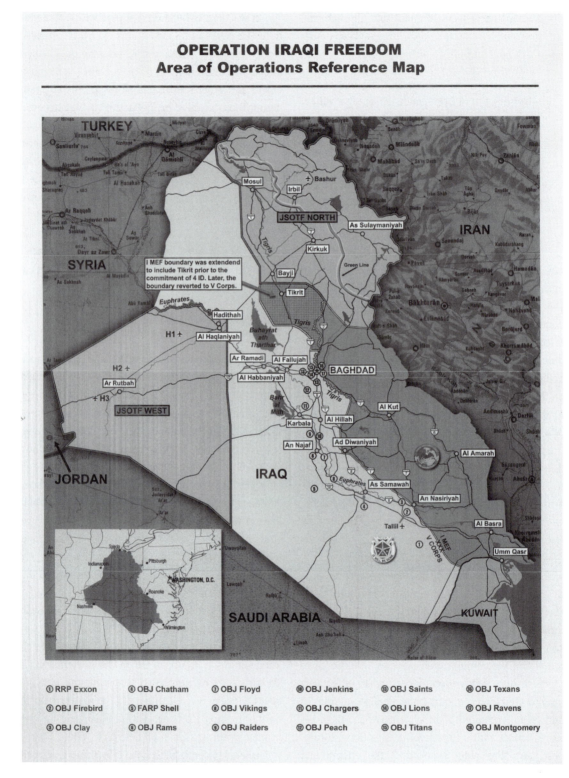

① RRP Exxon	④ OBJ Chatham	⑦ OBJ Floyd	⑩ OBJ Jenkins	⑬ OBJ Saints	⑯ OBJ Texans
② OBJ Firebird	⑤ FARP Shell	⑧ OBJ Vikings	⑪ OBJ Chargers	⑭ OBJ Lions	⑰ OBJ Ravens
③ OBJ Clay	⑥ OBJ Rams	⑨ OBJ Raiders	⑫ OBJ Peach	⑮ OBJ Titans	⑱ OBJ Montgomery

Fig 17.1 Operation Iraqi Freedom, Area of Operations.

possible. A vertical envelopment with airborne forces was also possible. However, both approaches meant a much longer war, requiring considerable time to build up forces. Kuwait was thus of strategic importance, providing the primary staging area for the ground war and access to Iraq.

While the limited access problem dictated the axis of advance, the size of the ground force, and the timing of the operation—when to initiate the ground war (G-day) and when to initiate the air war (A-Day)—were sources of considerable friction. The initial invasion plan advanced by General Franks, CENTCOM Commander, was based on Operation Plan 1003, which itself was based in part on the successful 1991 invasion. It called for a large invasion force of 200,000 to 250,000 men attacking from Turkey and Kuwait, securing the northern and southern sectors of the country, winning and maintaining the support of the Kurds and Shia, and then advancing on Baghdad from the north and south. It also called for an air campaign that started weeks before the ground war to shape the battle space.[55] On 12 October 2002, the *New York Times* reported:

> Defense Secretary Donald H. Rumsfeld said today that he had ordered the military's regional commanders to rewrite all of their war plans to capitalize on precision weapons, better intelligence and speedier deployment. That way, he said, the military could begin combat operations on less notice and with far fewer troops than thought possible. . . .[56]

In January 2003, *Time* magazine reported:

> "Despite being told not to do it, [Franks] basically sent up a revised Gulf War I plan. Rumsfeld couldn't believe it," says a senior Pentagon official. . . . While Franks said he needed at least 250,000 troops, Rumsfeld wanted no more than 100,000. . . . The final number split the difference: war with Iraq could begin with as few as 150,000 US troops in the region. . . . Franks wanted Air Force bombers to pound Iraqi positions for 10 to 14 days before starting a ground war. . . . Rumsfeld balked at that request. . . . And Rumsfeld pushed his foot to the floor on a ground war too, insisting that once the real shooting starts, US tanks and

other armored vehicles should race ahead of their supply lines toward Baghdad in days, if not hours. . . .[57]

In a controversial article, Seymour Hersh observed that Rumsfeld had thrown out Franks' plan:

> Secretary of Defense Donald Rumsfeld and his inner circle of civilian advisers . . . had insisted on micromanaging the war's operational details. . . . On at least six occasions, the planner told me, when Rumsfeld and his deputies were presented with operational plans . . . he insisted that the number of ground troops be sharply reduced. . . .[58]

General Franks, in his book, disputes this assessment. Franks, however, was a man concerned with his own reputation and place in history. He wanted to be seen as the architect of the victory.[59] However, the official history of the US Army notes:

> The executors of Iraqi Freedom wanted more internal flexibility than the TPFDL tended to allow. . . . Unfortunately, dramatic changes on short notice in the midst of a wartime deployment did not work well. The finite physical hardware of airlift and sealift could not morph as quickly as force packages could be redesigned: hasty reconfigurations typically did not allow for appropriate combat service support. . . .

The Rumsfeld Way wasted time and money, and damaged morale. The authors of the Army's history found that:

> To many a guardsman and reservist, the result seemed to be chaos, with soldiers mobilized in accordance with the TPFDL waiting idly for weeks and months, rushing overseas only to find they had not been time-phased with the arrival of their equipment, or finding an imbalance between the scope of their mission and the resources available. The situation got worse when troops already away from their jobs and families for months awaiting deployment were told they would have to stay at least a year in Iraq to meet force requirements.[60]

Rumsfeld believed that a new approach to how America goes to war was necessary. He believed that in the aftermath of 9/11 all war plans had to be reassessed, to respond to the new terrorist threats and "rogue nations" possessing biological, chemical, and/or nuclear weapons. He believed that "too many of the military plans on the shelves of the regional warfighting commanders were freighted with outdated assumptions and military requirements, which have changed with the advent of new weapons and doctrine."[61] He believed that new doctrines, new technologies, and the RMA had dramatically changed the conduct of war. He believed that the Army was a dinosaur, unwilling to change, and incapable of looking beyond its traditional ways of doing things. Rumsfeld's beliefs, attitude, and prejudices against the Army mandated a new plan. Rumsfeld, however, was planning to fight the wrong war.

Franks' thinking and war plans were also off the mark. As Franks characterized his war plans: "This will be a campaign unlike any other in history . . . characterized by shock, by surprise, by flexibility and by the employment of precise munitions on a scale never before seen, and by the application of overwhelming force." Franks further noted that, "We would put our faith in maneuver."[62] However, it is more accurate to note that this was the type of plan Franks was forced to adopt. His initial plan called for considerably more ground combat power in the form of heavy Army divisions. He wanted overwhelming combat power. His initial plan called for an extensive air war prior to the ground war. He explained:

> During months of planning, the length of air operations in preparation for the ground attack had steadily decreased. Two months earlier, we had projected sixteen days and nights of air and SOF operations to 'shape the battlespace' before the first Coalition armor crossed the berm. Now our Abrams and Bradleys would already be deep inside Iraq when . . . airmen delivered a possible knockout blow to the regime in Baghdad on the night of Friday, March 21.[63]

Remarkably, Franks still believed a long air war was necessary. Given the extraordinarily one-sided armor battles in the first Persian Gulf War, and the degraded state of Iraqi armor forces, Franks displayed

an incredible lack of imagination in developing his operational plan. He didn't lack confidence in his Army. He lacked confidence in his ability to move beyond the limitations of his experience. Hence, he sought to replay the first Persian Gulf War. In Operation Desert Shield/Storm, Tommy Franks was a Brigadier General who served as the Assistant Division Commander for Operation and Maneuver in the 1st Cavalry Division, a heavy armor division out of Fort Hood, Texas. As such, he was intimate with Schwarzkopf's operational plan. The safest thing for him to do was to duplicate it as closely as possible. Like Omar Bradley, during World War II, who also lacked confidence, and used the Sicily invasion plan as a model for the Normandy invasion, Franks took the Schwarzkopf plan as a model for the second Iraq invasion.[64] In both cases the situation and enemy were very different.

The extended air campaign was dropped for a number of reasons. First, it wasn't necessary. Ground forces could slice through Iraqi armor formations considerably faster and cheaper than airpower. Second, Franks and the Pentagon concluded that Saddam Hussein would anticipate a replay of the first Gulf War. Hence, he would initiate the destruction of Iraq's oil fields and infrastructure as soon as the air campaign began. Those fields were supposed to pay for the war and finance the Iraqi recovery. To preclude their destruction, it was argued that the extensive air campaign had to be eliminated. The oil fields had to be seized in the opening hours of the war. Third, Franks concluded that by operating in an unexpected manner, tactical and operational surprise could be achieved. Finally, the air campaign had actually started long before the initiation of hostilities on 20 March.

The air campaign actually started in the summer of 2002, when Rumsfeld directed UN-sanctioned air patrols to conduct operations that focused on the destruction of Iraq's air defense system. Between June 2002 and March 2003, roughly 4,000 sorties were flown to destroy radar and communication systems, surface-to-air missiles, and other threats to allied airpower. And, during the twelve years of combat air patrols in the two Iraqi no-fly zones, the US and UK had periodically attacked the Iraqi integrated air defense system, slowly eroding its capabilities. Air

Force General Moseley observed: "We've been involved in Operation Northern Watch well over 4,000 days ... [and] Southern Watch for well over 3,800 days.... We've certainly had more preparation, pre-hostilities, than perhaps some people realize."[65] Franks and others in Washington hoped that the ground war would be unnecessary, and that the air campaign alone would achieve the political objective by killing Saddam Hussein and many of his most senior advisors.

In the open desert, the Iraqi forces were extremely vulnerable to long-range fire from American air and ground forces. Even though American forces were vastly outnumbered, expectations for rapid victory in the desert were high. The major concern was the fight for Baghdad, and possibly other Iraqi cities. Military operations in urban terrain greatly diminish the effectiveness of American technology, since airpower is considerably less effective in those situations. In urban ground war, the range of engagements is substantially reduced. Fighting is at close quarters and the killing typically takes place within a 50-foot radius. Small arms and infantry dominate the battlefield, and operations are manpower intensive. Ammunition and water are used at a higher rate than in other forms of combat, and it takes considerably more manpower to secure an area. And once an area is secure it has to be guarded, or the enemy will backtrack and reoccupy the area.

Command and control is difficult in urban terrain. Operations are decentralized. Greater initiative is required at the small unit level. Tanks and other vehicles are channeled through narrow streets, making them more vulnerable to attack. Resupplying and the evacuation of wounded and dead are extremely difficult and hazardous. In this environment, it is better for the defenders to wound a man than to kill him. Wounded soldiers force other soldiers to risk their lives retrieving and evacuating them. The likelihood of killing innocent civilians increases greatly, as does the likelihood of alienating the people. Civilians are exposed to war, and can be used as shields. The destruction of hospitals, schools, public facilities, mosques, and cultural sites becomes unavoidable, and with the destruction of each building, the people become angrier and more willing to fight. Guerrilla warfare becomes more likely. Civilians become

soldiers and enemy soldiers can simply change their clothing and appear as civilian noncombatants. Caches of weapons can be planted throughout a sector, making it possible for an unarmed civilian to rapidly become a guerrilla fighter. Children can be used as sources of intelligence for enemy fighters. Booby traps and snipers become important instruments of war, greatly impeding the attackers. Finally, tall buildings provide excellent perches for harassing and sniper fire. The psychological strain on soldiers of combat in urban terrain is enormous. The sights and sounds of the battlefield are up close and personal.

There is one major factor that decisively influences the ability of a state to fight urban, guerrilla, and insurgency warfare. The fighters must be believers. They must believe in some ideology, religion, and/or leader. With the decentralized nature of these types of wars, soldiers or guerrillas who do not believe in the cause for which they are fighting can simply quit, take off their uniforms, hide their weapons, and go home. Combatants in urban terrain have to act on their own initiative. Hate and anger are great motivators. Foreigners ransacking your home are great motivators. Enemy forces that are seen as invaders and occupiers can ignite the passions that move soldiers and civilians to fight with great tenacity. The primary concern of the soldiers and marines in the coalition forces was that the war would devolve into a fight for every building, every street, and every block in Baghdad. The fact that Iraq was not a nation reduced the ability of Saddam Hussein's regime to fight such a war. However, coalition forces did not want to create a nation by alienating the Iraqi people. Saddam Hussein's strategy for war was, at least in part, based on getting Americans to fight in the cities, where they might inflict heavy casualties on Iraqi civilians and structures. Such destruction, with the help of the media, had the potential to influence Iraqi, American, and world opinion. In other words, the conduct of the war could put the people under so much pressure that it created a nation willing to fight. The US could also lose the war for the hearts and minds of the people. Urban terrain offered Saddam Hussein the greatest opportunity to inflict heavy casualties on US forces.

A large part of the war was over before the first shot was fired. Special Forces were deployed months before the opening of major combat to shape the battlefield, develop and assist indigenous forces (the Kurds and Shiites), locate key facilities and leaders, enhance the accuracy and lethality of airpower, and conduct PSYOPs. Information operations included electronic warfare, computer network attack, deception plans, psychological operations, and operational security.

PSYOPs operations deserve special attention. In OIF, they were on a scale and sophistication never conducted before. They were designed to influence the behavior of Iraqi generals and key leaders, soldiers, and civilians. In the run up to the war, PSYOPs were used to shape the battlefield. The very name of the operation, Iraqi Freedom, was part of the PSYOPs plan to inform the Iraqi people that the war was not against them, but the regime of Saddam Hussein. Leaflet drops, radio and television broadcasts, and email were part of a multimedia campaign. EC–130E Commando Solo aircraft of the Air Force National Guard's 193rd Special Operations Wing out of Harrisburg, Pennsylvania, broadcast messages on commercial AM/FM, short wave radio bands, and VHF/UHF television. The mobile radio broadcast system and mobile television broadcast system operated out of Kuwait. A translated excerpt of a Commando Solo broadcast informed:

> People of Iraq. The standard of living for Iraqis has dropped drastically since Saddam came into power. Every night, children go to sleep hungry in Iraq. The sick suffer from ailments that are easily treatable in the rest of the world. Saddam has built palace after palace for himself and has purchased fleets of luxury cars—at the expense of the Iraqi people. . . . Saddam has exploited the Oil for Food Program to illegally buy weapons and materials intended to produce nuclear, biological, and chemical weapons and for lavish gifts for his elite regime members. . . . Saddam has built monuments to promote his legacy at your expense. . . . How much longer will this corrupt rule be allowed to exploit and oppress the Iraqi people?[66]

Other themes encouraged Iraqi soldiers to desert, and warned them not to use WMDs, not to destroy the oil infrastructure, and not to damage the environment. Civilians were warned to stay at home

and not to interfere. In the days just prior to the invasion, 20 million leaflets were dropped. Leaflets repeated the same themes as the broadcasts. One stated: "Any unit that chooses to use weapons of mass destruction will face swift and severe retribution by Coalition forces. Unit Commanders will be held accountable if weapons of mass destruction are used." Iraqi generals and key leaders were called and emailed. Starting in January 2003, the Pentagon "began sending thousands of e-mail messages to commanders, promising protection for those who comply with the order to not use weapons of mass destruction against allied forces."[67] They were told to keep their units at home. Even President Bush and his cabinet took part in the PSYOPs campaign, threatening Iraqi generals on television, endeavoring to separate them from Saddam Hussein, telling them not to follow Saddam Hussein's orders to use WMDs, and that if they did there would be severe consequences. After the war, General Tommy Franks, "revealed that senior Iraqi officers accepted bribes for a promise not to engage coalition forces. Consequently, US and UK forces met light resistance in many locations that might have otherwise been heavily defended. 'I had letters from Iraqi generals saying: I now work for you,' General Franks said."[68]

The biggest strategic planning failure of the coalition forces was not having in place a significant plan to win the peace. Because Rumsfeld's Pentagon believed that US forces would be welcomed into an Islamic nation, a Middle East state, as liberators, it thought only about the conventional war. Because so little thought had gone into post-conflict planning, numerous horrendous decisions were made that facilitated the rise of the insurgency.

Opposing Forces

The Iraqi Army in 2003 was considerably smaller and less capable than in 1991.[69] While a considerable number of the force had survived the 1991 war, their effectiveness had been significantly degraded over the years. By 2003, Iraqi forces were poorly trained and equipped. Their inability to purchase new equipment or repair parts made inoperable, "deadlined," many vehicles, causing their cannibalization—taking parts from one vehicle to make another operational.

The absence of French and Soviet technical advisors damaged the ability of Iraqi forces to maintain their tanks, infantry fighting vehicles, and other equipment. The lack of ammunition for training eroded their ability to accurately engage targets with artillery, small arms, and main tank guns. The lack of field training damaged their ability to construct defensive fighting positions, maneuver forces, conduct operations in urban terrain, or employ weapons of mass destruction.

Saddam Hussein employed four types of forces: the regular army, the Republican Guard, the Special Republican Guard, and the *fedayeen* (martyrs). The most formidable force was the Republican Guard (RG). It numbered roughly 60,000 soldiers, and had priority for equipment, training, and other resources. The RG was believed to be capable of generating significant combat power. It was organized into six divisions: three stationed north of Baghdad along the main highway leading to Turkey, and three stationed south along the main highways leading to Kuwait. Those forces north of the city formed the I Corps and those south of it, the II Corps. Two RG divisions—one from each corps—defended in the immediate vicinity of Baghdad, forming an outer perimeter. Expanding out from Baghdad, the other divisions were located in the vicinity of major cities, for example Tikrit and Mosul. Saddam Hussein expected Turkey to cooperate with the US, providing access from the north. Inside Baghdad was the Special Republican Guard, a force of roughly 15,000 soldiers. It was responsible for the defense of the city. These men were lightly armed, but were believed to be well trained and equipped. They were selected because of their loyalty to Saddam Hussein, and were commanded by Saddam Hussein's son Qusay. The regular Army (RA) was in the worst condition. It numbered between 150,000 and 200,000 soldiers, organized into seventeen divisions. It was believed that these forces, for the most part, would not fight, and if they did would be incapable of generating significant combat power. Much of their equipment was old and obsolete, and desertion was common, particularly among the Shia. Saddam Hussein, a Sunni, could not trust these forces. Still, there were armor divisions among the RA forces that were capable of doing considerable damage. CENTCOM could not dismiss them.

The presence of RG forces to some degree strengthened the will of the RA forces.

According to General Franks, the *fedayeen* was, "a group of ill-trained but fanatical regime loyalists; *Al Quds*, local Baath militia commanded by party leaders and national Baath Party militia members; and the volunteers known as the 'Lions of Saddam,' a group of Sunni boys eighteen and younger who had received rudimentary military training."[70] These forces were based on the ideology of suicide bombers, and the operational doctrine of fast hit-and-run shock raids akin to those attacks employed by Somali warlords against US Army Rangers in Mogadishu in 1990.[71] The *fedayeen* fought in pickup trucks mounted with machine guns and other light weapons, such as RPGs, rocket grenades. They were called "technicals," a term that originated in Mogadishu. These forces were ineffective against M1s and Bradleys, but could do considerable damage to thin skinned vehicles, such as trucks and Humvees. CENTCOM had not planned to fight the "technicals." Franks wrote:

> Our lack of HUMINT [human intelligence] had given us a nasty surprise: We'd had no warning that Saddam had dispatched these paramilitary forces from Baghdad. Our analysts had seen reconnaissance images of pickup trucks, their cargo bays covered by tarps, and civilian buses loaded with passengers moving south, but this had raised no concerns.

The strength of the *fedayeen* was unknown. Franks estimated as many as 40,000 fighters. These forces created more concern due to the element of surprise than from real military effectiveness.

* * * * *

American invasion forces consisted of two corps commands, the V US Army Corps and the 1st Marine Expeditionary Force (MEF), both of which were under the command of Lieutenant General David D. McKiernan's Third Army. McKiernan, not Franks, was the Coalition Forces Land Component Commander. The axis of advance was from Kuwait to Baghdad, with the Army conducting the main attack on the left flank and the Marines conducting the supporting attack on the right. In reality, there was no main attack or supporting attack. It was a 300-mile race to

Baghdad with the expectation that the two forces would remain within supporting distance of one another. The prize was the capture or killing of Saddam Hussein, an event that national and world media would cover extensively. Given the historic relationship between the Army and Marine Corps, Americans could expect a competitive race, with issues such as supporting distance secondary matters.

Lieutenant General William Wallace commanded V Corps. It was based on the 3rd Infantry Division (Mechanized) out of Fort Stewart, Georgia, commanded by Major General Buford C. Blount III, like Franks, a native of Texas. The 101st Airborne Division (Air Assault) under the command of Major General David H. Petraeus, and a brigade of the 82nd Airborne Division under the command of Major General Charles H. Swannack, Jr., supported the operation. In addition, the 10th and 5th Special Force Groups (SFG), the Ranger Regiment, the 4th PSYOP Group, and the 173rd Airborne Regiment were deployed. The Army deployed 233,342 soldiers, including 8,866 National Guardsmen and 10,683 reservists, roughly half the active Army and half the total forces deployed. When the operation kicked off, the Army was not fully deployed; hence, its total personnel count is a bit misleading. The equipment for a third corps-size organization based on the 4th ID (Mechanized) out of Fort Hood, Texas, was still at sea.[72] The Army's V Corps was also not fully deployed and ready for combat when the operation was initiated. Combat forces and combat service support forces were still in various stages of deployment. This influenced the conduct of the operation.

Lieutenant General James T. Conway, USMC, commanded the 1st MEF, a joint and combined force of 81,500 men, based on the 1st Marine Division, which consisted of three regimental combat teams (RCT), under the command of Major General James Mattis, and the 1st (UK) Armoured Division, under the command of Major General Robin Brims. The UK division consisted of the 7th Armoured Brigade, the 16th Air Assault Brigade, and the 3rd Commando Brigade. A brigade size force from the Second Marine Division formed Task Force Tarawa. The Marines deployed 74,405 marines, including 9,501 reservists. In reference to the command situation and joint and combined operations, Conway concluded, "It worked

and was jointness in its finest sense. I had a solid relationship with General McKiernan. The staffs had the inevitable friction over pop-up issues, but level heads always prevailed."[73] Conway's total ground combat forces numbered 115,000 marines and soldiers, and 26,000 British soldiers.

The air forces deployed for OIF included those of the US Air Force, Navy, Marine Corps, and Army, and those of coalition nations: the Royal Air Force, Royal Australian Air Force, and Canadian Air Force. The US Air Force, however, provided more than half of the combat aircraft employed (fifty-one percent), and almost half of the support aircraft (forty-five percent). Air Force Lieutenant General T. Michael Moseley headed CENTCOM's Air Forces, serving as Combined Force Air Component Commander. The Air Force deployed 293 fighters, including F–15s, F–16s, and F–117s; 51 bombers, including B–52s, B–1s, and B–2s; 182 tankers, including KC–10s and KC–135s; 111 Airlift aircraft, including C–130s, C–17s, and C–21s; 60 intelligence, reconnaissance and surveillance (IRS) aircraft, including E3Bs, E8Cs, EC–130, RC–135s, and U–2s; 131 SOF aircraft, including MH–53s, UH–60s, and HH–60s, and UAVs, including Predators and Global Hawks. The Air Force deployed 54,955 airmen, including 7,207 National Guardsmen, and 2,084 reservists. The 4th Air Support Operation Group (ASOG) provided the Army's V Corps close air support, performing not as a supporting arm, but as a co-combatant.[74] The 3rd Marine Aircraft Wing (MAW), and Naval aviation supported the 1st MEF.

Speaking in March 2004, Admiral Vern Clark outlined the Navy's contribution to Operation Iraqi Freedom:

> A year ago, we had 164 Navy ships and almost 78,000 sailors at sea in support of OIF and the global war on terrorism. . . . In all, 221 of our then 306 ships, about 73% of our total force, were under way. Seven of 12 carrier strike groups, 9 of 12 expeditionary strike groups, 33 of 54 attack submarines, and some 600 Navy and Marine Corps tactical aircraft were forward deployed in support of the national commitment and policy.[75]

Some of these forces were for Operation Enduring Freedom in Afghanistan; however, the vast majority supported OIF. The carriers, *USS Abraham*

Lincoln, Theodore Roosevelt, Constellation, Harry S. Truman, Carl Vinson, George Washington, and *Nimitz* supported OIF. The Navy provided 293 fighters, primarily F–18s and F/A–18s, and the Marine Corps 130 fighters, primarily F–18s. Navy aviation flew more than 7,000 sorties. The Navy's surface warships and submarines launched more than 800 Tomahawk cruise missiles. Navy expeditionary warships deployed 60,000 Marines. Navy SEALs conducted convert operations. Navy Special (mine) Clearance Teams cleared 913 nautical miles of waterways, using dolphins and other resources. While transporting the Army to the battlefield is not a Navy responsibility, it was involved in delivering equipment and other materials to Kuwait. The Navy was able to "surge" during the operation, stressing men and machines.[76]

The Air War

The air war did not open as planned. The CIA believed it had pinpointed the location of Saddam Hussein, his sons Qusay and Uday, and other senior leaders. This information caused Bush to approve a raid to kill them. The Air Force rapidly deployed two F–117 Nighthawks, stealth fighters, from Qatar, each loaded with two EGBU–27 precision-guided bombs (laser guided bombs enhanced with guidance systems that used Global Positioning satellites). The Navy responded by firing dozens of Tomahawk missiles from six warships.[77] The decapitation strike failed. Saddam and his sons lived. (The CIA's evidence may have been based on one of Saddam Hussein's many look-a-likes.) Still, Major Mark J. Hoehn, one of the F–117 pilots, concluded, "We knocked the regime off balance, and we kept them off balance. Whether or not we got [Saddam], he was never a significant factor after that."[78]

Intelligence also caused Franks to advance the ground war. Reconnaissance and satellite images appeared to show that Iraqi forces were preparing to torch the Rumilyah Oil Fields—an operation that would have taken substantially more than twenty-four hours. Franks advanced the ground war eight-and-a-half hours from 0600 Friday, 21 March, to 2130, 20 March, to get forces into the field as soon as possible. The Marines were able to secure the fields before substantial damage occurred. The air campaign, "shock

and awe," was not moved up, and went off as scheduled at 2100, 21 March.

In the first few days of the air campaign, the Air Force and Navy deployed their full array of airpower, flying 15,000 sorties against enemy targets. B–52s flying out of Britain launched cruise missiles. Submarines and surface ships launched more than 800 Tomahawk cruise missiles. F–117s flying out of al-Udeid Air Base, Qatar, dropped precision-guided bombs. F/A–18 flying from carriers in the Persian Gulf and Mediterranean, and Air Force F–15Cs and F–16s flying out of Kuwait dropped and launched precision munitions. B–2s flying out of Diego Garcia in the Indian Ocean dropped JDAMs (joint direct attack munitions) and other ordnance. B–1Bs attacked targets with precision-guided weapons. KC–135s refueled Air Force, Navy, and coalition aircraft. C–17s delivered men and material. C–130Js provided theater transport. E–8C Joint JSTARS radar aircraft provided twenty-four-hours-a-day battlefield reconnaissance. EC–130Es broadcast AM/FM radio and VHF/UHF television messages critical to limiting Iraqi casualties. MH–53M from the 21st SOS, Special Operations Forces, supported special and conventional operations. By every standard, the air forces employed demonstrated capabilities unparalleled in the history of warfare.

Outer space was used as never before in war. The array of satellites and their capabilities was as impressive as the airpower employed.[79] Major General Franklin J. Blaisdell, the Air Force director of space operations and integration during OIF, observed, "We are so dominant in space that I pity a country that would come up against us." Global positioning system satellites directed precision-guided weapons on target through sandstorms, rain, and wind. Imaging radar satellites detected and pinpointed the movement of Republican Guard forces so they could be destroyed by airpower. Satellites listened in on Iraqi communications, providing useable battlefield information. Satellites provided photographic information for planning and conducting special operations; provided communications facilitating command and control, reducing the response time of shooters; provided weather data for pilots and Navy ships; directed UAVs such as the Predator and Global Hawk; and even facilitated logistical efforts, tracking supplies and making possible more precise coordination of the delivery of supplies.

The initial targets included the enemy's command and control facilities, suspected locations of their top leaders, and Republican Guard headquarters. More specifically, the Ministry of Information, the Baghdad Presidential Complex, the Council of Ministers Building, the Republican Palace, Al-Salam Palace, Al-Sijood Presidential Palace, and the Ministry of Planning were all targets. The effort was to destroy control facilities, the brain, and by so doing paralyze the arms and legs, the fighting forces. In the first forty-eight hours of the air war, over 1,500 targets across Iraq were struck. *Time* recorded:

> For the allied command, the hope remains that the mere demonstration of American air power will persuade large numbers of Saddam's best trained and most loyal soldiers, the Republican and Special Republican Guard, to surrender before the US and British forces begin a siege of Baghdad. A senior Administration official told *Time* that the military has "killed a significant number of the Republican Guard, we're trying to break their will and get them to go home." Defense officials predicted last week that up to a quarter of the Republican Guard troops would surrender if the details were worked out. "They're using the psychological instrument to collapse [the enemy's] will through intimidation and the creation in his mind of inevitable defeat."[80]

Airpower, the "shock and awe" campaign, did not produce the immediate collapse many expected and hoped for. While it produced partial paralysis of the brain, the limbs, the Iraqi ground combat forces, were still active. The ground war was still necessary.

With the advance of the V Corps and 1st MEF, tactical airpower dominated the air war effort. By all estimates, Army and Air Force operations achieved a higher level of proficiency than in any previous war. The 3rd ID and 4th ASOG (Air Support Operations Group) fought integrated battles against Iraqi armor formations. One Army observer concluded:

> V Corps' Cobra II drive to Baghdad during Operation Iraqi Freedom (OIF) broke fresh ground in a number of areas, but perhaps none

so important as the conduct of joint operations. . . . It was not merely the parallel functioning of two armed services; it was the almost flawless operation of a thoroughly integrated combat-arms team. Army officers of the V Corps staff described the result in superlatives: it was the best, most efficient, most effective and most responsive air support the Air Force has ever provided any US Army unit.[81]

And *Air Force Magazine* noted that: "Gulf War II . . . took integration to new highs, and now some view it as the distinguishing feature of the warfare, US. Style. . . ." Vice Admiral (retired) Arthur K. Cebrowski, director of the Pentagon's Office of Force Transformation, concluded, "When the lessons learned come out, one of the things we are probably going to see is a new air-land dynamic. . . . It is as if we will have discovered a new sweet spot in the relationship between land warfare and air warfare."[82] The conventional war was considered a major success for "jointness" between the Army and the Air Force because of the "unprecedented degree of air-ground coordination."[83] In the V Corps area of operation the 4th ASOG conducted 886 battlefield-shaping missions and 606 close air support missions. In urban terrain the Air Force destroyed 225 buildings, 105 bunkers, and 226 various other targets. Army artillery and airpower were closely coordinated.

Special Operations, PSYOPs, Iraqi memories of Operation Desert Storm, and the psychological influence of the air campaign probably deserve the lion's share of the credit for strategic decisiveness in the conventional war of OIF. The vast majority of Iraqi forces decided not to fight, and many of those forces that fought did so without determination. However, it must be remembered that Iraq was not a unified, cohesive *nation*. It was a *state* with deep fractures that precluded a more total war effort from the Iraqi people.

The air war in OIF was not the first network-centric war. It was, however, considered a positive step in that direction. In *Air Force Magazine* it was noted that:

> Air warfare tactics are on the verge of what many believe will turn out to be a far-reaching revolution. . . . OEF in Afghanistan and OIF in Iraq pioneered a more extensive use of airborne networks to distribute senior information, share tactical messages, and exert command and

control over forces. The May 2003 end of major combat operations in Iraq led the Air Force Chief of Staff, Gen. John P. Jumper, to observe, "We've learned the value of things such as networking." The power of nearly all major strike platforms— from B–2 bombers to A–10 attack aircraft—was multiplied by fresh intelligence-surveillance-reconnaissance (ISR) data or updated CAOC [combined air operations center] communications and tracking.... In OIF the "networking was crude."[84]

Jumper further noted that, "It was machine-to-machine interfaces, but it was crude. Our kids did it on the chat networks at the speed of typing, not the speed of light."

The Ground War

On 20 March 2003 the Army's 3rd Infantry Division and 101st Airborne Division, and the 1st Marine Division and 1st UK Armoured Division crossed into Iraq to destroy the armed forces of Iraq that decided to fight, and to remove Saddam Hussein from power. The Army's V Corps advanced from Kuwait up the Euphrates River valley south of Nasiriyah, to Samawah, to Najaf, to Hillah and Karbala, and into Baghdad, while the 1st MEF advanced from Kuwait up Route 1 north, between the Euphrates and Tigris Rivers to Numaniyah and Route 6, and into Baghdad. The Army entered the city from the southeast and the Marines from the northeast. The V Corps' lead division, the 3rd ID, moved through the desert and along unimproved roads, parallel to the Euphrates River, securing logistical and air bases, and the road networks, which comprised its lines of communication (LOC). The 1st Marine Division had better roads, but more urban terrain to move or fight through. By 9 April 2003, organized resistance had ended. Both the Army and Marine Corps attribute the success of the operation to bold, rapid maneuver warfare.

Neither the Army nor the Marine Corps sought to maneuver to find, fix, and destroy the enemy's main force. They maneuvered to avoid enemy forces. The objective was Baghdad. Hence, they bypassed enemy strong points, leaving behind elements to eliminate or contain these forces. The lead elements would keep going, no matter what.

In hindsight either the Army or Marines' ground force could have won the conventional war without the other. The vast majority of Iraqi forces decided not to fight. One Army assessment concluded:

> Of course, no plan survives contacts with the enemy, and the Iraqi defenders offered a few surprises of their own. The widely expected mass capitulation of the regular army never materialized. Generally, they did not surrender or even vigorously defend. Instead, the majority of Iraqi soldiers just melted away, offering relatively light, if any, resistance. Yet, it was unclear whether this was a deliberate tactic to preserve the force, the result of the extended PSYOP campaign, the result of the ongoing attacks on their command and control systems, the result of their fear of coalition combat power, or simply as close as the soldiers could come to a formal capitulation given the tight control imposed by the layers of security services.[85]

By just melting away, Iraqis kept the weapons and ammunition required to fight the insurgency war that emerged soon after the conventional war ended. Instead of the expected 50,000 prisoners of war, only 6,200 surrendered or were captured. When the conventional war ended, the US had suffered 122 killed, the British thirty-three. The real war had become the insurgency war, which by November 2005 had killed over 2,000 soldiers and marines.

A comprehensive history of the Army and Marine Corps advance north is not possible in these few pages.[86] However the Army's assessment of the campaign can be found in the 3rd ID's After Action Report, which in part read as follows:

> The division succeeded in its tenacious attack over 600 kilometers (km) from Kuwait to Baghdad, through storms of biblical proportion and constant enemy resistance, specifically because of its bold and decisive maneuver and ability to command and control on the move. Brigade combat team (BCT) and division command posts (CPs) separated and formed smaller more mobile command posts in preparation for the continuous attack.... The continuous attack across 600+ kilometers forced the division to fight in multiple directions and with units in

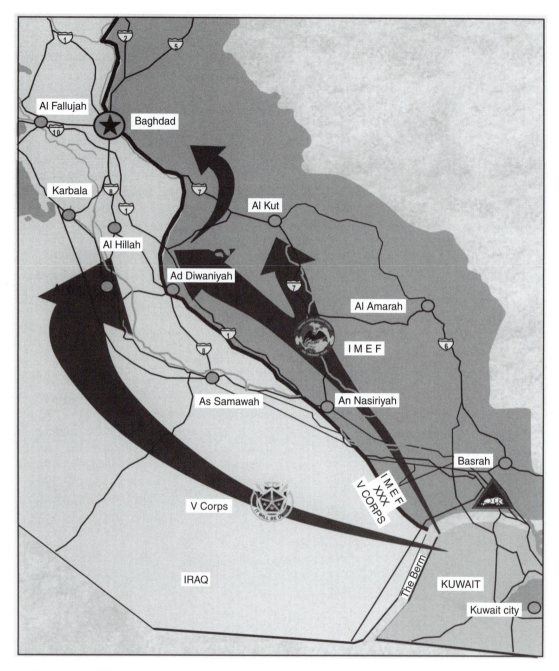

Fig 17.2 Operation Iraqi Freedom, V Corps (Western Axis) and 1st MEF (Eastern Axis) maneuver toward Baghdad.

contact often up to 200 kilometers apart. A key to this successful attack was the early resourcing of the maneuver elements with requisite forces to shape and destroy the enemy, as well as conduct all the other necessary function to be successful. By executing a mission focused task organization of engineers, artillery, air defense artillery (ADA), military police (MPs), logistics assets, and other, the division attempted to give the BCTs all of the assets they would need to influence every aspect of their fight.[87]

In the conventional war, there was no way for US forces to lose. Still, there were surprises that required adaptation. The Army did not plan to fight the *fedayeen* irregular forces. As a consequence, it had to

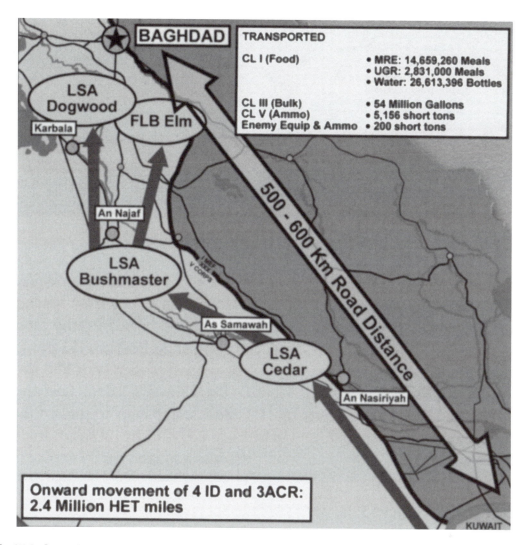

Fig 17.3 Operation Iraqi Freedom, V Corps Logistics Line of Communication.

employ its light infantry—the 82nd and 101st Airborne Divisions—to secure its LOC and clear towns along its axis of advance. At Samawah, Hillah, Karbala, and other towns, the airborne and air assault soldiers fought in urban terrain. These were time-consuming battles that occupied infantry forces that might have been needed for the much-anticipated battle for Baghdad.

For a detailed assessment of the Marine campaign see Bing West's *The March Up: Taking Baghdad with the 1st Marine Division*. Bing wrote:

The plan was the first major test of the maneuver warfare doctrine, designed for commanders to defeat an enemy by clever movement rather

than by brute force that relied on two-sided attrition. . . . As the supporting effort in Iraqi Freedom, the MEF by design confronted more Iraqi divisions than did the Army. The MEF was supposed to draw off Iraqi forces so that Army Fifth Corps could get to Baghdad faster and with less opposition. . . . There were six Iraqi divisions guarding the area assigned to the Marines, stretching roughly from the Euphrates River east to the Iranian border. . . . Saddam had four divisions stacked along that route, with a fifth in the southern Rumalia oil fields and a sixth near Baghdad. . . . After a day's fighting . . . General Mattis suddenly shifted the division 100 kilometers to the west and attacked up two highways between the Euphrates and Tigris Rivers. . . . General Mattis advanced

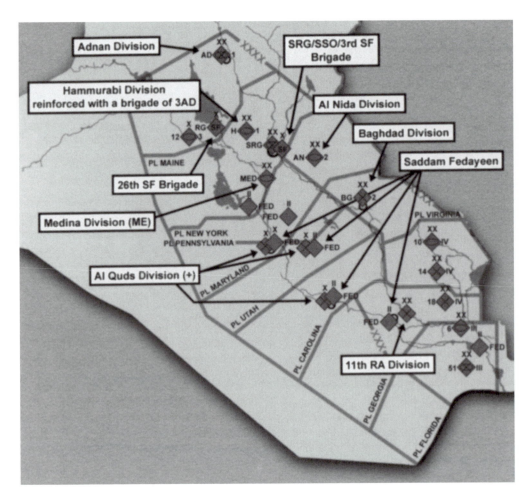

Fig 17.4 Operation Iraqi Freedom, Iraqi Force Disposition.

three regimental combat teams, each with about 1,000 vehicles, in a 100 kilometer single file up two highways.... After a spectacular "run and gun" tank charge of 110 kilometers in two days, General Mattis had his division poised at the Baghdad Bridge.[88]

The 1st Marine Division was employed as if it were a heavy armor division. This should not have been done, the consequence of inter-service rivalry. The division was not equipped to fight another armor division. The Marine Corps is still primarily a light infantry force. It generates the greatest combat power in urban, jungle, and mountainous terrain, and littoral regions. It would have contributed significantly to the much-anticipated, Stalingrad-like battle for Baghdad, had it occurred. Another Army heavy armor division should have been used in the secondary effort in the march to Baghdad. A

fully operational, trained Republican Guard division equipped with T–72 tanks and BMPs would have stopped the Marines with heavy losses. Marines are not trained or equipped to fight such a force. The Marines, however, were determined that OIF would not be a repeat of Operation Desert Storm, where it became obvious they were not necessary.

Every Marine killed in an amphibious track vehicle in the march to Baghdad was a victim of inter-service rivalry. Employing light, thin-skinned amphibious track vehicles hundreds of miles from the sea was ridiculous. The M–2 Bradley fighting vehicle offers considerably greater firepower, protection, and survivability. However, as in other operations over the past fifty years, it became more important to divide the operational pie evenly than to employ forces in accordance with the function for which they were designed. The degraded state of Iraqi forces, their

Fig 17.5 Operation Iraqi Freedom, Iraqi Force Disposition, Northern Iraq.

decision not to fight with tenacity (for whatever reason), and the dominance of American airpower minimized casualties, but that does not negate the fact that the Pentagon employed the wrong forces structure.

The Marine Corps too had a few surprises. The *fedayeen* and the fight for Nasiriyah consumed time and manpower on the way to Baghdad. However, Task Force Tarawa, along with the British 1st Armour Division, was able to assume responsibilities for actions in southern Iraq, allowing the 1st Marine Division to continue north to Baghdad. On 23 March, as the lead elements, the 5th and 7th RCTs of the 1st Marine

Division, advanced north toward Diwaniyah, Task Force Tarawa, under the command of Brigadier General Richard Natonski, kicked off an attack to clear An Nasiriyah. The bridges there were critical to Marine operations. The *fedayeen* decided to fight for the city, and so built up their forces. This was the first fight of the war where the Iraqis fought with determination. The Marines used TOW and Javelin antitank weapons to knockout the T–55s blocking their way. The *fedayeen* responded with RPGs (rocket-propelled grenades) to knock out amphibious track vehicles. The fighting went on for several days. After suffering heavy casualties, the *fedayeen* decided to give up the city. The Marines suffered eighteen killed and numerous wounded.

On 24 March, the Apache helicopters of the 101st Airborne Division's 11th Aviation Regiment conducted a deep attack far in advance of ground units, sustaining heavy damage. Several aircraft were downed, and two pilots captured. Franks noted:

> Thirty Apaches had launched. . . . Twenty-nine made it back with some degree of damage. . . . In the end only one of the Regiment's Apache units reached its objective, a long oasis where thirty T–72 Republican Guard tanks were dug in. But the ground fire was so intense that the gunships had to withdraw before firing a single missile. . . . Not a single tank or artillery piece of the Medina Division was damaged in the attack.[89]

The attack was controversial.[90] Some argued that Army tactics were at fault. Some argued that the doctrine was fatally flawed. And still others argued that the technology was too fragile to survive on the modern battlefield, particularly in deep operations. It was also argued that Air Force fixed-wing aircraft would have better performed this mission. A pilot from 1st Battalion (Attack), 3rd Aviation Regiment described the situation the Apaches faced in OIF:

> The fight that raged around us in the opening days of the ground war was not at all like Desert Storm. Enemy air defense and anti-aircraft artillery (AAA) units had demonstrated adaptability and improved in tactics, especially in their ability to target attack helicopters, since then. The enemy placed weapon systems beneath tree lines and palm canopies, and they tucked them into urban areas to exploit Apache vulnerabilities. On more than one occasion, the enemy employed an obviously lucrative target, a T–55 or T–72 tank, in the open as bait, with the expectation of drawing Apache helicopters into an air defense ambush. Near many ambush positions, observer teams in Arab civilian attire triangulated aircraft locations and directed mortar and anti-aircraft artillery fires. . . . The battlefield had changed as well. Our aviators flew into battle expecting to fight Iraq's fielded military forces, mainly armor and artillery. . . . In 2003, however, the Iraqis tucked their conventional weaponry

inside city blocks, among family dwellings and behind human shields.[91]

New enemy tactics diminished the operational effectiveness of the Apache. The Apache was designed for the deep strike mission on the European battlefield. However, in Operation Desert Storm it demonstrated a high degree of effectiveness in deep operations, destroying Iraqi tanks and other high-value targets. Urban terrain and the light it generates diminish the Apache's effectiveness by greatly reducing its standoff range and rendering its night vision devices useless. Still, none of the arguments against the Apache influenced the Army's commitment to the aircraft. They flew throughout the conventional war, successfully carrying out numerous missions, including close combat.

On 25 March, Army Rangers, Special Forces, and soldiers from the 82nd Airborne Division jumped into Northern Iraq to secure an airfield. The following night the 173rd Airborne Brigade based in Vicenza, Italy, conducted a night jump into Northern Iraq to seize the airfield at Bashur.[92] Within twenty-five minutes, more than 1,000 soldiers were on the ground. Seventeen C–17s supported the operation. The remainder of the brigade air landed. In a few days, over two thousand soldiers and almost 400 vehicles, including an armor company of five Abrams and Bradley fighting vehicles, were on the ground prepared for action. The mission was to link up with Kurdish forces to support the operation of the Combined Forces Special Operations Component Commander (CFSOCC). These forces were also part of the deception plan to cause Saddam Hussein to leave significant forces north of Baghdad.

Fifty miles south of Baghdad on 25 March, the 3rd ID stopped. General Wallace, the V Corps commander, explained: "I've got to give my best military judgment, given the weather, the long lines of communication, and given that we have to pull up our long line of logistics. . . . We've got to take this pause. We're still fighting the enemy every night." The terrain, force structure, supply situation, unanticipated *fedayeen* attacks on the LOC, brutal weather conditions, incomplete logistical preparation, insufficient reserve forces, expected stiff enemy resistance around and in Baghdad, and fatigue made the halt necessary. The

3rd ID and V Corps were stretched across more than 250 miles of desert. They were fighting in several directions, and their Apaches were grounded because of the sand storm. At this juncture, intelligence identified two Iraqi armor columns. This intelligence was made public, causing grave concern among the professional soldiers (an example of how communications technology and the media can influence events on the battlefield).

Retired generals appeared on national television to tell the American people that Rumsfeld and Franks had gone in too light, with insufficient forces. Retired General Barry M. McCaffrey, who had commanded the 24th Infantry Division in Operation Desert Storm, stated: "Their assumptions were wrong. . . . There is a view that the nature of warfare has fundamentally changed, that numbers don't count, that armor and artillery don't count. They went into battle with a plan that put a huge air and sea force into action with an unbalanced ground combat force."[93] McCaffrey was right, and many old soldiers publicly supported his views. However, this was an argument that stretched all the way back to Bradley and Ridgway and the opening years of the Cold War. Old soldiers had been making this argument for six decades. While McCaffrey's comments angered Franks, had he recalled his initial plans and the size of the force he had requested and argued for, he too would have concluded that McCaffrey was right.[94] Had the majority of Iraqi armor forces decided to fight, one heavy division could have faced as many as six Iraqi armor divisions. While the Marine Corps had increased the number of Abrams in its formations, in desert terrain it could not produce the combat power of a single armored cavalry regiment. And, had the Iraqis employed the chemical weapons they were "believed" to possess, the tactical efficiency of both the Army and Marine forces would have been significantly degraded.

It was during that horrendous sandstorm that the most significant Air Force action took place. JSTARS radar aircraft identified two separate columns of enemy armor forces south of Baghdad, oriented toward the 3rd ID. The Iraqi forces were stationary trying to ride out the storm. They were elements of the Hammurabi and Medina Republican Guard Divisions. The 3rd ID, with two brigades forward, was substantially outnumbered. During those tense days the Air Force took on the Republican Guard. Franks wrote:

> By 2000 hours, B–52s, B–1s, and a whole range of Air Force, Marine, and Navy fighter-bombers would be flying above the dense ochre dome of the sandstorm, delivering precision-guided bombs through the zero-visibility, zero-ceiling weather. I was confident that we were looking at the end of organized Iraqi resistance. . . . Strike aircraft of all sizes were moving over a wide curve kill zone that stretched from Al Kut in the Tigris Valley in the east to the Karbala Gap in the west. The sand continued to blow. The Republican Guard units were hunkered down, and they were destroyed in place, tank by BMP fighting vehicle by artillery piece. The bombardment that lasted from the night of March 25 through the morning of March 27 was one of the fiercest, and most effective, in the history of warfare.[95]

Lieutenant General Daniel P. Leaf, US Air Force, worked directly with General McKiernan to coordinate the effort. General Moseley observed: "The strikes on those formations have been devastating and have been decisive in breaking them up."[96] On 5 April, he commented, "I'll tell you up front that our sensors show that the preponderance of the Republican Guard divisions that were outside of Baghdad are now dead." Employing primarily precision weapons (sixty-eight percent), the Air Force demonstrated a capability only glimpsed in Operation Desert Storm: the ability to rapidly destroy enemy armor forces in detail.[97] The Air Force's attacks sped up and facilitated the attack of ground forces into Baghdad.

The Iraqis also facilitated their own rapid defeat. As in the first war, Iraqi generals proved incompetent. Saddam Hussein and his senior leaders failed to develop a coherent, integrated defensive system. Given the time and manpower available, the Iraqis could have constructed an in-depth defense that attrited coalition forces as they advanced towards Baghdad. One embedded reporter wrote:

> In this war Iraq had a choice of weapons—and it chose badly. The Iraqis had mortars and lucrative

targets at every road junction, yet they rarely fired, perhaps from fear of the counterbattery radars. . . . The Iraqis had ample weapons, but they did not have the will to use them. The plain fact was that in the countryside the Iraqi army had not consistently shown up to fight. . . . Overall it had been a paramilitary fight, meaning the Iraqis lacked military organization. Without such organization, a force cannot defend a city. Contrary to the fears of senior American staffs overseeing the battle, the Iraqi military wasn't digging in to defend Baghdad.[98]

Saddam Hussein also had interior lines. He should have been able to move his forces faster than the coalition. However, senior Iraqi leadership may have intentionally ceded the conventional war, in preparation for the unconventional war.

The halt enabled the men of the 3rd ID and 1st Marine Division who had been on the move almost continuously since the 20th to get a bit of rest, perform necessary maintenance, and reload and refit. While the halt was controversial, and there was some friction between the Army and Marine Corps over its length, it was a prudent move. During the halt, the Army and Marines secured their supply line, consolidated forces, and cleared up troubled areas along their route of march. Had the much-anticipated battle for Baghdad actually taken place, these actions would have proven critical for continuous operations.

On 31 March, the 3rd ID and 1st Marine Division continued the advance north. Bing, who accompanied the Marines, characterized Marine operations:

Instead of [orders] to seize the city, the verbal order from the Coalition Force Land Component Commander (CFLCC) was to conduct raids into Baghdad. This was prudent for the Army's Fifth Corps to the west, which had tanks but few infantry. With tanks and perhaps four times as many infantry (6,000 dismounted riflemen), however, raids back and forth across a war-damaged bridge did not make sense to I MEF and 1stMarDiv. The Marines had come to Baghdad to seize and liberate it, not to lay siege to it. So the MEF divided East Baghdad into 36 zones, designated "targets of interest" in each zone, and sent the three regiments across the bridge with

orders to "raid" from one target to the next until they occupied all the zones.[99]

Bing's words indicate that the orders of the senior Army commander were for the most part ignored—a practice that went back to World War II.

On 4 April, elements of the 3rd ID moved to secure Saddam International Airport just outside the city. The following day, the 3rd ID conducted probing attacks, or what Franks called "thunder runs," into Baghdad.[100] The lead elements fought through a series of ambushes, but found no significant organized resistance and no major armored formations. David Zucchino, an embedded reporter with the 3rd ID, in his narrative, *Thunder Run*, described the actions of a mechanized company:

It seemed to him [the company commander] presumptuous to invade a hostile metropolis of 5 million people ... without a detailed breakdown of enemy forces and defense. . . . Even so, the first thunder run had given Conroy and his men a certain level of confidence, and they believed their tanks and Bradleys could blow through the city center the same way they had blown past the Iraqi defense. . . .

The advance of the Marine Corps may have motivated these innovative tactics. They may have also been a function of the lack of respect for the Iraqi Army, the experience in fight thus far, and pressure from the CENTCOM/Rumsfeld to keep going as fast as possible. Still, thunder runs were bad tactics. Zucchino continued:

Conroy was still uncertain what to expect inside the city, though he was not particularly surprised when he spotted two Iraqi armored personnel carriers just beyond an overpass. They were backing up and turning around, trying to get in position to fire on the approaching convoy. The carriers— they were Russian-made BMPs—were outfitted with 105mm short-barrel guns, which fired skinny little rounds that were not capable of penetrating an Abram's armor but could disable a tank if they struck in the rear engine compartment. Conroy ordered his gunner to hit one of the BMPs with a main gun round. Then he radioed back and told a tank commander from his third platoon to take care of the other one. The gunners squeezed the trigger before the BMPs could turn around. The vehicles burst into flames. Their ammunition racks ignited and their turrets popped off—a spectacular show of exploding metal brought a round of cheers from the crews.[101]

The experience of another mechanized company went as follows:

Cyclone Company had been at the circle for just five minutes when a white car streaked across the bridge.... Barry could see three men inside. One of them was pointing a machine gun out a window. Barry gave the order to fire. Three tanks opened up, including Barry's own Abrams. The sedan caught fire and crashed. Two men climbed out and both went down, killed instantly by coax [machine gun]. Thirty seconds later, a white Jeep Cherokee sped down the bridge span. Coax and. 50-caliber rounds shattered the windshield. The Cherokee exploded. The fireball was huge—so big that Barry was certain the vehicle had been loaded with explosives.... This was a suicide car.

And they kept coming—sedans, pickups, a Chevy Caprice, three cars in the first ten minutes, six more right after that. The tanks destroyed them all. It was incomprehensible. Barry kept thinking: *What the hell is wrong with these people?* They were trying to ram cars into tanks. It was futile—absolutely senseless. It was like they *wanted* to die, and as spectacularly as possible. Barry hated slaughtering them. And that's what it was—slaughter.

The battles, while dangerous, were extremely one sided, and some soldiers were reluctant to kill Iraqi suicide fighters. They simply had no other option. The anticipated Stalingrad-like battle for Baghdad never took place. While a number of intense close quarter firefights took place, resistance was uncoordinated and relatively light. One soldier noted, "By the end of April 8 and the beginning of April 9, we were sort of looking at each other as if to say 'Is that it?'"

On 9 April, the Marines entered Firdos (Paradise) Square, where newly "liberated" Iraqis were endeavoring to pull down an enormous statue of Saddam Hussein. The Marines, using a tank recovery vehicle, assisted the Iraqis. These impressive scenes were shown around the world, and marked the end of major conventional combat operations in Iraq. (Arab news sources argued that the entire event was staged with an American and a "pre-Saddam Hussein Iraqi flag" on hand for the numerous assembled television cameras and reporters.) Still, the conventional war was fought with professionalism, valor, and determination. The British military historian John Keegan wrote:

Americans had achieved a pace of advance unprecedented in history, far outstripping that of the Germans towards Moscow in the summer of 1941.... The campaign thus far had achieved extraordinary results, the farthest advance at speed over distance ever recorded and the disintegration of an army twice the size of the invading force. Superior equipment and organization supplied many of the reasons why such success had been won. Besides material and technical factors, however, moral and psychological dimensions had been at work. Daring and boldness had played parts in the campaign as significant as dominance in the air, greater firepower or higher mobility on the ground.[102]

The Marine Corps attributed its success to its maneuver warfare doctrine, which was based on a decentralized system of command, the commander's intent, and mission statement orders. The Army's assessment was similar. Rumsfeld could claim it was his doctrine, and Franks his plan. However, the major reasons for the low casualties and successful conventional campaign lie not in the actions of the US, but in the social, political, military, and cultural dimensions of Iraq.

The US and UK fought a state, an individual and his personal army, not a culturally cohesive people, not a nation. As a consequence, the Iraqi people, and for the most part the Iraqi Army, did not show up to fight. Keegan later wrote: "Saddam's utter collapse shows this has not been a real war."[103] He concluded that in the ground war US and UK forces fought, "the Ba'ath Party militia, effectively a sort of political Mafia, equipped with nothing more effective than

BAGHDAD

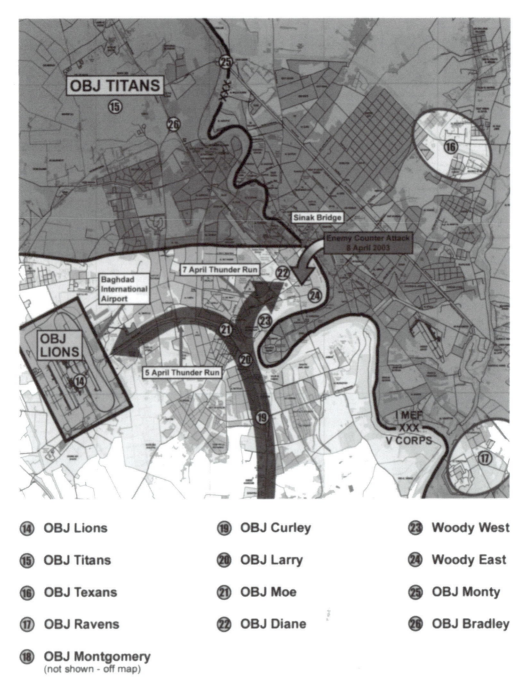

⑭	**OBJ Lions**	⑲	**OBJ Curley**	㉓	**Woody West**
⑮	**OBJ Titans**	⑳	**OBJ Larry**	㉔	**Woody East**
⑯	**OBJ Texans**	㉑	**OBJ Moe**	㉕	**OBJ Monty**
⑰	**OBJ Ravens**	㉒	**OBJ Diane**	㉖	**OBJ Bradley**
⑱	**OBJ Montgomery** (not shown - off map)				

Fig 17.6 Operation Iraqi Freedom, Thunder Runs into Baghdad.

hand-held weapons." While this is an overstatement, it is a fact that Saddam Hussein lacked the support of the Iraqi people and that for the most part the Iraqi Army did not fight for him. The people and army were not vested in his government or political system. In addition, Arab armies were incapable of generating the combat power of Western armies in conventional operations, and years of neglect had eroded the

Iraqi war machine to the point that much of it was inoperable. The Iraqi Army lacked sufficient confidence in its equipment and weapons to stand and fight. The psychological warfare campaign, while brilliantly conceived and well executed, worked in large part because of the divisions in Iraqi society, because Saddam Hussein did not have the loyalty of most of his regular Army, and because Saddam Hussein's brutality and injustice had destroyed his legitimacy and the legitimacy of the state.

The precision bombing campaign worked because it did not alienate the Iraqi people from the coalition. It worked by keeping the people divided and not creating the unity of purpose that maintained Britain in 1940 and the Vietnamese in the 1960s. The bombing campaign was not sufficiently painful to cause the Iraqi people to unite in opposition to the United States. The Special Forces campaign worked in much the same way. By preserving Iraqi infrastructure and limiting damage, the coalition forces worked to keep the Iraqi people from becoming alienated. The air and ground components also produced outstanding results by fighting only those forces that decided to fight. What, then, is the verdict on the Rumsfeld doctrine? Did his doctrine prove its effectiveness in a conventional war? Yes and no.

In every war since the Vietnam War, the US has fought forces vastly inferior to its own. But, more importantly, the US has fought individual dictators—Manuel Noriega, Saddam Hussein, and others—or fought wars in which American ground forces were not deployed or decisively engaged (Kosovo and Somalia).[104] The outcomes of these conventional struggles were never in doubt. Hence, against states and dictators the Rumsfeld doctrine has proven effective. Still, in the case of Operation Iraqi Freedom, Rumsfeld took significant risk. In hindsight, either the Army or the Marine forces alone could have produced a victory, but had just the Republican Guard and Special Republican Guard fought loyally and tenaciously, and had Saddam Hussein's system produced a few good generals, they could have made the US pay dearly for Baghdad. The "Rumsfeld doctrine" would *not* have worked against a unified nation-state fighting a more total war. Still, the conventional war was an impressive victory for US forces.

18.

THE SECOND PERSIAN GULF WAR: OPERATION IRAQI FREEDOM II, THE COUNTERINSURGENCY WAR, 2003–2010

In the postinvasion political debate much has been made of the lack of intelligence about WMD. The WMD assessments were clearly wrong. *But the far more important error was in understanding the political and social circumstances inside Iraq.* Leaders in the White House and especially the Department of Defense were extraordinarily ignorant about Iraq. They were either unaware of their own ignorance or decided that knowledge was unimportant and could be supplied by the best guesses of select Iraq exiles—predominantly the Iraqi National Congress (INC), which was built by and around Ahmad Chalibi (who also declared confidently that WMD stocks were in Iraq). *There was far better information within the intelligence community on internal Iraqi dynamics.* However, the political leaders did not solicit the intelligence community for deeper analysis on such matters. Administration leaders pressed the intelligence community for information on Iraq's WMD and links to al-Qaeda, but did not ask about the viability of imposing external opposition groups on Iraq. In fact, the CIA was explicitly blocked from participating in postconflict planning.[1]

—Charles Duelfer, *Hide and Seek*, 2009

Postconflict planning has historically been a function of headquarters at echelons above corps, and continuing problems with more recent operations are at least partly attributed to the generally small scale of American interventions. Difficulties also result from the fact that for at least the latter half of the 20th century, US military leaders and planners focused predominantly on winning wars, not on the peacekeeping or nation building that comes afterward. The unpleasant result of the war in Southeast Asia magnified this shortcoming, as the services developed doctrines, force structure, and attitudes designed to fight major conventional war and avoid another experience like Vietnam. But national objectives can often be accomplished only after the fighting has ceased; a war tactically and operationally "won" can still lead to strategic "loss" if transition operations are poorly planned or executed. The ironic truth about Phase IV operations is that the American military would rather not deal with them . . .

—Conrad Crane, "Phase IV Operations," 2004

On 1 May 2003, President Bush declared an "end of major hostilities." The announcement was premature. He and Secretary of Defense Rumsfeld had badly misjudged the situation in Iraq, which degenerated into an insurgency war (OIF II). While the conventional war in Iraq (OIF) was unnecessary, the insurgence war that emerged in its aftermath could have been avoided. In the early stages of the insurgency there were opportunities to contain it.

The counterinsurgency war can best be understood by dividing it into three phases, each distinguished by shifts in strategy and changes in leadership. From June 2003 to June 2004, during OIF II, Phase one, the insurgency emerged and grew while Lieutenant General Ricardo Sanchez was Commander of the Combined Joint Task Force 7 (CJTF-7). Phase two, the US counterinsurgency war to stabilize Iraq, prevent civil war, destroy terrorists, and build Iraqi security forces, took place under the leadership of General George William Casey, Jr., commander of the Multi-National Force-Iraq (MNF-I) from July 2004 to January 2007. The final phase of the counterinsurgency war, known as "the surge," took place under the leadership of General David Petraeus, commander of the MNF-I from January 2007 to September 2008; and General Raymond Odierno, commander MNF-I from September 2008 to September 2010. In the final months of Odierno's command, President Barak Obama ended Operation Iraqi Freedom, initiating the phased withdrawal of US forces, and giving the democratically elected Iraqi government primary responsibility for the security and stability of Iraq.

Numerous arguments have been advanced to explain the emergence of the insurgency in Iraq. All of them point to failures in US Phase IV, post-conflict operations. Consider the following explanations: the American sense of moral righteousness; the Army's efforts to forget the experience of the Vietnam War; the Army's reluctance to implement nation-building strategies and campaigns; the Army's offensive-oriented, "can do" culture; the "de-professionalization" of the Army; the services' intense, almost singular focus on Phase III Conventional Combat Operations, which caused them to fail to adequately plan for and resource post-conflict operations; poor, unimaginative leadership; erroneous assumptions about the Iraqi people welcoming the Americans as liberators; faulty intelligence about the state of Iraqi infrastructure and oil industry; ignorance of Iraqi culture and social structure and the sectarian divisions that separated the peoples of Iraq; and ignorance of the psychological damage to the Iraqi people caused by decades of brutal leadership under Saddam Hussein. All these and numerous other arguments have been advanced.[2] However, the fundamental problem was a familiar one: *too few soldiers on the ground to do what was necessary*.

We never get it completely right. There are always unanticipated and unknown factors that influence the conduct and outcome of military operations, and the more foreign the culture, the greater the *friction*. However, with sufficient numbers of soldiers, insufficient knowledge, poor intelligence, and poor planning can be overcome. Leaders have the flexibility and opportunity to react to problems when they

have sufficient numbers of soldiers on the ground. With several more divisions, the looting and chaos in Iraqi cities, particularly Baghdad, could have been stopped. With more soldiers, Iraqi stocks of weapons and ammunition could have been located and guarded. With more soldiers, the government buildings, infrastructure, and priceless artifacts in Iraqi museums could have been protected and saved from destruction. With several more divisions the presence of US forces would have been felt in the major cities. The people of Iraq would have felt safe in their homes and business, and the terrorists, criminals, and other wrongdoers would have felt threatened and uncertain. With more soldiers, the US could have established positive control, and business activities could have resumed almost immediately. Governmental workers could have returned to their offices and gone about the business of running the country. With more soldiers on the ground the story of Iraq could have been very different. Paul Bremer, Bush's lead man in Iraq, concluded: "In my view the Coalition's got about half the number of soldiers we need here and we run a real risk of having this thing go south on us."[3] Bremer came to this conclusion too late to stop the emergence of the insurgency. In hindsight he accepted the findings of the RAND report, which concluded, "The population of Iraq today is nearly 25 million. That population would require 500,000 troops on the ground to meet a standard of 20 troops per thousand residents. This number is more than three times the number of foreign troops now deployed to Iraq."[4]

This recommended troop strength was a force larger than the entire regular Army of the United States on 9/11. These forces did not all have to be Americans. They could have been Canadian, French, German, and/or Japanese allied forces. However, without them, military, civilian, and political leaders had little or no ability to influence the situation as it deteriorated. All they could do was watch in horror as looters, criminals, and later terrorists caused chaos and destroyed the infrastructure of the country. All they could do was watch helplessly as sectarian violence started to reshape the neighborhoods of Baghdad and other cities. The millions of traumas caused by post-conflict fighting will influence Iraqis socially and politically for decades to come, and will slow the progress towards reconciliation and a stable, constitutional democracy.

The failure to learn and adapt also damaged the US war effort. After the threats were identified, the US failed to react, failed to rapidly redeploy soldiers and marines to Iraq in sufficient numbers to stop the bleeding and reverse the situation. Military and civilian leaders in the Bush Administration seemed incapable of understanding what they were looking at. Bush, Cheney, and Rumsfeld, like Johnson and McNamara, did not understand the war they committed the United States to fight. Hence, for more than a year after the insurgency started in Iraq, the Bush Administration insisted that the Army and Marine Corps were not fighting an insurgency war.

While the Army and CENTCOM deserve some blame for the numerous failings for OIF, the Bush Administration has earned the lion's share.[5] It adopted an old idea in a new package. Network-centric warfare, war with advanced technologies, primarily airpower, was supposed to win the war without committing large numbers of ground troops. Consider the words of General Anthony Zinni:

> The Bush administration came in with an idea of transforming the military into something lighter, smaller, quicker—whatever. The bill payer was going to be heavy ground units [Army divisions]. Nobody listened to the military commanders in chief.... We are now involved in culture wars. We do not understand the cultures in this region of the world.... I have spent the past 15 years in this part of the world. And every time I hear people in D.C. talk about this region, they demonstrate they do not have a clue....[6]

Secretary of Defense Rumsfeld insisted on going in light, with a small force, in part to prove the new level of effectiveness caused by the RMA and the transformation of US forces. For personal, political, and ideological reasons, Rumsfeld was incapable of employing the most knowledgeable and experienced people for the reconstruction of Iraq. Finally, Rumsfeld's vision for post-war Iraq was built on erroneous assumptions that produced horrendous decisions. The assumption that Americans would be welcomed as liberators, the assumption that the Iraqi regular Army was unnecessary, the assumption that the country could be run effectively *without* the Ba'athist bureaucracy of Saddam Hussein, the assumption that the Iraqi infrastructure needed only minor repairs, the assumption that the war would pay for itself, the assumption that the Sunnis and the Shias would not start killing each other with the removal of Saddam Hussein—these and other incorrect assumptions destroyed the ability of the US to meet the expectations of the people of Iraq, and hence, to gain their support. These assumptions produced decisions that decimated the government bureaucracy, destroyed the security forces, and dumped hundreds of thousands of angry people into an economy that could not employ them. These numerous bad

Fig 18.1 Vice President Dick Cheney talking with Secretary of Defense Donald Rumsfeld.

Fig 18.2 General Tommy Franks.

decisions facilitated the growth of the insurgency. As a consequence, "the coalition of the willing" made its task much more difficult and costly, and diminished the probabilities of creating a stable, democratic, capitalist Iraq that could serve as a model for other Arab states.

Because political leaders are mostly ignorant of the nature and type of the wars they decide to fight, they are absolutely incapable of explaining those wars to the American people, and hence, incapable of sustaining their support. However, since in 1973 the American people removed themselves from the conduct of the wars of the United States, their support was not as critical as it was during the Vietnam War. Still, the Bush and Rumsfeld vision of war was culturally regular. They believe that a revolution in military affairs had transformed the American conduct of war. They believed that with advanced technology and new doctrine they could dictate the course of the war and the peace that followed. They believed significant ground forces were unnecessary. They were wrong.

The Media, Public Opinion, and War

In twenty-first-century wars the media is of greater strategic importance to the outcome of war than ever before. New forms of electronic communication and imaging technologies have made it possible for any individual with a cell phone, whether civilian or soldier, to capture a moment and transmit it at the speed of light. With access to the Internet and email, anyone can send and distribute information, documents, maps, graphics, photographs, sounds, and other materials almost instantly to millions of people. Current affairs websites, "blogs," Twitter, Facebook, YouTube, and other online social media and services connect people as never before. They provide new means for the public to get and distribute information. They provide means for unified action and means for people to assemble and act in hours. With these new technologies and information outlets, public opinion can be transformed in hours, and social movements initiated in days. In February 2011, a "revolution" took place in Egypt that ousted the 30-year government of President Hosni Mubarak. Twitter, Facebook and other online sources made it possible for the movement to spread in days. In addition, it is no longer just the American media that is of strategic importance. Al Jazeera, Abu Dhabi TV, and other Arab news networks have influenced Arab public opinion in ways that have damaged the US efforts in Iraq.

The strategic importance of the media was demonstrated by the Abu Ghraib prison scandal in 2004, during which American soldiers were captured on camera torturing and abusing Iraqi prisoners.[7] Thousands of images were digitized and flashed around the world, showing up on the Internet and on the pages of Arab newspapers. The images, admittedly reprehensible, angered Arabs, reinforcing their views of the Bush Administration, the armed forces of the United States, and Americans. These images damaged the prestige and credibility of the US, supported the claims of terrorists and insurgents, and hurt the war effort in Iraq.

The Pentagon, armed forces, CENTCOM, and major subordinate commands now recognize the strategic importance of the media, and seek to use the media as a resource to facilitate the achievement of military and political objectives. In February 2003, the Pentagon created Public Affairs Guidance for the conduct of Operation Iraqi Freedom: "The Department of Defense policy on media coverage of future military operations is that media will have long-term, minimally restrictive access to US air, ground, and naval forces through embedding."[8] And FM 3–61, Public Affairs Fundamentals, states: "Public Affairs fulfills the Army's obligation to keep the American people and the Army informed and helps establish the conditions that lead to confidence in America's Army and its readiness to conduct operations in peacetime, conflict and war."[9] The White House and Pentagon had to the sell the war, and the services were still in the business of selling themselves.

In OIF, the Pentagon modified an old system to fit the new realities of war. It developed a system of "embedded reporters," journalists who accompanied soldiers into battle. This was not new. Gordon Gaskill, a war correspondent during World War II, who landed at Omaha Beach with the Big Red One on 6 June 1944, provided Americans with one of the most vivid accounts of the battle.[10] What was new was the attachment of reporters to units for the duration of the movement or operation. Because more recent wars have involved considerable movement, and because the battlefields are hostile, reporters can't move around unescorted. Too often there is no "frontline." For a given operation, news agencies requested access to operational units. Their selected, trained reporters registered with a given service (Army, Marine Corps, Air Force, and Navy), and were then attached to a unit. Foreign reporters were also embedded with American forces.

By almost all assessments, the media policies of the Pentagon during conventional operations in Iraq produced outstanding results for the armed forces, the media, and the American people.[11] Lieutenant General James Conway, USMC, responding to the question, "What is your opinion of OIF media coverage in general, and the embedded reporter concept?" stated: "I would give 'OK' grades to both—especially the embedded concept. I think that's a home run and the wave of the future."[12] An assessment from the perspective of Army Special Forces concluded:

> Some of the most exciting news reported during Operation Iraqi Freedom has been the result of the Department of Defense program to embed media with frontline troops, including special operations forces (SOF). Embedding has allowed reporters and camera crews to not only record

operations and events, but to some extent experience the action themselves. Such intimacy has given the media and the public new insight into the lives and the trials of SOF personnel. The close cooperation has also provided leaders and troops with the opportunity to learn how best to work with the media and turn the attention to their advantage.[13]

These views were a long way from the attitudes and beliefs about reporters and the media that dominated the military in the wake of the Vietnam War. But did they represent a fundamental change in the relationship between the military and the media, or was it a temporary change based on almost complete success in the conventional campaign? For the most part, things went well in the conventional war. The enemy fought a bit, but then "melted away." The conventional war was dramatic and short. American casualties were low. The statue episode, during which Marines helped Iraqis pull down a statue of Saddam Hussein, received worldwide coverage and made Americans feel good and optimistic. Conway and others optimistically predicted, "there will be a US commitment for at least another year or two. I don't think it's going to be all that long."[14]

The happy times and the gloating were short lived. When the insurgency war started, the Bush Administration, Pentagon, and Army started complaining about the media. They complained that the good being done was being overlooked, that all the successes achieved such as opening schools, restoring electricity and water, and so on, went almost unreported, but every insurgency attack, every suicide bomber, every roadside bomb, every dead American was reported with great alacrity. A few months after the conventional war, Rumsfeld complained:

> I picked up a newspaper today and I couldn't believe it. I read eight headlines that talked about chaos, violence, unrest. . . . And here is a country that's being liberated, here are people who are going from being repressed and held under the thumb of a vicious dictator, and they're free. And all this newspaper could do, with eight or 10 headlines, they showed a man bleeding, a civilian, who they claimed we had shot—one thing after another. It's just unbelievable how

people can take that away from what is happening in that country.[15]

An Army battalion commander lamented:

The international media is a powerful tool for the insurgents, who rely on spectacular attacks that may kill a limited number of people but will splash blood all over the television screens. Our work with city councils and our efforts to rebuild the infrastructure of Iraq and promote democracy, however, have gone largely untold, and that is what the majority of our soldiers are doing.[16]

The happy times were an aberration, a function of something that rarely happens in war: the enemy, at least temporarily, quit. The cultural norms of neither the military nor the media had changed significantly. Ultimately, however, the White House and Pentagon had little to be concerned about. By the summer of 2005, the deaths of thirty or forty Iraqis and two or three American soldiers or marines were no longer front-page news. The professional Army and Marine Corps were fighting the insurgency war, causing little or no disturbance to the lives of most Americans. And although public support for the war declined, and a majority of Americans came to believe that they had been misled about the causes of the war, it meant little to the course and conduct of the war, and the soldiers and marines fighting it.

*   *   *   *   *

The Department of Defense National Media Pool system, developed in 1985, was employed in OIF. However, the system was not employed consistently. It had been modified, contracted, or expanded for every war. In Operation Enduring Freedom in Afghanistan, media access to the fighting was limited. In OIF, the Bush Administration was considerably more confident, and hence, access was greatly expanded. The system for dealing with the media is less a function of established regulations and principles, and more a function of the disposition and attitudes of the Administration at the time of the conflict.

Still, in OIF, the press enjoyed greater access to operational units than in previous post-Vietnam wars. Once the conventional war ended, reporters had the freedom to move around Baghdad and other cities. However, as the insurgency grew in strength, it became more dangerous for reporters to move independently, and they did so at their own risk. Several reporters were kidnapped and executed by insurgents. According to the International News Safety Institute, fifty-one media workers were killed in Iraq by August 2004, after seventeen months of war. In January 2006 that number had risen to sixty-one.[17]

The system of embedding reporters had unanticipated results. It created a subtle psychological effect that tended to diminish the ability of reporters to remain objective. They were welcomed into units with young Americans trying to do a dirty job. They developed relationships with those soldiers and marines. They bonded with the men of the unit, possibly developing the group identity. A PAO captain wrote:

According to protocol, the reporters were the equivalent of majors and, therefore, outranked me. I tried my best not to yell at them, but they regularly infuriated me. They brought way too much gear. They had to be told over and over to close the doors of their work tent at night to maintain light discipline. They apparently were incapable of picking up after themselves. The list goes on. In spite of all of this, I liked them.[18]

This response was mutual. And these relationships made it difficult for many reporters to report objectively. General Franks, in briefing a few days into the war, stated: "I am a fan of it [embedding reports]." He indicated that it was good for the world to see the professionalism and humane conduct of American soldiers and marines. He believed that the system would help create a favorable public opinion environment, possibly gaining support for the war.

The embedding system made worse the tunnel vision effect that frequently occurs when covering tactical operations. Reporters only saw the actions of one or two units. Thus, they could report only on the tactical situation they witnessed. Media networks patched these vignettes together to form a larger picture. Still, it was a tactical view of the war, and at most, an operational view, resulting in an overall skewed record of events for the home viewer. The strategic picture was not visible at the unit level. The system of embedded reporters gave the services considerable control over what reporters saw. This does not mean reporters were manipulated. News agencies provided some of their reporters with elaborate vehicles and trained technicians to transmit directly from the field. As a result, American viewers could watch operations happen almost in real time from their living rooms.

The strategic situation was put out to reporters several times daily from the media operations centers (MOCs) in the theater and at the Pentagon briefing room. Since Operation Desert Storm, the services and Pentagon have been aggressive in getting their story out, recognizing that ambiguity creates opportunities for misunderstanding. Secretary of Defense Rumsfeld became a regular on national television, and somewhat of a celebrity as he cowed reporters with his acerbic, matter-of-fact manner. CENTCOM and the Pentagon actively fed the media, endeavoring to anticipate every possible question and respond to them before they were asked. Media operation centers were focal points for the news media during military operations.

*   *   *   *   *

Tactically and operationally, the performance of the press has improved since the dark days of the Vietnam War. Strategically, however, in 2002 and 2003 the media did an extraordinarily poor job, worse than its horrendous performance during the Tet Offensive in 1968. Instead of questioning and investigating the need for a second war in Iraq, it sold war to the American people. The US, in essence, went to war based on an unsubstantiated claim that Iraq had weapons of mass destruction. This unsubstantiated story was sold to Americans by the media. The press never seriously challenged the claim or tried to substantiate it. It accepted and repeated the claims made loudly and frequently by President Bush and Vice President Cheney that Iraq had nuclear capabilities and had worked with terrorist organizations. Reports that there were no weapons of mass destruction in Iraq went almost unreported.[19] The question of what constituted weapons of mass destruction was rarely asked. (Chemical weapons, which are not WMDs, were lumped together with nuclear weapons. There is no comparison in the destructive power of these

weapons.) By the fall of 2002, the Bush Administration and the media had convinced a staggering sixty-nine percent of the American people that Saddam Hussein was responsible for the 9/11 attacks on the US, with no real evidence to support this conclusion.[20] How did they come to believe this, and why was there no rebuttal?

In the last years of the twentieth century a new phenomenon emerged in the US. With the advent of the 24-hour cable news stations and "talk-radio," the White House, Pentagon, and State Department had limitless, gratis access to the public, and thus, the ability to manipulate and distort public opinion as never before. With this access, administrations had the ability to "spin" the story, the ability to make truths look like lies, and lies look like truths. "Talking heads" and so-called "authorities" told the story the way they wanted it understood, with little—and in some cases no—regard for the truth. They told their story frequently, aggressively, and through numerous media. By so doing, they were able to make people see things that were not there and to make people believe things for which there was no proof. If a story, even a lie, is told often enough and wrapped in the authenticity of government officials and the authority of respected news anchors, it can be turned into a fact accepted by the American people. The FOX News Network, owned and operated by the staunch conservative Rupert Murdoch, perfected these techniques, becoming an ally of the White House in its aggressive campaign to sell war to the American people.[21] Political parties infiltrated "news organizations" and found sympathetic producers who were willing to spin stories. Twenty-four-hour, cable news programs and "neoconservative" talk radio personalities aggressively sold the war in Iraq to the American people. But, this is only part of the problem.

The American people lack sufficient knowledge of the world outside of the United States to make informed decisions, and because they are no longer responsible for conducting the wars of the United States, they have little incentive to get informed. One student of the recent performance of the media wrote:

> It is difficult for Americans to make knowledgeable judgments about the existence of civilization-related clashes if the public knows little about the

civilization in question. Although the news media should not bear the entire burden of teaching the public about the world—the education system also has major responsibilities, which it consistently fails to fulfill—news coverage is a significant element in shaping the public's understanding of international events and issues. Aside from their occasional spurts of solid performance, American news organizations do a lousy job of breaking down the public intellectual isolation. The breadth of news coverage depends on news organizations' own view of the world, a view that is often too narrow . . . .[22]

According to media analyst Andrew Tyndall, in 1989, ABC, CBS, and NBC on their evening news shows presented 4,032 minutes of coverage about other countries. In 2000 that dropped to 1,382 minutes. With the war in Afghanistan, and the move towards war in Iraq, news coverage increased to 2,103 minutes in 2002.[23] Americans are too poorly informed to make judicious decisions on issues of war, and cannot depend on the media, or the American government, to provide them with honest information. Misinformation and ignorance are threats to democracy.

What Went Wrong: The Insurgency War[24]

Iraq, arguably "the cradle of civilization," had many attributes that should have made it a paradise on Earth. Rich in oil resources and fertile land, with an educated, talented population, Iraq had all the attributes necessary for advanced civilization, wealth, prosperity, and happiness. However, other factors can influence the ability of a state to succeed, such as its leadership, the system of government, military forces, cultural, religious, and ethnic divisions, and the "neighborhood" of state. Iraq, like many of the states of the Middle East, has not realized its potential, and its people have long been denied the fulfillment of their aspirations. Extensive physical and psychological damage, largely unseen by American political and military leadership, facilitated the descent into chaos and the rise of the insurgents and terrorists that hurt the US efforts to restore and transform Iraq.

Consider the condition of Iraq in 2003, when the second American invasion and subsequent occupation took place. Iraq's economy had been in a state of decline for decades. The Iran-Iraq War (1980–1988) and first Persian Gulf War (Operation Desert Storm, 1990–1991) had nearly bankrupted the country. The economy was based primarily on the production and exportation of oil. In 1991, Iraq produced 3.5 million barrels per day. During the thirteen years of UN sanctions, that dropped as low as 700,000 barrels per day and stopped completely during the invasion. Iraq was also agriculturally rich. The Tigris and Euphrates Rivers provided it with an abundance of arable land. However, by 2001, the embargo and drought had destroyed the ability of the country to feed its people. Twenty-two percent of the children in Iraq suffered from malnutrition. At maximum production, the electrical grids in Iraq could produce only fifty percent of the electricity needed. In potable water, Iraq was only capable of producing sixty percent of what its people required. One observer noted that: "the residents of Baghdad dumped 500 metric tons of sewage into the Tigris River every day, which went south to all the towns and cities down south for them to use as cooking water, drinking water, washing water, and that type of thing."[25] The greed, destructive policies, and wars of Saddam Hussein and the UN embargo that was the result, destroyed the ability of Iraq to sustain its people. What had taken decades to destroy could not be fixed overnight, not even with the power and attention of the United States.

There was also enormous, unseen psychological damage. The people of Iraq suffered from PTSD. Arguably, the entire region suffered from varying degrees of PTSD. Iraqis had been traumatized by years of brutal war and the brutality of Saddam Hussein. Deep ethnic and sectarian divisions also separated the people of Iraq. The Kurds and the Shia majority had long and deep roots of hate and anger against the Sunni regime of Saddam Hussein. The military strength of the loyal Republican Guard and the ruthless brutality of Saddam Hussein and his Ba'ath Party kept the hate and anger and the aspiration of the Kurds and Shias well buried. The American invasion uncovered and exposed these roots, resulting in explosions of emotion, the search for justice, revenge and retribution, and hopes for a new era of opportunities and a new and better way of life. The Iraqi people expected a great deal from America, the victor; they expected too much in fact. Bremer correctly assessed the situation this way:

> Every adult Iraqi had indeed been shocked and awed by the speed and precision with which the Coalition had crushed Saddam Hussein's vaunted Republican Guard and overthrown the Baathist regime. After such a display of super-power might, many expected us to work similar miracles once the tanks stopped rolling. If we could destroy individual artillery pieces at the height of a blinding sandstorm, why couldn't we provide reliable electric power or a steady supply of gasoline? And of course as each day passed with the heavily armed Coalition unable to cor-rect seemingly basic economic problems, the resolve and confidence of Iraqi insurgents and foreign terrorist increased.[26]

The people of Iraq expected the victors to fix their problems, to usher in a new era. The victors expected to go home. They had failed to recognize and understand the physical condition of Iraq and the psychological conditions of its people. As a conse-quence, a power vacuum emerged. In hindsight, Bush recognized that he and his advisors had badly mis-judged the situation: "There was one important con-tingency for which we had not adequately prepared. In the weeks after liberation, Baghdad descended into a state of lawlessness. I was appalled to see looters carrying precious artifacts out of Iraq's national museum and to read reports of kidnappings, murder, and rape." To explain this descent, Bush wrote:

> Part of the explanation was that Saddam had released tens of thousands of criminals shortly before the war. But the problem was deeper than that. Saddam had warped the psychology of Iraqis in a way we didn't fully understand. The suspicion and fear that he had cultivated for decades were rising to the surface.[27]

Long-held anger and hate were released by the American invasion. The reduction in American forces and the redeployment of American command struc-tures created opportunities for foreign terrorist groups, such as al-Qaeda, Shia insurgents, Sunni mili-tia, criminals, and individuals with grudges against their neighbors who happened to be of a different

sect. Add to this situation long disgruntled neighbors, the Shia of Iran and the Sunni of Syria, and enormous stocks of weapons and ammunitions that once belonged to the Iraqi Army and Republican Guard.

On 14 June 2003, newly promoted Lieutenant General Ricardo S. Sanchez took command of the V Corps, which was designated as Combined Joint Task Force 7 (CJTF-7), the senior-most military head-quarters in Iraq. Sanchez described his situation:

> We had gotten a few things up and running in Baghdad, but for the most part, everything around the country was still shut down. Some police stations were open but none were effective. Distribution of fuel and electricity was sporadic, at best. A food-rationing system was not yet in place. The political and economic sys-tems of the country were in dire straits. Banks were not open. Commerce was nonexistent. The judicial system had disappeared. There was no national government council yet established, and local councils were few and far between. The mission at hand was daunting.[28]

General Ricardo S. Sanchez received consider-able criticism for the emergence of the insurgency in Iraq during his watch. Some of it was deserved; most of it was not. Rumsfeld observed: "Sanchez would have to lead a force more than ten times that size [of an Army division], work with numerous coalition nations, and command a headquarters that he had never been trained or prepared to assume [in order to have been completely successful]."[29] The Army had selected its most junior Lieutenant General for the biggest job in the Army in 2003. Sanchez can be blamed for a lack of foresight, a failure to anticipate, and for a failure to adapt and respond quickly to the growing insurgency. However, even if he had perfect intelligence and foresight, he still lacked the resources, manpower, and authority to influence the situation dramatically. He also lacked the attention of, and access to, Rumsfeld and Bush that were required to refocus significant resources needed for security, sta-bility, and nation-building. In his book, *Wiser in Battle*, Sanchez responded to his critics. He was angry and disappointed at the outcome of his tenure as com-mander in Iraq (and possibly for not being selected for his fourth star). Sanchez could rightly argue that he was set up to fail: "With both CENTCOM and CFLCC leaving Iraq, V Corps was going to have to operate at the theater strategic level, for which it possessed no expertise, as well as the operational and tactical level across the country."[30] He further noted that:

> This abrupt turnaround was another monumental blunder that created significant strategic risk for America.... Whatever the reasons for CFLCC's disengagement, the foreseeable consequences were daunting. In country, we would no longer have the staff-level capacities for strategic- or operational-level campaign planning, policy, and intelligence. All such situational awareness and institutional memory would be gone with the departure of the best available Army officers who had been assigned to CFLCC for the ground war. The entire array of established linkages was dismantled and redeployed. Furthermore, V Corps had no coalition operations and ORHA/CPA-related staff capacity.... And finally, the loss of our strategic level national intelligence capacities would cause serious problems that would lead to part, to future problems at Abu Ghraib.[31]

Sanchez had significant shortages of critical, trained personnel: engineers for reconstruction, MPs to run prisons and interrogate prisoners, intelligence collection and analysis personnel, and logisticians. This shortage of trained personnel was one of the reasons frequently cited for the infamous Abu Ghraib prisoner abuse incident, which so badly damaged American credibility and efforts to earn the support of the Iraqi people.[32] There were also significant shortages of personnel trained in Arabic and people who understood the history and culture of Iraq. In addition, according to Jay Garner, the man initially selected to lead the civilian occupation of Iraq, there was no reconstruction strategy: "I'm going to tell you, there's no strategy for Iraq. There was never one when I was there, and I haven't seen one since I left. But, we have to have one."[33] While acknowledging that mistakes had been made, the Rumsfeld Pentagon disagreed with this assessment.[34] Wolfowitz, responding, stated: "There is a lot of talk that there was no plan.... There was a plan, but as any military officer can tell you, no plan survives first contact with

reality."[35] Some Army leaders agree with this assessment, but conclude that their plans and strategy were ignored by Rumsfeld, Wolfowitz, and other senior political leaders.[36]

Domestic politics and infighting within the Bush Administration hindered the development of a post-conflict strategy for Iraq. In the year prior to the invasion, the US Department of State organized a study group, *The Future of Iraq Project*, which included Iraqi exiles, to study post-Saddam Iraq. It produced a report that addressed "reconstruction of shattered infrastructure, the creation of free media, the preservation of antiquities, the administration of justice ..., the development of the moribund economy, and most important, the formation of a democratic government." The 2,500-page report represents the most comprehensive effort produced by the Bush Administration to prepare for the future of Iraq. Sanchez and Garner, however, never saw the report. Friction between the Powell Department of State and the Rumsfeld Department of Defense over jurisdiction and authority diminished the ability of the two branches of government to effectively work together.[37]

At the Pentagon, Douglas J. Feith, the Under-Secretary of Defense for policy, and head of the Office of Special Plans, was responsible for post-conflict planning.[38] Rajiv Chandrasekaran, an observer of the US Phase IV operations in Iraq, noted that:

> Feith's office conducted its postwar planning with utmost secrecy. There was little coordination with the State Department or the CIA, or even with post-conflict reconstruction experts within the Pentagon, and there was an aversion to dwelling on worst-case scenarios that might diminish support for the invasion. Feith's team viewed the mission as a war of liberation that would require only modest postwar assistance. They assumed the Iraqis would quickly undertake responsibility for running their country and rebuilding their infrastructure.[39]

Part of the justification for the war was that the reconstruction of Iraq would cost the American people almost nothing, because of the state's oil wealth. That justification for the war influenced planning, causing the selective use of intelligence and ultimately the development of unrealistic assumptions and expectations.

Retired Lieutenant General Garner, while agreeing to lead the post-conflict reorganization of Iraq under the direction of CENTCOM, which placed his organization under Lieutenant General David McKiernan, the commander of the CFLCC, had little authority to select and direct his team. Garner created and headed the Office of Reconstruction and Humanitarian Assistance (ORHA) to temporarily run and manage the affairs of Iraq.[40] ORHA consisted of three groups: humanitarian assistance, reconstruction, and civil administration.[41] ORHA worked with the CFLCC Phase IV planning team. Arguably, Garner's organization was also set up to fail. It had less than three months to prepare for operations in Iraq, and lacked the talent, information, and resources needed to succeed. USAID was available to assist in the planning, but this resource belonged to the Department of State, and hence, was not fully engaged. Feith noted that:

> ORHA's purpose was to serve as a team of expert assistants for Franks—an organized set of civilians to help him fulfill his post-Saddam duties. The ORHA staff would include officials who had been working on postwar planning in Washington over the last year or so. Their various agencies would assign them temporarily to the new office at the Pentagon; and, a few weeks later, the whole group would deploy to Kuwait, where they would prepare to move into Iraq as soon as circumstance permitted.

Feith insisted that: "ORHA was created to become part of CENTCOM and to help in Phase IV planning and operations, not to supplant it in any way."[42] But, the withdrawal of Army forces, particularly CFLCC, meant ORHA had to take on responsibilities far beyond its capacity.

ORHA lacked the resources and authority to achieve the objectives of the Bush Administration. It was plagued with personnel problems. Rumsfeld told Garner to fire some of the people he considered the most knowledgeable and talented, because they were from the Department of State.[43] Garner later stated that:

> my ... number one [problem], the infighting before I left between DoD and State Department. The warfare between Rumsfeld and Powell

permeated everything we did. Well, I fault Rumsfeld and Powell for that. I mean, they're big guys; they should not operate that way. But really, I fault Condoleeza Rice for that. . . . Her job is to get the two of them and say, "Hey, if you can't get along, then we're going to meet in the President's office before the sun sets in Washington." And to my knowledge she didn't do that.

Rice, in 2005, succeeded Powell as Secretary of State. In the in-fighting campaigns, Rumsfeld usually won. In the White House, he enjoyed the advice and support of his close friend Vice President Dick Cheney. Personal animus, political affiliations, party loyalty, interagency disagreements, and neoconservative ideological correctness insured that the best people and best ideas did not rise to the top. The Bush Administration was incapable of producing the best from America, because it insisted that significant parts of America were ineligible to participate.[44] Artificial limited war made it possible to ignore the traditions and ways of thinking and acting common in total wars.

While the early days of America's occupation of Iraq are considered a "fiasco" by most observers, there were some successes. People did not starve. There was no plague, no epidemics, and no genocide or mass murders. Garner delineated the priorities and successes of ORHA and the Army:

> The first one was to get the ministries back to a functioning level countrywide. The second was to pay salaries, nationwide—that's salaries to all the public servants, the police, and the army. Number three was to restore the police, the court and prison systems. Number four was to restore basic services to Baghdad. . . . Number five was to end the fuel crisis. I don't know if you remember that, but there was no fuel. All cooking in Iraq is done with propane, so we had to bring propane in. Plus, there wasn't gas to move vehicles around. . . . The sixth thing was to purchase the harvest. Now, the wheat was ready to harvest—the wheat, barley, and other things. So we needed to purchase all that and to also re-establish the food distribution system. We needed to install interim town councils in every city of 100,000 or more. That's 26 cities. And then, we needed to

meet the public health needs and avoid epidemics. And, by and large, we accomplished most of these priorities.[45]

Given the sectarian divisions and the hatred of the Ba'athists by the Kurds and Shia, there was a real threat for civil war and mass disorder. Sanchez and Garner deserve some credit for what did not happen. Still, Garner was soon out of a job, his organization disbanded.[46] Ambassador L. Paul Bremer III, who headed the Coalition Provisional Authority (CPA), arrived in Baghdad 12 May 2003 to replace him.[47] The CPA answered directly to the Pentagon and Rumsfeld. However, Bremer also had direct access to the President.[48] He was provided $18.4 billion and given primary responsibility for the stabilization and reconstruction of Iraq. His objective was "the development of the Iraqi Interim Authority, with the goal that it would exercise substantial authority as soon as possible."[49] Bremer did not command coalition forces, but he noted that, "the US Central Command ... had orders from the president and Rumsfeld to coordinate their operations with the CPA."[50] Bremer threw out significant parts of the plans and programs developed by Garner and the CFLCC planning team. For the most part he ignored his commanding general. Sanchez noted that he "refused to take any corrective actions," and "listened to us and walked away."[51] Sanchez further explained:

When Bremer communicated his plan back to Washington, people at the Department of Defense expressed some uneasiness about it, but everybody acquiesced to his wishes. At this point in time, it appeared to me that Washington was distancing itself from all things related to Iraq. No one was focusing, scrutinizing, or analyzing the impact of decisions that were coming out of CPA. Meanwhile, Ambassador Bremer was changing the entire political strategy of the coalition. And it became very clear to me that we were going to be stuck in Iraq for a much longer time than we had all anticipated.[52]

James Stephenson, former USAID Mission Director in Iraq, seconded this assessment, "it became evident early on that Ambassador Bremer was not receptive to advice and was actively hostile to any that went against his own judgment." Stephenson continued:

I do not fault Bremer alone for the spectacular mistakes made by the CPA, DOD, and White House.... He was not responsible for the generally poor quality of the personnel whom DOD hired for the CPA. I do fault him, however, for accepting their counsel, for arrogance and hubris that seemingly emboldened him to continue on a course that was so obviously misguided, and for ignoring fifty years of US experience in post-conflict nation building.[53]

In May Bremer issued three significant orders that damaged the ability of the coalition to stabilize Iraq. The first was for "de-Ba'athification," to remove the bureaucracy and administrators of Saddam Hussein who had been responsible for running the country. This meant the loss of institutional knowledge in the form of the people who understood how things worked. The second order formally dissolved the Iraqi Army and Ministry of Defense. This meant the elimination of Iraq's most important security forces. With these orders, Bremer in essence fired

Fig 18.3 President George W. Bush (right) and Ambassador L. Paul Bremer.

400,000 knowledgeable, experienced people, most of whom had no allegiance to Saddam Hussein, and put them into an economy that offered few other job opportunities. To explain the disbandment of the Iraqi Army, Bremer's top security advisor, Walter Slocombe, noted that there was no way to quickly weed out supporters of Saddam Hussein. He further noted that during the looting:

> They didn't just steal stuff that was not nailed down, they stole the toilet fixtures and they stole the pipes and the tile in the latrine. There was literally no place to feed anybody, no place to house them, no place for them to take care of essential bodily function. And as we build up the (new) Iraqi army, we're having to go around to old Iraqi military bases and at very considerable expense reconstruct them simply so as to have basic facilities.[54]

Sanchez noted, "In one fell swoop, Bremer had created a 60 percent unemployment rate and angered hundreds of thousands of people." The final Bremer order was to discard Garner's plan for putting Iraqis back in charge of Iraq at the local and political levels. Garner stated: "Then, on Friday, they brought in the Iraqi leadership group we had put together and they were told, 'We're the government here. You're not going to be the government. Go home.'" Garner concluded that: "So, on Saturday morning when we woke up, we had somewhere between 150,000 and 300,000 enemies we didn't have on Wednesday morning, and we had no Iraqi face of leadership to explain things to the Iraqi people. We began to pay significantly for those decisions."[55]

Bremer's assessment of this period differs in significant ways. He notes that the Iraqi Army and Ba'athist bureaucracy had in large part dissolved themselves during the invasion. Still, he issued the orders that disbanded institutions that he later had to recreate at considerable expense. Garner observed that:

> What happened, as you saw, months later the CPA began to try to rectify that. The first thing that happened ..., they put in the Committee of 25—they brought that back in order to have an Iraqi face in leadership. Then, later on, they

started a very slow but measured process of bring back elements of the army. And finally, a few months ago, they started bringing back some of the Baathists that they had de-Baathified.[56]

On 7 July General John P. Abizaid took command of CENTCOM. Abizaid, the son of Arab Americans, spoke Arabic and held a master's degree from Harvard in Middle East Studies. Less than two weeks after assuming command, he declared that the US was engaged in a guerrilla war with supporters of the former regime of Saddam Hussein and foreign Muslims extremists who had been recruited to fight for al-Qaeda and other terrorist organizations. By 31 October, a Sunni-based insurgency raged, 120 Americans had been killed, and 1,100 wounded. The primary weapons were improvised explosive devices (IEDs). By the end of the year, OIF had cost 450 American lives and 8,000 wounded.

There were many sources of the insurgency. Iraqi expectations from their "liberators" were much too high. The coalition forces' new enemies were lack of time, resources, and know-how. They also had to contend with ethnic and sectarian divisions within Iraq, the long hatred of the Ba'athist regime, Islamic fundamentalists, foreign terrorist organizations, and interference from Iran and Syria. Ancient ethnic and sectarian divisions and traditional rivalries long contained by military forces and the brutality of Saddam Hussein's regime were unleashed by the American invasion. Revenge, long sought by the majority Shia population and the Kurds against the Sunnis and Ba'athist Party of Saddam Hussein, was, to some degree, realized in the lawless environment created by the invasion. Terrorist groups from outside the country, including al-Qaeda, were able to cross the porous borders into Iraq to attack American forces, emplace improvised explosive devices, and exploit sectarian divisions to create a larger war. The criminal elements in Iraq were let loose by the ousted regime of Saddam Hussein to prey on the people, loot, and spread disorder. Iran, a natural ally to the Shia, was able to strengthen its position in Iraq, and supported the various Shia movements directed toward the formation of government and the creation of militia forces. Tens of thousands of unemployed and underemployed soldiers and government officials from the disbanded Iraqi Army and Ba'athist bureaucracy, and the prevalence of large stocks of weapons and ammunition looted from unsecured stocks, fed the insurgency. The de-Ba'athification of Iraq removed the institutional knowledge necessary to get the country up and running again. The lack of basic services angered and frustrated the Iraqi people. Islamic fundamentalist ideology coupled with Western arrogance, and ignorance of the situation, culture, and language, helped produce a protracted insurgency war.

On 14 December 2003, the fugitive Iraqi President Saddam Hussein was captured hiding in a "spider hole." Hopes that his capture would change the dynamic of the situation in Iraq were not realized.

The Multi-National Force-Iraq: New Leadership, New Strategy, New Commitment

On 2 March 2004, five bombs exploded in Iraqi cities, killing 250 people and wounding 500. A few weeks later in Fallujah, insurgents ambushed and killed four US contractors who worked for the private security firm Blackwater. Their bodies were mutilated and hung from a bridge. Next, Mahdi Army militia in Sadr City ambushed soldiers of the 1st Cavalry Division, killing 8 and wounding 60.[57] They took over key sections of An Najaf, Al Kut, and Karbala. In November, the Marines, supported by the Army, initiated the second battle for Fallujah.[58] The close-quarter, urban battle raged for seven weeks. The Marines secured the city, killing 14,000 insurgents. Ninety-five marines and soldiers were killed and another 1,000 wounded. Improvised explosive devices (IEDs) continued to take a heavy psychological and physical toll on US forces. In 2004, attacks rose to an average of forty to sixty incidents per day.[59] Throughout 2004 and 2005, violence in Iraq escalated. The Army and Marine Corps redeployed more soldiers and Marines to Iraq to fix what had gone wrong.

On 15 May 2004, Multi-National Force-Iraq (MNF-I) came into existence and CJTF-7 was deactivated. The mission of the new command was to:

Conduct offensive operations to defeat remaining noncompliant forces and neutralize destabilizing influences in Iraq in order to create a secure environment. [To] organize, train, equip, mentor, and certify credible and capable Iraqi security forces in order to transition responsibility for security from Coalition forces to Iraqi forces. Concurrently, [to] conduct stability operations to support the establishment of government, the restoration of essential services, and economic development in order to set the conditions for a transfer of sovereignty to designated follow-on authorities.[60]

On 1 July 2004, General George Casey assumed command of MNF-I from Lieutenant General Sanchez. Donald Wright and Timothy Reese in their book *On Point II*, noted that the creation of MNF-I and the appointment of General Casey:

showed DOD's commitment to providing the right mix of senior leadership, manpower, and other resources to the campaign in Iraq. The more robust structure and staffing of MNF-I subordinate commands that followed Casey's posting to Iraq were of particular importance. They gave the Coalition's new theater-strategic headquarters in Iraq the type of capacity and capabilities that CJTF-7 had never enjoyed.

Just two days prior to the change of command, the CPA was dissolved, and Iraq once again became a sovereign country under the authority of the Iraqi Interim Government. Ambassador John Dimitri Negroponte assumed responsibilities for American civilian leadership in Iraq on 30 June 2004. He worked closely with Casey to stabilize and save Iraq.

On 5 August, Casey issued a new strategy and doctrine for Army operations in Iraq:

In partnership with the Iraqi Government, MNF-I conducts full spectrum counter-insurgency operations to isolate and neutralize former regime extremists and foreign terrorists, and organizes, trains and equips Iraqi security forces in order to create a security environment that permits the completion of the UNSCR 1546 process on schedule.[61]

Casey sought to employ a "security force-centric" counterinsurgency doctrine. His objective was not to fight a Vietnam-style "insurgent-centric" war,

Fig 18.4 General George W. Casey (left).

not to focus primarily on finding and killing the enemy, and not to escalate the war with the deployment of more and more US forces. His objectives were to stabilize the country with deployed forces, build Iraqi security forces and governmental institutions as quickly as possible, and turn the war over to the Iraqis, i.e., *the Iraqiazation of the war*. With an all-volunteer force, the type of war fought in Vietnam was not possible. Hence, a third objective was to minimize the commitment of US Army forces, which Casey knew were overcommitted. Victory, in the classic sense of the word, was not an objective. In 2004, as the situation in Iraq continued to deteriorate, the Army started reorganizing for a protracted counterinsurgency war.

*   *   *   *   *

The new modular Army force made it possible for the Army to fight two protracted wars in Iraq and Afghanistan, without significantly expanding the size of the Army, or, more importantly, without calling on the American people to serve.[62] On 28 January 2004, Army Chief of Staff, General Peter J. Schoomaker, explained the new Army modular force to the House Armed Service Committee. Responding to Representative Ike Skelton, he stated:

> There's no question the Army is stressed.... What we are doing is trying to transform the Army simultaneously with meeting the security

commitments of the nation.... Right now I've been authorized by the Secretary of Defense to grow the Army by 30,000 people within the authority that he has under emergency powers, that he has under the law, Title 10. And to do that, to buy the opportunity to restructure the Army, which is what we're doing ... [We're] looking at modulizing the Army, standardizing it, developing an Army that's more lethal, more agile, more capable of meeting the current and future operating environment tasks ....[63]

Schoomaker outlined a fundamental change in the way the Army operated. Responding to Skelton's statement that, "My own view is that the solution lies more in the neighbor of 40,000 [additional soldiers], based upon testimony going back to 1995," Schoomaker stated:

> I'm adamant that that is not the way to go, that if we can structure the Army in a way through this temporary growth, and when we look for internal efficiencies ... we think we can get 10,000 spaces through military-to-civilian conversion. We think by stabilizing the Army, where we don't move the Army every two to three years on an individual basis, but we keep people in place, develop cohesive, stable units where spouses can work, where kids can go to school, where people can invest in homes and develop

equity, stabilize this force—it's better for the fighting force, it's better for the families, and it will increase our retention.[64]

Under this new modular Army force, the individual replacement system, employed in World War II, Korea, and Vietnam, passed into history. The new modular Army got rid of the last vestige of the citizen-soldier Army. The all-volunteer force created a military cluster. And although it was too small to do all that it was asked to do, the fact that it was a self-contained unit precluded the acrimonious national debate that characterized the Vietnam War. To make up for the resultant deficiencies in manpower, the Army reorganized itself. It civilianized thousands of jobs to get more deployable soldiers. It redeployed major units from Korea and Europe. It converted artillery units into MP units and got rid of air defense battalions. It deployed Reserve and National Guard forces in ways for which they were not designed. The Army also reorganized the National Guard. Schoomaker, in reference to the National Guard, told the committee: "we want to go from [the] 15 enhanced brigades that we have today to 22—increase their level of readiness . . . and increase their capability to become part of a broader rotation base. . . ." Schoomaker concluded, "[T]his is the biggest internal Army kind of restructuring we have done in 50 years."

Each of the Army's ten divisions was reorganized into four expeditionary brigade combat teams (BCTs), each with its own organic artillery, signal and reconnaissance, and engineering and sustainment units. There are three types of combined arms maneuver brigades: infantry, heavy (armor and mechanized infantry), and Stryker. These brigades replaced the division as the Army's basic building block. The intent was to make the Army more combat ready, adaptable, deployable, and sustainable. The new organization increased the number of regular Army deployable brigades from thirty-three to forty-three. These units were to train, deploy, fight, and then redeploy to the United States as cohesive combat teams. The new system greatly enhanced the combat effectiveness of the Army, and made it possible to rotate brigades into and out of Iraq, Afghanistan, and other parts of the world, rather than worry about losing individual soldiers, as in the old system. Divisional

headquarters became more like Corps headquarters. BCTs were attached and detached to the headquarters as needed. For example, the 82nd Airborne Division Headquarters could have attached heavy BCTs from the 1st Cavalry Division or the 1st Armor Division depending on their needs. The Army modular force also went a long way toward standardizing equipment and personnel. A unit deployed to Iraq accepted the equipment of the unit that was redeploying to the United States with little loss of momentum. The Army was also better able to tailor force for contingency operations and the needs of the geographic combatant commanders. Training was standardized at the national training centers. Under the old organization, each division had a unique table of organization and equipment. This meant that training had to be tailored to the units of each division that rotated through the centers. These types of inefficiencies were eliminated. The 3rd Infantry Division at the National Training Center at Fort Irwin, California, was the first unit to test the new organization. Following that, the rest of the active Army was transformed, and then the National Guard and Reserves, giving the Army more than 70 deployable BCTs.

* * * * *

On 30 January 2005, Iraq held its first free national election in fifty years. The Sunnis, for the most part, boycotted the election. Still the turnout was high, and the election remained a cause for optimism. Violence, however, continued to escalate. In the latter part of 2005, the Bush Administration outlined a new strategy for victory, and initiated a campaign to explain the war to the American people in an effort to halt their declining support for it. The fact that no weapons of mass destruction were ever found damaged the credibility of the Bush Administration. In a speech delivered on 12 December 2005, President Bush informed the American people that the US and Iraqi people had reached the "turning point" of the war. "There is still a lot of difficult work to be done," he stated, "But thanks to the courage of the Iraqi people, the year 2005 will be recorded as a turning point in the history of Iraq, the history of the Middle East, and the history of Freedom."

Again Bush's pronouncement was premature. The "turning point" had not yet been reached. The

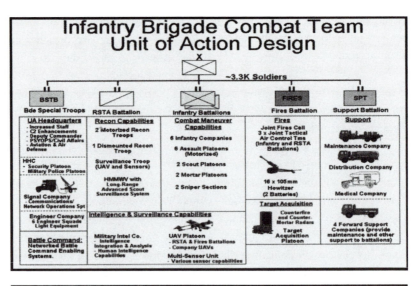

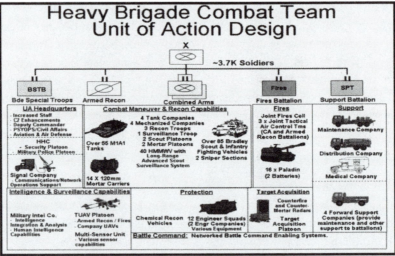

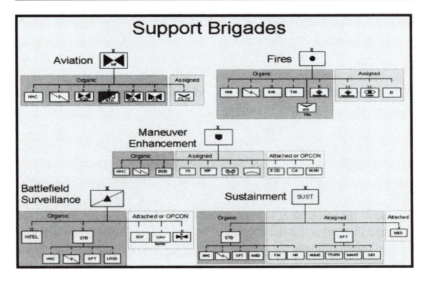

Fig 18.5 Army Brigade Combat Team.

war would require still more effort, more resources, more soldiers and marines, and many more sacrifices. Three days later in a primetime television address, Bush stated: "To retreat before victory would be an act of recklessness and dishonor, and I will not allow it." In Bush's vision, "victory" included: "Short term, Iraq is making steady progress in fighting terrorists, meeting political milestones, building democratic institutions, and standing up security forces. Long term, Iraq is peaceful, united, stable, and secure, well integrated into the international community, and a full partner in the global war on terrorism."[65] Bush still believed that Iraq could be the seed for the growth of democracy throughout the Middle East.[66] He went on to identify the enemies—the rejectionists, Saddamists, and terrorists—and to describe them and their status:

> The rejectionists are ordinary Iraqis, mostly Sunni Arabs who miss the privileged status they had under the regime of Saddam Hussein.... We believe that, over time, most of this group will be persuaded to support a democratic Iraq.... The Saddamist are former regime loyalists who harbor dreams of returning to power, and they are trying to foment anti-democratic sentiment amongst the larger Sunni community. Yet they lack popular support and, over time, they can be marginalized and defeated by the people and security forces of a free Iraq. The terrorists, affiliated with or inspired by al-Qaida, are the smallest, but most lethal, group. Many are foreigners.... They are led by a brutal terrorist named Zarqawi, al-Qaida's chief of operations in Iraq, who has stated his allegiance to Osama bin Laden.[67]

The terrorists, in Bush's view, were the most significant enemy and the major problem. However, the more basic problem was among the Iraqi people themselves. The ancient rivalry between the Shias, Sunnis, and Kurds threatened to fracture the country into three separate states. Terrorists sought to exploit these ancient rivalries to expand the war and their power. Bush outlined his assessment of the enemy's objectives:

> The terrorists' stated objective is to drive US and coalition forces out of Iraq and gain control of

that country and then use Iraq as a base from which to launch attacks against America, overthrow moderate governments in the Middle East and establish a totalitarian Islamic empire that reaches from Spain to Indonesia.

Bush emphasized that it was essential to take the offensive and fight the terrorists in Iraq. Otherwise, the US would have to fight them in other parts of the world and at home. Another enemy that Bush well understood, but did not mention, was the disaffection and the alienation of the Iraqi people. Could the US win the hearts and minds of the Iraqi people?

In November 2005, President Bush made known his *National Strategy for Victory in Iraq*. The thirty-five-page document delineated three integrated tracks: political, economic, and security. The political objective was: "To help the Iraqi people forge a broadly-supported national compact for democratic government, thereby isolating enemy elements from the broader public." The intermediate objectives were: First, to "**Isolate** hardened elements from those who can be won over ... by countering false propaganda and demonstrating to the Iraq people that they have a stake in a viable, democratic Iraq." Second, to "**Engage** those outside the political process and invite in those willing to turn away from violence through ever-expanding avenues of peaceful participation. And third, to "**Build** stable, pluralistic, and effective national institutions that can protect the interests of all Iraqis and facilitate Iraq's full integration into the international community."[68]

The economic objective was: "To assist the Iraq government in establishing the foundations for a sound economy with the capacity to deliver essential services." The intermediate objectives were: First, to "**Restore** Iraq's neglected infrastructure...." Second, to "**Reform** Iraq's economy ... so that it can be self-sustaining...." And third, to "**Build** the capacity of Iraqi institutions to maintain infrastructure, rejoin the international community, and improve the general welfare of all Iraqis."

The third and most important "track" of Bush's strategy was security. Security was a prerequisite for political and economic development. The security objective was: "To develop the Iraqis' capacity to secure their country while carrying out a campaign to defeat the terrorists and neutralize the insurgency." The three intermediate objectives were: First, to "**Clear** areas of enemy control by remaining on the offensive, killing and capturing enemy fighters and denying them safe-haven." Second, to **Hold** areas freed from the enemy control by ensuring that they remain under the control of a peaceful Iraqi government with an adequate Iraqi security force presence. And third, to "**Build** Iraqi Security Forces and the capacity of local institutions to deliver services, advance the rule of law, and nurture civil society."

Bush's, and hence, General Casey's, major strategy in 2005 was the "Iraqiization" of the war. Similar "tracks" had been employed in Vietnam under General Abrams. And the basic problems in Iraq were the same as those in Vietnam: security, time, loyalty, allegiance, and selflessness. Without the willingness of the Iraqis to join with others and selflessly fight to defend the American-established government, the US could not succeed in its mission. No matter how many weapons and resources the US provided Iraq, and no matter how well the Army trained Iraqi forces, if they were not loyal to the government, they could not withstand the test of battle. The US undertook the monumental task of transforming the apolitical *subjects* of Saddam Hussein into active *citizens* of the new American-made Iraqi republic. Neutrality was not enough. In a new democracy struggling to achieve legitimacy, the active participation of a significant portion of the population is required.

The development of loyal citizens requires time, commitment, sacrifice, and leadership. The establishment of a capitalist democracy was not a task that could be achieved purely with material, technical skill, and efficient organization. It required an understanding of the cultural tenets that created cohesion among people, so as to not violate them, and to create new institutions that affirm them while achieving coalition political objectives. The creation of such institutions was a task that had taken generations for most Western nations. It was not going to happen overnight in Iraq. And there were other problems. Clear, hold, and build sounded good, but who was going to do the "holding" and the "building?" US forces were still too few to perform the first task. There were too few soldiers and marines and loyal Iraqi security forces to maintain security, making it impossible to

convince the Iraqi people that the presence of US forces created peace and stability as opposed to chaos and violence. In fact, in the early months of 2006, polls showed that many Iraqis believed that the presence of US forces was causing violence instead of preventing it.

*   *   *   *   *

Iraq is not Vietnam, and in 2005 there were a number of factors that worked for the Bush Administration and against the insurgency. Iraq's desert terrain is much more favorable to American methods of operation, facilitating combat operations and control of the flow of men and materials. American technologies made it possible for US forces to control more space with fewer soldiers than was possible during the Vietnam era. Technologies, such as UAVs, improved the ability of coalition forces to find and target insurgency forces and to operate with greater efficiency, achieving greater economy of force. Thus, US and coalition forces were better able to isolate the battlefield and the insurgents. The Iraqis are divided between three major groups, and only one group, the Sunnis, were united against the US. The Sunnis have no military equivalent to the PAVN, or the leadership from Hanoi, nor do they have the material wealth of the PRC and SU, or the charismatic leadership of a Ho Chi Minh. The material wealth of the US, rapidly and efficiently applied, could palpably improve the living conditions of the average Iraqi, helping win the support of the people. There are certain basic conditions for life that all people want: safe homes, good schools, good hospitals, a basic standard of living, a functioning criminal justice system, and a future for their children. The US could help the Iraqis produce these basic conditions in Iraq, and many Iraqis knew this. Iraqi soldiers, provided they remained loyal to the government and were in fact militarily effective, had the greatest potential to save Iraq, to gain the support and confidence of the people, and defeat the insurgency. *The question was: could we build this new Iraqi Army fast enough?*

Special Forces methods and techniques have improved significantly since the Vietnam War, and PSYOPs and information operations were considerably more sophisticated in 2005 than in 1965. Winning the information war was essential to success in Iraq.

By bringing the UN and allies more intimately into the war, the US gained some degree of legitimacy in the eyes of the world. And American allies, particularly the British, could help dissipate some of the ire directed at the US from the Arab world. The US, with the assistance of European allies, had the ability to cut off much of the funding to insurgency forces and to influence regional states such as Syria and Iran. The almost complete removal of the American people from the conduct of the war gave the Bush Administration greater freedom to prosecute the war. Bush did not have the problems that Johnson and Nixon faced trying to explain the Vietnam War to the American people, and trying to conduct the war in ways that maintained the people's support. The situation in Iraq at the end of 2005 was not completely beyond repair. It was still possible to produce a stable, democratic, government.

There was, however, another side to this equation that could potentially work against the United States. Historically, the US has *not* been a force for democracy in the region. In fact, the exact opposite is true.[69] US support for Arab monarchies, essentially dictators, and for Israel aligned it against the Arab people, much in the way its support for the French aligned it with European imperialism, and against the people of Vietnam. In addition, most people recognize that the US is primarily interested in the region because of its oil reserves. The US forces in Iraq were essentially occupation forces. Their presence could help unite the various tribal and sectarian entities against a common enemy—the US. In this respect, the objectives of insurgent and terrorist forces were more similar and unifying than those sought by the United States. The opposition fought for the removal of American forces from their backyard and from their homes. However, terrorists, while Arab, were also outsiders, who killed Iraqis and destroyed Iraqi homes, businesses, and even mosques. The terrorist forces also fought to establish an Islamic government, a form of government many Iraqis did not want. While Iraqi insurgents fought over the division of resources and for political power, Iraq was still their home. Its destruction benefitted neither the Sunni nor Shia. Thus, the potential also existed to separate the terrorists from the insurgents. The US had an opportunity to realign the forces arrayed against it. *Thus, the second question was: how to exploit this opportunity?*

In 2005, Bush was concerned about keeping congressional support for the war. In Congress, there was talk of cutting off funding. Strategically, the US was on the defense. While it was able to conduct limited offensive operations, it could not control the cities, towns, and border regions. It could not gain sufficient intelligence to disarm the insurgency forces, and it could not capture terrorist leaders. Iraqis, who endeavored to support the Americans and the new Iraqi government, were dying in increasing numbers, and the anger, discord, and killing between the Sunni and Shia populations was expanding, threatening civil war. While American casualties were relatively low, the US was spending roughly $8 billion per month in Iraq. Deficit spending created an enormous drag on the economy that threatened recession. Americans were poorer in real dollars in 2005 than they were in 2000 when Bush took office. The Army, as in Vietnam, could not be defeated in the field. However, time, deficit spending, and the expenditure of hundreds of billions of dollars down what some people believed was a bottomless pit, threatened to destroy the support of the American people and Congress. In other words, the war could be lost in the United States. *The third question was: could the Bush Administration maintain congressional support for the war?*

The New Way Forward: New Strategy, Leadership, Doctrine, and Tactics

On 22 February 2006, Sunni extremists destroyed the al-Aakari Golden Mosque, an important Shia holy site. Rumsfeld observed that: "the bombing of the Samarra mosque was the most strategically significant terrorist attack in Iraq since liberation, seemingly designed by al-Qaida to trigger an all-out Sunni-Shia civil war." He further noted that: "The event marked the ascendance of Shia militia and a new stage of sectarian conflict.... In the wake of Samarra, the Shia militias began a campaign of ruthless ethnic cleansing."

In December 2006, *The Iraq Study Group Report* was published.[70] Former Secretary of State James A. Baker III and former US congressman from Indiana,

Lee H. Hamiltion, co-chaired the group. The report noted that:

> The Iraqi government cannot now govern, sustain, and defend itself without the support of the United States. Iraqis have not been convinced that they must take responsibility for their own future. Iraq's neighbors and much of the international community have not been persuaded to play an active and constructive role in supporting Iraq. The ability of the United States to shape outcomes is diminishing. Time is running out.[71]

When the report was published, 2,900 Americans had been killed in Iraq and another 21,000 wounded. Approximately 141,000 soldiers and marines were fighting there along with 16,500 soldiers from 27 states of the "coalition of the willing" (the largest contingent, 7,200 soldiers, was from the United Kingdom). The US had spent roughly $400 billion dollars on the war, and was still spending an estimated $8 billion per month. And after all this sacrifice and commitment of resources, the situation in Iraq was still deteriorating. Obviously something had to change. In the opening letter to the Iraq Study Group, Baker and Hamilton noted that:

> No one can guarantee that any course of action in Iraq at this point will stop sectarian warfare, growing violence, or the slide toward chaos. If current trends continue, the potential consequences are severe. Because of the role and responsibilities of the United States in Iraq, and the commitments our government has made, the United States has special obligations. Our country must address as best it can Iraq's many problems. The United States has long-term relationships and interests at stake in the Middle East, and needs to stay engaged.[72]

The report made a number of recommendations, the most important of which was that: "new and enhanced diplomatic and political efforts in Iraq and the region, and a change in the primary mission of US forces in Iraq that will enable the United States to begin to move its combat forces out of Iraq responsibly." This was a call for the "Iraqization" of the war, an element of US strategy that was already well established. The report noted the declining condition of the services: "US military forces, especially our ground forces, have been stretched nearly to the breaking point by the repeated deployments in Iraq, with attendant casualties ..., greater difficulty in recruiting, and accelerated wear on equipment."[73] The Study Group argued that:

> The Iraqi government should accelerate assuming responsibility for Iraqi security by increasing the number and quality of Iraq Army brigades. While this process is underway, and to facilitate it, *the United States should significantly increase the number of US military personnel*, including combat troops, embedded in and supporting Iraqi Army units. As these actions proceed, US forces could begin to move out of Iraq.[74]

The Study Group clearly had the Vietnam War in mind, concluding that: "The United States must not make an open-ended commitment to keep large numbers of American troops deployed in Iraq." Prior to the publication of the report, troop strength in Iraq had been strenuously debated and increased several times. Generals Abizaid and Casey opposed the deployment of additional forces. Some civilian leaders also opposed escalation. Rumsfeld recalled that: "The skepticism of senior military leaders, however, was mild in comparison with the opposition within the State Department. Rice argued that surging more US troops would further antagonize American allies and erode domestic political support."[75]

In January 2007, President Bush, responding to the *The Iraq Study Group Report*, stated, "It is clear that we need to change our strategy in Iraq." In the State of the Union Address he delineated another new strategy for Iraq. First, however, recognizing that the war no longer had the support of the majority of the American people, he argued that the US could not "cut and run": "This is not the fight we entered in Iraq, but it is the fight we're in. Every one of us wishes this war were over and won. Yet it would not be like us to leave our promises unkept, our friends abandoned, and our own security at risk." He believed that, "On this day, at this hour, it is still within our power to shape the outcome of this battle. Let us find our resolve, and turn events toward victory."[76]

Bush then outlined his third new strategy for Iraq: "We're carrying out a new strategy in Iraq—a plan that demands more from Iraq's elected government, and gives our forces in Iraq the reinforcements they need to complete their mission." The most controversial element of Bush's new strategy was the "surge," which called for an additional 20,000 troops. Bush stated:

> In order to make progress toward this goal, the Iraqi government must stop sectarian violence in its capital. But the Iraqis are not yet ready to do this on their own. So we're deploying reinforcements of more than 20,000 additional soldiers and Marines to Iraq. The vast majority will go to Baghdad, where they will help Iraqi forces to clear and secure neighborhoods, and serve as advisers embedded in Iraqi Army units. With Iraqis in the lead, our forces will help secure the city by chasing down the terrorists, insurgents, and the roaming death squads.[77]

Bush's new strategy integrated many of the recommendations from *The Iraq Study Group Report*. However, Bush's tenacity and perseverance deserves recognition. He was determined to not go down in history as the second American President to lose a war. He was not going to be like Johnson or Nixon. However, given the mood of the country, would this have been possible with a conscripted Army?

Bush put a new commander in charge of operations in Iraq. General David H. Petraeus took command of the Multi-National Force-Iraq on 27 January 2007. A year later, in April 2008, Ambassador Ryan Crocker could state: "One conclusion I draw from these signs of progress is that the strategy that began with the Surge is working." And in *US News and World Report*, Linda Robinson wrote:

> By June 2008, Iraq was calmer than it had been since April 2004. The war was not over, but it clearly had reached a new stage. When Gen. David Petraeus took command a year and a half earlier, Iraq was on fire. The majority in the United States believed there was no way to avoid an ignominious defeat such as America had not suffered in a quarter century. Petraeus, with the help of many others, pulled Iraq back from the

brink of civil war and created an opportunity for the next administration to bring the war to a soft landing.[78]

The US Army, Marine Corps, and coalition forces, under the leadership of General David Petraeus, reversed the situation in Iraq, turning what many Americans believed was another Vietnam-style debacle into a fragile, but lasting and stable peace. To do this, Petraeus had to change the way the Army operated, and employ new counterinsurgency doctrine. He had to transform the culture of war that had evolved since the Vietnam War, which placed the protection of soldiers before the mission. In Iraq, soldiers would ultimately have to dismount, close with, and engage the people, not with weapons at the ready, but with the intent to learn, gain information, and secure them from threats. Finally, the Army had to learn to rely on Iraqis themselves to solve the problems of Iraq.

*   *   *   *   *

To succeed in Iraq, the Army and Marine Corps had to rethink the way they fought. Lieutenant General David Petraeus, as Commander of the Combined Arms Center, was primarily responsible for the development of the Army and Marine Corps' new counterinsurgency doctrine published in FM 3–24 *Counterinsurgency*.[79] Petraeus formed a diverse team of civilian and military experts, led by retired Lieutenant Colonel Conrad Crane, to write the manual.[80] He worked closely with the Marine Corps, particularly General James Mattis, and incorporated concepts and tenets from the Marine Corps's small wars manual. One reviewer concluded: "this field manual is not simply a refinement on the margins of US practice; given where the military has been since Vietnam, it is paradigm shattering."[81]

Petraeus earned a Ph.D. in International Relations from Princeton University. His dissertation was on the US Army in Vietnam. In 2003, he commanded the famed 101st Airborne Division in Operation Iraqi Freedom. The division covered the advance of the 3rd Infantry Division (Mechanized) and fought significant battles at Karbala and Najar. Petraeus later earned recognition for his conduct of stability operations in Mosul and Niveveh Provinces. His enlightened tactics and policies and engagement with the people enhanced his reputation as the Army's expert in counterinsurgency and stability operations. Following an assignment as the first commander of the Multi-National Security Transition Command-Iraq, and the NATO Training Mission-Iraq, June 2004 to September 2005, Lieutenant General Petraeus took command of the Combined Arms Center at Fort Leavenworth, Kansas. In October 2006, he published an article in *Military Review* titled, "Learning Counterinsurgency: Observations from Soldiering in Iraq," in which he delineated lessons learned from his studies and experiences in Iraq. Petraeus's observations were incorporated into the Army's new counterinsurgency manual. In 2007, Bush selected Petraeus to implement his new "surge" strategy in Iraq. Petraeus's success earned him command of the US Central Command (2008–2010), and under the Obama Administration, command of Operation Enduring Freedom in Afghanistan (2010–2011).

Insurgency and counterinsurgency are as old as war itself. These are enormous topics.[82] No effort is made in these few pages to delineate the ideas that are products of this form of war. However, some discussion is necessary to understand the wars in Iraq and Afghanistan. An **insurgency**, according to the Department of Defense, is:

> an organized movement aimed at the overthrow of a constituted government through the use of subversion and armed conflict. Stated another way, an insurgency is an organized, protracted politico-military struggle designed to weaken the control and legitimacy of an established government, occupying power, or other political authority while increasing insurgent control.[83]

And a **counterinsurgency** (COIN) is: "military and paramilitary, political, economic, psychological, and civic action taken by a government to defeat insurgency." FM 3–24, while accepting these definitions, was quick to note that they are "a good starting point, but they do not properly highlight a key paradox: though insurgency and COIN are two sides of a phenomenon that has been called revolutionary war or internal war, they are distinctly different types of operations." The objective of insurgents and counterinsurgents is the support and loyalty of the people.

The effort on both sides is earn the willing support of the people, to discredit the other, to destroy the legitimacy of the other, and earn legitimacy in the eyes of the people. FM 3–24 noted that, "Political power is the central issue in insurgencies and counterinsurgencies; each side aims to get the people to accept its governance or authority as legitimate."[84]

Counterinsurgency operations frequently require knowledge sets different from those common to conventional operations, such as language skills, cultural understanding, and historical information on a population. Soldiers and marines fighting insurgents must frequently act and think in ways that are in direct opposition to the norms of conventional military operations. Several of General Petraeus's "observations" emphasize these objectives and elucidate the difficulties in conducting COIN operations:

Observation Number 10 ... that *success in a counterinsurgency requires more than just military operations.* Counterinsurgency strategies must also include, above all, efforts to establish a political environment that helps reduce support for the insurgents and undermines the attraction of whatever ideology they may espouse.... In certain Sunni Arab regions of Iraq, establishing such a political environment is likely of greater importance than military operations, since the right political initiatives might undermine the sanctuary and assistance provided to the insurgents.

Observation Number 9, *cultural awareness is a force multiplier,* reflects our recognition that knowledge of the cultural "terrain" can be as important as ... knowledge of the geographic terrain. This observation acknowledges that the people are, in many respects, the decisive terrain ....

Observation Number 4 reminds us that *increasing the number of stakeholders is critical to success.* This insight emerged several months into our time in Iraq as we began to realize that more important than our winning Iraqi heart and minds was doing all we could to ensure that as many Iraqis as possible felt a stake in the success of the new Iraq.

Observation Number 11 *Ultimate success depends on local leaders*—is a natural reflection of Iraqi sovereignty and acknowledges that success in Iraq is, as time passes, increasingly dependent on Iraqi leaders ....

Observation Number 3 is that, in an endeavor like that in Iraq, *money is ammunition*. In fact, depending on the situation, money can be more important than ammunition—and that has often been the case in Iraq since early April 2003 when Saddam's regime collapsed and the focus rapidly shifted to reconstruction, economic revival, and restoration of basic services.

Observation Number 2 is that, in a situation like Iraq, the liberating force must *act quickly, because every Army of liberation has a half-life* beyond which it turns into an Army of occupation. The length of this half-life is tied to the perceptions of the populace about the impact of the liberating force's activities.[85]

Petraeus delineated a "people-centric" (or population-centric) strategy and doctrine, as opposed to an "insurgent-centric" doctrine, which emphasized killing the enemy, or a "security forces centric" doctrine that focused on the "Iraqization" of the war—the preferred American approaches. Petraeus noted that before deciding to conduct an operation, commanders needed to perform a "cost-benefit analysis," by asking "Will this operation take more bad guys off the street than it creates by the way it is conducted?" He quoted General John Galvin, who stated:

> The ... burden on the military is large. Not only must it subdue an armed adversary while attempting to provide security to the civilian population, it must also avoid furthering the insurgents' cause. If, for example, the military's actions in killing 50 guerrillas cause 200 previously uncommitted citizens to join the insurgent cause, the use of force will have been counterproductive.

In other words, sometimes the best solution was to do nothing, or something that caused the least possible damage. This was a hard lesson for Americans to learn. Petraeus's words focused on the people of Iraq and the actions of US soldiers to influence the people. Not one of his observations was devoted to finding, fixing, and killing the enemy. Nor was his focus on force-protection.

In an article titled, "Principles, Imperatives, and Paradoxes of Counterinsurgency," several of the authors of the COIN manual delineated the counterintuitive nature of this form of warfare. They wrote:

> The more you protect your forces, the less secure you are.... The more force you use, the less effective you are.... Sometimes doing nothing is the best reaction.... The best weapons for counterinsurgency do not fire bullets.... Them [security forces] doing something poorly is sometimes better than us doing it well.... If a tactic works this week, it will not work next week; if it works in this province, it will not work in the next.... [And,] Tactical success guarantees nothing.[86]

This kind of thinking represented a cultural shift for the armed forces of the United States.

In COIN, armed forces are not enough. The Army and Marine Corps lacked the skills, talents, and resources to do all that was necessary to succeed in Iraq. Petraeus recognized that other government agencies were essential for success. A "whole-of-government-approach" was required. Economic development, the formation of governmental institutions, and the physical reconstruction of damaged infrastructure were not areas of specialization common to the Army. Criminal investigation, land and water usage, and numerous other areas also required civilian experts. COIN required the support of many agencies of government that have not traditionally deployed to war. The FBI, USAID, the Department of State, the Department of Agriculture, and other such agencies were required on the battlefields in COIN. The interagency process, however, was in its infancy in OIF, and this was evident throughout. Still, the process of cultural change required for these independent agencies to cooperate on the battlefield was significantly advanced in Iraq.

In COIN both sides are engaged in what were once called propaganda campaigns. The Army now uses the term *information operations*. The side that tells the story first usually wins the advantage. The Army's system of getting approval from senior commanders for public pronouncements gave the insurgents and terrorists a huge advantage. The chain of command slowed the Army's responses, and allowed the enemy to tell the story its way. The Army had to fundamentally change the way it communicated. To get the message correct and to tell the story first, the Army had to depend on sergeants and lieutenants responding immediately on the spot to any and every event that had media attention. To tell the story without offending the audience's cultural understanding was absolutely necessary. This required educating soldiers.

COIN required patience, long-term commitments, manpower, knowledge, training, education, and a willingness to accept casualties and expend resources in a profligate manner. While the Army and Marine Corps remained understaffed in Iraq, and repeated combat tours wore heavily on regular and reserve forces and their families, the two services grew into highly effective, extremely knowledgeable, proficient combat forces. Protracted war was a new experiment for the all-volunteer forces. However, the ability to learn to do things smarter, to do them again and again, greatly enhanced the ability of the United States to achieve political objective through COIN operations. The consequences of this experiment are still being revealed, and not everyone agrees that the new COIN doctrine is the solution to irregular warfare. Colonel Gian Gentile was one of the most vociferous opponents of the Army's new "COIN way of war." He wrote:

> It is time for the Army to debate FM 3–24 *critically*. . . . The simple truth is that we have bought into a doctrine for countering insurgencies that did not work in the past, as proven by history, and whose efficacy and utility remain highly problematic today. . . . Yet that theory has shaped a new way of war and has seduced analysts . . . and senior Army officers, and other influential members of the defense community into believing it to be proven in practice.[87]

* * * * *

In May 2007, in a report to the Pentagon, General Petraeus described the operational environment as "the most complex and challenging" he had ever seen. He noted that:

> al Qaeda, extremist militias, and Sunni insurgent groups seek to destroy what Iraqi

leaders are trying to build. Political parties with ethnosectarian interests, limited government capacity, and corruption add additional challenges, and exceedingly unhelpful activities by Iran and Syria-especially those by Iran . . . compound the enormous problems facing the new Iraq.[88]

Petraeus continued:

> Iraq is, in fact, the central front of al Qaeda's global campaign and we devote considerable resources to the fight against al Qaeda Iraq. We have achieved some notable successes in the past two months, killing the security emir of eastern Anbar province, detaining a number of key network leaders, discovering how various elements of al Qaeda Iraq operate, taking apart a car bomb network that had killed 650 citizens of Baghdad, and destroying several significant car bomb factories. Nonetheless, al Qaeda Iraq remains a formidable foe . . . The extremist militias in Iraq also are a substantial problem and must be significantly disrupted. . .[89]

Given the complexity of the environment, no single chapter can accurately describe the multitude of tasks and diversity of operations undertaken by US forces in Iraq. Nor is it appropriate to give all the credit for the transformation to General Petraeus and his leadership team. Much of the success was a function of actions taken and institutions built by General Casey and his team. The "surge" of an additional 20,000 troops (actually 30,000) acting alone was not enough to reverse the situation in Iraq. However, the addition of hundreds of thousands of effective, loyal Iraqi security forces working and cooperating with US forces greatly multiplied their effectiveness. In June 2007, US troop strength in Iraq reached 160,000, (the "surge"). However, the majority of the surge came from Iraq. In October 2007, Petraeus wrote:

> One of the principal reasons for the steady, albeit slow, improvement in the capability of the 350,000-strong Iraqi Security Force has been our strong partnership effort, Multi-National Security Transition Command advisers increase ministerial capacity by mentoring senior Iraqi leaders in

the ministries of Interior and Defense, helping them develop, resource and employ their forces. Multi-National Corps-Iraq and its division headquarters ensure unity of effort by working closely with their counterparts, the Iraqi corps and division headquarters. Transition teams, as well as our units, partner with the Iraqi Army and National Police brigades and battalions that share their battle space while civilian police advisers and military police elements mentor the local Iraqi police. Across Iraq, our troopers are fighting and shedding blood alongside their Iraqi comrades-in-arms.[90]

The psychological implications of the surge may have been as important as the physical presence of additional US forces. The surge was, in part, a confidence-builder. It indicated to the Iraqi people and their security forces that the US was staying; that it was committed to a secure, democratic Iraq. This new confidence made them more willing to commit and sacrifice. These forces gave the Iraqi people a choice.

In Anbar Province in 2006, Iraqi Sunnis rejected terrorism, rejected al-Qaeda's violence and leadership, and accepted the presence and assistance of US forces. This dramatic and courageous transformation became known as the *Anbar Awakening* (later the Sunni Awakening). The 1st Brigade of the 1st Armored Division, the "Ready First Combat Team," was at the center of the Anbar Awakening. Major Neil Smith and Colonel Sean McFarland, the commander of the 1st BCT, 1st AD, wrote: "When we arrived in Ramadi in June 2006, few of us thought our campaign would change the entire complexion of the war and push Al-Qaeda to the brink of defeat in Iraq."[91] To explain his counterinsurgency operations in Anbar province, General McFarland used a combustion engine analogy.[92] The indigenous population was the fuel; his forces, the Ready First BCT, was the oxygen; the spark was provided by the enemy. Al-Qaeda's excessive violence, particularly the murder of Sheik Khalil, started the combustion process, which resulted in accelerating the relationship between US forces and the indigenous population.

To facilitate the growth of this new relationship, McFarland deployed his forces among the people in combat outposts. Securing and strengthening tribal

leaders and their people was his primary concern. To do this, he needed local Iraqi security forces to partner with American soldiers and Marines. McFarland established relationships of trust with the local sheiks, providing them with money and fuel to distribute to their people, and they in turn provided him with the intelligence and manpower needed to provide security around the clock. Smith and McFarland noted that:

> We ... took some extraordinary measures to ensure the survival of tribal leaders who 'flipped' to our side. We established neighborhood watches that involved deputizing screened members of internal tribal militias as 'Provincial Auxiliary Iraqi Police,' authorizing them to wear uniforms, carry weapons, and provide security within the defined tribal area.[93]

When one tribe flipped, it created the conditions for others to flip in order to gain the same security and economic advantages provided by US forces. Through the sheiks, money and fuel became effective weapon systems. Smith and McFarland concluded that, "the enemy overplayed its hand and the people were tired of Al-Qaeda."

Al-Qaeda's assassinations of sheiks caused new, more aggressive leaders to rise to positions of tribal leadership. Smith and McFarland observed that "a growing concern that the US would leave Iraq and leave the Sunnis defenseless against Al-Qaeda and Iranian-supported militias made these young leaders open to our overtures." As confidence grew, both sides became more trusting and able to take on more challenging and complex operations and projects. Smith and McFarland concluded that: "Our willingness to adapt our plans based on the advice of the sheiks, our staunch and timely support for them in times of danger and need, and our ability to deliver on our promises convinced them that they could do business with us."[94] Reconstruction and economic development began almost concurrently with the establishment of new security relationships. Benefits to the community strengthened the local sheiks, and as a consequence, the relationships of the community with American forces. And the personal relationship between the sheiks and US commanders promoted good governance. This cycle was employed again and again with considerable success.

General Patraeus studied the Anbar Awakening. He took the lessons learned there and incorporated them in other locations. He deployed American forces strategically to provide the oxygen necessary to initiate combustion in other parts of the country, particularly Baghdad, the center of gravity in Iraq. In counterinsurgency operations, how soldiers were employed mattered. A hundred soldiers out patrolling the streets and engaging the people can be more effective than a hundred soldiers mounted in M1 Abrams Tanks and M2 Bradley Fighting Vehicles. In February 2007, General Petraeus told his soldiers and marines: "Secure and serve the population. The Iraqi people are the decisive 'terrain.' Together with our Iraqi partners, work to provide the people security, to give them respect, to gain their support, and to facilitate establishment of local governance, restoration of basic services, and revival of local economies." Petraeus described US strategy as follows:

> The campaign is pursued along four related lines of operational-security, economic, diplomatic and political. We work with our Iraqi counterparts to help secure the population and foster economic development. Security and economic progress, in turn, give Iraqi leaders a chance to resolve the tough issues that have divided them and to develop their governmental institutions. . . . In addition, our actions along the four lines of operation are bolstered by supporting initiatives in the areas of reconciliation, capacity building, rule of law, good governance and strategic communications.[95]

In the summer of 2007, the Iraqi people reached a critical juncture at which they rejected terrorism and violence against their own people. This was the "tipping point." Petraeus observed that:

> The most encouraging development has been seeing Iraqis increasingly reject extremist groups and the violence they visit on the Iraqi people. For example, in Anbar Province and some other areas of the country, local tribes are turning away from al Qaeda and other extremist groups and towards the government of Iraq. Not surprisingly these areas are becoming decidedly more peaceful.[96]

On 10 September in a report to Congress on the situation in Iraq, Petraeus summarized the actions taken to calm Iraq:

> One reason for the decline in incidents is that Coalition and Iraqi forces have dealt significant blows to Al Qaeda-Iraq. The Al Qaeda and its affiliates in Iraq remain [but] dangerous, [but] we have taken away a number of their sanctuaries and gained the initiative in many areas.
>
> We have disrupted Shia militia extremists, capturing the head and numerous other leaders of the Iranian-supported Special Groups . . . .
>
> Coalition and Iraq operations have helped reduce ethno-sectarian violence, as well as bringing down the number of ethno-sectarian deaths substantially in Baghdad and across Iraq. . . . The overall [number of] civilian deaths has also declined . . . .
>
> Iraq Security Forces have also continued to grow and to shoulder more of the load. . . . Iraqi elements have been standing and fighting and sustaining tough losses, and they have taken the lead in operations in many areas.
>
> Additionally, in what may be the most significant development of the past 8 months, the tribal rejection of Al Qaeda that in Anbar Province and helped produce such significant change there has now spread to a number of other locations as well.[97]

Petraeus confidently predicted, "I believe that we will be able to reduce our forces to the pre-surge level of brigade combat teams by next summer without jeopardizing the security gains that we have fought to achieve." In December, Petraeus announced that violence was down sixty percent. However, 2007 was the deadliest year of the war—852 soldiers and marines died.

A number of the major themes that run through the story of this astonishing reversal in Iraq are worth noting:

1. New, inspired learning, and adaptive leadership taking command under deteriorating conditions,
2. Cultural transformation in the Army, which required soldiers to accept greater risk in order to secure the population.

3. Retraining and reorganization of the Army to conduct population-centric counterinsurgency operations while fighting two wars (Iraq and Afghanistan).

4. Shifts in the cultures of the Pentagon, White House, and Congress, away from the overemphasis on force protection and the intolerance for American casualties, toward greater emphasis on protecting and securing the population, greater engagement with the people, and primary focus on achievement of the mission.

5. The adoption of "the whole-of-government" approach to war; that is, the integration of government agencies, such as the Department of State, USAID, the Department of Agriculture, the FBI, and other agencies, into Army and Marine Corps operations, and the expansion of interagency process and planning.

6. A new level of jointness, a new level of cooperation between the services, born out of necessity because the Army and Marine Corps were too small. The Navy and Air Force supported operations in Iraq and Afghanistan that took them away from their primary instruments of war. And, the Army and Marines cooperated and integrated their forces in ways that were not possible in World War II, Korea, Vietnam, or Operation Desert Storm.

7. The employment of private military firms to do what the Army and Marine Corps could no longer do for themselves, including carrying weapons and providing security. The privatization of warfare may be the future of warfare.

8. Comprehension and focus on the human terrain and use of the political tactics to transform a state that contained three nations into a fledgling modern nation-state.

The war in Iraq caused a cultural transformation in the way Americans thought about and conducted war, much of which was extraordinarily healthy for the United States and the world. The belief widely held by foreign states that Americans could not take casualties and would leave the battlefield before the mission was accomplished if sufficiently bloodied, was destroyed in Iraq.

In 2008, Barack Obama was elected President of the United States. Senator Obama (Democrat from Illinois, 2005–2008) had argued that the war in Iraq was unnecessary and had been poorly executed by the Bush Administration. Candidate Obama proposed a timetable for the withdrawal of US forces from Iraq. The Iraq government accepted this timetable, which, to some degree, locked both sides into an agreement. In office, President Obama retained Bush's Secretary of Defense Robert Gates, and selected Hillary Clinton for Secretary of State. His charge to both was to end the war, and withdraw US forces. On 16 September 2008, General Raymond T. Odierno took command of the MNF-I, and General Petraeus was promoted to the US Central Command, responsible for the wars in both Iraq and Afghanistan. From December 2006 to February 2008, Odierno had commanded the Multi-National Corps-Iraq (MNC-I), the second-most senior command position in Iraq and the command most responsible for implementing Petraeus's new counterinsurgency strategy and doctrine. Odierno continued the campaign strategy initiated by Petraeus, and was now responsible for overseeing the phased withdrawal of US forces. The question that haunted many political and military leaders was: was it too soon? Were the Iraqi government and security forces ready to take responsibility for their own security? The rapid withdrawal of US force could jeopardize all that had been accomplished.

Campaign rhetoric is rarely transformed directly into policy. Candidates usually do not have to face the hard realities that frequently influence, if not determine, foreign and military policies. In regard to the wars in Iraq and Afghanistan, however, President Obama was able to keep his campaign promises. Because of the enhanced security situation and because of the new professionalism of the Iraqi security forces in 2010, the majority of US forces could be safely withdrawn. On Tuesday night, 31 August 2010, in an address from the Oval Office, President Obama informed the American people that the US war in Iraq was over: "Tonight I am announcing that the American combat mission in Iraq has ended, Operation Iraqi Freedom is over." The President did not declare victory. To do so would have been premature. In September 2010, General Odierno stated: "It's going to be three to five years post-2011 before we really understand where Iraq is going and how successfully we've actually been in pushing Iraq forward." The outcome of the war will not be known for a number of years.

However, the prospects are good. During this period, it is important for the United States to remain engaged. To abandon Iraq completely would be a mistake akin to that made in Afghanistan following the evacuation of the Soviet Union, when the US withdrew its support for the insurgents fighting against Soviet occupation.

Rumsfeld's War

Approximately 1.5 million servicemen served in Iraq during OIF. Many served multiple tours, and 4,423 died. More than 32,000 were wounded. In 2003, the armed forces of the United States were not prepared to fight an insurgency war and carry out nation-building operations. And as the situation in Iraq deteriorated, the Pentagon was forced to take measures to increase the size of ground forces, and to change its force structure. Congress, too late to immediately influence events in Iraq, increased the authorized strength of the Army and Marine Corps. However, in 2005, both the Army and Marine Corps were struggling, and in some months failing, to meet their monthly recruitment goals, and both services were overcommitted. As recruitment became more difficult, standards were lowered, and age limits were expanded. As the insurgency expanded, the popularity of the war declined, and more and more American parents decided Iraq was not worth the commitment of the lives of their sons and daughters.

To make up for the shortage in manpower, the Pentagon redeployed Army units from Korea and Europe. It called up inactive reservists, and mobilized substantial numbers of guard and reserve units, placing many of these "weekend warriors" in situations for which they were untrained or poorly trained. It created new reenlistment bonuses to encourage soldiers and marines to stay in the service. "Stop loss" policies were put into effect. The service tours of regular soldiers and marines were extended beyond contractual obligations, and scheduled retirements were cancelled. The Pentagon initiated plans to "rebalance the force," with the objective of civilianizing more than ten thousand military positions in order to create additional deployable brigades. The Air Force and the Navy took over jobs in various parts of the world, traditionally carried out by the Army and Marine Corps. The Army initiated plans to reorganize into brigade-centric forces to increase the number of deployable units. Some units extended the tours of duty in Iraq to eighteen months, and soldiers home for eight to twelves months were scheduled to rotate back to Iraq. The Army deployed soldiers who were trained for specific jobs into roles for which they were not trained. For example, artillerymen were deployed as infantrymen and truck drivers. The Pentagon deployed civilians to combat theaters. It sought to employ the resources of government and non-government agencies, and allied military forces and agencies to free up American ground forces for more combat-related jobs. However, it made no effort to call upon the American people to serve. There was no draft. The White House and Pentagon simply increased the burden on the military cluster.

As a consequence of these actions, predictably, the quality and morale of the regular Army, National Guard, and Reserves started to deteriorate. The repeated, extended tours damaged the cohesiveness of Army families, and in June 2005, *USA Today* reported, "The number of active-duty soldiers getting divorced has been rising sharply with the deployments to Afghanistan and Iraq."[98] In 2004, the officer corps divorce rate shot up seventy-eight percent. One chaplain stated, "We've seen nothing like this before. It indicates the amount of stress on couples, on families, as the Army conducts the global war on terrorism."[99] As the retention of good soldiers became more difficult, the ability to get rid of bad soldiers became more difficult.[100]

To help with the manpower shortage the Pentagon started "outsourcing" the war, employing private military firms (PMFs), civilian contractors such as Blackwater, Global Risks, DynCorp International, MPRI, L3, SAIC, and Halliburton, and the individuals they hired, to provide security, logistical support, maintenance, and training.[101] By July 2004, more than 20,000 contractors were in Iraq. A few years later there was a "surge" of contractors. Allison Stranger in her study, *One Nation Under Contract*, noted that: "In Iraq in 2007, more than 180,000 government contractors were on the ground, compared to 160,000 US soldiers."[102] The industry boasted over $100 billion in annual sales.[103] Many of these contractors were carrying out "mission-critical" tasks, which the services had traditionally insisted were exclusively military functions. These private contractors/soldiers suffered more casualties than any of the armed forces of Bush's "coalition of the willing."[104] PMFs were both domestic and foreign firms. In Iraq, men from more than 30 nationalities were employed by PMFs. PMFs are not in the official chain of command, and as private firms they do not answer to the President or Congress. Peter Singer noted: "Their customers also ranged across the moral spectrum from 'ruthless dictators, morally depraved rebels and drug cartels' to 'legitimate sovereign states, respected multinational corporations, and humanitarian NGOs.'"[105] Yet US governmental officials recognize that if the services provided by PMFs under the Logistics Civilian Augmentation Program (LOGCAP) were eliminated, it would bring about the "complete collapse of the support infrastructure" for OIF. Singer observed:

> [I]t is more a "coalition of the billing" than the "willing" . . . . Iraq is where the history books will note that the [PMF] industry took full flight. Iraq is not just the biggest US military commitment in a generation but also the biggest marketplace in the short history of the privatized military industry. In Iraq, private actors play a pivotal role in great-power warfare to an extent not seen since the advent of the mass nation-state armies in the Napoleonic Age . . . .[106]

As the missions and tasks required of the armed forces of the United States expand, and the obligations of American citizens continue to decline, PMFs will grow in importance and numbers.

PMFs displace and conceal the cost and trauma of war. PMF casualties in Iraq were frequently not Americans. PMFs have no requirement to report killed or wounded to the Pentagon or press. They reduce the political cost of war for the decision-makers in Washington. They diminish the need for the President to explain the war and seek the support of the American people. PMFs are, in fact, a new form of mercenaries. Patriotism does not matter. PMFs have no obligation to maintain operational security, to not reveal intelligence, to not change sides, or to not act selfishly. Terrorist organizations can employ PMFs. In fact, they can employ the very same individual contractors who work on American installations throughout the world.

*　*　*　*　*

The conduct of the war in Iraq was primarily a function of Donald Rumsfeld's technological vision of war. McNamara had "graduated response." Rumsfeld had "shock and awe." Neither worked. Some Army leaders argued against the Rumsfeld vision of war.[107] General Shinseki told the Senate Armed Services Committee it would take "several hundred thousand troops to secure Iraq." Many senior leaders in the Army and Marine Corps would have fought a very different war, one with greater ground forces, logistical preparation, and concern for winning the support of the Iraqi people.[108] Rumsfeld and his deputy, Wolfowitz, contradicted Shinseki, stating respectively, "The idea that it would take several hundred thousand US forces I think is far off the mark," and "wildly off the mark."[109] Rumsfeld and Wolfowitz were wrong. They also argued that the Iraqi people would welcome US forces as liberators. Wolfowitz stated, "It is entirely possible that in Iraq, you have the most pro-American population that can be found anywhere in the Arab world. . . . If you're looking for a historical analogy, it's probably closer to post-liberation France."[110] Wolfowitz and Rumsfeld assumed that as soon as the Iraqi people fully understood that Saddam Hussein was gone they would put down their weapons and rally to the Americans. They were wrong about this as well. In June 2003, Rumsfeld told reporters: "I guess the reason I don't use the term guerrilla war is that it isn't . . . anything like a guerrilla war or an organized resistance."[111] Rumsfeld's words contradicted the words of Army General Abizaid, who stated the US faced "a classic guerrilla-type campaign."

Rumsfeld and Wolfowitz were wrong about the number of forces required, the time it would take, the nature of the war, and the cost of the war.[112] They advanced a unilateral approach to the war. They argued that allies were not necessary, that US forces alone could do the job. After the conventional war, they continued this record of misjudgment and failures. They disbanded what was left of the Iraqi Army—forces General Franks believed had the potential to provide security before the insurgency gained ground.[113] They focused resources on finding weapons of mass destruction. They missed opportunities to redirect the forces, to focus them on fighting the growing lawlessness, to securing stocks of weapons and ammunition that were later used to kill Americans, and to stopping the looting and uncontrolled destruction of property, which threatened to destabilize the country. With a larger force, many of the problems that created the conditions for the insurgency to grow could have been avoided. One uniformed Pentagon official observed: "We are repeating every mistake we made in Vietnam."[114]

By the end of 2004, it was evident that the Army and Marine Corps were too small to provide security for Iraqis. It was evident that ground combat forces lacked the type of training and equipment required for the type of war they were fighting. It was evident that the insurgency forces were gaining in strength and effectiveness, and that the situation was deteriorating. It was evident that the US had acted almost unilaterally, had gone to war again without its European allies, and, as a consequence, American ground forces would again assume the heaviest burden and make the greatest sacrifices.[115] It was evident that the new Iraqi security forces were incapable of fighting the insurgency forces without the backing of US ground forces. And above all, it was evident that the most advanced technologies ever produced by mankind could not reverse the situation, and that the only possible way to restore Iraq was with additional ground forces. Hundreds of billions of dollars of the most sophisticated machines that science and engineering had ever produced could not stop a poorly trained, poorly equipped, poorly educated, insurgent guerrilla force. Yet Rumsfeld was culturally regular, his vision of war, based on the application of advanced science and technology, was what the American people expected and paid for.

19.
THE AMERICAN CULTURE OF WAR AND THE FUTURE OF WARFARE

In capitalist countries, as Lenin pointed out, in times of war the conflict between the government and the people, the people and the army, and the army and the government becomes more acute. . . . Past military experience shows that the harder the trials of a country, the more boldly are manifested the opposing tendencies. It is for this reason that modern bourgeoisie military theoreticians, fearing a disruption of the equilibrium between the social strata of their country . . . strive for methods of warfare and strategic concepts which would guarantee the quickest conclusion of war, and preclude popular objection to war. In fitting their military strategy to limited moral resources, bourgeois military theoreticians advance various theories such as those of "limited war" and "small professional armies." The political scheme of these theories is to convince the public that war will require few sacrifices and will be limited as to scope, methods, and aims, so that it can be won by a small professional army without involving the entire nation.[1]

—Marshal of the Soviet Union, V.D. Sokolovsky, 1968

Recently, we surpassed the combined duration of World War I, World War II, and Korea. In that time, almost 5,500 men and women have given their lives and over 37,000 others have been wounded in action. It's because of men and women like these—and more than 13,000 Soldiers who have been decorated for valor since 9/11—that the American people can go about their daily lives, prosper and thrive. . . . When this war began in 2001, we had a great Army. But . . . it was too small to do what the Nation asked us to do. And so, we found ourselves out of balance—so weighed down by our commitments in Iraq and Afghanistan that we couldn't do the things that we knew we needed to do to sustain this All Volunteer Force for the long haul and to build the capability to do other things.[2]

—General George Casey, Army Chief of Staff, 2010

To better understand the American culture of war that produced the practices evident in Afghanistan and Iraq, it is useful to look at ourselves through the eyes of our enemy. The former Soviet Union expended enormous resources studying the American practice of war. Soviet professionals identified tensions between the people and the army, the people and the government, and the army and the government. These tensions were greatly amplified during periods of war. In the United States, and many Western nations, these tensions led to the elimination of *the people* from the conduct of the war of the state. In 2010, Army Chief of Staff General George Casey drew a clear distinction between the American people and men and women of the armed forces, who have committed their lives to the security of the state. The military cluster, "the small professional army," fought the two long wars in Afghanistan and Iraq. The American people "prospered and thrived" at home, having no obligations to serve during periods of war.

The American Culture of War

The most significant development in the conduct of war in the twentieth century was the elimination of the American people from the conduct of the wars of United States. After the terrorist attacks on the United States on 11 September 2001, the Bush Administration went to war, promising a campaign that was global in scope. In two long wars in Afghanistan and Iraq, the armed forces were overextended. Soldiers and marines served multiple tours in combat, infecting the professional force with post-traumatic stress disorder at levels unseen before. Commanders in both countries were incapable of implementing accepted operational doctrines and comprehensive strategies because they had too few troops. The security situation in both countries deteriorated, largely because of insufficient "boots on the ground." And yet the President of the United States made no effort to call upon the American people to serve in the armed forces. This was a historic first. At war, when the Army and Marine Corps were pressed to the limits of their capabilities, no effort was made to call upon the American people to serve in the armed forces. The inaction of the President and Congress confirmed this new American practice of *war without the people* initiated in 1973 in the final days of the Vietnam War, when the American people rejected the idea of fighting *artificial limited wars* with a national, conscripted army.

The transformation of the American practice of war caused the transformation of the American practice of citizenship. It has been argued throughout this work that five major factors influenced the American practice of war: 1. the development of *nuclear weapons* and *advanced airpower*, which created *artificial limited war*, 2. the ugly, dehumanizing, personal nature of traditional *ground warfare*, which goes against the cultural and constitutional norms that inform Americans that man is not a means to an end, but the end; 3. the expectations of the American people for ever expanding levels of consumption and a better life; 4. the assumption of new roles and responsibilities in world affairs, responsibilities for the security of foreign nations and states thousands of miles from our borders, and for peoples who have no historic relationship or cultural affinity to the American people; and 5. the advent of a new form of *militarism*. The

transformation of the American practice of war, and as a consequence, practice of citizenship, has made the United States more of a *state* than a *nation*.

*   *   *   *   *   *

Witnessing the birth of the modern nation-state, Carl von Clausewitz endeavored to capture the essence of the revolution in warfare that was a consequence of the French Revolution. Clausewitz wrote:

> At a total phenomenon [war's] dominant tendencies always make war a paradoxical trinity—composed of primordial violence, hatred, and enmity, which are to be regarded as a blind natural force; of the play of chance and probability within which the creative spirit is free to roam, and of its element of subordination, as an instrument of policy, which makes it subject to reason alone.
>
> The first of the three aspects mainly concerns the people; the second the commander and his army; the third the government. The passions that are to be kindled in war must already be inherent in the people, the scope which the play of courage and talent will enjoy in the realm of probability and chance depends on the particular character of the commander and the army; but the political aims are the business of government alone.[3]

The modern nation-state—the birth of which Clausewitz observed—no longer exists. In developed Western, capitalist, democracies "the nation" in the classic sense of the word no longer functions. The people have been removed from the conduct of the war. The concept of citizenship in the United States has evolved in such a way that the people no longer have a significant part to play in the wars of the United States. In this regard the United States is more *state* than *nation*. The schedule of responsibilities Americans owe their country has deteriorated to almost nothing from World War II to the present, and the ability of the United States to produce combat soldiers has diminished significantly. Michael Walzer, writing during the final years of the Vietnam War, believed that a new concept of citizenship had evolved in the United States. He endeavored to delineate this new reality:

> The extraordinary transformation in social scale which has occurred in the past century and a

half has created a radically different kind of political community—one in which relations between individual and state are so attenuated (at least their moral quality is so attenuated) as to call into question all the classical and early democratic theories of obligation and war. The individual has become a private man, seizing pleasure when he can, alone, or in the narrow confines of his family. The state has become a distant power, captured by officials, sometimes benevolent, sometimes not, never again firmly within the grasp of its citizens.[4]

Walzer creates a new status of citizenship: "*resident aliens at home*," in which the people have no obligation to fight the wars of the nation-state. He argues that people that have voluntarily "dropped out" of the political life of the nation have only one obligation to the state—to defend society against immediate destruction. Just as foreigners residing in most Western states have no obligation for military service to that state, and also have no right to participate in the political system, individual "alienated residents" who *do not* participate in their own nation-state's political system, which in the US is roughly half of all eligible voters, have no obligation to go to war to defend the state or its interests abroad. He argues that the state had lost its legitimacy to an indeterminate number of citizens, and with the loss of legitimacy went the loss of obligation to defend the state. Walzer concluded: "He [the resident alien at home] has incurred limited, essentially negative duties to the state that regulates and protects his social life. He is bound to respect the regulations and to join at critical moments in the protection. But that is all he is bound to do."[5] While there is no legal basis for this new category of "resident alien," Walzer recognized that the significance of the nation-state to large clusters of people living in the United States had declined considerably since World War II.[6] Many Americans were no long willing to fight for the nation-state in artificial limited wars, wars such as the Korean War and the Vietnam War, wars that *did not directly and immediately threaten* the borders of the United States. This is the new reality of the United States. The people of the United States no longer have a significant part to play in the state's decision for war and its conduct of war. Clausewitz's "trinity" of war is no longer a useful analytical tool for understanding war.

In many ways the US has returned to the political-military system that prevailed in Europe during the seventeenth and eighteenth centuries, the period of the absolute monarch, when an elite ruling class, the aristocracy, gave small professional armies military objectives and fought limited wars for political, economic, and territorial gains. Wars were limited by the rate of march of soldiers and the speed of horse-drawn wagons; by climate, weather, and geography, by the rate of musket fire and the willingness of soldiers to employ bayonets, by the ability of a given population to sustain soldiers and the ability of kings to pay for arms, by the ability of noble lords to mobilize soldiers while seeing to the need to produce crops to sustain his people, and by the political objectives and visions of commanders and kings. Wars during the period of the absolute monarch were limited by very real social, political, economic, cultural, technological, and organizational constraints of the time. War was the business of the nobility and their small professional armies. The other clusters of society, the majority, had nothing to do with war.

Robert R. Palmer, in a description of Europe during the "old regime" (the period of the absolute monarchs, prior to the French Revolution and the grant of citizenship to all the people of a state), wrote:

> A "good people" was one that obeyed the law, paid its taxes, and was loyal to the reigning house [in our time, that would be the Republican or Democratic Parties]; it need have no sense of its own identity as a people, or unity as a nation, or responsibility for public affairs, or obligation to put forth a supreme effort in war.[7]

Palmer further noted that:

> *The tie between the sovereign [king] and subject was bureaucratic, administrative, and fiscal, an external mechanical connection of ruler and ruled, strongly in contrast to the principle brought in by the Revolution, which, in its doctrine of responsible citizenship and sovereign people, effected an almost religious fusion of the government with the governed . . . .*

The people, according to Palmer, "felt that they participated in the state, that they derived great advantages from their government, and therefore, should fight for it loyally and with passion."[8] "Religious fusion" and the "passion" to fight loyally for the government, in the age of artificial limited war, existed in relatively few Americans at the end of the twentieth century, too few to impose conscription, too few to meet the needs of the armed forces in two long wars, and too few to achieve the too numerous missions administrations have placed on the services. The United States at the dawn of the new century is more a "state," a political, bureaucratic body, than a "nation," a culturally cohesive body. What explains this incredible transformation?

Artificial Limited War

Nuclear weapons and airpower promised to transform the conduct of war, and, by so doing, they transformed the American practice of citizenship. Nuclear weapons and airpower caused the development of artificial limited war, war in which governments artificially placed limitations on the means employed, the geographic areas of engagement, the resources committed, the time invested, and, most importantly, the commitment of the emotional and psychological energy, the passions (primordial violence, hatred, and enmity) of their people. It was the passions of the people—their involvement, their commitment—that drove war towards the unlimited end of the spectrum of war, towards total war, during the French Revolution and wars of Napoleon. The US Civil War, World War I, and World War II each grew in violence and intensity, each consumed more and more people and resources, each produced higher casualties and greater destruction. However, in World War II, two new technologies changed the conduct of war, causing humanity to *try* to step back from the brink of total destruction.

Airpower and nuclear weapons guaranteed a new level of destruction, a level of destruction that called into question human existence. These new technologies created the ability for a single airplane with a single bomb to destroy a city of hundreds of thousands of people. The firebombing of Japan, followed by the bombing of Hiroshima and Nagasaki with atomic bombs, were stark evidence of the effectiveness of these new technologies. Hundreds of thousands of people were killed instantly. The people had no chance to fight back; no chance to defend themselves; no chance to do anything except die in

place. These technologies took the humanity out of warfare. They took away the engagement, the struggle, the hopes, the passions, the anger, and the hate. After the carnage in Japan, this fact slowly became evident to many of the peoples of the world. These two technologies caused many to believe that mass armies and navies were obsolete. No army could survive the release of such destructive power as that witnessed at Bikini Island in 1952, the first test of the "super bomb," the hydrogen bomb, with a yield greater than 20 megatons. The war against Japan, that last year of World War II, confirmed a new American paradigm for war, a new American practice of war. The traditional American practice of war with mass, conscripted armies conducting offensive operations to destroy the enemy's main army *seemed* obsolete.

New Roles in World Affairs

In the aftermath of World War II, the United States took on more and more international responsibilities, believing that the policy of isolationism during the interwar period had failed to maintain peace. The Truman Administration, following the vision and plans of the Roosevelt Administration, advanced the United Nations, entered into new mutual defense agreements, and became responsible for the security of millions of people outside of the United States. Witnessing Stalin's retention of the massive World War II Soviet Army and the Soviet development of nuclear weapons and airpower, the US and USSR began a period of Cold War, a period of hostile coexistence wherein each side prepared for total nuclear war and fought artificial limited, proxy wars. Still, between 1945 and 1950, the United States all but got rid of its Army, determining it was no longer necessary in an age of airpower and nuclear weapons. In June 1950, Communist North Korea violently attacked South Korea. The US Army that had numbered over six million men organized in 89 divisions in 1945, now numbered less than 600,000 men organized into ten relatively poorly trained and poorly equipped divisions. The first phases of the Korean War were considered a policing action—not war. Four understrength US Army infantry divisions, performing occupation duties in Japan, were deployed to stop the advance of the North Korean People's Army (NKPA) down the Korean peninsula. But, the NKPA, trained and equipped by the Soviet Union, was not a gang of criminals to be policed. The first US units in Korea suffered humiliating defeats, and the police action quickly became a real war against a minor power.

In September, General Douglas MacArthur conducted a turning movement that landed one Marine and one Army division behind the NKPA at Inchon. Within weeks the NKPA was destroyed as an organized fighting force. The Truman Administration, failing to recognize the new world created by nuclear weapons and airpower, employed traditional practices, and sought traditional political objectives: to complete the destruction of the enemy's army and destroy the government of North Korea. The original limited war political objective, to save South Korea, gave way to total war political objectives, the reunification of the two Koreas and the total destruction of North Korea as a separate political entity. This new political objective was unacceptable to the newly established People's Republic of China (PRC), which shared a contiguous border with North Korea. In October, US forces crossed the 38th parallel into North Korea, ignoring the warning of the PRC. In November, the People's Liberation Army (PLA) entered North Korea, initiating a new war with a major, nuclear power—the United States. The PRC disguised its army as a volunteer force. The PLA was supported by the USSR, which had acquired nuclear weapons in 1949. The Korean War created the conditions for the first nuclear war. The PLA struck violently, inflicting heavy casualties on the US Army, and causing the longest retreat in its history. MacArthur informed the President this was a new war.

It is at this moment that *artificial limited war* came into existence. Truman established the precedent that has been followed by every nuclear power since. While Americans were fighting and dying in large numbers against a numerically superior enemy, the President of the United States decided *not* to employ the power of United States to destroy the PLA and bring the war to a quick end. He decided not to deploy nuclear weapons and confined the attacks with airpower to the borders of Korea. He decided to fight an *artificial limited war*. He decided to pay the cost of the Korean War, the cost for the survival of South Korea, with the lives of American soldiers and marines,

airmen and sailors. How could the President explain this to the American people? He couldn't.

Artificial limited war created a paradox in the American mind. The word "war" held significant cultural, historic, and mythological contents. In the American mind it meant commitment to something greater than oneself. It meant sacrifice and emotional attachments. It meant national unity and national effort. It meant the focus of the energy of the nation on some great vision of a better future. It meant offensive actions, offensive operations. It meant dramatic actions and great generals and political leaders. It meant Washington, Grant, Lee, Sherman, Eisenhower, and Patton. It meant Gettysburg, Omaha Beach, Iwo Jima, and the Battle of the Bulge. It meant the nation in arms. Americans thought they knew what "war" meant. Truman's new practice of war, which placed artificial limitations on the passions of the people and the means and resources employed, could not be reconciled with the American cultural understanding of war. As a consequence, Americans started to withdraw their support for war.

Artificial limited war presented the American people with an inexplicable contradiction. Some Americans were asked to give all, to commit their most precious resource, life, to a war, while the US government held back the employment of resources that could have ended the war in hours and days, as opposed to months and years. Limited war was only limited at the strategic and operational level. At the tactical level, the bullets, grenades, artillery, and bombs still killed and wounded. And there was nothing limited about dying. In the midst of the Korean War, after General Mathew B. Ridgway stopped the retreat, and again initiated offensive operations aimed at the destruction of the PLA, the US stopped major offensive operations and went on the strategic defense in the vicinity of the 38th parallel in Korea. This act, the assumption of the *strategic defense*, told the American people and the world the US was now fighting for limited objectives. Again, the President had placed artificial limitations on the American practice of war: a US Army that held substantial offensive capability voluntarily assumed the strategic defense and fought a protracted war of attrition. This was un-American. How could the President explain this to the American people? He couldn't, and for two long, bloody years support for the war among the American people deteriorated. The American people were unwilling to fight a strategically defensive, protracted war of attrition. On the strategic defense there was no way to win. Eisenhower ultimately ended the Korean War by threatening the use of nuclear weapons, threatening a return to the practice of total war. The American practice of war in Korea violated too many tenets of the American culture of war.

The Korean War was short and, considered by many, an aberration. The Korean War, however, represented the future of warfare. The paradox of the Korean War grew into a cultural crisis during the Vietnam War. The entire ground war in Vietnam was fought on the strategic defense. The Cold War was a strategically defensive war. It was based on the "policy of containment." However, strategically defensive Cold War was tolerated by the American people because of the knowledge that the next war would be total nuclear war, and because no Americans were fighting and dying.

Militarism and Consumption

At the same time the United States entered the new era of artificial limited war it entered an unprecedented buildup for total nuclear war. The preparation for war with the Soviet Union touched every American life, creating a new form of American militarism. Americans witnessed and participated in the greatest arms race in human history. New technologies, new capabilities, new levels of destructive power continued to enter the inventories of both superpowers. Throughout the 1950 and 1960s, Americans knew they were preparing for a total nuclear war with the Soviet Union, and that airpower and nuclear weapons were the primary instruments. They witnessed incredible developments in technologies. They witnessed the development of rocket technologies, supersonic aircraft, satellite technologies, television and communication technologies, and they envisioned a future where "starships" travelled the galaxy and wars were conducted from their clean high-tech bridges with lasers and photon torpedoes. Americans not only accepted this arms race, they expected their government, scientists, engineers, universities, and military leaders to win it. They expected to have the best

weapons and the most advanced military technologies. They expected to be the first to the moon, and then on to other planets. War, real science and technology, and science fiction were merged. Americans came to accept high defense budgets, billion dollar weapon systems, and top secret research and development programs. At the same time, the United States maintained a small conscripted Army that many believed was obsolete and would play only a minor role in future wars.

This arms race and buildup was paralleled by unprecedented economic expansion, unprecedented prosperity, and *unprecedented consumption*. Americans started to enjoy a new standard of living. American expectations from life expanded with every mile of the new interstate highway system, and with every new airport and jet airliner added to the American landscape. Home ownership, automobile and television ownership, and annual vacations became parts of the "American dream." Commercial advertisements told Americans to consume. Shopping and consumption, getting and consuming, became the major American activity. The quality of life in the United States reached levels unknown to large populations of humanity in all previous centuries. A new tenet of American citizenship became the right to ever increasing levels of consumption. These new levels of consumption had ramifications for the American people, both physical and psychological. Without doubt, Americans in 2001 were, physically and psychologically, less able to perform as combat soldiers than in 1941.

In the early 1960s the United States went to war in Vietnam, accepting the responsibilities that came with its new role in world affairs. During the Vietnam War, the precedent established by President Truman was maintained. The Vietnam War was an *artificial limited war*. The US Army and Marine Corps fought the entire war on the strategic defense—a protracted war of attrition. There was no possibility of strategically offensive operations to destroy the enemy's main army in its homeland. North Vietnam's contiguous border with the PRC assured that the United States would not invade. This meant the war was necessarily protracted. The war was to be won with airpower, but not with nuclear weapons and not in accordance with the Air Force's strategic bombing doctrine. The Air Force employed a new limited war airpower doctrine called "graduated response." It did not work. It did not convince the enemy he could not win. Artificial limited war, as practiced in Korea and later Vietnam, exhausted the will of the American people. Each year of the Vietnam War, American support deteriorated.

The war did not fit into either of the American paradigms for war. It did not fit into the traditional American practice of war, with large, conscripted armies conducting offensive operations to destroy the enemy's main army, or the new technological vision of war from the air. Each year of the war the contradiction grew in intensity. The longer the war went on, the greater the estrangement between the American people and the Army and the American people and the government. Between 1968 and 1972 the war in Vietnam exploded into a conflict in the United States: the American people vs. the US government and Army. In 1969, the Nixon Administration started the slow withdrawal of US forces, handing power back to the South Vietnamese, the Vietnamization of the war. And in 1973, the American people removed themselves from the conduct of the wars of the United States. The all-volunteer force came into existence.

Artificial Limited War caused the Establishment of the All-volunteer Forces

It asked some Americans to sacrifice everything as if they were fighting a total war, while other Americans sacrificed nothing. It asked some Americans to sacrifice everything, while the government limited the means employed. Some Americans were asked to commit their most precious possessions, their sons and daughters, to a war the United States government did not intend to win. The national consensus and national unity that was the norm in total war was almost completely absent in artificial limited wars. The passions of the people were intentionally kept in check by the government, which recognized that the involvement of all the people could push war towards the extremes, towards total war, and possibly towards nuclear war. During the Vietnam War, American discontent with artificial limited war grew until the war effort was no longer sustainable. The American people withdrew their support for the war, which meant

they withdrew their sons and daughters from the war, by not supporting the draft. The all-volunteer force would fight the future wars of the United States.

With the collapse of the Soviet Union, the checks on US offensive strategy and operations were gone. The US no longer had to conform its behavior to take into consideration the nuclear arsenal and military capabilities of the Soviet Union. The employment of US forces greatly increased. The Institute of Land Warfare noted in 2000 that:

> The United States employs its Army around the world to promote stability, prevent conflict, and deter aggression. There are routinely more than 140,000 Army personnel forward stationed or deployed around the world. They are conducting an average of 300 separate missions in 70 different countries. . . . The Army is in more places doing more missions than ever before. Since 1989, the average frequency of Army contingency deployments has increased from one every four years to one every 14 weeks. Some of these (Bosnia for example) have evolved into ongoing commitments. The Army today is more than one-third smaller than it was in 1989. In practical terms, that means the number of active divisions has been reduced from 18 to 10. The increasing number and scope of these operations . . . lead to repetitive deployments for individual servicemembers . . . and significantly greater wear and tear on equipment.[9]

The United States now had a new, long-service professional fighting force that was not dependent on the will of the American people. The political costs of war for the President and Congress decreased significantly. The production of new airpower technologies, such as stealth aircraft and precision missiles, and the development of new doctrines, such as "network-centric warfare," created the illusion that wars could be fought and won quickly and cheaply. The airpower paradigm that emerged during World War II was still influencing decisions in Washington, even though it has never proven decisive.

In the wake of the terrorist attacks on the United States, this new American practice of war was confirmed. Less than one percent of the 300 million American "citizens" carried the burden of two long wars in Afghanistan and Iraq. The American under-standing of *citizenship* had been transformed. President Bush asked nothing of the American people. He gave them tax cuts and told them to continue their normal practices of consumption. War, a practice that once required national unity, sacrifice, commitment to something beyond oneself, love of country, and the emotions and passions of the people, now required almost nothing from the people. In artificial limited war the *survival* of the United States was not directly threatened.

Clausewitz's trinity of war no longer serves as a useful analytic tool for understanding war in the twenty-first century. The people have been removed from the equation of war, and artificial limited war is now the primary practice. But, is this practice of war sustainable?

*   *   *   *   *

The issue of *militarism* requires special consideration, because it is invisible to most Americans, and yet an accepted cultural norm. Americans willingly expend hundreds of billions of dollars annually on the means for war, but do not show up to fight. This suggests that Americans derive great satisfaction and value from the production and maintenance of the means of war, apart from the value these weapon systems bring to national security. Americans are not militaristic in the sense that they love war. They are militaristic in the sense that, for multiple reasons, they love the means of war. During the Cold War, militarism became part of American culture, not just the American culture of war. The production of military equipment, the development of new technology, and the sustainment of military facilities is not simply a function of military necessity. It is a function of the needs of congressmen and women to get reelected, the needs of regional economies and specific communities to sustain jobs, the needs of various industries, and the needs of the self-image of American people. During the Cold War the military became big business. Today the United States is the largest arms producer and dealer on Earth. Many of the best minds and best scientific institutions in America are committed to the production of weapons systems and military-related technologies. Many universities depend on defense, or defense-related contracts and

grants to maintain their institutions. Many states depend on defense dollars to maintain their economies. The standard of living in certain areas of the country is directly influenced by the production or cancellation of a particular weapon system, or the movement of specific military units. The most powerful position in the United States after the President is that of Secretary of Defense, who in 2010 managed a budget of over $600 billion, considerably more than the gross domestic product of most states on Earth. The military forces of the United States are employed in almost half of the countries on Earth, directly influencing the actions of their governments, and American forces indirectly influence in the actions of all states on Earth.[10] Every year the American film industry produces movies that highlight the capabilities of American war machines and forces. Military force is the American answer to hostile aliens, monsters, rogue asteroids, natural disasters, manmade disasters, and just about every other calamity that can afflict a people. Consider the following examples of American militarism:

> Supporters of the C-17 [Globemaster III strategic airlifter] have been quietly lobbying to add five more of the big transports to the FY11 defense authorization bill. Last year, ramrodded by the late Pennsylvania Rep. John P. Murtha (D-Pa), lawmakers added 10 US Air Force C-17s to the planned "buy" at a cost of $2.5 billion. Boeing assembled the C-17 at a Long Beach, Calif. facility that manufactures no other product. Supporter of continued C-17 production for US forces say the program supports 30,000 jobs and that loss of the C-17 factory would be a devastating blow to the declining US industrial base. They've had their way until now—winning Congressional add-ons that over several years paid for 43 C-17s that the last two administrations said they didn't want and the Air Force said it didn't need.[11]

Consider the following community response to the movement of military forces:

> On July 29, [2010] the Pentagon announced that it would deactivate Holloman's [Air Force Base, N.M.] two F-22 squadrons, the 7th and 8th

Fighter Squadrons. . . . The Pentagon's announcement sought to reassure the community around Holloman with the news that the base would soon receive two F-16 Fighter Falcon squadrons and would inherit the FTU [formal training unit] mission for the F-16. One local press wag called this a "consolation prize." Local leaders including Krumm, Rep. Harry Teague, Gov. Bill Richardson and Alamogordo Mayor Ron Griggs all put a smiley face on the news by insisting that the transition from F-22 to F-16 would mean more jobs and greater prosperity for the region. One public official said that the FTU mission would result in more military people appearing in town temporarily, filling hotels and restaurants.[12]

Finally, consider the production plans for Navy attack submarines:

Beginning next year [2011], the Navy plans to double the production rate to two submarines per year for $2.5 billion apiece. The work is split between Electric Boat and Northrop Grumman Shipbuilding-Newport News in Virginia. The Navy intends to build a class of 30 ships to replace the aging Los Angeles-class attack submarines. In the next 30 years, the plan is to buy 25 at a cost of $63 billion. The production ramp-up of the Virginia class is being closely watched as it is happening amid growing concerns about the Navy's ability to finance big-ticket programs over the long term. The Virginia class, as well as most ship programs, will be competing for funds with what is expected to be a flat budget. Adding to the fiscal challenges are plans to begin building yet another new submarine to replace the Ohio-class ballistic missile boomers. This ship potentially could wreck the Navy's budget, analysts predict. The Congressional Budget Office estimates the lead ship of the Ohio replacement class in 2019 will cost $13 billion, with the total cost for the 12-ship class reaching $99 billion.[13]

With the collapse of the Soviet Union, it is difficult to know exactly what threat these vessels are being built to defeat.[14]

It is the job of military leaders to define the threats and request the resources necessary to defeat them. In the military mind, more is always better. It is the job of political leaders to weigh the threats and

the resources requested against the competing needs of the people. It is the job of the people to insure that the political leaders are doing their job and striking the appropriate balance between all the competing needs of the society. However, when the political leaders and the people argue for military capabilities in excess of that requested by military leaders, the military is serving needs beyond that of national security. And when the military is permitted to expend resources for weapons systems for which there is no enemy to fight, then militarism has infected the government and the people. The military in the United States serves political, economic, social, psychological, and cultural purposes that have nothing to do with national security.

American militarism is not simply a national problem; it is a global problem. The existence of military capabilities influences the decision for war and the objectives sought through war. The Bush Administration's decision for war in Iraq was based partly on the fact the war looked easy. It looked so easy that the George W. Bush Administration, unlike the George H.W. Bush Administration, sought total objectives and few allies. It sought the total destruction of the Iraqi government. Given the US experience in Operation Desert Storm, given the expansion in our airpower capabilities, given the so-called revolution in military affairs, "network-centric war" and "shock and awe," the Bush-Rumsfeld-Cheney team thought the war would be a piece of cake, and prematurely declared victory aboard the *USS Abraham Lincoln*. The irony is that this supposedly high-tech war, this war that was supposed to be won by airpower, evolved into another primitive ground war where soldiers and marines had to physically close with the enemy and kill them, and then learn to work with the local populations.

During the Cold War, the American people became addicted to defense spending. Arguably, the United States needs enemies to maintain its economy and keep its people employed and happy. Americans also became enamored with military hardware, jet aircraft, huge aircraft carriers, submarines, and so on. However, this love affair with the military did not include the conduct of ground warfare. It did not include the type of warfare we are most likely to fight in the future: conventional, ground combat, guerrilla and counterinsurgency combat, stability operations and nation-building. There was nothing high-tech, sophisticated, or glamorous about an infantry division, small unit warfare, or counterinsurgency campaigns. There were few high-tech, high-paying jobs for maintaining ground combat forces. And there were few congressmen and women supporting the retention of significant ground forces. As a consequence, the United States has maintained insufficient military capacity in ground forces and considerably more capacity than necessary in air and some types of naval forces. As a consequence, during each war we are forced to make major adjustments, relearn old lessons, and suffer unnecessary losses to meet the realities of the battlefield.

This New American Militarism is Unsustainable

It wastes limited resources, and precludes the United States from responding effectively to crises and conflicts in various parts of the world. The pace of deployments is more likely to increase than decrease. Irregular warfare, humanitarian crises, environmental security, globalization, climate change, economic crises, "the bottom billion," and other manmade and natural disasters that afflict humanity guarantee that the armed forces of the United States are going to be busy well into the middle of the twenty-first century. What the United States will need for these crises is well-trained, well-equipped, well-educated soldiers and marines, not stealth bombers and fighters, not precision missiles and nuclear weapons.

The Future of Warfare

The way the services think about national security has to evolve. The White House and Pentagon are always in a reactive mode. Currently, there are conflicts in states in Africa, the Middle East, Asia, Central and South America. These conflicts can spread and become regional wars. The interconnectedness of humanity on Earth will not permit Western nations to ignore this carnage, or wait until they explode across borders. Economic crises in foreign states are erupting into violence. These are potentially national security problems. Environmental change and climate change are creating emergency situations that have

the potential to emerge as national security problems. Water shortages have caused conflicts in the Middle East and Africa that have erupted into violence, which have the potential to influence the entire region. Energy shortages and disputes over oil and its distribution have caused conflicts that also have the potential to erupt into regional conflicts. Population growth and the exposure to other cultures via the Internet have produced millions of young men with expectations that are not being met by their governments and economies. These young men are potential resources for terrorist organizations and movements that are anti-democratic, anti-American, and anti-West. Economic development in foreign states with rising expectations is a matter of national security. Communicable diseases in a globalized world threaten the health of the American people, and could produce new crises that influence national security. Concepts of human security are changing the way nations and states respond to conflict in various parts of the world. The armed forces need to think, plan, train, and educate in new ways to be effective in this rapidly changing world.

* * * * * *

In 2009, Secretary of Defense Robert Gates informed the American people and the armed forces that:

> What is dubbed the war on terror is, in grim reality, a prolonged, worldwide irregular campaign— a struggle between the forces of violent extremism and those of moderation. Direct military force will continue to play a role in the long-term effort against terrorists and other extremists. But over the long term, the United States cannot kill or capture its way to victory. *Where possible, what the military calls kinetic operations should be subordinated to measures aimed at promoting better governance, economic programs that spur development, and efforts to address the grievances among the discontented, from whom the terrorists recruit.* It will take the patient accumulation of quiet success over a long time to discredit and defeat extremist movements and their ideologies . . . .

The recent past vividly demonstrates the consequences of failing to address adequately the dangers posed by insurgencies and failing states.

Terrorist networks can find sanctuary within the borders of a weak nation and strength within the chaos of social breakdown. A nuclear-armed state could collapse into chaos and criminality. The most likely catastrophic threats to the US homeland—for example, that of a US city being poisoned or reduced to rubble by a terrorist attack—are more likely to emanate from failing states than from aggressor states. . . . *Whether in the midst of or in the aftermath of any major conflict, the requirement for the US military to maintain security, provide aid and comfort, begin reconstruction, and prop up local governments and public services will not go away.*[15]

Gates's words were reflected in US National Defense Strategy: "US dominance in conventional warfare has given prospective adversaries, particularly non-state actors and their state sponsors, strong motivation to adopt asymmetric methods to counter our advantages. For this reason, we must display a mastery of irregular warfare comparable to that which we possess in conventional combat." This is no small task. Still, the National Defense Strategy and the words of the Secretary of Defense are ample recognition that irregular warfare (IW) has become as strategically important to national security as traditional, conventional warfare.[16] (IW encompasses counterterrorism operations, guerrilla warfare, foreign internal defense, counterinsurgency, and stability operations.) Given these new priorities, Gates directed the DOD and the services to:

1. Identify and prevent or defeat irregular threats from state and non-state actors.
2. Extend US reach into denied areas and uncertain environments by operating with and through indigenous foreign forces.
3. Train, advise, and assist foreign security forces and partners.
4. Support a foreign government or population threatened.
5. Create a safe, secure environment in fragile states.[17]

The Army and Marine Corps have been performing these missions in Afghanistan, Iraq, and other parts of the world since 9/11. Gates's directive gives formal recognition to those efforts and further delineates roles and responsibilities. But, the services are being asked to do too much, and they do not possess all the skills, talents, and resources needed to succeed in these complex environments.

Before this directive and strategy were put into effect, the armed forces had initiated a fundamental reorientation away from conventional warfare and state-to-state military operations, and towards counterinsurgency and stability operations, counterterrorism operations, nation-building, and humanitarian intervention. The creation of the Army and Marine Corps Counterinsurgency Center, the Joint Center for International Security Forces Assistance, and Peace Keeping Stability Operations Institute; and the new Army/Marine Corps manuals FM 3–24 Counterinsurgency (2006), FM 3–07 Stability Operations (2008), FM 3–0 Operations (2008), and FM 3–07.1 (2009) Security Force Assistance, are indicators of this transformation in thinking about the conduct of war.[18] The introduction to the Army's new Stability Operations manual states:

Today, the Nation remains engaged in an era of persistent conflict against enemies intent on limiting American access and influence throughout the world. This is a fundamental clash of ideologies and cultures, waged across societal abysses separating rich ethnic and religious traditions and profound differences in perspective. The Nation is embarking on a journey into an uncertain future where these precipitous divides threaten to expand as a result of increased global competition for natural resources, teeming urban populations with rising popular expectation, unrestrained technological diffusion, and a global economy struggling to meet the mounting demands from emerging market and third world countries.

The character of this conflict is unlike any other in recent American history, where military forces operating among the people of world will decide the major battles and engagements. *The greatest threat to our national security will not come from emerging ambitious states but from nations unable or unwilling to meet the basic needs and aspirations of their people.*[19]

The services have also adopted a more holistic approach to the conduct of war, accepting the need for a whole-of-government approach in a complex environment. Jointness, the integration of the talents, capabilities, and resources of the services, to create synergies in operations is not enough. Other governmental agencies, such as the Department of State, US Agency for International Development, Defense Intelligence Agency, Central Intelligence Agency, Federal Bureau of Investigation, Department of Justice, Drug Enforcement Administration, and the Department of Agriculture have critical roles to play. To achieve IW objectives and improve operational effectiveness, some of these agencies were integrated into strategic and operational plans in Iraq and Afghanistan. These agencies possess talents, skills, and abilities that are not found in the armed forces, but are greatly needed in many developing regions. As a result of these changes and new learning, the services are developing and integrating a new vocabulary, the vocabulary common to the United Nations, the Red Cross/Red Crescent, the US Agency for International Development, and other such agencies. Terms such as capacity building, comprehensive approach, interagency coordination, whole-of-government approach, security force assistance, conflict transformation, rule of law, fragile state, vulnerable state, crisis state, and other such terms are now being heard in the halls of the Command and General Staff College, the War Colleges, the service academies, and other military schools and training centers. *Still, the whole-of-government approach is not enough.*

Irregular warfare is in part a function of globalization, environmental change, and the aspirations of people. This rapidly changing environment requires us to look at security issues in new ways. Consider three concepts: *human security, environmental security,* and *expeditionary economics.*

Human security tenets are slowly becoming accepted in states and nations and by peoples in all parts of the Earth. The United Nations, the United States, NATO, and other alliances have committed resources and military forces in support of human security objectives. Consider the approach of the former Secretary-General of the UN, Kofi Annan:

Currently, most analysts, following Kofi Annan (2000), agree that human security encompasses both freedom from want and freedom from fear.

Broadly speaking, human security as freedom from want describes a condition or existence in which basic material needs are met, and in which there is a reasonable expectation that protection will be afforded during any crisis or downturn—natural or man-made—so that survival is not threatened. Human security as freedom from fear describes a condition of existence in which human dignity is realized, embracing not only physical safety but going beyond that to include meaningful participation in the life of the community, control over one's life and so forth. This suggests a radical account of politics as freedom from domination/exploitation, not simply the freedom to choose as advocated by the liberal tradition. Thus, while material sufficiency lies at the core of human security, in addition, the concept encompasses non-material dimensions to form a qualitative whole. In other words, human security embraces the whole gamut of rights, civil and political, economic and social, and cultural.[20]

The concept of "human security" is based on the belief that *all* human beings have the right to some basic level of security, for example, the right to live, the right to not be attacked, the right to speak, the right to associate, the right to gather for peaceful demonstrations, the right to food, water, and shelter, the right to medicine and medical treatment, the right to work, and the right to education and training.[21] In a book entitled, *The Bottom Billion: Why the Poorest Countries Are Failing and What Can be Done About It*, Paul Collier advanced the concept of human security and called for action.[22] The "bottom billion" live in the poorest states on Earth. Death through war, famine, ethnic cleansing, criminal and gang activities, natural disasters, and other forms of violence is common. The peoples of places such as Haiti, Ethiopia, Somalia, Laos, Burma, Afghanistan, and many others reside at the bottom. Collier has called for action:

To date, we have largely been bystanders in this struggle. We can do much more to strengthen the hand of the reformers. But to do so we will need to draw upon tools—such as military interventions, international standards-setting, and trade policy—that to date have been used for other purposes. The agencies that control these instruments have neither knowledge of nor interest in the problems of the bottom billion.[23]

The indicators show that this is changing, that the major Western powers are starting to realize that globalization, in part, means the exportation of conflicts and diseases, corrupt ideologies and extremist religious beliefs; and that, as a consequence, actions need to be taken before these situations explode into future 9/11s. Mary Kaldor, in an article titled, "Human Security in Complex Operations," observed that:

> Violence and resentment, poverty and illness, in places such as Africa, Central Asia, or the Middle East travel across the world through terrorism, transnational crime, or pandemics. Instead of allowing insecurity to travel, we need to send security in the opposite direction. The kind of security that Americans and Europeans expect to enjoy at home has to spread to the rest of the world. We cannot any longer keep our parts of the world safe while ignoring other places. The world is interconnected through social media, transportation, and basic human sympathy. In other words, human security is about the blurring of the domestic and international . . . .[24]

Kaldor asks for a broader vision of security. She defined "human security" as follows:

> Human security has a multifaceted definition which includes the security of individuals rather than states; security from both violence and economic and environmental threats; and security that is established through law rather than through war. It is a concept that can facilitate both the way one understands complex operations and how one designs the toolkit for addressing these risks and dangers.[25]

Kaldor, citing a UN Development Program report, wrote: "The report identified seven core elements, which together made up the concept of human security: economic security, food security, health security, environmental security, personal security, community security, and political security."[26] If all governments accepted these tenets of human security advanced by the United Nations, then governments that had the power to act would have the obligation to act. Under these conditions, the United States and other governments would have had to act to stop the genocide in Rwanda, the famine in Ethiopia and North Korea, and the political persecution in Iran and Syria and in other states.

The tenets of human security are extensions of the ideas that led to the creation of the United Nations, and efforts to preclude holocausts, such as that carried out by Nazi Germany against Jews in World War II. Kaldor noted that "the idea [is] that the international community has a responsibility to protect people threatened by genocide, ethnic cleansing, and other massive violations of human rights when their governments fail to act."[27] Kaldor and others who advance the tenets of human security are asking us to change the way we think about states and nations, about the use of armies and navies, and about the relationships between people and the conduct of war. She writes: "human security is about the everyday security of individuals and the communities in which they live rather than the security of borders; it is about the security of Afghans and Americans and Europeans, not just the security of the United States and Europe."[28] War is still the ultimate determinant of human activity on Earth. Perhaps Kaldor and others who support her views are being a bit naïve to think otherwise; yet, there are indicators that this way of thinking about security has found acceptance.

The Obama Administration has, to some degree, without formally doing so, accepted the tenets ·of human security. In March 2011, President Obama committed US forces to operations in Libya in order to preclude the anticipated massacre of rebellious, civilians, opponents of the Libyan dictator Muammar Qaddafi. Two months after the commencement of military operations, the Obama Administration justified its actions:

> The bottom line is this operation has achieved a great deal . . . in terms of saving lives; in terms of pushing back Qaddafi's forces and degrading his capabilities and his ability to threaten his own people; in terms, again, of building international support to isolate and pressure Qaddafi; and to pursue a goal that is profoundly in the interest of the Libyan people and the United States, which is an end to the targeting of civilians in Libya and ultimately, of course, a Libya that is more reflective of the aspirations of its own people.[29]

Libya did not attack the United States. Libya was not a threat to the security of the United States. In fact, the Qaddafi government had recently renounced its earlier efforts to acquire nuclear weapons, and was seeking accommodation and trade with the United States, United Kingdom, and Europe. The stated mission of the armed forces was not the destruction of the enemy's main army, or the destruction of the enemy's government. While Obama called for Qaddafi to leave Libya, he stressed that the mission was not regime change, but to preclude a massacre, a humanitarian crisis. The United States, with the approval provided by a United Nations resolution, and in concert with its European allies, initiated military operations in Libya to provide *human security*. The big question is: can this policy be applied universally? Is the United States going to commit military forces to guarantee the human security of all peoples of the Earth, and, if not, how do administrations determine when to intervene and when not to intervene? What are the requirements for military intervention to provide human security? Kaldor delineated six principles of human security: the primacy of human rights, legitimate political authority, multilateralism, the bottom-up approach, regional focus, and clear and transparent civilian command. These principles, however, do not translate into political guidance or policies for the governments of Western nations. Something more is needed.

· *Environmental security* issues are growing causes for wars. Chris King, an environmental scientist, in a document titled, "Understanding International Environmental Security: A Strategic Military Perspective," defined "environment security" as follows:

Environmental security is a process for effectively responding to changing environmental conditions that have the potential to reduce peace and stability in the world. Environmental security involves identifying the critical issues and accomplishing environmentally related actions to prevent and/or mitigate anthropogenically induced adverse changes in the environment and minimize the impacts of the range of environmental disasters that could occur.

One does not have to accept the predictions of the global-warming, dooms-dayers to recognize that environmental issues are real and a growing cause of regional conflict. States, nations, and peoples are fighting over water resources, arable land, land that is not inundated with water, and environmental degradation that is making the land in some regions unlivable. Environmental scientists are asking political and military leaders to see the world through very different eyes. Consider the words of Norman Myers: "National security is not just about fighting forces and weaponry. It relates to watersheds, croplands, forests, genetic resources, climate and other factors that rarely figure in the minds of military experts and political leaders, but increasingly deserve, in their collectivity, to rank alongside military approaches as crucial in a nation's security."[30]

Without a sustainable environment, peace cannot exist. In Central Command and Africa Command regions, environmental security issues are among the major causes of conflict. Joint Forces Command, in an annual document, *The Joint Operating Environment* (JOE), has identified ten "Trends Influencing the World's Security" that pose challenges for the United States in the years and decades ahead.[31] They include: demographics, globalization, economics, energy, food, water, climate change and natural disasters, pandemics, cyber, and space. The JOE study notes that: "The world's future over the coming quarter of a century will be subject to enormous disruption and surprises, natural as well as man-made."[32] We need to prepare for these "disruptions and surprises." The expanding population, rising expectations, energy scarcity, water scarcity, climate change, and natural disasters are making environmental security issues, national security issues that will involve the armed forces.

Environmental security is not just a strategic issue, it also an operational and tactical problem. In 2008, the Army commissioned a study through the RAND Corporation, titled: "Green Warriors: Army Environmental Considerations for Contingency Operations from Planning Through Post-Conflict."[33] The study concluded that:

environmental considerations—including clean water, sanitation, hazardous-waste management— can be important for achieving overall US objectives during reconstruction and post-conflict operations, including both short- and long-term stability. If not properly addressed in planning or operations, environmental considerations can increase the costs of an operation and make it more difficult for the Army to sustain the mission.[34]

The study group that prepared the report, while identifying the significance of environmental issues, noted that, "Yet, environmental considerations are not well incorporated into Army planning or operations in any phase of an operation;" and that "The Army needs to bring about a cultural change regarding the ways environmental issues are viewed and handled in contingencies. Such change is difficult and will require a broad-based effort that includes changes in doctrine, training, and equipment."[35]

Every time significant Army forces enter a region, an environment, it necessarily changes it, sometimes significantly and in ways we cannot see and understand. The impact, however, is usually negative, and the relationship between the hearts and minds of indigenous people and the environment is direct. When we use their water it affects them. When we process our waste it affects them. When we damage their fields it affects them. When we destroy or fail to identify and protect cultural resources it affects them. The RAND study bluntly stated: "It does no good to win the war only to forfeit the peace."[36] Currently, relatively few resources are devoted to understanding the environments in which the Army operates, or the rapidly changing "trends" identified in the JOE, or trying to find new ways to fix problems before they become disasters that require greater military involvement and the commitment of more resources. Stealth bombers and attack submarines will not provide the solutions. The Pentagon and the Services lack the knowledge, expertise, and facilities to analyze environmental security issues and develop strategies that mitigate environmental problems.

Expeditionary economics is a military matter. Without economic development, counterinsurgency and stability operations cannot succeed. The US Army and Marine Corps in Iraq and in Afghanistan have devoted considerable time and resources to the development of the economies of these countries. Both the COIN manual (FM 3–24) and the Stability Operations manual (FM 3–07) address the significance of economic development. In the COIN manual, under the heading, "Support Economic Development," it states: "Without a viable economy and employment opportunities, the public is likely to pursue false promises offered by insurgents.... Unemployed males of military age may join the insurgency to provide for their families."[37] In the Stability Operations manual, under the heading "Support to Economic and Infrastructure Development," it states: "Military tasks executed to support the economic sector are critical to sustainable economic development. The economic viability of a state is among the first elements of society to exhibit stress and ultimately fracture as conflict, disaster, and internal strife overwhelms the government.... Economic problems are inextricably tied to governance and security concerns."[38] And, under the heading "Economic Stabilization and Infrastructure," the manual directs practitioners to: "Implement programs that encourage trade and investment with initial emphasis on host-nation and regional investors, followed at a later stage by foreign investors."[39] While recognizing the importance of economic development in counterinsurgency and stability operations, the Army and Marine Corps have few resources and expertise to advance economic development in foreign countries. Some insist this is not a matter for the services. However, it is a mission-essential task in IW.

Carl Schramm, in an article titled, "Expeditionary Economics: Spurring Growth After Conflicts and Disasters," wrote: "Economic growth is critical to establishing social stability, which is the ultimate objective of these counterinsurgency campaigns and disaster-relief efforts."[40] Schramm noted that, "A central element in the failure to establish robust economies in war-torn or disaster-stricken countries is the prevailing doctrine of international development, according to which strong economies cannot emerge in poor countries." He concluded that: "It is imperative that US military develop its competence in economics. It must establish a new field of inquiry that treats economics reconstruction as part of any successful three-legged strategy of invasion, stabilization or pacification, and economic reconstruction. Call this expeditionary economics." The key is to get some form of economic activity started, to promote entrepreneurship, to provide the people with the minimum assistance necessary to make money.

As noted, the Army and Marine Corps are already involved in the economic development of failed states. Provincial reconstruction teams (PRTs) are part of the effort to get economic activities started in war-torn areas. The services have published "handbooks," such as, "Commander's Guide to Money as a Weapons System," and "Agribusiness Development Teams in Afghanistan," to help soldiers and marines use money more effectively to counter the appeal of the insurgents.[41] In the former handbook, in the Introduction it states:

> Warfighters at brigade, battalion, and company level in a counterinsurgency (COIN) environment employ money as a weapons system to win the hearts and minds of the indigenous population to facilitate defeating the insurgents. Money is one of the primary weapons used by warfighters to achieve successful mission results in COIN and humanitarian operations.[42]

Tactical commanders work with PRTs and are provided "Commander's Emergency Response Program" (CERP) money to influence events in their areas of operation. However, if the use of money does not translate into economic development, it is only a temporary fix that will ultimately result in failure. The handbook notes that one of the "specific uses for the CERP" is "economic, financial, and management improvement. Projects to improve economic or financial security."

Many soldiers object to the use of the term "money as a weapons system." Money does not kill or wound, or provide the psychological effects of M-4s or M-16s. And the distribution of foreign aid is not traditionally what soldiers do. Still, money can make the employment of real weapons less necessary in some cases, and thus, save lives. Soldiers and marines are doing things they have no education and little training to do. We are expending enormous resources to improve the lives of people in failed states with little understanding of theories and practices of economic development. However, no one else can do the job. Physical security is a prerequisite for economic security. Soldiers and marines must provide some basic level of physical security before initiating activities to provide economic security. But, they cannot wait until they have absolute security. What is a *permissive environment* for soldiers and marines is an untenable environment for UN and USAID workers and other non-combatant, external agents. We should not expect soldiers to become economists; hence, we need to provide soldiers with economists and the basic skills needed to succeed in developing regions threatened by extremist elements and failed governments.

*   *   *   *   *   *

War is not going to go away. However, the nature of warfare is changing. The type of warfare the United States is most likely to engage in will not directly threaten the survival of the state. While the United States needs to maintain conventional armor and mechanized forces and conventional naval and air forces, well trained and equipped, ready to fight, it also needs to maintain significant Army and Marine ground forces, infantry, capable of engaging in operations ranging from humanitarian assistance, to counterinsurgency operations, to full-scale infantry combat. Like it or not, the armed forces are the face of the United States in all parts of the planet. They have to engage with the people. Flying over the land or sailing by will not achieve political or humanitarian objectives. Significant ground forces are absolutely necessary. The presence of US forces on the ground creates security, stability, and opportunity. However, Army and Marine Corps leaders have to accept the fact they will never have enough soldiers and marines to do all that is required, and that political leaders will continue to put them in situations that stretch their forces and intellect. The Army and Marine Corps will remain relatively small forces, and the American people will remain uninvolved and uncommitted.

The whole-of-government approach is not enough. A broader vision is required. Only America's universities can provide the research necessary to fix the problems that are facing humanity. Only America's universities possess the capacity to train and educate large numbers of servicemen and women in the skills, knowledge, and expertise they need to function effectively in the multi-cultural, diverse environment in which they are most likely to fight in the future. *A new relationship between the services and America's universities is absolutely necessary to meet the multiple commitments and multiple types of demands that are certain in future complex environments.*

The services need to fundamentally change the way they *educate* officers, NCOs, and enlisted men and women. Learning and adapting has to become a continuous process in the professional military education of all the services. Hierarchical, objective-driven organizations, with long histories of success operate on principles and well-established systems of belief that create norms of behavior, predictability, and a strong reluctance to take risks, to try new methods, and to take on new challenges. Hierarchical structures pass down orders to subordinate organizations. Original ideas, creative thinking, independent thinking and actions are suppressed. Technology, doctrine, rank structure, regulations, laws, standard operational procedures, command selection and promotion systems, training, and service culture produce conformity that inhibits the ability of service men and women to think "outside of the box." The structure and the systems create predictability, but diminish responsiveness and dynamism.

The future will not look like the past. Managing conflicts between well-established nations and states, with regular armies and navies will be only one of many requirements placed upon the services. Many of the future requirements of the armed forces will demand new, creative, responsive solutions and leadership. Today Army and Marine forces are distributed over great distances, requiring decentralized chains of command. Captains and lieutenants, sergeants, and even corporals are making decisions that influence the lives of indigenous peoples. These forces are required to act independently, to respond immediately, to think outside of the box, and to make decisions with minimal guidance from senior leaders. We need to better prepare and better educate our soldiers and marines to make the right decisions in these complex, diverse environments.

Officers and NCOs need to be given time to matriculate from universities, time to be exposed to the diversity common on America's campuses, time to discuss and debate ideas, time to understand and appreciate other cultures, languages, religions, and ideologies, and time to think, reflect, and learn. Every day of the work week, hundreds, even thousands, of servicemen and women, in and out of uniform, need be on the campuses of America's universities. And on every major military installation with deployable forces and/or education responsibilities, professors, faculty members, and graduate students in significant numbers ought to be working with military leaders at all levels to assist in pre-deployment education, such as language, culture, and history, and to help senior leaders research new solutions to problems they are likely to face in foreign lands. The Army and Marine Corps should orient each of their divisions and brigades towards specific regions of the Earth, so they can learn the history, culture, and languages of the peoples who live there. We need to have not just the best-equipped, best-trained military on Earth. We need to have the smartest, best-educated military on Earth, the smartest soldiers and marines ever deployed. Education is a force multiplier.

Given the relatively small size of our armed forces, the world-wide responsibilities of the United States, the consistent pressure from Congress to cut the size of ground forces, and the long service of soldiers, sailors, airmen, and marines, we absolutely need and can have the best-educated, smartest armed forces on Earth. The failure of the services to fully exploit these tremendous resources—America's universities—to educate and train servicemen and women and to provide the critical research they need to address complex problems will result in strategic failures that cost lives, damage the United States politically, and cost enormous, precious resources.

NOTES

Introduction

1. General George W. Casey, "Chief of Staff of the Army Statement on the Army's Strategic Imperatives," before the Senate Armed Services Committee United States House of Representatives, 15 November 2007, http://www.army.mil/-speeches/2007/11/15/6144-chief-of-staff-of-the-army

2. Robert Oppenheimer, "Atomic Weapons and American Policy," Foreign Affairs, XXXI: 4 July 1953, 529 (italics added). Quoted in Lawrence Freedman, *The Evolution of Nuclear Strategy* (NY: St. Martin's Press, 1983), 94.

3. It is important to recognize the United States is a democratic nation. Its people have a say. The people of the Soviet Union had no say in the national defense policies of the country. In addition, they were traumatized by the experience of World War II. They accepted, without question, the defense policies of their government.

4. Michael J. Weiss, *The Clustered World* (Boston: Little, Brown, 2000), 10, 258.

5. Andrew Marshall with the support of Rumsfeld developed a plan called "A Strategy for a Long Peace," 12 February 2001. The plan cut two active duty heavy divisions, like the 3rd ID that invaded Iraq in 2003, and four Army National Guard Divisions.

6. Peter Boyer, "A Different War: Is the Army Becoming Irrelevant?" *The New Yorker*, 1 July 2002, 54–67.

Chapter 1

1. Robert O'Connell, "The Origins of War," *Experience of War*, ed. Robert Cowley (New York: Laurel, 1992), 11.

2. John A. Vasquez, *The War Puzzle* (New York: Cambridge University Press, 1993), 196, 197.

3. Cultural theories have been used to examine and explain the behavior of nations in war throughout recorded history. J. Hector St. John de Crevecoeur in 1782 published a letter entitled "What is an American," in which he wrote: "Men are like plants; the goodness and flavor of the fruit proceeds from the peculiar soil and exposition in which they grow. We are nothing but what we derive from the air we breathe, the climate we inhabit, the government we obey, the system of religion we profess, and the nature of our employment." In "Letters from an American Farmer (New York: E.P. Fox, Duffield, 1904), 56. See also: Richard Maxwell Brown, *No Duty to Retreat: Violence and Values in American History and Society* (Norman: University of Oklahoma Press, 1991); Richard Slotkins, *Regeneration Through Violence: The Mythology of the American Frontier, 1600–1860* (New Hampshire: Wesleyan University Press, 1973); and *Gunfighter Nation* (New York: Harper, 1986); John Shy, "The Cultural Approach to the History of War," *The Journal of Military History* Special Issue 57 (October 1993) 13–26; Colin Gray, *The Geopolitics of Super Power* (Lexington: University Press of Kentucky, 1988) and *War, Peace and Victory* (New York: Simon and Schuster, 1990); Ken Booth, *Strategy and Ethnocentrisim* (New York: Holmes and Meier, 1979); and Ken Booth, "The Concept of Strategic Culture Affirmed," *Strategic Power: USA/USSR*, ed. Carl G. Jacobsen (London: Macmillan, 1990).

4. Bronislaw Malinowski, "An Anthropological Analysis of War," *War: Studies from Psychology, Sociology, Anthropology*, rev. ed., ed. Leon Bramson and George Goethals (New York: Basic Books, 1968), 256.

5. Clifford Geertz, *The Interpretation of Cultures: Selected Essays* (New York: Basic Books, 1973), 5.

6. Philip Babcock Gove, *Webster's Third New International Dictionary of the English Language Unabridged* (Springfield, Massachusetts: G. & C. Merriam Company, 1971), 552.

7. Charles H. Coates and Roland J. Pellegrin, *Military Sociology: a Study of American Military Institutions and Military Life* (Maryland: Social Science Press, 1965), 26, 27.

8. Colin Gray, *War, Peace, and Victory* (New York: Simon and Schuster, 1990), 45, 46.

9. Pierre Bourdieu, *Outline of a Theory of Practice* (London: Cambridge University Press, 1985).

10. Bourdieu, *Outline of a Theory of Practice*, 72, 78.

11. Bourdieu, *Outline of a Theory of Practice*, 15.

12. Richard Maxwell Brown, *No Duty to Retreat* (Norman: University of Oklahoma Press, 1991), 37.

13. Samuel Stouffer, et al., *The American Soldier* (New Jersey: Princeton University Press, 1949), 131–135.

14. Frederick Jackson Turner, "The Significance of the Frontier in American History," *The Turner Thesis: Concerning the Role of the Frontier in American History*, ed., George Roger Taylor (Boston: D.C. Heath and Co., 1956), 2. Also, see: Frederick Jackson Turner, *The Frontier in American History* (New York: Holt, Rinehart and Winston, 1962) and *Frontier and Section: Selected Essays of Frederick Jackson Turner* (New Jersey: Prentice Hall, 1961).

15. Gray, *The Geopolitics of Super Power*, 43. Also see: Colin Gray, "Strategy in the Nuclear Age: The United States, 1945–1991," *The Making of Strategy*, ed. Williamson Murray, MacGregeor Knox, and Alvin Bernstein (New York: Cambridge University Press, 1994), 579–611.

16. Colin S. Gray, *Modern Strategy* (New York: Oxford University Press, 1999), 129.

17. Vasquez, *The War Puzzle*, 206, 207.

18. Vasquez, *The War Puzzle*, 202.

19. Vasquez, *The War Puzzle*, 207.

20. Victor Davis Hanson, *Carnage and Culture* (New York: Random House, 2001), 7.

21. John A. Lynn, *Battle: A History of Combat and Culture* (Boulder, Colorado: Westview Press, 2003), xiv.

22. Hanson, *Carnage and Culture*, 4. John Lynn in the introduction to his book, *Battle*, is critical of the way in which Hanson uses the concept of culture. He believes that emphasizing *The Western Way of War*, causes Hanson to, "Ultimately . . . replace the notion of an all encompassing universal soldier not with variety and change but with a universal and eternal *Western* soldier and, by implication, with an equally universal and stereotyped non-Western, or 'Oriental,' warrior." Lynn concluded that Hanson's work was "deeply flawed."

23. Russell F. Weigley, "American Strategy from Its Beginnings through the First World War," *Makers of Modern Strategy*, ed. Peter Paret (Princeton, New Jersey: Princeton University Press, 1986), 408.

24. D.W. Brogan, *The American Character* (New York: Alfred A. Knopf, 1944), 150. In a chapter entitled, "The American Way in War," Brogan wrote: "Space determined the American way in war, space and the means to conquer space. Into empty land the pioneers moved, feeling their way slowly, carefully, timidly if you like. The reckless lost their scalps; the careful, the prudent, the rationally courageous survived and by logistics, by superiority in resources, in tenacity, in numbers."

25. Norvell De Atkine, "Why Arab Armies Lose Wars," *Armed Forces in the Middle East: Politics and Strategy*, ed.

by Barry Rubin and Thomas A. Keaney (London: Frank Cass, 2002), 23–40.

26. Kenneth M. Pollack, "The Influence of Arab Culture on Arab Military Effectiveness" (Ph.D, Massachusetts Institute of Technology, 1996), 259–261, 759.

27. Kenneth M. Pollack, *Arabs at War* (Lincoln: University of Nebraska Press, 2002), 574. Also see, Raphael Patai, *The Arab Mind*, revised edition (New York: Hatherleigh Press, 2002).

28. For example, in the Yom Kippur War in 1973, Egypt, under the leadership of Anwar Sadat, employed new strategy and doctrine against Israel that took into consideration the attributes of the Egyptian and Israeli cultures. By doing so Egypt fought a very limited conventional war, with modest military objectives, and a major political war, which involved the superpowers. Sadat achieved his political objectives.

29. Albert Axell and Hideaki Kase, *Kamikaze: Japan's Suicide God's* (New York: Pearson Education, 2002).

30. Victor Davis Hanson, *Ripples of Battle* (New York: Doubleday, 2003), 15, 16. Hanson put this tenet in historical context: "But rarely do we appreciate battles as human phenomena or the cumulative effects—the ripples—that change communities for years, or centuries even, well after the day's killing is over. . . . In this regard I plead guilty to the classical notion—more or less continuous since Herodotus and Thucydides to the close of the nineteenth century—*of the primacy of military history*. In theory, of course, all events have equal historical importance. . . . Yet in reality, all actions are still not so equal. We perhaps need to recall the more traditional definition of the craft of history—a formal record of past events that *are notable or worthy of remembrance*. Whereas *I Love Lucy* might have transformed the way thousands of Americans in the 1950s and 1960s saw suburban life, women's roles or Cubans, it still did not alter the United States in the manner of Yorktown, Gettysburg, or Tet—in creating, preserving, or almost losing an entire society."

31. Adam Smith, *The Wealth of Nations* (New York: The Modern Library, 1937), 739. Adam Smith wrote: "Even though the martial spirit of the people were of no use towards the defence of the society, yet to prevent that sort of mental mutilation, deformity, and wretchedness, which cowardice necessarily involves in it, from spreading themselves through the great body of the people, would still deserve the most serious attention of government; in the same manner as it would deserve its most serious attention to prevent a leprosy or any other loathsome and offensive disease . . . from spreading itself among them. . . ."

32. William McDougall, "The Instinct of Pugnacity," reprinted in *War*, ed. Leon Bramson and George W. Goethals (New York: Basic Books, 1964), 33–64. McDougall wrote: "The Germanic tribes were perhaps

more pugnacious and possessed of more military virtue in a higher degree than any other people that has existed since. They were the most terrible enemies … they could never be subdued because … they loved fighting, that is, because they were innately pugnacious." McDougall's thesis is flawed because he attributes differences in the "instinct of pugnacity" to race. He argues that some races, like some dogs, are naturally more aggressive than others. While his observation that some nations have been more warlike than others is essentially correct, he failed to recognize that culture, not race, was the primary cause, and that culture was influenced by numerous factors, and that as a consequence, the so-called "instinct of pugnacity" was not a permanent condition. Japan and Germany are noteworthy for the cultural change that was initiated out of the trauma of World War II. In the year 2000 both nations were considered among the least pugnacious on the planet.

33. Michael C. Desch, "Explaining the Gap: Vietnam, the Republicanization of the South, and the End of the Mass Army," in *Soldiers and Civilians*, ed. Peter D. Feaver and Richard H. Kohn (Cambridge, Massachusetts: MIT Press, 2001), 290–324, 295.

34. Michael J. Weiss, *The Clustered World* (Boston: Little, Brown and Company, 2000), 10, 11, 21, 22.

35. Weiss, *The Clustered World*, 13, 14. Weiss defined clusters: "Clusters, which were created to identify demographically similar zip codes around the US, are now used to demarcate a variety of small geographic areas, including census tracts (500–1,000 households) and zip plus four postal codes (about ten households). Once used interchangeably with *neighborhood type*, however, the term *cluster* now refers to population segments where, thanks to technological advancements, no physical contact is required for cluster membership.... The cluster system serves as a barometer in this changing world, monitoring how the country is evolving in distinct geographical areas."

36. Norvell De Atkine, "Why Arab Armies Lose Wars," 26.

37. L. Luca Cavalli-Sforza, Paolo Menozzi, and Alberto Piazza, *The History and Geography of Human Genes* (Princeton, New Jersey: Princeton University Press, 1994), Introduction. Also, see Steve Olson, *Mapping Human History* (New York: Houghton Mifflin, 2002), 3–7. Olson wrote: "Every single one of the 6 billion people on the planet today is descended from the small group of anatomically modern humans who once lived in eastern Africa.... Human groups are too closely related to differ in any but the most superficial ways. The genetic study of our past is revealing that the cultural difference between groups could not have biological origins. Those differences must result from the experiences individuals have had.... Genetic research is now about to end our long misadventure with the idea

of race. We now know that groups overlap genetically to such a degree that humanity cannot be divided into clear categories."

38. Francis Crick, *The Astonishing Hypothesis* (New York: Charles Scribner's Sons, 1994), 10.

39. Jeffrey Kluger, "Ambition: Why Some People Are Most Likely to Succeed," *Time*, 14 November 2005, 48–59. Kluger noted that: "Ongoing studies of identical twins have measured achievement motivation—lab language for ambition—in identical siblings separated at birth, and found that each twin's profile overlaps 30% to 50% of the other's. In genetic terms, that's an awful lot...."

40. David H. Hackworth, *About Face* (New York: Simon and Schuster, 1989), 47.

41. Henry G. Gole, Colonel US Army Retired, "Combat in Korea: Reflections by a once young soldier," Unpublished paper (italics added).

42. It is important to disassociate the capacity to engage in battle from the predisposition for pugnacity. Individuals with zero capacity to risk their lives can be extremely bellicose. Also, the Army and Marine Corps do not produce warmongers, quite the contrary.

43. L. Luca Cavalli-Sforza, Paolo Menozzi, and Alberto Piazza, *The History and Geography of Human Genes* (New Jersey: Princeton University Press, 1994), 6.

44. Jean-Jacques Rousseau, *Emile or On Education*, ed. Allan Bloom (New York: Basic Books, 1979), 221.

45. For a survey of the literature on the role of hunting in human development see: Matt Cartmill, *A View to a Death in the Morning: Hunting and Nature Through History* (Cambridge, Massachusetts: Harvard University Press, 1993). Much of this literature has been discredited because of developments in genetic science. Also, see: Barbara Ehrenreich, *Blood Rites: Origins and History of the Passions of War* (London: Virago Books, 1997).

46. Infantry Journal Staff, "Army Ground Forces," *Infantry Journal*, June 1946, 17–23.

47. William H. Kelly, Major US Army, "War Neuroses," *Infantry Journal*, August 1946, 20, 21.

48. Lord Moran, *Anatomy of Courage* (New York: Avery Publishing, 1987), 151.

49. Charles MacDonald, "The Qualities of a Soldier," *The Army Information Digest*, December 1950, 7–13.

50. Audie Murphy, *To Hell and Back* (New York: Henry Holt and Co., 1949), 13, 14.

51. Dwight D. Eisenhower, *Crusade in Europe* (New York: Garden City, 1948), 454, 455.

52. John C. McManus, *The Americans at D-Day* (New York: Tom Doherty Associates Book, 2004), 98, 99.

53. Within the US Army and Marine Corps at all times there have been systems for the elimination of men considered unfit. No sergeant or officer with average intelligence who has trained soldiers for war for more than six months believes that all men are created equal. The ability to observe men in difficult, strenuous

circumstances over long periods of time rapidly destroys this myth. The elimination of soldiers from combat arms, and the Army, was (is) routine. The means of elimination were long ago established and institutionalized. The system for producing combat soldiers from the point of entry to the battlefield was a constant process of weeding out. Even in the late 1960s and early 1970s, when the nation and Army were desperate to find and draft men to send to Vietnam, the Army recognized that some men were "un-trainable" and eliminated them.

54. Philip Babcock Grove, *Webster's Third New International Dictionary of the English Language* (Massachusetts: G&C Merriam, 1971).

55. Victor Krulak, Lt. Gen. USMC, *First to Fight* (Annapolis: Naval Institute Press, 1984), xv.

56. It is human nature to compare, and assess value based on some scale, which is at least in part culturally imbued. Hence, no matter how much an individual has, it is relative to what others have. Perceived disparity causes people to covet, and disparities in power, disparities between the weak and the strong, motivate actions to take what is coveted. Fighting to get is fundamental to human existence. For a more complete analysis and bibliography of the unchanging factors in human nature, the human condition, and war, see Adrian R. Lewis, "Causes of War," *Reader's Guide to Military History*, ed. Charles Messenger (London: Fitzroy Dearborn Publishers, 2001), 81–85.

Chapter 2

1. Harry Truman, *Memoirs of Harry S. Truman 1945*, Vol. I (New York: A Da Capo Paperback, 1955), 506.

2. John Shy, *A People Numerous and Armed*, Revised ed. (Ann Arbor: University of Michigan Press, 1991), 279, 280.

3. Robert E. Osgood, *Limited War* (Chicago: University of Chicago Press, 1957), 29, 30.

4. T.R. Fehrenbach, *This Kind of War* (New York: MacMillian, 1989), 161.

5. US Army, N.A. Skinrood, Colonel US Army, Officer Assignment Division, Subject: Data for Comment on Recommendation of Reserve Officers Association, Main Library, USMA.

6. Numerous studies have characterized the American way of war. See: Maurice Matloff, "The American Approach to War, 1919–1945," *The Theory and Practice of War* (New York: Prager, 1965), 213–243; John Shy, *A People Numerous and Armed*, 272, 273; Russell Weigley, *The American Way of War*, Colin Gray, *The Geopoliticals of Super Power* (Lexington: University Press of Kentucky, 1988); and others.

7. For the studies on the adaptability of the US Army see: Michael Doubler, *Closing with the Enemy* (Lawrence,

Kansas: University Press of Kansas, 1994); Stephen E. Ambrose, *Citizen Soldiers* (New York: Simon and Schuster, 1997); and Russell Hart, *Clash of Arms* (Boulder, Colo.: Lynne Rienner, 2001).

8. The tenet was restricted to white men until the latter half of the twentieth century. Males of other racial groups were believed to lack the martial spirit and even the physical capabilities of white men.

9. Dwight D. Eisenhower, President, Inaugural Address, 20 January 1953, Congressional Record.

10. George M. Fredrickson, *The Black Image in the White Mind* (Middletown, Connecticut: Wesleyan University Press, 1971), 99. Also, see David Roediger, *Working Toward Whiteness* (New York: Basic Books, 2005).

11. Herbert McClosky and John Zaller, *The American Ethos: Public Attitudes toward Capitalism and Democracy* (Cambridge, Massachusetts: Harvard University Press, 1984), 82, 83.

12. McClosky and Zaller in *The American Ethos*, 85.

13. Russell Weigley, *History of the United States Army*, Enlarged Ed. (Bloomington: Indian University Press, 1984), 16.

14. Alexander Hamilton, *The Federalist: A Commentary on the Constitution of the United States*, No. 25, ed. Robert Scigliano (New York: The Modern Library, 2000), 155. Hamilton's military papers are found in volumes 6 & 7 of his collected Works, ed. Henry Cabot Lodge, Federal Ed., 12 vols. (New York: 1904).

15. Weigley, *History of the US Army*, 154.

16. Emory Upton, *The Military Policy of the United States* (Washington: GPO, 1917), VII.

17. US Army Ground Forces, "AGF Job: To Build Units Fit to Fight," *Infantry Journal*, June 1946, 17–23.

18. US Army, CMH Pub 104–9, *The Personnel Replacement System in the US* (Washington, D.C.: US GPO, 1988), 247–253.

19. Russell Weigley, "The American Military and the Principle of Civilian Control from McClellan to Powell," *The Journal of Military History* SPECIAL ISSUE 57, October 1993, 52. Charles Kirkpatrick in his study, *Writing the Victory Plan*, uses slightly different figures. He uses the figure of 138,389,000 for the population of the United States.

20. Charles B. MacDonald, "The Qualities of a Soldier," *The Army Information Digest*, December 1950, 7–13. U.P. Williams, Lieutenant Colonel US Army, "They May Not Die—But They Wither Fast," *Military Review*, July 1950, 17–23. Audie Murphy, *To Hell and Back* (New York: Henry Holt and Co., 1949), 13, 14.

21. Frank Pace, Jr., Secretary of the Army, "The Army and Public Service" based on the Stafford Lecture, "Public Service, Present and Future," *Army Information Digest*, July 1952, 3 (emphasis added).

22. D.J. Carrison, Cdr. US Navy, "Our Vanishing Military Profession," *Military Review*, June 1954, 59–62.

23. Christopher Buckley, "Viet Guilt: Were the Real Prisoners of War the Young Americans Who Never Left Home?" *Esquire*, September 1983, 68–72. Buckley quoted Myra MacPherson of the *Washington Post*, who wrote: "Now there is some meager measure of reconciliation; some who used to taunt them (the homecoming soldiers) at army camps and airports—the student deferred taunting those less privileged draftees of those who felt compelled to serve their country—admit guilt and shame."

24. Manton Eddy, Lt. Gen. U.S.A., "Military Power and National Policy," *Army Information Digest*, April 1950, 42–46.

25. Flavius Vegetius Renatus, *The Military Institutions of the Romans*, translated from the Latin by Lt. John Clarke, Reprinted in *Roots of Strategy*, ed. T.R. Phillips (Harrisburg, PA: Stackpole Book, 1985), 77. Vegetius advanced this thesis: "Fisherman, fowlers, confectioner, weavers, and in general all whose professions more properly belong to women should, in my opinion, by no means be admitted into the service. On the contrary, smiths, carpenters, butchers, and hunts-men are the most proper to be taken into it. On the careful choice of soldiers depends the welfare of the Republic." See page 79.

26. James H. Toner, "American Society and the American Way of War: Korea and Beyond," *Parameters*, Vol. XI, No. 1, Spring 1981, 78–89 (italics added).

27. Robert E. Osgood, *Limited War* (Chicago: University of Chicago, 1957), 33 (italics added).

28. Andrew Bacevich, *The Limits of Power* (New York: Henry Holt, 2008), 173.

29. Mortimer B. Zuckerman, Editor-in-Chief, *U.S. News & World Report*, October 27, 2008, 92.

30. David Halberstam, *The Fifties*, x (italics added).

31. John A. Hannah, Assistant Secretary of Defense (Manpower and Personnel), "Doctrine for Information and Education," *Army Information Digest*, July 1953, 3–7.

32. Dwight Eisenhower, *Mandate for Change* (New York: Doubleday, 1963), 484, 485.

33. James B. Twitchell, *Living It Up: Our Love Affair with Luxury* (New York: Columbia University Press, 2001), 4, 5, 28–38. Twitchell presented research that showed that the vast majority of the nation's college students aspired to be millionaires with all the prestige and privilege that wealth produces. Very few millionaires show up on battlefields. Also see Michael J. Weiss, *The Clustered World* (Boston: Little, Brown, 2000).

34. Nowhere was this more evident than the compensation the 9/11 Commission awarded the families of the victims of 9/11. There was no pretence of equality. Each life was assigned a value, and janitors were worth considerably less than corporate executives.

35. Dwight Eisenhower, *Mandate for Change* (New York: Doubleday, 1963), 484, 485.

36. Results of the National Health and Nutrition Examination Survey (NHANES) 1999–2000, www.cdc.gov/nccdphp/dnpa/obesity/trend/maps/index.htm. Also see, Susan Brink, "Eat This Now!" *U.S. News and World Report*, 28 March 2005, 56–58. Brink noted: "A national team of researchers reported in last week's *New England Journal of Medicine* that obesity already reduces the current life expectancy in the United States by four to nine months." During the last three decades of the twentieth century obesity increased dramatically, afflicting America's children. The percentage of children and adolescents who were defined as overweight doubled between 1970 and 2000. Diabetes, high blood pressure, and numerous other serious bodily disorders were on the rise as a result of weight gain.

37. Michelle Andrews, "The State of America's Health," *U.S. New & World Report*, February 2009, 9–12.

38. Infantry Journal Staff, "Once Again . . ." *Infantry Journal*, October 1945, 6, 7.

39. Alexis de Tocqueville, *Democracy in America* (New York: The Modern Library, 1981), 333, 338.

40. See Michael Sherry, *The Rise of American Air Power: The Creation of Armageddon* (New Haven: Yale University Press, 1987); and Eric Katz, "On the Neutrality of Technology," *Death by Design: Science, Technology, and Engineering in Nazi Germany* (New York: Longman, 2006), 291. *Technology is not value free.* Katz wrote: "The popular view that science is value-free has also come under attack in this time period. Indeed, one way to characterize the postmodern age in which we live is by acknowledging as a basic idea that all human creations—both ideas and physical artifacts—are the products of a particular culture and history and that they are endowed by the creative process with the specific values and purposes of the culture of subculture (race, class, gender) that created them. No human creation is morally neutral or value-free because all are the product of a particular culture and worldview."

41. Richard Overy, *Why the Allies Won* (New York: W.W. Norton, 1995), 104, 105.

42. *Liberty*, 5 December 1931, 31. Quoted in Richard Overy's *Why the Allies Won*, 105.

43. See Martin Gilbert, *The First World War: A Complete History* (New York: Henry Holt, 1994).

44. See Alfred F. Hurley, *Billy Mitchell: Crusader for Air Power* (Bloomington: Indiana University Press, 1975).

45. Quoted in "The Strategic Bombing Survey."

46. Alfred P. Sloan Foundation, "Preface to the Sloan Technology Series," reprinted in Richard Rhodes, *Dark Sun: The Making of the Hydrogen Bomb* (New York: Simon and Schuster, 1996), 13. "Technology is the application of science, engineering, and industrial organization to create a human-built world. It has led, in developed nations, to a standard of living inconceivable a hundred years ago. The process, however, is not free

of stress; by its very nature, technology brings change in society and *undermines convention*. It affects virtually every aspect of human endeavor: private and public institutions, economic systems, communication networks, political structure, international affiliations, the organization of societies and the condition of human lives. The effects are not one-way; just as technology changes society, so too do societal structures, attitudes and mores affect technology. But perhaps because technology is so rapidly and completely assimilated, the profound interplay of technology and other social endeavors in modern history has not been sufficiently recognized."

Chapter 3

1. Arthur G. Trudeau, Lieutenant General US Army, Chief of Research and Development, "Man—The Ultimate Factor," *Army Information Digest*, November 1959, 10.

2. Henry H. Arnold, General Army Air Force, "Air Strategy for Victory," *Flying*, XXXIII, No. 4, October 1943, 50.

3. Jan C. Smuts, Lieutenant General British Army, "The Second Report of the Prime Minister's Committee on Air Organization and Home Defense against Air Raids," 17 August 1917. Quoted in Phillip S. Meilinger, Colonel USAF, *The Paths of Heaven: The Evolution of Airpower Theory* (Maxwell Air Force Base, Alabama: Air University Press, 1997), 43.

4. The list of historical works on the air war is extensive. A list of additional readings on the subject can be found on the companion website for this book. Wesley F. Craven and James L. Cate, *The Army Air Forces in World War II*, 7 vols. (Chicago: University of Chicago Press, 1953); Richard J. Overy, *The Air War, 1939–1945* (New York: Scarborough Books, 1980); Ronald Schaffer, *Wings of Judgment: American Bombing in World War II* (New York: Oxford University Press, 1985); Michael S. Sherry, *The Rise of American Air Power: The Creation of Armageddon* (New Haven, CT: Yale University Press, 1987); Conrad C. Crane, *Bombs, Cities, and Civilians: American Airpower Strategy in World War II* (Lawrence, KS: University Press of Kansas, 1993); Geoffrey Paret, *Winged Victory: The Army Air Force in World War II* (New York: Random House, 1993); Tami D. Biddle, *Rhetoric and Reality in Air Warfare: The Evolution of British and American Ideas about Strategic Bombing 1914–1945* (Princeton, NJ: Princeton University Press, 2002); Benjamin F. Cooling, ed., *Case Studies in the Achievement of Air Superiority* (Washington, DC: GPO, 1994); Robert A. Pape, *Bombing to Win: Air Power and Coercion in War* (Ithaca, NY: Cornell University Press, 1996); John Buckley, *Air Power in the Age of Total War* (Bloomington: Indiana University Press, 1999); John Gooch, ed., *Airpower: Theory and Practice* (London:

Frank Cass, 1995); Alfred C. Mierzejewski, *The Collapse of the German War Economy, 1944–1945: Allied Air Power and the German National Railway* (Chapel Hill: The University of North Carolina Press, 1988); and Robert F. Futrell, *Ideas, Concepts, Doctrine: Basic Thinking in the United States Air Force 1907–1960* (Maxwell Air Force Base, Alabama: Air University Press, 1989); Stephen L. McFarland, *America's Pursuit of Precision Bombing, 1910–1945* (Washington, D.C.: Smithsonian Institution Press, 1995). Biographies and autobiographies also provide important information and insights: Sir Arthur Harris, Marshal of the R.A.F., *Bomber Offensive* (California: Presidio Press, 1990); Richard G. Davis, *Carl A. Spaatz and the Air War in Europe* (Washington, D.C.: Center of Air Force History, 1993); Curtis E. LeMay with MacKinlay Kantor, *Mission with LeMay: My Story* (New York: Doubleday, 1965); Henry H. Arnold, *Global Mission* (New York: Harper and Brothers, 1949); Thomas M. Coffey, *HAP: The Story of the U.S. Air Force and the Man Who Built It, General Henry H. "Hap" Arnold* (New York: Viking, 1982); Dik A. Daso, *Hap Arnold and the Evolution of American Airpower* (Washington, D.C.: Smithsonian Institution Press, 2000); Thomas M. Coffey, *Iron Eagle: The Turbulent Life of General Curtis LeMay* (New York: Crown, 1986); Charles Griffith, *The Quest: Haywood Hansell and American Strategic Bombing in World War II* (Maxwell Air Force Base, Alabama: Air University Press, 1999); Dik A. Daso, *Hap Arnold and the Evolution of American Airpower* (Washington, D.C.: Smithsonian Institution Press, 2000); and Winston S. Churchill, *The Second World War*, 6 vols. (Boston: Houghton Mifflin, 1949).

5. For the history of the Army in World War II see: Stephen Ambrose, *Citizen Soldiers* (New York: Simon and Schuster, 1997); Michael Doubler, *Closing with the Enemy* (Lawrence, Kansas: University Press of Kansas, 1994); James M. Gavin, *On to Berlin* (New York: Viking Press, 1978); Peter S. Kindsvatter, *American Soldiers* (Lawrence, Kansas: University Press of Kansas, 2003); Charles MacDonald, *The Mighty Endeavor* (New York: Oxford University Press, 1969); Charles MacDonald, *A Time for Trumpets* (New York: Bantam Books, 1984); Peter R. Mansoor, *The G.I. Offensive in Europe* (Lawrence, Kansas: University Press of Kansas, 1999); S.L.A. Marshall, *Men against Fire* (Gloucester, Mass: Peter Smith, 1978); Audie Murphy, *To Hell and Back* (New York: Henry Holt, 2002); Williamson Murray and Allan R. Millett, *A War to be Won* (Cambridge, Massachusetts: Belknap Press, 2000), Geoffrey Perret, *There's A War to be Won* (New York: Random House, 1991), and Russell Weigley, *Eisenhower's Lieutenants* (Bloomington: Indiana University Press, 1990). Also see the official histories of the US Army in World War II.

6. It is worth noting that no service is worse than the Army at telling its story. The marines can land on an island,

spend five days in combat, and it is enshrined in myth and legend. An Army division can land in Europe, spend more than 300 days in combat, suffer over 100 casualties, fighting what was arguably the finest army in World War II, and no one in America knows the name of the division. This practice made little difference during most of the nation's history, but during the Cold War it hurt the Army, and consequently the nation. America's failure to understand war is, in part, a function of the Army's failure to explain it.

7. Rangers are specially trained to operate behind enemy lines to conduct raids that destroy enemy command and control facilities, unit headquarters and logistical bases; to rescue captured soldiers; and to conduct reconnaissance patrol. They are also used to seize and hold objectives behind enemy lines, such as airfields and other high value targets, until more substantial forces can be deployed. Ranger units have been part of the Army since the American Revolution; however, modern Rangers can also conduct airborne, air assault, and light infantry operations. Rangers also conduct special operations typically in conjunction with Special Forces.

8. Charles E. Heller and William A. Stofft, ed. *America's First Battles 1776–1965* (Lawrence, Kansas: University Press of Kansas, 1986).

9. Russell Weigley, *The American Way of War* (Bloomington: Indiana University Press, 1973), 142, 143. Brian M. Linn, Eric M. Bergerud and others are critical of Weigley's thesis, believing that it is too simplistic, that it failed to explain the American conduct of numerous more limited wars. However, in regard to total wars, Weigley's work is valid. Russell Weigley described war as practiced by General U.S. Grant: "Grant proposed a strategy of annihilation based upon the principle of concentration and mass, hitting the main Confederate armies with the concentrated thrust of massive Federal forces until the Confederate armies were smashed into impotence. . . . In the spring of 1864 he took the field with the Army of the Potomac. . . . It was the grim campaign to destroy the Confederacy by destroying Lee's army. . . . His method of achieving the destruction of the enemy army was not to seek the Austerlitz battle [a single decisive Napoleonic battle] . . . but rather an extension of the concept of battle until the battle became literally synonymous with the whole campaign: he would fight all the time, every day, keeping the enemy army always within his own army's grip, allowing the enemy no opportunity for deceptive maneuver, but always pounding away until his own superior resources permitted the Federal armies to survive while the enemy army at last disintegrated."

10. Charles E. Kirkpatrick, *An Unknown Future and a Doubtful Present* (Washington, DC: CMH, 1990), 107.

11. US Army, FM 100–5 Field Service Regulations, Operation (Washington, DC: War Department, 1941), 5.

12. US Army, *Field Service Regulations, Operations*, FM 100–5 (Washington, DC: War Department, 1941), 18.

13. US Army, FM 22–10 Leadership (Washington, DC: Department of the Army, 1951), 5.

14. US Army, AFHQ, Training Memorandum Number 22, Training to Kill, 20 March 1943, RG 407, Box 148, Archive II.

15. Joseph Balkoski, *Beyond the Beachhead* (Machanicsburg, PA: Stackpole Books, 1999), 89, 86.

16. Weigley, *Eisenhower's Lieutenant*, 27.

17. Intelligence Annex to Army Group B War Journal, 23 October 1944, pp. 1–3, Microcopy T–311, Roll 1, Combined Arms Research Libaray, Ft. Leavenworth, Kansas. Also reprinted in Peter R. Mansoor, *The G.I. Offensive in Europe* (Lawrence, Kansas: University Press of Kansas, 1999), 184, 185.

18. Adrian Lewis, *Omaha Beach* (Chapel Hill: University of North Carolina Press, 2001), Chapters 5 and 6.

19. The term "Blitzkrieg" was created by the Allies, not the Germans. And some historians argue that Blitzkrieg was a myth developed to explain the fall of France. See the works of Robert Doughty. Also see: Robert Citino, *Quest for Decisive Victory: From Stalemate to Blitzkrieg in Europe, 1899–1940* (Lawrence, KS: University Press of Kansas, 2002).

20. Gen. Willis Crittenberger, "Armor's Role in National Security," *Army Information Digest*, July 1953, 35–41.

21. Combat power is the cumulative force of all the resources: technologies, doctrines, talents, skill, intelligence, genius, luck, cultural understanding, and every other factor, that influences the ability of a unit to destroy enemy forces. Combat power consists of not only palpable, measurable components, such as tanks and airplanes; but also, intangible components, such as courage, esprit de corps, patriotism, and numerous other very real but invisible factors. Combat power changes moment to moment and is different with every enemy, every geographic region, every culture, and every society. Relative combat power is measured in the heads of commanders and political leaders, not on computers.

22. Reprinted in "British and American Approaches to Strategic Bombing: Their Origins and Implementation in the World War II Combined Bomber Offensive," in *Airpower*, ed. John Gooch (London: Frank Cass, 1995), 92. The complete text is in AIR 6/19, Public Record Office, London.

23. John Lukacs, *Five Days in London May 1940* (New Haven: Yale University Press, 1999), 104, 184; Gerhard Weinberg, *A World at Arms* (New York: Cambridge University Press, 1994), 142.

24. Winston Churchill, *The Second World War: Their Finest Hour* (Boston: Houghton Mifflin, 1949), 458.

25. Harris, *Bomber Offensive*, 54.

26. Winston Churchill, *The Second World War: The Hinge of Fate* (Boston: Houghton Mifflin, 1950), 281.

27. Charles P. Snow, *Science and Government* (London: Oxford University Press, 1961), 47–51.

28. Christopher Browning equated the bombing of Germany and Japan with other atrocities, including the Holocaust. Browning wrote: "Other kinds of atrocity, lacking the immediacy of battlefield frenzy and fully expressing official government policy, decidedly were 'standard operational procedures.' The fire-bombing of German and Japanese cities, the enslavement and murderous maltreatment of foreign laborers in German Camps and factories ... the reprisal shooting of a hundred civilians for every German soldier killed by partisan attack ... these were not the spontaneous explosions or cruel revenge of brutalized men but the methodically executed policies of government." Browning, *Ordinary Men* (New York: Harper Collins, 1998), 161.

29. *The U.S. Strategic Bombing Survey*, "Summary Report, The Civilians."

30. John Buckley, *Air Power in the Age of Total War* (Bloomington: Indiana University Press, 1999), 15. Buckley noted: "It has been argued that Germany and Japan were able to resist air bombardment on such a huge scale because of the nature of their regimes—authoritarian, regimented and conditioned by excessive propaganda. However, before the Second World War, similar analysts claimed that totalitarian dictatorships were brittle and especially prone to morale-sapping air raids, saddled as they were with alien and unnatural forms of government which evoked little deep-rooted support. Conversely, liberal democracies could endure the excesses of total war. ... Airpower was simply not capable of bringing about the destruction of whole modern societies in the manner envisaged in the interwar era. ..."

31. Bernard Brodie, *Strategy in the Missile Age* (Princeton: Princeton University Press, 1965), 132, 133.

32. Robert A. Pape, *Bombing to Win* (Ithaca: Cornell University Press, 1996), 24.

33. Quoted in Jerome Kuehl, *Stalingrad, The World at War*, Video (New York: Thames Television).

34. Richard Overy, *Why the Allies Won*, (New York: W.W. Norton, 1995), 132, 133.

35. Overy, *Why the Allies Won*, 132.

36. US Strategic Bombing Survey, "Narrative Summary," in Maurer Maurer, ed., *The U.S. Air Service in World War I*, 4 Vols. (Washington, DC: Office of AF History, 1978), Vol. IV, 501–2. Reprinted in Tami Davis Biddle's "British and American Approaches to Strategic Bombing: Their Origins and Implementation in the World War II Combined Bomber Offensive," in *Airpower*, by John Gooch, 108.

37. Conrad Crane, *Bombing Cities and Civilians* (Lawrence, Kansas: University Press of Kansas, 1993), 19.

38. John Shiner, *Foulois And The U.S. Army Air Corps 1931–1935, The United States Air Force General Histories* (Washington, DC: Office of Air Force History, 1983), 216.

39. Crane, *Bombs, Cities, and Civilians*, 118.

40. W. Hays Parks, "'Precision' and 'Area' Bombing: Who Did Which, and When?" in *Airpower*, ed. John Gooch, 148.

41. *The U.S. Strategic Bombing Survey*, "Summary Report, The Civilians."

42. Alfred Mierzejewski, *The Collapse of the German War Economy, 1944–1945* (Chapel Hill: University of North Carolina Press, 1988), 178–182.

43. W. Hays Parks, "'Precision' and 'Area' Bombing: Who Did Which, and When?" in *Airpower*, ed. John Gooch, 146. Parks concluded that: "... the image conveyed by the word precision is inappropriate to describe USAAF heavy bomber practice. Enemy defences kept the American daylight bombers from achieving the results they sought, and the consistently poor European weather regularly forced the Americans to bomb using radar aids—a practice that inevitably led to unsatisfactory results as the Americans were not as well trained, equipped, or experienced as the British in radar-bombing techniques."

44. Crane, *Bombs, Cities, and Civilians*, 11.

45. Historians and airmen have produced numerous studies on the fire bombing of Japan, including: Martin Caidin, *A Torch to the Enemy* (New York: Ballantine, 1960); Wilbur H. Morrison, *Point of No Return: The Story of the Twentieth Air Force* (New York: Times Books, 1979); Robert Guillain, *I Saw Tokyo Burning: An Eyewitness Narrative from Pearl Harbor to Hiroshima*, trans. William Byron (Garden City, New York: Doubleday, 1981); Haywood Hansell, Jr., *Strategic Air War Against Japan* (Maxwell Air Force Base, Ala.: Airpower Research Institute, 1980); Haywood S. Hansell, Jr., *The Strategic Air War Against Germany and Japan: A Memoir* (Washington, DC: Office of Air Force History, 1986); Kevin Herbert, *Maximum Effort: The B–29s Against Japan* (Manhattan, Kansas: Sunflower University Press, 1983); Hoito Edoin, *The Night Tokyo Burned* (New York: St. Martin's Press, 1987); Curtis E. LeMay and Bill Yenne, *Superfortress: The Story of the B–29 and American Air Power* (New York: McGraw-Hill, 1988); E. Bartlett Kerr, *Flames Over Tokyo* (New York: Donald I. Fine, 1991); Kenneth Werrell, *Blankets of Fire: U.S. Bombers Over Japan During World War II* (Washington, DC: Smithsonian Institution Press, 1996); and Daniel Haulman, *Hitting Home: The Air Offensive Against Japan* (Washington: Air Force History and Museums Program, 1999).

46. Richard Frank, *Downfall: The End of the Imperial Japanese Empire* (New York: Random House, 1999), 13.

47. Frank, *Downfall*, 19.

48. Curtis LeMay, *Mission With LeMay: My Story* (New York: Doubleday, 1965), 347–352.

49. Crane, *Bombs, Cities, and Civilians*, 33.

50. John Dower, *War Without Mercy* (New York: Pantheon Books, 1986), 11.

51. Otto D. Tolischus, "False Gods-False Ideals," *Marine Corps Gazette*, November 1944, 14–21. This line of thought was not unique. See: Samuel B. Griffith, Lieutenant Colonel USMC, "The Man Suntzu," *Marine Corps Gazette*, August 1943, 3–6; and George Amburn, Corporal USMC, "A Marine Considers the Jap," *Marine Corps Gazette*," July 1945, 19.

52. Greg Kennedy, "Anglo-American Strategic Relations and Intelligence Assessments of Japanese Air Power 1934–1941," *The Journal of Military History*, Vol. 74, No. 3, July 2010, 737–773.

53. Quoted in Martin Caidin, *A Torch to the Enemy: The Fire Raid on Tokyo* (New York: Ballantine, 1960), 23.

54. Bernard Brodie, *Strategy in the Missile Age*, 138, 139.

55. Gerald Linderman, *The World Within War* (Cambridge, Mass.: Harvard University Press, 1997), 150.

56. Pape, *Bombing to Win*, 10.

57. Pape, *Bombing to Win*, 124.

58. Frank, *Downfall*, 347.

59. Frank, *Downfall*, 348. The historiography on the decision to drop the atomic bombs is extensive. See: Thomas Allen and Norman Polmar, *Codename Downfall* (New York: Simon and Schuster, 1995); Gar Alperovitz, *Atomic Diplomacy* (New York: Penguin Books, 1985); Herbert Feis, *Japan Subdued* (Princeton, NJ: Princeton University Press, 1961); Richard Frank, *Downfall*; Akira Iriye, *Power and Culture* (Cambridge, MA: Harvard University Press, 1981); Martin Sherwin, *World Destroyed* (New York: Alfred Knopf, 1975); John Skates, *The Invasion of Japan, Alternative to the Bomb* (Columbia: University Press of South Carolina Press, 1994; Paul Fussell, *Thanks God for the Atomic Bomb and Other Essays* (New York: Summit Books, 1988); Vincent C. Jones, *Manhattan: The Army and the Atomic Bomb, U.S. Army in WWII* (Washington, DC: CMH, 1985); Barton Bernstein, "The Atomic Bomb Reconsidered," *Foreign Affairs* 74 (January–February 1995), 135–142; Barton Bernstein, "Roosevelt, Truman, and the Atomic Bomb, 1941–1945: A Reinterpretation," *Political Science Quarterly* 90 (Spring 1975), 23–69. Thomas T. Hammond, "'Atomic Diplomacy' Revisited," *Orbis* 19 (Winter 1976), 1403–28. For a more comprehensive bibliography see, Samuel J. Walker, "The Decision to Drop the Bomb," *Diplomatic History*, 14 (1993), 97–114.

60. Quoted in part in, Harry Truman, *Memoirs*, Vol. I (New York: A Da Capo Paperback, 1986), 422; and Robert Donovan, *Conflict and Crisis* (New York: W.W. Norton, 1977), 96.

61. Steve Call, *Selling Air Power: Military Aviation and American Popular Culture after World War II* (College Station: Texas A & M University Press, 2009), 2.

62. Ernest King, *U.S. Navy at War, 1941–1945* (Washington, DC: Department of the Navy), 169–170.

63. *Unification of the Armed Forces: Hearings before the Committee on Naval Affairs, United States Senate*, 79th Congress, 2nd Session, 79.

64. Julian S. Corbett, *Some Principles of Maritime Strategy* (Annapolis, Maryland: Naval Institute Press, 1911); Alfred T. Mahan, *The Influence of Seapower Upon History* (New York: Hill and Wang, 1957).

65. Alexander De Seversky, *Victory Through Air Power* (New York: Simon and Schuster, 1942), 182–183.

66. For studies on the Marine Corps and Marine culture, see Allan Millett, *Semper Fidelis*; Craig M. Cameron, *American Samurai*; Holland Smith, *Coral and Brass* (New York: Charles Scribner's Sons, 1949); and Victor H. Krulak, Lieutenant General USMC, *First to Fight: An Insider View of the Marine Corps* (Annapolis, Maryland: Naval Institute Press, 1984).

67. The issue of inter-service rivalry is discussed more fully in subsequent chapters.

68. See Robert Burrell, "Breaking the Cycle of Iwo Jima Mythology," *The Journal of Military History*, Vol. 68, No. 4, 2005, p. 1161.

69. There is much myth about the development of amphibious warfare doctrine during World War II. The Marine Corps is typically given too much credit and the Navy, the Army, and the British too little credit. In fact, two amphibious warfare doctrines were developed: the Central Pacific Marine-Navy doctrine and the British-US Army Mediterranean Theater doctrine. See: Adrian Lewis, *Omaha Beach*, Chapter 2, and George Carroll Dyer, Vice Admiral US Navy, *The Amphibians Came to Conquer: The Story of Admiral Richmond Kelly Turner* (Washington, DC: US GPO, 1991), 202–203. Dyer quoted Turner, who wrote: "No one Service invented amphibious warfare. The Marines contributed much (patterned on Japanese methods) to its development in recent years. But so also did the Navy, including Naval Aviation. Furthermore, beginning in 1940, the Army contributed a great deal. We should not forget that the biggest operation of all—Normandy—was very largely a US Army and British affair. The Marines had nothing to do with the European and African landings, and the US Navy was not the controlling element."

70. Marines fought in American Expeditionary Forces under General Pershing during World War I. However, the US did not enter the war until 1917, and the war ended in 1918.

71. The 2nd Marine Division was activated on 1 February 1941 at San Diego, CA. It fought at Guadalcanal for 178 days, Tarawa, five days, Saipan twenty-five days, and Tinian for eight days.

72. The 4th Marine Division fought for four islands: Kwajalein, Saipan, Tinian, and Iwo Jima.

73. See: Dower, *War Without Mercy* (New York: Pantheon Books, 1986).

74. Roosevelt and the War Department recognized that the Pacific was a secondary theater, and that the only way for Japan to achieve victory was for Germany to win the war in Europe. If the Germans lost, there was no way for Japan to win.

75. Frank, *Downfall*, 140–147.

76. Frank, *Downfall*, 140–147.

77. The Navy and Marines argued that speed was necessary to reduce the vulnerability of Navy vessel supporting landing operations; however, the principle of speed was more a function of the Navy's desire to advance to the next operation, than tactical or operational necessity.

78. Quoted in Norman Cooper's "The Military Career of General Holland M. Smith, USMC," Ph.D. dissertation, University of Alabama, 1974, 119.

79. Smith, *Coral and Brass*, 14, 17, 52.

80. Cameron, *American Samurai*, 148.

81. The battle for Peleliu went on for seventy-five days. The Army's 81st Infantry Division relieved the 1st MD.

82. See Jon T. Hoffman, Lieutenant Colonel, USMC, *Chesty* (New York: Random House, 2001), 289.

83. Cameron, *American Samurai*, 135. Cameron's study focuses specifically on the 1st Marine Division; however, he states that the attitudes and cultural tenets identified are common to a lesser or greater degree throughout the Marine Corps.

84. Allan Millett, *Semper Fidelis*, Revised and Expanded Edition (New York: The Free Press, 1991), 460.

85. Cameron, *American Samurai*, 155, 135. Cameron explained: ". . . Army troops, as a result of their basic organization and indoctrination, were generally less well suited to the Pacific War than the marines. . . . The Army's orientation toward fighting an extended, attritional type of warfare as was necessary in Europe and the larger landmasses . . . required an emphasis on conserving manpower and unit effectiveness that was inimical to the type of combat necessary to seize small, heavily fortified islands." The second argument: "maintained that the marines were more effective than their Army counterparts on an individual level because they possessed an aggressiveness and spirit lacking in the soldiers. It was not simply that the Marine Corps provided its men with better training, the argument ran, but that the Marines recruited from men who were better than the soldiers in every respect." Cameron concluded: "This attitude was carefully cultivated by the Marine Corps through recruit indoctrination, promotion, and public relations." Cameron's work was much maligned. Still, his chapter on Marine attitudes towards the Army is well documented.

86. Cameron, *American Samurai*, 150. At Peleliu 12,000 Japanese fought the First Marine Division to the point that it became combat-ineffective. Consider the following exchange between the senior operational commander, General Geiger, and the 1st Marine Division Commander: "Shocked by what he had seen, Geiger met with Rupertus, told him that he considered the 1st Marines [Regiment] to be ineffective as a fighting unit, and suggested that Puller's men be replaced with an Army regiment. 'At this,' Coleman observed, 'General Rupertus became greatly alarmed and requested that no such action be taken, stating that he was sure he could secure the island in another day or two.' Geiger finally overruled Rupertus, and by the afternoon of the twenty-third elements of the 321st RCT were already relieving units of the 1st Marines."

87. Charles Kirkpatrick, *An Unknown Future and A Doubtful Present* (Washington, DC: CMH, 1990), 101–115.

88. Russell Weigley, "The American Military and the Principle of Civilian Control from McClellan to Powell," *The Journal of Military History*, Special Issue 57, October 1993, 54.

89. Robert Palmer, *The Mobilization of the Ground Army* (Washington, DC: Historical Section, Army Ground Forces, Study No. 4, 1946). Also see: Kent R. Greenfield, Robert Palmer, and Bell Wiley, *The Army Ground Forces: The Organization of Ground Combat Troops, United States Army in World War II* (Washington, DC: Historical Division, US Army, 1947), and Robert Palmer, Bell I. Wiley, and William Keast, *The Army Ground Forces: The Procurement and Training of Ground Combat Troops, United States Army in World War II* (Washington, DC: Office of the Chief of Military History, Department of the Army, 1948).

90. By comparison, the Germans with a population of 79.5 million, manned 304 divisions, the USSR with a population of roughly 170.5 million, manned over 400 divisions. The strength of German division changed during the war from 17,734 men in 1939 to 12,700 in 1944. See I.C.B. Dear and M.R.D. Foot, *The Oxford Companion to World War II* (New York: Oxford University Press, 1995), 1207.

Chapter 4

1. Dwight Eisenhower, *Crusade in Europe* (New York: Doubleday, 1948), 456.

2. T. R. Fehrenbach, *This Kind of War* (New York: MacMillan, 1963), 454.

3. Taylor, *Uncertain Trumpet*, 3, 4.

4. Eisenhower, *Crusade in Europe*, (emphasis added) 455, 456.

5. Winston Churchill, *The Second World War: The Grand Alliance* (Boston: Houghton Mifflin, 1950), 443, 444.

6. Churchill, *The Grand Alliance*, 444 (italics added).

7. *Public Papers of the Presidents of the United States, Harry S. Truman, April 12 to December 31, 1945* (Washington, DC: GPO, 1961), 549.

8. George Kennan, "The Sources of Soviet Conduct," *Foreign Affairs*, vol. XXIV, No. 4 (July 1947), 566–582 (Italics added).

9. See John Lewis Gaddis, *We Now Know: Rethinking the Cold War History* (New York: Oxford University Press, 1997); Ralph B. Levering, Vladimir O. Pechatnov, Verena Botzenhart-Viehe, and C. Earl Edmondson *Debating the Origins of the Cold War: American and Russian Perspectives* (New York: Rowman and Littelfield Publishers, 2002); Walter LaFeber, *America, Russia, and the Cold War 1945–2006* (Boston: McGraw Hill, 2006); Geoffrey Roberts, *Stalin's Wars: From World War II to Cold War, 1939–1953* (New Haven: Yale University Press, 2006); and Robert L. Beisner, *Dean Acheson: A Life in the Cold War* (New York: Oxford Univesity Press, 2006). See the bibliography for a more complete list of works on the Cold War.

10. For a perspective on the carnage and suffering see: Elena Kozhina, *Through the Burning Steppe: A Memoir of Wartime Russia, 1942–1945*, trans. Vadim Mahmoudov (New York: Riverhead Books, 2001), 31.

11. American Psychiatric Association, *Diagnostic and Statistical Manual of Mental Disorders*, 4th edn (Washington, DC: Published by the American Psychiatric Association, 1994), 424, 425. According to the APA manual, people suffering from PTSD display some of the following behaviors: "Individuals with PTSD may describe painful guilt feelings about surviving when others did not survive or about the things they had to do to survive. Phobic avoidance of situations or activities that resemble or symbolize the original trauma may interfere with interpersonal relationships. . . . The following associated constellation of symptoms may occur and are more commonly seen in association with an interpersonal stressor . . . impaired affect modulation; self-destructive and impulsive behavior; dissociative symptoms; somatic complaints; feelings of ineffectiveness, shame; despair, or hopelessness; feeling permanently damaged; a loss of previous sustained beliefs; hostility; social withdrawal; feeling constantly threatened; impaired relationships with others; or a change from the individual's previous personality characteristics."

12. Susan J. Linz, edited, *The Impact of World War II on the Soviet Union* (New Jersey: Rowman & Allanheld, 1985).

13. For example, the behavior of Israel absolutely cannot be understood without knowledge of the PTSD caused by the Holocaust. Consider these words: "Ben Gurion's vision of an Israel secured against existential threats has now been realized. Though nuclear weapons have not been officially acknowledged, they have greatly contributed to Israel's image as the strongest nation in the Middle East. The Jews of Israel will never be like the Jews in the Holocaust. Israel will be able to visit terrible retribution on those who would attempt its destruction." See: Avner Cohen, *Israel and the Bomb* (New York: Columbia University Press, 1988), 342.

14. Omar Bradley, General US Army, Chief of Staff, statement before the House Foreign Affair Committee, "The Strategy of Map," *Army Information Digest*, Sept. 1949, 8–10.

15. Louis Johnson, Secretary of Defense, statement before the House Foreign Affairs Committee, "Military Assistance For Mutual Security," *AID*, September 1949, 3–7.

16. Omar Bradley, Chief of Staff US Army, "One Round Won't Win the Fight" *AID*, April 1949, 31–35.

17. Bradley, "One Round Won't Win the Fight" *AID*, April 1949, 31–35.

18. Report of the President's Air Policy Commission, "Survival in the Air Age," Washington, DC, US GOP. Parts of the report were published in *Army Information Digest*, March 1948, 38–46. The members of the commission were: Thomas K. Finletter, Chairman, formerly Special Assistant to Secretary of State Cordell Hull; George P. Baker, Vice-Chairman, Professor of Transportation, Harvard Graduate School of Business Administration; Palmer Hoyt, Publisher, *Denver Post*; John A. McCone, President, Joshua Hendy Iron Works; and Arthur Whiteside, President, Dun and Bradstreet.

19. The President's Air Policy Commission, "Survival in the Air Age."

20. Carl Spaatz, General USAF, "The World of Strategic Air Force," *AID*, October 1948, 17–19. From a report by the USAF Chief of Staff to the Secretary of the Air Force, 30 June 1948.

21. Carl Spaatz, USAF, "The World of Strategic Air Force," *AID*, October 1948, 17–19.

22. Harry Truman, *Memoirs of Harry Truman*, Vol. II (New York: A Da Capo Paperback, © 1956), 306.

23. From a statement by the Secretary of Defense before the Senate Armed Services Committee on 25 March 1948. Extracts from the address were published under the title, "Armed Forces Needed to Keep the Peace," in *AID*, May 1948, 57–58.

24. J. Lawton Collins, General US Army, "The Postwar Military Establishment and its Manpower Problems," 17 Jan. 1947, 1–5, Collins' Papers, The Cold War Army, Box 25, File 4, Eisenhower Library.

25. Collins, "The Postwar Military Establishment," 5 (italics added).

26. Omar Bradley and Clay Blair, *A General's Life* (New York: Simon and Schuster, 1983), 474.

27. Bradley, "Our Military Requirements—III" *AID*, July 1948, 74–78. From an address by General Bradley before the House Armed Services Committee on 14 April 1948.

28. James Forrestal, Secretary of Defense, "First Report of the Secretary of Defense," December 1948. Also published as "The State of the National Military Establishment," *Military Review*, April 1949, Vol. XXIX, No. 1, 3–13.

29. Walter Millis, ed., *The Forrestal Diaries* (New York: Viking Press, 1951), 552. In May, Forrestal killed himself.

30. Quoted in Edward A. Kolodzie, *The Uncommon Defense and Congress, 1945–1963* (Columbus: Ohio State University Press, 1966), 58.

31. Omar Bradley, CJCS, "Toward a Long-Range Manpower Policy," *AID*, March 1951, 11–15. Extracted from statements made before the Preparedness Subcommittee of the Senate Armed Services Committee on the Problem of Military Manpower, 22 Jan. 1951.

32. J. Lawton, Collins, General US Army and Chief of Staff, US Army during the Korean War, "Our Global Responsibilities," *AID*, Feb. 1952, 3–6.

33. For a more complete study of UMT see James Gerhardt, *The Draft and Public Policy* (Columbus: Ohio State University Press, 1971).

34. Walter Mills, ed. *The Forrestal Diaries*, 388. Forrestal recorded in his diary on 8 March 1948 that: "The effect of the Finletter report and of the Brewster Hinshaw Board [this was the parallel Congressional Aviation Policy Board which reported on 1 March] *has been to convince the country that by a substantial increase in appropriations for Air, there would be no necessity for UMT* . . . (italics added)."

35. W. Stuart Symington, "Facing Realties," *AID*, May 1950 (emphasis added).

36. The Soviet atomic bomb was based on the American design. A German-born scientist, Klaus Fuchs, had stolen the plans.

37. On 22 Sept. 1949 the Soviet Union exploded its first atomic bomb, followed by Britain on 3 Oct. 1952, France on 13 Feb. 1960, and the PRC on 16 Oct. 1964. For decades these five powers were members of an exclusive club; however, India, Pakistan, and Israel later joined the club. Other states will eventually also acquire nuclear weapons.

38. Robert L. Beisner, *Dean Acheson: A Life in the Cold War* (New York: Oxford University Press, 2006), 236–251.

39. Paul H. Nitze was the primary author and Director of the Policy Planning Staff in the State Department.

40. NSC–68, "Report to the President Pursuant to the President's Directive of 31 January 1950," 7 April 1950, FRUS 1950, 1:235–92. Reprinted in *US National Security Policy and Strategy: Documents and Policy Proposals*, ed. Sam Sarkesian with Robert Vitas (New York: Greenwood Press, 1988), 38–43. Quoted in Steven L. Rearden's *History of the Office of the Secretary of Defense: The Formative Years, 1947–1950*, Vol. I (Washington, DC: US GPO, 1984), 528–531.

41. Robert McBane, Major US Army, "The Proposed Defense Budget," *AID*, May 1949, 54–60.

42. Collins, "The Postwar Military Establishment," 8.

43. Curtis LeMay, General US Air Force, with MacKinlay Kantor, *Mission with LeMay: My Story by General Curtis E. LeMay* (New York: Doubleday, 1965), 431 (italics added).

44. Dean Acheson, *The Korean War* (New York: Norton, 1969), 40, 41.

45. Harry Truman, "The President's Stand on Korea," *AID*, August 1950, 3–9. Fifty-two of the fifty-nine member nations support action to restore peace in Korea.

46. Matthew Ridgway, *Soldier: The Memoirs of Matthew B. Ridgway* (New York: Harper, 1956), 191.

47. J. Lawton Collins, *War in Peacetime* (Boston: Houghton Mifflin, 1969), 69, 70.

48. Jim Dan Hill, *The Minute Man in Peace and War* (Harrisburg, Pennsylvania, 1964), 500.

49. See Jeffrey Barlow, *Revolt of the Admirals* (Washington, DC: Naval Historical Center), 1994. The Revolt of the Admirals was an organized movement to subvert the will of civilian political leaders, who had cancelled the construction of the super carrier—the *USS United States*.

50. Between 1 January and 30 June 1950 the authorized strength of the regular Army was cut from 677,000 to 630,000 to meet budgetary limits. In January 1950, the actual strength was 638,824. By June, the month the Korean War started, it had dropped to 591,487, or 38,513 below the authorization.

51. Dwight Eisenhower, "The Long Pull for Peace" *AID*, April 1948, 33–41. From the "Final Report of the Chief of Staff General of the Army Dwight D. Eisenhower."

52. Eisenhower, "The Long Pull for Peace," 33–41.

53. Eisenhower, "The Long Pull for Peace," 33–41.

54. Omar Bradley, Gen. US Army, CJCS, "The Path Ahead," *AID*, Oct. 1950, 24–26.

55. General Frederick J. Kroesen, "Korean War Lessons," *Army*, August 2002, 7.

56. Blair, *The Forgotten War*, 4–9, 29.

57. Mark Clark, Gen., Chief of Army Field Forces, "The Payoff in Training," *AID*, Jan. 1950, 3–8.

58. J. Lawton Collins, Chief of Staff US Army, "Men, Materiel and Money," *AID*, July 1953, 8–16.

Chapter 5

1. Douglas MacArthur, General US Army, *Reminiscences* (New York: A Da Capo Paperback, 1985), 335.

2. The CPV are also known as the Chinese Communist Forces, or CCF.

3. The next time the Army employed offensive, campaign-winning doctrine, the burden of war rested on the military "cluster," a relatively small group of military professionals, and airpower was still considered the dominant instrument in war.

4. For discussions on the origins of the Korean War see Bruce Cummings, *Korea's Place in the Sun: A Modern History* (New York: W.W. Norton, 1997); *The Origins of the Korean War*, Volume I, *Liberation and the Emergence of Separate Regimes* (Princeton: Princeton University Press,

1981); Volume II, *The Roaring of the Cataract* (Princeton: Princeton University Press, 1990); and, edited, *Child of Conflict: The Korean-American Relationship, 1943–1953* (Seattle: University of Washington Press, 1983). And see, Carter J. Eckert, et al., *Korea: Old and New: A History* (Seoul: Il-chokak, 1990); Kathryn Weathersby, *Soviet Aims in Korea and the Origins of the Korean War*, Working Paper No. 8, Cold War International History Project (Washington, DC, 1993); and Allan Millett, *The War for Korea 1945–1950: A House Burning* (Lawrence: University Press of Kansas, 2005).

5. Mathew B. Ridgway, *The Korean War* (New York: A Da Capo Paperback, 1967), 2.

6. Sergei N. Goncharov, John W. Lewis, and Xue Litai, *Uncertain Partners: Stalin, Mao, and the Korean War* (Stanford, California: Stanford University Press, 1995), see Chapter 5, "The Decision for War in Korea," 130–168, specifically 144.

7. Figures on the size of the NKPA vary considerably from a low of 100,000 to a high of 165,000 men. When the 120,000 men of the Soviet 25th Army withdrew from North Korea, they left behind all their equipment. The NKPA also inherited the equipment of the defeated Japanese 34th and 58th Armies. Stalin provided more weapons and equipment to NKPA than it did to the PLA during the Chinese Revolution.

8. Harry S. Truman, *Memoirs of Harry S. Truman, 1946–52: Years of Trial and Hope*, Vol. II (Garden City, New York: A Da Capo Paperback, 1956), 338, 339.

9. Douglas MacArthur, General US Army, *Reminiscences* (New York: A Da Capo Paperback, 1964), 332, 333 (emphasis added).

10. Matthew B. Ridgway, *The Korean War* (New York: A Da Capo Paperback, 1967), 21, 22.

11. James F. Schnabel, *United States Army in the Korean War Policy and Direction: The First Year* (Washington, DC: US Army, CMH, 1972), 78. Douglas MacArthur, General US Army, *Reminiscences* (New York: A Da Capo Paperback, 1964), 334.

12. MacArthur, *Reminiscences*, 331.

13. Truman, *Memoirs of Harry S. Truman, 1946–52: Years of Trial and Hope*, Vol. II, 463.

14. Truman, *Memoirs*, Vol. II, 341.

15. For an excellent study on the campaign for Pusan see: Uzal W. Ent, *Fighting on the Brink: Defense of the Pusan Perimeter* (Paducah, KY: Turner Publishing Co., 1996).

16. Wilson A. Heefner, *Patton's Bulldog: The Life and Service of General Walton H. Walker* (Shippensburg, Pennsylvania, 2001), 134. Also see "Old Pro," (cover story on General Walker) *Time Magazine*, Vol. LVI, No. 5, 31 July 1950, 18–20.

17. Thomas E. Hanson, "The Eighth Army's Combat Readiness Before Korea: A New Appraisal," *Armed Forces & Society*, Vol. 29, No. 2, Winter 2003, 176. Also see: Thomas E. Hanson, *Combat Ready? The Eighth US Army on the Eve of the Korean War* (College Station: Texas A&M University Press, 2010).

18. US Army, Eighth US Army, War Diary, Section I: Prologue, 25 June 1950 to 12 July 1950, RG 407, Box 1081, NA II.

19. US Army, EUSA, "Strength of Units of Eight Army," 30 June 1950, RG 407, Box 1081, NA II.

20. Roy K. Flint, "Task Force Smith and the 24th Division: Delay and Withdrawal, 5–19 July 1950," *America's First Battles 1776–1965*, ed., Charles E. Heller and William A. Stofft (Lawrence, Kansas: University Press of Kansas, 269–272.

21. Jim D. Hill, *The Minute Man in Peace and War: A History of the National Guard* (Harrisburg, Pennsylvania: Stackpole, 1964), 506, 507.

22. William F. Dean, *General Dean's Story: as told to William L. Worden* (New York: Viking Press, 1954, 17.

23. Leon B. Cheek, Jr., Lieutenant Colonel, Artillery, "Korea, Decisive Battle of the World," *Military Review*, March 1953, 20–26.

24. This order was controversial. See Schnabel, *Policy and Direction*, 126; and D. Clayton James, *The Years of MacArthur: Triumph and Disaster 1945–1964* (Boston: Houghton Mifflin, 1985), 446. James recorded the assessment of General Almond that Walker's "to stand or die" order was motivated by MacArthur's order to Walker not to withdraw from Taegu. Also see: Courtney Whitney, Major General US Army, *MacArthur: His Rendezvous with History* (New York: Knopf, 1956), 344. Whitney made a similar argument.

25. Edward M. Almond, Lieutenant General, US Army and MacArthur's Chief of Staff in Japan, "Conference on United Nations Military Operations in Korea, 29 June 1950—31 December 1951," Carlisle, Pennsylvania, Army War College, 8.

26. US Army, Office, Chief of Army Field Forces, Training Bulletin No. 1, Combat Information, 20 March 1953, MHI.

27. Fritzsche, Carl F., Brigadier General US Army, "Physical Fitness—A Must!" *Army Information Digest*, July 1955, 41–43.

28. For the official US Army history account see: Roy E. Appleman, *South to the Naktong, North to the Yalu, US Army in the Korean War* (Washington, DC: Center of Military History, 1986), 194. Appleman wrote: "The tendency to panic continued in nearly all the 24th Infantry operations west of Sangju. Men left their positions and straggled to the rear. They abandoned weapons on positions. On one occasion the 3rd Battalion withdrew from a hill and left behind 30-caliber and 50-caliber machine guns, 8 60-mm mortars, 4 3.5-inch rocket launchers, and 102 rifles." It is hard to believe that soldiers—no matter how poorly trained and motivated— left their rifles, their only form of protection; however, Appleman's major argument was in keeping with the

general feelings of the time—black men are racially inferior lacking the qualities of character necessary to make good soldiers. For another assessment by a black officer who fought with the 24th Regiment in Korea see: Charles M. Bussey, Lieutenant Colonel US Army, *Firefight at Yechon* (New York: Brassey's Inc., 1991). Bussey wrote: "After my firefight at Yechon the colonel told me that I should receive the Medal of Honor, but because I was a 'Negro,' he could not let that happen. Other controversy has raged over the role and performance of black soldiers in Korea. The white press emphasized stories about Negroes bugging out. In those early days in Korea, the black 24th Infantry Regiment performed better than the regiments of the white 24th Infantry Division and just as well as the other regiments that came later to Korea. The US Army's official history of the first part of the Korean War . . . by Roy E. Appleman, strikes me as unfair and not representing what I saw personally. His book suggests that the Negro soldiers and their units were no good. The official history cites twenty-four instances of poor behavior by the 24th Infantry that I served in. Mr. Appleman was never in the combat zone, and some of the interviews upon which his account is based took place as much as five years afterward. Mr. Appleman interviewed only one black officer and no black enlisted men. He never talked to me." This controversy was addressed in William T. Bowers, William M. Hammond, and George L. MacGarrigle's *Black Soldier White Army: The 24th Infantry Regiment in Korea* (Washington, DC: US Army Center of Military History, 1996).

29. Blair, *The Forgotten War*, 554, 555.
30. Dr. William Glenn Robertson, *Counterattack on the Naktong, 1950, Leavenworth Papers* (Leavenworth, Kansas: US Army Command and General Staff College, December 1985), 108.
31. MacArthur, *Reminiscences*, 346.
32. US Army, Headquarter X Corps War Diary, Operation Chromite, 15 August to 30 September, General Edward M. Almond, RG 407, Box 1089, NA II.
33. For the Marine Corps interpretation of the Inchon Landing see the Marine Corps' official history by Lynn Montros and Nicholas Canzona, *US Marine Operations in Korea 1950–1953, The Inchon-Seoul Operation*, Vol. II, USMC (Washington, DC: Historical Branch, G–3, US Marine Corps, 1955; Robert Debs Heinl, Jr. Colonel USMC, *Victory at High Tide: The Inchon-Seoul Campaign* (New York: J.B. Lippincott, 1968); and Edwin H. Simmons, Brigadier General USMC, *Over the Seawall: Marines at Inchon, Marines in the Korean War Commemorative* (Wash. DC: GPO, 2000).
34. From Walt Sheldon's interview with Galloway, for *Hell or High Water: MacArthur's Landing at Inchon* (New York: Macmillan, 1968), 49. Quoted in Ronal Carpenter's "Did MacArthur Save the Marines?" *Proceedings*, Vol. 126/8/1,170, August 2000, 66.

35. See, Adrian R. Lewis, *Omaha Beach: A Flawed Victory* (Chapel Hill: University of North Carolina Press, 2001).
36. For an excellent study of tidal conditions as Inchon see: Harold A. Winters, *Battling the Elements: Weather and Terrain in the Conduct of War* (Baltimore: The Johns Hopkins University Press, 1998), 207–214.
37. MacArthur, *Reminiscences*, 349. See also, D. Clayton James, *The Years of MacArthur: Triumph and Disaster 1945–1964* (Boston: Houghton Mifflin, 1985), 469.
38. Admiral Robert L. Dennison, Oral History Interviewed by John T. Mason, 3/27/1973, Annapolis, Maryland: US Navy Institute Oral History Program, Dennison #5, 203.
39. Reserve Officers of Public Affairs Unit 4–1, *The Marine Corps Reserve: A History* (Washington, DC: Division of Reserve, Headquarters, US Marine Corps, 1966) 164.
40. Ronald H. Carpenter, "Did MacArthur Save the Marines?" *Proceedings*, Vol. 126/8/1,170, August 2000, 70.
41. Lynn Montross and Captain Nicholas A. Canzona, USMC, *US Marine Operations in Korea 1950–1953, The Inchon-Seoul Operation*, Volume II (Washington, DC: Historical Branch, G–3, Headquarters US Marine Corps, 1955), 134–136.
42. Montross, *The Inchon-Seoul Operation*, 129.
43. Robert D. Heinl, Colonel USMC, *Victory at High Tide* (New York: Lippincott, 1968), 38, 39.
44. Stanley Sandler, *The Korean War: No Victors, No Vanquished* (Kentucky: University of Kentucky Press, 1999) 92, 93. See: Alonzo Hamby, "Public opinion: Korea and Vietnam," *Wilson Quarterly*, Summer 1978; Karl G. Larew, "Inchon Not a Stroke of Genius or Even Necessary," *Army*, December 1988; and Bruce Pirine, "The Inchon Landing: How Great Was the Risk?" *Joint Perspectives*, 3 Summer 1982.
45. Ridgway, *The Korean War*, 44.
46. Schnabel, *Policy and Direction*, 176.
47. Hal D. Steward, Major US Army, Headquarters, 1st Cavalry Division (Infantry), "Rise and Fall of an Army," *Military Review*, February 1951, 32–35.
48. US Army EUSAK, War Diary, 1 September 1950 to 30 September 1950, RG 407, Box 1101, NA II.
49. Quoted in Rosemary Foot, *The Wrong War: American Policy and the Dimensions of the Korean Conflict, 1950–1953* (Ithaca, New York: Cornell University Press, 1985), 71.
50. Quoted in Max Hastings, *The Korean War* (New York: Simon and Schuster, 1987), 118 (emphasis added). Also see, Matthew B. Ridgway, *The Korean War* (New York: A Da Capo Paperback, 1967), 45; and Allen Guttmann, ed., *Korea and the Theory of Limited War* (Boston: D.C. Heath, 1967), 9.
51. Schnabel, *Policy and Direction*, 199.
52. Rosemary Foot in her book, *The Wrong War*, (74–87), provides the best assessment of the American decision to cross the 38th parallel. Foot wrote: "As for China, Washington concluded that it was unlikely to enter the

war because of the PRC's inappropriate and low military capability, its domestic problems, its desire to take its seat in the U.N., and it reluctance to become further dependent on Moscow, militarily and diplomatically."

53. Truman, *Memoirs*, vol. II, 362. Schnabel, *Policy and Direction*, 200. NCS 73/1 (29 July) and NSC 73/4 (August) delineated the actions to be taken if the Chinese entered the War: "as long as action by UN military forces now committed or planned for commitment in Korea offers a reasonable chance of successful resistance, such action should be continued and extended to include authority to take appropriate air and naval action outside of Korea against Communist China."

54. James, *Triumph and Disaster 1945–1964*, 488, 489; and Ridgway, *The Korean War*, 45.

55. Quoted in Schnabel, *Policy and Direction*, 194.

56. Truman's recollection of this meeting differs from MacArthur's. See, Truman, *Memoirs*, 366; and Major General Courtney Whitney, *MacArthur: His Rendezvous with History* (New York: Alfred A. Knopf, 1956), 392. General Whitney, who was at Wake Island during the conference, wrote: "MacArthur promptly replied that his answer would be purely speculative, but that his guess would be 'very little.' He then explained this viewpoint. Obviously he could only speak from a military standpoint, with a political decision. But as a backdrop to his military speculation, MacArthur proceeded from the premise . . . that there was no evidence from Peiping even suggesting that Red Chinese intervention was under serious consideration."

57. For a concise assessment of CPV see, Scott R. McMichael, Major US Army, *A Historical Perspective on Light Infantry*, CSI, Research Survey No. 6 (Ft. Leveanworth, KS: US Army Command and General Staff College, 1987), 51–80. For a more detailed study see: Alexander George, *The Chinese Communist Army in Action: The Korean War and Its Aftermath* (New York: Columbia University Press, 1967).

58. Quoted by James H. Tate, "The Eighth Army's Winter Campaign," *Army Information Digest*, August 1951, 42–57.

59. Quoted in Whitney, *MacArthur*, 421.

60. Oral Reminiscences of Governor W. Averell Harriman, Interviews with D. Clayton James, 20 June 1977, RG–49, MacArthur Archives and Library, Norfolk, Virginia.

61. *Public Papers of the Presidents of the United States Harry S. Truman, January 1 to December 31, 1950* (Washington, DC: GPO, 1965), 741–743.

62. Joint Chiefs of Staff directive to General Douglas MacArthur. Reprinted in *Reminiscences*, MacArthur, 377.

63. MacArthur response to the Joint Chiefs of Staff on 30 December 1950. Reprinted in *Reminiscences*, MacArthur, 379.

64. JCS response to MacArthur's proposal for expanding the war. Reprinted in *Reminiscences*, 380.

65. Quoted in *Life* magazine, 12 May 1952, 111.

66. Matthew B. Ridgway, *The Korean War* (New York: A Da Capo Paperback, © 1967), 83.

67. Ridgway, quoted in, Roy E. Appleman, *Ridgway Duels for Korea* (College Station: Texas A&M University Press, 1990), 7.

68. Ridgway, *The Korean War*, 85.

69. Quoted in James F. Schnabel, "Ridgway in Korea," *Military Review*, March 1964, 7.

70. Margaret A. Mallman, Captain US Army, "Korean Brawn Backs the Attack," *Army Information Digest*, December 1951.

71. Quoted in James F. Schnabel, "Ridgway in Korea," *Military Review*, March 1964, 7.

72. Ridgway, *Soldier*, 206, 207.

73. Quoted in Schnabel, "Ridgway in Korea," *Military Review*, 11.

74. Quoted in *Life* magazine, 12 May 1952, 114 (cover story). Also see, Ridgway, *Soldier*, 208.

75. Dennis J. Vetock, *Lessons Learned: A History of US Army Lesson Learning* (Carlisle Barracks, PA: US Army Military History Institute, 1988), 76.

76. US Army, EUSAK, G–2, Periodic Intelligence Report, No. 150, Inclosure No. 2, RG 407, Box 1133, NA II.

77. S.L.A. Marshall, *Infantry Operations and Weapons Usage in Korea* (London: Greenhill Books, 1988), 5–7, 128–130, 133–135.

78. Russell A. Gugeler, *Combat Action in Korea* (Washington, D.C.: Office of the Chief of Military History, 1970), 100.

79. Fehrenbach, *This Kind of War*, 393–394.

80. Appleman, *Ridgway Duels For Korea*, 258.

81. US Army, Office, Chief of Army Field Forces, Training Bulletin No. 1, Combat Information, 20 March 1953, MHI.

82. Quoted in "American Society and the American Way of War: Korea and Beyond," by James H. Toner, *Parameters*, Vol. XI, No. 1, Spring 1981, 78–89.

Chapter 6

1. Curtis E. LeMay, *Mission With LeMay* (New York: Doubleday, 1965), 463, 464 (italics added).

2. Robert Futrell, *The US Air Force in Korea 1950–1953* Revised Edition (Washington, DC: Office of Air Force History, 1983), 193.

3. Futrell's book, *The US Air Force in Korea*, is the standard work on the airpower in the Korean War. For a more recent study see, Conrad A. Crane, *American Airpower Strategy in Korea 1950–1953* (Lawrence: University Press of Kansas, 2000).

4. John W. R. Taylor, "What Has Korea Taught Us?" *Military Review*, August 1954, 86–89. Taylor observed, "Their [the U.N. Air Force's] failure to stem the flood of the North Korean invasion in 1950 and the later Chinese

onslaught was regarded by some armchair critics as proof of the inability of air power to play a significant role in tactical warfare. The critics chose to forget that the enemy in Korea was usually an infantry man, moving without vehicles and artillery, at night, carrying only a rifle and a bowl of rice, over mountain trails where the front line was never held long enough to permit proper close air support. . . ." In other words, the Air Force was unprepared for the type of war it had to fight in Korea.

5. Walton S. Moody, *Building A Strategic Air Force* (Washington D.C.: Air Force History, 1995), 396.

6. Curtis LeMay, General US Air Force, *Mission with LeMay: My Story* (New York: Doubleday, 1965), 462, 463.

7. See Alan Stephens, "The Air War in Korea, 1950–1953," in *A History of Air Warfare* (Washington, DC: Potomac Books, 2010), 27–52.

8. Crane, *American Airpower Strategy in Korea 1950–1953*, 21, 22.

9. Quoted in Futrell, *The US Air Force in Korea, 1950–1953*, 186 (italics added).

10. Allan R. Millett, "Korea, 1950–1953," *Case Studies in the Development of Close Air Support*, ed. Benjamin Franklin Cooling (Washington, DC: Office of Air Force History, USAF, 1990), 374. Lieutenant General George E. Stratemeyer commanded the FEAF until June 1951, and General O.P. Weyland for the remainder of the war (italics added).

11. Millett, "Korea, 1950–1953," *Close Air Support*, 350, 351.

12. Admiral Charles D. Griffin, Oral History Interview by John T. Mason, 4/14/1970, Annapolis, Maryland: US Navy Institute Oral History Program, #5 Griffin, 231.

13. Futrell, *The United States Air Force in Korea 1950–1953*, 705. Futrell argued that, the differences in performance between the Air Force and Marine Corps was the result of "fundamental philosophical differences between the USAF-Army and the Marine systems of air-ground operations." The Army tended to rely more heavily on its artillery than the Marine Corps ground force, resulting in different techniques for deploying close air support.

14. For a description of the system see Futrell, *The US Air Force in Korea*, Chapter 3. "Drawing the Battleline in Korea," 77.

15. Edward M. Almond, Lieutenant General US Army, "Mistakes in Air-Support Methods in Korea," *US News and World Report*, 6 March 1953, 58–61.

16. Edward M. Almond Papers, *Senior Officer Debriefing Program*, interviewed by Captain Thomas G. Fergusson, Anniston, Ala., six tape series of typed transcripts (Carlisle Barracks, Pennsylvania: US Army Military History Institute, 25–30 March 1975), Tape 5, 57.

17. The F–80 was the Army Air Forces' first jet, and the F–86 was the Air Forces' first swept-wing fighter. It was rushed to Korea to take on the Soviet-made MIG jet fighter flown in large part by Soviet pilots. See Marcelle

Size Knaack, *Encyclopedia of US Air Force Aircraft and Missile Systems*, vol. 1, *Post World War II Fighters 1944–1973* (Washington, DC: Office of Air Force History, 1978), 23, 52.

18. Admiral John J. Hyland, Jr., Oral History Interviewed by Paul Stillwell, 5/31/1984, Annapolis, Maryland: US Naval Institute Oral History Program, #6 Hyland, 379.

19. Millett, *Close Air Support*, 359.

20. Millett, *Close Air Support*, 381.

21. William W. Momyer, General US Air Force, *Airpower in Three Wars (WWII, Korea, Vietnam)* (Maxwell Air Force Base, Alabama: Air University Press, April 2003), 128.

22. Futrell, *The United States Air Force in Korea 1950–1953*, 695, 696.

23. Xiaoming Zhang, *Red Wings Over the Yalu: China, The Soviet Union, and the Air War in Korea* (College Station: Texas A&M University Press, 2002), 122.

24. Zhang, *Red Wings Over the Yalu*, 138.

25. Crane, *American Airpower Strategy in Korea*, 176.

26. Andrew M. Jackson, Admiral US Navy, Oral History Interview 2/7/1972, US Naval Institute, Annapolis, Maryland, Jackson # 5, 173–182.

27. Norman Friedman, *US Aircraft Carriers: An Illustrated Design History* (Annapolis, Maryland: Naval Institute Press, 1983), 256. The Naval historian, Norman Friedman, wrote: "The revival of carrier construction was very much a consequence of the Korean War. The North Koreans attacked on 25 June 1950, vindicating Forrest Sherman's plea that one carrier be maintained in the Far East at all times. On 11 July the Joint Chiefs agreed to postpone further consideration of reductions in the carrier force level, and the following day Secretary of Defense Johnson, the man who had killed the [USS] *United States*, offered Admiral Sherman a new carrier."

28. B.S. Bhagat, Brigadier British Army, "Military Lessons of the Korean Conflict," *Military Review*, December 1952, 71–79.

29. Gen. O.P. Weyland, "The Air Campaign in Korea," *Air University Quarterly Review* 6 (Fall 1953), 27–28. Quoted in Crane, *American Airpower Strategy in Korea*, 171.

30. J. Thomas Schneider, Chairman, Personnel Policy Board, Office of the Secretary of Defense, "The Need for Understanding," *Army Information Digest*, June 1951, 3–6.

31. Floyd L. Parks, Major General, "Army Public Relations— A Review of 1952," *Army Information Digest*, March 1953, 3–13.

32. *The Big Picture* film series started in 1951 with thirteen half-hour programs devoted to the Eighth Army in Korea. Of the 111 television stations, ninety-seven broadcast the program. The Army Signal Corps produced the series and distributed it without cost. It was believed that the program reached ninety percent of the viewing audience, estimated at 50 million viewers. It was considered one of the Army's most successful pub-

lic relations programs. In 1955 there were only 35 million televisions in the United States; however, each week 50,000 new sets went into American homes. Television was rapidly becoming the most ubiquitous and important means of communicating with the public. Additionally, it was estimated that 75 million people attended 20,000 theaters in the United States each week in 1952. A "hit" picture could reach as many as 40 million people. The objectives of the Army Motion Picture Section were to help the American people gain a better understanding of war, Army life, and the sacrifices, hardship, and courage of soldiers. The Home Town News Center was established in July 1951 in Kansas City, Missouri. Its purpose was to "improve, supervise, and control the flow of informational material to home town news media" in accordance with AR 360–20. At the end of the war, in 1953, the Center was in contact with more than 11,950 newspaper, radio, and television editors.

33. Karl A. Von Voigtlander, Major US Army, "The War for Words," *Army Information Digest*, January 1953, 54–59.

34. Edward F. Witsell, Major General US Army, Adjutant General, "The Casualty Report Tells the Story," *Army Information Digest*," November 1950, 7–10.

35. M.P. Echols, Colonel US Army, "Information in the Combat Zone," *Army Information Digest*, April 1951, 60–64.

36. Von Voigtlander, "The War for Words," 56 (italics added).

37. Von Voigtlander, "The War for Words," 57 (italics added).

38. Mathew B. Ridgway, *The Korean War* (New York: Doubleday, 1967), 73.

39. Floyd L. Parks, Major General US Army, "The Commander and the Press," *Army Information Digest*, May 1953, 17–20.

40. Julius O. Adler, Major General USAR, "The Free Press—Weapon of Democracy," *Army Information Digest*, June 1953, 17–21 (italics added).

41. Douglas MacArthur: Testimony Before the Armed Services and Foreign Relations Committees of the Senate, 26–28. Reprinted in *Korea and the Theory of Limited War*, ed. Allen Guttmann (Boston: D.C. Heath, 1967), 17, 18.

42. Quoted in George C. Mitchell's *Matthew B. Ridgway*, 93, 94. Ridgway later stated: "As a soldier, I do not question the right of the President, as Commander in Chief, to relieve any officer with whose views and actions he disagrees. . . . I do feel that this dismissal could have been handled with more grace."

43. The Joint Chiefs of Staff, Memorandum for the Record, CJSC Omar N. Bradley, Subject: Relief of General Douglas MacArthur, 25 April 1951. Washington, DC: JCS Declassification Branch, 8 June 1977. Bradley wrote: "I felt that proper action was to let General Marshall write a personal and confidential letter to General MacArthur, pointing out the difficult position in

which he was placing the government. We went so far as to draft a copy of such letter. I furnished part of the draft and General Marshall filled in the rest of it."

44. The Joint Chiefs of Staff, Memorandum for the Record, CJSC Omar N. Bradley, Subject: Relief of General Douglas MacArthur, 25 April 1951. Washington, DC: JCS Declassification Branch, 8 June 1977.

45. Douglas MacArthur, *Reminiscences* (New York: McGraw Hill, 1964) 403.

46. MacArthur, *Reminiscences*, 404.

47. MacArthur, *Reminiscences*, 404.

48. Almond, "Mistakes in Air-Support Methods in Korea," 58–61.

49. Harry S. Truman, "Limiting the War in Korea is Essential to Avoid a World War," *The Korean War: Interpreting Primary Documents*, edited Dennis Nishi (New York: Greenhaven Press, 2003), 95–97.

50. For Ridgway's assessment of the relief of MacArthur see, George C. Mitchell, *Matthew B. Ridgway: Soldier, Statesman, Scholar, Citizen* (Mechanicburg, PA: Stackpole Books, 2002, Chapter 9.

51. George Q. Flynn, *The Draft, 1940–1973* (Lawrence: the University Press of Kansas, 1993), 104–109. See: Irving W. Hart, Lieutenant Colonel US Army "On Extending Selective Service," *Army Information Digest*, May 1950, 31–35. All the Chiefs of the services argued for extending the draft.

52. Irving W. Hart, Lieutenant Colonel US Army, "On Extending Selective Service," *Army Information Digest*, May 1950, 31–35.

53. The Selective Service Act of 24 June 1948 obligated enlisted men to serve for twenty-one months on active duty and afterward to remain in the inactive reserve for five years. In the event of emergency men in the inactive reserve could be recalled to active duty. If a man enlisted for one year of active duty as an eighteen-year-old, he had a six-year obligation in the inactive reserve. And, if a man served thirty-three months on active duty he acquired no reserve obligation. Reservists were recalled to fight the Korean War, 140,000 from the National Guard and 230,000 from the Organized Reserve Corps. Congress revised these requirements several times during the 1950s.

54. Elva Stillwaugh, Major US Army, "Personnel Policies in the Korean Conflict," Washington, DC: Department of the Army, Office of the Chief of Military History, 22.

55. J. Lawton Collins, Chief of Staff, US Army, "Our Global Responsibilities," *Army Information Digest*, February 1952, 3–6. Based on an address at the annual autumn Convocation at Tulane University in 1952.

56. In fact, the Army released 809,000 in 1953, and the Selective Service provided 746,000. The end strength was 1,533,815.

57. J. Lawton Collins, "Men, Materiel and Money" *The Army Information Digest*, July 1953, 8–16.

58. Frink, J.L., Jr., Lieutenant Colonel, US Army, "The Shipment of Replacements in Groups," *Military Review*, August 1950, 45–51.

59. Alexander M. Haig, Jr., General US Army, *Inner Circles: How America Changed the World, A Memoir* (New York: Warner Books, 1992), 68, 69.

60. Charles C. Moskos, Jr., *The American Enlisted Man* (New York: Russell Sage Foundation, 1970), 10.

61. Stillwaugh, "Personnel Policies in the Korean War," 29.

62. Hill, *The Minute Man in Peace and War*, 507.

63. Charles G. Cleaver, 1st Lieutenant US Army, "History of the Korean War Personnel Problems" Prepared in Military History Section Headquarters, Far East Command, Tokyo, Japan, 15 August 1952, Washington, DC: US Army Center of Military History, 75 (italics added).

64. Cleaver, "Personnel Problems," 74.

65. Patterson, William H. Lieutenant Colonel, US Army, "The Personnel Function Within the United States Army," *Military Review*, January 1951, 16–24.

66. David Curtis Skaggs, "The KATUSA Experiment: The Integration of Korean Nationals into the US Army, 1950–1965," *Military Affairs*, April 1974, 53–58.

67. Cleaver, "Personnel Problems," 93, 94. And see: Herbert H. Andrae, Lieutenant Colonel, US Army, "Rotation," *Military Review*, November 1950, 21–28.

68. Lloyd R. Moses, Colonel US Army, "The Training of Loss Replacements," *Military Review*, December 1951, 37–44.

69. U.P. Williams, Lieutenant Colonel US Army, "They May Not Die—But They Wither Fast," *Military Review*, July 1950, 16–23 (emphasis added).

70. Charles E. Kirkpatrick, *An Unknown Future and a Doubtful Present: Writing the Victory Plan of 1941* (Washington, DC: Center of Military History, 1990), 78, 98.

71. Samuel Stouffer, et al, *The American Soldier: Combat and its Aftermath* (NJ: Princeton University Press, 1949), 3–4.

72. J. Lawton Collins, "Men, Materiel and Money" *The Army Information Digest*, July 1953, 8–16.

73. Mark Clark, *From the Danube to the Yalu* (Summit, PA: TAB Books, © 1954), 187, 192.

74. John Montgomery, Jr., "Unit Rotation—The Long View," *Military Review*, Sept. 1951, 11–14.

75. Clark, *From the Danube to the Yalu*, 192 (emphasis added).

76. Cleaver, "Personnel Problems," 101, 110. Cleaver wrote: "Large-scale rotation not only involved a rapid turnover of basic soldiers but also removed from the theater key men whose training required a long time, i.e., specialists, officers, and noncommissioned leaders. . . . Nobody knew how long basic soldiers could continue to replace trained men, including noncommissioned officers and specialists, at a rate of 20,000 a month before the saturation point would be reached." Still, General Van Fleet concluded: "this high enlisted rotational turnover has had a highly beneficial effect on the combat effectiveness of Eighth Army."

77. Stillwaugh, *Personnel Policies in the Korean War*, Chapter 4, "Rotation," 38. Also see: Roger W. Little, "Buddy Relations and Combat Performance," *The New Military: Changing Patterns of Organization*, ed. Morris Janowitz, (New York: Norton, 1964), 197.

78. S.L.A. Marshall, *Pork Chop Hill: The American Fighting Man in Action, Korea, Spring, 1953* (New York: William Morrow, 1956), 14.

79. Anthony Herbert, *Soldier* (New York: Holt, Rinehart and Winston, 1973), 57.

80. Little, "Buddy Relations and Combat Performance," 221.

81. Stillwaugh, *Personnel Policies in the Korean War*, Chapter 4, "Rotation," 39.

82. Quoted in Jim Dan Hill, *The Minute Man in Peace and War*, 512.

83. Marshall, *Pork Chop Hill*, 18. Marshall concluded: ". . . I could not believe in the policy of individual rotation then in use. . . . To my mind, it was ruinous to morale and to good administrative order within an armed force. Whatever it gave the soldier, it sacrificed most of the traditional values, such as earned promotion and citation, pride in unit, and close comradeship."

84. Andre Fontaine, "You and I, USA," *Army Information Digest*, December 1953, 14–25.

85. Floyd Parks, General US Army, "Defense Begins at Home," *Army Information Digest*, Jan. 1953, 11.

86. J.P. Womble, Rear Admiral US Navy, "The Womble Report On Service Careers," *Army Information Digest*, February 1954.

87. Clausewitz, *On War*, 593.

88. Matthew B. Ridgway, *The Korean War* (New York: A Da Capo Paperback, © 1967), 192.

89. Quoted in Morris MacGregor, Jr., *Integration of the Armed Forces, 1940–1965* (Washington, DC: CMH, 1985), 312.

90. Bernard C. Nalty, *Strength For the Fight: A History of Black Americans in the Military* (New York: Macmillan, 1986, 242, 243. See: MacGregor, Jr., *Integration of the Armed Forces 1940–1960*; and Gail Buckley, *American Patriots: The Story of Blacks in the Military From the Revolution to Desert Storm* (New York: Random House, 2001).

91. Quoted in Senate, Hearing Before the US Senate Committee on Armed Services, *Universal Military Training*, 80th Congress, 2nd session, 1948, 995–996.

92. Ridgway, *The Korean War*, 193.

93. Office of Deputy Assistant Secretary of Defense for Equal Opportunity and Safety Policy, Department of Defense, *Black Americans in Defense of Our Nation* (Washington, DC: US GPO, 1985), 66.

94. Walter Hermes, *Truce Tent and Fighting Front, The United States Army in the Korean War* (Washington, DC: Office of the Chief of Military History, 1966), 58. For a recent

assessment of Marine Corps operations in the final phases of the war see Bernard C. Nalty, *Outpost War: US Marines from the Nevada Battles to the Armistice, Marines in the Korean War Commemorative Series* (Washington, DC: GPO, 2003).

95. Ridgway, *The Korean War*, 167. Robert Osgood, *Limited War* (University of Chicago Press, 1957), 185.

96. Van Fleet was a veteran of the Normandy invasion and operations in Western Europe. His son, an Air Force pilot, was killed during a mission over North Korea.

97. Ridgway, *Soldier*, 219.

98. Charles Turner Joy, Admiral US Navy, *How Communists Negotiate* (New York: Macmillan, 1955), 173–174.

99. Futrell, *The US Air Force in Korea*, 648.

100. Msg, V0022, Gen. O.P. Weyland to Gen. Earle Patridge, 19 Jan 1954, Weyland Official Correspondence, 50/00/00–53/00/00, File 168.7104–50, AFHRA, Maxwell Air Force Base, Ala. Quoted in Crane, *American Airpower Strategy in Korea*, 171.

101. Washington Headquarters Services, Directorate of Information Operations and Reports.

102. J. Lawton Collins, *War in Peacetime: The History and Lessons of Korea* (Boston: Houghton Mifflin, 1969), 312.

103. Department of the Army, *Semiannual Report of the Secretary of the Army* (Washington, DC: GPO, 1951), 2.

Chapter 7

1. John Foster Dulles, "Policy for Security and Peace," Department of State Bulletin, Vol XXX, 29 March 1954, *American Foreign Policy*, ed., Harold Karan Jacobson (New York: Random House, 1960), 376.

2. Clay Blair, *The Forgotten War* (New York: Times Book, 1987), 971.

3. John Foster Dulles, "Policy for Security and Peace" in *American Foreign Policy*, 371.

4. Dulles, "Policy for Security and Peace," 374, 375.

5. Department of State, National Security Policy: NSC 162/2, 30 October 1953, *Foreign Relations of the United States, 1952–1954*, vol. II, part 1, pp. 577–597, and in *US National Security Policy and Strategy: Documents and Policy Proposals*, ed., Sam C. Sarkesian with Robert A. Vitas (New York: Greenwood Press, 1988), 48–52.

6. Dwight D. Eisenhower, *Mandate for Change: The White House Years, 1953–1956* (New York: Doubleday, 1963), 82. Eisenhower wrote: "I thought the decision to intervene was wise and necessary."

7. Eisenhower, *Mandate for Change*, 180.

8. Stephen E. Ambrose, *Eisenhower: The President* (New York: Simon and Schuster, 1984), 144.

9. Dwight D. Eisenhower, "The President's News Conference on March 17, 1954," *US National Security Policy and Strategy: Documents and Policy Proposals* (New York: Greenwood Press, 1988), 55–58.

10. James M. Gavin, Lieutenant-General US Army, *War and Peace in the Space Age* (New York: Harper, 1958), 150.

11. Quoted in Emmett J. Hughes, *The Living Presidency* (New York: Coward-McCann and Geoghegan), 15, 16; and E. Bruce Geelhoed, *Charles E. Wilson and Controversy at the Pentagon 1953 to 1957* (Detroit: Wayne State University Press, 1979), 102.

12. Eisenhower, "The Long Pull for Peace" *The Army Information Digest*, April 1948, 33–41.

13. John F. Kennedy, "Conventional Forces in the Atomic Age," *The Strategy of Peace* (New York: Harper, 1959), 184.

14. Mark W. Clark, General US Army, *From the Danube to the Yalu* (Summit, PA: TAB Books, © 1954), 196.

15. Matthew B. Ridgway, *Soldier: The Memoirs of Matthew B. Ridgway* (New York: Harper, 1956), 275.

16. Ridgway, *Soldier*, 191.

17. Ridgway, *Soldier*, 312.

18. Matthew B. Ridgway, "Trends in Modern Warfare," *Army Information Digest*, January 1950, 63.

19. On 11 September 2001, the US Air Force was incapable of deploying and sustaining one armor brigade into Afghanistan or anywhere else.

20. John F. Kennedy, US Senator, "Conventional Forces in the Atomic Age," *The Strategy of Peace*, ed. Allen Nevin (New York: Harper, 1960), 184–185.

21. Ridgway, *Soldier*, 296, 311.

22. Ridgway, *Soldier*, 286.

23. Wallace C. Magathan, Jr., Lieutenant Colonel US Army, "In Defense of the Army," *Military Review*, April 1956, 3.

24. James E. Cross, "What is the Army's Job?" *Military Review*, June 1956, 43.

25. H.P. Storke, Major General US Army, "Speak Up for the Army," *Army Information Digest*, July 1959, 2–9.

26. Charles C. Moskos, Jr., *The American Enlisted Man* (New York: Russell Sage Foundation, 1970), 18.

27. Ridgway, *Soldier*, 316.

28. Maxwell D. Taylor, *Swords and Plowshares* (New York: W.W. Norton, 1972), 170.

29. Maxwell D. Taylor, Army Chief of Staff, "Development of Basic Guidance for Army Programs," *Army Information Digest*, June 1957, 3–19.

30. Maxwell D. Taylor, *The Uncertain Trumpet* (New York: Harper, 1959), 5, 6.

31. Robert E. Osgood, *Limited War* (Chicago: University of Chicago Press, 1957); Henry A. Kissinger, *Nuclear Weapons and Foreign Policy* (New York: Harper & Brothers, 1957).

32. Taylor, *Swords and Plowshares*, 171.

33. T.A. Weyher, Brigadier General US Army, "What's New in Firepower," *Army Information Digest*, May 1957, 3–8.

34. Taylor, *Swords and Plowshares*, 152, 153.

35. Theodore C. Mataxis and Seymour L. Goldberg, *Nuclear Tactics: Weapons, and Firepower in the Pentomic Division, Battle Group, and Company* (Harrisburg,

Pennsylvania: The Military Service Publishing Company, 1958), 104.

36. Paul F. Yount, Major General US Army, "Transportation For Tomorrow's Army," *Army Information Digest*, February 1958, 12–19.

37. Maxwell D. Taylor, "The Army of the Future," *Army Information Digest*, January 1957, 15, 16.

38. US Army, "US Army Deterrent Force" *Army Information Digest*, March 1958, 35–40. The Army noted: "The use of small-yield nuclear weapons by tactical forces for a tactical purpose would not necessarily transform limited war into general war. However, the clear abandonment by either side of the 'least possible destruction' principle [of limited war] would greatly increase the likelihood of general war."

39. William C. Westmoreland, *A Soldier Reports* (New York: Doubleday and Co., 1976), 32.

40. Maxwell D. Taylor, "The Race for Technological Superiority," *Army Information Digest*, August 1959, 23, 24, and 26.

41. James E. Hewes, Jr., *From Root to McNamara Army Organization and Administration 1900–1963* (Washington, DC: Center of Military History, 1975), 306, 307.

42. Andrew J. Bacevich, *The Pentomic Era: The US Army Between Korea and Vietnam* (Washington, DC: National Defense University Press, 1986), 98, 99.

43. Harry H. Ransom, "Scientific Manpower and National Strategy," *Military Review*, December 1956, 57–62.

44. Paul Dickson, *Sputnik: The Shock of the Century* (New York: Walker, 2001), 2, 3, 4, and 224.

45. Lyman L. Lemnitzer, General US Army, "Looking Ahead with the Army," *Army Information Digest*, June 1959, 14 (italics added).

46. Bruce C. Clarke, General US Army, "Strengthening Our Readiness Capabilities," *Army Information Digest*, June 1959, 15.

47. Moody, *Building a Strategic Air Force*, 416, 417.

48. In 1957, to insure that the bombers were not caught on the ground, SAC implemented a new alert and readiness system. Bombers were loaded with nuclear bombs and maintained in the air. A second strike force was placed on a 15-minute alert status. While the system was modified over the years, and the numbers of aircraft in the air varied with the level of tension between the superpowers, the program was eventually eliminated. The stress on aircraft and men were enormous. Still, SAC maintained a "go to war" state of readiness throughout the Cold War.

49. Michael R. Beschloss, *Mayday: Eisenhower, Khrushchev and the U–2 Affair* (New York: Harper and Row, 1986), 5.

50. On 1 May 1960, Gary Powers' U–2 was downed over the SU, creating a major diplomatic crisis—the pilot lived—ending the U–2 overflights of the SU, ending any chance of a new relationship with the SU in the immediate future, and embarrassing the Eisenhower Administration in its last year in office. That same year

the first images from a satellite provided the US with intelligence. This technology was in its infancy, but its promise for the future was enormous. The Soviets were also developing this technology.

51. Conrad Crane, *American Airpower Strategy in Korea 1950–1953* (Lawrence: University Press of Kansas, 2000), 172.

52. Quoted in Norman Friedman, *US Aircraft Carriers: An Illustrated Design History* (Annapolis, Maryland: Naval Institute Press, 1983), 244.

53. Friedman, *US Aircraft Carriers*, 248.

54. Friedman, *US Aircraft Carriers*, 244.

55. The need for bigger aircraft to employ nuclear weapons and the advent of the jet aircraft placed new demands on the carrier, making most of the Navy's World War II fleet obsolete. Aircraft carrier design was the function of a series of tradeoffs between the size and weight of aircraft, the numbers of aircraft, the endurance and capabilities of the ship, and the maximum cost that Congress was willing to fund. The intensity of aircraft carrier operations increased with the speed of aircraft. The increased weight and size of jet aircraft demanded greater space, larger elevators, larger hangars, and an overall more muscular ship. The increased rate of fuel consumption and ultimately the more varied types of ordinance, including missiles, also created new demands for space.

56. The British-designed, angled deck made possible the employment of larger aircraft, a forward park space for aircraft, a safer operational environment, and theoretically the ability to launch and recover aircraft simultaneously. The ship employed the British-designed steam catapult to launch aircraft, and mirror landing air system to facilitate the recovery aircraft. Elevators were located at the edge of the deck, as opposed to the center elevators of World War II. With the exception of larger size, the *USS Ronald Reagan*, commissioned in 2003, looked very much like the *Forrestal*. Over the years, the propulsion system changed with the advent of small nuclear reactors. The *USS Enterprise*, commissioned in 1961, was the first nuclear-powered aircraft carrier. Nuclear power meant aircraft carriers could sail for years without refueling. New aircraft, missiles, radar, communication systems made the carrier more capable primarily in the tactical role. With the development of the nuclear-powered submarine (SSN) and the submarine-launched ballistic missile (SLBN), the strategic nuclear mission of the aircraft carrier was considerably diminished. Aircraft carriers are employed primarily in the tactical support of ground forces and in sustained bombing campaigns coordinated by the Air Force.

57. Brodie, *Strategy in the Missile Age*, 394.

Chapter 8

1. Omar N. Bradley, General US Army, "Address at the third National Industry Army Day Conference,"

4 February 1949. Published as "Creating a Sound Military Force," *Military Review*, August 1949, Vol. XXIX, No. 2, 3–6.

2. William C. Westmoreland, *A Soldier Reports* (New York: Doubleday and Co., 1976), 121.

3. Anthony C. Zinni, General USMC, "A Commander Reflects," *US Naval Institute Proceedings*, Vol. 126/7/1,169, July 2000, 35.

4. Walter Goerlitz, *History of the German General Staff: 1657–1945* (New York: Praeger, 1957). T.N. Dupuy, *A Genius for War: The German Army and General Staff, 1807–1945* (NJ: Prentice-Hall, 1977). Gordon A. Craig, *The Politics of the Prussian Army 1640–1945* (London: Oxford University Press, 1955). Hans Rosenberg, *Bureaucracy, Aristocracy and Autocracy: The Prussian Experience 1660–1815* (Cambridge, Massachusetts: Harvard University Press, 1958).

5. The German system was incompatible with America's culture, political system, and geographic circumstances. While aspects of the German system were adopted in the nineteenth century following the impressive victories of Helmuth von Moltke (1800–1891), in the twentieth century it became "an object of hatred, fear, and revulsion."

6. National Security Act of 1947, United States Statutes at Large. Reprinted in *US National Security Policy and Strategy: Documents and Policy Proposals*, edited, Sam C. Sarkesian with Robert A. Vitas (New York: Greenwood Press, 1988), 9–15. See also *Department of Defense: Documents on Establishment and Organization 1944–1978*, 35–50.

7. Harry S. Truman, "Message to the Congress—19 December 1945," *The Department of Defense: Documents on Establishment and Organization 1944–1978* (Washington, DC: Office of the Secretary of Defense, Historical Office, 1978), 11–15.

8. David I. Walsh, Committee of Naval Affairs, United States Senate, Carl Vinson, Chairman, Committee of Naval Affairs, House of Representatives, Letter to the Secretary of the Navy outlining their objections to S. 2044, *The Department of Defense: Documents on Establishment and Organization 1944–1978* (Washington, DC: Office of the Secretary of Defense, Historical Office, 1978), 18–20.

9. Allan R. Millett, *Semper Fidelis: The History of the United States Marine Corps* (New York: The Free Press, 1991), 457, 458.

10. Quoted in Millett, *Semper Fidelis*, 460.

11. Paul Y. Hammond, *Organizing for Defense: The American Military Establishment in the Twentieth Century* (Connecticut: Greenwood Press, 1961), 228, 229.

12. James V. Forrestal, *The Forrestal Diaries*, edited by Walter Millis (New York: Viking Press, 1951), 270.

13. *Life*, 5 June 1944, 41–44.

14. Forrestal served as a naval aviator in World War I. He served as Undersecretary of the Navy in the Roosevelt Administration and in 1944 was promoted to Secretary of the Navy. During World War II Forrestal fought hard to secure the resources required to build the world's largest navy. See: Omar N. Bradley and Clay Blair, *A General's Life: An Autobiography by General Omar N. Bradley* (New York: Simon and Schuster, © 1983), 497.

15. Millett, *Simper Fidelis*, 464.

16. Sam Sarkesian, *US National Security Policy and Strategy: Documents and Policy Proposals* (New York: Greenwood Press, 1988), 9, 10.

17. James Forrestal, *The Forrestal Diaries*, edited Walter Millis (New York: The Viking Press, 1951), 392, 393 (emphasis added).

18. Forrestal, *The Forrestal Diaries*, 393.

19. Omar Bradley and Clay Blair, *A General's Life* (New York: Simon and Schuster, 1983), 492. The copyright on this book was 1983. Bradley died in April 1981; hence, he did not approve the final version of this book. The final chapters were written with extensive work from author Clay Blair.

20. Carl A. Peterson, Lieutenant Colonel US Army, "Ground Forces—Key to Survival," *Military Review*, August 1956, 3–5.

21. The nation's fleet of C 5A transports is rapidly aging, with nothing comparable to replace it under construction. The new C 17 does not have the same capabilities.

22. Victor H. Krulak, Lieutenant General USMC, *First to Fight: An Inside View of the US Marine Corps* (Annapolis, Maryland: Naval Institute Press, 1984, xv.

23. Senate Armed Services Committee, National Security Act Amendments of 1949, Hearing, 81st Congress, 1st Session, p. 9. Quoted in Hammond, *Organizing for Defense*, 239.

24. Louis Johnson, Secretary of Defense, "Strengthening the Defense Team." *Army Information Digest*, October 1949, 3–14.

25. National Security Act Amendment of 1949, US Statutes, Vol. 63, part 1, 1950, 579–583, reprinted in *US National Security Policy and Strategy*, ed. Sam C. Sarkesian (New York: Greenwood Press, 1988), 15. Also see, *Department of Defense, Documents on Establishment and Organization 1944–1978*, ed. Alice C. Cole, Alfred Goldberg, Samuel A. Tucker and Rudolph A. Winnacker (Washington, DC: Office of the Secretary of Defense, 1978). See also, "National Security Act Amended," *Army Information Digest*, September 1949, 59–60.

26. Louis Johnson, Secretary of Defense, "Strengthening the Defense Team." *Army Information Digest*, October 1949, 3–14.

27. Omar N. Bradley and Clay Blair, *A General's Life*, 498. The copyright on this book was 1983. Bradley died in April 1981; hence, he did not approve the final version of this book. The final chapters were written with extensive work from author Clay Blair.

28. Bradley, *A General's Life*, 595.

29. Sam Sarkesian, *US National Security Policy and Strategy: Documents and Policy Proposals* (New York: Greenwood Press, 1988), 18, 19, 23, 24.

30. Public Law 85–599, Department of Defense Reorganization Act of 1958, reprinted in *US National Security Policy and Strategy*, ed. Sam C. Sarkesian (New York: Greenwood Press, 1988), 22.

31. "Why Was the US Unarmed?" *Time Magazine*, Vol. 56, October 2, 1950, 18.

32. Clay Blair, *The Forgotten War: America in Korea 1950–1953* (Times Books, 1987), 4–6.

33. *The Officer Guide*, 20th edition, 1954, 263.

34. S.L.A. Marshall, *The Armed Forces Officer*, 1950, 8. Matthew B. Ridgway, *The Korean War*, 1967, 234. General W.R. Peers, Memorandum for: The Chief of Staff, US Army, Subject: The Son My Incident, 1970.

35. Senate Subcommittee of the Appropriations Committee, *Department of Defense Appropriations*, FY 1951, 8/12, 1950, 15–16 (italics added). Also quoted in Edward A. Kolodziej, *The Uncommon Defense and Congress*, 1945–1963, 114.

36. Collins, *War in Peacetime*, 72.

37. J. Lawton Collins, Army Chief of Staff, *War in Peacetime: The History and Lessons of Korea* (Boston: Houghton Mifflin, 1969), 73.

38. Collins, *War in Peacetime*, 74.

39. Lloyd J. Matthews and Dale E. Brown, edited, *Assessing the Vietnam War* (Washington, DC: Pergamon-Brassey's, 1987).

40. Matthew B. Ridgway, *Soldier: The Memoirs of Matthew B. Ridgway* (New York: Harper, 1956), 288.

41. Maxwell D. Taylor, General US Army, *The Uncertain Trumpet* (New York: Harper, 1959), 19.

42. John K. Singlaub, Major General US Army with Malcolm McConnell, *Hazardous Duty: An American Soldier in the Twentieth Century* (New York: Summit Books, 1991), 381–405. General Singlaub publicly voiced his disapproval of President Carter's plan to withdraw the 2nd Infantry Division from Korea. Carter immediately recalled him to the US and personally informed him, "General I've lost confidence in your ability to carry out my instructions. So I've asked the Secretary of Defense to have you reassigned. . . . I have decided, however, not to have you disciplined." Of course, reassignment was punishment, and Singlaub had no chance for another promotion.

43. William C. Westmoreland, General US Army, *A Soldier Reports* (New York: Doubleday, 1976), 135, 136.

44. Westmoreland, *A Soldier Reports*, 417.

45. Russell Weigley, "The American Military and the Principle of Civilian Control from McClellan to Powell," *The Journal of Military History*, Speical Issue 57, October 1993, 27–58.

46. Samuel P. Huntington, *The Soldier and the State: The Theory of Politics of Civil-Military Relations* (Cambridge, Massachusetts: The Belknap Press, 1985), 83.

47. Keith D. Mc Farland, "The 1949 Revolt of the Admirals," *Parameters*, Vol. XI No. 2, June 1981, 57. See: Jeffrey G. Barlow, *Revolt of the Admirals: The Fight for Naval Aviation, 1945–1950* (Washington, DC: Naval Historical Center, 1994).

48. Bradley, *A General's Life*, 510.

49. See Lynn Montross, Major Hubard D. Kuokka, USMC, and Major Norman W. Hicks, *US Marine Operations in Korea 1950–1953*, Volume IV, *The East-Central Front* (Washington, DC: Headquarters, US Marine Corps, 1962), 187. Montross, et al, wrote: ". . .the atomic bomb of Hiroshima rendered obsolescent in 10 seconds a system of amphibious assault tactics that had been 10 years in the making. Obviously, the concentrations of transport, warships, and aircraft carriers that had made possible the Saipan and Iwo Jima landings would be sitting ducks for an enemy armed with atomic weapons."

50. Quoted from Eisenhower's Diary in Omar Bradley and Clay Blair, *A General's Life*, 499.

51. Louis Johnson, Secretary of Defense, "Progress in Defense," extracted from "The Second Report of the Secretary of Defense," *Army Information Digest*, February 1950, 11–22.

52. Baer, *One Hundred Years of Sea Power*, 313. Note, Bradley specifically mentioned large-scale amphibious operations such as the Normandy and Sicily invasions. He did not argue that small-scale operations were no longer practical. Bradley is frequently misquoted.

53. Quoted in E. Bruce Geelhoed, *Charles E. Wilson and Controversy at the Pentagon 1953 to 1957* (Detroit: Wayne State University Press, 1979), 138.

54. For a more complete discussion on the "Revolt of the Admirals" see: Paul Y. Hammond, "Super Carrier and B–36 Bombers: Appropriations, Strategy and Politics," in *American Civil-Military Decisions: A Book of Case Studies*, ed. Harold Stein (Alabama: University of Alabama Press, 1963); Andrew L. Lewis, LCDR, USN, "The Revolt of the Admirals," Master's Thesis, Air Command and Staff College, Air University, Maxwell Air Force Base, Alabama, April 1998; Norman Friedman, *US Aircraft Carriers* (Annapolis, Maryland: Naval Institute Press, 1983).

55. Nick Kotz, *Wild Blue Yonder: Money, Politics and the B–1 Bomber* (Princeton, NJ: Princeton University Press, 1988), 3, 4.

56. Keith Smith, Lieutenant General USMC (Retired), "V–22 Is Right for War on Terrorism," *US Naval Institute Proceeding*, Vol. 128/1/1,187, January 2002, 42–44. Also see: Richard Whittle, *The Dream Machine: The Untold History of the Notorious V–22 Osprey* (New York: Simon & Schuster, 2010).

57. H.R. McMaster, *Dereliction of Duty: Lyndon Johnson, Robert McNamara, the Joint Chiefs of Staff, and the Lies that Led to Vietnam* (New York: Harper Collins, 1997), 333, 334.

58. Douglas Kinnard, "A Soldier in Camelot: Maxwell Taylor in the Kennedy White House," *Parameters*, Vol. XVIII No. 4, December 1988, 15.

59. Senator Barry Goldwater, "The Joint Chiefs of Staff and Unified Commands" from a series of six, senate floor speeches. Ninety-Eighth Congress, 1983.

60. See Andrew Bacevich, *The New American Militarism: How Americans are Seduced by War* (New York: Oxford University Press, 2005).

61. Alfred Vagts, *A History of Militarism: Civilian and Military*, revised edition (New York: The Free Press, 1959), Introduction, 15–17 (italics added).

62. Vagts, *A History of Militarism*, 14. Consider the words of Alfred Vagts, published in his classic work, *A History of Militarism*: "Armies may protect society, if they prepare intelligently for defense; they may threaten it if they lose a sense of proportion between their own interests and those of the rest of society. . . . Militarism is thus not the opposite of pacifism; its true counterpart is civilianism. Love of war, bellicosity, is the counterpart to love of peace, pacifism; but militarism is more, and sometimes less, than love of war."

63. Alfred Vagts, *A History of Militarism: Civilian and Military*, Revised Edition (New York: Free Press, 1959), 16, 17. More recently Andrew Bacevich added to our knowledge of militarism in America with his book, *The New American Militarism: How Americans are Seduced by War* (New York: Oxford University Press, 2005).

64. Gordon Adams, *Iron Triangle, the Politics of Defense Contracting* (New Brunswick, NJ: Transaction Publishers, 1982). Also see: Ron Matthews and Curie Maharani, "The Defense Iron Triangle Revisited," *The Modern Defense Industry*, ed. Richard A. Bitzinger (Santa Barbara, California: ABC Clio, 2009), 38–55.

65. Allan R. Millett, *Semper Fidelis: The History of the United States Marine Corps*, Revised and Expanded Edition (New York: Free Press, 1991), 520. "As the Eisenhower administration pressed for further economies and reductions in defense spending in 1954 and 1955, the Corps sensed that the FMF would fall victim to the budget officers. . . . Headquarters turned to Congress and was again successful in minimizing the impact of the Eisenhower austerities."

66. Michael S. Sherry, *The Rise of American Air Power: The Creation of Armageddon* (New Haven: Yale University Press, 1987), x, xi.

67. Matthew B. Ridgway, General US Army, "Army Troop and Public Relations," *Army Information Digest*, August 1954, 3–5.

68. Cecil J. Gridley, Colonel US Army, "A Battle for Men's Minds," *Army Information Digest*, November 1954, 3–8 (italics added).

69. Maxwell D. Taylor, General US Army, *Swords and Plowshares* (New York: Norton, Co., 1972), 171.

70. *New York Times*, 27 June 1957, 8. Wernher von Braun, the intellectual power behind the Army's missile program noted: "The Jupiter involves several hundred million dollars of taxpayers' money. One hundred percent security would mean no information for the public, no money for the Army, no Jupiter. . . . The Army has got to play the same game as the Air Force and the Navy."

71. Peter G. Boyle, *Eisenhower: Profiles in Power* (New York: Longman, 2005), 122.

72. Jim G. Lucas, *Washington Daily News*, 29 July 1959, quoted in Hearings, *Employment of Retired Military and Civilian Personnel*, p. 473. Also quoted in Samuel P. Huntington, "Interservice Competition and the Political Roles of the Armed Services," *The American Political Science Review*, Vol. 55, No. 1 (March 1961), 40–52.

73. Stephen E. Ambrose, *Eisenhower, The President*, Vol. 2 (New York: Simon and Schuster, 1984), 612.

Chapter 9

1. John F. Kennedy, US Senator, "The Missile Gap," 14 August 1958, in *The Strategy of Peace* by John F. Kennedy, ed. Allen Nevin, (New York: Harper, 1960), 38, 39.

2. Carl von Clausewitz, *On War*, edited and translated by Michael Howard and Peter Paret (Princeton, NJ: Princeton University Press, 1976), 313.

3. Clausewitz, *On War*, 75.

4. Brodie, *Strategy in the Missile Age*, 325–327 (italics added).

5. Basil Liddell-Hart, "Are Small Atomic Weapons the Answer?" in *Deterrent or Defence*, 1960. Quoted in Michael Carver, "Conventional Warfare in the Nuclear Age," *Makers of Modern Strategy*, ed. Peter Paret (NJ: Princeton University Press, 1986), 785.

6. Robert Oppenheimer, "Atomic Weapons and American Policy," Foreign Affairs, XXXI: 4, July 1953, 529 (italics added). Quoted in Lawrence Freedman, *The Evolution of Nuclear Strategy* (New York: St. Martin's Press, 1983), 94.

7. US Army, USMA, *Cadet Notebook* (West Point: Department of History, 1989–1990), 19.

8. Matthew B. Ridgway, *The Korean War* (New York: Da Capo Press, 1967), 245.

9. US Army, FM 100–5 *Field Service Regulation Operation* (Washington, DC: Department of the Army, 1954), 7 (italics added).

10. US Army, FM 100–5 *Field Service Regulation Operation* (Washington, DC: Department of the Army, 1949), 21.

11. Henry Kissinger, "Military Policy and Defense of the 'Grey Areas,' " *Foreign Affairs*, April 1955, vol. 33, No. 3, 427.

12. Henry Kissinger, *Nuclear Weapons and Foreign Policy* (New York: Harper, 1957), 143.

13. Robert E. Osgood, *Limited War: The Challenge to American Strategy* (Chicago: University of Chicago Press, 1957), 1, 2.

14. Osgood, *Limited War*, 191.

15. Osgood, *Limited War*, 183.

16. Kissinger, "Defense of the 'Grey Areas,' " 421, 427.

17. Osgood, *Limited War*, 22–27.

18. Osgood, *Limited War*, 271. Kissinger, "Defense of the 'Grey Areas,' " 421. Osgood quoted Kissinger.

19. Osgood, *Limited War*, 55, 56.

20. The Kennedy Administration and the Pentagon under the leadership of Robert McNamara later adopted a strategy of "graduated response" that was based on these same tenets of war.

21. Osgood, *Limited War*, 242, 243, 270.

22. Osgood, *Limited War*, 186.

23. Kissinger, "Defense of the 'Grey Areas,' " 420, 421.

24. Henry Kissinger, *Nuclear Weapons and Foreign Policy* (New York: Harper and Row, 1962), and *The Necessity for Choice* (New York: Harper and Row, 1961). Bernard Brodie, *Strategy in the Missile Age* (Princeton: Princeton University Press, 1959). Albert Wohlstetter, "The Delicate Balance of Terror," *Foreign Affairs* 37, 2 (January 1959). Herman Kahn, *On Thermonuclear War* (Princeton: Princeton University Press, 1961).

25. Douglas Kinnard, "A Soldier in Camelot: Maxwell Taylor in the Kennedy White House," *Parameters*, Vol. XVIII No. 4, December 1988, 13–24.

26. John F. Kennedy, US Senator, "The Missile Gap," 14 August 1958, in *The Strategy of Peace* by John F. Kennedy, edited by Allen Nevin (New York: Harper, 1960), 39 (emphasis added).

27. Robert E. Osgood, *Limited War: The Challenge to American Strategy* (Chicago: University of Chicago Press, 1957), chapter II, "The American Approach to War."

28. John F. Kennedy, US Senator, "Conventional Forces in the Atomic Age," *The Strategy of Peace*, edited by Allen Nevin (New York: Harper, 1960), 183–185.

29. Maxwell D. Taylor, *The Uncertain Trumpet* (New York: Harper, 1959), 6 (italics added).

30. Quoted in Lawrence Freedman, "The First Two Generations of Nuclear Strategists," *Makers of Modern Strategy* (Princeton: Princeton University Press, 1986), 752.

31. Bernard Brodie, *Strategy in the Missile Age* (Princeton: Princeton University Press, 1965), 394.

32. John F. Kennedy, President of the US, "Radio and Television Report to the American People on the Berlin Crisis, July 25, 1961," *US National Security Policy and Strategy: Documents and Policy Proposals*, edited Sam C. Safkesian (New York: Greenwood Press, 1988), 119–123.

33. James E. Hewes, Jr., *From Root to McNamara: Army Organization and Administration 1900–1963* (Washington, DC: Center of Military History, 1975), 321, 358.

34. Quoted in James M. Roherty, *Decisions of Robert S. McNamara: A Study of the Role of the Secretary of Defense* (Florida: University of Miami Press, 1970), 98.

35. H.R. McMaster, *Dereliction of Duty: Lyndon Johnson, Robert McNamara, the Joint Chiefs of Staff, and the Lies that Led to Vietnam* (New York: Harper Collins, 1997). Civilian military theorists published more books and articles on nuclear war than the senior-most military leaders. This does not mean that they had a clearer vision of war or more comprehensive understanding of strategic planning. The strategic thinking of generals and admirals was not readily available to the public. It was, however, published in speeches, addresses to Congress, and in their actions and programs initiated within the limits of their authority. The writings of senior Army and Air Force leaders, delineated in this work, show a clear capacity for strategic thinking.

36. Curtis E. LeMay, *Mission with LeMay* (New York: Doubleday, 1965), 5, 553.

37. Alain C. Enthoven and K. Wayne Smith, *How Much is Enough: Shaping the Defense Program, 1961–1969* (New York: Harper and Row, 1971), 89.

38. Enthoven, *How Much is Enough*, 93, 95.

39. Bernard Brodie, *Strategy in the Missile Age* (Princeton, New Jersey: Princeton University Press, 1965), 9–11.

40. General Anthony Zinni was sent to Israel to negotiate peace between the Israelis and Palestinians.

41. The Army is more oriented toward the leadership of men under the most trying human conditions. The Air Force and Navy are more oriented toward perfecting the employment of machines. The way they do business in peacetime changes little during war. A reading of Air Force General Curtis LeMay's books reveals an opposition to most Army and Navy initiatives. Airpower was his preferred solution to every problem.

42. Charles G. Cooper, Lieutenant General USMC, "The Day It Became the Longest War," *US Naval Institute Proceedings*, May 1996, 77–80.

43. James M. Roherty, *Decision of Robert S. McNamara: A Study of the Role of the Secretary of Defense* (Florida: University of Miami Press, 1970), 105.

44. Robert S. McNamara, *The Essence of Security: Reflections in Office* (New York: Harper and Row, 1968), x, xi (emphasis added).

45. McNamara, *The Essence of Security*, 60 (emphasis added).

46. McNamara, *The Essence of Security*, 59.

47. CONARC was established on 1 February 1955 under command of General John E. Dahlquist at Fort Monroe, Virginia. The new command replaced the Office, Chief of Army Field Forces (1948), which replaced the World

War II Army Ground Force (1942), which replaced General Headquarters, United States Army (1940).

48. For organizational charts of the ROAD Armored Division see, Jonathan M. House, *Toward Combined Arms Warfare: A Survey of 20th Century Tactics, Doctrine, and Organization*, Combat Studies Institute, Research Survey No. 2 (Fort Leavenworth, KS: US Army Combined and General Staff College, 1984), 158. Also see: William A. Brown, Major US Army, "ROAD Doctrine: Battalion in the Defense," *Infantry*, Vol. 52, No. 1, (Jan–Feb 1962), 31–37.

49. Allan R. Millett, Colonel, USMC, *Semper Fidelis: The History of the United States Marine Corps*, Revised and Expanded Edition (New York: The Free Press, 1980), 452–454.

50. Lynn Montross, *Cavalry of the Sky: The Story of US Marine Combat Helicopters* (New York: Harper and Brothers, 1954). Montross is the author of the official history of *US Marine Operations in Korea* Volumes I–V. He presents a balanced view of the war and the employment of the helicopter.

51. John W.R. Taylor, "What Has Korea Taught Us?" *Military Review*, August 1954, 86–89.

52. Tolson, *Airmobility 1961–1971*, 5.

53. Quoted in Robert A. Doughty, "The Evolution of US Army Tactical Doctrine, 1946–76," (Fort Leavenworth, Kansas: Combat Studies Institute, 1979), 28, 29.

54. Bergerson, *The Army Gets an Air Force*, 112, 113.

55. Bergerson. *The Army Gets an Air Force*, 114.

56. McNamara, *The Essence of Security*, 82, 83.

57. Hamilton H. Howze, General US Army, "Tactical Employment of the Air Assault Division," *Army*, September 1963, 36–53.

58. Howze, "Tactical Employment of the Air Assault Division," 38.

59. Howze, "Tactical Employment of the Air Assault Division," 52, 53.

60. Bergerson, *The Army Gets an Air Force*, 148. Bergerson concluded: "This growth [of Army aviation] is not dependent on charisma. The Army aviators were by no means in the thrall of charismatic leadership; rather, they made good use of opportunistic, politically astute, and properly credentialed officers. In deciding to allow into the movement senior officers marked by others for positions of power, the direction of Army aviation was set."

61. One of the most significant contributions of the helicopter has gone unnoticed. It is a symbol of American humanitarian assistance, a symbol of American goodwill. In many parts of the world the presence of American helicopter signals relief from floods, hurricanes, famines, and other natural and man-made disasters.

62. As the war in Iraq degenerated into an insurgency war, the Army started to look again at the counterinsurgency doctrine employed in Vietnam. As a consequence, a plethora of new articles and a new field manual were published. See *Military Review* from 2005 to 2011, FM 3–24, Counterinsurgency, December 2006, and FM 3–07, Stability Operations, and FM 3–07.1 Security Force Assistance.

63. For a brief but excellent study of revolutionary warfare see: John Shy and Thomas W. Collier "Revolutionary War," *Makers of Modern Strategy*, ed. Peter Paret (Princeton, NJ: Princeton University Press, 1986), 815–862.

64. Bernard B. Fall, "The Theory and Practice of Insurgency and Counterinsurgency," *Naval War College Review*, April, 1965, 271. Also see FMI 3–7.22 Counterinsurgency Operations (Washington, DC: Headquarters, Department of the Army, October 2004), 1–1.

65. Fall, "The Theory and Practice of Insurgency and Counterinsurgency," *Naval War College Review*, 272.

66. Clausewitz, *On War*, 480.

67. William C. Westmoreland, General US Army, "Address before a Joint Session of Congress, April 28, 1967," *Department of State Bulletin*, 15 May 1967, 738–741. Reprinted in Sarkesian's *US National Security Policy and Strategy*, 153–157.

68. Mao Tse-tung, *Selected Military Writings of Mao Tse-tung* (Peking: Foreign Language Press, 1967), 229, 230 (emphasis added).

69. Mao Tse-tung, *Selected Military Writings*, 249.

70. Clausewitz, *On War*, 248 (emphasis added).

71. Vo Nguyen Giap, *People's War People's Army: The Viet Cong Insurrection Manual for Underdeveloped Countries* (New York: Frederick A. Praeger, 1962). See Douglas Pike's, *People's Army of Vietnam* (New York: Da Capo Press, 1986), and *Viet Cong: The Organization and Techniques of the National Liberation Front of South Vietnam* (Cambridge, Massachusetts: The MIT Press, 1966); The Military History Institute of Vietnam, *Victory in Vietnam: The Official History of the People's Army of Vietnam, 1954–1975*, trans. Merle L. Pribbenow (Kansas: University Press of Kansas); and, Bernard B. Fall, *Hell in a Very Small Place: The Siege of Dien Bien Phu* (New York: A Da Capo Paperback, 1966.

72. Pike, *PAVN*, 226.

73. Francis John Kelly, Colonel US Army, *US Army Special Forces 1961–1971, Vietnam Studies* (Washington, DC: Department of the Army, 1973), 5, 6.

74. Alfred H. Paddock, Jr., *US Army Special Warfare: Its Origins*, revised edition (Lawrence: University Press of Kansas, 2002), 156.

75. Andrew F. Krepinevich, Jr., *The Army and Vietnam* (Baltimore: The Johns Hopkins University Press, 1986) 100–107.

76. Paddock, *US Army Special Warfare*, 157.

77. Krepinevich, *The Army and Vietnam*, 112.

78. Douglas S. Blaufarb, *The Counterinsurgency Era: US Doctrine and Performance, 1950 to the Present* (New York: The Free Press, 1977), 100.

Chapter 10

1. Harold Moore, *We Were Soldiers Once . . . And Young* (New York: Random House, 1992), 314, 315.

2. William Westmoreland, "Vietnam in Perspective," *Military Review*, Vol. LIX, No. 1, Jan. 1979, 36.

3. Guenter Lewy, *America in Vietnam* (New York: Oxford University Press, 1978), 85. Lewy wrote: "The same basic criticism has been made by the British expert. 'The American forces,' Sir Robert Thompson has written, 'fought a separate war which ignored its political and other aspects, and were not on a collision course with the Vietcong and North Vietnamese, who therefore had a free run in the real war.' There was much talk about the significance of the 'other war,' about winning the hearts and minds of the people, the importance of defeating the enemy's insurgency through political and social reform and so forth, but in reality pacification took a back seat and the efficacy of psychological operations was commonly measured by the number of leaflets dropped and the number of loudspeakers broadcasts made. . . . The Kennedy administration had tired hard to get the military [the Army] to develop an understanding of and capacity for counterinsurgency. The nature of guerilla warfare and the measures necessary to meet this challenge were studied at the Special Forces School at Fort Bragg and the war colleges, but the military never developed counterinsurgency capabilities on any major scale." McNamara supports this argument in his book, *In Retrospect*. Also see, Andrew Krepinevich, *The Army and Vietnam* and John Nagl, *Counterinsurgency Lessons from Malaya and Vietnam*.

4. For a discussion of the range of arguments that explain American defeat in Vietnam see: Geroge C. Herring, "American Strategy in Vietnam: The Postwar Debate," *Military Affairs* 46 (April 1982), 57–63. Also see: William E. DuPuy, "Vietnam: What We Might Have Done and Why We Didn't Do It," *Army*, 36 (February 1986), 22–40; Harry Summers and Russell Weigley, "Lessons from Vietnam: A Debate," *Vietnam as History* (Washington, DC: Wilson Center/University Press of America, 1984); Jeffrey Clarke, "On Strategy and the Vietnam War," *Parameters* 56 (Winter 1986), 39–46; Bruce Palmer, Jr., *The 25-Year War* (New York: Simon & Schuster, 1984); Harry Summers, Jr., *On Strategy* (Carlisle, Pennsylvania: US Army War College, Strategic Studies Institute, 23 March 1982); Andrew Krepinevich, Jr., *The Army and Vietnam*; U.S.G. Sharp, *Strategy For Defeat* (San Rafael, California: Presidio Press, 1978); and William Westmoreland, *A Soldier Reports* (New York: Doubleday, 1976). For a more complete bibliography on the Vietnam War see the "Selected Bibliography").

5. See Stanley Karnow, *Vietnam: A History* (New York: Penguin Books, 1997), chapters 1–3.

6. President Roosevelt opposed the reestablishment of the French empire in Southeast Asia. In a letter to Secretary of State Cordell Hull in January 1944 he wrote: "I saw Halifax [the British ambassador to the US] last week and told him . . . that it was perfectly true that I had, for over a year, expressed the opinion that Indo-China should not go back to France . . . it should be administered by an international trusteeship. France has had the country . . . one hundred years, and the people are worse off than they were at the beginning." Quoted in Ronald Spector, *Advance and Support* (New York: Free Press, 1985), 22. FDR believed that imperialism was one of the causes of war, and opposed it. Truman had a different vision and believed that maintaining the alliance in Western Europe was of the utmost importance.

7. Dean Acheson, *Present at the Creation* (New York: W.W. Norton and Co., 1969), 671, 672.

8. George Eckhardt, *Command and Control 1950–1969, Vietnam Studies* (Washington, DC: Dept. of the Army, 1974), 6.

9. Dwight D. Eisenhower, "The Importance to the United States of the Security and Progress of Viet-Nam: Address at Gettysbury College, Gettysburg, Pennsylvania, 4 April 1959. Published in Committee of Foreign Relations, US Senate, *Background Information relating to Southeast Asia and Vietnam* (Washington, DC: US GPO, 1967), 96–97. See also: Eisenhower, *Public Papers of the Presidents of the United States: Dwight D. Eisenhower, 1953* (Washington, DC: GPO, 1958), 381–390.

10. For a discussion on Eisenhower's decision not to intervene, see Spector, *Advance and Support*, chapter 11, "The Question of Intervention," 191–214.

11. Matthew Ridgway, *Soldier: The Memoirs* (New York: Harper and Brothers, 1956), 275–278.

12. Halberstam, *The Fifties*, 408. In a discussion on intervention between Winston Churchill and Admiral Arthur Radford, CJCS, the Admiral was informed that in 1947 Britain had given up India, its most important imperial possession, without fighting a war. There was no way Britain was going to fight a war to save a French possession. Besides, Churchill reasoned that the most important task was to defuse tensions with the Soviet Union.

13. A reproduction of the agreement is in Department of State, *American Foreign Policy, 1950–1955: Basic Document*, Department of State Publication 6446, 2 vols. (Washington, DC: GPO, 1957), 1: 750–767. Quoted in Spector, *Advice and Support*, 219.

14. John Kennedy, "Conference of the American Friends of Vietnam June 1, 1956," *The Strategy of Peace*, ed. Allan Nevins (New York: Harper and Brothers, 1960), 64.

15. *US–Vietnam Relations*, XI, 331–342. Quoted in David Kaiser, *American Tragedy*, 106.

16. Maxwell Taylor, "The US Commitment in Viet-Nam: Fundamental Issues: Statements by Secretary Rusk and

General Maxwell Taylor Before the Senate Committee on Foreign Relations" 17 February 1966, *Background Information Relating to Southeast Asia and Vietnam* (Washington, DC: US GPO, 1967), 207.

17. Ball was appointed Under Secretary of State for Economic Affairs and later Under Secretary of State in the Kennedy Administration. In the Johnson Administration Ball was the "devil's advocate." Quoted in Robert J. McMahon, *Major Problems in the History of the Vietnam War*, 2nd edition (Lexington, Massachusetts: D.C. Heath, 1995), 217, 218.

18. Lyndon Johnson, *The Vantage Point: Perspectives on the Presidency 1963–1969* (New York: Holt, Rinehart, and Winston, 1971), 148.

19. Dwight D. Eisenhower, "Letter from President Eisenhower to President Diem October 1, 1954," *US National Security Policy and Strategy*, ed. Sam Sarkesian (New York: Greenwood Press, 1988), 133, 134.

20. The Treaty was signed in Manila in September 1954. Australia, France, New Zealand, Pakistan, the Philippines, Thailand, Britain, and the United States signed the agreement. Committee on Foreign Relations, US Senate, *Background Information Relating To Southeast Asia and Vietnam*, 3rd Revised Edition (Washington, DC: GPO, 1967), 85.

21. Article 16 of the Accord prohibited the introduction into Vietnam of troops and other military personnel that had not been in the country at the time of the ceasefire. Articles 17–19 contained restrictions regarding weapons, equipment, ammunition, bases, and military alliances. The introduction of new types of arms, ammunition, and materiel was forbidden. Exchanges of weapons piece-by-piece were permitted. An International Control Commission (ICC) was established to monitor compliance. See George S. Eckhardt, *Command and Control 1950–1969*, *Vietnam Studies* (Washington, DC: Dept. of the Army, 1974), 15. Spector, *Advance and Support*, 260–262.

22. Clark M. Clifford, "A Viet Nam Reappraisal: The Personal History of One Man's View and How It Evolved," *Foreign Affairs*, July 1969 Vol. 47, No. 4, 601–622.

23. President Kennedy, Exchange of Message between President Kennedy and President Ngo Dinh Diem of the Republic of Viet-Nam, 14 Dec. and 7 Dec. 1961, *Background Information Relating to Southeast Asia and Vietnam* (3rd revised edition) Committee of Foreign Relations, US Senate (Washington, DC: GPO, July 1967), 99–100.

24. This increase in personnel violated the 1954 Geneva settlement.

25. Francis Kelly, Colonel US Army Special Forces, *US Army Special Forces 1961–1971: Vietnam Studies* (Washington, DC: Department of the Army, 1973), 4–7. Special Forces were first deployed to Vietnam in 1957. The 1st Special Forces Group trained the Vietnam

Army at the Commando Training Center in Nha Trang. This was a small effort, but it was embryonic in the creation of Vietnamese Special Forces units.

26. Neil Sheehan, *A Bright Shining Lie* (New York: Random House, 1988), 203–265.

27. David Halberstam, *The Making of a Quagmire*, Revised edition (New York: Alfred A Knopf, 1988), 72, 79.

28. Halberstam, *The Making of a Quagmire*, 24.

29. It has been argued that Kennedy had planned to withdraw from Vietnam. McNamara in his book, *In Retrospect* (New York: Times Book, 1995), 102, wrote that: "Johnson felt more certain than President Kennedy that the loss of South Vietnam had a higher cost than would the direct application of US military force, and it was this view that shaped him and his policy decisions for the next five years." He further stated in a film entitled "The Fog of War," that Kennedy planned to withdraw from Vietnam, removing all 16,000 advisors by 1965. Other students of the war have also advanced this thesis. David Kaiser, *American Tragedy* (Cambridge, Massachusetts: The Belknap Press, 2000), Chapter 5. Kaiser wrote: "Kennedy never regarded Southeast Asia as a propitious place to deploy American power." While Kennedy may have been reluctant to deploy additional forces, he still expanded America's commitment.

30. For the most comprehensive study of the Gulf of Tonkin incident, see Edwin E. Moise, *Tonkin Gulf and the Escalation of the Vietnam War* (Chapel Hill: The University of North Carolina Press, 1996).

31. Moise, *Tonkin Gulf and the Escalation of the Vietnam War*, 205, 239, 240. Moise charged: "There is evidence that a number of senior American officials could provide no rational motive for the action they believed Hanoi had taken on the night of 4 August. They tended to read Hanoi's motives as a mirror of their own—based more on pride than on concrete national interest, and reacting to immediate changes in the short-term situation rather than to long-term goals." He quotes William Bundy: "The Administration simply had no clear theory at all, did not know what to make of the attacks, and in default or any coherent motive could only conclude that Hanoi wished to make a gesture of how strong and tough it was." Hanoi believed that the Johnson Administration fabricated the incidents to "carry the war to the North."

32. Committee on Foreign Relations, US Senate, *Background Information*, 120–122.

33. Committee on Foreign Relations, US Senate, *Background Information*, 126 (emphasis added). Also published in Alexander Bloom and Wini Breines, ed. *"Takin' it to the Streets:" A Sixties Reader* (New York: Oxford University Press, 2003), 162, 163.

34. Ronald H. Cole, Walter S. Poole, James F. Schnabel, Robert J. Watson, and Willard J. Webb, *The History of the Unified Command Plan 1946–1993* (Washington, DC:

Office of the Chairman of the Joint Chiefs of Staff, 1995), 2. Also see, John T. Correll, "Disunity of Command," *Air Force Magazine*, 88, January 2005, 34–39; and Ian Horwood, *Interservice Rivalry and Airpower in the Vietnam War* (Fort Leavenworth, Kansas: Combat Studies Institute Press, 2006.

35. Maxwell Taylor, Ambassador to Vietnam, "The US Commitment in Viet-Nam: Fundamental Issues: Statements by Secretary Rusk and Gen. Maxwell Taylor before the Senate Committee on Foreign Relations, *Department of State Bulletin*, vol. LIV, No. 1393, 7 Mar. 1966, 1–17. Also published in *Background Information*, 194–214.

36. For a comprehensive study of airpower in Vietnam, see Mark Clodfelter, *The Limits of Air Power: The American Bombing of North Vietnam* (New York: The Free Press, 1989). Also see Wayne Thompson, "Operations over North Vietnam, 1965–1973," in *A History of Air Warfare*, ed. John Andreas Olsen (Washington, DC: Potomac Books, 2010), 107–126.

37. Michael Beschloss, *Reaching for Glory* (New York: Simon and Schuster, 2001), 175.

38. Quoted in Townsend Hoopes, *The Limits of Intervention*, New Edition (New York: W.W. Norton, 1973), 19.

39. Marshall Michel III, *Clashes: Air Combat Over North Vietnam 1965–1972* (Annapolis: Naval Institute Press, 1997), 1, 2.

40. Walter J. Boyne, "Route Package 6," *Air Force Magazine*, November 1999, 56–61. Also see: Kenneth Bell, *100 Mission North: A Fighter Pilot's Story of the Vietnam War* (Washington, DC: Brassey's, 1993).

41. Summers, *Vietnam Almanac*, 74. Sharp, *Strategy for Defeat*, 4.

42. Sharp, *Strategy for Defeat*, 4.

43. Berger, ed., *The United States Air Force in Southeast Asia*, 81, 82.

44. Francis Kelly, *US Army Special Forces 1961–1971, Vietnam Studies* (Washington, DC: Dept. of the Army, 1973), 161.

45. John Schlight, *The US Air Force in Southeast Asia, The War in the South: The Years of the Offensive 1965–1968* (Washington, DC: Office of Air Force History, 1988), 292.

46. Walter Boyne, *Beyond the Wild Blue* (New York: St. Martin's Press, 1997), 153, 154.

47. McNamara and his "whiz kids" had adopted the Robert Osgood theory of limited war outlined in 1957. See Robert Osgood, *Limited War* (Chicago: University of Chicago Press, 1957), 242.

48. Beschloss, *Reaching for Glory*, 199.

49. U.S.G. Sharp, *Strategy for Defeat* (San Rafael, California: Presidio Press, 1978), 2.

50. William Westmoreland, *A Soldier Reports* (New York: Double & Co., 1976), 410.

51. Quoted by John Correll, "Rolling Thunder," *Air Force Magazine*, 88, March 2005, 58–65.

52. Clodfelter, *The Limits of Air Power*, 138.

53. Beschloss, *Reaching for Glory*, 347.

54. Robert McNamara, "Tuesday, April 20, 1965, 7:15 P.M." *Reaching for Glory*, ed., Beschloss, 282.

55. President Johnson, "to Robert McNamara, June 21, 1965," Beschloss, *Reaching for Glory*, 343.

56. John A. Cash, John Albright, and Allan W. Sandstrum, *Seven Firefights in Vietnam* (Washington, DC: Office of the CMH 1985), 22. US Army After Action Report, Ia Drang Valley Operation, 1st Battalion, 7th Cavalry, 14–16 November 1965, (Headquarters, 1st Battalion, 7th Cavalry, 1st Cavalry Division (Airmobile), APO San Francisco, California 96490, Infantry School, Fort Benning, Georgia).

57. US Army Infantry School, Operations of the 1st Battalion, 7th Cavalry, 1st Cavalry Division (Airmobile), In the Airmobile Assault of Landing Zone X Ray, Ia Drang Valley, Republic of Viet Nam, 14–16 November 1965 (Personal Experience of a Company Commander).

58. George Herring, "The 1st Cavalry and the Ia Drang Valley, 18 Oct.–24 Nov. 1965," *America's First Battles 1776–1965*, ed., Charles Heller and William Stofft (Lawrence: University Press of Kansas, 1986), 300–326.

59. Harold Moore, *We Were Soldiers Once . . . And Young* (New York: Random House, 1992), 314, 315.

60. The Military Institute of Vietnam, *Victory in Vietnam: The Official History of the People's Army of Vietnam, 1954–1975*, trans. Merle L. Pribbenow (Kansas: University Press of Kansas, 2002), 171.

61. The Military Institute of Vietnam, *Victory in Vietnam*, 171.

62. The Republic of Korea provided the largest contingent of forces to assist the US and RVN: two divisions, one ROK Marine brigade, and support units. A total of 4,407 ROK soldiers and marines were killed in action.

63. Clausewitz, *On War*, 595, 596.

64. US Army, Headquarters, USMACV, Directive Number 525–4, Tactics and Techniques for Employment of US Forces in the Republic of Vietnam, W.B. Rosson, Major General, Chief of Staff, 17 September 1965, Westmoreland History files, 29 Aug–24 Oct 1965, US Army CMH, Washington, DC. Reprinted in John Copland's "Winning the Vietnam War: Westmoreland's Approach in Two Documents," *The Journal of Military History*, 68, April 2004, 553–574.

65. Quoted in Edward Doyle and Samuel Lipsman, *America Takes Over 1965–67* (Boston, MA: Boston Publishing Co, 1982), 60. Also see, USMACV, Directive Number 525–4, Tactics and Techniques for Employment of US Forces in the Republic of Vietnam.

66. Archer Jones, *Elements of Military Strategy: An Historical Approach* (London: Praeger, 1996), 174.

67. William Corson, *The Betrayal* (New York: W.W. Norton, 1968), 176–181.

68. Victor Krulak, *First to Fight* (Annapolis: Naval Institute Press, 1984), 189, 183.

69. Krulak, 188.
70. William C. Holmberg, Major USMC, "Civic Action," *Marine Corps Gazette*, June 1966, 20–28.
71. See: Lewis W. Walt, General USMC, "Civil Affairs," *Marine Corps Gazette*, September 1968, 11; H. G. Lyles, Captain USMC, "Civic Action Progress Report," *Marine Corps Gazette*, September 1969, 52; George Wilson, MSgt. et al, "Combined Action," *Marine Corps Gazette*, October 1966, 28–31; Holmberg, "Civic Action," 20–28. Articles, published after the war, are also useful. See: Raymond C. Damm, Jr., Lt. Col., "The Combined Action Program: A Tool for the Future," *Marine Corps Gazette*, October 1998, 49–53; T.P. Schwartz, "The Combined Action Program: A Different Perspective," *Marine Corps Gazette*, February 1999, 63–72; Charles L. Armstrong, Lt. Col., USMC, "Combined Action Program Variations in El Salvador," *Marine Corps Gazette*, August 1990, 36–39.
72. Samples, J.E., 1st Sgt., USMC, "Civic Action vs. Fighting," *Marine Corps Gazette*, 50 August 1966, 10.
73. Jones, *Elements of Military Strategy*, 180.
74. Quoted in Lewis Sorley's *Honorable Warrior: General Harold K. Johnson and the Ethics of Command* (Lawrence, Kansas: University Press of Kansas, 1998), 227.
75. Sorley, *Honorable Warrior*, 237.
76. The hamlet evaluation system was a questionable method of rating hamlets and villages to ascertain the level of pacification. See "Measuring Hamlet Security in Vietnam, Report of the Special Study Mission," Committee on Foreign Affairs, House of Representatives, 90th Congress (Washington, DC: US GPO, 1969).
77. Kelly, *US Army Special Forces 1961–1971*, 165. Kelly noted: "In many instances the success or failure of an operation was validated by the statistical considerations attending it. The usual method of determining the efficacy of psychological operations, for example, was by counting the number of leaflets dispensed or the number of loudspeaker broadcasts made."
78. David Hackworth, *About Face* (New York: Simon and Schuster, 1989), 572, 573. Also see: Douglas Kinnard, *The War Managers* (NJ: Avery Publishing, 1985, 72–75.
79. Powell, *My American Journey*, 149.
80. Dave Palmer, *Summons of the Trumpet* (New York: Ballantine Books, 1978), 180, 182 (italics added).
81. Roy Flint, General US Army, "Experience of a Battalion Commander in Vietnam," Oral History taken by the 25th Infantry Division in Vietnam after a command tour. Used at West Point to educate cadets. For an excellent, detailed study of the combat operations of the 25th Infantry Division, see Eric Bergerud, *Red Thunder Tropic Lightning: The World of a Combat Division in Vietnam* (Boulder: Westview, 1993).
82. Herring, *America's Longest War*, 4th edition, 233.
83. Quoted in Bergerud, *Red Thunder Tropic Lightning*, 112.
84. Quoted in Bergerud, *Red Thunder Tropic Lightning*, 295.
85. Quoted in John J. Tolson's *Airmobility 1961–1971*, 65.
86. John Hay, Jr., *Tactical and Materiel Innovations, Vietnam Studies* (Washington, DC: Dept. of the Army, 1974), 11.
87. Palmer, *Summons of the Trumpet*, 180, 182.
88. Kelly, *US Army Special Forces*, 166.
89. Powell, *My American Journey*, 145.
90. Palmer, *The 25-Year War*, 205.

Chapter 11

1. Robert Elegant, "How to Lose a War: Reflections of a Foreign Correspondent," *Encounter*, August 1981, 73–90.
2. Hammond, *The Military and the Media*, 385–387.
3. Winant Sidle, Major General US Army, "A Battle Behind the Scenes: The Gulf War Reheats Military–Media Controversy," *Military Review*, Vol. LXXI, No. 9, September 1991.
4. Peter Braestrup, *Big Story: How the American Press and Television Reported and Interpreted the Crisis of Tet 1968 in Vietnam and Washington* (New Haven: Yale University Press, 1978). William M. Hammond, *The Military and the Media 1962–1968* (Washington, DC: US Army CMH, 1988).
5. Hammond, *The Military and the Media*, 138.
6. Hammond, *The Military and the Media*, 140.
7. Hammond, *The Military and the Media*, 144.
8. John Mueller, *War, Presidents, and Public Opinion* (New York: John Wiley, 1973), 167. Also see: Peter Braestrup, *The Big Story* (New Haven: Yale University Press, 1977); Daniel C. Hallin, *The "Uncensored War"* (New York: Oxford University Press, 1986); Clarence Wyatt, *Paper Soldiers: The American Press and the Vietnam War* (Chicago: University of Chicago Press, 1995); and Hammond, *The Military and the Media*.
9. George Herring, "The 1st Cavalry and the Ia Drang Valley, 18 October–24 November 1965," *America's First Battles 1776–1965*, ed. Charles E. Heller and William A. Stofft (Kansas: University Press of Kansas, 1986), 320. Herring wrote: "Army spokesmen refused to admit an ambush."
10. Moore, *We Were Soldiers Once . . . And Young*, 25.
11. Lewis Sorley, *Honorable Warrior: General Harold K. Johnson and the Ethics of Command* (Lawrence, Kansas: University Press of Kansas, 1998), 212.
12. Harry G. Summers, Jr., *On Strategy: The Vietnam War in Context* (Carlisle Barracks, Pennsylvania: Strategic Studies Institute, 23 March 1982), 22. Summers wrote: "The student draft deferments, along with the decision not to ask for a declaration of war and not to mobilize our reserve forces, were part of a deliberate Presidential policy not to arouse the passions of the American people. The effect of this was that we fought the Vietnam War in *cold blood*."

13. Palmer, Jr., *The 25-Year War*, 204, 205.

14. Kelly, *US Army Special Forces*, 163, 164.

15. Robert N. Young, Major General US Army, Assistant Chief of Staff, G–1, "Rotation Plus Stability: Operation Gyroscope," *Army Information Digest*, March 1955, 2–5. See also: William O. Quirey, Lieutenant Colonel, US Army, "ROTATION," *Military Review*, November 1954, 31–35; John P. Morgan, Major, US Army, "Turn and Return," *Army Information Digest*, September 1958, 13–18.

16. William O. Quirey, Lieutenant Colonel, US Army, "ROTATION," *Military Review*, November 1954, 31–35.

17. Major John P. Morgan, "Turn and Return," *Army Information Digest*, September 1958, 13–18.

18. Bergerud, *Red Thunder*, 115.

19. Bruce Palmer, Jr., *The 25-Year War* (New York: Simon and Schuster, 1984), 205.

20. Douglas Kinnard, *The War Managers* (Wayne, NJ: Avery Publishing, 1985), 111.

21. See: George Flynn, *The Draft, 1940–1973* (Lawrence, Kansas: University Press of Kansas, 1993); Robert Griffith, Jr., *The US Army Transition to the All-Volunteer Force 1968–1974* (Washington, DC: CMH, 1997); Christian Appy, *Working-Class War: American Combat Soldiers and Vietnam* (Chapel Hill, The University of North Carolina Press, 1993); James Gerhardt, *The Draft and Public Policy* (Columbus: Ohio State University Press, 1971); and Michael Foley, *Confrontation: The War Machine: Draft Resistance During the Vietnam War* (Chapel Hill: The University of North Carolina Press, 2003).

22. Newsweek, "The Draft: The Unjust vs. the Unwilling," *Newsweek*, 11 April 1966, 30–34.

23. Christian Appy, *Working-Class War*, 6.

24. Colin Powell, General US Army, *My American Journey* (New York: Random House, 1995), 148.

25. Alexander Haig, Jr., *Inner Circles* (New York: Warner Books, 1992), 185.

26. Quoted in Eric Bergerud, *Red Thunder, Tropic Lightning* (Boulder: Westview Press, 1993), 272.

27. Quoted in Bergerud, *Red Thunder*, 265.

28. Joe P. Dunn, "Draft," in *The Encyclopedia of the Vietnam War*, ed., Spencer Tucker (New York: Oxford University Press, 1998), 107.

29. Michael Shafer, "The Vietnam Era Draft: Who Went, Who Didn't and Why It Matters," *The Legacy: The Vietnam War in the American Imagination* (Boston: Beacon Press, 1990), 67.

30. Shafer, "The Vietnam Era Draft," *The Legacy*, 67–69.

31. Shafer, "The Vietnam Era Draft," *The Legacy*, 69. I was drafted in 1972. At Ft. Polk, Louisiana, in basic training there were men from Mississippi that signed their names with an X.

32. Marilyn Young, *The Vietnam War 1945–1990* (New York: Harper Collins, 1991), 320.

33. Robert Griffith, *The US Army's Transition to the All-Volunteer Force, 1968–1974* (Washington, DC: CMH, 1995), 158.

34. Michael Beschloss, *Reaching for Glory* (New York: Simon and Schuster, 2001), 141.

35. See Kara Dixon Vuic, *Officer, Nurse, Woman: The Army Nurse Corps in the Vietnam War* (Baltimore: The Johns Hopkins University Press, 2010).

36. Flynn, *The Draft*, 229.

37. George Bush and Brent Scowcroft, *A World Transformed* (New York: Vintage Books, 1998), 486.

38. Martin Luther King, Jr., "Declaration of Independence From the War in Vietnam," *"Takin' it to the Streets:" A Sixties Reader*, ed., Alexander Bloom and Wini Breines (New York: Oxford University Press, 2003), 186–191.

39. Fact Sheet: Negro Participation in the Armed Forces and in Vietnam, Tab. C to Memo, Director of Military Personnel Policy to Chief of Staff, subj: Evaluation of Marshall Report Pertaining to Negro Distribution and Casualties. Casualty figures are from Tab. C. "Extract from the Report of the National Advisory Commission on Selective Service." Copies in CMH. Harry G. Summers, Jr., in his book, *Vietnam War Almanac* (New York: Facts on File Publications, 1985), 98, wrote: "Ironically, the Vietnam war was the first war in which black American servicemen and women participated on an equal basis with whites, and initially they paid a high price for that long-sought goal. Although black service personnel made up 10.6% of the total US force in Vietnam, compared with 13.5 percent proportion of military-age blacks in the general population, a disproportionate number of black servicemen initially served in front-line combat units. As a result, they at first suffered a higher percentage of combat fatalities than whites. In 1965–66 black soldiers constituted over 20 percent of the US battlefield deaths. The Army and Marine Corps took specific personnel actions to overcome this problem . . . and by 1967 the proportion had declined to just over 13 percent." Also see: Charles C. Moskos and John Sibley Butler, *All That We Can Be: Black Leadership and Racial Integration the Army Way* (New York: Basic Books, 1996).

40. B.G. Burkett and Glenna Whitley, *Stolen Valor: How the Vietnam Generation Was Robbed of its Heroes and its History* (Dallas, Texas: Verity Press, 1998), 454.

41. Arnold Barnett, Timothy Stanley and Michael Stone, "America's Vietnam Casualties: Victims of a Class War?" *Operations Research 40* (September–October 1992): 856–866, 865.

42. Flynn, *The Draft*, 233.

43. For discussions on both sides of this issue see the following works: James Fallows, "Low-Class Conclusions," *The Atlantic Monthly*, April 1993, 38–42; "Conscription: The Fairness Doctrine," *The Economist*, 12 January 1991, 21; George Flynn, *The Draft 1940–1973*; Newsweek, "The Draft: The Unjust vs. the Unwilling," *Newsweek*, 11 April 1966, 30–34; Eric Bergerud, *Red Thunder*, "James Fallows Reflects on the Draft's

Inequities (1969), 1975," *Major Problems in the History of the Vietnam War*, 2nd Edition, ed. Robert J. McMahon (Lexington, Massachusetts: D.C. Heath, 1995, 477–480; James Gerhardt, *The Draft and Public Policy* (Columbus: Ohio State University Press, 1971); Buckley, "Viet Guilt" *Esquire*, September 1983, 68–72; and *Vietnam Veterans Memorial/Directory of Names*, Vietnam Veterans Memorial Fund, Washington, DC (June edition).

44. Quoted in Flynn, *The Draft*, 231.

45. Flynn, *The Draft*, 227.

46. Powell, *My American Journey*, 144. See Seymour M. Hersh, *My Lai 4: A Report on the Massacre and its Aftermath* (New York: Random House, 1970); and James S. Olson and Randy Roberts, *My Lai: A Brief History with Documents* (Boston: Bedford/St. Martin's, 1998) for a history and analysis of this event.

47. "We Refuse to Serve" *"Takin' it to the Streets*," 195–196.

48. See Maurice Isserman and Michael Kazin, *America Divided: The Civil War of the 1960s* (New York: Oxford University Press, 2000).

49. Noted in Hoopes, *The Limits of Intervention*, 97.

50. Robert McNamara, *In Retrospect* (New York: Random House, 1991), 266–269.

51. McNamara, *In Retrospect*, 273.

52. Xiaoming Zhang, "The Vietnam War, 1964–1969: A Chinese Perspective," *The Journal of Military History*, Vol. 60, No. 4, October 1996, 731–762.

53. Westmoreland, *A Soldier Reports*, 332.

54. Quoted in George C. Herring, *America's Longest War*, 4th edition (Boston: McGraw Hill, 2002), 232.

55. Quoted in Peter Braestrup, *Big Picture: How American Press and Television Reported and Interpreted the Crisis of Tet 1968 in Vietnam and Washington* (New Haven: Yale University Press, 1977), 135.

56. Braestrup, *Big Picture*, 118.

57. Peter C. Rollins, "Television's Vietnam: The Visual Language of Television News,*" Journal of American Culture* 4 (1981), 114–135.

58. Rollins, "Television's Vietnam," 114–135.

59. Westmoreland, *A Soldier Reports*, 334.

60. Braestrup, *Big Picture*, 471.

61. Elegant, "How to Lose a War," 73–90.

62. Braestrup, *Big Picture*, 471.

63. George Herring, *America's Longest War*, 2nd edition (New York: McGraw Hill, 1979), ix.

64. Lewis W. Walt, General USMC, "Civil Affairs," *Marine Corps Gazette*, September 1968, 11.

65. Austin Hoyt, Martin Smith, and Richard Ellison, *Vietnam A Television History*, Volume 4, *Tet 1968* (Boston: WGBH Boston Video, 1983).

66. *Vietnam A Television History*, Volume 4, *Tet 1968*. For an assessment on the performance of the ARVN, see Andrew Wiest, *Vietnam's Forgotten Army: Heroism and Betrayal in the Army* (New York: New York University Press, 2008).

67. For more complete studies on the Tet Offensive see: William Thomas Allison, *Tet Offensive: A Brief History with Documents* (New York: Routledge, 2008); Don Oberdorfer, *Tet* (New York: Doubleday, 1971); James H. Willbanks, *The Tet Offensive: A Concise History* (New York: Columbia University Press, 2007).

68. Clifford, "A Viet Nam Reappraisal," 601–622.

69. Abrams departed Vietnam in June 1972 to assume the position of Army Chief of Staff. He died on 4 September 1974.

70. Richard Nixon, "Vietnamization," 3 November in *Vietnam and America*, ed., Marvin E. Gettleman, Jane Franklin, Marilyn B. Young, and H. Bruce Franklin (New York: Grove Press, 1995), 434, 436.

71. Richard Nixon, *The Memoirs of Richard Nixon* (New York: Simon and Schuster, 1990), 348.

72. Jeffrey Kimball, *Nixon's Vietnam War* (Lawrence, Kansas: University of Kansas Press, 1998), 41.

73. Nixon, *The Memoirs*, 298.

74. H.R. Haldeman, *The End of Power* (New York, 1975), 81.

75. Davidson, *Vietnam at War*, 612–615.

76. Lewis Sorley, *A Better War: The Unexamined Victories and Final Tragedy of America's Last Years in Vietnam* (New York: Harcourt, 1999), 23.

77. Jeffrey Clarke, *Advice and Support: The Final Years* (Washington, DC: CMH, 1988), 362, 363.

78. Herring, *America's Longest War*, 4th edition, 291.

79. Spencer Tucker, *The Encyclopedia of the Vietnam War* (New York: Oxford University Press, 1998), 58.

80. Mark Clodfelter, *Limits of Air Power: The American Bombing of North Vietnam* (New York: Free Press, 1989), 166–176. Phillip Davidson, *Vietnam at War* (New York: Oxford University Press, 1988), 699, 705.

81. John Sherwood, *Afterburner: Naval Aviators and the Vietnam War* (New York: New York University Press, 2004), 2.

82. Herring, *America's Longest War*, 308.

83. Clodfelter, *Limits of Air Power*, 161, 166.

84. For the Air Force's interpretation of the effectiveness of this bombing campaign see: Raymond W. Leonard, "Learning from History: Linebacker II and US Air Force Doctrine," *The Journal of Military History*, Vol. 58, No. 2, April 1994, 267–303; Sherwood, *Afterburner*, 2; and Earl H. Tilford, Jr., *Setup* (Maxwell Air Force Base, Alabama: Air University Press, June 1991), 263.

85. Arnold R. Isaacs, *Without Honor: Defeat in Vietnam and Cambodia* (Baltimore: Johns Hopkins University Press, 1983), 61. Isaacs noted: "Before the agreement was even signed, the legend began to be created: the bombing had done it. . . . Yet the events did not really show that the bombing forced North Vietnam to any new decision." This work contains an excellent analysis of the Paris Agreement.

86. Davidson, *Vietnam at War*, 723.

87. Fred Wilcox, *Waiting For an Army To Die: The Tragedy of Agent Orange* (New York: Vintage, 1983).

88. Tucker, ed., *The Encyclopedia of the Vietnam War*, 64.

89. Powell, *My American Journey*, 148.

90. Roy A. Werner, Captain USAR, "Down the Road to Armageddon?," *Military Review*, vol. LV No. 7, July 1975, 30, 31.

91. For contrast see, Walter Millis, *The Martial Spirit* (Chicago: Elephant Paperbacks, © 1931).

Chapter 12

1. US Army, FM 100–5, Operations (Washington, DC: Department of the Army, 5 May 1986), 14–17.

2. Glosson, *War With Iraq*, 289.

3. The second President Bush endeavored to copy this formulation of the world with his "Axis of Evil" State of the Union address.

4. The B–2 was not ready for service in the first Persian Gulf War.

5. Buster Glosson, *War With Iraq: Critical Lessons* (Charlotte, NC: Glosson Family Foundation, 2003), 26.

6. Glosson, *War With Iraq*, 12.

7. Glosson, *War With Iraq*, 291.

8. Glosson, *War With Iraq*, 289.

9. Glosson, *War With Iraq*, 129.

10. The assassination of political leaders was not legal by national and international law. The US, thus, used terminology that disguised its true intent.

11. Glosson, *War With Iraq*, 291, 292.

12. Glosson, *War With Iraq*, 27.

13. Glosson, *War With Iraq*, 21.

14. Glosson, *War With Iraq*, 14.

15. Diane T. Putney, "From Instant Thunder to Desert Strom: Developing the Gulf War Air Campaign's Phases," *Readings in American Military History*, ed., James M. Morris (NJ: Pearson, 2004), 367–378. Also see, John A. Warden, III. *The Air Campaign: Planning for Combat* (Washington, DC: National Defense University Press, 1988).

16. Paul H. Herbert, Major US Army, *Deciding What Has to Be Done: General William E. DePuy and the 1976 Edition of FM 100–5 Operations* (Fort Leavenworth, Kansas: Combat Studies Institute, July 1988), 1.

17. Romie L. Brownlee and William J. Mullen III, *Changing an Army: An Oral History of General William DePuy, USA Retired* (Washington, DC: US Army Center of Military History, 1979), 190.

18. John Romjue, *From Active Defense to AirLand Battle: The Development of Army Doctrine 1973–1982* (Ft. Monroe, Virginia: Historical Office US Army Training and Doctrine Command, June 1984).

19. In 1973 Army Chief of Staff General Abrams sent Major General Starry to Israel to study the armored warfare battlefield and to incorporate lessons learned into the design of the M1 main battle tank.

20. General Don Starry, "Reflections," *Camp Colt to Desert Storm: The History of US Armored Forces*, ed., George F. Hofmann and Don A. Starry (Lexington: The University Press of Kentucky, 199) 549, 550 (italics added).

21. US Army, FM 100–5, Operations (Washington, DC: Department of the Army, 5 May 1986), 14–17. FM 100–5 defined these terms: "Initiative means setting or changing the terms of battle by action. It implies offensive spirit in the conduct of all operations.... In the attack, initiative implies never allowing the enemy to recover form the initial shock of the attack. Agility—the ability of friendly forces to act faster than the enemy—is the first prerequisite for seizing and holding the initiative. Such greater quickness permits the rapid concentration of friendly strength against enemy vulnerabilities. This must be done repeatedly so that by the time the enemy reacts to one action, another has already taken its place, disrupting his plans and leading to late, uncoordinated, and piecemeal enemy response.... Depth is the extension of operations in space, time, and resources. Through the use of depth, a commander obtains the necessary space to maneuver effectively; the necessary time to plan, arrange, and execute operations; and the necessary resources to win. Momentum in the attack and elasticity in defense derive from depth.... Synchronization is the arrangement of battlefield activities in time, space, and purpose to produce maximum relative combat power at the decisive point. Synchronization includes but is not limited to the actual concentration of forces and fires at the point of decision." For an excellent discussion of the development of AirLand Battle Doctrine, see Richard Swain, "AirLand Battle," in *Camp Colt to Desert Storm*, 360–402.

22. US Army, FM 100–5, *Operations* (Washington, DC: Department of the Army, 29 April 1977), 8–2.

23. Anne Chapman, *The Army's Training Revolution 1973–1990* (Fort Monroe, Virginia: US Army Training and Doctrine Command, 1991). Also see: DePuy, *Changing an Army*, 182, 183. Starry benefited from the work conduct under DePuy's leadership. Starry initiated a number of studies to transform Army training: the Review of Education and Training of Officers (RETO), the Army Training Study, and the Long Range Training Base Study.

24. This was a semiofficial Air Force doctrine because General W.L. Creech, TAC Commander, could not speak for the entire USAF, and TAC was not a warfighting command. It provided forces for the theater commanders.

25. One A–10 pilot, Douglas N. Campbell, recalled: "In the late 1980s I flew A–10 weapons and tactics tests as part of the Air Force's fighter test unit at Nellis Air Force Base, Nevada. In so doing, I went from relative isolation inside my A–10 wing to active exposure to the rest of

the tactical air force. The encounter was unpleasant, because the A–10 was not popular with many fighter pilots. To them, its slow speed and ugliness made it a tactical liability and a visual embarrassment. I also arrived as the Air Force tried to replace the A–10s with modified F–16 fighters for the close air support role." See, Douglas Campbell, *The Warthog and the Close Air Support Debate* (Annapolis, Maryland: Naval Institute Press, 2003), x.

26. Robert Sunell wrote: "In spite of criticism, the M1 tank, although evolutionary, included many revolutionary innovations that would make it one of the most survivable tanks ever produced. First was the special armor package that provided unprecedented crew protection from both chemical and kinetic energy weapons. Second, the ammunition compartment was designed to blow out and away from the crew should a detonation occur. . . . Third was the fire control system, which included a ballistic computer that stabilized the tank cannon, allowing the crew to shoot on the move. This ballistic computer system—along with the Abram's exceptional thermal sight—played a key role later in the Gulf War. The fourth innovation was the turbine engine and the mobility it provided. The enhanced transmission and suspension system provided high cross-country speed with acceptable crew comfort." The M1 had a 105mm gun. It was up-gunned to a 120mm smoothbore gun in the M1A1 upgrades.

27. For a short but excellent summary of the design and production of the M1 see, Robert J. Sunell, "The Abrams Tank System," ed. Hoffmann and Starry, *Camp Colt to Desert Strom*, 432, 473. The British developed Chobham armor. Snell wrote: "Chobham armor's layers of ceramic, steel, and titanium, laminated between layers of ballistic nylon would resist penetration by both kinetic- and chemical-energy ammunition." Studies have shown that while front armor of the M1s sustained hits from enemy tanks, not one was destroyed during the war. Firepower was a problem in the first production model of the M1, which mounted a 105-mm main gun. The Army recognized its limitations, but in order to keep the cost down, and thus the tank palatable to Congress, the Army stuck with the same gun that was in the M60 tank. The main gun problem was corrected in later models by adopting the German 120-mm smooth-bore gun, which gave the M1A1 greater range, accuracy, and destructive power. In the Gulf War all Army divisions were equipped with M1A1s, with the exception of one brigade of the 1st ID.

28. James Kitfield, *Prodigal Soldiers* (Washington, DC: Brassey's, 1995).

29. It added vertical take-off and landing cargo and troop carrier aircraft to its inventory. This aircraft makes it possible for the Marines to project power deep into the interior of a country, to move far beyond the littoral

regions. It also made possible intra-theater sustainability. However, the V–22 Osprey is enormously expensive and has been plagued with technical problems.

30. USMC, FMFM1 *Warfighting* (Washington, DC: Headquarters USM.C., 6 March 1989), 58, 59, and 29.

31. FMFM 1–1 *Campaigning* (Washington DC: Headquarters US Marine Corps, 25 January 1990), 64, 65.

32. Kenneth Estes, "Mounted Warfare in the Marine Corps," *Camp Colt to Desert Storm*, ed. George Hoffmann and Donn Starry, 484.

33. Harry Summers, retired Colonel US Army, was the author of an influential book, *On Strategy: The Vietnam War in Context* (Carlisle Barracks, Pennsylvania: US Army War College, 1981). He used Clausewitz's work, *On War*, to explain the defeat of the United States in Vietnam.

34. William Westmoreland, "Vietnam in Perspective," *Military Review*, Vol. LIX No. 1, Jan. 1979, 34, 35.

35. At West Point I had the opportunity to teach a course on the evolution of US Army doctrine. During that course I was fortunate to have a number of combat arms officers talk to my cadets. As they spoke a number of things came through consistently. They had committed their lives to this war and these people. They had lost good friends and soldiers that had served under their command, creating in some cases a sense of survivor's guilt. They had killed for their country, and in almost every case had disagreed with the conduct and administration of the war. However, ultimately, they had failed. The effort had been in vain. Vietnam was lost. And, there had been no monuments built to the memories of those who died, no welcome home, and no victory parade, until more than a decade after the war. While the evidence is anecdotal, it does not require a huge leap of faith to come to these conclusions.

36. Westmoreland, "Vietnam in Perspective," 34 (italics added).

37. Charles C. Moskos, Jr., *The American Enlisted Man*, 10.

38. Reprinted in Michael Handel, *Masters of War* (London: Frank Cass, 1992), 311 (italics added).

39. Carl von Clausewitz, *On War*, ed. and trans. by Michael Howard and Peter Paret, 81.

40. Colin Powell, General US Army, *My American Journey* (New York: Random House, 1995), 149, 434.

41. In April 1980, the US Army's Delta Force, supported by the Navy, Air Force, and Marines, tried to rescue fifty-two Americans held hostage in Tehran since the Islamic Revolution in November 1979. In the Iranian desert before the rescue operation commenced a helicopter collided with a C–130 aircraft, killing eight servicemen, and ending the rescue operation. It was a miserable failure and surprisingly amateurish given the quality and experience of individuals involved.

42. Anthony Zinni, Gen. USMC, "A Commander Reflects," *Proceedings*, Vol. 126/7/1,169, July 2000, 35.

43. National Security Act of 1947, US Statutes at Large. Reprinted in *US National Security Policy and Strategy: Documents and Policy Proposals*, ed., Sam Sarkesian with Robert Vitas (New York: Greenwood Press, 1988), 9–15.

44. David Jones, Written Statement of the Chairman of JCS, Hearings before the Investigations Committee of the Committee of Armed Services House of Representatives, 97th Congress, "Reorganization Proposal for the Joint Chiefs of Staff, April–August, 1982, 52–60 (italics added).

45. Publish Law 99–433, 99th Congress, 1 October 1986. Reprinted in part in *US National Security Policy and Strategy: Documents and Policy Proposals*, ed. Sam Sarkesian, 25.

46. Publish Law 99–433, 99th Congress, 1 October 1986. Reprinted in part in *US National Security Policy and Strategy: Documents and Policy Proposals*, 31.

47. General Frank Pace, Chairman of the Joint Chiefs of Staff, "The 16th Chairman's Guidance to the Joint Staff: Shaping the Future," 1 Oct. 2005. Available online at the Pentagon's website.

48. For a comprehensive discussion on the passage of this Act, see James Locher III, *Victory on the Potomac: The Goldwater-Nichols Act Unifies the Pentagon* (College Station: Texas A&M Press, 2002).

49. Quoted in James Locher III, "Goldwater-Nichols: Fighting the Decisive Battle," *Joint Forces Quarterly*, Summer 2002, 38–47.

50. Locher III, "Goldwater-Nichols: Fighting the Decisive Battle," 38–47.

51. Locher III, "Goldwater-Nichols: Fighting the Decisive Battle," 38–47.

52. Edward Meyer, "The JCS—How Much Reform is Needed," *Armed Forces Journal International*, April 1982, 82–90. Reprinted in Hearings before the Investigations Committee of the Committee of Armed Services House of Rep., 97th Congress, "Reorganization Proposal for the JCS," April–August, 1982, 7–14.

53. Hammond, *Organizing for Defense*, 256–259.

54. See Charles Cogan, "Desert One and Its Disorders," *Journal of Military History*, Vol. 76, No. 1, Jan. 2003, 201–216.

Chapter 13

1. George Bush and Brent Scowcroft, *A World Transformed* (New York: Vintage Book, 1998), 354.

2. For the Army's view of Operation Desert Storm, see: Robert H. Scales, Jr., *Certain Victory: The US Army in the Gulf War* (Washington, DC: Brassey's, 1994); Stephen Bourque, *Jayhawk! The VII Corps in the Persian Gulf War* (Washington, DC: Department of the Army, 2002); H. Norman Schwarzkopf, *It Doesn't Take a Hero* (New York: Bantam Books, 1992); Colin Powell, *My American Journey* (New York: Random House, 1995); Harry Summers, Jr., *A Critical Analysis of The Gulf War* (New York: Dell Book, 1992); and Tom Clancy with General Fred Franks, Jr., US Army, *Into the Storm* (New York: Berkeley Books, 1998). For the Air Force's view, see: Buster Glosson, *War With Iraq: Critical Lessons* (Charlotte, NC: Glosson Family Foundation, 2003); Richard Hallion, *Storm Over Iraq: Air Power and the Gulf War* (Washington, DC: Smithsonian Institute Press, 1992); William Andrews, *Airpower Against an Army* (Maxwell Air Force Base, Alabama: Air University Press, February 1998); and Tom Clancy with General Chuck Horner, General US Air Force, *Every Man a Tiger* (New York: G.P. Putnam's Sons, 1999). For the view from the White House, see: George Bush and Brent Scowcroft, *A World Transformed* (New York: Vintage Books, 1998). For critical analysis, see: Michael R. Gordon and General Bernard E. Trainor, USMC, *The General's War: The Inside Story of the Conflict in the Gulf* (Boston: Little, Brown and Co., 1995); US News & World Report, *Triumph without Victory* (New York: Random House, 1992); and Anthony Cordesman and Abraham Wagner, *The Lessons of Modern War: Volume IV: The Gulf War* (Boulder, Colorado: Westview Press, 1996).

3. Bush and Scowcroft, *A World Transformed*, 484

4. The Iran-Iraq War has also been called the "Persian Gulf War." For this study the Persian Gulf War refers only to Operation Desert Storm.

5. USMC, Fleet Marine Force Reference Publication (FMFRP) 3–203, Lessons Learned: The Iran-Iraq War, Vol. I, M.P. Caulfield, Maj. Gen. USMC (Washington, DC: Headquarters USMC, 10 December 1990), 65. Also see: Abbas Alnasrawi, *The Economy of Iraq* (Westport, Conn.: Greenwood Press, 1994).

6. In 1979 Mohammad Reza Shah was over thrown in an Islamic Fundamentalist Revolution, establishing the Islamic Republic of Iran, a theocracy under the leadership of Ayatollah Ruhollah Khomaini.

7. Michael Klare, "Arms Transfers to Iran and Iraq during the Iran-Iraq War of 1980–88 and the Origins of the Gulf War," *The Gulf War of 1991 Reconsidered*, ed., Andrew Bacevich and Efraim Inbar (London: Frank Cass, 2003), 3–24, 17. Also see: Gregory Gause, "Iraq's Decision to Go to War, 1980 and 1990," *Middle East Journal* 56, 2002, 47–70; Musallam Ali Musallam, *The Iraqi Invasion of Kuwait: Saddam Hussein, His State and International Power Politics* (London: British Academic Press, 1996); and Con Coughlin, *Saddam: His Rise and Fall* (New York: Harper, 2005), 214–216.

8. Iraq claimed the territory on the grounds that it had been part of the Iraq Ottoman province of Basra.

9. Quoted in Edward Atkeson, "Iraq's Arsenal: Tool of Ambition," *Army*, Vol. 41, No. 3, Mar. 1991, 22–30.

10. PBS Frontline, *The Long Road to War* (PBS Video, 1999).

11. Gordon and Trainor, *The General's War*, 20–22.

12. Klare, "Arms Transfers to Iran and Iraq during the Iran-Iraq War of 1980–88 and the Origins of the Gulf War," 3–24, 16. This is an excellent summary of the causes of the war.

13. C.G. Jacobsen, *The New World Order's Defining Crises* (Vermont: Dartmouth Publishing Co, 1996), 27.

14. In 1985, the Reagan Administration secretly sold arms to Iran, the funds from which were used to assist the Contras. This duplicity became known at the Iran-Contra Affair. The West also supported Israel's acquisition of nuclear weapons, creating a double standard, one for Western nations and another for non-Western nations. See Avner Cohen, *Israel and the Bomb* (New York: Columbia University Press, 1998), 341. Cohen wrote: "It would have been nearly impossible for Israel, technologically and financially, to develop a plutonium-based nuclear infrastructure on its own." Thus the West created the motivation for Iraq, Iran, Egypt and other Middle East states to seek nuclear weapons.

15. Dilip Hiro, *The Longest War: The Iran-Iraq Military Conflict* (New York: Routledge, 1991).

16. Quoted in John F. Antal, Major US Army, *The Iraqi Army, Forged in the Fire of the Gulf War* (Leavenworth, Kansas: US Command and General Staff College), 17, 18.

17. John F. Antal, Major US Army, "The Sword of Saddam: an Overview of the Iraqi Armed Forces," Distributed at the US Military Academy, in 1990. Also see: US Army Battle Command Training Program, "Iraq: 'How They Fight' World Class OPFOR," (Fort Benning, Georgia: US Army Infantry School, 1990). Figures on the size, organization, and technology of the Iraq armed force vary slightly because of differences in sources of information.

18. USMC, Fleet Marine Force Reference Publication (FMFRP) 3–203, Lessons Learned, 99.

19. Atkeson, "Iraq's Arsenal: Tool of Ambition," 26, 27.

20. US Army Command and General Staff College, "Identifying the Iraqi Threat and How They Fight," Cdr, USCAC, Attn: ATXL-CST-C, LTC Bisles, Fort Leavenworth, Kansas, 66027.

21. Stephen Pelletiere, Douglas Johnson II, and Leif Rosenberger, *Iraqi Power and US Security in the Middle East* (Carlisle, Pennsylvania: US Army War College, Strategic Studies Institute, 1990), ix.

22. Richard Jupa and James Dingeman, "The Republican Guards: Loyal, Aggressive, Able," *Army*, vol. 41, No. 3, March 1991, 54–62.

23. USMC, Fleet Marine Force Reference Publication (FMFRP) 3–203, Lessons Learned, v.

24. Schwarzkopf, *It Doesn't Take a Hero* 467.

25. The British and French deserve the lion's share of the credit for political and military turmoil and misery that has plagued the Middle East for a century. However, the US also deserves some credit. In 1953 the CIA-British backed coup in Iran overthrew the Mossadegh government, installing a dictatorship under the Shah, who insured that the oil flowed at prices acceptable to the US and Britain.

26. Effraim Karsh and Inari Rautsi, *Saddam Hussein: A Political Biography* (New York: Free Press, 1991).

27. Antal, "The Iraqi Army," 17.

28. Bush and Scowcroft, *A World Transformed*, 360.

29. Bush and Scowcroft, *A World Transformed*, 418.

30. Egypt for example was released from its $7 billion debt.

31. Bush and Scowcroft, *A World Transformed*, 418.

32. Bush and Scowcroft, *A World Transformed*, 332, 333.

33. Israelis correctly argue that when Israel was formed there was no "Palestinian nation." The act of creating Israel also created a unified Palestine. The people were formed into a nation by opposition to the formation of Israel. Israel has also concluded that the only way it will ever be secure in the Middle East is by bringing about a cultural transformation. Arab nations and states need to adopt Western values and ethics, capitalism and democracy. The US has more recently adopted the Israeli view of the Middle East, and is engaged in a fight to transform the Middle East by planting seeds of democracy and capitalism.

34. CENTCOM had no permanently assigned units. Horner commanded the 9th Air Force at Shaw AFB, South Carolina, which was designated to provide airpower for CENTCOM operations.

35. The area became known as the "black hole" because of the secrecy and the long working hours. Officers that went in seemed to never be seen again.

36. Quoted in Diane T. Putney, "From Instant Thunder to Desert Storm: Developing the Gulf War Air Campaign's Phases," *Air Power History* 41–3, (Fall 1994), 38–50.

37. Glosson, *War With Iraq*, 55.

38. Glosson, *War With Iraq*, 203, 204. Glosson quoted a discussion he had with Schwarzkopf: "Unless you tell me differently, I'm going to ignore any request that Waller makes that violates your direct guidance to me, or where the conditions have changed and the intel that he was using to make that decision is no longer accurate, or the target is no longer there." Waller too would have supported this statement.

39. Glosson, *War With Iraq*, 35.

40. Hallion, *Storm Over Iraq*, 254. Hallion wrote: "Unfortunately, some naval proponents charged after the war that naval aviation could have been used more significantly, but the CENTAF staff had been unwilling to do so." One student of the air campaign noted: "Navy integration into ATO was limited, mostly for technical reasons, and the Marines referred to the JFACC as the joint force 'air coordinator' instead of the 'air component commander.'" See John T. Correll,

"The Strategy of Desert Storm," *Air Force*, vol. 89, No. 1, 26–33.

41. Robert H. Scales, *Certain Victory: The US Army in the Gulf War* (London: Brassey's, 1994), 106.

42. Bush and Scowcroft, *A World Transformed*, 381.

43. Bush and Scowcroft, *A World Transformed*, 381.

44. The V and VII Corps were stationed in Germany. The III Corps was at Fort Hood, Texas. Each corps consisted of two heavy divisions, armor or mechanized, and an armored cavalry regiment, which could generate almost two-thirds the combat power of a heavy division.

45. William F. Andrews, Lieutenant Colonel USAF, *Airpower Against an Army: Challenge and Response in CENTAF's Duel with the Republican Guard* (Maxwell Air Force Base: Air University Press, 1998), 24.

46. Andrews, *Airpower Against an Army*, 25.

47. Bourque, *Jayhawk!*, 184.

48. John A. Nagl, "A Tale of Two Battles," *Armor*, Vol CI, No. 3, May–June 1992, 8.

49. A World War II battle where the 101st Airborne was completely surrounded during the Battle of the Bulge. The division did not surrender.

50. Correll, "The Strategy of Desert Storm," 26–33.

Chapter 14

1. Richard Hallion, *Storm Over Iraq: Air Power and the Gulf War* (Washington, DC: Smithsonian Institution Press, 1992), 1.

2. Eric C. Ludvigsen, "The 'Expansible' Army," *Army*, Vol. 41, No. 4. April 1991, 27–29.

3. Glosson, *War With Iraq*, 26.

4. Glosson, *War With Iraq*, 20, 21.

5. *US News and World Report*, noted, "On the final night of the war—within hours of the cease-fire—two US Air Force bombers dropped specially designed 5,000-pound bombs on a command bunker fifteen miles northwest of Baghdad in a deliberate attempt to kill Saddam Hussein. This, despite President Bush's repeated denials that Washington had ever targeted Saddam Hussein personally." See: US New and World Report, *Triumph without Victory: The Unreported History of the Persian Gulf War*, viii.

6. Andrews, *Airpower Against an Army*, 23. Andrews noted that: "Much of the planning was quantitative in nature, using computer models and spreadsheets. The Checkmate [planning cell] calculations considered multiple quantitative and qualitative factors. Quantifications included munitions available in the theater, aircraft numbers, sortie rates, target types, objectives, and expected success per sortie (based on Saber Selector, and advanced computer program modeling weapons deliveries)." Also see John Andreas Olsen, "Operation Desert Storm, 1991," in *A History of Air Warfare*, ed.,

John Andreas Olsen (Washington, DC: Potomac Books, 2010), 177–200.

7. President Bush and others praised the patriot missile system during the war. Out of forty-two fired, it was believed that forty-one had hit their targets. Post-war studies showed that they were actually considerably less effective.

8. See Gulf War Air Power Survey. See also, Barry R. Schneider, "Counterforce Targeting: Capabilities and Challenges," *Counterproliferation Papers Future Warfare Series* No. 22 (Maxwell Air Force Base, Alabama: Air University, August 2004), 13–19.

9. Glosson, *War With Iraq*, 33, 212.

10. Glosson, *War With Iraq*, 193.

11. Gordon and Trainor, *The General's War*, 318.

12. Schneider, *Counterforce Targeting*, 14.

13. United States General Accounting Office, *Operation Desert Storm: Evaluation of the Air Campaign*, GAO/NSIAD–97–134 (Washington, DC: GPO, June 1997) 158.

14. Glosson, *War With Iraq*, 185–189, 197.

15. Glosson, *War With Iraq*, 195.

16. For a comprehensive study of the Navy during Operation Desert Storm see: Edward J. Marolda and Robert J. Schneller, Jr., *Shield and Sword: The United States Navy and the Persian Gulf War* (Annapolis, Maryland: Naval Institute Press, 2001).

17. The Navy League of the US, "White Papers: The Sea Services' Role in Desert Shield/Storm," Congressional Record, Vol. 137, No. 108, Washington, 16 July 1991.

18. Hallion, *Storm Over Iraq*, 255.

19. Hallion, *Storm Over Iraq*, 256.

20. For a personal account of the Marine F/A–18 air war see: Jay A. Stout, *Hornets Over Kuwait* (Annapolis, Maryland: Naval Institute Press, 1997).

21. Schwarzkopf, *It Doesn't Take a Hero*, 434, 435.

22. Hallion, *Storm Over Iraq*, 253.

23. There was a minority view in the Air Force: "Iraqi weapons systems were diminished by CENTAF attacks. That there was ground fighting, and in some cases very intense fighting, suggests the 50 percent attrition figure was not of primary importance. Lt. Gen Frederick Franks, VII Corps commander remarked, '50 percent didn't mean much to Capt. McMaster' (a company commander at 73 Easting). Airpower's value to the RGFC battle seems to reside in the options it took away from the enemy commander. Constrained logistics meant he couldn't go far or fight long; damaged C2 meant he couldn't coordinate his actions; airpower blinded his artillery and pinned his units, setting the Republican Guard for the coup de grace to be administered by combined air and ground forces during phase IV." See, Andrews, *Airpower Against an Army*, 70, 71.

24. GAO, Operation Desert Storm: Evaluation of the Air Campaign, 30, 31. This is the best study available on the air war in Operation Desert Storm.

25. The Army was willing to support the Marine Corps acquisition of M1A1s, however, the Marine Corps decided not to transition just before going into hostilities.

26. Scales, *Certain Victory*, 41, 42.

27. Peter C. Langenus, Colonel US Army, "Moving an Army: Movement Control for Desert Storm," *Military Review*, Vol. LXXI, No. 9, September 1991, 40–51. Also see: Jimmy D. Ross, Deputy Chief of Staff for Logistics, "Victory: The Logistics Story," *Army*, Vol 41, No. 10, October 1991, 128–140.

28. Schwarzkopf, *It Doesn't Take a Hero*, 453, 454.

29. Schwarzkopf, *It Doesn't Take a Hero*, 455.

30. Schwarzkopf, *It Doesn't Take a Hero*, 456.

31. Gordon and Trainor, *The General's War*, 267–288. They wrote: "Khafji was one of a series of border engagements at the end of January that took Schwarzkopf and his top commanders completely by surprise. Although characterized at the time as a minor skirmish, the two-day clash was the war's defining moment. Schwarzkopf's failure to grasp the significance of Khafji was one of the general's greatest oversights. His war plan was never revised to take account of the lessons of the battle and that omission contributed mightily to the escape of the Republican Guard when the allies' land offensive was launched more than three weeks later." They concluded that: "the ground generals who controlled the war— Schwarzkopf and Powell—were not inclined to accept the notion that an invading army could be destroyed from the air. . . . The consequences . . . an incomplete victory. . . ." Also see: David Morris, *Storm on the Horizon: Khafji—The Battle that Changed the Course of the Gulf War* (New York: Free Press, 2004).

32. Schwarzkopf, *It Doesn't Take a Hero*, 461.

33. Bourque, *Jayhawk!*, 292, 293.

34. Clancy with General Fred Franks, Jr., *Into the Storm: On the Ground in Iraq*, 339, 340.

35. For a detailed account of the battle see: Douglas Macgregor, *Warrior's Rage: The Great Tank Battle of 73 Easting* (Annapolis, Maryland: Naval Institute Press, 2009).

36. US Army, CMH and Defense Advanced Research Project Agency, "The Battle of 73 Easting 26 Feb. 1991: A Historical Introduction to a Simulation," Michael D. Krause, Colonel US Army, 2 May 1991.

37. Richard Bohannon, "1–37 Armor in the Battle of 73 Easting," *Armor*, Vol. CI, No. 3, May–June 1992, 11–17. The 2nd ACR also fought a battle that has been called "73 Easting."

38. Scales, *Certain Victory*, 261, 262.

39. Scales, *Certain Victory*, 293.

40. Cordesman and Wagner, *The Lessons of Modern War, Volume IV: The Gulf War*, 651.

41. Macgregor, *Warrior's Rage*, xii.

42. Quoted in Clancy, *Every Man a Tiger*, 469.

43. Cordesman and Wagner, *The Lessons of Modern War: The Gulf War*, Vol. IV, 651. Note: Tom Clancy uses different estimates in his works. See *Every Man a Tiger*, 468.

44. Bourque, *Jayhawk!*, 291.

45. Cordesman, *The Lessons of Modern War*, 651. Also see, Bourque, *Jayhawk!*, 456.

46. Powell, *My American Journey*, 519–521.

47. Schwarzkopf, *It Doesn't Take a Hero*, 469, 470.

48. Thomas Mahnken, "A Squandered Opportunity? The Decision to End the Gulf War," in *The Gulf War of 1991 Reconsidered*, ed. Andrew Bacevich (London: Frank Cass, 2003), 121–148.

49. Mahnken, "A Squandered Opportunity," 143. Also see: Jeffrey Record, *Hollow Victory: A Contrary View of the Gulf War* (Washington, DC: Brassey's, 1993); and Gordon and Trainor, *The General's War*.

50. Gordon and Trainor, *The General's War*, 477.

51. Bush and Scowcroft, *A World Transformed*, 489.

52. Quoted in Jeffrey Record, *Dark Victory: America's Second War Against Iraq* (Annapolis, Maryland: Naval Institute Press, 2004), x.

53. Powell wrote: "Norm Schwarzkopf was, deservedly, a national hero. And the criticism that the fighting had stopped too soon had chipped his pedestal. He did not like it. . . . Schwarzkopf had been a party to the decision, and now he seemed to be distancing himself from it." (*My American Journey*, 525).

54. For a more detailed discussion see, Hans Blix, *Disarming Iraq* (New York: Pantheon Books, 2004).

55. Stephen D. Cooper, "Press Controls in Wartime: The Legal, Historical, and Institutional Context," *American Communication Journal*, Vol. 6, Issue 4, Summer 2003, 2–22. Cooper noted: "During the war, journalists were denied free access to the theater of operations during deployment and combat, and were restricted by a system of military escorts, pooled coverage, and military review of copy for it potential to disclose classified information." This work has an excellent "Works Cited and Notes" section.

56. George Bush, *A World Transformed*, 17.

57. US Army FM 3–61.1 Public Affairs Operation (www.globalsecurity.org/military/library/policy/army/fm/3-61.1 Chapter 2, page 1 of 6.

58. Winant Sidle, Major General US Army, "A Battle Behind the Scenes: The Gulf War Reheats Military-Media Controversy," *Military Review*, Vol. LXXI, No. 9, September 1991, 52–63.

59. Pete Williams, Assistant Secretary of Defense (Public Affairs), "Statement Before the US Senate Committee on Government Affairs," reprinted in *The Media and the Gulf War: The Press and Democracy in Wartime*, ed., Hedrick Smith (Washington, DC: Seven Locks Press, 1992), 33–44.

60. Sidle, "A Battle Behind the Scenes," *MR*, 57.

61. Sidle, "A Battle Behind the Scenes," *MR*, 58.

62. FM 3–6.1, Appendix X.

63. US News and World Report, *Triumph Without Victory*, ix.

64. Eric C. Ludvigen, "The 'Expansible' Army," *Army*, Vol. 41, No. 4, April 1991, 27–29.

65. Daniel Bolger, *Death Ground: Today's American Infantry in Battle* (Novato, CA: Presidio, 2000), 17–19.

Chapter 15

1. Peter Riesenberg, *Citizenship in the Western Tradition: Plato to Rousseau* (Chapel Hill: University of North Carolina Press, 1992), 73, 80.

2. Michael Weiss, *The Cluster World* (Boston: Little, Brown, 2000), 10–15.

3. David M. Kennedy, "Sons, Brothers, Soldiers" *The Dallas Morning News*, Sunday, 31 July 2005, 4P.

4. James R. FitzSimonds and Jan M. Van Tol, "Revolution in Military Affairs," *Joint Forces Quarterly*, Spring 1994, No. 4, 24–31. FitzSimonds and Van Tol wrote: "Information processing has always been part of warfare. In the future, however, it may be central to the outcome of battles and engagements. If so, establishing information dominance over one's adversary will become a major focus of the operational art. Information warfare is still an ill-defined term. However, it might encompass a range of concepts. . . ."

5. Quincy Wright, *A Study of War* (Chicago: University of Chicago, 1965), 977.

6. Ole R. Holsti, "Of Chasm and Convergence: Attitudes and Beliefs of Civilian and Military Elites at the Start of the New Millennium," *Soldiers and Civilians: The Civil-Military Gap and American National Security*, ed. Peter D. Feaver and Richard H. Kohn (Cambridge, Massachusetts: MIT Press, 2001), 27.

7. Thomas E. Ricks, "The Widening Gap Between the Military and Society," *The Atlantic Monthly*, Vol. 280, No. 1, July 1997, 66–78.

8. Gordon Trowbridge, "Today's Military: Right, Republican and Principled," *Marine Corps Times*, 5 January 2004, 13–15.

9. Aaron Gilbert, Corporal US Marine Corps, serving on the *USS Saipan*, Persian Gulf, March 2003. The poem is entitled "THE MARINE (italics added)." Available at stutzblackhawk@bellsouth.net.

10. Beth Bailey, *America's Army: Making the All-Volunteer Force* (Cambridge, Massachusetts: Belknap Press, 2009), see chapter 1, "Individual Freedom and Obligations of Citizenship." Also see, Robert K. Griffith, Jr., *The US Army's Transition to the All-Volunteer Force, 1968–1974* (Washington, DC: Center of Military History, United States Army, 1997).

11. US National Commission on Terrorist Attacks Upon the US, *The 9/11 Commission Report* (New York: W.W. Norton, 2003), 334–338. Also see: Richard Clarke, *Against All Enemies* (New York: Free Press, 2004), 30–31. Clarke, in a conversation with Powell, stated: "Having been attacked by al Qaeda, for us now to go bombing Iraq in response would be like our invading Mexico after the Japanese attacked us at Pearl Harbor."

12. George W. Bush, "Address to a Joint Session of Congress and the American People," White House, Washington DC, 20 September 2001, www.whitehouse.gov/news/release/2001/09/

13. Richard Kohn, "The Erosion of Civilian Control of the Military in the United States Today," *Naval War College Review*, Vol LV, No. 3, Summer 2002, 8–59.

14. Carl Builder, *The Masks of War: American Military Styles in Strategy and Analysis* (Baltimore, 1989), 3.

15. Weigley, "The American Military," 28.

16. Colin Powell, CJCS, "Why Generals Get Nervous," *New York Times*, 8 October 1992, A35, col. 4.

17. Holsti, 97.

18. Samuel Huntington, "Interservice Competition and Political Roles," *The American Political Science Review*, Vol. 55, No. 1, March 1961, 40–52.

19. Quoted in Flanagan, "The 100-Hour War," *Army*, 24.

20. Morris MacGregor, Jr., *Integration of the Armed Forces 1940–1965* (Washington, DC: Center of Military History, 1985), 291–342. While Truman demonstrated the political courage to publish the executive order, he lacked the courage to implement it. The armed forces ignored the order until the Korean War.

21. Michael Gordon and Bernard Trainor, *Cobra II: The Inside Story of the Invasion and Occupation of Iraq* (New York: Pantheon Books, 2006), 4.

22. Gordon Sullivan, "Force XXI," *The Collected Works of the Thirty-second Chief of Staff United States Army: June 1991–June 1995* (Washington, DC: CMH, 2004), 316.

23. James Cross, "What is the Army's Job?" *Military Review*, June 1956, 43–47 (italics added).

24. Peter Mansoor, *Baghdad at Sunrise* (New Haven: Yale University Press, 2008), 107, 109. Such accounts of Operation Iraqi Freedom now fill the shelves of bookstores across the country. In the last years of the Vietnam War and the period immediately following it numerous books were published, some of which were good, that sought to identify and explain the causes of defeat. We are now going through such a period in regard to Operation Iraqi Freedom, a war that most Americans now believe was poorly executed and unnecessary.

25. Thomas G. Mahnken, "Transforming the US Armed Forces: Rhetoric or Reality," *Naval War College Review*, Summer 2001, Vol. LIV, No. 3, 86–99.

26. The debate on the RMA has been ongoing for more than a decade. The professional journals of all the services over the last ten years have articles addressing network-centric warfare, jointness, information dominance, digital communications, precision-guided munitions, the

"system of systems," and other such topics. See: *Proceedings; Joint Forces Quarterly;* and *US Army War College Quarterly, Parameters; Naval War College Review, Army, Air Force,* and others.

27. See Art Cebrowski, Vice Admiral USN., and John Gartska, "Network-Centric Warfare: Its Origins and Future," *Proceedings,* Jan. 1998, 28–35; and William Owens, Admiral USN, *Lifting the Fog of War,* and "The Once and Future Revolution in Military Affairs," *Joint Forces Quarterly,* Summer 2002, 55–61.

28. John Tirpak, "The Network Way of War," *Air Force,* Vol. 88, No. 3, March 2005, 26–31.

29. Preston Lerner, "Robots Go to War," *Popular Science,* Vol. 268, No. 1, January 2006, 42–49.

30. Andrew Marshall, with the support of Rumsfeld, developed a plan called "A Strategy for a Long Peace," 12 February 2001. The plan cut two active duty heavy divisions, like the 3rd ID that invaded Iraq in 2003, and four Army National Guard divisions. The other services were also to have reductions in force. Had these cuts gone into effect, the situation in Iraq in 2005 would have been much worse. The Navy acquired the F/A 18E/F Super Hornet, the Air Force, F/A 22 Raptor, and the Marine Corps, Joint Striker Fighter (JSF). The Navy and Air Force were also to acquire the JSF.

31. Quoted in Michael Evans, "Dark Victory," *Proceeding,* September 1999, Vol. 125/9/1,159, 35.

32. Andrew Bacevich, "Neglected Trinity: Kosovo and the Crisis in US Civil-Military Relations," in *War Over Kosovo,* eds., Andrew Bacevich and Eliot Cohen (New York: Columbia University Press, 2001), 155.

33. Gabriel Kolko, *Another Century of War?* (New York: The New Press, 2002), 76.

34. Michael Evans, "Dark Victory," 33–37.

35. See Christopher Haave, Col. USAF, and Phil Haun, Lt. Col. USAF, *A–10s Over Kosovo: The Victory of Airpower Over a Fielded Army* (Maxwell Air Force Base, Alabama: Air University Press, December 2003). In the "Foreword" it states: "This event marked a milestone for airpower, as it was, arguably, the first time airpower alone was decisive in achieving victory in combat."

36. Bacevich, 159.

37. Sean MacFarland, "Addendum: Anbar Awakens," *Military Review,* May–June 2008, 77–78.

38. FM 3–0, *Operations* (Washington, DC: Headquarters Department of the Army, February 2008).

39. John Romjue, *American Army Doctrine the Post-Cold War* (Ft. Monroe: TRADOC, 1997), 113–119.

40. The US Atlantic Command morphed into the Joint Forces Command (JFCOM) responsible for joint doctrine and training; however, it was later reestablished as the US Northern Command (NORTHCOM). The Unified Command Plan (UCP) is reviewed every two years in accordance with the National Security Act of 1947 and the Title 10 US Code 161. The review establishes military combatant commands and the missions, functions, and geographic area of operation (AOR) of each. The UCP is changed based on changes in the National Security Strategy (NSS) and National Military Strategy (NMS). Under the 2002 UCP, the JFCOM was responsible for transformation, experimentation, joint training and interoperability for all the services. The command is to introduce new doctrine and streamline future military operations.

41. Robert M. Gates, Secretary of Defense, Speech delivered at Maxwell-Gunter Air Force Base, to the Air War College, April 15, 2009, www.defenselink.mi/speeches.

42. The F–22 incorporates stealth and Harrier VTOL technologies and the most advanced radar systems. Hence, it is capable of seeing enemy aircraft before its presence is detected, allowing it to launch missiles at greater range and well before opposing aircraft. As a consequence, it is argued that one F–22 can take on as many as five F–15s. It is also faster and more agile than any of its competition, including the F/A–18. Since World War II the difference between Air Force and Navy fighter aircraft has been marginal, with the Navy sometimes producing a better fighter. However, the F–22 represents a significant advancement. The F–22 is also an F/A–22, a ground attack aircraft or F/B–22. This dual role helps justify its tremendous cost.

43. The Defense Advanced Research Project Agency (DARPA) has been working on and testing the Boeing X–45C and Northrop Grumman X–47B. See Bill Sweetman, "Is This the Future of Air Combat," *Popular Science,* vol. 267, no. 1, July 2005; and Nathan Brasher, US Navy, "Unmanned Aerial Vehicles and the Future of Air Combat," *Proceedings,* July 2005, Vol. 131/7/1,229, 36–39. The UAV has a number of hurtles to cross before it can compete with piloted aircraft. These include landing on aircraft carriers, air-to-air refueling, and sharing air space with military and civilian aircraft. In addition, tactical and operational doctrines have to be developed. However, the biggest hurdle facing the UCAV are the cultures of the Air Force and Navy, which hold that nothing will ever replace manned aircraft.

44. Department of Defense Directive 5100.1, 1 August 2002.

45. James Paulsen, "Naval Aviation Delivered in Iraq," *Proceeding,* June 2003, Vol. 129/6/1,204, 34–37.

46. Bing West and Ray Smith, *The March Up* (New York: Bantam Books, 2003), 220.

47. L.R. Roberts and J.P. Farnam, USMC, "Airborne Recon Supported Marines' Advances in Iraq," *Proceedings,* Vol. 130/6/1,216, June 2004, 40–43.

48. Frank Mulcahy, "High-Speed Sealift: Is a Joint Mission," *Proceedings,* Vol. 131/1/1,223, 34–37.

49. Sean M. Herron, "Joint High Speed Vessel: Opportunities to Revolutionize Strategic Power Projection," *Defense Transportation Journal,* Vol. 66, No. 5, September 2010,

12–23. The Army was programmed to purchase five joint high-speed vessels, and the Navy twelve.

50. Edward J. Walsh, "Navy-Army High-Speed Ship Program Moving Forward," *US Naval Institute Proceedings*, Vol. 136/12/1,294, December 2010, 88.

51. FM 3–0, Chapter 1, Page 8 of 15.

52. Col. John Warden III, US Air Force, "Special Review," *Proceedings*, Vol. 130/9/1,219, Sept. 2004, 66.

53. See Richard Whittle, *The Dream Machine: The Untold History of the Notorious V–22 Osprey* (New York: Simon and Schuster, 2010) for the history of the troubled development of the aircraft.

54. US Army, "A Statement of the Posture of the US Army 2003," General Eric K. Shinseki, Committees and Subcommittees of the US Senate and House of Representatives, First Session, 108th Congress.

55. The maintenance requirements for vehicles designed for amphibious assault; that is, to traverse water and littoral regions, increased as they performed tasks for which they were not designed.

56. Fontenot, *On Point*, 64.

57. Quoted in Joseph L. Galloway, "General Tommy Franks Discusses Conducting the War in Iraq," Knight Rider Washington Bureau, 19 June 2003. Also quoted in Jeffrey Record, *Dark Victory*, 103.

Chapter 16

1. Osama Bin Laden, et al, "Declaration of the World Islamic Front for Jihad Against the Jews and Crusaders," 23 February 1998. Quoted by Michael Knapp, "The Concept and Practice of Jihad in Islam," *Parameters*, Vol. XXXIII, No. 1, Spring 2003, 82–94. The word "jihad" literally means "to struggle" or "strive;" in Islam "to struggle in the way of God." A jihad is a "holy struggle." A "fatwa" is a formal and authoritative Islamic legal decree on civil or religious issues that is formulated and promulgated by a mufti, a qualified and respected Islamic theologian-jurist who has the authority to interpret Islamic law. It is based on the Qur'an. See Mir Zohair Husain's *Islam and the Muslim World* (Iowa: McGraw-Hill, 2006).

2. "The National Security Strategy of the United States" (Washington, DC: The White House, 9 September 2002), www.whitehouse.gov/nsc/nssall.html.

3. See *The 9/11 Commission Report: Final Report of the National Commission on Terrorist Attacks Upon the United States* (New York: W.W. Norton, 2003), 47.

4. Todd Sandler and Walter Enders, wrote: "the attacks on September 11, 2001 ... had significant costs that have been estimated to be in the range of $80 to $90 billion when subsequent economic losses in lost wages, workman's compensation, and reduced commerce are included...." See, "Economic Consequences of Terrorism in Developed and Developing Countries: An Overview," in *Terrorism, Economic Development, and Political Openness*, ed., Philip Keefer and Norman Loayza (New York: Cambridge University Press, 2008).

5. Osama Bin Laden's body was buried at sea: a brilliant idea to preclude any efforts to use his remains to continue the war against Americans.

6. See: Thucydides, *The Peloponnesian War*, ed., Robert B. Strassler (New York: Touchstone Books, 1996); and Donald Kagan, *On the Origins of War* (New York: Doubleday, 1995).

7. For a discussion on the differences between preemptive war and preventive war see Harry S. Laver, "Preemption and the Evolution of America's Strategic Defense," *Parameters*, Summer 2005, 107–120.

8. See Byman, D.L. "Al-Qaeda as an Adversary: Do We Understand Our Enemy?" *World Politics*, Vol. 56, No. 1, October 2003, 9, www.alanalexandroff/Byman.com. Osama Bin Laden, Bin Laden Speech, *Aljazeera*, www.english.alijazeera.net. P.L. Bergen, *Holy War: Inside the Secret World of Osama Bin Laden* (New York: Simon and Schuster, 2002), 303. D. Benjamin and S. Simon, *The Age of Sacred Terrorism* (New York: Random House, 2002), 490.

9. Osama Bin Laden, *Bin Laden Speech*, Aljazeera (October 30, 2004), www.english.aljazeera.net.

10. In 2011, the Egyptian people initiated a democratic revolution that spread to Yemen, Libya, Tunisia, Saudi Arabia, Syria, Jordan, Lebanon, Morocco, Algeria, and other Middle East States. These revolutionary movements were pro-democracy and became known as the "Arab Spring." In some cases these movements were brutally contained. The question is: for how long?

11. George W. Bush, "Address to a Joint Session of Congress and the American People," White House, Washington, DC, 20 September 2001, www.whitehouse.gov/news/release/2001/09/print/20010920-8.

12. In 2009 at Fort Leavenworth, Kansas, General David Petraeus noted that seventy to eighty percent of the officer corps of the Army was suffering from PTSD.

13. The bibliography on terrorism is too extensive to delineate here; however, the following works are a good place to initiate a study of this complex practice of war: M. Crenshaw, *The Logic of Terrorism: Terrorist Behavior as a Product of Strategic Choice*; Russell Howard, James Forest, and Joanne Moore, *Homeland Security and Terrorism: Reading and Interpretations* (New York: McGraw Hill, 2006); Brigitte L. Nacos, *Terrorism and Counterterrorism: Understanding Threats and Responses in the Post–9/11 World*, 2nd edition (New York: Penguin, 2007). For an extensive bibliography see: *Terrorism and Counterterrorism: An Annotated Bibliography* (Dr. James Forest, USMA Combating Terrorism Center), www.teachingterror.com/bibliography.

14. See Todd Sandler and Walter Enders, "Economic Consequences of Terrorism in Developed and Developing Countries: An Overview," *Terrorism, Economic Development, and Political Openness*, ed., Philip Keefer and Norman Loayza (New York: Cambridge University Press, 2008).

15. Michael Howard, "Mistake to Declare this a "War," *RUSI Journal*, December 2001, 1–4.

16. *National Strategy for Combating Terrorism* (Washington, DC: The White House, 2003), 2.

17. The Department of Homeland Security (DHS) was created. The Transportation Security Administration (TSA) was created. And other functions of government were reorganized.

18. Aryn Baker and Loi Kolay, "The Longest War," *Time*, 20 April 2009, 27.

19. See Paul Collier, *The Bottom Billion* (New York: Oxford University Press, 2007); and The United Nations, "The Millennium Development Goals Report," 2008.

20. For a discussion on human terrain system see "My Cousin's Enemy is My Friend: A Study of Pashtun 'Tribes' in Afghanistan," Afghanistan Research Reachback Center White Paper, TRADOC G2 Human Terrain System, United States Army, (Fort Leavenworth, Kansas, September 2009). For a discussion on provincial reconstruction teams see, FM 3–07, *Stability Operations* (Washington, DC: Headquarter Department of the Army, 6 October 2008), F–1. For a discussion on Security Force Assistance see, FM 3–07.1 *Security Force Assistance* (Washington, DC: Headquarters, Department of the Army, 1 May 2009).

21. In 2002, the Bush Administration put into practice a new National Security Strategy, the "Bush doctrine of war," which called for "preemptive war," but in essence amounted to "preventive war," which is illegal under the laws of war. The introduction stated: "And, as a matter of common sense and self-defense, America will act against such emerging threats before they are fully formed.... Finally, the US will use this moment of opportunity to extend the benefits of freedom across the globe." See "Full Text: Bush's National Security Strategy," *New York Times*, 20 Sept. 2002; and David Sanger, "Bush's Doctrine for War," *New York Times*, 18 March 2003. Sanger wrote: "President Bush thus turned America's first new national security strategy in 50 years—the doctrine of pre-emptive military action against foes—into the rationale for America's latest war."

22. *National Security Strategy of the United States of America* (Washington, DC: The White House, 17 September 2001), 9, 10, www.whitehouse.gov/nsc/nssall.html.

23. Douglas J. Feith, *War and Decision: Inside the Pentagon at the Dawn of the War on Terrorism* (New York: Harper, 2008), 507. The Patriot Act, which made it possible for governmental agencies to listen to American telephone communications with people in foreign countries, calls into question the extent to which the Bush Administration sought to preserve "our way of life." For an assessment on the moral compass of the Bush Administration, see: Jane Mayer, *The Dark Side: The Inside Story of How the War on Terror Turned into A War on American Ideals* (New York: Doubleday, 2008).

24. Lou Dubose, and Jake Bernstein, *Vice: Dick Cheney and the Hijacking of the American Presidency* (New York: Random House, 2006), 114, 115.

25. Donald Rumsfeld, *Known and Unknown: A Memoir* (New York: Sentinel, 2011), 423, 424.

26. Thomas C. Schelling, "The Diplomacy of Violence," *The Use of Force*, 3rd edition, ed., Robert J. Art and Kenneth N. Waltz (New York: University Press of America, 1983), 3.

27. Bernard Brodie, *Strategy in the Missile Age* (Princeton, New Jersey: Princeton University Press, 1959), 392.

28. Michael Walzer, *Just and Unjust Wars* (New York: Basic Books, 1977), 76, 77.

29. George W. Bush, "President Bush Outlines Iraqi Threat," www.whitehouse.gov/news/release/2002/10/print/20021007-8.... For a detailed analysis of Bush's speech see: Institute for Public Accuracy, "Detailed Analysis of October 7, 2002, Speech by Bush on Iraq," www.accuracy.org/article.php?articleId=1029.

30. Bush endeavored to make the war more palatable to those who opposed "preventive wars" by arguing that a surprise attack from Saddam Hussein was possible: "President Bush today offered a new argument for acting quickly against Iraq, saying that Saddam Hussein 'has a horrible history' of striking without warning." David Sanger, "Bush Tells Critics Hussein Could Strike at Any Time," *New York Times*, 5 October 2002, www.nytimes.com/2002/...1/middleeast/06IRAQ.html?todaysheadlines.

31. Jeffrey Record, "The Bush Doctrine and War with Iraq," *Parameters*, Vol. XXXIII, No. 1, Spring 2003, 4–21.

32. Jeffrey Record, "The Bush Doctrine and War with Iraq," *Parameters*, Vol. XXXIII, No. 1, Spring 2003, 4–21.

33. Quoted in James Kitfield, "Fractured Alliance," *National Journal*, 26 April 2003, 721; and Record, *Dark Victory*, 42.

34. Jeffrey Record, "The Bush Doctrine and War with Iraq," *Parameters*, Spring 2003, 4–21 (italics removed).

35. *Dallas Morning News*, 25 September 2001. David Sanger of the *New York Times*, on 5 October 2002, reported that: "Some allies and Iraq's Arab neighbors today stepped up their criticism of Mr. Bush's pressure to confront Mr. Hussein, and to confront him quickly. President Hosni Mubarak of Egypt, who has openly split with Mr. Bush over the strategy, warned in an interview published in Cairo that the United States has not thought through the consequence of an attack that would remove Mr. Hussein from office. He said that such a move could lead to civil war 'because of the ethnic and

religious diversity of this country.' The result, he said, could be a 'partition of Iraq.'" David Sanger, "Bush Tells Critics Hussein Could Strike at Any Time."

36. George H.W. Bush volunteered for service in the Navy on his 18th birthday. He was the youngest pilot in the Navy when he received his wings. He flew fifty-eight combat missions in World War II, and was shot down by Japanese antiaircraft gunfire. He parachuted in the Pacific and was rescued by a US submarine. He attended Yale University, where he was a member of Phi Beta Kappa, and the captain of the baseball team. His son, George W. Bush, also became a fighter pilot. He joined the Air National Guard in May 1968, the year of the Tet Offensive in Vietnam. He completed flight training and was stationed at Ellington Air Force Base in the vicinity of Houston, Texas. He did not serve in Vietnam. He later attended Yale University, again following the path of his father.

37. See Peter Singer, *The President of Good and Evil: The Ethics of George W. Bush* (New York: Dutton, 2004); Stephen Mansfield, *The Faith of George W. Bush* (New York: Penguin, 2003); and the four volume works of Bob Woodward, *Bush at War, Plan of Attack, State of Denial: Bush at War Part III*, and *The War Within* (New York: Simon and Schuster, 2008).

38. See: Stephen Hayes, *Cheney: The Untold Story of America's Most Powerful and Controversial Vice President* (New York: Harper Collins, 2007); Lou Dubose and Jake Bernstein, *Vice: Dick Cheney and the Hijacking of the American Presidency* (New York: Random House, 2006); and Jane Mayer, *The Dark Side: The Inside Story of How the War on Terror Turned into a War on American Ideals* (New York: Doubleday, 2008).

39. Bush was referring to actions taken by the Clinton Administration.

40. Woodward, *Bush at War*, 38, 39.

41. Joseph C. Wilson, "What I Didn't Find in Africa," *New York Times*, 6 July 2003, www.nytimes.com/ 2003.../06WILS.html. Wilson wrote: "Did the Bush administration manipulate intelligence about Saddam Hussein's weapons program to justify an invasion of Iraq? Based on my experience with the administration in the months leading up to the war, I have little choice but to conclude that some of the intelligence related to Iraq's nuclear weapons program was twisted to exaggerate the Iraqi threat." Also see, David Sanger, "Bush Claim on Iraq Had Flawed Origin, White House Says," *New York Times*, 8 July 2003. Sanger wrote: "The White House acknowledged for the first time today that President Bush was relying on incomplete and perhaps inaccurate information from American intelligence agencies when he declared in his State of the Union speech, that Saddam Hussein had tried to purchase uranium from Africa." And see Michael Duffy and James Carney, "A Question of Trust," *Time*, 21 July 2003, 22–26.

42. Walsh, "Bush 2.0," 22. Also see Walsh, "Another Step Closer to War," *US News and World Report*, 21 October 2002, 30.

43. Paul Burka, "The Man Who Isn't There," *Texas Monthly*, February 2004, 78–115.

44. Kenneth T. Walsh, "Bush 2.0," *US News and World Report*, 24 January 2005, 16–23.

45. See also: Raymond Bonner, "US Can't Locate Missiles Once Held in Iraq Arsenal," *New York Times*, 8 October 2003, www.nytimes.com/2003/10/08/international/ middleeast/08MI.... Douglas Jehl and David Sanger, "Powell's Case, a Year Later: Gaps in Picture of Iraq Arms," *New York Times*, 1 February 2004, www.nytimes. com/2004/02/01/international/middleeast/01W.... And, James Risen, "Ex-Inspector Says C.I.A. Missed Disarray in Iraqi Arms Program," *New York Times*, 26 January 2004, www.nytimes.com/2004/01/26/ international/middleeast/26KA....

46. Public Law 107–296—NOV. 25, 2002, 116 STAT. 2135, 107th Congress, Title I—Department of Homeland Security, www.dhs.gov/.

47. President George W. Bush, *The Department of Homeland Security*, June 2002, www.dhs.gov/.

48. The mission of the Transportation Security Authority (TSA) is to: "protect the Nation's transportation system to ensure freedom of movement for people and commerce." In the aftermath of the 9/11 attacks the Bush Administration established the TSA. Its primary purpose was to prevent future attacks, by identifying terrorists before they boarded airplanes. The TSA changed the way Americans travelled. Long lines at security checkpoints became the norm for Americans. Invasions of privacy were accepted with only occasional disruptions by angry travellers. Americans accepted inconveniences and headaches every time they travelled. And hours were literally stolen from their lives every time they travelled by Osama Bin Laden and his al-Qaeda terrorist organization. In March 2003, TSA was transferred from the Department of Transportation to the Department of Homeland Security.

49. Janet Napolitano, "Department of Homeland Security," *Defense Transportation Journal*, April 2011, 61.

50. President George W. Bush, *The Department of Homeland Security*, June 2002, 3, www.dhs.gov/

51. The Directorate for Science and Technology is the "primary research and development arm" of DHS.

52. See *The 9/11 Commission Report: Final Report of the National Commission on Terrorist Attacks Upon the United States* (New York: W.W. Norton, 2003). The jets were American and United Airlines Boeing 767s.

53. United Nations Security Council Resolution 1378 (2001), Adopted by the Security Council at its 4415th meeting, on 14 November 2001, S/RES/1378 (2001).

54. See David Isby, *Afghanistan: Graveyard of Empires: A History of the Borderlands* (New York: Pegasus Books, 2010).

55. The CIA provided the Mujahideen, resistance forces, weapons, ammunition, and other resources needed to fight the Soviets. Stinger missiles that brought down Soviet MI-24 Hind helicopter gunships were considered particularly effective. See: J. Bruce Amstutz, *Afghanistan: The First Five Years of Soviet Occupation* (Washington, DC: National Defense University, 1986), 192–197. Also see: Ali Ahmad Jalai and Lester W. Grau, *The Other Side of the Mountain: Mujahideen Tactics in the Soviet-Afghan War* (Quantico, Virginia: US Marine Corps Studies and Analiyisis Division, 1995); and Lester W. Grau, ed., *The Bear Went Over the Mountain: Soviet Combat Tactics in Afghanistan* (Fort Leavenworth, Kansas: Foreign Military Studies Office, 2005).

56. For a discussion of Central Asia after the collapse of the Soviet Union see: Charles Hawkins and Robert R. Love, eds., *The New Great Game: Chinese Views on Central Asia* (Fort Leavenworth, Kansas: Foreign Military Studies Office, 2006).

57. Louis Dupree, *Afghanistan* (NJ: Princeton University Press, 1973), xx.

58. On 23 May 2011, CNN news reported that Mullah Mohammed Omar was reported dead. The report was not confirmed, nor did it state how he died.

59. The word "Taliban" means "student." See: Ahmed Rashid, *Taliban* (New Haven: Yale University Press, 2000) for an in-depth study of this movement, organization, and government.

60. David Isby, *Afghanistan* (New York: Pegasus, 2010), 5.

61. Norman Friedman, *Terrorism, Afghanistan, and America's New Way of War* (Annapolis, Maryland: Naval Institute Press, 2003), 212.

62. Friedman, *Terrorism, Afghanistan, and America's New Way of War* (Italics added), 212.

63. Richard B. Andres, Craig Willis, Thomas E. Griffth, Jr., "Winning with Allies: The Strategic Value of the Afghan Model," *International Security*, 30.3 (2005/06), 124–160.

64. Isby, *Afghanistan*, 6.

65. Donald Rumsfeld, *Known and Unknown: A Memoir* (New York: Sentinel, 2011), 360.

66. Robin Moore, *The Hunt for Bin Laden: Task Force Dagger* (New York: Random House, 2003), 128. For a more comprehensive study of Special Forces Operations in Afghanistan in the early years of the war see: Charles H. Briscoe, Richard L. Kiper, James A. Schroder and Kalev I. Sepp, *Weapon of Choice: US Army Special Operations Forces in Afghanistan* (Fort Leavenworth, Kansas: Combat Studies Institute, October 2003).

67. Sean Naylor, *Not a Good Day to Die: Untold Story of Operation Anaconda* (New York: Berkley Caliber Books, 2005), 15, 16.

68. Dexter Filkins, "Pakistanis Say US Is Allowed in Border Area," *New York Times*, 24 April 2002.

69. Sean Naylor, *Not a Good Day to Die* (New York: Berkley Caliber Books, 2005), 22.

70. UNSCR 1386 authorized the deployment of multinational forces in Afghanistan to create the conditions for self-sustaining peace. On 11 August 2003 NATO assumed leadership of the ISAF.

71. www.isaf.nato.int/mission.html.

72. In September 2006 the government of Pakistan signed a treaty ceding control of the FATA's Northern Waziristan region to Taliban-linked tribal authorities. This region became a wilderness for terrorism. Many suspected that Osama Bin Laden was hiding there. See, Imtiaz Gul, *The Most Dangerous Place: Pakistan's Lawless Frontier* (New York: Viking, 2010).

73. Raymond Bonner, "Tribal Leaders in Pakistan Warn the US to Keep Out," *New York Times*, 25 March 2002, www.nytimes.com/2002/03/25/international/asia/25STAN.html.

74. Imtiaz Gul, *The Most Dangerous Place: Pakistan's Lawless Frontier* (New York: Viking, 2010), xii.

75. Bob Woodward, *Obama's Wars* (New York: Simon and Schuster, 2010), 3.

76. Jeffrey A Sluka, "Death From Above: UAVs and Losing Hearts and Minds," *Military Review*, May–June 2011, 70–76.

77. Quoted in Sluka, "Death From Above," *Military Review*, 73.

78. Sluka, "Death From Above," *Military Review*, 70–76.

79. Aryn Baker and Loi Kolay, "The Longest War," *Time*, 20 April 2009, 29.

80. Aryn Baker and Loi Kolay, "The Longest War," *Time*, 20 April 2009, 29. Baker and Kolay wrote: "That's one reason failure in Afghanistan is not an option. An Afghan businessman adds another. He lived through the resistance to the Soviets in the 1980s, only to see the US abandon Afghanistan when they left. Another betrayal, he thinks, could produce the same blowback that helped lead to 9/11. "If Afghanistan is sold out again," he says, "you would be basically giving 60% of the nation into the hands of the people who want to destroy the West. And I can tell you that these young Afghans are ingenious, they are creative and they know how to use computers. I can guarantee you that they will find infiltration routes into the US and Europe within four years. There won't be another chance for the West to get it right."

81. Antonio Giustozzi, "The Neo-Taliban Insurgency: From Village Islam to International Jihad," *Afghanistan Transition under Threat*, ed. Geoffrey Hayes and Mark Sedra (Canada: Wilfrid Laurier University Press, 2008). Also see: Antonio Giustozzi, *Koran, Kalashnikov and Laptop: The Neo-Taliban Insurgency in Afghanistan* (New York: Columbia University Press, 2008).

82. Craig C. Colucci, Captain, US Army, "Committing to Afghanistan: The Case for Increasing US Reconstruction and Stabilization Aid," *Military Review*, Vol. LXXXVII, No. 3, May–June 2007, 38–45.

83. Barack Obama, Plan for Ending the War in Iraq, Obama/Biden Campaign Website 2008, *The Encyclopedia of Middle East Wars: The United States in the Persian Gulf, Afghanistan, and Iraq Conflicts, Volume Five, Documents*, 1869.

84. Headquarters International Security Assistance Force, "General Stanley A. McChrystal, Commander's Initial Assessment," Kabul, Afghanistan, 30 August 2009, 2–11.

85. Headquarters International Security Assistance Force, "General Stanley A. McChrystal, Commander's Initial Assessment," Kabul, Afghanistan, 30 August 2009, 2–11.

86. President Obama, Obama Afghanistan Speech Text, 1 December 2009, www.huffingtonpost.com/2009/12/01/Obama-afghanistan-speech-text-excerpts_n_37608.

87. President Obama, Obama Afghanistan Speech Text, 1 December 2009, www.huffingtonpost.com/2009/12/01/Obama-afghanistan-speech-text-excerpts_n_37608.

88. Headquarters International Security Assistance Force, Kabul, Afghanistan, General Stanley McChrystal, ISAF Commander's Counterinsurgency Guidance.

89. Headquarters International Security Assistance Force, Kabul, Afghanistan, General Stanley McChrystal, ISAF Commander's Counterinsurgency Guidance.

90. Headquarters, US Forces-Afghanistan, International Security Assistance Force, Kabul, Afghanistan, Memorandum, Subject: Counterinsurgency Training Guidance, 10 November 2009.

91. McChrystal, Commander's Initial Assessment, 2–12.

92. Barak A. Salmoni and Paula Holmes-Eber, *Operational Culture for the Warfighter* (Quantico, VA: Marine Corps University, 2008), 36. They have in essence produced a field manual on culture.

93. Nathan Finney, Captain, US Army, *Human Terrain Team Handbook*, September 2008, 2. This effort has not escaped controversy. Anthropologists at various universities have been critical of these efforts.

94. Nathan Finney, *Human Terrain Team Handbook* 2, 3.

95. The services need to rely on the vast reservoirs of knowledge available at universities. The services need to form intimate relationships with the best universities, with the most knowledgeable faculty on a given region. The services need to release their officers and NCOs to study on campus, exposing them to a diversity of people and ideas.

96. The September 2010 edition of *The Week* featured a characterization of President Hamid Karzai with the caption "King of Corruption." The article, titled "The fight against corruption in Afghanistan," in part stated: "A frustrated President Obama summoned Defense Secretary Robert Gates and other top advisors this week to formulate a new way of dealing with Afghan President Hamid Karzai, who has stymied US-led efforts to clean up the rampant corruption in his regime. In a recent week, Karzai blocked several international investigations of graft in his government, amid continuing allegations that members of Karzai's inner circle, including two of his brothers, are involved in drug-trafficking, bribery, and smuggling cash to foreign havens like Dubai." See, *The Week*, 24 September 2010, 4.

97. General James Mattis, USMC, was nominated by Secretary of Defense Robert Gates to replace General Petraeus. Mattis took command of CENTCOM on 11 August 2010.

98. These figures vary depending on the source. The figures used are from the ISAF website; however, Admiral James G. Stavridis, Commander of United States European Command and Supreme Allied Commander of NATO, wrote: "There are currently 49 countries on the ground in Afghanistan providing roughly 150,000 troops." See: James Stavridis, "The Comprehensive Approach in Afghanistan," www.ndu.edu/press/comprehensive-approach-afghanistan.html.

99. US Senate, Committee on Armed Services, "Hearing to Receive Testimony on the Situation in Afghanistan," Washington, DC, Tuesday, 15 March 2011, 9.

100. Volney F. Warner, "Afghanistan: Context and What's Next," *Joint Force Quarterly*, Issue 56, 1st Quarter 2010, 18–24.

101. Warner, *Afghanistan*, 19.

102. John J. Malevich and Daryl C. Youngman, "The Afghan Balance of Power and the Culture of Jihad," *Military Review*, March–April 2011.

103. Bing West, "The Way Out of Afghanistan," *Military Review*, March–April 2011, 89–95. West believed the following model was the best approach: "In the 2010 battle for Marja, Golsteyn was advising a battalion of 400 Afghan soldiers. But he had only ten mature Special Forces sergeants, too small a team for sustained combat. So the Marines placed under his command a rifle platoon, engineers, and fire support specialists. Thus, a captain commanded an advisor task force rather than a team, but his force enabled the Afghan battalion to perform credibly on its own." This was a new version of the combined action platoon doctrine employed by the Marine Corps in Vietnam. Also see Bing West, *The Wrong War: Grit, Strategy, and the Way Out of Afghanistan* (New York: Random House, 2011).

104. President Obama, "Remarks by the President on the Way Forward in Afghanistan," 22 June 2011, www.whitehouse.gov/the-press-office/2011/06/22/remarks-president-way-forward-afgh.

105. See Christopher D. Kolenda, "Winning Afghanistan at the Community Level," *Joint Force Quarterly*, Issue 56, 1st Quarter 2010, 31; John Nagl, "A Better War in Afghanistan," *Joint Force Quarterly*, Issue 56, 1st Quarter 2010, 32–39; and Seth G. Jones, "Community Defense in Afghanistan," *Joint Force Quarterly*, Issue 57, 2nd Quarter 2010, 9–15. Also see: Committee on Foreign Relations United States Senate, "Evaluating US Foreign Assistance to Afghanistan, June 8, 2011" (Washington, DC: US Government Printing Office, 2011). The report noted that: "According to the World Bank, an estimated 97 percent of Afghanistan's gross domestic product (GDP) is derived from spending related to the international military and donor community presence. Afghanistan could suffer a severe economic depression when foreign troops leave in 2014 unless the proper planning begins now." In other words, when the US pulls out of Afghanistan the economy will probably collapse. The report concluded that: "However, insecurity, abject poverty, weak indigenous capacity, and widespread corruption create challenges for spending money." And, for sustaining the government.

Chapter 17

1. Ali A. Allawi, *The Occupation of Iraq: Winning the War, Losing the Peace* (New Haven: Yale University Press, 2007).

2. Seymour Hersh, "Offense and Defense," *New Yorker*, 7 April 2003, 43.

3. The air campaign against Iraq had gone on for almost a decade. Targets in Iraq were periodically attacked and destroyed.

4. Charles Duelfer, *Hide and Seek: The Search for Truth in Iraq* (New York: Public Affairs, 2009), xii.

5. Duelfer, *Hide and Seek*, xii.

6. George W. Bush, *Decision Point* (New York: Crown Publishers, 2010), 223, 224.

7. Samuel Huntington, "The Clash of Civilization," *Foreign Affairs*, 72 (Summer 1993), 22–49, 29.

8. Samuel Huntington, *The Clash of Civilization and the Remaking of World Order* (New York: Simon and Schuster, 1996), 20.

9. Bernard Lewis, *What Went Wrong? The Clash Between Islam and Modernity in the Middle East* (New York: Harper Collins, 2002), 151.

10. Lewis, *What Went Wrong?* 153.

11. Michael T. Klare, *Blood and Oil* (New York: Henry Holt, 2004), xiv–xvi.

12. Mohammed Aldouri, Iraqi Ambassador to the UN, "In Iraq's Word: White House Seems to be Caught in 'Hysteria of War'," *New York Times*, 17 October 2002.

13. Ali A. Allawi, *The Occupation of Iraq* (New Haven: Yale University Press, 2007), 459 (italics added).

14. Rashid Khalidi, *Resurrecting Empire: Western Footprints and America's Perilous Path in the Middle East* (Boston: Beacon Press, 2004), x–xii.

15. Chalmers Johnson, *The Sorrows of Empire: Militarism, Secrecy, and the End of the Republic* (New York: Henry Holt, 2004), 3, 4. Johnson wrote: "Americans like to say that the world changed as a result of the September 11, 2001, terrorist attacks on the World Trade Center and the Pentagon. It would be more accurate to say that the attacks produced a dangerous change in the thinking of some of our leaders, who began to see our republic as a genuine empire, a new Rome, the greatest colossus in history, no longer bound by international law, the concerns of allies, or any constraints on its use of military force."

16. Andrew Bacevich, *The New American Militarism* (New York: Oxford University Press, 2005), 10, 11.

17. Andrew Bacevich, *American Empire* (Cambridge, MA: Harvard University Press, 2002), Chapter 8.

18. Bacevich, *The New American Militarism*, 176.

19. John Mearsheimer and Stephen Walt, "The Israel Lobby," *London Review of Books*, Vol. 28, No. 6, 23 March 2008, http://www.lrb.co.uk/v28/n06/print/mear01_.html. Mearsheimer and Walt were brutally attacked by the supporters of Israel.

20. The US has been doing the "paying" for decades. For the millions of dollars the Jewish lobbies give to members of Congress each year, Israel has received more than $140 billion.

21. John J. Mearsheimer and Stephen M. Walt, *The Israel Lobby and US Foreign Policy* (New York: Farra, Straus and Giroux, 2007), 5.

22. See Alan Dershowitz, "Debunking the Newest—and Oldest—Jewish Conspiracy: A Reply to the Mearsheimer-Walt 'Working Paper.'" Also see Benny Morris, "The Ignorance at the Heart of an Innuendo: And Now From Some Facts," *The New Republic Online*, 8 May 2006, http://www.tnr.com/docprint.mhtml?I=20060508&s=morris050806.

23. John Keegan, *The Iraq War* (New York: Alfred A. Knopf, 2004), 96.

24. "Text of President Bush's Speech," *Christian Science Monitor*, 12 Dec. 2005, http://www.csmonitor.com/earlyed/earlyUS1212a.htm.

25. Peter J. Boyer, "The Believer: Paul Wolfowitz Defends his War," *New Yorker*, November 2004, www.newyorker.com/printables/fact/041101fa_fact. See also: Bret Stephens, "Man of the Year," *Jerusalem Post*, Rosh, Hashana, 2003.

26. Project for the New American Century, Letter to President William J. Clinton, 26 January 1998, Subject: Removal of Saddam Hussein's Regime, www.newamericancentury.org/iraqclintonletter.htm. Donald Rumsfeld also signed this document.

27. The Project for the New American Century, *Rebuilding America's Defense: Strategy, Forces and Resources For A*

New Century, September 2000, 1150 Seventeenth Street, N.W., Suite 510, Washington, DC, 20036.

28. Jamie Risen and David Johnston, "Spy Case Renews Debate Over Pro-Israel Lobby's Ties to Pentagon," *The New York Times*, 6 September 2004, www.nytimes.com/2004/09/06politics/06spy.html?pagewant.... It was further noted that this same group was also pushing the US toward a possible war with Iran: "To Israel, Iran represents a grave threat to its national security. Pushing the United States to adopt a tougher line on Tehran is one of its major foreign policy objectives, and Aipac has lobbied the Bush administration to support Israel's policies."

29. "In the President's Words: 'Free People Will Keep the Peace of the World.'" Transcript of President Bush's speech to the American Enterprise Institute, AEI, Washington, DC, 26 Feb. 2002. Quoted in Jeffrey Record, "Bounding the Global War on Terrorism," Strategic Studies Institute (Carlisle PA: US Army War College, Dec. 2003), 20.

30. George W. Bush, "In Bush's Words: 'Advance of Democratic Institutions in Iraq Is Setting an Example'," *New York Times*, 23 Sept. 2003, www.nytimes.com/2003/09/24/international/middleeast/24PT (italics added).

31. Condoleezza Rice, "Transforming the Middle East," *Washington Post*, 7 Aug. 2003.

32. An investigative report published in *Newsweek* concluded that: "they described the Office of the Vice President, with its large and assertive staff, as a kind of free-floating power base that at times brushes aside the normal policymaking machinery under National Security Advisor Condoleezza Rice. On the road to war, Cheney in effect created a parallel government that became the real power center." It was further noted that: "Cheney often teams up with Defense Secretary Donald Rumsfeld to roll over National Security Adviser Rice and Secretary of State Colin Powell." See "How Dick Cheney Sold the War" *Newsweek*, 17 Nov. 2003, 34–40. Also see: "Dick Cheney: The Man Behind the Curtain," *US News and World Report*, 13 Oct. 2003, 26–32.

33. Project for a New American Century website, www.newamericancentury.org/iraq-082602.htm. p5.

34. *New York Times*, "Full Text: In Cheney's Words," www.nytimes.com/2002/international/middleeast/26WEB-CHENEY.htm.

35. The debate was broadcast on National Public Radio. See *New York Times*, 6 Nov. 2002, for "Text of the US Resolution of Iraq." Macho male egos may have played some part in the debate. Intellectually, the female senators and representatives tended to give the strongest arguments against war.

36. Every nation on Earth produces "Hitlers." The major differences between these individuals and Hitler's Germany are: one, they do not normally become heads of state; and two, that if they do become head of state, it is a state incapable of generating tremendous combat power. If the US goes to war to remove all the so-called "Hitlers" on Earth, the armed forces are going to be extremely busy.

37. "Excerpts from the Debate in the Senate on Using Force Against Iraq," *New York Times*, 10 September 2002, www.nytimes.com/2002/10/09/politics/09STEX.html. "Excerpts from House Debate on the Use of Military Force Against Iraq," *New York Times*, 10 September 2002, www.nytimes.com/2002/10/09/politics/09HTEX.htm.

38. See Richard W. Stevenson with Julia Preston, "Bush Meets Blair Amid Signs of Split on U.N. War Role," *New York Times*, 31 January 2003, www.nytimes.com/2003/.../international/middleeast/01PREX.html. They wrote: "American officials have said the resolution adopted unanimously by the Security Council in November, No. 1441, not only calls for Iraq to comply immediately with demands that it disarm but also sanctions the use of force against Mr. Hussein's government by stating the Iraq 'will face serious consequences' if it does not give up its weapons of mass destruction. 'Should the United Nations pass a second resolution, it would be welcomed if it is yet another signal that we're intent on disarming Saddam Hussein,' Mr. Bush said as a joint news conference with the prime minister. 'But 1441 gives us the authority to move without any second resolution, and Saddam Hussein must understand that if he does not disarm, for the sake of peace, we along with others will go disarm Saddam Hussein.' "

39. David E. Sanger, "Iraq Makes U.N. Seem 'Foolish,' Bush Asserts," *New York Times*, 29 October 2002. See "Text: Bush's Speech on Iraq" *New York Times*, 18 Mar. 2003.

40. See George W. Bush, *Decision Point* (New York: Crown Publishers, 2010), 91. Also see: Tim Russert, *Meet the Press*, MSNBC Transcript for 16 March 2003, www.msnbc.com/news/886068.asp?cpl. On *Meet the Press* on 16 Mar. 2003, when asked by Tim Russert: "What could Saddam Hussein do to stop war?" Cheney replied: "Well, the difficulty here is it's—he's clearly rejected, up till now, all efforts, time after time. And we have had 12 years and some 17 resolutions now. Each step along the way he had the opportunity to do what he was called upon to do by the U.N. Security Council. Each time he has rejected it. I'm not sure now, no matter what he said, that anyone would believe him. We have ... been down this effort now for six months in the U.N. with the enactment of 1441. We asked for a declaration of all his WMDs come clean. He refused to do that. He's again, continued to do everything he could to thwart the inspectors. I'm hard-put to specify what it is he could do with credibility at this stage that would alter the outcome."

41. Seymour Hersh, *Chain of Command* (New York: Harper Collins, 2004), 188.

42. In a fifty-page intelligence estimate Tony Blair, Britain's Prime Minister, argued that Iraq could launch chemical and biological weapons within "45 minutes," that "intelligence shows that the Iraqi program is almost certainly seeking an indigenous ability to enrich uranium to the level needed for a nuclear weapon," and that Iraq was trying to acquire significant quantities of uranium from unspecified countries in Africa. See: Warren Hoge, "Blair Says Iraqis Could Launch Chemical Warheads in Minutes," *New York Times* 24 Sept. 2002, www.nytimes.com/2002/09/25/international/middleeast/25BRIT.html. Also see: Patrick Tyler, "Britain's Case: Iraqi Program to Amass Arms 'Up and Running,'" *New York Times*, 24 Sept. 2002, www.nytimes.com/2002/...1/middleeast/25ASSE.html.

43. Powell's speech before the UN was shown on national television.

44. Kevin Whitelaw, "Getting It Dead Wrong," *US News and World Report*, 11 April 2005, 32–33.

45. George Tenet, *At the Center of the Storm: My Years at the CIA* (New York: Harper Collins, 2007), 305.

46. Tenet, *At the Center of the Storm*, 302.

47. Tenet, *At the Center of the Storm*, 341.

48. Judith Miller and Julia Preston, "Blix Says He Saw Nothing to Prompt a War," *New York Times*, 30 Jan. 2003, www.nytimes.com/2003/01/31/international/middleeast/31BLIX.html. Also see, Hans Blix, "Report to the Security Council by the Chief U.N. Weapons Inspectors," *New York Times*, 15 Feb. 2003, www.nytimes.com/2003...5BTEX.htlm. Before the war started there were challenges to the US intelligence estimates. Hans Blix, the UN Chief inspector for Iraq's WMD, challenged Powell's assessment of the findings of the inspectors. "Mr. Blix took issue with what he said were Secretary of State Colin L. Powell's claims that the inspectors had found that Iraqi officials were hiding and moving illicit materials within and outside of Iraq to prevent their discovery. He said that the inspectors had reported no such incidents." The International Atomic Energy Agency (IAEA) demonstrated that documents showing Iraq had tried to purchase uranium from overseas were forged. And it disputed CIA allegations that aluminum tubes were for a nuclear program. The State Department intelligence sources also challenged the CIA's assessments.

49. Tenet, *At the Center of the Storm*, 332, 333.

50. At this point in time with the fighting still in progress, no definitive history of the war is possible. Hence, the objective here is to outline only what is known about the conventional campaign, and to consider some of the salient factors in the insurgency war. A number of works have appeared on the war. See: Gregory Fontenot, E.J. Degen, and David Tohn, *On Point: The US Army in Operation Iraqi Freedom* (Washington, DC: Office of the Chief of Staff, 2004); Williamson Murray and Robert H. Scales, Jr., *The Iraq War: A Military History* (Cambridge, Massachusetts: The Belknap Press, 2003); John Keegan, *The Iraq War* (New York: Alfred A. Knopf, 2004); Jeffrey Record, *Dark Victory: America's Second War Against Iraq* (Annapolis, Maryland: Naval Institute Press, 2004). Michael Gordon and Bernard Trainor, *Cobra II: The Inside Story of the Invasion and Occupation of Iraq* (New York: Pantheon Books, 2006). The Gordon and Trainor book is the most comprehensive study available to date. Also see, US Army, Third Infantry Division (Mechanized) After Action Report, Operation IRAQI FREEDOM, available online.

51. Vego, Milan, "Learning from Victroy," *Proceedings*, Vol. 129/8/1,206, August 2003, 32–36.

52. "Chasing the Ghosts," *Time*, 26 September 2005, 33–40.

53. Harlan Ullman and James Wade, *Shock and Awe: Achieving Rapid Dominance* (Washington, DC: Center for Advanced Concepts and Technology, 1996), xv.

54. Mark Thompson, "Opening With a Bang," *Time*, 17 March 2003, 32–39.

55. Battle space expands the concept of battlefield to include air and sea, and even space where satellite technologies greatly influence the American conduct of war.

56. Thom Shanker and Eric Schmitt, "Rumsfeld Orders War Plan Redone for Faster Action," *New York Times*, 12 October 2002, www.nytimes.com/2002/10/13/international/middleeast/13MILI.html.

57. Mark Thompson and Michael Duffy, "Pentagon Warlord," *Time*, January 2003, 22–29.

58. Seymour Hersh, "Offense and Defense," *New Yorker*, 7 April 2003, 43.

59. James Conway, Lt. Gen. USMC, "'We've Always Done Windows,'" *Proceedings*, Vol. 129/11/1, 32–34. Conway, while arguing that only Franks can answer the question of Rumsfeld's micromanagement approach, gave an indication that supported Hersh's assessment. He stated: "We spent probably about six weeks, over three different conferences, preparing the time-phased force deployment data. When it came time to deploy, it actually was done by requests for forces. And each of those was scrutinized, not necessarily by Secretary of Defense Rumsfeld, but by his office. They were lumped and approved in 'groupments' of forces for deployment. Not the way we would typically do things; perhaps not the way we would advocate doing them in the future."

60. Richard Stewart, *American Military History*, Volume II, *The US Army in the Global Era, 1917–2003.* (Washington, DC: US Army Center of Military History, 2005), 496.

61. Shanker, "Rumsfeld Orders War Plans Redone for Faster Action."

62. Franks, *American Soldier*, 444, 465.

63. Franks, *American Soldier*, 439, 440.

64. See Adrian Lewis, *Omaha Beach: A Flawed Victory* (UNC Press, 2001).

65. Quoted in Suzann Chapman, "The 'War' Before the War," *Air Force*, 87, February 2004, 52–57. Operation Southern Watch, commenced on 26 August 1992. It protected the Shia from Saddam's repression. Operation Northern Watch started on 1 January 1997. It protected the Kurds. These operations were training grounds for Air Force and Navy pilots, and familiarized commanders with the battle space.

66. Cherilyn Walley and Michael Mullins, "Reaching Out: Psychological Operations in Operation IRAQI FREEDOM," *Veritas*, Journal of Army Special Operations History, PB 31-05-1, Winter 2005, 36–41.

67. Matthew French, "DOD Aims PSY-Ops at Iraqi Officers," *Federal Computer Week*, 24 Mach 2003.

68. OIF Information Operation Lesson Learned—First Look http://www.cadre.maxwell.af.mil/warfarestudies/iwac/Downloads/W250%20Reading.doc.

69. Fontenot, *On Point*, 99.

70. Franks, *American Soldier*, 486.

71. Mark Bowden, *Black Hawk Down* (New York: Penguin Books, 1999).

72. For a complete Order of Battle for Combined Forces Land Component Command see Fontenot, *On Point*, 441. Also see, US Army, Third Infantry Division (Mechanized) After Action Report, OIF, 2003.

73. James Conway, Gen. USMC, "'We've Always Done Windows,'" *Proceedings*, Vol. 129/11/1, 209, Nov. 2003, 32–34.

74. Robert Dudney, "The Gulf War II Air Campaign by the Numbers," *Air Force*, 86, July 2003, 36–41.

75. Scott Turner, "US Navy in Review," *Proceedings*, Vol. 130/5/1,215, May 2004, 80–82.

76. Michael Malone, Vice Admiral; James M. Zortman, Rear Admiral; and Samuel J. Paparo, Commander US Navy, "Naval Aviation Raises the Readiness Bar," *Proceedings*, Vol. 130/2/1,212, 39–41.

77. Romesh Ratnesar, "Awestruck," *Time*, Special Edition, 21 March 2003, 38–53. Under international law it is illegal to target the leader of a country for assassination.

78. Adam Herbert, "The Baghdad Strikes," *Air Force*, 86, July 2003, 46–50.

79. Robert S. Dudney, "Space Power in the Gulf," *Air Force*, 86, June 2003, 2.

80. *Time*, 21 March 2003, 52, 53. Retired Army General Robert Scales was quoted in the article.

81. Charles Kirkpatrick, "Joint Fires as They Were Meant to be: V Corps and the 4th Air Support Operations Group During OIF," Land Warfare Papers (Arlington, VA: The Institute of Land Warfare, Oct. 2004).

82. Rebecca Grant, "Hand in Glove," *Air Force Magazine*, 86, July 2003, 30–35.

83. Fontenot, *On Point*, Introduction.

84. Rebecca Grant, "Air Warfare in Transition," *Air Force Magazine* 87, December 2004, 46–50.

85. Fontenot, et al, *On Point*, 102.

86. For a detailed assessment of the Army's view of the campaign see *On Point*, by Gregory Fontenot, et al.

87. US Army Third ID (Mechanized) After Action Report: OIF, 2–5.

88. Bing F.J. West, "Maneuver Warfare: It Worked in Iraq," *Proceedings*, Vol. 130/2/1,212, 36–38.

89. Franks, *American Soldier*, 497, 498.

90. Richard Newman, "Ambush at Najaf," *Air Force* 86, Oct. 2003, 60–63.

91. David Rude and Daniel Williams, "The 'Warfighting Mindset' and the War in Iraq," *Army*, 53, July 2003, 35–38. The Apache, AH–64D Longbow, carries 16 Hellfire missiles each capable of knocking out a tank, is able to fly under the enemy's radar, and is capable of tracking and processing over a hundred targets at once. These targets could be relayed to other aircraft and weapons systems.

92. Thomas Collins, Lt. Colonel, US Army, "173rd Airborne Brigade in Iraq," *Army*, 53, 43–46.

93. Michael Gordon, "The Test for Rumsfeld: Will Strategy Work?" *New York Times*, 1 April 2003.

94. Franks, *American Soldier*, 511.

95. Franks, *American Soldier*, 503.

96. Grant, "Hand in Glove," *Air Force*, 34.

97. Ironically the impressive television pictures that had been so influential in the first Persian Gulf War were not available for the more spectacular and decisive campaign of the second Gulf War. This was because in OIF the Air Force employed more precision weapons that were guided by global positioning satellites. Laser-directed precision weapons required visual target identification. They made possible the impressive television pictures. The Air Force destroyed the Iraqi armor division with systems that required no visual identification, systems that cut through the sand storm as if it wasn't there.

98. West and Smith, *The March Up*.

99. F.J. Bing West, "Maneuver Warfare: It Worked in Iraq," *Proceedings*, Vol. 130/2/1,212, 36–38.

100. Franks, *American Soldier*, 517.

101. David Zucchino, *Thunder Run: The Armored Strike to Capture Baghdad* (New York: Grove, 2004), 117, 118.

102. John Keegan, *The Iraq War* (New York: Alfred A. Knopf, 2004), 186, 193.

103. John Keegan, "Saddam's Utter Collapse Shows This Has Not Been a Real War," *London Daily Telegraph*, 8 April 2003.

104. Operation Just Cause, the invasion of Panama in December 1989, was to remove General Noriega. The war in Iraq in 2003 was primarily to change the regime.

Chapter 18

1. Charles Duelfer, *Hide and Seek: The Search for Truth in Iraq* (New York: Public Affairs, 2009), xii.

2. For a critical review of the Army see: Nigel Aylwin-Foster, General British Army, "Changing the army for counterinsurgency operations," *Military Review*, November–December 2005, http://findarticles.com/p/articles/mi_ mOPBZ/is_6_85/ai_n27865529/pg_14/?tag=content; coll. For a rebuttal see: Kevin C.M. Benson, "OIF Phase IV: A Planner's Reply to Brigadier Aylwin-Foster," *Military Review*, March–April 2006, 61–68.

3. L. Paul Bremer III, Ambassador, *My Year in Iraq* (New York: Simon and Schuster, 2006), 106.

4. Bremer, *My Year in Iraq*, 10. Rajiv Chandrasekaran, in his book, *Imperial Life in the Emerald City*, noted that Bremer believed that "we've got as many soldiers as we need here right now." The Army and Marine Corps *Counterinsurgency Field Manual* FM 3–24, accepted this figure, noting that, "such calculations remain very dependent upon the situation." See FM 3–24, paragraph 1–67. See also: Donald Rumsfeld, *Known and Unknown: A Memoir* (New York: Sentinel, 2011), 661–663.

5. See Tony Zinni, General USMC, *The Battle for Peace: A Frontline Vision of America's Power and Purpose* (New York: Palgrave MacMillan, 2006); and David S. Cloud and Eric Schmitt, "More Retired Generals Call for Rumsfeld's Resignation," *New York Times*, 14 April 2006, front page story.

6. Tony Zinni, General USMC, "Understanding What Victory Is," *Proceedings*, Vol. 129/10/1,208, Oct. 2003, 32, 33.

7. Mark Mazzetti, Julian Barnes, and Edward Pound, "Inside the Iraq Prison Scandal," *US News and World Report*, 24 May 2004, 18–30. See Christopher Graveline and Michael Clemens, *The Secrets of Abu Ghraib Revealed: American Soldiers on Trial* (Washington, DC: Potomac Books, 2010).

8. Secretary of Defense, "Public Affairs Guidance (PAG) on Embedding Media During Possible Future Operations/Department in the US Central Command Area of Responsibility (AOR)," 10 Feb. 2003.

9. Army FM 3–61.1 Public Affairs Operations (Fort Mead, MD: Army Public Affairs Center), Chapter 1.

10. Gordon Gaskill, "Bloody Beach," *American Magazine*, September 1944.

11. Dan McSweeney, Captain USMC, "Clowns to the left of me ...," *Proceedings*, Vol. 129/11/1,209, Nov. 2003, 46–48. McSweeney wrote: "I would be surprised if our reporters did not consider the embedment program a success. Being stuck in the middle with these reporters showed most of us that while there are worlds of difference between the military and the media, both groups share many traits."

12. Conway, "We've Always Done Windows," 32–34.

13. Cherilyn A. Walley, "SOF and the Media During Operation Iraqi Freedom," *Veritas*, Journal of Army Special Operations History, PB 31–15–1, Winter 2005, 32–36.

14. Conway, "We've Always Done Windows," *Proceedings*, Nov. 2003, 32–34. Conway credited Marine Corps doctrine with creating the conditions for peace.

15. Donald Rumsfeld, Secretary of Defense, televised Pentagon News Briefing, 11 April 2003.

16. Lt. Col. David Hubner, 1st Battalion, 77th Armor, "Commanders in Iraq: Some Lessons Learned," ed., Dennis Steel, *Army 55*, June 2005, 24–30.

17. The Committee to Protect Journalists noted that from 1955 to 1975, sixty-six journalists had been killed in Vietnam, compared to sixty-one in Iraq from March 2003 to January 2006.

18. McSweeney, "Clowns to the left of me ...," 47.

19. See Hans Blix, *Disarming Iraq* (New York: Pantheon Books, 2004). Blix headed the UN weapons inspection team. In his book he traces the move to war, showing that the Bush Administration wanted war. Weapons of mass destruction were a ruse. He also shows that the American media did little to challenge the supposed reasons for war.

20. Dana Milbank and Claudia Deane, "Hussein Link to 9/11 Lingers in Many Minds," *Washington Post* (6 Sep. 2003), A–1.

21. See the documentary film, *OUTFOXED: Rupert Murdoch's War on Journalism*, produced and directed by Robert Greenwald. Murdoch's media networks gave him access to 280 million Americans. In 1996 Roger Ailes, the former media strategist for Nixon, Reagan, and Bush, Sr., presidential campaigns, became FOX News CEO and Chairman. The film makes the argument that viewers of FOX News are the most misinformed viewers.

22. Philip Seib, "The News Media and the 'Clash of Civilizations,'" *Parameters*, vol. XXXIV, No. 4, Winter 2004–05, 71–85.

23. Howard Kurtz, "For Media After Iraq, A Case of Shell Shock," *Washington Post*, 28 April 2003, A1.

24. The number of works on what went wrong is extensive and growing. See: Thomas E. Ricks, *Fiasco: The American Military Adventure in Iraq* (New York: Penguin Press, 2006); and his sequel, *The Gamble: General David Petraeus and the American Military Adventure in Iraq, 2006–2008* (New York: Penguin Books, 2009). Also see: Rajiv Chandrasekaran, *Imperial Life in the Emerald City: Inside the Green Zone* (New York: Vintage Books, 2006); Ali A. Allawi, *The Occupation of Iraq: Winning the War Losing the Peace* (New Haven: Yale University Press, 2007); Ricardo Sanchez, Lieutenant General US Army, *Wiser in Battle: A Soldier's Story* (New York: Harper Collins, 2008); and L. Paul Bremer III, *My Year in Iraq:*

The Struggle to Build a Future of Hope (New York: Simon and Schuster, 2006). For a perspective from the White House see: Bob Woodward, *State of Denial: Bush at War Part III* (New York: Simon and Schuster, 2006) and *The War Within: A Secret White House History 2006–2008* (New York: Simon and Schuster, 2008). For the Army's perspective see: Donald P. Wright and Timothy Reese, *On Point II: The United States Army in Operation IRAQI FREEDOM May 2003–January 2005* (Fort Leavenworth, Kansas: Combat Studies Institute Press, June 2008).

25. Jay M. Garner, "Iraq Revisited," *Turning Victory Into Success: Military Operations After the Campaign*, ed. Brian M. De Toy (Fort Leavenworth, Kansas: Combat Studies Institute Press, September 2004), 253.

26. L. Paul Bremer III, *My Year in Iraq* (New York: Simon and Schuster, 2006), 112.

27. Bush, *Decision Points*, 258.

28. Ricardo S. Sanchez, Lieutenant General US Army, *Wiser in Battle: A Soldier's Story* (New York: Harper Collins, 2008), 197.

29. Rumsfeld, *Known and Unknown*, 500.

30. Ricardo S. Sanchez, Lieutenant General US Army, *Wiser in Battle: A Soldier's Story* (New York: Harper Collins, 2008), 188.

31. Sanchez, *Wiser in Battle*, 180, 181.

32. See Christopher Graveline and Michael Clemens, *The Secrets of Abu Ghraib Revealed: American Soldiers on Trial* (Washington, DC: Potomac Books, 2010).

33. Jay M. Garner, "Iraq Revisited," *Turning Victory Into Success*, ed. Brian M. De Toy (Fort Leavenworth, Kansas: Combat Studies Institute Press, September 2004), 266.

34. Donald Rumsfeld, *Known and Unknown: A Memoir* (New York: Sentinel, 2011), 717.

35. See: Peter Slevin and Dana Priest, "Wolfowitz Concedes Iraq Errors," *Washington Post*, Thursday, 24 July 2003, A01, www.washingtonpost.com/ac2/wp-dyn/A37468-2003jul23?Ia..

36. Kevin C.M. Benson, "OIF Phase IV," *Military Review*, November December 2005, 61–68.

37. Peter Slevin and Dana Priest, "Wolfowitz Concedes Iraq Errors," *Washington Post*, Thursday, 24 July 2003, A01, www.washingtonpost.com/ac2/wp-dyn/A37468-2003jul23?Ia.. They wrote: "But after Bush granted authority over reconstruction to the Pentagon, the Defense Department all but ignored State and its working group."

38. See Douglas J. Feith, *War and Reconstruction: Inside the Pentagon at the Dawn of the War on Terrorism* (New York: Harper, 2008).

39. Rajiv Chandrasekaran, *Imperial Life in the Emerald City* (New York: Vintage Books, 2006), 33.

40. Feith, *War and Reconstruction*, 349. On 20 January 2003 President Bush signed the charter creating the ORHA.

41. For a comprehensive study of the ORHA see, Gordon W. Rudd, *Reconstructing Iraq: Regime Change, Jay Garner, and the ORHA Story* (Lawrence: University of Kansas Press, 2011).

42. Feith, *War and Reconstruction*, 349.

43. Garner, "Iraq Revisited," 262.

44. See Rumsfeld's assessment in his book *Known and Unknown*, 503.

45. Garner, "Iraq Revisited," 260, 261.

46. Rumsfeld, *Known and Unknown*, 502. Of Garner, Rumsfeld wrote: "he had done his job well and had formed a good working relationship with the emerging Iraqi leaders . . ."

47. L. Paul Bremer III, *My Year in Iraq: The Struggle to Build a Future of Hope* (New York: Simon and Schuster, 2005.

48. Rumsfeld, *Known and Unknown*, 506.

49. Rumsfeld, *Known and Unknown*, 505.

50. Bremer, *My Year in Iraq*, 4.

51. Sanchez, *Wiser in Battle*, 185.

52. Sanchez, *Wiser in Battle*.

53. James Stephenson, *Losing the Golden Hour: An Insider's View of Iraq's Reconstruction* (Washington, DC: Potomac Books, 2007), 20, 21. Stephenson delineated what was needed in Iraq: "Through trial, error, failure, and success, all practitioners—Western government, the United Nations, the World Bank, bilateral aid agencies, nongovernmental organizations, and contractors—had learned there are three critical elements of stabilization and reconstruction: security, democracy, and economic growth. All are relative terms, depending on conditions in a particular country, and all are moving targets that are changing and require constant adjustment."

54. Matt Kelley, "Pentagon plans for Iraqi army dissolved in postwar chaos," Boston News.Com www.boston.com/dailynews/294/wash/Pentagon_plans_for_Iraq.

55. Garner, "Iraq Revisited," 265.

56. Garner, "Iraq Revisited," 265, 266.

57. Muqtada al-Sadr was a powerful Shia religious leader who directed the Sadriyun, which included the Mahdi Army militia.

58. See Richard S. Lowry, *New Dawn: The Battles for Fallujah* (New York: Savas Beatie, 2010),

59. Wright and Reese, On Point II, 315. Mine resistant ambush protected (MRAP) vehicles were part of the American response to IEDs. To counter the IED threat the Pentagon developed a family of mine resistant ambush protected, MRAP vehicles. These vehicles were effective, but took time produce and deploy.

60. Donald P. Wright and Timothy R. Reese, *On Point II: Transition to the New Campaign: The US Army in Operation Iraqi Freedom, May 2003–January 2005* (Fort Leavenworth, Kansas: Combat Studies Institute, June 2008), 176.

61. Wright and Reese, *On Point II*, 177.

62. In an influential work, *Breaking the Phalanx: A New Design for Landpower in the 21st Century* (Westport, Connecticut: Praeger, 1997), part of the RMA debate, Douglas A. Macgregor argued for the reorganization of

the Army into "mobile combat groups." The basic combat unit was to shift from the division to the brigade, which was self-sustaining, and that could be augmented with additional forces. Part of the lesson was to get forces to the battlefield faster, and to take advantage of advanced technologies.

63. Hearing of the House Armed Service Committee, Subject: Operation Iraqi Freedom Force Rotation Plan, Washington, DC: 2118 Rayburn House Office Building, 28 January 2004. 10, 11.

64. Hearing of the House Armed Service Committee, Subject: Operation Iraqi Freedom Force Rotation Plan, Washington, DC: 2118 Rayburn House Office Building, 28 January 2004. 10, 11.

65. National Security Council, *National Strategy for Victory in Iraq*, November 2005.

66. In 2011 revolutionary movements in Egypt, Yemen, Libya, and other Middle East countries caused many to believe the Bush Administration had in fact laid the groundwork for fundamental change throughout the region.

67. Text of President Bush's Speech, Source Associated Press and *The Christian Science Monitor*, 12 December 2005, www.csmonitor.com/earlyed/earlyUS1212a.html.

68. The population of Iraq was sixty percent Shiite Arab, twenty percent Sunni Arab, seventeen percent Sunni Kurd, and three percent others.

69. During the Iraq-Iran War the US helped arm Iraq. The US has propped up the royal families in Saudi Arabia and Kuwait. The US unofficially, and along with other Western nations, assisted Israel with its nuclear development program, giving Arab nations in the region a legitimate reason to seek similar technology. The US arms Israel. Its policies in the region have not been balanced, making it totally impossible for the US to act as a neutral party in regional discussions.

70. James A. Baker, III, and Lee H. Hamilton, et al., *The Iraq Study Group Report: The Way Forward—A New Approach* (New York: Vintage Books, 2006).

71. Baker, *The Iraqi Study Group Report*, 32.

72. Baker, *The Iraq Study Group Report*, ix, x.

73. Baker, *The Iraq Study Group Report*, 76.

74. Baker, *The Iraq Study Group Report*, xvi (italic added).

75. Rumsfeld, *Known and Unknown*, 715.

76. President George W. Bush, *State of the Union Address*, 23 January 2007.

77. President George W. Bush, *State of the Union Address*, 23 January 2007.

78. Linda Robinson, "Seeking an Iraq Endgame," *US News and World Report*, September 1–8 2008, 38. Also see: Linda Robinson, *Tell Me How This Ends: General David Petraeus and the Search for a Way Out of Iraq* (New York: Public Affairs, 2008).

79. The Army's new manuals have not escaped controversy, particularly FM 3–24 Counterinsurgency. Edward Luttwak, a noted military historian, has been critical of the manual. In 2007 in *Harper's* he argued that manual constituted military "malpractice." US Army FM 3–0 Operations (Washington, DC: Headquarters Department of the Army, 27 February 2008), D–1. FM 3–0 Operations defined doctrine as: "a body of thought of how Army forces intend to operate as an integral part of a joint force. Doctrine focuses on how to think—not what to think. It establishes the following: How the Army views the nature of operations, Fundamentals by which Army forces conduct operations, [and] Methods by which commanders exercise command and control. Doctrine is a guide to action, not a set of fixed rules."

80. The writers included Eliot Cohen, John A. Nagl, Jan Horvath, David Kilcullen, and other noted scholars.

81. Sarah Sewall, "Introduction to the University of Chicago Press Edition: A Radical Field Manual," *The US Army and Marine Corps Counterinsurgency Field Manual* (Chicago, Illinois: The University of Chicago Press, 2007, xxxv.

82. The bibliography on counterinsurgency warfare is extensive; hence, only a few works are identified. See the "Annotated Bibliography" in FM 3–24 for a more complete list of works. See: Andrew Birtle, *US Army Counterinsurgency and Contingency Operations Doctrine 1860–1941* (Washington, DC: US Army Center of Military History, 2003) and *US Army Counterinsurgency and Contingency Operations Doctrine 1942–1976* (Washington, DC: US Army Center of Military History, 2006); Bernard B. Fall, *Viet-Nam Witness 1953–66* (New York: Frederick A. Praeger, 1966); David Galula, *Counterinsurgency Warfare: Theory and Practice* (Westport, Connecticut: Praeger Security International, 2006); Ernesto (Che) Guevara, *Guerrilla Warfare* (New York: Monthly Review Press, 1961); David Kilcullen, *Counterinsurgency* (New York: Oxford University Press, 2010); Mao Tse Tung, *Selected Military Writings* (Peking: Foreign Language Press, 1967); John Nagl, *Learning to Eat Soup with a Knife: Counterinsurgency Lessons from Malaya and Vietnam* (Chicago: University of Chicago Press, 2002; T.E. Lawrence, *Seven Pillars of Wisdom: A Triumph* (New York: Anchor, 1991); Douglas Pike, *PAVN: People's Army of Vietnam* (New York: Da Capo Press, 1986) and *Viet Cong* (Cambridge, Massachusetts: MIT Press, 1966); and Robert Taber, *War of the Flea: The Classic Study of Guerrilla Warfare* (Washington, DC: Potomac Books, 2002).

83. FM 3–24 Counterinsurgency, paragraph 1–1.

84. FM 3–24 Counterinsurgency, paragraph 1–2.

85. David H. Petraeus, Lieutenant General US Army, "Learning Counterinsurgency: Observation from Soldiering in Iraq," *Military Review, Special Edition, Counterinsurgency Reader* (Fort Leavenworth, Kansas: Combined Arms Center, October 2006), 45–55.

86. Eliot Cohen, Conrad Crane, Jan Horvath, and John Nagl, "Principles, Imperatives, and Paradoxes of Counterinsurgency," *Military Review*, March–April 2006, 49–53.

87. Gian P. Gentile, "Time for the Deconstruction of Field Manual 3–24," *JFQ*, issue 58, 3rd quarter 2010, 116–117. Also see: Gian Gentile, "A Strategy of Tactics: Population-centric COIN and the Army," *Parameters*, Autumn 2009, 5–16; and "The Imperative for an American General Purpose Army That Can Fight," *Orbis*, Summer 2009, 457–470.

88. David Petraeus, General US Army, "The Central Front," *The Weekly Standard*, 7 May 2007, Vol. 12, Iss. 32; 7 (Summary of Petraeus's Report).

89. David Petraeus, General US Army, "The Central Front," *The Weekly Standard*, 7 May 2007, Vol. 12, Iss. 32; 7 (Summary of Petraeus's Report).

90. David Petraeus, General US Army, "Iraq: Progress in the Face of Challenge," *Army*, Oct. 2007, Vol. 57, Iss. 10, 115–6.

91. Neil Smith, Major US Army, and Colonel Sean MacFarland, Colonel US Army, "Anbar Awakening: The Tipping Point," *Military Review, Special Edition, Counterinsurgency Reader II* (Fort Leavenworth, Kansas: Combined Arm Center, August 2008), 65–76.

92. From an interview with General McFarland at Fort Leavenworth on 8 March 2011.

93. Smith and McFarland, "Anbar Awakening," 67.

94. Smith and McFarland, "Anbar Awakening," 75.

95. David Petraeus, General, US Army, "Iraq: Progress In the Face of Challenge," *Army*, Oct. 2007, Vol. 57, Iss. 10, 115–6. Petraeus added: "Support gained through diplomacy with Iraq's neighbors and the international community helps reinforce and complement progress in the security, economic, and political arenas."

96. David Petraeus, General, US Army, "Iraq: Progress in the Face of Challenge," *Army*, Oct. 2007, Vol. 57, Iss. 10, 115–6.

97. General David H. Petraeus, *Report to Congress on the Situation in Iraq*, 10–11 September 2007.

98. Gregg Zoroya, "Soldiers' divorce rates up sharply: Separation, stress erode marriages," *USA Today*, 8 June 2005, front page.

99. Quoted by David Crary in "Army divorce increase with deployments," *Denton Record*, Thursday, 30 June 2005, 3A.

100. Jim Tice, "Keeping soldiers in service," *Army Times*, 13 June 2005, 8, 9.

101. See Peter Warren Singer, *Corporate Warriors: The Rise of Privatized Military Industry* (Ithaca: Cornell University Press, 2003), 230–242. Halliburton was particularly controversial because Vice President Dick Cheney formerly led the firm, which received $6 billion dollars in no-bid contracts. Charges of abuse of power, a lack of oversight, and price gouging have been made. Also see: Deborah D. Avant, *The Market for Force: The Consequence of Privatizing Security* (New York: Cambridge University Press, 2005).

102. Allison Stranger, *One Nation Under Contract: The Outsourcing of American Power and the Future of Foreign Policy* (New Haven: Yale University Press, 2009), 84.

103. Paul R. Verkuil, *Outsourcing Sovereignty: Why Privatization of Government Functions Threatens Democracy and What We Can Do About It* (New York: Cambridge University Press, 2007).

104. Patrick Radden Keefe, *Defense and Arms, Iraq: America's Private Armies*, 2004.

105. Peter Singer, *Corporate Warriors: the Rise of the Privatized Military Industry* (Ithaca: Cornell University Press, 2003), 9.

106. Peter Singer, "Warriors for Hire in Iraq," *Defense*, Brookings Institution (15 April 2004). Singer noted the American taxpayer was the biggest employer of PMFs, a $100 billion dollar industry, and that the US government had signed over 3,000 contracts in the last decade. These PMFs employ lobbyists, and expend tens of millions of dollars annually to buy influence in Washington.

107. Bernard Weinraub with Thom Shanker, "Rumsfeld's Design for War Criticized on the Battlefield," *New York Times*, 1 April 2003. Weinraub noted, "Lt. Gen. William S. Wallace, the V Corps Commander, who said the military faced the likelihood of a longer war than many strategists had anticipated."

108. Seymour M. Hersh, "Annals of National Security, Offense and Defense: The battle between Donald Rumsfeld and the Pentagon," *The New Yorker*, 7 April 2003, 43–45. Also see, Seymour M. Hersh, *Chain of Command: The Road from 9/11 to Abu Ghraib* (New York: Harper Collins, 2004).

109. Eric Schmitt, "Pentagon Contradicts General on Iraq Occupation Force's Size," *New York Times*, 27 February 2003. Rumsfeld's Pentagon was in many ways like McNamara's Pentagon, with civilian "whiz kids," exerting undue influence. While Army officers cannot publicly say what they think, the critical works that have come out of the Army War College, and the words of General Shinseki and others are indicators of the dissatisfaction in the Army for the Rumsfeld conduct of the war.

110. Dr. Paul Wolfowitz, Deputy Secretary of Defense, *Philadelphia Inquirer*, 17 November 2002.

111. *Time*, 26 September 2005, 49.

112. One study compared the cost of the war in Iraq with the cost of the war in Vietnam: "consider that late last summer the Pentagon was spending $5.6 billion per month on operations in Iraq, an amount that exceeds the average cost of $5.1 billion per month (in real 2004 dollars) for US operations in Vietnam between 1964 and 1972." In 2005 the war in Iraq was costing $6 billion per month. The Bush Administration told the American people the war would cost about $70 billion.

In January 2006 one study predicted that the war in Iraq could cost as much as a thousand billion dollars, or US $1 trillion. See, David Isenberg, "Iraq, the Mother of All Budget Busters," *Asia Times*, 14 January 2006.

113. Franks, *American Soldier*, 441. Franks wrote: "A functional plan and policy to pay Iraqi military units so they can be immediately co-opted and put to work for the Coalition of reconstruction."

114. *Time*, 26 September 2005, 46.

115. Only the British provided significant forces, 30,000 to 40,000 combat soldiers and air support. The other thirty nations of Bush's "coalition of the willing" provided almost nothing that enhanced combat power.

Chapter 19

1. V.D. Sokolovsky, Marshal of the Soviet Union, *Military Strategy*, 3rd edition (Alexandria, Virginia: Defense Logistical Agency, Defense Technical Information Center, 1968), 41.

2. George Casey, Army Chief of Staff, "A Message from the Chief of Staff," *Echoes*, May–Aug 2010, 1.

3. Carl von Clausewitz, *On War*, ed. and trans., Michael Howard and Peter Paret (New Jersey: Princeton University Press, 1976).

4. Michael Walzer, *Obligation: Essays on Disobedience War and Citizenship* (Cambridge, Massachusetts: Harvard University Press, 1970), 99.

5. Walzer, *Obligations*, 114.

6. Walzer hastens to add: "there are no states willing to admit the reality of alienation among their inhabitants or to recognize the alienated resident as a moral person." Also see: Michael Weiss, *The Clustered World* (Boston: Little, Brown, and Company, 2000).

7. R.R. Palmer, "Frederick the Great, Guibert, Bulow: From Dynastic to National War," *Makers of Modern Strategy*, ed. Peter Paret (NJ: Princeton University Press, 1986), 92.

8. Palmer, "Fredrick the Great . . . ," *Makers of Modern Strategy*, 92, 119.

9. Institute of Land Warfare, "The Way Ahead" (Arlington, Virginia: Association of the United States Army, July 2000), 5. Had the Soviet Union existed neither Gulf Wars would have taken place.

10. Gordon R. Sullivan and Michael V. Harper, *Hope is not a Method* (New York: Broadway Books, 1996), 7. In 1996, General Sullivan, the former Army Chief of Staff, observed that: "In the years after the Berlin Wall came down, the Army's operational commitment tripled."

11. Robert F. Dorr, "No More C–17s for the Air Force?" *The Year in Defense*, http://theyearindefense.com/ aerospace/no-more-c-17s-for-the-air-force, August 2010, 3.

12. Robert F. Dorr, "F-22s Fly 'Bittersweet' Final Missions at Holloman Air Force Base," http://theyearindefense. com/aerospace/f-22s-fly-bittersweet-final-missions-at-holloman-air-force . . . , August 2010.

13. Grace V. Jean, "Shipyards Speed Up Submarine Production Amid Concerns About Navy's Future Budgets," *National Defense*, July 2010, Volume XCV, No. 680, 30–33.

14. The Chinese are building fleets of relatively inexpensive diesel submarines. The idea of swarming US Naval forces with overwhelming numbers has been advanced. However, the US is not going to overcome this numerical disadvantage by building $2.5 billion boats.

15. Robert M. Gates, "A Balanced Strategy: Reprogramming the Pentagon for a New Age," *Foreign Affairs*, January/February 2009, www.foreignaffairs. org/20090101 facessay88103/robert-m-gates/ . . . (italics added).

16. This has been greatly debated. Many military leaders believe that it is a mistake to invest considerable training time and resources in a form of warfare that can never actually threaten the survival of the United States, while diminishing capabilities in conventional warfare that can make a decisive difference in the survival of states such as South Korea.

17. See DOD Directive 3000.05 (28 November 2005).

18. These manuals have not escaped controversy, particularly FM 3–24 Counterinsurgency. Edward Luttwak, a noted military historian, has been critical of the manual. In 2007, in *Harper's*, he argued that the manual constituted military "malpractice."

19. William B. Caldwell, IV, Lieutenant General, Commander, US Army Combined Arms Center, FM 3–07 Stability Operations, October 2008, vi (italics added). Also see, *Human Terrain Team Handbook*, September 2008, and *Military Review*, Special Edition, *Counterinsurgency Reader I and II* (Fort Leavenworth, Kansas: US Army Combined Arms Center, October 2006 and August 2008).

20. Caroline Thomas, "Globalization and Human Security," *Globalization, Development and Human Security*, ed., Anthony McGrew and Nana K. Poku (Cambridge, UK: Polity Press, 2008), 108, 109.

21. For a more comprehensive study on human security see: Anthony McGrew and Nana K. Poku, ed., *Globalization, Development and Human Security* (Cambridge, UK: Polity Press, 2008).

22. Paul Collier, *The Bottom Billion* (New York: Oxford University Press, 2007). Also see Paul Collier, *War, Guns, and Votes: Democracy in Dangerous Places* (New York: Harper, 2009).

23. Collier, *The Bottom Billion*, xi.

24. Mary Kaldor, "Human Security in Complex Operations," www.ndu.edu/press/human-security-complex-operations.html, 2/28/2011, 3. Also see, Mary Kaldor, *New & Old Wars: Organized Violence in a Global Era* (Stanford, California: Stanford University Press, 2001).

25. Kaldor, "Human Security," 3.

26. Kaldor, "Human Security," 2.

27. Kaldor, "Human Security," 2.

28. Kaldor, "Human Security."

29. Lynn Sweet blog, "Obama White House on the defense of Libya attacks, From an administration official," http://blogs.suntimes.com/sweet/2011/06/Obama_white_house_on_defen.html.

30. Quote in a paper by Chris King titled "A Strategic Analytic Approach to Environmental Security for NATO," given at the NATO Security Science Forum on Environmental Security, Brussels, Belgium, 12 March 2008.

31. US Joint Forces Command, *The Joint Operating Environment 2010* (Suffolk, VA: Joint Forces Command, 18 February 2010).

32. JFC, *The Joint Operating Environment*, 12.

33. David E. Mosher, Beth E. Lachman, Michael E. Greenberg, Tiffany Nichols, Brian Rosen, and Henry H. Willis, *Green Warriors: Army Environmental Considerations for Contingency Operations from Planning Through Post-Conflict* (Santa Monica, California: RAND Corporation, 2008.

34. Mosher, "Green Warriors," iii.

35. Mosher, "Green Warriors," xvii.

36. Mosher, "Green Warriors," xviii.

37. FM 3–24 Counterinsurgency (Washington, DC: Headquarters, Department of the Army, December 2006), 5–17.

38. FM 3–07 Stability Operations (Washington, DC: Headquarters, Department of the Army, October 2008), 2–12.

39. FM 3–07 Stability Operations, 2–8.

40. Carl J. Schramm, "Expeditionary Economics: Spurring Growth After Conflicts and Disasters," *Foreign Affairs*, May/June 2010, 89–99.

41. US Army, "Handbook No. 09–27, Commander's Guide to Money as a Weapons System" (Fort Leavenworth, Kansas: The Center for Army Lessons Learned, April 2009); "Handbook No. 10–10 Agribusiness Development Teams in Afghanistan" (Washington, DC: The National Guard Agribusiness Development Team Coordination Office, November 2009).

42. Handbook No. 09–27, 1.

INDEX

How We Are Changed by War: A Study of Letters and Diaries from Colonial Conflicts to Operation Iraqi Freedom

D.C. Gill

The prolonged conflict in Iraq has shown us war's transformative effect. Civilians rivet themselves to events happening halfway around the world, while young soldiers return home from battlefields, coping with the memories of those events.

How We Are Changed by War examines our sense of ourselves through the medium of diaries and wartime correspondence, beginning with the colonists of the early seventeenth century, and ending with the diaries and letters from Iraqi war vets. The book tracks the effects of war in private writings regardless of the narrator's historical era, allowing the writers to 'speak' to each other across time to reveal a profound commonality of cultural experience. Finally, interpreting the narratives by how the writers conveyed the content adds a richer layer of meaning through the lenses of psychology and literary criticism, providing a model for any society to examine itself through the medium of its members' informal writings.

ISBN 10: 0-415- 87310-9 (hbk)
ISBN 10: 0-415- 87311-6 (pbk)

America and the Vietnam War: Re-Examining the Culture and History of a Generation

Andrew Wiest, Mary Kathryn Barbier, and Glenn Robins

The Vietnam War was one of the most heavily documented conflicts of the twentieth century. Although the events themselves recede further into history every year, the political and cultural changes the war brought about continue to resonate, even as a new generation of Americans grapples with its own divisive conflict.

America and the Vietnam War: Re-Examining the Culture and History of a Generation reconsiders the social and cultural aspects of the conflict that helped to fundamentally change the nation. With chapters written by subject area specialists, *America and the Vietnam War* takes on subjects such as women's role in the war, the music and the films of the time, the Vietnamese perspective, race and the war, and veterans and post-traumatic stress disorder. Features include:

- chapter summaries
- timelines
- discussion questions
- guides to further reading
- a companion website with primary source documents and tools (such as music and movie playlists) for both instructors and students.

Heavily illustrated and welcoming to students and scholars of this infamous and pivotal time, *America and the Vietnam War* is a perfect companion to any course on the Vietnam War Era.

ISBN 10: 0-415-99529-0 (hbk)
ISBN 10: 0-415-99530-6 (pbk)

Triumph Revisited: Historians Battle for the Vietnam War

Andrew Wiest and Michael Doidge

"[T]he book provides, in a relatively brief format, an excellent introduction to, and overview of, the major controversies and conflicts in the historiography of the early years of the Vietnam War … Recommended"— *Choice*

"In *Triumph Revisited*, Wiest and Doidge have collected Moyar's critics (and there are many) to explain why the standard explanations for the United States' failure in Vietnam—its exaggerated Cold War fears, its hopeless client, and its incoherent strategy—remain compelling. Moyar is allowed a spirited defense. The collection demonstrates the importance of debate as a way of illuminating important issues and questioning established positions."— *Foreign Affairs*

More than thirty years later, the Vietnam War still stands as one of the most controversial events in the history of the United States, and historians have so far failed to come up with a definitive narrative of the wartime experience. With competing viewpoints already in play, Mark Moyar's recent revisionist approach in *Triumph Forsaken* has created heated debate over who "owns" the history of America's war in Vietnam.

Triumph Revisited: Historians Battle for the Vietnam War collects critiques of *Triumph Forsaken* from both sides of this debate, written by an array of Vietnam scholars, cataloguing arguments about how the war should be remembered, how history may be reconstructed, and by whom. A lively introduction and conclusion by editors Andrew Wiest and Michael Doidge provide context and balance to the essays, as well as Moyar's responses, giving students and scholars of the Vietnam era a glimpse into how history is constructed and reconstructed.

ISBN 10: 0-415- 80020-4 (hbk)
ISBN 10: 0-415- 80021-1 (pbk)

Chemical Warfare during the Vietnam War: Riot Control Agents in Combat

D. Hank Ellison

Chemical Warfare during the Vietnam War documents the use of antipersonnel chemical weapons throughout the Vietnam War, and explores their effectiveness under the wide variety of circumstances in which they were employed. The short, readable account follows the US program as it progressed from a focus on the humanitarian aspects of non-lethal weapons to their use as a means of augmenting and enhancing the lethality of traditional munitions. It also presents the efforts of the North Vietnamese to both counter US chemical operations and to develop a chemical capability of their own.

Chemical Warfare during the Vietnam War is a comprehensive and thoroughly fascinating examination of riot-control agents during the Vietnam War.

ISBN 10: 0-415- 87644-5 (hbk)
ISBN 10: 0-415- 87645-2 (pbk)